Craft, Industry and Everyday Life:
Finds from Medieval York

By Patrick Ottaway and Nicola Rogers

Published for the York Archaeological Trust by the
Council for British Archaeology

2002

Contents

List of Figures

List of Tables

Volume 17 Fascicule 15

Craft, Industry and Everyday Life: Medieval Finds from York

By Patrick Ottaway and Nicola Rogers

With contributions by G.D. Gaunt, T. Horsley, M.E. Hutchinson, J. Jones, J.G. McDonnell, C. Mortimer, E. Paterson, S. Rees, D. Starley, R. Tyson, P. Walton Rogers, K. Wiemer

Key words: craft, dress accessories, horse equipment, household equipment, industry, medieval, metallography, metalworking, textile production, tools, vessel glass, York

Introduction

This comprehensive report represents a landmark in the publication of medieval finds from excavations in York. It encompasses very large assemblages of medieval artefacts of a wide variety of materials, including iron, non-ferrous metal, stone, jet, amber, fired clay, glass and textile. These were recovered from four major sites in York, excavated during the 1970s and 1980s, at 16–22 Coppergate, 46–54 Fishergate, Bedern Foundry (hereafter known as the Foundry) and the College of the Vicars Choral of York Minster at Bedern (hereafter Bedern), and also from smaller sites in the vicinity of 16–22 Coppergate (Coppergate watching brief and 22 Piccadilly) and Bedern (2 Aldwark and Bedern Chapel). In total, approximately 6,000 stratified medieval objects are discussed; the bulk of these finds are of metal, either iron (c.3,000 objects, not including c.2,500 nails), or non-ferrous metals (c.2,000). Some categories of medieval finds from these sites are not included here, as they either have been or are to be published elsewhere in the *Craft, Industry and Everyday Life in Anglo-Scandinavian and Medieval York* series of finds fascicules; these relate to finds of bone, antler, ivory and horn (*AY* 17/12), wood and woodworking (*AY* 17/13) and leather and leatherworking (*AY* 17/16 in prep.). Collectively, these fascicules provide expert, up-to-date analysis and comment on a broad range of medieval objects, adding considerably to the number of medieval finds from the city which have been published, the only previous report relating specifically to finds of this period having appeared in 1982 (*AY* 17/4).

Both 16–22 Coppergate and 46–54 Fishergate have produced substantial assemblages of pre-Conquest material, some of which have already been published. Groups of Anglo-Scandinavian material from Coppergate already published comprise the textiles (*AY* 17/5), the pottery (*AY* 16/5) and the iron and ironworking evidence (*AY* 17/6), although a small number of additional Anglo-Scandinavian iron objects have come to light since publication of the last-named fascicule and are included in a special section below (pp.3005–12). Another fascicule in the *Craft and Industry* series includes Anglo-Scandinavian finds of other materials (*AY* 17/14). Reports relating to non-ferrous metalworking (*AY* 17/7) and textile-working (*AY* 17/11) from all post-Roman periods have also appeared. Anglian and late 10th–12th century finds from Fishergate have been published in *AY* 17/9.

Although the main theme of this volume is the medieval period, it should be noted that the periods of occupation at the various sites from which the finds derive are not quite the same. At 16–22 Coppergate, occupation was continuous from the late 9th century through to the post-medieval period, but the vast majority of the finds in this volume come from contexts of c.1100–1500. The site at 22 Piccadilly and the Coppergate watching brief also produced medieval artefacts from contexts with a similar date range. The finds in this volume from the three other major sites, the Foundry, Bedern and 46–54 Fishergate, come from medieval contexts of which the earliest date is usually at least c.100–150 years later than the earliest medieval contexts examined at Coppergate. The college at Bedern was established in 1252 and the excavation did not examine much in the way of pre-college levels. The sequence at Bedern continued into the post-medieval period, although the archaeology of the site after the decline of the college in the later 16th century was not examined in detail. As in the case of Bedern, the pre-13th century archaeology of the adjacent Foundry site was not examined, but a sequence of deposits and structures of later medieval and post-medieval date was carefully recorded. At 46–54 Fishergate, where settlement of both the Anglian period and the 11th–12th century was also recorded, the finds in this volume come largely from the excavation of the Gilbertine Priory of St Andrew which was founded in 1195 and dedicated in 1202; it was dissolved in c.1538, when it underwent extensive stripping and demolition.

The first part of this report presents evidence relating to craft and industrial activities on all the sites. Non-ferrous metalworking at the Foundry has been discussed in some detail in the excavation report (*AY* 10/3, 186–200), but further evidence of some of the products and waste from the Foundry and its environs came to light during the preparation of this report, and is included here. Some of the metal tools recovered point to leather, wood and textile working, and the evidence for agricultural and fishing activity is also presented. The second section brings together all the items relating to the everyday life of the inhabitants of the sites. This includes objects used in eating and cooking, fittings attached to buildings and furniture, items relating to security arrangements, personal and dress accessories, items relating to reading and writing, objects with ritual or recreational use, and items of horse equipment. Finally there is a discussion of the significance of the chronological and spatial distributions of the objects, and the differing natures of the site assemblages, allowing a comparison to be made between the ecclesiastical sites of Bedern and St Andrew's Priory, Fishergate, and the secular sites at 16–22 Coppergate, 22 Piccadilly and 2 Aldwark. A comprehensive catalogue completes the report.

Authorship of this report has been divided on the basis of materials. Patrick Ottaway has catalogued and reported on the ironwork. In addition, some preliminary cataloguing work on the Foundry and

Bedern ironwork was undertaken by Dr Ian Goodall. Metallographic examination of iron knives was undertaken by Dr David Starley (formerly Ancient Monuments Laboratory, English Heritage, now Royal Armouries, Leeds) with additional items examined by Dr J.G. McDonnell (Bradford University) and Dr Karen Wiemer (Cambridge University). Mineralised organic remains on iron objects were examined by Jacqui Watson (Ancient Monuments Laboratory, English Heritage), whose report is lodged in the YAT archive. Nicola Rogers is responsible for the cataloguing and discussion of the bulk of the remaining material, with the exception of the vessel glass, reported on by Dr Rachel Tyson, textiles and textile tools by Penelope Walton Rogers, analysis of non-ferrous metalworking at the Bedern sites by Dr Catherine Mortimer, lithological identifications by Dr G.D. Gaunt, and gemstone identifications by Marjorie Hutchinson and Susan Rees. Alison Goodall made a study of the copper alloy and lead alloy objects from the Bedern sites, and provided a basis for the catalogue entries for this material, as well as some useful points for discussion. The concluding discussion has been written jointly by the two main authors.

The material discussed in this report, together with copies of all appropriate records, will be deposited at the Yorkshire Museum, York, under the Museum and YAT accession codes 1976–81.7 (16–22 Coppergate), 1982.22 (Coppergate watching brief), 1987.21 (22 Piccadilly), 1978–80.14.III (2 Aldwark), 1973–9.13.X (Bedern south-west), 1978–80.14.II/IV (Bedern north-east), 1973–6.13.I/II (Bedern Foundry), 1974–5.13.III/IV (Bedern south-west, long trench), 1980.20.I/II (Bedern Chapel) and 1985–6.9 (46–54 Fishergate).

Archaeological Introductions to the Sites

Excavations at 16–22 Coppergate
(Fig.1301)

By R.A. Hall

The data recovered have been attributed to six broad periods (Table 265); the evidence presented here relates to the mid 11th–14th/15th centuries. During this time the site was sub-divided into four tenement plots which, in general, were more densely occupied as time passed.

Table 265   Summary of archaeological development at 16–22 Coppergate

Period	Date	Characteristics
1	late 1st–late 4th century or later	Roman timber and stone buildings; late Roman cemetery. Limited survival of organic materials
2	5th–mid 9th century	Apparent desertion. Homogeneous loamy deposits which did not preserve organic materials
3	mid 9th–late 9th/early 10th century	Rubbish disposal, suggesting occupation close by. Post/stake and wattle alignments, possibly boundaries. Organic materials preserved only in pit cuts
4A	late 9th/early 10th century–c.930/5	Realignment of boundaries, suggesting that Coppergate was laid out by this period. Possible buildings at Coppergate frontage. Organic materials preserved mainly in pit cuts
4B	c.930/5–c.975	Four tenements distinguishable, with post and wattle buildings at Coppergate frontage. Evidence for ironworking and other trades on a commercial scale. Organic-rich deposits nearer to Coppergate; organic content thinning to zero towards River Foss
5A	c.975	Near Coppergate frontage only. Layers between structures of Periods 4B and 5B; probably mixture of occupation deposits, dump deposits and soil from 5B semi-basements
5B	c.975–early/mid 11th century	Perpetuation of boundaries. Introduction of sunken-featured structures in double row at street frontage. Organic-rich deposits as in Period 4B
5Cf	mid–later 11th century	Organic-rich deposits at street frontage, associated with buildings which survive only in Tenement D
5Cr	mid–later 11th century	Post-built structure closest to River Foss sealed by earliest in a succession of dump deposits. Little organic material surviving
6	later 11th–16th century	No remains surviving at street frontage, but area to rear increasingly built up above later dump deposits. New methods of building and rubbish disposal, leading to reduction in organic content of deposits

Site history and a summary

The site of 16–22 Coppergate lies on the spur of land between the Rivers Ouse and Foss. It is bounded to the west by Coppergate, a street leading towards the only bridge across the Ouse in the medieval period, and to the east by the banks of the Foss.

The earliest occupation on the site, designated Period 1 (Table 265), was in the Roman era. There is some evidence that there were temples in the immediate vicinity, and there may also have been a variety of commercial and residential establishments constructed of both timber and stone. The site also contained a small late Roman cemetery. At the present stage of research there seems no reason to suppose that Romano-British activity continued in this area much beyond c. AD 400, and from then until the mid 9th century the site seems to have been unoccupied (Period 2). This period was marked stratigraphically by the accumulation of up to 1m of grey silty clay loam soils; there was no evidence for structures. All of the pottery in these layers was Roman, with the exception of a small quantity of Anglo-Scandinavian sherds which are believed to be intrusive.

A later 8th century helmet, found only 9m beyond the excavation's perimeter during construction work in 1982, lay within a wood-lined shaft. This was, per-

Fig.1301 *Plan showing position of (1) 16–22 Coppergate; (2) area of Watching Brief, zones 1–7 (shown in green); (3) 22 Piccadilly, a–d correspond to Trenches 1–4; and (4) St Mary, Castlegate. (Based on the 1982 Ordnance Survey 1:1250 National Grid Plans. Reproduced from Ordnance Survey mapping with permission of Ordnance Survey on behalf of Her Majesty's Stationery Office, © Crown Copyright MC 100012225.) Scale 1:1250*

haps, a mid–late Anglian well, and may possibly relate to a contemporary settlement nucleus, either on the ridge now represented by Nessgate/Castlegate, and/or around what may be an early ecclesiastical foundation at St Mary's, Castlegate (Fig.1301, 4). The final backfilling of the shaft is dated to the Anglo-Scandinavian period on the basis of a characteristic suite of accompanying palaeobiological remains (pp.870–81, *AY* 17/8).

Above the clean grey loams which mark the four and a half centuries interpreted as Anglian desertion of the site, a band of dirtier grey silty clay loams was recognised, and into these was cut a series of features. One of the earliest of these features was a sequence of hearth/oven/kiln bases represented by a horizontal setting of re-used Roman tiles, perhaps used in glassworking. An archaeomagnetic determination of 860 ± 20 was obtained from these features. This is the single most precise indication of the date when this period of renewed use of the site began, although it is not possible to relate it to either a definitely pre-Viking (i.e. pre-866) or post-Viking date with conviction. It does seem, however, that the assemblage of Anglian pottery from the site is best seen as in a direct typological and thus chronological succession with that from the Anglian occupation site at 46–54 Fishergate (*AY* 7/1; *AY* 16/6, 650–1) where occupation is thought to cease in the mid 9th century.

Apart from one porcupine sceat of c.720–40, found in an 11th century layer at the river end of the site, all of the nine other identifiable Anglian coins from the site are of 9th century date (*AY* 18/1, 51–3). All were found in contexts stratigraphically later than that with the archaeomagnetic determination of 860 ± 20. Such coins occur in hoards found in York which may be interpreted as a response to the Viking attack of 866. This evidence suggests that activity and settlement in this area recommenced in the middle of the 9th century. There is no stratigraphic or artefactual evidence to indicate that there was protracted Anglian activity before that time.

Other features in this period included pits containing domestic debris and some containing human skeletal remains. The latest features of this period were a series of post-holes, some apparently forming alignments at an angle to the later tenement lines, and an accompanying cobble spread at the south-

west of the area. It is conceivable that these features represent the remains of a building, although this is not certain. This entire horizon, Period 3, is dated c. AD 850–900 on the basis of a combination of archaeomagnetic and numismatic evidence; in later periods, dendrochronological data provide a greater level of chronological precision.

Sealing the post-holes, cobble spread and other features of Period 3 were deposits into which were inserted wattle alignments which anticipated the alignment of the subsequent tenements and structures, but which do not themselves form obviously coherent structures. These alignments and their associated layers and features are assigned to Period 4A and dated c. AD 900–930/5. These layers were very similar to those of Period 3 and, like those, were not particularly conducive to the survival of organic artefacts.

The next phase on the site, Period 4B, is marked by the division of the area into four tenements, designated A–D, and if the street Coppergate was not in being before it must have been laid out at this time. The tenements were defined by wattle fences, whose lines fluctuated only very slightly over the succeeding millennium; towards the River Foss end of the site, however, there was no trace of any continuation of the fences discovered nearer to Coppergate. Each tenement contained buildings of post and wattle construction, positioned with their gable-ends facing the street. All had been truncated towards their front by the subsequent widening of Coppergate; the greatest surviving length was 6·8m, and they averaged 4·4m in width. The buildings on Tenements A and B had been substantially disturbed by the digging of semi-basements for the Period 5B buildings, but those on Tenements C and D were very largely intact. The buildings had to be repaired or replaced frequently, for they were vulnerable to fire as well as to natural decay, but successive refurbishments varied little in their dimensions and position. Hearths were found on the long axes of the buildings in Tenements B, C and D; any trace in A was destroyed by later intrusion, and even in B only vestiges remained.

Only one rank of buildings stood in each tenement and their lengthy backyards were not built up but used for rubbish disposal and other ancillary functions. A sequence of superimposed floor levels built up by gradual accumulation within each building. Their accompanying artefacts allow the activities within each tenement to be followed with varying degrees of assurance. Metalworking seems to have been the predominant activity, with the manufacture of items in iron, copper alloy, lead alloy, silver and gold. A notable feature was the quantity of crucibles recovered with their important corroborative evidence for the range and variety of metalworking techniques (*AY* 17/6; *AY* 17/7). Occupation was evidently intensive, generating organic-rich occupation deposits which accumulated rapidly, in particular in and around the buildings, and which accounted for a continual rise in ground level. Deposits which were rich in organic remains extended to approximately half-way down the excavated area in the direction of the River Foss.

In the later 10th century the remains of the latest phase of post and wattle structures at the street frontage were covered to a depth of up to 1m. This horizon, which was not traced in the yard areas behind the buildings, is interpreted as resulting in part from the upcast in digging out the sunken structures of Period 5B, and partly as a deliberate dump of makeup or levelling material. It thus accumulated very quickly, probably within a period of weeks or months, and contained a mixture of material of c.975 and before.

The dating of Period 5A is dependent on the dendrochronological analysis of timbers from the immediately succeeding plank-built semi-basement structures of Period 5B. These were erected at the Coppergate end of each tenement, sometimes in two closely spaced ranks; as in Period 4B, organic-rich deposits were concentrated in the vicinity of these buildings, and the organic content of the deposits decreased riverwards. As in the buildings of Period 4B, successive layers of silty loam characterised the superimposed floors. Manufacturing continued at this period, although new trades were practised.

On Tenement D sufficient overlying stratification remained undisturbed to show that the latest of the Period 5B sunken buildings was eventually replaced by structures built at ground level. The chronology of these subsequent buildings is imprecise: they can be assigned only approximately to the mid 11th century. They and their associated stratification are designated as belonging to Period 5Cf. A series of approximately contemporary mid 11th century lev-

els was also identified at the rear of the site, associated with and sealing a post-built structure, the latest timber of which has been dated through dendrochronology to 1014–54. These levels, which did not preserve their organic component, are designated Period 5Cr. They were themselves covered by a series of dumps of silty clay loam interleaved with evidence for sporadic activity, and dated to the Norman period.

Within the Anglo-Scandinavian stratification there is clear evidence from coins and pottery for the displacement of objects from the context where they were originally deposited and their redeposition in later layers. The principal mechanism of this movement was the cutting of pits, wells and the like, and, more particularly, the digging out of the sunken element in the Period 5B buildings, which penetrated earlier levels and redistributed the soil removed from them. In the case of the precisely dated coins it can be seen that, in the Anglo-Scandinavian levels, coins sometimes occur in contexts dated 75–100 years later than their striking (*AY* 18/1, 24), although their wear patterns do not suggest circulation for this length of time and there is evidence that they were hoarded. Study of the pottery from Anglo-Scandinavian levels has shown that sherds of both Roman wares and of handmade middle Saxon type which are unlikely to have been produced after c. AD 850–900 are found residually throughout the era, another testimony to the redistribution of earlier material (*AY* 16/5, fig.144).

At the Coppergate street frontage, no buildings survived later than those attributed to Period 5Cf. The earliest surviving building of Period 6 was a late 11th/12th century post and wattle structure incorporating a hearth at the rear of Tenement C. It adjoined the only length of contemporaneous property boundary which could be identified. Other, probably structural, features attributed to this time include a hearth and a group of large posts at the excavated rear limit of Tenement A.

In the 12th–12th/13th century the building at the rear of Tenement C was replaced with a series of superimposed post and wattle structures incorporating hearths/ovens. This complex, which stood within well-defined fenced property boundaries which could be traced towards the middle of the site, is tentatively interpreted as a bakery or malting house. The end of a post and wattle structure on the adjacent Tenement B was also recorded, as was a further set of possibly structural features, including hearths, at the rear limit of Tenement A. A very fragmentary possible structure, represented by a post alignment, was noted towards the front end of Tenement C.

The tenement plots were occupied more extensively in the 13th–13th/14th centuries, although the only evidence for buildings on Tenement A was, once more, from its rear, where a series of post-holes and sill walls defined a structure. Towards the rear of Tenement B a building was erected which had its principal uprights supported by padstones; alongside it a cobbled surface providing an access way replaced and extended over the fence line that had earlier separated Tenement B from Tenement C. A relatively long building, constructed on pile-cluster foundations, now stood on Tenement C; it is unclear whether it extended to the riverside limit of excavation, or whether a separate structure occupied that part of the tenement plot. Meanwhile, at the riverward end of Tenement D, there is some evidence for a structure represented most tangibly by a line of posts to the north-east of a series of deposits which have the characteristic of internal floor deposits. It is the combination of these two sets of features which define the structure shown on Fig.1302. Towards the Coppergate end of the plot a stone-built structure with substantial horizontal timber foundations in parts, may also have been erected within this period.

A very similar layout of buildings was maintained into the 14th–14th/15th centuries, although most individual structures were rebuilt during this time. A new building represented by post-holes now occupied the rear of Tenement A, and the Tenement B padstone building was also rebuilt. The long building on Tenement C continued in use initially but was then demolished; an alley surface was laid down between it and the building on Tenement D. Later, a ditch, redefining the Tenement C–D property boundary, was cut within the limits of the earlier long Tenement C building. Evidence for a contemporary building over the rear of Tenement D was now unequivocal, with the construction of a rubble sill wall. The stone cellared building nearer the frontage may have remained in use.

The latest coherent archaeological evidence is dated to the 15th–15th/16th century. A much more substantial, stone-built, structure, was now erected in the centre/rear of Tenement A; its full extent is not known. More recent disturbance has removed contemporary stratification from most of Tenement B, and there was no trace of any building within the undisturbed portion at the riverward end of this property. A new, relatively long building represented by rubble sill walls was built at the centre/front of Tenement C, and there were also robbed out traces of another, smaller structure nearer to the river, with a ditch defining the property boundary to one side and a wall to the other. The earlier Tenement D buildings continued in use at this time.

A series of dendrochronological and archaeomagnetic determinations provide a fairly precise chronology for a majority of the buildings; ceramic and numismatic data support and extend this information.

Although the number and size of these buildings varied throughout the later medieval and earlier post-medieval centuries, their intermittent presence sealed the deposits below and temporarily protected them from damage caused by intrusive pits. Furthermore, the introduction both of levelling deposits before the erection of some of the buildings, and of dump deposits which indicate the disposal of a quantity of rubbish in a single event, served to raise the ground level and offer some protective cloak or masking against erosion and disturbance. Conversely, changes in building techniques and materials, notably the increasing use of stone and then brick wall footings, and tiled roofs, contributed to a gradual diminution in the amount of organic debris being generated and deposited on the site during the later medieval period. From the 13th–13th/14th century onwards, access alleyways rather than fence lines sometimes marked the boundaries of tenement plots. Concomitantly, these stone surfaces also sealed underlying deposits, temporarily protecting them from intrusion and degradation. Nonetheless, the digging of wells, cess-pits and other features throughout the medieval and post-medieval centuries did bring some earlier material to the surface.

Recovery of evidence

The excavation, directed by R.A. Hall, took the form of a continuous archaeological campaign of five years and four months during 1976–81. Resources were provided principally by the Ancient Monu-

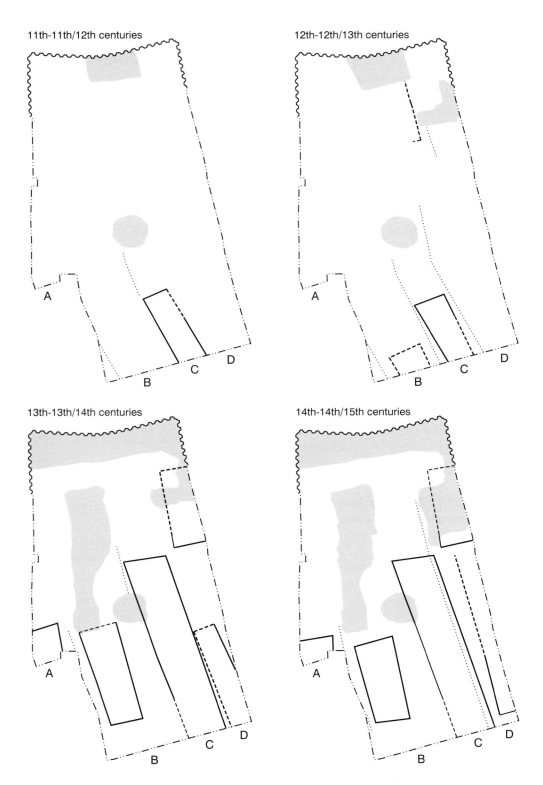

11th-11th/12th centuries

12th-12th/13th centuries

13th-13th/14th centuries

14th-14th/15th centuries

Fig.1302 *(above and facing) Plans of the site at 16–22 Coppergate showing the area of deposits excavated for Period 6. Scale 1:500. The insertion of perimeter shoring after the removal of most Period 6 deposits slightly lessened the excavated area*

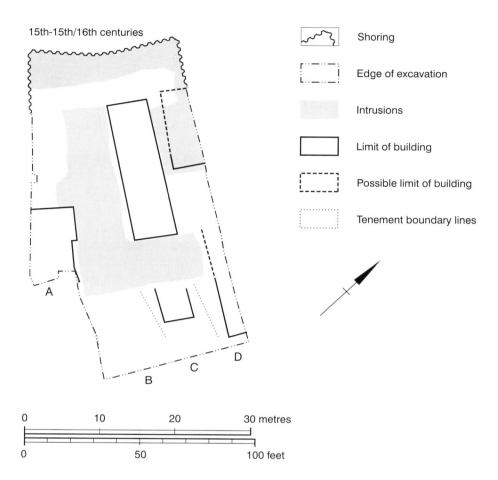

15th-15th/16th centuries

A B C D

	Shoring
	Edge of excavation
	Intrusions
	Limit of building
	Possible limit of building
	Tenement boundary lines

0   10   20   30 metres

0   50   100 feet

ments Inspectorate of the Department of the Environment (now English Heritage), the Manpower Services Commission, the British Academy and a host of private individuals and corporations.

Mid 10th century to late medieval deposits were investigated over the entire excavated area, which comprised c.1000m². Owing to a shortage of funding, the earliest levels, dating from the Roman period to the early/mid 10th century (i.e. up to and including what is described above as Period 4A), were not examined right across the c.1000m² open in the subsequent levels. Instead, a strip measuring approximately 20·7 × 5m across the Coppergate street frontage and a contiguous strip up to 12m wide and 37m long, running down the southern half of the site

towards the River Foss, were excavated to natural soils.

Layers attributable to Periods 1 and 3 were recorded throughout these strips. A well-defined Period 2 horizon existed only in the street frontage strip; elsewhere, because of stratigraphic interruptions and an overall thinning of these earlier layers as they ran eastwards from the street frontage, Period 2 contexts could not be isolated with certainty. Therefore, although some deposition of soil must have taken place throughout Period 2, remains of this period are of limited extent. Similarly, the Period 4A horizon, while extending right across the frontage, could not be traced convincingly down the southern strip beyond a point where diagnostic features petered out. It is thus conceivable that a small amount of soil build-up which took place during Period 4A on that part of the southern strip to the east of the limit of identifiable 4A features has been subsumed into Period 4B, which was investigated over the entire excavated area.

For reasons outlined above, the deposits designated as Period 5A were limited in extent to the front part of the site. Deposits of Period 5B were traced across the entire area excavated. Deposits of Period 5Cf and 5Cr were limited to the front- and rear-most portions of the excavation respectively, and no contemporary levels could be stratigraphically isolated in the central part of the excavation. Layers of Period 6, a designation that encompasses all deposits of the Anglo-Norman to post-medieval/early modern eras, covered the entire excavated area except where removed by more recent disturbances. As noted above, structures which could be attributed to Period 6 were not in evidence at the modern street frontage, but structures were found across the rest of the excavated area (Fig.1302). Survival of these remains was affected in places by modern (19th and 20th century) disturbance, particularly that related to occupancy of part of the site by Cravens, the Victorian and later sweet factory. These variations in the size of area excavated must be borne in mind in any chronological/quantitative analysis of the artefactual evidence.

The characteristics of the demolition site that was handed over for investigation, notably the varying extent of modern intrusions, coupled with the logistics of excavation and the continual financial uncertainties, dictated the strategy and tactics employed throughout the excavation process. Anglo-Scandinavian deposits were revealed below modern cellars within a few days of excavation commencing, yet elsewhere on the site later medieval deposits were still being investigated two years later.

During the redevelopment of 1981–3 a continuous watching brief over an extended area, running down to the present edge of the River Foss, was maintained under the direction of N.F. Pearson. The results of this exercise are incorporated into the report below.

The structures and strata recorded in the Coppergate excavations will be published in AY 6, 7, 8 and 10. Biological evidence from the Anglo-Scandinavian deposits has been published in AY 14/7 and the Anglo-Scandinavian animal bones have been published in AY 15/3; biological evidence from medieval deposits will be published in AY 14 and the medieval animal bones have been published in AY 15/5. The Anglo-Scandinavian pottery has been published in AY 16/5 and the medieval pottery will appear in a subsequent fascicule in AY 16. A series of artefact reports is being published in AY 17. The post-Roman coins and numismatica are included in AY 18/1. Roman coins will appear in AY 18/2.

The Watching Brief

By N.F. Pearson

The Coppergate watching brief embraced the whole of the 2·02ha area of the Coppergate Shopping Centre redevelopment from the Castlegate frontage in the west to Piccadilly in the east. Observations were also made in the areas of 16–22 Coppergate not explored during the main excavation campaign, that is, strips to the west, east and south of the open area. A watch was also kept at 14 Coppergate, where the rear of the property was redeveloped in 1984 only after the construction of the rest of the shopping centre had been completed. Recording also took place to the rear of the former Market Tavern, 24 Coppergate, where a medieval building on the Coppergate street frontage was refurbished as part of the development.

Observation and recording was carried out in often adverse conditions during ground preparation and building works undertaken by Wimpey Construction plc. The ground preparation works were undertaken largely by machine, under archaeological supervision. Where significant archaeological deposits were disturbed, work was suspended to allow recording, or, where appropriate, small-scale excavation. To facilitate recording the redevelopment area was split into discrete zones (Fig.1301).

The principal Roman features encountered included the fragmentary remains of a largely robbed-out stone building recorded between the Coppergate excavation and 14 Coppergate (Zone 1). This has tentatively been interpreted as a warehouse, on the basis of its proximity to the River Foss. In the helmet pit area (Zone 3), four pits were excavated in addition to a linear feature. In the Fossbank area (Zone 6), a red gritstone wall was observed briefly during machine clearance. It was well constructed with individual blocks measuring 0·8 × 0·6 × 0·4m. No other associated material was seen and although it was clearly structural in nature its north-east/south-west alignment precludes it from being interpreted as a river wall.

The only feature from the site which may be attributable to the Anglian period is the pit containing the Coppergate helmet (see p.2675).

From the Anglo-Scandinavian period, the west wall of Structure 5/1 (Period 5B), which had already been examined during the main excavation, was uncovered in the area between the Coppergate excavation and 14 Coppergate (Zone 1). Associated tenement boundaries and pits were also recorded. Between the Coppergate excavation and the Market Tavern public house (Zone 2), further well-preserved timber buildings and associated features, attributed to Periods 4B and 5B, were recorded.

The recorded medieval features included structural remains, fence lines, riverside reclamation, the outer defences of York castle, and parts of the cemetery of All Saints, Pavement. From the post-medieval and early modern periods the most significant discoveries were part of the cemetery of St Mary, Castlegate, traces of the canalisation of the River Foss, and part of the footings for the Victorian prison in the Castle Yard.

Excavation at 22 Piccadilly

By R. Finlayson

When the site of the ABC Cinema at 22 Piccadilly was to be developed an excavation was carried out to examine, in four trenches, some of the material which would be destroyed by the new development (Fig.1301, 3). The site lay to the south-east of the tenements excavated on Coppergate, in an area between them and the River Foss. From these limited areas of excavation some interpretation of the changes in topography and depositional regimes relating to the River Foss could be made. Trench 4 was within the course of the River Foss prior to its canalisation in or after 1793. A steeply sloping bank of natural sandy clay in Trench 3 is likely to have been a part of the river bank. Trenches 1 and 2 were located to the west of this bank and demonstrated intensive occupation of the area from the 1st century to the 16th century; later deposits had been truncated by the foundation

of the ABC Cinema (Table 266). Many of the deposits were dumps and build-up material containing domestic and industrial waste which provided important information about craft activities, the utilisation of resources, diet and living conditions.

Roman activity comprised what was probably a drainage ditch, aligned at right angles to the modern day River Foss. The cut silted up and filled with material c. AD 280 (AY 16/8). During the 9th–12th centuries there were a series of attempts to make the area close to the Foss usable. Periods when the area was in use and timber features were built were interspersed with periods when activity declined. Flood deposition, the decay of vegetation, and the dumping of domestic and industrial waste material all resulted in an accumulation of deposits. Particular evidence was found of a glass industry, small pelt preparation, horn and antler working, and butchery on a commercial as well as a domestic scale.

The first timber feature in Trench 1 was a fence parallel to the present course of the River Foss. This fence was no longer in use when a dump and buildup of organic material covered the whole area. Environmental evidence suggests the area was wet grassland, and associated pottery is consonant with a 9th century date. A further series of fences were constructed with two elements aligned parallel to the River Foss, and an alignment intersecting them at right angles. Pottery in associated dump and buildup deposits also dates from the first half of the 9th century.

In Trench 3 there were indications of an attempt at revetment to try to prevent soils slumping towards the sloping bank in the second half of the 10th century. A second phase of constructional activity in Trench 3 is represented by wattle which broadly followed the contour of the land, forming an open U shape. A similar U-shaped construction was found on the south-west bank of the River Ouse at North Street (YAT 1993.1; Fig.1314, 11, p.2702), also dated to the 11th century.

In Trench 2 timber fences and revetments indicate that some land management and manipulation of the course of the River Foss is likely to have taken place during the late 10th–early 11th century. There was evidence for the natural accumulation of material, for a deliberate raising of the ground surface,

Table 266   Summary of archaeological development at 22 Piccadilly

Period	Date	Description
Natural		Sandy clay
1	Roman	Riverine deposition, drainage ditch at right angles to the Foss, silting of ditch and dumping
2	9th century	Small pit and fill, riverine deposition, fence parallel to the Foss, dump and build-up material, two fence lines at right angles to each other, peaty and silty clay build-up and dump
3	10th century	Riverine deposition, silty clay, organic build-up and dump, timber revetment of river bank, silty clay, organic build-up and dump
4.1	975–early/mid 11th century	U-shaped timber revetment and wattle fence on river bank, silty clay and organic build-up and dump, fence
4.2	later 11th century	Renewal of intersecting fences, organic build-up and dumped large sawn timbers, timber revetment of river bank, silty clay build-up and dump
4.3	mid–late 12th century	Riverine deposition, compact peat build-up, small pit cuts, river bank timber revetment, silty clay build-up and dump, clay levelling on river bank
5.1	13th century	Pit cut with organic fill, drainage channel, soak-away?, peaty build-up, levelling
5.2	early–mid 14th century	Clay and peaty build-up and dump, rubbish pits
6	15th–early 16th century	Drainage? cut, organic build-up and dump, pit cut, barrel-lined well
7	15th century–modern	Levelling, concrete

for fences and for possible revetments, but there was evidently continued periodic waterlogging of the area. Dumped material included concentrations of smashed crucibles with glass making waste (*AY* 17/14), a number of glass beads (ibid.) and antler waste (*AY* 17/12).

A broadly similar series of activities and structures continued into the later 11th century. Glass beads, numerous worked goat horncores, antler waste, two bone skates, an increased amount of crucible waste, and a dump of large sawn timbers were recovered from this material and reflect the continuation and range of craft activity (*AY* 17/12 and *AY*

17/14). A series of revetment timbers found closer to the river in Trench 3, and a fence line in Trench 1, both dated to the same period.

In the 12th century the area continued to be used for the disposal of rubbish although glass industry waste ceases to appear. However, the soil now included a higher proportion of inorganic material, including demolition debris, although peaty deposits also continued to accumulate. The area continued to be used for the disposal of domestic and industrial waste throughout the medieval period, with some evidence for drainage in the form of cuts and a large soakaway. The latest significant feature found on the site was a cask-lined well dating to the 15th or 16th century (*9190–2*, *AY* 17/13). Later deposits had been truncated by the foundations of the ABC Cinema.

Excavations at Bedern (Fig.1303)

By R.A. Hall

The College of the Vicars Choral

Bedern, an area of notorious slums in the 19th century, lies c.105m south-east of York Minster. The name survived into the 1970s as that of a minor street, formerly a cul-de-sac, approached through a medieval gatehouse fronting on to Goodramgate, and giving access to the obvious remains of Bedern Chapel and the considerably less obvious traces of a medieval stone and timber hall. These three structures were the only survivals from the College of the Vicars Choral of York Minster. The college was established in 1252. The office of Vicar Choral derived from the obligation upon absentee canons to appoint personal deputies to take their place in the choir of York Minster. Throughout the 14th century the college housed 36 vicars but it began to decline from the end of the 15th century. In 1574 the vicars ceased to dine in common, although the college was not formally dissolved until 1936.

An important documentary archive provides evidence for diverse aspects of the college, both as an institution and as a group of men (with, after the Reformation, wives and families) living a communal life (Harrison 1952; Tringham 1993). However, much remained undocumented about the college's topographical and structural development, and about the daily lives of the vicars. In 1968 Lord Esher recommended that the existing light industrial usage of the area be replaced by housing. York City Council subsequently purchased land in Bedern and promulgated redevelopment of the vicinity. It was this which prompted the initiation by York Archaeological Trust of a campaign of excavations which eventually lasted from 1973 to 1980.

The total depth of stratification hereabouts, and the nature of Roman–early Norman occupation and activity, was tested in excavations of a long trench (see below), and beneath some modern cellars (*AY* 3/3; *AY* 14/5). The upper levels of the long trench contained a sequence of deposits and structures which can often be firmly linked either with those in the area to the north-east occupied by the Vicars Choral or those to the south-west in the area occupied by a foundry. Clay-loam layers dating to the 11th and 12th century were seen only in the long trench, however. Here too was evidence for the robbing of the Roman fortress wall in the 12th century, and for a series of pits, clay floors and other features indicating 12th century occupation (Period 1A). See Table 267.

The largest portion of available resources and effort was devoted to the precinct of the College of Vicars Choral, as defined on the 1852 Ordnance Survey map of York. In total, an area of 2,500m² was investigated, representing about 30% of the estimated college precinct at its maximum extent. Various parts of the site were designated different area codes. These are used in the catalogue and may be summarised as follows:

Bedern long trench (1973–5.13.III/IV; SE 60545207)
Bedern Foundry (1973–6.13.I/II; SE 60515208)
Bedern south-west (1976–9.13.X; SE 60535209)
Bedern north-east (1978–9.14.II; SE 60535213)
Bedern north-east (1979–80,14.IV; SE 60555212)
Bedern Chapel (1980.20.I/II/III; SE 60505214).

Modern deposits were usually machined off; excavation by hand then continued to a fairly uniform depth of 1·5m below the modern ground surface. This self-imposed limit was designed to allow the recording of all deposits which would be destroyed by the redevelopment campaign. Fortuitously, this depth of strata encompassed all archaeological remains from the 13th century onwards and thus included the entire span of the archaeological record for the College of the Vicars Choral. Virtually all material was recovered by hand, the excavation pre-dating the introduction of routine riddling/sieving on York sites.

During the first half of the 13th century it appears that Bedern was subject to light agricultural usage, with a series of drainage gullies and ditches representing property boundaries running back from Goodramgate, and some slight garden structures (Period 1). In the mid 13th century this land was acquired by the college, which erected its first buildings on either side of an open courtyard, running back from Goodramgate, which was to become Bedern Close. On the north-east side of the close a large building — the great hall — was constructed; on the south-west side a stone building and a smaller timber-

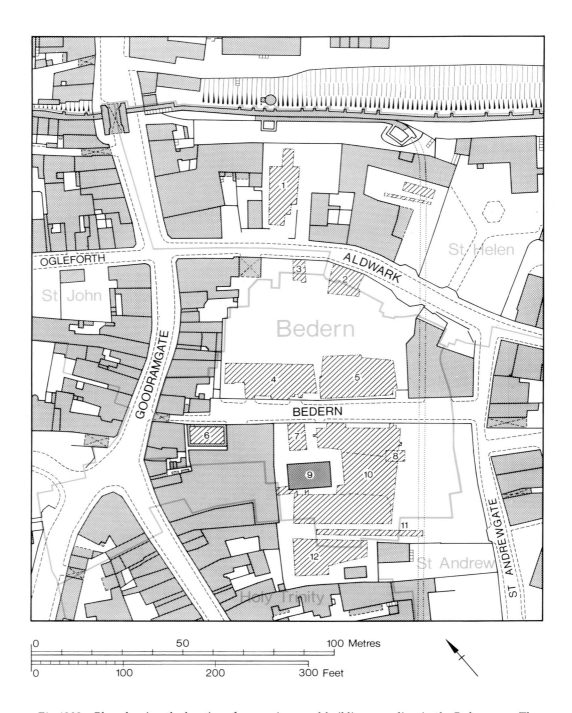

Fig.1303 *Plan showing the location of excavations, and building recording in the Bedern area. The outline of the parish boundaries (in green) defining the precinct of the College of the Vicars Choral is based on the 1852 Ordnance Survey map. (1) 1–5 Aldwark; (2) 2 Aldwark; (3) Cellar, 1976.14.I; (4) Bedern north-east, 1978–9.14.II; (5) Bedern north-east, 1979–80.14.IV; (6) Bedern Chapel, 1980.20.I/II; (7) Cellar, 1976.13.IV; (8) Cellar, 1976.13.VI; (9) Bedern Hall, 1980.13.XV; (10) Bedern south-west, 1976–9.13.X (11) Bedern Trench III/IV (long trench), 1973–5.13.III/IV; (12) Bedern Foundry, 1973.13.I/II. (Reproduced from Ordnance Survey mapping with the permission of Ordnance Survey on behalf of Her Majesty's Stationery Office, © Crown Copyright MC 100012225.) Scale 1:1250*

framed structure were built (Period 2). As the college expanded the vicars required more accommodation. A second hall was constructed along the south-west side of the close, although this appears to have been short-lived, and a smaller structure was built behind it (Period 3). By the late 13th century (Period 4) there were further buildings at the south-west end of Bedern. In the early 14th century the chapel was constructed and there were major changes to the buildings on the south-west side of the close (Period 5). In the middle of the 14th century the college reached the peak of its prosperity; the great hall was rebuilt, apparently to provide separate residences; new individual residences were also built on the south-west side of the close (Period 6). There was major building activity throughout the precinct from the mid 14th to the early 15th century (Period 7), creating a second courtyard to the south-west, and coinciding with attempts to revive the corporate life of the college. The great hall was now rebuilt in stone, and a new stone-built communal hall was constructed south-west of the close, with adjacent service accommodation, kitchen block, archive room and college gardens. The chapel was enlarged and a number of new houses were built. A bridge may also have been built across Goodramgate at this time. A stone wall now marked the limit of the precinct to the south-east, whilst the south-western development of the college was constrained by the continued presence of a medieval foundry. From the mid 15th to the early 17th century (Period 8) there was less new building work although the existing structures continued to be modified as the vicars increasingly lived away and sub-let their houses to lay tenants. During the post-medieval period Bedern became a notorious slum (Period 9).

Analysis of the record of complex floor deposits has shown that there was considerable reworking of many contexts, and much disturbance of earlier layers by subsequent activities. Nonetheless, the development of the buildings — their sub-divisions, rebuildings and renovations — can be clearly traced. Furthermore, they can normally be dated to within 50 years, and sometimes can be equated with building campaigns precisely dated on the basis of documentary evidence. Medieval buildings survived, albeit in increasingly remodelled forms, until the early 17th century. By the mid 17th century, however, many of the medieval buildings had been demolished and replaced.

Table 267 Summary of phasing at sites within the College of Vicars Choral at Bedern (including Bedern long trench, Bedern south-west, Bedern north-east and Bedern Chapel)

Period	Date
Period 0	Roman, Anglian, Anglo-Scandinavian
Period 1A	11th–12th century (applies only to the long trench)
Period 1	early–mid 13th century
Period 2	mid 13th century
Period 3	mid–late 13th century
Period 4	late 13th century
Period 5	early 14th century
Period 6	mid 14th century
Period 7	mid 14th–early 15th century
Period 8	mid 15th–early 17th century
Period 9	mid 17th century onwards

Some buildings within the college precinct, such as the chapel, continued in collegiate use into the post-medieval period. As the number of vicars in the college shrank, and as the remaining vicars increasingly lived outside the precinct, more buildings in Bedern were put to secular uses. This post-medieval/early modern stratification was often recorded to different standards from those employed when dealing with the medieval strata, depending upon the nature, integrity and perceived value of the deposits.

Bedern Foundry

An area of medieval and post-medieval industrial activity adjacent to the college precinct was examined in detail (SE 60515208; Fig.1303, **12**), concentrating on a former narrow lane running off Goodramgate. From the mid–late 13th century to the late 15th–early 16th century the site was occupied by a complex of workshops, which were frequently repaired, remodelled or rebuilt. Many of them were associated with walls, pits and hearths. This occupation and activity was separately phased, and was designated Periods 1–5 (Table 268). From Period 2, the late 13th–early 14th century onwards, deposits of clay mould fragments and other casting debris

Table 268 Summary of phasing at Bedern Foundry

Period	Date
Period 0	late 12th–early 13th century
Period 1	mid–late 13th century
Period 2	late 13th–early 14th century
Period 3	14th century
Phase 1	early 14th century
Phase 2	early–mid 14th century
Phases 3–5	mid–late 14th century
Phase 6	late 14th century
Period 4	15th century
Phases 1–2	early 15th century
Phases 3–4	early–mid 15th century
Phases 5–9	mid–late 15th century
Period 5	late 15th–early 16th century
Phase 1	late 15th century
Phases 2–4	late 15th–early 16th century
Period 6	mid 16th–mid 17th century
Period 7	mid 17th–20th century

Table 269 Summary of phasing at 2 Aldwark

Building phases	Date
Building 1	late 13th–early 14th century
Building 2	
Phase 1	early–mid 14th century
Phase 2	later 14th–early 15th century
Phase 3	15th century
Building 3	late 15th–16th century

were sometimes found. These indicate that founding was carried out, and that the foundry's main products were cauldrons and other domestic vessels. Structures with substantial stone walls were erected c.1300 and remained in use throughout the 14th century (Period 3); c.1400 all the buildings in the foundry complex were rebuilt and the alleyway was both extended and linked, via a 90° continuation, to the property of the adjacent College of the Vicars Choral (Period 4). In the later 15th–early 16th century (Period 5) there was another phase of building development; the earlier ground plan was, however, retained. During Period 6 (mid 16th–mid 17th century) metal-working furnaces and hearths were replaced by a series of ovens, and the deposition of foundry waste ceased. Some parts of the complex apparently became derelict, but the remainder functioned as a bakery, a usage attested in the name Baker's Lane. From the mid 17th to the 20th century (Period 7) light industrial usage dominated the area.

2 Aldwark

This site (SE 60585214), designated as Area III of the main site of Bedern north-east (1978–80.14.III; Fig.1303, **2**), lies within the medieval walled city, near the junction of Aldwark with St Andrewgate (see *AY* 10/2, 89–112). A series of medieval structures and associated features was investigated. A discrete phasing system exists for 2 Aldwark (see Table 269).

The excavations of medieval tenements at 2 Aldwark have already been published in *AY* 10/2. The pottery from the site is described in *AY* 16/3. Bedern Foundry has been published in *AY* 10/3. Roman occupation in the Bedern area has been discussed in *AY* 3/3. The coins have been published in *AY* 18/1; the pottery will be published in *AY* 16/9. The structural report for the College of Vicars Choral site has been published in *AY* 10/5. The considerable number of re-used architectural fragments recovered from the excavations have been published in *AY* 10/4. Historical research on the tenemental history of the Bedern and Aldwark area will be published in *AY* 20.

Excavation at 46–54 Fishergate (Fig.1304)
By R.L. Kemp

The site comprised two adjacent open areas and a series of narrow trenches totalling c.2,500m² (SE 60655115). It lay directly to the east of the confluence of the Rivers Ouse and Foss, west of the medieval street Fishergate (modern Fawcett Street and George Street) which may be on the line of a Roman road from Foss Bridge, and to the south of the Walmgate medieval suburb. This is also where the east-west morainic ridge across the Vale of York meets the River Ouse, and forms a natural crossing point. The sequence of development is discussed below and summarised in Table 270.

The earliest recorded deposits from the site were the natural clays with pebble and cobble inclusions typical of the glacial drift under much of York (Period

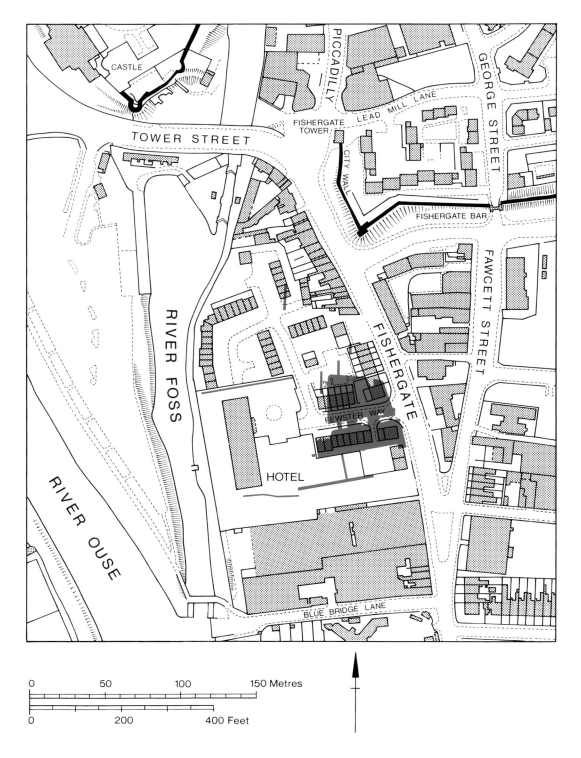

Fig.1304 *Plan showing the position of the excavations (in red) at 46–54 Fishergate. (Reproduced from Ordnance Survey mapping with the permission of Ordnance Survey on behalf of Her Majesty's Stationery Office, © Crown Copyright MC 100012225.) Scale 1:2500*

Table 270 Summary of archaeological development at 46–54 Fishergate

Period	Description	Characteristics
1	Natural subsoil	Till and fluvio-glacial sands, and clays with gravel
2 1st–4th century	Roman agricultural activity	Plough scores, minor ditches, mixed natural deposit containing abraded Roman pottery
3a Late 7th/early 8th–early 9th century	Part of Anglian trading settlement	Properties delineated by ditches and lines of pits, and containing structures, pit groups, ?middens
3b Later 8th or early 9th century	?Levelling of first settlement	Period 3a pits and structures covered by distinctive horizontal charcoal-laden deposit spread; site possibly re-organised
3c Within first half of 9th century	Re-occupation of settlement area	Major ditch and a few pit groups (no discernible structures)
3z Late 7th/early 8th–mid 9th century	Features not linked to Periods 3a–c	Pits, ditches etc. (probably belong to Period 3a)
4a Late 10th/first half of 11th century	New settlement established	Structure in south-eastern corner and pits/post-holes to south-west. Latest pottery in fills is Stamford ware
4b Mid 11th–?mid 12th century	Cemetery and church (south-west), new building (south-east)	Burials and possible timber church in south-west, replacement structure to south-east
4c ?Later 11th or 12th century	Church possibly rebuilt in stone (south-west)	Construction deposits over Period 4b burials
4d 12th century	Continued use of cemetery and settlement	Burials in cemetery area, pits and post-holes over structures in the south-east
4z 11th–12th century	Features not linked to Periods 4a–d	Pits, burials etc.
5 1142/3–1195	St Andrew's in the possession of Newburgh Priory	Historical reference only. Period not distinguished archaeologically

1). Shallow scores in the surface of the natural subsoil and two shallow, meandering ditches associated with much abraded Roman pottery probably represented ploughing and either field boundaries or drains (Period 2). An even, site-wide, deposit of disturbed natural clay also contained abraded Roman sherds and was interpreted as tilth containing material from middens possibly spread as manure.

The Roman surface was cut by an extensive complex of pits, ditches and post-holes dated by pottery, coins and artefacts to between the very late 7th or

Table 270 (*contd*)

Period	Description	Characteristics
6a 1195–late 13th century	Gilbertine priory in original form	New monastic complex built in stone. Burials
6b Late 13th–early 14th century	First modifications to priory	Minor adjustments within church and rebuilding of cloister alley. Road/yard south of nave. Burials
6c Early–mid 14th century	Substantial alterations to priory	Complete rebuilding of church and east range, substantial changes in north range. Burials
6d Late 14th–15th century	Further modifications to priory	New fittings in church, alterations in east and north ranges, buttresses in cloister alley
6e 15th/16th century	Continued use and modifications to site	Adjustments to north range. Well, cess pit etc. in southern part of site
6f 16th century	Final modifications in north range	Adjustments to partitions in north range
6z 13th–16th century	Features not linked to Periods 6a–f	Pits, burials, agricultural/horticultural deposits, hearths etc. Ditches north of priory area
7a c.1538	Demolition of church, cloisters and east range	Robbed wall foundations, heavy layer of rubble, window glass, limekiln
7b c.1540	Demolition of north range	Partially robbed wall cores
7c Second half of 16th century	Secular occupation of west range	Pits containing much animal bone, artefacts and pottery cut through robbed walls of north range
8 c.17th–19th century	Orchards	Extensive layer of dark loam
9 c.1870–1900	Early glass factory	Brick foundations
10 c.1900–1984	Modern glass factory	Modern buildings, concrete floors, services, pipes etc.

early 8th century and the mid 9th century (*AY* 7/1). Over part of the site, two sets of features were stratigraphically separated from each other by an extensive horizontal deposit.

The first signs of occupation comprised a series of boundary ditches, pits and structures (Period 3a). This settlement is thought to represent a small part of the trading *wic* from which *Eoforwic* or Anglian

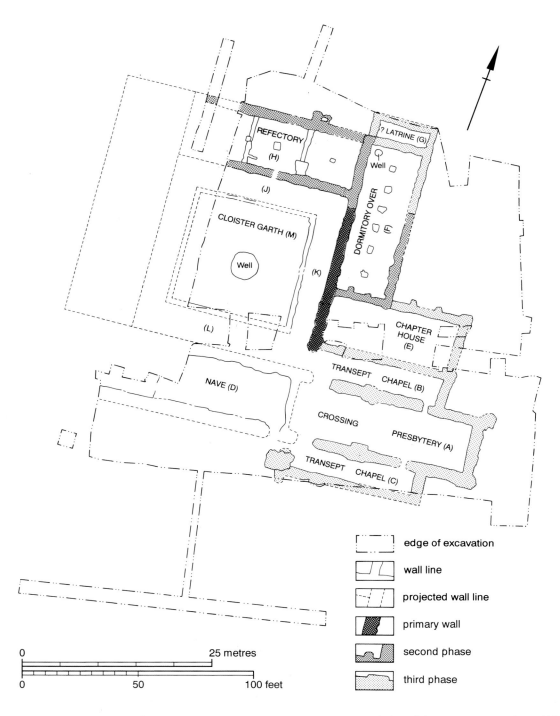

Fig.1305 *Order of construction of the original (Period 6a) priory and reconstructed plan of the west range at 46–54 Fishergate. (Room notation explained in AY 11/2). Scale 1:500*

York derives the second part of its name. The settlement appears to come to an abrupt end with evidence for structures being rapidly dismantled and pits systematically backfilled. All were covered by a highly distinctive charcoal-laden deposit (Period 3b). The finds generally resembled those of Period 3a and the

layer appears to represent the contents of Period 3a middens and other debris systematically spread across the dismantled and levelled settlement, with a large amount of charcoal introduced to the upper surface perhaps for purposes connected with hygiene or health (*AY 7/1*). The charcoal-laden deposit was

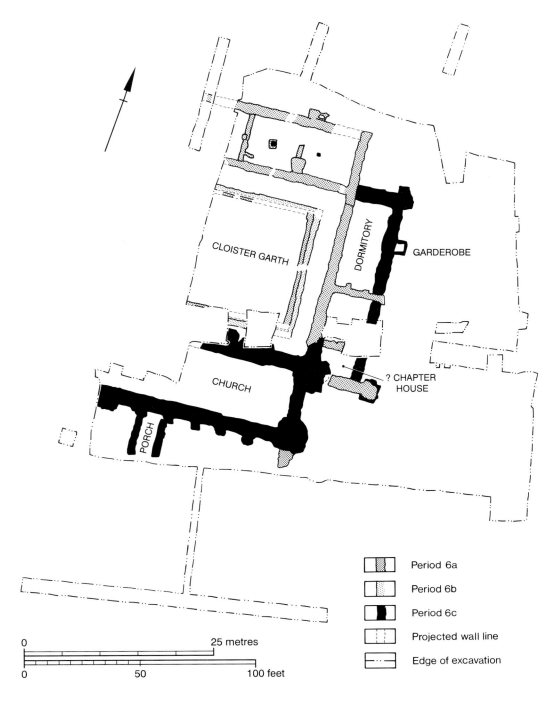

CLOISTER GARTH

DORMITORY

GARDEROBE

CHURCH

PORCH

? CHAPTER
HOUSE

	Period 6a
	Period 6b
	Period 6c
	Projected wall line
	Edge of excavation

0   25 metres

0   50   100 feet

Fig.1306 *Plan of the priory in Period 6c. Scale 1:500*

cut by a new boundary ditch associated with a number of pit groups (Period 3c). This new settlement was less intense and less extensive than that seen in Period 3a, but the assemblages from the two periods are generally similar.

This more limited settlement may have continued into the later 850s but, from the evidence of both coinage and pottery, it is unlikely to have been occupied long after the Viking capture of York in 866. The site remained abandoned until c.1000 and produced none of the distinctive pottery assemblages of the later 9th and 10th centuries.

Evidence for the re-occupation of the site comprises a series of refuse pits and structures dated by pottery to the late 10th or early 11th century (Period 4a). In the south-western corner of the site the pits were superseded by a cemetery associated with a possible timber church (Period 4b). This church may have been replaced in stone on an adjacent site, perhaps in the second half of the 11th century (Period 4c), and burials continued in the cemetery area throughout the 12th century (Period 4d). The church is most likely to have been that dedicated to St Andrew, which was in the hands of Hugh FitzBaldric in 1086 (Domesday Book; Burton in *AY* 11/2). In the south-eastern part of the site a sequence of superimposed structures and pits (Periods 4a, b and d), spanning the 11th and 12th centuries, was broadly contemporary with deposits in the south-west.

The Period 4 features were part of a settlement that may have belonged to a continuous ribbon suburb represented by a string of early churches on either side of medieval Fishergate. This route, running south from Foss Bridge, may have had Roman origins; it declined in importance, particularly after the postulated suburb was cut in two by the erection of the Walmgate section of the city defences in the 12th or 13th century.

The church of St Andrew, Fishergate, receives further historical reference in 1142/3, when it is recorded as being in the hands of Newburgh Priory (Period 5), and at the end of the 12th century it formed the basis of the donation to the Gilbertine Order for their new priory (Period 6). The archaeological deposits which presumably belonged to Period 5 form a continuous series with those of Period 4, and it was not possible to separate them stratigraphically.

Levels attributed to both Periods 3 and 4 were sealed beneath a single deposit of imported earth interpreted as the remains of a foundation platform for the new priory of St Andrew of the Order of St Gilbert of Sempringham, begun in 1195 and dedicated in 1202. The original structures (Period 6a) comprised a cruciform church to the south of the cloister, probably with a low central tower, north and south transepts with eastern chapels, a presbytery and an aisleless nave; a chapter house with possible west-

ern vestibule; an eastern dormitory with latrines to the north; and a northern refectory (Fig.1305). All were linked by a continuous alley around the cloister garth. A presumed western range had been destroyed by the modern factory. Architectural fragments and an extensive assemblage of window glass broadly confirmed the historical date of construction and both showed some Cistercian influence. There was evidence that both the church and chapter house were glazed from the outset.

The priory underwent certain modifications (Period 6b) including the rebuilding of the cloister arcade and minor works in the church, which can be tentatively dated by coins and pottery to the late 13th or early 14th century.

In the 14th century there was an extensive programme of alterations in which the church, east range and chapter house were rebuilt, and the undercroft of the north range, previously used for storage, was possibly converted for use as a ground floor refectory or as domestic apartments (Period 6c; Fig.1306). An historical reference to funding of certain building works at the priory in c.1335 by Henry Burghersh, Bishop of Lincoln, may provide a context for these alterations. This rebuilding in the latest architectural styles inevitably necessitated the re-fenestration of the church in contemporary style.

The priory continued to be altered and adapted in minor ways (Periods 6d–f), until its dissolution in 1538 (Period 7a). The buildings were demolished and a lime kiln was built in the cloister garth using elements of the cloister arcade. This heralded the wholesale robbing of the entire complex for building materials, including the customary interest in lead from both roofs and windows. Clearly the windows of the priory had been stripped primarily for their lead came, and a considerable assemblage of glass fragments was excavated from a heap in the nave of the final church. It was the absence of came that suggested this was a lead robber's working area, and that the glass represented waste following this process.

The northern range may have been used as stables and/or a store during early demolition operations until it was also demolished and robbed of all usable building materials (Period 7b). The final period of occupation is marked by rubbish pits, cut through the western end of the north range, which can be dated to the later 16th century; it is possible that the missing west range provided living quarters at this time (Period 7c).

The site was virtually abandoned and used as an orchard (Period 8) until it was partly occupied by an extension of the adjacent glass factory in the later 19th century (Period 9). By the 20th century the entire site was under intensive industrial use (Period 10).

The Fishergate excavations are published in detail in *AY* 7/1 (Anglian period) and *AY* 11/2 (medieval period, including the architectural fragments from all periods); the pottery is in *AY* 16/6; Anglian and other finds are in *AY* 17/9; the window glass is in *AY* 11/3; and the coins will be in *AY* 18/2. The animal bones appear in *AY* 15/4, while all other biological remains were scarce and are therefore reported in brief in the appropriate fascicules.

Conservation Report

By J. Jones, with a contribution on objects from 22 Piccadilly by E. Paterson

Introduction

Conservation of the finds for this fascicule was undertaken by staff and students at the York Archaeological Trust Conservation Laboratories between 1973 and 1997. The variety of approaches taken reflects the changes and advances in the discipline during this time (see pp.1516–19, *AY* 17/10). These approaches also reflect the differences in preservation between the sites. The conservation strategy adopted during the preparation of this fascicule required a sharp focus because it was clear that the entire assemblage could not be conserved to meet current publication standards in the time and with the resources available.

The material from excavations at 46–54 Fishergate had been conserved in the late 1980s and early 1990s (pp.1218–23, *AY* 17/9). The conservation of osseous materials, wood and leather from all the sites reported here are discussed in *AY* 17/12, *AY* 17/13 and *AY* 17/16 (in prep.) respectively. Of the other objects from these sites, those made of iron constituted the largest and most significant assemblage, and they were therefore chosen to receive a full assessment and an investigative programme of conservation for this fascicule.

Iron

Coppergate

Much of the ironwork from medieval contexts at 16–22 Coppergate and the watching brief site had been conserved and studied at the same time as that from Anglo-Scandinavian contexts during preparation of *AY* 17/6; the burial environment, subsequent corrosion, storage requirements and techniques used to investigate and protect the artefacts are discussed there (pp.466–71).

The aims of the current project were, firstly, to ensure that all 2,000 or so iron objects from medieval contexts at Coppergate had been X-rayed and, secondly, to select those requiring further investigation. Some 500 items were selected for conservation for one or more of three reasons: to enable identification

of objects not identifiable from X-rays; to allow accurate illustration; to reveal non-ferrous inlay or plating. Objects with surviving traces of mineral-preserved organic materials and remains of non-ferrous metals (platings, inlays, brazing metal, solder and metalworking debris) were sent to the Ancient Monuments Laboratory for analysis and identification. Both paper and electronic records were updated and the ironwork was securely packed and stored in desiccated boxes. The conservation and external consultants' records, along with any photographs, X-radiographs, slides and video footage, form an important part of the site archive.

The corrosion found on those objects which had not previously been conserved was similar to that described by O'Connor in *AY* 17/6, but ten further years of storage had caused some additional deterioration. Areas of the surface had begun to flake off, exposing a bright orange powdery corrosion above the bare metal core, often accompanied by small crusty spheres exuding a yellow-brown liquid (Turgoose 1982). These reactions require only oxygen and water to continue, so a rigid adherence to dry storage (<15%RH) is essential to the survival of the assemblage, although this has been difficult to achieve in practice whilst the objects were being studied.

Selective removal of corrosion using the air abrasive usually allowed the identification of objects and exposed any non-ferrous plating for analysis. This close examination often yielded further technological observations. For example, non-ferrous globules and metalworking debris were found incorporated in corrosion on *11921* and *11964*, solder was found on *12991* and a serrated edge was revealed on sickle *12980* (see Fig.1351, p.2746).

Some 300 objects were cleaned for illustration and they presented some additional problems. Unfortunately, some information has been lost on the objects which had been treated either chemically or electrolytically in the 1970s to strip away corrosion and this cannot be retrieved (see *12643* on Fig.1456 and compare with the same key as it is today on Fig.1457, pp.2878–9). However, improved X-radiography and air abrasive equipment have revealed new information on many other objects. For example, handle remains were found on awl *11506*; plating, and details of leaf spring and case construction were found on padlocks such as *12563*, *12572* and *12597* (Fig.1448, p.2871); the shape of stem and bits was clarified and decoration exposed on keys such as *12599*, *12608* and *12658*. Hardened cutting edges (*11854*), piled structures (*11809* and *11855*), notches on the tang to secure the handle (*11853*; Fig.1358, p.2755) and stamped decoration (*11854*; Fig.1358) were found on knives.

The entire collection of iron objects has not been systematically surveyed, their original condition is not well documented, the treatment details vary, the storage history is not known, and changes have not been recorded or measured. A quantitative condition survey and assessment of the collection is recommended for the future.

22 Piccadilly

Twenty-five iron objects from Anglo-Scandinavian and medieval contexts at 22 Piccadilly were selected for investigative conservation. The corrosion products were very similar to those on objects from Coppergate. The crusts varied considerably in appearance and texture but the most predominant corrosion product appeared to be vivianite, suggesting a similar low-oxygen, high-phosphate burial environment. Preservation of the metal core and surface detail varied. The metal core survived almost intact on a small number of objects with thin and relatively non-disruptive corrosion crusts. However, patchy or complete depletion of the metal core has occurred in a large proportion of objects, as has a noticeable disruption of surface detail.

An important factor affecting the condition and interpretation of the material from Piccadilly was the extent of active post-excavation corrosion. Eighty-eight percent of the assemblage showed signs of active corrosion, almost certainly the result of a breakdown in dry storage conditions. Information surviving in the replacement corrosion has been put at risk. Most objects displayed cracking, distortion and flaking, and revealed characteristic spots of bright orange powder at the metal surface and 'weeping' from cracks.

Corrosion removal helped to confirm the identification of many items and revealed a variety of technological details. Evidence of metalworking in the form of tool marks survives on a number of objects: vessel handle *13037* (Fig.1393, p.2809) has large hammer marks and *13019*, a small punch, is heavily distorted by hammering towards its narrow end (Fig.1328, p.2721). File marks survive on knife blades *13036* and *15324*. Another knife blade (*15335*) and an axe-head (*13020*) have hardened cutting edges visible in the replacement corrosion.

Blobs of non-ferrous metal, and traces of lead and copper, within the corrosion crust on a small punch (*15323*) are likely to be the debris from metalworking. Non-ferrous plating was detected on a number of objects and other forms of decoration were revealed: incised decoration (*15324*; Fig.1554, p.3005), applied strips of wire (*13045*; Fig.1442, p.2865), grooves (*13034*, *15333*) and bevelled edges (*13036*, *15330*) on knife blades.

Mineral-preserved organic material survives on a number of items. Part of the wood stake survives inside ferrule *13044*, remains of a knife handle survive on the tang of *15333*, and wood survives on the inside of one of the large hinge fittings.

Bedern

Iron from the College, Foundry and Chapel sites at Bedern contrasted markedly in appearance with that from Coppergate and Piccadilly. It was generally covered in very extensive orange-brown corrosion deposits, often incorporating stones, tile, charcoal, bone, straw, seeds, etc. This corrosion was thick, dense, well attached and often difficult to remove. In many cases (e.g. *13267*) the entire metal core had corroded (Turgoose 1982, 6), leaving only a hollow 'cast' of the object preserved in a large lump of corrosion. The blue vivianite and lustrous sulphides seen on the ironwork from phosphate-rich, waterlogged, anoxic environments on Coppergate were not present on the artefacts from Bedern. Post-excavation corrosion was often severe due to fluctuating and varied storage regimes, and many objects had fragmented. It was common to find twenty or more fragments per bag; sometimes they had passed the point of redemption and the X-rays provide the only complete record.

Some conservation was undertaken in the 1970s, as in the case of Coppergate. In 1987 Dr I. Goodall began a programme of research, requiring selective cleaning and new X-rays to answer specific queries. A dozen objects with tinned surfaces were treated at this time using tannic acid (p.1220, *AY* 17/9). A recent examination of these found two-thirds in excellent condition, with no visible corrosion. The remaining one-third have a few small patches of bright orange powder, confirming that this treatment alone does not provide reliable protection.

In 1995, 30 boxes stored as bulk finds were found to contain iron objects. Some 600 items were revealed by a programme of X-radiography, nearly doubling the assemblage of ironwork from the Bedern sites. These included a file (*13687*; Fig.1331, p.2723), a spoon auger (*13692*), awls (*13164, 13709*), locks (*14056–7*; Fig.1448, p.2871), keys (*14084*; Fig.1452, p.2874), knives (*13792*; Fig.1363, p.2758), arrowheads (*13293, 14164*) and a Jew's harp (*14117*; Fig.1517, p.2949). Some 220 objects were selected for further investigation using the criteria discussed above for Coppergate. Because of the very dense corrosion, few of the Bedern objects were completely cleaned for illustration, and X-radiographs were consequently very important.

As with the Coppergate material, many technological observations were made during the conservation phase. Small spheres of non-ferrous metal and fragments of hammer scale were incorporated in many of the corrosion products, which could help to indicate areas of metalworking on site (e.g. *13771*).

Other materials

The vast majority of objects made from materials other than iron which are discussed in this fascicule were not examined by a conservator as part of the publication project; they have only had initial stabilisation treatment or conservation at the time of excavation. The methodology described by Spriggs in *AY* 17/14 (pp.2467–9) also applies here. There was no investigative strategy behind the selection for conservation, so many objects which might yield further information about craft or industry may not have been investigated, especially if their condition was very poor or fragmentary, or if they were believed to represent industrial waste.

With the exception of the non-ferrous metal objects from 22 Piccadilly, the copper alloys were rou-

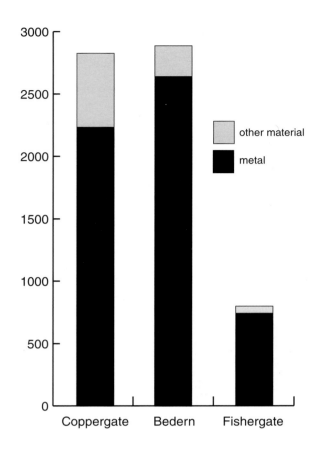

Fig.1307   Comparison of the ratio of finds of metal to finds of other inorganic materials from Coppergate, Bedern (all sites) and Fishergate

tinely stabilised and lacquered in the 1970s and 1980s. Alison Goodall began a programme of research on the Bedern material in 1986–7 and a large number of objects were investigated at that time; those revealing surface coatings were sent for XRF analysis. Copper alloy is not X-rayed routinely, however, so hidden decorative features, surface coatings and constructional details may not have been explored or recorded.

Ten copper alloy objects and one lead alloy object from 22 Piccadilly were selected for investigative conservation. Some were selectively cleaned to reveal specific surface details, such as the heads of pins (*13066–8*); others merited full removal of corrosion for research or illustration (*13076, 13060, 13054* and *13061*). Three objects were sent for XRF analysis (*13066, 13068* and *13060*). Ring *13061* shows a casting flash.

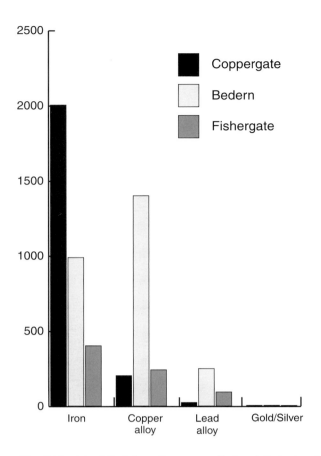

Fig.1308   *Metal finds from Coppergate, Bedern (all sites) and Fishergate*

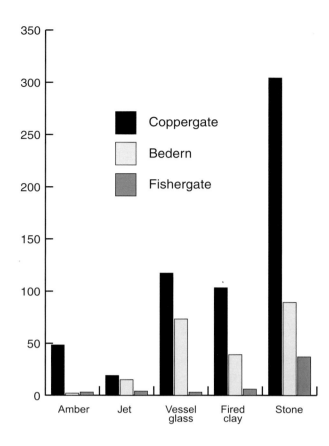

Fig.1309   *Non-metal finds from Coppergate, Bedern (all sites) and Fishergate*

The non-ferrous metalworking debris and slag from Bedern has been studied by C. Mortimer (see pp.2708–12), but no other slag has been included. It is known, however, from the study of finds from Fishergate (p.1220, *AY* 17/9) that heavily corroded objects are often misidentified on site as slag, and that a selective programme of X-radiography can help to distinguish them.

Discussion

One of the duties of a conservator, in addition to examining each individual object, is to view the assemblage as a whole and to help determine whether any biases have been introduced by differential preservation of materials on site, by retrieval techniques, or by selection for treatment (Ancient Monuments Laboratory 1995). The introduction of computerised databases has made this overview possible. Figures 1307–13 are based on total numbers of objects selected for research at the start of the project, some of which have not been catalogued.

Figure 1307 compares the ratio of metals to other inorganic materials and their total quantities by site (all the Bedern sites are considered as one). Metals comprise the largest proportion of artefacts from each assemblage, despite differing burial environments. Fishergate produced many fewer finds from the medieval period than the other two sites, even though more extensive sieving was undertaken on that site. The surviving metals from Fishergate do not appear to be in any worse condition than those from Bedern, so the soil conditions are unlikely to explain this fact. Fishergate covered a similar area to Bedern, although the volume of deposits was far less than at Coppergate. The relatively small number of objects from Fishergate probably relates to the character of the settlement and the location of the excavation trenches within the church and other priory buildings rather than in areas used for refuse disposal.

Figures 1308–9 examine the collection by material. Coppergate has consistently higher proportions

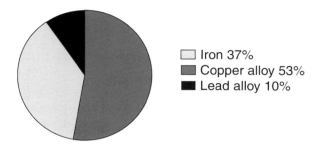

Fig.1310   *Ratio of ferrous to non-ferrous metals at all Bedern sites before the addition of ironwork from bulk finds*

Iron 37%
Copper alloy 53%
Lead alloy 10%

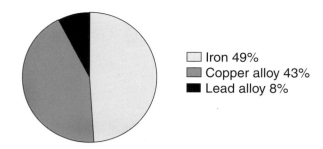

Fig.1311   *Ratio of ferrous to non-ferrous metals at all Bedern sites after the addition of ironwork from bulk finds*

Iron 49%
Copper alloy 43%
Lead alloy 8%

of all non-metals than the other sites. The Bedern sites have most copper alloy and Coppergate the highest proportion of ironwork. Again, these differences cannot be explained by burial conditions. It is possible that difference in the ratio of ferrous to non-ferrous metals between Bedern and Coppergate may point to a functional difference between the ecclesiastical and secular site assemblages.

Figures 1310–13 show the effect of adding bulk finds. They illustrate how a bias can be introduced by selective treatment of finds. At the time of excavation these bulk finds from all the Bedern sites were not considered worth recording individually as small finds or by X-radiography. The results of the current X-radiographic programme have, however, proved of value (see above) and bring the ratio of ferrous to non-ferrous finds from Bedern much more in line with that at Fishergate (Fig.1312). None the less, even after the addition of the ironwork from the Bedern

bulk finds, the two sites occupied entirely or in part by ecclesiatical institutions have a much greater percentage of non-ferrous metals than the secular Coppergate site (Fig.1313).

Very few lead alloy objects from Fishergate received treatment, but Buckingham (*AY* 17/9) notes that all the lead was examined in the laboratory, selectively treated in order to retrieve maximum information, and properly packed and stored, so this assemblage is less of a cause for concern than might at first be expected. Fired clay and stone were not treated in the laboratory, but their robust nature generally requires little stabilisation or consolidation, although packing and storage requirements may not have been addressed. Details of the treatment of iron objects were not available on database at the time of writing. This aspect of the finds assemblage could be examined in the future.

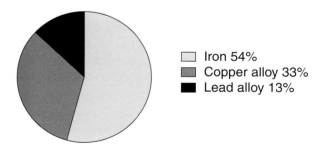

Fig.1312   *Ratio of ferrous to non-ferrous metals at Fishergate*

Iron 54%
Copper alloy 33%
Lead alloy 13%

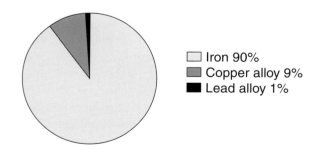

Fig.1313   *Ratio of ferrous to non-ferrous metals at Coppergate*

Iron 90%
Copper alloy 9%
Lead alloy 1%

Summary

The conservation work for this fascicule has encompassed 25 years of research and development. During this time significant information has been recorded about the assemblages from the sites under consideration. The artefacts catalogued here are now held as far as possible in stable storage environments, but many productive areas of research remain to be explored in the future. The collection of medieval iron slag and the database of XRF analyses of alloys, plating metals and solders could be used in a systematic study of metalworking technology. More work could be done to identify factors involved in site formation and to assess the effect of burial environment on artefacts. Finally, because a wide variety of experimental treatments have been used on this collection, a review of the current condition of each artefact could lead to improvements in contemporary conservation practice.

Fig.1314 *Other sites in York mentioned in the text*

1   County Hospital
2   York Minster
3   St Mary's Abbey
4   21–33 Aldwark
5   St Andrew's Church, St Andrewgate
6   12–18 Swinegate
7   St Andrewgate
8   Parliament Street sewer trench

9   34 Shambles
10   11–13 Parliament Street
11   North Street
12   Lloyds Bank, Pavement
13   Church of St Mary Castlegate
14   Skeldergate
15   Baile Hill

Craft and Industry

The first part of this fascicule deals with the evidence for a range of crafts and industries. The distinction between the two is not always easy to make in a medieval context as even in the later medieval period manufacturing was usually household-based and required little capital investment in equipment (Swanson 1989, 127). A craft is, however, taken to be a small-scale manufacturing activity using little or no specialist equipment while an industry produced goods on a relatively large scale and employed a certain amount of fixed equipment such as hearths or water tanks in a specialist workshop, not necessarily the residence of the workers who included people beyond the owner's immediate family. In the former category may be placed such activities as bone working, woodworking and certain aspects, at least, of textile production. In the latter category may be included some forms of metalworking, such as that practised at the Foundry, pottery making (not included in this fascicule) and aspects of textile production, such as fulling and dyeing. Building may be described as an industry on account of the scale

1   Newcastle upon Tyne
2   Durham
3   Ripon
4   Wharram Percy
5   York
6   Beverley
7   Kirkstall Abbey
8   Hull
9   Sandal Castle
10 Goltho
11 Nottingham
12 Chester
13 Derby
14 Dudley Castle
15 Leicester
16 King's Lynn
17 North Elmham
18 Norwich
19 Weoley Castle
20 Bordesley Abbey
21 Northampton
22 Eynsham Abbey
23 Oxford
24 London
25 Blunden's Wood
26 Newbury
27 Ospringe
28 Canterbury
29 Winchester
30 Gomeldon
31 Salisbury
32 Southampton
33 Battle Abbey
34 Exeter

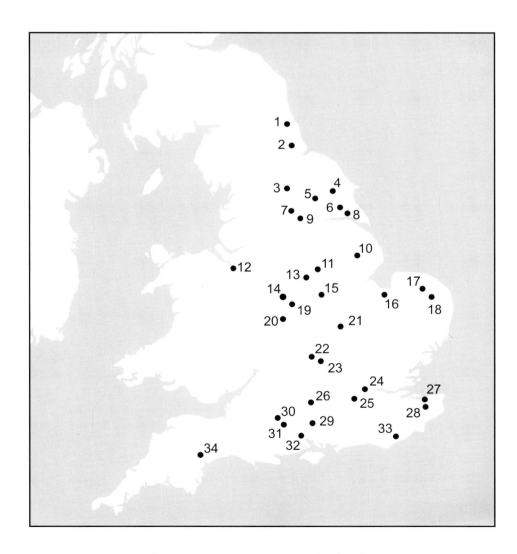

Fig. 1315   *Map of Britain showing main sites mentioned in the text*

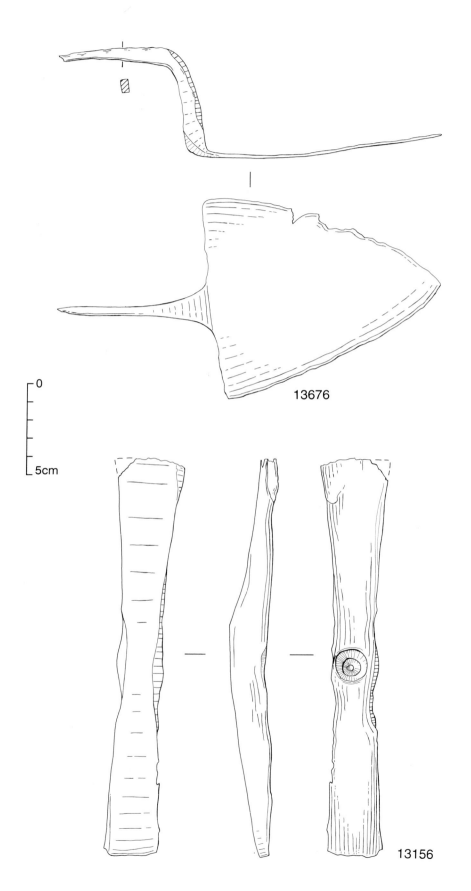

13676

13156

0

5cm

Fig.1316 *Builders' tools: trowel*
13676 *from Bedern; pickaxe head*
13156 *from the Foundry. Scale 1:2*

of operations, although most of those employed in it were unskilled or semi-skilled and performed routine tasks (ibid., 82).

Building

A small number of tools associated with building construction were recovered from across the sites, and may relate to construction and/or demolition of structures identified by excavations at the sites, and described in the relevant fascicules: *AY* 10/3, *The Bedern Foundry*; *AY* 10/5, *The Vicars Choral of York Minster: The College at Bedern*; *AY* 10/6, *Buildings and Land Use at and around Medieval Coppergate*; and *AY* 11/2, *The Church and Gilbertine Priory of St Andrew, Fishergate*.

Building tools (Fig.1316)

Trowels

There are four trowels, two from Bedern (*13676*, mid 14th–15th century context and *13675*, mid 14th century context), one from an unstratified deposit at Coppergate (*11459*) and one from Fishergate (*14858*, 13th century context). They are of similar form and size and would have been used by masons, bricklayers or plasterers. Each has a cranked tang and *14858* has the remains of the wooden handle surviving. They also have large triangular blades suitable for spreading mortar or plaster and *13675* was found in a mortar floor deposit in Building 16 at Bedern (Period 6; *AY* 10/5, p.454).

Pickaxe heads

13156, found in an early 14th century context at the Foundry, is probably a pickaxe head. It has a wedge-shaped tip at each end. In the centre there is a socket which, curiously, does not go through the complete thickness of the object perhaps to avoid weakening it. Presumably a wooden handle was positioned in the socket and then secured by cords or some other means. This is an unusual object and there appear to be no comparable examples. It was probably used for digging foundations or demolishing walls.

14859 is large pickaxe head, 435mm long, from a dissolution period context at Fishergate and may even have been one of the tools used to demolish the priory buildings.

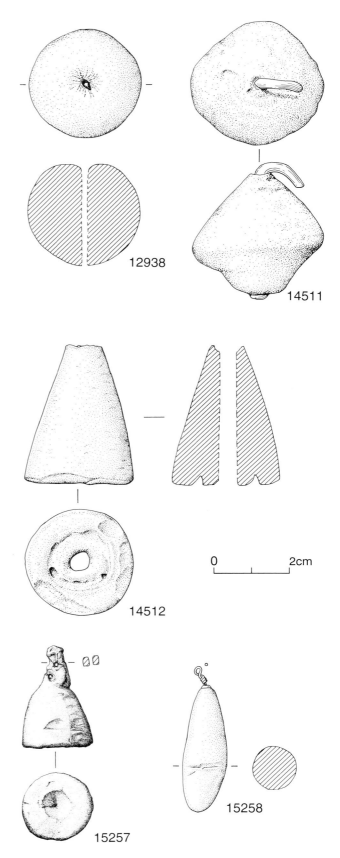

Fig.1317 *Plumb-bobs 12938 from 16–22 Coppergate, 14511–12 from Bedern, 15257–8 from 46–54 Fishergate. Scale 1:1*

Plumb-bobs (Fig.1317)

A varied group of lead alloy weights, *12938, 14511–12, 15257–8*, are united by the common factor of having a means of suspension; all may have been used as plumb-bobs. Two weights make use of copper alloy for suspension: the biconical example (*14511*) has a copper alloy staple running through it, forming a suspension hook at one end; inside the lead the staple has a more flattened section to prevent it from twisting or sliding out. Weight *15258* has an elongated oval shape, and a copper alloy twisted wire suspension loop. The other Fishergate plumb-bob (*15257*) has an integral loop formed by perforating the drawn out and flattened upper end. *14512*, of a similar conical shape, is axially perforated, as is the spherical *12938*.

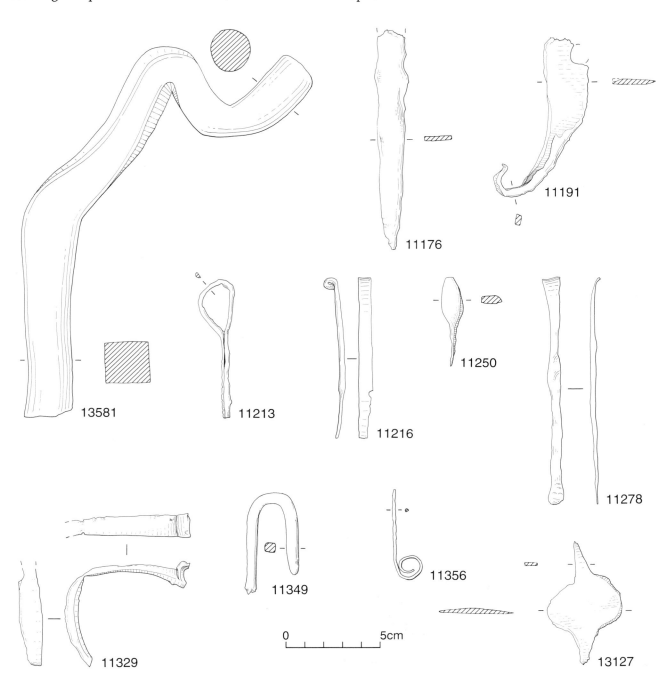

Fig.1318 *Debris from ironworking in the form of bars, strips and plates: 11176, 11191, 11213, 11216, 11250, 11278, 11329, 11349, 11356 from 16–22 Coppergate; 13127 from the Foundry; 13581 from Bedern. Scale 1:2*

Although any of the above could have functioned as hanging weights, similarly shaped objects have been identified elsewhere as plumb-bobs (Jones 1990, 304–6, fig.71a; Moorhouse and Wrathmell 1987, 136, fig.71, 231). Several of the York examples, including both from Fishergate, were recovered from construction levels; 15257 came from a Period 6a levelling deposit, close to the spot where an iron trowel (14858) was found, both perhaps lost during building works (see above). 15258 came from soil dumped within the chancel during preparation for a new floor in Period 6b. One of the Bedern plumb-bobs (14511) was also retrieved from levels associated with a new building, Building 11, constructed in the late 13th–early 14th century.

Metalworking

The evidence for metalworking exists as debris from both ironworking and non-ferrous metalworking and also a small number of tools.

Ironworking (Fig.1318)

Coppergate produced c.300 items which may be classified as bars, strips or plates according to the criteria given in AY 17/6 (pp.492–502), which are that bars and strips have a maximum width to thickness ratio less than 4:1, but bars are distinguished from strips by having a product of width and thickness over 300mm². Plates have a maximum width to thickness ratio greater than 4:1.

Some of the items from medieval contexts are probably fragments of finished objects which can no longer be identified, but the majority are likely to be offcuts or partly forged items from the smithing process (e.g. 11191, 11213, 11216, 11278, 11329, 11349). Since there is little evidence for metalworking on the Coppergate site in the medieval period, they are likely to be residual from the Anglo-Scandinavian period. The Foundry, Bedern and Fishergate have also produced a few bars, strips and plates. At the first two sites they are likely to be fragments of broken objects and at the latter some may be residual from smithing activity in the Anglian period. Of particular interest, however, is 13581, a very large misshapen bar (245mm in length with a cross-section 26 × 26mm) from a late 14th–early 15th century context at Bedern (Fig.1318). This is probably freshly smelted iron intended for use in a smithy, but how it came to be deposited at Bedern is unknown. No smithy is known of in the College of the Vicars Choral, although smithing may have taken place from time to time to answer the needs of construction works. For a representation of medieval ironworking in progress see Fig.1319.

Non-ferrous metalworking

A comprehensive account of non-ferrous metalworking in both the Anglo-Scandinavian and medieval periods at 16–22 Coppergate has already been published, concluding that a wide range of metals

Fig.1319   Ironworking hearth, c.1340, from The Romance of Alexander *(Bodleian MS Bodl. 264, fo.82r)*

were worked, particularly in the Anglo-Scandinavian period (pp.816–17, *AY* 17/7). A similar range of metals appear to have been worked on a smaller scale in the Anglian and 11th–12th century periods at Fishergate (pp.1232–9, *AY* 17/9). The archaeological report on the Foundry includes details of the metalworking practices carried out there based on analysis of mould fragments and metalworking debris such as slag and spillages (*AY* 10/3), but a larger-scale qualitative analysis survey of the metal waste from both the Foundry and Bedern has since been carried out and the results are presented below. Evidence for non-ferrous metalworking at medieval Fishergate, 22 Piccadilly and 2 Aldwark is also included below.

Bedern and the Foundry

Analysis of material from high-temperature processes, including a re-examination of material from the Foundry

By Catherine Mortimer

Introduction

Structural and artefactual evidence revealed during the 1973–6 excavations showed that large copper alloy vessels were cast at the Foundry site during the medieval period (13th to 16th centuries). Some of this material was discussed in a previous study of the site (*AY* 10/3, 195–200). An assessment of the metalworking debris at the site (Bayley 1993) suggested that a large-scale qualitative analysis survey of the metal waste could be used to discover what types of alloy were used at or near the site, and that a small number of quantitative analyses would determine precise compositions, as previous analytical programmes had provided only partial answers. This work would allow some assessment of the type of artefacts which could have been produced at the site. An assessment of the distribution of different types of technological debris over the whole of the Bedern area was also requested. The collation of further details about the mould and crucible fragments was recommended, where possible.

Methods

The entire extant collection associated with high-temperature processes from Bedern and the Foundry comprised over 40kg of debris, packed into more than 500 bags and boxes; this was examined and the contexts, material identifications and weights entered into a spreadsheet. Where small find numbers had been assigned, these were also recorded; most of the material had been bulk-finded, however. Two tables (Appendices 1 and 2) which record this information are not published here but have been placed in the YAT archive.

This report does not discuss all of the material found at the site. Much more material is known to have been excavated, but is not now extant. Furthermore, there are a number of factors which mean that accurate quantification, even of the extant material, is difficult. Some material types are poorly represented because they were friable, for example, the less highly fired or vitrified pieces, such as moulds and copper dross (copper alloy material, now heavily corroded). As the original packaging was less than ideal, these pieces are often poorly preserved. Many of the samples were mixed and it was sometimes impractical, if not impossible, to sort out different types of material, especially where the material was fragile. As far as was possible, the major component of mixed contexts was identified and the material ordered in the spreadsheet accordingly. Two balances were used, those at YAT being accurate to 5g, and those at the Ancient Monuments Laboratory (AML) to 1g. Some of the samples are extremely small and light, and a nominal weight (of 5g or 1g) was entered into the spreadsheet for these. The recovery rate of some of the smallest samples must have been affected by their visibility in the earth — bright red pieces of accidentally formed glass were easily seen during excavation, but dark-coloured ('black') ones may have been more frequently overlooked. Similarly, it seems probable that small ceramic fragments would have been overlooked or not collected, and that small amounts of ash or charcoal would have been ignored. From this database, a range of material was selected as being suitable to address the questions posed by the assessment.

Non-ferrous metal waste

A variety of drops, spillages, dross and other non-ferrous waste was available for examination, totalling 5·3kg of copper alloy material and 0·76kg of lead-rich material (excluding one large piece of litharge cake). The majority of this material is likely to relate to casting operations, although in the case of many of the smaller fragments, it is not possible to determine their origin with any accuracy.

Table 271 XRF analysis of copper alloy waste from the Foundry

Note: 'Leaded copper with antimony' often has tin at low levels, as well as the lead, so this alloy category could probably be merged with the 'leaded bronze with antimony'.

Key: Cu = copper; Zn = zinc; Pb = lead; Sn = tin; Sb = antimony

	Frequency
Leaded bronze with antimony (Cu-Pb-Sn, tr Sb)	27
Leaded bronze (Cu-Pb-Sn)	14
Leaded copper (Cu-Pb)	13
Leaded copper with antimony (Cu-Pb, tr Sb)	8
Quaternary (Cu-Pb-Sn-Zn)	5
Leaded brass (Cu-Zn-Pb)	4
Copper	1

Qualitative analysis of waste from the Foundry

Some atomic absorption analysis had been carried out earlier (Ranson 1977), but the element suite analysed for was not complete; significantly it omitted antimony and arsenic (noted by Bayley and Richards in *AY* 10/3, 189). Non-destructive X-ray fluorescence (XRF) analysis of a selection of 72 pieces of copper alloy waste shows that a range of copper alloys were being worked at the site.

Some late medieval vessels (e.g. cauldrons) have been analysed previously (Blades 1995; Brownsword and Pitt 1981) and it has been shown that these are often made from copper alloys containing relatively small amounts of tin, large amounts of lead and significant quantities of antimony. This composition reflects the use of copper that originally came from a source with high levels of antimony. Similar alloys with high levels of arsenic were also occasionally used. These alloys would have been suitable for many large cast artefacts, but not for bells, which are always made from low-lead, high-tin bronzes (e.g. Tylecote 1976, 72). Although arsenic was not noted as a major alloy component in the metals tested here, this may reflect the difficulty of detecting arsenic in leaded copper alloy using XRF (lead Lα and arsenic Kα peaks overlap significantly and arsenic is rarely present in high enough quantities to allow the arsenic Kβ peak to be used). Also arsenic is a volatile element which tends to be lost on melting or re-

melting copper alloys. A fragment of copper alloy apparently still trapped in its mould (Bedern north-east, sf832, context 4346) is unfortunately too small to allow the artefact to be identified, but this has a leaded bronze with antimony composition.

A broad range of other alloys were used for other types of artefacts at this time, depending on the metallurgical properties required. As the majority of the fragments examined here are drops and spills, such as might be found on a casting site, it is not surprising that most of the alloys are relatively lead-rich, since leaded alloys are easier and cheaper to cast.

It should be noted that it is difficult to predict the original, uncorroded, alloy composition of an artefact from qualitative analyses of the surfaces of corroded artefacts, as the corrosion products are often enriched or depleted in some elements, compared to the interior.

Quantitative analysis of waste from the Foundry

Three pieces of copper alloy waste from the Foundry (sfs447, 1378 and 1478) had been sectioned and mounted in bakelite blocks for metallographic analysis during previous work on the Bedern material. As the chemical analyses performed during this earlier work were thought to exclude analysis for antimony, arsenic and other significant elements, these three pieces were re-examined and re-analysed using the energy-dispersive X-ray analysis (EDX) facility of the scanning electron microscope (SEM).

Table 272 EDX analysis of three copper alloy samples from the Foundry (average of three analyses per sample). Figures quoted to the nearest 1% and normalised to 100%

Key: Cu = copper; Zn = zinc; As = arsenic; Pb = lead; Sn = tin; Sb = antimony

	Cu	Zn	As	Pb	Sn	Sb
Sf447	78	0	2	6	0	14
Sf1478	76	0	0	19	4	1
Sf1378	77	1	0	3	18	1

All three samples were extremely heterogeneous and accurate quantitative analysis of the bulk samples was very difficult; approximate EDX analyses are given in Table 272. Sf447 was porous and contained several different metallic phases. Bulk analysis indicated that copper, antimony, arsenic and lead were present, with antimony, arsenic and lead all being important alloying components. Sf1478 is a heavily leaded tin bronze, with a large proportion of the lead lying in discrete pools (any lead over 0·1% does not dissolve in copper). Sf1378 is a high-tin bronze with an as-cast dendritic structure clearly visible. Given this heterogeneity, further sampling and analysis of similar metallic material from the site would be very time-consuming.

The qualitative and quantitative results presented here (added to the SEM-EDX result in *AY* 10/3, 189) confirm the supposition that arsenic and antimony were important elements in many, but not all, of the copper alloys used at the site.

Lead-rich waste was also found on the site, in smaller quantities, but in many of the same range of forms as the copper alloys (e.g. drops and spillages). XRF carried out on two samples from Bedern south-west (sf1972, context 5120; no sf number, context 5293) indicated that they were predominantly lead, with traces of tin and copper.

Crucibles

Twenty-six contexts within the extant corpus contained crucible debris, weighing 1·7kg, of which 0·724kg came from the Foundry. This is clearly only a fraction of the amount which might be expected from a site where a large number of artefacts were

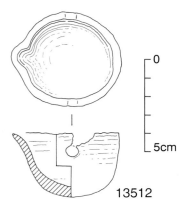

Fig.1320 *Crucible* 13512 *from Bedern. Scale 1:2*

cast. The comparative lack of crucibles at the Foundry has been commented upon previously (*AY* 10/3, 198). Unfortunately, the six crucibles listed in *AY* 10/3 had been lost by the time this report was written so no further analysis was possible.

At least three different types of crucible were observed, including a thick-walled type, for example, *13514* (possibly late or post-medieval), and a thinner-walled type which was sometimes given an extra outer layer, for example, *13510*. Although only fragments survive, the thick-walled type of crucible may have been approximately the same size as the large flat-bottomed examples seen in post-medieval contexts elsewhere (e.g. Bayley 1992, fig.5). Accidentally formed glasses of various colours and vitrification containing copper alloy specks (now corroded to green) were often seen on the exterior of crucibles.

Two of the small crucibles from Bedern are complete (*13508*, Period 1A; *13512*, Period 6); these and the remaining extant crucibles with small find numbers have been looked at by **Dr A.J. Mainman** who has studied the fabrics and comments:

13512 *has a pouring lip, and also suspension holes, formed before firing, on two opposing sides to enable the crucible to be tilted for pouring using some method of suspension (Fig.1320). It is made of a gritty unglazed fabric, apparently related to the local ubiquitous gritty ware (current 11th–13th centuries). The form is unique, however, so this dating may not apply. It was found in a mid 14th century deposit. The fragmentary 13511 is made of Stamford ware or a similar fine white fabric, as are 13509–10 and 13513; if they are Stamford ware they are likely to date from the 10th or more probably the 11th century, all thus being residual in their 13th–late 14th century contexts. 13515 is a small body sherd made of a vitrified sandy fabric, while the fabrics of 13508 and 13514 are too vitrified to be identified.*

XRF analysis of metal found on seven crucibles and crucible fragments showed that they had been used to melt quaternary alloys (copper alloyed with zinc, lead and tin) and, possibly, leaded brasses. No examples of copper alloys with high concentrations of arsenic and antimony were discovered by this method. This is not surprising, since the crucibles analysed are all too small to have been used in casting large artefacts, such as cauldrons, but would instead have been used to cast small artefacts. Large and small cast artefacts demand different properties of the metal used to make them and it is known that different alloys were used for them at this period (Blades 1995). Only crucibles with distinctive copper alloy metal specks or lumps were analysed in this study, as surface XRF analysis of those crucibles which only have vitrification is likely to give a misleading impression of the alloys melted in them, as some elements are preferentially absorbed into the crucible surface whilst others are not (cf. Bayley et al. 1991, 397),

There seem to be no marked patterns of chronological or spatial distribution in the crucibles. Small quantities come from Periods 2–6 at the Foundry and Periods 1–2 and 4–8 at Bedern. The majority of the material from Bedern appears to come from the area south-west of Bedern Close, but small amounts come from the area north-east of the close and from the site at 2 Aldwark.

Moulds

Very few of the 13,000 clay mould fragments examined by Ranson (1977) were available for inspection. Those which were available are mainly those illustrated in the excavation report (AY 10/3, fig.81) together with a few more nondescript fragments, which have been severely abraded during storage (as well as during deposition). This means that it is not possible to expand on the range of forms already recorded. The surviving mould fragments suggest that the vessels being made would have been comparable with those cast in the nearly complete mould found at Prudhoe Castle, Northumberland (Wilthew 1986).

Altogether, clay mould material from 28 contexts was examined, totalling 3·8kg (compared with over 200kg examined by Ranson in 1977). The majority of the moulds associated with vessel casting had no evidence of any metal adhering, which meant that any XRF analysis of the surface of these pieces could be misleading. Two of the moulds which did have small amounts of copper alloy trapped in their surfaces were analysed using XRF (Foundry context 156; Bedern south-west, context 6262) and on this basis were thought likely to have been used for casting leaded bronzes.

A small piece from a possible stacking mould of clay was found (Bedern south-west, context 1614). Large-scale production of small artefacts, such as buckles, was achieved by making large stacks of piece moulds and casting them in a single operation (cf. Armitage et al. 1981).

Two moulds made from lithographic stone which were found at Bedern were analysed by XRF to investigate any metal traces left from use. It is likely that low melting temperature metals would be cast in this type of mould. Suitable metals might include lead-tin alloys although, in this case, the results of XRF analysis are difficult to interpret because of the very low levels of metals present. In one case (13436) lead was detected around the sprue area, and traces of copper were found in the area of the artefact impressions. In the other (13437), a plug of metal proved to be tin-rich with a trace of copper but this is most probably a locating peg, judging by its position (see below).

Furnace structure debris

A tuyère was discovered in a mixed sample bag (Bedern south-west, context 5292) and, as it has copper alloy specks trapped within the slagging, this must have been involved in the copper alloy melting process. XRF of the copper alloy areas showed the presence of copper, lead and a small amount of tin.

Accidentally formed glasses

A range of accidentally formed glasses were found at the site, as separate lumps or droplets as well as on crucibles. Some of these glasses were coloured red or reddish-brown by the presence of copper. Others appeared black, due to the intensity of the colouration; one example that was analysed using XRF (Bedern south-west, context 5146) was lead-rich, with tin, zinc and traces of copper also present. An opaque green 'glass' formed in the same way (Bedern south-west, context 7585) was found to be lead-rich, with traces of copper and iron. Glasses can be formed in any high-temperature process where silica is fluxed, for example, by the presence of alkalis (giving fuel ash slags) and lead oxides (giving high-lead glasses). Such circumstances would prevail in copper alloy melting, where the silica in the crucible walls would be fluxed with lead from the copper alloys where it is open to the air. There is no evidence for deliberate glassmaking at the site.

Ironworking slags and other iron-rich material

A total of 6·4kg of ironworking slag, most of it not diagnostic of either smelting or smithing, was found in the re-examination work. Ironworking residues are often present on a non-ferrous casting site, as a result of activities such as tool-making and tool-mending. Iron-rich concretion was frequently found; in some cases this may be related to iron-working but iron panning may also be involved.

Litharge

A large piece from a litharge cake, *14509*, was found in a late 15th–early 16th century level in the south-east part of the garden area of Bedern. This is a by-product of silver purification or refining, but may be residual in this context; litharge cakes are well known from Middle and Late Saxon/Viking deposits, but not from medieval contexts, possibly because, by this period, chemical separation techniques were used rather than cupellation (J. Bayley, pers. comm.).

Other high-temperature debris

Several other types of high-temperature debris were found on site: ash, fuel (charcoal and possibly coke), cinder, fired clay, re-used tiles and vitrified furnace/hearth lining. These types of material are not always connected with non-ferrous metal casting but, in a number of cases, splashes of copper-rich dross indicate that they were at least in the vicinity of high-temperature copper alloy working. Given the dominance of copper alloy melting amongst the high-temperature work at the site, it seems quite possible that many of the remaining pieces of high-fired ceramic debris also relate to non-ferrous metalworking.

Conclusions

Analysis has shown that copper alloy casting at this site used a range of copper alloys. These included some alloys which contained high concentrations of antimony and/or arsenic, of a type known to have been used for casting large vessels, and others which were leaded bronzes and zinc-rich alloys, suitable for a wide range of casting work, including small artefacts. There is one example of an alloy suitable for casting bells, but this alloy could also have been used to cast other artefacts. Red, brown, black and green glasses were accidentally formed during heating and melting of the non-ferrous metals. The mould evidence indicates casting of small trinkets and large vessels. Other metalworking activities in the area include small-scale ironworking (probably smithing, perhaps related to manufacture or maintenance of

iron tools used in copper alloy casting) and silver purification or refining.

Other evidence of non-ferrous metalworking at Bedern and the Foundry

In addition to the material studied by Dr Mortimer, other elements likely to be related to non-ferrous casting and other metalworking were recovered at the Foundry and Bedern; these include failed castings, sheet fragments and offcuts, strips, bars, rods and wires. The two stone moulds noted above are also discussed below in more detail.

Casting moulds of stone (Fig.1321)

Both stone mould fragments (*13436–7*) were found at Bedern; *13436* derived from an early–mid 13th century pit fill, *13437* from a late 13th century spread backfilling pits and a gully north-west of Building 10. These moulds have been lithologically identified by **Dr G.D. Gaunt** who comments:

The two moulds are made of chalk from the Upper Cretaceous Chalk Group, the nearest outcrops of which are in the Yorkshire Wolds. 13436 is sufficiently coarse-grained (although still fine-grained in absolute terms) to imply a source in the Ferriby Chalk Formation, which encompasses the lowest c.26m of the Chalk Group and contains several layers that are relatively slightly coarser-grained than the rest of the succession.

Both moulds formed one part of multi-piece moulds, as keying holes indicate, and both appear to have been used on both faces. *13436* may have been used to cast decorative discs, perhaps counters, presumably of lead or pewter, while *13437* may have produced metal beads similar to a ribbed pewter bead recovered from an early 15th century deposit in London (Egan and Pritchard 1991, 316, fig.209, *1585*). A 13th century stone mould for making similar beads was found in Lund (Bergman and Billberg 1976, 207, fig.151).

Failed castings (Figs.1322–3)

Nothing that could have been produced by these moulds was found at Bedern, but failed castings of other small metal objects confirm part of Dr Mortimer's analyses which noted the use of alloys and clay moulds indicating the casting of small artefacts. These failed castings comprise two belt loops with external rivets (*14381*), three unfinished buckles with

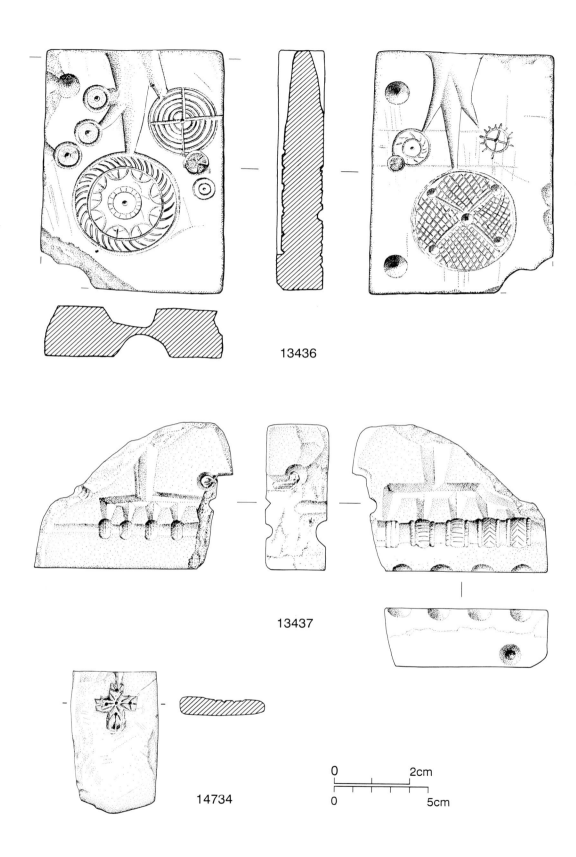

Fig.1321 *Casting moulds of stone: 13436–7 from Bedern; 14734 from 46–54 Fishergate. Scale 1:1, 14734 1:2*

Fig.1322 *Failed castings: (top to bottom)* 13340 *and* 13341 *from the Foundry;* 14381 *and* 14373 *from Bedern. Actual length of* 13340 *42·2mm*

Fig.1323 *Failed castings from St Andrewgate: (from left, clockwise) sfs500, 216, 198, 446 and 217. Actual length of sf500 38·5mm*

forked spacers recovered from the Foundry (*13340–1*) and from Bedern (*14315*), and unfinished forked spacers from strap-ends found in late 15th–early 16th century deposits at Bedern (*14370, 14373*). A site at St Andrewgate nearby (1995.89 YORYM; Fig.1314, 7) produced similar miscastings including two belt loops (sfs216–17), recovered from a 14th century rubbish pit, and five forked spacers from buckles, including two cast together which came from the backfill of a possible late 14th–early 15th century quenching pit (sf500), a late 15th–early 16th century ditch or robbed out wall backfill (sf198), and material redeposited in the 18th century (sf58). A double-looped rectangular buckle (sf446) was also found in a late 15th–early 16th century context. The small number of failed castings, no doubt the result of efficient recycling, spread over all parts of the Bedern area and at St Andrewgate nearby, unfortunately make it difficult to pinpoint the area(s) of production of these small objects. It is unclear whether these castings result from work on several sites close together, or originate from one site, from which they have been scattered or removed and dumped.

Further details of the failed castings and illustrations are found in the relevant discussion of the completed pieces (see pp.2902–3 and Figs.1476–7).

Other metalworking debris (Figs.1324–5)

Scrap metal produced by smithing, comprising non-ferrous bars, rods, sheet offcuts and fragments, strips and wires, was also recovered from the Foundry and Bedern sites, and may represent discarded fragments which have escaped recycling. For definitions of the differing elements of scrap, see pp.780–8, *AY* 17/7.

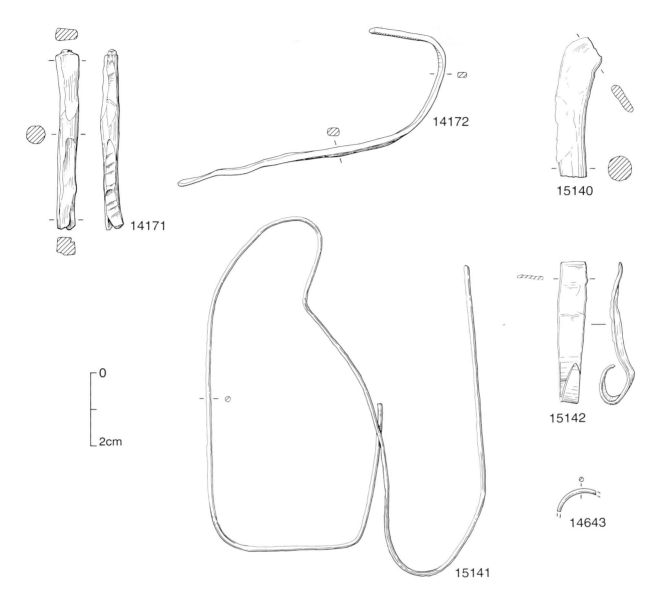

Fig.1324 *Copper alloy scrap 14171–2 from Bedern, 15140–2 from 46–54 Fishergate; silver wire 14643 from Bedern Chapel. Scale 1:1*

No copper alloy ingots were identified, but bars which have been hammered out of ingots, such as *14171*, were recovered. These in turn were further worked into rods, sheet and strips. Lengths of copper alloy wire, formed either by hammering down rods or by drawing, were also recovered; these may relate to pin-making (see p.2718). Offcuts of copper alloy sheet (e.g. *14172*) were a product of the working of sheet. Apart from three bar fragments hammered out of ingots and found at Bedern (e.g. *14510*), all the lead alloy scrap took the form of sheet fragments, offcuts or strips. The Bedern Chapel site pro-

Table 273 Distribution of non-ferrous waste from the Foundry and Bedern

	g	%
Foundry	1503	30.4
Bedern south-west including trench III/IV	3416	69.1
Other areas	25	<1.0
Total	4944	

Table 274 Distribution of non-ferrous scrap from the Foundry and Bedern (in grams)

	Copper alloy	Lead alloy	Total	% of whole
Foundry	81	17	98	29.9
Bedern	193	37	230	70.1
Total	274	54	328	

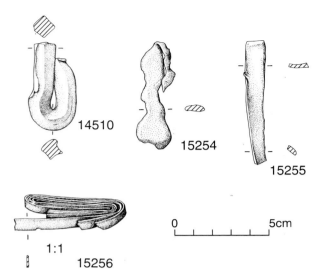

Fig.1325 *Lead alloy scrap* **14510** *from Bedern and* **15254–6** *from 46–54 Fishergate. Scale 1:2,* **15256** *1:1*

duced no copper alloy or lead alloy scrap, but a tiny fragment of silver wire, *14643*, perhaps part of a wire for decorative application, was retrieved from early 15th century floor levels.

Chronological and spatial distribution of the metalworking debris

Of the material analysed which could be assigned both to a part of the site and to a chronological period, distribution by site was as shown in Tables 273–6.

Tables 273–4 show an exact agreement between the totals of waste and scrap across the sites. Distribution across the sites chronologically is not so exact, however, as Tables 275–6 show.

One possibility concerning the origin of the material found on the Bedern site is that it was generated in the Foundry, but comparison of the data from the two sites shows that this need not be the case. Although relating exactly the sequence on the Foundry site to that on Bedern is not possible, it may be noted firstly that there is very little material from Bedern corresponding to the peak in the data for Period 2 in the Foundry, the period in which the first evidence for hearths was found (*AY* 10/3, 163). Secondly, the peak in Bedern Period 7 (corresponding to Period 4, phases 1–4, on the Foundry) does not correspond to a peak in the Foundry data. This allows the suggestion that some working of non-ferrous metal took place in the College precinct. As far as Bedern

Table 275 Non-ferrous waste and scrap by period at the Foundry (three unstratified pieces of scrap not included)

Period	Waste		Scrap	
	g	%	g	%
2 (late 13th–early 14th cent.)	525	35.0	3	3.15
3 (14th cent.)	26	1.7	8	8.40
4 (15th cent.)	209	14.0	19	20.00
5 (late 15th–early 16th cent.)	113	7.5	8	8.40
6 (mid 16th–mid 17th cent.)	438	29.0	37	38.90
7 (mid 17th–20th cent.)	192	13.0	20	21.05
Total	1503		95	

Table 276 Non-ferrous waste and scrap at Bedern by period

Period	Waste		Scrap	
	g	%	g	%
1–3 (early–late 13th cent.)	34	1.0	35	15.2
4 (late 13th cent.)	19	5.0	7	3.0
5 (early 14th cent.)	9	25.0	20	8.7
6 (mid 14th cent.)	284	8.5	28	12.2
7 (mid 14th–early 15th cent.)	1342	39.5	44	19.1
8 (mid 15th–early 17th cent.)	1621	47.5	90	39.1
9 (mid 17th cent. onwards)	107	3.0	5	2.2
Total	3416		230	

Periods 8 and 9 are concerned, this overlaps with the last period in which metalworking is thought to have taken place in the Foundry (Period 5), but continues into later times. It is possible, therefore, that as much as half of the material from Bedern came from contexts post-dating the end of metalworking in the Foundry. The same pattern is seen at the Foundry itself, where 42% of the waste material and 60% of the scrap came from contexts deposited after metalworking on the site is thought to have ceased (Periods 6–7) and must therefore be residual.

Unfortunately, the other metalworking evidence, in the form of moulds and faulty castings, is very limited and appears scattered both chronologically and spatially, failing to clarify the picture presented by the metal debris and scrap.

2 Aldwark

This site produced a few pieces of scrap metal, although no other metalworking debris was recovered. The copper alloy scrap comprised an offcut (*14692*), sheet fragments (*14693–4*), a strip (*14695*) and wire (*14696*). Only one lead alloy offcut of sheet (*14729*) was recovered.

46–54 Fishergate

A flat-bottomed crucible of medieval or later date (*4611*, p.1233, *AY* 17/9) and a stone casting mould, *14734*, both found unstratified, and some non-ferrous metalworking debris and scrap from medieval levels suggest possible metalworking on the site, although some of the material could be residual from Anglian metalworking (pp.1232–9, *AY* 17/9).

Table 277   Copper alloy working debris from Fishergate (Period 6)

Period	Casting	Offcuts	Sheet	Rods	Wire	Total
6a	4	2	7	2	3	18
6a/6b	1	1	–	–	1	3
6b	33	1	2	–	–	36
6b/6c	1	–	–	–	–	1
6c	20	1	1	–	2	24
6d	1	1	–	–	1	3
6e	–	1	4	–	–	5
6z	–	1	1	–	1	3
Total	60	8	15	2	8	92

Stone casting mould (see Fig.1321, p.2713)

14734 is one half of a two-piece stone mould, used for casting small cross-shaped objects, perhaps mounts for books. Although unstratified, a mould for making book mounts would most likely have been in use during the priory's lifetime; copper alloy book mounts were also found on the site (see pp.2939–40). **Dr G.D. Gaunt** comments:

On the evidence of its highly compacted nature, 14734 is probably from a Lower Palaeozoic (in effect Ordovician or Silurian) source in southern Scotland or Cumbria. There are some similar Carboniferous rocks in northern England, however, notably in the Wensleydale Group (formerly Yoredale sequence) of the northern Pennines. In view of the worn edges, this mould may have been made from a locally found flattish erratic, whatever the original source rock.

Table 278   Copper alloy working debris from Fishergate (Period 7)

Period	Casting	Offcuts/strips	Sheet	Bars	Rods	Wire	Total
7a	5	2	1	1	–	2	11
7b	1	–	1	–	–	2	4
7c	–	4	1	–	1	–	6
Total	6	6	3	1	1	4	21

Table 279 Lead alloy manufacturing debris from Fishergate (Period 6)

Period	Run-off	Offcuts	Sheet/strips	Total
6a	8	1	9	18
6a/b	2	1	4	7
6b	2	2	1	5
6c	2	1	2	5
6e	3	4	–	7
6z	3	1	1	5
Total	20	10	17	47

Table 280 Lead alloy manufacturing debris from Fishergate (Period 7)

Period	Run-off	Offcuts	Sheet	Total
7a	4	16	7	27
7c	14	1	3	20
Total	18	17	10	45

Casting debris and scrap metal (Figs.1324–5)

Tables 277–80 present a breakdown by period of the copper alloy and lead alloy metalworking debris and scrap from Fishergate, including *15140–2* and *15254–6*. The tables show that the majority of the copper alloy debris from Period 6–7 contexts (83·6%) comes from Period 6 levels, particularly Periods 6a–6c, when the priory was constructed and underwent major reconstruction; some of the debris may have been Anglian in origin and cast up to medieval levels during these works. By contrast, almost 50% of the lead alloy derives from Period 7 activity, when the priory buildings were robbed and the windows knocked out and stripped of their lead (*AY* 11/2, 216). Any lead roofing would also have been removed (see below).

22 Piccadilly

Some scrap metal was recovered from this site. It comprised a copper alloy sheet fragment (*13052*), strips (*13053–5*) and wire (*13056–9*), and a lead alloy bar (*13071*), rod (*13072*) and sheet fragment (*13073*).

Pin-making

There is no clear evidence for pin-making at any of the sites, although all sites produced small quantities of rods and wires (see p.2715) which may represent the early stages of pin-making; a pinner's bone found at Fishergate (*8167*) indicates possible pin-making on that site in the post-medieval period (pp.1992–3, *AY* 17/12).

Metalworking tools

Tongs (Figs.1326–7)

There are two pairs of tongs: *13677* (mid 14th–early 15th century context) from Bedern and *14860* (early–mid 14th century context) from Fishergate. Tongs were a basic smithing tool used for holding pieces of metal at all stages in the fabrication process. *13677*, at 160mm long, is the larger; its jaws are curved in cross-section having concave inner faces. This is an unusual feature as the jaws are usually flat, as on *14860*.

13677 has ball-shaped expansions at the tips of its arms. They would have allowed a chain to be held between them to keep the arms in tension while the smith carried out sustained or repetitive actions. The tongs could also be put down without the forging slipping from its jaws (Goodall 1980b, 9–10). On *14860* an incomplete chain survives attached to a loop at the tip of one arm, the other, now missing, probably had a ball-shaped tip.

Hammer heads (Fig.1326)

There are five hammer heads. These include *13157* (late 13th century context) and *13158* (mid–late 15th century context) from the Foundry which may have been used in the metalworking processes carried out on the site. In addition, *11461* (12th–13th century context) comes from Coppergate and *13678* (mid 14th–early 15th century context) comes from Bedern. These two are also likely to have been used in metalworking, probably non-ferrous rather than ferrous in view of their size. *13678* and probably *13158* have a single wedge-shaped arm surviving while *13157* has one arm with a rounded cross-section and one which appears to taper to a point. *11461* has one arm with a

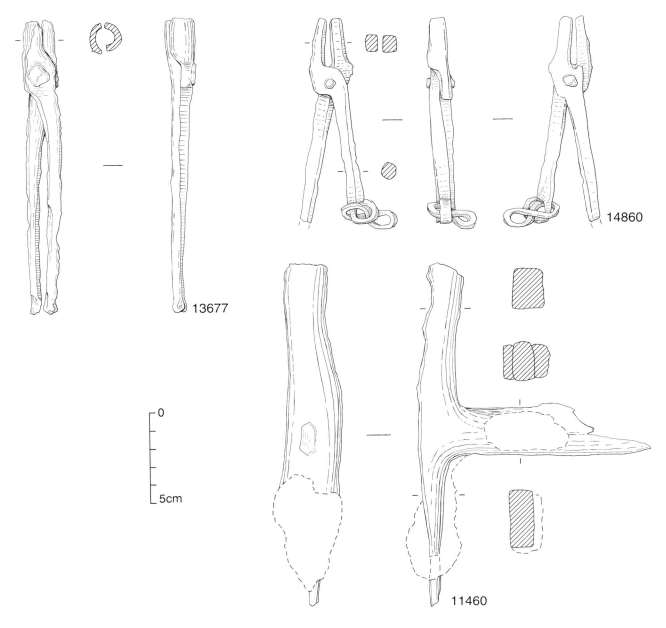

Fig.1326 *Tongs 13677 from Bedern and 14860 from 46–54 Fishergate; hammer 11460 from 16–22 Coppergate. Scale 1:2*

sub-rectangular cross-section and the other is wedge-shaped. It is similar to a small hammer from an Anglo-Scandinavian context at Coppergate (*2203, AY 17/6*), but need not be residual.

11460 (late 15th/early 16th century context) from Coppergate is a large hammer with a length between the arm ends of 200mm. One arm has a subrounded cross-section and the other had a claw tip. Two projections from the eye grip the remains of the wooden

handle with the aid of a rivet. This is probably a carpenter's rather than a metalworker's tool, although it could also have been used by a farrier, the claw serving to remove nails from horses' hooves. Claw hammers are common from contexts dated to the 12th century onwards, but the riveted projections may be a late and post-medieval feature. A similar, if smaller, hammer head to *11460* came from a late 15th century context at Northampton (Fig.1315, **21**; Goodall 1979, 272, fig.119, *61*).

Fig.1327 *Metalworking tools: (left to right) punches* 11463 *from 16–22 Coppergate,* 14864 *from 46–54 Fishergate,* 11465 *from 16–22 Coppergate,* 12973 *from the Coppergate watching brief,* 13681 *from Bedern,* 11464 *from 16–22 Coppergate,* 14863 *from 46–54 Fishergate,* 11468 *from 16–22 Coppergate; tongs* 14860 *from 46–54 Fishergate and* 13677 *from Bedern. Actual length of* 13677 *160mm*

Punches (Figs.1327–9)

In all there are 24 punches of varying sizes and forms, and in varying states of completeness. They may all have been used for metalworking, either ferrous or non-ferrous, and *14863* (15th–16th century context) from Fishergate has non-ferrous metal adhering to it. Where heads survive they are usually burred, indicating appreciable use.

Punches usually taper over all or most of their length to tips which are pointed, rounded or wedge-shaped. In cross-section they are usually rectangular or sub-rectangular.

The largest punch is *13159* (late 13th century context) from Bedern Foundry which is 240mm in length and could have been hand-held by a blacksmith to make holes in hot iron. Another substantial punch is *13681* (mid 14th–early 15th century context) from Bedern which is 155mm long and up to18mm thick. The cross-section of the upper third is rounded while that of the rest is rectangular.

Coppergate has produced three medium-sized smiths' punches: *11464* (early 12th century context), *11465* (13th–14th century context) and 11468 (12th–13th century context). Others come from Piccadilly (*13018*, late 11th–12th century context) and Fishergate (*14863*, 15th–16th century context, and *14864*, 13th–16th century context). *11465* is unusual in narrowing sharply from the centre to the head which, like the heads of most others, is burred as a result of use. In cross-section the corners of *11464* are rounded and a channel runs down the centre of the wider faces. On *11465* similar channels can be seen and in cross-section the narrower faces are convex. *14864* is parallel-sided to just below its mid-point after which it tapers and has a rounded cross-section. *14863* is a relatively flat tool which tapers to a rounded tip. *12973* (undated medieval context from the Coppergate watching brief) and *13160* (from a 14th century context at the Foundry) are slim punches, probably used in non-ferrous metalworking. *13680* (mid 14th century context) from Bedern was of similar size to the objects already described in this paragraph, but has a pro-

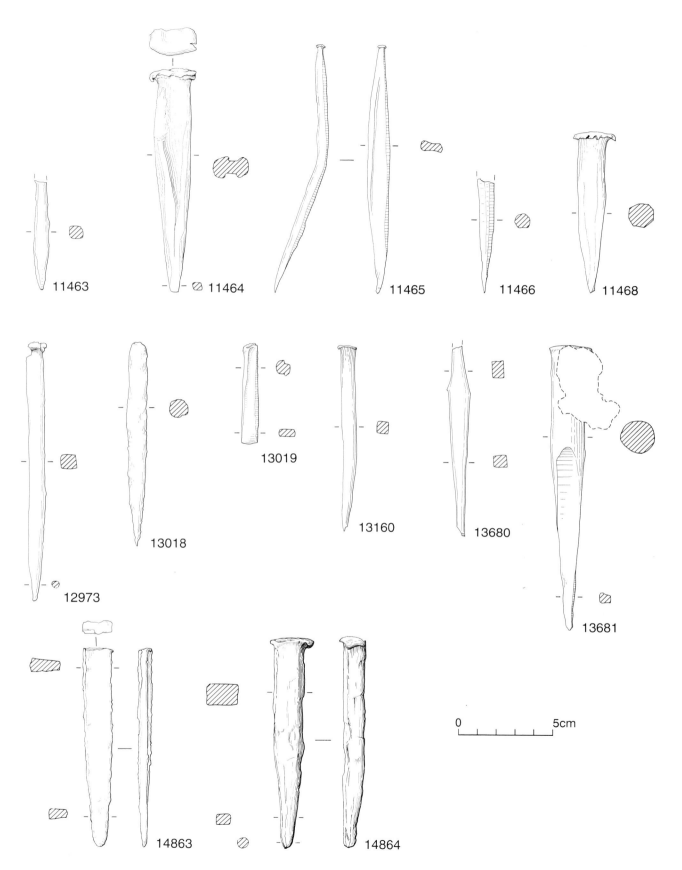

Fig.1328 *Punches 11463–6, 11468 from 16–22 Coppergate, 12973 from the Coppergate watching brief, 13018–19 from 22 Piccadilly, 13160 from the Foundry, 13680–1 from Bedern, 14863–4 from 46–54 Fishergate. Scale 1:2*

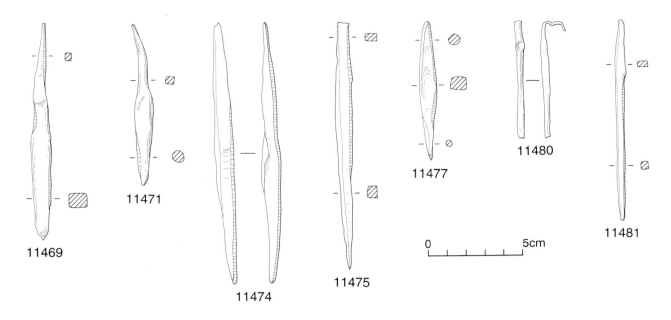

Fig.1329 *Tanged punches 11469, 11471, 11474–5, 11477, 11480–1, all from 16–22 Coppergate. Scale 1:2*

nounced neck, although its head is broken off. In use this punch could have been gripped below the head by tongs or wires to protect the smith while working hot iron.

Tanged punches (Fig.1329)

There is a group of seventeen iron objects which have two arms which taper away from the centre (*11469–83* from 16–22 Coppergate; *13686* from Bedern; *14865* from 46–54 Fishergate). They are more robust than the awls (see p.2728) which in other senses they may resemble. In most cases one arm probably served as a tang which was set in a wooden handle and the other served as the working arm. Some have arms of equal length while others have one arm, thought to be the tang, shorter than the other. It is difficult to determine the use of these objects, but some may have been metalworking punches while others were probably used by carpenters as reamers for enlarging and cleaning out augered holes in timber (Goodall 1980b, 34) or by stonemasons for trimming millstones.

The largest item in this group is *11474* (mid 12th century context), 144mm long. The other tanged punches are typically c.100mm in length, although the shortest is *11480* at 65mm. Tangs, or presumed tangs, always have a rectangular cross-section but

the working arm can have a rounded cross-section. It is common (e.g. *11469* and *11471* from Coppergate) to find a shoulder between the tang and working arm which would have stopped the handle slipping down. *11469* (post-medieval context) is likely to be a mill pick and resembles an object identified as such from a 14th century context at King's Lynn (Fig.1315, **16**; Goodall 1977, 295, fig.134, 39).

Files (Figs.1330–1)

There are three items identified as files, but they are very different from each other. *11484* from a late 13th century context at Coppergate is complete. It has a slightly curved blade with a short tang. There are what appear to be teeth on the concave edge and on the lower part of one face, although the other face has no teeth. This could be an unfinished object which was discarded during manufacture. It is similar to a tanged file of 10th–11th century date from Thetford, Norfolk (I.H. Goodall 1984, 77, 10) although this object has a straight blade. *13687* (mid 15th–early 17th century context) from Bedern is an incomplete blade fragment of a metalworking file with fine cross-cut teeth on one face and on both edges. *14866* from a dissolution (16th century) period context at Fishergate is an incomplete blade with fine diagonal grooves on one face. It is possible that this is an intrusive object of later date.

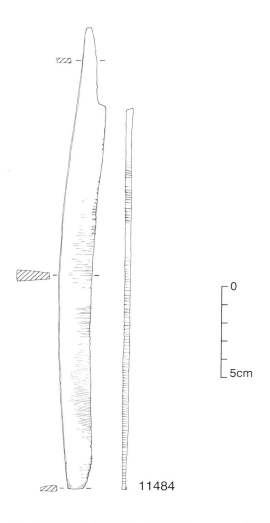

Fig.1330 *File* 11484 *from 16–22 Coppergate. Scale 1:2*

0

5cm

11484

Chisels

There are four chisels, the largest being *14867* from a late 13th–early 14th century context at Fishergate which is 250mm long. It has a heavily burred head and could have been either a stonemason's or blacksmith's tool. In the latter case it would have been hand-held to cut hot iron.

A substantial chisel, probably a metalworker's tool, is *13161* (post-medieval context) from the Foundry, 155mm long. *13688* (mid 14th–early 15th century context) from Bedern is smaller than the other chisels and could have been used for either metalworking or woodworking.

Fig.1331 *Detail of file* 13687 *from Bedern, showing cross-cut teeth*

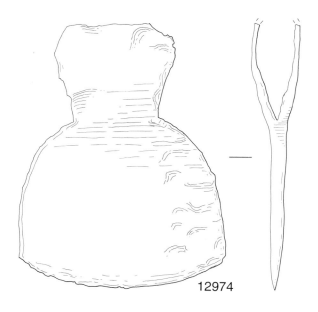

12974

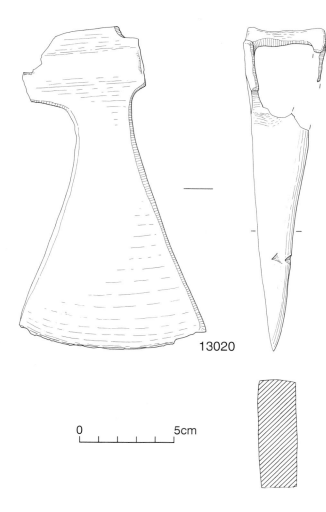

13020

0 |___|___|___|___|___| 5cm

Woodworking

The ironwork includes a small number of woodworking tools which may be set alongside the evidence for medieval wooden artefacts and timber structures, principally from Coppergate where ground conditions favoured preservation, although not to the same extent as in the Anglo-Scandinavian contexts. The wooden artefacts are considered in detail by Carole Morris in *AY* 17/13 and they include parts of buckets, tubs and casks, two garderobe seats, and tools for agriculture and textile manufacture. The medieval timber structural remains, including evidence for carpentry techniques and tool marks, will be considered in *AY* 10/6.

Woodworking tools

Axes (Figs.1332–4)

There are only two axes from the ironwork assemblage, which may reflect the assiduous recycling of a tool with a valuable steel content. *13020* from a 15th–early 16th century context at Piccadilly is a very well-preserved, heavy-duty woodman's axe, 178mm in length. It has an asymmetrical cross-section showing that it could have been used for trimming timbers (Ypey 1981) and the socket has a flat top which would allow use as a hammer. Further discussion of

Fig.1332 *Axes* 12974 *from the Coppergate watching brief and* 13020 *from 22 Piccadilly. Scale 1:2*

Fig.1333 *Noah building the Ark using woodworking tools, c.1420–30 (Bodleian Library, MS Barlow 53 R)*

Fig.1334 *Axe 13020 from 22 Piccadilly. Actual length 178mm*

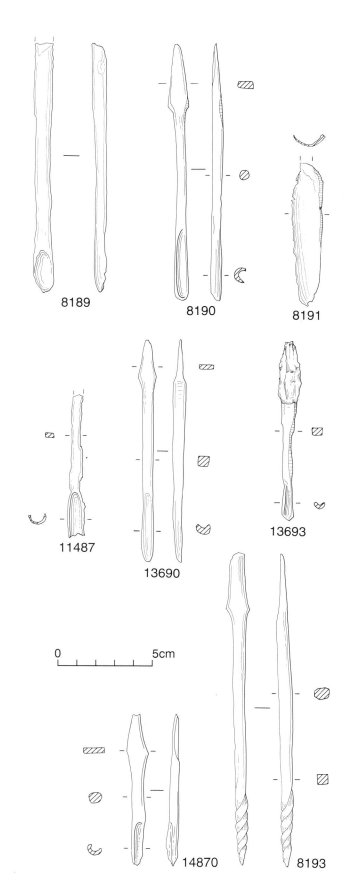

the use of axes appears in *AY* 17/13 (pp.2104–6, 2108–9). This axe is probably residual in its context, being similar to many woodman's axes of the 10th–12th centuries including that from 11–13 Parliament Street in York (Fig.1314, **10**; p.190, *961*, *AY* 17/4). *12974* from the Coppergate watching brief site is a light axe, bet-

Fig.1335 *(right) Spoon augers 8189–91 and 11487 from 16–22 Coppergate, 13690 and 13693 from Bedern, 14870 from 46–54 Fishergate; twist auger 8193 from 16–22 Coppergate. Scale 1:2*

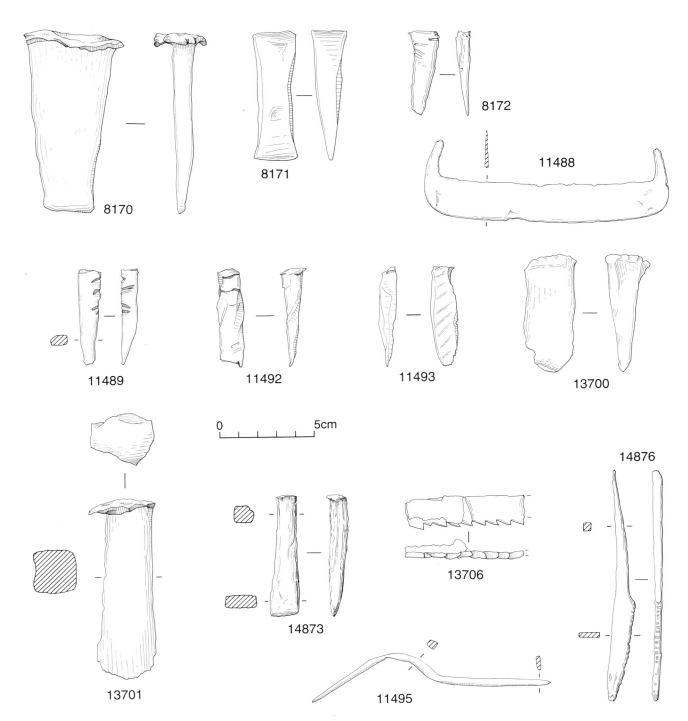

Fig.1336 *Woodworking tools: drawknife 11488 from 16–22 Coppergate; wedges 8170–2, 11489, 11492–3 from 16–22 Coppergate, 13700–1 from Bedern, 14873 from 46–54 Fishergate; saw blade 13706 from Bedern; tanged chisel 11495 from 16–22 Coppergate; and rasp 14876 from 46–54 Fishergate. Scale 1:2*

ter described, perhaps, as a chopper. Its blade is symmetrical in cross-section and in face view it has a waist below the socket above two rounded shoulders. The cutting edge is convex. This object is probably postmedieval in date.

Spoon augers (Figs.1335, 1337)

There are sixteen spoon augers (also known as spoon bits) or parts of spoon augers. The spoon auger was used for boring or enlarging holes in wood and was one of the medieval woodworker's most important tools. He would probably have had a set of varying sizes as can be seen in the 10th century Mästermyr tool chest (Arwidsson and Berg 1983) and in the finds of both pre- and post-Conquest periods from York (for Anglo-Scandinavian examples see pp.532–6, *AY* 17/6). Further discussion of the use of spoon augers appears in *AY* 17/13 (p.2113).

The largest augers from medieval contexts are *8189–90* (both mid 13th century contexts) from Coppergate which are c.140mm in length. Blades *8191* (13th–14th century context) and *8192* (mid 12th century context) are, however, from larger tools, probably comparable to the largest of the Anglo-Scandinavian examples which are over 300mm in length (pp.532–6, *AY* 17/6). At the other end of the scale the smallest example is *14869* (early–mid 14th century context) from Fishergate which is only 63mm

long. The larger blades are 15–16mm wide and the narrower 7–10mm.

The form of medieval spoon augers is very standardised and little changed from pre-Conquest times. Shafts have a sub-rectangular cross-section and the tang widens away from the shaft with upward sloping shoulders before tapering to a wedge-shaped tip. The handle was set transversely as shown in Fig.207, *AY* 17/6.

Twist auger (Figs.1335, 1337)

8193 from a 12th–13th century context at Coppergate is an example of a twist auger, a tool used like a gimlet to start holes in wood (see p.2114, *AY* 17/13). This is an unusual object for which there is no known parallel in a medieval context, although the tip of another was found in an Anglo-Scandinavian context at Coppergate (*2267*, *AY* 17/6).

Fig.1337 *Woodworking tools: (left to right) augers 13693 from Bedern, 8190 from 16–22 Coppergate, 14870 from 46–54 Fishergate; twist auger 8193 from 16–22 Coppergate; wedges 8171 and 8170 from 16–22 Coppergate; wedges 13700 and 13701 from Bedern; rasp 14876 from 46–54 Fishergate; and (at bottom) drawknife 11488 from 16–22 Coppergate. Actual length of rasp 127mm*

Drawknife (Figs.1336–7)

11488 is a drawknife from a 13th century context at Coppergate. It consists of a flat blade with a short tang projecting from each end of the cutting edge. The object would have been used for the chamfering, rounding and trimming of wooden objects.

Wedges (Figs.1336–7)

Twenty-five objects have been identified as wedges. Wedges of various sizes were used for tree-felling, wood-splitting (see pp.2106–8, *AY* 17/13) and to secure the wooden handles on iron tools. Wedges typically have wide blades which narrow slightly, if at all, from head to tip, but they can be difficult to distinguish from chisels, especially when damaged or corroded.

Wedges used for heavy-duty work must include *13701* (mid 14th–early 15th century context) from Bedern (104mm long, 33mm wide and 25mm thick), *8170* (12th–13th century context) from Coppergate (100mm long, 47mm wide and 12mm thick) and *8171* (11th–12th century context) from Coppergate (71mm long, 23mm wide and 18mm thick). The first two have heavily burred heads as a result of use, as do a number of the other wedges. These are smaller, being typically 50–70mm long with a width of c.15mm and thickness of c.8mm. The smallest wedge is *14872* (30mm long) from an early–mid 14th century context at Fishergate and was probably used for a tool handle as can be seen, for example, on a T-shaped axe from London (Pritchard 1991, 135, fig.3.14).

Saw blade (Fig.1336)

13706 from a mid 14th–early 15th century context at Bedern is an incomplete saw blade with set teeth. This object probably represents a small piece of evidence for a change in woodworking practice in York, as Morris comments in *AY* 17/13 (p.2104) that there is little evidence for the use of saws in Britain until the late medieval period.

Rasp (Figs.1336–7)

Fishergate produced a carpenter's file or rasp (*14876*) from a 13th century context. It appears rather like a knife with the top of the tang being in line with the back of the blade. There are teeth on one edge (c.4 per cm). Teeth were more widely spaced on a rasp than on a metalworker's file to prevent them clogging up

and the tool would have been used for smoothing or shaping wood. Comparable objects are rare, but *14876* appears to be similar to a rasp of 12th–13th century date from Wroughton Copse, Fyfield Down, Wiltshire (Goodall 1980b, 34).

Woodworker's chisel (Fig.1336)

11495 is a woodworker's chisel with a crank-shaped tang and narrow blade which comes from an early 12th century context at Coppergate. A discussion of the use of woodworking chisels appears in *AY* 17/13 (p.2110).

Leatherworking

An assemblage of leatherworking tools, principally awls and currier's knives, is described below and they may be set alongside a number of leather artefacts from medieval contexts which will be discussed in detail in *AY* 17/16. The majority of these artefacts come from Coppergate, where ground conditions favoured preservation of leather, although not to the same extent as in the Anglo-Scandinavian contexts. Medieval leatherwork includes offcuts, shoes, straps, knife sheaths and scabbards.

Leatherworking tools

Awls (Figs.1338–9)

There are some 50 probable awls, of which 31 come from Coppergate. Although about 75% of the Coppergate awls come from 12th–13th century contexts, their find-spots were not concentrated in any one part of the site. In addition, there was an awl from Bedern Foundry and there were seven from Bedern, six from Fishergate, three from Piccadilly and one from Aldwark.

Awls are usually taken to be leatherworking tools, but some of the objects under discussion here could have been used in woodworking, bone working or other crafts. The awls have two tapering arms usually of equal length, although four examples (*11506, 11509, 11513, 11520*) have one arm shorter than the other, but are too thin to be considered as tanged punches (see p.2722). One arm of an awl served as a tang and would have been set in a wooden handle, but if the working arm broke the arms could have been reversed as happened to an awl from an Anglo-Scandinavian context from Coppergate (p.552, *AY* 17/6).

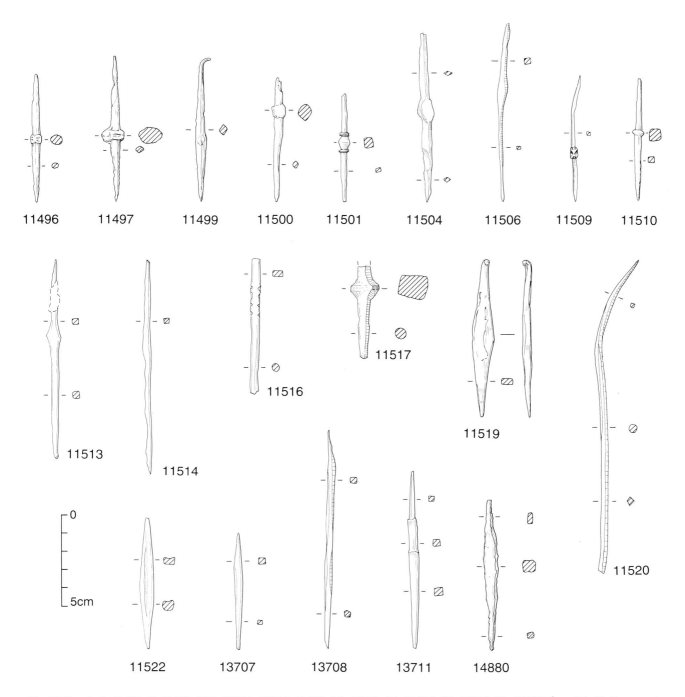

Fig.1338 *Awls 11496–7, 11499–501, 11504, 11506, 11509–10, 11513–14, 11516–17, 11519–20, 11522 from 16–22 Coppergate, 13707–8 and 13711 from Bedern, 14880 from 46–54 Fishergate. Scale 1:2*

Awl arms usually have diamond-shaped or rectangular cross-sections. The former is especially adapted to leatherworking as it allows a cleaner cut to be made in the material than an awl with a rectangular cross-section (Attwater 1961, 28). There are fourteen awls with both arms of diamond-shaped cross-section and another (*11523*) has one arm with a diamond-shaped and one with a rectangular cross-section. This group includes the two longest medieval awls, *11503* and *13021*, 131 and 130mm long respectively, which are comparable to the larger awls of diamond-shaped cross-section from Anglo-Scandinavian contexts (e.g. *2713*, *AY* 17/6).

Fig.1339 (left to right) Awls 11496, 11497, 11500, 11501, 11509 and 11505, all from 16–22 Coppergate. Actual length of 11496 70mm

Medieval awls commonly have a feature in the centre between the arms which was intended to prevent the handle slipping down, but also provided an opportunity for simple decoration. Some, such as

11506, 11513 and 11526 from Coppergate, have a simple expansion between the arms. 11504 (11th–12th century context) from Coppergate has a flattened and widened area between its arms similar to those seen on Anglo-Scandinavian awls (e.g. 2722 and 2726, AY 17/6). Most common is some form of collar. This is roughly circular on 11510 (early 14th century context) and 11511 (mid 12th century context) from Coppergate, and rectangular on 13709 (early 14th century context) from Bedern. A circular collar with a central groove can be seen on 11496 (post-medieval context), 11497 (mid 13th century context) and 11508 (early 13th century context) from Coppergate. 11500 (early 13th century context) and 11509 (12th–13th century context) from Coppergate have small block-like collars. On 11509 each face of the block has a saltire or similar motif formed by punch marks. 11501, from the same context as 11500, has a biconical moulding flanked on each side by a collar.

Similar collars do not occur on any of the Anglo-Scandinavian awls from York and may therefore be a post-Conquest innovation, although no other examples are known from medieval contexts in England. Moulded collars can, however, be seen on a 10th century awl from Goltho, Lincolnshire (Fig.1315, 10; I.H. Goodall 1987, 178, fig.156, 25), and Århus, Denmark (Andersen et al. 1971, EYA, BCS). Circular collars very similar to those on the Coppergate awls can be seen on 12th century awls from Lund, Sweden (Mårtensson 1976, fig.143).

Currier's knives (Figs.1340–1)

There are twelve knives from Coppergate which were specialist tools used for cutting and paring leather. They are distinguished from other knives by

Fig.1340 Currier's knife 11537 from 16–22 Coppergate. Actual length 176mm

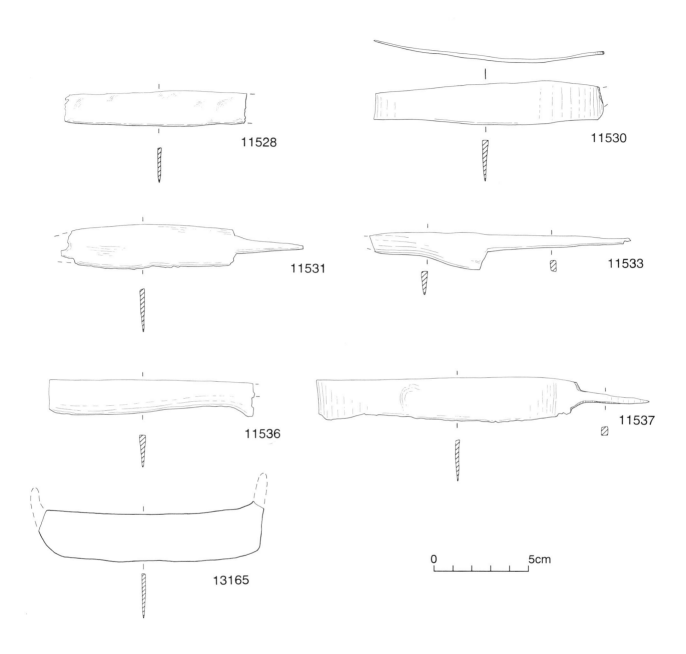

Fig.1341 *Currier's knives 11528, 11530–1, 11533, 11536–7 from 16–22 Coppergate; leatherworker's slicker 13165 from the Foundry. Scale 1:2*

having blades which are unusually thin, but relatively wide. The Coppergate examples all have blades with straight ends; no example has the projecting spike sometimes seen on these objects (Goodall 1980b, 59).

Most of the Coppergate currier's knives have lost their tangs; obviously a point of weakness lay at the junction of blade and tang. Of the three complete examples, *11537* is the longest at 176mm. The blades have lengths between 95mm and 137mm, except for that of *11533* (identification not entirely certain) which has a blade only 61mm long. Blade widths lie between 18mm and 28mm. Blade backs are usually straight, but can be slightly S-shaped. The cutting edges often show signs of heavy wear, being markedly S-shaped or concave.

Examples of currier's knives were found in all four Coppergate tenements. The earliest contexts to produce currier's knives were late 11th–12th century (*11533* and *11536*) and the remainder come from contexts dated up to as late as the 15th–16th century (*11527*). No comparable knives come from pre-Conquest contexts at York or elsewhere and the type appears to be a post-Conquest innovation.

Slicker (Fig.1341)

13165 (15th century context) from the Foundry is an incomplete leatherworker's slicker (or sleaker). It originally had a flat blade with tangs at 90° to the back at each end. Slickers were used in the tanning process to force out the dirt retained under the hair roots just below the grain layer of a hide and to shave the flesh side until the surface was smooth, ensuring leather of even thickness (Goodall 1980b, 58).

Textile production

By Penelope Walton Rogers, Textile Research, York (UK)

Introduction

A large collection of textile-manufacturing tools from 16–22 Coppergate has already been described in *AY* 17/11, and individual categories of textile tool from this site have been reviewed separately in *AY* 17/12 (pp.1964–71), *AY* 17/13 (pp.2325–37) and *AY* 17/14 (pp.2530–3). The later part of the Coppergate collection, from Period 6 (the 11th–17th centuries), has provided a useful standard with which to compare the smaller groups of material from medieval Bedern, 2 Aldwark, 22 Piccadilly and Fishergate. The well-dated series from 9th to 11th century Coppergate has also made it possible to identify a number of redeposited Anglo-Scandinavian artefacts at the other sites. The evidence from Bedern, Aldwark, Piccadilly and Fishergate will be described here in order of manufacture, from raw materials through to finished products, using the Coppergate material for comparison. The artefacts and their phases have been summarised in Table 281.

Raw materials: wool, flax and dyes

Two whittled wooden pegs, 105 and 74mm long (*9196*, *9198*), and a fragment of a third (*9197*) from 15th/16th century levels at Piccadilly have been identified as bale pins (*AY* 17/13). A further eighteen bale pins were recovered from Coppergate, from deposits ranging in date from the 12th/13th to the 16th centuries (pp.1716–18, *AY* 17/11). These bale pins were used to fasten the packs of merchandise, especially wool, carried by pack ponies. No examples of the raw wool itself were found at any of the sites other than Coppergate (pp.1713–15, *AY* 17/11; pp.301–11, *AY* 17/5), but a small number of sheep keds from Period 6 at Piccadilly confirm that fleeces were passing over this site in the 15th/16th century (contexts 2008 and 3003, Carrott et al. 1995, 8, 34).

At Bedern there were also some seeds of the flax plant, *Linum usitatissimum* L., from the College of the Vicars Choral (Hall et al. 1993a, 14) and from the Foundry (Hall et al. 1993b, 13). The flax plant is, of course, the source of the flax textile fibre and the seeds can represent residue from flax preparation. No seedpods or stems were recovered, however, and the presence of food plants in the same deposits suggests that the flax seed (linseed) was in this instance being used in cooking. Dyeplants have been found only at Piccadilly, mainly in a well fill dated to the 15th/16th century (context 2008). Woad, *Isatis tinctoria* L., was the chief component of this material, although weld, *Reseda luteola* L., and greenweed, *Genista tinctoria* L., were also present (Carrott et al. 1995, 8, 32). Blue flecks deposited on some calcareous material in context 2008 were examined by absorption spectrophotometry and proved to be indigotin, the colorant found in woad-dyed cloth (Walton Rogers, report in YAT archive). Bran was found in the same context. This deposit is, then, almost certainly the waste from a woad vat, the bran having been used to ferment the dye and the calcareous material to make it soluble. The colours produced would have been blue (woad), yellow (weld and greenweed) or green (blue and yellow combined).

Fibre processing (Fig.1342)

Iron spikes which will have come from either wool combs or flax heckles were present at Bedern, Piccadilly and Fishergate, in relatively small numbers (Table 281) when compared with the 194 spikes from medieval Coppergate (revised from 195 in Table 145, *AY* 17/11). The difficulties in distinguishing between teeth from wool combs and spikes from flax heckles have been reviewed elsewhere (pp.1727–31, 1796–9, *AY* 17/11) but the main diagnostic features may be summarised as follows. Wool comb teeth were gen-

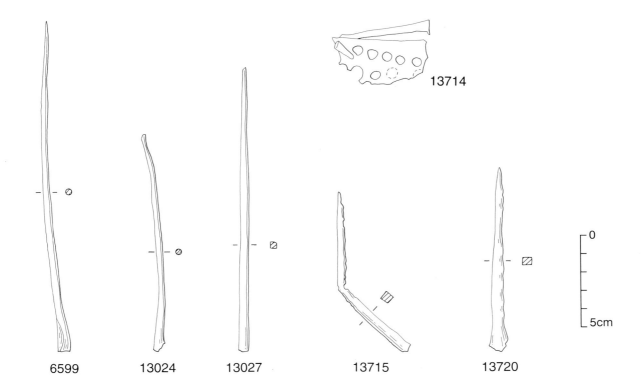

Fig.1342 *Tools used in fibre processing: part of a wool comb 13714 from Bedern (drawn from X-ray); iron spikes 6599 from 16–22 Coppergate, 13024 and 13027 from 22 Piccadilly, 13715 and 13720 from Bedern. Scale 1:2*

erally 90–110mm long until the end of the 12th century, when they lengthened to as much as 186mm. Flax heckle spikes were variable in length and diameter, but seem to have been mainly 60–110mm long. Wool comb teeth often had rounder sections than flax heckle spikes, although this is not a universal rule. The remnants of an iron plate or casing at the base of the spike is almost certainly diagnostic of a wool comb.

With this in mind, the iron casing with two rows of five holes from early 15th century deposits at Bedern (*13714*) can confidently be identified as from a wool comb, as can a spike with the remains of an iron base-plate from the 15th century Foundry (*13168*). Other spikes, 86–106mm long, with more angular cross-sections, from 11th/12th and 13th century levels at Bedern (*13715–16, 13719–20*) and the Foundry (*13166*), are more likely to be from flax heckles. Finally, some long spikes with rounded sections from Bedern (*13730*), Piccadilly (*13024, 13027*) and Fishergate (*14892*) are more typical of the late

form of wool comb. The remaining spikes are difficult to categorise and have been designated simply 'comb/heckle spikes'.

Patrick Ottaway comments on the production of the iron spikes:

The spikes may be described as thin tapering iron strips of either rounded or rectangular cross-section with pointed tips, unlike nails of the Anglo-Scandinavian and medieval periods which usually have wedge-shaped tips. The most distinctive feature of a spike is the stepped (or 'bearded') head created when it was severed from the parent bar during forging. The smith partly cut the iron with a chisel, but did not cut the whole way through it to avoid dulling the chisel on the anvil; final breakage was therefore achieved manually, leaving the step.

The short-toothed wool combs of the early period were used one in either hand, in order to straighten and align wool fibres prior to spinning (illustrated in Fig.797, p.1723, *AY* 17/11). When the heavier long-

Table 281 Textile equipment from Bedern, the Foundry, Fishergate and 22 Piccadilly

Five items from 2 Aldwark (14668–70, 14697–8) are described in the text, but not listed here.
For the textile equipment from 16–22 Coppergate, see AY 17/11.

Bedern, including Bedern Chapel	The Foundry	22 Piccadilly	Fishergate
Period 1A, 11th/12th century 1 iron spike 2 iron needles 2 copper alloy needles *Period 1, early–mid 13th century* 1 iron spike 1 iron needle *Period 2, mid–late 13th century* 1 iron spike 1 bone spindle whorl 1 iron needle *Period 3, mid–late 13th century* 2 iron spikes 1 iron needle *Period 4, late 13th century* 3 iron spikes 1 bone thread reel *Period 5, early 14th century* 1 iron needle 1 copper alloy needle 1 iron scissors *Period 6, mid–late 14th century* 1 iron spike 1 iron needle	*Period 2, late 13th–early 14th century* 1 iron spike 3 chalk spindle whorls 1 copper alloy thimble *Period 3, late 14th century* 2 iron spikes	*Period 4, c.975–11th/12th century* 2 iron spikes *Period 5.1, 13th century* 3 iron needles *Period 5.2, early–mid 14th century* 1 iron spike 2 iron needles	*Period 6a, 1195–late 13th century* 12 iron spikes 3 stone spindle whorls 1 bone spindle whorl 2 clay loom weights 1 bone pin-beater 1 copper alloy supposed couching needle 2 iron shears 3 iron needles *Period 6a/6b* 11 iron spikes 1 stone spindle whorl 1 clay loom weight 2 iron needles 1 copper alloy needle 1 iron shears *Period 6b, late 13th/14th century* 2 iron spikes *Period 6c, early–mid 14th century* 3 iron spikes 1 stone spindle whorl

Bedern, including Bedern Chapel	The Foundry	22 Piccadilly	Fishergate
Period 7, late 14th–early 15th century 6 iron spikes 1 iron wool comb casing 2 chalk spindle whorls 1 limestone spindle whorl 3 copper alloy needles 6 iron shears 1 iron tenter hook	*Period 4, late 14th–early 15th century* 4 iron spikes		*Period 6z, 13th–16th century* 1 iron needle 1 copper alloy needle 2 iron tenter hooks
Period 8, mid 15th–early 17th century 2 iron spikes 2 bone spindle whorls 1 bone single-ended pin-beater 1 copper alloy needle 4 copper alloy thimbles 3 iron shears	*Period 6, mid 15th–early 17th century* 1 chalk spindle whorl 1 clay loom weight 4 copper alloy needles 1 copper alloy thimble	*Period 6, 15th–early 16th century* 3 wooden bale pins dyeplants: woad, weld, greenweed 2 iron spikes 1 iron needle	*Period 6e, 15th/16th century* 1 copper alloy thimble 1 iron tenter hook
Period 9, mid 17th century onwards 1 chalk spindle whorl 1 bone spindle whorl 4 copper alloy needles 1 copper alloy netting needle	*Period 7, mid 17th century onwards* 1 iron spike 1 iron needle 1 copper alloy knitting needle	*Period 7, 15th century or later* 1 iron spike	*Period 7a, c.1538* 1 iron needle 1 copper alloy thimble 1 iron shears

toothed combs arrived, one of them had to be fixed to a post or bench. The raw wool was mounted on the teeth of the fixed comb and then the second comb was drawn through the fibres. To aid the process, oil was applied to the wool and the combs heated as shown in a 15th century French edition of *Livre des Femmes Nobles et Renommées* by Jean Boccace (Giovanni Boccaccio) (Fig.1343).

In contrast, the spikes of flax heckles are set in clusters in solid wooden blocks with the teeth pointing upwards. A bundle of prepared flax stems is held at one end and brought down smartly on to the block of spikes, and then tugged towards the 'heckler' so that the stems tear longitudinally (Fig.799, p.1726, *AY* 17/11; a woman heckling flax is also illustrated in another edition of Boccaccio's work, *De Claris Mulieribus*, MS Royal 16 Gv. fo.56). Progressively finer-toothed heckles are used until the flax has been processed down to fine individual filaments, and is ready for spinning.

Spinning (Fig.1344)

The five stone spindle whorls from Periods 6a–c at Fishergate are all Anglo-Saxon in form and the single bone example may also be a redeposited artefact (p.1268, *AY* 17/9). There are no authentically medieval whorls from this site, nor are there any from 22 Piccadilly. At Coppergate spinning equipment was much more common. There was a small wooden spindle, *6697*, from a 12th/13th century deposit and 61 stone, twelve bone, two antler, two clay and three potsherd whorls from medieval levels (Table 146, *AY* 17/11). The potsherd whorls are redeposited Roman artefacts and the stone whorls include at least fifteen which are the Anglo-Saxon form, Form A; some of the bone femur-head whorls may also be redeposited artefacts (see below). A further five or six cylindrical and bun-shaped stone whorls represent Form B, a type which spans the period of the Norman invasion and which was probably still in use in the 12th century. Two ornamented antler whorls, *6692–3*, may be compared with other medieval examples (p.1743,

Fig.1343 *A woman using long-toothed wool combs in MS Fr.598 fo.70v, Bibliothèque nationale, Paris. Two more combs are warming by the container of coals at her feet. Cliché Bibliothèque nationale de France, © BnF.*

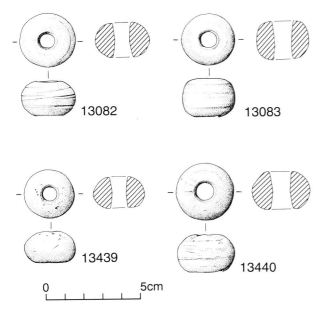

Fig.1344 *Globular medieval spindle whorls, Form C. Chalk whorls 13082–3 from the Foundry and 13439 from Bedern, limestone whorl 13440 from Bedern. Scale 1:2*

AY 17/11), but the clay whorls, *6582–3*, are more unusual and difficult to date.

The remaining Coppergate stone whorls are the globular or near-globular whorls, designated Form C, which are typical of eastern England in the medieval period (pp.1736–41, *AY* 17/11). They have been lathe-turned more frequently than the earlier whorls from the same site and their weights are more standardised, at 15–32g. Decoration is rare, although one example, *6571*, has painted red bands. They are all made from types of limestone and chalk — especially the latter — which are available in the Yorkshire-Humberside region (identification by G.D. Gaunt).

At Bedern (including the College, Chapel and Foundry) there were twelve spindle whorls from deposits ranging in date from the 13th to the 17th century or later (Table 281). Seven of the eight stone whorls are the globular Form C, which, as already noted, is typical of the medieval period. Like the Coppergate whorls, they are made from chalk and limestone, and are lathe-turned. Those which are complete and can be weighed are especially light, at 14–23g, which suggests they have been used for some very fine spinning. The eighth stone whorl, *13438*, is

made from chalk in a flattened barrel shape categorised as Form B (see above) and it is likely that this whorl, from a post-medieval context, is a redeposited artefact. The remaining four whorls from the Bedern area are all made from cattle femur-heads (*AY* 17/12). One, *8015*, is from a 13th century deposit and the others, *8016–18*, from post-medieval levels. Bone whorls of this sort were common in the 10th and 11th centuries, but diminished in numbers through later centuries (pp.1741–3, *AY* 17/11; p.1966, *AY* 17/12) so that these, too, are likely to be residual artefacts.

As well as the spindle whorls, there are some loose ends of half-spun linen yarn, *14585*, from 11th/12th century Bedern. These probably represent waste ends cut off and discarded by the spinner and provide useful confirmation of the evidence of the flax heckle spike, that flax was being processed and spun on the site in the Anglo-Norman period.

Weaving

The fragments of loom weights from medieval levels at Fishergate (three examples), Coppergate (two) and the Foundry (one) are all undoubtedly residual Anglo-Saxon or Anglo-Scandinavian artefacts. They are rare finds in York, when compared with the many hundreds recovered from Early and Middle Anglo-Saxon sites, probably because the warp-weighted loom with which they were used had largely gone out of use before the town started on its 10th century period of growth (p.1753, *AY* 17/11). A fragment of double-ended pin-beater from Fishergate, Period 6a, *5527*, would have been used with the same loom as the loom weights and must also be a residual find (pp.1269–70, *AY* 17/9).

Other artefacts connected with weaving were more common on Anglo-Scandinavian sites in York, but they seem to have become rarer from the late 11th century onwards, as weaving became a specialist guild craft (pp.1827–9, *AY* 17/11). At Coppergate, medieval levels yielded an iron blade from a toothed weft-beater, *6608* (Fig.1345), and a single-ended bone pin-beater, *6675*, both of which would have been used with the two-beam vertical tapiter's loom, on tenement A; a wooden heddle cradle *6654* and heddle rod *6655*, came from a webster's horizontal cloth loom, on tenement B (pp.1757–66, 1815, *AY* 17/11). There is also a coarse-toothed wooden object, probably the blade from another weft-beater, *6653*, which

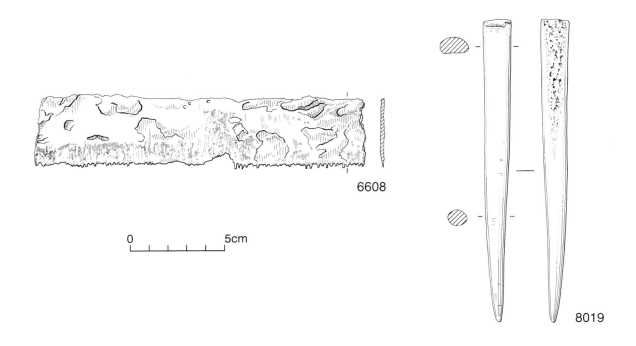

0   5cm

6608

8019

Fig.1345 *Tools used in weaving: toothed weft-beater 6608 from 16–22 Coppergate; bone pin-beater 8019 from Bedern. Scale 1:2*

may have been used with a two-beam vertical loom for the production of sacking.

There is only one other artefact connected with weaving from the other four sites, a long single-ended pin-beater which was recovered from post-medieval levels of the College garden at Bedern (*8019*) (Fig.1345). It has been cut from a cattle or horse long bone (S. O'Connor, pers. comm.) and the shaft and tip are smooth and highly polished, while the square end has been left with a roughly chopped edge. This is one of the two types of single-ended pin-beater used with the two-beam vertical loom (Walton Rogers 2001). At 166mm, it is longer than most pin-beaters from outside York, but *6678* from 12th century Coppergate (probaby residual Anglo-Scandinavian: p.1815, *AY* 17/11) is the same and there are roughouts for pin-beaters of similar length, *6676* and *7040*, from late Anglo-Scandinavian levels of the same site (*AY* 17/12). There are as yet no single-ended bone pin-beaters from England dated later than the 13th century and it is almost certain that the Bedern example is another redeposited artefact.

Finishing and laundering (Fig.1346)

There was no evidence for cloth finishing at any of the sites under discussion. Some small iron hooks — five from Coppergate (*6609–12* and *11730*), one from the Foundry (*13174*), one from Bedern (*13733*) and three from Fishergate (*14911–13*) — are similar to the 'tenter hooks' used to stretch cloth after fulling,

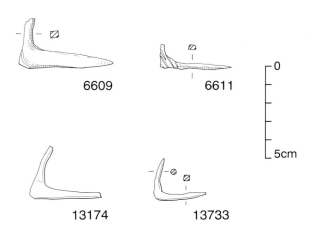

6609   6611

13174   13733

0

5cm

Fig.1346 *Iron tenter hooks or hooks for suspending wall hangings 6609 and 6611 from 16–22 Coppergate, 13174 from the Foundry (drawn from X-ray), 13733 from Bedern. Scale 1:2*

but identical hooks were also used to hang tapestries and other wall hangings. Without any supporting evidence for cloth finishing at Bedern, Fishergate or Coppergate, their use for suspending hangings seems more likely. No glass slick-stones for smoothing garments after laundering were recovered from any of the sites, apart from Coppergate, where there were fifteen fragments of examples from medieval deposits (pp.1772, 1775–9, *AY* 17/11).

Cutting and stitching (Figs.1347–8)

Needles were present at all sites and thimbles, shears and scissors were also well represented (Table 281). In the large collection of needles from Coppergate, it was possible to see an increased use of copper alloy in relation to iron in the medieval period (Table 150, *AY* 17/11). The evidence given in Table 281 suggests that the use of copper alloy rose over the period in question; taking all four sites together, there are thirteen iron and three copper alloy needles dated to the 11th–13th centuries, and eight iron and fourteen copper alloy dated to the 14th century or later. **Patrick Ottaway** adds:

Iron needle heads were made in one of two ways (Rollins 1981, 7). In the first the head was flattened and the eye then punched through it. As can be seen on 11733 (Fig.1347) this could be a two-stage process with a preliminary indentation made by a punch with a wedge-shaped tip and then the hole pierced by a punch with a rounded tip. Alternatively, the head was formed by flattening the end of the strip and splitting it with a small chisel. The bifurcated ends were then splayed out and the ends closed and welded to form the eye. Punching usually results in a round eye while the second method of head manufacture results in an elongated lentoid eye. In Anglo-Scandinavian contexts 65% of needles had punched eyes and 35% had eyes made in the second way.

These figures mask a rise in the use of punched round or oval eyes during the Anglo-Scandinavian period, which has been noted at Coppergate and other sites outside York (p.547, *AY* 17/6; pp.1781–7, *AY* 17/11). By the medieval period, punched eyes seem to have become standard and of the needles represented in Table 281, only one iron needle, from Period 6 at Piccadilly, *13032*, can be confidently identified as the split-and-welded type which was typical of early Anglo-Scandinavian Coppergate. The remaining iron and all of the copper alloy needles in

the table, where identifiable, have punched eyes. The 74 needles from Period 6 at Coppergate were mostly typical hand-sewing needles of medium to coarse gauge, 40–60mm long for iron and 50–80mm long for copper alloy. Amongst these was a leatherworking needle with a triangular cross-section, *6632*, three fine needles, probably used in silk-work (iron *6615* and copper alloy *6626–7*), and six especially large ones, 110–75mm long, which may have been used to stitch sacking (p.1785, *AY* 17/11).

The needles from Bedern, Piccadilly and Fishergate are similarly 37–60mm long for iron and 45–80mm long for copper alloy. One example in copper alloy from Bedern (*14179*) is 109mm long, approaching the size of the sacking needles from Coppergate (*6614, 6616–17, 6619, 11733*). Most would have been used in ordinary needlework, although one in iron from Piccadilly (*13031*) is as fine as the silk-working ones from Coppergate, and two copper alloy examples with triangular sections at the tip from Bedern (*14176–7*) and one from the Foundry (*13299*) may have been used for leather. This does not necessarily imply that a specialist leather-worker was working on the site. At a time when leather garments were commonplace, a leather-working needle for running repairs was probably an essential component of the housewife's workbox.

Eight copper alloy thimbles (Fig.1347), used to help push the needle through the cloth, have been described by **N.S.H. Rogers**:

Eight copper alloy thimbles were recovered from Fishergate (15146–7), the Foundry (13302–3) and Bedern (14185–8). The earliest example from the group, an open-topped tailor's thimble, 13302, also represents one of the earliest firmly dated thimbles recovered in England (Egan 1998, 265); it was found in a late 13th–early 14th century layer associated with a possible casting pit at the Foundry. The two other ring thimbles recovered from the Foundry and Bedern (13303, 14188) both came from mid 16th to 17th century deposits; 13303 has the maker's mark 'H' stamped into it, possibly indicating manufacture in Nuremburg, Germany (Holmes 1985, 3). The three domed thimbles found at Bedern (14185–7) all derive from garden soil of the mid–late 15th century; the small size of 14186 suggests that it may have been made for a child. Both the Fishergate thimbles are also domed; 15146, found in a Period 6e (15th–16th century) cess pit, has an unusual detachable leather lining, made from a strip of leather

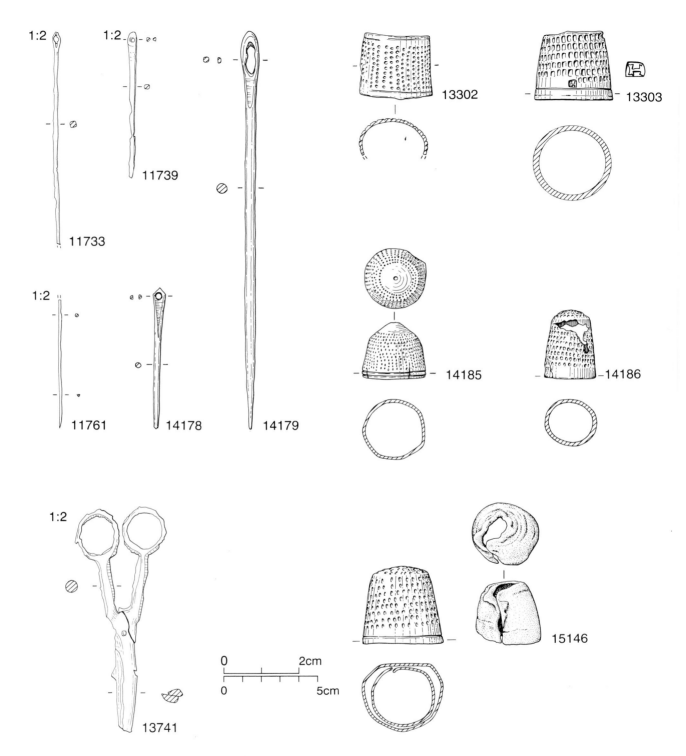

Fig.1347 *Iron needles 11733, 11739, 11761 from 16–22 Coppergate; copper alloy needles 14178–9 from Bedern; copper alloy thimbles 13302–3 from the Foundry, 14185–6 from Bedern, 15146 from 46–54 Fishergate (with leather lining); iron scissors 13741 from Bedern. Iron objects scale 1:2, copper alloy objects scale 1:1, detail of 13303 2:1*

sewn into a sub-dome shape, clearly preserved as a result of damp burial deposits. Only one other example of a lined thimble is known to the author, this having been recov-ered by a metal detector user in Loversall, South York-shire. Inside the Loversall thimble, an off-white coarse linen fragment of irregular shape was corroded to the top (P.

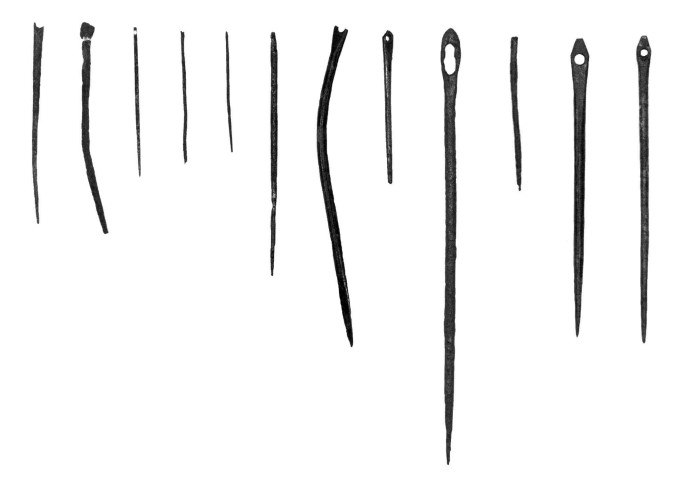

Fig.1348 Needles (from left to right) 13734 and 13736 from Bedern (iron), 13030, 13029 and 13031 from 22 Piccadilly (iron), 14174, 14177–9 from Bedern (copper alloy), 13738 from Bedern (iron), 14175 and 14180 from Bedern (copper alloy). Actual length of 14180 77mm

Walton Rogers, pers. comm.). It seems most likely that these linings were inserted as padding to narrow the size of the thimble, although other functions, such as relieving the pressure on the nail or avoiding the feel of cold metal on arthritic fingers, cannot be discounted (E. Holmes, pers. comm.). Although these two thimbles appear to be the only examples so far discovered, the use of padding or linings may not have been uncommon, their insubstantial nature and manufacture from organic materials probably explaining their absence archaeologically.

Finally, iron shears were recovered from Coppergate (six), Fishergate (four), Bedern (nine) and 2 Aldwark (two) (Table 281; see also pp.2749–51 and Figs. 1353–4). The six from Coppergate (revised from five in Table 150, *AY* 17/11) are spread over the period from the 11th/12th to the 14th/15th century but the nine examples from Bedern cluster in late 14th and 15th century deposits. Shears may have been used

for all sorts of household tasks, of which cutting cloth is just one possibility. The Bedern blades are relatively standard, at 52–80mm long, while the Coppergate shears were more variable, with blades from 35 to 125mm long. The smallest of these may well have been used in textile crafts such as needlework or hand-spinning. A pair of iron scissors, *13741*, has also been found in early 14th century levels at Bedern. Scissors were a comparative rarity in the medieval period (Øye 1988, 107–9), although there is an example of a pair from late 12th century Lurk Lane, Beverley, E. Yorkshire (Fig.1315, **6**; Armstrong and Tomlinson 1991, 136).

Netting (Fig.1349)

A small netting needle or shuttle, *14184*, was found in a post-medieval deposit at Bedern. It is 87mm long and made from a thin copper alloy rod

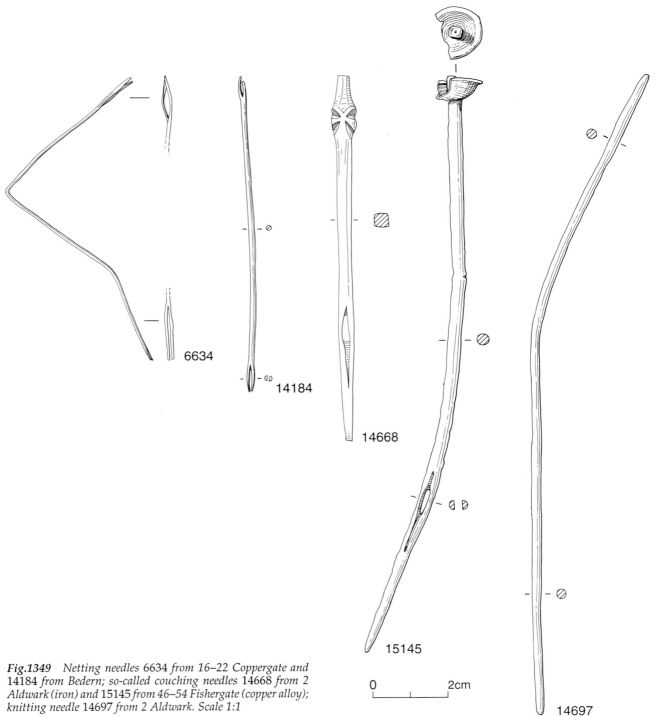

Fig.1349 *Netting needles* 6634 *from 16–22 Coppergate and* 14184 *from Bedern; so-called couching needles* 14668 *from 2 Aldwark (iron) and* 15145 *from 46–54 Fishergate (copper alloy); knitting needle* 14697 *from 2 Aldwark. Scale 1:1*

0 _____ 2cm

which has been split into a fork at either end. A similar netting needle, 111mm long, was recovered from late 14th or early 15th century Coppergate (*6634*, pp.1789–90, *AY* 17/11) and there are further examples, 101–47mm long, of the same date from London

(Crowfoot et al. 1992, 147). In view of the quantity of redeposited material at Bedern, it is tempting to see *14184* as a residual late medieval artefact, but in fact silk netting continued to be made in later periods. An almost intact example of a silk and cotton hairnet was found inside the wall of a 16th century cottage at Aysgarth, North Yorkshire (kindly shown to the author by the owners), and similar netting needles, in white metals, can still be found in Victorian and Edwardian workboxes. The post-medieval date for the object, in this instance, could be correct.

So-called couching needles (Fig.1349)

Two similar items, one in copper alloy from late 12th or 13th century Fishergate (*15145*) and the other in tin-plated iron from late 14th century Aldwark (*14668*), are examples of the objects sometimes known in the archaeological literature as couching needles. Both have a sturdy stem which tapers to a blunt point at one end, where the stem is pierced by a long slit. Both are ornamented at the other end, the iron example with a moulded triangular design resembling a four-petal flower (the top of this one is missing) and the copper alloy example with a hollow hemisphere, which was probably originally a complete sphere. The copper alloy example is longer than the iron one, but they seem generically the same and presumably had the same function.

Two further examples of these items, in copper alloy, are known from medieval Winchester (Fig.1315, **29**). In their report on the Winchester finds, Biddle and Elmhirst (1991) list others from Britain and the Continent, ranging in date from the 8th to the 13th century. To these may be added a further example reportedly from Roman levels at Angel Court, London (Wheeler 1930, 105, pl.XLII), although its spherical head has much in common with the later finds. A number of tentative identifications for these objects have arisen over the years. Couching needles, suggested by Biddle and Elmhirst (1991, 807–15), seems highly unlikely, in view of the fine nature of medieval couched embroidery and the large diameter of the objects. There is another tool used in couched embroidery, a 'broche', used to lay the gold thread on top of the fabric, which loosely resembles these items, but a broche generally has an open, forked end (Groves 1973, 91). Use as hair pins should not be disregarded. Similar ornamented pins were worn in the 17th century, although in these the slit is further towards the pin head. Margeson, in discussing the Norwich finds, refers to a Dutch portrait in which a woman wears such a pin at the left temple, with a jewel suspended from the slit (Margeson 1993, 8–9).

Biddle and Elmhirst's second suggestion that these objects are lawyers' bodkins, used to pass ribbon and cords through legal documents, is inviting. Their illustration of the Winchester examples alongside a modern lawyer's bodkin shows striking similarities in size and shape between the three (Biddle and Elmhirst 1991, pl.LV). The distribution of the English finds may also support this view. One of the Winchester examples comes from the bishop's palace at Wolvesey and the other from The Brooks, an area of tenements close to, and probably servicing, the Cathedral. Similarly, the Aldwark example was found near to the Minster and the College of the Vicars Choral, and the Fishergate object is from the earliest phase of the priory. Ecclesiastical establishments of this sort would have generated any number of legal documents and the clerks who compiled them may well have been housed nearby.

Knitting (Figs.1349–50)

Two copper alloy rods with a rounded point at either end, *14697–8*, were recovered from the same late 14th century layer, possibly a floor, in the tenement at 2 Aldwark. A fragment of a third rod of post-medieval date came from the Foundry (*13304*). A.R. Goodall has suggested that these are double-ended knitting needles, used in sets of four or five for knitting in the round. The dimensions of the Aldwark examples — both are c.180mm long and *14697* is 2·6mm diameter (British knitting needle No.12) while *14698* is 1·9mm diameter (British No.14) — match those of a set of 1940s steel needles, 180mm long and size No.14, which the author used to knit a replica of a late 15th century wool cap from Newcastle upon Tyne (Fig.1315, **1**; Walton 1981, 199–200). The early date of the Aldwark examples, however, requires a brief review of the evidence for the arrival of knitting in this country.

Knitting with multiple needles and a continuous thread is generally believed to have been brought to southern Europe by the Arabs. The earliest survivals of the craft are fine knitted goods in silk, found across Europe in high-status burials of the 13th and 14th century (Rutt 1987, 39–52; Schmedding 1978, 90–1, 284–8; Flury-Lemberg 1988, 18; Cardon 1993, 38–9). In the early stages knitting may have been a specialist craft, but the number of 14th century Italian and south German paintings depicting the Virgin Mary knitting (Turnau 1983, 383–5; Rutt 1987, 44–50) sug-

Fig.1350   *Copper alloy knitting needles: (left to right) 14697–8 from 2 Aldwark; 13304 from the Foundry. Actual length of 13304 133·2mm*

London and Newcastle are, of course, ports, where foreign goods may be expected, and there are records of knitted garments being imported in Italian galleys at this time (Crowfoot et al. 1992, 74). Indeed, analysis of the Newcastle fragment showed it to have been made of a south European wool and dye (Walton 1981). There is therefore no definite evidence that the craft was practised in England until 1465, when a certain Marjoria Claton of Ripon was described as a 'cappeknytter' (Buckland 1979, 23, citing Ripon Chapter Acts, SS **64**, 1875, 120).

From this point on, knitters begin to appear with increasing frequency in documents and by the 16th century knitting was obviously well established in the Yorkshire countryside (Sellers 1974, 412–13; Hartley and Ingilby 1978, 6ff). In 1590 the burgesses of York even set up a knitting school for poor children, in a house in St Saviourgate (ibid., 9). Medieval York had close connections with the Continent and it is quite likely that the craft of knitting reached York as soon as anywhere in England. Until, however, further evidence such as medieval knitted goods has been found in the city, it is impossible to be sure that the metal rods from Aldwark were really used for this purpose.

Summary of evidence for textile production

At Fishergate all the tools associated with yarn and cloth production can be shown to be residual Anglo-Scandinavian artefacts or dumped material probably brought in from outside the area. Only needlework, represented by needles and thimbles, is likely to have been practised at the priory. At 22 Piccadilly, there is also only limited evidence for the textile crafts before the late 15th or 16th century, but at this stage wool seems to have been brought on to the site and presumably dyed in the woad vat which was clearly operational at this time. The wool comb spikes from this site could have been used to open out the fleece before dyeing, although they come from the periods immediately before and after the dye vat evidence.

gest that it soon became a woman's domestic craft. By the end of the 14th century more ordinary wool knitting was reaching the towns of northern Europe. The earliest examples from Britain are dated to the late 14th century and are from three waterfront sites in London (Crowfoot et al. 1992, 72–5). There is also a single piece from Newcastle upon Tyne dated to the first half of the 15th century (Walton 1981, 200).

There is also evidence for woad dyeing nearby at 17–21 Piccadilly in the late 14th century (Alldritt et al. 1991, 9). This part of Piccadilly lies on the periphery of a zone focused on the parish of St Denys, Walmgate, where a number of dyers are known to have been resident in the late 14th (Leggett 1971) and 15th century (Fig.857b, *AY* 17/11; Goldberg 1992, 64–71).

The Bedern area contrasts with Fishergate and Piccadilly. Here flax seems to have been prepared and spun in the Anglo-Norman period, followed by flax and wool processing, and spinning in later phases. There was no dyeing or weaving there, but needlework is well represented by needles, thimbles and shears. Yarn production and needlework are typically the skills of the medieval housewife and their presence at the College of Vicars Choral may indicate that female domestic servants were working there.

Medieval Coppergate, as described in *AY* 17/11, was for a while home to specialist artisans — tapiters on one tenement and websters on another — although there is no evidence for them after the early 13th century. The dyers who had been active during the Anglo-Scandinavian period had left the site even earlier, in the mid 11th century. The archaeological evidence suggests that there may have been a shift from guild crafts to a trade in wool over the 12th to 14th centuries, at a time when historical evidence shows the Coppergate-Pavement area becoming increasingly a focus for merchants and drapers. The domestic crafts of yarn production and needlework, however, continued to be practised on the site until the 14th century or later.

Jet working

Worked and unworked fragments of jet, shale and other jet-like materials such as cannel coal, lignite or other fossil coal (described as non-jet as they cannot be more positively identified), as well as finished objects, were found across the York sites. Material identification was undertaken by Ian Panter; the methods he used are described in *AY* 17/14 (pp.2470–3).

Evidence of possible jet working was found in medieval levels at 16–22 Coppergate, where worked and unworked fragments of jet (*11066–7, 11069–72*), as well as a cross-shaped roughout, possibly an unfinished pendant (*11068*), were recovered.

Four fragments (*11069–72*) derive from late 11th–12th century dumped deposits; the roughout, *11068*, was found in the 13th century demolition spread B6d6, associated with Building B6d1, and other fragments (*11066–7*) in early 14th century occupation deposits in B6f, the building which replaced B6d1. The relative proximity of pieces *11066–8* may indicate a common origin, possibly pointing to jet working on the site; the unworked pieces from earlier contexts (*11069–72*) may be from earlier jet working or could be residual from possible jet working in the Anglo-Scandinavian period (see pp.2498–500, *AY* 17/14).

Other jet objects recovered from medieval levels at Coppergate include finger-rings (*11073–7*, see p.2928) and dice (*11078–9*, see p.2949). Two cross pendants (*9862–3*) found in 12th century levels, but possibly of earlier date, have been published in *AY* 17/14 (pp.2590–1).

Jet, non-jet and shale offcuts and fragments were also recovered from Fishergate (*14772*), the Foundry (*13104–6*) and Bedern (*13492, 13503, 13505*). The non-jet fragment from Fishergate (*14772*) was found in priory demolition levels, while the Bedern pieces derive from the earliest levels, e.g. *13492* from Period 1A, through to late to post-medieval deposits (e.g. *13104*) and are too few to indicate any working on site, although jet and non-jet objects including rosary beads and knife handles (see p.2759) were also found there.

Agriculture

Well before the medieval period much of the foodstuff required to feed the population of York was imported to the city, mainly from farms in the surrounding countryside. However, citizens throughout the centuries would have augmented their purchases with any food which they could grow in their gardens and backyards. Some of the agricultural tools described here could well have been used in this type of small-scale cultivation. It is known that many of the vicars had their own gardens within the college precinct at Bedern; there was also a common garden where vegetables and herbs were grown and vines were cultivated. In 1328–9 a spade and a shovel were purchased for use in this garden (YMA, VC 6/2/10). From the early 14th century, at least, there was an orchard within the college garden. See *AY* 10/5, 578–9 for further details. Some wooden agricultural tools

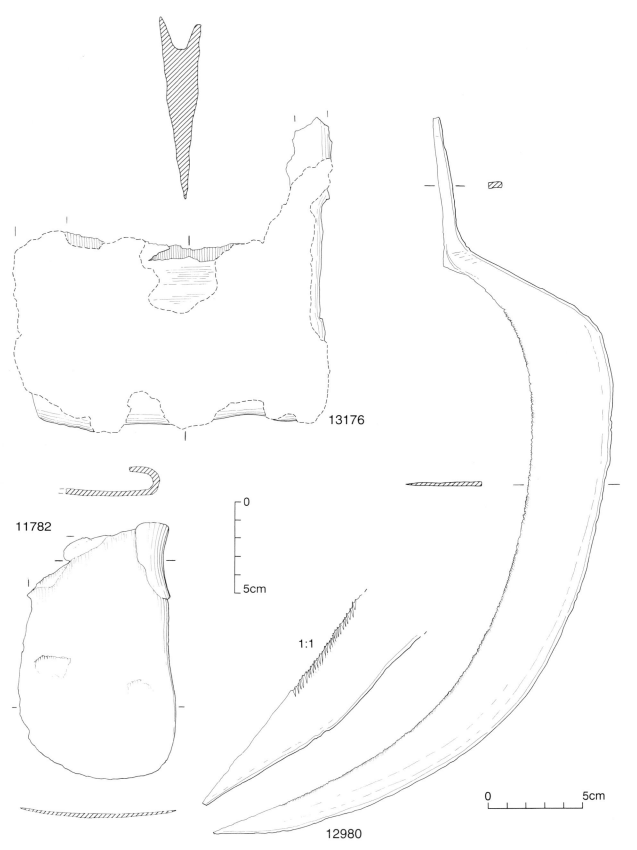

13176

11782

0

5cm

1:1

12980

0   5cm

Fig.1351 *Iron spade sheaths* 11782 *from 16–22 Coppergate and* 13176 *from the Foundry; iron sickle* 12980 *from the Coppergate watching brief. Scale 1:2*

from York have been published in *AY* 17/13 (pp.2315–24), including a spade with a rounded tip from 16–22 Coppergate (*8969*) to which an iron spade sheath very like *11782* would have been fitted.

Agricultural tools

Spade sheaths (Fig.1351)

There are three iron spade sheaths, two from Coppergate, *11782* (mid 13th century context) and *11783* (unstratified), and one (*13176*) from a post-medieval context at the Foundry. Medieval spades usually had a wooden blade with some form of sheath or edging to prevent wear. One would expect the blade to slot into a mouth at the base of the sheath, but *11782* simply covered the whole of the rear of the blade and was apparently held in place at the top by two lugs, although one would have thought it also needed securing at the tip. Narrow spade blades with rounded tips similar to that to which *11782* was attached are shown in the Bayeux Tapestry and other medieval illustrations, but it is not possible to tell how their sheaths were attached. *11783* is fragmentary and its original form is unclear. *13176* has a straight tip, slightly concave mouth and an arm on each side which ran up the sides of the wooden blade, terminating in an attachment lug. Many similar examples have been found in 15th–17th century contexts, including Sandal Castle, W. Yorkshire (Fig.1315, 9; I.H. Goodall 1983, 242, fig.5, 52).

Sickle (Fig.1351)

A 15th–16th century context in the Coppergate watching brief produced a complete sickle 410mm long (*12980*). The blade has been filed to create a toothed edge which would saw the stalks of grain or grass as it was pulled towards the user.

Pitchfork tines

13742 (mid 15th–early 17th century context) from Bedern is an incomplete tanged pitchfork or hayfork c.200mm long, of which one tine and the stub of a second survive. *11784* is a single tine from Coppergate, 167mm long and of diamond-shaped cross-section.

Pruning hook

14921 from a 13th century context at Fishergate may be the incomplete blade and tang of a pruning or weed hook.

Fishing

Analysis of fish bones in the medieval period from the sites under discussion revealed a change in the pattern of consumption throughout York from the Anglo-Scandinavian period, with a move from freshwater to marine fish (*AY* 15/5, 375). This was particularly noticeable at Coppergate, less so at Fishergate, possibly because as an out-of-town riverside location it continued to be a convenient place to collect and process freshwater fish (ibid., 399). Equipment recovered from the sites provides evidence of both sea and river fishing.

Fishing equipment

Iron fish hooks were found at Coppergate, and possible lead alloy fishing weights were found at Coppergate (*12939–40*), Bedern (*14513*) and 2 Aldwark (*14730*). Fishergate also produced artefactual evidence of fishing, in the form of lead alloy (*15259–64*) and stone (*14754–5*) weights.

Fish hooks (Fig.1352)

There are eight fish hooks from medieval contexts at Coppergate which may be set alongside seven from Anglo-Scandinavian contexts on the site (pp.600–1, *AY* 17/6). The longest is *11787* which at 79mm long is 24mm longer than the longest pre-Conquest example. There is then a range of sizes down to the smallest which is 28mm long. The terminals do not always survive, but three are looped and three are flattened. Two hooks (*11791–2*) have barbed tips. Medieval fish hooks are not common finds, but those from Coppergate may be compared with a group of fourteen or so from Great Yarmouth which are about 60–80mm long. Several of these are barbed and most appear to have flattened terminals (Rogerson 1976, fig.53); they were presumably used for sea fishing off the Norfolk coast.

Net sinkers (Fig.1352)

Six lead alloy net sinkers from Fishergate (*15259–64*) are elongated oval weights, made from rolled lead alloy sheet and with axial perforations, used to weigh down the lower edges of hand nets during fishing. Examples were also recovered from Anglian and 11th–12th century deposits at the site (*5477–83*, p.1320, *AY* 17/9). *15259–62* were all found in Period 6a deposits; *15259–60* were found together in a soil dump pre-dating the construction of the east cloister

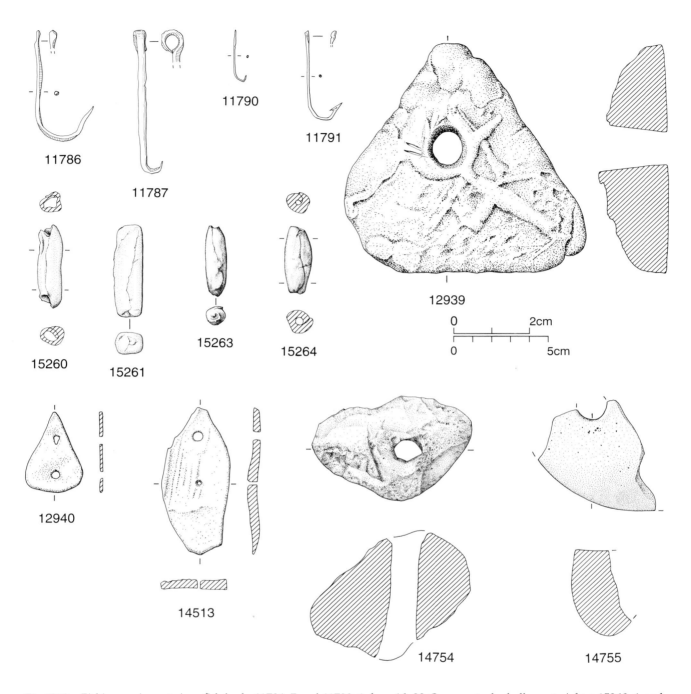

Fig.1352 *Fishing equipment: iron fish hooks 11786–7 and 11790–1 from 16–22 Coppergate; lead alloy net sinkers 15260–1 and 15263–4 from 46–54 Fishergate; lead alloy net weights 12939–40 from 16–22 Coppergate and 14513 from Bedern; stone net weights 14754–5 from 46–54 Fishergate. Scale 1:2; lead alloy net weights 1:1*

alley, *15262* was found in cemetery soil, and *15261* was recovered from a possible floor level within the nave, in which a stone net sinker (*14754*) was also found. The remaining two weights derive from late priory (*15263*) and dissolution (*15264*) deposits.

Two possible lead alloy net weights from Coppergate are both triangular with suspension holes: *12940* derives from 12th/13th century levelling or dumping, while *12939* was found in an early 15th century well construction cut backfill. Though more roughly shaped, *14513* from Bedern may be another example. All resemble others recovered from the wreck of a 15th century vessel in London (Steane and Foreman 1988, 162, fig.15, *32–3*). Also made from rolled lead alloy sheet, *14730* comes from a late 14th–early 15th century level at 2 Aldwark, a site some way from the river; it is possible that this object may have arrived in imported soil.

Stone net weights (Fig.1352)

The site at Fishergate produced three stone net sinkers from Anglian and 11th–12th century levels (*4459–61, AY 17/9*). A flint object made of an erratic cobble with a natural perforation (*14754*) was found in a Period 6a floor level, alongside the lead sinker (*15261*); it may have had the same function. **Dr G.D. Gaunt** comments:

14754, being made of flint, originated in the Upper Cretaceous Chalk Group, which forms the Yorkshire and Lincolnshire Wolds, so provenance from these regions, or from derived glacial and/or beach deposits in adjacent areas is assumed. Flint occurs only in the two middle divisions of the Chalk Group, in upward order the Welton and Burnham formations, and the flint in these is characteris-tically of nodular and tabular form respectively (Wood and Smith 1978, 272–5).

Also from Fishergate, *14755* is a fragmentary perforated stone, which may also have been a net weight, although, being made of chalk, its longevity as such seems questionable (see also *4462*, p.1321, *AY 17/9*). It was recovered from Period 6a/6b cemetery soil. **Dr G.D. Gaunt** comments:

As with 14754, 14755 originated in the Upper Cretaceous Chalk Group, although its shape suggests a secondarily derived beach cobble.

Other tools

Shears (Figs.1353–4)

Twenty-one items have been identified as iron shears or parts of shears. Shears were used for a range of tasks including sheep shearing, cloth manufacture, leatherworking and also for cutting hair and personal toilet.

The larger shears may have been used for sheep shearing. Blades *13746* (108mm long) from a late

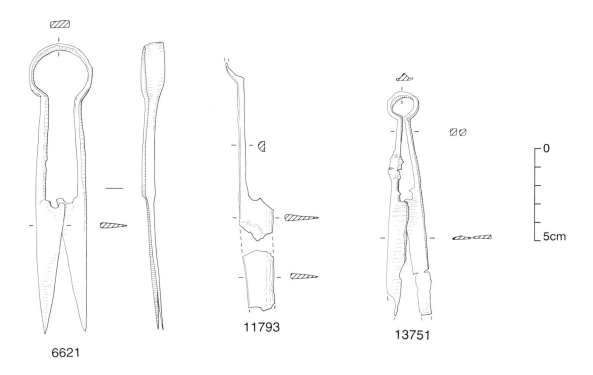

Fig.1353 *Iron shears 6621 and 11793 from 16–22 Coppergate, 13751 from Bedern. Scale 1:2*

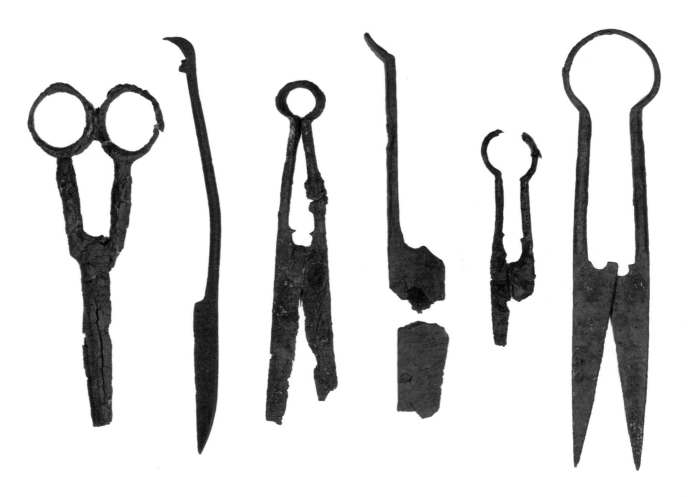

Fig.1354 *(left to right) Iron scissiors 13741 from Bedern; iron shears 15324 from 22 Piccadilly (Anglo-Scandinavian), 13751 from Bedern, 11793, 6622 and 6621 from 16–22 Coppergate. Actual length of 6621 158mm*

14th–early 15th century context at Bedern and *6620* (125mm long) from a mid 12th century context at Coppergate must have come from shears over 200mm in length and would be among the larger medieval shears recorded.

Of medium size, as far as medieval shears are concerned, with a length of 158mm, is one complete pair from Coppergate (*6621*, mid 13th century context). A fragmentary half of a pair (*11793*, 12th–13th century context) from Coppergate was probably of similar size. Slightly smaller is *13751* (late medieval context) from Bedern and an incomplete pair, *6622*, from a 15th century context at Coppergate was probably similar in size.

As far as form is concerned, all the blades appear to have straight backs which curve in at the ends to the tip. They therefore correspond to the knife blade back form C (see p.2752). *13743* (late 14th–15th century context) from Bedern has a cutting edge which is bevelled. There is some variation in the form of the shoulder at the junction of blade and stem. This is usually concave, but there are four examples with an extra 'cusp' (e.g. *6622* and *13751*). Others have straight sloping shoulders, but unique are the shoulders on *6621* (mid 13th century context) which are horizontal, but have a little U-shaped cut in them. There are internal nibs below the bow on *11796* from Coppergate (mid 15th century context). The bows that survive are the simple loops one would expect, but that of *6622* is unusual in having a triangular cross-section.

Knives

There are 235 tanged knives from medieval contexts on the sites under discussion, of which some are complete or nearly so, but many more are incomplete or fragmentary. One hundred and two knives come from Coppergate, 24 from the Foundry, 66 from Bedern and 37 from Fishergate, not including an additional 25 knives which came from Period 4 (11th–12th century) contexts at this last site (*AY* 17/9). Another six knives come from the small sites included in this volume.

The knives may be divided into those with a whittle tang and those with a scale tang. In the former case the knife has a tapering tang which was driven into the handle and in the latter the handle was formed from scale plates which were riveted to the tang. The whittle tang group is by far the largest, there being only 21 certain scale tang knives, all of which come from the Foundry or Bedern. The scale tang knife was introduced to Britain in the mid 13th century and its occurrence at Bedern is not surprising given that the occupation sequence there begins in earnest in the 13th century, but it is curious that no examples were found at either Coppergate or Fishergate as both have occupation deposits of the late and post-medieval periods. Finally, there are two probable knives which appear to have had iron tangs made in one piece with the blade.

Whittle tang knives (Figs.1355–63)

The whittle tang knives from medieval contexts have been classified according to the principles established for the Anglo-Scandinavian knives from Coppergate (pp.559–61, *AY* 17/6). Terms used in description are given in Fig.226, *AY* 17/6. In the first instance this involves the creation of groups based on the form of the blade back as this is the feature which has usually been least subject to wear and

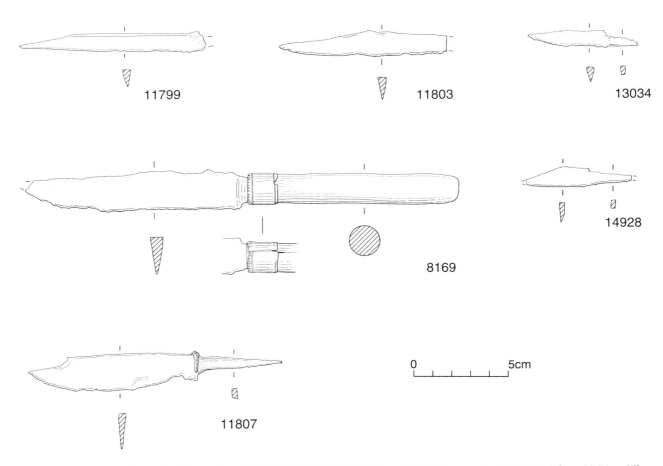

Fig.1355 *Iron knives of blade back form A and B: 11799 (A1), 11803 (A2) from 16–22 Coppergate; 13034 (A3) from 22 Piccadilly; 8169 (Ai) and 14928 (A2) from 46–54 Fishergate; 11807 (B) from 16–22 Coppergate. Scale 1:2*

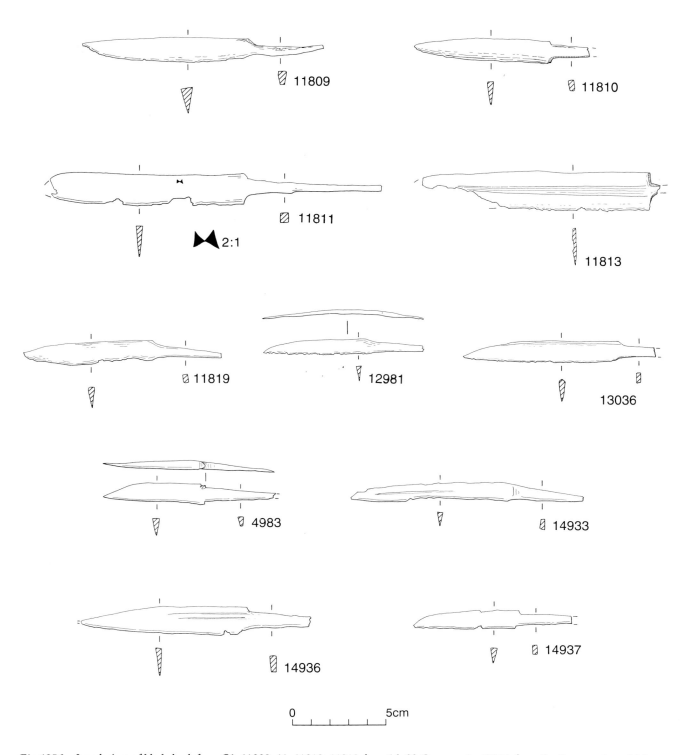

Fig.1356 *Iron knives of blade back form C1: 11809–11, 11813, 11819 from 16–22 Coppergate; 12981 from the Coppergate watching brief; 13036 from 22 Piccadilly; 4983, 14933, 14936–7 from 46–54 Fishergate. Scale 1:2*

damage during use. Classification involves the use of a straight edge to establish whether a blade back has two straight parts meeting at an angle (form A), a straight rear and curved front part (if concave, form B; if convex, form C), a wholly curved back (form D)

or a wholly straight back (form E). Secondly, providing it is unbroken, any knife with a blade back which is wholly straight or had a straight rear part (all forms except D) may be placed on a horizontal line between the tip of the blade and the mid-point of the tip of the tang to determine whether the straight part is horizontal or slopes up or down. Subsequent to the consideration of back form, cutting edge form, surface features and dimensions may be analysed.

In all there are seventeen knife blades with back form A, the 'angle-back' (Fig.1355); this is c.14% of the 123 knives for which a back form could be determined. The commonest variant was form A2 (ten examples) in which the rear part of the back rises to the angle; there were five examples of form A1 in which rear part is horizontal. The angle between the line of the rear part of the back and the front part is usually c.20°, but *11806* is unusual in having an angle of only 4°.

In Anglo-Scandinavian contexts at Coppergate 19% of knives had back form A (pp.562–5, *AY* 17/6). Although some of those in medieval contexts will probably be Anglo-Scandinavian in origin and those in medieval contexts at Fishergate may be Anglian in origin, it appears that angle-back blades remained current until the late 12th century. Another three have, for example, been recorded from contexts of this date in London (Cowgill et al. 1987, 78–80, 4–6).

There is only one knife of blade back form B (*11807*) which comes from a 12th–13th century context at Coppergate (Fig.1355). This may be residual, but the form is not common in the pre-Conquest period either, Anglo-Scandinavian contexts at Coppergate producing only two specimens (p.565, *AY* 17/6). *11807* is also unusual in having a very pronounced convex cutting edge.

The most numerous back form in the medieval period is C, of which there are 69 examples. This represents c.56% of knives with determinable back forms, a very similar percentage to that in Anglo-Scandinavian contexts at Coppergate (55%). There are three variants (C1–3). There are 24 examples of back form C1 (Fig.1356) on which the rear part is horizontal before it curves down to the tip and 22 examples of back form C3 in which the rear part of the back slopes down before it curves away to the tip. For C2 see below. On 20 blades the variant cannot be determined with certainty (Ci) (Fig.1357). It is likely that blades with back form C3 (Fig.1357) originally had back form C1 when they were made, but have been worn in such a way as to cause the back to slope down (see p.570, *AY* 17/6). This may in turn be

related to metallographic structure in the sense that blades with a steel core or similar structure (which are the most common in the medieval period) as opposed to a steel strip welded to an iron back could be worn more heavily before becoming redundant (pp.598–9, *AY* 17/6, and see p.2766 for types of metallographic structure).

Back form C2, in which the rear part rises before curving down to the tip, occurs on only two knives, *14939* from a 13th century context at Fishergate and *13754* from a post-medieval context at Bedern, both of which may be residual as the form appears more common in pre-Conquest than post-Conquest contexts; ten, for example, were recovered from Anglo-Scandinavian contexts at Coppergate (p.570, *AY* 17/6).

There are 28 examples of blade back form D in which the back curves over the whole length of the blade (Fig.1358). Twenty came from Coppergate where they make up c.28·5% of knives of which the blade back form can be determined which compares with 24% in the Anglo-Scandinavian contexts (p.572, *AY* 17/6). Some medieval examples may be residual, but the form clearly remained current throughout the medieval period.

There are only two knife blades (*11867–8*), both from 13th century contexts at Coppergate, with backs which appear to run straight from the shoulder to tip (back form E; Fig.1358). *11868* has a blade of average size, but *11867* is an unusually large knife (length 215mm) with a very broad blade on which the cutting edge sweeps up sharply to the tip. It probably had some specialist function. Knives very similar in form and dimensions come from a medieval context at North Elmham Park, Norfolk (Fig.1315, **17**; Goodall 1980a, 510, fig.265, 24), and a 15th–16th century context at Somerby, Lincolnshire (Mynard 1969, 83, fig.12, IW60).

13772 from a mid–late 13th century context at Bedern has an unusually shaped blade back which runs straight from the shoulder for 15mm and then slopes down sharply before sloping away more gently to the tip (Fig.1358). No obvious parallel suggests itself. Finally, *14958* is a knife from a 13th century context at Fishergate which has a blade with a most unusual curled-over tip (Fig.1358). No comparable knives are known from Britain, but one has been recorded in a medieval context at Ytre Moa in Norway (Bakka 1965, fig.7).

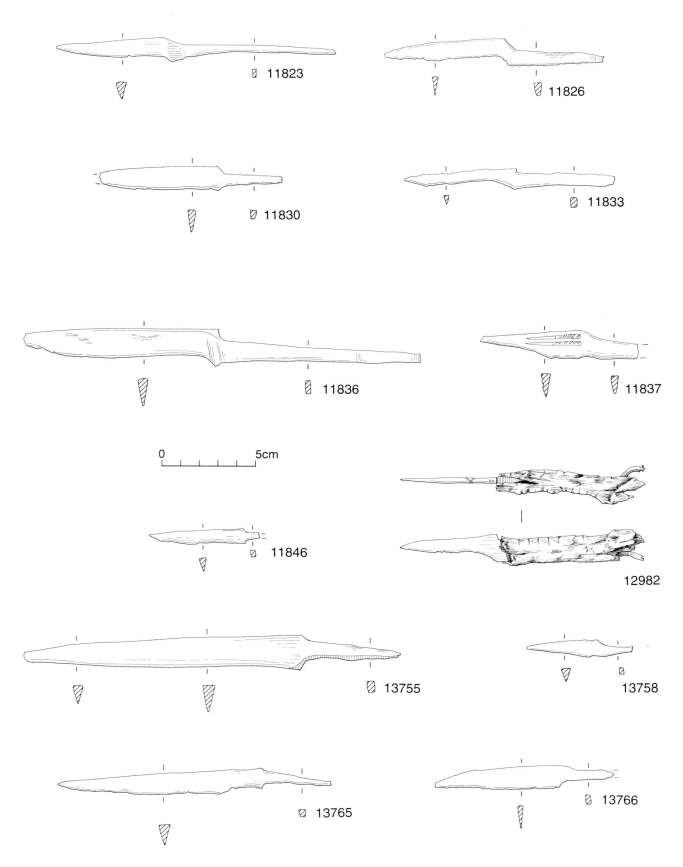

Fig.1357 *Iron knives of blade back form C3 and Ci: 11823 (C3), 11826 (C3), 11830 (C3), 11833 (C3), 11836–7 (C3), 11846 (Ci) from 16–22 Coppergate; 12982 (C3) from the Coppergate watching brief; 13755 (C3), 13758 (C3), 13765–6 (Ci) from Bedern. Scale 1:2*

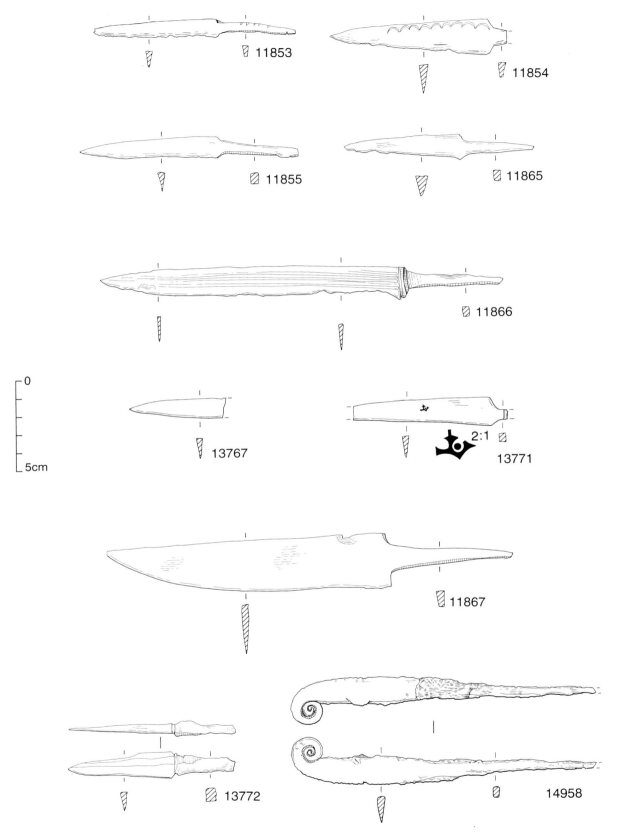

Fig.1358 *Iron knives of blade back form D: 11853–5, 11865–6 from 16–22 Coppergate, 13767 and 13771 from Bedern; iron knife of blade back form E: 11867 from 16–22 Coppergate; iron knife with a blade of unusual form 13772 from Bedern; iron knife with curled over blade tip 14958 from 46–54 Fishergate. Scale 1:2*

Cutting edges

The medieval knives exhibit the usual range of cutting edge forms identified on the Anglo-Scandinavian knives from Coppergate (pp.572–4, *AY* 17/6). As originally made, a blade probably had a cutting edge which was either straight, straight before curving up slightly to the tip or, more rarely, slightly convex over its whole length. The effect of wear was in many cases to create a reverse S-shape. This is the result of sharpening with a hone stone. The S-shape is usually quite slight, but can be very marked on occasions (e.g. *11826* and *11833*). Wear may also create a concave cutting edge or other less regular shapes.

Surface features

A number of knives exhibit what may be described as surface features. Some may have been intended as decoration, but others, as in the case of cutlers' marks, may have been primarily intended to designate the product of a particular smith.

There are eight examples of knives with simple horizontal, incised grooves near the top of the blade faces. In five cases (*11799, 11862, 11895, 13762, 14934*) there is one groove on each face, but on the blade of *14936* from Fishergate there are two grooves on one face and one on the other, while on *11880*, an unusually long and narrow blade from a mid 13th century context at Coppergate, there is a groove on only one face. These simple horizontal grooves are a feature first seen on knives in the early Anglo-Saxon period and are common on knives from middle Anglo-Saxon and late Anglo-Saxon/Anglo-Scandinavian contexts (pp.579–81, *AY* 17/6). Their existence on the knives referred to above may indicate that these objects are residual in their medieval contexts.

In the case of *11813* from Coppergate (13th century context) a shallow channel c.5mm wide runs along the centre of each face of the blade from shoulder to tip (Fig.1356, p.2752). A similar feature can be seen on a knife from a late 11th–early 12th century context at Winchester (Goodall 1990, fig.254, *2709*).

A knife, originally having an angle-back blade, which is almost certainly Anglo-Scandinavian in origin, is *11837* (early 13th century context) from Coppergate which has two grooves on each face inlaid with copper wire twisted into a herringbone

pattern (Fig.1359). This feature can be seen on a number of other knives, almost always with an angle-back blade, found in pre-Conquest contexts at, for example, Canterbury (Fig.1315, **28**; Saunders 1978, 25–63, fig.11, *13*), Cheddar (Goodall 1979c, 264, *31*), London (Pritchard 1991, 124–7, *1*), Oxford (Fig.1315, **23**; Durham 1977, fig. 25, *5*) and Winchester (Goodall 1990, 841, *2654*).

Two whittle tang knives and one blade fragment from Bedern have incised and inlaid designs. On *13777* from an early 14th century context at Bedern there are eleven surviving crosses between two horizontal grooves (Figs.1360, 1363). On *13792*, an incomplete blade from a mid 15th–early 17th century context at Bedern, the left face had a row of lozenges within a curvilinear scrollwork pattern set between two pairs of horizontal lines; the inlay has been identified as mercury gilded silver (Fig.1361). **Tim Horsley** writes:

Visual inspection indicated that the blade was inlaid with a white metal, becoming yellow in colour towards the tang. Analysis of the two differently coloured areas showed them both to be rich in silver, with the yellow metal richer in gold. Mercury was also detected in both areas. Closer examination revealed traces of keying, visible where the metal inlay has worn down exposing alternate bands of inlay and the iron of the blade. It appears that following the preparation of a portion of the blade by keying, a thin silver wire was laid on this area in the desired pattern. To attach this wire to the knife, it was then hammered, a process which flattened both the silver wire and the keying. Once secured to the blade, the silver pattern was gilded using mercury, to give the appearance of a solid gold overlay. During use, the gold has become partially worn off exposing the silver wire, except in the area next to the handle where the blade was slightly better protected.

The blade fragment *13184* from a post-medieval context at the Foundry has a concave channel on both faces, each inlaid with silver wire in a running loop pattern (Fig.1362). A similar pattern in mercury gilded silver wire can be seen on a knife from the County Hospital site in York (YAT 1983.19, sf166; Fig.1314, **1**).

Inlaid knives of medieval date are not common, although other examples have come from London. Inlaid crosses similar to those on *13777* can be seen on two blades from late 14th century contexts (Cowgill et al. 1987, *73, 92*). A looped pattern set in concave channels similar to *13184* can be seen on a knife

Fig.1359   Detail of 11837, an iron knife from 16–22 Coppergate, showing inlaid copper wire

Fig.1361   Detail of 13792, an iron knife from Bedern, showing
inlay of mercury gilded silver

from a late 13th century context (ibid., 25). Another
blade fragment with a similar pattern comes from a
15th–early 16th century context at Oxford (Goodall
and Hinton 1977, 142, fig.25, 5). In view of their rarity, it may be significant that two of the York inlaid
knives come from the College of Vicars Choral at
Bedern where some, at least, of the residents were
probably of higher social status and greater wealth
than those of contemporary Coppergate where no
examples were found. It may also be noted that two
other iron objects, possibly from horse equipment,
treated with mercury gilding come from the Foundry (13279) and Bedern (14122).

Similar in inspiration to the grooves discussed
above are, perhaps, a line of nine semi-circles punched

into the top of each blade face of 11854, a knife from
a late 13th century context at Coppergate (see
Fig.1358). No exact parallel for this feature suggests
itself.

There are three examples of knife blades, all of
back form C, from 13th–early 14th century contexts
at Fishergate with small notches cut into the back at
the shoulder (4999 and 14933–4). In addition, it may
be noted that there are two at the shoulder of an
unstratified blade from Coppergate (11904). Ten examples of similar notches were found on blades in
Anglo-Scandinavian contexts at Coppergate. Evidence from York and elsewhere suggests they are
probably a pre-Conquest feature which can occur on
blades of both back form A and C (pp.581–2, AY

Fig.1360   Detail of 13777, an iron knife from Bedern, showing
inlaid crosses

Fig.1362   Detail of 13184, an iron knife from the Foundry,
showing inlaid silver wire

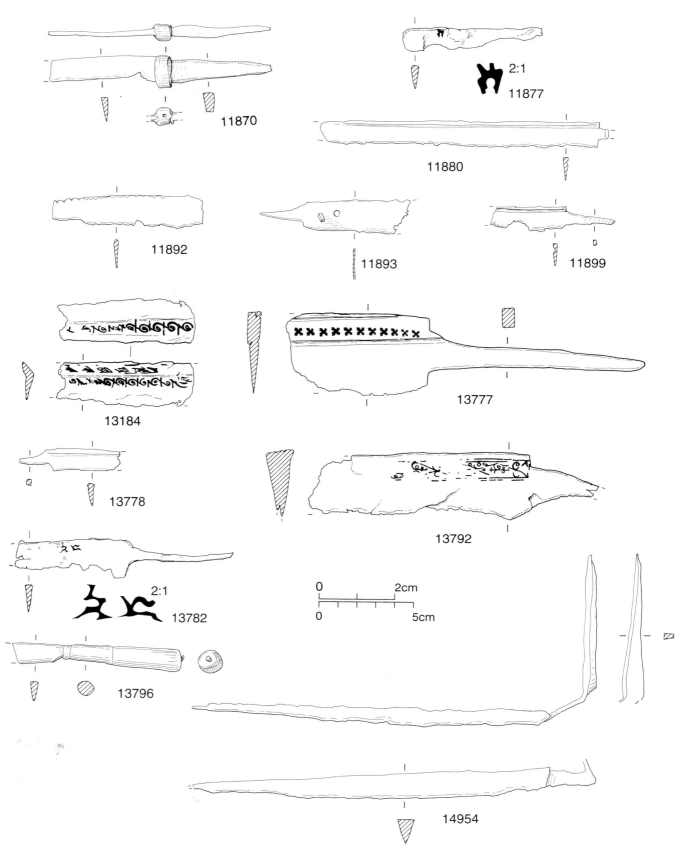

Fig.1363 *Knives of indeterminate blade back form:* 11870, 11877, 11880, 11892–3, 11899 *from 16–22 Coppergate;* 13184 *(inlaid with wire in a running loop pattern) from the Foundry;* 13777 *(with eleven inlaid crosses),* 13778, 13782, 13792 *(inlaid with mercury gilded silver) and* 13796 *(with antler handle) from Bedern;* 14954 *from 46–54 Fishergate. Scale 1:2,* 13184, 13777 *and* 13792 *1:1*

17/6). The three knives from Fishergate may be Anglian in origin and residual in their contexts.

On a knife from Fishergate (*4983*) the back is worked into a little V-shaped tip above the shoulder. This feature can also be seen on an Anglo-Scandinavian knife from Coppergate (p.581, Fig.230, *2822, AY* 17/6) and probably indicates that *4983* (see Fig.1356) is residual in its medieval context.

Chamfering of the edges of the blade back can be seen on *13036* from a late 11th–12th century context at Piccadilly. This is another feature which may be primarily pre-Conquest as there are ten examples from Anglo-Scandinavian contexts at Coppergate (p.579, *AY* 17/6) and another from an Anglo-Scandinavian context at Piccadilly (*15330*).

Inlaid cutler's marks occur on the blades of three whittle tang knives, two (*13771* and *13782*) from mid 14th–early 15th century contexts at Bedern, and one from a post-medieval context at Coppergate (*11877*). Cutler's marks first appear on knives in the late 13th–early 14th century and were usually inlaid until the early 16th century (Hayward 1957, 5).

Tangs and handles (Figs.1358, 1363–4)

There is a bolster between the tang and handle of two knives (*11866* and *11890*), both from late 11th century contexts at Coppergate. The feature suggests, at first sight, that these knives are late or post-medieval in date and must be intrusive in their contexts, but another knife with a bolster from an 11th century context was found in Winchester (Goodall 1990, 844, *2699*). There is a brass collar at the junction of blade and tang on *11870* from a post-medieval context at Coppergate.

Few handles survive as other than mineralised remains, but a fine ivory example can be seen on *8169* (late 13th–early 14th century) from Fishergate which also has a copper alloy collar at the junction of blade and tang. An unstratified, but probably late or post-medieval, knife from Coppergate (*11901*) has a bone or ivory handle.

In addition to the knife handles of bone and antler (pp.1971–3, *AY* 17/12) and wood (see pp.2282–5, *AY* 17/13) published elsewhere, and the traces of organic materials found in situ on some of the knives discussed above, two jet handle fragments found at Bedern

(*13493–4*) may also have acted as knife handles. Both are socketed and would therefore have been used on whittle tang knives, although elsewhere jet seems rarely to have been used for this purpose. No jet handles were found on an extensive collection of medieval knives from London, for instance (Cowgill et al. 1987), and only one example from a 10th century deposit was noted at Winchester (Hinton 1990e, 865, fig.261, *2881*). The Bedern handles derived from contexts of mid 14th–early 15th century date.

Hilt-plates (Fig.1364)

Recovered from Coppergate (*12858–9*) and Bedern (*14189*), these copper alloy plates were positioned at the blade end of the handle on a whittle tang knife; they are commonly found separated from knives, although occasionally in situ (e.g. Goodall 1990, fig.254, *2704*; fig.256, *2803*). They were used only with whittle tang knives, which were in use throughout the medieval period (Goodall 1980b, 86). The three York examples were found in deposits dating from the 11th–14th century.

Dimensional patterns

Although not usually considered in any detail in the study of knives, dimensional patterns are potentially very significant for determining the date of knife assemblages and the function of individual knives or groups of knives (Ottaway 1990). There follows a summary of the data for the medieval knives from the sites under discussion, although it

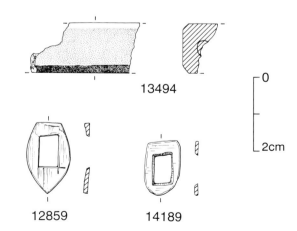

Fig.1364   Jet handle fragment 13494 from Bedern; copper alloy hilt-plates 12859 from 16–22 Coppergate and 14189 from Bedern. Scale 1:1

should be noted that it is not particularly revealing as, firstly, there are relatively few knives which are unbroken, and, secondly, a number of the knives from medieval contexts at Coppergate and Fishergate are probably residual from earlier periods.

The longest knife from a medieval context is *14954* from Fishergate which now measures 296mm but was originally slightly longer. It is possible that the object is residual from Anglian contexts and, although its form is now difficult to determine because of damage, it would, if Anglian, be of sufficient size to be described as a small *seax* or single-edged weapon (see Fig.1363). Four other knives are over 200mm long (*11836*, *11866–7* and *13755*), but do not come within 80mm of *14954*. The smallest unbroken knives are *13758* at 58mm and *14928* at 59mm. The longest blade belongs once again to *14954* at 188mm and smallest complete blade to *14928* at 34mm. The greatest maximum width of blade can be found on *11867* which measures 31mm (for a further note on this knife see p.2753).

The average length of 50 knives from medieval contexts which survive unbroken was 113·72mm, the average length of 96 unbroken blades was 71·60mm and the average maximum width of those blades 12·78mm. This may be compared with the data for knives from the Anglo-Scandinavian period at Coppergate (pp.574–8, *AY* 17/6) in which the average length for 78 unbroken knives was 120·46mm, for 127 unbroken blades was 66·92mm and the average maximum width of those blades was 14·13mm. The difference between the Anglo-Scandinavian and medieval figures for total length and length of blade is probably due to a greater number of relatively small knives in the medieval assemblage. There are seven unbroken knives from medieval contexts shorter than the Anglo-Scandinavian minimum length of 81mm.

In addition to data for the dimensions quoted above, three ratios between the dimensions of the knives from medieval contexts may also be considered. The average ratio between the total length of blade and the distance from the shoulder to the point where the back begins to slope down (back form A) or curve (back forms B and C) to the tip is 1·68:1, but this figure hides a marked difference between the average for knives of back form A (2·01:1) and of back form C (1·62:1). The average figure for the Anglo-

Scandinavian knives from Coppergate was 1·78:1, but this again hides a distinction between the knives of back form A (1·99:1) and back form C (1·70:1). The difference in overall average may be accounted for by a higher proportion of back form A knives in the Anglo-Scandinavian sample than in the medieval sample (25/95–13/72).

The average ratio of length of blade to maximum width of blade in the medieval assemblage is 5·68:1 which compares well with 5·18:1 for the Anglo-Scandinavian knives from Coppergate. In the latter assemblage there was a marked distinction between the figure for knives of back form A at 4·37:1 and back forms C and D at 5·40:1 and 5·18:1 respectively; in other words knives of back form A are relatively wider in relation to length than those of other forms. In the medieval period the average figures for back forms C (5·91:1) and D (5·36:1) are also higher than for back form A (5·27:1), but not markedly so.

The average ratio of total length to length of blade in the medieval sample was 1·77:1 which is almost exactly the same as for Anglo-Scandinavian knives from Coppergate (1·76:1). The figures again hide a distinction between knives of back form A and those with the other principal back forms. For the medieval period the average for A is 1·55:1 and for C is 1·91:1, while for D it is1·51:1. For the Anglo-Scandinavian period the average for A is 1·59:1, for C 1·80:1 and for D 1·83:1. In both periods the distinction is a result of a group of knives of back form C (and D in the Anglo-Scandinavian) which have tangs longer than the blades (i.e. a ratio greater than 2:1). In the medieval contexts there are six examples, all except one from Coppergate. The greatest ratio of total length to length of blade is 2·65:1 (*12982*, Fig.1357). The only example not from Coppergate is *14958*, the unusual knife from Fishergate with a curved-over tip. Knives with long tangs appear to be an innovation of the 9th century; they have been recorded in many other late Anglo-Saxon/Anglo-Scandinavian assemblages (Ottaway 1990). Remarkably, no knife with a tang longer than the blade has been recorded by the author in a securely dated middle Saxon context. The Coppergate medieval knives with long tangs may all be Anglo-Scandinavian in origin and residual in their contexts, but this cannot be conclusively determined as there is no comparative dimensional analysis of securely dated medieval knives.

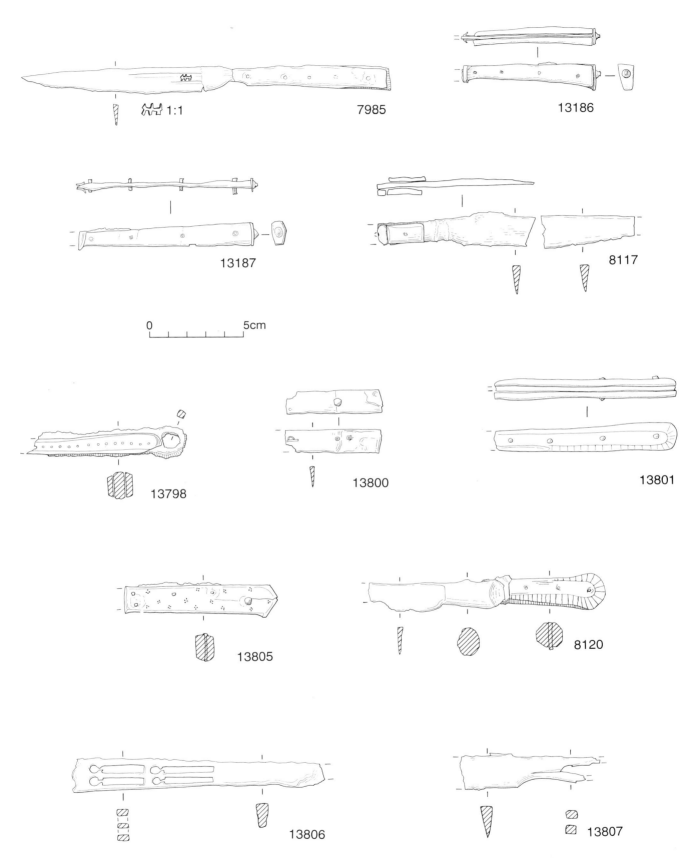

Fig.1365 *Scale tang knives: 7985, 13186–7 from the Foundry; 8117, 13798, 13800–1, 13805 from Bedern; 8120 from Bedern Chapel; knives with iron tangs: 13806–7 from Bedern. Scale 1:2, detail of 7985 1:1*

In conclusion, a brief dimensional analysis does not suggest a great difference in the size and proportions of knives in the Anglo-Scandinavian and medieval periods. This may be due to the effect on the statistics of a number of earlier knives which were residual in their medieval contexts and a more distinctive medieval pattern may emerge when knives of secure medieval date are studied.

Scale tang knives (Fig.1365)

In only a few cases do the blades of scale tang knives survive in anything like a complete state and there are ten tangs for which there is no blade surviving at all. It is possible that some of the blades without tangs from Bedern and the Foundry came from scale tang knives, but this is not certain. As far as blade form is concerned, it may be noted that *13192* from a post-medieval context at the Foundry has the characteristic rounded rear seen on many scale tang knives of late medieval or early post-medieval date (Ottaway forthcoming).

There are inlaid cutlers' marks on three blades: *7985* (post-medieval context) from the Foundry, *8117* (mid 14th century context) and *13800* (mid 14th–early 15th century context), both from Bedern. On *13800* it is clear that the mark is in the form of a P. There are brass shoulder plates brazed onto *13187* and riveted to *13193*, both from post-medieval contexts at the Foundry, and riveted to *13803* from a mid 15th–early 17th century context at Bedern. A bolster divides the blade and tang of *8120* from a post-medieval context at Bedern Chapel of a form which confirms that it is not residual. *13798* (mid 14th–early 15th century context) from Bedern survives as a tang only which has an eye at the end for suspension from a belt.

The scale plates were attached to the tangs by iron rivets on *13189* and *13192*, both from post-medieval contexts at the Foundry, by non-ferrous rivets on *13190* (post-medieval context) and *13798* from Bedern, and by tubular non-ferrous rivets on *13797* (mid 14th–early 15th century context), *13801* (late medieval context) and *13804* (post-medieval context) from Bedern, and *13187* (post-medieval context) from the Foundry. Where they survive, the scale plates are wooden (*13187*) or bone (*8117, 8120, 13189, 13798*).

The earliest scale tang knife is *8117* from a mid 14th century context at Bedern, and there are nine from mid 14th–early 15th century contexts at Bedern and the Foundry. Although the earliest scale tang knives at, for example, Winchester (Goodall 1990, 838–9) may be 13th century, it seems that they were not regularly made until rather later. It is very striking that there are no scale tang knives from Coppergate, in spite of the fact that substantial deposits of the 13th–14th century were excavated and numerous knives were found in them. It may also be noted that the earliest recorded scale tang knives in a large corpus of knives from London were from early–mid 14th century contexts (Cowgill et al. 1987, 26, 86, fig.58, 63–4) and in another large corpus from Norwich (Fig.1315, **18**) from contexts dated no earlier than 1400 (Goodall 1993, 128).

Knives with iron tangs (Fig.1365)

There are two unusual objects (*13806–7*) which appear to have been knives with iron tangs, both from post-medieval contexts at Bedern. *13806* has a stub of blade and the tang, which appears to be complete, is pierced by four rectangular chambers with cusped heads. It is, perhaps, possible that these chambers were originally filled with bone, wood or other material, but nothing now survives. The blade of *13807* is also largely missing and the tang is incomplete, but the two surviving 'prongs' are thought to have been part of some sort of pattern akin to that of *13806*. No parallels readily suggest themselves for these objects.

Key to Table 282 (facing)

Date: context date
Period: analyses of knives from Fishergate Period 4 are published in *AY* 17/9 (pp.1277–304)
Macro: macrostructure, for types see below
Micro: microstructure: B = bainite, F = ferrite, NP = nodular pearlite, Pe = pearlite, Ph = ferrite with phosphorous ghosting, SC = spheroidised cementite, TM = tempered martensite, UB = upper bainite
Hardness: average value recorded for each structural element, using Vickers scale, HV
Examined by: D = D. Starley, G = J.G. McDonnell, K = K. Wiemer

Table 282 Iron knives examined metallographically from medieval contexts in York

No.	Period	Date	Blade back form	Macro	Micro	Hardness	Examined by
16–22 Coppergate							
11533	6	early 12th	?currier's knife	5	TM	379	G
11803	6	early 12th	A2	1e	first: Ph second: SC	182 172	K
11811	6	15th–16th	C1	2a	back: Ph edge: TM	191 475	D
11814	6	12th	C1	1c	back: Ph edge: TM	224 603	K
11817	6	late 11th	C1	0	F	93	G
11818	6	late 11th	C1	1d	first: F/Ph second: Pe	182 239	G
11830	6	13th	C3	1c	back: Ph/F core: SC	170 324	K
11834	6	late 11th	C3	1a	flanks: F/Ph core: TM	248 391	G
11860	6	early 14th	D	1e	first: Ph second: Pe	139 140	K
11862	6	early 13th	D	1a	sheath: F/Pe edge: TM	173 620	G
11888	6	13th–14th	Indeterminate	2a	back: Ph edge: TM centre: pattern welded Pe/Ph	201 569	K
11894	6	12th–13th	Indeterminate	1c	back: Ph edge: SC	197 187	D
Bedern							
13766	9	mid 17th	Ci	1c	back: Ph/F edge: TM	166 650	D
13767	1	early–mid 13th	D	2b	back: Ph edge: TM centre: Ph/TM (pattern-welded)	168 525	D
13782	7	mid 14th– early 15th	Indeterminate	4	core: Ph/F/UB outer: TM/B	214 565	D
46–54 Fishergate							
4981	4z	11th–12th	A1	2b	back: F edge: SC	183 321	K
4995	4z	11th–12th	Indeterminate	2b	back: F/Ph edge: SC	185 286	K
4997	4z	11th–12th	C1	0	Ph	165	K
5005	4z	11th–12th	C2	2a	back: Ph edge: TM	203 755	K
5028	4b	11th–12th	Indeterminate	1a	flanks: Ph core: TM	303 519	K
14937	6a/b	late 13th/ early 14th	C1	2b	back: F edge: TM/B/NP	116 563	D
14940	6c	early–mid 14th	C3	1a	centre: TM/B/NP sides: F/Pe	587 133	D

Metallographic Examination

Twenty-one knives from medieval contexts and one (*13766*) from a post-medieval context were examined metallographically. As a result of developing research priorities and the intermittent availability of resources, the work has been undertaken in three separate stages (designated Groups 1–3 below) by three different researchers over a fifteen-year period. Five knives (Group 1) from medieval contexts were examined by Dr J.G. McDonnell in 1983–4 as part of a programme of metallography aimed largely at studying ironwork from the Anglo-Scandinavian period (*AY* 17/6). In 1992–3 ten knives (Group 2) were examined by Dr Karen Wiemer as part of her research for a PhD thesis at the University of Cambridge (Wiemer 1993). Five of these knives which came from 11th–12th century contexts 46–54 Fishergate were published in *AY* 17/9 (pp.1277–1304), along with knives from Anglian contexts. The results from examination of the remaining five knives from Coppergate are published below. Finally, another seven knives were examined by Dr David Starley in 1998 (Group 3). A summary of the data appears in Table 282. The results of the examination by each of the specialists are published in self-contained sections below, but the introduction written by David Starley serves as an introduction to them all.

Introduction

By David Starley

The knives were examined visually and by X-radiography before sampling. The purpose of X-radiography was partly to help determine the condition of the object prior to sampling, but also non-destructively to detect structural features such as the presence of weld lines and pattern-welding. This information was used to decide where to remove samples from the blades. On the original X-radiograph the welds show as dark (X-ray transparent) lines, because of the presence of low-density material, either entrapped slag and scale or corrosion which has penetrated at these points of weakness. Most of the York blades examined showed longitudinal weld lines running along the length of the blade, suggesting a likelihood of butt-welded edged blades. However, without metallographic examination these could have been confused with the bands of slag and corrosion typically found in archaeologically recovered ancient iron artefacts. *11888* from Coppergate and *13767* from Bedern were notable for a band of dia-

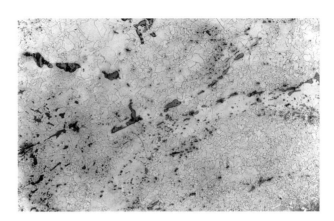

Fig.1366 *Micrograph of ferritic iron (×52), nital etched, showing even, light-coloured crystals*

gonally striated metal running through the centre of the blade, indicating a pattern-welded blade.

Metallographic examination

By David Starley

Iron alloys used in the medieval period can be divided into three broad categories: ferritic iron, phosphoric iron and steel. All three types contain slag inclusions. The properties and basic microstructure of these alloys are described below.

Ferritic iron (Fig.1366): Pure iron without significant impurities. Relatively soft and easily worked, but liable to bend and, if used as a cutting edge, would be rapidly blunted. Recognised in an etched microstructure as plain white crystals.

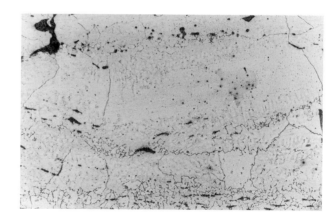

Fig.1367 *Micrograph of phosphoric iron (×52), nital etched, showing enlarged crystal size and watery 'ghosting'*

Fig.1368 Micrograph of tempered martensite (quenched steel), nital etched (×100)

Phosphoric iron (Fig.1367): Even at trace levels, phosphorus (typically of the order of 0·1 to 0·3%) entering the iron during smelting may significantly harden the metal without disadvantageously affecting its toughness. In the etched microstructure phosphoric iron can be recognised qualitatively due to 'ghosting'. This effect, caused by differential hardness between higher and lower phosphorus regions, gives the ferrite grains a 'watery' appearance, with bright areas which may be difficult to bring into sharp focus with the microscope. The effect of phosphorus on the properties of the iron can be directly measured, by carrying out microhardness testing on the surface of the polished specimen. Chemical or physico-chemical analysis of the metal will allow quantitative measurement of the phosphorus content.

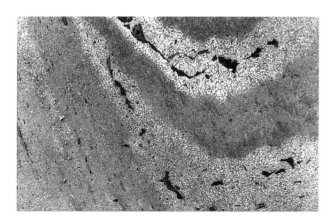

Fig.1369 Micrograph of pattern welding (×52), nital etched, showing alternate bands of phosphoric iron (light etching) and steel (dark etching)

Steel is iron containing small amounts of carbon, typically 0·2 to 1%. It has advantages in being both tougher and harder than iron. Additionally, and very importantly, it can be hardened to a greater extent by appropriate heat treatment. Heating followed by quenching in water gives considerable hardness, but may make the artefact brittle. This can be avoided either by subsequently tempering the artefact, i.e. reheating, but to a lower temperature than it was quenched from, which helps relieve stresses within the structure. Alternatively, a less severe 'slack' quench can be used, cooling not in water but in a less thermally conductive medium such as oil. The microstructures of steel reflect the amount of carbon present, the severity of quenching and the effects of reheating. With 0·8% carbon, the eutectic composition, steel which has not been heat treated consists entirely of a dark-etching phase known as pearlite. Occasional steels which exceed this carbon content contain both pearlite and iron carbide. More common are lower-carbon steels which contain both pearlite and the carbon-free phase, ferrite. The ratio of these phases directly relates to the composition, thus a 0·4% carbon steel contains 50% pearlite and 50% ferrite, whilst at 0·2% carbon the proportions will be 25% and 75% respectively.

When rapid cooling takes place, a range of other crystalline structures tends to form instead of pearlite, of which the two most common phases are bainite, and (for very rapid cooling) martensite (Fig.1368). Unfortunately the presence of these phases prevents any accurate estimation of the amount of carbon in the alloy.

If the artefact is reheated to a sufficiently high temperature, perhaps accidentally in a fire or because tempering was carried out for an excessive time, further changes will take place to both quenched and slow-cooled steel. Iron carbide (Fe_3C or cementite) becomes visible. In less severe cases the pearlite may be described as agglomerated. Longer heating will result in a structure in which 'spheroidised iron carbide' is present. In extreme cases the iron carbide will diffuse to form a separate phase at the ferrite grain boundaries.

As well as identifying the alloys used and the heat treatments applied to them, metallography enables the method of construction to be determined. The main requirement of a blade is that it should have a hard cutting edge so that it can be sharpened and will hold the edge. Secondly, the blade should be sufficiently tough to prevent it breaking in use. Hardness should not be at the expense of brittleness, and a wholly martensitic blade is not ideal as it tends to be brittle. A skilful smith can combine steel and iron in a number of ways, such that the edge of the blade is composed of steel and can be hardened, but that the main body of the knife (the back) is of a low-carbon alloy that is not prone to brittleness. Such a composite blade has the additional advantage that steel, which until post-industrial revolution times was an expensive commodity, could be used more sparingly. Sometimes an additional requirement of knives was that they should be particularly visually pleasing. The use of dissimilar metals, when polished and lightly etched, can give a distinctive appearance to the surface of the blade. The best known technique is known as 'pattern-welding' in which the blade is built up of contrasting alloys, twisted together then welded into the blade (Fig.1369).

The typology for metallographic structures of knives used in this study was originated by Tylecote and Gilmour (1986, 2–3). Of relevance to this report are the following types (Fig.1370):

0:    all ferritic or phosphoric iron, no steel edge
1a: steel core flanked by ferritic and phosphoric iron, i.e. core or sandwich welded
1c: steel core inserted as a tongue into the iron back
1d: steel forms a flank on one side of blade
1e: steel forms one-half of section
2a: steel cutting edge scarf-welded to ferritic or phosphoric back
2b: steel cutting edge butt-welded to the iron back
4:    steel forms a sheath around an iron core
5:    all steel.

The analyses

Group 1

By J.G. McDonnell

Methods of analysis

Sections were taken by either spark erosion or by cutting with a jeweller's piercing saw. Usually a wedge-shaped section was removed (Fig.1371), maximum length 25mm, determined by the mounting method. All specimens were mounted in hot-setting conducting bakelite producing 30mm diameter discs, normally less than 10mm thick. Polishing followed standard procedures from coarse grits to a one micron diamond pad finish. Specimens were examined in the as-polished condition and then etched in nital (2% nitric acid and alcohol). Phosphorous distribution was examined using Stead's reagent (1g $CuCl_2$ + 4g $MgCl_2$ +1 ml HCl in 100ml alcohol). Specimens were examined at low-power magnification to determine the overall structure. Detailed examination was made at magnifications up to ×1000 (oil immersion). The terminology used to describe the structures is given by Tylecote and Gilmour (1986, 4–18, 262–3). Macrohardness and microhardness testing was carried out on prepared surfaces.

Probable currier's knife 11533

X-radiography showed that there was little effect from corrosion, and no overall structural details except for the usual horizontally orientated slag lines in the tang, and small cracks (<5mm in length) running vertically down from the knife back. A single half-section was removed (Fig.1371).

In the unetched condition vertically orientated slag lines were observed, but there was no strong

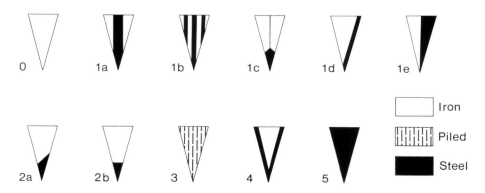

Fig.1370   *Schematic cross-sections of knife types (after Tylecote and Gilmour 1986, fig.1)*

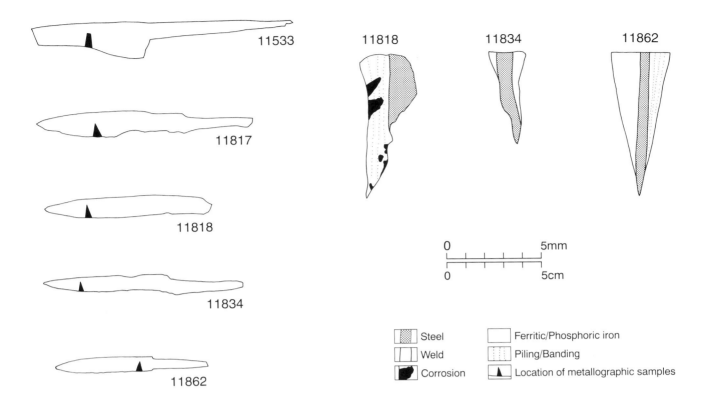

Fig.1371 Location of metallographic sections and schematic cross-sections for Group 1 knives. Knives scale 1:2, cross-sections 5:1

evidence of banding. In the etched condition the over-all method of manufacture was not readily apparent, the entire section being tempered martensitic steel (400HV, 379HV; mean of four readings), but showing some carbon content variation (probably due to the presence of localised areas containing phosphorus, 180HV, 233HV, ASTM 8).

Knife *11533* was either of all-steel manufacture (Type 5), or was a butt-welded knife (Type 2) with the butt-weld high up the knife back, but there was no evidence for such a weld in the X-radiographs. The presence of the microcracks in the knife back would support an all-steel interpretation.

Knife *11817* (Fig.1372)

Knife *11817* was corroded and part of the cutting edge was absent, due either to wear, corrosion or fracture. X-radiography confirmed that corrosion had penetrated the knife, and also showed extensive slag banding. A single half-section was removed (Fig.1371).

In the unetched condition vertically orientated slag lines were observed. In the etched condition the knife section was ferritic with some grain boundary carbides present (Fig.1372). There was no evidence of a steel cutting edge. A second section was therefore removed, but it also had the same structure. The cutting edges of both specimens were corroded, and there were sharp changes of angle in the cross-sectional profile of the cutting edge. It is therefore possible that a steel butt-welded cutting edge had corroded or worn away. The irregular profile of the cutting edge of the knife would suggest extensive wear or breakage of the cutting edge. The microhardness tests showed a slight increase from the back of the section (124HV) to the tip (157HV). The overall mean Vicker's Hardness was 93HV. The grain size was consistent (ASTMS 4/5). There was no change in grain size at the tip of the knife indicative of it being used as the cutting edge; this lends further support to the argument for erosion by wear or corrosion of an applied cutting edge. These results indicate the use of a ferritic rather than a phosphoric iron.

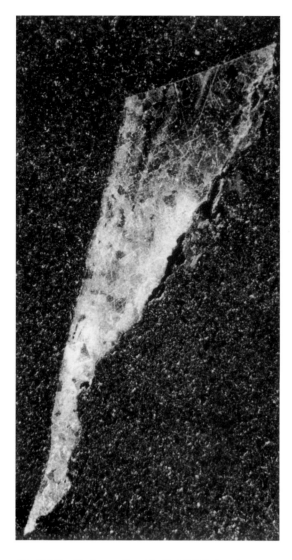

Fig.1372 Early medieval knife 11817 *showing macro-structure Type 0 (×26)*

Fig.1373 Early medieval knife 11818 *showing manufacture Type 1d (×26)*

Knife *11817* was ascribed to macrostructure Type 0, but there was some evidence to suggest that a butt-welded cutting edge had been present. This would suggest that, rather than being unfinished, the knife had been heavily used.

Knife *11818* (Fig.1373)

X-radiographs showed extensive corrosion mid-way along the cutting edge, and horizontal slag banding. A single half-section was removed.

Examination of the unetched specimen showed heavy corrosion penetrating inwards from the faces of the blade, especially in the lower part (cutting edge area) of the section. Slag inclusions were present throughout the section, and slag lines were present on one side of the knife. When etched the overall structure was that of two strips welded together in the vertical plane (Figs.1371, 1373). The first iron contained the slag lines and was a piled structure of bands of ferritic/phosphoric iron (151HV, 215HV, ASTM 6) and ferrite plus grain boundary carbides (181HV, ASTM 6). The second iron was a fine de-graded (partially spheroidised) pearlitic structure (186HV, 260HV) that coarsened at the tip to pearlite plus ferrite (237HV, 274HV).

2768

Knife *11818* was manufactured according to Type 1d (one steel flank). The presence of a distinct central weld line would indicate the latter method of manufacture. The knife had not been heat treated, and was therefore of poor quality.

Knife *11834*

Knife *11834* had a concave profile at the tang/blade interface, possibly enhanced by corrosion. X-radiography showed the presence of some corrosion penetration. A single half-section was removed (Fig.1371).

In the unetched condition a pattern of slag inclusions indicative of Type 1 manufacture was present. There were no distinct slag lines that could be interpreted as weld lines, but the slag inclusions were concentrated in a central band. In the etched condition the Type 1 method of manufacture was confirmed (Fig.1371). The two flanks were ferritic/phosphoric iron, but had undergone considerable carbon diffusion, thus giving a structure varying from ferrite/phosphoric (200HV, ASTM 8) to tempered martensite and fine nodular pearlite (244HV, 300HV). One of the flank/core weld lines was a white/yellow line (indicative of nickel or arsenic enrichment). The central core was a slack quenched steel with a tempered martensitic structure degrading to bainite in parts (353HV, 454HV–366HV). It had undergone slight decarburisation near the flank welds.

Knife *11834* was a good-quality knife manufactured according to the Type 1a method.

Knife *11862*

The knife had been slightly bent near the tang/blade junction. The X-radiographs showed the presence of slag lines at this point. There was some cor-rosion of the tang but no other features were determined. A single half-section was removed. In the unetched condition some corrosion was present at the top of the section. The metal was generally clean except for one area of vertically orientated small slag inclusions. On one side of the section five converging lines (parallel to the face of the knife) could be distinguished because they were more reflective. When etched the knife was a Type 1a (Fig.1371), with a sandwiched steel blade, which at the tip had a tempered martensitic structure. This degraded higher up the knife section to a pearlite plus ferrite structure. The lines observed on one side of the knife in the unetched condition resulted from the steel core and several thin bands of ferrite plus pearlite in the predominantly ferritic sheath. The other side of the core was ferritic, but some carbon diffusion, from the core, had occurred during welding. The knife showed preferential wear on one side. The hardness results are shown in Table 283.

Knife *11862* was a good-quality knife with an effectively heat-treated cutting edge.

Analyses of metal matrix composition of Group 1 knives is given in Table 284.

Group 2

By Karen Wiemer

Methods of analysis

Wedge samples were cut using a low-speed oil-cooled rotary saw and were vacuum mounted in cold-setting resin. The location of the sample sections is noted in Fig.1374. The samples were ground on silicon carbide paper, polished to one micron diamond finish and examined optically using a metallurgical microscope before and after etching in 2% nital (2% nitric acid in alcohol). Grain sizes are given as ASTM grain size numbers and were measured by comparison using a standard ASTM grain size eyepiece. Microhardness was measured using a Leitz RZD-DO tester with a 100g load, and lowering and dwell times of 15 seconds each. Minor element concentrations were established by electron microprobe analysis using a Cameca SX 50 and a link wavelength dispersive spectrometer. Trace (tr) is used to denote average concentrations of less than 0·20% weight. For further analysis and discussion of these knives see Wiemer 1993.

Table 283 Knife *11862*, hardness values

		ASTM	HV	HV
Sheath	Ferrite	5–6	180	166
Cutting edge	Pearlite plus ferrite		277	247
Cutting edge	Tempered martensite		532	707

Table 284 Analyses of metal matrix composition of Group 1 and Group 2 knives from 16–22 Coppergate

a = ferritic iron; (a) = high arsenic metal; (b) = lightly carburised iron or decarburised steel; c = steel; (d) = weld metal;
p = phosphoric iron; p(b) = lightly carburised phosphoric iron

Cat. no.	Iron type	P	S	Mo	Ti	V	Cr	Mn	Co	Ni	Cu	Zn	As	Fe	Total
11533	c	0.01	0.00	0.00	0.00	0.00	0.00	0.00	0.01	0.04	0.00	0.00	0.00	99.47	99.54
11533	p(b)	0.20	0.01	0.00	0.00	0.00	0.00	0.00	0.04	0.11	0.02	0.00	0.00	100.03	100.42
11533	b	0.25	0.01	0.00	0.00	0.00	0.00	0.00	0.05	0.15	0.02	0.00	0.00	100.34	100.81
11803	p	0.28	0.02	0.00	0.00	0.00	0.00	0.00	0.02	0.04	0.00	0.00	0.00	99.64	99.99
11803	p	0.36	0.02	0.00	0.00	0.00	0.00	0.00	0.00	0.01	0.00	0.00	0.00	100.34	100.73
11803	a(b)	0.04	0.02	0.00	0.00	0.00	0.00	0.00	0.00	0.05	0.00	0.00	0.00	99.84	99.95
11814	c	0.22	0.01	0.00	0.00	0.00	0.01	0.00	0.03	0.07	0.00	0.00	0.01	98.92	99.26
11814	c	0.18	0.01	0.00	0.00	0.00	0.00	0.01	0.02	0.05	0.00	0.00	0.00	99.66	99.93
11814	p(b)	0.07	0.00	0.00	0.00	0.00	0.00	0.00	0.01	0.05	0.00	0.00	0.01	100.23	100.37
11814	p(b)	0.10	0.01	0.00	0.00	0.00	0.00	0.00	0.00	0.03	0.06	0.00	0.00	100.40	100.60
11814	p	0.07	0.01	0.00	0.00	0.00	0.00	0.01	0.01	0.04	0.00	0.00	0.00	99.99	100.13
11814	p	0.09	0.00	0.00	0.00	0.00	0.00	0.00	0.00	0.02	0.05	0.00	0.00	100.78	100.94
11814	p	0.08	0.00	0.00	0.00	0.00	0.00	0.00	0.00	0.05	0.00	0.00	0.00	101.07	101.21
11817	a	0.06	0.01	0.01	0.00	0.00	0.00	0.00	0.02	0.06	0.02	0.00	0.01	100.25	100.43
11818	c	0.12	0.01	0.02	0.00	0.00	0.00	0.00	0.01	0.05	0.08	0.01	0.03	98.30	98.63
11818	p	0.19	0.00	0.00	0.00	0.00	0.00	0.00	0.04	0.07	0.03	0.00	0.06	99.15	99.54
11830	c	0.05	0.01	0.01	0.00	0.00	0.00	0.01	0.00	0.01	0.00	0.00	0.00	94.38	94.46
11830	c	0.06	0.02	0.01	0.00	0.00	0.00	0.00	0.00	0.00	0.00	0.00	0.05	92.88	93.01
11830	p	0.10	0.00	0.01	0.00	0.00	0.00	0.00	0.01	0.02	0.00	0.00	0.00	90.58	90.72
11830	p	0.08	0.01	0.00	0.00	0.00	0.00	0.00	0.00	0.01	0.00	0.00	0.00	95.56	95.66
11830	p	0.12	0.01	0.00	0.00	0.00	0.00	0.00	0.00	0.03	0.00	0.00	0.00	88.30	88.46
11830	p(d)	0.12	0.00	0.02	0.00	0.00	0.00	0.00	0.00	0.05	0.00	0.00	0.03	93.19	93.40
11834	c	0.07	0.02	0.00	0.00	0.00	0.00	0.02	0.01	0.02	0.00	0.00	0.00	97.59	97.73
11834	p	0.14	0.02	0.00	0.00	0.00	0.00	0.00	0.01	0.03	0.02	0.00	0.06	98.98	99.26
11834	a	0.01	0.01	0.00	0.00	0.00	0.00	0.00	0.01	0.04	0.00	0.00	0.02	99.83	99.92
11834	d	0.02	0.02	0.00	0.00	0.00	0.00	0.00	0.04	0.23	0.02	0.00	0.15	98.50	98.97
11860	p(a)	0.11	0.00	0.00	0.00	0.00	0.00	0.00	0.00	0.02	0.02	0.00	0.89	99.65	100.68
11860	a(b)	0.04	0.00	0.01	0.00	0.00	0.00	0.00	0.00	0.02	0.10	0.00	0.10	99.25	99.52
11862	c	0.05	0.03	0.00	0.00	0.00	0.00	0.00	0.02	0.00	0.00	0.00	0.00	99.76	99.86
11862	p	0.16	0.01	0.00	0.00	0.00	0.00	0.00	0.04	0.00	0.00	0.00	0.00	101.11	101.31
11862	p	0.30	0.01	0.00	0.00	0.00	0.00	0.00	0.03	0.00	0.00	0.00	0.00	100.23	100.57
11888	c	0.02	0.01	0.00	0.00	0.00	0.00	0.01	0.01	0.06	0.02	0.00	0.00	98.88	99.00
11888	p	0.53	0.01	0.00	0.00	0.00	0.00	0.00	0.02	0.06	0.00	0.00	0.00	99.13	99.75
11888	p(b)	0.10	0.01	0.00	0.00	0.00	0.00	0.02	0.04	0.05	0.00	0.00	0.00	99.53	99.75
11888	p	0.27	0.00	0.00	0.00	0.00	0.00	0.00	0.01	0.05	0.00	0.00	0.00	99.97	100.29

Knife *11803* (Fig.1375)

The blade of knife *11803* was broken and no part of the tang remained. The cutting edge was jagged and unevenly worn. In the X-radiograph, the metal of the back appeared very clean. The cutting edge was irregular with limited areas of fine, rounded corrosion possibly owing to steel microstructures. No weld line was apparent. The X-radiograph indicated a possible Type 1 knife.

The polished samples contained many vertical bands of dark and medium stringers and elongated inclusions. Some contained a lighter second phase. Corrosion entering at the cutting edge had divided

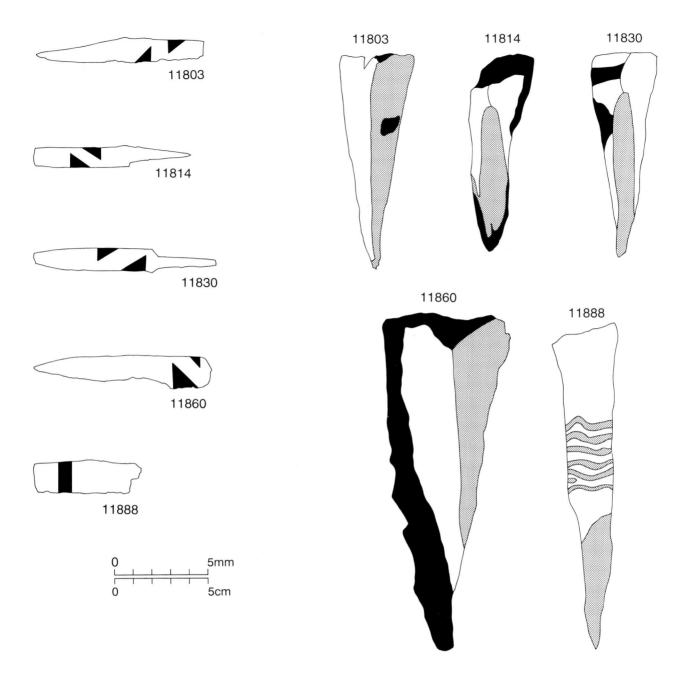

Fig.1374 *Location of metallographic samples and schematic cross-sections for Group 2 knives (for key see Fig.1371, p.2767). Knives scale 1:2, cross-sections 5:1*

the tip into approximately six layers of metal. The metal of the back contained more internal corrosion than that of the edge. Etching (Fig.1375) revealed that the blade consisted of a piece of phosphoric iron joined vertically along the mid-line of the knife to a piece of low-carbon steel. The sharp boundary between the two layers indicated 'half sandwich' or

Type 1e manufacture. The iron was high in phosphorus (%P = 0·15 to 0·45; average = 0·32) and divided into roughly three layers of varying grain size (ASTM 3–4) with the finer grains associated with a slightly higher carbon content. There was much ghosting in the metal of the back. The steel contained mostly dark inclusions. It was low in carbon (%C <0·3) and con-

2771

Fig.1375 (left) Knife 11803 *showing Type 1e manufacture* (×15)

sisted of ferrite and completely spheroidised cementite. The iron contained cementite as grain boundary films in the higher carbon bands. The average hardness of both layers was similar: HV0·1 = 172 and 175 for iron and steel respectively, and both were present at the cutting tip. The maximum hardness measured was in phosphoric iron at the back of the knife (HV0·1 = 191). Corrosion had attacked the iron and steel evenly at the cutting edge but internal corrosion was greater in the iron of the knife back. With the exception of phosphorus, the iron and steel were low in minor elements. The hardness of the iron was reflected in its phosphorus content (Tylecote and Gilmour 1986, 9).

The blade of knife *11803* was made by jointing a layer of steel and phosphoric iron by Type 1e manufacture. The low carbon content of the steel precluded a hard, quenched edge. Given the distribution of the phases, the steel appeared to have been air cooled when first made to produce grains of ferrite and pearlite. The knife had since been over tempered and carbon was present only as spheroidised cementite in the steel and grain boundary films in the iron. The iron and steel had similar low hardness. This knife was not made to a high standard.

Knife *11814*

Corrosion was spalling off knife *11814* and the tip of the blade was missing. The edge appeared worn below the shoulder. The X-radiograph did not reveal any welds or structures in the back. Rounded corrosion patterns were visible in thin areas of the cutting edge and it was hypothesised that the knife was of

Table 285 Hardness values and minor element levels for knife *11803*

	ASTM	Hardness (HV0.1)	P	S	Co	Ni
			(weight %)			
Phosphoric iron, edge	4	168	0.28	0.02	0.02	0.04
Phosphoric iron, back	3–4	182	0.36	0.02	–	tr
Steel	8	172	0.04	0.02	–	0.05

Table 286 Hardness values and minor element levels for knife *11814*

	ASTM	Hardness (HV0.1)	P	S	Co	Ni	Cu
			(weight %)				
Steel, left-hand side	6–7	206	0.07	–	tr	0.05	–
Steel, right-hand side	<8	265	0.10	tr	–	0.03	0.06
Steel core, edge		603	0.22	tr	0.03	0.07	–
back		380	0.18	tr	0.02	0.05	–
Knife back, steel		224	0.07	tr	tr	0.04	–
iron	4–5	159	0.09	–	–	0.02	0.05
iron	3	152	0.08	–	–	0.05	–

Type 1 manufacture. Two samples were removed (Fig.1374).

Corrosion divided the edge sample in half. It had entered at the cutting tip and had formed preferentially around large, elongated and irregular slag inclusions of a medium darkness. The metal was otherwise clean with a few lighter, small round, subround and irregular inclusions; it seemed to consist of several vertical layers. A layered structure was also apparent in the section cut from the knife back.

Etching revealed three steel layers. The middle layer was a hypoeutectoid steel (%C = c.0·6 to 0·8) which contained the most carbon and internal corrosion. It formed a tempered martensite cutting edge (max.HV0·1 = 636) but did not extend to the back of the knife. The hardness decreased away from the tip and the microstructure consisted of tempered martensite and/or bainite and ferrite. At the back of this layer, extensive decarburisation has resulted in a structure of carbide colonies and ghosting ferrite (HV0·1 = 251). Some decarburisation had occurred along both weld joins. The sheaths each contained ferrite, Widmanstätten ferrite and tempered martensite or bainites. The carbon content varied within each layer and the steel microstructures throughout the sample were not very homogeneous possibly owing to the phosphorus present in the metal. The phosphorus level of the steel core was relatively high (%P = 0·12 to 0·34) but had not precluded effective carburisation of the metal. The prior austenite grain size was coarsest in the left flank and finest in the right one. The right sheath had been worn away more than the left. The latter was also less decarburised and formed part of the back of the knife. The left sheath was heavily corroded in the knife back and seemed to end midway along the back section. Three pieces of phosphoric iron above and beside the core formed the remainder of the back of the knife. Ferritic grain growth had occurred in this metal and there was ghosting around carbide regions.

Knife *11814* was of Type 1c manufacture and consisted of three layers of steel with pieces of phosphoric iron added at the back. There was much

Table 287 Hardness values and minor element levels for knife *11830*

	ASTM	Hardness (HV0.1)	P	S	Mo	Ni	As
			(weight %)				
Iron, left-hand side	3–5	151	0.08	tr	–	tr	–
Iron, right-hand side	3	143	0.10	–	tr	0.02	–
Iron, knife back	3	170	0.12	tr	–	0.03	–
Steel core, edge		324	0.05	tr	tr	tr	–
back		320	0.06	0.02	tr	–	0.05

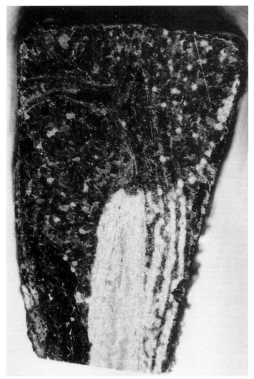

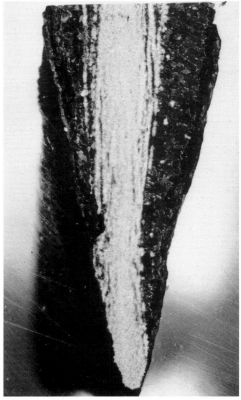

Fig.1376   *Knife* 11830 *showing Type 1c manufacture (×15)*

internal corrosion in the steel core. The knife had been heated to above the upper critical temperature and then probably slack quenched to produce a tempered martensite cutting edge. The metal of the core was high in phosphorus and its microstructure was not homogeneous. It had, however, been successfully carburised and the steel at the cutting tip was estimated to be of eutectoid composition. Knife *11814* was manufactured to a high standard with a very good edge hardness.

Knife *11830* (Fig.1376)

The tip of knife *11830* was missing. The tang was bent near the shoulder, and it widened and flattened at the end. The cutting edge was in good condition and followed a shallow S curve below the shoulder. The X-radiograph showed a crack running parallel to the back of the knife for half the length of the blade. This was avoided during sampling. No other structures were visible in the back. The cutting edge was slightly serrated in profile and had a rounded corrosion pattern. Samples were cut from the edge and back of the knife (Fig.1374).

Both polished sections contained vertical inclusion bands with cleaner metal at the sides. Inclusions were concentrated in the centre of the blade and into the cutting edge. These were dark stringers and elongated inclusions. To one side, a row of lighter, dendritic, two-phase, irregular inclusions revealed a possible weld join to metal that had only a few small spheroidal and subround inclusions. On the other side of the section, corrosion had entered the sample along one inclusion band.

Etching (Fig.1376) revealed sandwich type manufacture with iron sheaths joining above a steel core (Type 1c). The edge was a medium-carbon steel and consisted of ferrite and partially degraded, tempered carbide (%C = c.0·3 to 0·5; max.HV0·1 = 355). A white line surrounding the core was due to a slightly higher phosphorus concentration in this area. The flanks consisted of equiaxed phosphoric iron into which carbon had diffused unevenly from the core during working. Evidence of grain growth and spheroidised carbide at ferrite grain boundaries further indicated that the knife had been over tempered. The iron and steel used were low in minor elements with the exception of phosphorus.

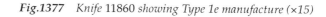

Fig.1377   *Knife* 11860 *showing Type 1e manufacture* (×15)

Knife *11830* was of Type 1c manufacture with a medium-carbon steel edge and phosphoric iron sheaths. The original microstructure of the steel was probably martensite or martensite and bainites which would imply quench hardening. At some point in its history, either intentionally or unintentionally, the knife had been spheroidise annealed resulting in a reduction in the hardness the edge. The hardness of the edge was adequate, but may initially have been much greater.

Knife *11860* (Fig.1377)

Knife *11860* was in poor condition. The blade was broken and split at the base of the tang. The end of the blade had been re-attached during conservation. The cutting edge was S-shaped owing to corrosion or wear. The X-radiograph indicated that most of the blade had mineralised and cracked. Some metal remained near the tang. It had neither a clearly fibrous nor a rounded corrosion pattern. The cutting edge profile was very irregular. Heavy mineralisation limited the amount of information which could be obtained from the X-radiograph and prevented speculation on the method of manufacture.

The unetched metal was clean with some parallel, vertically oriented stringers and small spheroidal and subround inclusions. A few contained a second, light phase, but most inclusions were of a single, medium oxide. The inclusions were larger and more irregular to one side of the knife back.

Table 288   Hardness values and minor element levels for knife *11860*

	ASTM	Hardness (HV0.1)	P	Mo	Ni	Cu	As
				(weight %)			
Iron	2–5	139	0.11	–	0.02	0.02	0.89
Steel	5–6	140	0.04	tr	0.02	0.10	0.10

Etching (Fig.1377) revealed two layers of metal joined along the centre of the blade cross-section. One layer was of coarse-grained, equiaxed, phosphoric iron with some low-carbon steel bands. The phosphorus content varied widely (%P = 0.04 to 0.24) and the iron was high in arsenic (%As = 0.51 to 1.27). The second layer consisted of medium-grained ferrite and pearlite colonies. The cementite lamellae in the pearlite had started to degrade and the oxide surrounding the metal contained white, corrosion-resistant, carbide particles. The carbon content of the steel was low (%C = c.0.2 to 0.3).

Knife *11860* was made by Type 1e manufacture and consisted of a layer of phosphoric iron joined to a piece of low-carbon steel of approximately the same hardness (max.HV0.1 = 149 and 158 respectively). Iron formed the remaining cutting edge. The knife had been slow-cooled to produce grains of ferrite and relatively coarse pearlite. It was subsequently held below the eutectoid temperature sufficiently long for the cementite lamellae to begin to spheroidise. Even without this softening heat treatment, knife *11860* would not have been a high-quality tool.

Knife *11888* (Fig.1378)

Knife *11888* was a fragment of a blade having an indeterminate back form. The cutting edge was in good condition and was slightly concave. A join could be seen running the length of the blade. The X-radiograph showed two welds dividing the blade into three horizontal layers. No structures were obvious in the back. The middle section had an irregularly hatched, fibrous corrosion pattern which is characteristic of pattern-welded structures. The edge had a slightly scalloped profile. The corrosion pattern was rounded along the edge and fibrous below the weld. One slice was cut through the width of the blade to obtain a

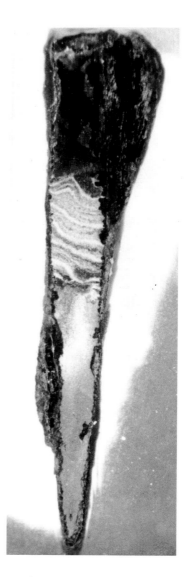

Fig.1378 *Knife* 11888 *showing Type 2 manufacture with pattern-welded insert (×9)*

Table 289 Hardness values and minor element levels for knife *11888*

	ASTM	Hardness (HV0.1)	P	S	Mn	Co	Ni	Cu
			(weight %)					
Steel tip	3–5	569	0.02	tr	tr	tr	0.06	0.02
Middle	8, <8	268	0.53	tr	–	0.02	0.06	–
Carburised iron		260	0.10	tr	0.02	0.04	0.05	–
Iron back	1, >1	201	0.27	–	–	tr	0.05	–

complete cross-section (Fig.1374). One of the welds cracked along its length during sampling.

The unetched sample contained three horizontal layers. The metal of the back was cleanest, with a couple of larger, dendritic grey inclusions and a few small irregular inclusions. A string of small to medium, irregular, multi-phase inclusions indicated a weld below this section. Corrosion had entered the metal just above the weld and extended through half the cross-section; this would explain the break during sampling. Oxide along the weld and surrounding the sample was cracked. The middle section contained roughly horizontal bands of small, medium to dark inclusions of various shapes. A row of very irregular inclusions of a medium oxide containing a light, globular, dendritic phase indicated a weld below this layer. The metal of the edge had the most and the largest slag inclusions. These were large, vertically oriented and consisted of several phases. There were also some very dark inclusions around which much internal corrosion had formed.

Etching (Fig.1378) confirmed a three-layer structure. Very coarse-grained, equiaxed phosphoric iron made up the knife back. There was much ghosting along grain boundaries and the ferrite appeared to have undergone grain growth. The middle section was roughly pattern-welded and consisted of alternating bands of low- to medium-carbon steel and phosphoric iron. The inclusions were concentrated in the steel. There was ghosting in the iron around inclusions and carbide. The edge consisted of quenched and tempered steel with a tempered martensite microstructure at the edge (max.HV0·1 = 605). The carbon content decreased away from the cutting tip and there was much decarburisation at the join to the pattern-welded section.

Knife *11888* was of Type 2 manufacture and consisted of three horizontal layers. A medium to high carbon steel edge was scarf-welded to a pattern-welded middle section. Coarse-grained phosphoric iron formed the back of the knife. The blade was slack quenched to produce a tough, tempered martensite cutting edge. The fragment of this knife which remained indicated that it had been made to a high standard and was a high-quality tool.

Analyses of metal matrix composition of Group 2 knives may be found in Table 284 (p.2770).

Group 3

By David Starley

Sampling, metallographic preparation and microhardness testing

As far as possible each blade was sampled twice, with a narrow wedge cut from both edge and back of the knife and sufficient overlap to match the two sections. This was carried out in five of the knives but unfortunately, for two more severely corroded examples, *13782* and *14940*, the metal was only sufficiently well preserved to obtain samples from the back of the knife. The most heavily corroded sample *14940* was cut with an aluminium oxide blade on a low-speed water-cooled saw. The remaining artefacts were sampled with a combination of jeweller's piercing saw and junior hack saw. The cut sections were then mounted in thermosetting phenolic resin and prepared using standard metallographic techniques: grinding on successively finer abrasive papers then polishing with diamond impregnated cloths. The specimens were examined on a metallurgical microscope in both the 'as polished' (unetched) condition and after etching in 2% nital.

The results of the metallographic examination are represented visually in Fig.1379. A Shimadzu microhardness tester was used to determine the hardness of different phases within the metallographic structure, which helped both to identify the alloy present and to provide a direct measure of the effectiveness of the blades for cutting.

Microanalysis

Microanalysis was undertaken to provide compositional data which could show whether the iron and steel in composite blades came from similar sources. Some differences in composition should be expected from the conditions required to produce steel; a reducing atmosphere which encourages carbon to pass into and remain within the iron will also tend chemically to reduce iron oxide within the inclusions to metallic iron, making the inclusions more glassy. In addition to this, significant differences may also be apparent for minor and trace elements which may relate to the composition of ore from different geological sources or geographical areas.

Analysis of the metal matrices and inclusions within the iron was undertaken on a LEO 440i SEM

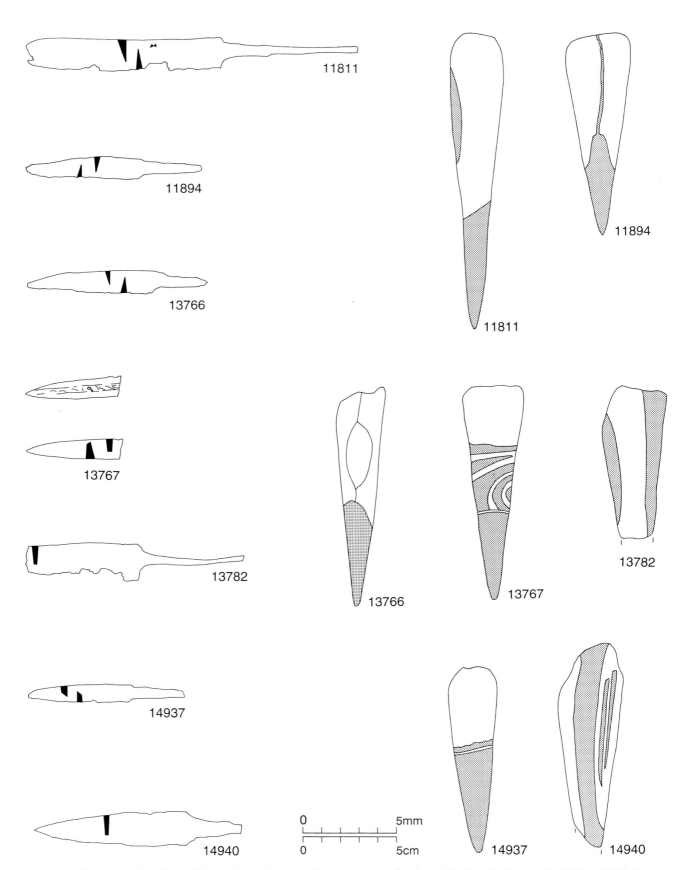

Fig.1379 *Location of metallographic sections and schematic cross-sections for Group 3 knives (for key see Fig.1371, p.2767). Knives scale 1:2, cross-sections 5:1*

Table 290 Composition of metal matrices of Group 3 knives from York (rhs = right-hand side; lhs = left-hand side)

| Site and cat. no. | Sample information | | Composition (wt% element) | | | | | | | SEM |
	AML ref.	Matrix	section	P	S	Fe	Co	Ni	Cu	ref.
Coppergate 11811	960028	phosphoric	back	0.27	nd	99.73	nd	nd	nd	ykm01
			back	0.16	nd	99.84	nd	nd	nd	ykm02
			edge	0.26	nd	99.74	nd	nd	nd	ykm03
			mean	0.23	nd	99.77	nd	nd	nd	
		steel	edge	nd	nd	98.55	nd	nd	1.45	ykm04
			edge	nd	nd	98.89	nd	nd	1.11	ykm05
			mean	nd	nd	98.72	nd	nd	1.28	
Coppergate 11894	960029	steel	edge	nd	nd	100.00	nd	nd	nd	ykm06
			edge	nd	nd	100.00	nd	nd	nd	ykm07
			mean	nd	nd	100.00	nd	nd	nd	
		phosphoric	back	0.37	nd	99.63	nd	nd	nd	ykm08
			back	0.22	nd	99.78	nd	nd	nd	ykm09
			mean	0.30	nd	99.70	nd	nd	nd	
Fishergate 14940	960030	steel	core	nd	nd	100.00	nd	nd	nd	ykm10
			core	0.08	nd	99.93	nd	nd	nd	ykm11
			mean	0.04	nd	nd	nd	nd	nd	
		ferrite		0.17	nd	99.83	nd	nd	nd	ykm12
Fishergate 14937	960031	ferrite	back	nd	nd	100.00	nd	nd	nd	ykm14
			edge	nd	nd	100.00	nd	nd	nd	ykm15
			mean	nd	nd	100.00	nd	nd	nd	
		steel	back	nd	nd	100.00	nd	nd	nd	ykm16
			edge	nd	nd	100.00	nd	nd	nd	ykm17
			mean	nd	nd	100.00	nd	nd	nd	
Bedern 13767	960032	steel	edge	nd	nd	100.00	nd	nd	nd	ykm18
			edge	nd	nd	100.00	nd	nd	nd	ykm19
			mean	nd	nd	100.00	nd	nd	nd	
		white weld line	edge	nd	nd	99.50	nd	0.38	nd	ykm20
		pattern weld (phos)	back	0.34	nd	99.66	nd	nd	nd	ykm21
		pattern weld (steel)	back	nd	nd	100.00	nd	nd	nd	ykm22
		phosphoric	back	0.15	nd	99.75	nd	nd		ykm23
			back	0.18	nd	99.72	nd	nd		ykm24
			mean	0.17	nd	99.83	nd	nd		
Bedern 13782	960033	phosphoric		0.09	nd	99.78	nd	nd	nd	ykm25
				0.12	nd	99.88	nd	nd	nd	ykm26
		mean		0.11	nd	99.89	nd	nd	nd	
		steel (rhs)		0.10	nd	99.76	nd	nd	0.14	ykm27
		steel (lhs)		nd	nd	99.86	nd	nd	nd	ykm28
		mean		0.05	nd	99.88	nd	nd	0.07	
Bedern 13766	960034	ferrite (lhs)		0.21	nd	99.79	nd	nd	nd	ykm29
		ferrite (rhs)		nd	nd	99.88	nd	nd	nd	ykm30
		ferrite (centre)		0.12	nd	99.73	nd	nd	nd	ykm31
		mean		0.11	nd	99.89	nd	nd	nd	
		steel		nd	nd	100.00	nd	nd	nd	ykm32

Table 291 Composition of inclusions in Group 3 medieval knives from York

rhs = right-hand side; lhs = left-hand side

| Site details | AML ref. | Sample information | | Inclusion size (length x width, in mm) | Composition (wt% oxide) | | | | | | | | | | | | SEM ref. |
		section	matrix		Na₂O	MgO	Al₂O₃	SiO₂	P₂O₅	S	K₂O	CaO	TiO₂	Cr₂O₃	MnO	FeO	
Coppergate 11811	960028	edge	steel	30 x 3	nd	1.6	5.8	20.6	0.7	0.3	3.0	2.9	0.4	nd	0.5	63.8	YK001
	960028	edge	steel	30 x 5	nd	1.5	7.2	47.0	0.7	nd	5.9	8.8	nd	nd	9.8	19.4	YK002
	960028	edge	steel	20 x 4	nd	1.4	8.2	52.2	nd	0.4	6.5	8.3	0.5	nd	10.8	11.6	YK003
	960028	edge	steel	10 x 3	nd	1.6	8.6	38.5	0.5	nd	4.6	3.2	0.4	nd	3.2	39.1	YK004
	960028	edge	steel	15 x 15	nd	2.5	8.4	43.3	0.5	nd	4.5	4.4	0.4	nd	12.4	23.4	YK005
	960028	edge	phosphoric	100 x 10	nd	nd	7.8	9.2	7.7	1.5	0.4	1.1	nd	nd	nd	72.2	YK006
	960028	edge	phosphoric	80 x 15	nd	nd	2.2	8.9	5.7	0.9	0.2	0.7	nd	nd	nd	81.3	YK007
	960028	edge	phosphoric	70 x 30	nd	0.2	2.3	10.0	4.8	1.2	0.2	0.9	nd	nd	nd	80.3	YK008
	960028	back	phosphoric	100 x 30	nd	nd	2.1	6.5	3.2	1.3	0.2	0.4	nd	nd	nd	86.3	YK009
	960028	back	phosphoric	200 x 40	nd	0.2	2.7	8.0	4.4	1.3	nd	0.8	nd	nd	0.1	82.4	YK010
	960028	back	phosphoric	40 x 30	nd	nd	2.1	11.4	1.6	1.3	nd	0.3	nd	nd	nd	83.3	YK011
	960028	back	phosphoric	50 x 30	nd	nd	6.2	8.3	4.1	2.5	0.2	1.3	nd	nd	nd	77.4	YK012
	960028	back	phosphoric	60 x 60	nd	0.1	3.4	7.8	3.8	1.2	nd	1.1	nd	nd	nd	82.5	YK013
Coppergate 11894	960029	edge	steel	20 x 3	0.6	0.7	11.3	53.2	nd	0.1	6.2	5.3	0.7	nd	0.4	21.3	YK014
	960029	edge	steel	20 x 10	0.4	0.9	13.2	45.0	nd	nd	4.8	4.2	0.5	nd	0.7	30.0	YK015
	960029	edge	steel	15 x 10	0.5	1.1	15.2	53.4	nd	nd	5.9	4.6	0.5	nd	0.5	18.0	YK016
	960029	edge	steel	35 x 6	0.5	1.2	15.3	50.4	0.3	nd	5.4	4.7	0.5	nd	0.5	20.9	YK017
	960029	back	steel	30 x 10	0.3	0.9	14.2	47.6	0.3	nd	4.9	4.3	0.6	nd	0.4	26.3	YK018
	960029	edge	phosphoric/ferritic	90 x 50	nd	2.0	14.2	35.1	3.5	0.3	2.6	5.0	0.6	nd	2.8	33.9	YK019
	960029	back	phosphoric/ferritic	60 x 10	nd	1.5	12.6	31.6	3.3	0.4	2.9	4.8	0.8	nd	2.9	38.9	YK020
	960029	back	phosphoric/ferritic	150 x 100	nd	2.0	14.0	34.6	3.2	0.1	2.6	5.0	0.5	nd	2.5	35.3	YK021
	960029	back	phosphoric/ferritic	60 x 15	nd	1.8	14.3	35.7	2.4	nd	3.0	6.0	0.8	nd	3.6	32.1	YK022
	960029	back	phosphoric/ferritic	30 x 20	0.2	2.7	15.4	40.6	nd	nd	3.2	6.1	0.7	nd	3.0	27.9	YK023
Fishergate 14940	960030	edge	ferrite	20 x 20	nd	0.4	3.7	9.7	14.4	nd	0.4	1.6	nd	nd	0.6	69.1	YK024
	960030	edge	ferrite	15 x 6	nd	0.5	0.4	10.4	17.0	0.8	0.3	0.7	nd	nd	0.4	69.2	YK025
	960030	edge	ferrite	100 x 10	nd	0.6	4.5	11.8	9.0	0.5	0.5	2.1	nd	nd	0.6	70.3	YK026
	960030	edge	ferrite	25 x 10	nd	0.2	0.7	10.4	8.7	0.5	0.1	0.9	nd	nd	0.1	78.2	YK027
	960030	edge	ferrite	25 x 12	nd	1.3	2.7	14.2	8.5	0.5	0.4	5.8	nd	nd	1.2	65.2	YK028
	960030	edge	ferrite	100 x 10	nd	1.5	4.9	15.3	1.7	0.3	nd	1.0	nd	nd	1.1	74.0	YK029
	960030	centre	steel	30 x 20	nd	1.4	8.5	51.9	nd	nd	3.9	4.0	0.4	nd	2.2	27.5	YK031
	960030	centre	steel	20 x 5	0.2	1.9	8.2	48.2	nd	nd	5.0	6.1	0.7	nd	2.1	27.4	YK032
	960030	centre	steel	20 x 6	nd	1.5	8.0	48.5	nd	nd	4.2	4.2	0.6	nd	1.3	31.3	YK033
	960030	centre	steel	20 x 15	0.1	1.6	8.6	55.5	nd	nd	4.2	4.8	0.6	nd	2.0	22.3	YK034
	960030	centre	steel	15 x 12	nd	0.9	5.3	31.1	2.5	0.2	2.8	3.3	0.3	nd	1.5	51.8	YK035
	960030	centre	steel	20 x 10	0.1	2.3	10.0	52.0	nd	0.1	4.5	8.0	0.7	nd	2.0	20.2	YK036

Site details	AML ref.	Sample information		Inclusion size (length x width in mm)	Composition (wt% oxide)													SEM ref.
		section	matrix		Na$_2$O	MgO	Al$_2$O$_3$	SiO$_2$	P$_2$O$_5$	S	K$_2$O	CaO	TiO$_2$	Cr$_2$O$_3$	MnO	FeO	
Fishergate 14937	960031	edge	steel	10 x 8	0.8	1.2	6.0	64.2	nd	nd	3.9	7.5	0.3	nd	nd	15.9	YK037
	960031	edge	steel	30 x 12	0.1	0.9	4.3	53.8	nd	nd	2.8	6.1	0.4	nd	0.1	31.3	YK038
	960031	edge	steel	25 x 10	0.8	1.1	6.5	59.8	nd	nd	4.4	7.2	0.5	nd	nd	19.4	YK039
	960031	edge	steel	20 x 20	0.8	1.0	5.5	58.5	nd	nd	4.0	7.6	0.3	nd	nd	22.1	YK040
	960031	edge	steel	30 x 20	0.7	1.0	5.9	62.2	nd	nd	2.7	6.6	0.4	nd	nd	20.3	YK041
	960031	edge	steel	40 x 20	1.2	1.2	6.3	73.0	nd	nd	4.4	8.9	0.3	nd	nd	4.3	YK042
	960031	edge	ferrite	15 x 12	nd	0.4	0.4	nd	nd	nd	nd	nd	nd	nd	nd	99.2	YK043
	960031	edge	ferrite	20 x 20	nd	0.4	0.4	0.9	nd	nd	nd	nd	nd	nd	nd	98.1	YK044
	960031	back	ferrite	40 x 20	nd	0.4	1.8	8.3	nd	nd	0.9	2.5	nd	nd	nd	86.0	YK045
	960031	back	ferrite	60 x 30	nd	0.8	0.4	0.5	nd	nd	nd	nd	nd	nd	nd	98.3	YK046
	960031	back	ferrite	80 x 10	0.5	0.4	14.4	28.7	nd	nd	10.2	9.2	0.4	nd	nd	36.0	YK047
	960031	back	ferrite	60 x 20	0.3	0.3	11.2	19.5	0.4	nd	9.1	6.8	0.2	nd	0.3	51.7	YK048
Bedern 13767	960032	edge	steel	30 x 10	0.3	1.0	5.1	37.0	0.7	nd	3.0	2.9	0.6	nd	1.4	47.8	YK049
	960032	edge	steel	30 x 20	0.2	2.4	7.5	53.8	0.2	nd	6.1	4.5	0.7	nd	2.0	22.2	YK050
	960032	edge	steel (weld line)	150 x 40	nd	0.1	0.2	nd	nd	nd	nd	0.3	nd	nd	0.1	99.2	YK051
	960032	pattern weld	weld-steel	12 x 12	0.2	2.3	7.4	61.8	nd	nd	3.5	6.4	0.5	nd	1.3	16.3	YK052
	960032	pattern weld	weld-steel	10 x 5	nd	1.9	6.1	36.3	0.4	nd	3.2	4.7	0.4	nd	1.0	45.8	YK053
	960032	edge	steel	60 x 30	nd	2.7	6.9	47.8	nd	nd	4.5	3.9	0.4	nd	1.9	31.7	YK054
	960032	edge	steel	90 x 10	nd	1.5	5.2	39.3	nd	nd	4.1	2.7	0.4	nd	1.9	44.6	YK055
	960032	back	pattern weld	100 x 18	nd	nd	0.5	5.3	0.6	nd	0.3	nd	nd	nd	nd	93.3	YK056
	960032	back	pattern weld	60 x 10	nd	nd	nd	nd	0.5	nd	nd	nd	nd	nd	nd	99.5	YK057
	960032	back	pattern weld	10 x 5	nd	3.1	9.6	40.6	0.7	nd	2.9	6.4	0.5	nd	0.8	35.3	YK058
	960032	back	phosphoric	20 x 20	nd	0.7	3.8	13.8	7.6	1.1	1.1	2.7	nd	nd	0.4	68.7	YK059
	960032	back	phosphoric	100 x 80	nd	1.2	8.1	18.9	3.6	0.4	2.8	4.9	0.3	nd	0.9	58.7	YK060
	960032	back	phosphoric	30 x 20	nd	0.9	2.2	16.6	6.3	nd	0.8	3.0	nd	nd	0.4	69.6	YK061
	960032	back	phosphoric	30 x 20	nd	3.3	14.3	31.1	2.5	nd	3.9	8.2	0.4	nd	1.6	34.4	YK062
	960032	back	phosphoric	40 x 8	nd	nd	0.2	11.7	2.0	nd	nd	0.1	nd	nd	nd	85.9	YK063
	960032	back	phosphoric	10 x 10	nd	4.4	16.9	38.3	5.2	nd	5.2	10.3	0.8	nd	3.0	16.0	YK064
Bedern 13782	960033		steel (rhs)	20 x 7	0.3	1.3	6.0	51.3	nd	nd	7.5	11.7	0.6	nd	8.7	12.7	YK065
	960033		steel (rhs)	10 x 10	nd	1.1	7.2	50.5	nd	nd	4.9	11.7	0.6	nd	6.2	17.7	YK066
	960033		steel (rhs)	100 x 10	0.2	3.4	10.8	53.1	nd	nd	10.6	9.2	1.0	nd	7.2	4.6	YK067
	960033		steel (rhs)	10 x 3	nd	0.5	5.8	34.9	0.9	nd	1.8	1.0	0.6	nd	2.2	52.3	YK068
	960033		steel (lhs)	20 x 5	nd	1.4	3.8	30.1	7.0	1.2	2.4	7.3	0.5	nd	13.6	32.8	YK069

Site details	AML ref.	section	matrix	Inclusion size (length x width in mm)	Na$_2$O	MgO	Al$_2$O$_3$	SiO$_2$	P$_2$O$_5$	S	K$_2$O	CaO	TiO$_2$	Cr$_2$O$_3$	MnO	FeO	SEM ref.
13782 contd	960033		steel (lhs)	10 x 3	nd	1.7	4.7	31.4	1.6	0.3	3.1	7.0	0.5	nd	10.7	39.3	YK070
	960033		phosphoric	7 x 4	nd	0.6	2.9	10.9	4.3	0.3	0.3	1.2	0.3	nd	3.4	75.9	YK071
	960033		phosphoric	40 x 20	nd	0.3	1.8	16.8	8.2	1.7	1.1	3.3	0.2	nd	0.4	66.1	YK072
	960033		phosphoric	50 x 20	nd	0.3	2.8	16.1	10.9	1.4	1.1	3.8	0.3	nd	0.4	62.7	YK073
	960033		phosphoric	10 x 4	nd	0.1	nd	nd	1.2	nd	nd	nd	nd	nd	nd	98.7	YK074
	960033		phosphoric	100 x 10	nd	0.2	3.5	18.6	7.4	0.5	0.7	4.1	0.1	nd	0.5	64.2	YK075
	960033		phosphoric	70 x 15	nd	0.3	1.7	16.1	3.9	0.7	0.2	1.0	nd	nd	0.2	75.8	YK076
	960033		phosphoric	150 x 100	nd	0.1	5.8	12.6	11.1	0.9	0.7	6.9	0.3	nd	0.3	61.2	YK077
Bedern	960034	edge	steel	8 x 4	0.1	0.9	2.3	38.4	0.8	0.3	1.6	8.0	nd	nd	0.2	47.3	YK078
13766	960034	edge	steel	30 x 4	0.1	0.8	2.3	29.2	0.6	0.3	1.9	9.0	nd	nd	0.4	55.5	YK079
	960034	edge	steel	30 x 5	0.3	1.5	4.3	44.7	1.3	0.4	2.9	10.0	0.2	nd	0.3	34.3	YK080
	960034	edge	steel	10 x 6	0.4	2.5	7.8	39.5	nd	nd	4.2	13.2	0.8	nd	1.1	30.6	YK081
	960034	back	steel	9 x 5	nd	0.2	0.9	22.0	2.3	0.3	0.8	4.3	nd	nd	0.2	69.2	YK082
	960034	back	steel	7 x 4	nd	0.5	1.1	28.7	1.9	0.2	0.8	3.5	nd	nd	0.3	63.0	YK083
	960034	back	ferrite (lhs)	50 x 30	nd	0.3	9.3	18.7	5.1	1.0	1.8	0.8	0.4	nd	3.4	59.1	YK084
	960034	back	ferrite (lhs)	40 x 9	nd	0.4	13.9	22.1	4.6	0.4	1.9	0.4	0.5	nd	3.2	52.7	YK085
	960034	back	ferrite (lhs)	80 x 8	nd	0.3	2.9	21.4	3.4	0.3	0.3	nd	nd	nd	2.1	69.4	YK086
	960034	back	ferrite (lhs)	30 x 10	nd	0.2	1.2	14.5	10.8	0.4	1.3	1.3	nd	nd	1.5	68.9	YK087
	960034	back	ferrite (lhs)	30 x 8	nd	nd	13.2	11.7	8.0	0.3	1.5	1.4	0.6	nd	2.5	60.7	YK088
	960034	back	ferrite (rhs)	40 x 5	nd	nd	0.6	0.6	nd	nd	nd	nd	nd	nd	0.3	98.6	YK089
	960034	back	ferrite (rhs)	30 x 4	nd	nd	0.3	1.2	0.2	nd	nd	0.3	nd	nd	nd	98.1	YK090
	960034	back	ferrite (rhs)	25 x 4	nd	2.0	13.4	32.2	3.7	0.2	2.6	8.8	0.9	nd	2.1	34.1	YK091
	960034	back	ferrite (rhs)	100 x 7	nd	0.4	3.6	6.9	2.6	nd	0.5	1.6	0.3	nd	0.6	83.4	YK092
	960034	back	ferrite (rhs)	60 x 10	nd	1.4	2.1	16.6	0.4	0.2	1.3	12.8	0.2	nd	1.7	63.3	YK093
	960034	back	ferrite (centre)	40 x 15	nd	3.0	9.7	26.2	9.2	0.9	2.3	5.9	0.5	nd	2.9	39.5	YK094
	960034	back	ferrite (centre)	40 x 15	nd	2.8	9.3	24.9	7.2	0.8	2.0	5.7	0.5	nd	2.7	44.1	YK095
	960034	back	ferrite (centre)	80 x 30	nd	2.1	4.6	20.6	6.3	1.0	0.9	3.5	0.2	nd	2.0	58.9	YK096
	960034	back	ferrite (centre)	20 x 7	nd	2.1	7.0	22.1	9.6	1.3	1.4	3.8	0.4	nd	2.4	49.8	YK097
	960034	back	ferrite (centre)	15 x 7	nd	2.5	7.9	22.8	8.3	1.1	1.4	4.2	0.3	nd	2.4	49.1	YK098
	960034	back	weld line	20 x 12	nd	nd	nd	1.0	0.4	nd	nd	0.2	nd	nd	nd	98.3	YK099
	960034	back	weld line	100 x 5	nd	nd	nd	1.2	0.4	nd	nd	1.4	nd	nd	nd	96.9	YK100
	960034	back	weld line	200 x 20	nd	0.1	1.4	5.8	22.7	1.0	1.9	1.7	nd	nd	1.3	64.3	YK101
	960034	back	weld line	80 x 20	nd	nd	0.3	0.8	nd	nd	nd	nd	nd	nd	nd	98.9	YK102

Composition (wt% oxide)

fitted with Oxford ISIS energy-dispersive X-ray analyser (EDXA) with thin window. This was able to detect all elements above boron in the periodic table. The advantages of SEM-based EDX analysis lie in the ability of the technique to undertake analysis at high magnifications on selected small areas, such as specific phases or mixtures of phases. The method is therefore highly suitable for heterogeneous archaeological materials. The sample was viewed in back-scattered mode before quantitative analysis was undertaken. This mode enhances atomic number contrast, rather than topography, allowing phases within the inclusions to be differentiated. Phases containing elements with higher atomic numbers, such as the iron in wüstite, appear lighter than low atomic number phases, such as glasses, with fayalite appearing as an intermediate mid-grey. Composition was determined over each inclusion as a whole rather than individual phases within them.

It should be noted that the technique can only be used to detect elements, not compounds. Figures quoted in Table 290, which refer to the weight percentage of oxide, are derived from assumptions about the stoichiometry (i.e. the combining tendency) of each element. Minimum detectable levels vary from element to element: for oxides of sodium (Na), magnesium (Mg), aluminium (Al), silicon (Si), phosphorus (P), potassium (K), calcium (Ca) and titanium (Ti) these are approximately 0·1wt%, and for sulphur (S) and manganese (Mn) about 0·15wt%. Sensitivity is slightly greater for the pure metals within the iron matrix, but few impurity elements are present even at these levels. For the York knives, the most frequent impurity detected was phosphorus, with occasional traces of copper and nickel. Analyses of matrices are given in Table 290 and of individual inclusions in Table 291.

Results of examination

Knife 11811

X-radiography revealed frequent striations along the length of the blade, but no distinct line which could positively be identified as a weld line. A probable cutler's mark was also visible, appearing as two equilateral triangles with points touching (Fig.1379).

Metallographic examination of the unetched sample showed the presence of slag inclusions. Throughout most of the blade these were of irregular, elongated shape, containing two phases, and occupied 3% of the volume of the artefact. Towards the cutting edge of the blade very few (<1%) inclusions were present and these were of very small size.

Etching revealed that the blade was constructed of two components: the back of the blade was almost entirely coarse-grained (ASTM 2) ferrite with ghosting indicating the presence of phosphorus. A small area on one side of the back showed a slightly higher carbon content. By contrast the edge of the blade was of tempered martensite (see Fig.1368, p.2765), with a high hardness. An oblique weld line separated the two zones.

The differences in hardness between iron and steel are evident. However, to put these values in perspective, it should be noted that the 190HV value for phosphoric iron is of the order of 40–80 units higher than a pure, ferritic iron. Also the hardness of the steel is probably 100–200 units lower than an untempered steel.

Microanalysis further differentiated the two components. The iron in the back was shown to have a

Table 292   Hardness values for knife 11811

Phosphoric iron Knife back		Tempered martensite Knife edge	
	163.6HV		497.8HV
	177.7HV		473.0HV
	196.8HV		503.0HV
	189.3HV		424.5HV
	225.1HV		477.8HV
Mean	190.5HV		475.2HV

mean phosphorus content of 0·23%, but no other impurities, whilst the steel contained no phosphorus but 1·28% copper. The latter probably arose from contamination during working, but it might have resulted from an ore source containing traces of copper. Inclusions also showed distinct differences between the two alloys. As noted above, some of these differences are due to the conditions required for steel production. However, other significant differences are also present. Those in the steel contain much manganese whilst those in the phosphoric iron contain sulphur. The analytical results strongly suggest different sources for the two metals. Higher levels of sulphur in the phosphoric iron may suggest the use of mineral coal in the early working of this metal.

Interpretation

A high-quality Type 2a blade in which a steel edge had been scarf-welded to a phosphoric iron back. The blade had subsequently been quenched and tempered to give a mean edge hardness of 475HV. Differences in composition suggest geographically and possibly technologically different origins for the two alloys.

Knife *11894*

No weld lines were visible in the X-radiograph.

In the unetched condition a marked contrast in the inclusion content and composition was visible between the edge and the back of the knife. The edge contained less than 1% of single-phase elongated inclusions whilst the back had 5% of single- and dual-phase inclusions. These were often angular and were elongated or in the form of stringers.

When etched the back of the blade was shown to be mostly phosphoric iron (see Fig.1367, p.2764) with a large grain size (ASTM 1), although small areas contained a mixture of finer-grained ferrite (ASTM 5) with agglomerated cementite (Fe_3C). The edge contained two phases, ferrite and spheroidised/agglomerated cementite. The co-existence of these phases without the products of either slow cooling (pearlite) or rapid quenching (bainite and martensite) is significant. The alloy is a steel but one that has been held at high temperatures for longer periods than is metallurgically beneficial. Two possible explanations may be suggested. Firstly, an incompetent smith may have misjudged the heat treatment of the blade. More probably, considering the deliberate selection of materials and the skill that has been used in forging the blade, the knife could have been accidentally reheated at a later date, perhaps by being dropped in a fierce fire or in the conflagration of a building. The result, as shown by the microhardness figures, is a blade in which the edge is even softer than the back.

Microanalysis confirmed that the difference between the two components was restricted to their phosphorus content — the back contained 0·3%, the edge none. The inclusions in both parts are relatively similar for the oxides of calcium, aluminium and titanium, but the back is notably high in the oxides of magnesium, manganese and, predictably, phosphorus.

Interpretation

A Type 1c blade in which a steel 'tongue' had been skilfully inserted into a phosphoric iron back. At some time, probably later in the knife's history, the blade had been severely heated, without subsequent

Table 293   Hardness values for knife *11894*

Phosphoric iron	213.1HV	Ferrite/spheroidised	185.7HV
Knife back	180.0HV	pearlite	165.2HV
	181.1HV	Knife edge	198.0HV
	199.3HV		206.0HV
	210.2HV		182.2HV
Mean	196.7HV		187.4HV

Table 294 Hardness values for knife *13766*

Ferritic/phosphoric iron		Martensite	
Knife back	163.3HV	Knife edge	612.4HV
	159.5HV		641.7HV
	168.2HV		681.8HV
	156.7HV		673.0HV
	180.0HV		641.7HV
Mean	165.5HV		650.0HV

quenching, such that its effectiveness was severely reduced. The composition of the two components suggests that the phosphoric iron and steel derived from different sources.

Knife *13766*

The X-radiograph strongly suggested three bands within this knife, but with no evidence of twisting associated with pattern-welding.

Metallographic examination of the unetched sample showed the contrast between the few inclusions in the edge of the knife (<1% subround to elongated, single phase) with greater numbers in the back (3% elongated, single and dual phase). The nital etch revealed the edge to be of tempered martensite, with a V-shaped weld line and some carbon diffusion across it into the low-carbon back. The back itself was of very unusual composite construction with two sides enclosing a central core. Very faint ghosting was noted in places with very variable grain size (ASTM 7 to 1). This, together with the slightly elevated hardness values for the low-carbon region, indicates that some phosphorus is present.

Of the three sections in the back, one side (left in Fig.1379, p.2778) and the core contained some phosphorus, but none was detected in the other side or in the steel edge. The phosphorus content in the inclusions mirrored that of the matrices, but few other trends were evident, except that the central low-carbon region contained significant levels of sulphur and magnesium.

Interpretation

A Type 1c with steel cutting edge inserted into a low-carbon back. The complexity of the back may have resulted from an attempt to create a decorative effect. However, the metals are so similar that this could not have been particularly effective and the recycling of small fragments may be a more probable explanation for the observed structure. The blade has been heat treated and the cutting edge showed the highest hardness of all the blades examined.

Knife *13767*

The X-radiograph showed three zones in the knife: an edge, a back and, between the two, a band of metal

Table 295 Hardness values for knife *13767*

Phosphoric iron		Tempered martensite	
Knife back	159.5HV	Knife edge	559.8HV
	156.7HV		553.7HV
	186.9HV		503.0HV
	171.3HV		530.3HV
	166.2HV		477.8HV
Mean	168.1HV		524.9HV

with diagonally oriented striations characteristic of the twisted portions of pattern-welded blades.

In the unetched sample the position of weld lines were shown by lines of inclusions. Overall the blade contained about 2% inclusions, but in some areas these occupied much less volume. Near the edge the inclusions were dark grey, often fractured and of elongated to stringer morphology. In the pattern-welded region and back, inclusions were more variable in form, being angular and irregular but rarely as elongated.

After etching the sample the three regions of the blade were identified as a tempered martensite edge, a phosphoric iron back and a central pattern-welded region in which bands of tempered martensite alternated with bands of phosphoric iron (see Fig.1369, p.2765). Some diffusion of carbon into the phosphoric iron bands had occurred. A light-etching band marked the location of the weld between the edge and pattern-welded region.

Microanalysis of the metal showed the steel in the edge and in the pattern-welded region to be similarly free of impurities. All the low-carbon material contained phosphorus. In the pattern-welded region this was double (0·34%) that of the back (0·17%). This may be the result of deliberate selection; phosphorus tends to block the diffusion of carbon and hence would provide maximum visual contrast between two metals. Inclusion composition was very variable and added no useful information. The similarity to *11888*, where the pattern-welded zone incorporated a particularly high phosphorous iron, may be noted.

Interpretation

Technologically this blade is a Type 2b, with a steel blade and iron back. However, it is notable in also having a central pattern-welded region, which would have required considerable skill, given the small size of the knife. Quenching and tempering had given a good, though not especially hard, edge. The smith made use of at least two alloys: steel and phosphoric iron. It also seems likely that a further, particularly phosphorus-rich iron was used in the pattern-welded region. This is a high-quality blade, being both serviceable and aesthetically pleasing.

Knife *13782*

Only the back of this heavily corroded knife had survived sufficiently well to allow it to be sampled. However, even in the corroded region possible weld lines were apparent. A trace of non-ferrous metal can be associated with the cutlers' marks.

The unetched sample was seen to contain a large number of inclusions (5%) in a band running down through the centre. These were large, of irregular shape, generally elongated and contained multiple phases. By contrast the surviving outside regions contained only 1% of inclusions and they tended to be smaller, dark grey, of single phase and of elongated or stringer morphology.

Etching revealed the outer surface of the blade to be tempered martensite with some bainite and the centre to be a banded structure including ferrite with phosphorus ghosting and a feathery structure, probably upper bainite, which suggests that this central

Table 296 Hardness values for knife *13782*

Low-carbon bainite	193.0HV	Tempered martensite	519.1HV
Knife core	186.9HV	Bainite	591.9HV
	184.5HV	Knife sides	530.3HV
	254.4HV		657.0HV
	250.6HV		524.7HV
Mean	213.9HV		564.6HV

region contains areas with some carbon, though probably not more than 0·1 or 0·2%, the lower of which would be consistent with hardness values around 250HV.

Compositionally, low levels of phosphorus were found to be present in the low-carbon region and in the steel on one side of the blade (right-hand side in Fig.1379, p.2778). This side also contained traces of copper, perhaps linked to the non-ferrous speck seen on the X-radiograph. The other steel component showed no trace of impurities. Surprisingly the steel on the opposite side (left on Fig.1379) contained high-phosphorus inclusions. This was distinguished from the phosphoric iron by high levels of oxides of magnesium, titanium and manganese, and from the other steel by high sulphur and high manganese.

Interpretation

The interpretation of the blade is made less certain by the advanced state of the corrosion, which had oxidised the edge of the blade. However, it appears most probable that the blade corresponds to Type 4 in which the steel forms a sheath around a phosphoric iron core. Quenching and tempering had been used to ensure an effective cutting edge. However, as different sources of steel are suggested for the two sides of the blade, these may have been prepared and welded onto the core separately rather than wrapping a single sheet around.

Knife *14937*

X-radiography revealed distinctive narrow bands running parallel to the edge of the knife, indicative of a butt-welded edge.

Microscopic examination of the unetched sample identified several lines of slag stringers along weld lines. One of these was later found to correspond with the join between the steel edge and iron back; the others would have originated during earlier working of the iron. The back of the knife contained variable concentrations of inclusions, up to about 5% by volume and generally small and grey. The edge contained fewer (1%) but larger inclusions of subround to elongated form.

The etched structure confirmed the position of a butt-weld. The edge of the blade consisted of tempered martensite at the extreme edge, through bainite and nodular pearlite to pearlite near the weld. The back was entirely ferritic (see Fig.1366, p.2764) with a grain size of ASTM 6, except for a region near the weld into which carbon had diffused. The weld was further distinguished by a light-etching band.

Analysis of the metal matrices found no impurity elements present at detectable levels. Many of the inclusions in the back of the knife were almost pure iron oxide, being entrapped scale. Others were unusually high in the oxides of aluminium, potassium and calcium. Otherwise the inclusions in both components were free of phosphorus, manganese and sulphur.

Interpretation

A high-quality Type 2b blade with a steel edge butt-welded to an iron back. The whole has subsequently been quenched and tempered or slack quenched. The composition of the iron and steel are similar, but not particularly distinctive, and a similar or the same source of ore cannot be ruled out.

Table 297   Hardness values for knife *14937*

Ferritic iron		Tempered martensite	
Knife back	112.5HV	Knife edge	513.7HV
	114.2HV		634.2HV
	108.2HV		591.9HV
	127.7HV		508.3HV
	119.5HV		566.0HV
Mean	116.4HV		562.8HV

Knife 14940

No unambiguous weld lines were visible in the X-radiograph. Because the edge of the blade was severely corroded only a single sample was taken from the back of the blade.

Before etching, microscopic examination of the inclusions within the section showed their presence to vary considerably from 1 to 3%. They were of elongated or stringer morphology and generally mottled appearance, although some were seen to contain two phases.

Etching showed the blade to be of sandwich construction. At high magnification the microstructure of the dark-etching band through the centre was shown to vary from tempered martensite towards the edge of the blade to nodular pearlite and bainite nearer to the back of the blade. The difference in structure is due to the thickening of the blade towards its back, which would therefore have cooled less quickly when the blade was quenched. The sides of the blade were heterogeneous in carbon content, being predominantly ferrite (ASTM 5) but with some bands of pearlite. The banded nature of this metal may indicate that the iron had been piled to give it more uniform properties.

Microhardness shows a much greater contrast in hardness between blade and back compared with *11894*.

Analysis, surprisingly, found some phosphorus at one point in the steel but not as much as in the iron where 0·17% was detected. The latter suggests that this alloy borders on being classed as phosphoric iron. However, given the low hardness values and lack of ghosted structure, its initial classification as

ferritic iron was retained. Inclusion composition showed the usual concentration of glass-forming oxides in inclusions in the steel phase, although the concentration of phosphorus and, significantly, sulphur is greater in the iron. As mentioned on p.2784, the sulphur may be due to the use of coal in the early working of the bloom, or bars of metal. Interestingly, the phosphorus content of the inclusions is very high at up to 17%. This suggests that a high-phosphorus ore was used, but smelted at relatively low temperatures such that the phosphorus, which partitions between the metal and slag during smelting, passed largely into the slag.

Interpretation

A Type 1a sandwich welded blade in which two heterogeneous, but largely ferritic, iron plates flank one of steel. The whole has been effectively heat treated by quenching and tempering to provide a hard edge on a tough back. The sandwich blade, whilst less sparing of steel than the butt- or scarf-welded knife, has the advantage that long-term resharpening will never reach a point whereby the steel edge is entirely worn away. Few oxides show significant compositional differences between the iron and steel, though for the former, the high content of phosphorus pentoxide suggests a different ore source whilst its sulphur content may result from the use of mineral fuel during bloom or bar smithing.

Discussion

By David Starley (with additional material by Patrick Ottaway)

Scientific examination of the medieval knives from Coppergate, Bedern and Fishergate using metallography, SEM-based microanalysis, X-radiography and microhardness testing allowed a much greater

Table 298 Hardness values for knife *14940*

Ferritic iron		Tempered martensite	
Knife back	134.0HV	Knife edge	585.3HV
	138.4HV		454.5HV
	119.5HV		634.2HV
	140.0HV		649.5HV
	133.3HV		612.5HV
Mean	133.0HV		587.2HV

level of understanding of the artefacts than non-destructive examination alone could have achieved. In particular it has enabled determination of the iron alloys available to metalworkers, an assessment of the forging and heat treatment techniques of the smiths and a measure of the effectiveness of the knives in use. The unusually good preservation of the knives was an important factor in successfully sampling and examining the blades.

Looking firstly at the range of alloys, with the exception of *4997* and the heavily worn blade *11817*, all the blades incorporated steel in such a way that it formed part of the cutting edge. Steel has the important property of being amenable to hardening; appropriate heat treatment results in high hardness which allows a sharp edge to be retained. Like most knives and other edged tools and weapons, the York knives also incorporated other iron alloys. Low-carbon iron has the practical advantage of not becoming brittle due to heat treatment but retaining its toughness. It would also have had the economic benefit of being cheaper. Six blades contained pure 'ferritic' iron, nine phosphoric iron and six a mixture of the two with only one constructed entirely of steel.

The use of microanalysis in the project allowed the alloys to be studied in greater depth. Few elements were present in the iron matrix in sufficient quantity to be quantified by the energy dispersive detector of the scanning electron microscope used by Starley for Group 3 (Table 291, pp.2780–2), although the phosphorus levels of the phosphoric iron, and occasional copper and nickel contents were above the limits of detectability. The greater sensitivity attainable by the wavelength dispersive spectrometer used by Wiemer for Group 2 (Table 284, p.2770) provided a more reliable quantification of impurities within the metal. Slag inclusions, which are a characteristic component of early iron, provided further compositional data on which to compare the individual components within the blades.

Data from microanalysis provided useful evidence relevant to a major topic of discussion in ferrous archaeometallurgy: the manufacture and supply of steel. On the one hand there is documentary evidence for importation of steel as a separate commodity, even as a frequent occurrence in 15th century London (Childs 1981). Little attempt has been made to match accounts, such as the 'authoritative opin-

ion' from 1577 which stated that 'as for our steele it is not so good for edge tools as that of Colaine' (i.e. Cologne) (Hopkins 1970, 125), with the composition of renaissance, medieval or earlier blades from archaeological sites.

Not only is the geographical origin of steel open to question but also its technological origin. Many archaeometallurgists believe that traditional bloomery processes were adapted to produce a more steely bloom when required, or that a heterogeneous bloom could be separated into high- and low-carbon parts. A third option is for iron to be carburised by heating it in a highly reducing, carbon-rich atmosphere so that carbon was absorbed into the metal. This carburising principle can be divided into two basic processes. The first is cementation, in which iron bars were converted to steel, then worked into artefacts. Later it formed the basis of a major industry, but the earliest historical evidence of it in Europe comes from Germany in the late 16th century (Barraclough 1976). The second process, which we now know as case carburisation or case hardening, is recorded earlier than this. Theophilus' *On Divers Arts*, written in about 1100, describes the hardening of files by heating in a carburising medium of ox horn and salt (Hawthorne and Smith 1963, 93). This reference has been used by numerous scholars to suggest that this was usual method of producing steel. However, in this technique carbon penetration is very slow and therefore more appropriate to objects like files in which a very hard, but only very thin surface layer is required. Such a layer would soon be lost when a knife was resharpened.

As mentioned above, it is recognised that the composition of inclusions in steel will differ from those in low-carbon iron. This is a function of the highly reducing conditions required for the absorption and retention of carbon; these will also reduce iron oxide in the inclusions to metallic iron, with a corresponding increase in concentration of the other elements present. However the York data from Group 3 showed that for six of the seven knives the composition of the inclusions, and often the iron matrices, was sufficiently different to be certain that the alloys came from different sources. For the seventh blade (*14937*) the compositions of iron and steel were not sufficiently distinctive that either differences or similarities could be used to say whether their sources were related. The marked compositional differences contrast with Wiemer's microprobe analyses of the Anglian knives from 46–54 Fishergate which show most, though not all, knives to have similar trace element contents in the different metallic phases (pp.1277–308, *AY* 17/9). It might be thought possible to use these differences to source the artefacts but attempts to do this have achieved very limited success due to a number of difficulties inherent in iron production. These have been summarised (Starley 1992, 55) as:

1. The wide variety of raw materials, particularly ores, which are available
2. The ubiquity of ore sources and their lack of characterising features
3. A lack of complementary data from production sites
4. The heterogeneous composition of artefacts
5. The alteration of composition by subsequent processing
6. The possible reworking of scrap
7. The deliberate or accidental addition of non-essential components.

Given these possible obstacles, it is not possible to suggest the origin of the alloys, or of the knives if the latter were imported ready-made to the city. What can be suggested, and it is an important step forward, is that the iron and steel have different origins and these differences are likely to be geographical. However, technological differences, probably including the use of coal in smithing (shown by the presence of sulphur in inclusions), are also likely to be a factor. The results from the knife analyses do appear to provide evidence of widespread trade in specialist ferrous alloys during the later medieval period.

The second purpose of the investigation was to study the techniques used by the smiths for forging and heat treating the blades. Other metallographic studies have shown that the preferred method of construction technique appears to vary over time as much, perhaps, for cultural as for practical reasons. Anglian and middle Anglo-Saxon knives tend to be butt-welded (Tylecote and Gilmour Type 2), whilst in the Anglo-Scandinavian period they are usually either butt-welded or are variants of the 'sandwich' construction technique (Tylecote and Gilmour Type 1). Relatively little metallographic work has been undertaken on medieval blades, and the York material presented a rare opportunity to extend our understanding of smithing techniques forward in time.

Twenty-two objects from the three sites provide a small data set from which to draw conclusions. However, some trends were apparent even allowing for the fact that some of the knives may have been residual, in other words they were originally deposited in contexts of an earlier date to that in which they were found. First of all it is apparent that quite a variety of techniques were used to combine the iron and steel components of the blade. Of the Type 1 variants there were four sandwich construction (Type 1a), four inserted steel tongues (Type 1c), one steel flank (Type 1d) and two half sandwich (Type 1e). There were two examples of a scarf-weld (Type 2a), one of which has a pattern-welded core, and four horizontal butt-welds (Type 2b) including another with a pattern-welded core. In addition, there was one probable all-steel (Type 3) and one wrapped steel (Type 4) specimen, while two have no surviving steeled cutting edge. If the knives from medieval period contexts in York are compared to those from the Anglo-Scandinavian period at Coppergate in broad terms, we find that in the former the ratio of Type 1 to Type 2 is 11:7 while in the latter it is 18:18 (p.598, Table 37, *AY* 17/6). In both periods other types are rare. These figures may not immediately suggest a great difference in manufacturing technique between the two periods. However, if knives from Anglian contexts at 46–54 Fishergate (Table 111, *AY* 17/9) and from Coppergate pre-Period 4B (i.e. pre-c.925) are compared with those from later Anglo-Scandinavian and medieval contexts at Coppergate, Fishergate and Bedern we find that in the former group the corresponding ratio is 2:15 while in the latter it is 16:8. The conclusion arrived at in *AY* 17/9 (p.1308) that a significant period of change in approach to knife manufacture, not only in York but in England, occurred in the mid 10th century seems to be confirmed by these data. The character of this change is that of a replacement of a near uniform approach in the middle Anglo-Saxon/Anglian period to one of greater diversity, but not of the wholesale replacement of one method of manufacture by another. Although variants of Type 1 are more common than Type 2 from the mid 10th century onwards, knives with Type 2 structure were still made.

The final aim of the metallographic study was to assess the quality and effectiveness of the blades. Ideally a blade should have maximum hardness at its edge, but with greater toughness in the main body. Almost all the blades examined had been constructed

in such a way as to achieve this, although by different combinations of steel and low-carbon iron alloys. Only two (*11817* and *4997*) had no detectable steel cutting edge, but this may have been lost and so they may originally have been better tools than they now seem to be.

Direct measurement of the effectiveness of the blades was provided by microhardness testing. Results from this often showed high hardnesses of 450 to 600HV. For most knives, metallography and microhardness results testify to the skill and understanding of the smith in first quenching the blade to harden the steel edge, then tempering it by reheating to toughen it. For the exceptions the microstructure indicated that the blades had been reheated to a much too high temperature so that the hardness was adversely affected. This could have resulted from an error of judgement by the smith, although the damage may well have been done long after manufacture.

Pattern-welded knives

Particular mention should be made of the two pattern-welded blades *11888* and *13767* (from 13th–14th century contexts at Coppergate and Bedern respectively). Despite their small size these knives had been built up with considerable skill from three components: a steel edge, a moderately phosphoric back and, between these two, a twisted combination of steel and highly phosphoric iron. When ground, polished and etched the sides of the blades would have showed a pleasing decorative effect, making them highly desirable objects.

In addition to these, two other pattern-welded whittle tang knives from medieval contexts were identified by X-radiography. They are *11866* from a late 11th century context at Coppergate which, as noted above, is also unusual in having a bolster between blade and tang and in its large size (length 213mm), and *13778* from an early 14th century context at Bedern.

The origins of pattern-welding of knives, as opposed to swords and other weapons, probably lie in the middle Anglo-Saxon period and many examples are known in late Anglo-Saxon/Anglo-Scandinavian contexts including two from Coppergate (p.598, *AY* 17/6, *2756*, *2892*). It is now becoming apparent that pattern-welding remained a decorative device until

perhaps the 13th century or even later if *13778* is not residual in its context. Another post-Conquest example from York was found in a 12th century context at St Andrewgate, York (Fig.1314, **7**; YAT 1995.89, sf595), and others come from 13th century contexts in London (Cowgill et al. 1987, *4*, *7*) and at Eynsham Abbey (Fig.1315, **22**; Ottaway forthcoming, sf209; Fell and Starley forthcoming), while an example from a 14th century context comes from Winchester (Goodall 1990, 852, fig.256, *2809*; Tylecote 1990, 150, fig.30). Pattern-welding is usually associated with blades of back form A whether in the pre-Conquest or post-Conquest period and so it is unusual to find it on knives of back form D in the cases of *11866* and *13767*.

Pivoting knives (Fig.1380)

Medieval contexts at Coppergate produced five pivoting knives (*11907–11*) and the Foundry one (*13199*). The way in which these knives worked is shown in Fig.243, *AY* 17/6. When a blade was in use the notch on the opposite side of the pivot rested on a rivet which was also one of two holding the sides of the handle-cum-case together. This rivet counteracted upward pressure on the blade's cutting edge. All those from medieval contexts are to a greater or lesser extent incomplete, but *11910* was clearly the largest with a surviving length of 164mm. The longer of its two blades has a back which becomes concave towards the tip and the shorter blade has an angle back. In these respects it is similar to three pivoting knives published in *AY* 17/6 (*2976–8*). The backs of the longer blades of *11909*, *11911* from Coppergate and of *13199* from the Foundry also become concave, but the backs of the shorter blades of the two Coppergate knives are straight before curving down to the tip (missing on *13199*). On *11907* both blade backs have this form.

One face of *11909* (late 11th/early 12th century context) has the remains of two parallel grooves inlaid with brass and copper wires. A similar pattern of inlay can be seen on two pivoting knives from 9th–11th century contexts at Winchester (Goodall 1990, 837, fig.251, *2644*, *2648*). As noted above, similar inlay can also be found on other knives of pre-Conquest date and it is likely that *11909* is residual in its context.

There are four pivoting knives from Anglo-Scandinavian contexts at Coppergate and those from medieval contexts are also likely to be of pre-Conquest origin. Pivoting knives appear to be cur-

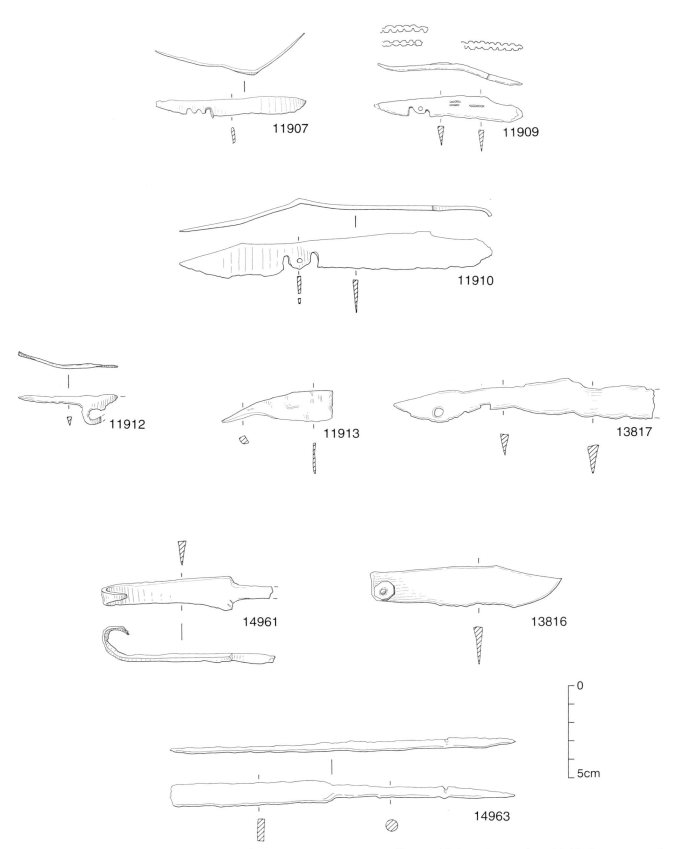

Fig.1380 *Pivoting knives 11907, 11909–10 from 16–22 Coppergate; miscellaneous blades 11912–13 from 16–22 Coppergate and 13817 from Bedern; paring knife 14961 from 46–54 Fishergate; folding knife 13816 from Bedern; sharpening steel 14963 from 46–54 Fishergate. Scale 1:2, details of inlay on 11909 scale 2:1*

rent in the 8th–11th centuries and do not occur on medieval sites where there is no pre-Conquest occupation.

Other blades (Fig.1380)

There are a few incomplete blades from knives or other sorts of tools of which the original form cannot now be determined. They include *11912*, a small object from a 13th century context at Coppergate, which exists as a thin tapering blade attached to an incomplete pierced component on which it may have swivelled; a second blade may have projected from the other side of it. *11913* from a 12th century context at Coppergate is an incomplete blade with a convex back which flows straight into the tang. This then curves below the level of the cutting edge and thickens to a wedge-shaped tip. *13817* from a late medieval context at Bedern is a very corroded slightly curved blade, broken at one end and pierced just before the tip.

Paring knife (Fig.1380)

14961 from a 16th century context at Fishergate is a knife with a deliberately curved blade which was probably used for paring or gouging and would have been ideal for cleaning out and trimming horses' hooves.

Knife mood

14962 from a 13th century context at Fishergate is a knife-like object, but the 'blade' does not have a cutting edge. This may be a knife which has been discarded during the smithing process prior to sharpening and if so can be described as a knife 'mood' or blank.

Folding knife (Fig.1380)

13816 is a blade from a mid 14th–early 15th century context at Bedern which is unfortunately broken at the rear end, but does not appear to be coming to a tang; rather it seems to widen slightly. It is suggested that this is the blade of a folding knife, possibly with an incomplete thumb piece, which rotated on the rivet which passes through it near the rear and also presumably through the end of a case. No trace of this survives. On one blade face a brass octagonal washer is set on the end of the rivet; the other face is obscured by corrosion. Folding knives are rare in medieval contexts, but two others, one in a boxwood case, have been found in London (Cowgill et al. 1987, 106, *309–10*).

Possible sharpening steel (Fig.1380)

14963 from a 13th century context at Fishergate is similar to *14962* in the sense that it has a spatulate blade' which does not have a cutting edge; in addition it has a tang of rounded cross-section which tapers to a point. This object is probably Anglian and may be compared to a number of similar spatulate objects of this date which defy identification. Helen Geake has suggested that they may be steels, i.e. knife sharpening tools, because they have often been found near knives in Anglo-Saxon graves (Geake 1995, 90–2). Sharpening, however, was usually done with a hone. Another suggestion is that they are strike-a-lights, although again this does not explain the form of the 'blades'. Furthermore, whether as a steel or a strike-a-light, it has to be assumed that the tang would have been set in a wooden handle so as to allow the user a firm grip. However, if they were intended to be given handles the tangs would have a rectangular rather than the usual rounded cross-section as seen on *14963*. In view of this, it may be suggested that these spatulate tools were intended to be gripped with the 'blade' while the 'tang' was actually used as a pointed tool.

Hones (Figs.1381–2)

These were recovered from all the sites, and in particular in considerable numbers from Coppergate. **Dr G.D. Gaunt** comments:

As with all the other stone artefacts included in this report, lithological examination was by hand lens and low-power stereo microscope in reflected light, supplemented for a few items where higher magnification was required by the use of a petrological microscope also in reflected light; none of the artefacts was thin-sectioned.

Fifty-seven hones from Coppergate (*10881–937*), three from the Foundry (*13084–6*), fourteen from Bedern, including two from 2 Aldwark (*13441–52, 14656–7*), and seven from Fishergate (*14735–41*) are made of quartz-muscovite schist. Twenty-two hones from Coppergate (*10938–59*), two from 22 Piccadilly (*13007–8*), one from the Foundry (*13087*) and three from Bedern (*13453–5*) are of quartz-muscovite phyllite. Three objects from Coppergate (*10977–9*) made of other stone types are also possible hones. Three schist hones (*10885, 10890, 10937*) and two phyllite hones (*10939, 10942*) from medieval Coppergate were used for metamorphic dating or natural remanent magnetisation measures by Crosby and Mitchell (1987). Medieval levels at Fishergate also produced three phyllite hones, thought to be residual and published in *AY 17/9 (4449–51)*.

The schist hones are of Norwegian Ragstone type for which a source in the Eidsborg area of central southern Norway is suggested by thin-section petrological and archaeological evidence (Ellis 1969, 149–50; Moore 1978, 65–8). The phyllite hones have, with few exceptions, a consistent lithology that equates them with the hones of Purple phyllite type as described by Ellis (1969, 144–7), and referred to by Moore (1978, 68) as Blue phyllite. Archaeological distributions suggest a source in the Norwegian Caledonide outcrops according to Crosby and Mitchell, but provenance in the Scottish Highlands or Shetland Islands cannot be precluded. See pp.2484–5, *AY 17/14*, for more detailed lithological information about the sources of schist and phyllite hones.

All the other hones are from British sources. Four of them (*10966–7, 14742–3*) are highly compacted sandstones and siltstones from the Lower Palaeozoic successions (in effect Ordovician and Silurian) of southern Scotland and/or Cumbria, and another five sandstone hones (*10968–71, 13458*) are either from these sources or from northern Pennine Carboniferous sources. One slate hone, *10976*, derives from the Lower Palaeozoic successions in either Cumbria or northern Wales. An appreciable number of moderately to well-compacted sandstone hones (*10960–5, 13456–7, 14745*) are referable to Coal Measures or other Upper Carboniferous sources in the eastern Pennines. In addition, four fine-grained muscovite-laminated sandstone hones, *10972–5*, are attributable

to Elland Flags-type sandstones in the Yorkshire Coal Measures, although it is possible that some or all of them may have been made from old Roman roofing stones found in situ in York. One other hone, of fine-grained calcareous sandstone, *14744*, was derived from Middle or Upper Jurassic sources, almost certainly in north-eastern Yorkshire.

The imported hones

At the three main sites under discussion there appears to have been contemporaneous use of the different stone types amongst the hones; at all, however, the imported schists and phyllites predominated. At Coppergate, schist hones represented c.59% of the total, and phyllites c.20%, but this dominance by the imported stones was also true of the Anglo-Scandinavian Periods 4B–5B (pp.2485–91, Tables 229–30, *AY 17/14*), and it is possible that a proportion of the hones in medieval levels at the site are residual from the earlier Anglo-Scandinavian activity. Similarly at Fishergate, it is unclear how many of the schist hones may be residual; it could be argued that none of those from Period 6 levels was associated with life in the priory, all three coming from Periods 6a–6b cemetery soil (*14735–7*), while the remainder came from 16th century destruction levels. But, at Bedern, where pre-medieval activity is much more restricted, the imported hones still significantly outnumber the sandstone examples, by a factor of 6:1, and they are concentrated in Periods 4–7 (late 13th–early 15th century) deposits; moreover, only imported hones occurred at the Foundry. This evidence from Bedern in particular does suggest that schist hones continued to represent a significant trade from the Anglo-Scandinavian period on into the medieval period in York; phyllite hones may also

Table 299   Hones by stone type (* = already published in *AY 17/9*)

	Schist	Phyllite	Sandstone/ siltstone	Slate	Total
Coppergate	57	22	16	1	96
22 Piccadilly	–	2	–	–	2
Foundry	3	1	–	–	4
Bedern, including Aldwark	14	3	3	–	20
Fishergate	7	3*	4	–	14
Total	81	31	22	1	135

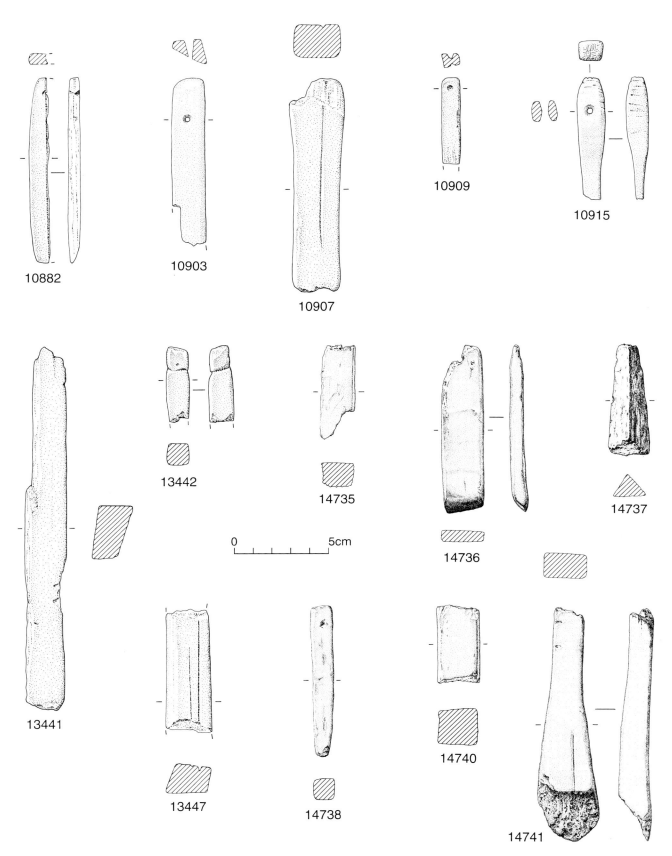

Fig.1381 *Schist hones:* 10882, 10903, 10907, 10909, 10915 *from 16–22 Coppergate;* 13441–2, 13447 *from Bedern;* 14735–8, 14740–1 *from 46–54 Fishergate. Scale 1:2*

10909

10915

10882

10903

10907

13441

13442

13447

14735

14736

14737

14738

14740

14741

0   5cm

have continued to appear in the 11th century, although as at many other sites, their use tailed off after the 12th century (see for example Lurk Lane, Beverley; Foreman 1991, 106).

Hones of metamorphic rock are thought to have been first brought to this country by the Scandinavians in the 10th century (Ellis 1969, 149), schist hones rapidly becoming the dominant type used, particularly in the north and east of the country (Crosby and Mitchell 1987, 489). Ellis noted a general fall off in the numbers of schist hones from c.1300 onwards (1969, 182), but a subsequent study of English honestones by D.T. Moore indicated that schist, or Norwegian Ragstone, was the most popular stone type in use throughout the entire medieval period (1978, 70), and the York hones bear this hypothesis out. Excavations at medieval sites in Beverley (Foreman 1991, 106), Norwich (Margeson 1993, 197–202), Hull (Watkin 1987, 190), and Winchester (Ellis and Moore 1990, table 48, 283–4) have produced schist hones in considerable numbers, too.

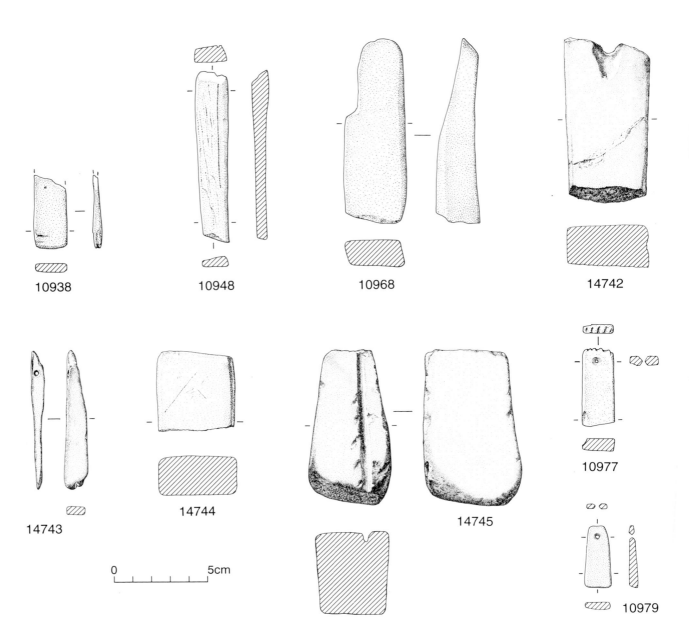

10938   10948   10968   14742

14743   14744   14745   10977   10979

0 _____ 5cm

Fig.1382 *Phyllite hones* **10938, 10948** *from 16–22 Coppergate; sandstone hones* **10968** *from 16–22 Coppergate,* **14742–5** *from 46–54 Fishergate; possible hones* **10977** *and* **10979** *from 16–22 Coppergate. Scale 1:2*

The hones exhibit a range of shapes, sizes and sections, which may, to some extent, be linked to the rock from which they were fashioned. This relationship between stone type and shape was tested at Winchester, where it was shown, perhaps unsurprisingly, that amongst the complete examples, the more coarsely grained sandstone hones tended to be wider and thicker than those of the smaller-grained schist and phyllite (Ellis and Moore 1990, 869). This led to the suggestion that sandstone hones may have been used for sharpening agricultural and other large blades, with the slighter schist hones employed for small blades and craftsmen's tools (ibid.). In a study of other York hones, MacGregor proposed an alternative differentiation, however, hypothesising that the coarser sandstones may have been for initial blade sharpening and the finer schists and phyllites for fining the cutting edge (p.79, *AY* 17/3). Apart from blades, the York hones were also used to sharpen points of tools, such as needles (see p.2739). This is more of a feature of hones from Bedern; 33% from that site (*13444–8, 13455*) had sharpening grooves, while at Coppergate, only c.5% (*10885, 10887, 10907, 10933, 10948, 10976*) exhibited these features. These figures suggest that the main function of the Coppergate hones was to keep knife blades keen, and point to craft/industrial type activity, while those at the ecclesiastical institution may have had a more domestic role.

A small number of hones have perforations for suspension; sometimes these survive complete (*10903, 10915, 10977–8*), but they were clearly a point of weakness, and many other examples (*10882, 10893, 10909, 13449*) have been left incomplete for fear of breakage, or have indeed broken through at that point (e.g. *10943*).

Rotary grindstone (Fig.1383)

A fragmentary rotary grindstone, *14746*, was found at Fishergate in a Period 7c dump of domestic waste associated with post-dissolution activity. Originally mounted on a horizontal axle, it had a diameter of c.180mm and a smooth grinding edge; it shows signs of having been burned or perhaps re-used in a hearth. Three grindstone fragments found in Period 6 contexts at Coppergate (*9636–8*) were considered residual, and are included in *AY* 17/14.

Dr G.D. Gaunt comments: 14746 *is made of a fine-to medium-grained sandstone, which may tentatively be*

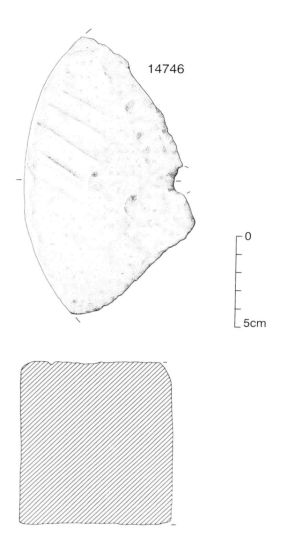

Fig.1383 Fragment of a rotary grindstone 14746 from 46–54 Fishergate. Scale 1:2

attributed to the Millstone Grit sequence, although it could be from the Coal Measures, the nearest outcrops of which are in the Leeds-Castleford area.

Sandstone rotary grindstones of varying sizes, used for sharpening blades and other cutting edges, have been found previously in York. The Parliament Street sewer trench (Fig.1314, **8**; YAT 1976–7.11) produced one with a diameter of c.90mm (*683, AY* 17/4), while larger examples, probably dating from the Anglo-Scandinavian period, were found in excavations at Lloyds Bank, Pavement (Fig.1314, **12**; YAT 1972.21) (diameter c.540mm, *378, AY* 17/3), and Barclays Bank on High Ousegate (diameter c.265mm, Radley 1971, 42). Apart from the grindstones from

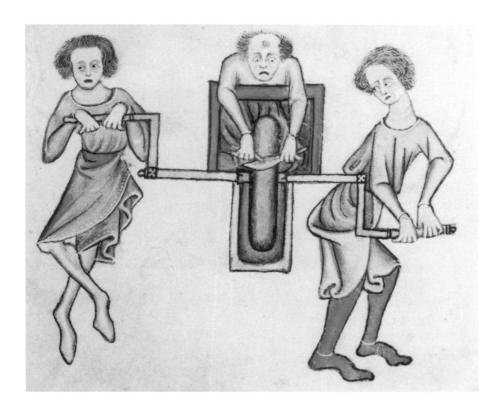

Fig.1384 Two men turning a rotary grindstone whilst a third sharpens his knife (BL Add MS 42130 fo.78b)

medieval contexts at Coppergate, a further 26 were found in Anglo-Scandinavian levels, ranging in diameter from c.50mm to c.220mm, the majority being c.50–80mm across (73·7%) (*AY* 17/14). Elsewhere in Britain, these tools seem to be rare, although a single example with a diameter of c.230mm was recovered from excavations on the High Street, Exeter (Fig.1315, **34**), in association with 12th century pottery (Allan 1984, *S21* , 298, fig.166), and three were recovered from 13th–14th century deposits at the deserted medieval village of Gomeldon, Wiltshire, two with diameters of c.250–300mm (Musty and Algar 1986, 152, fig.11, *5–7*). The recovery of *14746* from waste associated with post-dissolution activity at Fishergate indicates that it could derive from any time during the existence of the Gilbertine priory, or even from pre-priory activity on the site.

Haematite

Eleven fragments of haematite of the 'reddle' variety were recovered from Period 6 contexts at Fishergate (*14747–53*) and a single fragment from a late 13th century deposit at 22 Piccadilly (*13009*). The lithology of haematite is commented upon by Dr G.D. Gaunt in *AY* 17/9 (p.1316).

Reddle had a number of applications, including use as a pigment or paint, in cosmetics and as jeweller's rouge to polish metal. At Fishergate, the majority of the haematite found in medieval contexts derives from levelling and construction deposits associated with the building of the priory, and it is most likely that these fragments are residual from earlier levels which produced almost 70 fragments (p.1316, *AY* 17/9).

Everyday Life

Domestic

Food preparation

Rotary querns

Rotary querns were used widely during the middle and later Saxon periods throughout north-western Europe, as archaeological finds have shown, but documentary evidence indicates that prohibitions on their use in England began during the 12th century, resulting in a decline in their use (Biddle and Smith 1990, 882). Consequently, finds of querns from medieval contexts need to be treated with caution; the substantial size and hard-wearing nature of these stone artefacts frequently results in their survival into later levels, and often their re-use.

Fragments of rotary querns were recovered from medieval levels at Coppergate, Fishergate and Bedern; those from Fishergate were all deemed to be residual in their medieval contexts, and have been described in *AY* 17/9 (pp.1321–9). Six finds from the Foundry (*13088–93*), two from Bedern (*13459–60*), 49 from Coppergate (*10980–11028*) and one from 22 Piccadilly (*13010*) are discussed here.

Dr G.D. Gaunt comments upon the Bedern, Coppergate and Piccadilly querns:

13092–3 and 11026–8 are the only examples made of sandstone, and all probably derive from the Millstone Grit sequence in the Pennines; all the other quern fragments are made of vesicular lava of Mayen type from the north-eastern part of the Eifel region of Germany. Further geological information is given in AY 17/9: on Mayen lava (p.1322) and on Millstone Grit sandstones (p.1329).

All of the querns are of similar forms to those found at Fishergate (pp.1321–9, *AY* 17/9). Four of the pieces recovered from the Foundry came from partition slots or walls (*13089–91, 13093*), while a fifth (*13088*) came from a floor surface composed largely of tile and other fragments; this suggests that they had been found and re-used during various phases of construction work on the site in the medieval period. On Bedern, *13459* was found within the stone packing of a post, while *13460* was recovered from modern levels and had traces of mortar adhering to it, indicating that it had also been used in construction.

Of the 49 finds from Coppergate's medieval levels, fourteen (*11000, 11002–3, 11005–8, 11011–12, 11018, 11020–1, 11024* and *11027*) were recovered from in or around Building Cd1, a 12th century bakery which underwent a number of rebuilds, and a further seven (*10990–6*) from a boundary ditch C6e2 which was dug near the then abandoned building C6d1 and may have contained deposits from within the demolished bakehouse. Many of the quern fragments were clearly re-used — nine were found in post-holes, presumably used as packing, and another was set into one of the ovens. Those recovered from the earliest structural phases may be residual from Anglo-Scandinavian activity, which also produced many quern fragments (see pp.2547–52, *AY* 17/14). Other querns used during rebuilding, including seven from post-holes, may be fragments of querns used previously in the bakery to prepare the flour — some charred grains found within the building point to such a process there.

Of the other fragments, two were found in a mid 17th century hearth (*10980–1*); most of the others derived from 11th–14th century build ups and dumps.

Re-used lava quern fragment

11025 may be a lava quern fragment, re-used as a rubbing or smoothing stone; it was found in 13th–14th century levels at Coppergate.

Mortars (Figs.1385–6)

Fragments of these large durable stone vessels and their pestles, used for pounding or grinding food-stuffs and other materials, were found on all the York sites: Coppergate produced four mortars (*11029–32*); the Foundry produced five (*13094–8*); twelve mortar fragments were found at Bedern (*13461–72*) and a single one at 22 Piccadilly (*13011*). Two possible pestles were retrieved from Bedern (*13473*) and Fishergate (*14756*).

Dr G.D. Gaunt comments upon the mortars and pestles.

The majority of the mortar fragments (thirteen) are of Permian Lower Magnesian Limestone, which crops out along the western edge of the Vale of York from Ripon southwards to beyond Doncaster, the nearest outcrops to York being in the Tadcaster-Wetherby area. Large quantities of this dolomitic limestone were used for building and monumental carved items in Roman York, almost all being of the oolitic-relict oolitic-microcellular varieties; in contrast, when used for building purposes in medieval York, mainly fine-grained varieties, obviously from different quarries, were employed. The Lower Magnesian Limestone mortars from Bedern and 22 Piccadilly are of the relict oolitic-microcellular type, as is the possible trough, 13474 (see p.2827), indicating the probable re-use of Roman building stone here. Buckland notes that building stone of Millstone Grit from Roman York was re-used in Anglo-Saxon churches in the adjacent region (Buckland 1988, 245–6); the Millstone Grit mortar, 13466, may also represent re-use of Roman building stone. The other sandstone mortars, 13094–5, are attributable to a range of Carboniferous and Jurassic sources. The two remaining mortars (13461–2) and pestle (13473) are made from limestones that, despite some differences, have lithologies broadly indicative of Mesozoic origins, in effect from Middle or Upper Jurassic or, much less likely, Lower Cretaceous successions. In detail, however, the lithologies of pestle 13473 and mortar 13461 are not closely comparable to limestones in these successions in Yorkshire or the eastern Midlands but are suggestive of those in the Upper Jurassic Portland and Purbeck sequences respectively, in Dorset. 13462 may also have a southern provenance. The possible pestle from Fishergate, 14756, is of bioclastic limestone, typical of shell debris-rich layers called coquinas that occur in Middle and Upper Jurassic limestones in northeastern Yorkshire, Lincolnshire and in the eastern Midlands and Cotswolds. The nearest sources to York are the Whitwell Oolite of the Howardian Hills and the Millepore Bed of the Yorkshire coastal area, both Middle Jurassic, and the Upper Jurassic Coralline Oolite which crops out around the northern and western flanks of the Vale of Pickering. This pestle would probably have been used to grind soft materials.

The four mortars from Coppergate (11029–32) are made from textural varieties of Permian Lower Magnesian Limestone that are neither oolitic nor relict oolitic, and are not markedly microcellular, so they are not suggestive of re-use of former Roman building stone. Three of the mor- *tars contain sparse fossils, probably signifying sources in the lowest strata of the limestone, and therefore near the western edge of its outcrop.*

Most of the mortars share certain features such as lugs or lips with runnels, moulded projections, and ribs on the wall exteriors; as well as providing strength to the mortar body, the ribs and lips may have enabled the mortar to be set into a table top, and kept in a firm position, allowing both hands to be used for grinding (Drinkwater 1991, 169). Rough bases, such as that seen on 13466, may have been designed for grinding coarse substances, with smoother bases used to produce pastes (ibid.).

These features are typical of mortars of sandstone or limestone found elsewhere in medieval England, such as King's Lynn (Dunning 1977), Winchester (Biddle and Smith 1990), Wakefield (Butler 1983), Hull (Watkin 1987) and Beverley (Foreman 1991). More unusual are the pierced handles seen on fragments from 22 Piccadilly and the Foundry (13011; 13098). These are characteristic of imported mortars of Caen stone, a Middle Jurassic fine-grained, micropelletal limestone that is often, but incorrectly, described as 'oolitic' (Ashurst and Dimes 1990, 121). Such mortars occur most commonly in the south and east of England. Also found on a number of mortars of Purbeck marble at King's Lynn, it has been suggested that this feature was copied from Caen stone mortars (Dunning 1977, 324–5). Although no Caen stone mortars are known in York or elsewhere in the north of England, Purbeck limestone mortars were clearly imported to Bedern (see above), and this feature may have been introduced to York via this trade. As Dr Gaunt's report makes clear, however, local stone was used most frequently, a pattern repeated at other sites in the north of England: local stone was used exclusively as at Sandal Castle, Wakefield (Butler 1983, 330), or for the majority of mortars, as at two sites in Hull (Watkin 1987, 190) and at Lurk Lane, Beverley (Foreman 1991, 107).

Pestles (Fig.1386)

The fragmentary 13473 appears to be roughly contemporary with the earliest mortars, having been recovered from a Period 2 (mid 13th century) deposit at Bedern. 13473 has a rounded base as seen on modern pestles. The identification of 14756 as a pestle is less convincing. If it once served this purpose, it has subsequently been cut down, resulting in a very

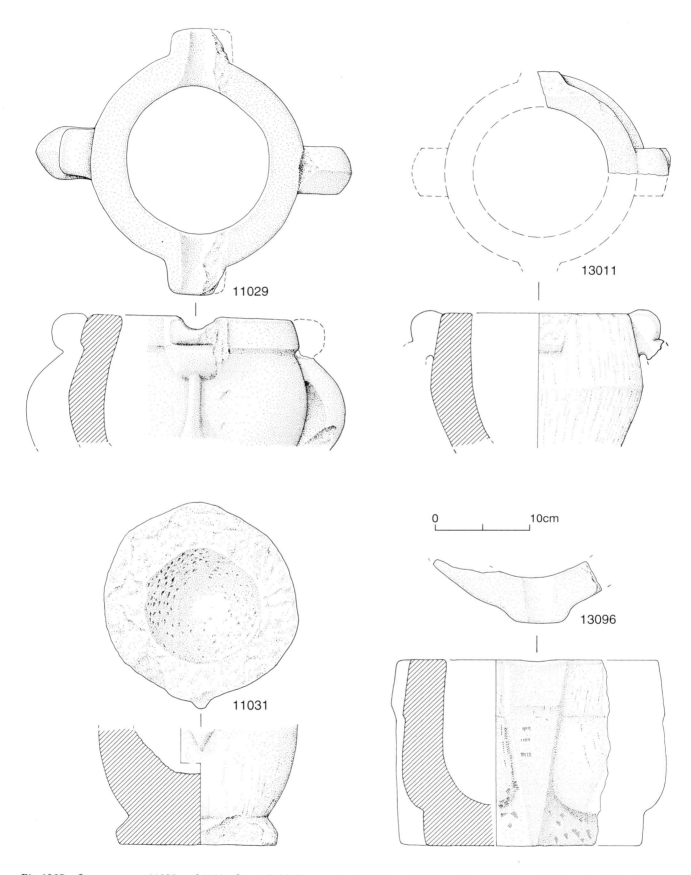

Fig.1385   *Stone mortars* 11029 *and* 11031 *from* 16–22 *Coppergate;* 13011 *from* 22 *Piccadilly;* 13096 *from the Foundry. Scale* 1:4

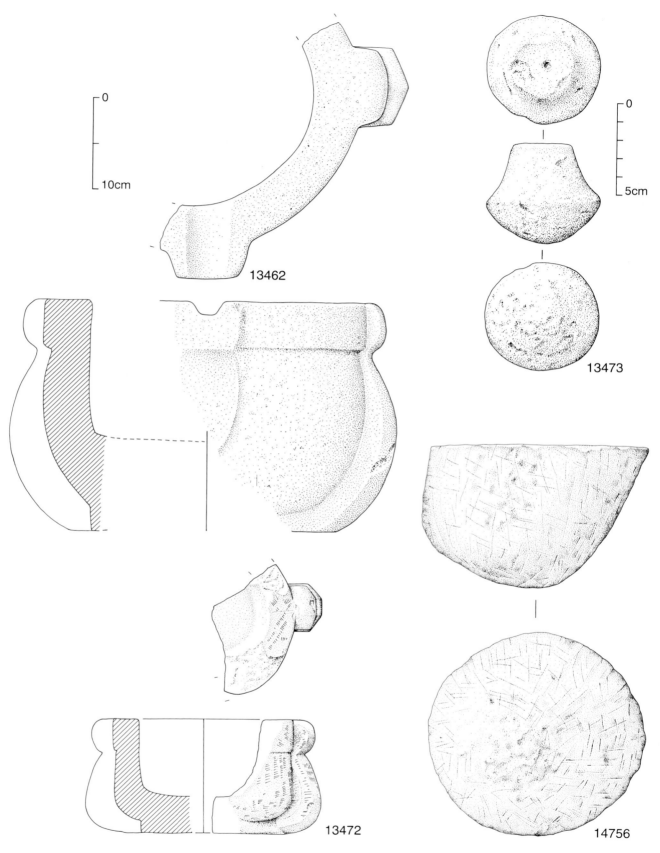

Fig.1386 *Stone mortars* 13462 *and* 13472 *from Bedern; stone pestles* 13473 *from Bedern and* 14756 *from 46–54 Fishergate. Mortars scale 1:4, pestles 1:2*

0

10cm

0

5cm

13462

13473

13472

14756

smooth upper face. *14756* derives from a 15th–16th century cess pit close to the south door of the church at St Andrew's Priory, Fishergate. Stone pestles have rarely been found archaeologically, and medieval examples have only been identified with certainty in the Ostend area of Belgium (Dunning 1977, 323), although another possible medieval example resides in the Salisbury and South Wiltshire Museum (Dunning 1991, 172, fig.47, *18*). The scarcity of stone pestles indicates that other less durable materials must also have been used for this purpose; illustrations in the Luttrell Psalter (c.1340) show a large, possibly wooden, pestle being used in conjunction with a stone mortar (see Fig.1389, p.2805). *13473* is made of the same Purbeck limestone as mortar *13461*, which also derives from a 13th century context, suggesting that mortars and pestles may have been imported together to the region.

Uses of mortars and pestles (see Fig.1389)

It is generally accepted that mortars are a 13th century introduction, when they appear to supersede the use of rotary querns for grinding foodstuffs (Biddle and Smith 1990, 890–1). In addition to domestic use, mortars and pestles have also been illustrated as tools used in the preparation of drugs (James 1902, 26, *1044*), a possible function for some of those found at Bedern, perhaps, where other chemical and medical equipment including urinals and alembics have been recovered (see p.2826).

The period during which mortars were made and used is less well understood; as with rotary querns (see above) this is partly due to their durability and consistent re-use in later contexts such as walls, or hearths, as noted at King's Lynn (Dunning 1977, 321), and Gomeldon, Wiltshire (Musty and Algar 1986, 151), and also seen at York. Five of the mortar fragments from the Foundry and Bedern were found in walls (*13095–7; 13465–6*), while at Coppergate *11029* was used in the packing of a building foundation pit, and *11030* and *11032* were recovered from levelling/ dumps.

Cutlery

Many of the knives discussed above were probably used at the table (see Fig.1389) as well as serving as craft tools. In addition to these, a few other table cutlery items were found.

Spoons (Fig.1387)

A copper alloy spoon with leaf-shaped bowl and long handle was found at Bedern (*14190*). A typology of medieval spoons in Ward Perkins 1940 (130) suggests that the leaf-shaped bowl on metal spoons is indicative of a late 13th–14th century date (ibid., 129, pl.XXVI, *1*, pl.XXVII, *1*); this accords with the

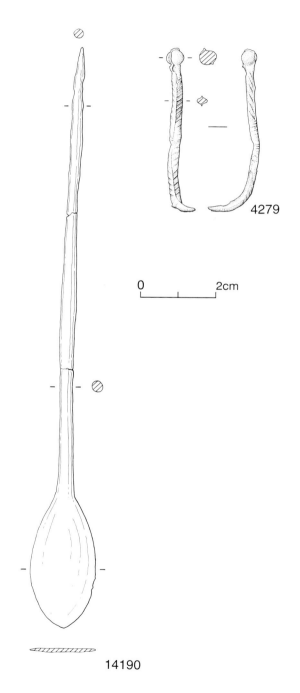

Fig.1387 Copper alloy spoon 14190 *from Bedern; unfinished lead alloy spoon handle* 4279 *from 16–22 Coppergate. Scale 1:1*

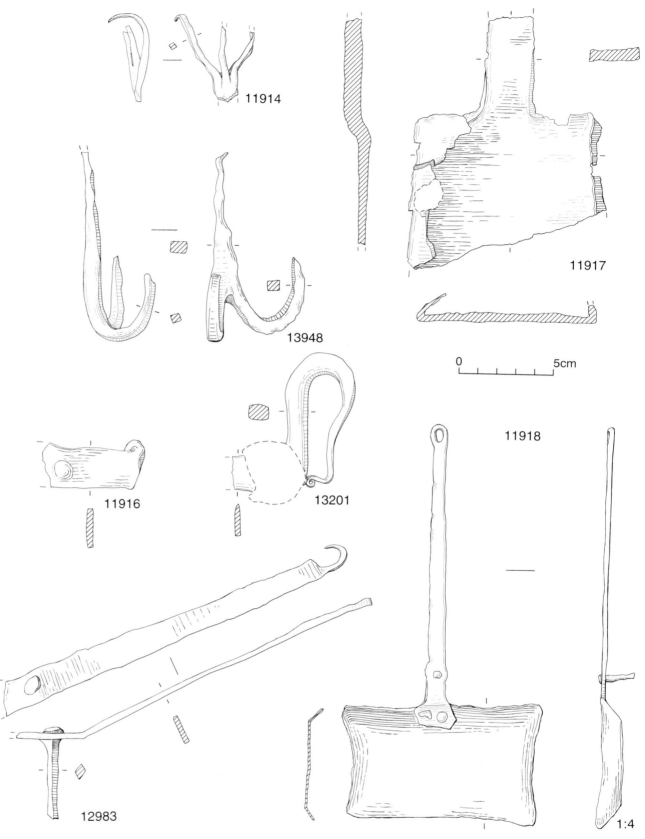

Fig.1388 *Iron flesh hooks* 11914 *from 16–22 Coppergate and* 13948 *from Bedern; iron strike-a-lights* 11916 *from 16–22 Coppergate and* 13201 *from the Foundry; iron shovels* 11917–18 *from 16–22 Coppergate; shovel handle* 12983 *from the Coppergate watching brief. Scale 1:2,* 11918 *1:4*

recovery of *14190* in a mid 14th century post-hole in the residential Building 5. Metal spoons are more commonly found in pewter (see for example Brisbane 1990, 832–3) or lead/tin (Egan 1998, 245) than copper alloy, and *4279*, found in an early 14th century dump at Coppergate and previously published as an unfinished lead alloy pin (p.780, Fig.340, *AY 17/7*), appears rather to be an unfinished and fragmentary spoon handle, still retaining casting flashes. This identification was first suggested by Egan (1998, 245), and closer inspection of the diamond-sectioned stem of *4279* with its chevron decoration reveals its similarity to pewter spoon handles found in London (ibid., 248, fig.194). Metal spoons appear to have been rare in the medieval period; wooden spoons would have greatly outnumbered metal examples, as recent discoveries in Europe have begun to show (Morris and Margeson 1993, 136; *AY 17/13*). Despite this, of six wooden spoons found at Coppergate (*8895–9, 9174*), only one derives from medieval levels (*8899*); a single wooden example was also found in a mid–late 13th century level at Bedern (*9234*) (see *AY 17/13*).

Hearth-related equipment

Flesh hooks (Figs.1388–9)

11914 from a 12th–13th century context at Coppergate is part of a small iron flesh hook which would have been used to extract meat and other items from cooking vessels. The shank is largely missing, but there are three prongs, as is usual, which were curved over at their tips. Goodall (1980b, 159) notes that hooks of this form would have had a short angled stem set in a wooden handle and that they were probably replaced by hooks of a different form after the 13th century.

13948 is a substantial tanged double hook of iron from a late medieval/post-medieval context at Bedern which was probably a flesh hook.

Strike-a-lights (Fig.1388)

There are three iron strike-a-lights which would have been used with flints to create a spark to ignite tinder: *11915* (early 15th century context) and *11916* (13th century context) from Coppergate, and *13201* (late medieval context) from the Foundry. *11916* has a looped terminal at the surviving end of the striking plate; it resembles a strike-a-light from a context dated 1270–1350 at London (Egan 1998, 121, *337*).

Fig.1389 *Kitchen scene showing (left to right) the use of a flesh hook and skimmer, knives, and wooden pestle with stone mortar (BL Luttrell Psalter, fo.207)*

2805

11915 is L-shaped and is pierced in the centre of the striking plate to allow suspension from a belt by means of a thong. *13201* is incomplete.

Shovels (Figs.1388, 1390)

There are two iron shovels, one complete (*11918*) and one incomplete (*11917*) from 13th–14th century and post-medieval contexts at Coppergate, respectively. An additional handle comes from the watching brief (*12983*). The handle, which has a looped end, is attached to the blade by being nailed on to a roughly oval expansion from the back of the blade. Near the base of the handle a short downwards projection has been fitted which would have allowed the object to be left at rest without the contents of the blade tipping out. *12983* is the handle of a similar shovel to *11918*. *11917* has a blade and handle, both of which are incomplete, made in one piece.

Medieval iron shovels are rare, but were probably used where an open fire and great heat, as in a hearth or baker's oven, prevented the use of a wooden tool. An incomplete iron shovel was found in a 13th–14th century glass furnace at Blunden's Wood, Surrey (Fig.1315, **25**; Wood 1965).

Vessels

Iron

Fragment *13818* from Bedern may be part of something like a cauldron.

Wooden bucket with iron fittings (Figs.1391–2)

8742 is a wooden bucket made of nine oak staves and a single-piece circular base. It was found in an early 15th century well at Coppergate (see also pp.2225–6, 2230–2, *AY* 17/13). Three iron bands run around the bucket at top, centre and base. Attached to the top of the bucket were two handle suspension fittings in the form of a pair of straps joined by a U-shaped loop. The handle is pierced in the centre to accommodate a swivelling suspension fitting to which three figure-of-eight-shaped chain links are attached.

A number of complete medieval buckets bound by iron hoops have been found in wells elsewhere (Goodall 1980b, 165–6) including a late 12th–13th century example from Duffield Castle, Derbyshire, with similar suspension fittings to *8742* (Dunning 1974, 104–5, fig.13), an example dated 1270–1600 from Weoley Castle, West Midlands (Fig.1315, **19**), with a handle set in holes in the staves rather than in iron fittings, but with an attached swivel hook and chain (Taylor

Fig.1390 *Iron shovel* 11918 *during excavation. Scale unit 10mm*

2806

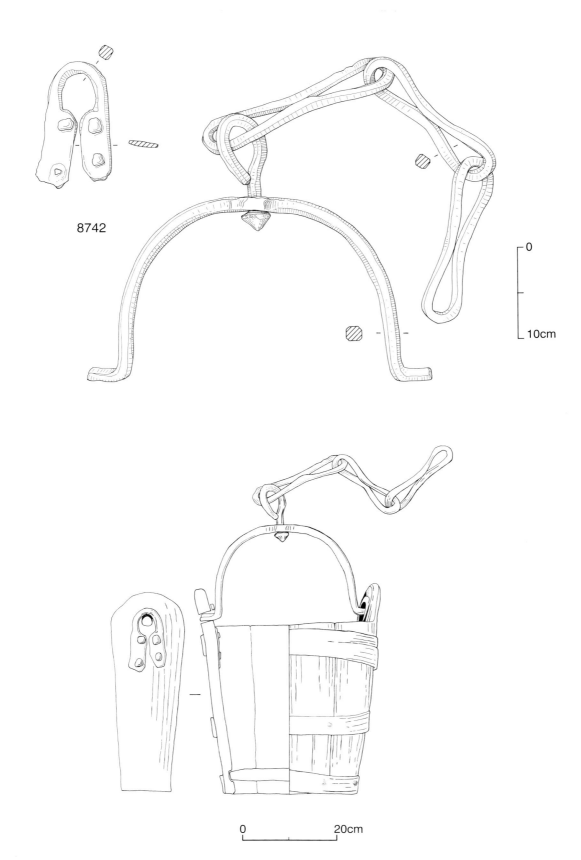

Fig.1391 *Wooden bucket with iron fittings 8742 from 16–22 Coppergate. Scale 1:8, details of iron fittings 1:4*

8742

0

10cm

0   20cm

Fig.1392   *Wooden bucket with iron fittings 8742 in situ in an early 15th century well at 16–22 Coppergate. Scale unit 10cm*

1974), and a late 15th century example from Kilton Castle, Redcar and Cleveland, with similar suspension fittings to *8742* and a handle with attached swivel hook (Goodall 1980b, 260, J139, fig.119). Another bucket handle with a swivel fitting attached, dated 12th–15th century, from Llanstephan Castle, Dyfed, was recorded by Goodall (ibid., 262, J157, fig.120) who also records two very similar, if slightly smaller suspension fittings to those on *8742* from Newbury, Berkshire (Fig.1315, **26**; ibid., 260, J144–5, fig.119).

Iron vessel handles (Fig.1393)

In addition to the handle of wooden bucket *8742*, there are two smaller vessels handles (*11919–20*) from Coppergate. They are incomplete, but were probably similar in size and form, both being made from a spirally twisted bar. *13037* from Piccadilly (late 11th century context) is probably, but not certainly, a vessel handle which incorporates a spirally twisted component set between two plain ones.

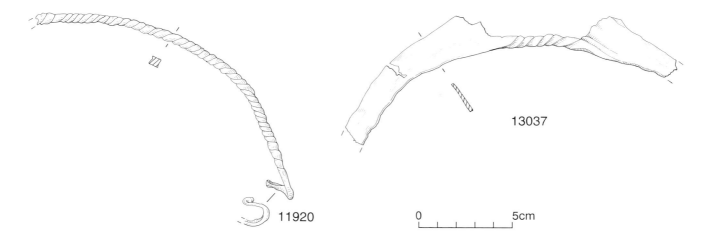

Fig.1393 *Iron vessel handles* 11920 *from 16–22 Coppergate and* 13037 *from 22 Piccadilly. Scale 1:2*

Non-ferrous

Cast vessels

Analysis of the mould material found at the Foundry indicated the casting of non-ferrous bells and vessels on the site (*AY* 10/3, 186–9), and so it is unsurprising that a number of fragments of cast vessels of copper alloy (*13305–15*) and lead alloy (*13406–7*) were recovered there, many of which may be failed castings from the Foundry's operations (*AY* 10/3, 189), although the majority occurred in post-Foundry contexts (ibid., 195). Copper alloy (*14191–208*) and lead alloy fragments (*14514–15*) were also found at Bedern. No cast vessel fragments were found on the other sites.

Copper alloy vessels (Fig.1394)

The following text on copper alloy vessels draws heavily on a report produced by A.R. Goodall.

The most commonly encountered medieval metal vessel forms are tripod cauldrons and skillets, used in cooking, and ewers or jugs (Egan 1998, 161), but confident attribution of excavated fragments to particular forms is rarely possible. Possible fragments from three-legged skillets were recovered from both the Foundry and Bedern, all in 15th century deposits; *13305* from the Foundry and *14194* from Bedern both comprise a leg and foot with a broad medial rib, while another fragment, *14201*, may be from the handle of a skillet. Three-legged skillets, like that from Stanford in the Vale, Berkshire (Dunning 1962, 98–100), have a suggested date centring on the 14th century. The slender, triangular-sectioned leg with a well-made foot, *14193*, from late 15th–early 16th century levels at Bedern, may have come from a skillet or from a tripod ewer like that shown in Roger van der Weyden's painting of the Annunciation, c.1440 (Theuerkauff-Liederwald 1975, 179) or like examples in Carlisle Museum (Brownsword, Pitt and Richardson 1981, 49–55). The Foundry also produced what appears to be the foot from a tiny vessel, *13307*, and the handle or leg of a vessel, *13306*, both from mid 16th–mid 17th century contexts.

Further fragments coming mainly from the rims or bodies of cast cooking vessels or dishes were found on the Foundry site (*13308–15*) and at Bedern (*14191–2, 14195–200, 14202–8*). *13313* has part of a raised rib on its inner face and several fragments (*13311–12, 14203*) have soot blackening on their outer surfaces (*AY* 10/3, 189). The length of slightly curved, cast strip (*14200*) may be from a handle. *14208* has a raised lug on the surface and may be from the body of a mortar. *14198* is from a shallow vessel, such as a plate or dish, perforated just below the rim; *14197* is a rim fragment from a cooking vessel; and *14191* appears to be from the base of a small cast vessel. Body fragment *14206* may be from a bell or a vessel. Rim fragment *14199* has broken across a perforation which may indicate a repair.

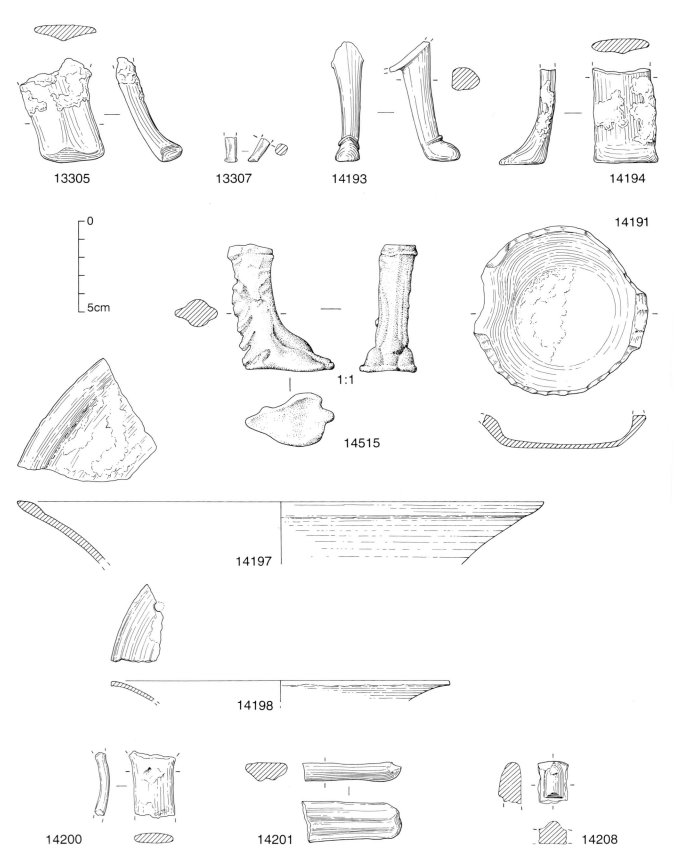

13305   13307   14193   14194

0

5cm

14191

1:1

14515

14197

14198

14200   14201   14208

Fig.1394 *Parts of cast copper alloy vessels 13305, 13307 from the Foundry; 14191, 14193–4, 14197–8, 14200–1, 14208 from Bedern; leg and foot of a cast lead alloy vessel 14515 from Bedern. Scale 1:2, 14515 1:1*

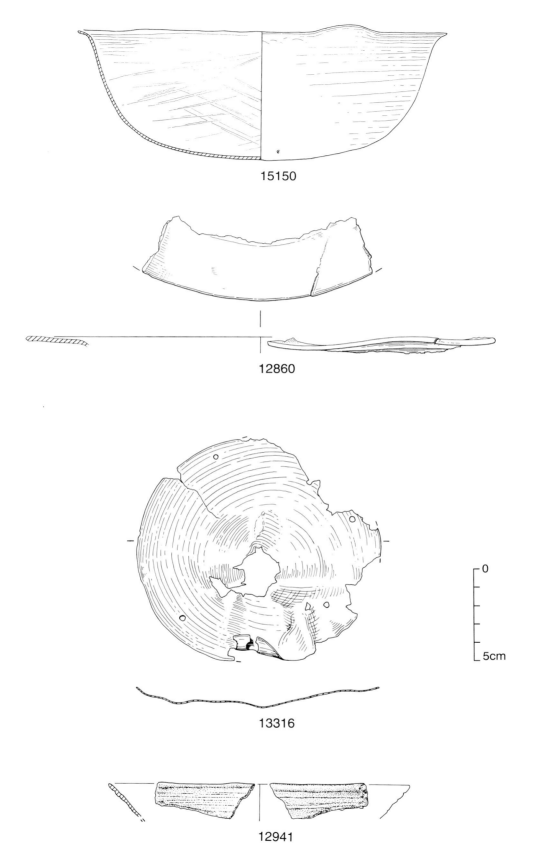

15150

12860

13316

0

5cm

12941

Fig.1395 *Complete bowl of copper alloy sheet* 15150 *from 46–54 Fishergate; fragments of copper alloy sheet vessels* 12860 *from 16–22 Coppergate and* 13316 *from the Foundry; rim fragments of pewter sheet vessel* 12941 *from 16–22 Coppergate. Scale 1:2*

Many of these fragments may have been destined for recycling. Others clearly represent scrap, including several joining sections, now twisted, of a rim with perforations from an unknown vessel, *14195*.

Lead alloy vessels (Fig.1394)

Fragments of cast lead alloy vessels were also found at both the Foundry and Bedern (*13406–7* and *14514–15*). *13407* consists of some 35 fragments of a shallow bowl, while *14515* appears to be the leg from a small vessel, with a zoomorphic clawed foot and a fringe of hair at the back of the leg. Although these fragments may have been destined for recycling, there was no evidence of the casting of lead alloy vessels at the Foundry.

The origin of these non-ferrous cast vessel fragments is unclear, but it is quite possible that most derive from the Foundry's operations, despite the recovery of the majority from the College; movement of people and deposits across the boundary between the Foundry and College from the 15th century has previously been noted (*AY* 10/3, 203), with industrial debris found in pits in the vicars' garden. Vessel fragments found in Period 7 (*14192, 14195–6, 14205–6*) and Period 8 (*14198, 14201, 14208*) levels at Bedern are also concentrated in the garden and kitchen area to the south-west of the College; these may indicate where they were used, but could also suggest movement from the Foundry to the south-west (see Fig.1303, p.2686). The Foundry may have been supplying the College with some of its products, although there is no documentary evidence of such a relationship (ibid.). The Foundry itself produced only four vessel fragments from deposits associated with its operation (*13305, 13311, 13313–14*), with *13313* being found in a clay loam containing c.2kg of mould debris; the relative lack of discarded vessel fragments may indicate their disposal at some distance from the workings, and/or efficient recycling.

Sheet vessels

Copper alloy bowl (Figs.1395–7)

A virtually complete bowl of copper alloy sheet, *15150*, was found at Fishergate in a layer associated with levelling the ground prior to the construction of the north range in the early 13th century. Originally hemispherical with an out-turned rim, it is now slightly misshapen and has holes in the base and one side; circumferential ridges indicate that it was

dressed over a former during manufacture (see Fig.1397). The unworn exterior suggests that the bowl itself may have been a liner for a vessel, perhaps made of wood, so its main function may have been to hold liquid. Complete metal vessels are rare survivals, although another sheet metal bowl, also of 13th century date though somewhat larger than *15150*, was found in excavations at Full Street, Derby (Fig.1315, **13**; Hall and Coppack 1972, 38–9, fig.6, *10*). Fragments of copper alloy sheet vessels are common finds, however, particularly on ecclesiastical sites — see for example the Austin Friars, Leicester (Fig.1315, **15**; Clay 1981, 130, fig.46, *6–14*); some of these bowls may have had ritual functions such as penitential washing of hands (Zarnecki et al. 1984, 254). The context of *15150* indicates that this example almost certainly pre-dates the Gilbertine priory, but it may be associated with the 11th–12th century church of St Andrew, Fishergate, which was recorded in Domesday Book and mentioned in a charter of 1142/3 (*AY* 11/2, 49); possible traces of a timber and a stone church were recovered during excavations (ibid., 72).

Other fragments of sheet vessels comprise rim fragments of copper alloy (*12860, 13316, 14209–10, 15148–9*) and pewter (*12941*). *13316* is an incomplete shallow dish, but irregularly spaced perforations close to the circumference and holes cut into the edge are of uncertain function.

Fig.1396 *Top view of copper alloy bowl* **15150** *from 46–54 Fishergate. Actual diameter 210.8mm*

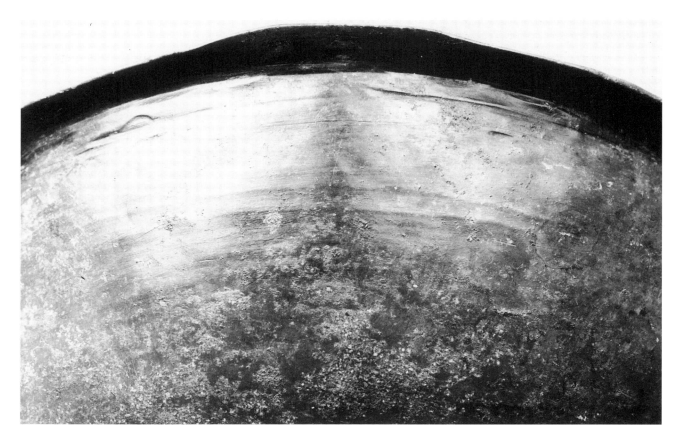

Fig.1397 *Detail of copper alloy bowl* 15150 *showing turning marks*

Copper alloy box (Fig.1398)

An unusual though clearly incomplete rectangular brass box with legs, *13004*, was recovered from the Coppergate watching brief. Found in 15th–16th century dumped soil, it retains substantial parts of two sides, and less of the other two; one of the shorter sides is decorated with a cast four-legged animal with a large snout and tail, while one of the long sides has some simple openwork and a large perforation, as well as stamped ring-and-dot motifs. Both of the less intact sides also appear to have had openwork within them. Three of its original four legs remain, the shapes of which, with their expanded feet, are similar to those found on 15th–16th century non-ferrous cauldrons or skillets. An integral ledge along the sides indicates a lid or shelf may originally have slotted in, probably sliding in from the side with the animal motif, and a possible function as a brazier or food-warmer has been suggested (D. Gaimster, pers. comm.), although there are no obvious signs of heat

having been used. Dr Gaimster also notes that the box may be of European origin, as it resembles less ornate examples found in late medieval Flemish paintings, notably Dieric Bouts's (1415/20–1475) scene of the *Ordeal by Fire* in the series the *Justice of the Emperor Otto* now in the Museum of Ancient Art, Brussels.

Patches (Fig.1399)

12861, 13317, 14211–15, 14699 and *15151–4* are copper alloy sheet metal patches, used as repairs to sheet metal vessels. The majority have elongated slots, some of which still contain sheet rivets, cut from strips of sheet and used in the same way as modern brass paper fasteners; the arms of the clip are initially folded together and after insertion into the slot they are folded outwards and flattened to secure the patch. *14699* also has inscribed decoration. *15154* appears to have been folded over a vessel rim and has a small rivet hole rather than a slot for attach-

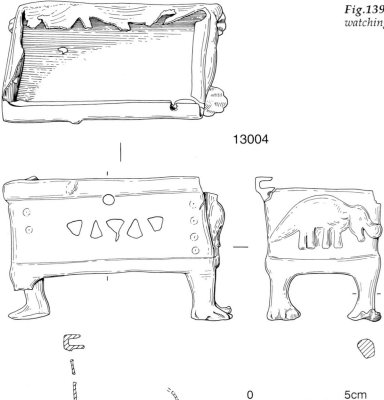

13004

ment. Individual copper alloy sheet rivets were also found (*13318, 14216–18*).

Possible lead alloy vessel patches include a large piece of slightly curved lead alloy sheet with perforations around the edge from 2 Aldwark (*14731*) and a smaller patch from 22 Piccadilly (*13074*).

Lead plugs to repair ceramic vessels

Found attached to a sherd of a highly decorative green glazed vessel of York ware (A.J. Mainman, pers. comm.), *13408* is a plug of lead which appears to have been used as a repair; while York ware dates to the late 12th–13th centuries, the object was found in a late 15th century deposit at the Foundry. Two similar plugs were found in an early 15th century context at Bedern (*14516–17*).

Pot lids

Large stone and ceramic discs which may have acted as pot lids but are more likely to be counters are discussed on p.2951.

Glass vessels (Figs.1401–6)

By Dr Rachel Tyson

Introduction (Fig.1400)

Excavations at the sites in York under discussion uncovered glass vessel fragments dating from the 12th to the end of the 15th century.

In England the discovery of medieval glass vessels has been restricted to high-status sites in prosperous areas of towns, religious sites, castles, palaces and manors (see Tyson 2000). The glass is found in relatively small quantities, partly because it decays severely when it is buried, so any finds are significant. Glass of three compositional types was made in this period. High-lead glass was made in northwestern Europe, probably Germany, in the 13th and early 14th century, and products included bright yellow, green and opaque red tablewares. Soda glass was made from the 13th century onwards in a wide area further south including southern France, Italy, Spain and the eastern Mediterranean. These vessels

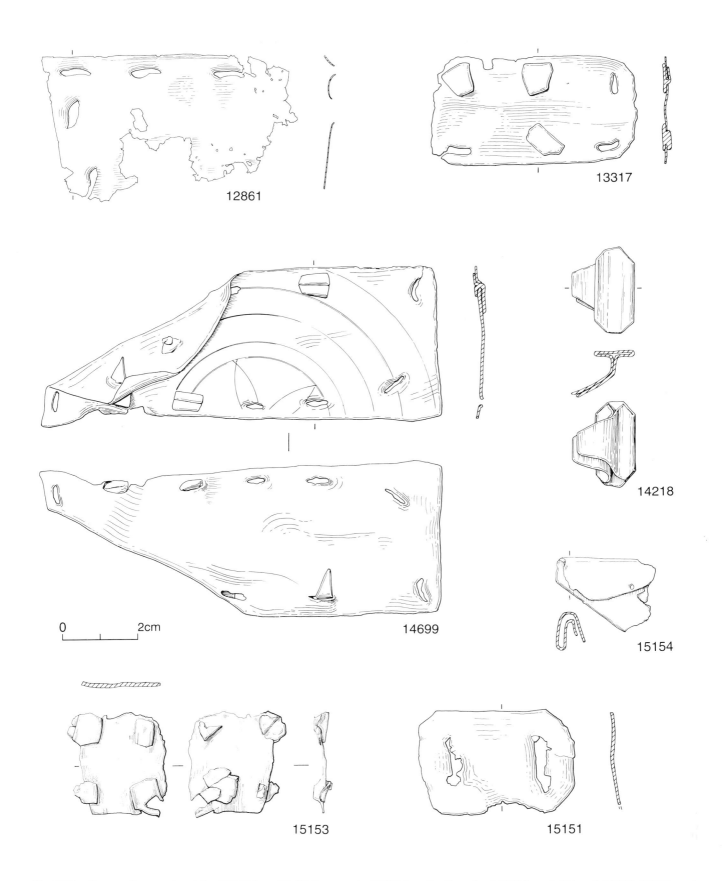

Fig.1399 *Copper alloy repair patches* 12861 *from 16–22 Coppergate,* 13317 *from the Foundry,* 14699 *from 2 Aldwark,* 15151, 15153–4 *from 46–54 Fishergate; copper alloy sheet rivet* 14218 *from Bedern. Scale 1:1*

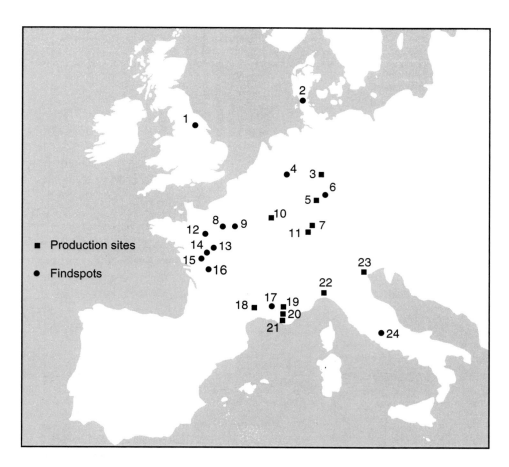

Fig.1400   Map of Europe showing the main sites mentioned in the glass report

1. York	9. Etampes	17. Châteauneuf-de-Gadagne
2. Ribe	10. Argonne	18. La Seube
3. Kaufunger Forest	11. Black Forest	19. Cadrix
4. Neuss	12. Le Mans	20. Rougiers
5. Spessart	13. Langeais	21. Planier
6. Würzberg	14. Brain-sur-Allones	22. Monte Lecco
7. Baden Würtemberg	15. Parthenay	23. Venice/Murano
8. Chartres	16. Charroux	24. Farfa

included colourless or greenish tablewares, which are found in Britain, and, although utilitarian vessels were made for the local population, they would not have been exported. Potash glass was concentrated in northern Europe. Decorated tablewares of green and sometimes colourless glass were exported to England from the Continent, while English glass-houses produced simpler utilitarian wares. There is no irrefutable evidence that tablewares were made in England before 1500.

While potash glass was made in Europe from the 9th or 10th century, little conclusive evidence can be found for glass vessels in England after the Norman Conquest until the later 12th century. Coppergate is one of the few sites to have yielded 12th and 13th century glass. One fragment, *11149*, comes from a late 11th century context, but since the complete vessel form remains unknown it is not possible to verify whether the context date can be relied upon. Although a large proportion of the 38 Coppergate vessels were extremely fragmentary and undiagnostic, there were a number of fragments decorated with applied trails, and a base which is likely to have come from a rare early footed goblet (*11131*). The Bedern and Foundry sites produced 55 vessels (48 from

Bedern, seven from the Foundry) which consisted of an extensive range and quantity of all three compositional types of glass in use between the 13th and 15th century. Three vessels from 2 Aldwark on the edge of the Bedern precinct may have come from the College of Vicars Choral, or possibly from the tenements of Aldwark. Only three medieval vessels were excavated from Fishergate, and one fragment from 22 Piccadilly.

The stratigraphy of Bedern appears to be quite disturbed, with fragments of a high-lead glass jug (*13538*) scattered in contexts of three different periods as well as in unstratified deposits. Many vessels can be shown by their style to be earlier than the dates of the contexts in which they were found. The glass from the remaining sites is more consistent with the dating of the contexts in which it was found.

High-status tablewares

An impressive quantity and range of decorative tablewares were excavated at Bedern, including a goblet (*13536*) and jug or serving flask of yellow high-lead glass (*13538*), two beakers with painted enamel decoration (*13531–2*), a blue painted bowl (*13535*), and two colourless bowls with blue-trailed decoration (*13533–4*). These all date to the 13th and 14th centuries, when medieval tableware was at its peak in the variety of decorative styles used. A few coloured fragments including one from a blue ribbed bowl (*13113*) found at the Foundry probably come from decorative vessels of the 15th century. Coppergate produced some slightly earlier 12th to 13th century decorated vessels including a number of green glass fragments with applied trailed decor-ation which may come from several forms (e.g. *11139–40*) and the base of a footed goblet (*11131*); similar goblets have been found in France,

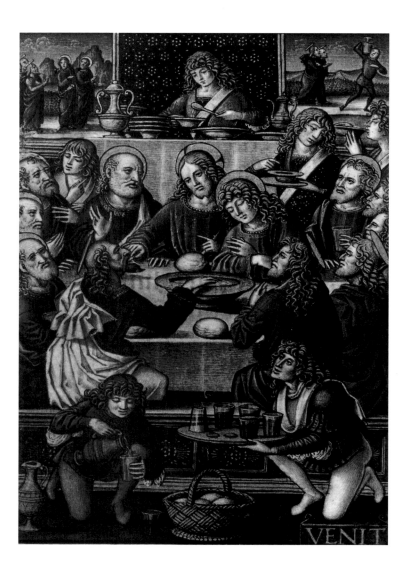

Fig.1401   *Glass vessels in use c.1500,* Sforza Hours *(BL Add MS 34294, fo.138v)*

2817

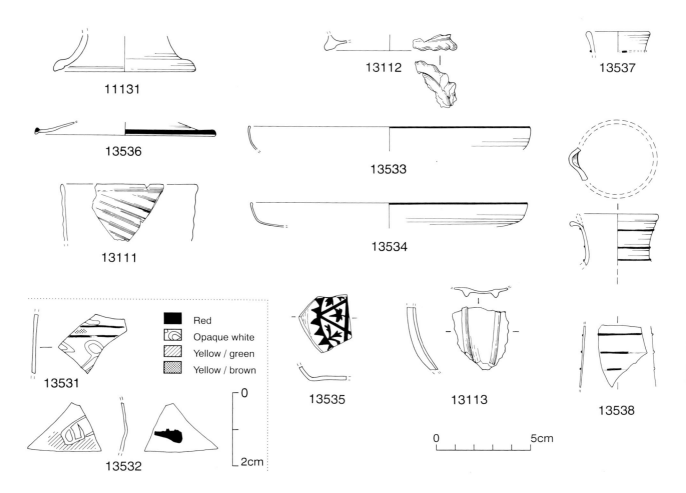

Fig.1402 *(above and facing) Vessel glass fragments: base rim fragments of footed goblets 11131 from 16–22 Coppergate and 13536 from Bedern; beaker fragments with enamelled decoration 13111 from the Foundry, 13531–2 from Bedern; bowl fragments 13112 from the Foundry, 13533–4 (with blue trail around rim) and 13535 (blue glass with black decoration) from Bedern; bowl or goblet fragment 13113 from the Foundry; fragments from jugs or pouring flasks 13537–8 from Bedern; other fragments of tableware or decorated vessels 11139–40, 11142 from 16–22 Coppergate; fragments of flasks or urinals 11143 from 16–22 Coppergate, 13549, 13558 and 13560 from Bedern; fragment of glass tubing from an alembic 13561 from Bedern; undiagnostic fragment 11152 from 16–22 Coppergate. Scale 1:2, 13531–2 1:1*

but this is the first identified in England. A fragment from a yellow high-lead glass goblet (*11130*) was also found, a type present in the 13th and early 14th centuries, and, given the early nature of the other Coppergate glass, it is likely that this fragment dates to the 13th century.

Medieval manuscript illustrations of contemporary feasts suggest that drinking vessels were used in a communal capacity in the 13th and 14th centuries, as seen in a 14th century dining scene where the ten figures shown share four glass goblets (Foy and Sennequier 1989, pl.IX, 214–15, *165*). Books of etiquette give instructions on the use of drinking ves-

sels with respect to sharing the cup. *The Babees Book* in a 15th century English translation of the original 13th century Latin instructs:

*Whanne ye shalle drynke, your mouthe clence with
A clothe; Youre handes eke that they in no manere
Imbrowe the cuppe, for thanne shulle noone be lothe
Withe yow to drynke that ben withe yow yfere*
(Furnivall 1868, 255–6).

(When you drink, clean your mouth with a cloth, as well as your hands, so that they do not dirty the cup. Then nobody will be unwilling to drink with you who has done so before).

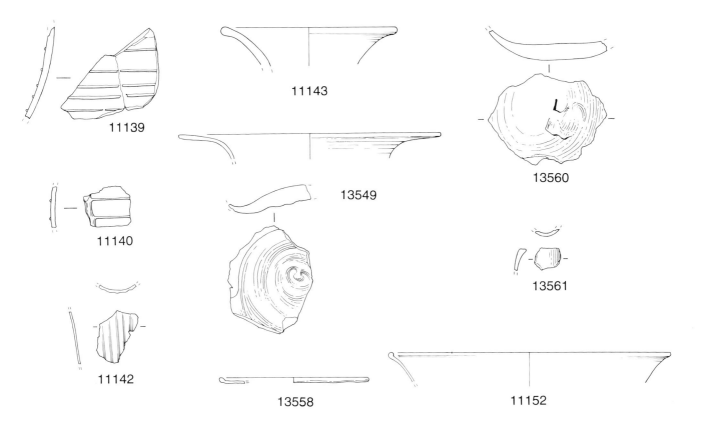

11139

11143

13560

11140

13549

13561

11142

13558

11152

Diners who shared vessels and food with one another were said to be 'mess' companions. The number of people and vessels shared in each mess varied with rank, household and occasion (Henisch 1976, 175–6). It is likely that high-status vessels such as glass tablewares were restricted to the most important in a household, perhaps some or all of those on the high table. In the iconography of the later 14th and 15th centuries increased numbers of drinking vessels are seen in relation to the diners, becoming almost equal in quantity. A late 14th century miniature of the Wedding of Cana shows ten glass beakers on the table or being refilled and approximately eleven guests (Foy and Sennequier 1989, *192*, pl.XIV). A Last Supper scene from the *Sforza Hours*, dating to c.1500, shows a relatively large concentration of glass beakers, implying individual use (Fig.1401, BL Add Ms 34294 fo.138v). However, most of these illustrations are Italian or French. It cannot be assumed that this change in table manners and attitudes occurred at the same time in England. Indeed, a description of England written by a Venetian in c.1496 observes disdainfully that the English were:

very sparing of wine when they drink it at their own expense. And this, it is said, they do in order to induce their other English guests to drink wine in moderation also; not considering it any inconvenience for three or four persons to drink out of the same cup (Sneyd 1847, 21).

It can therefore be suggested that the table vessels used at Coppergate and Bedern may have been shared amongst a number of diners and restricted to the more important figures.

Stemmed goblets (Fig.1402)

A green glass base rim fragment folded under at the edge, *11131*, came from a 12th to 13th century context at Coppergate, and is likely to come from a footed goblet of that date. It is the only example of this type known in England. Green glass goblets with comparable hollow bases folded in at the edge have been found in France dating to the same period, including two with wide drinking bowls decorated with mould-blown fins from Etampes and Langeais (Foy and Sennequier 1989, 162–3, *85–6*), and another two, one with a horizontal flange on the bowl and one an undecorated footed goblet, from Châteauneuf-de-Gadagne in southern France (ibid., 163–5, *87–8*). A more ornate goblet with a conical foot folded in at the edge below a solid stem section decorated with suspended trailing from Brain-sur-Allones is dated to the late 13th to early 14th century (ibid., 175, *103*). These French finds come from a variety of site types and contexts (see Fig.1400 for locations), including a grave at Châteauneuf-de-Gadagne, suggesting that the glass may have been used as a chalice rather than as a table vessel. While a few examples of glass from French sites come from contexts which indicate a liturgical use (ibid., 357–9), this is not true of medieval glass from England. The concentration of this goblet type in France suggests that these vessels were probably made there. The only evidence from production sites consists of some similar footed bases found at the southern French glasshouses of Planier and Rougiers (Fig.1400, **20–1**) where production is known to have taken place in the 13th century, and may have started slightly earlier (Foy 1985, 20–4). It is possible that other rim fragments excavated at Coppergate may also have come from this vessel type.

Fragments from two goblets of yellow high-lead glass have been found in York. A small trailed fragment from a goblet bowl was excavated at Coppergate (*11130*), while the lower part of a hollow stem and base with a blue trail around the rim edge was found at Bedern (*13536*). High-lead glass vessels were recognised as a medieval type in 1987 (Baumgartner and Krueger 1988, 161–2), previously having been attributed to the Roman or post-medieval periods, while those excavated from medieval contexts were assumed to be made of soda glass. Forms found include beakers, goblets, jugs and possibly bowls dating to the 13th or early 14th century (ibid., 161–75). They are bright (almost fluorescent) yellow, green or occasionally opaque red, decorated with trails and prunts of the same colour or contrasting blue, green or opaque red glass. Since 1987 an increasing number have been recognised in Britain including hollow-

stemmed goblets from Knaresborough Castle (North Yorkshire), Old Sarum Castle (Wiltshire), St Mary's Street in Bedford, Westgate in Southampton, Bordesley Abbey (Worcestershire) and Durham (Tyson 2000, 58–61). The first four of those listed have surviving base rims, all of which have a green or blue trail around the rim edge, as does the Bedern fragment. Of the 33 high-lead glass vessels known in England, all but two are yellow, the exceptions being an opaque red beaker base from Ludgershall Castle in Wiltshire (Henderson 2000, 174–5, no.47, fig.6.52), and another similar fragment from Seaford in East Sussex (Tyson 2000, 78, 83, 85, no.g116, fig.12). Lead glass vessels are highly decorative, and it is almost certain that both York goblets would originally have had trailed or prunted decoration on the bowl. Compositional analysis of lead glass vessels from Europe shows that they contain up to 84% lead oxide (Wedepohl et al. 1995), which is extremely high compared with modern lead crystal which contains c.30–35%.

No production sites have yet been found. However, finds are concentrated in a band from England across the Low Countries to Germany. Isotopic analysis of the lead from three fragments excavated in Germany shows that the lead came from relatively local sources in the Harz mountains, the northern Eifel and eastern Bavaria (Wedepohl et al. 1995, 81–2). While this convincingly suggests that lead glass was made in Germany, it remains possible that it may have also been made in other countries including England, but further research and analysis is required.

Fragments from a jug or flask of yellow high-lead glass from Bedern are discussed below (*13538*).

Beakers (Fig.1402)

Two fragments of colourless glass with enamelled decoration were excavated at Bedern (*13531–2*). These belong to a type produced in the late 13th and early 14th century, the majority of which are beakers, although a few stemmed goblets are known (Baumgartner and Krueger 1988, 126–60). Coloured enamel was painted on the inner and outer surfaces; the decoration incorporated a range of themes, the majority being heraldic or religious scenes, featuring figures, animals or coats of arms, usually with an inscription or pattern painted in a band around the top. Fragment *13531* shows a fraction of the inscription close to the beaker rim with the characteristic red-yellow-red border lines below it. Below this is a small part of the main depiction which cannot be identified. Fragment *13532* is not from such a recognisable part of the vessel, but the painted element bears a strong resemblance to the train of a robed figure on a beaker found in Ribe, Denmark (Fig.1400, **2**), and a partial resemblance to a similar robe on a fragment from Foster Lane in London (Baumgartner and Krueger 1988, 137–8, *85–6*). Robed figures are common on these beakers, especially in religious scenes, where haloed figures are flanked by columns and plants (ibid., 129–38). There is evidence that these beakers were made in Venice/Murano (Fig.1400, **23**) in the late 13th to mid 14th century. One example from the British Museum, known as the 'Aldrevandin beaker', bears the inscription '+MAGISTER ALDREVANDIN ME FECI(T)' (Master Aldrevandin made me) (Tait 1979, 16–17, pl.1). Remarkably, Venetian documents record an 'Aldrovandino, fiolario' (glassmaker) on Venice's glassmaking island of Murano in 1331. Other Venetian glassmakers and enamel painters are recorded in association with descriptions of this style between c.1280 and 1351 (Whitehouse 1981, 172; Clark 1983, 155). Further enamelled beakers have been excavated in England from Launceston Castle and Restormel Castle in Cornwall, Dale Abbey in Derbyshire, Wolvesey Palace, Winchester, and a large group from a goldsmith's pit in Foster Lane, London (Clark 1983; Tyson 2000, 89–94, fig.10 and frontispiece). They are found throughout Europe, always in high-status contexts (Baumgartner and Krueger 1988, 126–60). The heraldic depictions on some suggest that they may have been specifically commissioned by clients, although many others feature recurring designs.

13111 from the Foundry comes from a beaker of green glass with optic-blown twisted ribbing. The gather of glass would have been placed in a ribbed mould before blowing and twisting the vessel to its full size, creating faint 'wrythen' ribs. This type of beaker is found between the 14th and 16th centuries, for example, in 14th century Exeter (Charleston 1984, 265–6, no.G12) and 15th century Germany (Baumgartner and Krueger 1988, 303, *351*). Most green examples are made of potash glass, and, while it is possible that some were made in the forest glasshouses of England, they are also common in other regions of Europe, particularly Germany, where there is more evidence for the production of a range of potash glass beakers.

Bowls (Fig.1402)

An unusual and interesting piece is a fragment of blue glass from the flattened centre of a bowl, with black painted decoration (*13535*, Fig.1403). This decoration consists of a circular border with serrated outer edges, with a six-pointed hexagram (or possibly a pentagram) star made up of two interlacing triangles within the border. There is foliate decoration within and between the points of the star. The centre of the star has not survived, but may have had additional decoration. Two glass fragments with comparable decoration have been found in England (Tyson 2000, 135–7, nos.g346–7, fig.26). A flask or lamp cover from Victoria Street, London, has a blue glass roundel marvered into the side, painted with a brownish iridescent pigment, with a circular serrated border containing a shield with a faint (perhaps originally gilded) eagle in the centre, a heraldic bird on top and a dragon on either side. The foliage on the corners of the shield is very similar to that on the York fragment. Another probable flask fragment of blue glass from Weoley Castle, West Midlands, is decorated in pale blue enamel and gilt. Again, it has a circular serrated border with an internal seven-arched border with a small trefoil motif on each cusp. Within each arch is the faint trace of a foliate design, which may have originally been gilt, with similarities to the foliage on the York fragment. In the centre is a heraldic beast within a smaller circular border.

Fig.1403 *Fragment of blue glass with black painted decoration from the centre of bowl* **13535** *from Bedern. Actual width of fragment 24mm*

None of these fragments came from well-dated deposits.

No closely comparable vessels are known outside England. However, all the decorative elements can be found on other artefacts from western Europe in the 13th and 14th centuries. Heraldic birds, beasts and shields are common decorative devices at this date, and the serrated circular border is found in Gothic art. A pair of 13th century French bronze enamelled gemellions (shallow bowls for rinsing hands at the table) in the British Museum have circular serrated borders with heraldic shields and mythical creatures in the centre (Cherry 1991, 39, fig.49). The cusped arches on the Weoley fragment are common on Gothic window glass. The hexagram and pentagram found on the York fragment had a symbolic significance in the Near East where they represented the Seal of Solomon and were used as protective talismans (Spencer 1983, 81). They were also used as general decoration in western Europe. For instance, they are found on 13th century ceramic floor tiles from Newminster Abbey, Northumberland (Eames 1980, vol.2, *2070–2*). It is unlikely that the hexagram on the York bowl fragments had any symbolic significance to the College of the Vicars Choral. Vessels made entirely of blue glass are relatively rare in medieval Europe. Blue decoration is frequently found on colourless glass vessels, including late 13th to 14th century bowls with blue lenses marvered onto the base which have been found on southern French production sites (Foy and Sennequier 1989, 236, *213*, pl.XVIII). However, no fragments with comparable decoration to these three blue painted vessels have been found on any furnace sites. It is probable that they are western European, perhaps French Gothic, and were produced in the 13th century or the first half of the 14th. The York bowl would have been a distinctive and valuable vessel.

13533–4 both come from very delicate colourless shallow bowls with a blue trail applied around the rim, originally with an S-shaped profile, turning inwards and down on the lower half of the bowl. These bowls are of a type commonly found in Europe and England. Other examples have blue trailed decoration and colourless drops on the lower body, often with a pincered foot ring, such as those from Southampton (Fig.1315, **32**) and Nottingham (Fig.1315, **11**; Tyson 2000, 104, 106–9, figs.16–17). None of the lower section of these two bowls from York survives. They

may have had no further decoration, similar to a bowl excavated at the glass production site at Cadrix in southern France which only has a blue rim trail (Foy and Sennequier 1989, 234, *207*). Bowls of this type dating to the late 13th and 14th centuries have been found on a number of glasshouse sites in southern France, including Cadrix, La Seube, Planier and Rougiers (Fig.1400, **18–21**; ibid., 75–83). Colourless vessels with blue trails were also made in Italy, with beakers with blue rim trails found on the glass production site at Monte Lecco (Fig.1400, **22**) dating to around 1400 (Whitehouse 1981, 168–9). While there is no physical evidence that bowls of this type were also made at Italian glasshouses, it is likely.

The exact function of these 'bowls' is controversial. It has been suggested that they may have been used as cups, bowls or table lamps (Foy 1985, 46). The rim diameters of published examples range from 111mm (Cadrix) to 398mm (Farfa Abbey, Italy; Fig.1400, **24**), which suggests that if they all had the same function, they would most likely have served as bowls for different types and quantities of foodstuffs.

13112 is a fragment from a base ring which has had small 'feet' pulled out all around the circumference, from either a beaker or small bowl of colourless glass with a greenish tinge. Imported bowls of the late 13th and 14th century often have an applied tooled base ring, such as those found in Southampton (Tyson 2000, 107–8, fig.17). This feature is also found on beakers of the late 13th to 14th century in Europe, the most common of which are colourless (or with a greenish tinge) with blue trailed decoration or small colourless prunts (Baumgartner and Krueger 1988, 181–3, 186–9, 195–9). It is also seen on greenish glass European beakers of the late 14th and 15th century or later, with prunted or optic-blown decoration (ibid., 297–8, 337–40, 342).

Bowl or goblet (Fig.1402)

A fragment of blue glass from the Foundry, *13113*, has mould-blown vertical ribs and may come from a bowl or a goblet. Blue glass vessels were produced in Venice and other *façon de Venise* workshops across Europe in the second half of the 15th century (Tait 1979). Those at the higher end of the market were often decorated with gilt and coloured enamel, and used as ceremonial vessels. A blue goblet bowl dating to the late 15th century was excavated at the

Austin Friars, Leicester, which also had vertical mould-blown ribs, with an applied rilled ring around the basal angle of the bowl (Mellor and Pearce 1981, 139). However, the Leicester goblet and other 15th century goblets have a relatively straight vertical wall profile, while the curvature on the York fragment is much greater, perhaps indicating a bowl. Bowls, with or without pedestal bases, often had vertical ribs, with enamel decoration in the centre of the bowl and around the rim, leaving the ribs themselves undecorated (Tait 1979, 29–33, 37).

Jugs or pouring flasks (Figs.1402, 1404)

A number of yellow high-lead glass fragments from the same vessel were recovered from contexts associated with late 13th–mid 14th century deposits in and around the possibly residential Building 10 at Bedern; they include part of a pouring lip, and body fragments with blue-green trailing (*13538*). The production and dating of high-lead glass is discussed on p.2814. High-lead glass jugs are not as common as goblets, but one is known from Neuss in Germany (Fig.1400, **4**) which has a handle but no pouring lip (Baumgartner and Krueger 1988, 172, *137*); the trailed lower part of a lead glass bulbous vessel which may be from a flask or jug was found at Middle Pave-

ment, Nottingham (Tyson 2000, 116–17, no.g256, fig.20). Potash glass jugs with applied trailing, a pouring lip, and handle, are more common, including one from High Street C, Southampton (Charleston 1975, 216–17, *1489*). *13537* is a rim fragment also from a yellow lead glass vessel with green-blue trailing, with a diameter of only 36mm. This is much smaller than most jugs, although the circumference is usually oval and the overall diameter may have been larger. The body fragment of *13538d* has a diameter of only c.40mm, so it is possible that these fragments are indeed all from the same vessel, with a relatively narrow neck. Vessels with pouring lips do not always have handles, but often resemble flasks rather than jugs, having a long narrow neck, pouring lip and a bulbous body, such as a colourless and blue-trailed flask with a pouring lip from Wool House, Southampton, which has an irregular rim diameter of up to c.75mm (ibid., 218–19, *1521*). The fragments from the Bedern vessel may therefore not necessarily come from a handled jug, but may be from a pouring or serving flask, performing the same function.

Other tableware/decorated vessels (Fig.1402)

A number of heavily weathered fragments of green glass decorated with applied trailing were ex-

Fig.1404   Fragments with blue-green trailing of jug or pouring flask 13538 *from Bedern*

cavated from Coppergate. The largest fragment is from a slightly flaring body wall with five parallel horizontal trails (*11139*). Others also have parallel horizontal trails at varying intervals, between 0·3 and 2·0mm wide. *11140* has a wavy vertical trail crossing two horizontal trails. All of these trailed fragments are from 12th to 13th century contexts, except *11137* which is from a 15th to 16th century layer but is so similar that it must belong with these 12th and 13th century fragments.

Trailed green glass vessels of the 12th and 13th centuries are the most common style of decorated vessels of this date. They include bowls with vertical or inturned rims, 'vases' with inturned rims, beakers with slightly everted rims, and flasks or bottles. These characteristically have parallel horizontal trails, sometimes with a zig-zagging design running across or below. Bowls decorated in this manner with inturned and everted rims include those excavated in Chartres, Parthenay and Le Mans in France (Fig. 1400, **8, 15, 12**; Foy and Sennequier 1989, 171–2, *98–100*). Trailed 'vases' with inturned rims have been found in a tomb in Charroux, France (Fig.1400, **16**; ibid., 178–9, *108 a–b*). Similar vessels with inturned and slightly everted rims have also been excavated in 12th to 14th century contexts in Germany (Baumgartner and Krueger 1988, 106–10, 114–17, *50–3, 59–60, 63–4*). These include a beaker from Würzberg (Fig.1400, **6**) with a slightly everted rim, with closely comparable trailing to *11140* with a wavy vertical trail crossing horizontal trails (ibid., 114, *60*). Other forms which these fragments may come from include flasks with zig-zagging trails over or below horizontal trails (Foy and Sennequier 1989, 179–83, *109–12*; Baumgartner and Krueger 1988, 110–13, *55–8*). It is probable that most of these vessels were made in Germany or northern France in the 12th to 13th century, with trailed beakers continuing to be made into the 14th century. Some rim fragments excavated at Coppergate may come from the vessels represented by the trailed body fragments.

Trailed 12th and 13th century glass vessels are less well represented in England than on the Continent. The inturned rim of a bowl with horizontal trails was found in Beverley (Henderson 1992, 135–7, *95*), while trailed flasks have been excavated at Tynemouth Priory, and Watling Court and Stothard Place in London (Tyson 2000, 131–3, nos.g327–9, fig.25). Smaller trailed fragments are more common, including those

from Cathedral Green, Winchester (Charleston 1990, 940, *3284*), Bishopsgate and Botolph Street, Norwich (Haslam 1993, 97–8, *604–5*), and St Albans Abbey (Tyson 2000, 184–5, nos.g1292 and g1316). While some of these vessels are likely to have been tablewares, others may have had liturgical uses, particularly since a large proportion were excavated from religious sites and tombs. Two small trailed fragments of glass were also found at Bedern (*13539, 13542*).

The early 12th century treatise *De Diversis Artibus*, written by an author calling himself Theophilus who has tentatively been identified as a German monk, includes a chapter on glassmaking. Theophilus provides instructions for making potash glass from wood ashes, and gives a brief description of applying threads to glass vessels:

> *... take a little glass out of the furnace in such a way that it trails a thread behind itself and lay this on the vessel in the place you have selected. Turn it around close to the flame so that the thread adheres...* (Hawthorne and Smith 1963, chapter 10, 58).

Potash glasshouses have been excavated in the Rhine-Meuse areas of Germany and in northern France, including Spessart (Baumgartner and Krueger 1988, 28–30), Baden-Württemberg (ibid., 35), the Kaufunger forest (ibid., 39), the south-west Black Forest (ibid., 37–8), and the Argonne region (Foy and Sennequier 1989, 67–9) (see Fig.1400 for locations). Potash glass was also made in England (Charleston 1991, 254–6), but no evidence has yet been found on any of these glasshouse sites for this early vessel type.

11142 consists of small fragments of an originally pale green or colourless vessel with vertical fluting, probably from a flask neck of a type made from the 14th to the later 15th or early 16th century (Mentasti et al. 1982, 66–7, *42*; Foy and Sennequier 1989, 313, *340*). These fluted vessels were widely produced in Europe — in Italy and other centres of *façon de Venise* glass in France and the Netherlands.

In addition to these diagnostic types of tableware, small fragments of colourless glass (*13540*), blue glass (*13543*) and dark red/purple glass (*13541*) were excavated. These are likely to come from tableware vessels. The colourless fragment could date from the 13th century onwards, while coloured glass was most common in the 15th and early 16th centuries (Tait 1979).

Utilitarian vessels

Glass was also used to make simple utilitarian vessels for lighting, uroscopy, storage, distilling and other industrial functions. These vessels were made of green potash glass at English glasshouses, such as a well-researched group in the Surrey/Sussex Weald for which there is documentary evidence dating from c.1240 (Kenyon 1967, 26). Glasshouses are also known to have been situated in Shropshire, Staffordshire, Cheshire and probably Essex, and it is likely that

Fig.1405   *A mid 15th century illustration showing physicians examining glass urinals (BL MS Aug. vi, fo.66,* Propriété des Choses*)*

many more existed in Britain (Charleston 1991, 255–6). Although some may have been involved purely in the production of window glass, fragments of hanging lamps, flasks and urinals have been found on others, such as the glasshouse at Blunden's Wood in Surrey (Fig.1315, **25**), whose last firing has been dated to c.1330 (Wood 1965). It is likely that consumers would have used utilitarian vessels from a relatively local source.

In common with decorative glass, finds from utilitarian glass vessels are also limited to prosperous town sites, religious establishments, castles and manors. In the case of the simpler local potash glass vessels this cannot entirely be due to the intrinsic value of the glass, although its fragility makes it less economical than other materials, but culturally it must have been associated with the more prosperous or educated.

Flasks and urinals (Fig.1402)

A number of rim and base fragments of flasks and urinals of heavily weathered green potash glass were excavated from the York sites. Glass uroscopy vessels were used to examine the colour and consistency of urine, the principal method of medical diagnosis from the 13th to the 17th century. One 15th century medical manuscript illustration shows twelve urinals with different coloured contents and the diagnosis for each (Foy and Sennequier 1989, 332, 374, pl.XXIX), while other illustrations often depict doctors examining a patient's urinal (Fig.1405). The urinal had a wide everted neck, often with the rim turned in at the extreme edge, a bulbous body and a convex rounded base. The convex bases found at Coppergate and Bedern (*11147–8, 13546, 13550, 13559–60*) are most likely to come from urinals. The kicked bases and wide everted rims found at all the York sites may come from urinals or a variety of flasks (*11143–6, 11149, 13014, 13544–5, 13548–9, 13551–5, 13557–8*). Flasks with different combinations of wide or narrow necks, and kicked or convex bases, had diverse uses. Various flask shapes are specified in medieval documents for the preparation of herbal, alcoholic and medicinal recipes, and colouring pigments, sometimes in combination with distilling equipment (Moorhouse 1993). They were probably also used for general domestic purposes including storage, and possibly at the table. On religious sites they may have had liturgical uses. Some of the rims and kicked bases from Coppergate may come from

decorative trailed vessels, given the number of trailed body fragments of the 12th and 13th centuries when utilitarian vessels were less numerous.

Possible distilling equipment (Fig.1402)

A piece of tubing, *13561,* was excavated at Bedern. This may come from the spout of an alembic, or possibly a flask neck. The alembic was the upper vessel in the distilling set, which also consisted of the cucurbit and the receiver (Fig.1406; Moorhouse et al. 1972, 88–9). Glass and pottery distilling vessels were often used in combination, and a number pottery fragments recovered from Bedern have been interpreted as parts of such apparatus (Jennings 1991, 30–4; *AY* 10/5, 402). Large deposits of glass distilling vessels have been found on monastic sites such as Pontefract Priory and castles such as Sandal (Moorhouse et al. 1972, 89–98; Moorhouse 1983). Distillation was used for the preparation of alcoholic, herbal, medical and craft recipes, and alchemy is known to have been practised in monasteries and castles as a philosophical discipline (Moorhouse et al. 1972, 84–7). Most excavated glass distilling vessels date to the 15th century or later, although writers such as Chaucer in *The Canon's Yeoman's Tale* (lines 760–7, 791–4) confirm that glass distilling vessels were in use in England by the 14th century, perhaps earlier.

Undiagnostic fragments (Fig.1402)

A number of vessel glass fragments of medieval appearance but not attributable to any particular

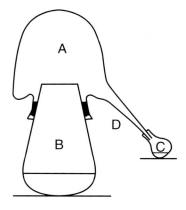

A=alembic
B=cucurbit
C=receiver
D=spout

Fig.1406 *Reconstruction of glass still with alembic (after S. Moorhouse; see Blair and Ramsay 1991, fig.121)*

Table 300 Undiagnostic glass vessels by context date

Site	11th–12thc.	12thc.	12th–13thc.	13thc.	13th–14thc.	14thc.	14th–15thc.	15thc.	Later or unstratified
16–22 Coppergate	1	2	4	8	1		1	1	
Foundry								3	1
Bedern			2			4	4		3
2 Aldwark									3
46–54 Fishergate							1		1

vessel form were also excavated from medieval and post-medieval contexts on the York sites. Most of these were made of heavily weathered green potash glass, and are likely to have come from flasks, urinals, distilling equipment or hanging lamps, although it is possible that some rims came from tablewares. The quantities and context dates from each site are summarised in Table 300.

Conclusion

The York sites discussed here include contrasting assemblages of glass which rank York archaeologically as one of the most significant British cities for medieval glass vessels, with some unique examples. Coppergate produced fragments from green trailed vessels and a probable footed goblet dating to the 12th or 13th century, and from a 13th century high-lead glass goblet, amongst the earliest 'high medieval' glass in England. Some of the most prestigious decorative vessels of the 13th and 14th centuries were used at the College of Vicars Choral. The glass also included a number of different utilitarian vessels. It is regrettable that the disturbed stratigraphy at Bedern contributes little to the dating of the glass, and the distribution across the site reveals little about the areas of use of the glass. Fragments from seven glass vessels were recovered from the Foundry site on the south-west fringe of the Bedern precinct. It was clearly not a prime area for the use or disposal of vessel glass. There was movement of people and rubbish across the Bedern boundary (*AY* 10/3, 203), and, since the fragments include high-status tablewares, they must have strayed from the College where other valuable glass was found. Nine undiagnostic potash glass fragments from three vessels were excavated from 2 Aldwark, an area consisting of tenements on the northern edge of Bedern, some owned by the Vicars Choral. While these fragments may have also strayed from the College, the tenement in-habitants included 'citizens and craftsmen of York and members of the Yorkshire knightly class' (*AY* 10/2, 55) who may have owned a small amount of glass themselves.

The Bedern assemblage compares more closely with the glass from secular castles and palaces of the period than with the more abstinent monastic sites, such as the poorer priory at Fishergate which produced only three utilitarian vessel glass fragments. Although only one flask/urinal rim was found at 22 Piccadilly, the nature of the other sites where glass has been found indicates that this was probably a relatively wealthy or high-status site.

Stone vessel (Fig.1407)

A large but fragmentary rectangular vessel, possibly a trough, was found at Bedern (*13474*) in a mid 14th century deposit within the residential Building 14.

Dr G.D. Gaunt writes: 13474 *is made of relict oolitic dolomitic limestone from the Permian Lower Magnesian Limestone; see p.2800 for the origins of this stone type.*

Structural items and fittings
Iron nails

All the sites under discussion produced large quantities of nails, details of which are available in archive. Only nails with plated or unusual heads have been catalogued and discussed here.

Plated nails (Fig.1408)

There are 41 tin- or tin/lead-plated nails from Coppergate, one from Piccadilly, eight from the Foundry and 72 from Bedern. Analysis of plated nails from the Foundry and Bedern was undertaken as part

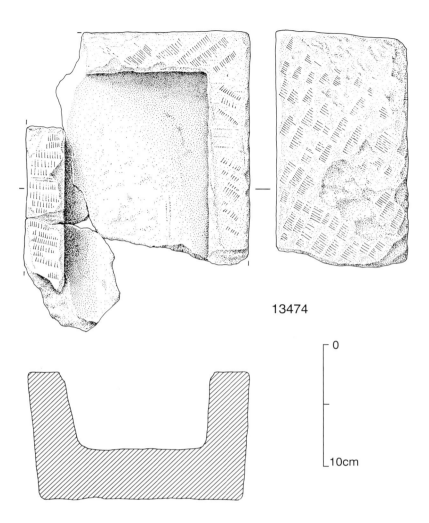

Fig.1407 *Stone vessel, 13474, possibly a trough, from Bedern. Scale 1:3*

13474

0

10cm

of a BA dissertation by E.L. Bowron (1996) which revealed that of 80 nails examined the plating metal in 39 cases was lead, in 30 cases a tin/lead alloy, and in eleven cases pure tin. Another three from Copper-gate plated with only lead were recorded (*11921, 11942, 11964*).

All these nails usually have neatly rounded and/ or domed heads. Length varies between c.30 and 85mm. Tin-plating of nails appears to begin in the 8th century (p.1409, *AY* 17/9) and was widely used in the Anglo-Scandinavian period (pp.611, 614, *AY* 17/6). Few examples are known from medieval contexts other than in York, probably because the YAT policy of X-radiographing nails has not hitherto been widely followed elsewhere. As in the Anglo-Scandinavian period, tin-plated nails were probably used as much for decoration as for practical purposes and might have been found along with other tin-plated fittings, such as stapled hasps (see pp.2842–4) on chests and caskets.

Iron stud and bosses (Fig.1408)

There is a tin-plated iron stud from a late 14th–early 15th century context at Bedern (*13891*) which may have served as a nail, but has a head also intended to be decorative. It is dished and in the form of a six-petalled flower. *14672* from Aldwark is a stud or nail with an unusual pointed head.

Coppergate has produced two iron bosses which must have served a decorative purpose, perhaps on items of furniture. *11967* (late 11th century context) has a domed centre surrounded by a wide flange. *11966* (early 14th century context) is a faceted domed boss set on a shaft, now incomplete, which is plated. Above the boss the shaft is capped with a copper alloy finial.

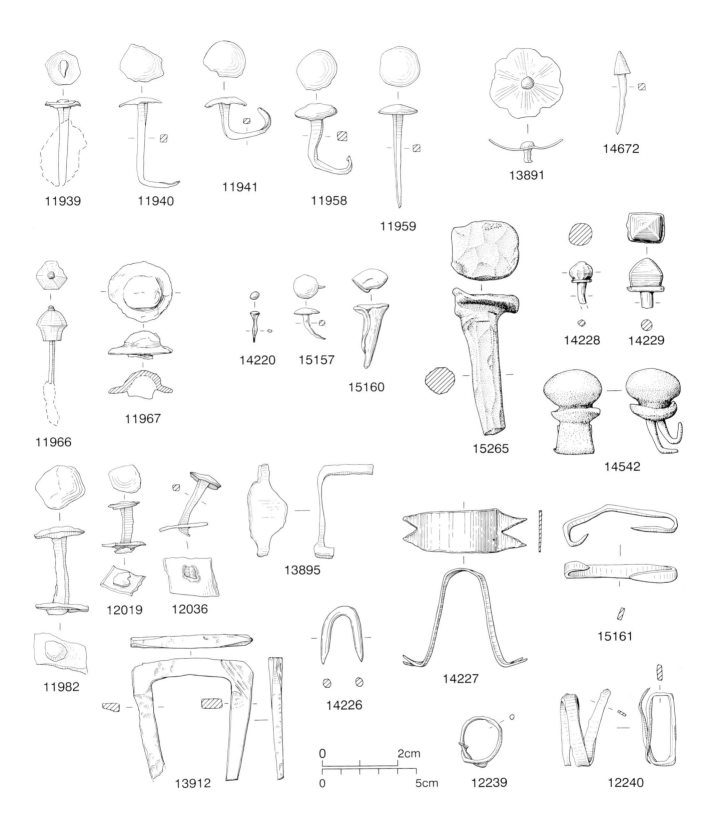

Fig.1408 *Tin-plated iron nails 11939–41, 11958–9 from 16–22 Coppergate; tin-plated iron stud 13891 from Bedern; iron nail with a pointed head 14672 from 2 Aldwark; decorative iron bosses 11966–7 from 16–22 Coppergate; copper alloy tacks 14220 from Bedern, 15157 and 15160 from 46–54 Fishergate; lead alloy nail 15265 from 46–54 Fishergate; copper alloy knops or finials 14228–9 and lead alloy knop 14542 from Bedern; iron clench bolts 11982, 12019, 12036 from 16–22 Coppergate; iron staples 13895 and 13912 from Bedern; copper alloy staples 14226–7 from Bedern and 15161 from 46–54 Fishergate; iron collars or clips 12239–40 from 16–22 Coppergate. Iron objects scale 1:2, copper alloy and lead alloy objects scale 1:1*

Non-ferrous metal rivets, tacks and nails (Fig.1408)

Individual and fragmentary rivets such as those used on belt fittings or strap attachment plates were found at Fishergate (*15155–6*), the Foundry (*13319*) and Bedern (*14219*); tacks, perhaps used on fine carpentry or caskets, were also recovered (*12862, 14220–1, 14223, 15157–9*). *15160* is another possible tack (compare to Margeson 1993, 77, fig.42, *470*). *14222* appears to be a fragmentary copper alloy nail. A lead alloy nail, *15265*, was found at Fishergate.

Non-ferrous knops (Fig.1408)

14228–30 are decorative copper alloy knops or finials, possibly used on small pieces of furniture; they were all found in 14th–15th century contexts at Bedern. Found in a late 13th century context, *14542* is a lead alloy knop with projecting flanges for attachment.

Clench bolts (Fig.1408)

Medieval contexts at Coppergate (including the watching brief) produced 129 iron clench bolts or fragments of clench bolts, Fishergate produced 43, Piccadilly two, but only one was recorded from Bedern. How clench bolts were used for joining timbers in ships, doors and other items is described in a discussion of 86 clench bolts from Anglo-Scandinavian contexts at Coppergate in *AY* 17/6 (pp.615–18). The vast majority of clench bolts from medieval contexts are, like the Coppergate Anglo-Scandinavian examples, 25–45mm in length, although the longest measures 95mm (*12984*). Again, as in the Anglo-Scandinavian assemblage, diamond-shaped roves and rectangular or square roves occur in about equal numbers.

Staples (Fig.1408)

Staples were principally used to join pieces of wood together, either in furniture or structures, and to hold fittings such as chains, hasps and handles in place. A more detailed review of the use of staples in the pre-Conquest period, which is also relevant for the post-Conquest period, may be found on pp.622–3 of *AY* 17/6.

As in the Anglo-Scandinavian period, there are several forms of staple, but there is a basic division between those which are rectangular and those which are U-shaped. Amongst the rectangular staples the most numerous (76 from Coppergate) are those where the wider faces of the arms are at 90° to the faces of staple itself. These are usually relatively small and light objects. Some have inturned or out-turned arms, many with clenched tips, as a result of being fixed into place.

Rectangular staples which have arms with their wider faces in the same plane as the faces of the staple itself tend to be relatively robust. This applies in particular to a group of eight very distinctive staples from Bedern with a flattening and slight rounding of the corner between head and arms (*13905–12*). It is not possible to generalise about their length because few are complete, but they are either 45–8mm or 60–5mm in width. Although they come from contexts of different periods, they all, with one exception, come from the south-western part of the Bedern site and it is possible that they originally belonged to a group which were made specially for some construction episode on the site.

U-shaped staples with the wider faces of their arms at 90° to the faces of the staple itself are, like their rectangular counterparts, numerous (51 from Coppergate) and relatively small and light compared to the seven which have their wider faces in the same plane of the staple itself.

A number of copper alloy staple-like objects were found on the various sites (*12863, 13320, 14224–7, 15161–3*). Considerably less robust than those of iron, and mainly formed from strips with tapered and bent over tips, their functions are uncertain, although one possible application is visible on plumb-bob *14511* which has a non-ferrous staple acting as a suspension loop (see p.2706 and Fig.1317).

Clips (Fig.1408)

Coppergate has produced six oval or round clips or collars. They are either similar to small rectangular staples, but with overlapping arms (e.g. *12240*), or are circular with the strip ends wrapped around each other (e.g. *12239*).

Wall anchors (Fig.1409)

12245 from a 13th century context at Coppergate is probably a form of wall anchor used in conjunc-

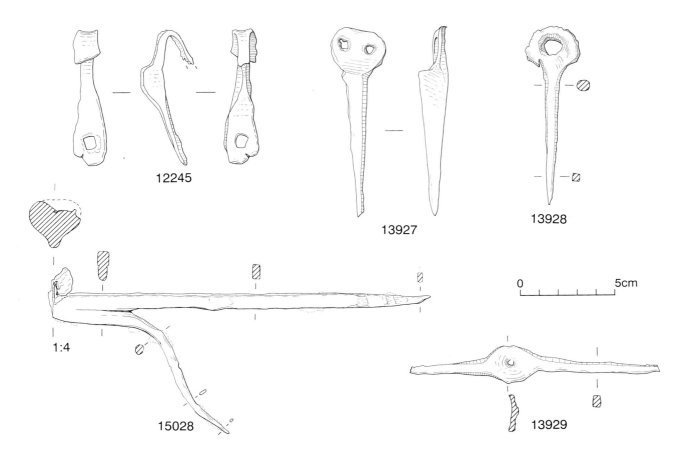

Fig.1409 *Iron wall anchors 12245 from 16–22 Coppergate and 13927 from Bedern; iron eyed bar 13928 from Bedern; iron gutter support 15028 from 46–54 Fishergate; iron window bar 13929 from Bedern. Scale 1:2, gutter support 1:4*

tion with a staple, timber dog or some other form of binding for joining two timbers and preventing movement between them (Fig.1410). It exists as an iron strap, now bent in the centre and incomplete, which has a pierced terminal at one end and probably had another at the broken end. There is an asymmetrical projection from one face. The object would probably have been set vertically and nailed onto a structural timber. A staple or similar object would then have joined the two timbers and been held in place by resting on the flat surface of the projection on *12245*. Fittings which worked in the same way can still be seen on buildings today, although they are usually post-medieval (O'Neil 1953, pl.LXIa, C).

Three very similar objects are wall anchors of typical late medieval–early post-medieval form: *12246* from a 16th century context at Coppergate and *13926–7*, both from post-medieval contexts at Bedern. Each consists of a large tanged spike which is flattened

into a terminal at the wider end; that of *13927* is pierced twice, but the others are unpierced. These objects were used to attach wood to masonry and brickwork. The shank was driven into the mortar joint and the head rested against the wood holding it in place (Goodall 1980b, 105).

Iron eyed bar (Fig.1409)

13928 from a late medieval context at Bedern is an object 98mm in length with a tapering shank and at the thicker end an eye 28mm in diameter. Its function is uncertain, but it presumably was used to support or hold other objects in place.

Iron gutter support (Figs.1409, 1411)

15028 is a gutter support bracket from a dissolution period deposit at Fishergate which may originally have come from one of the priory buildings. It has a long tapering shank with a downward project-

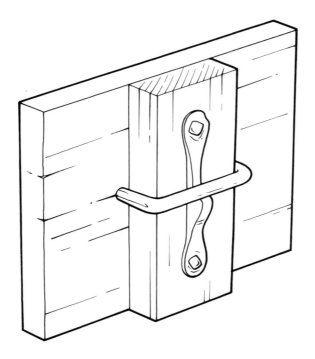

Fig.1410 *Diagrammatic reconstruction showing how a wall anchor was used, based on* 12245

ing tapered S-shaped arm at the thicker end and an upward projecting oval plate attached. Similar brackets can still be seen on medieval buildings in York today, although they are not themselves of medieval date, including, for example, Lady Row, Goodramgate, and St Andrew's Church, St Andrewgate (Fig.1314, **5**).

Iron window bar (Fig.1409)

13929 from a late medieval context at Bedern is a horizontal window bar with a central piercing to hold a vertical member.

Roofing lead (Fig.1412)

The dismantling of the priory at Fishergate included the stripping of lead from the roofs and windows, as indicated by the recovery of fragments of both types during the excavations. Roofing lead fragments were also recovered from contexts associated with building alterations during the priory's use.

Flashing

A very large strip of lead flashing, *15266*, which surprisingly escaped recycling, was recovered from a levelling deposit associated with minor modifications to the east range in Period 6d (late 14th–early 15th century), and was presumably removed from the roof during the alterations.

Offcuts of roof lead

These are typically rectangular strips with nail holes, possibly the result of cutting around the nails in order to lift off large areas of roofing sheet in one piece (Foreman 1991, 158). Apart from one offcut found in Period 6b grave fill (*15267*) and one unstratified offcut (*15275*), all derive from demolition layers, from the robbing of the church (*15268–72*) and from demolition period occupation at the west end of the north range (*15273–4*). Bedern also produced offcuts of roofing lead, all from Period 6–7 deposits (*14518–21*).

Window lead (Fig.1412)

Fragments of window lead or 'cames' were recovered from all the sites, in quantity from 46–54 Fishergate (see Table 301) but in small numbers from the other sites (*12942, 13075, 13409–17, 14522–37, 14644–50*).

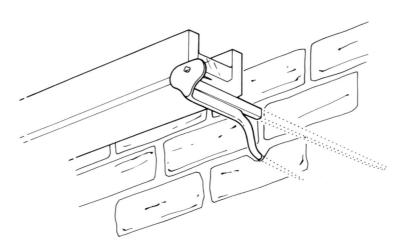

Fig.1411 *Diagrammatic reconstruction showing how a gutter support was used, based on* 15028

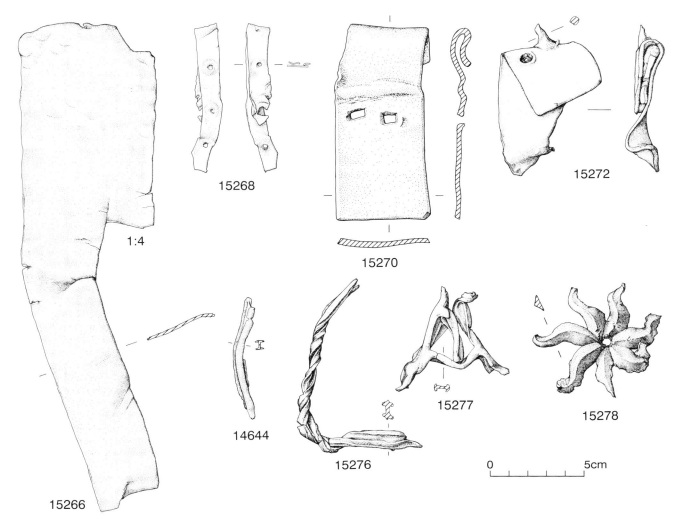

Fig.1412 *Roofing lead 15266, 15268, 15270, 15272 from 46–54 Fishergate; lead window cames 14644 from Bedern Chapel, 15276–7 from 46–54 Fishergate; gilded cast lead star 15278 from 46–54 Fishergate. Scale 1:2, 15266 1:4*

All fragments are characterised by H-shaped sections and the vast majority have been cast, the method of manufacture recorded by Theophilus, and in use until replaced by lead mills in the mid 16th century (Knight 1986, 31). Casting ridges along the sides of the cames were usually trimmed off, but are sometimes visible, as on the twisted up fragment *15276*. Only *14535* shows clear traces of milling, indicating that it must belong to post-College activity on the site. Several fragments retain traces of solder, used to attach them to linking cames, and occasionally the shape of a quarry is indicated by cames which are still joined (e.g. *13412, 15277*); a piece of glass remains within the leads of *14645* from Bedern Chapel. Possible window ties, which would have been soldered onto the leads and used to tie the window onto external iron window bars, include *13414* and *13417*. Both lead strips and lengths of copper wire are known to have been used as ties to attach completed window panels to the iron window bars or saddle bars which supported them (Archer 1985, 9; Gibson 1989, 264); some of the split cames found at Fishergate may have been used in this way (see Axworthy Rutter 1990, 119), as may small fragments of copper wire found on all the sites (see p.2715).

Distribution of the cames

At 46–54 Fishergate, the recovered cames undoubtedly represent a tiny fraction of the original used in the construction of the windows of the priory, as the vast majority must have been melted down during the priory's destruction.

As Table 301 shows, 60·6% of the cames derived from just three phases of the priory's existence. Two-thirds of these (40·6% of the total) derived from Period 7a priory demolition contexts, in deposits of Phases 225 (robbing of the south range including the church) or 331 (demolition of the eastern range, which contained the chapter house and dorter). Some cames were associated with a heap of window glass in the east-central part of the church which appeared to have been swept into a pile to enable the picking out of lead (*AY* 11/2, 216). Some of the roofing lead offcuts were also found here (*15271–2*), suggesting that other sources of lead were also brought to these heaps. The other concentration of cames (20%) comes from Phase 130 (Period 6e), a cess pit which also contained large amounts of 13th and 14th century window glass and other structural metalwork, and which related to alterations to the south of the church during the last years of the priory (*AY* 11/2, 203–7).

The few finds from Bedern were scattered across both the Foundry and the College sites, although all fragments (apart from the post-medieval milled lead came) are likely to derive from the College buildings. Little can be said about which buildings they were originally part of, although *14644* comes from a levelling deposit associated with 15th century extensions to the chapel, work which is known to have included reconstruction of the windows (see *AY* 10/5, 471).

The Coppergate cames derived from deposits ranging in date from the early 12th (*12947*) to 17th century (*12943*).

Lead star (Fig.1412)

A gilded cast lead star, *15278*, which would have been incorporated into a decorated vault or ceiling, was found in trample created by the Period 7a robbing of the chapter house; for further discussion of this object, see *AY* 11/2, 307–8.

Hinge pivots (Fig.1413)

There are 68 iron hinge pivots of which 49 come from Coppergate (including one from the watching brief), twelve from Bedern, two from the Foundry, one from Aldwark and four from Fishergate. A hinge

Table 301 Lead came fragments by phase at Fishergate

Phase	Period	no. of fragments
119	6a	1
319	6a	1
323	6b	2
216	6c	1
519	6c	2
327	6d	1
130	6e	19
131	6e	2
137	7a	1
225	7a	44
329	7a	1
331	7a	31
442	7a	1
443	7a	1
444	7b	1
804	7c	8
806	7c	5
226	8	1
333	8	9
527	8	9
335	10	1
021	11	1
228	11	7
336	11	1
449	11	1
609	11	1

pivot consists of a shank and a slightly shorter guide arm at 90° to it. They were usually used for hanging doors, gates or shutters. The shank was driven into the jamb, frame or wall and the guide arm fitted into the eye of the hinge strap, often of the U-eyed type (see p.2839). A characteristic feature found on most hinge pivots (e.g. *12256*) is the slight flattening or, in a few cases, nipping at the elbow during manufacture to make a vertical face for striking the shank when setting the object in place. *12292* has a shank of which the end has been clenched to make it secure. As an indication of the variation in size of the objects from medieval contexts, shanks measure between c.45mm and 114mm in length, a similar range to that of the 38 Anglo-Scandinavian examples from Coppergate (pp.635–7, *AY* 17/6).

Latch rests (Fig.1413)

There are ten iron objects identified as latch rests, ranging from 50–105mm in length, consisting of a

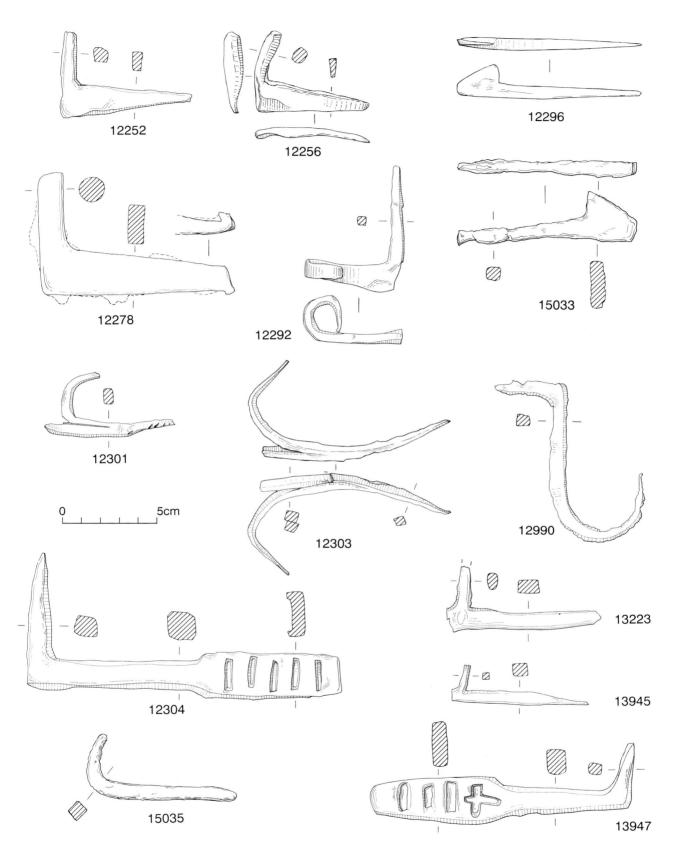

Fig.1413   *Iron hinge pivots* 12252, 12256, 12278, 12292 *from 16–22 Coppergate; iron latch rests* 12296 *from 16–22 Coppergate,* 15033 *from 46–54 Fishergate; iron wall hooks* 12301, 12303–4 *from 16–22 Coppergate,* 12990 *from the Coppergate watching brief,* 13223 *from the Foundry,* 13945 *and* 13947 *from Bedern,* 15035 *from 46–54 Fishergate. Scale 1:2*

tapering tang which is widened out into a triangular catch at the thicker end. Egan (1998, 54) has cast doubt on the identification of these objects and suggests that they are simply a form of hook as no suitable latches are known from medieval contexts. At all events, this humble object appears to be a medieval innovation as no pre-Conquest examples are known. The earliest York examples are from 13th century contexts at Coppergate.

It may be noted that seven wooden items described as brackets, of which two are from medieval contexts and five from Anglo-Scandinavian contexts, were found at Coppergate (pp.2361–5, *AY* 17/13). They appear to have functioned in same way as envisaged for the iron latch rests.

Iron hooks

Wall hooks (Fig.1413)

There are sixteen wall hooks. They can be a simple L-shape with a tapering tang (e.g. *13221* from the Foundry and *15035* from Fishergate), but more common are those with a shank which projects slightly forward of the hook arm (e.g. *12301*). This allows the object to be hammered into a wall without damaging it.

12304 from Coppergate (late 12th century context) and *13947* from Bedern (early–mid 13th century context) are very substantial hooks with expanded terminals to the tangs into which are punched shallow depressions. These hooks were used in masonry walls, the depressions providing a key for mortar. Similar objects are rare, but come from contexts associated with major masonry structures of medieval date including Clough Castle, Northern Ireland (Waterman 1954, 140, fig.12, *5*), and Portchester Castle, Hampshire (Hinton 1977, 201, fig.106, *42*).

12990 from a 16th century context in the Coppergate watching brief is a large, tanged, U-shaped wall hook.

S-hooks (Fig.1414)

There are nine S-hooks. They would have had a variety of possible uses such as hanging chains for pots and cauldrons, for holding tiles onto roofs (Goodall 1980b, 105) or for hanging butchered carcasses. This latter function would have suited the largest example *12310* from Coppergate which is 116mm long. *14677* from Aldwark is unusual in that one arm tip is flattened out into an oval terminal. *12991a* from the Coppergate watching brief may be an incomplete S-hook (or pot hook) which appears to bear traces of lead solder.

Swivel hooks (Fig.1414)

There are three small swivel hooks (*12315, 13949, 15038*), each of which is tin plated, and a fragment of

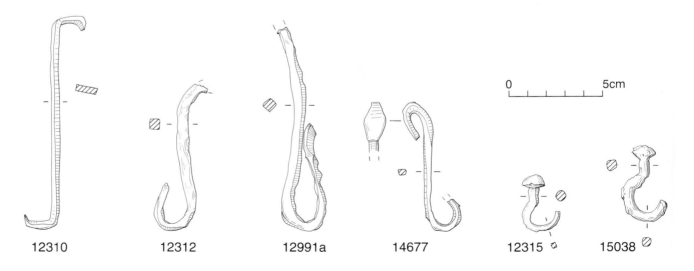

Fig.1414   *Iron S-hooks* 12310, 12312 *from* 16–22 *Coppergate,* 12991a *from the Coppergate watching brief and* 14677 *from 2 Aldwark; small iron swivel hooks* 12315 *from* 16–22 *Coppergate and* 15038 *from* 46–54 *Fishergate. Scale 1:2*

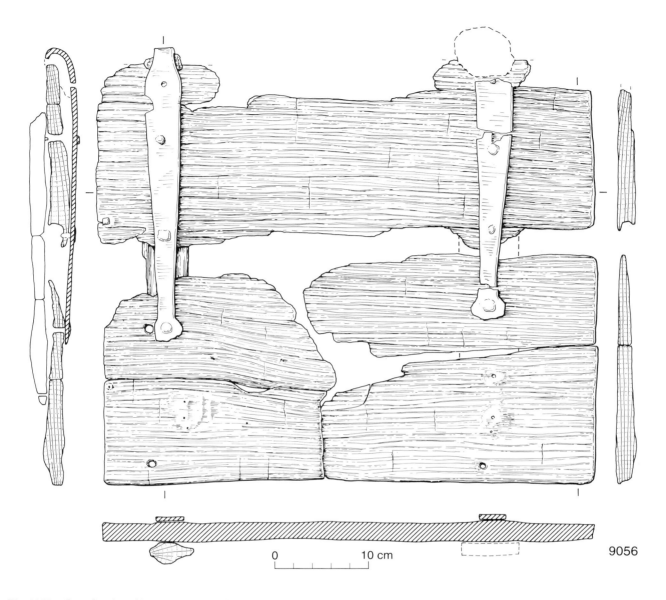

9056

Fig.1415 *Complete iron hinge straps on a wooden shutter from 16–22 Coppergate, 9056. Scale 1:4*

another (*15037*). Originally they would have been set in a ring or link and formed part of the gear for chains or other suspension equipment such as the elaborate tin-plated object with two hooks attached to it from a late 15th–early 16th century context at Winchester (Goodall 1990b, 826, fig.246, *2590*).

Socketed hook

12316 from Coppergate is a large socketed hook, c.103mm long, which is now very corroded. It exists as a socket, pierced for attachment to a handle or pole, which is flattened at the head into a wide L-shaped arm. It was possibly used as a boat hook.

Copper alloy hook

Found in a Period 1A deposit at Bedern, *14244* has a flattened pierced terminal, and hooked-up shaft of copper alloy.

Iron hinge straps (Figs.1415–17)

Hinge straps which have a looped eye at one end were used together with a hinge pivot to hang doors, shutters etc. Catalogued under this heading is a heterogeneous collection of objects, many of which are incomplete, but assumed to be hinge straps because of their size and form. Some may have been part of the particular type of hinge strap known as a U-eyed hinge (see p.2839).

Two complete examples of hinge straps 310mm long survive on a wooden shutter from an early 15th century context at Coppergate (9056; see also *AY* 17/13). *12318* from a post-medieval context at Coppergate is otherwise the largest strap in the assemblage with a length of 224mm. It is broken at the wider end where it starts to curve over and at the other end has a rounded pierced terminal which has

a pointed tip. This form of terminal is a very common feature on medieval structural ironwork, especially hinge straps and corner brackets. *13951* is a detached terminal, probably from a hinge.

13953 found in a mid 14th–early 15th century context at Bedern is a hinge strap with a closed eye at the end; this would have projected beyond the edge of the door to fit over the guide arm of the hinge pivot. *12320* from a 13th century context at Coppergate is another relatively long (175mm) but narrow strap

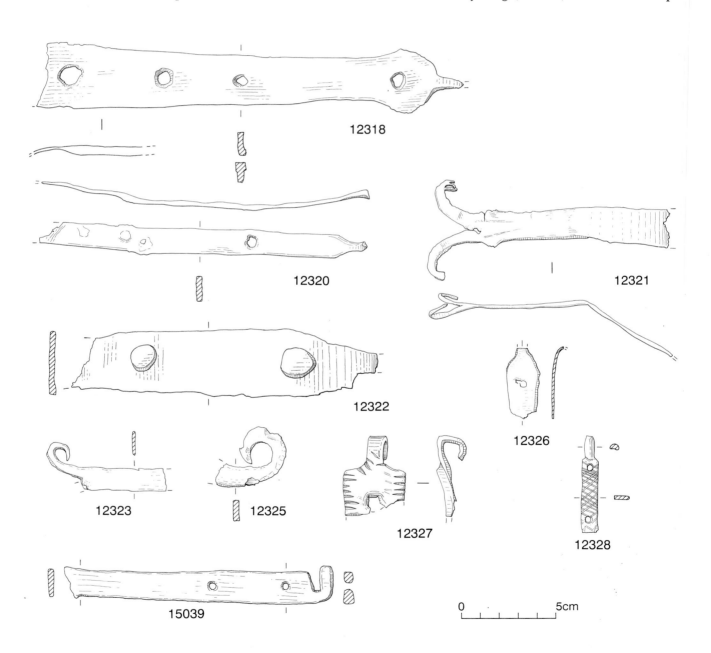

12318

12320

12321

12322

12326

12323

12325

12327

12328

15039

0   5cm

Fig.1416 *Iron hinge straps 12318, 12320–3 and 12325–8 from 16–22 Coppergate and 15039 from 46–54 Fishergate. Scale 1:2*

with an incomplete loop or eye. Straps *12321* (early 14th century context) and *12323* (early 12th century context) from Coppergate have or had bifurcated terminals with scrolled arms, another common medieval feature, especially on hinge straps. *13952* from a mid 14th–early 15th century context at Bedern has a bifurcated terminal, but there is also a central projection between the arms. *12325* is a detached scrolled arm.

A 15th–16th century context at Fishergate produced an unusual tin-plated hinge strap (*15039*) 142mm long, which has an arm at one end like the guide arm of a hinge pivot which would presumably have been set in an eye projecting from the door jamb. At the other end of the strap there would have been a rounded terminal.

Chests and caskets in the pre-Conquest period and until, perhaps, the early 13th century seem to have almost always employed two interlinked hinge straps of a very standardised basic form. One strap was fixed to the lid and had a U-shaped link at the head, as can be seen on the shutter hinge strap referred to above, while the other strap was fixed to the back of the container and had an eye at the head (pp.624–5, *AY* 17/6). Possible chest hinge straps from medieval contexts include *13954* from a mid 14th–early 15th century context at Bedern and *12317* from a 13th century context at Coppergate. *12319* from Coppergate is probably a strap from the back of a chest which has an eye formed by drawing out the head and looping it back over.

There are a number of small straps from hinges of the interlinked form which come from caskets. They include *12326* (13th–14th century context) from Coppergate and *15040* (15th–16th century context) from Fishergate which are plated. *12327–8*, both found in 12th–13th century contexts at Coppergate, and *13958* (mid 14th–early 15th century context) from Bedern are plated and also bear incised grooves or notches.

U-eyed hinge straps (Fig.1418)

There are 22 U-eyed hinge straps or fragments of such hinges. They were usually used with hinge pivots for the suspension of doors, gates and shutters. As in the Anglo-Scandinavian period (pp.637–9, *AY* 17/6), there are two principal forms.

In the first form, of which there are probably eight examples, the eye has a strap on each side. The straps have parallel sides and are or were pierced twice. In the second form there is a strap on one side and a terminal on the other side of the eye. The terminal of *12336* is rounded, but others have terminals which are round with a pointed tip as seen on *12330–4* from Coppergate. The strap of *12335* from a 12th century context at Coppergate has a bifurcated end and scrolled terminals. It is a smaller version of two large U-eyed hinges from Anglo-Scandinavian contexts at Piccadilly (*15341–2*; Figs.1556–7, pp.3010–11).

A third form of U-eyed hinge has a terminal on both sides of the eye as can be seen on *12337–8* from Coppergate.

Iron hasps (Fig.1419)

There are thirteen figure-of-eight-shaped hasps (eleven from Coppergate and one each from Bedern and Fishergate) which were used for fastening gates and doors. They would have articulated and been

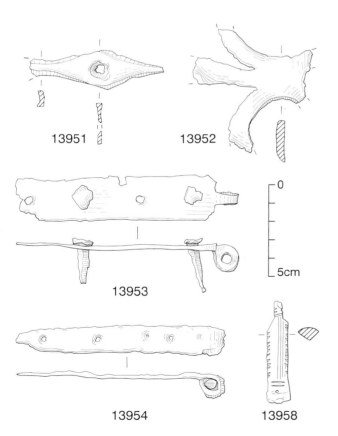

13951   13952

13953

0

5cm

13954   13958

Fig.1417 *Iron hinge straps* 13951–4 *and* 13958 *from Bedern. Scale 1:2*

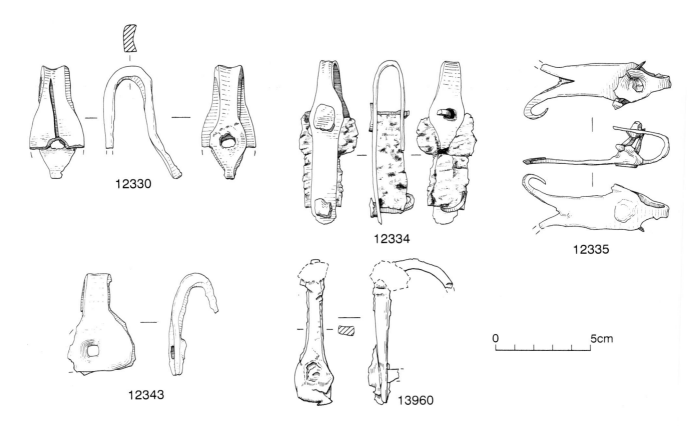

Fig.1418 *Iron U-eyed hinge straps 12330, 12334–5 and (incomplete) 12343 from 16–22 Coppergate, 13960 from Bedern. Scale 1:2*

held in place in the door jamb or gate post by a staple linked to a small loop at one end; the loops on *12351–2* have a rolled tip. The main body of the hasp was fitted over a staple on the door or gate itself and secured by a linch pin (see p.2851) or padlock. The examples under discussion are made from either plain or spirally twisted strips of iron. The eyes are usually of unequal size and the hasp is usually bent slightly at the waist, although *12348* is bent through 45° and *12355* through 90°. The latter could have been used to secure a chest lid, the end-loop being fixed to the top of the lid while the body fitted over a staple on the front of the container. The length of these hasps varies from 61mm (*15041*) to 152mm (*12346*). Figure-of-eight-shaped hasps have a long history which goes back to the Roman period and there is nothing typologically significant about the examples discussed here.

T-shaped hinge strap (Fig.1420)

12356 (mid 17th century context) is a plate, originally attached to a door jamb, with a looped projection on one side which would have articulated around a pin with a strap attached to a door or shutter. The use of this sort of pinned hinge for doors appears to begin in the late medieval period; early examples from late 15th–early 16th century contexts come from Norwich (Goodall 1993, 150–1, fig.111, 1177–8) and Ospringe, Kent (Fig.1315, **27**; Goodall 1979a, 132, fig.21, 61).

Casket and chest fittings

Small U-eyed hinge fitting (Fig.1420)

12357 from an early 12th century context at Coppergate is a small U-eyed hinge which has a rounded terminal each side of the eye and is tin plated. It was probably a casket fitting, although a fragment of what may have been a similar object has been identified as a belt fitting (*12715*, p.2896).

Pinned hinges (Fig.1420)

There are three examples from Bedern of small tin-plated parts of hinge straps which articulated

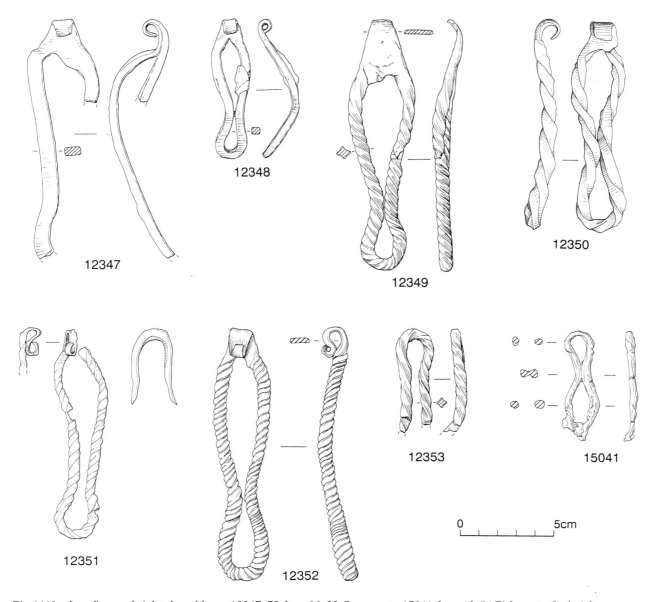

Fig.1419 *Iron figure-of-eight-shaped hasps 12347–53 from 16–22 Coppergate, 15041 from 46–54 Fishergate. Scale 1:2*

around a pin: *13964* (mid 14th century context), *13965* (mid 14th–early 15th century context) and *13966* (unstratified). These objects must all come from caskets. *12358* (mid 13th century context) from Coppergate may also be from a casket, but it is slightly different from the Bedern objects as the pin is held by an eye in the second strap and the object is not plated.

Copper alloy hinge fittings (Fig.1420)

Three such fittings were found in 14th and 15th century deposits at Bedern and all may have come from small boxes or caskets (*14241–3*). *14242* has been decoratively cut and incised, and the rivets for attachment reinforced on the reverse with narrow copper alloy strips.

Iron corner brackets (Fig.1420)

There are five identifiable corner brackets which are probably from caskets or chests. It may be noted that the surviving arm of *12359* from Coppergate had a rounded and pierced terminal with a pointed tip, a feature visible on many other medieval fittings including some of the corner brackets on the coffins

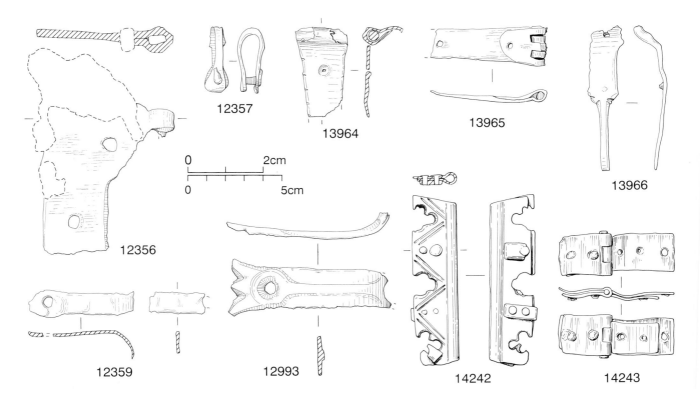

Fig.1420 *Iron T-shaped hinge strap 12356 from 16–22 Coppergate; small iron U-eyed hinge from a casket 12357 from 16–22 Coppergate; tin-plated iron pinned hinges 13964–6 from Bedern; copper alloy hinge fittings 14242–3 from Bedern; parts of iron corner brackets 12359 from 16–22 Coppergate and 12993 from the Coppergate watching brief. Iron objects scale 1:2, copper alloy objects scale 1:1*

from the medieval Jewish cemetery at Jewbury (*AY* 12/3, p.414). *12993* (undated medieval context from the Coppergate watching brief) is a robust corner bracket arm with a 'fish tail' end and a raised fillet running along the centre of one face.

Iron stapled hasps (Figs.1421–2)

There are sixteen stapled hasps (eight from Coppergate, seven from Bedern and one from Fishergate). A stapled hasp was used to secure the lid of a casket or chest. At the head it was attached to the lid and near its base a staple was attached which fitted into a slot in the face of the container by which it was secured by a sliding lock bolt (see p.2861). *12363* (mid 13th century context) from Coppergate and *13974* from Bedern (post-medieval context) are crank-shaped, showing that their chests had projecting lock plates.

The stapled hasps under discussion form a heterogeneous collection in a number of ways. First of all, some exist as single items while others consist of two components hinged together. Secondly, some

were attached to their containers by means of an eye or pierced terminal at the head while others were attached by a loop.

Of particular interest amongst those which exist as a single piece is *12367* from a late 11th century context at Coppergate. It is curved which suggests that it came from a chest with a convex lid. There is an eye at the head and the body is made from three spirally twisted strips. It has a copper alloy animal head below the eye and at the tip. The object has affinities with an all-iron stapled hasp from an Anglo-Scandinavian context at Coppergate (Fig.271, *3496*, *AY* 17/6), but with no other British stapled hasp. There are, however, many other stapled hasps with animal heads, largely from 9th–11th century contexts, in Scandinavia and Germany (pp.645–6, *AY* 17/6). *12367* is probably late Anglo-Scandinavian in origin, although it may well have been discarded in the late 11th century and need not therefore be residual. It may be noted, moreover, that iron animal-head terminals in an ostensibly Anglo-Scandinavian style appear on

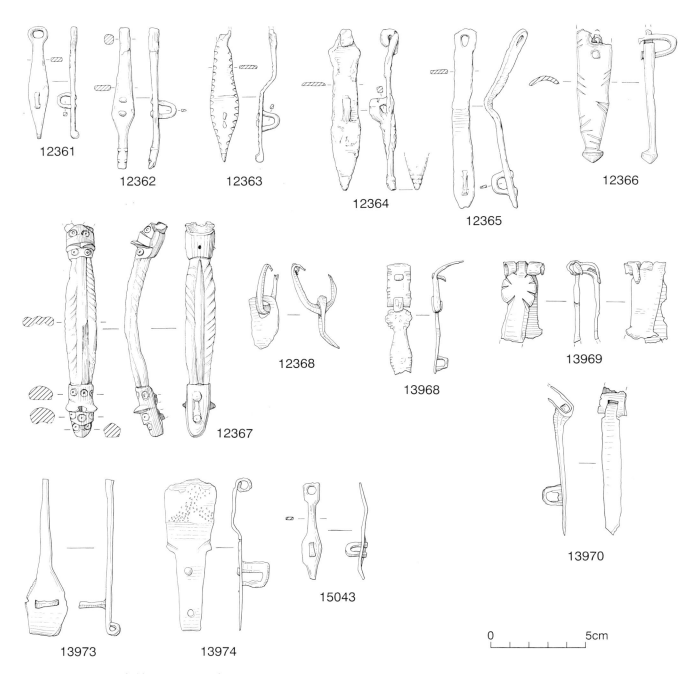

Fig.1421 *Iron stapled hasps 12361–8 from 16–22 Coppergate, 13968–70, 13973–4 from Bedern, 15043 from 46–54 Fishergate. Scale 1:2*

hinge straps of 13th century date fitted to cope chests in York Minster. The symbolism of the protective beast for a chest fitting is obvious and also appears in a highly stylised form on stapled hasp *12362*.

Of the other single-piece stapled hasps, pierced terminals are found at the head of *12361* (late 13th century context) and *12365* (early 13th century con-

text) from Coppergate, and *15043* (late 13th–early 14th century context) from Fishergate. Loops are found at the heads of two examples from Coppergate, *12363* (mid 13th century context) and *12364* (mid 16th century context), and one from Bedern, *13974* (post-medieval context). In most cases the main bodies of these objects are widened in the centre or immediately below it to accommodate the staple and as a result

Fig.1422 *Iron stapled hasps: (left to right) 12362, 12363, 12366, 12367 from 16–22 Coppergate; 13974 from Bedern; 15043 from 46–54 Fishergate; 13968 from Bedern. Actual length of 12362 82mm*

have a lentoid or lozenge shape. An exception is *12362* which narrows into a strip at the base, the tip having a relief moulding, probably as noted above a highly stylised animal head.

13973 from a late medieval/post-medieval context at Bedern is an unusual example of a single-piece stapled hasp in which the staple is set horizontally rather than vertically. This implies a lock bolt which moved in a perpendicular rather than a horizontal plane.

Amongst the hinged stapled hasps two from early 14th century contexts at Bedern (*13968–9*) are of in-

terest. They both have rounded areas at the head of the lower component of simple 'floreate' form. On *13968* there are six lobes and on *13969* there are six radial grooves around the edge.

Finally it may be noted that most of the stapled hasps are tin plated which confirms the impression that they had a decorative as well as a purely utilitarian function.

Iron handles (Fig.1423)

There are four drop handles from chests or caskets. *12369–70* from Coppergate have simple reverse L-shaped arms while *13975* from a mid 13th century context at Bedern has arms ending in loops with recurved tips. *15046* from Fishergate (13th–16th century context) has one surviving looped terminal and is plated. *15044* from a 13th century context at Fishergate is a large ring handle 88mm in diameter linked to a U-shaped staple by which was attached to a chest or door.

15045 from a 15th–16th century context at Fishergate is probably a handle, although it may simply have been the decorative terminal of a wooden shaft or pole. It consists of a tube at the head of which is a ring with internal cross-pieces. The object is plated with copper alloy. A similar item from an Anglo-Scandinavian context at Coppergate is tubular, formed into a circular eye at the head, and is also copper alloy plated (p.656, *3592, AY* 17/6). It is suggested that this was the handle from a sprinkler used in Christian rites. A medieval version would be an appropriate find in a Gilbertine priory.

Iron fittings (Figs.1424–5)

There are a large number of strips or plates which are or were probably pierced of widely varying size and form for which no exact function can be determined. This is often because they are incomplete or fragmentary. It may be surmised, however, that these objects are largely parts of bindings, hinge straps, corner brackets and other fittings from furniture or structures.

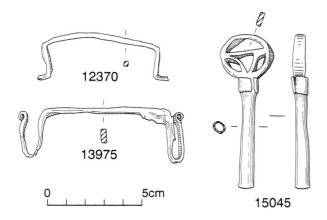

Fig.1423 *Iron handles: drop handles* 12370 *from 16–22 Coppergate and* 13975 *from Bedern; copper-plated handle, possibly from a ritual sprinkler,* 15045 *from 46–54 Fishergate. Scale 1:2*

While many of the objects catalogued under this heading have no features requiring comment, a few may be briefly noted. Amongst the larger items, *14004* from Bedern has a scrolled terminal at one end similar to those on hinge straps. Others of unusual form include *12385* and *12392* (Fig.1424)

Amongst the smaller objects a recognisable group exists as strips which have or had a pierced terminal at each end. The terminals are usually round, but other forms exist. These objects are usually plated and were probably casket fittings. Examples include *12444* (late 13th century context) from Coppergate, where the surviving terminal has small indentations around the face, and *14006* (13th century context) from Bedern on which the terminals have incised grooves cut into the edge of one face. Incised grooves are to be found on the surface of the strip between the terminals on *15061* from a late 13th–early 14th century context from Fishergate.

14009 (late 13th century context) from Bedern has D-shaped terminals. *12434, 12450* and *12453*, the last unusually plated with silver, all from 13th century contexts at Coppergate, have or had rectangular terminals. At one end of *12431* (now incomplete; late 14th–early 15th century context) from Coppergate is a roughly rectangular terminal and at the other end of what survives is a pierced oval panel; there are incised grooves either side of the holes. At each end of *12439* from Coppergate (12th–13th century context) there is a pierced, lobed terminal, one of which has a copper rivet and one an iron rivet in situ. The strip has short diagonal grooves arranged alternately on the edges of its upper face.

Other small plated fittings include *14017* (late medieval context) from Bedern with a pierced lozenge-shaped expansion. *14016* (late medieval context) from Bedern widens towards one end into which is cut a deep zig-zag and at the other end was a rounded terminal. *12448* and *12452* (both early 13th century contexts) from Coppergate are strips which may have been part of similar U-shaped fittings, if not the same object. They both have pierced U-shaped terminals projecting from the side near to their looped ends. *12452* has a second terminal at the head of the 'U'. One surface of both objects bears incised grooves.

13976 (early–mid 13th century context) from Bedern is more elaborate than most of the objects al-

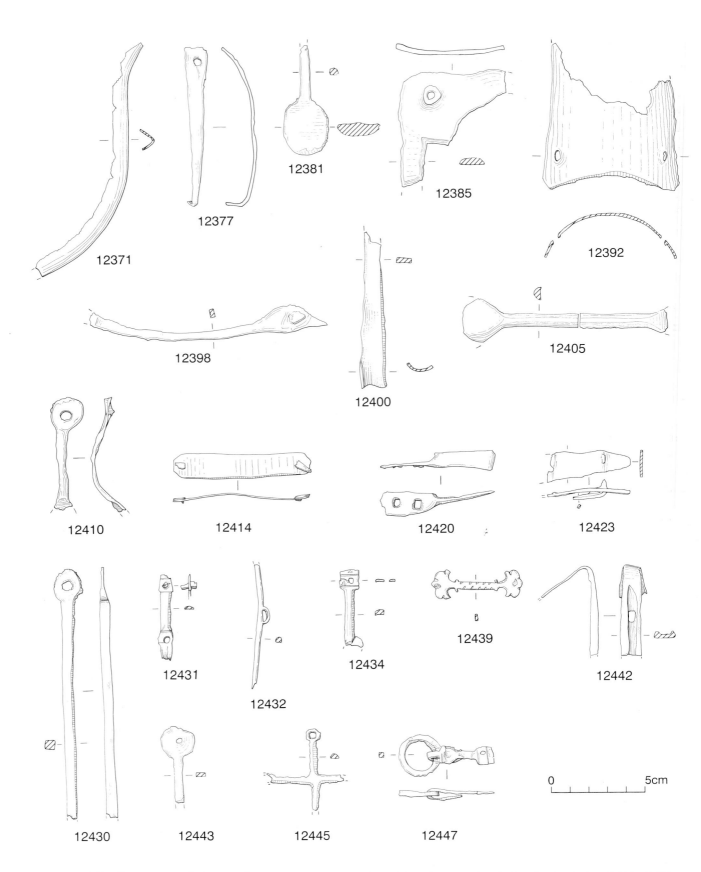

Fig.1424 *Miscellaneous iron fittings* 12371, 12377, 12381, 12385, 12392, 12398, 12400, 12405, 12410, 12414, 12420, 12423, 12430–2, 12434, 12439, 12442–3, 12445 *and* 12447, *all from* 16–22 *Coppergate. Scale* 1:2

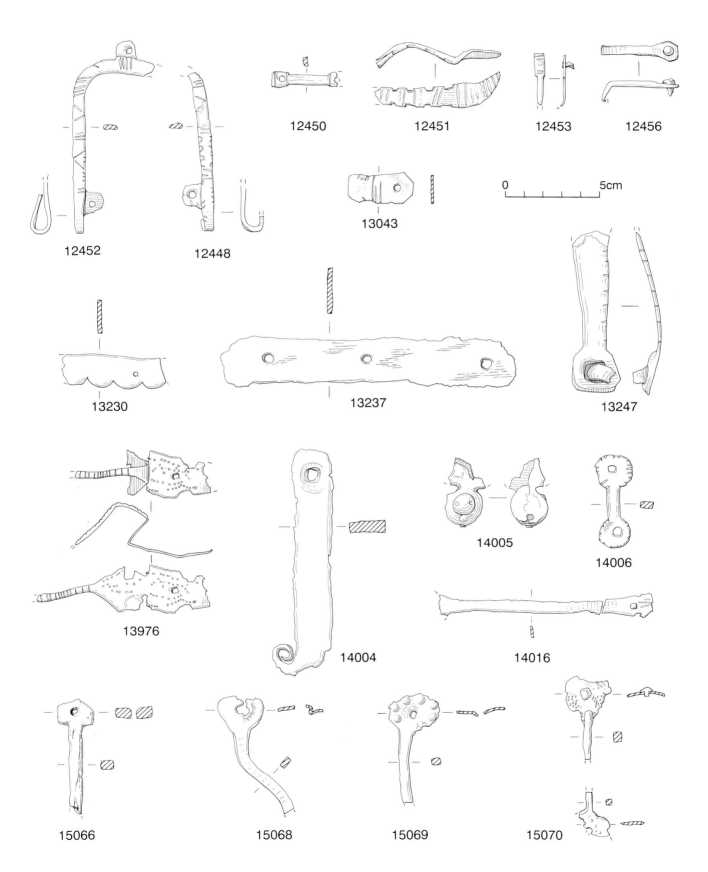

Fig.1425 *Miscellaneous iron fittings* 12448, 12450–3, 12456 *from 16–22 Coppergate;* 13043 *from 22 Piccadilly;* 13230, 13237, 13247 *from the Foundry;* 13976, 14004–6, 14016 *from Bedern;* 15066, 15068–70 *from 46–54 Fishergate. Scale 1:2*

ready described. It was originally U-shaped; one arm is a strip with incised diagonal grooves, the other arm widens out into a plate which is waisted near the broken end, pierced in the centre and has punched dots on its surface.

An unusual tin-plated object *12447* (early 15th century context) from Coppergate consists of two rectangular panels and then an oval panel joined by short lengths of strip; between the central rectangular panel and the oval panel it is folded over a small ring and the oval panel is riveted to the central rectangular panel. This was probably a casket fitting, the ring serving as a handle.

12445 from Coppergate (13th century context) is a small fitting in the form of a cross; presumably all four arms originally had pierced terminals. Finally, *12451* from Coppergate (12th–13th century context) was probably part of a small fitting, although no piercing survives. The sides are indented, it has grooves cut into its surface and is tinned.

Spirally twisted iron fittings (Fig.1426)

There a number of fittings, of unknown function, which consist of a spirally twisted strip and have or had one or two pierced terminals: *12459–62* from Coppergate, *14018* from Bedern and *15071* from Fishergate. Other incomplete spirally twisted strips from Coppergate (*12463–8*) may also have been part of such fittings, but no terminals now survive.

Non-ferrous binding strips or mounts (Fig.1427)

These were recovered primarily from the Foundry, Bedern and Fishergate (*13321–4, 14231–40, 15165–8*), with only two from Coppergate (*12864–5*). They may originally have been associated with boxes, caskets or other containers of wood or leather, of domestic or ecclesiastical nature, although use on books may also be a possible function for some (see pp.2939–40).

Found in Period 6a grave fill at Fishergate, *15165* is rectangular with a stepped profile, with traces of decorative tin plating on the upper face, and traces of wood around one of its three rivets. It may have had a functional as well as a decorative role on a small wooden box or casket. *15166–7* are strips which come from deposits associated with 14th century altera-

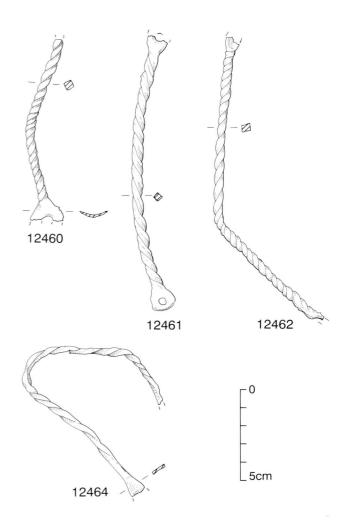

Fig.1426 *Spirally twisted iron fittings* 12460–2, 12464 *from 16–22 Coppergate. Scale 1:2*

tions to the priory, while *15168*, which appears originally to have bound something circular, comes from dissolution levels.

Five strips from Bedern (*14231–4, 14237*) are of U-shaped section, and, apart from *14237*, all derive from 12th–13th century features in the long trench. Such simple strips have been found elsewhere in both ecclesiastical (for example, Cathedral Green in Winchester; Hinton 1990d, 769, fig.219, *2330*) and domestic contexts (for example, Botolph Street, Norwich, Margeson 1993, 77, fig.43, *475*, and Rack Street, Exeter, A.R. Goodall 1984, 345, fig.193, *209*). The D-sectioned strips *14233–4, 14238* are more decorative; *14240* has a ring terminal, while *14236* has been silvered, and *14235* has beading and incised line decor-

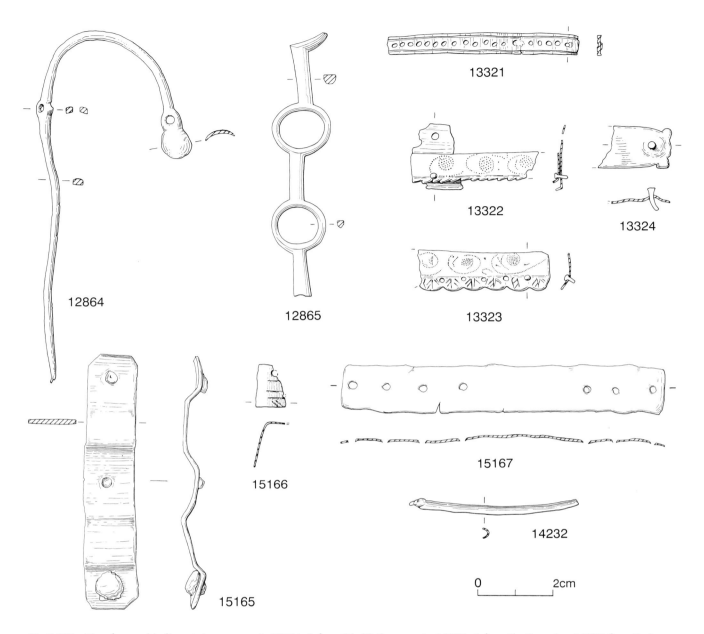

Fig.1427   *Non-ferrous binding strips or mounts* 12864–5 *from 16–22 Coppergate;* 13321–4 *from the Foundry;* 14232 *from Bedern;* 15165–7 *from 46–54 Fishergate. Scale 1:1*

ation. Both *14235* and *14236* were found in early 14th century deposits within the residential block, Building 5. These can be compared to gilded strips thought to be casket fittings, and found on 12th and 13th century manorial and castle sites, such as Goltho, Lincolnshire (A.R. Goodall 1987b, 173–6), and Castle Acre, Norfolk (Goodall 1982, 235–6, figs.43 and 44.1–23), and also on contemporary sites in Norwich (Margeson 1993, 75, fig.41, *457–9*).

Possible binding strips from the Foundry site include *13323* which has a pierced, scalloped edge with

traced and punched decoration on the surface; *13322* is possibly part of the same binding. Although *13323* is flat, a comparable strip from Winchester (Hinton 1990j, 1122, fig.364, *4316*) is folded along the straight edge, indicating a decorative edging. Also from the Foundry, *13321* from an early–mid 14th century context consists of two lengths of strip decorated with a row of punched dots between incised marginal lines, while *13324* is a short length of strip with a rivet through it surrounded by a repoussé roundel.

The two strips from Coppergate are both paralleled by examples from Winchester; *12865* from early 12th century levelling has decorative open circles (see Hinton 1990d, 773, fig.221, 2359), while *12864* from early 14th century occupation layers has a boss-like terminal and two attachment holes, similar to two strips from Winchester, identified as coffer-mounts (ibid., 766, fig.220, 2346–7).

Iron suspension fittings (Fig.1428)

There are eight vessel handle suspension fittings (e.g. *12471*) and two others on the bucket (*8742*, see pp.2806–7), all of which consist of a U-shaped eye of which the arms become straps pierced for attachment. Those associated with the bucket are, with lengths of 127 and 133mm, by far the largest and the others must come from smaller vessels.

Small U-eyed fittings (Fig.1428)

12469 is a small tin-plated object of uncertain function from Coppergate which consists of a swivel hook with domed head which is linked to what was probably a small U-eyed hinge fitting of which one arm survives (see p.2836). It has bevelled edges and two rectangular expansions to accommodate nail holes, one below the eye and one at the end. *12470* from Coppergate is a tinned fitting, now incomplete, which consisted of a U-shaped eye and two pierced triangular terminals of which one survives. Two similar objects were found in Anglo-Scandinavian contexts (*3483* and *3485*, *AY* 17/6) which suggests that *12470* is residual in its 16th century context. The function of these objects is uncertain, but they may have been used for holding drop handles in place on caskets and the like.

Swivel fittings (Fig.1428)

14021 is a curious iron object from an early 14th century context at Bedern for which there is no ready interpretation, although it may have been used as part of suspension gear for a vessel, perhaps a lamp. It consists of an incomplete link which at one end (the base?) appears to have had a rounded eye set in it and at the other (the head?) it is pierced. Set in the piercing is a strip with a spirally twisted loop at the head and a domed knop at the base.

12866, *13060* and *14245* are copper alloy swivel fittings with pierced heads. Small swivels might be used in conjunction with chains, or they could be from purse frames or dogs' collars.

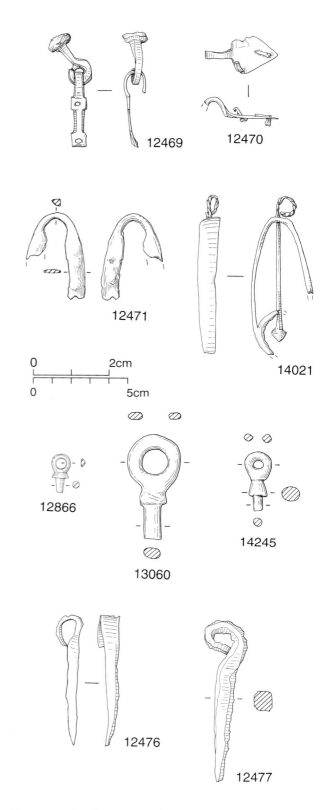

Fig.1428 *Small iron eyed fittings* 12469–70 *from 16–22 Coppergate; iron suspension fitting* 12471 *from 16–22 Coppergate; iron swivel fitting* 14021 *from Bedern; copper alloy swivel fittings* 12866 *from 16–22 Coppergate,* 13060 *from 22 Piccadilly and* 14245 *from Bedern; iron linch pins* 12476–7 *from 16–22 Coppergate. Iron objects scale 1:2, copper alloy objects scale 1:1*

Iron linch pins (Fig.1428)

There are two linch pins with looped heads from Coppergate which were probably used to secure chains or hasps: *12476* and *12477*.

Chain links (Fig.1429)

There are fifteen iron figure-of-eight-shaped chain links, ten from Coppergate, three from Bedern, one from the Foundry and one from Fishergate. In addi-

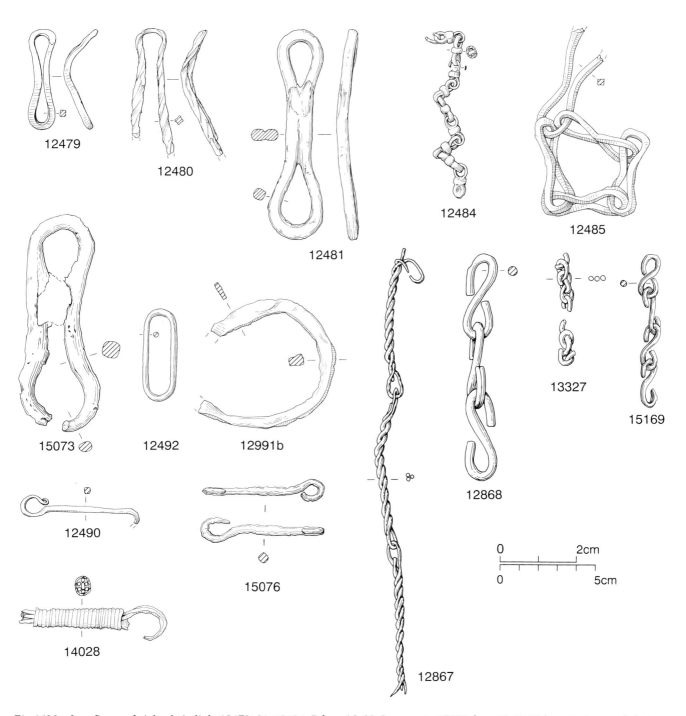

Fig.1429 *Iron figure-of-eight chain links 12479–81, 12484–5 from 16–22 Coppergate, 15073 from 46–54 Fishergate; iron oval chain links 12492 from 16–22 Coppergate and 12991b from the Coppergate watching brief; elongated iron chain links with a looped eye at each end 12490 from 16–22 Coppergate and 15076 from 46–54 Fishergate; iron chain link with wire wrapped around it 14028 from Bedern; copper alloy chain or chain links 12867–8 from 16–22 Coppergate, 13327 from the Foundry and 15169 from 46–54 Fishergate. Iron objects scale 1:2, copper alloy objects scale 1:1*

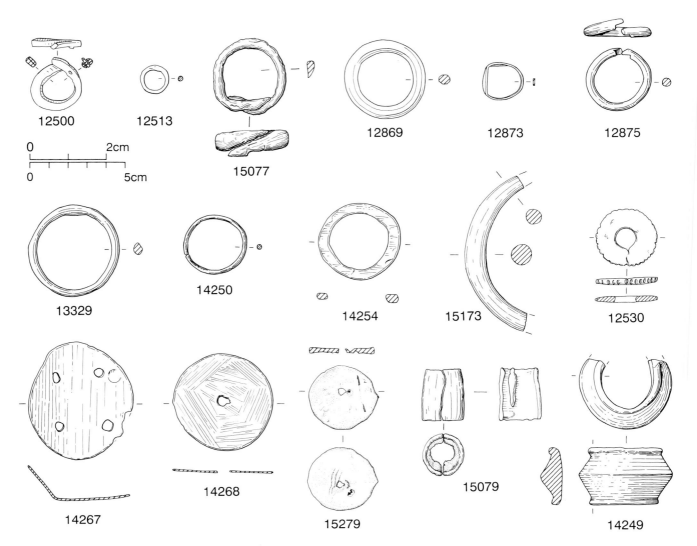

Fig.1430 *Iron rings* 12500, 12513 *from 16–22 Coppergate (possibly from chain mail),* 15077 *from 46–54 Fishergate; copper alloy rings* 12869, 12873, 12875 *from 16–22 Coppergate,* 13329 *from the Foundry,* 14250 *and* 14254 *from Bedern,* 15173 *from 46–54 Fishergate; iron washer* 12530 *from 16–22 Coppergate; copper alloy discs* 14267–8 *from Bedern; lead alloy disc* 15279 *from 46–54 Fishergate; iron collar* 15079 *from 46–54 Fishergate; copper alloy collar* 14249 *from Bedern. Iron and lead alloy objects scale 1:2, copper alloy objects scale 1:1*

tion, there is a group of five links (*12485*) and three formed the chain for the bucket (*8742*). These latter are by far the largest examples with lengths of 171–210mm. Otherwise the largest is *15073* from a 15th–16th century context at Fishergate with a length of 118mm. *12480* is unusual in being made from a spirally twisted strip and could be a hasp from which the end-loop has broken off (see Fig.1419, p.2841). *12484* is group of nine small figure-of-eight-shaped links. Each link has a small strip wrapped around its waist.

There are three oval links (*12991b, 15074–5*) and one (*12492*) with straight sides and rounded ends.

Many of the rings described below may also have been chain links.

12490 and *15076* are elongated links which have or had a looped eye at each end. They resemble the links found in two suspension chains from London, one dated 1350–1400, thought to have been used for lamps (Egan 1998, 132–3, *360–1*).

14028 (mid 14th–early 15th century context) from Bedern is probably a chain link which may have been figure-of-eight-shaped but has wire wrapped around it obscuring its form.

Fragments of copper alloy chain and of individual chain links were recovered from the main sites (*12867–8, 13325–7, 14246–8, 15169–72*) in deposits ranging in date from the early 13th (*12868*) to the mid 16th century (*12867*). Most of the chains are made of wire, but strip metal was also used; the most common designs of link are S-shaped, as on *13327* and figure-of-eight shape (e.g. *15169*). Chains such as these must have had a variety of functions, as dress fasteners in combination with hooks such as *15222* (see p.2921), and for suspension of objects including seal matrices, censers and scale pans (see below), although it is impossible to ascribe particular uses to short unattached lengths such as these.

Rings and washers (Fig.1430)

There is a heterogeneous collection of c.50 iron rings or ring fragments which may have been used in a number of ways as chain links, handles or even bridle cheek pieces. Meriting comment is *12526* from Coppergate made from a spirally twisted strip and tin plated; it may have been a casket handle. *12530* from Coppergate (13th–14th century context) may best be described as a washer; it is a disc with a hole in the centre, formed by curving a strip around and butt joining the ends. Grooves are cut into the edge of one face and it is tinned. No function immediately suggests itself.

Miscellaneous copper and lead alloy rings of various sizes were found in medieval deposits on all the sites (*12869–75, 12948, 13005, 13061, 13328–30, 14250–64, 14700–2, 15173–7*). A range of functions must be assumed for this disparate group, with the smaller finer rings such as *15176* with a diameter of 8·6mm clearly fulfilling a different role to that of the larger examples at over 30mm in diameter such as *14253*. The more substantial rings from 15th century and later contexts, such as *14263* and *14701* may have been used to hang curtains and other textiles (Hinton 1990h, 1095), while other possible functions include suspension of accessories such as knives or hones from belts, and handles on boxes or caskets.

Collars (Fig.1430)

15079 is a tubular iron collar from Fishergate, perhaps from a tool handle, to which it was clearly nailed. Copper alloy collars, also possibly from tool handles, comprise *14249*, an incomplete though originally substantial ring found in an early 15th century deposit at Bedern, and *15164* from a Period 6b grave at Fishergate, which shows signs of having been torn off in antiquity.

Non-ferrous discs (Fig.1430)

Discs of copper alloy (*12876, 14265–75, 14703*) and of lead alloy (*13418, 14538–41, 15279–80*) were found at all the main sites in contexts ranging in date from the early 12th century (*12876*) to the post-medieval period, although concentrated in 15th–16th century deposits. The majority are perforated, centrally or to one side, presumably for attachment as decorative elements to belts or caskets, or possibly for use as eyelets (see p.2855). Five lead alloy discs from medieval levels at Coppergate (*10594–8*) were thought to be residual from Anglo-Scandinavian activity and are published in *AY* 17/14 (pp.2563–4). Some of the lead alloy discs may have been used as weights (see p.2954).

Tubes/cylinders (Fig.1431)

There are twelve iron tubes which may have been either sheathing for wooden objects or incomplete objects of other types. They all have rounded cross-sections except for *14040* from a mid 14th century context at Bedern which has a rectangular cross-section. *15080* (13th–16th century context) from Fishergate is unusual in having a spiral incised groove on one end and copper alloy plating. Also plated with copper alloy are *13257* (15th century context) from Bedern Foundry and *14040* from Bedern.

Cylinders of copper alloy sheet were found at the Foundry, Bedern and Bedern Chapel sites (*13331, 14277–8, 14280–1, 14617*), and at Fishergate (*15178*). Their diameters range from c.6mm (*13331*) to c.11mm (*14277*) and they were recovered from late 13th (*14277–8, 15178*) to mid 14th century contexts (*14281*). Their functions are uncertain, but could be similar to those of chapes, large lace tags or ferrules (see below).

Ferrules (Fig.1431)

Two iron ferrules from Coppergate (*12538–9*, 13th–14th century contexts) were presumably set on the tip of wooden poles. *12538* is tin plated. *12539* is fragmentary but was part of a smaller object. Non-ferrous ferrules are not always distinguishable from chapes or simple cylinders, but the identification of the non-ferrous *9161* from a 16th–17th century dump

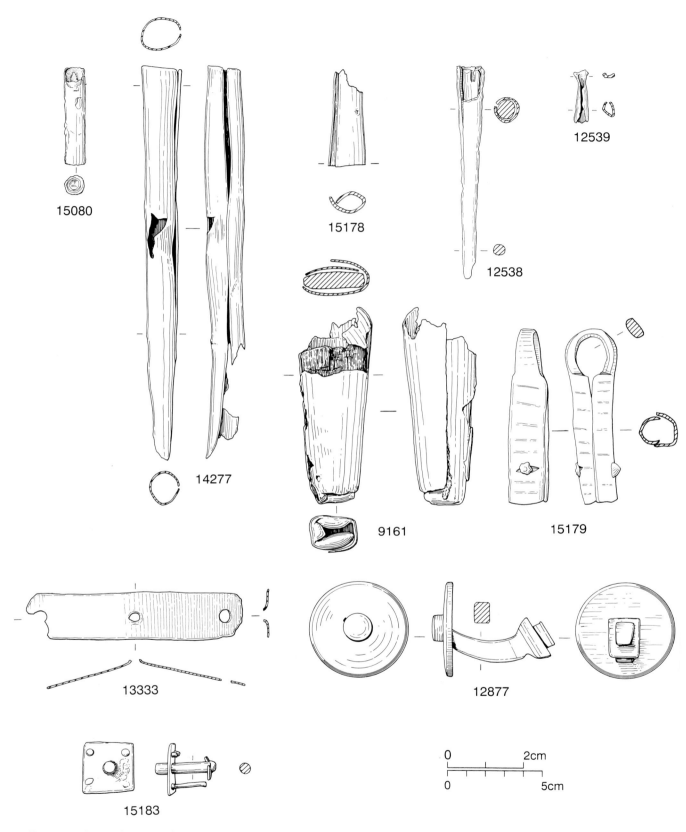

Fig.1431 *Iron tube* 15080 *from 46–54 Fishergate; copper alloy cylinders* 14277 *from Bedern,* 15178 *from 46–54 Fishergate; iron ferrules* 12538–9 *from 16–22 Coppergate; copper alloy ferrules* 9161 *from 16–22 Coppergate and* 15179 *from 46–54 Fishergate; copper alloy perforated strip* 13333 *from the Foundry; miscellaneous copper alloy fittings* 12877 *from 16–22 Coppergate and* 15183 *from 46–54 Fishergate. Iron objects scale 1:2, copper alloy objects scale 1:1*

at Coppergate is confirmed by the wood remains within, identified as beech (see p.2390, *AY* 17/13). Less certainly identified as copper alloy ferrules are *14276* from Bedern and *15179* from Fishergate; the latter was found in a Period 6a grave, is looped at one end and is similar to an object found in a late 11th–mid 12th century context at Goltho (A.R. Goodall 1987b, 176, fig.155, *67*).

Eyelets

13332 and *14618* were found in 15th–16th century deposits at the Foundry and Bedern Chapel, and are domed eyelets or washers from riveted mounts.

Miscellaneous perforated strips and fittings (Fig.1431)

Various perforated strips of copper alloy (*13333, 14282–6, 15180–2*) are of uncertain function, although some may be binding strip fragments. *12877*, found in an early–mid 13th century feature at Coppergate, comprises a disc with a rectangular-sectioned shank and rectangular washer. *15183*, from a 15th–16th century cess pit at Fishergate, also has a shank with rectangular plates at each end, one of which retains wood remains; the function of both these objects is uncertain.

Lighting

Medieval lighting equipment in the form of candle holders and lamps utilised ferrous and non-ferrous metals, stone and glass in their manufacture.

Iron candleholders (Figs.1432–3)

Coppergate, Bedern Foundry and Bedern produced a number of iron candleholders; there are three types, all of which were suitable for setting in a wooden base.

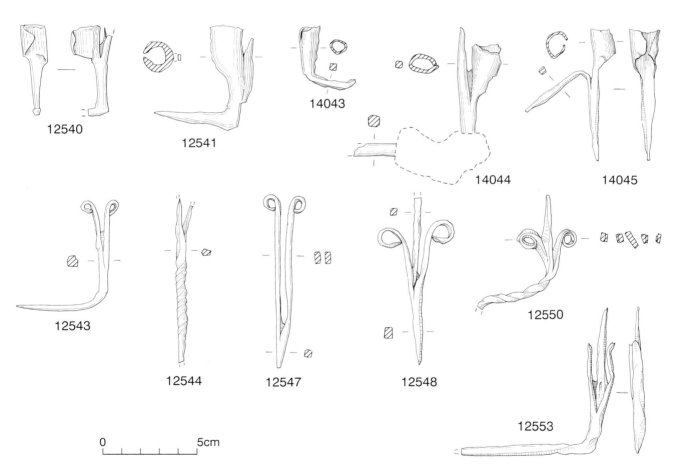

Fig.1432   *Iron candleholders: socketed candleholders 12540–1 from 16–22 Coppergate, 14043–5 from Bedern; bifurcated candleholders 12543–4 from 16–22 Coppergate; prickets 12547–8, 12550, 12553 from 16–22 Coppergate. Scale 1:2*

The first type has a socket (or cup) welded onto the head of a shank which can be either straight or L-shaped (e.g. *12540–1*). *14045* from a mid 14th–15th century context at Bedern is, however, unusual in being T-shaped in that the tang is set at 90° to the shank just below the socket. *14051* from a late medieval context at Bedern, which is also the largest candleholder in the assemblage with a length of 143mm, is unusual in having three additional arms with looped terminals attached to the shank. Although the socketed candleholder existed in the pre-Conquest period, there was only one from Anglo-Scandinavian contexts at Coppergate (*3675, AY 17/6*). This object was made in a different way to the medieval examples in that its socket was directly forged out of the shank rather than welded to it.

The second type of candleholder is the pricket of which Coppergate has produced ten, the Foundry one and Bedern one. A pricket has a spike on which the candle was impaled, two arms to hold it in place and a tapering shank which is usually straight but can be L-shaped (e.g. *12553* and *12556* from Coppergate and *14052* from Bedern). Two prickets from Coppergate have spirally twisted shanks: *12549* (13th–14th century context) and *12550* (late 12th century context).

Prickets are usually made of three pieces of iron welded together. The shank and one arm are often one piece of metal to which the spike and the other arm are welded, but sometimes (e.g. *13263* from a 15th century context at the Foundry) the shank and spike are a single piece to which the arms have been welded. The arms always have a looped or, more rarely, a rolled terminal (e.g. *12550*). Prickets are known in pre-Conquest contexts (*3677–8, AY 17/6*), but seem to become more common in those of the post-Conquest period.

The third type of candleholder resembles a pricket, but has no central spike. The candle was presumably wedged between the arms. There are six from Coppergate of which *12544* has a spirally twisted shank and *12543* has an L-shaped shank, whilst *12546* has both these features. Like the pricket, this type of candleholder also has its origins in the pre-Conquest period (*3680, AY 17/6*).

Copper alloy candleholders (Figs.1433–4)

A socket fragment from an unusual two-branched candlestick of a type incorporating both pricket and sockets (*14287*) was found in an early 14th century internal deposit in the residential Building 11 at the Bedern. Two-branched candlesticks similar to *14287*

Fig.1433 *Candleholders and prickets: (left to right) 12548, 12550, 12543, 12547 from 16–22 Coppergate, 14288 and 14045 from Bedern. Actual length of 12548 92mm*

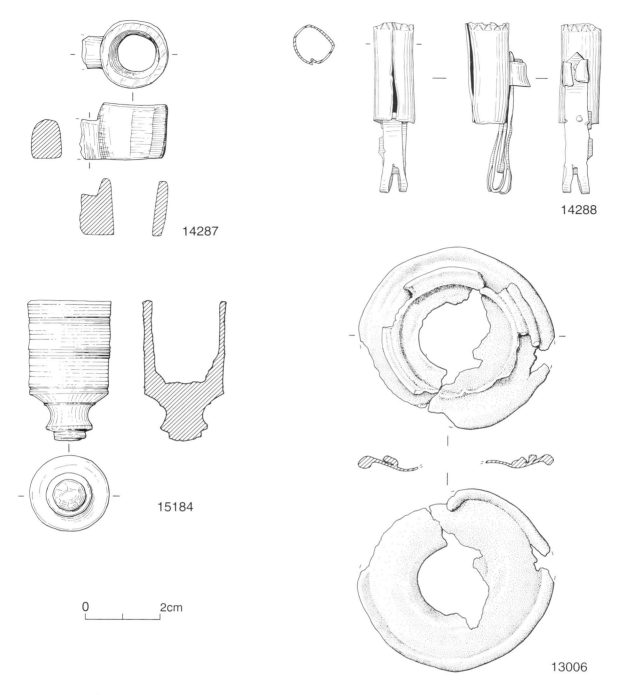

Fig.1434 *Copper alloy candleholders 14287–8 from Bedern, 15184 from 46–54 Fishergate; lead alloy drip tray for a candlestick 13006 from the Coppergate watching brief. Scale 1:1*

had tripod bases, a base form which dated from the 13th–mid 14th century (Michaelis 1978, 32, figs.11–12). A complete socket from a later type of double-branched candlestick, *15184* was found in dissolution levels in the east range of the priory at Fishergate; from the later 15th–early 16th century, the sockets for such candlesticks were made separately from the

branches, the short stubs at the ends fitting through holes in the branch (Brownsword 1985, 1).

Also found at Bedern, *14288* derives from an early 15th century spread laid down during alterations to Room 16A, and is from a hinged or folding candle-holder. The part of the candleholder which survives

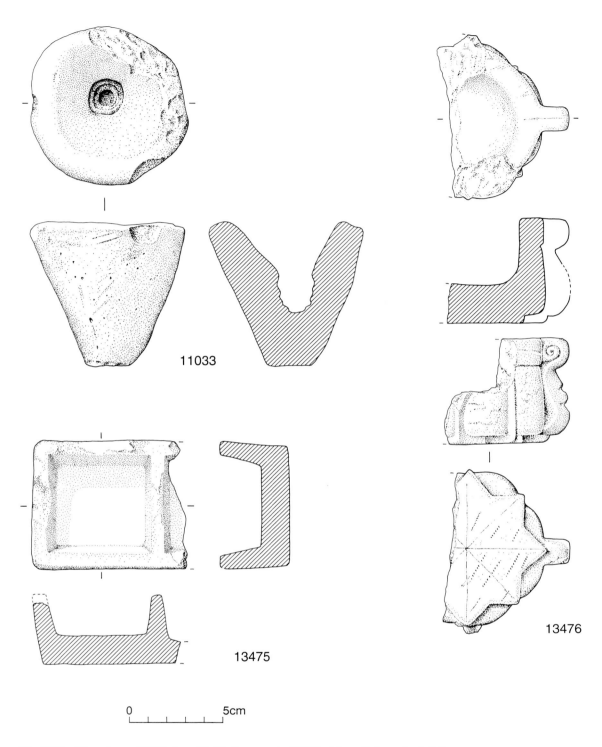

Fig.1435 *Stone lamps* 11033 *from 16–22 Coppergate,* 13475–6 *from Bedern. Scale 1:2*

comprises the socket and a hinge plate; the spike to which the socket would have been attached and which would have been wedged into a wooden surface is now lost. Parts of folding candlesticks have also been found at Billingsgate, London, and Hull, three examples coming from 14th century deposits (A.R. Goodall 1987a, 206, *214*), a fourth from Hull being unstratified (A.R. Goodall, pers. comm.).

Lead alloy candleholder (Fig.1434)

Possibly a drip tray from a pricket candlestick, *13006* derives from the St Mary Castlegate cemetery which was investigated during the 1982 Coppergate watching brief. Originally dished, there is a raised rim around the circumference on one face, while the central irregular hole marks the original position of the stick. Similar lead alloy drip trays have been recovered in London (see for example Egan 1998, 135–7, fig.103, *365*).

Stone lamps (Figs.1435–6)

Fragments of these substantial objects were found in medieval levels at 16–22 Coppergate (*11033–4*), the Foundry (*13099–100*), and Bedern (*13475–6*).

Dr G.D. Gaunt writes:

All of the Bedern lamps are made of Permian Lower Magnesian Limestone (see p.2800 for further information about this stone type). The two Coppergate lamps consist of oolitic limestone of Jurassic type. Possible sources include the Middle Jurassic Whitwell Oolite in the Howardian Hills and southern Hambleton Hills and its correlatives in the Millepore Bed in the Scarborough area, Cave Oolite in the South Cave area and Hibaldstow Limestone in northern Lincolnshire, and the Upper Jurassic Hambleton Oolite and Malton Oolite in the southern North Yorkshire Moors, Howardian Hills and southern Hambleton Hills.

The York lamps include both single and multiple reservoir types. Both lamps from Coppergate are simple inverted cones with flat bases and a single central well for the lamp oil; both were found in mid 13th century dumps. Another single lamp is *13476* from Bedern, but, unlike the Coppergate lamps, this example is circular with a moulded handle and other decorative mouldings on the exterior, and a decoratively shaped base. It comes from a mid–late 15th century context, and bears some similarity to an example found at Winchester (Barclay and Biddle 1990, 985, fig.308b, *3549*), also from a 15th century level.

The two lamps from the Foundry and the second from Bedern (*11033–4; 13475*) are all multiple types but of varying shapes: *13099* is cuboid with five circular reservoirs, the fragmentary *13100* was originally rectangular and appears also to have had five reservoirs. Only one square reservoir survives on the

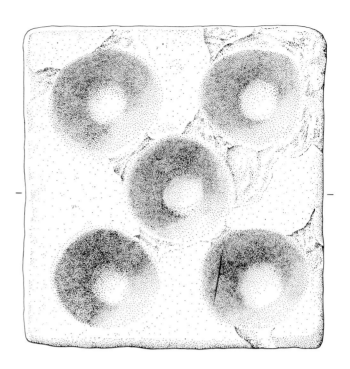

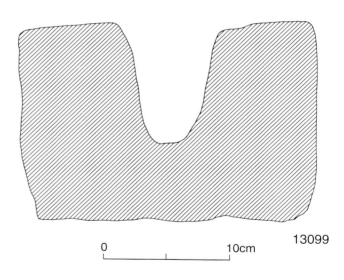

Fig.1436 *Stone lamp with five reservoirs* 13099 *from the Foundry. Scale 1:3*

rectangular lamp *13475*; its original complement is uncertain. Both *13099* and *13475* were recovered from early 15th century contexts, but, as with some of the stone querns and mortars (see pp.2799, 2803), *13099* had been re-used in building construction, in a padstone supporting a wall in the Foundry. The durability of these lamps makes dating difficult, but a

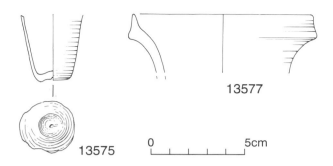

Fig.1437 *Glass hanging lamps: base 13575 and rim 13577, both from Bedern. Scale 1:2*

14th–early 15th century date seems likely, and a similar example from Salisbury was assigned the same approximate date (Drinkwater 1991, 173, fig.49, 36).

Multiple well lamps seem to have been less common than those with a single well. The few stone lamps found in London have all been of the single type (Ward Perkins 1940, 174–6), as were all those found in Winchester, where they were thought to have been used as stands for pottery lamps, which were also found in considerable numbers (ibid., 985–90). Multiple lamps have been recorded elsewhere, however (Robins 1937, 88–90; Evans 1969, 84), including one from St Mary's Abbey, York (Fig.1314, **3**; Yorkshire Museum accession nos.HB46–7), which has nine wells and is made of limestone. It has been suggested

that such lamps were particular to ecclesiastical sites (Robins 1937, 90).

Glass hanging lamps (Figs.1437–8)

Fragments of these were found at Bedern and Fishergate (*13575–8, 14777*) from contexts ranging from the mid 14th to the mid 16th century.

Dr Rachel Tyson comments:

These lamps have been found throughout England dating from the 13th to 16th centuries with almost half from religious sites, a substantial number from affluent town sites, and far fewer from castles and manors (Tyson 2000, 141–8). They are made of green potash glass, consisting of a long hollow stem rounded at the base with a prominent pontil mark on the underside. The stem flares out to form a bowl which usually has a vertical or slightly everted rim, sometimes slightly indented below the rim. A complete example dating to the 13th century has been found in Winchester (Charleston 1991, 259, fig.117). The thick base stub is the most common part of the lamp to survive. The lamp would have been suspended by chains or a harness around the base of the bowl. Hanging lamps can often be seen in manuscript illustrations hanging above altars, such as in a miniature of the Martrydom of Becket (British Library MS Harl. 5102, fo.32; Charleston 1991, 259, fig.118) or that hanging above Hugh of St Victor teaching in St Albans Abbey (Fig.1438). Similar lamps were also made of pottery although these would not have dispersed as much light as glass. The lamp would have been filled with oil or fat, making it more expensive to run

Fig.1438 *Probable glass hanging lamp, St Albans, late 12th century (detail from Bodleian Library, MS Laud misc. 409, fo.3v)*

than the cheaper alternatives of tallow candles or rushlights.

Two hanging lamp bases were found at Bedern (13575–6). Another was excavated at Fishergate (14777). Further fragments from Bedern come from an unusual potash glass form of thick glass, with the neck flaring out towards the rim, turned up at an angle to create a vertical band just below the rim (13577–8). They may come from hanging lamps. Not many rims are known in England which can be confirmed as belonging to lamps. However, a great variety of hanging lamp forms are found in medieval Europe and the eastern Mediterranean which demonstrate the number of vessels which could be used as lamps (Crowfoot and Harden 1931, pls.XXVIII–XXX), and the Bedern rims are of a form which would have been suitable for suspending in chains. One uncertainty is whether the glass of a lamp would be so thick (the Bedern fragments are at least 5mm thick), as most hanging lamps have thinner walls, presumably producing more light. Another possibility is that these two vessels may represent some kind of flask or container. Many different glass flask forms are found, both archaeologically and in manuscript illustrations, serving a wide range of functional and industrial purposes (see p.2826).

Locks and keys

Mounted locks

Bolt for lock with springs (Fig.1441)

12560 from a late 11th century context at Coppergate is a bolt from a lock in which it would have been held in place by leaf springs. A 'slide key' with a T-shaped bit was used to operate this type of lock, as described in *AY 17/6* (pp.660–1, Fig.282). The lock type does not appear to have been current after the 10th century and so *12560* is probably residual.

Lock mounted in wooden housing (Figs.1439–40)

There is a complete lock with a sliding bolt governed by a tumbler from a 16th century well at Coppergate (*9045, AY 17/13*). The lock chamber is carved out of a riven oak plank which was presumably part of a door. The iron parts are badly corroded, but all of them are recognisable. The chamber is crudely made, but incorporates space for the bolt, tumbler and, below them, at the rear, a plate bearing a spindle and possibly wards over which the key bit had to pass. There are two straps which were nailed

on to the rear to hold the bolt in place. Otherwise the lock chamber was probably open at the rear and the door could only be locked from the outside. The way this type of lock operated is described in *AY 17/6* (pp.657–8). The bolt is c.150mm long which gives an idea of the function of similar sized bolts found in excavation. It is considerably larger than a bolt c.60mm long found in a complete lock of the same type in a wooden housing from an Anglo-Scandinavian context at 6–8 Pavement (Fig.1314, **12**) which may have come from a chest (pp.80–1, *430, AY 17/3*).

There are three other bolts for this type of lock from medieval contexts. *12558* (mid 13th century context) from Coppergate and *15082* (15th–16th century context) from Fishergate, 207mm and 178mm long respectively, would also be from doors. *12559* from Coppergate is incomplete. If *9045* is of the same date as its context (16th century) it comes from near the end of the period in which this type of lock was widely used, a period which probably began in the 7th–8th century (p.660, *AY 17/6*; Ottaway 1996, 110). Medieval examples of the bolts are, however, numerous and while their use on doors is implied by the size of some specimens, there are examples of chest locks employing the bolts under discussion from, for example, London (Egan 1998, 104–8).

Iron ward plates (Fig.1441)

14053 from a mid 14th century context at Bedern and *15083* from a late 16th century context at Fishergate are ward plates. They were set in the centre of a lock chamber to govern the operation of keys which would have had bits with a central channel (see below).

Padlocks

Iron (Figs.1442–8)

There are 56 objects (37 from Coppergate) which were parts of barrel padlocks. The majority are probably parts of padlocks of three basic types, although it is not usually possible to assign the objects under discussion to a type as they are too fragmentary. One type of padlock had a key hole cut into one end of the case, and the second had a short T-shaped key hole cut partly into the end and partly into the side of the case; in both types the bolt hole was at the opposite end of the case. The way in which these two forms of barrel padlock operated is shown in Fig.1443. They both re-

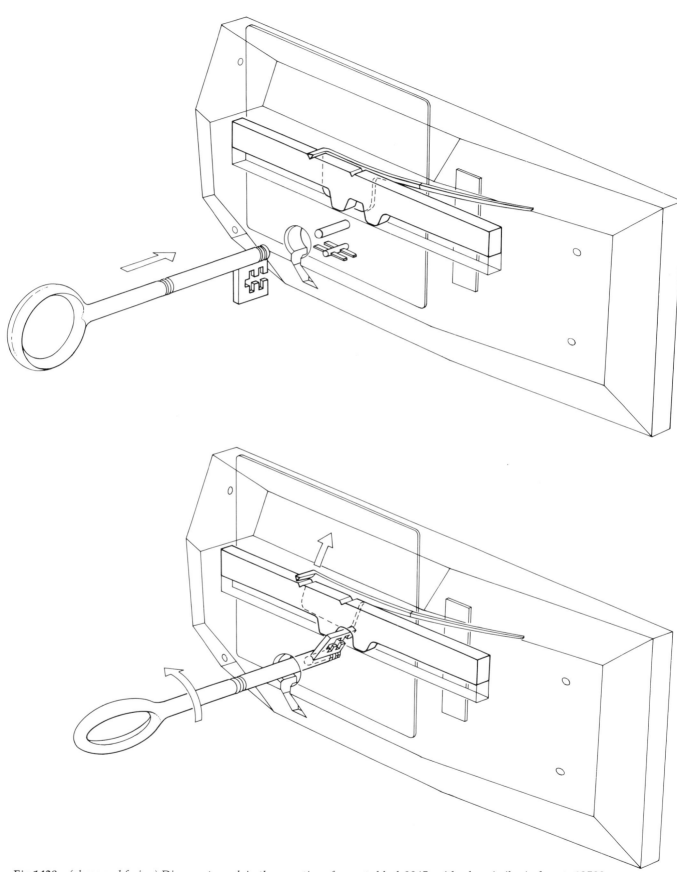

Fig.1439 *(above and facing) Diagram to explain the operation of mounted lock* 9045, *with a key similar in form to* 12599

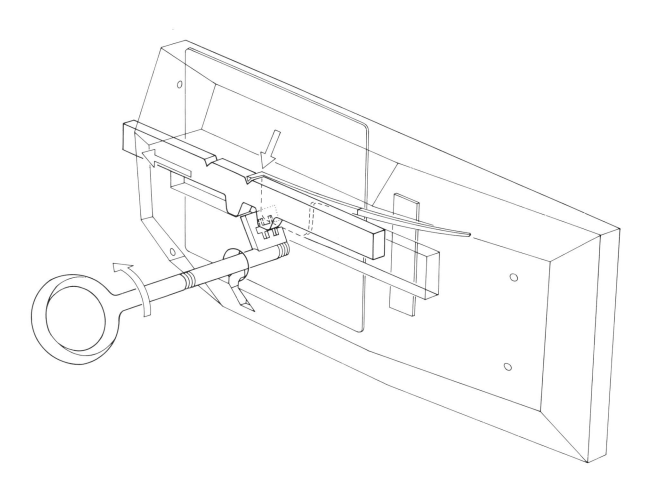

quire a key with its bit at an angle to the stem, of which there are a number of examples published below. A third type of medieval barrel padlock has an elongated T-shaped slot cut into the cylinder which worked in the way shown in Fig.1444. There are no examples of this type in the assemblage under discussion, although there are a number of suitable keys (see below).

12561–2 from Coppergate are padlocks of the first type, having cases with key holes cut into one end-plate, and 13045 from a late 11th century context at Piccadilly is probably of this type, although the end-plate with the key hole is missing. This is unlikely to be a residual pre-Conquest object as the surviving end-plate is recessed into the case rather than welded onto its end as was usual in the earlier period (see 3610, AY 17/6).

12563 from an early 14th century context and 12564 from a 12th century context, both at Coppergate, are cases of padlocks of the second type which have the short T-shaped key hole. Goodall (1980b, 125–6) notes that this type are usually from contexts with this date range.

The remaining padlock cases are too fragmentary to be assigned to a group. In all the examples where the end-plates survive, however, they are recessed into the case. Some cases have the tube for the arm of the bolt welded directly to the case including 12561 (12th–13th century context) and 12562 (early 12th century context) from Coppergate, while the others (e.g. 15085 from Fishergate) have, like 13045, the bolt arm tube separated from the case by a fin. This fin is sometimes pierced to allow suspension of the lock as can be clearly seen on 12563. All the cases are plated with brazing metals which are composed of various sorts of copper-based alloy. The brazing metal was also used to hold the components of the lock together and attach additional strips for decorative and strengthening purposes, usually along the sides of the case and around the ends.

The barrel padlock bolts exhibit some variation in respect of way the spine and springs are organised. In its simplest form the bolt develops into a spine at the base of which a pair of leaf springs is attached. The head of the spine is defined by a closing plate which, when the bolt is set in its case, covers and protects the bolt hole. The springs may be attached

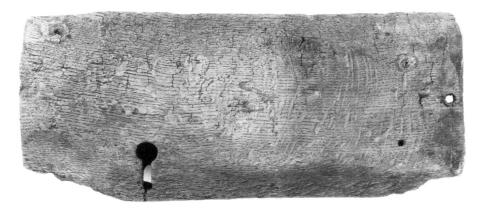

Fig.1440 *Front and back of complete lock in oak housing, 9045 from 16–22 Coppergate. Actual length of housing 320mm*

12558

12560

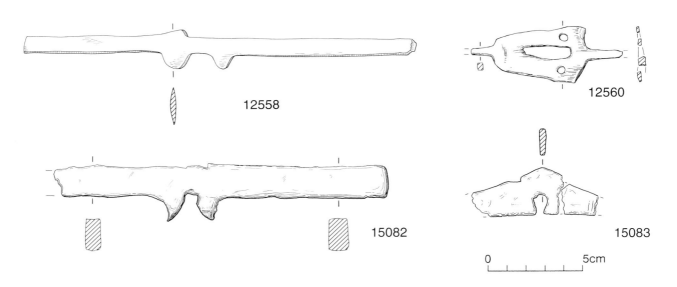

15082

15083

0   5cm

Fig.1441 *Iron bolts for locks* 12558 *and* 12560 *from 16–22 Coppergate,* 15082 *from 46–54 Fishergate; iron lock ward plate* 15083 *from 46–54 Fishergate. Scale 1:2*

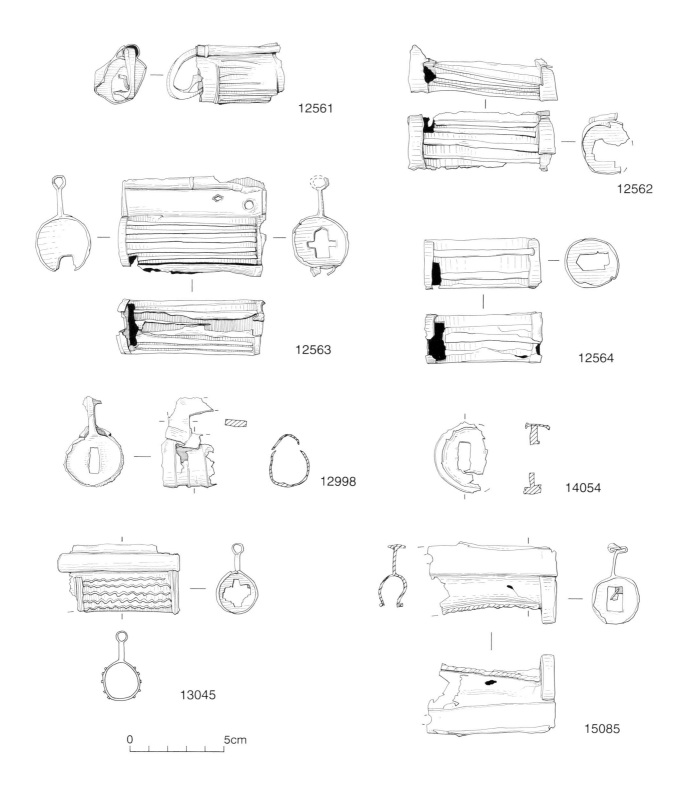

Fig.1442 *Iron barrel padlock cases* 12561–4 *from 16–22 Coppergate,* 12998 *from the Coppergate watching brief,* 13045 *from 22 Piccadilly,* 14054 *from Bedern,* 15085 *from 46–54 Fishergate. Scale 1:2*

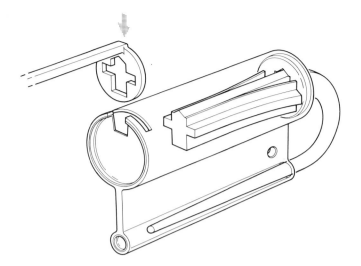 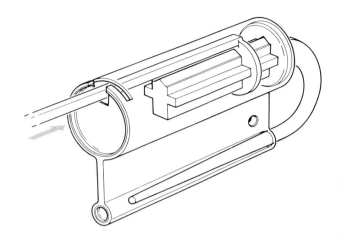

to the spine either by welding or by small rivets (e.g. *12579*). One or two additional spines may be added to make the lock more complex. This may be done by welding the additional spine to the base of the 'U' of the bolt above the closing plate before passing it through a hole in the plate. On *13265* from an early 14th century context at the Foundry there are two additional spines which are welded to opposing sides of the bolt while on *14057* from a mid 14th–early 15th century context at Bedern two spines have been made by splitting a single piece of metal which is welded to the bolt above the closing plate. On *14056* from a late 13th century context at Bedern the additional spine is welded onto the top of the U-shaped part of the bolt; this is unusual but not unparalleled. Additional spines usually have their faces at 90° to those of the original spine. Further complexity can be introduced by splitting the ends of the springs (e.g. *12579–80, 12593* from Coppergate).

Although details of the construction of the case, the mechanism and any decoration varied over time, the barrel padlock with an end key hole of recognisable post-Roman form has its origins in the 7th century, if not before, but that with the T-shaped slot was probably introduced to northern Europe in the 8th or 9th century. However, other English examples are usually from 12th–early 13th century contexts, such as those from King's Lynn (Goodall and Carter 1977, 291–2, fig.132, *1–2*). While the short T-shaped key hole may not have been current long after the

early 14th century, the padlock type with a key hole at the end of the case probably remained in use until the early post-medieval period.

12596 from a 13th–14th century context and *12597* from a late 12th century context, both from Coppergate, are examples of copper alloy-plated barrel padlocks which have a case with a projecting arm at one end and an L-shaped bolt. Both are small compared to most other padlocks but similar to examples made entirely of copper alloy (e.g. Egan 1998, 93, *244–5*). This type of padlock was presumably used for caskets. It is largely found in 13th–14th century contexts.

Coppergate has produced three bolts (*12572*, late 13th century context, *12594–5*, both 12th–13th century contexts) from padlock cases to which a U-shaped shackle was linked at one end. At the other end of the case the tip of the shackle would have fitted into a slot where it could be secured by the bolt which consists solely of a closing plate and spine with springs. Handling these bolts would have been difficult so a loop was sometimes added to the head as in the case of *12572*.

Copper alloy padlock (Figs.1448)

In addition to the iron padlocks, an almost complete copper alloy padlock with a swinging key hole cover on one face was recovered from an early 14th

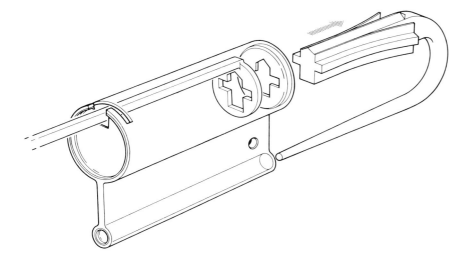

Fig.1443 (*left and facing*) *Reconstruction of barrel padlock with key hole at end,* 12563

century mortar spread within the residential Building 14 at the College of Vicars Choral (*14289*). Although iron padlocks could be plated (see for example *12596–7*), brazed or made with some copper alloy parts (Egan 1998, 91), completely non-ferrous padlocks appear to have been uncommon during the medieval period, although their failure to survive in numbers in the archaeological record could be the result of their generally small size (ibid., 92). Probably made for caskets, an identical padlock to *14289* was found at Castle Rising, Norfolk (Williams 1997, 93, fig.61, *30*); other similar examples come from urban sites such as London, where two were found in late 12th–late 13th century deposits (Egan 1998, 93), rural sites, such as the village of Goltho, deserted during the 14th century (Beresford 1975, 93, fig.44, *21*), and ecclesiastical contexts, such as the Greyfriars, Northampton (Williams 1978, 149, fig.22, *2*). See Fig.1315 for locations.

Keys

Iron keys for locks with sliding bolts and springs

There are three keys from medieval contexts of a type described as 'slide keys' in *AY* 17/6 (p.673) and *AY* 17/9 (p.1423), although not of the Roman type defined by Manning (1985, 92). *14683* from 2 Aldwark and those already published as *5238–9* from Fishergate (Fig.696, *AY* 17/9) are, like the bolt *12560* (see above) from the related lock type, likely to be residual from the Anglian or Anglo-Scandinavian periods.

Iron keys for mounted locks (Figs.1449–52)

Keys for locks like *9045* with sliding bolts and tumblers have hollow stems to fit over the spindle at the back. In the Anglian and Anglo-Scandinavian periods the keys were made from a single piece of iron and had a hollow stem (pp.668–9, *AY* 17/6). In addition, the bow was usually either circular or pear-shaped, and was wide and flat in cross-section; its tip was tapered and tucked into the head of the stem. The bit usually had simple rectangular ward cuts out of the sides and base. Two keys of this form come from medieval contexts at Coppergate (*12598* and *12600*) and they are probably residual.

In the medieval period keys often appear to have been made as three separate parts (bow, stem and bit) which were then welded together. Keys with hollow stems were still made throughout the medieval period and there are nineteen from the York sites under discussion. The bows are different from those of pre-Conquest date, however, in being forged from thin strips with rounded cross-sections. The bows are most commonly D-shaped, oval or circular, although those of *12602* from a 12th century context at Coppergate and *14064* from a mid 14th–early 15th century context at Bedern have the lozenge shape which occurs occasionally throughout the medieval period. Keys with bows of this form are shown in two stained glass windows of the first half of the 14th century in the nave of York Minster (the third window from the east in the north aisle and the third from the west in the south aisle, the Jesse Window) and in an illustration of St Peter in the *Bolton Hours*

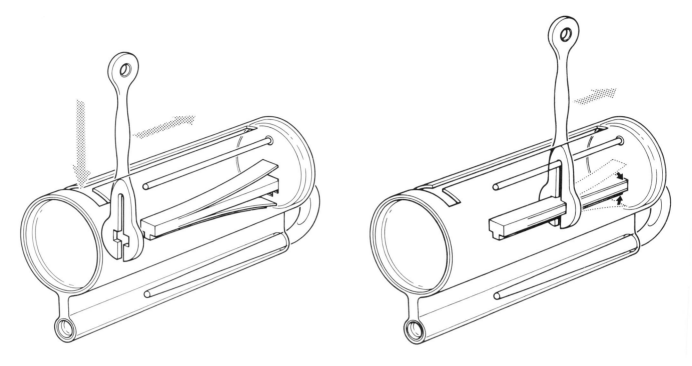

Fig.1444 *(above and facing) Reconstruction of barrel padlock* 13045, *using key* 12648

of c.1420–30 (Fig.1450, p.2873). The bits of hollow stem keys, as in the pre-Conquest period, are usually simple in form with cuts out of the sides and base, but some (e.g. *14070* from a late medieval context at Bedern) have a vertical central channel which divides the bit into two halves. This is not a medieval innovation as an Anglo-Scandinavian key from Coppergate (Fig.286, *3653, AY* 17/6) has a bit with a central channel, but it was more commonly used in the medieval period. It implies a lock with a central ward plate like *14053* (see above) over which the bit must pass. A number of hollow stem keys, including *12599, 12601* and *12603* from Coppergate, are plated and have incised grooves.

Fig.1445 *Iron barrel padlock case* 12563 *from 16–22 Coppergate. Actual length 79mm*

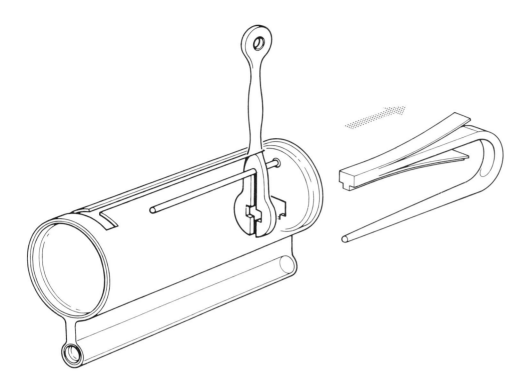

Keys with solid stems are relatively uncommon in late Anglo-Saxon/Anglo-Scandinavian contexts. They are usually small and used for casket locks of various forms including those with bolts and tumblers as referred to above. Large keys with solid stems similar in form to those with hollow stems and used in door locks only become common in the 12th century and are numerous in the medieval assemblages under discussion.

Based on the form of the bit, three sub-types can be identified. In the first two the stem projects beyond the bit. This implies a lock with some form of socket in which the key tip engaged rather than the spindle required by a key with a hollow stem. On some stems including those of *13268* (late 13th century context) from the Foundry and *14071* (mid–late 13th century context) from Bedern the tip is stepped in to enabled the key to be more easily fitted into place in the socket.

Fig.1446 Iron barrel padlock case 12564 from 16–22 Coppergate. Actual length 64mm

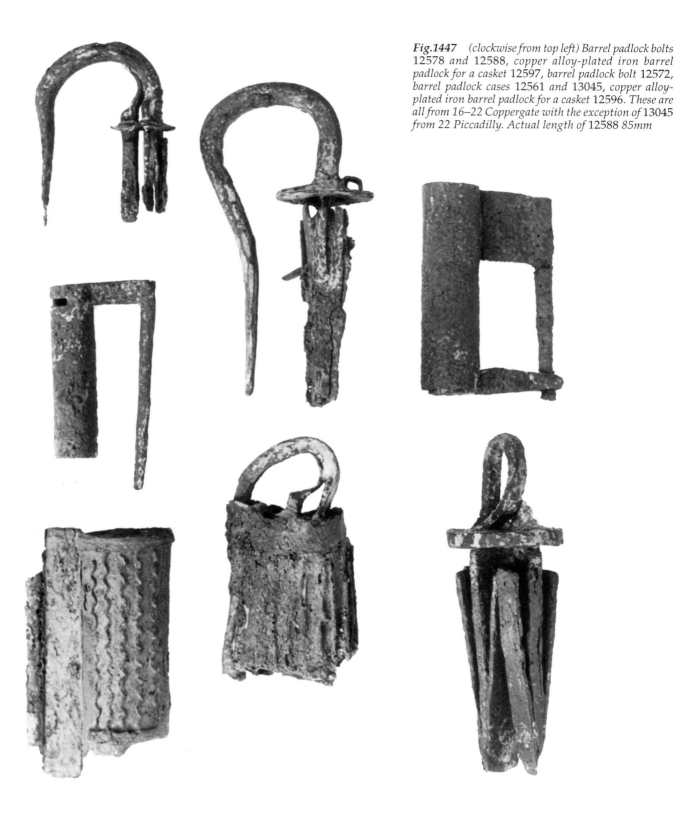

Fig.1447 (clockwise from top left) Barrel padlock bolts 12578 and 12588, copper alloy-plated iron barrel padlock for a casket 12597, barrel padlock bolt 12572, barrel padlock cases 12561 and 13045, copper alloy-plated iron barrel padlock for a casket 12596. These are all from 16–22 Coppergate with the exception of 13045 from 22 Piccadilly. Actual length of 12588 85mm

Fig.1448 (facing page) Iron barrel padlock bolts 12572, 12578–9, 12588, 12593–4 from 16–22 Coppergate, 13265 from the Foundry, 14056–7 from Bedern, 15087–8 from 46–54 Fishergate; copper alloy-plated iron barrel padlocks for caskets 12596–7 from 16–22 Coppergate; copper alloy padlock 14289 from Bedern. The toned areas on 12597 represent internal mechanism revealed by X-ray. Scale 1:2, 14289 1:1

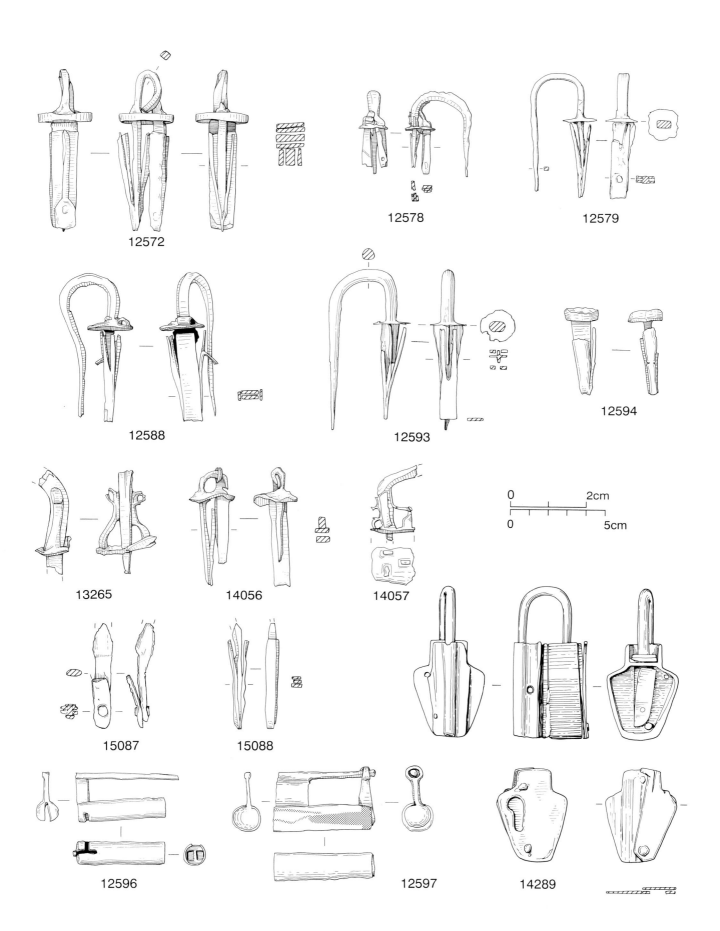

12572

12578

12579

12588

12593

12594

13265

14056

14057

0   2cm

0   5cm

15087

15088

12596

12597

14289

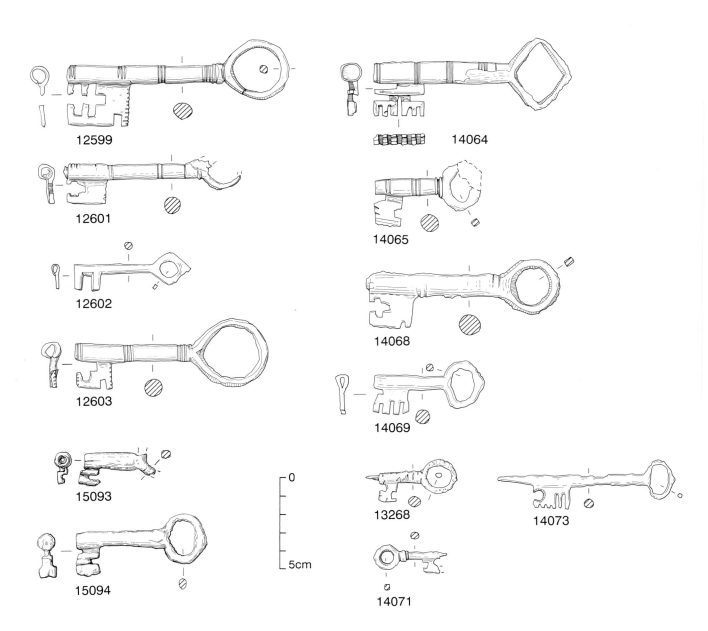

Fig.1449 *Iron keys with hollow stems for mounted locks* 12599, 12601–3 *from 16–22 Coppergate,* 14064–5, 14068–9 *from Bedern,* 15093–4 *from 46–54 Fishergate; iron keys with solid stems projecting beyond the bit which does not have a central channel* 13268 *from the Foundry,* 14071 *and* 14073 *from Bedern. Scale 1:2*

In terms of form, the bits of keys of the first sub-type (of which there are nine examples) have cuts in the sides and base. In the second sub-type the bit has a central vertical channel which divides it in two (e.g. *12606* from Coppergate, *14076* from Bedern, and *15096–7* from Fishergate). This sub-type remained current into the post-medieval period to which, on the basis of stem form, *14611* found unstratified at Bedern Chapel belongs.

On keys with a solid stem of the third sub-type the stem does not project beyond the bit, but between stem and bit there is a horizontal channel. All six examples from the York sites under discussion come from Bedern (e.g *14080*, mid 14th century, and *14084*, late medieval context) and there is none from Coppergate or Fishergate. This is a little surprising as keys of this type usually come from late 11th–13th century contexts.

Fig.1450 *An early 15th century representation of St Peter with the key of heaven from the* **Bolton Hours,** *c.1420–30 (Add. MS 2, fo.38r; reproduced by courtesy of York Minster Archive, © Dean and Chapter of York)*

Fig.1451 *(top to bottom, left) Keys for mounted locks 15097 and 15096 from 46–54 Fishergate, 14080 from Bedern, 15094 from 46–54 Fishergate, 14290–1 from Bedern; (top to bottom, right) 14064, 14076 from Bedern, 12606 and 12599 from 16–22 Coppergate. All are iron except 14290–1 which are copper alloy. Actual length of 15097 139mm*

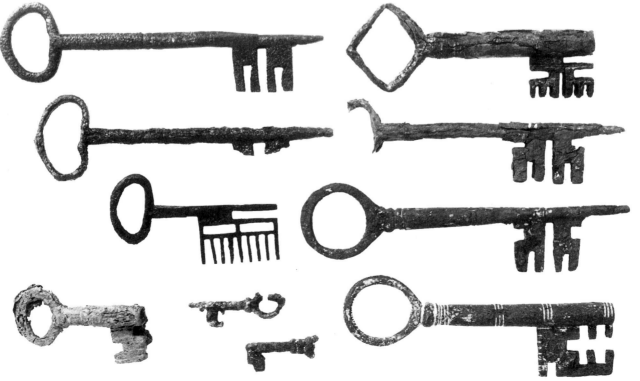

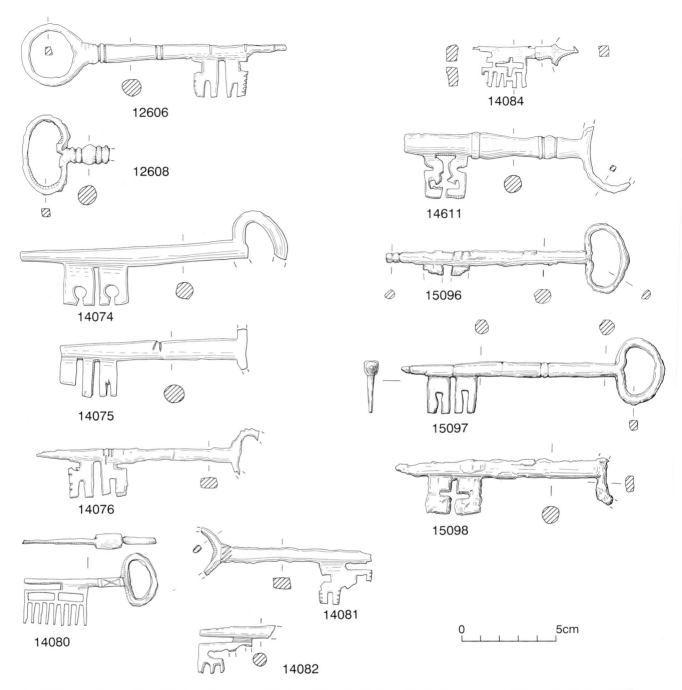

Fig.1452 *Iron keys with solid stems for mounted locks* 12606, 12608 *from 16–22 Coppergate,* 14074–6, 14080–2, 14084 *from Bedern,* 14611 *from Bedern Chapel,* 15096–8 *from 46–54 Fishergate. Scale 1:2*

Fig.1453 *(facing page) Iron barrel padlock keys with their bits at an angle to the stem* 12613–14, 12620, 12622, 12625, 12628–9, 12632, 12634, 12639 *from 16–22 Coppergate,* 12999 *from the Coppergate watching brief,* 14088 *from Bedern; copper alloy barrel padlock key with its bit at an angle to the stem* 12878 *from 16–22 Coppergate. Scale 1:2,* 12878 *scale 1:1*

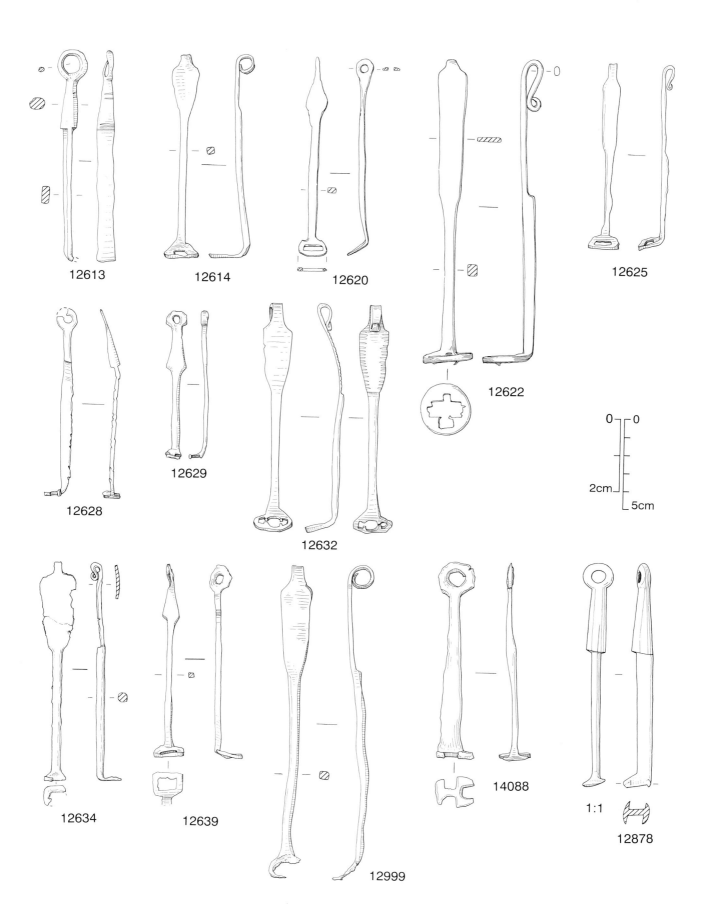

12613

12614

12620

12625

12622

12628

12629

12632

0 — 0

2cm —

5cm

12634

12639

12999

14088

1:1

12878

2875

The solid stem keys usually have D-shaped or oval bows, but *12608* and *13267* from post-medieval contexts at Coppergate and Bedern Foundry respectively, and *15096* from Fishergate (15th–16th century context) have the kidney-shaped bows which start to appear in the late medieval period and become common in the post-medieval era.

Finally, it may be noted that, as in the case of the hollow stem keys, there are many examples of keys with solid stems which have mouldings between bow and stem and bear incised grooves and non-ferrous plating.

Padlock keys (Figs.1443–4, 1453–7)

Iron

There are 56 barrel padlock keys from the sites under discussion. Of these, 36 have their bits at an angle of c.45°–90° to the stem. This implies use in a padlock of one of the first two types described above with a key hole at the end of the case. The bits are usually rounded, although that of *12625* is nearer rectangular and a number have cuts taken out of the sides of the bit (e.g. *12629*) which negates the roundedness to a greater or lesser extent.

The stems are usually widened and flattened near the centre, sometimes with an abrupt step (e.g. *12634*), to create a plate at the head which is usually more or less triangular (e.g. *12614, 12622, 12632* and *12999*), but can be diamond-shaped (*12620, 12639*) or oval (*12615*). Key *12628* (early 12th century context) and *12613* (13th–14th century context) are rather different in that near the head the stem steps out from its wider faces before tapering to the terminal. Terminals above triangular plates are usually looped, often with a recurved tip (e.g. *12622*). Terminals on the keys with diamond-shaped plates and on *12613* and *12628* are pierced. A similar copper alloy key to *12628*, *12878* comes from a 12th–13th century context at Coppergate (see below). Padlock keys with bits at an angle to the stem are usually undecorated, but *12632* (early 12th century context) has short grooves cut into the edge of one face of the plate at the top of stem and *12639* (unstratified) is tin plated.

Sixteen barrel padlock keys have their bits in line with the stem which implies that they were used in locks which had an elongated T-shaped key hole cut into the case. Surprisingly, perhaps, no locks of this

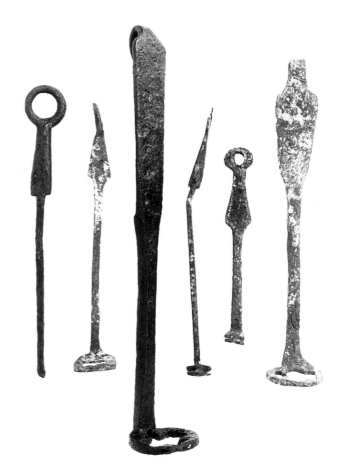

Fig.1454 *Iron barrel padlock keys with their bits at an angle to the stem: (left to right)* 12613, 12639, 12622, 12628, 12629, 12623, *all from 16–22 Coppergate. Actual length of* 12613 *116mm*

type were identified in the assemblage under discussion. As would be expected, the keys usually have a round bit (e.g. *12643, 12646, 12653* and *13047*) or, like *12642, 12645* and *12648*, a bit with a rounded component and an extension at the top which accommodated additional spines or springs in the lock. Rather different are the bits of *12640–1* which consist of four short projections, two on each side, from a spine at the base of the stem. Unusual also is the bit of *12647* which has an inverted T-shaped prong at the base of a D-shaped component.

The stems of these keys are usually rounded in cross-section, swell in the centre and have a moulding at head and base. Of these all except *12645, 12649* and *13047* have a spiral groove which is or was inlaid (e.g. *12640, 12642–4, 12653*). *13047* has a plain

Fig.1455 *Barrel padlock keys of very similar form: (left)* 12656 *in iron, (right)* 12878 *in copper alloy, both from 16–22 Coppergate. Actual length of* 12656 *67mm*

the bit in line with the stem from Bedern where occupation only began in earnest in the mid 13th century.

Four padlock keys from Coppergate (*12654–7*) have bits which are formed from four short teeth which project, two on each side, from the base of the stem. They all have stems which, like *12628* (see above), step out near the head before tapering to the base of the terminal. The terminals are, again like *12628*, pierced. *12655* has a spiral groove around the head of the stem which is inlaid with brass. Keys of this form elsewhere are usually from 12th–13th century contexts (Goodall 1980b, 140–1) and at Coppergate *12656* is from a mid 12th century context, *12655* is from a later 12th century context, *12654* is clearly residual in a 17th century context and *12657* is unstratified.

There are two box padlock keys from medieval contexts at the sites under discussion: *12658* from a mid 12th century context at Coppergate and one already published as *5242* from a 13th–early 14th century context at Fishergate (p.1423, Figs.696–7, *AY* 17/9). The operation of the form of box padlock with which these keys were used is shown in *AY* 17/6 (Fig.292). *5242* is relatively simple in form, but *12658* is a more elaborate object. It is tin plated and the central stem is spirally twisted and surrounded by a 'cage' of three additional strips with 'rope-work' down the sides.

Although the box padlock may have survived in use until the end of the 11th century, both the objects under discussion are probably residual. *5242* is presumably of Anglian origin and *12658* of Anglo-Scandinavian origin. *12658* is a more elaborate version of *3673* from an Anglo-Scandinavian context at Coppergate and there are many comparable examples from Scandinavia (p.677, *AY* 17/6). It should be noted that in *AY* 17/6 (Fig.291) *12658* is illustrated in error as *3673*; both keys are illustrated here in Fig.1458.

stem and on *12649* there are criss-cross grooves. *12646* has a near straight stem of rectangular cross-section. At the head of these keys there are or were pierced terminals of various forms. Set in the terminal of *12642* is a small ring by which the key was suspended from a belt.

The padlock with an elongated T-shaped key hole probably ceased to be current after the early 13th century and the date of the majority of the related keys from York and elsewhere seems to bear this out. *12649* is from a late 11th century context, but the remainder are from 12th–13th century contexts except for *12653* which is unstratified. It may also be significant that there are no examples of these keys with

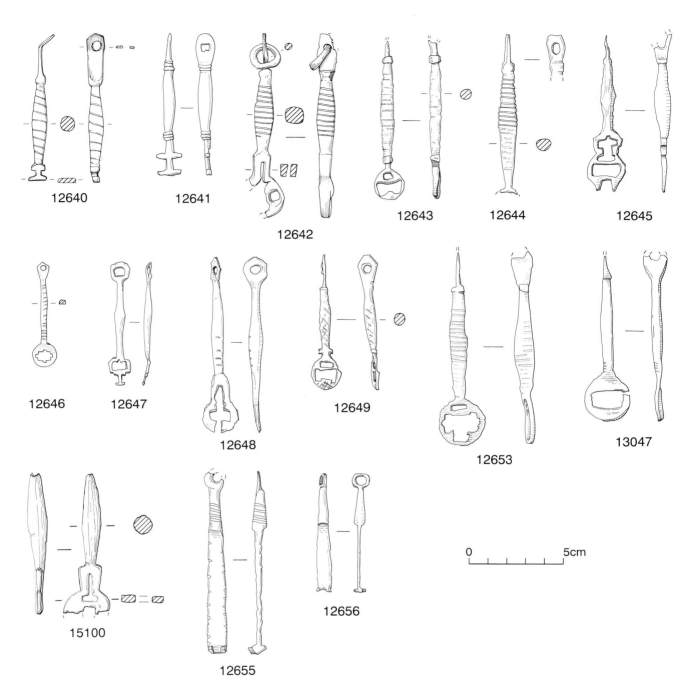

Fig.1456 *Iron barrel padlock keys with their bits in line with the stem 12640–9 and 12653 from 16–22 Coppergate, 13047 from 22 Piccadilly, 15100 from 46–54 Fishergate; keys with bits composed of short projections 12655–6 from 16–22 Coppergate. Scale 1:2*

Copper alloy barrel padlock key (Figs.1453, 1455)

A single copper alloy barrel padlock key with a circular bit at 90° to the stem was found in a 12th–13th century dumped deposit at Coppergate (*12878*); with its upper stem having an octagonal section, and its perforated terminal, it closely resembles iron key *12628*, with which it may be contemporary. Although the vast majority of such keys are made of iron, others of copper alloy are known: see an example from High Street, Hull (A.R. Goodall 1987a, 206, fig.118, *247*).

Fig.1457 *Iron barrel padlock keys with their bits in line with the stem: (left to right)* 12643, 12645, 12647, 12648, 12646, *all from 16–22 Coppergate. Actual length of* 12643 *89mm*

Iron latch keys (Fig.1459)

There are two so-called latch keys which were used in locks where the bolt was held in place with springs as in a padlock (Goodall 1980b, 154–5). *14090–1* both come from mid 14th–15th century contexts at Bedern. As can be seen on these examples, latch keys typically have a bow and short stem and then a bit which is multi-chambered. *14091* also has a projection from the tip of the bit which can be seen on examples elsewhere. Latch keys appear to have first been used in the late 12th century to judge by an example of this date from London (Egan 1998, 100–2, *267*), but the type usually seems to come from contexts of the late medieval period.

Casket keys (Fig.1460)

Two small copper alloy keys which were recovered from Bedern (*14290–1*) lack complete bows, but can be identified as probable casket or chest keys; several similar keys have been found in London (Ward Perkins 1940, 144, pl.XXX, *34–7*; Egan 1998, 111–12, fig.86, *294–8*), Norwich (Margeson 1993, 163, fig.120, *1311, 1313*), and Windsor, Berkshire (Mills 1993, 39, fig.18, *1*). *14290* was found in a mid 14th–early 15th century dump, while *14291* was unstratified.

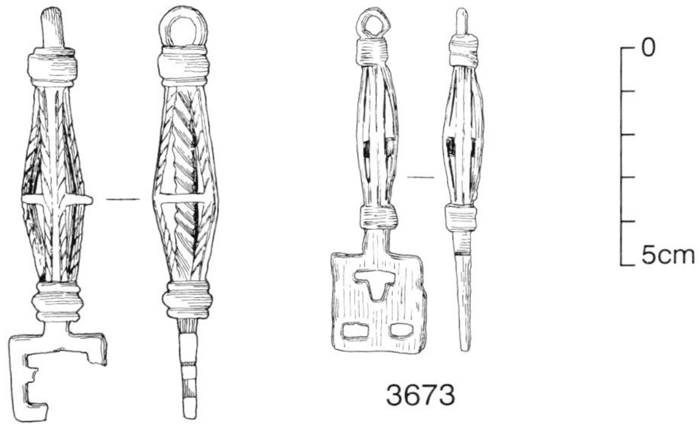

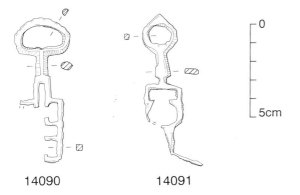

Fig.1458 *Iron box padlock keys* 12658 *(wrongly published in* AY *17/6) and* 3673, *both from 16–22 Coppergate. Scale 1:2*

Fig.1459 *Iron latch keys* 14090–1 *from Bedern. Scale 1:2*

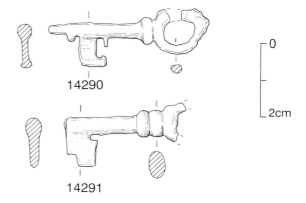

Fig.1460 *Copper alloy casket keys* 14290–1 *from Bedern. Scale 1:1*

Dress, dress accessories and personal ornament

Textile and yarn

by Penelope Walton Rogers, Textile Research, York (UK)

Introduction

No large collections of textiles from medieval York have as yet been published, but the small groups gathered together here, from Bedern, Fishergate and 22 Piccadilly, represent a useful cross-section of fabric-types in use in the medieval town. They may be compared with another small collection from 16–22 Coppergate which was published in *AY* 17/5. Since publication, some of the later stratigraphy at Coppergate has been revised, and the medieval textiles from that site, with revised dates, have therefore been included in Table 302.

The excavations at the three Bedern sites have yielded twenty separately itemised finds of textile and three of yarn, together with five braids or cords associated with copper alloy objects (see p.2885) and one imprint of a textile on a potsherd. Most of these come from the garden of the College of the Vicars Choral and the adjacent Foundry, with two from the Chapel and two from the centre of the College precinct. The textiles represent a full range of fabric-types, from coarse sackcloth, through wool clothing and household linen, to more prestigious textiles, such as silks and half-silks. In contrast, the small number of textiles from the Gilbertine priory at Fishergate represent only the middle range of clothing and household fabrics. The only textile from

medieval Piccadilly was another fragment of sack-cloth, but some linen textiles from late Anglo-Scandinavian levels have been included here for the sake of completeness.

Wool clothing fabrics

There are seven textiles from the Foundry, Bedern and Fishergate which are typical of wool clothing fabrics in the medieval and post-medieval periods. Five fragments, including an uncatalogued imprint on a pottery sherd, are woven in 2/1 twill (*14588, 14591, 15293–4*) and two in tabby (*14589–90*). There are also two clumps of yarn which have probably unravelled from a coarse wool textile of unknown weave (*14586–7*).

2/1 twill

One fragment from Bedern (*14588*) is an example of the most common textile type of the 11th to 14th centuries, with its 2/1 twill weave, yarn spun Z x S, and one matted face. Offcuts of similar fabrics, probably from a tailor's workshop, were found at Parliament Street, York (Fig.1314, **8**; YAT 1976–7.11; pp.232–4, *AY* 17/4), and others, clearly the remains of finished garments, have been recovered from many other sites in England (Crowfoot 1979; Crowfoot et al. 1992, 28). Three examples of the same fabric-type were recovered from medieval Coppergate (*1414–16*), the latest of which, from a 15th century pit, is almost certainly residual. The Bedern example is a good-quality, medium-weight fabric (cf. scatter diagrams Walton 1988, fig.30; Crowfoot et al. 1992, fig.13). A coarser example of the same weave has been impressed into the outer face of a sherd of Humber ware from the Foundry (context 880, Bay P4g), although this imprint is more likely to represent the clothing of the potter rather than any fabric worn at Bedern.

Two further fragments of 2/1 twill from the priory at Fishergate (*15293–4*) are from a part of the site loosely dated to the 13th–16th centuries. In fact, the 2/1 weave structure is almost unknown among 15th and 16th century wool textiles and only re-appears in fine 17th century worsteds of the type represented at Bedern by *14591*. The Fishergate pieces are there-

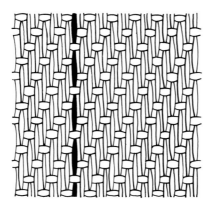

Fig.1461   Weave diagram of the 2/1 twills with single dark blue thread running through the warp from 46–54 Fishergate, 15293–4

Table 302 Textiles and yarn from Bedern, the Foundry and 16–22 Coppergate

Bedern, including Bedern Chapel	The Foundry	16–22 Coppergate Textiles Period 6: revised dating
Period 1A, 11th/12th century 14585 linen yarn, Z-spun, spinner's waste		*Late 11th or early 12th century* 1414 wool 2/1, 14Z x 7S, dyed ?orange
		12th century 1421 wool 2/2, 11Z x 8–10S, indigotin in Z only 1458 imprint of ?tabby in lead spill
Period 2, mid–late 13th century 14598 mineralised tabby, 18–20Z x 16–18I		*13th century* 1443 linen tabby, 20–22Z x 14–16Z 1444 linen tabby, 22Z x 22Z 1445 linen tabby, 20Z x 12Z, bleached
	Period 2, late 13th–early 14th century 13430 linen tabby, 2Z x 3prsZ, stitched 13428 linen tabby, 17–20Z x 12–14Z 13431 as 13430 13432 wool tabby, 2/Z-ply x 2–3/Z-ply	
Period 6, mid–late 14th century 14588 wool 2/1, 15Z x 10S, ?madder 14599 silk cord, Z2S	*Period 3, 14th century* 13434 silk yarn, Z2S, probably as 13435 13435 silk tabby ? prs x Z2S, madder 13427 wool tabby, 10Z x 12S, with striped band ('ray') 13433 silk tabby, 40Z x 36I, black dye	*Late 14th or early 15th century* 1417 wool tabby, 9Z x 9–10S, with striped bands ('ray'), madder 1457 silk yarn I2S
Period 7, late 14th–early 15th century 14589 wool tabby, 14Z x 14–16S, ?weld 14586 wool threads, S, coarse, red dye 14592 linen tabby, 12Z x 12–14Z 14600 wool cord, S2S 14489 mineralised cords, S-ply, inside bells 14587 wool threads, S, coarse		*15th century* 1416 wool 2/1, 12Z x 7S 1418 wool tabby, 13Z x 9–10S, madder 1419 wool tabby, 12–14Z x 12–14S 1420 wool tabby, 13–14Z x 13–14S, ?madder 1422 linen and wool tabby, 4 x 20S, madder and indigotin
Period 8, mid 15th–early 17th century 14590 wool tabby, 7–9 Z and S x 5S, red dye 14312 flax inside buckle 14354 silk tablet braid, 20 x 24 prs, on strap-end	*Period 6, mid 15th–early 17th century* 13429 linen tabby, 14Z x 12Z	
Period 9, mid 17th century onwards 14591 wool, ?2/1, 30–36Z x 18–20?S 14460 linen braid, in aiglet 14654 silk and silver tabby, 18S x 70Z	*Period 7, mid 17th century onwards* 13389 silk braid, in aiglet	*Unstratified* 1415 wool 2/1, 11Z x 6–7Z and S

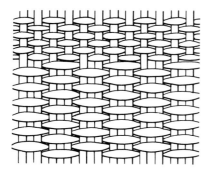

Fig.1462 Weave diagram of the tabby with extended tabby coloured bands from the Foundry, 13427

just inside the Bedern College precinct (*AY* 10/3, 172). The main fabric is a tabby weave of unremarkable quality, but across the middle of the fragment runs a narrow band of coloured stripes. The structure of the band in 2/2 extended tabby (Figs.1462–3) is such that the stripes form continuous lines, uninterrupted by the warp. The band is 12·5mm wide and made up of weft threads in the order, 11 red, 15 green, 2 red, 10 green, 2 red, 5 green, 4 undyed silk, 2 same colour as ground weave. The ground weave is now brown, but dye analysis shows it to have been given a weak dyeing with madder, which would have put it somewhere in the colour range of salmon, pale tan or apricot.

Another example of the same fabric-type has been recorded from a late 14th or early 15th century pit fill at 16–22 Coppergate (pp.383, 389–390, *1417*, *AY* 17/5). The Coppergate piece was poorly preserved (pl.XXXIVa, *AY* 17/5), but may be reconstructed as a natural white ground with bands over 25mm wide, striped in brown, red and white. The best-preserved band has weft threads in the order 2 red, 6 white, 6 brown, 18 red, 8 white, ≥4 brown (incomplete), but there are other bands with different arrangements of stripes. Some plied silk threads found in association

fore likely to belong to the 13th or 14th century. These fragments probably originated in the same cloth, as they have S-spun yarn in warp and weft, an unusual feature shared with only a small percentage of the large medieval collections of 2/1 twills from London (Crowfoot et al. 1992, 35). More uniquely, both the Fishergate pieces have a single dark blue thread running through the warp (Fig.1461). Most of the 2/1 twills recorded so far appear unpatterned, although a few simple checks have been found at Durham (Crowfoot 1979, 38–9) and London (Crowfoot et al. 1992, 31), and the 13th century ordinances of the London guild show that patterned fabrics formed part of the guild weaver's craft (*Liber Custumarum* **2**, 125). The Fishergate example, originally a white fabric with lines of dark blue fleck, is a new addition to our knowledge of these medieval patterns.

Tabby weave

As 2/1 twill became less popular for wool textiles during the course of the 14th century, its place was taken by tabby weave (pp.385–6, *AY* 17/5). The wool tabby weave textile (*14589*) from 15th century Bedern, with yarn spun Z x S, is a typical medium-quality wool clothing fabric of the late 14th to early 16th century (Walton 1981, 193–5; Crowfoot et al. 1992, 27, 45). This example seems to have been dyed yellow, but two of the three similar fabrics from 15th century Coppergate (*1417*, *1420*) had been dyed red. A coarser example from post-medieval levels of Bedern, *14590*, is more unevenly spun and woven and this, too, has been dyed red.

Tabby with coloured bands, known as 'ray'

A fragment of patterned wool textile (*13427*) was recovered during the Foundry excavations from mid–late 14th century layers of a large cess pit, situated

Fig.1463 Wool textile in tabby weave with a band of closely woven stripes in extended tabby weave, 13427 from the Foundry. Actual length 112mm

with the textile remains (*1457*) are identical with the silk yarn in the Bedern piece and it seems likely that they originally formed part of the striped bands.

Textiles with bands of colour in this distinctive weft-faced weave seem to have been current in northern Europe in the 13th and 14th centuries. Nine examples are recorded from Amsterdam and Dordrecht, Netherlands (Vons-Comis 1982, 156), five from Novgorod, Russia (Nahlik 1963, 252–4), and one from Lübeck, Germany (Tidow 1990, 168–9). By far the largest collection, with 91 separate items, comes from the 14th century dock at Baynard's Castle, London, not far from the site of the medieval Royal Wardrobe (Crowfoot et al. 1992, 52–68). Two late examples are also known from London, from Trig Lane and Swan Lane, both from the first half of the 15th century (ibid., 208–9).

The ground weave of these fabrics is remarkably standardised. Almost all have Z-spun warp and S-spun weft, and most fall within a narrow range of thread-count, 9–11 ´ 8–12 per cm. Patterns and colours, on the other hand, seem to be infinitely variable and it is impossible to find an exact match for either of the York pieces in any of the published collections. The London evidence, however, suggests that the arrangement of stripes within bands became increasingly complex through the course of the 14th century (ibid., 54). In this respect, the two York examples, with three-colour stripes plus silk in the bands, have most in common with the late 14th century group.

These fabrics with bands of colour have been identified as the documented medieval cloth, 'ray' (Crowfoot et al. 1992, 52). Certainly, in technical terms they match the Franco-Flemish descriptions of the 13th and 14th century cloth called 'roie' (Espinas 1913, 802–8), which was traded into England under the name of 'ray' (Buyse 1955, 177–201). To the English, however, 'ray' seems to have been a catch-all term, covering other striped fabrics, such as 'ray velvet', as well as Flemish roie (Beck 1886, 272–3). When the York weavers' guild in 1164 claimed a monopoly in rayed cloth, *panni reati* (York City MS, transcribed in Sellers 1974, 407), at this early date they were probably thinking of a simpler striped weave rather than the one described here. When the same charter was re-affirmed in 1347 (Calendar of the Patent Rolls Pat.20 Edw.III, pt.iii, m.19), the meaning of *panni reati*

may have changed, as Flemish rays became better known. Flemish cloths had been traded into York through much of the 13th and 14th centuries (Buyse 1955, 18, 127, 170–2), and rays were among those unloaded at Hull in 1391/2 (ibid., 98). Weavers from the Low Countries also settled in York during the course of the 14th century (Heaton 1965, 13–16). At the present stage it is impossible to say whether the two York examples of tabbies with coloured bands are original Flemish ray, or ray made in York using Flemish technology.

The 14th century documentary evidence concerning rays shows that they were one of the cheapest of the Flemish imports, although still a well-priced fabric on the English market (Buyse 1955, 181). They were relatively small cloths and used for simple garments requiring little cutting, such as hoods and surcoats, although there is also one instance of ray being used for bed furnishings (ibid., 184). Rays seem to have been worn by both sexes, and especially by the servants in wealthy households, as part of their livery (ibid., 184, 187–8, 197–8). By the second half of the 14th century 'raye hoddes' had also become the mark of 'bawdes and strumpettes' (Strutt **2** 1842, 217). The example of ray from Bedern is a torn fragment deposited in a College cess pit along with the remains of two half-silks (see below) and is perhaps more likely to come from the clothing of a servant at the College, rather than some local 'strumpette's' headgear.

Linens

Two linen textiles in tabby weave were recovered from the Foundry, one (*13428*) from a late 13th or early 14th century deposit, the other (*13429*) from mid 16th to early 17th century levels. A third example (*14592*) comes from the mid 14th or early 15th century garden of the Vicars Choral and a fourth (*15295*) from 15th/16th century Fishergate. There were some similar, and finer, linens from 13th century Coppergate (*1443* and *1445*, p.383, *AY* 17/5).

Linen fabrics such as these, in simple tabby weave without any ornament, were used for undergarments and for sheets, table cloths and other household textiles. Many of the York linens were probably made locally, as linen production had been established in the town since the 10th century (p.414, *AY* 17/5) and by 1518 linen weavers were numerous enough to form their own guild (*YMB* **2**, 242ff). Some waste ends of half-spun linen yarn, from 11th/12th century Bedern (*14585*), have been described above.

In passing, four unpublished examples of charred linen textiles from late Anglo-Scandinavian levels at 22 Piccadilly may be mentioned. These include fine (sf368), medium (sf570) and coarse (sf603) fabrics, comparable with the medieval group from Bedern and the Anglo-Scandinavian collection from 16–22 Coppergate (pp.345–59, *AY* 17/5). One item, however, is of especial interest. It is a small fragment of fine 2/2 diamond twill, sf1276, a high-quality representative of a fabric-type which has already been reported from the Anglo-Scandinavian period, but only in relatively small numbers (p.354, *AY* 17/5).

Sacking

There are three especially coarse textiles from the early 14th century Foundry, *13430–2*. One, (*13432*) is made from a hairy wool, the other two from a coarse plant fibre. Another example of the same fabric-type, made in cattle hair, comes from mid to late 12th century levels at 22 Piccadilly (*13079*). All are woven in tabby weave, but the wool and cattle hair examples are made with thick plied yarn in warp and weft, while the plant-fibre textiles have paired single threads in one direction. Both the plant-fibre examples have been stitched with a stiff sisal-like cord in an overcasting stitch.

Coarse textiles in plied yarn are a common textile-type of quayside and warehouse sites of northern Europe. Many examples, in goat hair, cattle hair and low-grade wool, have been recovered from medieval and post-medieval levels of ports such as Newcastle upon Tyne (Walton 1988, 82) and Bergen (Schjølberg 1984, 87–9). The contexts from which they come suggest that they may have been wrapping fabrics for merchandise (ibid.), which were sometimes re-used for other makeshift tasks. These fabrics are also found in monastic burials, where they are believed to represent the hair shirt of the penitent, but the identification as a wrapper or sacking seems more likely for the textiles recovered from the Foundry, and

also for the fragment from Piccadilly, which was not far from the medieval waterfront on the Foss.

Coarse textiles made from plant fibre are less common in the archaeological record, although this may be because plant fibres do not survive well in a damp climate. An example almost identical with the Bedern pieces has been recovered from late medieval layers of the barbican ditch at Oxford Castle (Crowfoot 1976, 274) and it is possible that such fabrics were more common than the surviving evidence suggests. They most probably represent another type of sacking.

Silks

A fragment of fine black tabby weave silk (*13433*) was recovered from an early 14th century pit fill at the Foundry. The piece is deeply dyed with a tannin-based dye such as oak galls, but has no pattern of any sort. The remains of an open-weave tabby (*14598*) from a mid–late 13th century pit within the College precinct may also be silk; the fibres are now mineralised, but the open, net-like weave, the fine yarn and the lack of twist in the yarn in one system are all typical of silk textiles. Another fragment of silk tabby (*14654*) was found under the floorboards at Bedern Chapel in a layer dated to the 17th century (*AY* 10/5, 649). This is a fine, lightweight textile with silver strip spun round a silk core (silver filé) for the warp and flat silver strip inserted into the weft (Fig.1464).

Plain silk tabbies such as *13433* and *14598* were simple fabrics, made in many silk weaving centres and available over a wide period of time. Silks were always a luxury and, although the plainer types may have been within the reach of a well-to-do burgher, the average artisan would have found it hard to afford such textiles. It is therefore curious that one of these fragments comes from the site of the Foundry.

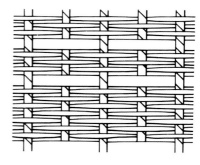

Fig.1464 *Weave diagram of silk and silver tabby from Bedern Chapel,* 14654

The silk and silver textile is much more compatible with its find-spot in the Chapel. The Church was always a great consumer of silks, especially those ornamented with silver and gold threads, for vestments and cloths associated with the liturgy.

Half-silks

Two groups of silk yarn, *13434–5*, both from mid–late 14th century levels of a cess pit just within the College precinct, are almost certainly the remains of half-silks, that is, textiles in which a silk weft has been combined with a linen warp yarn. In both cases the silk yarn lies in a flat plane, with regular imprints where the warp yarn, no longer present, originally crossed the weft. Similar remains have been recovered from Skeldergate (Fig.1314, **14**; YAT 1974.14, sf1072), although that piece is worked in single silk yarn, whereas the two Bedern examples are plied. All three appear to have been worked on a paired warp, one of the Bedern examples (*13435*) probably in an extended tabby weave, but the others in some more elaborate construction such as weft-faced twill.

In the 13th and 14th centuries most of the Mediterranean silk-weaving centres were still concentrating on all-silk textiles, although Spanish and Venetian workshops had begun to use a linen warp for some fabrics (May 1957, 60; Geijer 1979, 59, 145–6). These linen-silk textiles were generally weft faced, as the three York examples appear to be, so that the linen warp was hidden from view. Although half-silks were less costly than full silks, they were still handsome fabrics which could be used where a heavy material was required, for draperies and for the lining of the more elaborate kinds of silk or fur clothing (May 1957).

Belts or straps

The remains of two woven braids were found in 15th century levels at Bedern. The first is a poorly preserved silk tablet-woven braid, riveted into a copper alloy strap clasp, *14354* (see pp.2897–8). The braid is 12mm wide and has a central patterned zone, a tabby with warp floats worked on two-hole tablets, flanked on either side by a single four-hole cord; the raw warp ends of the braid have been tucked back under the braid before riveting. The second braid is represented by some linen threads visible in side view inside the belt plate of a copper alloy buckle (*14312*); the construction of this braid is hidden by the belt plate.

In the medieval period, flat braids, often patterned, were used for belts, girdles and straps such as those used to fasten spurs. Most surviving examples are constructed by tablet-weaving, a technique which produces a solid, inelastic band. The cheaper linen braids were probably the more common (Crowfoot 1950, Crowfoot 1954, Walton 1987), except in London, where silkwomen were employed to make these 'narrow wares' for the court and for other wealthy citizens (Dale 1934). A number of silk braids have been recovered from London sites (Crowfoot et al. 1992, 131–5), but outside the capital they are largely limited to church burials and sites such as Bedern with ecclesiastical connections.

Laces

Laces for fastening garments are represented by a thin tubular silk braid inside a post-medieval 'aiglet' or lace tag from the Foundry (*13389*) and a narrow, flat linen braid, folded lengthways into another post-medieval aiglet from the College (*14460*). *14599*, a silk cord from a 14th century cess pit at Bedern, may well be another garment lace, although it does not have a metal aiglet attached. Garment laces could be made in leather, silk or linen and constructed as braids, plaits, cords or simple tabby ribbons. The tubular silk braid *13389* appears to be tablet-woven, in the manner of the thin tubular braids from 14th century London (Crowfoot et al. 1992, 135–6). The flat linen braid *14460* is more like the broader silk ribbons from 17th century Dudley Castle, West Midlands, which had to be folded in order to fit into the aiglet (Walton Rogers unpublished). Laces such as these were used by both sexes for threading garment parts together, the aiglet helping to guide the lace through the eyelets (for corrrect terminology see Walton Rogers 1993).

Summary of the textile evidence

It has been noted above that three of the medieval textiles recovered during excavation of Bedern Foundry are in fact from that part of the site which lies just outside the Foundry and within the College grounds (*AY* 10/3, 172). If these three (*13427, 13433, 13435*) are amalgamated with the other textiles from within the College precinct, it becomes clear that most of the better-quality fabrics and the more luxurious textiles such as silks are concentrated within the area of the College, as is to be expected of a site with ecclesiastical connections. Several of the textiles come from pits, in at least one instance a cess pit. These are likely to be worn fabrics, torn up and re-used as latrine wipes. This may seem a cavalier attitude to expensive textiles, but it is clear from other sites, such as 17th century Dudley Castle, that the textile content of cess pits and garderobes tends to reflect the clothing and furnishings of the house to which they belong (Walton Rogers unpublished).

The medieval textiles from the Foundry itself consist of three coarse fabrics, probably sacking, two ordinary linens and one piece of silk. It has been remarked that a silk, even a plain one such as this, is a surprising find from an industrial complex. Julian Richards has, however, already noted that there was a certain amount of movement of both people and rubbish across the boundary between the College and the Foundry (AY 10/3, 151). Indeed, the College may have been landlord to the Foundry (ibid., 203) and individual members of the Vicars Choral may have visited the site.

The textile fragments from the priory at Fishergate are too few to allow any useful general comment. They are standard wool and linen fabrics, unremarkable except for the evidence for a blue fleck pattern in the two wool examples. The single piece of sacking from medieval Piccadilly is typical of waterfront sites, especially quaysides, of the period.

Raw animal fibre

There are five clumps of raw fibre from Bedern, all dated to the late 14th or early 15th century. The fibres have been examined by H.M. Appleyard, a specialist in animal coat fibres, who has identified three as goat hair (14593–4, 14596), one as horse hair (14595), and one as cattle hair (14597). The goat hair came from a layer of garden soil containing domestic debris, and the horse and cattle hair from rubbish pits dug into the same garden area (J. Richards, pers. comm.). It is possible that loose tufts of fibre from work-animals, or from pelts used for garments and furnishings, were swept from the house and stables and deposited on the garden or in the refuse pits. A single clump of animal fibre has been recovered from 15th/16th century Piccadilly (13078). This has been identified by the author as calf hair and it came from a group of deposits which yielded butchered cattle bones and perhaps also animal manure (Carrott et al. 1995, 8).

Buckles

Buckles of iron, copper alloy and, to a lesser extent, lead alloy were found on all the sites; the range of basic forms is common to the different metals used, although there was more decorative embellishment on the copper alloy buckles, perhaps indicating greater use of this material for buckles on clothing or in other very visible roles. The generally plainer iron buckles also probably served as dress fittings, but, some at least, were part of horse harness.

Annular buckles (Fig.1465)

The simplest buckle-frames are annular. There has been some confusion in the past as to the distinction in form between annular brooches and annular buckles (see Egan and Pritchard 1991, 64–5); in the analysis of the York assemblage, Egan's definition of brooch frames having a constriction or a hole for the pin, and buckle-frames lacking a constriction or hole, has been followed (ibid., 248). Employing these criteria, 12879–81 and 14292–4 have been identified as non-ferrous annular buckles. (For annular brooches from the York sites, see pp.2911–14).

Two of the buckles, 12880 and 14294, have pins with decorative mouldings; the pin on 14293 is plain. All three are similar in size with diameters of 41.5–45.1mm. While 14294 is likely to be residual in its Period 9 context, 12880 and 14293 derive from 14th–early 15th century levels, as do similar examples found in London (ibid., 58), and a slightly smaller but otherwise comparable buckle recovered from a burial at the Austin Friars in Leicester (Clay 1981, 133, fig.48, 24). The other annular buckle from Coppergate (12879), found in a 13th–14th century deposit, is somewhat smaller, with a diameter of only 14.7mm. Buckles of this size from the 14th–15th centuries have sometimes been identified as shoe buckles (ibid., 57), although they were more commonly made of iron or lead alloy (Grew and de Neergaard 1988, 75) (see below). Also from a 14th century context, the fragmentary 14292 is only tentatively identified as an annular buckle.

Shoe buckles (Fig.1465)

13419–22, 14544–7, 14651 and 15281 are small annular or sub-oval buckles of lead alloy; most have lost their pins, but those that survive, for example on 14545 and 15281 are of iron. Their diameters exhibit

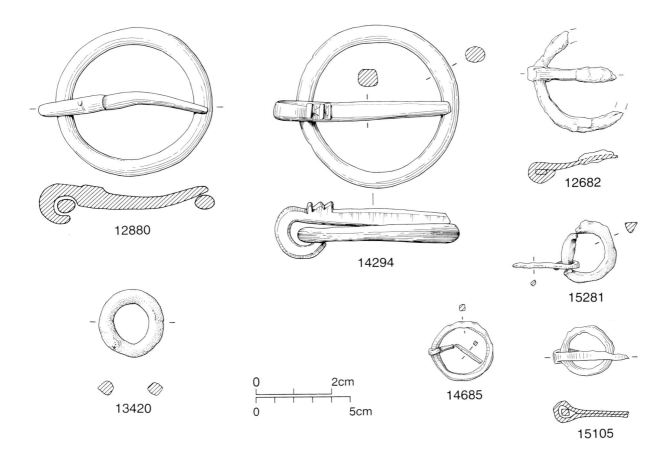

Fig.1465 *Annular buckles in copper alloy* 12880 *from 16–22 Coppergate,* 14294 *from Bedern, and in iron* 12682 *from 16–22 Coppergate; shoe buckles in lead alloy* 13420 *from the Foundry and* 15281 *from 46–54 Fishergate; shoe buckles in iron* 14685 *from 2 Aldwark and* 15105 *from 46–54 Fishergate. Scale 1:1, iron objects 1:2*

a narrow range from c.15mm (*13419*) to c.18mm (*14546*). Excavations in London have yielded large numbers of these small lead/tin buckles with iron pins (Egan and Pritchard 1991, 62–4), some of which were attached to shoes (Grew and de Neergaard 1988, 75–6, table 14), and all of which came from early–mid 15th century deposits. Similarly, the earliest examples of these from York come from early 15th century deposits (*14544–5*), the majority of the others coming from later 15th and 16th century levels.

There are also five small circular iron shoe buckles one each from Bedern (*14098*, late medieval–post-medieval context), Bedern Chapel (*14613*, post-medieval context), Aldwark (*14685*) and three from Fishergate (*15103*, 13th–14th century context, and *15104–5*, 15th–16th century contexts). Three of these buckles are tin plated. Iron shoe buckles are very com-

mon in medieval contexts of 13th century and later date, and their relative absence here is surprising.

Oval buckles (Fig.1466)

Only four iron buckles have oval frames: *15107* from a 13th–early 14th century context at Fishergate is a large buckle-frame with straight sides and rounded ends. The others are *12659*, which retains its buckle-plate, *12684* from Coppergate and *15106* from Fishergate.

Amongst the non-ferrous buckles, oval types lent themselves to a number of variations in shape and decoration, and they have been recovered in much greater numbers than their iron counterparts. One of the earliest examples amongst the York buckles is *14297* from a mid 13th century context at Bedern; it

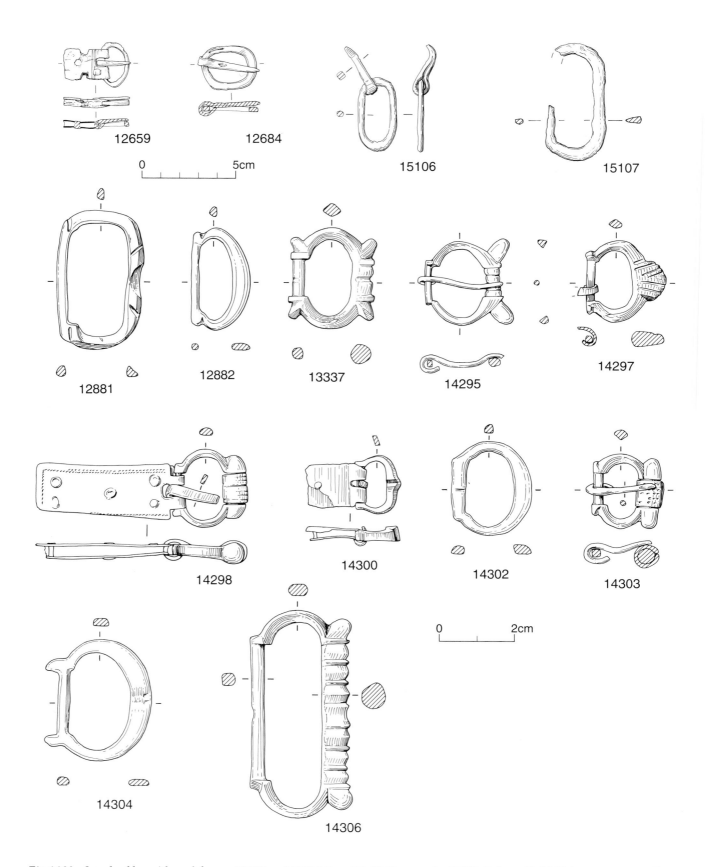

Fig.1466 *Iron buckles with oval frames* 12659 *and* 12684 *from 16–22 Coppergate,* 15106–7 *from 46–54 Fishergate; copper alloy buckles with oval frames* 12881–2 *from 16–22 Coppergate,* 13337 *from the Foundry,* 14295, 14297–8, 14300, 14302–4, 14306 *from Bedern. Iron objects scale 1:2, copper alloy objects scale 1:1*

has an expanded front and an almost lyre-shaped profile. A more ornate, but perhaps comparable, buckle was found with 13th century pottery at Riseholme, Lincolnshire (Thompson 1960, 106, fig.34.2). Unfortunately unstratified, *14305* also has an expanded front, and here the buckle-plate for attachment to the strap survives. Narrowed and often offset pin-bars are common features of oval buckles. They appear on simple oval buckles, such as *12882, 13334, 14299* and *14302,* on the lightly decorated *14296,* found close to another oval buckle *14297,* and on *12881.* They also appear on those with lipped front edges, of which *14300* is a good example. Their find-spots range in date from the 12th (*12882*) to the early 15th century (*14302*). They are also found on several buckles from Bedern which have moulded front edges; the earliest of these is *14295,* from a mid 13th century deposit, which has elaborate projecting knops, also seen on *13337* and the unstratified *14306.* Plainer mouldings appear on *13335* which retains a fragmentary buckle-plate and was found on the Foundry site. This type with mouldings is well known from 13th and 14th century contexts on other sites in Britain (see for example Atkin et al. 1985, 204, fig.35, *6*; Hinton 1990a, 517–19, fig.131, *1161, 1170–1*; Goodall 1991, 148–9, fig.114.590; Egan and Pritchard 1991, 72–4, fig.44) and on the Continent (Fingerlin 1971, 68–9, *51–72*). The belt buckle on the effigy of Berengaria, queen of Richard I, who died in 1230, seems also to be of this type (Egan and Pritchard 1991, 20, fig.10).

An oval buckle with small projections going back from the ends of the pin-bar, *14304* was found in post-medieval levels at Bedern, but comparable examples from elsewhere have derived from 14th century deposits. Two buckles from London, one still attached to pieces of the leather strap which was knotted around the buckle to leave the end hanging, are from a ceramic phase dated c.1350 to c.1400 (Egan and Pritchard 1991, 71–2), whilst a third was recorded by Ward Perkins (1940, 277, pl.76, *6*), and a fourth by Fingerlin (1971, 392, fig.450, *257*). The similarity of these buckles to the Lombardic letter 'C' (see for example a 14th century 'C' from the Dominican Friary, Chester; Lloyd-Morgan 1990, 166, 170, fig.104, *1*) is also noteworthy.

Two oval buckles have moulded front edges with knops with loose cylinders or rollers of sheet wrapped round them, the purpose of the cylinders

being to reduce chafing on the strap and to facilitate tightening the strap. On *14303* the roller is decorated with punched or traced lines, while that of *14298* has a grooved pin-rest. *14298* also retains its buckle-plate which has traced border decoration and five rivet-holes; it comes from a mid–late 13th century context, while *14303* is residual in a post-medieval context. A buckle of similar type was found at the bottom of a well at Lyveden, Northamptonshire, dated c.1250–1350 (Steane and Bryant 1975, 109, fig.42.18).

The fragmentary *14704* from 2 Aldwark is tentatively identified as a plain oval frame fragment.

Buckles with integral plates (Fig.1467)

There are two incomplete iron buckles which were made integrally with the buckle-plate, *12696* from a 13th–14th century context at Coppergate and *14104* from an early 14th century context at Bedern. They were probably part of spur fittings and the missing end would probably have had a hooked terminal.

Five non-ferrous buckles of this type were recovered, four having oval frames (*12884, 13336, 14307–8*) and one trapezoidal (*12883*). Although lacking a cylinder, the profile of *14307* and the five rivet holes on its integral plate closely resemble the oval *14298* (see above); it comes from a mid 14th century context at Bedern. The frame of *12884* is plainer though possibly gilded, while *12883, 13336* and *14308* all have decorative terminals to their plates; *14308* has an iron pin.

Copper alloy buckles with integral plates are not common, although a number have been found in London, where iron examples are more numerous (Egan and Pritchard 1991, 78, 106–9). The Baynard House site produced an iron buckle with trapezoidal frame which was attached to a spur strap, and this has led to the suggestion that these integral plate buckles may have been designed specifically for use with spurs (ibid., 109). Apart from a copper alloy example found at North Elmham (Fig.1315, *17*) in a pit dated 11th–12th century (Goodall 1980a, 503, fig.263, 20), most buckles of this type appear to come from 13th–14th century deposits: see for example *AY* 17/9, 1348–9, figs.650 and 651, *5313* (originally considered Anglian); Egan and Pritchard 1991, 109; Murray and Murray 1993, 189, fig.40, 188. The apparent 13th–14th century date range for this buckle type fits the contexts of the two Coppergate buckles

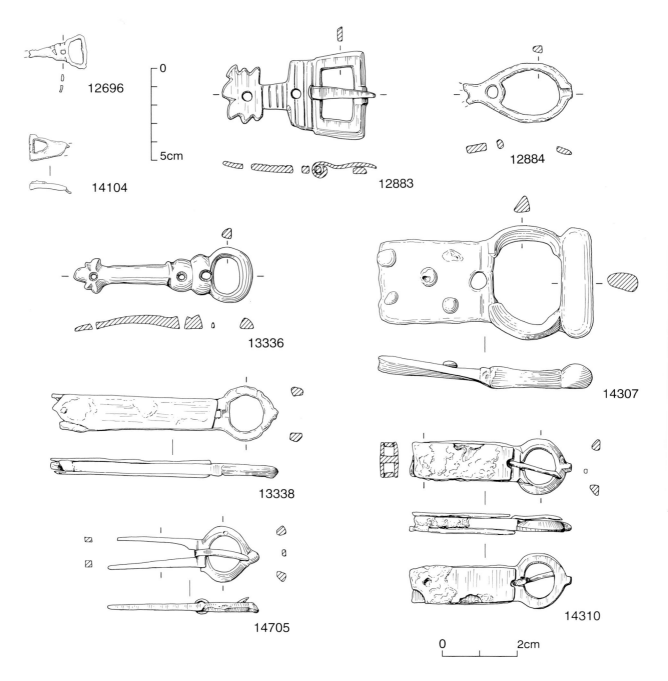

Fig.1467 *Iron buckles with integral buckle plates 12696 from 16–22 Coppergate, 14104 from Bedern; copper alloy buckles with integral buckle plates 12883–4 from 16–22 Coppergate, 13336 from the Foundry, 14307 from Bedern; copper alloy buckles with forked spacers 13338 from the Foundry, 14310 from Bedern and 14705 from 2 Aldwark. Iron objects scale 1:2, copper alloy objects scale 1:1*

and that of Bedern buckles; the Foundry buckle, which is from an early 15th century level, may be residual or possibly a late example.

Buckles with forked spacers (Fig.1467)

As with the buckles with integral plates, these were attached to the end of the strap by means of rigid plates, here a pair soldered onto a forked extension to the buckle-frame, and then secured to the end of the strap by rivets. All those in the York assemblage are copper alloy, and were recovered from sites in the Bedern area, including the Foundry (*13338–41*), the College (*14309–14*) and 2 Aldwark (*14705*). Although buckles of this type are sometimes decorated with rocked tracery and/or with circular openings with grooves at the mouth of the plate, all the York buckles are undecorated. The frames of all the buckles in this group do, however, have a characteristically pointed, sometimes almost ogival, front edge. *13338* has an exceptionally long fork and plates, while *14312* has linen threads preserved between the plates (see p.2885).

All the buckles of this type from Bedern derive from 15th century contexts, as does the 2 Aldwark buckle; one of the Foundry buckles (*13338*) comes from a late 15th–early 16th century deposit, the others being in post-medieval or unstratified levels. This concentration in 15th century layers does not accord with long-held opinion that they are essentially a 14th century form (Ward Perkins 1940, 268; Fingerlin 1971, 218, fig.336), nor with evidence from other sites, where they appear more commonly in 14th century levels (Hinton 1990a, 507, *1150, 1158–9*). Examples from London derived from 14th and early 15th century deposits, however (Egan and Pritchard 1991, 80), where it was noted that the decorative forms all came from 14th century levels, and the plain from 15th century contexts; this serves to bolster the dating of the York buckles to the 15th century.

Three failed castings of buckles with forked spacers were recovered from the Foundry (*13340–1*) and Bedern (*14315*); unfortunately, none appears to be from a well-stratified deposit (see pp.2712, 2714 and Fig.1322).

D-shaped buckles (Fig.1468)

This is the most common frame form amongst the iron buckles, of which there are nineteen examples. *14093* and *14096* (mid 14th–15th and late medieval contexts) from Bedern are similar in widening out from the straight side to the convex side. The frames range in size from a very substantial buckle, *12667*, 80mm long, which could have been a horse's girth buckle, to much smaller examples including *12661* from Coppergate and *15101* from Fishergate which have buckle-plates attached. *12665* is unusual in having a small loop on the curved side serving as a pin rest, and notched pin rests can be seen on *12663* and *12666*. *12670* has an expansion on the curved side for a pin rest. *12667* has a wedge-shaped cross-section on the curved side, while *12663* and *12664* have oblique rectangular cross-sections; both forms allow greater purchase for a leather strap.

Amongst the non-ferrous buckles, *14316* is possibly the earliest copper alloy buckle from any of the York sites under consideration, although it must be residual in its mid–late 13th century context. With its heavy D-shaped frame with much devolved zoomorphic heads at the ends of the pin-bar, it strongly resembles a buckle from Beverley, from a phase dated to the 10th to 11th century (A.R. Goodall 1991, 148–9, fig.114.583). Another comparable buckle, with a narrow plate, from Wharram Percy, North Yorkshire (A.R. Goodall 1979, 108, fig.55, *11*), has also been dated to the 11th century.

From a late 13th–early 14th century deposit, although in this instance from the Foundry, is *13342*. It has moulded stops at the ends of the pin-bar and a short folded-sheet plate with three rivet-holes unusually arranged in a line across the end of the plate. One of two non-ferrous D-shaped buckles from Fishergate, *15186* has a decorative polygonal knop at the front of the frame. Although from a post-medieval context, its similarity to a buckle from a context of the second half of the 14th century in London indicates a probable 14th century origin (Egan and Pritchard 1991, 94, fig.59, *421*). From an early–mid 14th century level at the Foundry, *13343* has a lipped frame; the other D-shaped buckles comprise *14317–18* from mid 15th–early 16th century levels at Bedern, and the fragmentary *15185* from Fishergate.

Rectangular, square and trapezoidal buckles (Figs.1469–70)

The rectangular form is the second most common form found amongst the iron buckles. The iron frames are usually small with sides under 35mm in length. *12680* is an incomplete tin-plated frame with small mouldings on one face.

Copper alloy buckles of the three forms considered under this heading were also recovered; they appear to be of 14th century origin. Two buckles from Fishergate (*15187–8*) and a third from Bedern (*14323*) possess square frames with moulded fronts, *14323* and *15188* retaining buckle-plates which contain a fragments of leather strap. *15187* was recovered from a deposit associated with the 16th century demolition of the priory, while the other two buckles came from post-medieval layers; all could derive, however, from the later 14th century, the period to which several similar copper alloy buckles from London are dated (Egan and Pritchard 1991, 96–7, fig.61). Two

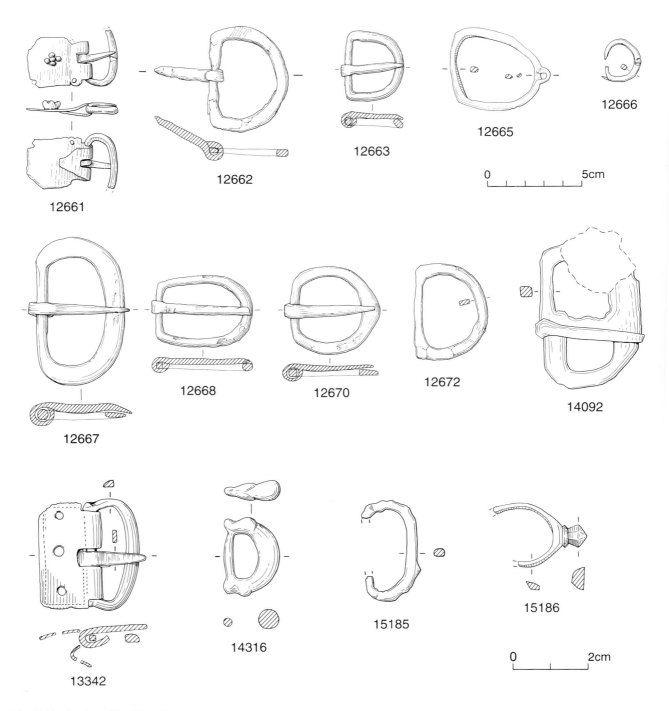

Fig.1468 *D-shaped buckles of iron 12661–3, 12665–8, 12670, 12672 from 16–22 Coppergate, 14092 from Bedern; D-shaped buckles of copper alloy 13342 from the Foundry, 14316 from Bedern, 15185–6 from 46–54 Fishergate. Iron objects scale 1:2, copper alloy objects scale 1:1*

large decorative rectangular buckles appear to be intrusive in their contexts. *15189* is a fragment of a trapezoidal buckle from Fishergate, which was originally gilded all over, and decorated with rocker-arm tracery. It came from a soil dump used to level the site before the construction of the priory in the early 13th century but a number of the levels within the dump were noted to have intrusive late 13th and 14th century pottery (*AY* 16/6, 626), and it seems likely that the buckle found its way in with this material.

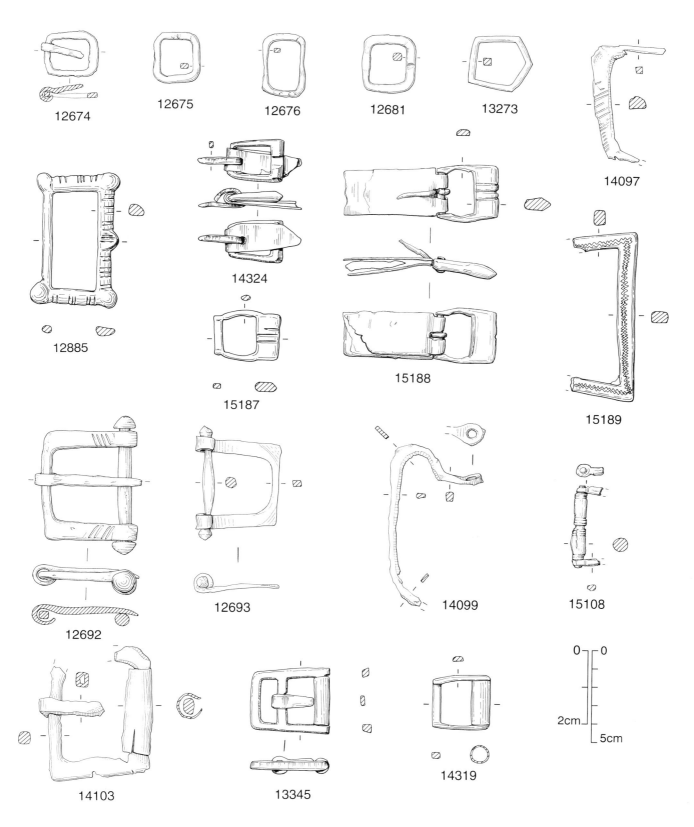

Fig.1469 *Rectangular, square and trapezoidal buckles: of iron* 12674–6, 12681 *from 16–22 Coppergate,* 13273 *from the Foundry,* 14097 *from Bedern; of copper alloy* 12885 *from 16–22 Coppergate,* 14324 *from Bedern,* 15187–9 *from 46–54 Fishergate. Iron buckle frames with rotating arms* 12692–3 *from 16–22 Coppergate,* 14099 *from Bedern,* 15108 *from 46–54 Fishergate. Buckles with rotating tubes: in iron* 14103 *from Bedern; in copper alloy* 13345 *from the Foundry and* 14319 *from Bedern. Iron objects scale 1:2, copper alloy objects scale 1:1*

Fig.1470 *Fragment of a trapezoidal buckle, originally gilded, decorated with rocker-arm tracery* 15189 *from 46–54 Fishergate. Actual length 46.3mm*

Rectangular iron frames with one end which rotates were part of horse trappings (Goodall 1980b, 173; Egan 1995, 57). Typically, the rotating end is held in looped terminals in the sides and has domed terminals. *12692* (late 12th century context) and *12693* from Coppergate have pins set on the end opposite the rotating arm, but *12690* (15th–16th century context) from Coppergate has a T-shaped pin which is set in the centre of the sides. *12692* has incised grooves and *12690* is plated. This form of buckle appears to be an innovation of the late 11th century and remained current until at least the 13th century. A mid 14th century context at Bedern has produced a T-shaped buckle-frame on which originally the shorter end rotated (*14099*). Buckles of this form have been found elsewhere in contexts of 12th–15th century date.

Two non-ferrous rectangular buckles also have rollers or revolving cylinders, a feature also seen on two oval buckles (*14303* and *14298*; see p.2889). *14319* is from an early 14th century deposit at Bedern. From an early–mid 15th century context at the Foundry, *13345* has an off-centre pin-bar with constriction for the pin, and a revolving cylinder on the front of the frame; it closely resembles a later 14th century example found in London (Egan and Pritchard 1991, 101, fig.64, *467*).

Simple frames with a central bar (Fig.1471)

There are four iron buckle-frames with an internal bar running between the sides to which the buckle-plate was originally attached. It is off-centre on *13271* from the Foundry (post-medieval context) and in the centre on *13270* (15th century context) and *13272* (late medieval/early post-medieval context) also from the Foundry, and *12660* (mid–late 14th century context) from Coppergate. *12660* and *13270* have similar elongated frames of which there are many late medieval examples in iron; the buckle-plate survives on both these York buckles.

Double-looped buckles (Fig.1471)

Also with a central bar, these copper alloy buckles differ from the iron buckles described above in hav-

Found in a 12th/13th century dump at Coppergate, *12885* has decorative projections and incised lines around the frame, and is also likely to be a 14th century buckle.

Both *14322* and *14324* retain buckle-plate fragments; unusually, *14322* has not been cast, but made from a strip which has been bent to form the front, top and bottom edges of the frame into which a separate pin-bar has been inserted. The fragmentary *14320* may be part of a square buckle, although it has an unusual rectangular projection below the pin-bar, possibly a remnant of casting which has not been removed. *13344* is a fragmentary rectangular buckle from an early 16th century deposit at the Foundry.

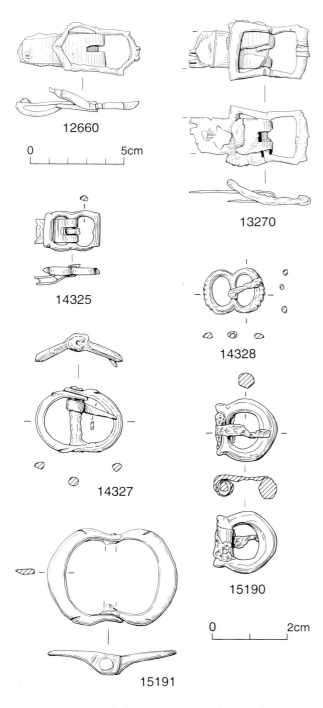

Fig.1471 *Iron buckle frames with a central internal bar 12660 from 16–22 Coppergate, 13270 from the Foundry; copper alloy double-looped buckles 14325, 14327–8 from Bedern, 15190–1 from 46–54 Fishergate. Iron objects scale 1:2, copper alloy objects scale 1:1*

ing two distinct loops to the frame. The earliest example from the York sites comes from an early 14th century layer at Bedern (*14325*); it has oval loops with straight ends and there is a folded-sheet buckle-plate

attached to the central bar. Of a similar size and shape, ample from the York sites comes from an early 14th century layer at Bedern (*14325*); it has oval loops with straight ends and there is a folded-sheet buckle-plate attached to the central bar. Of a similar size and shape, but from unstratified levels, *14328* has an iron pin, while *14706* has no surviving pin and is slightly larger. Lead alloy buckles of similar size and shape have been found on 15th century shoes (Egan and Pritchard 1991, 86–7, *353*), and it is possible that the two unstratified buckles may have had this function. However, Egan also notes a group of copper alloy buckles, which, like *14325*, have buckle-plates; he suggests these probably had a different function, no definite shoe buckles having been recovered with buckle-plates (ibid., 89). It may be that copper alloy buckles such as *14328* and *14706* shared this unknown use. Another possible double-looped buckle, *15190* from Fishergate, has an oval loop and the apparent remains of a second, and has an iron pin with a cylinder of copper alloy sheet under it. Its identification must be tentative, however, as only one loop survives, and its 13th century context is considerably earlier than those of other buckles of this type.

The remainder of the double-looped buckles are the larger type, sometimes called 'spectacle buckles', which are usually found in 15th century or later contexts (see for example Clay 1981, 133, fig.48, *32*; Harvey 1975, 260, *1789*; Hinton 1990a, 521, *1206, 1209*). Both *14327* and *15191* are composed of two semi-circular loops riveted together at the ends with an added central pin-bar; traces of corrosion indicate that *14326* and *15191* originally had iron pins, a not uncommon feature of these buckles (see Margeson 1993, 28, *152, 162*). *14326* derived from a late 15th to early 16th century deposit; the others were unstratified.

Buckle-pins (Fig.1472)

There are twenty iron buckle-pins (seventeen from Coppergate) now detached from their frames. For the most part they are similar in form to those still attached to buckles (e.g. *12701* and *15109*). However, *12698* has an unusual spirally twisted shank.

Five copper alloy pins which have separated from buckles have punched or cast decoration on them; all were found at Bedern. Three have cast mouldings just below the looped end (*14330–1, 14336*); these

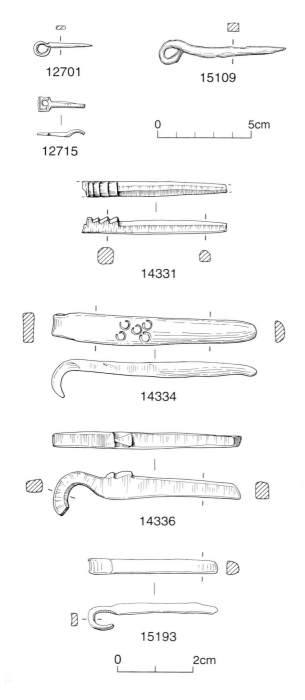

Fig.1472 *Iron buckle-pin 12701 from 16–22 Coppergate and 15109 from 46–54 Fishergate; iron belt fitting 12715 from 16–22 Coppergate; copper alloy buckle-pins 14331, 14334, 14336 from Bedern, 15193 from 46–54 Fishergate. Iron objects scale 1:2, copper alloy objects scale 1:1*

mouldings may not have been solely decorative, but would also have enabled a tight fit of the pin in the strap hole. *14330–1* are from 14th century levels, *14336* is unstratified. *14334–5* are similar but instead

of having moulded bosses, the widest part of the pin is decorated with punched rings or dots, the rings on *14334* having been gilded. The other unassociated pins are mostly of cut sheet or wire (*13346–7, 14329, 14332–3, 14337–8, 14620, 15192–3*). While the cast pins are most likely to have come from buckles, it is not impossible that some of the others may derive from annular brooches (see below).

Buckle-plates (Fig.1473; see also Figs.1466, 1468, 1471)

Buckle-plates provided a means of attaching a buckle to a strap, and were made by folding a plate over one side of the buckle-frame and riveting the ends together. Several of the buckles described above retained buckle-plates, but other buckle-plates were recovered which had lost their buckles.

The iron buckle-plates are essentially rectangular, although *12659* (12th–13th century context) from Coppergate has rectangular notches cut out of the sides while *12660* (mid 14th –mid 16th century context), also from Coppergate, and *13000* (14th century context) from the Coppergate watching brief site have rounded ends. *13270* (14th century context) from the Foundry and *12659* bear incised grooves. On one face of *12661* (late 12th century context) there is a small stud in the form of a five-petalled flower. *12714* (mid 13th century context) from Coppergate is unusual in that it is triangular; the surviving half has bevelled edges and towards the base there are two short protrusions on each side.

The copper alloy buckle-plates (*12886, 13348, 14339–52*) are also typically rectangular with a recess at each side of the fold for the buckle-frame and a slot or perforation for the buckle-pin. Some plates retain fragments of buckle-frames (*14348–9, 14352*) or buckle-pins (*14344*). The majority of the buckle-plates have become completely separated from their buckles, however. The number of rivets employed for attachment to the straps ranges from one at the lower end (*14342, 14352*) to five, a pair at each end and one centrally placed, as on *14350* which has traced border decoration. The oval buckle with moulded front (*14298*) from a mid–late 13th century deposit (see Fig.1466) retains buckle-plates similar to *14350*, and the similarity of their design may point to contemporaneity, although *14350* was recovered from a mid–late 15th century context. Traced or punched border decoration appears the most com-

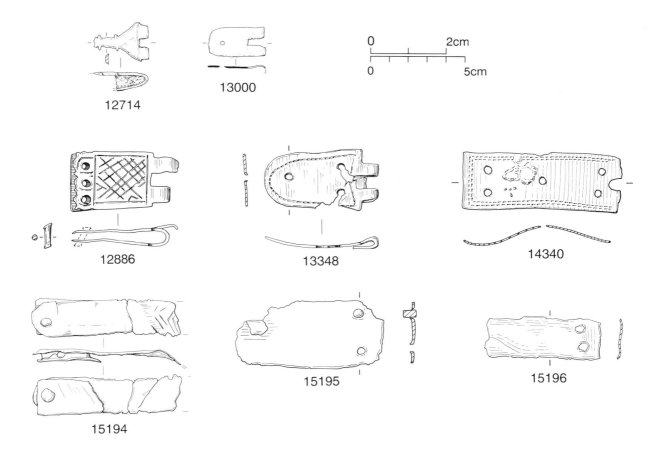

Fig.1473 *Buckle-plates without buckles: of iron* **12714** *from 16–22 Coppergate,* **13000** *from the Coppergate watching brief; of copper alloy* **12886** *from 16–22 Coppergate,* **13348** *from the Foundry,* **14340** *from Bedern; possible copper alloy buckle-plates* **15194–6** *from 46–54 Fishergate. Iron objects scale 1:2, copper alloy objects scale 1:1*

mon decorative technique applied to the York buckle-plates, as it is seen on *13348* and *14339–40*. More unusually, *12886* has cross-hatching and a scalloped lower edge. The remaining buckle-plates are undecorated.

Apart from the above, three plates from Fishergate (*15194–6*) are also possible buckle-plates. *15195–6* are both sub-rectangular sheets, broken at one end and with a pair of rivet holes at the other end, one of those on *15195* still containing a rivet; both were recovered from dissolution contexts. *15194* was found in a Period 6a pit, and comprises two incomplete plates riveted together at one end, one plate with incised line decoration. As all these are broken and lack the looped end and perforation for a buckle-pin, their identification as buckle-plates can only be tentative.

From 2 Aldwark, buckle-plate fragment *14707* was found close to buckle *14705* and may have origi-

nally belonged to it; a strap-end (*14710;* see below) was also found in the same context as the buckle, suggesting that the buckle and strap-end may have formed a set.

Belt fitting

12715 is an incomplete small tin-plated fitting from Coppergate which may originally have been riveted to a belt or strap and served to link it to some other item (see Fig.1472).

Copper alloy clasps

Strap clasps (Fig.1474)

A folding strap clasp (*14353*) and a plate with a bar mount attached (*14354*) represent the two parts of a clasp mechanism, in which the bar mount of the plate was inserted into the clasp frame, and held in place by the folding end of the clasp (this is illustrated clearly in Egan and Pritchard 1991, 116, fig.76). Although both *14353* and *14354* were recovered from Period 8/1 (mid–late 15th century) contexts in Area X at Bedern, they were found some distance apart and do not appear to belong to the same clasp. The frame of *14353* includes a forked spacer, and appears to be a clasp type that is contemporary with buckles and strap-ends of the same construction. At Bedern, this is certainly the case; as noted above, the vast majority of the forked spacer buckles were recovered from 15th century contexts at the College (see p.2891), and the same is true of the forked spacer strap-ends (see p.2902). Similar clasps to *14353* from London have also been dated to the late 14th and early 15th centuries (Egan and Pritchard 1991, 119–20, fig.78). Clasps lacking forked spacers but with simple plates

folded around the frame are also known, and *14355*, a folded plate which retains part of a frame and resembles a buckle-plate but lacks a hole for the pin, may originally have been attached to this type of strap clasp. Another possible example is *14358* which has a decorated plate. This clasp type has been recovered from contexts as early as the late 13th century in London (ibid., 116), as well as from 14th–15th century deposits in Winchester (Hinton 1990b, 540–2, fig.143, *1355*), and from Norwich (Margeson 1993, 38, fig.21, *251–5*). As with the London examples, *14355* comes from an earlier context (Period 6) than the forked spacer type clasps. The uses to which such clasps were put include fastenings on belts and other garments; *14354* retains a fragment of the silk tablet-woven braid to which it was originally attached (see p.2885).

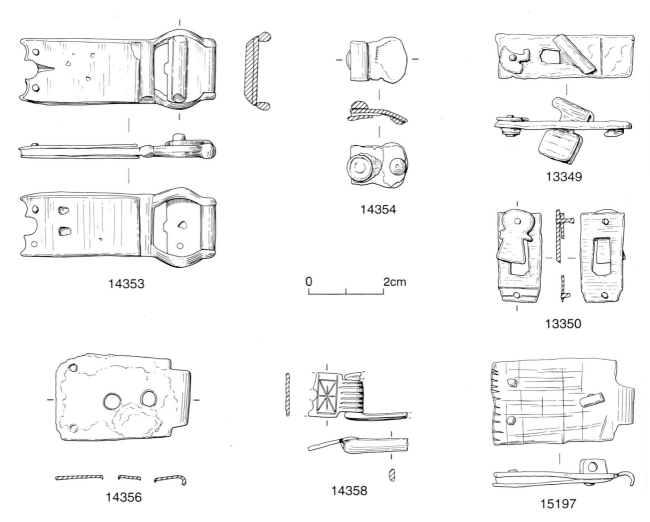

14353

14354

13349

13350

14356

14358

15197

0   2cm

Fig.1474 *Copper alloy clasps: strap clasps* 14353–4 *from Bedern; other clasps* 13349–50 *from the Foundry,* 14356 *and* 14358 *from Bedern,* 15197 *from 46–54 Fishergate. Scale 1:1*

Other clasps (Fig.1474)

Both found at the Foundry, *13349–50* appear to represent parts of another type of two-piece clasp. From an early–mid 14th century deposit, *13349* retains both components: a rectangular plate with rivets for attachment to a strap has a central longitudinal slot which contains the second element, a folded plate toggle which has been passed through the slot and then turned at 90° to form the fastening. *13350* also has a plate with a slot, but in this instance, there is a key hole-shaped device which pivots round, enabling a toggle (which has not survived) to be passed through the slot, turned and then held in place by the pivoting cover; this clasp came from a mid–late 15th century context. Two fittings which appear similar have been recovered from late 13th–mid 14th century deposits in London (Egan and Pritchard 1991, 120, fig.79); an undated example of the clasp with pivoting key hole-shaped cover in a private collection is still attached to a strap which is embellished with quatrefoil and sexfoil mounts (ibid.).

Other clasps include *14356–7* and *15197*, all of which have one hooked end, and two of which (*15197, 14357*) retain part of the leather straps to which they were originally attached. Clasps similar to *15197* have been found at other ecclesiastical sites, including St Augustine's Abbey, Canterbury (Henig 1988, 215, fig.69, *51*), and the Austin Friars, Leicester (Clay 1981, 133, fig.48, *33*); the hooked ends of all these fastenings may indicate use as book clasps (see pp.2936–9).

Iron belt hasps (Fig.1475)

There are four certain belt hasps from Coppergate. A belt hasp is like a buckle, but has no pin. *12719*

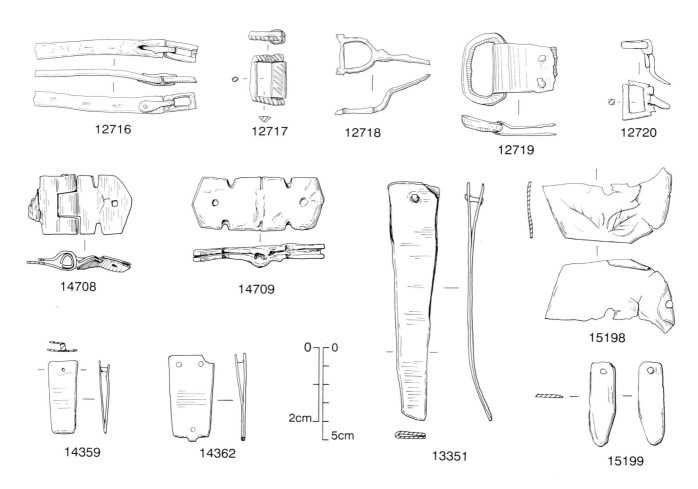

Fig.1475 *Iron belt hasps 12716–20 from 16–22 Coppergate; copper alloy hinged belt fittings 14708–9 from 2 Aldwark; copper alloy strap-ends made from one or two pieces of sheet 13351 from the Foundry, 14359 and 14362 from Bedern, 15198–9 from 46–54 Fishergate. Iron objects scale 1:2, copper alloy objects scale 1:1*

(early 13th century context) has a D-shaped frame and an attachment fitting similar to a buckle-plate is wrapped over the straight side. This fitting was originally riveted onto a belt end. Both hasp and fitting are tin plated. *12717* and *12720* (late 12th century contexts) are both quite small and more or less rectangular; in addition, both are plated. The ends of *12717* have a triangular cross-section and there are incised diagonal grooves cut into them; one side has a tube around it, also with grooves cut into it, to act as a runner. *12720* also bears incised grooves, not visible on the drawing. *12716* includes a small rectangular frame of which each end is recessed. This is attached to a length of narrow leather strap by means of a U-shaped fitting similar to *12717*. Both metal components are plated. *12718* is a curious D-shaped object with an elongated projection from the convex side which may also be belt hasp.

Copper alloy hinged belt fittings
(Fig.1475)

Found at 2 Aldwark, *14708–9* are both decoratively shaped with notched edges, and *14708* has been tin plated; they were both found in 15th–16th century levels. It has been suggested that hinged fittings such as these may have been used when two straps articulated together (Margeson 1993, 36, fig.21, *243*).

Copper alloy strap-ends (Figs.1475–6)

These dress accessories were attached to protect and embellish the tips of straps and girdles. Cast one-piece strap-ends, often decorated, are quite common finds on Anglo-Saxon sites, and many have been recovered from 8th–11th century contexts in York, including the sites at Fishergate (*5317–21*, *AY* 17/9) and Coppergate (*10421–4*, *AY* 17/14). Unlike their earlier counterparts, the medieval strap-ends found in York are made from sheet, and several different forms are represented amongst those found at the sites under discussion. Coppergate produced two from medieval deposits (*12889–90*), while seven were found at the Foundry (*13351–7*), fifteen at Bedern (*14359–69*, *14371–2*, *14374–5*), three at 2 Aldwark (*14710–12*) and four at Fishergate (*15198–201*). Two unfinished strap-ends were also found at Bedern (*14370*, *14373*).

The simplest forms of strap-end are made from one or two pieces of sheet. All the sites produced examples formed from one piece of sheet folded widthways and riveted at the open end, such as *14359*

from Bedern. A more uncommon type is made by folding a sheet lengthways, that is along one side, and one example of this was found in an early 14th century context at the Foundry (*13351*); similar examples from London also came from 14th century deposits (Egan and Pritchard 1991, 130, fig.85, *604–6*). The two-piece forms, such as *14362*, are commonly made from a pair of slightly tapering rectangular plates, sometimes cut to a point or ogee at the narrower end, and attached to the strap by rivets at the other end. An unusual variant of this form may be represented by *14363* from an early 15th century deposit at Bedern; it has been made from two approximately circular plates held together by a peripheral rivet with a large, gilded, domed head, and it retains mineralised leather between the plates. A considerably larger, but similar, circular strap-end was found in a late 14th century context in London (ibid., 135, *622*). Now very fragmentary, *15198* incorporates bent over edges for encasement of a strap, and an incised leaf design, so can tentatively be identified by its similarity to examples from London (ibid., 135–6, fig.87, *616–19*).

The most commonly found design amongst the York strap-ends, however, is made up of three pieces, comprising a pair of plates with a spacer plate between. These are both more substantial and more ornamental than the one- or two-plate strap-ends, almost invariably having a decoratively shaped tip. Most of the composite strap-ends are rectangular with forked spacer plates; *14711* is an example of a forked spacer plate which has become separated from its strap-end. One strap-end from 2 Aldwark (*14710*) may have a sheet spacer, a sub-rectangular plate with no fork; this type appears to be a 14th century form (ibid., 148). The Aldwark example comes from an early 15th century level. Two spacer plates with circular expansions were also recovered from Bedern; *14372* is rounded at the lower end, while the centrally expanded *14368* is fragmentary and possibly unfinished. In addition to variations in the shape of the plates, the tips also vary. *13352* has a simply shaped projection, *14711* has a collared knop, *14371*, decorated with cross-hatching, has been silvered and has more decorative acorn knops, and *14712* has a front plate decorated with traced zig-zag lines and a grooved circular opening at the top edge. Some textile survives between the plates of *14712*, indicating attachment to a fabric girdle or belt. Although unstratified, *14712* may be of similar date to *14364*,

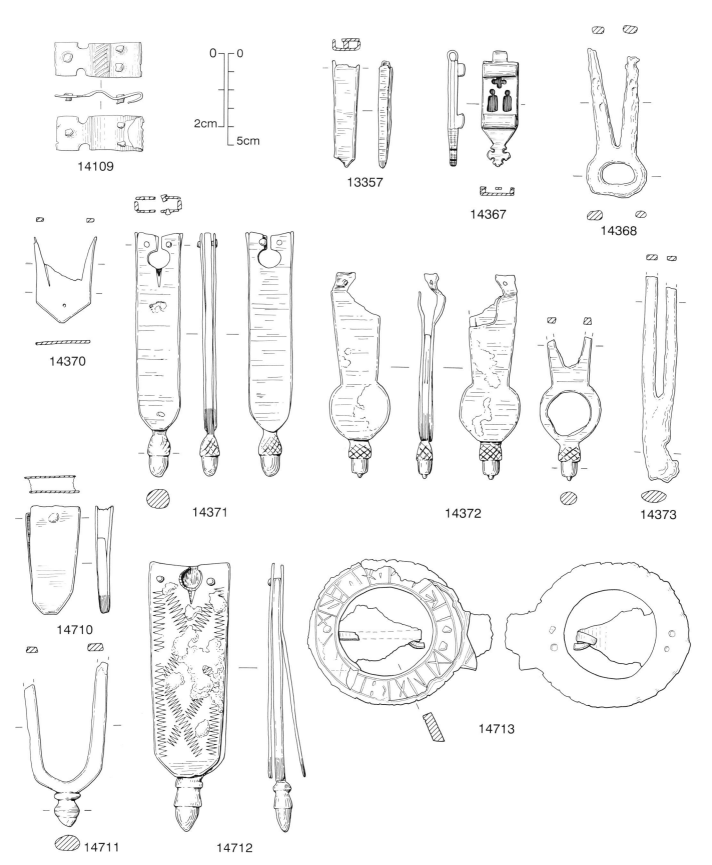

Fig.1476 *Iron strap-end 14109 from Bedern; copper alloy three-piece strap-ends 13357 from the Foundry, 14367–8, 14370–3 from Bedern, 14710–12 from 2 Aldwark; possible strap-end 14713 from 2 Aldwark. Iron object scale 1:2, copper alloy objects scale 1:1*

14109

0 ⌐ 0

2cm

5cm

13357

14367

14368

14370

14371

14372

14373

14710

14711

14712

14713

an incomplete plate with a similar circular opening, which was found in a context dating from the mid 14th to early 15th century. The forked spacer buckle *14312* (see above) was found together with strap-end *14371*, indicating that these items may have been produced as matching sets.

A very ornate strap-end (*14367*) comes from a mid 14th to early 15th century context at Bedern. It has a loop or hinge at one end formed from the fold of the plate, and a cruciform or trefoil-shaped terminal at the other; the plate has openwork decoration and two bar-mounts riveted onto it. There is a spacer plate in the middle. Comparable and contemporary strap-ends found in London (Egan and Pritchard 1991, 149, fig.97) and Wales (Manley and Lewis 1987, 271–2, fig.3, 1/7) have been made in a similar fashion but are decorated with acorn motifs; it is tempting to attribute the cross-shaped terminal of *14367* to its ecclesiastical context.

A study of the contexts from which the York strap-ends derive suggests that the simple one-piece strap-ends represent the earliest type; two of the three examples of this type recovered from Bedern came from mid–late 13th century deposits (*14359–60*), the third being from an early 15th century context (*14365*). This may be compared to similar strap-ends from London, which came from late 13th century and later levels (Egan and Pritchard 1991, 129). Roughly contemporary with the one-piece form, the two-piece strap-ends from York come from a 13th–14th century deposit at Coppergate (*12889*) and an early 15th century deposit at the Foundry (*13354*); this again accords with the range of find-spots of copper alloy strap-ends of this type from London (ibid., 135–6). The earliest forked spacer strap-end in the York series again comes from Coppergate, *12890*, deriving from a 12th–13th century levelling deposit. Comparison with London examples indicates that *12890* is likely to come from the later part of that date range, the earliest London forked spacer strap-ends being late 13th–early 14th century in date (ibid., 145), and the form itself is considered to belong to the 14th century, with few examples from later deposits (ibid.; Ward Perkins 1940, 268). The York composite strap-ends differ, however, from those from London in being concentrated within 15th and 16th century contexts: of fourteen forked spacer strap-ends from stratified contexts (all but one in the area of Bedern) in York, ten come from deposits of early 15th–early

16th century date. Moreover, there is clear evidence that these artefacts were being made in the area in the 15th–16th centuries, with two unfinished forked spacers deriving from late 15th–early 16th century deposits at Bedern (*14370, 14373*, see Fig.1322, p.2714); other buckle fittings were also being made in the area (see p.2714).

Possible strap-end (Fig.1476)

Found in a late 14th–early 15th century deposit at 2 Aldwark, *14713* is an annular two-piece object with a flat projection at one end, its exact form being somewhat obscured by organic adhesions. The flat back has a wavy edge, while the front is of plano-convex section, attached to the back by iron rivets. The adhesions attached to the inner edge of the object comprise mainly mineralised grass with fragments of an iron pin on a loop and traces of Z-spun textile. There is no constriction on the frame to take a pin, nor any attachment lug on the back, indicating that the pin is unlikely to have formed part of the object, but has become attached during deposition in the ground, and that it is therefore not a buckle or brooch. The projection on the side of the ring points to a strap-end type function (although the open centre seems unusual), and a fragment resembling the back plate of *14713* was recovered in London and identified as a strap-end fragment (Egan and Pritchard 1991, 132, fig.86, *615*). Unfortunately, the decoration on *14713* is now too worn to be confidently deciphered.

Iron strap-end (Fig.1476)

14109 from an early 14th century context at Bedern is a rectangular strap-end or belt hasp plate of which a little over half survives. At one end it is folded over and leather remains survive here around a pair of rivets; it is then broken. A semi-circular cut has been taken out of each side near the opposite end. The object is tin-plated and there are incised diagonal grooves in a central panel.

Strap-guides (Fig.1477)

These fittings (sometimes also known as belt slides) were used to secure the part of a strap which extended beyond the buckle, just as modern belts today generally have loops made as part of the belt. They are found in both iron and copper alloy.

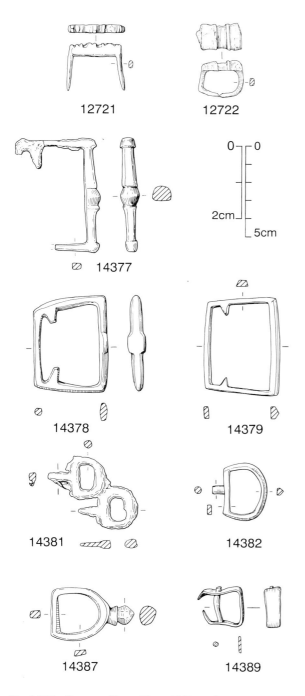

Fig.1477 *Strap-guides: of iron 12721–2 from 16–22 Copper-gate; of copper alloy 14377–9, 14381–2, 14387, 14389 from Bedern. Iron objects scale 1:2, copper alloy objects scale 1:1*

texts. The head of *12722* (late 11th century context) is composed of three small rectangular fields, that in the centre being recessed; the junction between them is marked by a groove and a raised strip. The form of the head is very similar to that of a strap-end from an Anglo-Scandinavian context (*3789, AY* 17/6). *12721* (mid 15th century context) has a narrow head with a pattern of notches cut into it. It is not plated and the clasp appears to be incompletely formed, features which suggest it may have been discarded during manufacture, as is suggested in the case of a few of the Anglo-Scandinavian examples (pp.688–9, *AY* 17/6).

Two types of copper alloy strap-guide have been identified by Egan and Pritchard (1991, 229), both of which are represented amongst the York material; a third possible strap-guide type was also recovered. All the strap-guides were found in the Bedern area (*13358, 14376–80, 14382–91, 14714*). The earlier of the two certain forms appears to be that with a rectangular or trapezoidal frame incorporating two opposed internal lugs close to one long edge. In London, these were found in late 12th–15th century deposits (ibid., 231–3). Bedern produced five of this type (*14376–80*), four of which derived from mid 13th to mid 15th century levels. These items have been found elsewhere, but have often been identified as buckle-frames (e.g. p.206, *729, AY* 17/4; Geddes and Carter 1977, 289, fig.130, *13*; Harvey 1975, 255, fig.240, *1725*).

The second form comprises oval, rectangular or trapezoidal loops with external rivets, as seen on *13358* and *14382–7*. All the Bedern loops have or had integral external rivets, which were used to fix the loop to the strap via a hole in the strap; a similar example but with an internal rivet was found in situ on the strap of an archer's wrist guard (Egan and Pritchard 1991, 229, fig.143). This form of loop appears to have been manufactured in the Bedern area, a faulty casting of two such loops having been found in a late 13th century deposit (*14381*; see Fig.1322, p.2714).

The third type consists of frames formed from a bent up strip with a separate internal bar parallel to one long edge (*14388–91, 14714*). These appear weaker than their counterparts, and their identification as strap-guides must remain tentative; apart from *14714* all these strap-guides come from early–mid 15th century contexts.

There are two iron strap-guides from Coppergate; these are of a form which appears to have been particularly associated with spur leathers and usually come from pre- or immediately post-Conquest con-

Chapes (Fig.1478)

These copper alloy objects were recovered from all the major sites under discussion (*12891, 13359, 14392–6, 14621, 15202*). All are made from sheet metal, rolled and with an overlapping soldered joint at the back; the bottom edges have been notched and folded inwards to close them. All are of a size to have been used to edge the lower end of a dagger sheath rather than a sword scabbard, and two chapes retain traces of the leather sheath within them (*14392, 14395*). All the chapes are of a similar form, being sub-triangular with a rounded tip. Some have an ornamental opening on the front face, such as *13359* and *14393*, and one shows traces of an ornamental band, now lost, around its upper edge (*12891*). Only one chape (*15202*) has been decorated with motifs, in this instance with crudely incised stars. Several chapes have been tinned, for example, *13359* and *14396*. This particular form of chape has previously been attributed to the later 14th–15th centuries (Ward Perkins 1940, 281) and this dating fits well with the contexts from which the York chapes derive; the earliest (*14392*) comes from a mid 14th century level, the others from early 15th century deposits or later.

Purse hanger (Fig.1479)

An incomplete copper alloy arched pendent mount, commonly called a purse hanger, was found

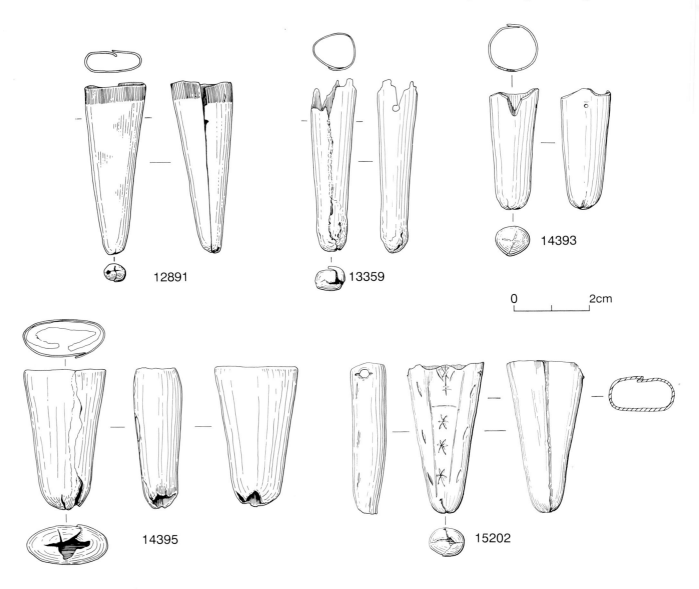

Fig.1478 *Copper alloy chapes* 12891 *from 16–22 Coppergate,* 13359 *from the Foundry,* 14393 *and* 14395 *from Bedern,* 15202 *from 46–54 Fishergate. Scale 1:1*

at Bedern (*14397*) in an early 15th century deposit. As the term indicates, these mounts were attached to belts or girdles for the suspension of purses or knives; similar examples from London retain the rectangular bar-mounts at each end with which they were affixed (Egan and Pritchard 1991, 219–23, *1196, 1198*). The London hangers come from contexts of similar date (ibid., 223) to the one from Bedern, but representations of these objects appear on sculptured statues and tombs as early as the 13th century in France (ibid., 219).

Copper alloy mounts and studs

Small and often decoratively shaped, these objects of copper alloy sheet would have been applied to various items of dress, such as belts, to other straps of leather or textile, such as harness, to books as decorative fittings, and to pieces of furniture, such as boxes and chests. Of varying shape, it is impossible to tell what the original function of individual mounts may have been, unless they have survived in situ, as have a number of the York mounts. They were attached via rivets, either integral or passing through one or more perforation, with eyelets securing them; in most cases, the rivets and eyelets have been lost (see also rivets and eyelets, pp.2830, 2855).

Circular mounts (Fig.1479)

The simplest mounts are plain and discoidal with a central perforation, and were found at Fishergate (*15203–4*) both incomplete, and at the Bedern sites (*13360, 14398, 14400–1*). *13360* and *14400–1* derived from 15th century contexts; all the others were from 13th century deposits. *14398* has been inserted into leather and retains an eyelet on the underside. Three decorated disc-shaped mounts, *13361, 14399* and *14715* share the same repoussé design of concentric rings. Two, *13361* and *14399*, derive from early–mid 15th century contexts, the third, *14715*, being unstratified; similar mounts from London were recovered from later 14th century deposits (Egan and Pritchard 1991, 179, fig.114, *927–8*). More unusual decoration is seen on two circular mounts from mid 15th to 16th century contexts, *14402–3*. *14403* has an incised chequer pattern within a plain border, while *14402*, made of thin copper alloy sheeting, has been cast with a relief design of a border of fleurs-de-lys surrounding a central shield bearing an illegible heraldic motif. The delicate nature of *14402* suggests

that it may originally have been attached to a casket rather than a belt or harness, although heraldic mounts are known to have decorated belts, as seen on the sword belt on the effigy of the Black Prince (died 1376) in Canterbury Cathedral (Egan and Pritchard 1991, 184, fig.116).

More numerous than the discoidal mounts are domed mounts, found on all the Bedern sites and at Fishergate, and deriving from contexts ranging in date from the 13th century to the post-medieval period (*13362–8, 14404–17, 14716–17, 15205–7*). Methods of attachment include integral rivets, as on *13368*, or central rivet holes for separate rivets, as on *13364*. On some examples, which lack either hole or rivet, it is unclear how the mount would have been attached, although traces of solder on one such mount, *15205*, indicate that some mounts with integral rivets were not made in one piece. Some mounts have been gilded (e.g. *14410*), others have tin/lead plating, such as *15206* with its decoratively cut circumference, and *13365* with a design of triple perforations. Several of the Bedern mounts, *14410, 14413* and *14416*, and *14717* from 2 Aldwark, retain eyelets or washers, with *14410* and *14416* still being attached to fragments of leather strap or belt. A leather strap from Coppergate (sf885) from a mid 14th century deposit also retains two hemispherical studs and holes for more (see *AY* 17/16 in prep.). The individual mounts range in diameter from 7·3mm (*14417*) to 22·2mm (*14409*), with over half being less than 10mm in diameter and only *14409* being more than 15mm across. Some of the smaller mounts may have been used on wooden furnishings such as boxes or in upholstery, but, as most lack the tips of their rivets, this function is hard to prove (see Egan and Pritchard 1991, 164). The functions of most of these mounts must remain a matter for conjecture.

In addition to the simple circular mounts, there are many variations on the theme. A triple-lobed design was recovered from the Bedern sites only (*13369, 14418, 14622*). Although the central lobes are perforated, it appears that the rivets for attachment were placed in the outer lobes, one of those on *14622* retaining its rivet. *14418* was found in a 15th century context, the others coming from post-medieval contexts. An apparently uncommon form, they have been noted in Lund, Sweden, as a 14th century type (Fingerlin 1971, 410, fig.110, *327*), and in a context dated c.1400–1600 in Norwich (Margeson 1993, 40, *276*).

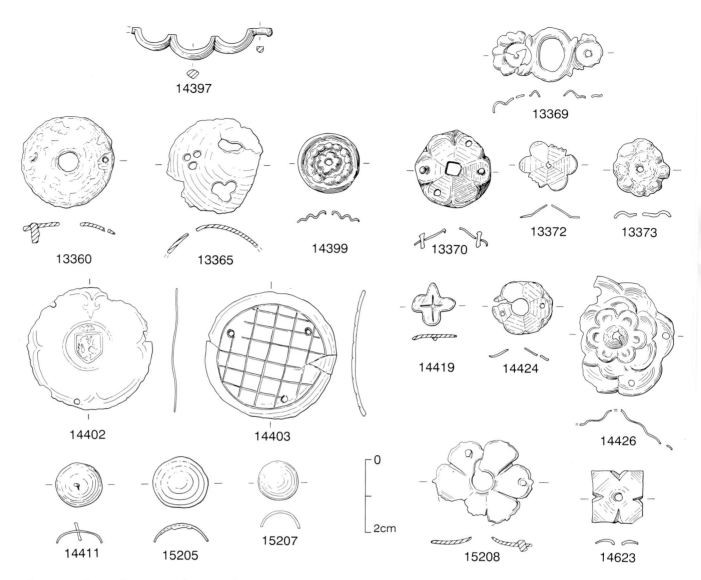

Fig.1479 *Incomplete copper alloy purse hanger* 14397 *from Bedern; copper alloy circular domed mounts* 13360 *and* 13365 *from the Foundry,* 14399, 14402–3, 14411 *from Bedern,* 15205 *and* 15207 *from* 46–54 *Fishergate; triple-lobed mount* 13369 *from the Foundry; petalled mounts* 13370, 13372–3 *from the Foundry,* 14419, 14424, 14426 *from Bedern,* 14623 *from Bedern Chapel,* 15208 *from* 46–54 *Fishergate. Scale* 1:1

Petalled mounts (Fig.1479)

A more common variant is the petalled mount, with examples in the York assemblage ranging from four petalled (quatrefoil) to eight (octofoil), the most common being six (sexfoil). All the quatrefoil mounts come from the sites in the Bedern area (*14419–22, 14623* and *14718*). *14419* with its flat head appears to be the earliest example in the group, coming from a late 13th century context; *14623* is similar, while *14420* may be unfinished. Three other quatrefoil mounts (*14421–2* and *14718*) have been stamped out to shape.

The sexfoil mounts are slightly more numerous than the quatrefoils, and were recovered at Fishergate (*15208*) and from the Bedern sites (*13370–2, 14423–5, 14624, 14719*). They exhibit a range of methods of attachment; apart from *14719* which may have had an integral rivet, now lost, all appear to have had one or more rivet holes. These could be central (e.g. *14624*) or in combination with a central perforation; sometimes there was one pair of peripheral rivet holes (e.g. *14425*), occasionally two (e.g. *13370*), with one pair perhaps replacing an earlier pair. Most of the mounts have a raised centre. This particular form of lobed mount appears fairly commonly on medieval sites across the country; see for example Harvey 1975, 258, fig.241, *1757*; Geddes 1985, 160, fig.51, *54–5*; A.R. Goodall 1983, 232, fig.1, *31*. In London, they are recorded from the mid 14th century onwards (Egan and Pritchard 1991, 190), but none of the York mounts comes from a context which is earlier than the mid 15th century.

Another mount from a mid 15th century deposit is *13373*, which is the only octofoil mount recovered. Even more ornate and the largest of the petalled mounts, *14426* comes from a 14th century context; this has three whorls, each of six petals, the petals having been punched out from the reverse face using tools with a C-shaped tip. The mount appears to have originally had two pairs of rivet holes as well as being perforated centrally. Three fragmentary repoussé mounts (*14427, 14715, 14720*) may also have originally been petalled; *14427* retained traces of gilding (not analysed).

Although none of the multifoil mounts from York was found in situ, this has been the case elsewhere, and these demonstrate the ornamental application of these mounts to articles of dress and also to books. For example, they adorn a strap with a forked spacer buckle which was found in the town ditch at Newgate, London (Ward Perkins 1940, 198, fig.63, *7*), while twelve similar mounts of lead/tin were found fixed to a large fragment of leather with a lobed edge (Egan and Pritchard 1991, 192, fig.121, *1028*). Spur straps have also been identified which are decorated with multifoil mounts (Clark 1995, 150–6, fig.112, *390*) although these mounts were made of tin-coated iron, and copper alloy mounts may not have been considered robust enough for such straps. Two books originally from the library at Bordesley Abbey, now in the Bodleian Library, Oxford, retain medieval bindings, and the outer cover of one of these (Ms. Laud Misc.606) preserves the outlines of eight- or ten-petalled fittings (Hirst et al. 1983, 201). Although the books are 12th century, the fittings were not necessarily original, but may have been contemporary with the 14th and 15th century mounts found in York. It should also be noted that sexfoil mounts attached not to leather but to non-ferrous strips have been recovered in London (Egan and Pritchard 1991, 242, fig.155, *1297*).

Rectangular mounts (Fig.1480)

Plain rectangular pieces of sheet with rivet holes for attachment to straps probably served as stiffeners for belts, or possibly as strap-ends. *14625*, unfortunately unstratified, retains two plates, decoratively notched around the edges and with part of the strap between them; it is very similar to an example from late dissolution levels at Battle Abbey in East Sussex (Hare 1985, 160, fig.50, *460*). Similar mounts with central perforations, such as *14432* and *15210*, were found in a series on a strap from London, although in this instance they were made of iron (Egan and Pritchard 1991, 197, figs.123–4, *1060*); the function of the central perforation is unclear. Although lozenge-shaped rather than rectangular, *14430* and *14548*, the latter made of lead alloy with a copper alloy coating, are otherwise similar. It is suggested that pairs of unperforated plates such as *12893, 12895–6, 14428, 14431* and *15209* may have acted to connect two lengths of strap (ibid., 227); of the York examples, only *15209*, which was recovered from Period 6c demolition derived material at Fishergate, retains both plates.

Square rather than rectangular, *13374* retains central rivets for attachment, and was probably a decorative mount (see straps below). Other possible mounts include *12894,* which has a brass front and lead back, and the rectangular *12892* and *14429*. Finally, a sub-trapezoidal mount with wood remains may originally have adorned a box or casket (*13375*).

Bar mounts (Fig.1480)

Bar mounts may be distinguished from other mounts by their narrowness and their tendency to extend the whole width of a strap. *13376* and *14433–7* are all bar mounts, and leather straps from Coppergate (sfs3006, 18851) and Bedern (sfs247, 1499) also bear several such mounts, some complete with circular roves (see *AY* 17/16 in prep.). The mounts are either cast (e.g. *13376*) or made of sheet (e.g. *14435*) and have plano-convex or U-shaped sections, with either a single central rivet or a rivet at each end; all are rectangular and undecorated apart from *14434* and *14437*. Found in a late 13th century deposit at Bedern, *14434* has a decoratively shaped edge and incised lines; an identical mount was found on Alms Lane, Norwich, in a late 15th century context (Margeson 1993, 40, fig.23, *277*), but may have been residual. A more common and apparently long-lived design is represented by *14437*, from an early

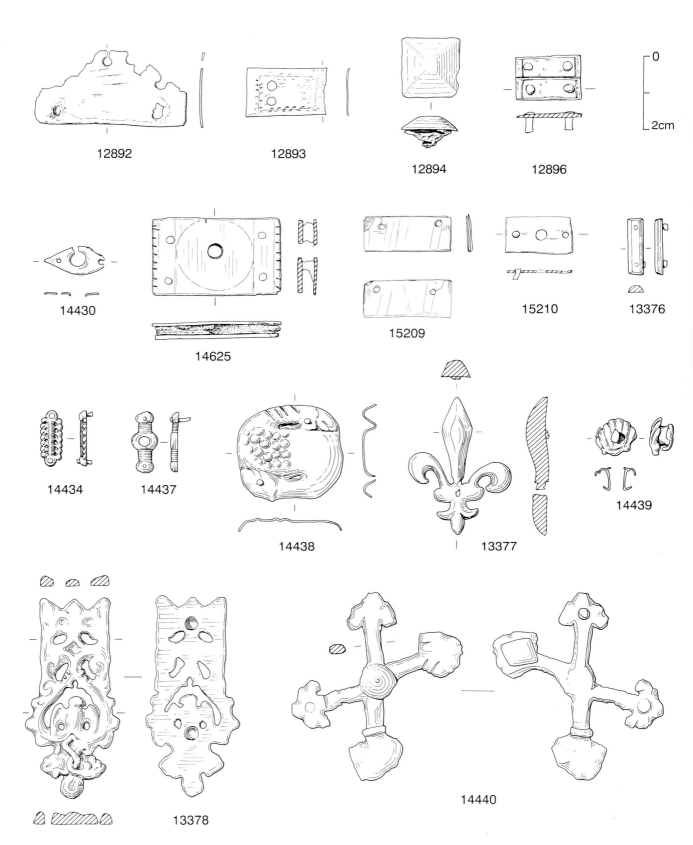

Fig.1480 *Copper alloy square, rectangular and lozenge-shaped mounts 12892–4, 12896 from 16–22 Coppergate, 14430 from Bedern, 14625 from Bedern Chapel, 15209–10 from 46–54 Fishergate; bar mounts 13376 from the Foundry, 14434 and 14437 from Bedern; S-shaped mount 14438 from Bedern; fleur-de-lys mount 13377 from the Foundry; scallop-shaped mount 14439 from Bedern; openwork mount 13378 from the Foundry; saltire mount 14440 from Bedern. Scale 1:1*

15th century context at Bedern. This has a circular perforated central expansion and decorative mouldings on the bars; similar mounts have been found in London in late 12th–early 14th century levels (Egan and Pritchard 1991, 213, fig.134, *1154–8*) and on several other sites, including Kirkstall Abbey, Leeds (Moorhouse and Wrathmell 1987, 132, fig.69, *176*), Lurk Lane, Beverley (A.R. Goodall 1991, 148, fig.114, *599*), Botolph Street, Norwich (Margeson 1993, 40, fig.23, *286*), and Winchester (Hinton 1990c, 543, fig.144, *1371*) (see Fig.1315 for locations).

S-shaped mount (Fig.1480)

The S-shaped mount from Bedern, *14438,* is made of repoussé sheet. The body of the 'S' is decorated with raised pellets and diagonal lines and there are small rivets in the ends. This common motif has been found elsewhere, for example in Norwich (Margeson 1993, 40, fig.23, *274*) and London (Egan and Pritchard 1991, 203, fig.127, *1085*), and is typically 15th century, being associated with the collars of SS, which were the livery of the House of Lancaster, and usually incorporated precious metals (Spencer 1985, 449–51).

Figurative and non-figurative mounts (Figs.1480–1)

The fleur-de-lys, as seen on the gilded mount *13377* from an early 15th century context at the Foundry, was another common medieval motif (see Egan and Pritchard 1991, 200, fig.126, *184*). Also from a 15th century context, but less certainly a mount, *14439* has a cylindrical shank with out-turned lower edge and a scallop-shaped head. A cast copper alloy decoratively shaped plate with openwork decoration, *13378,* may be a mount; it was found in a late 15th century deposit at the Foundry. The openwork incorporates a bird within a crocketed and scrolled frame and with a foliate terminal at the lower end, the upper end being notched. Although openwork strap-ends from the later medieval period are known (see for example Henig 1988, 215, fig.68, *48*), the lack of rivet holes suggests a different function, although holes for attachment are visible on the reverse. Perhaps originally attached to a casket or box, *14440* was found in an early–mid 14th century context at Bedern and is a saltire with arrow-shaped tips, two with rivet holes, and a central boss.

Mounts at strap joins (Figs.1482–4)

Two leather straps found in the Bedern area, one at the Foundry (sf1361) and one at the College (sf2101), clearly show the use of mounts at the point where two lengths of strap are joined together. The former was found in a mid–late 14th century deposit and comprises two pieces of strap with an overlapping join secured by two copper alloy baluster-shaped mounts, made of sheet and probably originally tinned, which are riveted at each end through both thicknesses of strap. Such a strap is likely to be part of a girdle, spur leather or fragment of decorative harness (*AY* 17/16 in prep.).

Small find 2101 is from an early 15th century pit in the College garden; it consists of several lengths of strap. On the cross-strap and on two other lengths of strap a series of quincunxes of rivets join two thicknesses of strap together, the central rivet also attaching a spoked wheel-shaped copper alloy mount. All the rivets have circular roves on the reverse face. The

Fig.1481   Gilded fleur-de-lys mount 13377 from the Foundry. Actual length 40.5mm

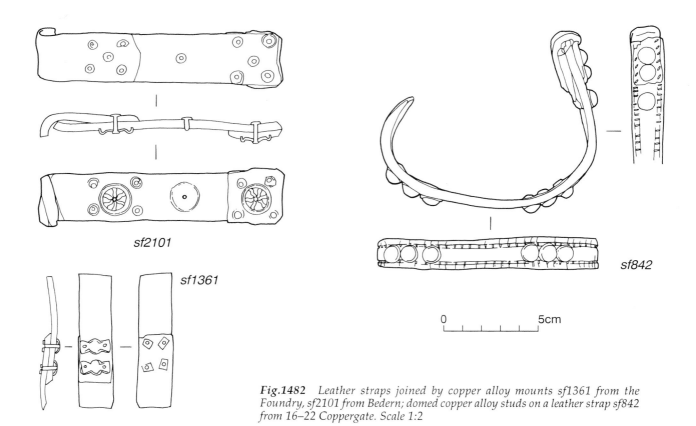

sf2101

sf1361

sf842

Fig.1482 *Leather straps joined by copper alloy mounts sf1361 from the Foundry, sf2101 from Bedern; domed copper alloy studs on a leather strap sf842 from 16–22 Coppergate. Scale 1:2*

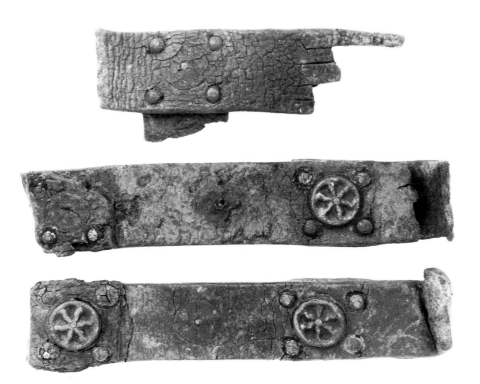

Fig.1483 *Leather strap with copper alloy mounts sf2101 from Bedern*

Fig.1484 Detail of spoked wheel-shaped copper alloy mount on leather strap sf2101. Actual diameter of mount 17mm

circular wheel-shaped mounts have wavy 'spokes' not dissimilar to the circular mounts with 'wavy star' designs from London (Egan and Pritchard 1991, *850*, fig.111), recovered from a context dated c.1350–1400. Although possibly associated with scabbard suspension, the fragment with the fixed junction, a feature not found on medieval belts, gives ground for reasonable doubt that this belongs to a belt and suggests a different function for the piece, such as horse harness (*AY* 17/16 in prep.).

Non-ferrous metal studs were also found on a lined strap of cattle hide from an early 15th century context at Coppergate; this has domed studs of pewter or some other lead/tin alloy (sf842; Fig.1482), and is particularly robust, its shape suggesting it may have been a dog collar (ibid.). A collar hung with bells appears on a dog illustrated in the St William window of York Minster (panel of Beatrice, the Dowager Lady Ros; Fig.1485).

Non-ferrous brooches

Annular brooches (Figs.1486–8)

Differentiating between plain annular buckles and annular brooches has long been a point of controversy; Egan has suggested that a critical factor is the presence or absence of a constriction for the pin on the frame, its presence indicating a brooch, its absence a buckle (Egan and Pritchard 1991, 248). Utilising this method, annular brooches of both precious and base metals were identified in the York assemblage. Bedern produced one brooch of gold (*14507*), and two of silver (*14505–6*). Brooches of base metal were recovered in larger numbers, with five of copper alloy (*12897–901*), and four of pewter (*12949–52*) being found at Coppergate, and two of copper alloy from Bedern (*14442–3*). Probable brooch pins of gold were found at Coppergate (*12936*) and the Foundry (*13405*), and of silver at Fishergate (*15252*), with a copper alloy brooch pin (*14444*) coming from Bedern.

Found in a Period 3 (mid–late 13th century) deposit outside the residential block, Building 9, at Bedern, *14507* is made of decoratively twisted multistrand gold wire, and has a pin with a multi-linear design, possibly defining a gripped or clasped hand where it loops around the frame. Two similar brooches, one of silver, the other of copper alloy, have been found in London in late 12th century contexts (Egan and Pritchard 1991, 256, *1339–40*). A simpler twisted copper alloy wire brooch (*12899*) appears to be contemporary, deriving from a 12th/13th century levelling or dump at Coppergate. The copper alloy brooch *14442* represents a related type, with twisted ornament on only half of the hoop, the other half being plain; it has been gilded to imitate a more expensive brooch. *14442* comes from a mid–late 13th

Fig.1485 Detail from the St William window, York Minster (panel 1e), showing a dog wearing a collar hung with bells (reproduced by courtesy of York Minster Archive, © Dean and Chapter of York)

century context at Bedern, and is a form found elsewhere in 13th century levels, for example at Lurk Lane, Beverley (A.R. Goodall 1991, 148–9, fig.114, *574*), and London (Egan and Pritchard 1991, 249, *1310*).

The gilded silver brooch *14506* is flat with a marked constriction for the pin, now missing, and has been divided up into seven wedge-shaped fields; four alternate fields are inscribed, the inscription reading *INRI* (identified by John Cherry). The inscription is an abbreviation of *I(H)ESUS NAZARENUS REX IUDEORUM*, a formula found in various forms on other ring brooches, including several in the collection of the National Museum of Antiquities of Scotland, all dated to the 14th century (Callander 1924, 169–70, fig.3). Perhaps originally the possession of a vicar, *14506* was found in a layer of mid–late 15th

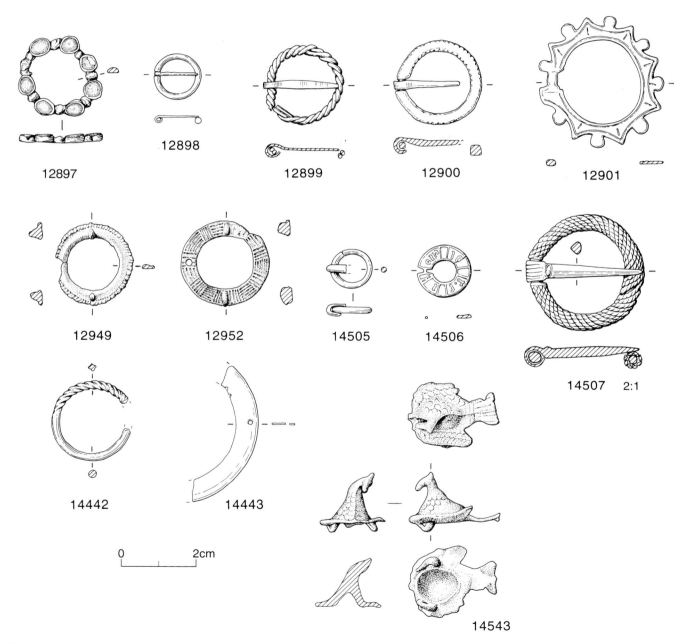

Fig.1486   *Annular brooches 12897–901 (copper alloy), 12949 and 12952 (pewter) from 16–22 Coppergate, 14442–3 (copper alloy), 14505–6 (silver) and 14507 (gold) from Bedern; cast lead bird-shaped brooch 14543 from Bedern. Scale 1:1, 14507 2:1*

century garden soil containing refuse including two tuning pegs (*8067–8, AY* 17/12) and other domestic rubbish, close to Building 27 (the evidence room).

The other silver brooch, *14505*, also from Bedern, is a simple miniature example, lacking most of its pin; it was found in Building 2 (of unknown function) in floor levels of the mid 13th century.

12897 is another imitation, in this instance of a brooch type set with gems, like the gold brooch found on Victoria Street, Manchester (Alexander and Binski 1987, 485–6, *651*). Made of copper alloy, it has seven raised settings containing enamel rather than gemstones. **M.E. Hutchinson** contributes the following:

This small brooch, originally c.24·0mm in diameter, is composed of seven roundels decorated with enamel, separated from each other by the metal backing which curves up between each enamelled circle like a small half-bead. AML Report 4354 identifies the metal as copper with some lead; the lead was probably added to produce a better casting. There is no sign of gilding. The pin appears to have been fixed round the brooch near one end of the smaller fragment, in place of an eighth enamelled roundel.

The decoration is vitreous enamel, melted into the setting. The enamelled decorations all have the same intended layout; an outer ring of opaque blue, then opaque white and, in the centre, red chips, possibly forming an irregular chequer of red and white enamel (Fig.1487). This area is covered with an iridescent layer of corroded glass, heav-ily lacquered, which makes it difficult to see the red chips or to attempt a beta-backscatter radiograph which might clarify the design.

12897 derives from an early 13th century levelling or dump at Coppergate, and is very similar to a brooch from Alms Lane, Norwich, found in a late 13th–14th century context (Margeson 1993, 15, fig.7, *58*).

Two pewter brooches, *12949* and *12952* (Fig.1488), the former recovered from late 13th century levelling or dumping, the latter from 11th–12th century levelling or dumping at Coppergate, are similar to *12901* in having raised projections as part of their design, although, despite careful scrutiny, no evidence was found of any material within them (M.E. Hutchinson, pers. comm.) and they may be bosses cast into the brooches, perhaps as imitation settings. Similar features are present on a number of pewter annular brooches from London (see for example Egan and Pritchard 1991, 252, fig.163, *1323*), and it has been suggested that they might originally have been painted to simulate stones, although analysis has so far failed to find any evidence for this (ibid., 258, 271). The two other pewter brooches, *12950–1*, are both from 13th century deposits, and both have moulded decoration; *12950* is decorated on the pin only, while *12951* has transverse ridges as seen on another London brooch of the early 13th century (ibid., *1322*).

Two copper alloy brooches (*12900–1*) have decorative edges, the former coming from a 12th–13th cen-

Fig.1487 *Detail of enamel setting in copper alloy brooch* **12897** *from 16–22 Coppergate*

Fig.1488 *Pewter brooch* 12952 *from 16–22 Coppergate. Actual diameter 23.5mm*

tury levelling/dump, the latter being unstratified. Considerably smaller, and plain, *12898* was found in a 13th–14th century context. A possible annular brooch fragment, *14443*, comprises an incomplete curved frame with a perforation possibly for a pin; it was found in an early 15th century deposit at Bedern.

Figurative brooch (Fig.1486)

A cast lead alloy bird-shaped brooch with projecting feathered neck, body and extended tail, *14543*, retains a loop and catch for a pin on its base. Although found unstratified at Bedern, a medieval date may be indicated by comparison with other lead alloy brooches with bird motifs found in 14th–15th century deposits in London (Egan and Pritchard 1991, 266, fig.172).

Brooch pins (Fig.1489)

None of the brooch pins can be assigned to any particular form of brooch, and so are not in themselves datable; all are of precious metal or give the

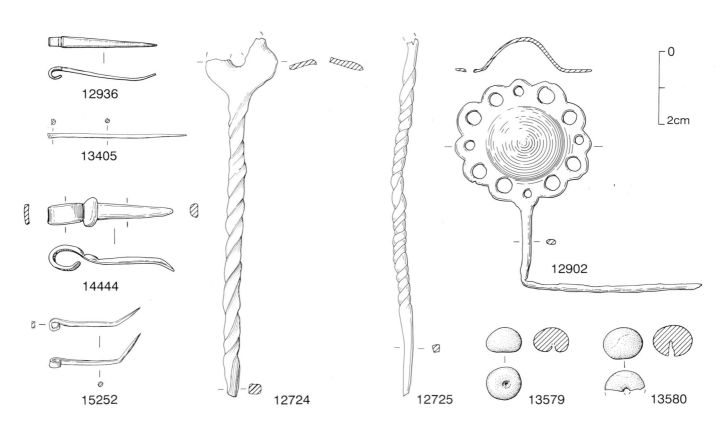

Fig.1489 *Brooch pins* 12936 *(gold) from 16–22 Coppergate,* 13405 *(gold) from the Foundry,* 14444 *(gilded copper alloy) from Bedern,* 15252 *(silver) from 46–54 Fishergate; iron dress pins* 12724–5 *from 16–22 Coppergate; possible copper alloy dress pin* 12902 *from 16–22 Coppergate; glass pin heads* 13579–80 *from Bedern. Scale 1:1*

appearance of precious metal through gilding. The two gold pins derive from a 14th–15th century dump at Coppergate (*12936*) and from a post-medieval context at the Foundry (*13405*), the silver pin from Fishergate (*15252*) is from a 13th century level, while the gilded copper alloy pin from Bedern (*14444*) comes from a mid–late 14th century context.

Dress pins (Fig.1489)

Copper alloy, and less commonly, iron dress pins, typically with relatively large diameter shanks and heads, are almost invariably pre-Conquest in date, although an unusual large copper alloy pin from Coppergate (*12902*) may be later (see below). Cast and often decorative copper alloy dress pins have been found in considerable numbers in York, for example, in Anglian deposits at Fishergate (*5337–5410*, pp.1361–7, *AY* 17/9) and at Anglo-Scandinavian Coppergate (see pp.2576–83, *AY* 17/14), while iron pins were also retrieved at Anglo-Scandinavian Coppergate (*3798–816*, pp.693–6, *AY* 17/6).

All the small iron pins from medieval contexts are probably residual from Anglian (Fishergate) or Anglo-Scandinavian (Coppergate and Bedern) contexts. Three have spherical heads (*14110, 15110* and *15115*) and are tin plated; *15111* has a spherical head and is not plated. *15112* and *15114* have sub-spherical lead heads. *15113* has a pointed head and is plated. There are also four pin shanks from medieval contexts at Fishergate already published in *AY* 17/9 as *5088–9, 5092–3*. For similar objects see *AY* 17/6 (p.693) and *AY* 17/9 (p.1367).

In addition, Coppergate has produced two possible iron pins c.100mm long with spirally twisted shanks (*12724* and *12725*) and in the case of *12724*, which is nearly complete, a pierced head. They may be compared with two possible pins with spirally twisted shanks from Anglo-Scandinavian contexts at Coppergate (p.696, Fig.300, *3804, 3809*, *AY* 17/6). *12723* which has a looped head may also be a pin.

The shank on *12902* indicates use as a possible dress pin, although the design of the prominent head suggests that it may have acted as a type of pin badge. A similar stylised flower forms the terminal to a 13th century casket mount from London (Egan 1998, 72, fig.50, *150*). *12902* was recovered from a mid 12th century dump.

Glass dress pin heads (Fig.1489)

Two blue glass pin heads were recovered at Bedern (*13579–80*). Although no longer attached to pins, their identity as pin heads rather than beads is indicated by perforations which fail to pierce both ends. The glass of neither pin head has been analysed, but glass pin heads found in London in late 12th century deposits were shown to be of high-lead glass (Egan and Pritchard 1991, 299, *1468–9*). Both high-lead glass beads and soda glass beads re-using Roman blue glass were being made in the 11th and 12th centuries in York on and around Coppergate (pp.2519–28, *AY* 17/14), an area that has also produced a green glass pin head (Radley 1971, 49). It is possible that both the Bedern pin heads derive from this industry; being blue they are more likely to be of soda glass.

Other copper alloy pins (Fig.1490)

Medieval pins made from copper alloy wire and with separately made heads have been found in quantity at all the sites discussed in this fascicule. They are much slighter in form than the earlier dress pin types. A total of 438 wire pins and pin shank fragments were recovered; 337 pins with heads have been classed according to head type, the remaining 101 being unclassifiable pin shank fragments (see below).

The vast majority of the pins with heads, representing approximately 90% (301 examples), have wire-wound heads, and were found on every site under discussion (see Table 303). Only one or two examples from each site have been catalogued.

Pins with wire-wound heads

As Table 303 shows, these simply made pins comprising a wire shaft with a head formed by wrapping wire once or twice around one end (see for example *12903* and *15211*) and occasionally stamped into a sub-globular shape, as on *13381*, were found in large numbers at the Foundry, Bedern and Fishergate. It can be seen from the table that of this total of 301, only 56 (18·6%) were stratified in pre-16th century deposits, the earliest being from 13th century contexts at Fishergate. A very similar picture was noted at Winchester, where 72 of a total of 371 pins (19·4%) came from pre-16th century levels, the earliest securely stratified examples also coming from 13th century contexts (Biddle and Barclay 1990, 561).

Table 303 Wire-wound pins by site and date

Site	13th c.	14th c.	15th c.	16th c.>	Unstrat.	Total
Coppergate	–	–	1	1	1	3
Piccadilly	–	–	3	1	–	4
Foundry	–	1	3	126	1	131
Bedern	–	–	29	42	17	88
Bedern Chapel	–	–	–	26	–	26
Aldwark	–	–	2	1	–	3
Fishergate	4	–	13	29	–	46
Total	4	1	51	226	19	301

Together with evidence from Southampton, where a small number of pins were also found in 13th century levels (Harvey 1975, 254–6, *1709, 1716, 1720, 1730*), the origin of these pins can be pushed back some 300 years earlier than had previously been thought (Tylecote 1972, 183). At both York and Winchester it is likely that some of the pins recovered from post-16th century contexts are residual from earlier activity, but, although statistical analysis of the Winchester pins suggested greater standardisation in the post-medieval period, it seems as yet impossible to differentiate medieval from post-medieval pins (Biddle and Barclay 1990, 560–71).

Pins with non-wire-wound heads

The 36 pins with other head types were found on all the sites except Bedern Chapel (see Table 304). As with the pins with wire-wound heads, only a few examples have been catalogued.

The pins with non-wire-wound heads may be divided into two main groups according to head type, although all share a similar construction, with their shanks fixed into the undersides of their heads. The majority (30) have globular or sub-globular heads (e.g. *12904–8, 13066–8, 13382–4, 14448–50, 14725, 15213–15*). The earliest example comes from a 13th century context at Fishergate (*15213*) but the majority derive from 14th and 15th century deposits as Table 304 shows. Most are plain but two examples have decoratively ridged heads (*14449* and *15214*), while analysis of material around the heads of *15213* and *14450* indicated the use of solder to attach the heads to the shank tops. Pins with more unusual head types (not included in Table 304) comprise *12909* from

Table 304 Globular-headed and other pins with non-wire-wound heads by site and date (* = lens-shaped head)

	11th–12th c.	13th c.	14th c.	15th c.	16th c.>	Unstratified	Total
Coppergate	1*	1*	5	4	2 + 1*	1	15
Piccadilly	–	–	–	3	–	–	3
Foundry	–	–	–	1*	2 + 1*	1	5
Bedern	–	–	4	2	2	–	8
Bedern Chapel	–	–	–	–	–	–	–
Aldwark	–	–	1*	1	–	–	2
Fishergate	–	1	–	–	2	–	3
Total	1	2	10	11	10	2	36

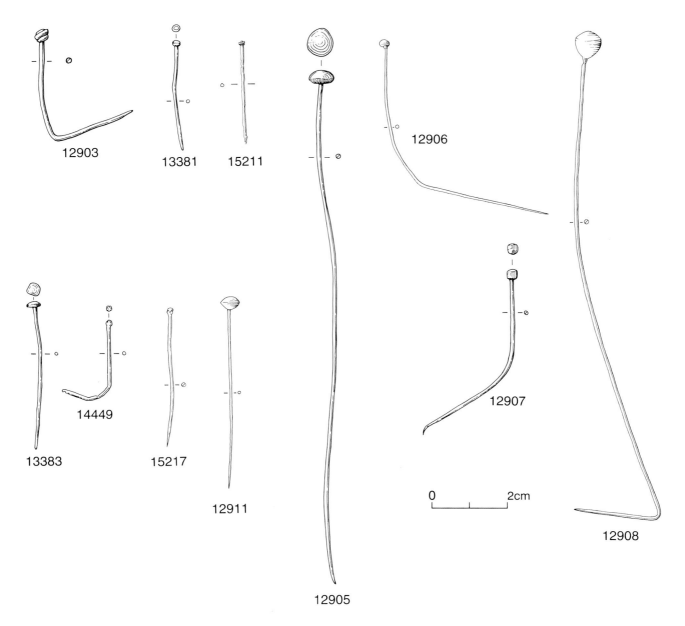

Fig.1490 Copper alloy pins with wire-wound heads 12903 *from 16–22 Coppergate,* 13381 *from the Foundry,* 15211 *from 46–54 Fishergate; copper alloy pins with globular or sub-globular heads* 12905–8 *from 16–22 Coppergate,* 13383 *from the Foundry,* 14449 *from Bedern; copper alloy pin with faceted head* 15217 *from 46–54 Fishergate; pin with lens-shaped head* 12911 *from 16–22 Coppergate. Scale 1:1*

mid 16th century levels at Coppergate which has an unusual lead alloy globular head, and three pins from Fishergate: *15216* from a Period 6b context has a head formed by small blobs which have been stuck to the shank top and then faceted, while from demolition levels *15217–18* both have faceted heads, the facets on *15217* standing proud of the head.

The second head type comprises two opposing hemispheres joined together, producing a lens-shaped head; the pin shank passes through a hole in the underside of the lower hemisphere. Six of these pins were found on the York sites (e.g.*12910–11*, *13385*), and, as Table 304 shows, two of those found at Coppergate represent the earliest examples of medieval pins from York. At Winchester, it was suggested that this pin type was a 14th or 15th century innovation, although of the eight such pins recovered, two came from considerably earlier contexts, one from a late 9th–10th century deposit, the other from a well-stratified late 11th century deposit (Biddle and Barclay 1990, 555, *1456–7*). The possibility that this is, in fact, a long-lived type was raised (ibid.), and it appears that the two pins from Coppergate (*12910–11*) support this supposition.

The tables above show that pins with wire-wound heads were the most commonly found across the York sites; there are marked differences, however, between the main sites, most notably between Coppergate and the others in the concentrations of pin types, as shown in Table 305.

Table 305 clearly shows the marked contrast between the assemblage of pins found at Coppergate and those found on the other main sites; it must be remembered, however, that Coppergate produced relatively few pins at all.

The function of both the wire-wound headed and other pins has been the subject of some debate; Biddle and Barclay chose to use the term 'sewing pins' for pins with wire-wound heads found in Winchester, although they noted that they also had other functions, most notably as dress fastenings, being used instead of buttons, and for fixing head-dresses in place (Biddle and Barclay 1990, 560). They considered the pins with non-wire-wound heads to be exclusively used as dress fasteners (ibid., 552). In Frances Pritchard's brief survey of pins from London, however, no functional distinction appears to be drawn between these two types, which she considers to have been primarily used to fix veils (Egan and Pritchard 1991, 297). Certainly clothing, in particular women's clothing, became more intricately folded and tucked during the 14th and 15th centuries, necessitating the use of pins in great numbers (Caple 1991, 243). The possible use of pins with wire-wound heads on shrouds has been posited (Bradley and Manning 1981, fig.8, *9*) but was discounted at Waterford, Ireland, where only seven pins were recovered on a site which contained over 1,200 burials (Scully 1997, 451). Similarly only three such pins were recovered from graves at Fishergate, where almost 300 burials were located (*AY* 12/2, 135, table 20).

Buttons (Fig.1491)

13277 from an early post-medieval context at the Foundry is probably a button made from tin-plated iron. Three copper alloy buttons were also recovered from Bedern (*14451–3*). All are, or were originally, spherical, being either hollow and cast in two pieces, as in the case of *14453*, or solid, one-piece castings; both types have looped shanks for attachment. The two one-piece buttons, *14451–2*, come from mid 13th–early 14th century deposits. It has been suggested previously that buttons were introduced into England during the 14th century (Newton 1980, 15), but recent finds of spherical buttons in 13th century contexts in London (Egan and Pritchard 1991, 272–6, *1376–9*, *1384–6*), together with the two Bedern examples, indicate an earlier introduction is likely, although at this date they may have been ornamental rather than fastenings (Biddle and Cook 1990, 571–2).

A copper alloy object with a loop at the back, *14454*, may also be an elaborately cast button although its design, depicting a bishop or archbishop with mitre and staff, seems rather elaborate for such a function. It was recovered from a mid–late 15th century deposit at Bedern.

Table 305 Pin head types expressed as percentages of all pins with heads (pin shank fragments were not catalogued)

	Wire-wound head	Globular head	Lens-shaped head	Total pins
Coppergate	16.6	66.8	16.6	18
Foundry	96.3	2.2	1.5	136
Bedern	86.9	13.1	–	95
Fishergate	93.8	6.2	–	49

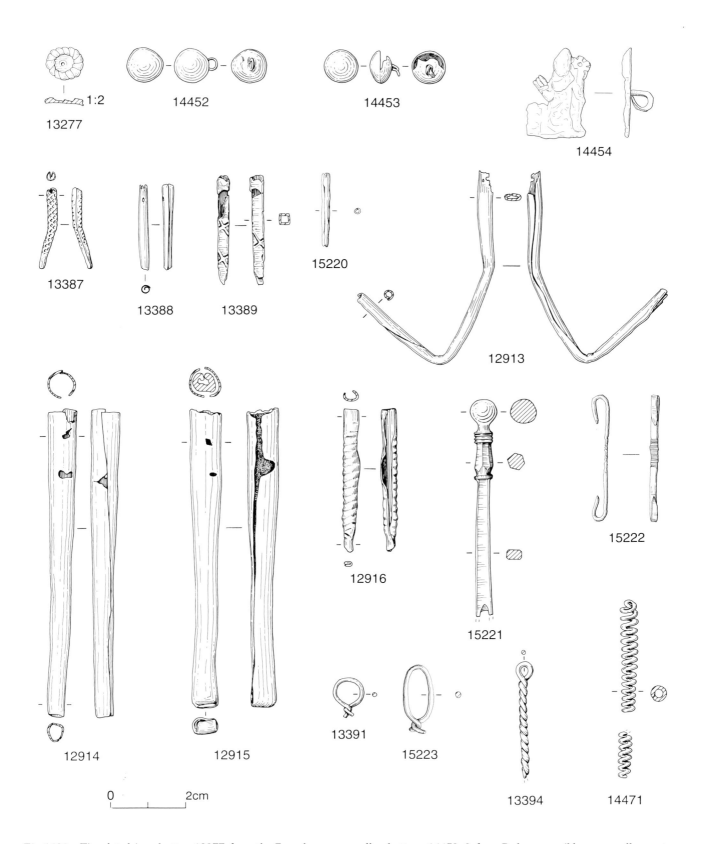

Fig.1491 *Tin-plated iron button* 13277 *from the Foundry; copper alloy buttons* 14452–3 *from Bedern; possible copper alloy cast button* 14454 *from Bedern; copper alloy lace tags* 13387–9 *from the Foundry,* 15220 *from 46–54 Fishergate; possible copper alloy lace tags* 12913–16 *from 16–22 Coppergate; possible lace or ribbon threader* 15221 *from 46–54 Fishergate; double hooked fastener* 15222 *from 46–54 Fishergate; wire loop fasteners* 13391 *from the Foundry and* 15223 *from 46–54 Fishergate; twisted wire loop* 13394 *from the Foundry; possible hair accessories* 14471 *from Bedern. Scale 1:1,* 13277 *scale 1:2*

Lace tags (Fig.1491)

These copper alloy objects were used on the ends of laces to prevent fraying and to facilitate threading; in the medieval period they were known as aiglets or points, the latter term also being used for the laces themselves, which were used to fasten clothing and accessories such as bags (see Egan and Pritchard 1991, 286). All the sites in York under discussion here produced lace tags, although only one from Coppergate has been confidently identified as such (*12912*), four others being possible examples (*12913–16*). The Foundry produced 23 tags (e.g. *13386–9*), while Bedern produced 33 (e.g. *14455–62*) and five came from Bedern Chapel (e.g. *14635–8*). Twenty-one tags were recovered at Fishergate (e.g.

15219–20) and one at 22 Piccadilly (*13069*). Only selected lace tags from each site have been catalogued.

A typology based on shape and seam identified four types of tag made of sheet within the York assemblage. These are a rolled tube with a butted or edge-to-edge seam (Type E), those with the seam edges folded inward (Type F), those with an overlapped seam (Type O), and those with a sub-square section (Type U). Apart from Type U, of which there is only one example (see below), all these types have been recognised elsewhere, for example, in Norwich (Margeson 1993, 22). Eight tags could not be typed. Table 306 shows at what periods these types occurred at Fishergate, the Foundry and Bedern. Type E was the most commonly recovered type, representing 60%

Table 306 Lace tags from the Foundry, Bedern and Fishergate by type and period

Bedern Foundry (NB one unclassified lace tag)

Period	1–5	6	7	Total
Type E	–	10	1	11
Type F	–	3	–	3
Type O	–	4	3	7
Type U	–	–	1	1
Total	–	17	5	22

Bedern (NB Seven unclassified lace tags)

Period	1–4	5	6	7	8	Post-med.	Unstrat.	Total
Type E	–	1	–	1	6	4	3	15
Type F	–	–	–	–	–	3	–	3
Type O	–	–	–	–	4	3	1	8
Type U	–	–	–	–	–	–	–	–
Total	–	1	–	1	10	10	4	26

Fishergate

Period	6a–d	6e	6f–z	7	8–11	Total
Type E	–	8	1	9	1	19
Type F	–	–	–	–	–	–
Type O	–	2	–	–	–	2
Type U	–	–	–	–	–	–
Total	–	10	1	9	1	21

of all the typed tags. The earliest occurrences of Type E were at Bedern (*14455*) in an early 14th century deposit and at 22 Piccadilly in 14th–15th century levels (*13069*); they occurred most frequently in 15th–16th century levels, however. Type O tags numbered 23 (28·75%); these all occurred in 15th–16th century or later contexts. There were eight examples of Type F (10% of all typed tags), and only one example of Type U; these both appear to be post-medieval types, occurring in mid 16th century and later deposits. Apart from one uncertain tag from Coppergate (see below), these post-medieval types were also the only ones to be decorated.

In their study of lace tags from London, Egan and Pritchard (1991, 281) noted a range in lengths of 25–40mm and so little variation that a standardised form could be recognised. Amongst the complete York tags all except the four from Coppergate noted above (*12913–16*) and a single tag from Bedern (*14456*) ranged in length from 16mm to 35mm and in diameter from 1·6 to 5mm. Of the four tags from Coppergate, three fall considerably outside these ranges, being 82–5mm in length, and all four derive from significantly earlier deposits, casting doubt on their identifications. A similar occurrence was noted amongst tags from London, however, where it was suggested that tags of c.40–100mm long may represent an earlier form which became less common after the middle of the 14th century (ibid., 290). This may also be true of the Coppergate tags, and suggests that the slightly larger tag from Bedern, although from a Period 8 deposit, may be residual.

Indications of the materials onto which tags were attached come from several examples which retain traces of textile or other organic material inside. Remnants of silk braid or cord were identified inside two tags, *13389* and *15219*, while another, *14460*, contained braid possibly made from hemp. No definite traces of leather were found in any of the York tags, despite such remains being found in tags elsewhere, such as London (Egan and Pritchard 1991, 282) and Winchester (Biddle and Hinton 1990c, 581). The use of rivets to attach the tags to their silk or leather points is also evident amongst the York tags, examples retaining rivets or their holes coming from every site.

Lace or ribbon threader (Fig.1491)

An incomplete copper alloy object, *15221*, found at Fishergate in deposits associated with 16th cen-
tury alterations to the priory's north range, has been identified by **Dr Carole Morris** as a possible lace or ribbon threader. She notes the following:

The broken end of 15221 had a hole through which one could pass a ribbon or thread; the tool end and thread could then be pushed through a hole, and the ribbon pulled through. It would act like a needle-threader or lace-maker's 'lazy-susan', and could have been used on fabric or on garments of the period (16th century) that needed lacing together, on jerkins, for example.

Double hooked fastener (Fig.1491)

Made from a copper alloy strip, *15222* was found in Period 7b destruction deposits in the refectory at Fishergate; similar examples have been found in contemporary contexts in Norwich and are thought to have been used with chains as clothes fasteners (Margeson 1993, 19, fig.9, *82*).

Wire loop fasteners (Fig.1491)

These simple copper alloy fastenings were found at the Foundry (*13390–3*), Bedern (*14463–5*) and Fishergate (*15223*), in deposits ranging in date from mid–late 15th century (*14463*) into the post-medieval period. The function of these items is uncertain, although possible uses include dress fasteners (Margeson 1993, 20) or chain links (Hinton 1990g, 1089, *4063*). As the find-spots of the York examples and others (e.g. Oakley 1979, 260, *115–20*) indicate, these are a late medieval to post-medieval type of fastener.

Twisted wire loops (Fig.1491)

These differ from the copper alloy wire fasteners in having an extended twisted shank with a pointed tip, and ten were recovered, all deriving from 15th–16th century deposits (*13070, 13394–6, 14466–9, 14639, 15224*). The function of these objects is uncertain; they have been interpreted as a form of lace tag (A.R. Goodall 1984, 339, fig.191, *125*) and as nail-cleaners or toothpicks (see for example Henig 1988, 216–17, fig.69, *61–2*; Margeson 1993, 63–4, fig.32, *400–1*).

Copper alloy wire hook and eye

Found in a mid–late 15th century deposit at Bedern, *14470* appears to be the hook from a hook and eye; such fastenings have been recovered from

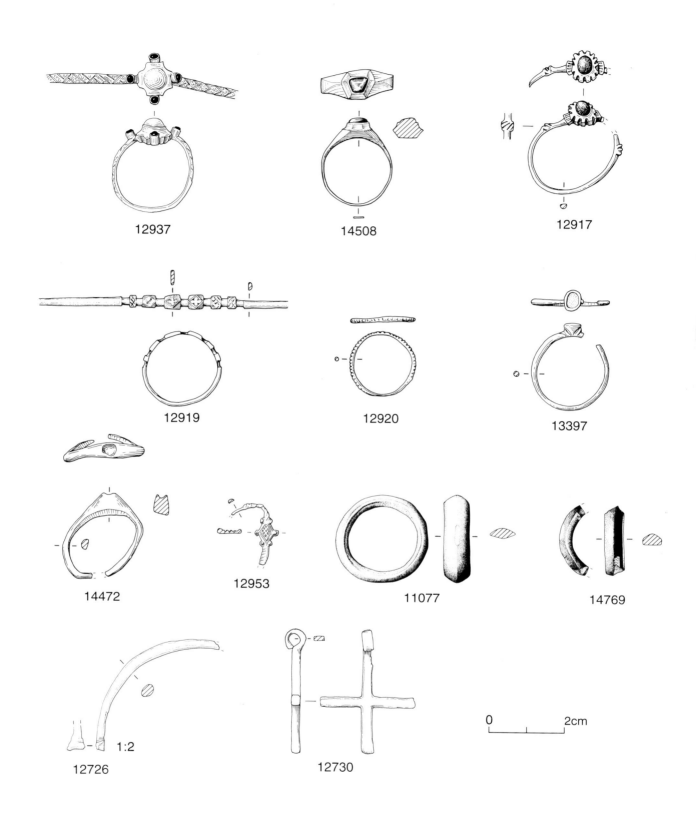

Fig.1492 *Finger-rings of gold and precious stones* **12937** *from 16–22 Coppergate and* **14508** *from Bedern; of copper alloy* **12917**, **12919–20** *from 16–22 Coppergate,* **13397** *from the Foundry,* **14472** *from Bedern; of pewter* **12953** *from 16–22 Coppergate; of jet* **11077** *from 16–22 Coppergate and* **14769** *from 46–54 Fishergate; tin-plated iron bracelet* **12726** *from 16–22 Coppergate; iron cross-shaped pendant* **12730** *from 16–22 Coppergate. Scale 1:1,* **12726** *1:2*

Norwich in deposits of similar date (Margeson 1993, 19, fig.10, *90*).

Possible hair accessories (Fig.1491)

Two fragments of coiled wire (*14471*) were found in a mid 15th century deposit at Bedern, and may have functioned as hair accessories; silk-covered coiled wire was sometimes used in medieval head-dresses, and fragments of such wire have been recovered from 14th–15th century contexts in London (Egan and Pritchard 1991, 294–6).

Jewellery

Finger-rings (Figs.1492–7)

Non-ferrous metal

Two gold finger-rings set with precious and semi-precious stones were recovered from medieval contexts at Coppergate (*12937*) and Bedern (*14508*). In addition, a finger-ring fragment of silver was recovered at Fishergate (*15253*), and ten rings of copper alloy were found, at Coppergate (*12917–22*), Fishergate (*15225*), at the Foundry (*13397*) and at Bedern (*14472–3*). A single pewter ring was found at Coppergate (*12953*).

Rings set with gems

The gold finger-rings *12937* and *14508* were examined by the archaeological gemmologist **M.E. Hutchinson**, who contributes the following:

12937 was examined by low-powered microscope and very few signs of wear were seen. It is a most attractive piece of jewellery. The head (front) of the ring is cruciform in shape, c.8·1mm across and set with a central pearl in a raised collet, which appears to be integral with the head. Four pink stones set on high collets are placed at the ends of the arms of the cross. There is no 'posy' engraved inside the shank, nor is there any evidence that the ring has been 'sized', that is, altered to fit. It corresponds roughly with a modern size 'T'. Analysis gives the surface of the ring a gold content of c.80%, slightly better than 18-carat gold which is 75% pure gold by weight.

The condition of the pearl is truly remarkable. Pearls have an organic component (conchiolin) as well as calcium carbonate (aragonite) and for a pearl to survive burial for 700 years and then to emerge from the ground not only almost completely undamaged and uneroded, but with its orient (mother-of-pearl multicoloured gleam) still in evidence is amazing. The pearl is roughly 5·6mm in diameter, but a portion is hidden by the setting. It is also partly brown in colour, but has been set so that this area is mostly concealed. This colour change is not unknown in pearls and the top, as mounted, is also slightly brown. It is probably a fresh-water pearl, as marine pearls were not readily available until the Portuguese discovered the route to the East and the Spanish reached the New World (Sprott 1984, 408). However, some marine pearls were probably traded or given as gifts earlier.

It is impossible to tell whether the pearl is complete, a half pearl or a blister pearl (a pearl which grows attached

Fig.1493 *Detail of pearl and garnets set in gold finger-ring* 12937 *from 16–22 Coppergate. Actual diameter of pearl 5.6mm*

to the nacreous lining of the shell and therefore has a part not covered with nacre, mother-of-pearl). One of the two latter options might be expected for reasons of economy. The setting gives no clues, as the pearl is about 5·6mm in diameter and the distance from the top of the pearl to the back of the head (the inside of the ring) is 6·1mm. Nor is it possible to tell whether the pearl is held purely by the setting, or whether it is part-drilled and held by a peg as in a modern pearl earring.

Camden's Britannia (1695, p.840d) states that pearls were found in the River Irt, in Cumberland. It also says on the same page, 'Muscle-Pearls (sic) are frequently found in other rivers hereabouts; as also in Wales and Foreign Countries'. They are certainly still fished in Scotland where they grow in the fresh-water mussel Margaritana margaritifera and, more rarely, the swan mussel Anadanta cygnea, though these are of no commercial value (Sprott 1984, 407).

Fig.1494 Details of both shoulders of gold finger-ring 12937 from 16–22 Coppergate. The decoration is neither symmetrical nor a mirror image

The pink stones were identified by their inclusions as natural stones, and examination of their absorption spectrum by hand-held visible-light spectroscope identified them as almandine garnets. They are slightly oblong and about 2·0mm long. Their irregular shape, combined with the fact that slight dips occur in their surfaces, strongly suggests that they are small polished pieces of water-worn gem gravel. Magnification reveals that they are not well polished, especially on the angle between top and side, but the small size of the stones prevents this detracting from their appearance. They are not claw set; the gold on the tops of the collets has been thinned and then rubbed over the margins of the stones. It is possible that the garnet on the shoulder which has the zig-zag design, rather than chevrons (see below), is a replacement, or has come out and been reset at some time, as it is set lower than the others, but the colour is a good match. The stones are unlikely to be foiled. They do not have the brilliance of foiled stones and it would be easier just to polish the inside of the mount before setting the stones. The black material round the pearl and the garnets is not a decayed silver foil, nor niello; this was confirmed by energy dispersive X-ray diffraction (ED-XRF). Under magnification it appears to be granular and the same as the patches of black material present on the surface of the head and on other pieces examined.

The shoulders are decorated with a black inlay, which has been identified as niello; it is not decayed silver inlay. An interesting feature is that the decoration is neither symmetrical, nor a mirror image on the two shoulders, but the design on one side is rotated through approximately 90°, as shown in Fig.1494. On one shoulder the design consists of five chevrons pointing away from the head, interspersed with small punched circles, frequently incomplete. On the other shoulder, the design is that of a zig-zag with other lines crossing it at an angle, going round part of the shank as a continuous design, rather than across it. Punched circles, frequently incomplete, are also incorporated.

12937 was recovered from a pit which related to areas of cobbling, possibly representing a path, between buildings on Tenement C; this period of activity is dated to the mid 13th century, a time when the wearing of gold rings was becoming popular (Oman 1974, 6). Such a fine ring with a high gold content and set with precious and semi-precious gems was clearly the possession of an individual of wealth; rings of this quality and value rarely appear in wills (Egan and Pritchard 1990, 329), and its loss, obviously accidental, must have been greatly regretted.

Examination of the inside of ring 14508 shows that it was made in two parts, the head and shoulders being one and the shank being the other. The joins can be seen clearly (see Fig.1495). The head of the ring, which is set with a watery, bluish, hexagonal stone in a closed setting, is expanded relative to the shank with the shoulders tapering to meet it in both directions. The shank is made of flat gold strip, 3·2mm wide at the back, and shows no sign of having been 'sized' or altered to fit.

The stone is not large, measuring roughly 5·0 × 4·7mm. Examination by low-powered microscope showed that it is parti-coloured blue and colourless, or possibly blue and pale yellow (though the obvious browny-yellow area is iron-staining reflecting from a fracture). It is this patchiness which gives the watery appearance. The stone (Fig.1496) has damage on two corners, in one case associated with an orangey-brown inclusion. A 'scoop' in the surface suggests that something undesirable, possibly a chip or an ugly inclusion, may have been ground out; the long curved facet on the longest edge of the stone also suggests that this stone presented problems to the polisher. Examination of the interior of the stone revealed growth lines, tension cracks and various inclusions, including a curious triangular one near to the surface and perpendicular to it. The back of the stone appears to be just chipped to shape, not polished, and this makes detection of a foil difficult as it causes reflections. However, a silvery gleam was no-

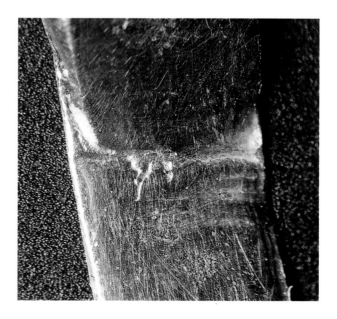

Fig.1495 *Detail of the inside of gold ring 14508 from Bedern showing the join between the two parts*

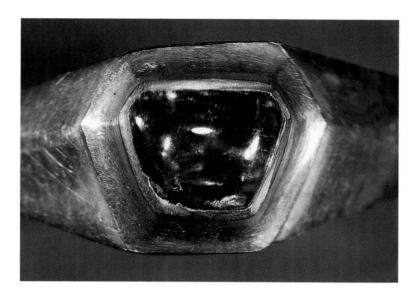

Fig.1496   Detail of the sapphire setting of gold ring 14508 from Bedern. Actual length of stone 5.0mm

ticed in one area and this may have come from a reflective foil. Previous analysis by the AML had identified a high percentage of aluminium in the stone. Examination by ED-XRF confirmed this, together with a trace of iron; there was no silica. When the stone's spectrum was examined with a hand-held visible-light spectroscope, the character-istic absorption spectrum of natural blue sapphire was seen. Natural blue sapphires are coloured by a small amount of titanium and iron. ED-XRF did not detect titanium, but the parts of the stone exhibiting a strong blue colour ap-pear to be deep in the stone. All this, together with the hexagonal shape of the stone and its appearance and col-our, identify the stone as a natural blue sapphire, the blue variety of corundum (Al_2O_3); it is probably a natural crys-tal of sapphire, the top of which has been polished. It is not possible to say definitely where this stone came from. Blue sapphires are found in the British Isles but have never been common. Sri Lanka is a possibility as many sapphires from there are parti-coloured.

14508 is poorly made by comparison with the pearl and garnet ring from Coppergate. The join be-tween the shoulders and the shank is clumsy on the inside and the shank is just a strip of gold joining the shoulders. However, it was a valuable ring set with a comparatively rare stone, so the lack of finish is somewhat surprising. It is set with a hexagonal sap-phire, and sapphire rings may have been particularly associated with ecclesiastics, with at least a dozen found in the graves of medieval bishops (Oman 1974, 46, 52, pl.13), some possibly representing the ring with which the bishop was consecrated. Elaborate pontifical rings, worn by bishops when celebrating masses, have also frequently included sapphires; see, for example, that of the mid 13th century archbishop of York, Walter de Gray (Cherry 1981, 64–5, *127*). *14508* was found in a mid 14th century deposit at Bedern (spread over foundations remaining from the demolition of the south-west aisle connecting wall in the residential Building 5), and is thus likely to be roughly contemporary with five gold rings set with gemstones found in London, including one set with a sapphire (Egan and Pritchard 1991, 327–9, fig.215, *1614*). Despite its poor finish and possible ecclesias-tical connections, a ring such as *14508* seems too grand to have belonged to one of the vicars.

Rings set with imitation gems

Medieval goldsmiths were exhorted not to set gems of glass or imitation stone into their rings, as a 15th century oath of the Goldsmiths' Company records (Reddaway and Walker 1975, 212–13). Rings of base metals were made in much greater numbers than their precious metal counterparts, however, and often imitated those of more precious metals in this manner, utilising glass settings; *12917* from a 12th–13th century levelling/dump at Coppergate is an example of one of these. **M.E. Hutchinson** contrib-utes the following:

This finger ring is very different from the gold ones described above. AML Report 4354 identified the metal as a high-zinc brass with lead and tin. The surface is now rough and degraded. The head of the ring has a decorative notched edge; there is no trace of gilding. The shank is detached at one side of the head and distorted. There are no shoulders as such, but there is a small cast-in, twisted decoration a short distance along the shank on each side of the head (Fig.1497).

The glass paste is an oval cabochon, c.4·6 × 3·7mm, very dull looking, with an extremely degraded surface; ED-XRF detected copper and zinc and a small amount of silica. However, a strong light passed through it showed that it was a transparent blue of medium tone. The material was identified as glass because bubbles could be seen and examination through a Chelsea filter showed the colourant to be cobalt. It is possibly intended to imitate a sapphire and probably has a foil behind it, but it is impossible to see anything through the glass, or between the edge of the glass and its setting (Fig.1497). Foils are common in closed settings and frequently tinted to improve the colour of both real and imitation stones, but even in 19th century jewellery they are very difficult to detect as they must be in close contact with the back of the stone to have the desired effect and they therefore tend to look like the back of the stone. The same granular black material as seen on 12937 is also present in the gap between the bezel and the glass. Under low magnification a band of metal corrosion products can be seen running round the base of the blue glass.

This may mark the site of a band setting, now gone, and probably accounts for the ED-XRF analysis mentioned above.

Compared to the gold rings, 12917 comes from the other end of the jewellery spectrum. It probably looked very pretty and golden when new, but as it was not gilded, the wearer's finger would eventually have gone green under the ring and it would have been exposed as cheap costume jewellery.

From the Bedern sites come 13397 and 14472 which have both lost their settings. 14472 has a stirrup-shaped hoop, originally set with an oval stone or glass paste. This hoop form was in fashion from the mid 12th to the 14th century (Murdoch 1991, 131) which indicates that 14472 is likely to be contemporary in its early to mid 14th century floor level in the residential Building 5. While base metal rings have often been found with glass settings in imitation of precious metal rings set with gems, as for example in London (Egan and Pritchard 1991, 326–7), others are known with gems, such as one from King's Lynn which was set with a garnet (Geddes and Carter 1977, 287, fig.130, 2). 13397 has been gilded to give the impression of being a more valuable ring, and was found in an early 14th century foundation pile at the Foundry.

Fig.1497 *Detail of finger-ring 12917 with blue glass setting from 16–22 Coppergate. Actual length of bezel 8.9mm*

Copper alloy rings without stones

Medieval rings in the form of simple bands were typically either cast or made of sheet (Egan and Pritchard 1991, 332); all the copper alloy hoops from Coppergate, which, apart from one unstratified example (12922), come from 11th–13th century levels, appear to be made from sheet. The majority of the Coppergate rings are brass, but 12918 is made of copper, and is small, possibly for use on an upper finger joint or for a child. Three of the rings are undecorated (12918, 12921–2) but the two others incorporate decorative features, simple grooving on 12920 and pairs of rectangular bezels on 12919 with incised decoration. In contrast, the simple bands from Bedern (14473) and Fishergate (15225) have been cast with ridge mouldings; the former derives from a late 15th/early 16th century context, the latter from 13th century cemetery soil.

Other rings

Only the sub-discoidal silver bezel of 15253 survives; it was found in Period 6a levelling deposits at Fishergate, and may pre-date the priory. The decoratively shaped pewter ring 12953 was recovered from a build-up deposit associated with a late 12th century structure at Coppergate. It has been cast with a lozenge-shaped bezel filled with cross-hatching, projections at each corner, and a moulding and grooves on the hoop; it shares the decorative characteristics of a number of pewter rings found in London (Egan and Pritchard 1991, 334, fig.218, 1630, 1632). The earliest of the London rings date to the early 13th century (ibid.), and all are noted to be small, as is 12953, suggesting use on upper joints, probably of little fingers, or by children (ibid., 335).

Jet and non-jet finger-rings (Fig.1492)

Finger-ring fragments of jet and non-jet (see p.2745 for explanation of the term) were recovered from medieval and unstratified deposits at 16–22 Coppergate (11073–7) and Fishergate (14769). At Coppergate, the stratified ring fragments (11073–6) were all recovered from 12th–13th century build up dump deposits, but they could be residual from earlier activity, with some fourteen jet finger-rings being recovered from Anglo-Scandinavian contexts (Roesdahl et al. 1981, 137, YAGJ8; pp.2587–8, AY 17/14). The Fishergate ring (14769) comes from an early 13th century grave fill and, as with the Coppergate rings, may derive from earlier activity on the site.

Bracelets (Fig.1492)

There is an incomplete tin-plated iron bracelet from a 13th–14th century context at Coppergate (12726) and a fragment of another from an 11th–12th century context at Piccadilly (13048). 12726 was originally penannular and part of one terminal survives. As no other medieval iron bracelets are known, both 12726 and 13048 are likely to be pre-Conquest in origin and may be set alongside a complete tin-plated iron bracelet or armlet and two fragments from Anglo-Scandinavian contexts at Coppergate (p.696, AY 17/6).

Pendants (Fig.1492)

12730 from a 12th–13th century context at Coppergate appears to have been an iron cross-shaped pendant which was suspended from a looped terminal. It is similar to an object of Viking Age date from Viborg, Denmark (Nielsen 1968, 48, fig.17), and may therefore be residual.

Two jet cross pendants from Coppergate have previously been identified as possibly Anglo-Scandinavian, despite their recovery from 12th century dumps (9862–3, pp.2590–1, AY 17/14). Further research, particularly on examples from Scotland, suggests that a 12th century date is more likely (Fraser Hunter, pers. comm.), and that these jet pendants are therefore medieval.

Gemstones (Fig.1498)

In addition to gemstones in situ on finger-rings, individual gemstones were recovered from the priory at Fishergate (14757–9) and Bedern (13477–8). 14757 was found in the fill of a Period 6a cut for the construction of the priory church, and 14758 derived from Period 6a/6b cemetery soil. 14759 was retrieved from Period 6z agricultural soil south of the priory, although it appears to be an intrusion from the Victorian period. From Bedern only 13477 is stratified; it was found in association with the Period 5 (early–mid 14th century) south-west wall of the possibly residential Building 10. The gemstones were studied by **Susan Rees**, who provides the following report.

The term 'gemstone' is used here to describe minerals which have been selected for their colour and physical properties for use in ornamentation. To establish that these were indeed gemstones, and not glass, and to identify the type of gemstone, the stones were examined under a bin-

ocular microscope at ×100 and ×160 using incident light and then transmitted light.

14757 is an irregular pebble shape, cloudy orange in colour. Under incident light the surface has a dull waxy lustre which has resulted from either natural weathering or handling. Under transmitted light natural flaws and cracks can be seen and the stone is cloudy and semi-opaque but a fairly uniform colour throughout. The orangey-brown colour and uniformity of opaqueness suggested that this stone was a cornelian.

14758 has been shaped and is deep purple in colour, ranging from deep to lighter hued patches. Initially it resembled a worn piece of coloured glass. Under incident light the surface can be seen to be randomly scratched and on one side in particular the surface is pitted and chipped. Under transmitted light patchiness and zoning of colour can be observed due to the alignment of some of the crystal planes, some areas appearing more transparent and lighter in colour than others. No air bubbles could be seen within the structure to indicate this might be glass, and a hardness test revealed the stone to be harder than glass. The appearance of the stone and its colour indicated that it was an amethyst from the quartz family.

14759 is a fragment of a stone that has been cut into a flat octagonal shape. The stone is a uniform shiny black-brown incorporating a thin band of opaque grey-blue that covers one face. Under reflected light the surface has a vitreous lustre, but both surfaces have random scratches on them. Under transmitted light the black layer is opaque and the blue-grey layer almost totally opaque. A hardness test showed the material to be harder than glass, and the pattern of the broken edge is not reminiscent of a glassy fracture. Because of the colour and banded nature of this stone it is most likely to be onyx, a quartz variety of chalcedony.

13477 is sub-rectangular. The base of the stone is slightly convex and the sides are also slightly convex and taper up towards a curved convex top. The stone is clear, colourless and has a glassy, glossy lustre. Under ×17 magnification the base of the stone is slightly worn, with a few short scratches. The top surface of the stone is not very worn and has one or two short old scratches. One of the short ends has a large conchoidal chip fracture which was initiated from the bottom edge. There is another much smaller chip fracture on one of the long edges, also initiated from the bottom edge. Both look like random accidental wear and damage. Fine but uneven polishing striations

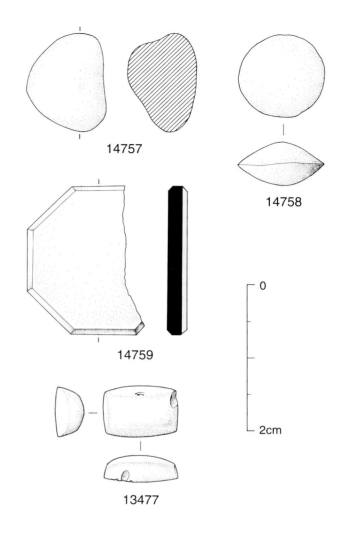

Fig.1498 *Gemstones: cornelian 14757, amethyst 14758 and onyx 14759 from 46–54 Fishergate; rock crystal 13477 from Bedern. Scale 2:1*

are visible on all of the bevelled sides suggesting shaping by hand. The facet edges are gently rounded and not sharp as in a modern stone. The stone has the transparency and colourless appearance of rock crystal (quartz), and a hardness of 7 suggesting quartz. XRF at the National Museums of Scotland revealed the almost exclusive presence of silica indicating that this was a natural material, not glass, and therefore rock crystal.

13478 is oval in shape with a gently convex base and sides which taper gently towards a bi-convex surface caused by a ridge running along the middle of the stone from short end to short end. The overall shape resembles that of an upturned boat or a hog's back shape. There are two small vertical chamfers/bevels in the middle of each long side of the stone which run from the bottom edge to halfway up the side of the stone and were presumably to help hold the stone into its setting. There are chips round the edges of these bevels but few elsewhere, suggesting these may have been caused by abrasion with the setting. Both top and bottom surfaces are finely worn and pitted. The stone is clear and colourless with a very slight pinky-grey tinge. Its lustre is glassy. Traces of a substance with a thin whitish-brown chalky appearance can be seen adhering to one side and part of the base of the stone; under ×16 magnification using a binocular microscope this can be seen to contain some largish particles of sand and grit. This substance is possibly the remains of mortar bound onto the stone during burial by some sort of mastic which could have been used to secure the stone into its setting. Also under magnification polishing/working marks in the form of parallel lines can be seen on the small vertical chamfers/bevels on the sides of the stone. Polishing marks can also be seen, but not as clearly, running in parallel lines along the length of the stone.

The stone has the transparency and colourless appearance of rock crystal (clear colourless quartz). Under magnification there are no air bubbles or other indications to point to this being glass, and the cleavage planes and the small specs on them indicating trapped moisture droplets during formation are typical of rock crystal. The stone has a hardness of 7 suggesting quartz. A refractive index was not possible because of the shape of the stone. To confirm the identity of the stone it was examined by XRF at the National Museums of Scotland. The almost exclusive presence of silica indicated this was a natural material and therefore rock crystal.

Uses and origins of the stones

The cornelian 14757 has not been worked, but may have been polished or naturally weathered; such stones are often found as waterworn pebbles. In the medieval period, many gemstones were incorporated into settings with very little change to their natural shape, and thus this stone could have been set into a piece of jewellery. Cornelians would have been imported from Russia, Germany or India; the Romans certainly used cornelians, however, and it is possible that this example may be a re-used stone from that period.

Amethysts such as 14758 have been used in jewellery since before the Roman period, and were amongst the most valued of gemstones until large resources were discovered in South America at the end of the 18th century. Beads of amethyst were used in necklaces and pendants in the 7th and 8th centuries, and were luxury items. Amethyst may have come to Britain from the eastern end of the Mediterranean via the Rhineland where it was used in the Roman period. The shape of 14758 is a double convex cabochon, the cabochon being one of the earliest and simplest ways of shaping a gemstone. The stone may have been chipped with a hammer of bone or stone using a hard surface as an anvil, the final shape being obtained by polishing with an abrasive. As with other gemstones, such as emeralds (for an emerald bead from Anglian Fishergate see 4574, pp.1376–7, AY 17/9), amethysts would have been valued, re-used and passed down over centuries. In the 13th and 14th centuries they were owned almost exclusively by wealthy laymen or clerics in Europe; the ecclesiastical nature of the Fishergate site in this period suggests that the stone could have been set into a gospel cover, a cross or reliquary in a simple bezel.

Onyx was very popular in the Roman period because of its layering of colour which could be exploited in carving cameos. There seems to be little evidence for the working of onyx after the Roman period, but Roman cameos were re-used in the medieval period when they were incorporated into jewellery. Onyx came back into fashion in the Victorian period because of its sombre colours; it was used in bracelets and brooches. 14759 has been cut into an octagonal shape and polished. The dark black-brown layer is not a natural colour in onyx, and it may have been dyed; because of its cryptocrystalline structure (sub-microscopic cryptopores and water content), onyx is able to absorb colour, and since the Roman period it has been coloured by heating it in substances such as honey. Since this stone is not carved into a cameo as onyx of the Roman period would have been, and because of its relatively sophisticated octagonal shape which is unusual for stones of the medieval period, 14759 may be intrusive from a later, possibly Victorian, context.

Rock crystal is found worldwide, but early sources may have been India, Egypt, Turkey, Spain, Cyprus or the Swiss and French Alps. Rock crystal was being used by the Greeks who gave it its name by calling it 'krystallos', which translated means ice, referring to its appearance. This stone was used from Greek and Egyptian periods onwards. It was prized in the Roman period and later for its optical qualities. From the early medieval period rock crystal was used for lenses, goblets, crystal balls and later chandeliers. The stone was also used as a gem in ecclesiastical relics and jewellery, before being largely superseded by glass from the 16th century onwards. The shape of 13478 is typical *of that used in the 12th and 13th centuries in church met-alwork and plate in Europe, for example in Paris where there were 'cristalliers' who specialised in working crystal as a gemstone itself, but also to imitate more precious gems by colouring and creating 'doublets'. This stone could thus be of medieval and ecclesiastical origins, and its size indicates it was set into something larger than a ring. Because of their transparency, such stones would be backed with silver, silver-gilt or gold foil to disguise the base of the setting and enhance the reflectance of the stone. The size of 13477 suggests that it could have been set with other stones in a larger object rather than on its own in a ring.*

Medical and toilet instruments

Copper alloy medical plates (Figs.1499–500)

Found in association with the skeleton of an adult male in the Period 6a/6b cemetery at Fishergate, *15226* comprises two fragments of copper alloy plate, both with perforations and with fragmentary remains of leather on them. They were recovered in the area of the right knee, where they appeared to have been placed one above and one below the knee, and where they had left staining on both the tibia and fibula (Knüsel et al. 1995, 376). The original shapes of the plates are unclear. In situ, one appeared to be sub-circular, while the other is more fragmentary; it is possible that both were originally discoidal. Analysis of the skeleton revealed that the individual, who may have been a member of the priory, and who appeared to have been approximately 60 years of age at death, had suffered a severe injury known as a rotary fracture-dislocation to his right knee (ibid., 371), possibly sustained after a severe fall, although early references to the playing of football amongst the Gilbertines might suggest an alternative cause of such an injury (Graham 1901, 158). This injury would have left the man with a noticeable limp and a chronic knee infection, and it is suggested that the plates represent medical intervention, primarily to provide support to the limb, and to enable the individual to continue to walk, although the copper may also have been employed for its apparent disinfectant property (Knüsel et al. 1995, 380). The use of such plates on a leg appears to be unparalelled within the archaeological record, although three instances of similar intervention on arms are recorded, all of Saxon or medieval date, two of which involve skeletons found

Fig.1499   Copper alloy medical plate fragments 15226 in situ near the right knee of an adult male skeleton from the Fishergate cemetery. Scale unit 10cm

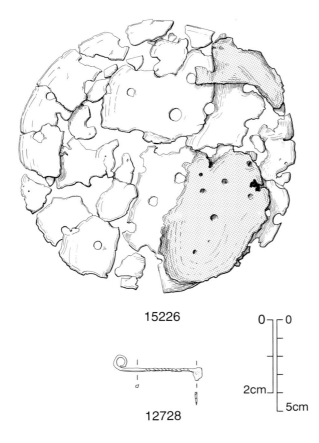

15226

12728

0 ⌐ 0

2cm ⌐

⌐ 5cm

Fig.1500 *Copper alloy medical plate with leather remains 15226 from 46–54 Fishergate, scale 1:1; iron fleam 12728 from 16–22 Coppergate, scale 1:2*

Copper alloy toilet instruments (Fig.1501)

Medieval double-ended toilet instruments often combined earscoops and toothpicks (Egan and Pritchard 1991, 379), and both Coppergate (*12923*) and Bedern (*14474–5*) produced simple non-ferrous examples. These have a scoop at one end and a flat pick at the other, and either plain (*14475*) or twisted (*12923, 14474*) shanks between; all came from late 14th–late 15th century deposits. A more unusual implement combining earscoop and toothpick was found in a Period 6b burial at Fishergate (*15227*); here, the toothpick end is bifurcated, and the centre of the shank is perforated, presumably indicating that this was originally part of a set. No exact parallels for *15227* have been found, but a three-piece set combining earscoop, bifurcated toothpick and tweezers attached via a rivet through their upper ends which was found in a later 14th century context in London (Egan and Pritchard 1991, 377, *1756*) contains the same elements, suggesting that *15227* may once have combined with tweezers. Related to the sets, but appearing to come from later deposits, are one-piece implements combining earscoop and toothpick with bifurcated ends; these typically have twisted wire decoration on the shank, and examples are known from several ecclesiastical sites including St Augustine's Abbey, Canterbury (Henig 1988, 216, fig.69, *59*), Battle Abbey (Geddes 1985, 162, *77*), and the infirmary at Kirkstall Abbey (Moorhouse and Wrathmell 1987, 132, *184/1959*).

Bone toilet sets were also found at Fishergate and Bedern (*8005, 8145*, p.1941, *AY 17/12*).

Copper alloy tweezers (Fig.1501)

These simply made implements, which are relatively common finds on medieval sites, were recovered from Coppergate (*12924–7*), Bedern (*14476*) and Fishergate (*15228–32*). Apart from *15229* which is an undecorated and slideless pair, and could be Roman (see Biddle 1990, 690 for discussion of the use of slides), all the tweezers appear to be medieval types.

within ecclesiatical institutions (ibid.). Perhaps this treatment was given by one member of the Gilbertine community to a fellow canon at the priory.

Iron fleams (Fig.1500)

There are two fleams from Coppergate, *12727* and *12728*, found in a 14th century and mid 12th century context respectively, and one (*14113*) from a mid 14th–early 15th century context at Bedern. A fleam is a bladed implement used for slitting veins to allow blood letting. The two Coppergate examples are almost identical in having spirally twisted shanks with looped terminals and small semicircular blades similar to those which can be seen on fleams used until the 20th century. The Bedern fleam is incomplete and has a plain shank. Other examples are rare, but there are two from mid–late 13th century contexts at Winchester, incorrectly identified as keys (Goodall 1990c, fig.330, *3857–8*).

Fig.1501 *(facing page) Copper alloy toilet implements 12923 from 16–22 Coppergate, 14474–5 from Bedern, 15227 from 46–54 Fishergate; iron tweezers 12729 from 16–22 Coppergate; copper alloy tweezers 12925–7 from 16–22 Coppergate, 15228–31 from 46–54 Fishergate; copper alloy cosmetic spoon 15233 from 46–54 Fishergate. Scale 1:1, 12729 1:2*

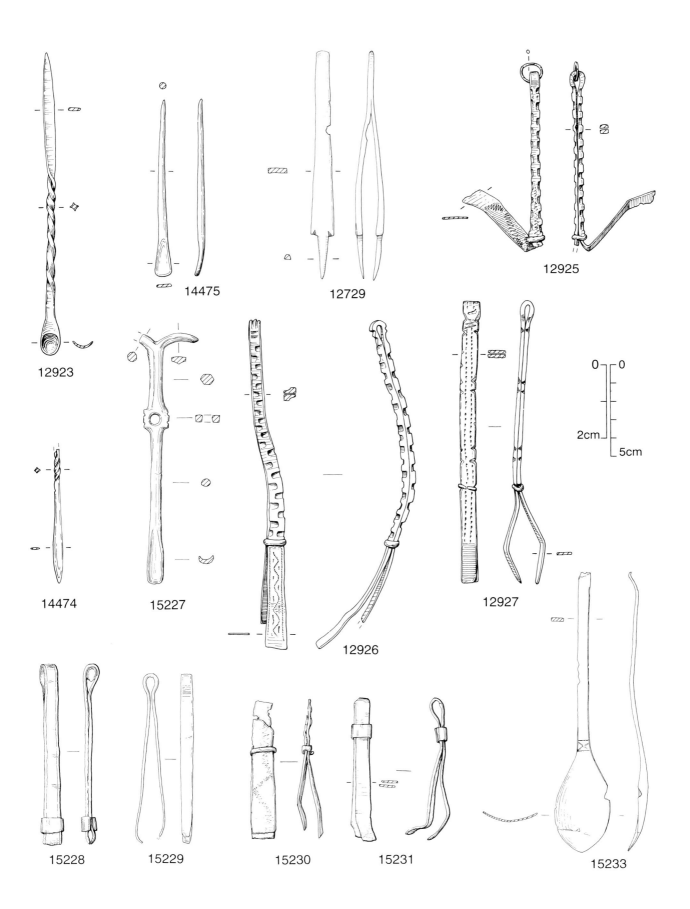

12923

14475

12729

12925

14474

15227

12926

12927

15228

15229

15230

15231

15233

0
0

2cm

5cm

2933

All the Coppergate tweezers derive from 12th–13th century deposits, and all have been decorated: *12927* has rouletting and notched tips, while *12924* and *12926* have a squared wave motif, cut deeply on *12926* which also has an incised zig-zag design below the slide; *12925* has a squared notch design with rocked tracery below the slide. In contrast, the medieval tweezers from Bedern and Fishergate are mostly plain, apart from *15230* which has rocked tracer ornament over it.

Iron tweezers (Fig.1501)

12729, from a mid 13th century context at Coppergate, is a pair of iron tweezers. Its arms are flat strips which widen slightly before stepping in to short pointed tips. There is a triangular indentation on each 'step'. A similar item comes from a late 13th–14th century context in London (Henig 1974, 191, fig.38, 55). The function of the York tweezers is uncertain, but Goodall has suggested that the London pair were used in cloth making to remove foreign matter from cloth before fulling (Goodall 1980, 54).

Copper alloy cosmetic spoon (Fig.1501)

An almost complete spoon (*15233*) with a shallow leaf-shaped bowl and flat rectangular stem was recovered from Period 6a cemetery soil at Fishergate. Spoons of copper alloy seem to be uncommon, but another example from London, dated to the 14th century, appears to be very similar to *15233* (Ward Perkins 1940, 133, pl.XXVI, no.1). The shallow leaf-shaped bowl resembles that of a fragmentary pewter spoon from Winchester (Brisbane 1990, 832, fig.248, *2625*), and of a silver spoon recovered from excavations at Taunton Castle in Somerset (Gray 1930, 157), both thought to be 13th century in date.

The size of *15233* suggests that it may have been used for cosmetic or medical purposes. Although somewhat larger than the scoops on the multi-functional sets, it is, however, considerably smaller than either the Winchester or London spoon. The upper end of the stem bends slightly before the break, and it seems possible that the spoon may originally have been attached to another implement as part of a set (see above).

Writing and literacy

Stylus (Fig.1502)

14115 is an iron stylus with a short flattened triangular eraser from a mid 14th–early 15th century context at Bedern. *14116* is a highly decorative tin-plated stylus found unstratified also at Bedern. The eraser is rounded with an open kidney-shaped centre and a straight top on which there are zig-zag grooves in pairs. At the head of the stem is a collar, each face with an incised saltire and in the centre a nick out of the edges. Around the stem were criss-cross grooves.

Lead alloy points (Fig.1502)

Lengths of lead, all with at least one pointed end, were found at Coppergate (*12954–5*), Bedern (*14549–67*) and Fishergate (*15282–6*); they functioned like pencils. Analysis of lead points found in Winchester indicated four different forms or classes (Biddle and Brown 1990, 736). Class I points have one pointed end and a gradual taper — at Winchester, these were found in 9th–13th century deposits. Classes II and III both have one pointed and one flattened end, differing only in having either a rounded (Class II) or squarish (Class III) cross-section. Class IV points are characterised by their forked upper end; at Winches-

Table 307 Classification of lead points by site

	Class I	Class II	Class III	Class IV	Total
Coppergate	–	1	1	–	2
Bedern	2	8	3	–	13
Fishergate	–	4	–	1	5
Total	2	13	4	1	20

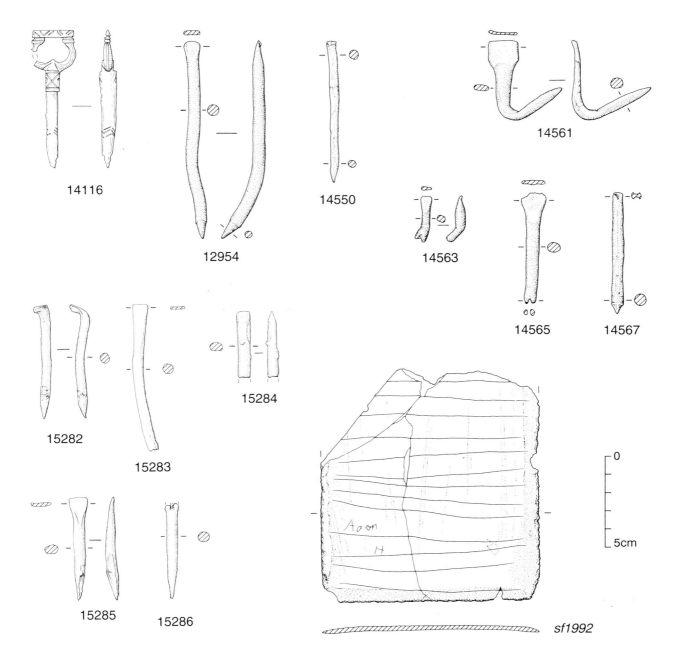

Fig.1502   *Tin-plated iron stylus* 14116 *from Bedern; lead alloy points* 12954 *from 16–22 Coppergate,* 14550, 14561, 14563, 14565, 14567 *from Bedern,* 15282–6 *from 46–54 Fishergate; possible writing slate sf1992 from Bedern. Scale 1:2*

ter two were found in late 11th to 12th century contexts (ibid., 744). All classes have been identified
amongst the 26 York points. Two examples of Class I
come from Bedern (*14549–50*), although both came
from contexts of the 14th century or later. Seventeen
points are of Classes II (*12954, 14551–8, 15282–5*) or
III (*12955, 14559–61*); these come from all the sites

from contexts ranging from the 11th century through
to post-medieval. The single Class IV point was found
in an unstratified context at Fishergate (*15286*), while
six points are unclassified (*14562–7*).

Analysis of the Winchester points showed all
classes were represented roughly equally, and it was

suggested that the functions of the points may differ according to type, the Class I and IV points being considered more likely to have been used for writing and ruling on manuscripts, although this was more confidently asserted in the case of the Class IV points, while it was suggested that Classes II and III might have been used by craftsmen such as carpenters (Biddle and Brown 1990, 737–8). At York, there were considerably fewer examples of Classes I and IV (three in total), while 17 of the points were of Classes II or III, suggesting that the majority of the points were not used in writing or manuscript production.

A closer look at the find-spots of these objects at Fishergate shows that the four Class II points all derive from levelling deposits of Periods 6a and 6b during the construction of and first modifications to the priory in the 13th and early 14th centuries. These may thus relate to the building work rather than the religious activities in the priory, and all may well have been used by craftsmen involved in the priory's construction, perhaps to make marks on wood, or for record-keeping on wax tablets. Similarly, three of the Class II and III points at Bedern (14551–2, 14554) appear in Period 2 and 3 deposits associated with the construction of the residential Building 6 and its replacement Building 9; another two of uncertain type (14562–3) came from a Period 2 construction spread associated with the residential Building 5.

Points of bone with iron tips which may be styli or possibly prickers for marking out lines on parchment were found at Coppergate (7067–68), Fishergate (8157–61) and Bedern (7971–75, 8036–57, 8122–23). Six possible pens made from bird radii were also recovered from Bedern, one from the Foundry (7976), the others from the area of the College (8058–62); all these bone points and pens are published in *AY* 17/12 (pp.1974–6).

Writing slate (Fig.1502)

A fragment of slate (sf1992 from Area 13.X), originally rectangular and the complete sides with bevelled edges, was identified as possibly medieval at a late stage and is a late addition to this report. It was recovered from a Period 8 (mid 15th–early 16th century) garden deposit at Bedern.

Dr G.D. Gaunt describes the slate as *dark grey, fissile along a cleavage which appears to coincide with original slightly undulating bedding. Lower Palaeozoic of northern Wales or, less likely, Cumbria.*

The slate, which is approximately 128 × 115 × 3·5mm, has irregularly spaced unruled transverse incised lines on both faces, with two letters ('A' and 'H') clearly visible towards one corner and on different lines. Fainter vertical lines are also apparent. The bevelled edges suggest a wooden frame was originally present.

The dating of this object is problematic. Its form is similar to slates known to have been used by children as recently as the 1930s (Dr G.D. Gaunt, pers. comm.), but the use of writing slates appears to go back at least to the time of Chaucer (Rhodes 1984, 121). According to Rhodes wooden-edged school slates are illustrated in a print of c.1740 (ibid.); few slates have been recovered from archaeological deposits of this period, however, although a number were found at the Franciscan Friary at Lewin's Mead, Bristol, dated to c.1500, and may have been used in the Friar's School (Webster and Cherry 1974, 189). The widespread use of slates in schools appears to date from the late 18th–19th centuries onwards (Rhodes 1984, 121), and it is quite possible that sf1992 is intrusive in its context (possibly from Bedern National School which was on the site c.1872–1941) although other material found with it includes a fragment of a medieval copper alloy skillet (14201) and no other recognisably post-medieval objects.

Copper alloy page-holder or clip
(Figs.1503–4)

A fragment from a clip to keep documents together or to hold down pages was found in a mid 14th century context at Bedern (14477). It represents the expanded tip of a pair of tweezers, and it has been tinned (see analysis details in the catalogue). These clips or holders have been found on other medieval sites, both secular such as Lower Brook Street, Winchester (Biddle and Hinton 1990b, 756, fig.215), and Swan Lane, London (Alexander and Binski, 1987, 384, 426), both from 13th century deposits, and ecclesiastical, for example, the reredorter of Bayham Abbey, East Sussex (A.R. Goodall 1983, fig.48, 14).

Copper alloy book clasps (Figs.1503, 1505)

Clasps which were probably used on books were recovered from Bedern (14478–80), Bedern Chapel

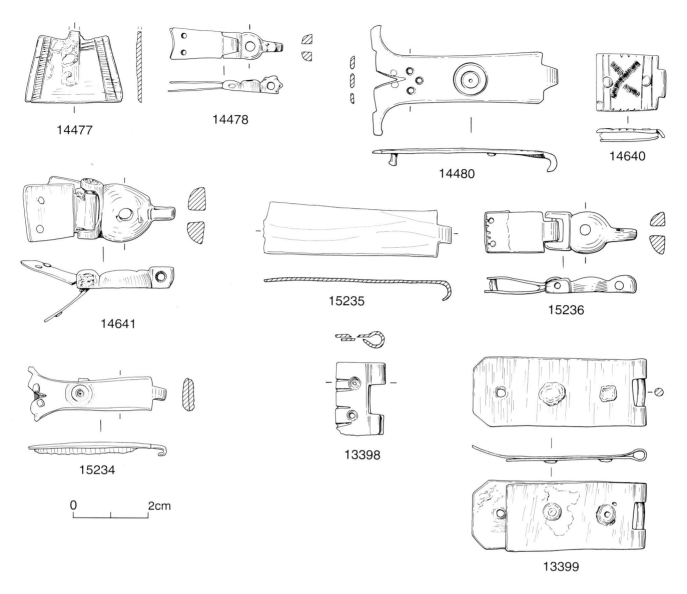

Fig.1503 *Fragment of copper alloy page holder* 14477 *from Bedern; copper alloy book clasps* 14478 *and* 14480 *from Bedern,* 14640–1 *from Bedern Chapel,* 15234–6 *from 46–54 Fishergate; copper alloy hinges which may have been used with book clasps,* 13398–9 *from the Foundry. Scale 1:1*

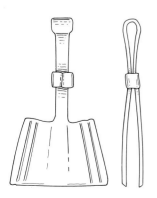

Fig.1504 *Reconstruction of a complete page holder, based on* 14477 *and an example from Winchester*

(*14640–1*) and Fishergate (*15234–6*). *14479–80* and *15234* are all examples of a type commonly found on both ecclesiastical sites, such as the Dominican Friary at Chester (Lloyd-Morgan 1990, 170, fig.104, *3–4*), Bordesley Abbey (Rahtz 1983, 181, fig.67, CA 96) and St Augustine's Abbey, Canterbury (Henig 1988, 179, fig.54, *3*; 215, fig.68, *49*), and on secular sites including 31–51 Pottersgate, Norwich (Margeson 1985, 58, fig.39, *28*), and Sandal Castle (A.R. Goodall 1983b, 235, fig.2, *113*). Other examples from York include

Fig.1505 *Detail of a book clasp from a statue of an apostle originally in the chapter house of St Mary's Abbey, York (reproduced by courtesy of the Yorkshire Museum)*

one from 21–33 Aldwark (Fig.1314, **4**; YAT 1973.5), probably associated with the church of St Helen-on-the-Walls, although originally identified as a Roman strap-end (MacGregor 1974, 9). A book at Sudeley Castle, Gloucestershire, which is dated 1429, possesses this type of book clasp (A.R. Goodall, pers. comm.), which has been recovered archaeologically from predominantly 15th and 16th century contexts. Apart from the unstratified *14480*, all the Fishergate and Bedern clasps also originate from deposits of this period. Of similar form to this type, *14640* and *15235* have hooked upper ends, but are more rectangular in shape.

Another type represented by *14478*, *14641* and *15236* has previously been published as a hinged fit-

ting associated with belts (see for example Ward Perkins 1940, pl.75, *13*; Clay 1981, 133, fig.48, *28*; Geddes 1985, 158, fig.50, *37*). Three examples from St Augustine's Abbey, Canterbury, were, however, described as possible book-fastenings (Henig 1988, 181, fig.54, *9–11*) and a statue from St Mary's Abbey in York (Fig. 1314, **3**) confirms this interpretation (see Fig.1505). The unidentified apostolic figure originally stood within the chapter house of the abbey and carries a book with a similar clasp. Although the statue is thought to date from the late 12th century (Wilson and Burton 1988, 19–20), the majority of these clasps have been recovered archaeologically from late 14th–15th century deposits, and a book in Erlangen library, Germany, which was bound in 1439 has a similar clasp, attached to a strap on the lower board with the perforation in the roundel fastened to a knob on the upper board (A.R. Goodall, pers. comm.). Another example was recognised from excavations at Ripon (Rogers 1997, p.149, fig.11, *33*).

Although these clasps have been found on secular sites, there is no doubt that they are particularly associated with ecclesiastical institutions, and it should be noted that neither Coppergate nor the Foundry site produced any of these items. Moreover, at Fishergate, one clasp came from the chapter house (*15236*) and another from a major deposit of robbing waste in the priory church (*15235*), indicating their association with books relating both to priory business and ritual.

Although no book clasps were recovered from the Foundry, two possible hinges for use with such clasps, both of copper alloy, were found on the site (*13398–9*). *13398* has an incompletely made rivet hole

and may have been discarded unfinished; it comes from a mid 16th–mid 17th century deposit at the Foundry.

Non-ferrous book mounts (Fig.1506)

In addition to the use of decorative clasps, books were sometimes provided with protective and/or ornamental mounts. *12928* from Coppergate, *14481–3* from Bedern, *14642* from Bedern Chapel and *15237–40* from St Andrew's Priory, Fishergate, and may all be from books. The conical or domed centres seem particularly characteristic of book mounts; domed mounts with lugs such as *14479* and *14483* appear to be plainer examples of a type identified in Amsterdam as book mounts (Baart et al. 1977, 403–4, 759–60), while similar examples can be seen on the early post-medieval *Commonplace Book of Henry Appleyard of Dunston* (Margeson 1993, 74–5, pl.XIII). The conical centres of the sexfoil mounts *14642* and *14482* may

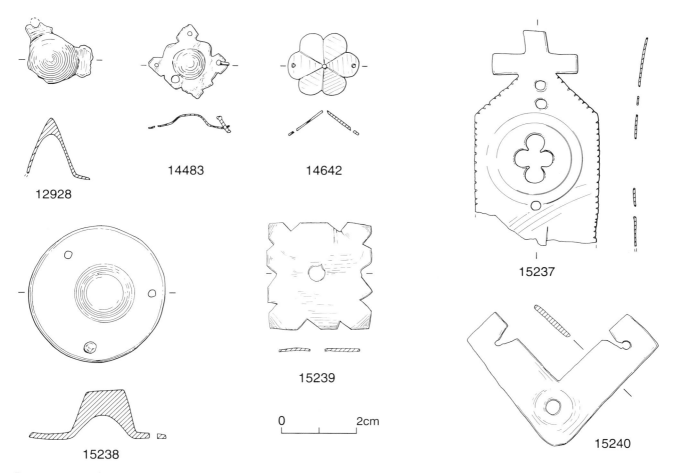

0   2cm

Fig.1506 *Non-ferrous book mounts* 12928 *from 16–22 Coppergate,* 14483 *from Bedern,* 14642 *from Bedern Chapel,* 15237–40 *from 46–54 Fishergate. Scale 1:1*

2939

similarly mark them out as book rather than belt mounts; the recovery of *14642* from a mid–late 15th century floor level within Bedern Chapel also points to a book-related function. Although recovered from a Period 4z pit at Fishergate, *15237*, with its shape of a church gable profile, seems most likely to be associated with the priory, and to be intrusive in its 11th–12th century context. A square mount with decoratively notched edges, *15239* was recovered from deposits relating to the demolition and robbing of the church in the mid 16th century, while a corner binding, *15240*, also possibly from a book, comes from later levels associated with the demolition of the priory.

Seal matrices (Fig.1507)

Copper alloy matrices used to stamp a seal in wax were recovered from Fishergate (*15241*) and Bedern (*14484–6*). A possible matrix made of stone was also found at Bedern (*13479*). See also Fig.1536 and p.2973 for a possible post-medieval type of lead alloy seal (*14582*) from Bedern.

Stone matrix

13479 depicts a stylised face at the centre, with an illegible legend, all surrounded by concentric circles; an incised quadrant is visible on the reverse face. The identification of this as a seal matrix is tentative, owing to its crudity, and also its material, which indicates a date no later than the end of the 12th century, when metal took over from bone and stone as the main material from which matrices were made (Alexander and Binski 1987, 396).

Dr G.D. Gaunt comments on *13479*:

This is made of Permian Lower Magnesian Limestone, which crops out along the western side of the Vale of York, although, as with other items made from oolitic/relict oolitic/microcellular varieties of this limestone in this report, it could have been made from former Roman building stone.

Copper alloy matrices

15241 found at the priory at Fishergate is in fact one-half of a well-engraved discoidal personal seal matrix. In the centre of the matrix a hawk or falcon is shown poised on a hand which holds its jesses; a second bird is visible to the side. Around this scene, within a billeted border, is the inscription OME : DEBELEBIO. The matrix has been deliberately cancelled by being cut in half, perhaps to prevent its use after the death of its owner, as with modern credit and bank cards; this was a not uncommon practice in the medieval period (Cherry 1992, 23–4). Interpretation of the inscription is uncertain, but it may that the first part is [S'TH]OME referring to the seal of Thomas of Belebio, although a colon would be expected betweeen the DE and the BELEBIO (J. Cherry, pers. comm.). There are two possible interpretations of the place name Belebio: Bielby which lies southeast of York near the road from Market Weighton (C. Daniell, pers. comm.) and Belby in the Liberty of Howdenshire (P.M. Stell, pers. comm.). Although it is unlikely that the Thomas who owned this seal can be identified with certainty, it could have been a clerk named Thomas de Beleby who in the 13th cemtury witnessed a charter by Sir Peter de la Hay (*EYC* **10**, 52, 97). The disc shape and motif is typical of this period (Alexander and Binski 1987, 396), and the matrix was recovered from soil overlying Period 6a and 6b stone coffins in the north transept of the church. It has been suggested that the matrix may derive from one of these earlier burials (*AY* 11/2, 161), and the date of the matrix would fit with this interpretation, although there would have been no need to break or cancel the matrix if it was to be buried with its owner. If the matrix does derive from a burial at the priory, one must assume that Thomas supported the priory and chose to be buried there.

The three copper alloy seal matrices from Bedern are all of the same faceted conical form, which first appears towards the end of the 13th century (Alexander and Binski 1987, 396), and both *14484* and *14485* retain looped handles, used for attachment to the person (ibid.). The device on *14484*, which has a circular matrix, is a squirrel with its tail curled up over its back; the inscription running round it reads 'I CRAKE NOTIS (NUTIS?), that is, 'I crack nuts'. While squirrels were sometimes seen in medieval art as women's pets, and a bawdy meaning could be read into this inscription, it has been suggested in relation to other examples that the cracking of nuts is an analogy for cracking open the seal (Alexander and Binski 1987, 277, 201). *14484* was found in an early–mid 14th century floor level in the south-easternmost bay of the residential Building 11, from which a jeton of Edward II (1307–27) was also recovered.

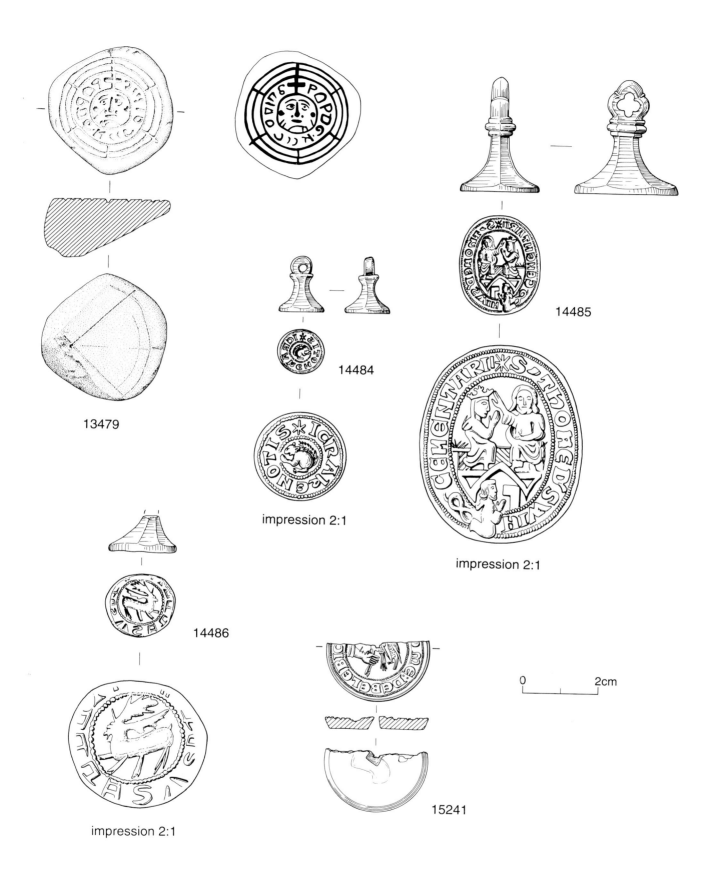

13479

14484

impression 2:1

14485

impression 2:1

14486

impression 2:1

15241

0   2cm

Fig.1507 *Seal matrices: of stone* 13479 *from Bedern; of copper alloy* 14484–6 *from Bedern and* 15241 *from 46–54 Fishergate. Scale 1:1, impressions 2:1 as indicated on illustration*

Another impersonal seal is *14486*, found in a post-medieval deposit. Unfortunately incomplete, lacking the upper end of its handle, it has a sub-circular matrix with a crudely cut stag device, and an incomplete inscription of ' ..(E)SV SEL ...'. A possible reading of this is IESV SELE PREVE, an inscription noted on a seal found near Bath, which has been dated c.1330 (Nelson 1936, 38, *78*).

The best-preserved matrix is *14485*, found in mid 16th century soil over pits within Building 18, but certainly residual in this context. It is a personal seal, with an oval matrix, the device showing a robed man, perhaps God, and a crowned kneeling woman, the Virgin Mary, with a smaller kneeling figure, probably the seal's owner, below. The inscription reads 'S'THOME DE SWIN CEMENTARIUS' and it was probably the seal of Thomas of Swine (8km northeast of Hull), stonemason.

Although devices on matrices were sometimes tailor-made for the customer (see for example the hare borne by a fish, belonging to Thomas Fishborne; Heslop 1987, 116), none of the devices employed on the York matrices is unique, and it is likely that most customers, particularly the less wealthy, selected their motif from a pre-existing range. Indeed, impersonal seals were almost certainly purchased ready made.

Fig.1508 *Detail from the St William window, York Minster (panel 2b), showing seals in use (reproduced by courtesy of York Minster Archive, © Dean and Chapter of York)*

Motifs of animals, such as the deer and squirrel, and birds, such as the hawk, became increasingly popular towards the end of the 13th century, when the range of designs appears to have broadened considerably (ibid.). The hawk device has been found locally on an example recovered by a metal detectorist at Bawtry, South Yorkshire (J. Halliday, pers. comm.), while the squirrel and his inscription has been particularly associated by some with women (Alexander and Binski 1987, 277, *201*). Motifs depicting suppliants and patron saints are most commonly found belonging to ecclesiastics and clerks (see Fig.1508), such as that of Roger de Farringdon, used in 1377 (ibid., 275, vi), but not exclusively so, as Thomas the Stonemason shows. A seal from an early 14th century context in a property on Blackfriargate, Hull, has a similar device but with an impersonal inscription (Goodall 1987a, 202, fig.116, *144*).

Seals, and the matrices in which they were formed, were of considerable importance in the literate medieval world, for they acted as validations of documents. An unbroken seal indicated that a document had not been tampered with, and authenticated its origin (Heslop 1987, 114). In legal terms, if an individual's seal appeared on a document, that individual was bound to honour the contents (ibid.); the use of a seal which was no longer valid could, however, be prevented by destroying the matrix (see above). Seals and their matrices reflected the status, and often the aspirations, of their owners. It was the right of all freemen to own a seal (Alexander and Binski 1987, 274), but differences in rank could be indicated by the materials from which a matrix was made, its size and the design employed on it. Although made of both precious and base metals, matrices of copper alloy such as those found in York were usually intended for the middle and lower end of the market (Heslop 1987, 115). The York matrices also illustrate that seals with personal inscriptions were not restricted to the higher echelons of society, but were equally available to craftsmen, such as Thomas the Stonemason.

Funerary and devotional objects

Chalices and paten (Figs.1509–11)

Pewter copies of silver sacramental chalices and patens have been found in many medieval graves. These copies were designed not for use in communion, but to accompany the burials of priests, as the

1229 constitutions of William of Blois, Bishop of Worcester, ordained (Oman 1990, 790). St Andrew's Priory at Fishergate is the only site of those under consideration where these objects were recovered; this is not surprising as it is also the only site on which associated burials were recovered.

A partially complete chalice and a paten, *15287*, were found buried with an adult male, 40–50 years old (*AY* 12/2, 157, burial 6128), in the Period 6a cemetery. The bowl of the chalice has lost fragments of the rim, which is pronounced and out-turned, but it is otherwise almost complete. The stem is broken below the single beaded knop as it begins to flare out, and fragments of the foot survive separately. The paten is complete apart from two fragments broken off the beaded rim, and it is slightly dished. There is a patch at the centre, which was clearly filled after the paten had been turned and then removed from the lathe. The chalice has also been made by lathe-turning, as indicated by the concentric circles visible on the bowl.

The chalice appears to be an approximate copy of a silver chalice of a design in use from the late 12th–late 13th centuries (Oman 1957, 41). While certainly the companion piece to the chalice, the paten cannot be independently dated by comparison with silver examples, as it does not have either the single or double central depressions typical of the two silver types (ibid., 47).

The chalice and paten were found lying over the stomach of the buried body, the arms of which may have been placed to hold the items (*AY* 12/2, 157). The chalice was in an upright position, but the original position of the paten is unclear; it may have been placed so that it covered the bowl of the chalice. The positioning of these items is paralleled at Winchester where ten of twenty pewter chalices recovered were found on the upper half of the body and appeared to have been buried in an upright position; in five cases, the paten had covered the chalice bowl (Biddle and Kjølbye-Biddle 1990, 791–3). This accords with known practice in the medieval period; according to the *Rites of Durham*, a prior was buried with 'a little challice of silver, other metell or wax, which was

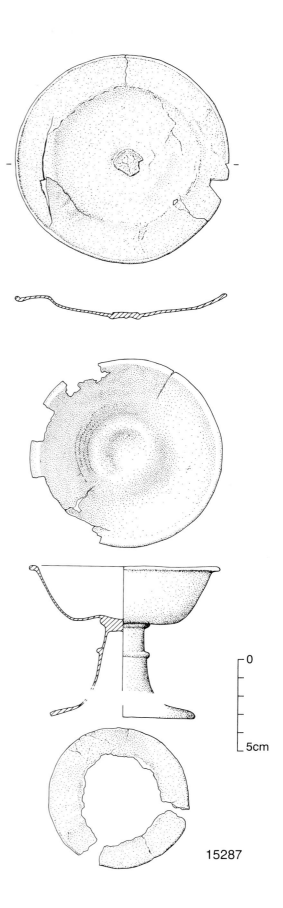

15287

Fig.1509 *Pewter chalice and paten 15287 from 46–54 Fishergate. Scale 1:2*

Fig.1510 *Pewter chalice 15287 from 46–54 Fishergate. Actual diameter of chalice bowl 102.5mm*

laid upon his brest within his coffine' (Fowler 1903, 51–7). The chalice would be upright because it often contained wine (Oman 1957, 40, n.1).

The identification of *15288* is uncertain, but the fragments may also derive from a chalice. The larg-

Fig.1511 *Pewter paten 15287 from 46–54 Fishergate. Actual diameter 112.1mm*

est fragment is a solid cylinder of pewter, with a pewter band around it, suggesting that it might be from the upper part of a chalice, where the bowl was attached to the stem (see Biddle and Kjølbye-Biddle 1990, figs.231–3). It was found in the upper half of a male grave (1428) of the Period 6b cemetery (*AY* 12/2, figs.45b–c), in the same area as *15287*. It is suggested that the Period 6a and 6b burials which include males, females and subadults in this area south of the church may represent a select group, and that the two males buried with pewter objects may have been priests serving at the priory, rather than canons (*AY* 11/2, 141).

A pewter chalice and paten similar to *15287* were recovered during clearance work at the church of St Mary Castlegate, York (Fig.1314, **13**; YAT 1974–5.25; *1250–1, AY* 17/4). Although the chalices differ slightly in design, they appear to be of the same general type. Silver examples have also been found in the graves of two 13th century archbishops of York (p.208, *AY* 17/4). Other pewter chalices and patens of this type have been found in graves in Lincoln Cathedral (Bruce-Mitford 1976, 138, fig.7, pl.V), Westminster Abbey (ibid., fig.6) and in Winchester (Oman 1990, 789–91).

Ampullae and pilgrim badges (Figs.1512–14)

Two flask-shaped ampullae, one largely complete (*12966*) and the other more fragmentary (*12965*), are both made of tin and were both recovered from Coppergate. *12966* is set within a trapezoidal plate; on the front face, an archbishop is depicted on the flask itself, his office represented by the mitre on his head, and the crozier and pallium which he grips in one hand, the other being raised in benediction. On the plate, to either side of the flask, are the clearly identifiable figures of St Peter, holding a key, and St Paul with a sword, with border decoration of small bosses around them. On the reverse face of the flask a striped figure with four wings appears to represent an angel. *12965* is of a different style, the flask being set in an openwork frame. Parts of both the flask and frame are now missing, but lentoid fields within the openwork, one on each side of the flask, appear to contain the same saintly figures of Peter and Paul, both associated with York Minster since the 8th century (Hall 1984, 145). It has been suggested that the archbishop's mitre on *12966* is of a type which was out of fashion by c.1200 (Wilson 1977, 24, n.25),

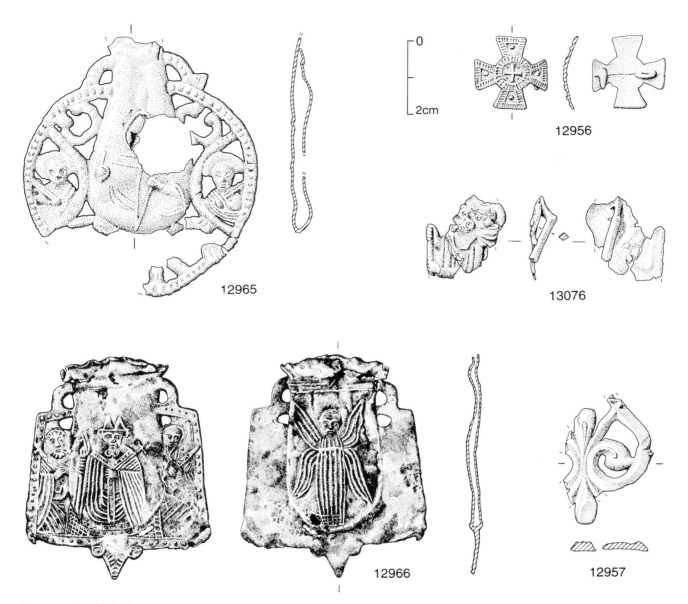

Fig.1512 *Tin flask-shaped ampullae 12965–6 from 16–22 Coppergate; pilgrim badge fragment 13076 from 22 Piccadilly; possible pilgrim badges 12956–7 from 16–22 Coppergate. Scale 1:1*

and that he may be identified as the 12th century Archbishop William of York, subsequently canonised as St William in 1227 (ibid., 8.). The cult status of St William, almost certainly seen as a northern rival to St Thomas of Canterbury, appears, however, never to have equalled that of his hugely successful southern counterpart. While many ampullae and pilgrim badges associated with St Thomas have been recovered (see for example Alexander and Binski 1987, 219–24, *43–65*), the two ampullae from Coppergate represent the only souvenirs to have survived St

William. Documentary evidence in the form of wills also indicate that even in Yorkshire, bequests for pilgrimages to Canterbury and to the shrine of Our Lady at Walsingham were far more popular than those to visit St William's shrine (Wilson 1977, 24, n.25).

Ampullae and pilgrim badges, initially made of tin and later of pewter, were souvenirs designed for pilgrims to particular shrines in England and also in Europe. Ampullae were designed to hold holy oil or water that had been in contact with a saint, and were

Fig.1513 *Tin flask-shaped ampulla set in an openwork frame 12965 from 16–22 Coppergate. Actual diameter 61.9mm*

Fig.1514 *Tin flask-shaped ampulla set in a trapezoidal plate 12966 from 16–22 Coppergate. Actual length 60.7mm*

being made in Canterbury by 1171, within a year of St Thomas Becket's murder (Alexander and Binski 1987, 219). Mass produced, ampullae were usually worn around the neck, suspended via the loops at the neck of the flask, and it seems very likely that the Coppergate ampullae are two examples of an item made in large numbers in York during the years following St William's canonisation. Unfortunately, only *12965* was found in a stratified context at Coppergate, deriving from a build-up deposit associated with an early 14th century timber-framed building at the rear end of Tenement B; it seems probable therefore, that this ampulla was made sometime during the 13th century, after 1227, or perhaps in the early 14th century. *12966* may be of a similar date, as its shape appears to imitate the 13th century reliquary shaped ampullae from Canterbury (Mitchiner 1986, 14–19, *1–7*; Alexander and Binski 1987, 219, *51–2*). Two other ampullae have been found in York (Yorkshire Museum, accession numbers 616.47, 617.47), while a two-piece stone ampulla mould recovered from 34 Shambles (Fig.1314, **9**; YAT 1974–5.12) was tentatively dated to the 15th century (*979*, pp.204–5, *AY* 17/4).

Pilgrim badge fragments were found at 22 Piccadilly (*13076*) and Bedern (*14568*). This souvenir type appears to have been introduced to England in the early 14th century (Alexander and Binski 1987, 219),

and, as its name implies, it was usually worn attached to clothing (Mitchiner 1986, 7). The fragmentary *13076* retains part of its clasp, and depicts St Christopher with his staff, and on his shoulder the Christ Child, unfortunately minus head, holding the orb of sovereignty in one hand, his other hand around the saint's neck. St Christopher was one of the most popular saints of the medieval period, supposedly offering protection against sudden death, and a representation of him could be found in almost every medieval parish church (Spencer 1998, 181). *13076* was found in a 15th–early 16th century dump of building debris in a disused barrel well, and may be contemporary with a badge retrieved from Butler's Wharf on the River Thames in London (ibid.). Unfortunately, the example from Bedern, *14568,* is too fragmentary to enable certain identification; its foliate decoration could derive from a badge or an ampulla with an openwork frame. The object was found in an early–mid 14th century deposit within Room 11B of the College, and was perhaps once the possession of a Vicar.

There are three further possible pilgrim badges. The cross-shaped pewter object *12956* from a 13th–14th century levelling/dump at Coppergate continues the cross theme in the central relief decoration, and there are remains of the catch plate and pin attachment loop on the reverse. From mid 16th century features at Coppergate, the lead alloy openwork fragment *12957* may also be from a badge. *14569* from Bedern is also fragmentary, but has a catch on the reverse and possible drapery in the design on the front face.

Non-ferrous metal bells (Fig.1515)

Two types of bell, open bells with an open mouth and a clapper, and rumbler bells which were closed and contained a pea, had a variety of functions in the medieval period. Both types are represented in the York assemblage, appearing at Coppergate (*12958*), the Foundry (*13400–1*), Bedern (*14487–90*), 2 Aldwark (*14727*) and Fishergate (*15242*). The only evidence of an open bell is the small gilded clapper recovered at Bedern (*14487*) in a late 13th century occupation level within Building 5 where Vicars were accommodated. Suggestions as to the possible functions for small open bells found at Winchester included use by priests visiting the sick, by lepers, in funeral processions, or during mass to warn the congregation of important moments in the consecration and benediction (Biddle and Hinton 1990a, 725). The gilding on *14487* suggests a ritual function may be the most likely in this case.

The copper alloy rumbler or 'pellet' bells come from later contexts than the open bell clapper, the earliest being from early to mid 15th century levels at Bedern (*14488–9*). They are made from two hemispheres of sheet metal, the edges folded over and sealing in an iron pea. Possible functions for these small bells include use on jesses on hawks, collars on hounds, and as dress decoration (Biddle and Hinton 1990a, 725–6). Although deriving from 15th century contexts on the York sites, elsewhere they have appeared as early as the 13th century (Harvey 1975, 254–5, *1711*, *1726*). Two small loops from Bedern, *14491–2*, may originally have suspended rumbler bells.

The pewter rumbler bell from an early 12th century dump at Coppergate (*12958*) and the copper alloy bell from Bedern (*14490*) which has been mercury

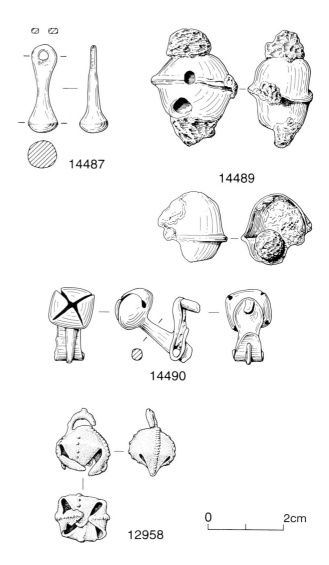

Fig.1515 *Gilded clapper from an open bell* **14487** *from Bedern; copper alloy rumbler bells* **14489–90** *from Bedern; pewter rumbler bell* **12958** *from 16–22 Coppergate. Scale 1:1*

gilded differ from the other bells in having a one-piece body, the lower edge having triangular projections which folded in at the base to seal in the pea. *14490* has a stud mounting and may have been used on harness, while *12958* has been decorated. Similar tin and pewter bells from London came solely from 13th century contexts (Egan and Pritchard 1991, 338, *1668–71*); they were considered a short-lived bell type exclusive to that century (ibid., 336), but the dating of the context of *12958* suggests that this type may in fact have originated earlier in the 12th century.

Rosary beads (Fig.1516)

Beads of jet (*13495–500, 14770–1*), shale (*13504*), non-jet (*13502*) and amber (*13506–7, 14775*) which were recovered from Fishergate and Bedern may all originally have formed parts of rosaries, strings of beads on which prayers were counted. The majority of the beads are globular, but others are annular or barrel-shaped. Bone rosary beads and bead waste from the two sites are published in *AY* 17/12 (pp.1944–5).

At Fishergate, all the beads which were recovered from levels associated with the priory's working life derive from Period 6a or 6b contexts (13th–early 14th century) in the northern and eastern ambulatories of the cloisters. This may indicate the area in which they were frequently used, although their phasing to the earliest periods of the priory may also indicate residuality from the Anglian period, which also produced beads of jet and amber (*4571, 4573, AY* 17/9). At Bedern the earliest contexts from which rosary beads were recovered date to the early 14th century. Fishergate also produced worked (*14773*) and unworked (*14774*) amber fragments.

Several of the beads were found together in the same context and may derive from the same string. On Fishergate these include two very similar globular jet beads (*14771*) found together in the same Period 6b deposit within the northern alley of the cloisters, and two amber beads (*14775*) recovered from the demolition deposit of a garderobe. Three globular jet beads (*13495–7*) were retrieved from a mid–late 14th century feature within Building 18 (of unknown function) at Bedern. A bead of jet-like material from Bedern (*13502*), found in an early–mid 14th century deposit within the residential Building 11, has basket-work decoration over it, and is paralleled by a jet bead found in a context of similar date during excavations on Blackfriargate, Hull (Watkin 1987, 190, fig.108, *13*).

Amber, jet and bone are known to have been used by Christians throughout medieval Europe to make rosary beads (Wilkins 1969, 45–7), and this identification has been put forward for beads of these materials found on other medieval sites, such as Winchester (Biddle and Creasey 1990, 660) and London (Egan and Pritchard 1991, 305; Mead 1977, 212). The earliest use of rosaries in England is thought to be during the 11th century (Biddle and Creasey 1990, 660), their popularity becoming more widespread during the 13th century (Wilkins 1969, 37). Individual rosary beads of jet and amber have been found elsewhere in York at 12–18 Swinegate (Fig.1314, **6**; YAT 1990.28, sfs1437, 2033) and Rawcliffe Manor (YAT 1993.5007, sf1374), while excavations at the site of a pumping station at North Street produced a group of 66 jet beads from a single late 13th/early 14th century context, including two beads which were apparently unfinished (Fig.1314, **11**; YAT 1993.1, sf33) (all unpublished).

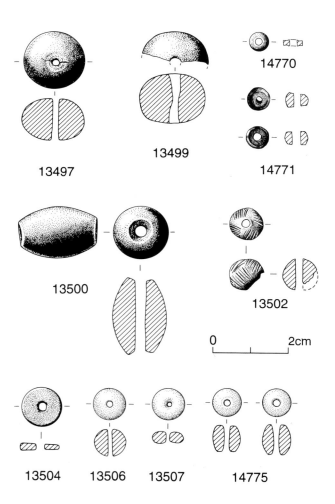

Fig.1516 *Rosary beads: of jet 13497, 13499–500 from Bedern and 14770–1 from 46–54 Fishergate; of a jet-like material 13502 from Bedern; of shale 13504 from Bedern; of amber 13506–7 from Bedern and 14775 from 46–54 Fishergate. Scale 1:1*

Other beads

An annular ceramic bead, *13530*, too crude to have formed part of a rosary, was found in an early 15th century context at Bedern. A discoidal object of stone with a small central perforation, *13480*, was found in a Period 5 level at Bedern. **Dr G.D. Gaunt** writes:

This object is made of either a biogenic (bioturbated?) limestone, similar (but not identical) to those in the Upper Jurassic Purbeck sequence of southern England, and closely comparable visually to 'Rouge Griotte' of Belgium, or an impure 'true' (i.e. metamorphic) marble of non-British origin.

13480 resembles a number of stone objects recovered from Anglo-Scandinavian deposits at Coppergate and identified as beads; fourteen similar beads came from Period 5B levels, including several of marble (*9767, 9772–4*, p.2598, *AY* 17/14). This suggests that *13480* may be residual from earlier levels at Bedern.

Music and recreation

Jew's harp (Fig.1517)

14117 is an iron Jew's harp from an unstratified context at Bedern. It has arms of the characteristic diamond-shaped cross-section, and a copper alloy reed set into a small recess at the head. Jew's harps of this form known elsewhere appear to be from 13th–16th century contexts. They include two from Wharram Percy (Fig.1315, **4**; Goodall 1979, 121, fig.63, 83) and one from London (Henig 1974, 195, fig.39, 83).

Gaming pieces

Dice (Fig.1518)

Dice of jet from 16–22 Coppergate (*11078–9*) and of stone from Fishergate (*14760*) were found in medieval contexts; the Coppergate dice both derive from 12th/13th century levelling/dumping deposits, while the Fishergate die was found in a pit fill asso-

ciated with the early–mid 14th century reconstruction of the priory.

Dr G.D. Gaunt comments on *14760*:

The chalk from which this die was made was probably obtained either from outcrops of the Chalk Group in the Yorkshire Wolds or from derived erratics in adjacent glacial, beach or river deposits.

On the jet dice the numbers are formed by ring-and-dot, those on *11078* being inlaid with calcium carbonate, those on *11079* inlaid with tin. Medieval dice generally employ one of two numbering systems: the one used from Roman times up to the present day has the spots arranged so that opposing sides add up to seven, but an alternative system also in use in the medieval period, certainly from the 13th–16th centuries, had one opposite two, three opposite four and five opposite six (Brown 1990, 692–3). As with the bone, antler and ivory dice (pp.1982–5, *AY* 17/12), the jet dice from York make use of both systems, *11079* using the conventional Roman numbering, *11078* the alternative. The crudely formed chalk die *14760* uses a third, possibly unique, unconventional numbering system, however, with one opposite three, two opposite six, and four opposite five.

Apart from the Coppergate dice, only one other jet die from an unspecified site has been recovered in York (RCHMY **1**, 144). Two medieval jet dice found at Winchester were both inlaid with tin, and, as at York, one was numbered conventionally, the other unconventionally (Brown 1990, 694). Lurk Lane, Beverley, produced a chalk die from a late 12th–13th century floor surface (Foreman 1991, 108), and a jet die from a late 13th–early 14th century floor (ibid., 122).

Gaming counters (Fig.1518)

Discoidal objects chipped or cut out of various materials including bone, antler, fired clay vessel sherds and tiles, and stone have been found previously on many medieval sites, and have generally been identified as playing pieces or counters (Carter 1977, 311; Mann 1982, 14). Coppergate, 22 Piccadilly, Fishergate and Bedern all produced these objects. Those of fired clay or stone from medieval deposits are considered here, while those of skeletal materials have been published in *AY* 17/12 (pp.1981–2) and those of wood in *AY* 17/13 (pp.2351–3).

Fig.1517 Iron Jew's harp 14117 *from Bedern. Scale 1:2*

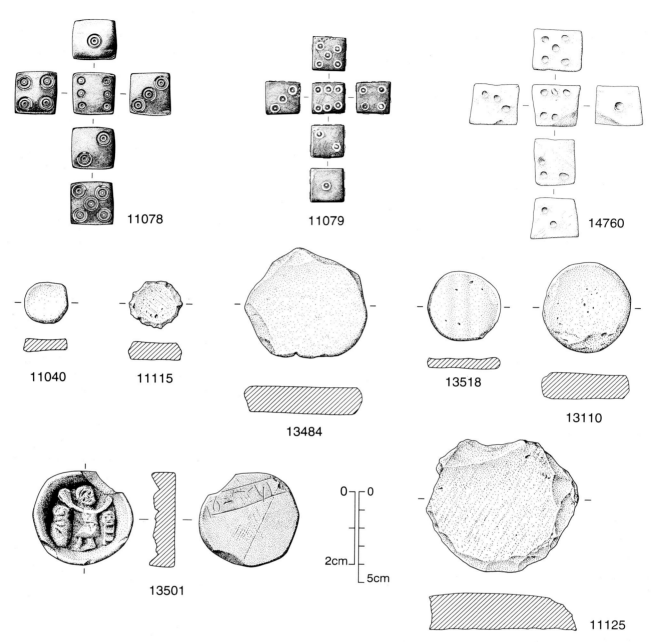

Fig.1518 *Dice of jet* 11078–9 *from* 16–22 *Coppergate and of chalk* 14760 *from* 46–54 *Fishergate; gaming counters* 11040 *(stone) and* 11115 *(tile) from* 16–22 *Coppergate,* 13484 *(stone) and* 13518 *(ceramic) from Bedern,* 13110 *(tile) from the Foundry; decorated jet disc* 13501 *from Bedern; counter or pot lid of tile* 11125 *from* 16–22 *Coppergate. Dice and jet disc scale 1:1; counters 1:2*

Counters of stone were found at Coppergate (*11035–41*), all from 12th–13th century deposits apart from *11035* which was from a 17th century demolition level, the Foundry (*13101–2*), Bedern (*13481–7*) and Fishergate (*14761*). Counters formed from ceramic vessel sherds came from Coppergate (*11085–105*), 22 Piccadilly (*13012*) and Bedern (*13516–19*). Tile counters came from Coppergate (*11106–21*), 22 Piccadilly (*13013*), the Foundry (*13108–10*), Bedern

(*13520–9*) and Fishergate (*14776*). A decorated jet disc (*13501*) found at Bedern may also be a gaming counter (see p.2952).

Stone counters

Dr G.D. Gaunt comments on the stone counters:

Six of the Foundry and Bedern counters, 13101–2, 13481–2, 13484, 13487, *and two from Coppergate,* 11036–

7, are made from fine-grained muscovite-laminated sandstones. Many such sandstones occur in the Coal Measures outcrops between Leeds and Derby, notably the Elland Flags of the Leeds-Bradford-Huddersfield areas and their more southerly correlatives. 11035 and 11038–9 are also probably from other typical varieties of sandstone in the Coal Measures, while 13483 is sandstone or congealed sand from an unknown source. 13485 is made of dolomitic limestone from the Permian Lower Magnesian Limestone, which crops out from Ripon southwards via Wetherby and Tadcaster to Doncaster and beyond. 11041 and 13486 consist of very fine-grained 'porcellanous' limestone which suggests an origin in one of the lithologically comparable thin limestones in the Middle or (less likely) Upper Jurassic successions of north-eastern Yorkshire, such as the Middle Jurassic Gormire (formerly Hydraulic) Limestone of the Howardian Hills and southern Hambleton Hills. The chalk counter 11040 probably derives from a similar source to the die 14760. The calcareous matrix and fossil content of 14761 implies either a marine sandstone from the Middle Jurassic of north-eastern Yorkshire or one of the sandstones in the Upper Jurassic Corallian Group of the same region.

Stone counters of sandstone and chalk were also recovered from Anglo-Scandinavian levels at Coppergate (see pp.2564–6, AY 17/14), and it is possible that some or all of those found in medieval levels are residual.

Fired clay counters

The ceramic counters derive from vessel sherds of the Roman to medieval periods. Some or all of those made from Roman sherds (11085–7, 13516) may be residual from the Roman period; counters made from Roman vessel sherds have been found in Roman contexts in York at Church Street (16–26, pp.2–3, AY 17/1), as well as at Colchester (Crummy 1983, 94). Coppergate also produced a number from Anglo-Scandinavian deposits (see p.2566, AY 17/14).

The two counters made of vessels from the Anglo-Scandinavian period both derive from Coppergate (11088–9), where similar counters were also recovered from Anglo-Scandinavian contexts (see p.2566, AY 17/14); as with the Roman counters, these may be residual in their medieval deposits.

Counters formed from medieval vessels were found at Coppergate, 22 Piccadilly and Bedern (11090–105, 13012, 13517–19) and derive from vessels which range in date from the mid/late 11th–16th

centuries (A.J. Mainman, pers. comm.). All the tile counters from Bedern and twelve of the Coppergate ones were chipped out of medieval roof tiles; four counters from Coppergate were made from Roman bricks (S. Garside-Neville, pers. comm.). Most of the counters have been roughly shaped, but occasionally they were more carefully finished off, with their edges and faces ground smooth (see for example 13110 and 13518). The tile counters are generally more crudely formed than the others.

Counters such as those from York are commonly found on medieval sites, including those of an ecclesiastical nature, although at Bedern games of chess and draughts, betting, gambling and throwing dice were strictly forbidden (Harrison 1952, 58). They were most likely used in the playing of tables, a range of games involving dice and counters on a board which was twice the size of a chess-board, hence the large size (up to c.70mm diameter) of the counters or tablemen (Brown 1990, 696). It has been suggested that the game of tables came to England in the 11th or 12th century (ibid.), although an antler counter roughout (7728, AY 17/12) was found in a context of undoubtedly pre-Conquest (Period 3) date at Coppergate, possibly pointing to the currency of the game in England before the arrival of the Normans.

Counters or possible pot lids (Fig.1518)

In addition to the counters, a number of stone and ceramic discs which appear too large to be tablemen (that is, with diameters of over 70mm) were recovered. Coppergate produced four of stone (11042–5), two of Roman brick (11122–3) and six of tile (11124–9), and Bedern one of tile (13529).

Dr G.D. Gaunt comments upon the stone objects:

The four stone objects are all made of Upper Carboniferous sandstones, probably from the Coal Measures. 11044–5 are specifically of Elland Flags-type sandstones in the Coal Measures.

While rather large to have been counters, they are probably too small to have acted as lids for any medieval pots (A.J. Mainman, pers. comm.), and their functions remain unclear. Similar objects were also found in Anglo-Scandinavian levels at Coppergate (9736, 9738, 9742, 9746, 9750, pp.2564–5, AY 17/14).

Jet disc (Fig.1518)

Unfortunately unstratified at Bedern, *13501* is a crudely decorated disc with a representation of the crucifixion in relief, the cross flanked by two figures, probably the Virgin and St John. There is also an illegible inscription cut into the reverse of the disc. Both the function and date of this object are unclear.

Trade and exchange

Scales (Fig.1519)

Evidence for commercial activity in the form of balances and scales is very limited. The only balances come from the Foundry (*13402–3*), while individual scale pans were recovered from Coppergate (*12929*), Bedern (*14493*) and Fishergate (*15243*). The more complete of the balances is *13402* which was found in an early 15th century context at the Foundry. Although a folding balance, it lacks its suspension stirrup. This type of balance is known in pre-Conquest contexts, with four examples being found at Anglo-Scandinavian Coppergate (*10405–6, 10410, 10412*, pp.2559–61, *AY* 17/14), but similar examples have also been found in medieval contexts, at Winchester (Biddle 1990, 917–18, fig.284, *3212*) and Norwich (Margeson 1993, 204, fig.155, *1573*). (*13403*) is fragmentary and came from a mid 15th–early 16th century context; it is impossible to determine whether it comes from a rigid or folding balance.

Although balances were found only at the Foundry, the recovery of scale pans at other sites indicates that balances may also have been used there. Two of

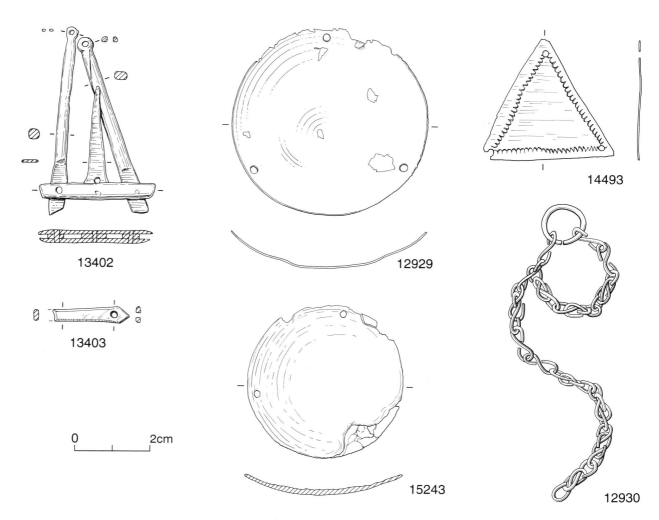

13402

13403

12929

14493

15243

12930

0   2cm

Fig.1519 *Folding balances* 13402 *and fragment of a balance* 13403 *from the Foundry; scale pans* 12929 *from 16–22 Coppergate,* 14493 *from Bedern and* 15243 *from 46–54 Fishergate; probable balance chain* 12930 *from 16–22 Coppergate. Scale 1:1*

the three scale pans (*12929, 15243*) are circular, the third (*14493*) being triangular. Both types would have been suspended by three chains attached via three holes, placed on the circumference of the circular pans and the corners of the triangular ones. It is unclear if there is any functional significance to the shape of the pans, both shapes being found throughout the medieval period (Biddle 1990, 918, *3217–23*; Margeson 1993, 205, *1576–81*), but the sizes of the pans, and the balances from the Foundry, suggest all were used for measuring small items or quantities of material, such as coins, precious metals or spices.

Balance chains (Fig.1519)

Although several lengths of non-ferrous chain were recovered from the sites under discussion (see pp.2852–3), only *12930* can be identified with confidence as probable balance chains; it comprises two lengths of S-shaped links attached to a ring at one end. If these chains were used with a balance, there would originally have been a third length which is now missing.

Weights

The majority of the weights found on the York sites are pan weights which would have been set in the pans of scales such as those described above; they are of copper alloy (*14728*), of lead alloy (*12960–4, 13077, 13423–5, 14570–8, 14652–3, 14732, 15290*) and of lead alloy with copper alloy coating (*15289*). A possible hanging weight (*12959*), for use with a steelyard, was found at Coppergate.

It should be noted that all measurements of weight are approximate, and that some weights were cleaned before being weighed while others were not. Although groups of weights from other cities such as London and Winchester have been studied in relation to the main medieval systems of measurement as currently understood (see Biddle 1990, 908–22; Egan 1998, 301–22), Egan has noted that attribution of archaeologically recovered weights to these systems is fraught with difficulties (ibid., 301). No attempt has been made here to do this with the York weights, not least because they have not all been treated to a standard in terms of cleaning and conservation, and some may more accurately reflect their original weights than others.

Pan weights (Fig.1520)

Recovered from early 13th century levelling deposits at Fishergate before the priory's construction, *15289* weighs c.73·4g. It is made of lead alloy, with a turned copper alloy shell and traces of iron staining, also seen on two weights from Winchester, thought to date from the 11th century (Biddle 1990, 910, 918–19, fig.280, *3192, 3195*). The iron residue may be from an iron pin used to hold the outer and inner clay moulds in place when casting the sheath by the lost-wax method (ibid., 910). Other examples found in Britain include Viking weights from the north-east coast of Ireland, and another dating from the 8th or 9th century in the Streeter collection (Kisch 1965, 83, fig.5 6), so *15289* appears likely to be residual in its medieval context.

Copper alloy

The only copper alloy weight, *14728*, is square, weighs c.4·2g and was found unstratified at 2 Ald-

Table 308   Lead pan weights (in ascending weight order by site)

Site	Cat. no.	Weight (g)	Treatment pre-weighing
16–22 Coppergate	*12964*	5.8	None
16–22 Coppergate	*12961*	8.5	None
16–22 Coppergate	*12962*	20.9	None
16–22 Coppergate	*12963*	27.2	None
16–22 Coppergate	*12960*	35.4	None
22 Piccadilly	*13077*	11.0	None
Bedern Foundry	*13424*	12.7	Cleaned
Bedern Foundry	*13423*	14.9	None
Bedern Foundry	*13425*	50.9	None
Bedern	*14574*	8.1	Cleaned
Bedern	*14572*	9.3	Cleaned
Bedern	*14571*	10.7	Cleaned
Bedern	*14575*	12.4	None
Bedern	*14577*	16.9	None
Bedern	*14570*	18.1	None
Bedern	*14576*	23.5	Cleaned
Bedern	*14573*	38.2	None
Bedern	*14578*	53.5	Cleaned
Bedern Chapel	*14653*	24.5	Cleaned
Bedern Chapel	*14652*	33.8	Cleaned
2 Aldwark	*14732*	19.8	None
2 Aldwark	*14733*	39.6	None
46–54 Fishergate	*15290*	14.5	None

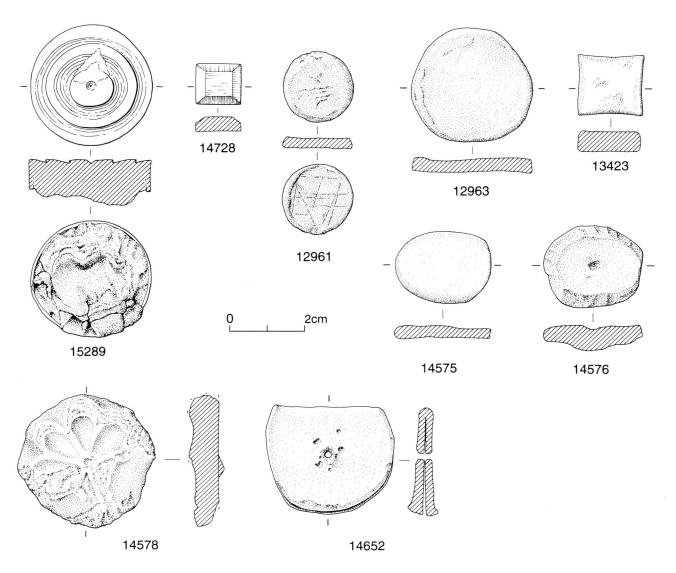

Fig.1520 *Weights* 15289 *from Fishergate,* 14728 *from 2 Aldwark,* 12961 *and* 12963 *from Coppergate,* 13423 *from the Foundry,* 14575–6 *and* 14578 *from Bedern,* 14652 *from Bedern Chapel. All the weights are of lead alloy except* 14728 *which is copper alloy;* 15289 *has a turned copper alloy shell. Scale 1:1*

wark; it was suggested that copper alloy weights of similar shape (but not similar weight) found in a late 14th century deposit in London (Egan 1998, 310, *978–9*) may be identified as bullion or goldsmiths' weights (see Biggs 1992, 15).

Lead alloy

The majority of these are circular or oval, either discoidal (*12960–2, 13077, 13425, 14570–3, 14575, 14653, 14732, 15290*) or of plano-convex section (*12963–4, 13424, 14574, 14576, 14733*), although identification of all these items as weights cannot be made with certainty. Most are plain, but both *13425* and

14732 are decorated with raised pellet motifs, while the stamped motifs on *14572* are unfortunately illegible. There are also square and rectangular weights (*13423, 14652*), and one octagonal (*14578*) which has an eight-petalled daisy impressed into its upper face. Apart from *14578* the shapes and motifs on all the lead weights from York are paralleled in London (Egan 1998, 310–20). The York examples range in weight from c.5·8g (*12964*) to c.53·5g (*14578*).

Hanging weight (Fig.1521)

The hanging weight *12959* is a crude bell shape, with an axial perforation; it was found in a mid 13th

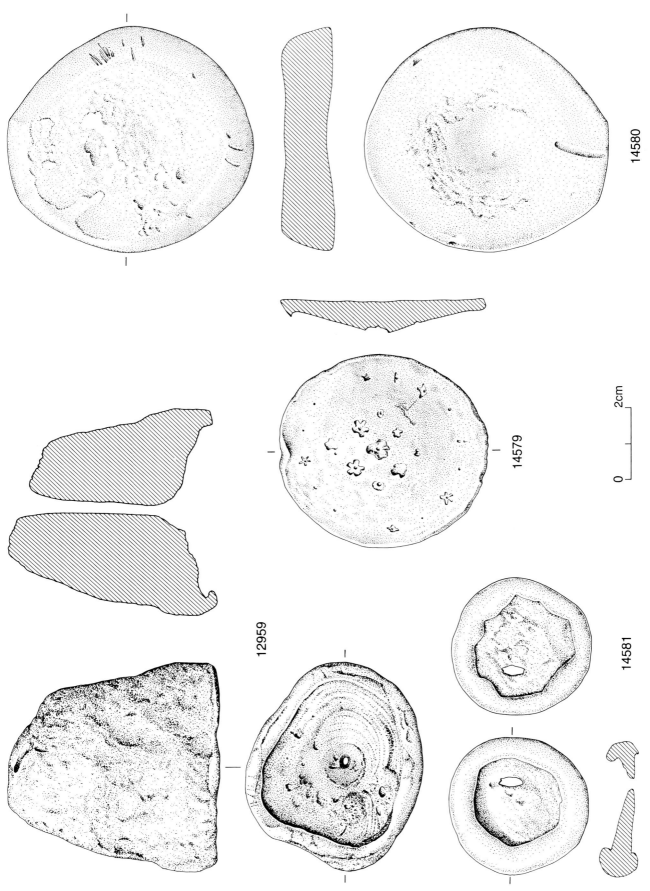

14580

14579

12959

14581

Fig.1521   *Lead hanging weight 12959 from 16–22 Coppergate; possible lead weights 14579–81 from Bedern. Scale 1:1*

0   2cm

century levelling deposit. Weighing approximately 600g, this weight appears likely to have had an industrial use.

Possible lead weights (Fig.1521)

Three miscellaneous circular or oval lead alloy objects from Bedern, *14579–81*, from deposits ranging from the 13th–late 15th centuries, may be weights. *14579* (113·1g) has been decorated with punched dots and stars, and *14580* (391·7g) has a notch on one surface. *14581* (68·4g) has thickened edges and a central recess.

Horse and riding equipment

Spurs

Prick spurs (Fig.1522)

12735 is a tin-plated iron prick spur from a late 11th century context at Coppergate. The surviving arm is straight and has a rectangular terminal pierced twice (LMMC Type Ai) with rivets in situ; the goad has an octahedral tip (LMMC Type 7). A straight arm suggests that the spur is pre-Conquest or immediately post-Conquest in date and a similar spur comes from an 11th century context at Walton, Buckinghamshire (Farley 1976, fig.39, 1). A similar goad can be seen on *12734*, also from a late 11th century context at Coppergate. This is a more or less complete spur which has arms which curve so as to fit snugly under the ankle bone. This feature was a development of the Norman period, as were the figure-of-eight-shaped terminals by which it was attached to the leathers. Similar terminals are visible on *12737* (13th–14th century context) and *12732* (post-medieval context) from Coppergate, both of which are prick spurs of simple form. *12732* has arms of triangular cross-section and *12737* has arms of the more usual D-shaped cross-section; in both cases the goads are missing.

Other fragments of prick spurs from Coppergate include *12731* (mid 13th century context), probably part of an arm which is very elaborately formed and finds no obvious parallel in Anglo-Scandinavian or medieval assemblages. *12736* (early 14th century context) is a neck and goad which is similar to Anglo-Scandinavian examples including *3832* from Coppergate (Fig.304, *AY* 17/6). *14121* from Bedern is probably a slotted arm terminal of common Anglo-Scandinavian form (p.699, *AY* 17/6).

Rowel spurs (Fig.1523)

The rowel spur, introduced to Europe in the 13th century, is represented by *14118* from a mid 14th–early 15th century context at Bedern. The surviving arm curves to a double-eyed terminal in which is set a fitting with a central disc and two opposing hooks which would link it to the leathers. This arrangement is typical of the late medieval period. Bedern has also produced two rowel boxes (the bifurcated section at the end of the goad which holds the rowel) from late medieval contexts: *14119* and *14120*.

A multi-point spur rowel, *12931*, unusually made of copper alloy rather than iron, was recovered from the base of a 15th–16th century well at Coppergate. Multi-point rowels, with points separated at the tips, appear to have been used contemporaneously with star rowels, which had separate points joined only at the centre (see *14120*); both types were in use from the 13th century up to the present day, and varied little in design, so it is rarely possible to date a rowel typologically (Ellis 1995, 147). Based on its context, a 15th–16th century date for *12931* seems probable. Rowel spurs can be seen on Fig.1534, p.2970.

Spur fittings (Fig.1523)

12738 from a mid 13th century context at Coppergate consists of a tapering hook with a sub-rectangular cross-section. At its base it widens out into two plates between which a strap would have been gripped. This was probably used for linking a spur to its leathers, although there appears to be no exact parallel. *12739* from Coppergate is a small fitting with a central eye and a hook at each end similar to that seen on *14118* which would also have linked a spur to its leathers. This comes from an early 15th century context and is characteristic of the period. *15117* is a similar object with a central domed element from a later 16th century context at Fishergate, but is probably 15th century in origin.

Iron bits

Snaffle bits and curb bits were used throughout the medieval period, snaffle bits usually having linked mouthpieces and ring cheek pieces whilst curb bits are more complex objects which allowed the attachment of extra reins and straps. The former were in general use for everyday riding while the latter, which allow greater control over the animal, were

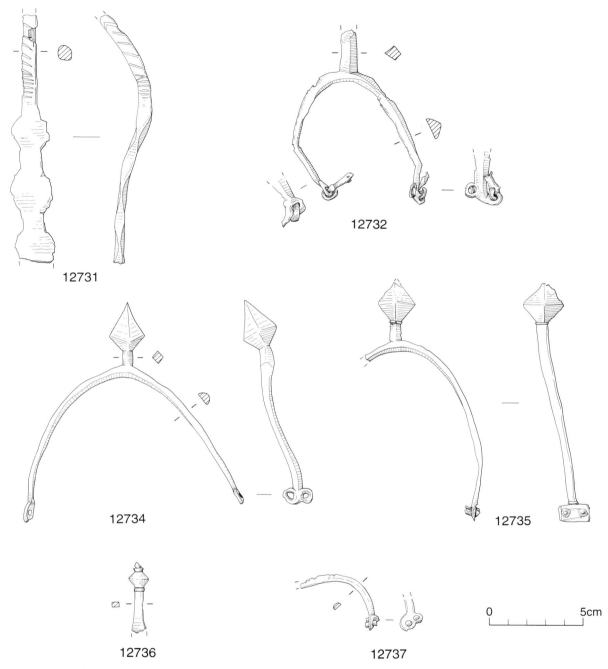

Fig.1522 *Prick spurs 12731–2, 12734–7, all from 16–22 Coppergate. Scale 1:2*

either used on war horses or in circumstances where the animal was led rather than ridden, as in the case of a packhorse or a horse on ceremonial parade.

Snaffle bits (Fig.1524)

There are two complete snaffle bits with ring cheek pieces, one from an 11th–12th century context at Coppergate (*12740*) and one of uncertain medieval date from 2 Aldwark (*14686*). The simpler in form is *12740*; the link eyes were made by folding over the ends of the shank while the cheek pieces are relatively small with a diameter of 39mm. Snaffle links from similar bits include *12742–4* from Coppergate. *14686* is an altogether more robust bit than *12740*. The link heads (i.e. where the cheek pieces

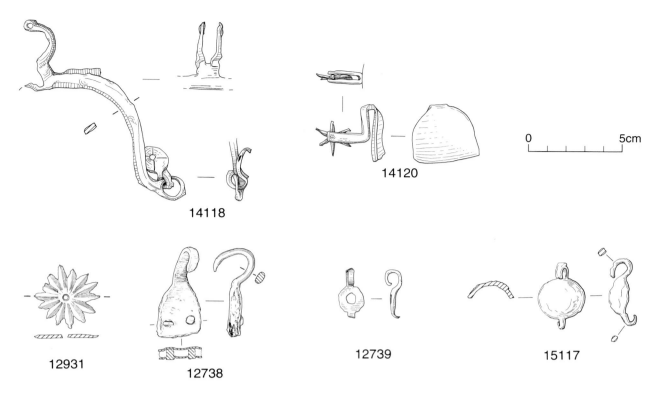

Fig.1523 *Parts of rowel spurs 14118 and 14120 (iron) from Bedern, 12931 (copper alloy) from 16–22 Coppergate; other spur fittings 12738–9 from 16–22 Coppergate and 15117 from 46–54 Fishergate. Scale 1:2*

were attached) are thickened and the eyes have probably been punched through them. The cheek piece rings have a diameter of 70mm. There are incised grooves at the head of the links and the whole object was tin plated. Similar bits come from a late 14th century context at Lochmaben Castle, Dumfries and Galloway (Macdonald and Laing 1974–5, 146, fig.10.1), and a late medieval context in London (Clark 1995, 49–50, 3).

12741 from a post-medieval context at Coppergate is one half of a bar bit. The surviving link is slightly curved and tapers towards the end where it joined the second link; at the other end it articulates with a straight bar at a point where the bar has a projecting eye. *12741* is probably residual as similar bits are known in medieval contexts from 12th century onwards. *12746* from Coppergate and *14123* from Bedern are strips with domed terminals which may be incomplete bars from similar bits. *12747* from a 13th–14th century context at Coppergate is a cheek piece from a bar bit on which the arms of the bar,

now incomplete, slanted away from the eye. It has incised grooves on the surface and is plated with copper alloy.

14687 from 2 Aldwark comprises a pair of tin-plated spirally twisted snaffle links which have oval eyes at each end. Similar links were found as part of a complete bit from a late 15th–early 16th century context at Ospringe, Kent (Fig.1315, **27**; Goodall 1979a, 132, fig.23, 111).

13049 from 22 Piccadilly (mid–late 12th century context) is a tin-plated double-eyed attachment link which would have joined the rein to the snaffle link. Similar objects are usually pre-Conquest (e.g. *3849*, *AY* 17/6), although they are also found in 11th–12th century contexts. They were probably used with bits which have some form of bar cheek piece as shown in Fig.1525; the characteristic thickening in the centre is to prevent the rein slipping once it has been tied. *14122* from an early–mid 13th century context at Bedern may be a similar object to *13049*. At one

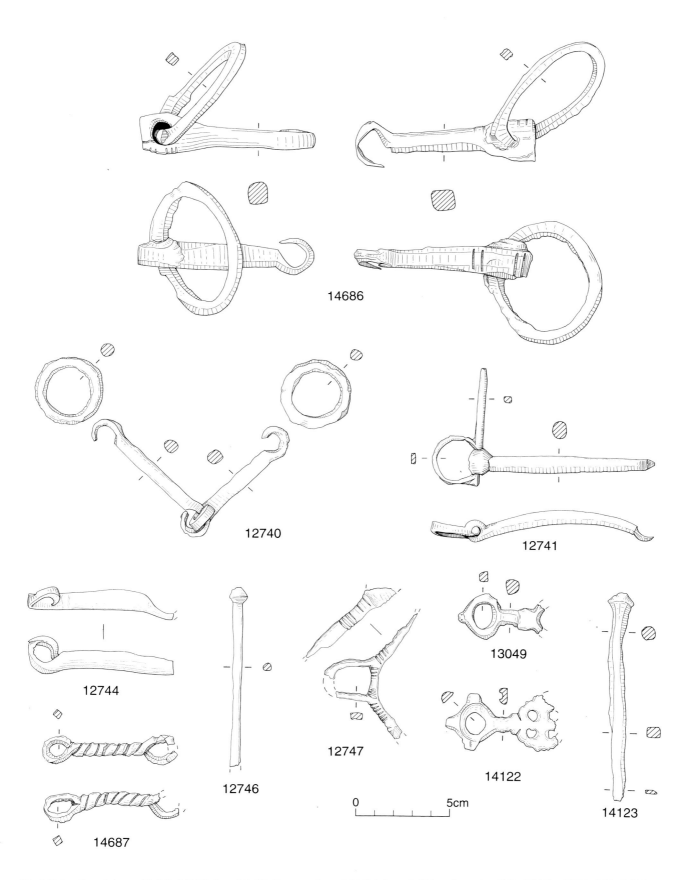

Fig.1524 *Complete snaffle bits* 12740 *from 16–22 Coppergate and* 14686 *from 2 Aldwark; parts of bits* 12741, 12744, 12746–7 *from 16–22 Coppergate,* 13049 *from 22 Piccadilly,* 14122–3 *from Bedern and* 14687 *from 2 Aldwark. Scale 1:2*

Fig.1525 *Reconstruction of a 10th–11th century horse bridle with a bit of a form known from Winchester (Waterman 1959, 75, fig.8.2) showing attachment link as* 13049 *and pendants as* 12752

end is an eye, but at the other is an incomplete disc pierced four times, probably for riveting to the rein. The object was probably part of a fairly expensive bridle as it is coated with mercury gilded silver.

Tim Horsley writes on the mercury gilding (see also p.2756): *The white-yellow metal was visible as a few small patches, but it is probable that either the whole object, or at least portions of it, were plated in this way.*

Curb bits (Fig.1526)

13001 (15th–16th century context) from Coppergate watching brief is part of a curb bit. Originally the object was symmetrical with a central strip which ran down the centre of the horse's nose; two strips curved away from the base of this strip to eyes which were linked to the mouthpiece of the bit. The vertical side members terminated in eyes which were attached to the reins. A more complete example of a very similar bit in copper alloy was recovered from

a possible 12th century context at Gloucester (Hurst 1986, 96, fig.40). *12748* from an early 15th century context at Coppergate is a detached side member.

12749, an incomplete object from a late 14th century context at Coppergate, is probably from a curb bit of a similar form. It consists of a flat mouth piece which at its unbroken end has a curved and spirally twisted strip projecting from it which terminates in a looped eye. Running up from the eye at 90° to the mouth piece are three spirally twisted strips, the central one being more robust than the others and broken. A photograph of a complete curb bit from Germany with a somewhat similar mouth piece and side link, dated to the first half of the 11th century, was published in the periodical *Archäologie in Deutschland* (Schäfer and Gross 2000, 33). This shows that the eye would have been linked to the bridle and the central spirally twisted strip would probably have curved forwards to connect in some way with a component similar to *13001*. The other strips running up from the eye would have been decorative. *12751* may be a fragment of a similar object.

12750 from an 11th–12th century context at Coppergate was originally a U-shaped object made from a strip of D-shaped cross-section; there are incised grooves on the convex face and it is tin plated. *13279* from a late 14th–early 15th century context at the Foundry was also U-shaped and has a looped terminal at the complete end; presumably there was a similar terminal at the broken end. Near the base of the U it is pierced twice. Like *14122* noted above, this object is plated with mercury gilded silver.

Tim Horsley writes on the mercury gilding: 13279 *has very small traces of gilded silver present in linear fragments. They appear to be the remains of gilded silver wire which, like the knife blade (13792) discussed on p.2756, had been arranged in a pattern. It is possible that it is not inlay, but traces of the plating surviving in keying, although keying is not visible elsewhere on the object.*

12750 and *13279* were probably parts of a type of curb bit of which a complete example, plated with non-ferrous metal, was found at Ludgershall Castle, Wiltshire (Goodall 2000, 153, fig.6.33, *242*). In this case a U-shaped component is linked to a bar set above the swivelling bar which went in the horse's mouth, but could drop down below the mouth and be linked to a lead rein or a martingale.

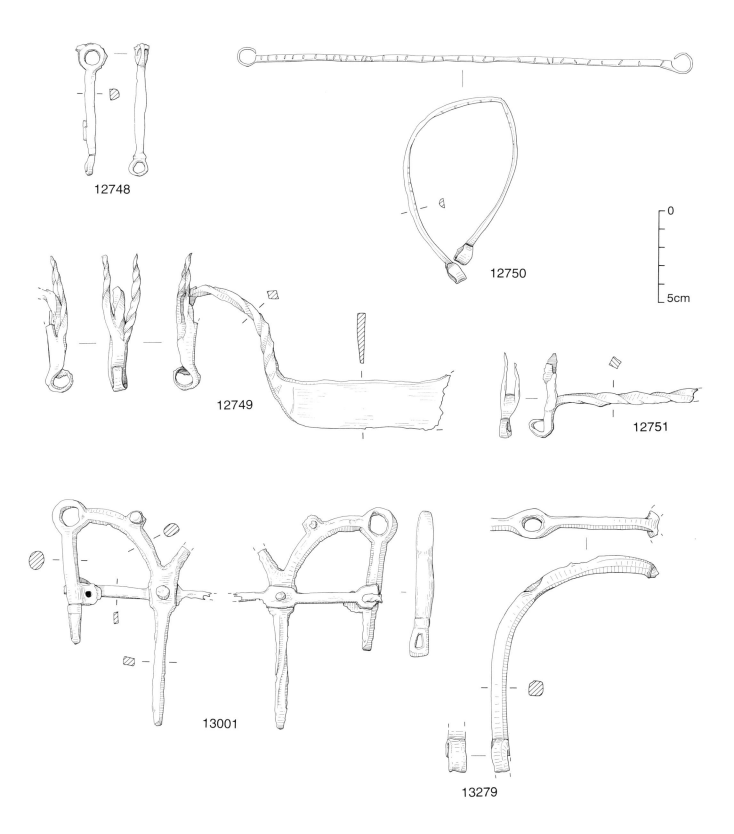

12748

12750

12749

12751

13001

13279

Fig.1526 *Parts of iron curb bits* **12748–50** *from 16–22 Coppergate,* **13001** *from the Coppergate watching brief,* **13279** *from the Foundry; probable bit component* **12751** *from 16–22 Coppergate. Scale 1:2*

0

5cm

Fig.1527   *Reconstruction of a later medieval bridle, incorporating* 13001 *from the Coppergate watching brief site*

Harness pendants (Figs.1528–9)

12752 from a 13th century context at Coppergate is a tin-plated iron harness pendant. It was attached to the end of a strap by means of a small rivet-like component which is linked to a triangular component. The latter has incised grooves in a diamond pattern on the surface. The object was probably used as shown in Fig.1525 which is based on a complete bridle found in a 10th century grave at Thumby-Bienebek, Germany (Müller-Wille 1987). *12752* is almost certainly Anglo-Scandinavian and may be compared with an object from Coppergate incorrectly identified as a hinge fitting (Fig.268, *3480, AY* 17/6).

Four copper alloy pendants (*14494–7*) and a pendant mount (*14498*) were recovered from Bedern, and two pendants from Fishergate (*15244–5*); they would

probably have been used as decorative attachments on harness. The pendants demonstrate a range of shapes, and most have been embellished with either enamelling (*14497*) or gilding (*14494–6, 15245*). Harness pendants are thought to have been used from the 12th century to the late 14th or early 15th century (Griffiths 1995, 62). The earliest examples included plain circular shapes such as *14496* and *15244* but during the 13th century a greater variety of shapes and increased use of gilding and enamelling became popular (ibid.). Perhaps dating to the 13th century, although unstratified, *15245* retains the circular shape but has been decorated with an irregular star surrounded by punched dots; it is also centrally perforated, possibly for a stud holding a decorative strap or ribbon (ibid., 65, *58–9*). *14495* is a quatrefoil with rocked tracer leaf decoration and gilding, and was recovered at Bedern from a mid–late 13th century clay loam dumped as levelling for the construction of Building 7, added to the residential block Building 5. The shield shape of *14494*, now incomplete, was another popular design, as seen on the horseman illustrated in the *Mappa Mundi* of c.1300 (ibid., 62, fig.46; see also Mitchiner 1986, 136–7, *392–5*). The use of heraldic devices was also common, such as the lion on *14497* which has been depicted in white enamel; although recovered from a late 15th–early 16th century deposit, it probably dates from the 13th or 14th century. A shield-shaped pendant found in Deanery Gardens, Ripon (Fig.1315, **3**), features an enamelled and gilt heraldic device (Rogers 1997, 149, fig.11, *39*).

Another shield-shaped copper alloy object which has been tinned may also be a harness pendant

(15246). It was found in a Period 6a/6b deposit at Fishergate, is incomplete and has a fragmentary lug at the back which may originally have joined at the top of the object forming a suspension loop. Another possible harness fitting is *14499*, which is shield-shaped with a long shank on the reverse. The shield bears traces of enamelling, the edges have been gilded and the design appears to be the heraldic symbol of the 'water bouget', a vessel for carrying water comprising two leather pouches hung from a yoke (Wheeler-Holohan 1931, 311). This symbol is part of the heraldic achievement of the Ros(s) family (see also Fig.1534, p.2970). Since *14499* does not incorporate the full coat of arms, however, attribution to this family cannot be made with certainty, although the family did use the single charge as a badge (H. Murray, pers. comm.). These shield-shaped items have been found elsewhere, including London, which

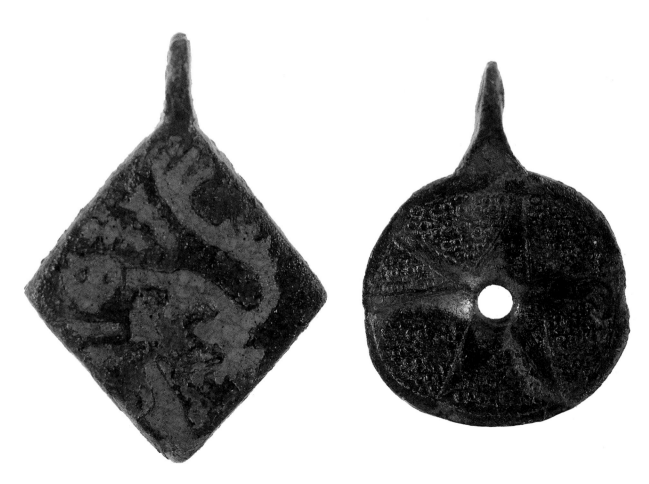

Fig.1528 *Copper alloy harness pendants: (left)* **14497** *with white enamelled lion 'passant guardant' from Bedern; (right)* **15245** *from Fishergate decorated with a six-pointed star within an incised circle, and traces of gilding. Actual length of* **14497** *46mm*

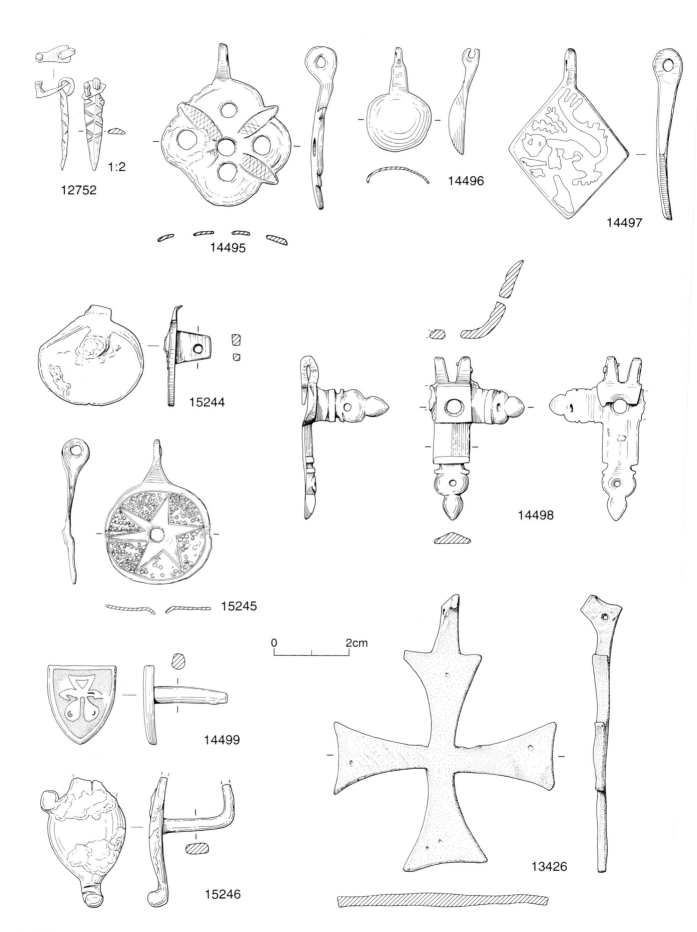

12752

1:2

14495

14496

14497

15244

15245

14498

0   2cm

14499

15246

13426

2964

produced two of a similar size to *14499*, both of which were decorated with the arms of England (Griffiths 1995, 69–71, fig.53, *77–8*). It is suggested that these fittings may originally have been mounts attached to stirrups, as found on an example from Oxfordshire (Griffiths 1989, 1, fig.4).

Pendants were suspended from harness via mounts to which they were attached by their integral perforated lugs; *14498* is a cruciform gilded mount, which originally had three arms with perforated terminals, the fourth arm being that from which the pendant would have been suspended (see Griffiths 1995, fig.52, *75*). Although both pendants and mounts were usually made of copper alloy, the pins holding the two elements together were often of iron. As a result loops often wore through and pendants were lost; many are recovered as isolated finds (ibid., 62–3; Hinton 1990f, 1047, n.1). A very similar mount to *14498* was recovered during metal-detecting near Saxton, North Yorkshire (J. Halliday, pers. comm.).

Found in a late 13th–early 14th century pit lining at the Foundry, *13426* is a large lead alloy pendant of cross formy shape, and another possible harness decoration.

Iron horseshoes (Fig.1530)

There are c.120 horseshoes or parts of horseshoes, of which 65 come from Coppergate. Where it can be determined, 42 of the Coppergate horseshoes plus three from the Foundry, seven from Bedern and four from Fishergate have the wavy outer side and countersunk holes characteristic of the late 11th–13th century. In the relatively narrow branches of the period (the average maximum width of those under discussion is c.22mm) the waviness is usually very marked compared to the pre-Conquest period when the wavy side and countersunk hole emerged, but on branches which were relatively wide (pp.707–9, *AY* 17/6). In the post-Conquest period horseshoes there are usually three countersunk holes in each arm, but *12756* has an additional hole on each side at the tip and in *13280* from a late 13th century context at the Foun-

dry, an unusually large shoe c.145mm in length, there were also four in each arm. In addition, horseshoes of the late 11th–13th century usually have a calkin formed by the end of the branch being turned over at 90° or folded back on itself (e.g. *12773*).

In the later medieval period horseshoes have smooth outer sides, the branches are usually slightly wider than hitherto and the holes are rectangular. Of the eight horseshoes from Coppergate with smooth sides, two are unstratified (*12801–2*), *12800* is from an early 12th century context and may be intrusive, *12796–7* from 13th century contexts, *12798* from a 13th–14th century context, *12799* from a 15th century context and *12795* from a post-medieval context. At Bedern horseshoes with smooth edges outnumber those with wavy edges 10:7 reflecting the later date of the occupation sequence.

Some 350 horseshoe nails were found at Coppergate, 30 at Fishergate and 22 at Bedern (details are held in the YAT archive). A little over half have D-shaped heads and most of the remainder probably had heads of this form, but are now worn into other shapes. Coppergate produced two eared heads characteristic of a 13th–14th century date (Goodall 1980b, 183). The average length of unbroken nails is 38mm (c.1½ inches). The average width of head was 15mm and length of head for unworn nails c.9·5mm, while thickness was usually 4–7mm.

Iron curry combs (Fig.1530)

12818 from a mid 12th century context at Coppergate is an incomplete curry comb which originally had a semi-cylindrical blade with two or three spirally twisted arms which were set in a wooden handle. *12819–20* are additional spirally twisted arms; to the latter a fragment of the blade is attached. The curry comb was used to groom a horse and a detailed review of its history in medieval England has been published by Clark (1995). *12818* appears to be one of the earliest curry combs from Britain and its dating seems to contradict the suggestion made by Clark (ibid., 163) that the semi-cylindrical blade was

Fig.1529 (facing page) *Tin-plated iron harness pendant* 12752 *from Coppergate; copper alloy harness pendants* 14495–7 *from Bedern,* 15244–5 *from 46–54 Fishergate; possible harness pendants* 14499 *from Bedern and* 15246 *from 46–54 Fishergate; mount for harness pendants* 14498 *from Bedern; lead alloy harness pendant* 13426 *from the Foundry. Scale 1:1,* 12752 *1:2*

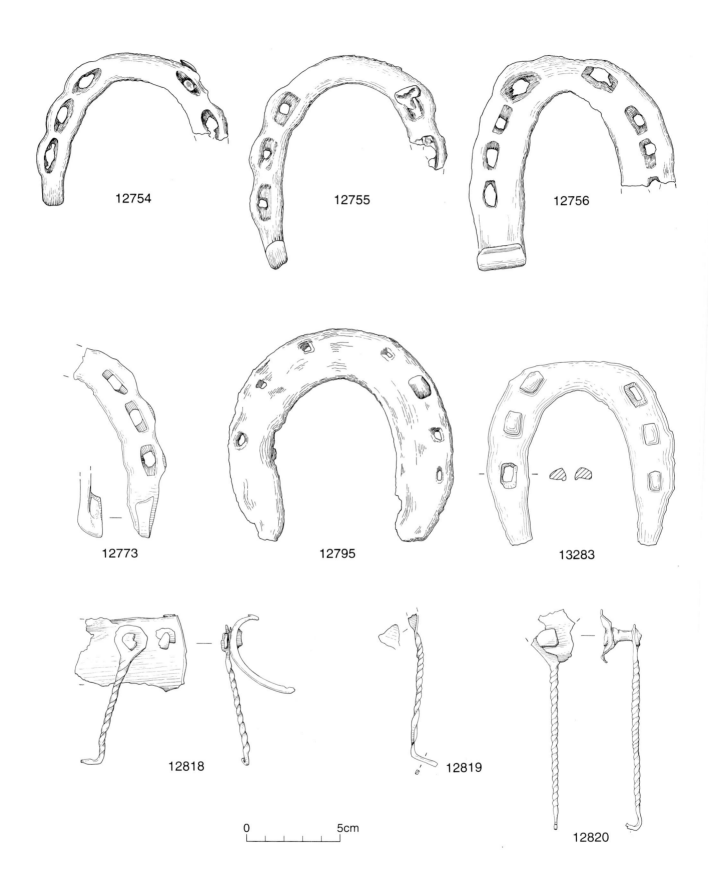

Fig.1530 *Iron horseshoes: with wavy outer side 12754–6, 12773 from 16–22 Coppergate, with smooth outer side 12795 from 16–22 Coppergate and 13283 from the Foundry; iron curry combs 12818–20 from 16–22 Coppergate. Scale 1:2*

a development of the 15th century, replacing an earlier form with a blade of angular cross-section.

Weapons and armour

Iron swords (Fig.1532)

There are two sword pommels and a guard, probably of Anglo-Scandinavian date, from medieval contexts at Fishergate which have been published as *5261–3* in *AY* 17/9 (pp.1431–3). *12821* from Coppergate is the tip of a sword blade.

Iron arrowheads (Figs.1531–2)

There are 44 arrowheads. *14153* from a late 13th century context at Bedern has a tanged leaf-shaped blade and is probably residual from the pre-Conquest period in which this form is common (pp.710–1, *AY* 17/6). All the other arrowheads are socketed including *14154* (early 14th century context) from Bedern, and *15128* (13th century context) and *15129* (late 13th–early 14th century context) from Fishergate which also have leaf-shaped blades. The latter two may be residual from the Anglian period — in which

socketed blades are usual — and the Bedern specimen may also be pre-Conquest, but all three could equally well be 11th–12th century.

The commonest blade form at Coppergate is triangular. *12826* (early 13th century context) has horizontal shoulders (LMMC Type 2). *12829* also has horizontal shoulders but the blade is unusually small; the socket appears to have been bent and damaged at the base in antiquity in some sort of secondary use. Other arrowheads, including *12827* (12th–13th century context), *12828* (late 12th century context), *12830* and *12832* have upward sloping shoulders (LMMC Type 1). *12831* (early 12th century context) has an unusually small blade with stepped shoulders. These arrowheads correspond to the 'multi-purpose forms' used for both hunting and warfare identified by Jessop (1996).

There are 21 barbed arrowheads of various forms. *12839* and *12841* both from 13th–14th century contexts at Coppergate and *15131* (early–mid 14th century context) from Fishergate have short rounded barbs and a collar at the junction of blade and socket. Short barbs as LMMC Type 13 can be seen, for ex-

Fig.1531 *Woman shooting a rabbit with a stunning arrowhead, from the early 14th century* Taymouth Hours *(British Library, Yates Thompson MS 13, fo.68v)*

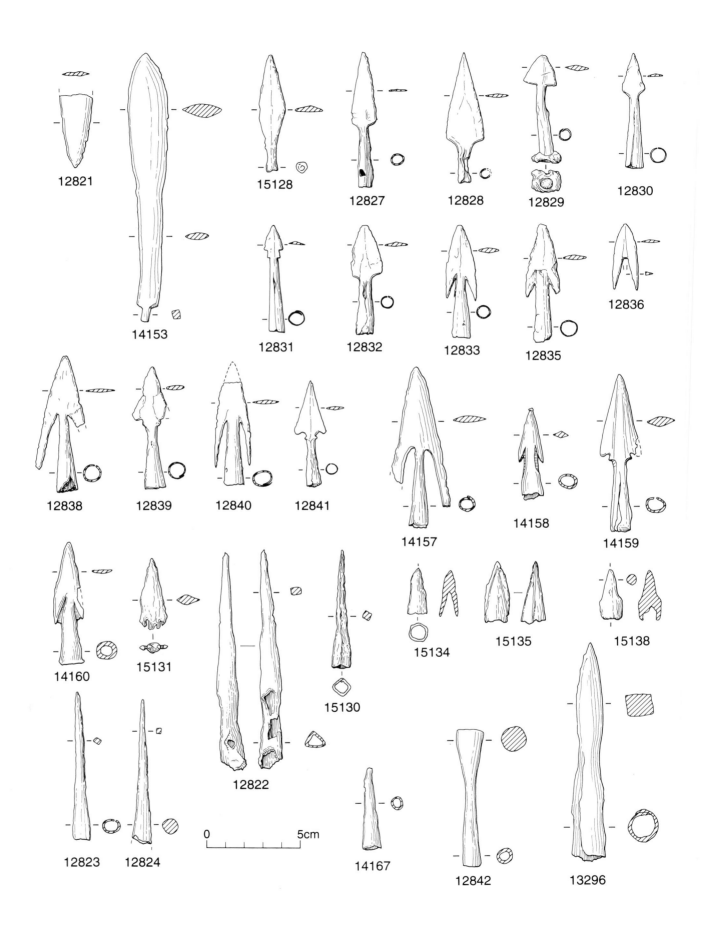

12821

14153

15128

12827

12828

12829

12830

12831

12832

12833

12835

12836

12838

12839

12840

12841

14157

14158

14159

14160

15131

12822

15130

15134

15135

15138

12823

12824

14167

12842

13296

0   5cm

2968

ample, on Coppergate examples *12833* (14th century context) and *12835* (mid–late 15th century context), on *14160* (late 14th–early 15th century context) and *14163* (late medieval context) from Bedern. These arrowheads are again thought likely to be multi-purpose by Jessop (1996). Long barbs which come down as far as or almost as far as the base of the socket (LMMC Type 14) can be seen on *12838* (mid 13th century context) and *12840* (12th–13th century context) from Coppergate and *14157* from an early 14th century context at Bedern. Jessop (ibid.) identifies arrowheads of this form as having a specialist use in hunting.

There are four small arrowheads which have a simple tapering blade of rectangular cross-section: *12823–5* (late 12th century, 13th–14th century and unstratified, respectively) from Coppergate, and *15130* (late 13th–early 14th century context) from Fishergate. A larger example is *12822* from Coppergate (13th century context). This form of arrowhead existed in the pre-Conquest period (p.714, *AY* 17/6), but was also apparently current for some considerable time afterwards.

Bullet-shaped arrowheads or tips used on long-bow shafts are represented by thirteen examples. The earliest is *15133* from a late 13th–early 14th century context at Fishergate, while *14167* is from a mid 14th century context at Bedern. The remaining five from Fishergate (*15134–8*) are from 15th–16th century contexts; *14169–70* are from late medieval contexts at Bedern and *13297* is from a post-medieval context at the Foundry. Two of the Fishergate examples (*15135* and *15137*) have a thin fin on opposing sides. All but two are, as is usual, plated with copper alloy. Numerous comparable late medieval examples come from Baile Hill, York (Addyman and Priestley 1977, 140, fig.10).

12842, from a 12th–13th century context at Coppergate, is probably an arrowhead used for stun-ning rather than killing game. It has two conical arms, one of which is socketed and slightly longer and thinner than the other, which is solid. An arrowhead of this type appears to be shown in an illustration from the early 14th century *Taymouth Hours* (Fig.1531).

Finally, *13296* from an early 15th century context at the Foundry is a heavy cross-bow bolt 115mm in length.

In addition to the arrowheads, a leather archer's bracer was recovered from a late 14th–late 15th century context at Coppergate (sf811, *AY* 17/16 in prep.). The bracer acted as a guard to protect the inside of the forearm from the sanp of the string when shooting a long-bow.

Iron mail (Fig.1533)

12843 from an early 14th century context at Coppergate exists as two pieces, one of twelve links and the other of five, of what may be mail. Some of the links have lapped welds. *12500* and *12513*, small rings from Coppergate, also appear to have had lapped welds and *12500* was riveted; they may also be from mail (see Fig.1430, p.2852).

Knuckle plates from plate armour gauntlets (Figs.1533–4)

Two copper alloy knuckle plates, *12932–3*, were recovered at Coppergate. Both are convex in shape to cover the main finger joint and have a longitudinal lozenge-shaped rib at the top of the curve; rivet holes at either side were for attachment of the plate to the gauntlet finger. During the 13th century, armoured protection for hands had been provided by mail mufflers (Edge and Paddock 1988, 81). From c.1330–40, hour-glass-shaped metal gauntlets were developed, which protected the wrist and main part of the hand, with narrow metal scales protecting the

Fig.1532 *(facing page) Tip of an iron sword blade* 12821 *from 16–22 Coppergate; iron arrowhead with a tanged leaf-shaped blade* 14153 *from Bedern; iron socketed arrowheads* 15128 *from 46–54 Fishergate (with a leaf-shaped blade),* 12827–32 *from 16–22 Coppergate (with triangular blades),* 12833, 12835–6, 12838–41 *from 16–22 Coppergate,* 14157–60 *from Bedern and* 15131 *from 46–54 Fishergate (with barbed blades),* 12822–4 *from 16–22 Coppergate and* 15130 *from 46–54 Fishergate (with simple tapering blades); bullet-shaped arrowheads or tips used on longbow shafts* 14167 *from Bedern and* 15134–5, 15138 *from 46–54 Fishergate; stunning arrowhead* 12842 *from 16–22 Coppergate; cross-bow bolt* 13296 *from the Foundry. Scale 1:2*

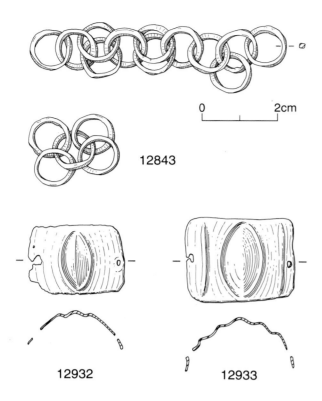

0   2cm

12843

12932   12933

Fig.1533 *Iron mail* 12843 *from 16–22 Coppergate; copper alloy knuckle plates* 12932–3 *from 16–22 Coppergate. Scale 1:1*

Fig.1534 *Detail from the St William window, York Minster (panel 1b), showing two sons of William, Lord Ros, wearing gauntlets (reproduced by courtesy of York Minster Archive, © Dean and Chapter of York)*

fingers. These were riveted to an internal cloth or leather glove, as the surviving gauntlets of Edward, the Black Prince (d.1376), illustrate (Waterer 1981, 86, fig.77). Finger scales such as *12932–3* overlapped the finger plates at the joint, being attached to the textile or leather glove via the rivet holes on each side, and enabled complete flexibility of the fingers. This style was maintained until the introduction of 'mitten gauntlets' during the 1430s (Griffiths 1990, 1084), but finger scales continued to be made for fingered gauntlets until the end of the 17th century.

12932–3 are identical apart from size, *12933* being slightly wider. Both have one damaged rivet hole, and although the rivets are absent, the size of the rivet holes and the lack of ferrous corrosion suggests slender copper alloy rivets were originally used, which are typical of the second half of the 14th century (Thom Richardson, pers. comm.). Both may be discarded plates, removed to allow the fitting of new covers, and their proximity to one another in the

ground suggests that they may have once belonged together (but see below). Similar finger-joint or knuckle plates of copper alloy or iron have been found along the Thames foreshore (Royal Armouries nos.III.2757, 4210, 4330–4; Thom Richardson, pers. comm.); another example was found in Winchester (Griffiths 1990, 1084).

While these knuckle plates are firmly dated to the later 14th century, they were both found in deposits of the 13th century. *12932* was recovered from a late 13th century levelling/dump deposit, while *12933* came from an early 13th century pit. It must be assumed that both are intrusive in their contexts: the early 13th century pit also contained intrusive late 14th century pottery (A.J. Mainman, pers. comm.). It has been suggested that *12932* may have originally been discarded in a late 14th century pit above the dump deposit (K. Hunter-Mann, pers. comm.).

Miscellaneous objects

Fossils

Various fossils were recovered from across the sites, including crinoid ossicles, bivalves, *Gryphaea*, corals, ammonites, belemnites, fossil echinoids and fossil brachiopods.

Dr G.D. Gaunt writes:

Many of these fossil types have been found previously in York (see AY 17/9, AY 17/14); geological information on Carboniferous crinoid ossicles, such as 11046 and 14762, known as St Cuthbert's beads, is given in AY 17/9 (pp.1386–7). The stellate ossicles of the Jurassic crinoid Pentacrinites *sp. as in 14658 are widespread, although rarely abundant, in limestones, some mudstones (mainly in the Lower Jurassic) and even a few sandstones (notably the Middle Jurassic Crinoid Grit of north-eastern Yorkshire, used in that region and sparsely in York for querns). They are not difficult to detach from weathered rock surfaces but do not normally survive as erratics in Quaternary deposits. As with Carboniferous crinoid ossicles, they possess perforated central canals, which, even if no longer open, are easily drilled to produce beads. Several species of the bivalve* Gryphaea *(e.g. 11048 and 13489) are common in the Jurassic rocks of eastern Yorkshire. Being thick-shelled and globose they are unusually robust for fossils, and large numbers have survived reworking into Quaternary deposits. The presence of* Gryphaea *at archaeological sites presumes some non-functional value, possibly related to their old English folk name of 'devil's toe-nails' and reputed medicinal value (Oakley 1965, 12). Belemnites such as 13491 occur in most Jurassic and Cretaceous rocks of marine origin and, as with* Gryphaea, *sometimes survive reworking into Quaternary deposits. Alternatively, 13491 which is largely unworn may have been extracted from a solid-rock site, most likely in north-eastern Yorkshire. The flattened surface on 13491 appears to be the result of artificial abrasion, possibly related to the production of a powder (once reputedly a cure for watery eyes in horses) or rasping (said to produce an odour with medicinal properties) (Oakley 1965, 14–15).*

Although a fragment of ironstone (14767) contains part of an indeterminate coarsely ribbed shell, an imprecise impression possibly of an ammonite or gastropod, and small spicular voids, none of these fossils appears sufficiently distinct to have had any use or significance, even as curiosities. The ironstone is lithologically similar to parts of the Lower Jurassic Cleveland Ironstone of north-eastern Yorkshire. The Cleveland Ironstone does not normally occur as erratics as far west as York, and any iron production from it would have been carried out near the ore source, so the reason for the presence of this isolated item at York is uncertain.

Unidentified objects

Iron (Fig.1535)

15139 from Fishergate is a strip with a hook or eye at the head which tapers into a bent loop at the other end. This may have been a key from a chatelaine similar to an example from an Anglian context on the same site (5243, AY 17/9).

Copper alloy (Fig.1535)

12934 is of plano-convex section, with both ends bent up, one with a perforated terminal, the other incomplete, and moulded decoration with ring-and-dot motifs on the convex face. The fragmentary 12935 appears to have been made up of five layers of metal, and has a shaped terminal and flat, sub-rectangular shank; both objects were found in 12th–13th century build-ups or dumps at Coppergate.

13404 was found in an early 15th century pit at the Foundry. Now in three fragments, its construction resembles a semi-circular strap-end with a spacer plate, but the object is also hinged with wire loops at each end of the hinge pin.

With a shaft of circular section, one bulbous and one squared off end, and a perforation close to the latter, 14500 derives from an early–mid 13th century deposit at Bedern. From an 11th–12th century context, 14501 is a strip with mouldings. A tongue-shaped piece of sheet with a slot and a notch in the upper end, 14503 was found in an early 15th century deposit at Bedern. 14504 may be a mount or some other sort of fitting; it is annular with raised projections at opposing sides on the reverse from which incomplete rivets extend. The fragmentary 14502 has an incomplete shaft with a finial at one end; it was found in an early 15th century deposit at Bedern.

15247 is a strip with one end roughly scooped, while 15250 is a narrow strip bent round to form a semi-circle with both tips bent out. 15249 comprises a shaft with one rectangular end, and 15251 appears to be a tube, most of which has been compressed flat, leaving a tiny socket at one end. 15248 is a decorative strip fragment which has solder traces on the reverse and thus seems likely to have been attached to another metal object.

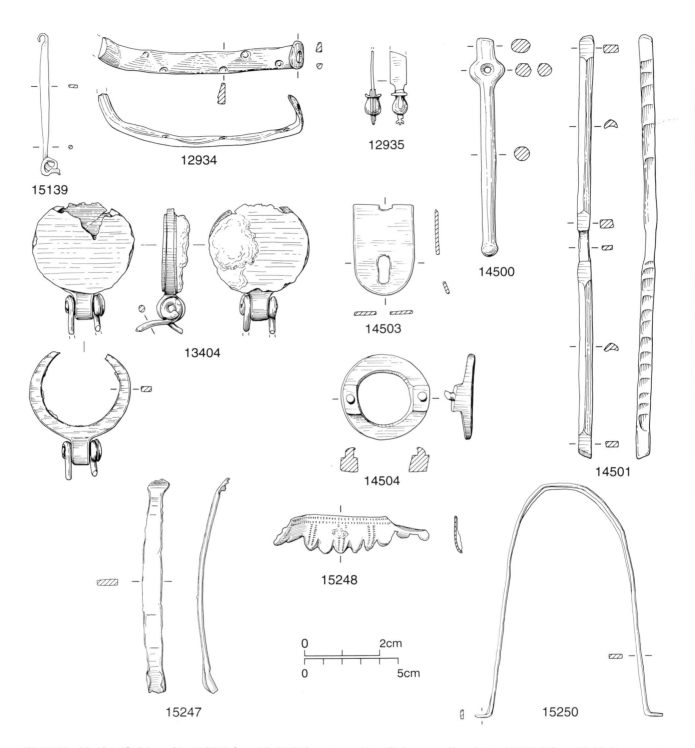

Fig.1535 *Unidentified iron object* 15139 *from 46–54 Fishergate; unidentified copper alloy objects* 12934–5 *from 16–22 Coppergate,* 13404 *from the Foundry,* 14500–1 *and* 14503–4 *from Bedern,* 15247–8 *and* 15250 *from 46–54 Fishergate. Scale 1:1, 15139 1:2*

Lead alloy (Fig.1536)

From a mid–late 15th century context at Bedern, *14584* is a flattened cylinder with one end sealed by a flap. *14582* was recovered from a mid–late 13th century pit underlying one of the walls of the residential Building 5 at the College. It comprises two sub-circular discs joined intermittently around the edges with a lip at one side on both faces. A very worn but slightly raised flower-like motif, possibly a fleur-de-lys, is visible on both faces although only under magnification. Despite its 13th century find-spot, this appears to be a post-medieval type of seal (G. Egan, pers. comm.), suggesting it must be intrusive in its medieval context. Found in a late 13th century deposit *14583* comprises a narrow shaft, with both ends broken; too narrow to be a point fragment, its function is uncertain.

Two unidentified lead alloy objects from Fisher-gate are *15291*, a strip of plano-convex section with both ends flattened, and *15292* which has a shaft of hexagonal section with one moulded end, the other end being broken.

Stone

Made of an igneous rock, probably basalt, the fragmentary *14768* from Fishergate has four polished faces, and may have been used as a smoothing stone; it was found in Period 6a levelling soil, and may be residual from earlier activity on the site.

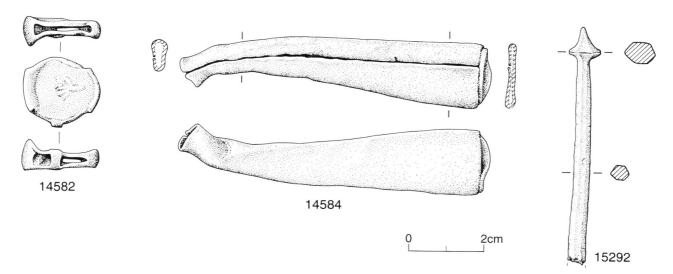

Fig.1536 *Unidentified lead alloy objects 14582 and 14584 from Bedern, 15292 from 46–54 Fishergate. Scale 1:1*

Intra- and Inter-Site Analyses

In this section consideration will be given to the evidence which the artefacts described and discussed above can provide for the changing character of occupation and activity on the sites from which they derive in the medieval period (mid 11th–16th centuries). This will be done largely by relating the quantification of the artefacts to the periods and site zones defined in the stratigraphic and structural analyses.

Introduction

It is difficult to assess how reliable a picture of the character of occupation and activity on a site at any particular time period in the past can be elicited from the assemblage of archaeological artefacts recovered there. In most cases the vast majority of objects used fail to appear in the archaeological record. Artefacts may simply disappear in ground conditions unsuitable for preservation. Alternatively, they may either have been disposed of in locations other than the site in question for a variety of practical and cultural reasons, or (and this is especially likely in the case of items made of precious metal) they may have been recycled. Furthermore, on multi-period urban sites such as those under discussion, the continual earthmoving operations attendant on building, pit digging and the like may have removed objects from their original place of deposition and left them in contexts which may be some distance away and/or of a much later date. In other words, on urban sites the level of residuality in contexts of any given period is likely to be high.

At 16–22 Coppergate major earthmoving episodes have probably led to a considerable bias in the data in that, on the one hand, the medieval street frontage areas had been removed by later activity and, on the other, large quantities of material had been dumped on the site in the late 11th–12th centuries, although this may not have come from very far away. In the Anglo-Scandinavian period, however, no such major episodes were identified and the finds may therefore be a more reliable guide to the character of occupation on the site at that time than in the post-Norman Conquest era. At the Foundry, Bedern and Fishergate there were no major episodes of removal or deposition of material, although contexts of all periods probably contain an appreciable residual component.

It should also be added that evidence for character of occupation and activity based on finds may be obscured by selective collecting strategies during excavation and by analytical strategies during post-excavation. Some evidence for the latter is noted in respect of horseshoe nails below.

In spite of all the conceptual and practical problems referred to above, it is none the less suggested that there are patterns in the data from the sites under discussion which hint at changes in the way these sites, or the parts of York in which they were located, were used over a period of over 500 years. This period may be extended to almost 1,000 years if the data from Anglian contexts at Fishergate (*AY* 17/9) and Anglo-Scandinavian contexts at Coppergate (*AY* 17/6) are also taken into consideration.

Particular reference will be made in this section to the analysis of the iron objects which make up the largest group in terms of material in the assemblage as a whole. Since object types made of iron, excluding dress fittings but including tools, structural fittings and weapons, were rarely made in other materials, they can be analysed as a self-contained group and make a distinct contribution to the study of the sites under discussion and especially the changing importance and character of craft activity.

The artefacts made of materials other than iron, namely non-ferrous metal, stone, fired clay, glass, jet and amber, fulfilled a wide variety of functions; unlike the ironwork, most of the artefacts made of these other materials are found in small numbers which do not readily lend themselves to useful distributional analyses. This comment does not apply to manufacturing debris, found in some quantity at both Coppergate and the Foundry, which has been studied and published elsewhere in *The Archaeology of York* series, in *AY* 17/7 and *AY* 10/3, although some further analysis of the Foundry material is included in this report (pp.2708–17). Where artefact types are present in what appear to be significant numbers, as in the case of the hones, some chronological and spatial analysis has been carried out.

Chronological analyses

Ironwork

The structure of the assemblage

While certain types of iron object, such as fibre processing spikes and knives, occur in sufficient numbers to allow their occurrence to be plotted through time in a statistically meaningful way, the vast majority do not. It has proved necessary, therefore, to consider the objects in larger groups broadly defined by function. For the purposes of the analysis below they have been assigned to nine groups (A–I) as follows.

A. *Bars, strips and plates*. This group includes, on the one hand, bar iron and smithing debris of the sort recorded in some quantity in Anglo-Scandinavian contexts at Coppergate (pp.492–506, *AY* 17/6), and, on the other, broken or incomplete objects which can neither be assigned to a well-defined type nor distinguished from smithing waste. Determining to which of the two sub-groups any particular item should be assigned is often impossible.

B. *Tools and implements*. This group includes all objects, apart from knives and comb teeth, used in processes of making or working. Objects used in fishing and agriculture are also included here, although there are very few examples in the assemblage.

C. *Fibre processing spikes*. As these items are both numerous and components of a larger object, the wool comb (or flax heckle), rather than tools in their own right, they are considered as a separate group.

D. *Knives*. As one of the most numerous objects in the ironwork assemblage, knives can be treated as a group in their own right. Some knives were no doubt craft tools, others personal items used in consuming food and other tasks, others again may have been multi-purpose artefacts, but it is rarely possible to assign a particular function to an individual specimen.

E. *Structural ironwork and fittings*. This large group includes objects which were usually nailed, stapled or driven into structures or furniture.

F. *Locks and keys*. These object types, with their distinct function, occur in sufficient numbers to be considered independently of Group E, although their principal use was for structures or furniture.

G. *Dress fittings and riding equipment*. This group includes objects worn about the person, although some, such as certain buckles, may have been horse equipment and so would properly belong in Group H, but this can not usually now be determined.

H. *Horse equipment*. The vast majority of the objects included under this heading are horseshoes and horseshoe nails, although there were also a few iron parts of bridles.

I. *Weapons and armour*. Items in this group are few in number and consist primarily of arrowheads.

Using these groups the chronological distribution of objects and the implication of that distribution for the character of occupation and activity may be considered for each of the principal sites in turn. Data used to produce Figs.1537–47 can be found in Tables 332–41 on pp.3161–4.

16–22 Coppergate

At Coppergate objects were recovered from contexts of all medieval and post-medieval dates from the late 11th century to the 19th, but the vast majority (90%) come from contexts of late 11th–mid 14th century date. It has proved difficult to date many individual contexts closely, but it has been possible for the purposes of this report to divide all the contexts on the site into the following broad chronological groups with a reasonable degree of validity as follows.

6i   late 11th–late 12th century
6ii   late 12th/early 13th–mid 13th century
6iii   late 13th–mid 14th century
6iv   late 14th–19th century

In Figs.1537–8, Tables 332–3 and the discussion which follows, data from Anglo-Scandinavian contexts originally published in *AY* 17/6 (see summary on pp.719–20) are included as it is by comparison of all the post-Roman periods on the site that the character of each is best understood.

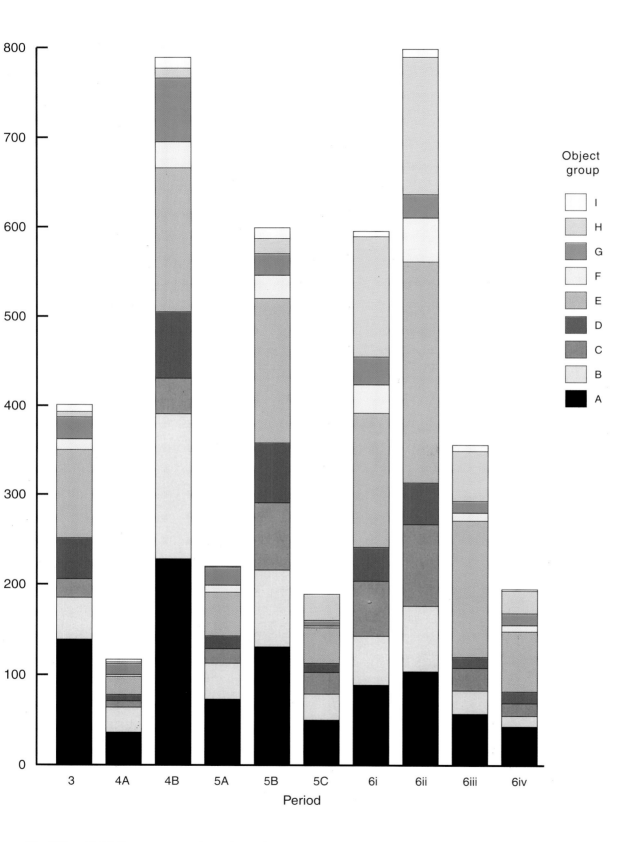

Fig.1537   *16–22 Coppergate: numbers of iron objects by group for the Anglo-Scandinavian and medieval periods*

2977

The Anglo-Scandinavian periods at Coppergate are as follows:

3   Mid 9th century–early 10th century
4A   Early 10th century–c.930/5
4B   c.930/5–c.975
5A   c.975 (finds largely residual)
5B   c.975–early/mid 11th century
5C   mid–later 11th century

Although the data need careful interpretation, a number of trends can be identified which may indicate the changing character of occupation and activity on, and in the environs of, the site. First of all, the relatively high percentages for Group A (bars, strips and plates) in Periods 3, 4A, 4B (34·5%, 30·5%, 29%) reflect what is known on other grounds, including the structural evidence, namely that ironworking was taking place on the site itself and in the immediate vicinity between the mid 9th century and the late 10th (*AY* 17/6). Period 5A material is largely residual from earlier periods and there must be a residual component in Periods 5B and 5C when there was no structural evidence for ironworking. The continuing absence of ironworking on the site is finally reflected in a drop in the Group A percentage in Period 6i (15%). In all the medieval contexts there will be residual material, but the Period 6 Group A assemblages probably have a higher proportion of broken and unidentifiable objects as opposed to waste from ironworking than hitherto.

As far as Group B, tools and implements, is concerned, the highest percentages are in Periods 4A and 4B (24% and 20·5%). These figures may be seen as complementary to the other substantial and varied evidence for crafts, including the working of iron and other metals, in the 10th century. Residuality may account for some of the Group B objects in Periods 5B and 5C, but there is no reason to doubt that craft activity continued on the site, although metalworking ceased. The apparent drop in the Group B percentage between Period 5C and Period 6i (15·5%–9%) is to some extent a result of the distorting effect of the high percentage of horse equipment on the data for the later period (see below), but, as will be shown

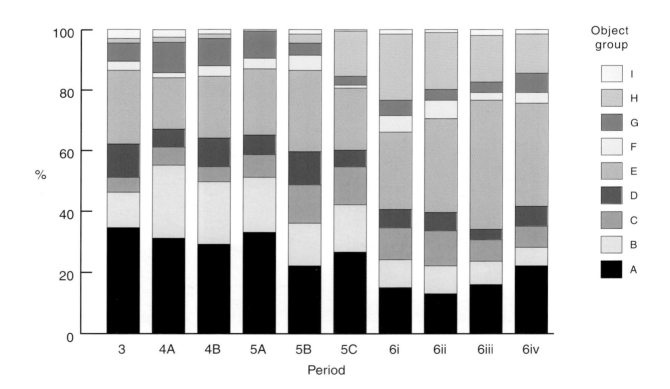

Fig.1538   *16–22 Coppergate: numbers of iron objects by group for the Anglo-Scandinavian and medieval periods expressed as percentages of the period totals*

in another way below, there does seem to have been a real decline in deposition of iron objects derived from craft activity between Periods 5C and 6i.

The percentages for Group C, fibre processing spikes, is highest in Periods 5B, 5C, 6i and 6ii (12·5%, 12·5%, 10·5%, 11·5%) but essentially the data indicate that fibre processing using hand-held combs was a widely practised urban craft in the 9th–13th centuries. The lower figures from 6iii and 6iv (both 7%) may result from the change in methods of wool processing in the later medieval period which used fixed installations in specialist workshops (pp.1721, 1827–9, *AY* 17/11).

The data in respect of Group D, knives, show that, as in the case of other tools, the highest percentage was recorded in the main Anglo-Scandinavian periods, and may thus provide support for the suggestion that some knives were specialist craft working tools (p.583, *AY* 17/6). Lower percentages in the medieval periods may be another indication of the decline in the importance of craft working in this part of York, although examples of the specialist currier's knife occur in medieval contexts (see p.2731–2).

The percentage score for Group E, structural ironwork and fittings, exhibits no great variation until Period 6ii when it rises from 25·5% in Period 6i to 31% before becoming 42·5 % in Period 6iii. The latter figure, at least, probably reflects the declining contribution of other groups especially the tools and implements in Groups B–D, to the assemblage.

The data for Group F, locks and keys, show little meaningful trend; evidently security was a consideration from the mid 9th century onwards.

The data for Group G, dress fittings and riding equipment, show the highest percentages in Periods 4A, 4B and 5A (10·5%, 9%, 9%). The figures can be seen to complement other evidence for the manufacture of tin-plated iron dress fittings and riding equipment on the site at this time (p.681, *AY* 17/6).

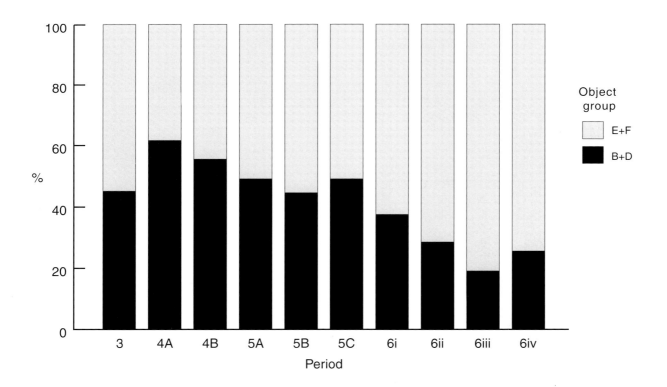

Fig.1539 *16–22 Coppergate: percentage of iron objects in the Anglo-Scandinavian and medieval periods in Groups B with D (tools, implements and knives) and E with F (structural ironwork, fittings, locks and keys)*

One of the most striking trends in the data concerns Group H, horse equipment, for which there are negligible percentages in all the Anglo-Scandinavian periods except for 5C in which there is a sharp rise to 15·5%. This is followed by a further rise to 22% in Period 6i. This illustrates very strikingly the introduction of the shoeing of horses in the early–mid 11th century (pp.707–9, *AY* 17/6) and its adoption as a standard practice from the 12th century onwards.

The number of weapons in Group I remains small in real and percentage terms in all periods and is made up largely of arrowheads except for a few sword fragments in the Anglo-Scandinavian periods.

It is not necessarily easy to determine clear trends in the inter-relationship of as many as nine groups of objects especially when, for example, a sharp rise in the numbers of one (Group H) halfway through the time period makes it difficult to compare the picture in respect of other groups before and after this rise. In the hope of gaining a rather clearer picture of the changing character of occupation and activity at Coppergate as reflected in ironwork, especially the impact of craft working, the data were re-examined solely in terms of the changing relationship between, on the one hand, the numbers of tools and implements (Group B) and knives (Group D), and, on the other, the numbers of structural ironwork and fittings (Group E) and locks and keys (Group F).

In general terms the data show a steady decline over time in the number of tools, implements and knives deposited in relation to structural ironwork and fittings (Fig.1539 and Table 334, p.3162). The figure for Period 4A (61·5% for B and D) is based on a relatively small number of objects and may, therefore, be unreliable. Overall, however, the high scores for the Anglo-Scandinavian periods clearly reflect the importance of craft working on the site, especially in Period 4B (55·5% for B and D) when the evidence for metalworking is particularly good. Figures for Period 5C (49% for B and D) are also based on relatively small numbers of objects, but it seems clear that a marked change in the character of deposition occurred between the mid 11th and late 12th century with objects from craft working becoming progressively a less significant component thereafter. One aspect of this already noted may be the decline in the importance of domestic preparation of wool for spinning.

46–54 Fishergate

In Tables 335–6/Figs.1540–1 the data on iron object numbers are shown for Fishergate, broken down into four main periods. The objects from Period 3 (Anglian) and Period 4 (11th–12th century) already published in *AY* 17/9 are shown alongside the data from Period 6a–c (c.1195–c.1350), roughly comparable to Periods 6ii and 6iii at Coppergate, and Periods 6d–e (late 14th–16th century). Not shown are 30 objects from Period 6z which are from medieval contexts, but are not more closely datable.

The percentages for Group A (bars, strips and plates) in the Anglian period (3) at Fishergate is comparable to that for the Anglo-Scandinavian periods at Coppergate and may be taken, along with the slag data, to suggest that ironworking was amongst the crafts practised on or near the site (pp.1224–30, *AY* 17/9; *AY* 7/2, 71–2), although no hearths were found.

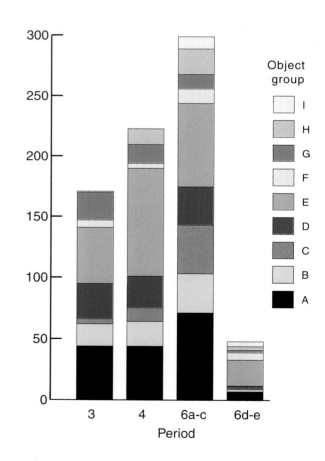

Fig.1540   *46–54 Fishergate: numbers of iron objects by group for the Anglian and medieval periods*

In the other periods there is little evidence for crafts and any Group A material is probably either residual from Period 3 or made up of broken and otherwise unidentifiable objects rather than waste derived from smithing.

The percentage of tools and implements (Group B) does not appear to change greatly through time. The figures are well below the highest for Anglo-Scandinavian Coppergate and cannot in themselves be used to indicate much in the way of craft activity on the site at any time.

Once again, the evidence provided by iron objects for the character of occupation and activity on the site was re-examined by considering the relationship between the numbers of tools, implements and knives (Groups B and D), and the numbers of structural iron-

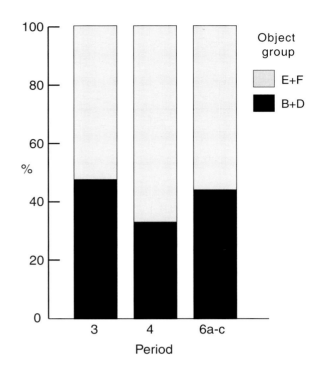

Fig.1542 *46–54 Fishergate: percentage of iron objects in the Anglian and medieval periods in Groups B with D (tools, implements and knives) and E with F (structural ironwork, fittings, locks and keys)*

work and fittings, and locks and keys (Groups E and F). This is shown in Fig.1542/Table 337.

It has to be said that these data do not present a particularly clear picture of change, although the percentage of Groups B and D is highest in Period 3 (47·5%). The corresponding figure for Period 4 (33%) suggests that craft activity did not play much of a role in activities on the site at this time, but a rise to 44% for B and D in Period 6a–c may hint at some craft activity somewhere in the priory precinct, if not in the area excavated; this is also indicated by the greater number of comb teeth (Group C) in the period (see Table 336), although tools of other materials related to textile working were few (see above).

Bedern

The data for the Foundry and Bedern sites may be considered together as there is little difference between them in terms of the composition of the iron-work assemblages (see below). Although some 11th–12th century occupation was recorded at the Bedern sites, the period yielded very few iron artefacts. For

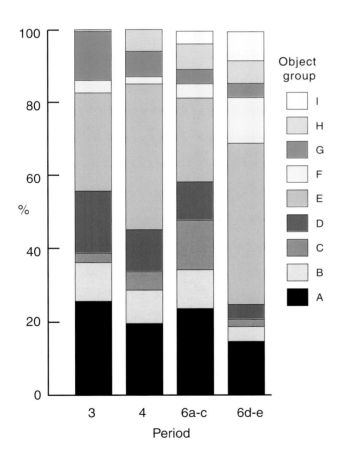

Fig.1541 *46–54 Fishergate: numbers of iron objects by group for the Anglian and medieval periods expressed as percentages of the period totals*

purposes of this analysis the contexts at Bedern can be broken up into four 'Finds Periods' (hereafter FP) corresponding to the site periods used in *AY* 10/3 and *AY* 10/5 as follows.

| | Site periods | | |
	Bedern	Foundry	Date
FP			
1	1–4	1–2	13th c.
2	5–6	3	early–late 14th c.
3	7	4.1–4.4	late 14th–early 15th c.
4	8–9	4.5–7	mid 15th c. and later

FP 1 and 2 correspond roughly to Coppergate Periods 6ii and 6iii and Fishergate Period 6a–c, while FP 3 and 4 correspond to Coppergate Period 6iv. In Figs.1543–4/Tables 338–9 the data on iron object numbers are shown for the two Bedern sites broken down into the four Finds Periods.

Although the numbers of objects from each period are, as at Fishergate, relatively small compared to the numbers from each period at Coppergate, some patterns similar to those found at the other two sites

appear in the Bedern data. The Group A (bars, strips and plates) percentage in FP 1–2 (18%) at Bedern compares well with the contemporary Coppergate periods, but in this case the material is probably made up almost entirely of broken objects rather than smithing debris as there is no other evidence for ironworking on the site. The Bedern percentages are, however, a bit lower than that for Fishergate Period 6a–c (23·5%), but there is no apparent reason for this unless residual Anglian smithing debris has enhanced the Fishergate figure. Tools and implements (Group B) in Bedern FP 1–2 (9% and 11%) score a little higher than in Coppergate Periods 6ii and 6iii, but the same as in Period 6a–c at Fishergate. The numbers and percentages of comb teeth are low in all the Bedern periods compared to the contemporary period assemblages from Fishergate and Coppergate which probably contain residual material. The Bedern data may, however, reflect the decline of hand combing in the later medieval period already noted. Knives (Group D) in Bedern FP 1 score higher (12%) than in Periods 6ii and 6iii at Coppergate and Period 6a–c at Fishergate, although in Bedern FP 2 the percentage (5·5%) is almost the same as in Coppergate

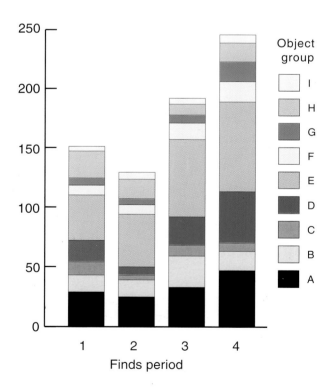

Fig.1543 *Bedern: numbers of iron objects by group for the medieval and late medieval/post-medieval periods*

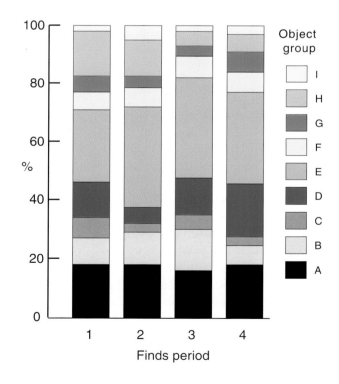

Fig.1544 *Bedern: numbers of iron objects by group for the medieval and late medieval/post-medieval periods expressed as percentages of the Finds Period totals*

Period 6ii (6%). Further comment relating to the data on tools and knives appears on p.2984.

The percentage of Group E (structural ironwork and fittings) for FP 2 (34·5%) compares well with Period 6ii figure at Coppergate (31%), although not with that for Period 6iii (42·5%). The figure for FP 1 (25%) at Bedern is lower than any of those just quoted, reflecting perhaps of the existence of relatively few buildings on the site in most of the 13th century (*AY* 10/5, 409–29), although it is similar to that for Period 6a–c at Fishergate (23%). The percentages for FP 3–4 at Bedern (34·5% and 31·5%) compare well with the contemporary Period 6iv at Coppergate (34%).

The only other group requiring comment is horse equipment (Group H) as figures for Bedern FP 1–2 (15·5% and 12·5%) are, taken together, lower than for contemporary Periods 6ii and 6iii at Coppergate (19%, 15·5%), although higher than Fishergate Period 6a–c (7%). The percentages from Bedern FP 3–4 (5% and 6%) are also lower than for Period 6iv at Coppergate (13%). One suspects that these discrepancies are a function of data collection and recording methods, especially at Bedern. Many horseshoe nails from Bedern probably lie unrecorded in bags containing nails of all types.

As at Coppergate and Fishergate, the evidence for the likely character of occupation and activity at Bedern as reflected in ironwork was re-examined in terms of the relationship between the numbers of tools, implements and knives (Groups B and D) and the numbers of structural ironwork and fittings, and locks and keys (Groups E and F). This is shown in Fig.1545/Table 340.

The relative percentages for FP 1 (41% for B and D, 59% for E and F) compare well with those for Fishergate Period 6a–c (44–56%). The figures for FP 2 at Bedern (27·5–72·5%) appear anomalous for this site. They are largely due to a smaller than expected number of knives. The figures compare well with medieval periods at Coppergate, however, especially with those of Period 6ii (28·5–61·5%). The percentages in FP 3 and 4 at Bedern (both 39–61%) appear rather different to those for the contemporary Coppergate Period 6iv (25·5–74·5%) and, as far as FP 3 is concerned, may be a reflection of the intensive building activity taking place on the site in the late 14th–early 15th centuries (*AY* 10/5).

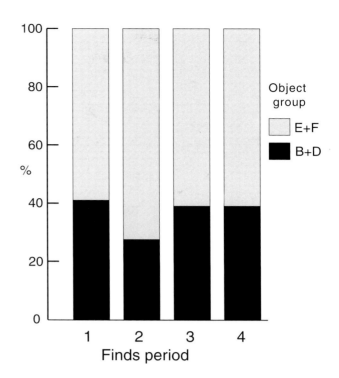

Fig.1545 *Bedern: percentage of iron objects in the medieval and late medieval/post-medieval periods in Groups B with D (tools, implements and knives) and E with F (structural ironwork, fittings, locks and keys)*

Conclusions

It has been suggested under each site heading that instead of relying on a consideration of all nine object groups, a clearer picture of trends in the character of occupation and activity, principally in respect of the extent of craft activity on or in the environs of those sites, emerges from a consideration of the relationship between, on the one hand, the numbers of tools, implements and knives (Groups B and D) and, on the other, the numbers of structural ironwork and fittings (Group E), and locks and keys (Group F). From the data a number of more general conclusions about the development of post-Roman York may be drawn (see pp.2998–3002). In Fig.1546/Table 341 the period assemblages discussed above are shown in descending order of the ratio between the percentage of tools and implements, and knives (Groups B and D), and the percentage of structural ironwork and fittings, and locks and keys (Groups E and F).

At first glance the most striking feature of the data presented in Fig.1546/Table 341 is probably the dis-

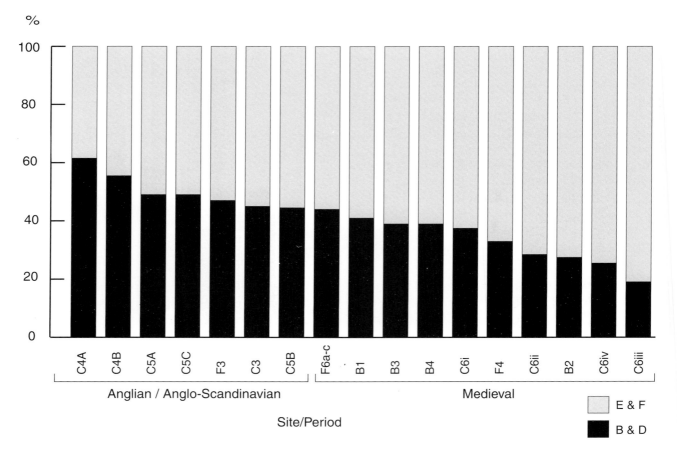

Fig.1546 *Coppergate (C), Bedern (B) and Fishergate (F): ironwork assemblages in descending order of numbers of tools, implements and knives (Groups B and D) as a percentage of the total numbers of objects in Groups B, D, E and F*

tinction between the Anglo-Scandinavian periods and one Anglian period, on the one hand, and the medieval periods on the other. Although the distinction is not marked by a sharp change, the implication is that the character of deposition and occupation on and around the sites under discussion in the Anglian and Anglo-Scandinavian periods was, to a greater or lesser extent, different from that in the medieval period. In the former, craft activity appears to have been more significant than in the latter.

The unusual character of Coppergate Periods 4A and 4B in particular may also be emphasised by the ratio of the number of knives to the number of tools (Fig.1547). In percentage terms the ratios for 4A and 4B (20:80% and 31:69%) are much lower than for any other site period in the list except for Coppergate Periods 5A and 5C, and Bedern FP 2, the first of which contains largely residual material. On this basis

Fishergate Anglian (Period 3) and Coppergate Periods 3 and 5B can be seen to be comparable to the medieval period groups. While knives may serve as both domestic and craft tools, the relatively low percentages of knives in relation to percentages of other tools appear to confirm the importance of craft activity at Coppergate for much of the 10th century. As far as the evidence of the iron objects is concerned, the decline seems to begin at the end of that century and continues into the 11th century and after the Conquest.

Objects made from materials other than iron

These artefacts have been looked at within object groups, but as the overall numbers of objects from all the sites are considerably smaller than those for the ironwork, a study of patterns of distribution of

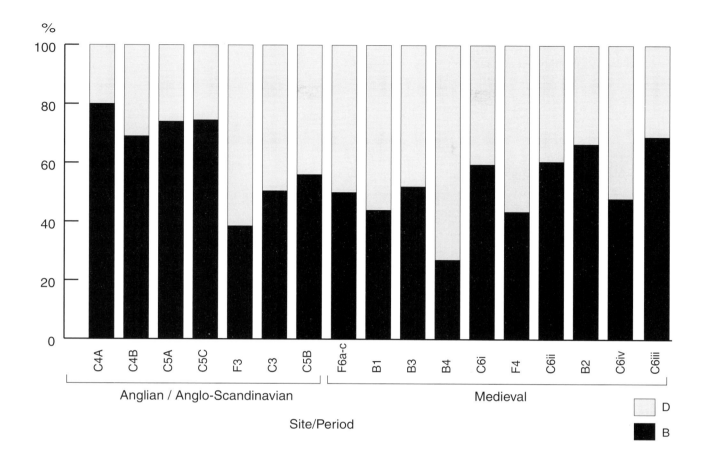

Fig.1547   Coppergate (C), Bedern (B) and Fishergate (F): percentage of knives (Group D) in Groups B and D combined

Table 309   Numbers of objects made from materials other than iron within functional groups by site

	Coppergate	Fishergate	Bedern
Craft tools	198	22	37
Fishing weights	2	8	–
Food preparation	54	7	79
Lighting	3	1	15
Dress accessories	19	30	144
Personal items	17	3	11
Medical	12	8	19
Writing	1	8	23
Devotional	5	9	20
Recreation	54	2	26
Trade (balances etc.)	8	3	20
Total	373	101	413

Table 310   Functional groups as percentages of object totals on each site

	Coppergate	Fishergate	Bedern
Craft tools	53.1	22.0	9.0
Fishing weights	0.5	8.0	–
Food preparation	14.5	7.0	23.4
Lighting	0.8	1.0	3.6
Dress accessories	5.1	30.0	34.8
Personal items	4.5	3.0	2.6
Medical	3.2	8.0	4.6
Writing	0.3	8.0	5.6
Devotional	1.3	9.0	4.8
Recreation	14.5	2.0	6.3
Trade (balances etc.)	2.1	3.0	4.8

In Tables 309–11, 313–18, 321–3 and 325 Bedern includes the College, the Foundry, the Chapel and 2 Aldwark.

this material has not been made in the same way as for the iron. Instead, certain groups of non-ferrous material have been analysed and results used to compare with those gained from analyses of the medieval ironwork.

Craft tools

These formed the major element in the Coppergate non-ferrous assemblage, but were of rather less significance at the other two sites as Tables 309–10 demonstrate.

Textile production

As Table 311 illustrates, medieval levels at Coppergate produced 75 spindle whorls and 24 copper alloy needles. The high number of artefacts associated with textile production may in part result from the Anglo-Scandinavian period, when the manufacture of textiles was a major activity (pp.1793–810, *AY* 17/11); it is probable that a number of the artefacts found in medieval levels are residual. Certainly, bone and antler spindle whorls recovered from medieval layers have been identified as probably Anglo-Scandinavian (pp.1965–6, *AY* 17/12). It has been suggested, however, that fibre processing, spinning and needlework were maintained from the Anglo-Scandinavian period into the early 14th century (p.1820, *AY* 17/11), and the recovery of significant numbers of iron fibre processing spikes (see p.2979) together with the whorls and needles noted here, and the bone and antler tools published elsewhere (pp.1964–71, *AY* 17/12), supports this view. In particular, the copper alloy needles, which were concentrated in mid 11th–late 13th century levels, indicate activity at that time, as very few were recovered from Anglo-Scandinavian contexts (Table 150, p.1778, *AY* 17/11). The complete absence of thimbles from Coppergate may be a reflection of the apparent decline in needleworking at the site from the early 14th century onwards, the time when metal thimbles are first beginning to appear elsewhere in York. It should be noted that while the non-ferrous material provides no evidence for fibre processing at Fishergate, the numbers of iron comb teeth recovered from late 12th–mid 14th century levels indicate this activity was occurring (see p.2981).

Hones

Small numbers of hones were found at the ecclesiastical sites, but medieval levels at Coppergate pro-

Table 311   Non-ferrous tools from the main sites

	Coppergate	Bedern	Fishergate
Whorls: stone/ fired clay	75	9	–
Thimbles	–	5	2
Needles	24	1	–
Total	**99**	**15**	**2**
Hones	99	22	11
Grindstones	–	–	1
Total	**99**	**22**	**12**
Lead weights	2	–	6
Stone weights	–	–	2
Total	**2**	**–**	**8**

duced 99, and it is instructive to look at these alongside the knives on which they were used. It has been noted that across the Anglo-Scandinavian and medieval periods the highest percentage of knives was recorded in the main Anglo-Scandinavian periods (see p.2979). Similarly, the hones were found in greater numbers in the main Anglo-Scandinavian periods than in the medieval period, with 126 coming from Period 4B alone (Table 312) as compared with the 99 retrieved from medieval contexts. A gradual falling off in the numbers of knives (and other craft working tools) from the late 12th century onwards was observed (see above); when Period 6 is subdivided (as defined on p.2976) and the hones looked at chronologically, this trend is repeated (Table 312).

Fishing weights

Artefactual evidence of fishing in the form of weights came, unsurprisingly, from the riverine sites, i.e. Fishergate and Coppergate (Table 311); Coppergate also produced iron fish hooks (see p.2747).

Domestic equipment (Table 313)

The querns and mortars involved in food preparation are of stone, many being particularly large pieces, and their recovery may in part be due to the re-use of a considerable number in walls, and as packing for post-holes (see pp.2799, 2803). It should also be noted that quern fragments were found in medieval levels at Fishergate but were all deemed residual (*4528–44, AY* 17/9).

Table 312 Hones at Coppergate by period

Period	Hones	% of all hones
3	22	5.45
4A	8	2.00
4B	126	31.40
5A	39	9.70
5B and C	107	26.70
Total	**302**	**75.25**
6i	45	11.25
6ii	29	7.20
6iii	11	2.75
6iv	13	3.20
Unstratified	1	0.25
Total	**99**	**24.75**

Of the 48 metal vessel fragments from the Bedern sites, seventeen (35%) derive from the Foundry; this is unsurprising in the light of its production of cauldrons and other domestic vessels (*AY* 10/3, 189), and many of the pieces found there may represent scrap for recycling. Medieval levels at Coppergate and Bedern also produced wooden vessels, including bowls (*8583–8612, 9202–6, 9226–30, AY* 17/13).

Similar numbers of glass vessels (assuming each fragment from a different vessel) were recovered from Coppergate and Bedern; these vessels included goblets and bowls, with some from Bedern described

Table 313 Finds of domestic equipment from the main sites

	Coppergate	Bedern	Fishergate
Food preparation			
Querns	48	9	–
Mortars/pestles	4	21	1
Stone vessels	–	1	–
Metal vessels/ fragments	2	48	6
Total	**54**	**79**	**7**
Glass tablewares	13	16	–
Table spoons	1	1	–

Table 314 Objects associated with lighting from the main sites

	Coppergate	Bedern	Fishergate
Non-ferrous holders	1	7	–
Stone lamps	2	4	–
Glass lamps	–	4	1
Total	3	15	1

as 'most prestigious decorative vessels' of high status (see p.2827). In contrast, only three undiagnostic fragments were found at Fishergate. In addition to the metal spoons recorded in Table 313, wooden spoons were also found at Coppergate and Bedern (*8999, 9234*, pp.2267–8, *AY* 17/13).

Lighting

Table 314 illustrates the point made earlier, that glass lamps, more delicate than their metal or stone counterparts, were found only on the ecclesiastical sites in York (see p.2860). Metal holders using candles were a cheaper and more commonly used form of lighting than the lamps using oil, and iron appears to have been the most frequently used metal, Coppergate producing eighteen iron candleholders, Bedern producing eleven and the Foundry five (see pp.2855–8). Although no metal candleholders were recovered from the priory at Fishergate, their use there seems probable.

Dress accessories

As Table 315 indicates, dress accessories — in particular buckles, strap-ends and strap-guides — were found in far higher numbers at Bedern than on any other site, and form the largest element in the entire non-ferrous assemblage from that site (c.35%). This concentration may be the result of the manufacture of such items in the area, with some of those found at Bedern perhaps being discarded products. It should be noted, however, that although fewer in number, the dress accessories found at Fishergate, where there is no evidence of manufacture in the area, represent c.30% of the non-ferrous assemblage found at the priory, a figure remarkably similar to that from Bedern; both contrast strongly with Coppergate, where dress acessories form only c.5% of the total

Table 315 Non-ferrous buckles and other dress accessories from the main sites

	Coppergate	Bedern	Fishergate
Buckles	11	88	16
Clasps	–	8	1
Strap-ends	2	24	4
Strap-guides	–	17	–
Chapes	1	7	1
Total	14	144	22

Table 317 Medical implements from the main sites

	Coppergate	Bedern	Fishergate
Urinal fragments	2	4	–
Urinal/flask fragments	5	11	–
Distilling equipment	–	1	–
Plate	–	–	1
Toilet implements	1	2	1
Tweezers	4	1	5
Spoon	–	–	1
Total	12	19	8

non-ferrous assemblage (see Table 310). These figures suggest metal dress accessories may have assumed greater importance as indicators of status on the ecclesiastical sites as compared to the secular Coppergate, or were simply more readily available. The items of personal jewellery, although few in number, offer a less clear contrast between the sites, however (see Table 316).

The only gold and silver objects from the sites were finger-rings and brooches. Table 316 shows that although all the sites produced at least one precious metal ring or brooch, five were found at Bedern, while a considerably higher number of base metal rings and brooches came from Coppergate.

Table 316 Non-ferrous finger-rings and brooches from the main sites

	Coppergate	Bedern	Fishergate
Gold			
Finger-rings	1	1	–
Brooches	1	2	–
Silver			
Finger-rings	–	–	1
Brooches	–	2	1
Other non-ferrous metal			
Finger-rings	7	3	1
Brooches	8	3	–
Total	17	11	3

Items associated with medical procedures

The unusual medical plate found at Fishergate points fairly conclusively to active medical interventions carried out at the priory (see pp.2931–2). The spoon may have been used to measure drugs, but the tweezers and toilet implements have less definite medical applications. While Bedern produced only three metal tweezers and toilet implements, a number of rim and base fragments of glass flasks and urinals were also found. As Dr Tyson has noted, the examination of urine was a medieval method of medical diagnosis. Flasks may have been used for the preparation of herbal, alcoholic and medicinal recipes and colouring pigments, sometimes in combination with distilling equipment. A piece of tubing (*13561*) may have come from the spout of an alembic, used in the preparation of alcoholic, herbal, medical and craft recipes, and possibly alchemy. While items associated with medical diagnosis are not unexpected on the ecclesiastical sites, their occurrence, albeit in small numbers, at Coppergate is more surprising.

Items associated with writing

It might have been expected that objects associated with books and writing would be recovered from the ecclesiastical sites, particularly from the College of Vicars Choral from which original written records still survive (see *AY* 10/5); as Table 318 shows, this is indeed the case. Several of the book fittings were found in specifically religious areas, such as the chapel at Bedern and the chapter house and church at Fishergate, although two of the twelve book fittings from Bedern came from the Foundry area. The concentration of all these items at Bedern and, to a

Table 318 Items from the main sites associated with literacy (italics denote published elsewhere)

	Coppergate	Bedern	Fishergate
Metal items			
Book fittings	1	12	8
Lead points	2	19	4
Seal matrices	–	4	1
Styli (iron)	–	2	–
Total	3	37	13
Items of skeletal material			
Styli/prickers	*2*	*27*	*5*
Pens	*–*	*6*	*–*
Total	*2*	*33*	*5*

Table 320 Lead points from the College of Vicars Choral at Bedern by period and area

	Bedern SW	Bedern NE (incl. 2 Aldwark)
FP		
1	4	2
2	2	3
3	2	4
4	–	2
Total	8	11

lesser extent, at the priory at Fishergate, reflects evidence provided by other items, including 22 bone styli/parchment prickers and five possible ink pens found at the College (five styli/prickers and one pen came from the Foundry), and a further five styli/parchment prickers found at Fishergate (pp.1974–6, *AY* 17/12). Two iron styli were also recovered at Bedern (Table 318). Lead points functioned like pencils, and may have been used for drawing lines on manuscripts, but study of the many points found suggests that the bulk of these were likely to have had a craft rather than a literary use; comparison with points from Winchester revealed that only two points from Bedern and one from Fishergate were of types associated with writing, the others probably used by craftsmen such as carpenters. This was confirmed by the finding of many points in levels associated with building construction (p.2936), and the differences in distribution across the site between the bone and iron writing equipment (Table 319) and the lead points (Table 320) indicates the likelihood of a craft rather than a literary use for most of the points.

As with the bulk of the points, the seal matrices appear to have no connection with the business of the members of the ecclesiastical institutions; the motifs on three of the metal seal matrices from the College and the priory (a squirrel, a stag and a hunting bird) appear secular, while the fourth, apparently depicting God and the Virgin Mary, belonged to a stonemason (Thomas de Swin) (see pp.2940–2).

Devotional and funerary objects

As with the writing equipment, these objects have particular associations with ecclesiastical life, and were found largely where they might have been expected. Apart from the bells, which may or may not have been involved in church ritual (see p.2947), the artefacts in Table 321 may be divided into two broad categories. Popular religious objects (ampullae and

Table 319 Prickers, pens and styli from the College of Vicars Choral at Bedern by period and area

	Bedern SW	Bedern NE (incl. 2 Aldwark)
FP		
1	2	–
2	5	1
3	10	2
4	4	4
Unstratified	2	1
Total	23	8

Table 321 Devotional and funerary objects from the main sites

	Coppergate	Bedern	Fishergate
?Reliquary settings	–	2	3
Ampullae	2	–	–
?Pilgrim badges	2	2	–
Bells	1	6	1
Chalices	–	–	2
Rosary beads	–	10	3
Total	5	20	9

Table 322 Musical instruments from the main sites (italics indicate published elsewhere)

	Coppergate	Bedern	Fishergate
Jew's harp	–	1	–
Tuning pegs	–	*12*	–
?stringed instrument	–	*1*	–
Whistles	*3*	–	–
Buzz-bones	*36*	*4*	*2*
Total	*39*	*18*	*2*

pilgrim badges) were found at the non-ecclesiastical Coppergate, as well as at Bedern; the more specifically institutional religious items were found at Bedern and Fishergate. These comprise the chalices which were found in burials at Fishergate, and are of the types regularly found in the graves of priests, and the rosary beads, although the latter were also used outside religious communities. Gemstones found at Fishergate and Bedern may derive from reliquaries.

Music

As an ecclesiastical institution with the prime function of providing deputies to sing in place of canons in the Minster, it is no surprise that artefactual evidence of music-making was found at Bedern. It was the only site to produce a metal musical instrument, the Jew's harp, but instruments or parts of instruments of bone and antler were also found there (pp.1979–80, *AY* 17/12). The tuning pegs would have been used to tune harps, lyres or fiddles, while the stringed instrument fragment was tentatively identified as coming from a zither or other keyboard instrument. In complete contrast, the lack of musical instruments at Fishergate reflects the Rule of the Order of St Gilbert that forbade all music, the organ and every kind of chant (Graham 1901, 74). Compared to the craftsman-made stringed instrument pieces from Bedern, the whistles and buzz-bones, found in large numbers at Coppergate in particular, were very simply made, probably as and when required, and in the case of the buzz-bones, appear to have been used only a few times before being discarded (p.1981, *AY* 17/12).

Finds from religious houses

Finds associated with literacy, devotion and music, as discussed above, are not exclusively linked to ecclesiastical institutions, but are characteristic of such sites. In a brief analysis of recurrent finds from religious houses, Thomas, Sloane and Phillpotts noted groups or types of objects found in excavations on sixteen sites of a religious nature (Thomas et al. 1997, 109, table 14). This survey showed that items with religious associations, clerical items relating to the production and use of documents, and a group of 'other' objects, in which were included musical instruments, appear consistently on ecclesiastical sites. In terms of the finds recovered, both the College at Bedern and the priory at Fishergate fit into this scheme, producing similar finds to many of the other sites noted. While this comes as no surprise, all these items being linked to the very 'raison d'être' of these institutions, it cannot be said that these types of finds identify such sites. This is made clear by the comparisons in the assemblages from York, where these religious sites are set against the secular sites of Coppergate and the Foundry. Objects with literary, religious and musical associations come from all

Table 323 Gaming finds from the main sites (italics indicate published elsewhere)

	Coppergate	Bedern	Fishergate
Stone, clay or jet gaming pieces			
Counters	52	26	1
Dice	2	–	1
Total	54	26	2
Antler, bone or wooden gaming pieces			
Counters	*6*	*1*	*–*
Dice	*12*	*8*	*2*
Total (all materials)	72	37	4

Table 324 Counters and dice of all materials from Coppergate by period and tenement (two unstratified items have not been included)

Tenement	Period 6i	6i–ii	6ii	6ii–iii	6iii	6iv	Total
A	–	–	1	2	1	3	7
AB	1	–	–	–	–	–	1
B	1	–	6	–	3	10	20
BC	–	–	1	–	–	1	2
C	2	–	11	–	1	1	15
CD	2	1	3	–	3	–	9
D	–	1	8	–	3	4	16
Total	6	2	30	2	11	19	70

the sites, although they may differ in terms of quantity and status. Further work needs to be done in comparing assemblages from ecclesiastical sites to those from contemporary secular sites in order to produce a more accurate account of what finds, if any, may typify a religious as opposed to a secular site.

Gaming

Both the jet dice from Coppergate are fairly elaborate examples with inlays; twelve bone, antler and ivory dice were also found in medieval levels at the site (pp.1982–4, AY 17/12). Bone dice were also found at the other sites. The majority of the counters are roughly cut from pottery sherds or tile fragments and appear predominantly hand-made; six counters of bone and ivory were also recovered at Coppergate (pp.1981–2, AY 17/12). Table 324 shows that gaming was clearly a favoured occupation at Coppergate from Period 6ii (late 12th–mid 13th century) onwards, with finds fairly evenly spread across Tenements B,

C and D. At the College of Vicars Choral, where rules of the 14th–early 15th century recorded that games of chess and draughts, betting, gambling and throwing dice were forbidden in the hall under a penalty of 3s. 4d. (Harrison 1952, 58), games of chance were nevertheless undertaken on the premises in the 14th century and later.

Balances and weights (Table 325)

All the surviving balances and parts of balances are small. Putting aside the possible weights from Bedern (14579–81), the pan weights from all the sites span a range from 4·2g (14728) to c.73·4g (15289), indicating use at all sites mainly for small and light materials, such as coins, precious metals, spices or drugs.

Intra-site spatial analysis

Another way of analysing the data reviewed above is in terms of a comparison between parts or zones of a single site rather than between sites. This has been done for Coppergate, Bedern and the Foundry, but not for Fishergate as no meaningful basis for a spatial division of the site suggested itself. The same caveats (p.2976) as were entered for the validity of the data in regard to chronological analysis apply and it should also be noted that the data are considered in regard to the medieval and post-medieval period as a whole. Numbers of objects are not large enough for a detailed correlation of spatial and chronological analyses. The results are therefore of a very generalised character, although some patterns emerge

Table 325 Balances and pan weights from the main sites

	Coppergate	Bedern	Fishergate
Balances	–	2	–
Scale pans	1	1	1
Balance chains	1	–	–
Weights	5	17	2
Total	7	20	3

which require comment. Data used to produce Figs. 1548–53 can be found in Tables 342–7 on pp.3164–6.

16–22 Coppergate

In the case of Coppergate a comparison of the four tenements (A–D) provides the most satisfactory basis for spatial analysis.

Ironwork

The data on numbers of iron objects are given in Fig.1548/Table 342. Some contexts cross the tenement boundaries and so the objects cannot be ascribed to one or the other, hence AB, BC and CD.

The data on object numbers may be analysed in two ways. The first, shown in Fig.1549/Table 343, is as object group percentages for each tenement assemblage (the objects from contexts designated AB are excluded as numbers are very small). This shows that 19% of the Tenement A assemblage is made up of Group A (bars, strips and plates) objects, 6% of the assemblage is made up of Group B (tools and imple-

ments) objects etc. The second method of analysis, shown in Fig.1550/Table 344, is as percentages of each object group by tenement. This shows, for example, that 7·5% of the Group A objects from medieval contexts come from Tenement A while 14% come from Tenement B etc.

Fig.1549 shows that in percentage terms the tenement assemblages do not vary greatly from the mean for the whole site (Table 343). In no case can it be suggested that the data imply a marked difference in the character of deposition and occupation between the tenements. Fig.1550 shows that there is no great variation from the mean in the proportions of the object groups which can be assigned to each tenement (Table 344) except in the cases where the groups are numerically relatively small (notably Groups F and I). Having said this, however, the percentage of Group D (knives) from Tenement B seems a little out of line at 25.5%, compared to a mean of 18.5% for the percentage of all medieval objects from the site assigned to this tenement, as does the percentage of Group G (dress fittings and riding equip-

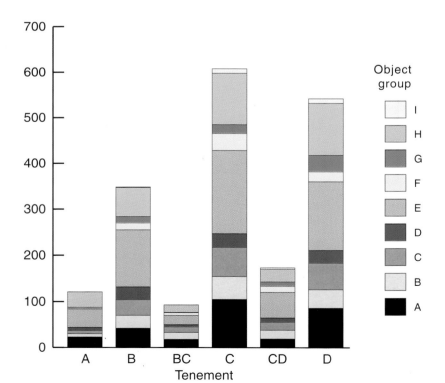

Fig.1548 *16–22 Coppergate: numbers of medieval iron objects in each group by tenement*

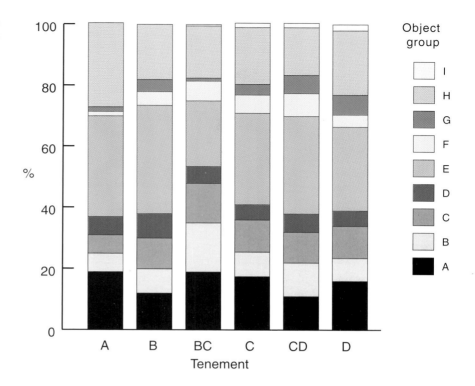

Fig.1549 16–22 Coppergate: object group percentages for each tenement assemblage

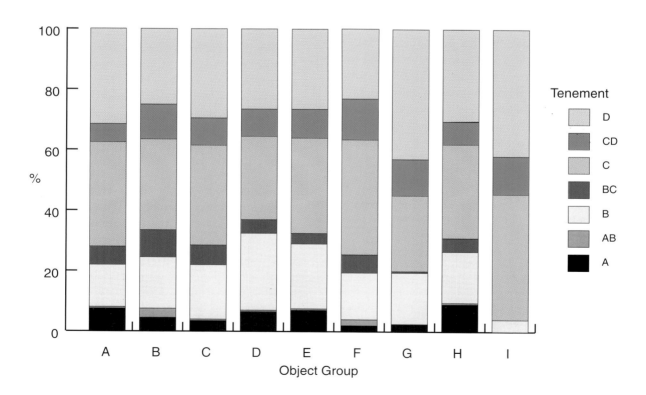

Fig.1550 16–22 Coppergate: iron object group breakdown by tenement (percentages)

Table 326   16–22 Coppergate: percentages of knives and hones within each tenement

Object type	A	AB	B	BC	C	CD	D	Unstrat.
				Tenement				
Iron knives	6.5	<1.0	25.5	4.5	27.5	9.0	25.5	–
Hones	6.0	1.0	17.0	6.0	36.0	16.0	16.0	1.0
All iron	6.5	<1.0	18.5	5.0	32.0	9.0	28.5	–

ment) from Tenement D at 43·5% compared to a mean of 28·5% for the tenement. In the former case there is no ready explanation, but in the latter the figure may have been increased by residual material in a tenement where it is thought that the manufacture of dress fittings was taking place in the Anglo-Scandinavian period (p.681, *AY* 17/6).

Objects of materials other than iron

Spatial analysis of the Coppergate hones across the tenements provides an interesting comparison with that of the knives and with other iron objects (Table 326).

It was noted above that the percentage of knives from Tenement B at 25·5% was rather out of line with the mean of all ironwork for the site (18·5%). Interestingly, the hones do not appear to copy the knife distribution as might have been expected, but across Tenements A–C seem more to reflect the mean for all the ironwork; in tenements CD and D, however,

where the knives follow the mean quite closely, the hones seem out of line with both.

The querns from Coppergate have also been analysed spatially and chronologically in Table 327. This illustrates a concentration of quern fragments on Tenement C in Period 6i; some of these fragments may have been used in the preparation of flour in a building interpreted as a possible bakehouse, where a number were found (see p.2799; also *AY* 10/6 forthcoming); an iron shovel (*11917*) for stoking or removing hot bread from an oven was also found there.

Bedern

The basis for intra-site analysis of object distribution at Bedern is a comparison of the Foundry with the areas of the College of the Vicars Choral excavated south-west and north-east of the street Bedern. The data for Bedern north-east include the objects from the neighbouring small site at 2 Aldwark.

Ironwork

The numbers of objects in each area and object group are relatively small compared to Coppergate, but, in general terms, a picture similar to Coppergate of low variability from the site mean emerges in both Figs.1552–3/Tables 346–7. Having said this, however, Fig.1552/Table 346 shows that Group B (tools and implements) form a noticeably higher proportion (14·5%) of the Bedern south-west assemblage than of the assemblages from the Foundry and Bedern north-east (8·5% and 8%). This should be seen alongside the data in Fig.1553/Table 347 which show that a markedly higher proportion of the tools and implements from the site as a whole come from Bedern south-west (57·5%) than from the other two areas

Table 327   Distribution of querns at Coppergate by period and tenement (none found in Tenement A)

Tenement	6i	6i–ii	6ii	6iii	6iv	Total
			Period			
B	5	–	2	1	1	9
BC	1	–	7	–	–	8
C	17	1	4	–	3	25
CD	1	–	–	–	1	2
D	1	–	2	1	–	4
Total	25	1	15	2	5	48

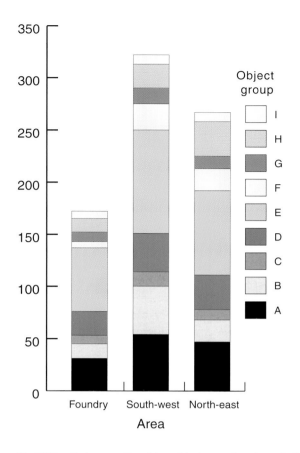

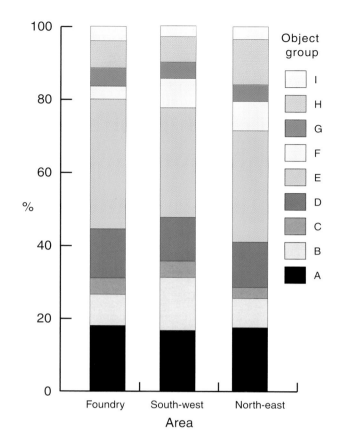

Fig.1551   Bedern: medieval iron objects, numbers in each object group by area

Fig.1552   Bedern: object group percentages for each area

(17·5% and 25%). These data are, perhaps, surprising as it would probably be expected that any figure above the mean for tools and implements would come from the Foundry, a site where other evidence has shown that manufacturing was taking place throughout the medieval period, although the evidence of copper alloy waste suggests that Foundry refuse was being deposited in the College precinct (see pp.2716–17). In a general sense this anomaly shows that this type of analysis has its limitations, at least when only a part of the artefact assemblage is considered. However, the value of this type of analysis is demonstrated by the implication, not immediately apparent from the structural archaeology, that tool-using activity, whether for building or crafts, in the College complex was primarily undertaken south-west of Bedern rather than north-east of it. The analysis of the finds chronologically (Tables 338–40)

suggests that this activity may have been particularly important in Site Period 7 (Finds Period 3) when there was a major episode of construction (*AY* 10/5).

Objects of other materials

The spatial distribution of the non-ferrous metal vessel fragments was studied to compare the Foundry, where such artefacts may have been made, with the College. Table 328 shows that the material found within the College was concentrated in the south-west area, that is the part nearest the Foundry; this matches up with evidence provided by other elements associated with non-ferrous metalworking, including the crucibles and the waste debris (see pp.2710–11), and suggests that some of the vessel pieces may have found their way in as the result of movement of material across the boundaries between the two sites (*AY* 10/3, 203).

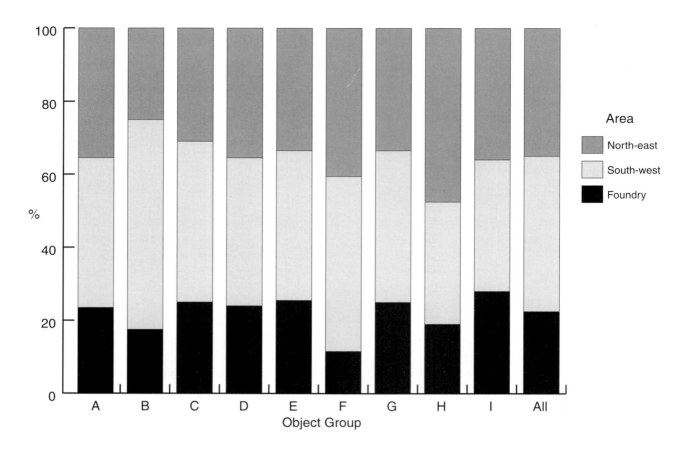

Fig.1553 *Bedern: medieval iron objects, percentage of objects by group in each area*

The increase in the amounts of material found in FP 3–4 may be a reflection of greater activity in vessel manufacture and/or less efficient recycling of waste.

Table 328 Spatial and chronological distribution of cast and sheet metal vessel fragments at Bedern (Bedern N.E. includes 2 Aldwark)

	Foundry	Bedern S.W.	Bedern N.E.	Total
FP				
1–2	2	4	1	7
3	5	8	2	15
4	10	11	4	25
Unstrat.	–	–	1	1
Total	17	23	8	48

Inter- and intra-site analyses: conclusions

Analysis of the chronological and spatial distribution data has suggested that it is possible to draw useful inferences on the changing character of occupation and activity on urban sites by means of simple quantification exercises. This appears to be particularly the case as regards the relative intensity of craft activity over time and between different areas. Clearly the degree of validity of these inferences depends, as noted above, on the extent of residuality in the finds, but trends may, none the less, be detectable in assemblages of large size. It is not usually possible, however, to base analyses on individual object types as their numbers are too small. Some higher order grouping of the sort presented above is necessary. In addition, one must be aware that the data can be biased, in ways which are not usually quantifiable, by a number of factors which include the collection policy during excavation and preservation conditions in the ground. Factors introducing a bias also include cultural attitudes to recycling and deposition in the past, and the effect of technological change which introduces new object types and renders others redundant.

These factors are, of course, of interest in their own right, but once their influence has been acknowledged, the analyses presented above still appear to indicate patterning in the data which may relate to real changes and distinctions in the character of occupation on the sites under discussion.

On the whole these patterns emerge from data in which the degree of variability from the relevant mean is low. This is probably, at least in part, because of the homogenising effect on artefact assemblages of any particular period or area as a result of redeposition caused by pit digging and other earth moving activities which are a continual accompaniment to the accumulation of urban archaeological deposits. However, it is also reasonable to infer that the character of occupation did not in fact change greatly during the course of the medieval and post-medieval period at or in the environs of any of the sites discussed above, and that there was no great distinction either between them or between zones within them. The impression derived from the artefacts, especially the ironwork, is of sites dominated by domestic activity accompanied by a low, if fairly constant, level of building work and craft activity, primarily leather, textile and wood working. This may be a very good reflection of the character of large parts of the medieval and post-medieval city in which it was usual for domestic activity and a range of small-scale craft activities to be conducted in the same locale. Evidence from other medieval towns suggests that only activities requiring fixed installations and/ or the use of heat and water, such as dyeing or fulling, were grouped in specific locations (Ottaway 1992, 188).

Only the Foundry of the medieval sites under discussion here can be considered a specialised manu-facturing area, but, as noted above, its function is not immediately implied by the artefacts other than metalworking waste found there. By contrast the potential of the type of analyses described above to determine the character of occupation and activity on a site is revealed when the medieval ironwork data are compared with those from the Anglo-Scandinavian period at Coppergate (see in particular Figs.1546–7, Table 341). Without needing to refer to the other archaeological evidence from the site, it is immediately clear that the character of occupation at Coppergate in much of the 10th century (Periods 4A and 4B) must have been markedly different from that in any subsequent period with a range of craft activities, including metalworking, being practised intensively. That 16–22 Coppergate was typical of Anglo-Scandinavian York in being a location for the practice of a number of different crafts, some, such as metalworking, involving the use of heat, is suggested by recent research. One can nonetheless envisage a fairly abrupt change in the character of this particular part of the city at the end of the 10th century or beginning of the 11th century as these heat-using crafts were moved to some safer location away from the increasingly crowded streets and tenements. Subsequently other crafts were practised in the area, but the ironwork suggests a steady decline in their importance to the local economy in the remainder of the Anglo-Scandinavian period and after the Norman Conquest.

It may be noted, finally, that as far as ironworking is concerned, the movement of blacksmiths to the urban periphery is also implied by the study of documentary sources for Winchester (Barlow et al., 1976, 434). By the 12th century most properties owned by blacksmiths were in the suburbs or close to the city gates. One reason for this is thought to be the rise in the shoeing of horses, city gates providing smiths with good opportunities for trade. As has been shown at Coppergate, and elsewhere, the occurrence of horseshoes rises dramatically in the 11th century and so the risk of fire may not have been the only consideration operating in York to take the smiths out of the town centre.

Economy and Society in Medieval York

The artefacts discussed in this fascicule have come from contexts dated between the 11th century and the early post-medieval period, although the date ranges are different on each site. The majority of finds from Coppergate and Piccadilly have come from 11th to mid 14th century contexts while the principal period of occupation at the Foundry and Bedern ran from the mid 13th century to the early post-medieval period, and at Fishergate from the late 12th to the mid 16th century. While the date range of the contexts from which the artefacts derive provides the basis for a wide-ranging overview of the development of many different object types over several hundred years, they also allow the character of occupation on the sites to be examined over the same period. This has, in turn, allowed some conclusions to be drawn about the economy and society of the medieval and early post-medieval city which may be set alongside those from other forms of archaeological evidence and from documentary sources. In this section a number of economic and social themes suggested by the finds will be discussed, beginning with the former.

As far as the distinction between craft and industry, two of the terms in the title of this fascicule, is concerned, this has already been touched on (p.2703). It was suggested that, although the dominant mode of production in the medieval city was, as described by Swanson (1989), small-scale and household-based, some activities could be properly identified as industrial because of both the large scale of manufacture and the use of fixed equipment for technically advanced activities using heat and/or water.

Using this definition, the best evidence for an industry on any of the sites under discussion comes from the Foundry where a large timber-framed building used for non-ferrous metalworking from the 13th to the 16th century was excavated. In addition to internal foundry structures, good evidence was found for the production of vessels, bells and possibly other non-ferrous artefacts (AY 10/3, 205; see above), although it is difficult to estimate the scale of production and how it may have varied over time. Much of the non-ferrous metalworking debris recovered from both the Foundry and Bedern sites probably derived from foundry activities, although, as noted on p.2717,

almost 50% of the material may be residual as it has come from contexts dated after the end of metalworking in the foundry. As far as metalworking tools are concerned, two punches, two hammer heads and a chisel have come from the foundry, a surprisingly small assemblage, perhaps, in view of the other evidence for production. Although heat-using activities may have been deliberately moved away from Coppergate at the end of the 10th century because of the danger of fire (p.2997), there is no reason to suggest that metalworking was unusual in the centre of medieval or early post-medieval York and the foundry's operations in this part of the city appear to have been augmented in the 15th and 16th centuries by further metalworkers based in the St Andrewgate area, clearly making non-ferrous dress accessories of various types (p.2714).

At Coppergate hearths for heat-using processes, principally metalworking, existed on the site in the 10th century (Period 4B), but there is nothing comparable in terms of fixed equipment from the later Anglo-Scandinavian and medieval periods. When contexts of the medieval period are compared to the Anglo-Scandinavian the former appears to have produced relatively little debris from certain types of manufacturing such as bone and antler (AY 17/12), non-ferrous metalworking (AY 17/7), or wood (p.2391, AY 17/13). Ironworking debris in the form of bars, strips and plates (p.2707) occurred in some quantity, but is probably largely residual Anglo-Scandinavian material. The tools from Coppergate suggest that textiles and leather goods were made in the immediate area, if not necessarily on the site itself, but there is no way of assessing the scale of production in the medieval period. Tools also suggest a certain amount of small-scale craft activity at Bedern in the medieval period, including leatherworking and textile manufacture, although metalworking and woodworking tools may pertain to the building work which continued almost uninterrupted between the mid 13th and early 15th centuries and sporadically thereafter (AY 10/5). Similarly at Fishergate there are metalworking and woodworking tools which may relate to building work rather than to manufacturing activities undertaken by the priors, and the appreciable number of iron bars, strips and plates may be largely residual from the Anglian period when ironworking probably took place on or near the site (*AY* 17/9). Some textile production and leather-working is also implied by the tools, presumably to supply the priory's immediate needs.

If we turn from production to the exchange side of the economy it may be suggested that a large proportion of the artefacts described above were exchanged at some point in their lives, whether in the sense of being bought and sold as part of commercial trade or passed from one hand to another in some other form of transaction. Medieval York is known from written sources to have been at the centre of an enormous range of exchange systems, many, if not the majority, purely local, but others regional and national, and others again international (Miller 1961, 41–7). There are a few objects which had a direct role in exchange, namely the balances and weights, and the sites have also produced a number of coins and tokens (*AY* 18/1), and wooden tally sticks (*9015–16*, *AY* 17/13). Having said this, it must be noted that the problem of studying exchange mechanisms and systems on the basis of archaeological material alone is that it is not usually possible to determine where artefacts were made unless their form or material has some distinctive character. In the medieval period the best archaeological evidence is usually derived from pottery both because of the possibility of establishing its source through examination of fabric and form, and because of the large quantity which is recovered, allowing statistically based trends of some validity to be established. As yet the medieval pottery from the sites under discussion in this fascicule has not been studied in any detail except in the case of the two Bedern sites. Jennings (*AY* 10/5, 401–2) has noted that importation from the York region and from the rest of Europe took place throughout the medieval and early post-medieval periods. In the 13th and 14th centuries wares from continental Europe are represented by a few Rouen-type vessels and rather more Saintonge ware jugs, including several polychrome examples. Towards the end of the 14th century and in the 15th century the emphasis of imported pottery moved from France to the Low Countries and the Rhineland.

In respect of other objects which can be sourced, we find regional trade represented by jet which was used for rosary beads and other objects. The material probably derived from the same source that was exploited by the inhabitants of Roman and Anglo-Scandinavian York, generally assumed to be the Yorkshire coast at Whitby; the raw material would then have been brought to York for finishing (p.1443, *AY* 17/9). Regional exchange is also implied by the majority of the fragments of mortar, an artefact type introduced during the medieval period, which are of Permian Lower Magnesian Limestone. The nearest outcrops to York are in the Tadcaster-Wetherby area, although some of the material may derive from the re-use of Roman building stone. Trade over a relatively long distance is implied by two mortars and a pestle which are made from limestones that may come from Dorset. The hones from British sources include examples made from stone types utilised at Fishergate in the Anglian period and at Anglo-Scandinavian Coppergate, including sandstones and siltstones from southern Scotland and/or Cumbria, and Coal Measures sandstones from the eastern Pennines (p.1313, *4437–9*, *AY* 17/9; p.2484, *4409*, *9307–63*, *AY* 17/14).

Some international trade contacts made before the Norman Conquest were apparently maintained afterwards. For example, the schist and phyllite hones found at all the sites almost certainly originated in Norway. Their initial appearance in York is thought to have been a result of Scandinavian invasion and settlement (see p.1315, *AY* 17/9). Similarly, the vast majority of the rotary querns are of lava from the Mayen region of Germany, also recorded in Anglian contexts at Fishergate (p.1322, *AY* 17/9) and Anglo-Scandinavian contexts at Coppergate (p.2551, *AY* 17/14). It is quite likely that the majority of the decorative glassware came from other parts of western Europe, particularly France, Germany and Italy. The amethyst from Fishergate and the rock crystals from Bedern would also have been imported from elsewhere in Europe, although they may have arrived at the York sites as ready-made objects of which the place of manufacture is unknown. Most of the amber has been shown to be from the Baltic (pp.2473–4, *AY* 17/14).

Having looked at the evidence for production and trade, the use of the artefacts discussed in this fascicule may be considered and we find that they give at least a glimpse of the lives of the people of medieval and early post-medieval York, and of the character of the buildings they lived in. Food preparation is represented by mortars and querns, and also by hearth equipment such as the iron flesh hook and strike-a-lights. The knives would, amongst many other purposes, have been used for preparing food and consuming it. Medieval illustrations show that knives were usually the only table implement, food being speared on the sharp tip prior to consumption. Folk would usually have washed their food down with water or ale, and graphic evidence for the use of an early 15th century well at Coppergate was found in the form of the bucket up-ended in it with part of the chain which had probably snapped during use (see Fig.1392). Wine may have been less frequently drunk, but the glass vessels from Coppergate and Bedern (p.2819) are thought to have been primarily for wine. Infected food and drink were one cause of illness in the medieval period and there is some evidence for medical practices including fleams for blood letting (p.2932) and vessels for the examination of urine samples (pp.2825–6).

Some stone houses are known to have existed in medieval York but buildings were, with the exception of churches and fortifications, generally timber-framed until the 14th century when a greater use of brick and stone began. Whether stone or timber was used, however, ironwork does not appear to have been employed in the main structure of buildings, but for doors, shutters and the like, and all the sites produced hinges and locks. Of particular interest was a wooden beam from a door with a lock set in it which came from an early post-medieval context at Coppergate (p.2861). As far as furniture is concerned the evidence is mainly for chests and caskets which probably occurred in a number of shapes and sizes. Some of the caskets, perhaps housing jewellery and personal items, were probably decorated with tinned iron and copper alloy fittings. It may be assumed that chests and caskets were routinely locked which explains the finds of padlocks and numerous padlock keys. Another aspect of the domestic regime to be revealed was lighting, effected by a range of iron candle holders plus stone and glass lamps, in addition to copper alloy candlesticks.

The personal appearance of the inhabitants of medieval York, especially of the 14th century and later, is well documented in the painted glass, sculpture and brasses to be found in the city's churches. However, these images frequently lack the details which can be supplemented by archaeological finds. Although some textile from clothing was found (pp.2880–5) the principal evidence for dress comes from such everyday items as buckles, clasps, strap-ends, brooches, buttons and assorted mounts. The variety of shapes and decorative motifs exhibited by these accessories indicates that such functional but visible fastenings were also viewed as a means of ornamenting the person.

The principal means of transportation in the medieval city was obviously the horse and the 11th century saw the introduction on a large scale of the horseshoe. This probably accompanied the increasing use of metalled streets which would have harmed an unshod animal. Horseshoes apart, items of horse furniture and riding equipment occurred in what might be considered surprisingly small numbers, although artefact assemblages from excavations in other medieval towns also produce very few. For example, in the assemblage of c.4,500 objects from medieval sites in Winchester published by Biddle (1990) there were only 22 pieces of bridle and 18 spurs or spur fragments.

When not at work, the inhabitants of medieval York would have spent a considerable amount of time on the observance of the Christian faith. One would expect some evidence for this in any substantial finds assemblage and not just in those from religious institutions. It is not surprising therefore that at Coppergate two flask-shaped tin ampullae were found along with an iron cross pendant and three possible pilgrim badge pendants, while Piccadilly produced a pilgrim badge fragment (p.2946). Although literacy was not the monopoly of the church, it is none the less significant that at Bedern items related to books (as well as religious ritual in the form of rosary beads) were well represented. In addition, a mid–late 15th century context at Bedern produced a gilded silver brooch (*14506*) inscribed *INRI*. At Fishergate the presence of a religious institution is reflected in the chalices and the rosary beads, and in the book fittings from the chapter house and church.

In their spare time the people of York clearly found time to play games including those using counters and dice which were even found in the College of the Vicars Choral. Despite the strictures against them (see p.2991), such recreations appear to have been common amongst the medieval religious community, as gaming boards found at a number of cathedrals attest (Cook 1961, 62). Musical recreation at Coppergate consisted of simply made whistles and buzz-bones (pp.1977–8, 1980 *AY* 17/12); at Bedern, the Jew's harp may have provided musical entertainment for the vicars (see p.2949), while the bone tuning pegs may derive from harps used in church (pp.1978–80, *AY* 17/12).

Determining the identity of the people who resided in, worked in or visited a place in the past, whether in terms of their gender, age, occupation, status or any other respect, is usually impossible in any but the broadest terms. It may be assumed, however, that the residents of the urban tenements at Coppergate were usually family groups. Unfortunately, very few if any artefacts can be said to be particular to women; for example, dress accessories and adornments predominantly associated with women today, such as brooches and finger-rings, were used equally by both sexes in the medieval period. At Bedern and Fishergate questions of the gender and age range of the residents should, in theory, be less problematic than at Coppergate and the Foundry because the vicars choral and the Gilbertine priors were supposed to be celibate, without either wives or children. However, neither of their institutions excluded female or child visitors, relations or servants who might lose or dispose of artefacts pertaining to their gender or age on the premises. At Bedern, moreover, it is known from documentary sources that by the 15th century there were frequent breaches of regulations regarding female visitors (*AY* 10/5, 614) and it is possible that the move from communal accommodation to single cells, which seems to have occurred in the mid 14th century, may have allowed greater freedom for illicit relationships. Although female items are difficult to identify, a few objects from Bedern, notably the pins, perhaps for fastening veils, and the possible hair accessories, may hint at their presence. For the Gilbertine priory at Fishergate we do not have the equivalent documentary evidence as for Bedern, but the presence of women with their children, at least as visitors attending the services, may be assumed. None of the sites produced any material that could be directly related to children.

Finally, the question of social status may be touched on. Research on documentary sources relevant to the Coppergate area shows that written evidence for the period before 1300 is rare, but possible owners of properties on the south-east side of the street in the 14th and 15th centuries have been identified (S. Rees Jones in *AY* 10/6, forthcoming). Reconstruction of two strings of neighbouring properties indicate a number of residences of wealthy and in-

fluential citizens, and mercantile families by c.1400. Some of the finds from Coppergate suggest, however, that it may have been a wealthy area before this. Individual high-status artefacts which stand out include, most notably, the stunning gold ring set with pearl and garnets (*12937*) found in a mid 13th century pit. High-status glass goblet fragments, of 12th–13th century date and probably made in France or Germany, have also been identified (*11130–1*).

We know something of the social standing of the vicars choral from documentary sources (*AY* 10/5, 381–3) which suggest that while they were possibly not in the highest echelons of the church hierarchy, they may be considered to have been people of some status and wealth compared to the majority of the population. When looking at this question in respect of the artefacts, however, it must be remembered that some may have been the property of people who worked in or visited the college premises. Having said this, there are some indications of wealth and there is no sense in which the College presents a picture of abstinent otherworldliness. This fits well with evidence provided by some documentary sources, notably wills, of personal wealth enjoyed by many of the vicars, at least by the 15th century (*AY* 10/5, 615) and perhaps for some time before this. In her report on the vessel glass, Dr Tyson noted (p.2827) that 'some of the most prestigious decorative vessels of the 13th and 14th centuries were used at Bedern . . . The Bedern assemblage compares more closely with the glass from secular castles and palaces of the period than with the more abstinent monastic sites'. Similarly, Penelope Walton Rogers, in comparing the textile fragments from the Foundry, Bedern and Fishergate, concluded (p.2886) that 'most of the better-quality fabrics and the more luxurious textiles such as silks are concentrated within the area of the College'. An assessment of the range of pottery from the site has suggested fewer cooking vessels than might be expected, but larger numbers of chamber pots which, with the implication that tedious trips to the privy were avoided, may be some small indicator of the vicars' superior life style! Individual high-status items of precious metal included a gold ring set with a sapphire (*14508*), a gold brooch found in a mid–late 13th century deposit (*14507*), and the gilded silver brooch (*14506*) inscribed *INRI*. A second silver brooch (*14505*) was found in floor levels of the mid 13th century. Amongst the ironwork there were two knife blades with gilded inlay, one from an early 14th century context and another probably of similar date, although found in a post-medieval context. It may be significant that the high-status items referred to above derive primarily from the 13th and 14th century levels at the College, the period during which it is recorded at its most prosperous and before the financial problems of the 15th century onwards (*AY* 10/5, 383–4). Even the horses had their own decorative harness pendants in the 13th and 14th centuries and, to judge by the cheek piece (*14122*) found, bridles might have included gilded iron components.

When considering the evidence from the Gilbertine priory it is necessary to enter similar caveats on the provenance of the finds as those entered for Bedern. However, the non-ferrous assemblage from the priory reveals an ecclesiastical establishment of a very different nature from the College of the Vicars Choral. The Gilbertines lived by the rule of St Augustine, which enjoined communal living and the renunciation of personal property (Graham 1901, 57), and in this context the evidence becomes completely explicable. The paucity of personal possessions, the lack of elaborate glass tablewares and the use of unremarkable pottery fabrics clearly reflect a more austere communal life which contrasts strongly with that enjoyed by the vicars choral. Unlike the College, St Andrew's was never a wealthy house; records of the 14th century include a grant for repairs by Bishop Henry Burghersh of Lincoln in 1335 because the priory was impoverished, and, throughout the 15th and 16th centuries, there are continual references to the priory's poverty (*AY* 11/2, 60). Life beyond the city walls in this small impoverished monastic community appears to have been very different from that in the relatively wealthy commercial and industrial zones around both Bedern and Coppergate in the heart of medieval York.

Future Research on Medieval Artefacts

In being one of a small group of publications under the heading *Craft, Industry and Everyday Life* which present a substantial assemblage of finds from medieval contexts in York for the first time (others being *AY* 17/12–13 and *AY* 17/16 in prep.), this fascicule represents an important landmark in the study of the city and of the medieval period in general. It is therefore legitimate to consider its implications for future research, whether on finds which have already been excavated or on finds which will come from future excavation. A number of finds assemblages of varying size and importance from medieval contexts in York remain unpublished. In addition, there is an ongoing excavation programme in the city which produces artefacts from medieval contexts on a regular basis.

The study of both unpublished and newly excavated finds will undoubtedly enhance the artefact type series established in this fascicule. In addition, objects will continue to provide information on the character and dating of occupation in those zones of the city from which they derive. Of particular value in this respect will be the identification, through waste products, part-made objects and tools, of manufacturing sites. A detailed knowledge of how manufacturing was organised and carried out is fundamental for understanding the development of the medieval city from its origins in the Anglo-Scandinavian period. While documentary sources may yield some information on where craftspeople resided and how their activities were organised, they pertain largely to the late medieval period. These sources are moreover largely silent on many subjects such as the character of raw materials and the techniques of manufacturing. For the medieval period as a whole, therefore, and especially before c.1400, the subject of craft and industry is primarily archaeological. The sites considered here have provided an insight into one important craft, that of bronze founding, an insight considerably enhanced by the metallographic analyses of the debris. In addition, the metallography of the iron knives has revealed important new data on the development of the blacksmith's craft in terms of the nature of the metal used and the methods of working it. In view of the small sample of knives examined (22, including five published in *AY* 17/9), however, these topics would clearly benefit from examination of other well-dated specimens. Further-

more, there is no certainty that knives are typical of edged tools as a whole, and examination of a range of other types would seem to be warranted.

Another important subject on which this fascicule has touched is the relationship between artefacts and the identity and status of the people who lived and worked on the sites on which they were found. As already noted, this is problematic especially when dealing with sites where there has been continual redeposition of material over many hundreds of years, which may destroy any distinctive character of an assemblage from a particular time period. Differences have, however, emerged between the major sites discussed above which appear to relate to the occupational roles and wealth of the residents and the conclusions here should provide points of departure for the study of other categories of material, notably pottery and biological samples. The characterisation of artefact assemblages with a view to determining the make-up of the population which generated them, in terms of age, gender and occupational structure, for example, appears to offer considerable research opportunities.

The study of medieval material culture, whose beginnings as an organised field of research lie, perhaps, in J.B. Ward Perkins's *London Museum Medieval Catalogue*, published in 1940, has developed over the last 60 years or so into a discipline which has made a substantial contribution to the study of the history of the period. Indeed it may now claim to be fed by many distinct sub-disciplines as will be readily appreciated in this volume. We have a sense, however, that the study of artefacts as a basis for our understanding of two particular, and related, topics, namely the development of medieval urbanism as an economic and social phenomenon, and daily life as experienced by the medieval townsperson, stands on the threshold of an exciting future, one in which new developments in scientific examination and computer-based techniques of statistical analysis will play a significant part alongside the more traditional skills of the typologist. Archaeologists in the great medieval cities of London, Norwich and Winchester, as well as a number of other towns, have already shown us the way towards that future, and it is with great pleasure that we feel a further, and not inconsiderable, step has been taken by this additional contribution from York.

Additional Anglo-Scandinavian Ironwork from 16–22 Coppergate, the Coppergate watching brief and 22 Piccadilly

Since the publication of *AY* 17/6 a number of additional iron objects from Anglo-Scandinavian contexts at 16–22 Coppergate have been identified as a result of the re-evaluation of the phasing of the site stratigraphy. In addition, there are a few Anglo-Scandinavian objects from the 22 Piccadilly site. Some of these objects warrant comment.

Tools and implements (Fig.1554)

Punches

15322–3 are small punches from early–mid 11th century contexts at 22 Piccadilly similar to two from Anglo-Scandinavian contexts at Coppergate (*2210, 2218, AY* 17/6). There is a trace of lead and copper on the broken end of *15323* which may give a clue to its use on non-ferrous metalworking.

Awl

15299 from Coppergate is an awl with arms of diamond-shaped cross-section similar to a number of others from Anglo-Scandinavian contexts at Coppergate (pp.552–4, *AY* 17/6).

Shears

15324 from 22 Piccadilly is a pair of shears of which the complete length (152mm) can be determined, although only one half survives. The stem is decorated with incised grooves and a saltire cross, and there is an internal nib below the bow. The grooves on the stem are an unusual feature, but can also be seen on a pair of probable 8th–9th century shears from Flixborough, Lincolnshire (Ottaway in prep., sf13503), while nibs can be seen on three 9th century shears from that site.

Knives

There are two additional Anglo-Scandinavian knives from 16–22 Coppergate, one from the watching brief and five from 22 Piccadilly. *15330* has back form A (the angle-back) and the edges of the back are chamfered, a feature which occurs on ten other Anglo-Scandinavian knives from Coppergate (p.579, *AY* 17/6). One knife, *15331*, has back form C1. Four knives have back form C3 (p.570, *AY* 17/6): *15307,*

15319, 15332 and *15333*. A finely cut groove runs along the top of each blade face of *15333* similar to those on many other Anglo-Scandinavian knives (pp.580–1, *AY* 17/6). The form of the blades of the two remaining knives (*15308* and *15334*) cannot be determined.

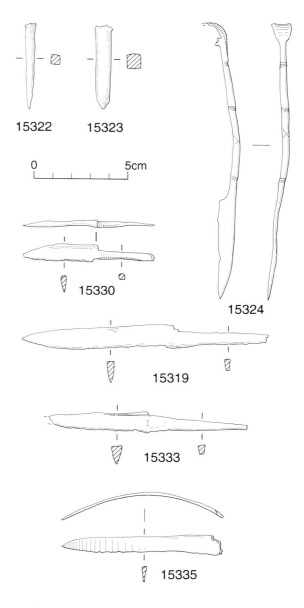

Fig.1554 *Finds from Anglo-Scandinavian contexts: punches 15322–3 from 22 Piccadilly, shears 15324 from 22 Piccadilly, knives 15319 from the Coppergate watching brief, 15330, 15333 and 15335 from 22 Piccadilly. Scale 1:2*

Metallurgy report

By Karen Wiemer

Three knives from Coppergate were examined by Karen Wiemer as part of the research for her PhD thesis (Wiemer 1993). In the case of *2891*, this knife has been discussed in *AY* 17/6 but its metallurgy report had not been completed by the time that fascicule was published and is therefore included here.

Knife *2891*

2891 was a small knife of back form A which appeared to be complete.

X-radiograph: Three horizontal layers and a weld line with a fibrous corrosion pattern above and along it were visible. Much of the mid-section of the edge had mineralised complicating interpretation of the x-radiograph. The region was avoided during sampling. A segment was cut from the back edge.

As-polished: Very clean metal made up both sections; only the tip contained many small, dark, subround and elongated inclusions. A horizontal 'V' of small, elongated, light and medium inclusions above the tip indicated a weld. A second band of finer inclusions, roughly parallel to the first, revealed another possible weld. The metal between and above these bands was clean. In the back, three arched lines of stringers and irregular inclusions indicated a layered structure. These were mostly medium to dark with some containing a lighter second phase.

Etched: The edge section consisted of three horizontal layers separated by two welds. The addition of a piece of steel around the edge of the blade had resulted in a yellow-white V-shaped weld line. The steel was a homogeneous mixture of over-tempered carbide, martensite and/or bainites, and a small amount of ferrite (C = c.0·5–0·7%; max. HV0·1 = 384). It was high in arsenic and higher in phosphorus than the much lower carbon steels in the knife back. The structure between the welds consisted of ferrite, some of which contained short needles, and degraded fine pearlite and tempered carbide. The upper weld line was less defined than the lower. The back consisted of two low-carbon steel layers with a narrow, slightly higher-carbon layer at the very back. A network of Widmanstätten ferrite revealed a coarse prior austenite grain size. A distinct, vertical, yellow-white, arsenic segregation line separated the two steel layers. This line and the two weld lines extended into the corrosion surrounding the blade. Microstructures throughout the sample had a granular appearance.

The thermal history involved slack quenching from a temperature well above the fully austentic and, at some point, spheroidise annealing. The welds were unusual and were neither butt nor scarf, and it was not clear just how this knife was assembled or how the edge and back sections related. The possibility that it was crudely pattern-welded with the structure of the sections resulting from the cut through the blade could not be supported by evidence from the sample sections or X-radiography. In order to resolve some of these questions, a complete

Table 329 Hardness values and minor element levels for knife *2891* (*hardness values for corresponding areas of the complete cross-section sample are given in parentheses)*

	Hardness* (HV0.1)	Element (wt%)					
		P	S	Mo	Co	Ni	As
Region							
Steel edge	363 (670)	0.13	0.02	tr	0.05	0.05	0.12
Steel between weld	186 (256)	tr	–	–	–	tr	0.03
Iron: back of edge section	187 (197)	0.02	–	–	–	–	0.03
knife back, right hand side	201 (194)	0.02	tr	tr	–	tr	0.04
knife back, left hand side	165 (174)	tr	–	–	–	–	0.04
Segregation line, back	–	tr	–	tr	tr	0.02	0.21

cross-section was removed through the of blade near the tip.

With the exception of the edge, the shape and distribution of inclusions was the same in the new and the original samples. The inclusions in the tip of the complete cross-section were dark but much larger, much more irregular in shape and more numerous than those in the first edge sample. A clear scarf-weld was defined by a string of small, irregular inclusions. Although etching revealed that the complete cross-section consisted of three horizontal layers, it made differences apparent. The tip consisted of tempered martensite (max.HV0·1 = 708) and fine nodular pearlite (HV0·1 = 452) with ferrite present only in a decarburised region near the weld. The steel was approximately eutectoid (C = c.0·8%). The associated segregation line was much less diffuse than in the first sample. Both upper welds followed a similar curve. The iron layer between the welds was narrower than the original edge section and was carburised throughout. Needles structures were absent. The most important difference was that the steel edge in the new section had been competently hardened and not over-tempered. The microstructures above the scarf-weld had a granular appearance and hardnesses similar to those of corresponding areas of the original samples. Unfortunately, because of the mineralised section at the middle of the edge, it was not clear from the radiographs whether a single piece of steel formed the cutting edge. The complete cross-section was taken after matrix analyses were completed, so its minor element levels are unknown. However, the differences in hardness, microstructure and inclusion distribution in the two edge samples might indicate that the cutting edge of the blade was not a single continuous piece.

It is difficult to reconcile the presence of both spheroidised and hardened structures in the edge. A possible explanation is that the hard, scarf-welded edge represents a partial or complete re-edging of the blade. The soft edge near the tang was either a region that was not repaired or was exposed when the new edge wore away. The former explanation is more likely as the shape of the edge shows no sign of wear. The three layers in this section arise from the remains of the original edge, and folding and layering in the iron used to make the back. The iron with the martensitic structures may represent only a small portion of the inhomogeneous iron bloom used to make the knife back. The complete cross-section consists of the new edge, and the iron knife back. The remnant of the original edge may be softer because the knife was over-tempered at some point before being repaired and/or because it was the more heavily tempered portion of a slack-quenched blade. Given that the steel in the cross-section near the tip must have been quenched from above the upper critical temperature, it would seem that only the tip of the blade was quenched, with tempering subsequently occurring due to heat flow from the uncooled parts of the blade. It is unlikely that the spheroidised edge represents a repair as the heat required to weld this would have tempered the whole blade, but the structure of the edge near the tip shows this did not occur. The corrosion at the middle of the edge may well support the idea of a partial repair since slag trapped in this region during the addition of a new layer near the end of the blade could be responsible for its preferential corrosion.

Interpretation

This was a Type 2 knife made using several pieces of low-, medium- and high-carbon steel, with at least two layers present in both the back and the edge. The carbon content was greatest at the tip. The edge contained two welds of unusual shape. A slice was cut through the whole blade to clarify the manufacture of the knife, and, although this section also contained two welds, the lower join was clearly a scarf-weld; the steel at the tip had a different thermal history and was much harder than the edge of the first section. The original knife appeared to have been competently quenched and tempered or slack-quenched from a temperature well above the upper critical temperature. The much harder edge near the tip was not heavily tempered and probably indicated that a portion of the blade was very competently repaired and rehardened after the original edge had worn away or broken.

Knife 15307 (Fig.1555)

The tang and very tip were broken. The cutting edge extended into the tang and followed a shallow S-curve to the end of the blade.

X-radiograph: The back was very clean with a slightly fibrous corrosion pattern and two clear slag lines near the tip. There was an indication of a rounded pattern along the cutting edge. No welds were apparent and it seemed likely that the knife was of Type 1 manufacture. Two wedges were removed.

As-polished: Both samples contained bands of vertically oriented inclusions with two-phase inclusions to one side of the section and dark elongated inclusions and stringers along the centre and in the tip. Lighter inclusions tended to be small and spheroidal or subround.

Etched: The edge was a variation of a three-layer sandwich having a steel core that did not extend through to the back, that is, Type1c. The cutting tip consisted of coarse, acicular, tempered martensite of approximately eutectoid composition (C = 0·6 to 0·8%; max. HV0·1 = 752). Behind the tip, a network of fine nodular pearlite surrounded the tempered carbide and revealed a prior austenite grain size that coarsened toward the knife back. White lines owing to high phosphorus rather than increased nickel or arsenic levels outlined the core. The grain size in the phosphoric iron flanks varied between the higher and lower carbon bands. Carbon had either diffused in from the core during manufacture or the sheaths had been made of piled iron and steel. Widmanstätten ferrite and tempered martensite or bainites were present in both. There was some ghosting in the iron of the back sample.

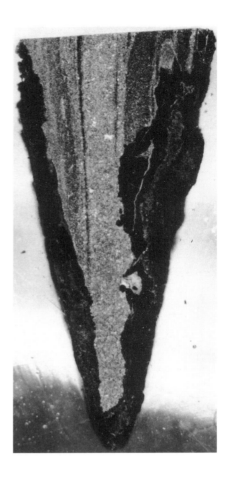

Fig.1555 *Knife 15307 (×20) showing Type 1c manufacture. The central weld line splits to hold an inserted steel blade*

Interpretation

This high-quality, Type 1c knife had an approximately eutectoid steel edge. The flanks consisted of high-phosphorus iron containing higher carbon, finer-grained bands owing either to carbon diffusion and segregation when the knife was made or to piling during the production of the iron used. The knife had been heated to above the fully austenitic temperature and rapidly quenched and lightly tempered,

Table 330 Hardness values and minor element levels for knife *15307*

	Hardness (HV0.1)	P	S	Mo	Co	Ni	As
Region							
Steel core: average	574	0.03	–	–	0.09	0.03	–
edge	701						
Iron and carbide sheaths	256	0.27	0.02	–	tr	0.03	–
Higher carbon areas	–	0.24	tr	tr	–	0.02	–
	483	0.14	tr	–	0.03	0.02	0.03

3008

possibly auto-tempered. The edge was the hardest of all the medieval knives sampled.

Knife *15308*

The knife had corroded extensively; it lacked a tip and portions of its back. It was not possible to ascertain a specific back form group. The edge was concave below the shoulder and straight, though jagged, elsewhere.

X-radiograph: The end of the blade had mineralised. There was a slight fibrous corrosion pattern in the back and limited regions of rounded corrosion along a roughly serrated cutting edge. No welds were apparent, so Type 1 manufacture was possible. Two samples were taken.

As-polished: The sections had similar inclusion distributions. A layer of corrosion entered at the back and continued through to the tip. The metal along the centre of the cross-section contained small, fine stringers which appeared to have been worked and broken while they were fluid. To one side, internal corrosion had formed preferentially around single-phase inclusions of a medium oxide which appeared to follow another metal layer. This iron layer contained large, two-phase, medium and light inclusions. The metal on the other side of the cross-section contained small spheroidal and subround inclusions many of which had cracked. A row of irregularly shaped inclusions marked a possible join.

Etched: The overall structure was a three-layer sandwich with corrosion splitting a central steel core. The microstructure had a granular appearance and consisted of over-tempered carbide, probably martensite or a mixture of martensite and bainites (C = 0·4 to 0·8%; max. HV0·1 = 278). Yellow-white lines resulting from increased nickel and colbalt levels ran along each side of the core and probably developed when the blade was smithed under oxidising conditions. Much carbon had diffused into the low-phosphorous iron sheath during welding. Its microstructure was coarser but otherwise similar to that of the core with the carbon content decreasing away from the weld. The 'ghosting' phosphoric iron of the second sheath had coarse, equiaxed grains which appeared to have undergone grain growth. Despite the high-phosphorous content, much carbon had diffused in from the core and was present as completely spheroidised carbide.

Interpretation

This was a Type 1a blade with a hypoeutectoid steel core and one phosphoric and one ferritic iron sheath. The microstructure of the steel and extensive carbon diffusion into both flanks indicated that the blade had been quenched from just above the fully austenitic temperature to produce a hardened edge. At some point after manufacture, however, the knife was sub-critically annealed for a sufficient length of time to precipitate and spheroidise cementite and cause ferritic grain growth. The knife appeared originally to have been made to a high standard but over-tempering had greatly softened the cutting edge.

Paring knife (Fig.1554)

15335 from 22 Piccadilly is the curved blade from what was probably a paring knife which would have

Table 331   Hardness values and minor element levels for knife *15308*

| Region | Hardness (HV0.1) | Element (wt%) | | | | | | |
		P	S	Mo	Co	Ni	Cu	As
Iron: 1eft hand side (ASTM 6,7)	189	0.33	0.02	–	0.03	0.06	tr	0.02
right hand side	242	0.05	–	tr	–	–	–	tr
Steel core:	264	0.07	tr	tr	0.06	0.14	–	0.08
Iron, knife back	170	0.19	tr	–	tr	0.05	–	tr
Segregation line	–	0.06	tr	–	0.15	0.75	0.05	0.33
Segregation line	–	0.12	tr	–	–	0.08	–	0.30

been ideal for cleaning out and trimming horses hooves. Two examples of 9th century date were found at Flixborough (Ottaway in prep.).

Strike-a-light

15329 from 22 Piccadilly has a tapering plate with a looped terminal at the wider end. It is similar to two strike-a-lights from Anglo-Scandinavian contexts at Coppergate (*3681–2, AY 17/6*) and others from 10th–12th century contexts.

Structural ironwork and fittings

(Figs.1556–7)

Pierced plate

15313 is a piece of crumpled plate pierced eight times, of no apparent function.

Hinge straps

Of particular interest are *15341–2* which are two very well-preserved examples from 22 Piccadilly with straps which have bifurcated and scrolled terminals. It is also possible to see details of the hammering marks left by the smith during forging. A pair of very similar hinges were found with a burnt and collapsed door of late Anglo-Saxon date in London (Horsman et al. 1988, 88–91, fig.84).

Stapled hasp

15343 from 22 Piccadilly is probably an incomplete stapled hasp. It was originally bent through 90° indicating that it was fitted to the lid of its container. Attachment was by means of a staple set in an eye at the head of the strap which was formed by drawing it out and then folding it back. Short grooves are cut into the edges of the face of the strap and it is tin plated.

Padlock key

15347 is a barrel padlock key from 22 Piccadilly with its bit at an angle to the stem similar to two from Coppergate (*3664–5, AY 17/6*) and other examples of pre-Conquest date from Winchester (Goodall 1990, fig.322, *3693–7*).

Dress fittings (Fig.1558)

Buckle

15348 is a small D-shaped buckle frame from 22 Piccadilly, similar to many others of 9th–10th century date.

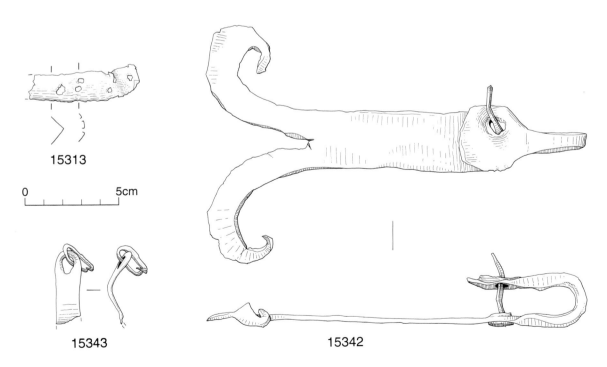

15313

0   5cm

15343

15342

Fig.1556 *Finds from Anglo-Scandinavian contexts: pierced plate* 15313 *from 16–22 Coppergate, U-eyed hinge with bifurcated strap* 15342 *from 22 Piccadilly, stapled hasp* 15343 *from 22 Piccadilly. Scale 1:2*

Fig.1557 *Anglo-Scandinavian U-eyed hinges with bifurcated straps:* 15341 *(top) and* 15342 *from 22 Piccadilly. Actual length of* 15342, *200mm*

Pins

15349 from 22 Piccadilly is a small iron pin with a spherical head made of tin. *15315* from Coppergate is a similar pin made entirely of tin-plated iron. Similar pins have already been noted in Anglo-Scandinavian contexts at Coppergate (p.693, *AY* 17/6).

Horse equipment

Horseshoes

There are three horseshoes to add to the small collection of Anglo-Scandinavian examples described in *AY* 17/6 (pp.707–9). *15350* from 22 Piccadilly is a branch with a smooth outer side, two countersunk holes and part of third. These features render it comparable to *3852*, *3854* and *3856* from Coppergate which may be taken as typical of the earliest horse-

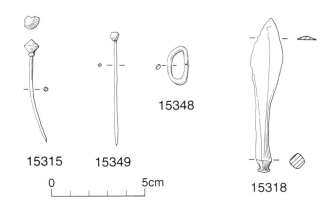

15315 15349 15348 15318

0   5cm

Fig.1558 *Finds from Anglo-Scandinavian contexts: pins* 15315 *from 16–22 Coppergate and* 15349 *from 22 Piccadilly, buckle frame* 15348 *from 22 Piccadilly, leaf-shaped arrowhead blade* 15318 *from 16–22 Coppergate. Scale 1:2*

shoes from England. *15316* from Coppergate is a branch tip which is clearly from a horseshoe with a wavy outer edge, a feature which emerges in the 11th century. Both *15316* and *15317*, the tip of another branch, have the turned-over calkin which again is commonly found on 10th–11th century horseshoes.

Weapons and armour

Arrowhead (Fig.1558)

15318 from Coppergate is a leaf-shaped arrowhead blade, originally tanged, which is similar to a number of others from Coppergate (pp.710–11, *AY* 17/6).

Catalogue

The catalogue numbers follow consecutively those on p.2660, *AY* 17/14, except for items previously catalogued in fascicules in *AY* 17 which appear at the start of relevant sections. Each entry ends with the small find number, prefixed sf, preceded by context number; a list of provenances appears on pp.3155–60. For terminology relating to non-ferrous plating on ironwork, see Appendix Two, pp.3167–8. If a catalogue entry incorporates more than one item or fragment, the dimensions given relate to the largest item. Entries for 16–22 Coppergate attributed to Period 6 are followed by a code denoting Tenement (A–D), Period (6), phase and sequence. Entries ending (modern) denote contexts associated with the buildings that preceded the Coppergate Development. It should be noted that since 1994 the Yorkshire Museum accession codes have been prefixed YORYM.

Abbreviations: L. = length; W. = width; T. = thickness; D. = diameter; H. = height; Wt. = weight

Finds from 16–22 Coppergate (1976–81.7)

All finds came from Period 6 contexts except those given as unstratified (u/s).

Stone

Spindle whorls

Where whorls are incomplete, measurement of the incomplete dimension is given in brackets [ ]. In these cases an estimated original weight has been added after the present weight.

Form A1

6543   Shaved spherical shape; decorated with five vertical zones of incised lines, one ladder and four herringbone design; brown surface discoloration. Chalk, white, very fine-grained; Chalk Group. D.34.3, T.21.7mm, Wt.30g; hole D.10mm 5231 sf1312 (C6c6, D6a7; mid 12th century) (*Fig.808*)

6544   Fragment only. Hemispherical shape with vertical-sided upper half; decorated with curving incised lines on all faces; brown surface discoloration. Chalk, white, very fine-grained; Chalk Group. D.33.3, T.20mm, Wt.14.1g 9572 sf2092 (D6a9; early 12th century) (*Fig.808*)

10829   Fragment only. Shallow cylindrical shape with rounded base; three encircling grooves on base, around hole. Chalk, white, very fine-grained; Chalk Group. L.36.0, W.13.8, T.14.2mm, Wt.[9.1, est.20]g 1263 sf237 (C6h4; early–mid 16th century)

10830   Shaved globular shape; undecorated. Chalk, white, very fine-grained; Chalk Group. D.34.8, T.19.0; hole D.10.1mm, Wt.15.7g 8304 sf1236 (A6z4; 13th century)

10831   Chipped, but almost complete. Hemispherical shape, with deep rilling around circumference; brown surface coating. Chalk, white, very fine-grained; Chalk Group. D.34.4, T.1.6; hole D.10.1mm, Wt.19.7g 3561 sf3336 (A6a1; late 11th century)

10832   Hemispherical shape; undecorated. Chalk, white, very fine-grained, with small fossil fragments; Chalk Group. D.37.9, T.14.0; hole D.8.8mm, Wt.11.6g 13119 sf3555 (A6z14; 15th–16th century)

10833   Flattened globular shape, with flat upper surface; decorated with encircling grooves. Limestone, pale grey, fine-grained, silty, with a few small bivalve casts and moulds, including one with fine reticulate ornament; 'granular' limestone, provenance uncertain. D.33.0, T.19.2; hole D.11.0mm, Wt.30.5g 12851 sf3691 (C6d23; late 12th century)

10834   Almost complete. Shaved hemispherical shape; undecorated. Chalk, cream to pale brownish-grey (possibly burnt), very fine-grained, with scattered individual and clustered larger 'grains', at least some of which are foraminifera; Chalk Group. D.34.0, T.17.5; hole D.11.3mm, Wt.[20, est.24]g 11530 sf4768 (B6g4; early 15th century)

10835   Fragment only. Globular with flat upper surface. Chalk, greyish white, fine-grained; Ferriby Chalk Formation of Chalk Group. L.27.0, T.16.0mm, Wt.[5.3, est.19]g 9362 sf18955 (D6a25; 12th/13th century)

10836   Shaved, flattened spherical shape; undecorated. Chalk, white with pale brownish-grey burnt patch, very fine-grained; Chalk Group. D.48.1, T.20.5; hole D.11.2mm, Wt.63.4g u/s sf3057

10837   Fragment only. Shallow cylindrical shape, with rounded base; undecorated. Chalk, white, very fine-grained; Chalk Group. L.31.1, T.11.1mm, Wt.[6.5, est.20]g u/s sf9315

Form A1 or A2

10838   Fragment only. Asymmetrical truncated biconical shape; incised lines all faces. Chalk, greyish-white, fine-grained; Chalk Group, possibly Ferriby Chalk Formation. L.13.5, W.11.4, T.[17.5]mm, Wt.[5.7, est.30+]g 2336 sf83 (A6z4; 13th century)

Form A1 or B

10839   Chipped but almost complete. Flattened globular shape, with concave upper surface; undecorated. Chalk, white, very fine-grained, with scattered foraminifera and part of an irregular nodule of dark grey flint; Chalk Group, possibly Welton Chalk Formation. D.36.8, T.14.1; hole D.10.4mm, Wt.23.7g 5348 sf1919 (C6e1, D6a16; 12th–13th century)

Form A1 or C

10840   Lower part only. Surviving piece hemispherical, original shape uncertain; undecorated. Limestone, medium to dark brownish-grey, fine-grained, silty, possibly slightly ferruginous, with scattered white short parallel streaks, some of which are small sub-rounded clusters of white calcite suggestive of degraded bivalve shells; 'streaky granular' limestone, provenance uncertain. L.28.2, T.18.6mm, Wt.[7.6]g 5484 sf1707 (C6e1, D6a16; later 12th century)

10841 Fragment only. Rounded lower part of a spherical or hemispherical whorl; undecorated; greyish-brown surface coating. Chalk, white, very fine-grained; Chalk Group. D.32.6, T.[7.9]mm, Wt.[9.0]g 10813 sf2784 (C6g1; early–mid 14th century)

10842 Incomplete. Spherical or hemispherical shape; decorated with encircling grooves. Chalk, greyish-white, fine-grained, intensely intruded superficially by dark blue to black shiny thin lath-like crystals, possibly vivianite; Chalk Group, possibly Ferriby Chalk Formation. D.34.7, T.[20.5]mm, Wt.[22.9]g 17024 sf4898 (C6c3; early 12th century)

Form A2

6550 Fragment only. Rounded truncated conical; undecorated. Chalk, white, very fine-grained; Chalk Group. D.25.4, T.18.9mm, Wt.9g 3537 sf4852 (A6c4; 12th century) (*Fig.806*)

6551 Truncated hemispherical shape; decorated with incised ring-and-dot, arranged in vertical pairs. Mudstone, dark grey, slightly fissile, silty, with numerous minute (c.0.2mm), pale to medium brown sub-angular to sub-rounded masses; probably Lower Palaeozoic or Upper Carboniferous. D.34.6, T.12mm, Wt.20g; hole D.10.2mm 1106 sf104 (D6y1; late 12th–13th century) (*Fig.808*)

10843 Fragment only. Rounded, shaved biconical shape; upper face concave; possible lathe marks. Chalk, white, very fine-grained; Chalk Group. L.17.4, T.13.5mm, Wt.[33.4, est.17]g 5245 sf2238 (D6d3; late 13th century)

10844 Almost complete. Shaved, rounded biconical shape; undecorated. Chalk, yellowish-grey/white, fine-grained; Chalk Group, possibly Ferriby Chalk Formation. D.36.9, T.19.7mm, Wt.[27.1, est.30]g 18331 sf5416 (B6a5, C6c3; early 12th century)

Form B

6564 Fragment only. Truncated biconical shape; incised zig-zag decoration in two zones. Chalk, white, very fine-grained; Chalk Group. L.33.9, T.19.8mm, Wt.14g 2901 sf681 (A6z1; 11th/12th century)

6565 Rounded cylindrical or shaved spherical shape; decorated with incised ladder decoration in six vertical zones. Chalk, white, very fine-grained, with scattered foraminifera; Chalk Group. D.26.9, T.24.1mm, Wt.20.2g; hole D.9.5mm 3493 sf3080 (A6c1; 12th century) (*Fig.808*)

6566 Fragment only. Shallow cylindrical; top and bottom decorated with fields of parallel incised lines. Chalk, white, very fine-grained; Chalk Group. D.36.9, T.12.1mm, Wt.11.6g u/s sf2368 (*Fig.808*)

10845 Cylindrical shape with rounded sides; undecorated. Limestone, pale grey (possibly pale bluish-grey within), fine-grained, silty; 'granular' limestone, provenance uncertain. D.30.6, T.15.5; hole D.10.0mm, Wt.20.6g 4008 sf176 (C6h8–11; 16th–late 17th century)

10846 Shaved globular shape; undecorated; possible lathe marks. Chalk, brownish-white, fine-grained; Chalk Group, possibly Ferriby Chalk Formation. D.40.3, T.22.0; hole D.11.2mm, Wt.45.8g 1585 sf282 (C6v1; late 11th–early 12th century)

10847 Fragment only. Shallow cylindrical shape; undecorated. Chalk, white, very fine-grained; Chalk Group. L.27.9, T.11.1mm, Wt.[5.2, est.21]g 11000 sf2901 (B6c7 early 13th century)

10848 Shaved, rounded biconical shape; undecorated. Chalk, white, very fine-grained; Chalk Group. D.30.0, T.23.0; hole D.11.5mm, Wt.22.7g u/s sf4616

Form B or C

10849 Chipped but almost complete. Irregularly cut, cylindrical shape, with curving sides and rounded upper and lower faces; undecorated. Chalk, white, very fine-grained; Chalk Group. D.39.6, T.18.4; hole D.10.7mm, Wt.31.6g 5981 sf2193 (C6c3, D6a5; late 11th/early 12th century)

10850 Fragment only. Shaved spherical shape; undecorated. Chalk, greyish-white, fine-grained; Chalk Group, possibly Ferriby Chalk Formation. L.32.6, T.23.2mm, Wt.[12.6, est.36]g 12422 sf3070 (D6e1; 13th/14th century)

10851 Shaved globular shape; encircling incised lines, possible lathe marks. Limestone, pale grey, fine-grained, silty, with a few traces of white short parallel streaks; 'granular' limestone, provenance uncertain. D.33.0, T.19.2; hole D.10.4mm, Wt.27.2g 13862 sf3601 (B6d2; 13th century)

10852 Fragment only. Truncated biconical shape; undecorated. Chalk, white, very fine-grained; Chalk Group. L.41.1, T.15.6mm, Wt.[15.0, est.33]g 15285 sf5297 (B6a1; late 11th century)

Form C

6568 Fragment only, decorated with incised ring-and-dot, arranged irregularly over surface. Chalk, white, very fine-grained; Chalk Group. L.28.7, T.20mm, Wt.7.3g 5975 sf3209 (C6c6; mid 12th century) (*Fig.808*)

6569 Flattened globular shape; undecorated; grey-brown surface discoloration. Chalk, greysih-white, fine-grained; Chalk Group, possibly Ferriby Chalk Formation. D.32.6, T.19.5mm, Wt.24.7g; hole D.10mm 5484 sf1720 (C6e1, D6a16; later 12th century) (*Fig.807*)

6570 Incomplete. Shallow, rounded biconical shape; lathe marks. Chalk, brownish-white, fine-grained; Chalk Group, possibly Ferriby Chalk Formation. D.35.9, T.17.4mm, Wt.18.1g 5442 sf2268 (C6e5; early 13th century) (*Fig.807*)

6571 Globular shape, decorated with three encircling bands of red paint and incised zig-zags between painted bands; central hole has been drilled and then redrilled. Limestone, pale grey, fine-grained, substantially dolomitic; probably Lower Magnesian Limestone but could be Upper Magnesian Limestone. D.27.1, T.20mm, Wt.18.2g; hole D.9.6mm 12496 sf3197 (D6a24; 12th/13th century) (*Fig.808*)

6572 Almost complete. Rounded biconical shape; decorated with incised grid-lines. Chalk, brownish-white, fine-grained, with some ?microbioclastic grains; Chalk Group, probably Ferriby Chalk Formation. D.34.7, T.25.1mm, Wt.32.2g; hole D.11.2mm 13902 sf4884 (B6c3; 12th/13th century) (*Fig.807*)

6573 Spherical; lathe marks. Chalk, brownish-white, fine-grained; Chalk Group, possibly Ferriby Chalk Formation. D.28, T.24.7mm, Wt.23.3g; hole D.10.2mm 13902 sf5114 (B6c3; 12th/13th century) (*Fig.807*)

6574 Rounded biconical; encircling incised lines, probably lathe marks. Chalk, greyish-white, fine-grained; Chalk Group, possibly Ferriby Chalk Formation. D.32.1, T.20.1mm, Wt.23.2g; hole D.9.6mm 4620 sf1268 (C6e9; mid 13th century) (*Fig.807*)

6575 Flattened globular shape; undecorated. Chalk, greyish-white, fine-grained; Chalk Group, possibly Ferriby Chalk Formation. D.28.6, T.14.4mm, Wt.15.4g; hole D.9mm 9224 sf3003 (C6e9; mid 13th century) (*Fig.807*)

6576 Fragment only. Globular shape; decorated with incised lines arranged in five encircling bands of ladder design.

Chalk, white with grey (possibly burnt) patches, fine-grained; Chalk Group, possibly Ferriby Chalk Formation. D.32, T.22.2mm, Wt.14g 9224 sf1331 (C6e9; mid 13th century) (*Fig.808*)

6577   Globular shape; lathe marks. Chalk, greyish-white, fine-grained; Chalk Group, possibly Ferriby Chalk Formation. D.29.5, T.20.4mm, Wt.22g; hole D.9.8mm 3258 sf1418 (A6g1; 13th/14th century) (*Fig.807*)

10853   Fragment only. Spherical shape; undecorated. Limestone, pale brownish-grey, fairly fine-grained, silty, with numerous white short parallel streaks, one with 'hooked' profile indicative of bivalve shell; 'streaky granular' limestone; provenance uncertain. L.20.5, T.23.2mm, Wt.[5.8, est.29]g 1506 sf378 (D6e9; mid 14th century)

10854   Globular shape; surface abraded but some possible lathe marks visible. Chalk, greyish-white, fine-grained; Chalk Group, possibly Ferriby Chalk Formation. D.31.4, T.21.8; hole D.11.0mm, Wt.25.7g 4658 sf769 (C6g19; mid 14th century)

10855   Fragment only. Spherical shape, tapering towards base; decorated with three encircling grooves. Chalk, white, very fine-grained; Chalk Group. L.16.5, T.17.0mm, Wt.[2.8, est.15]g 5064 sf935 (C6e9; mid 13th century)

10856   Chipped at one end. Globular shape; lathe marks. Chalk, brownish-white, fine-grained; Chalk Group, possibly Ferriby Chalk Formation. D.27.7, T.17.1; hole D.10.0mm, Wt.15.6g 9092 sf990 (D6e8; early 14th century)

10857   Biconical, slightly asymmetrical shape; undecorated. Chalk, white, very fine-grained; Chalk Group. D.34.8, T.21.1; hole D.10.3mm, Wt.24.5g 4620 sf1223 (C6e9; mid 13th century)

10858   Fragment only. Spherical shape; undecorated. Chalk, greyish-white, fine-grained; Chalk Group, possibly Ferriby Chalk Formation. L.23.0, T.24.8mm, Wt.[7.2, est.29]g 9213 sf1269 (D6e1; 13th/14th century)

10859   Fragment only. Globular shape; undecorated; possible lathe marks. Limestone, pale brownish-grey, fairly fine-grained, silty, with numerous white short parallel streaks and a few elongate, thin (<c.0.8mm) crystalline calcite 'beef' layers; 'streaky granular' limestone, provenance uncertain. L.3.2, T.2.2mm, Wt.[13.2, est.30]g 9323 sf1346 (D6d3; late 13th century)

10860   Fragment only. Globular shape; undecorated. Chalk, greyish-white, fine-grained; Chalk Group, possibly Ferriby Chalk Formation. D.34.0, T.25.1mm, Wt.[17.1, est.35]g 9224 sf1581(C6e9; mid 13th century)

10861   Fragment only. Globular shape; undecorated. Chalk, white, very fine-grained; Chalk Group. L.34.1, T.23.8mm, Wt.[12.6, est.29]g 9302 sf1615 (D6a26; 12th/13th century)

10862   Fragment only. Globular shape; four encircling incised lines. Chalk, brownish-white, fine-grained; Chalk Group, possibly Ferriby Chalk Formation. L.20.8, T.19.8mm, Wt.[6.6, est.33]g 9362 sf1658 (D6a25; 12th/13th century)

10863   Fragment only. Flattened globular shape; possible lathe marks; undecorated. Chalk, greyish-white, fine-grained; Chalk Group, possibly Ferriby Chalk Formation. L.29.4, T.16.8mm, Wt.[8.1, est.21]g 3362 sf1719 (A6ef; 13th century)

10864   Chipped at one end. Globular shape; undecorated. Limestone, pale brownish-grey, fine-grained, silty; 'granular' limestone, provenance uncertain. D.33.8, T.2.52; hole D.11.5mm, Wt.32.1g 5484 sf1857 (C6e1, D6a16; later 12th century)

10865   Flattened globular shape; lathe marks. Chalk, brownish-white, fine-grained; Chalk Group, possibly Ferriby Chalk Formation. D.35.2, T.19.0; hole D.10.1mm, Wt.30.2g 5484 sf2010 (C6e1, D6a16; later 12th century)

10866   Fragment only. Spherical shape; undecorated. Limestone, medium grey, fine-grained, silty; 'granular' limestone, provenance uncertain. L.25.9, T.23.0mm, Wt.[7.2, est.29]g 3392 sf2280 (A6f2; 13th century)

10867   Fragment only. Spherical shape; undecorated. Chalk, brownish-white, fine-grained; Chalk Group, possibly Ferriby Chalk Formation. L.25.0, T.22.2mm, Wt.[7.3, est.29]g 5348 sf2319 (C6e1, D6a16; 12th–13th century)

10868   Fragment only. Rounded biconical shape; decorated with encircling incised lines. Limestone, pale grey, fine-grained, with a thin (<0.5mm) dark grey recrystallised layer; 'granular' limestone, provenance uncertain. L.23.0, T.24.0mm, Wt.[7.0, est.30]g 11053 sf2624 (B6g2; 14th/15th century)

10869   Fragment only. Flattened globular shape; possible lathe marks. Limestone, pale brownish-grey, fine-grained, silty, with numerous white short, and a few long, parallel streaks; 'streaky granular' limestone, provenance uncertain. L.33.3, T.19.1mm, Wt.[13.1, est.29]g 12165 sf2941 (D6e3–7; 13th–early 14th century)

10870   Rounded cylindrical or sub-spherical shape; undecorated. ?Chalk, pale greyish-fawn, very fine-grained; probably Chalk Group. D.27.5, T.21.2; hole D.11.1mm, Wt.19.4g 11886 sf3058 (A6j35; 15th–16th century)

10871   Complete but in fragments. Flattened globular shape; undecorated. Chalk, greyish-white, fine-grained; Chalk Group, possibly Ferriby Chalk Formation. D.33.8, T.19.5; hole D.11.2mm, Wt.27.0g 13331 sf3309 (B6c3; 12th/13th century)

10872   Complete but surface abraded. Flattened globular shape. Chalk, greyish-white, fine-grained, with sub-angular to rounded ?microbioclastic grains, superficially intruded by scattered dark blue to black shiny thin lath-like crystals, possibly vivianite; Chalk Group, possibly Ferriby Chalk Formation. D.35.9, T.17.5; hole D.11.2mm, Wt.27.5g 13245 sf3379 (B6a7; early 12th century)

10873   Fragment only. Flattened globular, or rounded biconical shape; lathe marks. Chalk, greyish-white, fine-grained; Chalk Group, possibly Ferriby Chalk Formation. D.36.0, T.18.0mm, Wt.[15.0, est.30]g 11818 sf3503 (B6c2–6; 12th–early 13th century)

10874   Globular shape; undecorated. Chalk, greyish-white, fine-grained; Chalk Group, possibly Ferriby Chalk Formation. D.31.9, T.22.5; hole D.11.1mm, Wt.29.4g 13663 sf3519 (A6d1; 11th/12th century)

10875   Fragment only. Globular shape; undecorated. Chalk, greyish-white, fine-grained; Chalk Group, possibly Ferriby Chalk Formation. L.22.7, T.18.8mm, Wt.[4.9, est 20]g 16456 sf4572 (D6a9; early 12th century)

10876   Fragment only. Rounded biconical; undecorated. Chalk, white, very fine-grained; Chalk Group. L.36.8, T.27.4mm, Wt.[13.3, est.33]g 2286 sf5195 (C6v2; 12th century)

10877   Fragment only. Globular, tapering towards lower edge; undecorated. Chalk, white, very fine-grained; Chalk Group. L.31.8, T.17.2mm, Wt.[9.9, est.25]g 17697 sf5546 (B6a4, C6c2; late 11th/early 12th century)

10878   Fragment only. Flattened globular; undecorated. Chalk, white, very fine-grained; Chalk Group. L.18.6, T.19.0mm, Wt.[6.8, est.17]g 6339 sf5588 (D6a1; late 11th century)

Possible Form C

10879   Incomplete. ?Globular shape; lathe marks. Chalk, greyish-white, fine-grained; Chalk Group, possibly Ferriby Chalk Formation. D.29.1, T.19.4mm, Wt.[17.7]g 13899 sf4344 (B6f1; early 14th century)

Undetermined form

6578   Fragment only. Shallow cylindrical shape with incised zig-zag top and bottom. Chalk, white, very fine-grained;

Chalk Group. D.29.2, T.10mm, Wt.4.8g u/s sf12944 (*Fig.808*)

10880 Much abraded perforated stone object, possibly originally a spindle whorl, although central hole rather small. Original shape not clear. Chalk, greyish-white, fine-grained; Chalk Group, possibly Ferriby Chalk Formation. D.23.3, T12.1; hole D.6.0mm, Wt.[7.3]g 9017 sf836 (D6e11; mid 14th century)

Hones

Norwegian Ragstone type

10881 Irregularly rectangular, three sides dressed, both ends broken, perforation incompletely drilled from both sides at upper end. Schist, pale grey, fine-grained abundantly quartzitic, micaceous (mainly muscovite, sparse biotite), with sparse dark non-micaceous minerals. L.79, W.18, T.14.9mm 1114 sf140 (D6e10; mid 14th century)

10882 Of rectangular section, split axially, perforation drilled from both sides but not quite meeting. Three well-worn surfaces but split surface not used following split. Schist, as *10881* but slightly darker with a few calcite veins. L.106, W.10, T.17mm 1283 sf280 (C6z1; late 14th–early 15th century) (*Fig.1381*)

10883 Of rectangular section. One end sawn and split, other possibly sawn; four worn edges. Schist, pale grey, fine- to medium-grained, dominantly quartzitic (almost metaquartzite with elongate quartz), moderately micaceous (mainly muscovite, sparse biotite). L.45, W.24, T.26mm 4571 sf656 (C6e1–13; 12th/13th century)

10884 Of rectangular section. Both ends sawn, one on the diagonal. One worn surface, three roughly dressed, one with striations. Schist, as *10881*. L.68, W.35, T.25mm 1213 sf674 (C6z1; late 14th–early 15th century)

10885 Of rectangular section. Both ends broken away; a broad groove has been worn into the upper surface. Schist, pale grey, fine-grained, quartzitic (but not as abundantly as *10881*), micaceous (mainly muscovite, sparse biotite), with sparse dark non-micaceous minerals. L.55, W.35, T.20mm 1332 sf680 (C6x4; early 13th century)

10886 Fragment of rectangular section. Broken away at both ends; four worn surfaces. Schist, as *10885*, with sparse pale green ?chlorite. L.128, W.45, T.20mm 4604 sf738 (C6g19; mid 14th century)

10887 Fragment of rectangular section. Broken away at both ends. Narrow grooves worn into two unworn surfaces, one worn surface. Schist, as *10881*, with sparse pale green ?chlorite. L.75, W.30, T.25mm 9129 sf911 (D6e9; mid 14th century)

10888 Fragment of irregular section. One worn surface, other surfaces and both ends broken away. Schist, as *10881*, with sparse pale green ?chlorite. L.85, W.42, T.20mm 4620 sf923 (C6e9; mid 13th century)

10889 Of rectangular section. Broken away at both ends, three worn surfaces, one roughly dressed. Schist, as *10881*. L.75, W.24, T.11mm 4620 sf986 (C6e9; mid 13th century)

10890 Of rectangular section. One end broken away; two surfaces worn, two roughly dressed. Schist, as *10881*, with some slightly darker bands containing ?biotite. L.47, W.16, T.8mm 3098 sf1004 (A6ef; 13th century)

10891 Of rectangular section. Sawn at one end, broken away at the other; all four surfaces worn rounded. Schist, as *10883*, with few thin impersistent streaks possibly containing biotite. L.80, W.25, T.20mm 4620 sf1243 (C6e9; mid 13th century)

10892 Of rectangular section. Broken across both ends; all four surfaces worn. Schist, as *10885*. L.68, W.23, T.10mm 9224 sf1479 (C6e9; mid 13th century)

10893 Of rectangular section. Sawn across one end; four surfaces worn smooth, beginning of perforation on one surface. Schist, pale grey, very fine- to fine-grained (almost phyllite), quartzitic, micaceous (mainly or all muscovite), possibly Norwegian Ragstone type. L.70, W.16, T.10mm 5238 sf1492 (C6e5, D6a24; early 13th century)

10894 Of rectangular section. Worn smooth at both ends and on four surfaces, one end worn quite thin. Schist, as *10885*. L.115, W.23, T.15mm 5348 sf1525 (C6e1, D6a16; 12th–13th century)

10895 Fragment of approximately rectangular section. One end rounded, one broken across; three worn surfaces. Schist, as *10885*, L.98, W.33, T.20mm 9305 sf1705 (D6a24; 12th/13th century)

10896 Of rectangular section. Four worn surfaces partially broken/laminated away; sawn both ends, very long and thin. Schist, as *10885*. L.110, W.10, T.8mm 5484 sf1757 (C6e1, D6a16; later 12th century)

10897 Possible roughout. Both ends broken away but roughly shaped into a rectangle. Schist, as *10885*, with sparse pale green ?chlorite. L.135, W.50, T.22mm 5398 sf1825 (C6c6; mid 12th century)

10898 Of rectangular section. One end rounded, one broken away; four worn surfaces. Schist, as *10885*. L.110, W.35, T.8mm 9305 sf1879 (D6a24; 12th/13th century)

10899 Fragment of rectangular section. Both ends and two surfaces broken away; two worn surfaces survive. Schist, as *10885*, but slightly coarser (fine- to medium-) grained. L.63, W.25, T.21mm 5671 sf1889 (C6e6; early 13th century)

10900 Of rectangular section. Three worn surfaces survive; both ends roughly dressed. Schist, as *10881*, with sparse biotite and some pale green ?chlorite. L.50, W.20, T.22mm 3256 sf2049 (A6i2; 14th/15th century)

10901 Of rectangular section. Sawn and snapped across both ends, four worn surfaces. Schist, as *10881*. L.25, W.14, T.8mm 5348 sf2090 (C6e1, D6a16; 12th–13th century)

10902 Fragment, sub-rectangular, one side dressed, others naturally cleaved, both ends broken. Schist, as *10881*. L.95, W.32, T.17.8mm 9330 sf2145 (D6a26; 12th/13th century)

10903 Of triangular section, axial perforation, one end sawn and rounded, other broken away, three worn surfaces. Schist, as *10893*. Possibly Norwegian Ragstone type. L.92, W.21, T.12mm 5348 sf2173 (C6e1, D6a16; 12th–13th century) (*Fig.1381*)

10904 Fragment; surfaces uneven and both ends broken away. Schist, as *10893*, but slightly darker and with sparse pale green ?chlorite. Possibly Norwegian Ragstone type. L.30, W.20, T.10mm 5238 sf2203 (C6e5, D6a24; early 13th century)

10905 Fragment of rectangular section. Both ends sawn; two smooth surfaces, two roughly surfaces. Schist, as *10883*. L.28, W.11, T.12mm 5777 sf2302 (D6a17–23; late 12th–13th century)

10906 Fragment. All surfaces and ends broken away. One end possibly sawn and snapped. Schist, as *10885*, but slightly coarser (fine- to medium-) grained. L.80, W.25, T.6mm 5485 sf2312 (D6a16; mid 12th century)

10907 Of rectangular section, one end sawn and snapped, other end broken, all surfaces worn, with narrow sharpening grooves on two faces. Schist, as *10881*, but slightly coarser (fine- to medium-) grained, with sparse biotite and a few larger pale brown inclusions, possibly Norwegian Ragstone type. L.117, W.31, T.19mm 10119 sf2465 (C6h9; 16th–17th century) (*Fig.1381*)

10908 Fragment of rectangular section. One end sawn, one broken away; three worn surfaces, one broken away. Schist, as *10881*. L.74, W.33, T.15mm 11683 sf2866 (B6g3; early 15th century)

10909 Fragment of rectangular section, both ends sawn, four worn surfaces, incomplete perforation on both sides. Schist, as *10885*. L.49, W.11, T.10mm 13188 sf3380 (B6c4; 12th/13th century) *(Fig.1381)*

10910 Fragment of rectangular section. Both ends broken away, one smooth surface, another covered with possible ash glaze; two roughly dressed surfaces. Schist, as *10885*, with appreciable biotite. L.32, W.13, T.11mm 12727 sf3688 (D6a24; 12th/13th century)

10911 Of rectangular section. One end sawn diagonally, one end broken away; four worn surfaces and one partially broken away. Schist, as *10885*. L.58, W.20, T.19mm 12501 sf3916 (C6e7; early 13th century)

10912 Of roughly square section. Two worn surfaces, one end sawn on the diagonal; other broken away. Schist, as *10885*. L.55, W.25, T.20mm 13124 sf3986 (B6x1; 15th–16th century)

10913 Of rectangular section. Four worn surfaces; one end sawn and snapped, the other broken away. Schist, as *10885*. L.47, W.20, T.8mm 13442 sf3990 (B6f1; early 14th century)

10914 Fragment of rectangular section. Four dressed but not worn surfaces; both ends broken away. Schist, as *10881*, but slightly coarser (fine- to medium-) grained. L.26, W.17, T.10mm 11965 sf4002 (B6f6; 14th century)

10915 Of square section, one end sawn off, the other worn thin and snapped where worn, well-worn axial perforation, all surfaces worn smooth. Schist, as *10885*, but slightly darker. L.68, W.14, T.14mm 13949 sf4097 (B6c1; 12th/13th century) *(Fig.1381)*

10916 Fragment of irregular section. One worn surface, other surfaces and two ends broken away. Schist, as *10881*. L.83, W.17, T.8mm 12363 sf4118 (C6e5; early 13th century)

10917 Fragment of square section. Both ends broken away, one smooth surface; other surfaces broken away. Schist, as *10881*, but pale brownish-grey. L.75, W.27, T.20mm 16465 sf4432 (D6a19; late 12th century)

10918 Fragment of irregular section. One worn surface, other surfaces and both ends broken away. Schist, as *10885*. L.90, W.20, T.12mm 16612 sf4502 (D6a1; late 11th century)

10919 Of rectangular section. One end sawn off, one broken away where worn thin; four worn surfaces, worn perforation. Schist, as *10881*. L.47, W.17, T.10mm 6269 sf4696 (C6c1; early 12th century)

10920 Of rectangular section. Both ends roughly dressed, four worn surfaces. Schist, as *10885*. L.105, W.31, T.22mm 18047 sf4738 (B6c3; 12th/13th century)

10921 Of rectangular section. Both ends sawn, one worn edge. Schist, as *10885*. L.30, W.23, T.8mm 17591 sf4997 (C6c6; mid 12th century)

10922 Fragment of ovoid section. Broken away at both ends, rounded surface worn; flat underside not dressed. Schist, as *10881*. L.84, W.25, T.23mm 15033 sf5002 (C6v1; late 11th–early 12th century)

10923 Fragment of irregular section. One worn surface; both ends and other surfaces broken away. Schist, as *10885*, but slightly darker. L.36, W.14, T.10mm 6344 sf5310 (D6a1; late 11th century)

10924 Of triangular section. One end sawn, the other broken away. Two smooth surfaces, one roughly dressed. Schist, as *10881*, but slightly coarser (fine- to medium-) grained. L.48, W.21, T.15mm 17786 sf5379 (C6c2; early 12th century)

10925 Fragment only; two surfaces worn, two broken away, both ends sawn and then snapped. Schist, as *10885*. L.40, W.9, T.9mm 18668 sf5386 (C6d4; mid 12th century)

10926 Fragment of rectangular section. One end shaped round, the other broken away. Two worn surfaces, two roughly dressed. Schist, as *10881*, but slightly coarser (fine- to

medium-) grained. L.90, W.20, T.10mm 16734 sf5419 (C6a1, D6a1; late 11th century)

10927 Fragment of rectangular section. Sawn at both ends; four worn surfaces. Schist, as *10885*. L.28, W.10, T.9mm 17890 sf5420 (B6a1, C6a1; late 11th century)

10928 Fragment. Broken away at both ends and on three surfaces; one worn surface. Schist, as *10885*, with sparse biotite. L.45, W.22, T.14mm 16612 sf5452 (D6a1; late 11th century)

10929 Fragment. One end sawn, the other broken away. Two worn surfaces, two others not dressed. Schist, as *10885*. All surfaces except one appear worn and degraded (?weathered), suggesting ex-erratic (although erratics of this lithology are virtually unknown in England). L.42, W.15, T.11mm 18982 sf5585 (C6b2; 11th/12th century)

10930 Fragment of rectangular section. Broken away at both ends; four worn surfaces. Schist, as *10885*. L.60, W.30, T.18mm 2286 sf5625 (C6v2; 12th century)

10931 Of square section. Sawn at both ends; four worn surfaces. Schist, as *10885*. L.35, W.11, T.10mm 17890 sf5642 (B6a1, C6a1; late 11th century)

10932 Fragment of rectangular section. Split longitudinally, rounded at one end, the other broken away; three worn surfaces. Schist, as *10881*, but slightly coarser (fine- to medium-) grained, and with sparse biotite. L.55, W.20, T.18mm 18331 sf6040 (B6a5, C6c3; early 12th century)

10933 Fragment, sub-rectangular, of sub-square section, both ends broken, all sides dressed, three with grooves of U-shaped sectioned, one quite deep with sharpening scratch. Schist, as *10885*. L.46.8, W.19, T.18.3mm 6034 sf6155 (C6e2; 12th/13th century)

10934 Fragment of triangular section. One end sawn; three surfaces roughly dressed. Schist, as *10885*. L.21, W.12, T.9mm 6258 sf6231 (C6c3, D6a5; late11th/early 12th century)

10935 Fragment, ends broken, sides roughly cleaved, no signs of working. Schist, as *10881*. L.48.5, W.27.8, T.24.3mm 13964 sf6407 (B6a5; 11th/12th century)

10936 Fragment of square section. One end sawn, and the other broken away; two worn surfaces. Schist, as *10885*, but slightly darker. L.25, W.16, T.14mm 17787 sf7204 (C6c1; early 12th century)

10937 Fragment, both ends broken, three sides dressed, fourth roughly broken, broad groove of rectangular section cut into broken side. Schist, as *10881*. L.100, W.30, T.15mm u/s sf151

Purple Phyllite type

10938 Fragment, of rectangular section, four worn surfaces, sawn at one end, broken away at the other where worn thin, abandoned incompletely drilled perforation on one surface at thin end. Phyllite, medium grey, very fine-grained, quartzitic, micaceous (mainly or all muscovite). L.40, W.20, T.5mm 1229 sf386 (C6z1; late 14th–early 15th century) *(Fig.1382)*

10939 Possibly saw cut across top. One worn surface, the other end and other surfaces not dressed. Phyllite, as *10938*. L.74, W.17, T.8mm 1440 sf403 (C6x2; 11th/13th century)

10940 Fragment, ends and two sides roughly broken, other sides dressed. Phyllite, pale grey, very fine-grained, quartzitic, micaceous (mainly or all muscovite). L.28.9, W.26.3, T.8.9mm 4874 sf955 (C6g6; late 14th century)

10941 Of rectangular section. Both ends roughly dressed; four worn surfaces. Phyllite, as *10938*. L.55, W.12, T.13mm 9224 sf1317 (C6e9; mid 13th century)

10942 Of rectangular section, both ends sawn and snapped but already well worn on three surfaces, fourth surface broken away. Phyllite, pale to medium grey, very fine-grained, quartzitic, micaceous (mainly or all muscovite), with marked platy cleavage (giving laminated appearance). L.45, W.20, T.11mm 5348 sf2058 (C6e1, D6a16; 12th–13th century)

10943 Fragment, split longitudinally from axial perforation to end, possibly during drilling which was done from both sides. Phyllite, as *10938*. L.42, W.5, T.5mm 5981 sf2171 (C6c3, D6a5; late 11th/early 12th century)

10944 Fragment of irregular section. Broken away at both ends, four surfaces slightly worn. Phyllite, as *10938*. L.55, W.16, T.5mm 5981 sf2210 (C6c3, D6a5; late 11th/early 12th century)

10945 Of rectangular section. Both ends sawn and four worn surfaces. Phyllite, as *10938*. L.32, W.13, T.9mm 11458 sf2772 (B6c7; late 11th–early 12th century)

10946 Of approximately rectangular section. Both ends and part of one surface broken away; worn axial perforation. Phyllite, as *10938*. L.55, W.15, T.8mm 11965 sf3487 (B6f6; 14th century)

10947 Of triangular section. Three dressed but not worn surfaces, both ends broken away. Phyllite, pale to medium grey, very fine- to fine-grained (almost schist), quartzitic, micaceous (mainly or all muscovite). Possibly Purple Phyllite type. L.56, W.25, T.12mm 12501 sf3896 (C6e7; early 13th century)

10948 Of sub-rectangular section, one end sawn, other broken away, four worn surfaces, groove on one face. Phyllite, as *10940*. L.90, W.20, T.10mm 13571 sf3903 (B6a3; 11th/12th century) (*Fig.1382*)

10949 Fragment of roughly rectangular section. Two surfaces and both ends broken away, two worn surfaces. Phyllite, as *10938*. L.40, W.14, T.10mm 12647 sf3995 (D6c1; mid 13th century)

10950 Fragment of irregular section. Two worn surfaces, both ends broken away. Phyllite, as *10940*. L.48, W.23, T.8mm 16734 sf4498 (C6a1, D6a1; late 11th century)

10951 Fragment, sawn across diagonally at both ends. One worn surface, the others roughly dressed or broken. Phyllite, as *10938*, but slightly coarser (very fine- to fine-) grained (almost schistose). Possibly Purple Phyllite type. L.60, W.39, T.25mm 17009 sf4636 (B6a7; early 12th century)

10952 Fragment of irregular section. Part of one worn surface survives, the other surfaces and ends broken away. Phyllite, as *10938*. L.97, W.19, T.14mm 18284 sf4830 (B6a7; early 12th century)

10953 Fragment of rectangular section. One end broken away where worn very thin, the other end sawn and snapped across; four worn surfaces. Phyllite, as *10938*. L.35, W.20, T.5mm 18366 sf5453 (B6a5; 11th/12th century)

10954 Fragment of rectangular section. One end broken away where worn very thin, the other end sawn; four worn surfaces. Phyllite, as *10938*. L.52, W.20, T.6mm 2286 sf5619 (C6v2; 12th century)

10955 Fragment split longitudinally. Both ends sawn; three surviving worn surfaces. Phyllite, as *10938*. L.57, W.8, T.5mm 17890 sf5666 (B6a1, C6a1; late 11th century)

10956 Fragment of irregular section. Part of one worn surface survives, all other surfaces and ends broken away. Phyllite, as *10938*. L.40, W.22, T.10mm 17890 sf6002 (B6a1, C6a1; late 11th century)

10957 Fragment, tiny. Phyllite, as *10938*. L.14.5, W.11, T.2.7mm 17129 sf11453 (D6a2; late 11th century)

10958 Of square section, worn to spatulate form at one end, four worn surfaces. Phyllite, as *10938*, with sparse biotite. L.117, W.32, T.20mm 9224 sf18960 (C6e9; mid 13th century)

10959 Of rectangular section. Sawn at one end broken across the other end where worn thin. Four worn surfaces, axial perforation at top. Phyllite, as *10940*. L.44, W.9, T.4mm 5362 sf18961 (C6d8, D6a8; mid 12th century)

Sandstone

Upper Carboniferous

10960 Of multi-angled section. Broken away at one end and worn thin at the other; six worn surfaces. Pale grey, fine-grained with angular to sub-angular grains, well sorted and fairly well compacted. Upper Carboniferous, probably Coal Measures. L.60, W.30, T.25mm 3083 sf224 (A6i2; 14th/15th century)

10961 Of rectangular section. One end sawn, one broken across, three worn surfaces. Medium grey, fine-grained with angular to sub-angular grains, moderately to well sorted and fairly well compacted, with some scattered muscovite and sparse dark minerals and/or rock fragments; possibly fissile. Upper Carboniferous, probably Coal Measures. L.74, W.58, T.20mm 9057 sf897 (C6e11, D6e3; mid 13th century)

10962 Of square section. Three surfaces worn smooth, one roughly dressed; two ends sawn across. Medium grey, medium-grained with angular to sub-angular grains, fairly well sorted and fairly well compacted, with sparse muscovite and dark minerals and/or rock fragments. L.40, W.20, T.15mm 3256 sf1163 (A6i2; 14th/15th century)

10963 Of rectangular section. Three surfaces worn, one roughly dressed; one end sawn, one broken away. Pale brownish-grey, fine-grained with angular to sub-rounded grains, well sorted and fairly well compacted, with appreciable scattered muscovite. Upper Carboniferous, probably Coal Measures. L.44, W.25, T.18mm 5981 sf2220 (C6c3, D6a5; late 11th/early 12th century)

10964 Of approximately rectangular section, three worn surfaces, both ends sawn. Pale grey, very fine- to fine-grained and silty with sub-angular to sub-rounded grains, well sorted and fairly well compacted, with appreciable scattered muscovite. Upper Carboniferous, probably Coal Measures. L.72, W.35, T.20mm 13492 sf3972 (B6e1; late 13th century)

10965 Fragment of rectangular section. One end broken away, the other worn rounded. Pale grey, fine- to medium-grained with mainly angular grains, fairly well sorted and well compacted. L.42, W.35, T.20mm 16508 sf4184 (B6c2; 12th/13th century)

Lower Palaeozoic

10966 Of round section. Sawn and worn at one end, worn rounded at the other; part of one surface chipped away. Medium to dark reddish-grey, fine- to medium-grained with angular to sub-rounded grains, poorly sorted and highly compacted, with sparse muscovite and some white, red and dark minerals and/or rock fragments. Reddish colour possibly due to heat. D.22, L.62mm 1283 sf286 (C6z1; late 14th–early 15th century)

10967 Of irregular, natural shape and section; three worn surfaces. Medium to dark grey, very fine- to fine-grained with angular to sub-angular grains, well sorted and highly compacted, with some dark minerals and/or rock fragments, and ?siliceous matrix. L.105, W.54, T.54mm 9224 sf1325 (C6e9; mid 13th century)

10968 Of rectangular section, one end sawn, the other worn rounded, four worn surfaces. Medium to dark grey with thin pale grey layers, fine-grained (fine- to medium-grained in paler layers), with angular to sub-angular grains, well sorted and highly compacted with sparse muscovite and biotite and ?siliceous matrix; slightly fissile along ?low-angle cross-bedded layers. Lower

Palaeozoic or Carboniferous. L.100, W.34, T.17mm 11298 sf2674 (A6e5, B6e1; late 13th century) (*Fig.1382*)

10969 Of approximately ovoid section. Ends and surfaces well worn and rounded; large section broken away. Dark grey, fine-grained with angular to sub-angular grains, fairly well sorted and well compacted, with abundant scattered muscovite and biotite, sparse pale green ?chlorite, sparse dark minerals and/or rock fragments, sparse minute pyrites, and ?siliceous matrix. Lower Palaeozoic or Carboniferous. L.13, W.36, T.32mm 17360 sf4705 (C6d1; mid 12th century)

10970 Of rectangular section. Sawn across one end, worn thin at the other; six worn surfaces. Dark grey with thin medium grey layers, very fine-grained (fine-grained in paler layers) with indiscernible grain shapes, well sorted and highly compacted, with ?siliceous matrix. Lower Palaeozoic or Carboniferous; probably turbidite facies. Worn shape suggests erratic. Small glaze splash adhering. L.50, W.22, T.20mm 18074 sf4734 (B6c7; late 11th–early 12th century)

10971 Fragment of rectangular section. Ends and one surface broken away; three worn surfaces. Medium grey, fine- to medium-grained with angular to sub-angular grains, moderately sorted and well compacted, with appreciable scattered muscovite and some biotite, and sparse dark minerals and/or rock fragments. Lower Palaeozoic or (more probably) Carboniferous. L.75, W.42, T.40mm 16112 sf7235 (C6d21; late 12th century)

Coal Measures of Elland Flags type

10972 Of square section. Two surfaces worn smooth, two others dressed but not worn; both ends broken away. Pale grey, fine- to (slightly) medium-grained with angular to sub-rounded grains, moderately to well sorted and fairly well compacted, with fairly abundant muscovite partly concentrated on fissile laminae. L.30, W.14, T.15mm 4915 sf948 (C6e11; mid 13th century)

10973 Of square section, one face worn smooth, three others dressed but not worn, two ends sawn across. Medium grey, fine- to medium-grained with angular to sub-rounded grains, fairly well sorted and fairly well compacted with appreciable scattered muscovite and some bronze-coloured mica. L.35, W.15, T.16mm 9122 sf1060 (D6e1; 13th/14th century)

10974 Fragment, of hexagonal section, ends and two faces incomplete, the other faces dressed. Pale to medium grey, fine-grained with mainly sub-angular grains, fairly well sorted and well compacted, with appreciable muscovite concentrated on fissile laminae. L.40, W.35, T.19mm 3258 sf1830 (A6g1; 13th/14th century)

10975 Of rectangular section. One end sawn, one broken across; two smooth edges and two dressed but not worn surfaces. Pale brownish-grey, fine-grained with angular to sub-rounded grains, moderately to well sorted and fairly well compacted, with fairly abundant muscovite mainly concentrated on fissile laminae. L.65, W.29, T.15mm 3256 sf2366 (A6i2; 14th/15th century)

Other stone types

10976 Fragment, of rectangular section, one end and one surface broken away, other end worn away and other surfaces well worn, narrow groove in one surface. Slate (well-cleaved silty mudstone), medium grey, very fine-grained with some minute indeterminate mica. Lower Palaeozoic. L.50, W.47, T.10mm 5395 sf2201 (C6c6, D6a7; mid 12th century)

Possible hones

10977 Of rectangular section, axial perforation, sawn at one end, other end broken, all surfaces worn. Mudstone, dark grey, fissile, silty, with hardness not more than 6 on Moh's scale, probably insufficiently abrasive for use as hone. Probably Upper Carboniferous (i.e. Millstone Grit or Coal Measures). L.43, W.17, T.8mm 1096 sf187 (C6z1; late 14th–early 15th century) (*Fig.1382*)

10978 Of square section, upper end sawn square with perforation below, all faces dressed. Uncertain stone type; dark brownish-grey (with irregular paler greyish-brown and darker red streaks and patches), very fine- to ?fine-grained rock with hardness not more than 6 on Moh's scale, probably insufficiently abrasive for use as hone. Has appearance of slightly degraded igneous or meta-igneous rock. L.64.7, W.14.7, T.14.2mm 12944 sf3912 (B6c4, C6e6; early 13th century)

10979 Trapezoidal, ends rounded, of sub-rectangular section, suspension hole at upper end. Black, very fine-grained, ?slightly micaceous rock with hardness about 6 on Moh scale, probably insufficiently abrasive for use as hone. Basaltic appearance, probably tuff or Lower Palaeozoic indurated quartzitic siltstone or silty mudstone. L.35, W.15, T.3mm 16612 sf5412 (D6a2; late 11th century) (*Fig.1382*)

Rotary querns

Lava of Mayen type

10980 Fragment, of upper stone, part of perforation remaining. Pale to medium grey, vesicular, with porphyritic crystals of a white translucent mineral. Original size: D.360, L.150, T.40mm 4057 sf239 (C6h7; mid 17th century)

10981 Two fragments. Pale to medium grey, vesicular, with porphyritic crystals of a black mineral. L.170, T.60mm 4087 sf305 (C6h7; mid 17th century)

10982 Fragment of upper stone, edge and socket surviving. Medium to dark grey, vesicular, with porphyritic crystals of both white translucent and green minerals. D.560, T.20mm 4089 sf325 (C6h7; mid 17th century)

10983 Fragment. Medium grey, otherwise as *10980*. L.60, T.20mm 1472 sf486 (C6x2–6; 11th–mid 13th century)

10984 Fragment, possibly part of an edge. Pale to medium grey, vesicular, with two small (<10mm) rounded inclusions of sandstone. L.110, W.65, T.30mm 1765 sf803 (C6g18, D6f8; 15th/16th century)

10985 Fragment, probably of lower stone. Medium (slightly bluish-) grey, otherwise as *10982*. L.140, W.120, T.82mm 5484 sf1780 (C6e1, D6a16; later 12th century)

10986 Fragment with one edge surviving. Medium grey, vesicular, with porphyritic crystals of both black and green minerals. L.50, W.35, T.45mm 9305 sf1844 (D6a24; 12th/13th century)

10987 Fragment only. Medium grey, otherwise as *10980*. L.58, W.30, T.10mm 12563 sf3323 (D6e1; 13th/14th century)

10988 Fragment. Medium grey, vesicular. L.70, W.38, T.30mm 13567 sf3564 (B6a3; 11th/12th century)

10989 Fragment. Medium grey, otherwise as *10980*. L.38, W.32, T.12mm 12853 sf3732 (D6a22; 12th/13th century)

10990 Fragment. Medium grey, otherwise as *10980*. L.140, W.40, T.20mm 12985 sf3779 (C6e2; 12th/13th century)

10991 Two fragments. Medium to dark grey, otherwise as *10980*. L.50mm 12928 sf3856 (B6c2, C6e2; late 12th/early 13th century)

10992 Fragment, part of edge surviving. Pale to medium grey, otherwise as *10986*. L.80, W.35, T.42mm 12928 sf3863 (B6c2, C6e2; late 12th/early 13th century)

10993   Fragment. As *10987*. L.45, W.32, T.33mm 12928 sf3864 (B6c2, C6e2; late 12th/early 13th century)

10994   Fragment. Medium grey, vesicular. L.50, W.50, T.21mm 12928 sf3865 (B6c2, C6e2; late 12th/early 13th century)

10995   Fragment. As *10994*. L.42, W.30, T.14mm 12928 sf3866 (B6c2, C6e2; late 12th/early 13th century)

10996   Fragment, irregularly shaped. As *10994*. L.50mm 12928 sf3897 (B6c2, C6e2; late 12th/early 13th century)

10997   Fragment. As *10994*. L.41, W.34, T.15mm 12928 sf3898 (B6c2, C6e2; late 12th/early 13th century)

10998   Fragment. Pale to medium grey, vesicular, with porphyritic crystals of a green mineral. L.30, W.12, T.13mm 16072 sf4072 (C6e1; 12th/13th century)

10999   Fragment. Pale to medium grey, otherwise as *10986*. L.65, T.30mm 16072 sf4093 (C6e1; 12th/13th century)

11000   Fragment. Medium to dark grey, vesicular, with porphyritic crystals of white translucent, green and black minerals. L.50, W.34, T.24mm 16311 sf4138 (C6d22; late 12th century)

11001   Fragment. As *10998*. L.60, W.30, T.15mm 11440 sf4173 (B6g13; 16th–17th century)

11002   Fragment. Medium grey, otherwise as *10980*. L.95, W.55, T.105mm 16518 sf4182 (C6d22; late 12th century)

11003   Fragment. As *10998*. L.30, W.28, T.4mm 16617 sf4292 (C6d20; late 12th century)

11004   Two fragments. As *10988*. L.43, W.38, T.15mm 16556 sf4359 (B6a10, C6d8; mid 12th century)

11005   Three fragments, possibly of lower stone. As *10980*. L.160, W.150, T.85mm 16761 sf4392 (C6d20; late 12th century)

11006   Fragment. Medium to dark grey, otherwise as *10980*. L.140, T.100mm 16774 sf4400 (C6d20; late 12th century)

11007   Fragment. Pale to medium grey, otherwise as *11000*. L.185, W.92, T.35mm 16799 sf4494 (C6d20; late 12th century)

11008   Fragment. As *10988*. L.70, W.26, T.95mm 17065 sf4655 (C6d8–9; mid–late 12th century)

11009   Fragment. Medium to dark grey, otherwise as *10981*. L.40mm 17344 sf4675 (B6a5; 11th/12th century)

11010   Fragment of ?lower stone, with part of central perforation drilled from both sides. Medium to dark grey,vesicular. L.340, W.200, T.70mm 6282 sf4706 (D6a4; late 11th century)

11011   Eight fragments. Medium grey, otherwise as *10980*. L.60, W.60, T.25mm 17518 sf4729 (C6d20; late 12th century)

11012   Fragment. As *10994*. L.90, W.68, T.66mm 17511 sf4736 (C6d4; mid 12th century)

11013   Fragment. As *10994*. L.70, W.60, T.30mm 18047 sf4737 (B6c3; 12th/13th century)

11014   Fragment. Medium grey, otherwise as *10980*. L.70, W.50, T.42mm 6339 sf4746 (D6a1; late 11th century)

11015   Fragment with edge surviving, possibly a lower stone. Medium grey, otherwise as *11000*. D.280, T.75mm 15166 sf4795 (B6a7; early 12th century)

11016   Two fragments. Dark grey vesicular with (a) few large masses of dark greenish-grey radiating crystals, (b) few small porphyritic crystals of dark green and black minerals, and (c) an inclusion of black fibrous material, probably charred wood (suggesting basal part of a lava flow). L.136, W.107, T.45mm 17103 sf4836 (C6c6; mid 12th century)

11017   Fragment. As *10988*. L.80, W.70, T.65mm 18285 sf4841 (B6b3; 12th century)

11018   Eighteen fragments. Mainly medium grey, vesicular, a few fragments with small porphyritic crystals of a white translucent mineral, and some fragments with small porphyritic crystals of green and/or black minerals. L.150, W.62, T.25mm 17587 sf4842 (C6d1; mid 12th century)

11019   Fragment. Medium grey, otherwise as *10980*. L.130, W.38, T.24mm 17103 sf4845 (C6c6; mid 12th century)

11020   Fragment, of lower stone with part of perforation remaining. As *10980*. D.420, L.190, T.90mm 16892 sf4848 (C6d23; late 12th century)

11021   Fragment, part of grinding surface survives. As *10988*. L.160, W.100, T.100mm 16891 sf4923 (C6d3; mid 12th century)

11022   Fragment. Medium grey, otherwise as *10980*. L.52, W.25, T.12mm 17591 sf4996 (C6c6; mid 12th century)

11023   Fragment, irregularly shaped. As *10988*. L.106, W.30, T.13mm 13902 sf6878 (B6c3; 12th/13th century)

11024   Fragment. As *10988*. L.45, W.25, T.10mm 17587 sf14543 (C6d1; mid 12th century)

11025   Fragment, re-used as a rubbing stone, incomplete, of sub-oval section, one face worn very smooth. Pale grey, vesicular, but with vesicles that are more rounded than is usual in Mayen-type lava. L.85, W.30, T.30mm 11879 sf3366 (B6e2; 13th/14th century)

Sandstone

11026   Fragment with edge surviving. Pale to medium grey, fine- to medium- and slightly coarse-grained with mainly sub-angular grains, moderately sorted and moderately compacted. Millstone Grit. L.130, W.70, T.50mm 9224 sf2961 (C6e9; mid 13th century)

11027   Fragment of upper stone. Pale to medium grey, medium- to coarse-grained with mainly sub-angular grains, moderately sorted and moderately compacted. Millstone Grit. D.48, T.80mm 17033 sf4570 (C6d20; late 12th century)

11028   Fragment of upper stone, with central cone-shaped perforation. Pale to medium grey, medium- to (mainly) coarse-grained with angular to sub-rounded grains, poorly sorted and poorly compacted. Millstone Grit. T.35mm, perforation D.30mm 17397 sf4818 (B6a5; 11th/12th century)

Mortars

Lower Magnesian Limestone

11029   Incomplete, in 8 adjoining fragments, with a pair of opposed unpierced handles, and a pair of opposed sub-rectangular lips with rectangular runnels, supported by projection tapering into rib. Rim and majority of body survive, base broken away. Pale grey, fine-grained, slightly microcellular, mainly dolomitic. H.138.5, external D.300 (including handles), internal D.152mm 4304 sf525 (C6f1; late 13th century) (*Fig.1385*)

11030   Rim fragment, with sub-rectangular projection of plano-convex section. Greyish-white, fine- to medium-grained, mainly dolomitic, with a few small shell fragments and spicules. L.71.6, W.56.2, H.56mm 3098 sf878 (A6ef; 13th century)

11031   Incomplete, base and majority of body surviving, base circular, waist between base and body, part of triangular projection survives on one side, rim broken away. Pale grey, fine-grained, partly microcellular, dolomitic, with a few small geodes and small shell moulds. H.126, internal D.120, external D.226mm 9116 sf946 (D6e4; 13th/14th century) (*Fig.1385*)

11032   Body fragment, with part of projection on one side. Pale grey, fine-grained, mainly dolomitic, with a few small shell fragments and spicules. L.149.6, W.135.8, T.118mm 9224 sf1349 (C6e9; mid 13th century)

Lamps

11033 Inverted conical shape, with flat base, single central well. Limestone, greyish-white, fairly well sorted finely to medium oolitic; slightly friable. Middle or Upper Jurassic. D.87.7, H.84.2mm 1207 sf339 (C6x6; mid 13th century) (*Fig.1435*)

11034 Inverted sub-conical shape, flat base, with sub-oval well, rim and sides roughly faceted. Limestone, greyish-white, well sorted finely oolitic, with a few small shell fragments. Middle or Upper Jurassic. L.99.3, W.88.5, H.62.4, rim T.19.3mm 5239 sf1369 (C6e5; early 13th century)

Counters

Sandstone

11035 Edges dressed to form rough disc, both surfaces dressed. Sandstone, pale grey, fine-grained with sub-angular to sub-rounded grains, well sorted, and fairly well compacted, with scattered muscovite; probably fissile. Upper Carboniferous, probably Coal Measures. D.56, T.17mm 3109 sf276 (A6j28; early 17th century)

11036 Sub-discoidal, edges roughly dressed. Sandstone, medium grey, fine-grained with sub-angular to sub-rounded grains, well sorted and fairly well compacted, with appreciable muscovite largely concentrated on fissile laminae. Coal Measures of Elland Flags type. D.40, T.10mm 9305 sf1579 (D6a24; 12th/13th century)

11037 Fragment, sub-discoidal, surfaces laminated away. Sandstone, medium brownish-grey, otherwise as 11036. Coal Measures of Elland Flags type. D.38, T.8mm 5412 sf2177 (C6e1; 12th/13th century)

11038 Edges dressed to form rough disc, both surfaces dressed. Sandstone, medium grey, fine- to medium-grained with angular to sub-angular grains, moderately sorted and fairly well compacted, with sparse scattered muscovite and trace of thin bedding. Upper Carboniferous, probably Coal Measures. D.60, T.11mm 9248 sf2317 (D6c1; mid 13th century)

11039 Sub-discoidal, roughly chipped. Sandstone, pale grey with reddish colouration on one surface, fine- to medium-grained with mainly sub-angular grains, moderately sorted and well compacted, with sparse muscovite, pyrite, dark and red or reddened minerals and/or rock fragments. Upper Carboniferous, probably Coal Measures. Reddish colour suggests heat. D.47, T.15mm 17360 sf4698 (C6d1; mid 12th century)

Other stone types

11040 Sub-discoidal. Chalk, white, very fine-grained, with few forams. Chalk Group. D.23, T.7mm 3401 sf2611 (A6e2; early 13th century) (*Fig.1518*)

11041 Edges dressed to form rough disc. Limestone, pale grey, very fine-grained (almost porcellaneous), apparently thin bedded. Probably Middle Jurassic. D.60, T.16mm 15043 sf3874 (B6c6; early 13th century)

Pot lids or counters

Sandstone

11042 Edges dressed to form rough disc. Sandstone, pale to medium brownish-grey, otherwise as counter 11035. Upper Carboniferous, probably Coal Measures. D.87, T.16mm 9305 sf2039 (D6a24; 12th/13th century)

11043 Edges dressed to form rough disc, both surfaces dressed. Sandstone, pale brownish-grey, otherwise as counter

11035. Upper Carboniferous, probably Coal Measures. D.70, T.10mm 3549 sf3440 (A6c1; 12th century)

11044 Edges dressed to form rough disc, one surface dressed. Sandstone, as counter 11036. Coal Measures of Elland Flags type. D.88, T.17mm 17275 sf4732 (C6d11; late 12th century)

11045 Edges dressed to form disc, both surfaces dressed. Sandstone, pale to medium grey, otherwise as counter 11036. Coal Measures of Elland Flags type. D.70, T.16mm 18366 sf4929 (B6a5; 11th/12th century)

Fossils

Fossils 11050–1, 11055, 11057, 11062, 11065 were identified by Mr M. Mitchell; 11052–4 by Dr H.C. Ivemey-Cook; 11064 by Mr. C.J. Wood.

Crinoid ossicles

11046 Columnal, of reddish-grey silica with slight residual calcite. Wensleydale Group (formerly Yoredale sequence) or Harrogate Roadstone. 4620 sf1156 (C6e9; mid 13th century)

11047 Four joined together, of calcite. Carboniferous Limestone, Wensleydale Group (formerly Yoredale sequence) or Harrogate Roadstone. 11344 sf2882 (B6f7; 14th century)

Bivalves

11048 Of calcite. *Gryphaea arcuata*, Lamarck, Lower Jurassic. Worn condition suggests erratic. 12097 sf2781 (D6e9; mid 14th century)

11049 Of calcite. *Gryphaea arcuata*, Lamarck, Lower Jurassic. 16734 sf7203 (C6a1, D6a1; late 11th century)

Corals

11050 Compound, of calcite, *Lithostrotion junceum* (Fleming). Carboniferous Limestone. Worn shape indicates erratic. 18331 sf5373 (B6a5, C6c3; early 12th century)

11051 Simple, of calcite, *Dibunophyllum bipartitum* SS *bipartitum* (McCoy). Carboniferous Limestone. Worn shape suggests erratic. 6258 sf5677 (C6c3, D6a5; late11th/early 12th century)

Ammonites

11052 Half, of calcite, with pyritic surface, *Dactylioceras* cf. *tenuicostatum* (Young and Bird). Whitby Mudstone Formation of Lower Jurassic. 1442 sf428 (C6x2; 11th/13th century)

11053 Fragment, of calcite, *Dactylioceras* cf. *semicelatum* (Simpson). Whitby Mudstone Formation of Lower Jurassic. 5395 sf2132 (C6c6, D6a7; mid 12th century)

11054 Other half of 11052. 17890 sf5474 (B6a1, C6a1; late 11th century)

Chert

11055 Black, with cast of fossil brachiopod ?*Actinoconchus*, casts and moulds of small shell fragments, spicules and ?crinoid ossicle. Wensleydale Group (formerly Yoredale sequence). Some mortar adhering. 1404 sf2151 (D6y1; late 12th–13th century)

11056 Medium grey, with casts and moulds of radially and concentric-ribbed fossil brachiopods, and spicules. Wensleydale Group (formerly Yoredale sequence). 5906 sf2157 (C6c3; early 12th century)

Mudstones

11057 Medium grey calcareous, with cast and mould of fossil brachiopod *Productus SS* sp. Carboniferous Limestone. 6034 sf2256 (C6e2; 12th/13th century)

11058 Dark grey, fissile, calcareous, with fragment of fossil ostreaid bivalve. Jurassic. 16722 sf4411 (C6d12; late 12th century)

Limestones

11059 Cream to pale grey, poorly sorted finely to coarse oolitic, with fossil inoceramid bivalve and other shell debris. Middle or Upper Jurassic. 13147 sf3610 (B6u1; late 11th–early 13th century)

11060 Variably pale grey banded, largely silicified, with casts and moulds of fossil orthotetid brachiopod, other brachiopods, ?bivalves and minute fossil debris. Wensleydale Group (formerly Yoredale sequence) or lower part of Millstone Grit. 3493 sf3712 (A6c1; 12th century)

11061 Pale grey, poorly sorted fine to coarse oolitic, with scattered pisoliths, oncolithic layer on one surface, and fossil ostreaid bivalve. Middle or Upper Jurassic. 15594 sf4682 (C6c1; early 12th century)

11062 Pale greyish-yellow, largely silicified, with one large and abundant small fossil crinoid ossicles, traces of tabulate coral *Chaetetes* sp., four small wood fragments, ?ostracods, abundant spicules and other minute fossil debris. Wensleydale Group (formerly Yoredale sequence) or lower part of Millstone Grit. 18172 sf6887 (B6c1; 12th/13th century)

Other fossils

11063 Uncertain. Dark (slightly reddish in part) grey, very fine-grained, partly calcareous rock at surface, incorporating a few small shell fragments, spicules and ?ooliths. Weight suggests that interior consists of heavier material such as flint or ferruginous rock. Shape closely comparable to certain Jurassic and Cretaceous irregular conical echinoids with flattish inferior (i.e. basal) surfaces, but no trace of plates, spicule bases or other echinoid features. Either non-fossiliferous ferruginous nodule from (flat) base of nodule-producing layer, as occurs particularly in some calcareous mudstones in the Lower Jurassic, or iron-enriched or silicified echinoid with surface features worn away naturally (e.g. as erratic) or by long use as a poundstone (as some Mesozoic echinoids, notably *Clypeus*, are known to have been utilised). 1030 sf131 (C6i1; late 17th century)

11064 Echinoid of yellowish-grey flint with serpulid encrustation on surface. *Galerites* sp. or similar form such as ?*Echinogalerus*. Welton Formation or Burnham Formation of Chalk Group. Worn and battered condition indicates erratic. 13147 sf3526 (B6u1; late 11th–early 13th century)

11065 Brachiopod of calcite. ?*Productus productus* (Martin). Carboniferous Limestone. 17890 sf6589 (B6a1, C6a1; late 11th century)

Jet

Offcuts

11066 Sub-triangular, of rectangular section, all edges cut. L.21.7, W.20.7, T.4.5mm 11870 sf2954 (B6f3; early 14th century)

11067 Sub-rectangular, of rectangular section, one face and one edge sawn. L.30, W.19.5, T.4.5mm 11953 sf3267 (B6f3; early 14th century)

Roughout

11068 Of irregular Latin cross-shape, rectangular section, upper and lower ends appear broken. L.41.5, W.21.7, T.7.2mm 13427 sf3406 (B6d6; 13th century)

Fragments

11069 Of irregular shape and section. L.32.1, W.13.1, T.15.3mm 13638 sf3569 (B6c7; late 11th–early 12th century)

11070 Unworked, irregularly shaped. L.26.8, W.21.8, T.14.3mm 16612 sf4247 (D6a1; late 11th century)

11071 Unworked, irregularly shaped. L.55.2, W.40, T.21.4mm 17457 sf4825 (B6a5; 11th/12th century)

11072 Unworked, irregularly shaped. L.47, W.40.4, T.17.1mm 18331 sf5681 (B6a5, C6c3; early 12th century)

Finger-rings

11073 Fragment, of triangular section. L.24.5, W.8, T.5.6mm 5415 sf1799 (C6c6, D6a7; mid 12th century)

11074 Fragment, of irregular sub-plano-convex section. L.14.3, W.6.5, T.3.2mm 3493 sf3335 (A6c1; 12th century)

11075 Or bracelet fragment, of plano-convex section. L.12.4, W.11.7, T.2.7mm 13532 sf3498 (A6n3, B6c1; late 12th/early 13th century)

11076 Fragment, tiny, of sub-plano-convex section. L.5.5, W.6, T.3.9mm 17740 sf5170 (C6c3; early 12th century)

11077 Complete, of plano-convex section. D.23.9, section W.7.8, T.3.5mm u/s sf5381 (*Fig.1492*)

Dice

11078 Cuboidal, unconventionally numbered, 5:6; 3:4; 1:2, digits represented by ring-and-dot moitfs, with inlay. Analysis: inlay almost certainly $CaCO_3$. L.12.1, W.12, T.11.6mm 13532 sf3496 (A6n3, B6c1; late 12th/early 13th century) (*Fig.1518*)

11079 Sub-cuboidal, conventionally numbered, digits represented by inlaid ring-and-dot motifs. Analysis: tin inlay. L.9.7, W.9.5, T.9.4mm 13902 sf4954 (B6c3; 12th/13th century) (*Fig.1518*)

Fired clay

Spindle whorls

All cut to disc shape and central hole cut or drilled.

Form B

11080 Cylindrical with rounded sides; undecorated. Very sandy and with voids. D.41.2, T.17mm, Wt.32.8g; hole D.10.9mm 9252 sf1097 (D6e1; 13th/14th century)

11081 Irregular, shallow cylindrical (or thick disc); undecorated. Sandy. D.38.1, T.10.2; hole D.10.9mm, Wt.16.6g 4620 sf1137 (C6e9; mid 13th century)

Cut from pottery vessel sherds

11082 Fragment, approximately half. Sherd of mortarium base in samian ware. Central Gaulish, AD 170–200. D.27.2, T.7.4mm, Wt.3.8g; hole D.5.6mm 9122 sf1057 (D6e1; 13th/14th century)

11083 Complete. Base of beaker in grey/black fabric; mid 3rd century or later. D.35.4, T.11.6mm, Wt.16g; hole D.7.6mm 9789 sf2808 (D6f9; mid 14th century)

11084 Fragment including central hole. Wall sherd of samian ware. Central Gaulish, second half of 2nd century. D.41.2, T.5.7mm, Wt.9g; hole D.4mm 2284 sf4955 (B6u1; late 11th–early 13th century)

Gaming counters cut from pottery vessel sherds

Cut from Roman sherds

11085 Discoidal, smoothly chipped from flagon base. D.58, T.10mm 2128 sf749 (B6w1; 14th–early 15th century)

11086 Discoidal, roughly chipped from samian vessel sherd. D.22, T.10mm 8304 sf1270 (A6z4; 13th century)

11087 Discoidal, roughly chipped from grey ware sherd. D.30, T.8mm 12727 sf3679 (D6a24; 12th/13th century)

Cut from Anglo-Scandinavian sherds

11088 Discoidal, roughly chipped from grey ware sherd. D.30, T.11mm 5484 sf1800 (C6e1, D6a16; later 12th century)

11089 Discoidal, roughly chipped from grey ware sherd. D.50, T.10mm 3364 sf2233 (A6ef; 13th century)

Cut from medieval sherds

11090 Ovoid, chipped from splashed ware vessel sherd, edge partially ground. L.44, W.40, T.6.5mm 9057 sf867 (C6e11, D6e3; mid 13th century)

11091 Roughly chipped from splashed ware sherd. D.40, T.9mm 4915 sf947 (C6e11; mid 13th century)

11092 Roughly chipped from York or gritty ware sherd. D.50, T.13mm 1502 sf1339 (C6e11, D6e3; mid 13th century)

11093 Roughly chipped from gritty ware sherd. D.22, T.6mm 9305 sf1685 (D6a24; 12th/13th century)

11094 Discoidal, roughly chipped from splashed ware sherd. D.22, T.6mm 5415 sf1824 (C6c6, D6a7; mid 12th century)

11095 Roughly chipped from splashed ware sherd. D.50, T.8mm 9302 sf2307 (D6a26; 12th/13th century)

11096 Made from oxidised glazed ware sherd. D.50, T.7mm 10096 sf2452 (B6g13; 16th–17th century)

11097 Smoothly chipped from Brandsby-type ware sherd. D.30, T.5mm 10824 sf2718 (D6g2–3; mid–late 16th century)

11098 Roughly chipped from splashed ware sherd. D.50, T.7mm 10923 sf2727 (C6g1; early–mid 14th century)

11099 Roughly chipped from splashed ware sherd. D.30, T.5mm 9224 sf2811 (C6e9; mid 13th century)

11100 Roughly chipped from Humber ware sherd. D.42, T.8mm 11626 sf2872 (B6g4; early 15th century)

11101 Roughly chipped from splashed ware sherd. D.30, T.7mm 11554 sf2877 (B6g9; 15th/16th century)

11102 Roughly chipped from splashed ware sherd. D.25, T.4mm 11455 sf2897 (B6e1; late 13th century)

11103 Roughly chipped from York glazed ware sherd. D.60, T.5mm 12180 sf2912 (D6e5; early 14th century)

11104 Discoidal, roughly chipped from splashed ware sherd. D.30, T.8mm 9224 sf2974 (C6e9; mid 13th century)

11105 Discoidal, roughly chipped from York glazed ware sherd. D.25, T.5mm 12274 sf3063 (D6e1; 13th/14th century)

Gaming counters cut from ceramic tiles

11106 Roughly squared, abraded, chipped from tile. L.37, W.33, T.12mm 3093 sf291 (A6j29; 16th/17th century)

11107 Discoidal, roughly chipped from tile. D.60, T.13mm 3165 sf631 (A6j19; 16th century)

11108 Discoidal, smoothly chipped from tile. D.50, T.13mm 1502 sf964 (C6e11, D6e3; mid 13th century)

11109 Discoidal, roughly chipped from tile. D.50, T.13mm 4620 sf1237 (C6e9; mid 13th century)

11110 Discoidal, roughly chipped from tile. D.60, T.14mm 10758 sf2664 (B6g6; 15th century)

11111 Discoidal, roughly chipped from tile. D.60, T.13mm 10766 sf2680 (B6g4; early 15th century)

11112 Discoidal, roughly chipped from tile. D.55, T.15mm 10824 sf2682 (D6g2–3; mid–late 16th century)

11113 Roughly discoidal, made from tile. D.60, T.13mm 10880 sf2714 (B6g6; 15th century)

11114 Ovoid, roughly chipped from tile. L.62, W.50, T.15mm 11763 sf2884 (B6g4; early 15th century)

11115 Roughly discoidal, made from tile. D.30, T.10mm 12368 sf3054 (D6e3; 13th/14th century) (*Fig.1518*)

11116 Discoidal, roughly chipped from tile. D.60, T.14mm 13385 sf3436 (B6c1; 12th/13th century)

11117 Discoidal, roughly chipped from tile. D.60, T.16mm 12364 sf3882 (C6e6; early 13th century)

11118 Discoidal, roughly chipped from tile. D.40, T.12mm 16501 sf4175 (B6c1; 12th/13th century)

11119 Discoidal, roughly chipped from tile. D.40, T.9mm 16219 sf4303 (B6b1; 12th century)

11120 Roughly discoidal, chipped from tile. D.40, T.12mm 17241 sf4505 (C6d8; mid–late 12th century)

11121 Discoidal, roughly chipped from tile fragment. D.40, T.14mm 15840 sf5232 (B6c7, C6e7; early 13th century)

Gaming counters or pot lids

Cut from Roman brick

11122 Discoidal, roughly chipped from Roman brick. D.70, T.26mm 1585 sf298 (C6v1; late 11th–early 12th century)

11123 Discoidal, roughly chipped from Roman brick. D.70, T.15mm 15136 sf4147 (A6n2, B6a5; early 12th century)

Cut from ceramic tiles

11124 Discoidal, smoothly chipped from glazed tile fragment. D.50, T.17mm 5484 sf2062 (C6e1, D6a16; later 12th century)

11125 Discoidal, roughly chipped from tile. D.80, T.20mm 5755 sf2315 (D6a17–23; late 12th–12th/13th century) (*Fig.1518*)

11126 Discoidal, roughly chipped from tile. D.70, T.16mm 10097 sf2447 (B6g15, C6i3; 17th–18th century)

11127 Discoidal, roughly chipped from tile. D.70, T.16mm 13191 sf3439 (B6c3; 12th/13th century)

11128 Discoidal, roughly chipped from tile. D.70, T.13mm 15043 sf3875 (B6c6; early 13th century)

11129 Discoidal, roughly chipped from tile. D.70, T.17mm 13527 sf3977 (B6c7; late 11th–early 12th century)

Vessel glass

Tablewares and other decorated vessels

Goblets

Body

11130 Two adjoining body fragments from slightly convex body, probably a goblet bowl, with an applied horizontal pincered trail. Yellow high-lead glass, with some black surface weathering and dulling, otherwise bright. Body: D.70, T.<1, extant H.12mm 11958 sf3198 (B6f1; early 14th century)

Base

11131   Base rim fragment of weathered opaque brown, originally green, glass. Widely everted, and folded inside at edge to form a band 6mm wide. Probably from the foot of a stemmed goblet. Rim D.75.5, T.3–4mm 18194 sf4782 (B6c2; 12th/13th century) (*Fig.1402*)

Others

Rim

11132   Rim fragment of weathered opaque beige, originally green, glass. Rim diameter not measurable. Possible scar from a thin horizontal trail 4mm below rim edge. T.2mm 8304 sf1161 (A6z4; 13th century)

Body

11133   Eight small body fragments of weathered opaque brown, originally green, glass. Four fragments each have one thin horizontal applied trail. L.14, W.10, T.1.6–2, trail: W.0.4mm 5348 sf1547 (C6e1, D6a16; 12th–13th century)

11134   Three small adjoining body fragments of weathered opaque brown, originally green, glass. Thin horizontal trail applied across all three. Possibly from same vessel as 11133. Joined fragments L.21, W.20, T.1.4; trail: W.0.3mm 5348 sf1576 (C6e1, D6a16; 12th–13th century)

11135   Three body fragments, one made up of six adjoining fragments, of opaque weathered brown, originally green, glass. Two fragments each have one thin horizontal applied trail; the third has two parallel horizontal applied trails 20mm apart. L.35, W.25, T.3; trail: W.0.3–0.5mm 3362 sf1583 (A6ef; 13th century)

11136   Two adjoining body fragments of weathered opaque brown, originally green, glass. Five applied parallel horizontal trails, the third and fourth trails immediately next to each other. L.18, W.11, T.1.6; trail: W.0.6–0.9mm. Possibly from same vessel as 11133. 5348 sf2067 (C6e1, D6a16; 12th–13th century)

11137   Body fragment of weathered opaque mottled brown, originally green, glass. Two applied parallel horizontal trails 10.5mm apart. L.23, W.16, T.2–3; trail: W.1.1–1.8mm 19844 sf2518 (C6g17; 15th/16th century)

11138   Small body fragment of weathered opaque brown, originally green, glass. Part of an applied, probably horizontal, trail across it. L.18, W.14, T.3; trail: W.2mm 12762 sf3733 (C6e3 12th/13th century)

11139   Two large adjoining body fragments of weathered opaque brown, originally green, glass. Five parallel horizontal trails applied between 4 and 11mm apart. Extant H.50, T.2.8–3; trail: W.0.7–1.4mm 12363 sf3885 (C6e5; early 13th century) (*Fig.1402*)

11140   Body fragment of weathered opaque brown, originally green, glass. Two applied parallel horizontal trails, and one thicker slightly wavy trail crossing them at one end. L.24, W.21, T.2; horizontal trail: W.1, vertical trail: W.2mm 13242 sf3901 (B6c2; late 12th/early 13th century) (*Fig.1402*)

11141   Nine very small body fragments, originally joining, of weathered opaque brown, originally green, glass. Small part of a thin trail applied across one fragment. T.1, trail: L.4, W.1.2mm 2286 sf5084 (C6v2; 12th century)

11142   Five small body fragments of weathered opaque brown, originally colourless or pale green, glass. All have mould-blown vertical ribbed or fluted decoration. Possibly from a flask neck. D.<40, T.1.2–2, ribs 4mm apart. u/s sf2767 (*Fig.1402*)

Urinals/flasks

Rims

11143   Everted rim fragment of thick weathered opaque brown, originally green, glass. Slightly thickened at rim edge. Rim D.95, T.4.0–4.2mm 12912 sf3721 (C6e2; 12th/13th century) (*Fig.1402*)

11144   Thick widely everted rim fragment of green glass with mottled opaque brown surface weathering. Slightly thickened at rim edge. Rim D.170, T.3.5–5.0mm 17537 sf4758 (C6d8; mid–late 12th century)

11145   Three small adjoining fragments of an everted rim of weathered opaque brown, originally green, glass. Thickened at rim edge. Rim D.60, T.1.5–2.8mm 18366 sf5253 (B6a5; 11th/12th century)

Bases

11146   Fragment of opaque weathered brown, originally green, glass from the pushed in kick of a base. T.1–5mm 12276 sf3012 (D6e5; early 14th century)

11147   Fragment from the centre of a convex base of heavily weathered opaque mottled brown, originally green, glass. Pontil scar on underside. Extant D.28, T.1.5–5mm 13037 sf3166 (B6f4, C6g1; mid 14th century)

11148   Two adjoining fragments of weathered opaque mottled brown, originally green, glass fragment from a convex base. Negative pontil scar on underside. Extant D.55, T.1.5–4.0mm 12791 sf3724 (C6e3; 12th/13th century)

11149   Thick weathered opaque brown, originally green, glass fragment from the pushed in kick of a base. Part of a possible pontil scar visible on underside. T.3.5–6.0mm 16734 sf5001 (C6a1, D6a1; late 11th century)

Undiagnostic green glass fragments

Rims

11150   Three small fragments of an everted rim of thin weathered opaque brown, originally green, glass. Rim D. not measurable, T. at rim edge 0.3–1.3mm 5009 sf880 (C6e10; mid 13th century)

11151   Almost vertical rim fragment of opaque weathered brown, originally green, glass. Rim D.160+, T. at rim edge 0.9–2.8mm 9224 sf1461 (C6e9; mid 13th century)

11152   Everted rim fragment of weathered opaque brown, originally green, glass. Inturned at extreme rim edge, leaving a ridge around the inside edge. Rim D.150, T. at rim edge 1.0–2.5mm 11415 sf2729 (B6c7; early 13th century) (*Fig.1402*)

11153   Four small adjoining fragments of a slightly everted, almost vertical rim. Weathered opaque brown, originally green, glass. Slightly thickened at rim edge. Rim D.110–120, T.1.5–2.1mm 11458 sf3121 (B6c7; late 11th–early 12th century)

11154   Small fragment of rim of thick weathered opaque brown, originally green, glass. Rim D. not measurable, T.4mm 13160 sf3457 (B6c9; 13th century)

Body fragments

11155   Four adjoining fragments of weathered opaque brown, originally green, glass from the bulbous body of a vessel. L.43, W.35, T.1.5mm 4858 sf821 (C6f5; 13th/14th century)

11156 Seven very small body fragments of weathered opaque beige, originally green, glass. L.7, W.6, T.1mm 4915 sf913 (C6e11; mid 13th century)

11157 Fragment of body or base of weathered opaque brown, originally green, glass. L.16, W.12, T.4.5–5.5mm 5064 sf929 (C6e9; mid 13th century)

11158 Body fragment of weathered opaque brown, originally green, glass. L.11, W.11, T.1.2mm 3225 sf1807 (A6j2; 15th century)

11159 Fragment from the flaring curve of a vessel of weathered opaque brown, originally green, glass. L.28, W.21, T.2.2mm 11514 sf2751 (B6c2; 12th/13th century)

11160 At least ten small fragments of weathered opaque beige, originally green, glass fragments from the bulbous body of a vessel. L.15, W.13, T.1.2–2.0mm 11803 sf2921 (B6g1; 14th/15th century)

11161 Four very small body fragments of weathered opaque beige, originally green, glass. L.7, W.7, T.1mm 13454 sf3641 (B6d2; 13th century)

11162 Two very small body fragments of weathered opaque brown, originally green, glass. T.1mm 12841 sf3686 (C6e4; 12th/13th century)

11163 Fragment from the body or base of a vessel of weathered opaque brown, originally green, glass. L.23, W.21, T.4–5mm 15106 sf3783 (B6c5; early 13th century)

11164 Body fragment of weathered opaque brown, originally green, glass. L.16, W.12, T.3.2–3.5mm 17103 sf4816 (C6c6; mid 12th century)

11165 Five small adjoining very slightly curving body fragments of weathered opaque brown, originally green, glass. Adjoining L.25, W.13, T.1.5mm 17551 sf4897 (C6e3; 12th/13th century)

11166 Body fragment of weathered opaque brown, originally green, glass. L.17, W.15, T.2mm 18256 sf4901 (B6a7; early 12th century)

11167 Nine very small body fragments of weathered opaque beige, originally green, glass. T.1mm 13902 sf5225 (B6c3; 12th/13th century)

Iron

Blanks and scrap

For purposes of classification strips and bars have a maximum width to thickness ratio less than 4:1; bars a product of width and thickness over 300mm²; plates maximum width to thickness ratio greater than 4:1.

Bars

All have a rectangular cross-section.

11168 One end ragged and obliquely cut. L.62, W.32, T.9mm 5348 sf2088 (C6e1, D6a16; 12th–13th century)

11169 Broken at both ends. L.50, W.21, T.10mm 3093 sf15194 (A6j29; 16th/17th century)

11170 L.100, W.33, T.10mm u/s sf9

11171 Narrows, wider end roughly broken. L.72, W.30, T.8mm u/s sf13434

Plates

All are roughly rectangular unless otherwise stated.

11172 Triangular, slightly curved. L.50, W.15mm 2193 sf72 (A6z5; mid 12th century)

11173 Very corroded. L.58, W.23, T.2mm 1283 sf314 (C6z1; late 14th–early 15th century)

11174 Roughly rounded disc. D.22, T.1.5mm 4604 sf741 (C6g19; mid 14th century)

11175 Curved slightly, one straight side, rest irregular. L.59, W.44mm 4692 sf771 (C6g9–17; early 15th–15th/16th century)

11176 Narrows to pointed tip at one end; near the wider end, where broken, an expanded area with convex sides. L.120, W.18, T.3mm 4851 sf799 (C6e11; mid 13th century) (*Fig.1318*)

11177 Sides slightly raised on one face. Plated (quaternary: leaded gunmetal). L.68, W.16, T.5mm 9037 sf917 (C6e11; mid 13th century)

11178 L.50, W.14, T.2mm 1502 sf962 (C6e11, D6e3; mid 13th century)

11179 Broken at each end, sides with splits. L.58, W.9, T.1.5mm 5021 sf1036 (C6e10–11; mid 13th century)

11180 Cast iron. Triangular, slightly curved. L.74, W.48, T.13mm 3257 sf1059 (A6i2; 14th/15th century)

11181 Corroded. Narrows to a rounded end, was curved over at the other, now broken. L.137, W.26, T.4mm 4620 sf1138 (C6e9; mid 13th century)

11182 Narrows a little, sides irregular. L.60, W.37, T.4mm 9078 sf1142 (D6e1; 13th/14th century)

11183 Curved over at one end. L.55, W.16, T.3mm 4620 sf1193 (C6e9; mid 13th century)

11184 L.20, W.8, T.1mm 5245 sf1471 (D6d3; late 13th century)

11185 One half curved and widened irregularly. L.65, W.18, T.3mm 5484 sf1773 (C6e1, D6a16; later 12th century)

11186 Narrows, one side concave, broken at each end. L.22, W.11, T.1mm 9572 sf2363 (D6a9; early 12th century)

11187 Narrows to a point, irregular sides and faces, narrowed at the wider end. L.74, W.11, T.2mm 10022 sf2438 (C6i1; late 17th century)

11188 Narrows, folded over, broken at each end. L.35, W.15, T.3mm 9252 sf2502 (D6e1; 13th/14th century)

11189 L.35, W.9mm 12561 sf2514 (D6a3–25; late 11th–12th/13th century)

11190 Broken at each end. L.66, W.29, T.1mm 3235 sf2620 (A6g1; 13th/14th century)

11191 Two-thirds of the object tapers and is twisted to a curved-over tip. Broken at the other end. L.88, W.26, T.4mm 10944 sf2696 (D6e9; mid 14th century) (*Fig.1318*)

11192 Disc, slightly dished. Plated (possibly copper). D.27, T.2mm 11447 sf2752 (B6g13; 16th–17th century)

11193 Roughly triangular with a rectangular cut out of one corner. L.60, W.38, T.3mm 12018 sf2835 (D6e9; mid 14th century)

11194 Narrows, bent at the narrow end. L.56, W.15, T.2mm 11883 sf3016 (B6f3; early 14th century)

11195 L.39, W.10, T.2mm 5977 sf3033 (D6a7; 11th/12th century)

11196 Roughly broken at each end. L.60, W.32, T.3mm 12274 sf3056 (D6e1; 13th/14th century)

11197 Curved over into an L-shape, arms incomplete. Arms: L.48 and 47, W.24, T.3mm 11940 sf3171 (B6f1; early 14th century)

11198 L.76, W.16, T.3mm 5975 sf3210 (C6c6; mid 12th century)

11199 Broken at each end. L.54, W.17, T.2mm 12494 sf3211 (D6d1–2; late 13th century)

11200 Irregular shape. L.87, W.78, T.3mm 12485 sf3248 (D6c1; mid 13th century)

11201 Narrows. L.56, W.18, T.3mm 13315 sf3279 (B6c2; 12th/13th century–early 13th century)

11202 L.27, W.24, T.8mm 5975 sf3287 (C6c6; mid 12th century)

11203 Roughly triangular. L.38, W.33, T.10mm 12647 sf3446 (D6c1; mid 13th century)

11204 Broken at each end, one side convex. L.35, W.22, T.2mm 13454 sf3451 (B6d2; mid 13th century)

11205 Curved over at one end. L.31, W.10, T.2mm 12662 sf3453 (D6a26–d1; late 12th–mid 13th century)

11206 Curved over at one end and broken at the other. L.48, W.10, T.2mm 12671 sf3471 (D6a16; mid 12th century)

11207 Bent near one end. L.48, W.17, T.4mm 12863 sf3710 (C6e4; 12th/13th century)

11208 Flattened towards one end, sheared off at the other. Hammered surface. L.79, W.16, T.5mm 16410 sf4339 (D6a12; early 12th century)

11209 Narrows towards one end, flattened towards the other. L.155, W.20, T.6mm 16734 sf4394 (C6a1, D6a1; late 11th century)

11210 Slightly bent. Roughly triangular, thickened and severed at one end. Longest side has a marking out line. L.69, W.19, T.4mm 16612 sf4583 (D6a1; late 11th century)

11211 Irregular, central rib. L.61, W.48, T.6mm 17253 sf4656 (B6a7; early 12th century)

11212 L.20, W.15mm 15166 sf4794 (B6a7; early 12th century)

11213 Folded to form a loop at one end, below which the halves lie flush and one end is then folded over the other. L.76, T.3mm; loop: W.18 18256 sf4820 (B6a7; early 12th century) (*Fig.1318*)

11214 Curved, flattened slightly from one side to the other. L.69, W.30, T.6mm 2284 sf4932 (B6v1; 13th–early 14th century)

11215 Narrows, one side convex; broken at both ends, curved over at one. L.41, W.25, T.4mm 17787 sf5235 (C6c1; early 12th century)

11216 Slightly curved, tapers to one end where broken. At the other end is a rolled tip. L.90, W.9, T.3mm 15285 sf5265 (B6a1; late 11th century) (*Fig.1318*)

11217 Narrows slightly. L.76, W.15, T.4mm 6258 sf5425 (C6c3, D6a5; late11th/early 12th century)

11218 Narrows to a rounded end. Possible knife tang. L.38, W.9, T.2mm 17787 sf7223 (C6c1; early 12th century)

11219 L.21, W.15, T.3mm 17599 sf11428 (C6c6; mid 12th century)

11220 Roughly oval. L.44, W.18, T.3mm 17599 sf11437 (C6c6; mid 12th century)

11221 Five fragments. 17129 sf11447 (D6a2; late 11th century)

11222 One side convex. L.20, W.11, T.2mm 18194 sf11480 (B6c2; 12th/13th century)

11223 Narrows slightly. L.64, W.11, T.3mm 9248 sf14699 (D6c1; mid 13th century)

11224 Flattened to a roughly rounded tip at one end. L.33, W.12, T.5mm 5000 sf14739 (C6c6; mid 12th century)

11225 Narrows to a rounded end, the other end ragged. L.43, W.33, T.5mm 5331 sf14794 (D6a17; late 12th century)

11226 Curved over at one end, broken at both. L.65, W.25, T.3mm 1219 sf14930 (C6z1; late 14th–early 15th century)

11227 L.35, W.10mm 9224 sf14991 (C6e9; mid 13th century)

11228 Broken at one end, flattened to the other. L.49, W.15, T.7mm 10847 sf15117 (C6f1; late 13th century)

11229 One end broken, one side convex. L.27, W.12, T.3mm 3344 sf15255 (A6g1; 13th/14th century)

11230 Slightly curved, one side straight, the other side concave, widened and flattened at one end. Surfaces irregular. L.45, W.20, T.4mm 3235 sf15273 (A6g1; 13th/14th century)

11231 L.28, W.8, T.2mm 3235 sf15280 (A6g1; 13th/14th century)

11232 Two pieces, very corroded. L.65, W.13mm 2192 sf15343 (A6z4; early 12th century)

11233 L.44, W.13, T.2mm 11570 sf15409 (B6g1; 14th/15th century)

11234 (a) Roughly triangular, one side straight, others irregular. Four small indentations lie in a line parallel and adjacent to the straight side and there is one other. L.34, W.20mm; (b) Fragment with three small indentations in it. L.16, W.13mm; (c) Rolled up into a roughly shaped

tube. L.40, W.13mm. All have traces of plating (tin with trace copper, lead and zinc). 4620 sf15505 (C6e9; mid 13th century)

11235 Three straight sides, the fourth is broken. L.18, W.8mm 18331 sf15738 (B6a5, C6c3; early 12th century)

11236 L.66mm 10527 sf15905 (B6g11; early 16th century)

11237 Curved, broken each end; one face has concave facets along the sides. L.56, W.23, T.10mm 10464 sf15907 (C6g7; 14th/15th century)

11238 L.28, W.9, T.1mm u/s sf281

11239 Curved over at one end. L.36, W.14, T.2mm u/s sf333

Strips

All have rectangular cross-section unless stated.

11240 C-shaped. L.23, W.9, T.2mm 1284 sf244 (C6z1; late 14th–early 15th century)

11241 Flattened at one end. L.43, W.4, T.3mm 4125 sf312 (C6z1; late 14th–early 15th century)

11242 Slightly curved. L.48, W.4, T.4mm 4043 sf370 (C6z1; late 14th–early 15th century)

11243 L.43, W.4, T.4mm 4043 sf372 (C6z1; late 14th–early 15th century)

11244 Two strips. L.25, W.5, T.2mm 1609 sf415 (D6e1–3; 13th/14th century)

11245 Bent at 90° near each end. L.117; arms: L.27, T.3mm 3190 sf634 (A6j19; 16th century)

11246 Bent in the centre. L.42, W.3, T.2mm 4409 sf638 (C6g17; 15th/16th century)

11247 Slightly burred at one end. L.52, W.7, T.6mm 4604 sf740 (C6g19; mid 14th century)

11248 Bent over towards one end and tapers to a point at each end. L.200, W.13mm 9057 sf889 (C6e11, D6e3; mid 13th century)

11249 Roughly C-shaped. L.27, W.4, T.1mm 3232 sf965 (A6j8; 15th/16th century)

11250 One half has oval, spatulate shape, other half tapers to a point. L.48, W.12, T.5mm 1506 sf1041 (D6e9; mid 14th century) (*Fig.1318*)

11251 Slightly curved, rounded cross-section. L.110, W.6mm 4875 sf1056 (C6e11; mid 13th century)

11252 Flattened and widened slightly near one end. L.120, W.14, T.5mm 9252 sf1095 (D6e1; 13th/14th century)

11253 Slightly bent in the centre. L.180, W.9, T.2mm 9252 sf1114 (D6e1; 13th/14th century)

11254 Rounded cross-section. L.58, W.5mm 4620 sf1116 (C6e9; mid 13th century)

11255 L.55, T.2mm 4620 sf1129 (C6e9; mid 13th century)

11256 Tapers. L.71, W.10, T.3mm 9249 sf1131 (D6d2; late 13th century)

11257 Slightly curved, D-shaped cross-section, broken at each end. L.90, W.5, T.2mm 9078 sf1151 (D6e1; 13th/14th century)

11258 L.46, W.7, T.2mm 4620 sf1155 (C6e9; mid 13th century)

11259 Broken at each end. L.87, W.7, T.2mm 4620 sf1202 (C6e9; mid 13th century)

11260 L-shaped, one end curved and broken, the other end bent. Arms: L.65 and 50, W.9, T.3mm 4620 sf1225 (C6e9; mid 13th century)

11261 Folded in two. L.72, T.5mm 4620 sf1262 (C6e9; mid 13th century)

11262 Roughly triangular. L.51, W.15mm 9224 sf1334 (C6e9; mid 13th century)

11263 Slightly curved, tapers from one end to the centre, the thicker end is irregularly shaped. L.112, W.7, T.4mm 9224 sf1344 (C6e9; mid 13th century)

11264 Roughly C-shaped. L.170, W.7, T.2mm 9224 sf1381 (C6e9; mid 13th century)

11265 Diamond-shaped cross-section, becomes C-shaped at one end. L.53, W.4, T.4mm 9224 sf1435 (C6e9; mid 13th century)

11266 Curved and bent over at one end. L.75, W.5, T.1mm 9224 sf1441 (C6e9; mid 13th century)

11267 Curved. L.53, W.8, T.4mm 4620 sf1444 (C6e9; mid 13th century)

11268 C-shaped. L.22, W.2, T.1mm 5330 sf1478 (C6e5; early 13th century)

11269 L.35, W.6, T.2mm 5373 sf1507 (C6e7; early 13th century)

11270 Slightly curved, flattened towards one end. L.54, W.10, T.5mm 9330 sf1568 (D6a25; 12th/13th century)

11271 Tapers to a point. L.57, W.8, T.8mm 9305 sf1648 (D6a24; 12th/13th century)

11272 L.58, W.9, T.7mm 5373 sf1650 (C6e7; early 13th century)

11273 Slightly bent in the centre. L.75, W.5, T.5mm 5545 sf1663 (D6a17–23; late 12th–12th/13th century)

11274 Tapers to a point at one end, thicker end flattened. L.70, W.11, T.2mm 5415 sf1664 (C6c6, D6a7; mid 12th century)

11275 Tapers. L.73, W.10, T.10mm 5333 sf1768 (D6a17; late 12th century)

11276 Curved at one end, tapers to the other, widened slightly in the centre. L.76, W.14, T.2mm 5484 sf1842 (C6e1, D6a16; later 12th century)

11277 (a) Bent into a rough C-shape. L.245, W.7, T.2mm; (b) L.70, W.67, T.2mm 9305 sf1869 (D6a24; 12th/13th century)

11278 One end flattened, widened and curved over; the other rounded and spatulate; surfaces irregular. L.124, W.10, T.3mm 5348 sf1981 (C6e1, D6a16; 12th–13th century) (Fig.1318)

11279 L.31, W.7, T.1mm 5348 sf2048 (C6e1, D6a16; 12th–13th century)

11280 Two thin strips. L.32 and 25mm 9330 sf2135 (D6a25; 12th/13th century)

11281 L.48, W.5, T.5mm 5981 sf2205 (C6c3, D6a5; late 11th/early 12th century)

11282 Narrows to a point at one end, broken at the other. L.52, W.12, T.1mm 1572 sf2251 (D6y1; late 12th–13th century)

11283 Two strip fragments fused together. 9397 sf2264 (D6a17–23; late 12th–12th/13th century)

11284 Tapers slightly. L.39, W.13, T.6mm 9481 sf2295 (D6a14; mid 12th century)

11285 Tapers to a rounded end, at the other end it widens and thickens sharply before coming to a straight oblique cut. L.105, W.25, T.9mm 5238 sf2303 (C6e5, D6a24; early 13th century)

11286 A looped eye at one end, flattened and widened slightly before break at the other. Possibly a handle. L.81, W.12, T.3mm 3235 sf2386 (A6g1; 13th/14th century)

11287 Slightly curved, irregular sides and faces, tapers roughly towards the ends, one bent over, the other spatulate. L.125, W.8, T.3mm 11106 sf2404 (B6c8; early 13th century)

11288 C-shaped strip fragment. L.16, T.1mm 12147 sf2517 (D6e7; early 14th century)

11289 L.55, W.20mm 12147 sf2526 (D6e7; early 14th century)

11290 Badly corroded. Tapers to a wedge-shaped tip. At the thicker end it widens and has a roughly rounded terminal, now broken. L.129, W.13, T.8mm 10527 sf2576 (B6g11; early 16th century)

11291 Curved. L.87, W.4, T.2mm 10546 sf2592 (C6g6; late 14th century)

11292 Corroded. Curved. L.52, W.10mm 10560 sf2606 (B6g10; 15th/16th century)

11293 Curved near one end, rounded cross-section. Arms L.125 and 75, T.4mm 10264 sf2629 (D6f7; late 15th century)

11294 T-shaped, the cross-arm is wider, thicker and broken at one end. L.36, W.25, T.6mm 10822 sf2660 (D6f1; mid–late 14th century)

11295 Curved, rounded cross-section, broken at one end, looped over at the other. L.77, T.2mm 10634 sf2690 (B6f12; late 14th century)

11296 Double crank-shaped. L.82, W.12, T.3mm 11507 sf2753 (B6c6; early 13th century)

11297 Tapers to a rounded wedge-shaped tip at one end; at the other widens into what was probably a rounded terminal, now incomplete. L.108, W.20, T.4mm 12054 sf2773 (C6e11; mid 13th century)

11298 Tapers. L.77, W.13, T.6mm 11565 sf2780 (B6g3; early 15th century)

11299 Slightly curved, tapers, tip broken off, rounded cross-section. L.49, W.15mm 11680 sf2875 (B6g1; 14th/15th century)

11300 L.81, W.11, T.2mm 3539 sf2888 (A6d1; 11th/12th century)

11301 L.111, W.3mm 12257 sf2938 (D6e5; early 14th century)

11302 Bent into a C-shape, rounded cross-section. L.90, T.1mm 11803 sf2942 (B6g1; 14th/15th century)

11303 Slightly bent over in the centre. L.210, W.10, T.2mm 9224 sf2967 (C6e9; mid 13th century)

11304 Tapers at one end. L.172, W.9, T.5mm 9224 sf2970 (C6e9; mid 13th century)

11305 Looped-eye terminal at one end, the other end broken. L.130, W.16, T.2mm 9224 sf2981 (C6e9; mid 13th century)

11306 Bent at one end, rounded cross-section. L.80, W.2mm 12274 sf2987 (D6e1; 13th/14th century)

11307 Curves towards one end. L.64, W.7, T.2mm 12106 sf2991 (C6e9, D6e1; mid 13th century)

11308 Broken at one end, pinched at the other, bent in the centre. L.60, W.9, T.2mm 9224 sf3009 (C6e9; mid 13th century)

11309 Bent over at one end and curved at the other. L.62, W.10, T.6mm 11913 sf3028 (B6f1; early 14th century)

11310 Widens and ?bifurcates at the head, rounded cross-section. L.82, W.14mm 12422 sf3040 (D6e1; 13th/14th century)

11311 Rounded cross-section. L.38, T.7mm 12412 sf3065 (C6e5; early 13th century)

11312 Tapers towards each end. L.108, W.6mm 13302 sf3319 (B6f5, C6f6; early 14th century)

11313 Tapers, bent over at narrow end. L.55, W.16, T.2mm 12578 sf3327 (D6a16–19; mid–late 12th century)

11314 Curved and tapers to a wedge-shaped tip. L.69, W.14, T.10mm 12489 sf3337 (D6e1; 13th/14th century)

11315 Twisted and curved, very irregular in form. L.95, T.10mm 11857 sf3342 (B6f4; early 14th century)

11316 Tapers and is curved over at the tip. L.65, W.7, T.4mm 12412 sf3359 (C6e5; early 13th century)

11317 Rounded cross-section, broken at one end, at the other flattened and widened before tapering to a wedge-shaped tip. L.151, W.10, T.5mm 3460 sf3430 (A6c2; 12th century)

11318 Curves a little towards one end. L.68, W.8, T.2mm 11965 sf3468 (B6e1; late 13th century)

11319 L-shaped. Arms: L.49 and 18, T.6mm 13591 sf3479 (B6c9; 13th century)

11320 L.63, W.7, T.2mm 9224 sf3533 (C6e9; mid 13th century)

11321 One end rounded, the other broken. L.80, W.11, T.2mm 7782 sf3535 (D6y1; late 12th–13th century)

11322 Flattened at one end which is rounded. L.74, W.7, T.3mm 13660 sf3553 (A6n3, B6c1; late 12th/early 13th century)

11323 At one end flattened and widened as if to form a terminal. L.170, W.13, T.6mm 13454 sf3593 (B6d2; mid 13th century)

11324 Irregular surfaces due to hammering; flattened and widened at each end. L.124, W.15, T.4mm 13465 sf3633 (B6c1; 12th/13th century)

11325 Very corroded. L.65mm 13215 sf3722 (B6w1, C6z1; mid 13th century)

11326 L.70, W.6, T.4mm 12982 sf3760 (D6a18; late 12th century)

11327 Tapers to each end. L.165, T.8mm 3208 sf3764 (A6j1; 15th century)

11328 Elongated C-shape, broken at each end, tips curve forward a little (possibly a handle). L.87, W.5mm 12853 sf3790 (D6a22; 12th/13th century)

11329 Was curved, now bent, D-shaped cross-section, thickened at one end. Arms: L.55 and 50, W.12mm 13243 sf3816 (B6a7; early 12th century) (*Fig.1318*)

11330 Curved and narrows to one end, broken at the other. Possibly a part-made buckle as *12667*. L.74, W.14, T.5mm 9815 sf3861 (D6a22; 12th/13th century)

11331 Tapers to a point and is curved. Cross-section becomes rounded towards the tip. L.66, W.9, T.9mm 12619 sf3880 (D6a24; 12th/13th century)

11332 Tapers towards both ends, curved near one end, curled over at the other. L.65, T.4mm 12363 sf3884 (C6e5; early 13th century)

11333 Slightly bent, flattened and widened a little towards one end. L.123, W.6mm 12501 sf3890 (C6e7; early 13th century)

11334 Flattened and widened at one end. L.40, W.15, T.4mm 5975 sf3895 (C6c6; mid 12th century)

11335 Curved over at one end. L.83, W.7, T.3mm 12578 sf3910 (D6a16–18; mid–late 12th century)

11336 L.56, W.4, T.2mm 12839 sf3991 (C6d21; late 12th century)

11337 Tapers; flattened and curved over at the wider end. L.69, W.19, T.5mm 15124 sf4131 (B6a7; early 12th century)

11338 Tapers to a wedge-shaped tip and is slightly curved; roughly broken at the thicker end. L.77, W.18, T.9mm 15202 sf4156 (B6a1; late 11th century)

11339 Slightly curved, tapers to a rounded tip, broken at one end. L.140, W.13, T.3mm 16464 sf4157 (D6a19; late 12th century)

11340 L-shaped, diamond-shaped cross-section. Arms: L.57 and 28, T.9mm 16525 sf4218 (D6a13–14; mid 12th century)

11341 L.55, W.8mm 16731 sf4387 (C6d21; late 12th century)

11342 Tapers. L.68, W.15, T.9mm 16797 sf4631 (C6d17; late 12th century)

11343 L.66, W.8, T.4mm 17397 sf4828 (B6a5; 11th/12th century)

11344 Tapers to a wedge-shaped tip. L.153, T.3mm 13800 sf4859 (B6d2, C6e8; mid 13th century)

11345 Tapers irregularly to a point and is slightly twisted. Roughly rounded cross-section. L.131, W.7mm 18366 sf4905 (B6a5; 11th/12th century)

11346 One end turned over, the other broken. L.24, W.5, T.5mm 18256 sf4914 (B6a7; early 12th century)

11347 L.56, W.8, T.2mm 17551 sf4917 (C6c3; early 12th century)

11348 L.45, W.6, T.2mm 16734 sf5034 (C6a1, D6a1; late 11th century)

11349 U-shaped, one arm longer than the other and broken; the other has a rounded tip. L.55, W.28, T.7mm 6258 sf5041 (C6c3, D6a5; late 11th/early 12th century) (*Fig.1318*)

11350 Tapers. L.46, W.5, T.2mm 18134 sf5109 (B6c5; early 13th century)

11351 U-shaped, with a projection from the rear. L.42, W.17, T.6mm 6339 sf5129 (D6a1; late 11th century)

11352 Broken at one end. L.90, W.10, T.4mm 13902 sf5149 (B6c3; 12th/13th century)

11353 Tapers to a rounded tip (possibly a staple arm). L.35, W.11, T.3mm 17740 sf5152 (C6c3; early 12th century)

11354 Notch in centre of one face; comma-shaped strip welded to one end. Possibly from a lock. Plated (tin). L.61, W.28, T.2mm 18331 sf5209 (B6a5, C6c3; early 12th century)

11355 Tapers. L.35, W.5, T.2mm 17787 sf5213 (C6c1; early 12th century)

11356 A rolled terminal at one end and broken at the other. L.50, W.2; terminal: W.14mm 18366 sf5298 (B6a5; 11th/12th century) (*Fig.1318*)

11357 L.39, W.5, T.2mm 13902 sf5303 (B6c3; 12th/13th century)

11358 At one end flattened and widened into a plate which then narrows and is incomplete; at the other end tapers and the tip is spirally twisted. L.54mm 17890 sf5433 (B6a1, C6a1; late 11th century)

11359 Tapers a little to each end. L.55, W.13, T.10mm 17890 sf5441 (B6a1, C6a1; late 11th century)

11360 Bent. Triangular cross-section. L.78, W.9, T.5mm 16612 sf5443 (D6a1; late 11th century)

11361 Tapers to a spatulate wedge-shaped tip; sheared off at the thicker end. Irregular hammered surfaces. L.92, W.8, T.6mm 18331 sf5465 (B6a5, C6c3; early 12th century)

11362 Tapers; cut obliquely at the thicker end, rounded tip. L.73, W.11, T.11mm 17890 sf5535 (B6a1, C6a1; late 11th century)

11363 L.50, W.5, T.2mm 17890 sf5590 (B6a1, C6a1; late 11th century)

11364 Tapers; flattened at the wider end. L.39, W.5mm 6339 sf5591 (D6a1; late 11th century)

11365 Flattened and widened from one end to the other. The thicker end is cut obliquely. L.43, W.13, T.9mm 6258 sf5777 (C6c3, D6a5; late 11th/early 12th century)

11366 S-shaped, tapers, broken at the thicker end. Possibly a staple or a hook. L.61, W.6, T.6mm 17551 sf5928 (C6c3; early 12th century)

11367 Flattened and widened slightly towards one end. L.60, W.8, T.5mm 17551 sf5929 (C6c3; early 12th century)

11368 L-shaped, irregular thickness, longer arm curled over at tip. W.7, T.4mm; arms: L.64, W.34, 13964 sf6030 (B6c8; early 13th century)

11369 L-shaped. Arms: L.30 and 10, W.4mm 13964 sf6051 (B6c8; early 13th century)

11370 Broken at one end, at the other welded to an irregular oval plate. L.46, W.22, T.6mm 16612 sf6124 (D6a1; late 11th century)

11371 L.54, W.8, T.3mm 6291 sf6889 (C6c1, D6a3; late 11th/early 12th century)

11372 L.80, W.5mm 6258 sf6914 (C6c3, D6a5; late 11th/early 12th century)

11373 Curved at one end, broken at the other. L.30, W.4, T.2mm 16615 sf7378 (D6a3–9, late 11th century–early 12th century)

11374 Tapers. L.83, W.6, T.5mm 16734 sf11445 (C6a1, D6a1; late 11th century)

11375 Narrows slightly, burred tip. Possibly a small wedge. L.41, W.11, T.5mm 3362 sf14642 (A6ef; 13th century)

11376 L.57, W.3mm 5348 sf14644 (C6e1, D6a16; 12th–13th century)

11377 Rounded cross-section. L.57, T.2mm 3382 sf14654 (A6f2; 13th century)

11378 Narrows, slightly curved, roughly broken at each end. L.50, W.12, T.6mm 9122 sf14683 (D6e1; 13th/14th century)

11379 L.58, W.4, T.4mm 9252 sf14697 (D6e1; 13th/14th century)

11380 Narrows to a broken end. L.82, W.10, T.2mm 5206 sf14723 (B6c4, C6e6; early 13th century)

11381 Slightly irregular. L.77, W.6, T.4mm 5262 sf14725 (D6d1; late 13th century)

11382 Slightly bent. L.94, W.6mm 5000 sf14729 (C6c6 mid 12th century)

11383 L.91, W.3, T.4mm 5000 sf14733 (C6c6; mid 12th century)

11384 L.28, W.11, T.4mm 5000 sf14735 (C6c6; mid 12th century)

11385 One side convex, tapers from centre to each end, bent at one end. L.46, W.8, T.2mm 5000 sf14738 (C6c6; mid 12th century)

11386 L.28, W.11, T.2mm 5000 sf14742 (C6c6; mid 12th century)

11387 Flattened to a rounded wedge-shaped tip, stepped at the thicker end. Possible spring or nail. L.60, W.6, T.4mm 9330 sf14757 (D6a25; 12th/13th century)

11388 Narrows. L.44, W.9, T.5mm 5415 sf14774 (C6c6, D6a7; mid 12th century)

11389 Flattened slightly to one end. L.74, W.9, T.7mm 5230 sf14781 (D6a7; 11th/12th century)

11390 Rounded cross-section, one end wedge-shaped, the other split in two. L.85, T.5mm 5186 sf14785 (C6e7; early 13th century)

11391 L-shaped. Possibly an incomplete staple. Arms: L.47 and 21, W.6, T.4mm 5331 sf14793 (D6a17; late 12th century)

11392 Two strips, one bent at one end. L.25, W.8, T.2mm 3509 sf14807 (A6e1; early 13th century)

11393 L.55, W.5, T.5mm 18331 sf14820 (B6a5, C6c3; early 12th century)

11394 Tapers slightly, bent at narrow end. L.45, W.6, T.4mm 12180 sf14823 (D6e5; early 14th century)

11395 Rough U-shape. Possibly a collar or staple fragment. L.20, W.16, T.5mm 12278 sf14825 (D6e3; 13th/14th century)

11396 Tapers, curved over at 90° at the narrow end. L.80, W.12, T.2mm 5263 sf14832 (D6c1; mid 13th century)

11397 Tapers a little at each end. L.94, W.4mm 5263 sf14835 (D6c1; mid 13th century)

11398 Probably two strips welded together which have parted in the centre. L.68, W.10, T.8mm 12745 sf14846 (D6a24; 12th/13th century)

11399 Possible wedge. L.70, W.20mm 1141 sf14855 (C6i2; 17th/18th century)

11400 Bent in the centre. L.50, W.5, T.2mm 5484 sf14862 (C6e1, D6a16; later 12th century)

11401 Stepped head. Possibly a nail. L.40, W.5mm 12018 sf14863 (D6e9; mid 14th century)

11402 Possible comb tooth. L.57, W.6mm 12018 sf14864 (D6e9; mid 14th century)

11403 Narrows, one side straight, other slightly concave. L.59, W.8, T.2mm 11879 sf14868 (B6e2; 13th/14th century)

11404 Tapers, broken at thick end. L.96, W.12, T.5mm 12062 sf14885 (C6e10; mid 13th century)

11405 Flattened near one end, curved over and broken at the other. L.68, W.7, T.5mm 5348 sf14898 (C6e1, D6a16; 12th–13th century)

11406 Pinched off at one end. L.45, W.13, T.6mm 12125 sf14948 (D6e7; early 14th century)

11407 Flattened at one end. L.58, W.10, T.8mm 12179 sf14955 (D6e5; early 14th century)

11408 L.50, W.4, T.4mm 12791 sf14972 (C6e3; 12th/13th century)

11409 L.42, W.5, T.5mm 9305 sf15010 (D6a24; 12th/13th century)

11410 Flattened to a rounded wedge-shaped tip. Possible staple arm. L.45, W.8, T.2mm 9305 sf15011 (D6a24; 12th/13th century)

11411 L.81, W.6, T.4mm 9224 sf15013 (C6e9; mid 13th century)

11412 Curved at 90° near one end. Arms: L.54 and 17, W.6, T.34mm 9224 sf15020 (C6e9; mid 13th century)

11413 Narrows, curled over at the tip. L.43, W.13, T.2mm 9224 sf15021 (C6e9; mid 13th century)

11414 L.53, T.4mm 9224 sf15023 (C6e9; mid 13th century)

11415 L-shaped. Arms: L.20 and 19, W.4, T.2mm 9224 sf15025 (C6e9; mid 13th century)

11416 L.23, W.6, T.2mm 9224 sf15027 (C6e9; mid 13th century)

11417 L.31, W.10, T.4mm 4060 sf15070 (C6i1; late 17th century)

11418 L.39, W.5, T.2mm 4043 sf15072 (C6z1; late 14th–early 15th century)

11419 Roughly crank-shaped, broken at each end. L.66, W.11, T.6mm 4399 sf15082 (C6g18; 15th/16th century)

11420 Rounded cross-section, curves a little at one end. L.49, W.8mm 10779 sf15090 (C6f4–g4; early–late 14th century)

11421 Rounded cross-section, broken at each end (possibly modern). L.46, T.16mm 10280 sf15097 (B6g13, C6g17; late 15th/early 16th century)

11422 Flattened and widened at one end where ?broken over a hole. L.56, W.8, T.4mm 10758 sf15107 (B6g6; 15th century)

11423 Rounded cross-section, curved over at one end. L.43, T.3mm 10832 sf15118 (C6g1; early–mid 14th century)

11424 Tapers, thick end burred, other broken. L.63, W.10, T.5mm 10641 sf15127 (B6g4; early 15th century)

11425 L.34, W.8, T.8mm 16410 sf15151 (D6a12; early 12th century)

11426 L.38, W.7, T.3mm 16535 sf15155 (D6a9; early 12th century)

11427 Sides convex, thickest point off-centre, narrows to each end. L.60, W.9, T.4mm 16535 sf15156 (D6a9; early 12th century)

11428 Tapers, irregular faces. L.58, W.10mm 16734 sf15176 (C6a1, D6a1; late 11th century)

11429 Tapers slightly. L.108, W.18, T.10mm 17397 sf15187 (B6a5; 11th/12th century)

11430 Narrows slightly, one half has a rounded cross-section, thicker end flattened and bent. L.75, W.5mm 17040 sf15199 (D6a9; early 12th century)

11431 L.26, W.4, T.4mm 17787 sf15203 (C6c1; early 12th century)

11432 Roughly rounded cross-section, tapers to a point at each end. Possibly a tool. L.64, T.12mm 4591 sf15215 (C6g19; mid 14th century)

11433 Slightly curved at one end. L.67, W.10, T.3mm 4540 sf15228 (C6e13; mid 13th century)

11434 Rounded cross-section. L.123, T.6mm 4012 sf15241 (C6i3; 17th–18th century)

11435 Very corroded. L.79mm 4012 sf15243 (C6i3; 17th–18th century)

11436 Chisel cut at one end, broken at other. L.31, W.9, T.6mm 3493 sf15263 (A6c1; 12th century)

11437 Bent in two places, narrows towards each end. L.132, W.8, T.2mm 3235 sf15275 (A6g1; 13th/14th century)

11438 Slightly curved, broken at each end. L.96, W.14, T.5mm 11577 sf15309 (B6g12; early 16th century)

11439 Irregular shape, tapers to a wedge tip at one end and curved over, broken at the other. Possible hook or staple. L.83, W.14, T.8mm 11951 sf15325 (B6f3; early 14th century)

11440 One end rounded. L.57, W.3, T.3mm 1034 sf15328 (C6h3–4; early–mid 16th century)

11441 L.40, W.4, T.2mm 6281 sf15416 (D6a4; late 11th century)

11442 L.61, W.5, T.4mm 6257 sf15419 (C6c4; early 12th century)

11443 L.40, W.6, T.6mm 6257 sf15420 (C6c4; early 12th century)

11444 L.30, W.5mm 12191 sf15429 (D6e3–4; 13th/14th century)

11445 Tapers, curved over at 90° at the thicker end. L.74, W.4, T.4mm 3101 sf15526 (A6j25; 16th century)

11446 L.45, W.5, T.5mm 6257 sf15779 (C6c4; early 12th century)

11447 Tapers to wedge-shaped tip, broken roughly at the thicker end. Possible staple arm. L.47, W.11, T.7mm 5331 sf15783 (D6a17; late 12th century)

11448 Expands in the middle and is flattened and curved over at one end. Diamond-shaped cross-section. Possible awl. L.39, W.7mm 5539 sf15784 (C6e2–6; 12th/13th century)

11449 One end has a rolled tip, the other is recurved and broken. L.53, W.7mm u/s sf2403

11450 Slightly curved. L.71, W.4mm u/s sf3018

11451 Very corroded. Looped. L.33, W.15mm u/s sf3927

11452 L.40, W.8, T.5mm u/s sf5612

11453 C-shaped. D.25, W.10, T.4mm u/s sf6269

11454 Curved, widened and flattened at one end, broken at the other. L.73, W.10mm u/s sf7346

11455 Narrows. L.43, W.13mm u/s sf11556

11456 L.53, W.5, T.2mm u/s sf15124

Wire

11457 Incomplete large loop, twisted to form small loop at head. L.245 4252 sf496 (C6i4; 16th–19th century)

11458 Two strips spirally twisted together. L.142mm 4252 sf755 (C6i4; 16th–19th century)

Building tools

Trowel

11459 The blade has slightly convex sides which converge on a rounded tip. It has two sloping shoulders below the tang which is crank-shaped and probably tapered to a point. Blade: L.117, W.69; tang: L.62, W.14mm u/s sf20

Metalworking tools

Hammer heads

11460 One arm has a sub-rounded cross-section, the other has a rectangular cross-section and a claw tip, now damaged. Handle hole is oval, two projections from the junction of the arms run alongside and with the aid of a rivet grip the wooden handle of which a fragment remains. Wood is ash. L.200, W.25, T.25; projections: L.80mm 10333 sf2550 (B6g13, C6g15; late 15th/early 16th century) (Fig.1326)

11461 One arm is wedge-shaped and widens towards the face. The other arm has a sub-rectangular cross-section and tapers towards the face which is burred. The eye is a sub-rectangular shape (some wood remains in it). L.115, W.25, T.9mm 11416 sf2836 (B6c2–6; 12th/13th century–early 13th century)

Punches

11462 Possibly incomplete. Shaft has a rectangular cross-section and tapers to a wedge-shaped tip. L.61, W.11, T.6mm 4620 sf1127 (C6e9; mid 13th century)

11463 Shaft has a roughly rectangular cross-section and tapers to a blunt, pointed tip. Upper part of shaft also tapers slightly towards the head, which is slightly burred. L.60, W.8, T.8mm 5348 sf2053 (C6e1, D6a16; 12th–13th century) (Figs.1327–8)

11464 At its thickest at about one-third of the shaft's length down from the head; from here it tapers to a blunt tip and tapers upwards slightly to the head which is rectangular and burred. Cross-section immediately below the head is rectangular, but for much of the shaft's length the corners are rounded and each of the wider faces have a rough channel running down their centre, apparently made by folding-in of the edges. Narrower faces roughly convex. L.123, W.19, T.14mm 5981 sf2234 (C6c3, D6a5; late 11th/early 12th century) (Figs.1327–8)

11465 Shaft tapers towards a wedge-shaped tip and also towards the head which is burred. Wider faces of the shaft have a slight channel running down the centre; narrower faces are convex. L.139, T.9, W.6mm 12368 sf3061 (D6e3; 13th/14th century) (Figs.1327–8)

11466 Shaft has a sub-rectangular cross-section and tapers to a point; the head is missing. L.63, W.10, T.9mm 13037 sf3263 (B6f4, C6g1; mid 14th century) (Fig.1328)

11467 Shaft has a rectangular cross-section and tapers to a blunt rounded tip. L.97, W.10, T.7mm 13454 sf3637 (B6d2; mid 13th century)

11468 Shaft has a rounded cross-section and tapers to a point; the head is burred. L.91, W.17mm 13912 sf3658 (B6d2, C6e8; mid 13th century) (Figs.1327–8)

Tanged punches

Arms of approximately equal length

11469 Both arms have a rectangular cross-section and taper to a point. One arm markedly stouter than the other, there is a shoulder between them. L.117; arms: L.55 and 62; W.11, T.10mm 4081 sf290 (C6i1; late 17th century) (Fig.1329)

11470 Somewhat corroded. Both arms have a rectangular cross-section and tips are missing. One arm stouter than the other and there is a shoulder between them. L.114, W.10, T.10mm 4289 sf517 (C6i4; 16th–19th century)

11471 One arm tapers to a blunt rounded tip and has a rectangular cross-section which becomes rounded at the tip. The other arm is slightly curved, has a rectangular cross-section and tapers to a pointed tip. First arm stouter than the second, shoulder between them. L.90; arms: L.50 and 40, W.10, T.8mm 9481 sf1910 (D6a14; mid 12th century) (Fig.1329)

11472 One arm has a rectangular cross-section, tip missing. Other arm has a rectangular cross-section becoming rounded towards the tip which is blunt and rounded. Second arm stouter than the first and there is a shoulder between them. L.91; arms: L.48 and 43, W.10, T.9mm 13434 sf3596 (B6c9; 13th century)

11473 One arm has a rectangular cross-section and tapers to a point. Other arm has a sub-rectangular cross-section, tapers slightly and is squared off. L.95; arms: L.48 and 47, W.12, T.12mm 12928 sf3848 (B6c2, C6e2; late 12th/early 13th century)

11474 One arm has a rectangular cross-section and tapers to a wedge-shaped tip. Other arm has a rectangular cross-section becoming rounded at the tip which is blunt and rounded. L.144; arms: L.73 and 71, W.10, T.10mm 16525 sf4301 (D6a13–14; mid 12th century) (Fig.1329)

11475 One arm has a roughly rounded cross-section and tapers to a point; other arm has a rectangular cross-section and tapers to a wedge-shaped tip. L.137, W.10, T.8mm 17890 sf5460 (B6a1, C6a1; late 11th century) (Fig.1329)

11476 One arm has a rounded cross-section and tapers to a blunt, rounded tip; other has a rectangular cross-section and tapers to a wedge-shaped tip. L.67, W.9, T.6mm 18982 sf5576 (C6b2; 11th/12th century)

11477 In the centre it has a rectangular cross-section but both arms have rounded cross-sections and taper to blunt rounded tips. L.76; arms: L.44 and 32, W.9, T.8mm 13886 sf5997 (B6a3; 11th/12th century) (*Fig.1329*)

11478 Both arms taper to a pointed tip, one has a rectangular and the other a sub-rectangular cross-section. L.107mm 12496 sf14952 (D6a24; 12th/13th century)

Arms of unequal length

In some cases the shorter arm was clearly a tang and the longer the working arm.

11479 Working arm has a rounded cross-section and tapers to a rounded tip. Tang has a rectangular cross-section, tip curved over. L.109; working arm: L.74, T.8mm 5238 sf1392 (C6e5, D6a24; early 13th century)

11480 Working arm has sub-rectangular cross-section, there is a shoulder between it and the tang which is bent over or clenched at head. L.65, W.6mm 18331 sf6892 (B6a5, C6c3; early 12th century) (*Fig.1329*)

11481 One arm, which makes up about two-thirds of the object, has a rounded cross-section and tapers to a point, tip missing; other arm has a rectangular cross-section and a rounded tip. L.111, W.6mm 16734 sf11411 (C6a1, D6a1; late 11th century) (*Fig.1329*)

11482 Longer arm has a rounded cross-section and tapers slightly to a blunt tip; shoulder between it and the shorter arm which has a rectangular cross-section, now bent. L.75mm 5000 sf15867 (C6c6; mid 12th century)

11483 Tang has a rectangular cross-section, working arm somewhat corroded, sub-rounded cross-section and rounded end. Slight shoulder. L.101, T.12mm u/s sf1872

File

11484 Tanged with a curved blade, thickest in the centre, straight end. In section it narrows slightly from the convex to the concave side. Teeth occur on the concave side (c.8–9 per cm) and on the lower half of one face. L.255; blade: W.18, T.6mm 29325 sf10510 (D6d3; late 13th century) (*Fig.1330*)

Woodworking tools

Spoon augers

All the blades have a shallow U-shaped cross-section and rounded tips unless stated.

8189 Somewhat corroded. Blade sides slightly convex. Shaft has a rectangular cross-section, except near the blade where it becomes rounded. Tang missing. L.137; blade: L.33; bit: W.12, T.7mm 4788 sf797 (C6e13; mid 13th century) (*Fig.1335*)

8190 Blade widens slightly away from the shaft which has a sub-rounded cross-section. Tang widens upwards from the shaft with two sloping shoulders before tapering to a wedge-shaped tip. L.140; blade: L.36, W.8, T.6; shaft: W.6; tang: L.36, W.11mm 4850 sf854 (C6e1; 12th/13th century) (*Figs.1335, 1337*)

8191 Blade only. Tapers to a near pointed tip and the sides are slightly convex. Broken at the junction with the shaft. Slightly twisted suggesting a clockwise motion. L.77,

W.16, T.5mm 9641 sf3222 (D6e1; 13th/14th century) (*Fig.1335*)

8192 Blade only. Roughly parallel sides and, viewed from the front, appears slightly worn on the lower right hand side. L.55, W.45, T.15mm 16534 sf4179 (D6a13; mid 12th century)

11485 Blade incomplete, shank of rounded cross-section, flattened and widened to form narrowing tang with rounded tip. L.63, W.10, T.5mm 10022 sf2439 (C6i1; late 17th century)

11486 Corroded, in three pieces. Blade incomplete, shaft has a sub-rectangular cross-section, no shoulders before a tapering tang. L.124; blade: L.23, W.12; tang: L.35mm 12727 sf3678 (D6a24; 12th/13th century)

11487 Very corroded. Tang incomplete, blade tip missing. L.84; blade: W.10, T.7mm 3235 sf15274 (A6g1; 13th/14th century) (*Fig.1335*)

Twist auger

8193 Bit has five spirals and tapers to a point. Shaft has a sub-rounded cross-section which becomes rectangular towards the bit. Tang widens upwards from the shaft with two sloping shoulders before tapering to a wedge-shaped tip. L.171; bit: L.40; tang: L.33, W.12; shank: W.8mm 5348 sf1561 (C6e1, D6a16; 12th–13th century) (*Figs.1335, 1337*)

Drawknife

11488 Blade back convex, corners rounded. Cutting edge straight and two short tapering tangs project from each end of it. L.130; blade: W.21, T.2; W. over tangs: 35mm 11298 sf2673 (A6e5, B6e1; late 13th century) (*Figs.1336–7*)

Wedges

Rectangular cross-section unless stated.

8170 Wedge or chisel. Shaft tapers slightly and has a heavily burred head. L.100, W.47, T.12mm 5348 sf1999 (C6e1, D6a16; 12th–13th century) (*Figs.1336–7*)

8171 Shaft flares slightly towards the tip and expands slightly at the head. L.71, W.23, T.18mm 15136 sf4109 (A6n2, B6a5; early 12th century) (*Figs.1336–7*)

8172 Wedge or chisel. Shaft tapers slightly, head slightly burred. L.47, W.15, T.6mm 17551 sf5930 (C6c3; early 12th century) (*Fig.1336*)

11489 Incomplete? Shaft tapers slightly, one face curves towards the other at the tip. Three chisel cuts in one edge. L.53, W.13, T.7mm 4074 sf328 (C6h1; 15th/16th century) (*Fig.1336*)

11490 Shaft slightly curved, burred head. L.64, W.12, T.11mm 5348 sf1526 (C6e1, D6a16; 12th–13th century)

11491 Head missing; shaft tapers slightly. L.69, W.15, T.10mm 9330 sf1567 (D6a25; 12th/13th century)

11492 Wedge or chisel. Shaft has an irregular cross-section caused by being slightly twisted. Burred head. L.54, W.12, T.11mm 13454 sf3872 (B6d2; mid 13th century) (*Fig.1336*)

11493 Burred head, slight neck below it, sides convex. L.59, W.15, T.8mm 3362 sf14643 (A6e5; 13th century) (*Fig.1336*)

11494 L.51, W.17, T.10mm u/s sf15125

Tanged chisel

11495 Crank-shaped tang with a blade which widens slightly to the tip. L.125, W.8, T.4mm 15136 sf4159 (A6n2, B6a5; early 12th century) (*Fig.1336*)

Leatherworking tools

Awls

Both arms with a diamond-shaped cross-section

11496 Narrow collar with central groove around the centre. L.70, W.6mm 4252 sf940 (C6i4; 16th–19th century) (*Figs.1338–9*)

11497 Narrow collar with central groove around the centre. L.79, W.13mm 4620 sf1149 (C6e9; mid 13th century) (*Figs.1338–9*)

11498 One arm bent into a C-shape. L.101, W.6, T.5mm 4620 sf1302 (C6e9; mid 13th century)

11499 One tip curved over. L.78, W.6mm 9572 sf2093 (D6a9; early 12th century) (*Fig.1338*)

11500 One arm incomplete. Narrow block-shaped collar around the centre. L.68, W.8mm 3414 sf2227 (A6e1; early 13th century) (*Figs.1338–9*)

11501 Both arms incomplete. In the centre there is a biconical moulding flanked on each side by a collar. L.59, W.5mm 3414 sf2228 (A6e1; early 13th century) (*Figs.1338–9*)

11502 Both arms curved. L.88, W.4, T.3mm 13454 sf3584 (B6d2; mid 13th century)

11503 Tip of one arm missing. L.131, W.4mm 12501 sf3734 (C6e7; early 13th century)

11504 Tip of one arm missing. In the centre is a flattened and widened area. L.94, W.11mm 18366 sf4967 (B6a5; 11th/12th century) (*Figs.1338–9*)

11505 One arm incomplete, other tip missing. L.65, T.5mm 12915 sf14969 (D6a16; mid 12th century)

Both arms with rectangular cross-sections

11506 A little off-centre there is a shoulder between the arms. One is longer and thinner than the other. Wood remains adhere to the shorter arm. L.98, W.6mm 9224 sf1386 (C6e9; mid 13th century) (*Fig.1338*)

11507 L.109, W.6mm 11458 sf3092 (B6c7; late 11th–early 12th century)

11508 One arm incomplete, other curved. Double collar in the centre. L.83, W.5mm 5779 sf3274 (C6e6; early 13th century)

11509 Slightly off-centre is a small block expansion. On each face a large triangular indentation on the sides and at the ends two smaller indentations. L.71, W.5mm 12853 sf3738 (D6a22; 12th/13th century) (*Figs.1338–9*)

11510 Narrow collar around the centre. L.66, W.7mm 13442 sf3983 (B6f1; early 14th century) (*Fig.1338*)

11511 One arm tip missing. Narrow collar around the centre. L.65, W.5mm 5000 sf14740 (C6c6; mid 12th century)

11512 L.90, W.3, T.3mm 16734 sf15178 (C6a1, D6a1; late 11th century)

One arm with a rectangular and one with a rounded cross-section

11513 Slightly off-centre there is an expansion between the arms. Wood remains adhere to the arm of rounded cross-section. L.111, W.8mm 9305 sf1700 (D6a24; 12th/13th century) (*Fig.1338*)

11514 L.120, W.6mm 13454 sf3812 (B6d2; mid 13th century) (*Fig.1338*)

11515 Arm tips missing. L.75, T.4mm 12274 sf14877 (D6e1; 13th/14th century)

11516 Tang tip missing. Working arm has a rounded cross-section, tip missing. Between tang and working arm there are four triangular notches in each edge. L.75, T.6mm 11883 sf14928 (B6f3; early 14th century) (*Fig.1338*)

11517 Arm of rectangular cross-section is largely missing. Between the arms is a rectangular expansion. L.51, W.17mm 13527 sf14951 (B6c7; late 11th–early 12th century) (*Fig.1338*)

11518 L.58, W.4mm 3493 sf15265 (A6c1; 12th century)

Other awls

11519 Elongated lozenge shape. One arm end turned over into a hook. L.86, W.12mm 9346 sf1605 (D6a25; 12th/13th century) (*Fig.1338*)

11520 One arm has a sub-rectangular cross-section and is slightly curved near the tip; cross-section rounded in the centre. Second arm has a rectangular cross-section. L.172, W.5; arms: L.131 and 41mm 5348 sf1691 (C6e1, D6a16; 12th–13th century) (*Fig.1338*)

11521 One arm missing; the other has a diamond-shaped cross-section. L.71, W.4mm 18143 sf4748 (B6c3; 12th/13th century)

11522 One arm has a rectangular cross-section, the other a sub-rectangular cross-section. L.72, W.8, T.6mm 16734 sf5188 (C6a1, D6a1; late 11th century) (*Fig.1338*)

11523 One arm has a diamond-shaped cross-section, the other is incomplete and has a rectangular cross-section. L.79, W.4mm 18366 sf5261 (B6a5; 11th/12th century)

11524 Arms have a rounded cross-section, tips missing. L.73, W.6mm 5084 sf14727 (C6e11; mid 13th century)

11525 Arms have a rounded cross-section, tips missing. L.71, T.5mm 5348 sf14896 (C6e1, D6a16; 12th–13th century)

11526 Corroded. In the centre a short expansion. L.53, W.4mm 5264 sf15800 (D6c1; mid 13th century)

Currier's knives

All the blades have straight ends unless stated.

11527 Blade only, broken above the shoulder. Back had a slight S-shape. Cutting edge was convex. L.116, W.26, T.2mm 4931 sf839 (C6g18; 15th/16th century)

11528 Blade only, broken above the shoulder. Back has a slight S-shape. Cutting edge convex. L.95, W.20, T.1.5mm 9219 sf1021 (D6e3; 13th/14th century) (*Fig.1341*)

11529 Blade only. Back has a slight S-shape. Cutting edge straight. Concave shoulder, tang tapers slightly and is squared off. L.132; blade: L.95, W.20, T.3; tang: W.7, T.4mm 9224 sf1411 (C6e9; mid 13th century)

11530 Blade only, severed at the shoulder, slightly curved. Back convex. Cutting edge S-shaped. L.122, W.24, T.3mm 5404 sf2066 (C6e9; mid 13th century) (*Fig.1341*)

11531 Blade back slightly convex. Cutting edge now somewhat irregular, straight then convex and curves up sharply at the tip. Tang tapers to a point. L.137; blade: L.100, W.25, T.2; tang: W.10, T.3mm 13665 sf3603 (A6c5, B6a7; mid 12th century) (*Fig.1341*)

11532 End of blade. Back straight, cutting edge concave. L.45, W.21, T.1mm 13454 sf3811 (B6d2; mid 13th century)

11533 Blade bent in centre. Cutting edge a pronounced S-shape. Very slight shoulder. L.140; blade: L.61, W.22, T.5mm 15136 sf4035 (A6n2, B6a5; early 12th century) Metallurgy report (*Fig.1341*)

11534 Blade only. Back straight before curving down to the tip which is rounded and curved over. Cutting edge markedly concave. L.99, W.28, T.2mm 12363 sf4094 (C6e5; early 13th century)

11535 Blade fragment. L.68, W.28, T.2mm 16170 sf4110 (D6a16; mid 12th century)

11536 Blade only. Back has a very slight S shape. Cutting edge has a pronounced S-shape with an especially marked concave area near the rear. X-radiograph shows a weld between the back and cutting edge. L.109, W.19, T.3mm 18366 sf4985 (B6a5; 11th/12th century) (*Fig.1341*)

11537 Blade back and cutting edge have a gentle S shape. Tang tapers to a point. L.176; blade: L.137, W.26, T.3; tang: W.8, T.4mm 13902 sf5169 (B6c3; 12th/13th century) (*Figs.1340–1*)

11538 Incomplete blade only. Broken above the shoulder. The back becomes concave 60mm from the break, tip rounded. Cutting edge convex. L.77, W.18, T.2mm 7788 sf3364 (modern)

Textile tools

Fibre processing spikes

Rectangular cross-section

2431 Stepped head. L.72, T.5mm 16884 sf15137 (D6a9; early 12th century)

11539 Corroded. Stepped head. L.85, W.5mm 1445 sf365 (C6x2–6; 11th/13th century–mid 13th century)

11540 Bent in two places. Stepped head. L.117, W.4mm 1550 sf819 (D6e8; early 14th century)

11541 Stepped head, tip missing. L.108, W.7mm 9213 sf1002 (D6e1; 13th/14th century)

11542 Stepped head. L.105, W.5mm 5021 sf1029 (C6e10–11; mid 13th century)

11543 Bent near base, stepped head. L.134, W.10mm 9224 sf1330 (C6e9; mid 13th century)

11544 Stepped head. L.122, W.6mm 9302 sf1362 (D6a26; 12th/13th century)

11545 Tip missing. L.96, W.7mm 9274 sf1445 (D6a5–24; 11th/12th–12th/13th century)

11546 Badly corroded, in two pieces. L.82, W.3mm 5348 sf1489 (C6e1, D6a16; 12th–13th century)

11547 Stepped head. L.83, W.4mm 5238 sf1506 (C6e5, D6a24; early 13th century)

11548 Curved. L.74, W.4mm 5348 sf1511 (C6e1, D6a16; 12th–13th century)

11549 Curved near tip, stepped head, tip missing. L.73, W.4mm 5348 sf1514 (C6e1, D6a16; 12th–13th century)

11550 Stepped head. L.82, W.4mm 9330 sf1522 (D6a25; 12th/13th century)

11551 Badly corroded, in two pieces. L.63, W.5mm 9305 sf1677 (D6a24; 12th/13th century)

11552 Stepped head. L.117, W.8mm 5415 sf1726 (C6c6, D6a7; mid 12th century)

11553 L.106, W.6mm 9397 sf1776 (D6a17–23; late 12th–12th/13th century)

11554 Stepped head. L.105, W.5mm 5395 sf1883 (C6c6, D6a7; mid 12th century)

11555 Head missing. L.62, W.4mm 9305 sf1961 (D6a24; 12th/13th century)

11556 Stepped head. L.55, W.7mm 9224 sf2267 (C6e9; mid 13th century)

11557 Stepped head, slightly curved. L.131, W.5mm 5348 sf2332 (C6e1, D6a16; 12th–13th century)

11558 Stepped head. L.76, W.5mm 11458 sf2769 (B6c7; late 11th–early 12th century)

11559 Stepped head. L.83, W.6mm 5981 sf2924 (C6c3, D6a5; late 11th/early 12th century)

11560 Stepped head, tip missing. L.82, W.4mm 12148 sf2955 (D6e5; early 14th century)

11561 L.79, W.6mm 12412 sf3068 (C6e5; early 13th century)

11562 Stepped head. Tip missing. L.79, W.3mm 12412 sf3155 (C6e5; early 13th century)

11563 L.83, W.5mm 12411 sf3260 (C6e5; early 13th century)

11564 Stepped head. L.114, W.6mm 12561 sf3302 (D6a3–11; late 11th century–12th/13th century)

11565 Stepped head. L.104, W.7mm 15106 sf3780 (B6c5; early 13th century)

11566 Stepped head. L.71, W.5mm 12572 sf3823 (C6e1; 12th/13th century)

11567 L.80, W.7mm 13454 sf3844 (B6d2; mid 13th century)

11568 L.69, W.4mm 13465 sf3933 (B6c1; 12th/13th century)

11569 Bent near tip. L.81, W.4mm 16351 sf4083 (C6d18; late 12th century)

11570 L.82, W.4mm 16130 sf4150 (D6a16; mid 12th century)

11571 Stepped head. L.91, W.5mm 16612 sf4492 (D6a1; late 11th century)

11572 Stepped head. L.78, W.4mm 17040 sf4603 (D6a9; early 12th century)

11573 Corroded, head missing. L.92, W.6mm 13902 sf4874 (B6c3; 12th/13th century)

11574 Stepped head. L.79, W.5mm 18366 sf4909 (B6a5; 11th/12th century)

11575 Stepped head. L.91, W.7mm 9813 sf5006 (D6a25; 12th/13th century)

11576 Stepped head, lower part missing. L.53, W.5mm 6281 sf5296 (D6a4; late 11th century)

11577 Stepped head. L.87, W.6mm 15285 sf5304 (B6a1; late 11th century)

11578 Head missing. L.85, W.5mm 18331 sf5355 (B6a5, C6c3; early 12th century)

11579 Stepped head. L.85, W.7mm 17788 sf5696 (B6c4, C6c1; 12th/13th century)

11580 Head corroded. L.97, W.8mm 6339 sf5702 (D6a1; late 11th century)

11581 L.85, W.6mm 17627 sf5825 (C6c6; mid 12th century)

11582 Corroded. L.74, W.5mm 17551 sf5894 (C6c3; early 12th century)

11583 Corroded. Stepped head. L.89, W.6mm 16734 sf5921 (C6a1, D6a1; late 11th century)

11584 Corroded. L.68, W.5, T.5mm 13964 sf6159 (B6c8; early 13th century)

11585 Stepped head. L.72, W.4mm 16612 sf6435 (D6a1; late 11th century)

11586 Stepped head, incomplete. L.68, W.5mm 17699 sf6696 (C6c1; early 12th century)

11587 Stepped head, tip missing. L.77, W.6mm 17890 sf7234 (B6a1, C6a1; late 11th century)

11588 L.114, W.5mm 3233 sf14600 (A6g1; 13th/14th century)

11589 Stepped head. L.112, W.6mm 12503 sf14748 (C6e3; 12th/13th century)

11590 Head missing. L.91, W.7mm 5238 sf14777 (C6e5, D6a24; early 13th century)

11591 Stepped head. L.81, W.5mm 5230 sf14782 (D6a7; 11th/12th century)

11592 Stepped head. L.107, W.5mm 5186 sf14784 (C6e7; early 13th century)

11593 Stepped head. L.96, W.5mm 6258 sf14803 (C6c3, D6a5; late11th/early 12th century)

11594 Stepped head, tip missing. L.72, W.6mm 18331 sf14818 (B6a5, C6c3; early 12th century)

11595 L.96, W.6mm 5263 sf14835 (D6c1; mid 13th century)

11596 Stepped head. L.83, W.4mm 5348 sf14889 (C6e1, D6a16; 12th–13th century)

11597 Tip missing. L.59, W.3mm 5348 sf14891 (C6e1, D6a16; 12th–13th century)

11598 Stepped head. L.72, W.5mm 13686 sf14938 (B6c5; early 13th century)

11599 Stepped head. L.82, W.4mm 9224 sf15012 (C6e9; mid 13th century)

11600 Stepped head. L.90, W.6mm 9224 sf15016 (C6e9; mid 13th century)

11601 L.82, W.6mm 10771 sf15111 (B6g4; early 15th century)

11602 Stepped head. L.82, W.4mm 16410 sf15151 (D6a12; early 12th century)

11603 Stepped head, curved towards tip. L.90, W.6mm 16734 sf15182 (C6a1, D6a1; late 11th century)

11604 Stepped head. L.91, W.5mm 10265 sf15183 (D6h2; 16th/17th century)

11605 Stepped head. L.116, W.7mm 17397 sf15189 (B6a5; 11th/12th century)

11606 Stepped head, tip missing. L.94, W.7mm 17397 sf15195 (B6a5; 11th/12th century)

11607 Stepped head, tip missing. L.74, W.7mm 17040 sf15196 (D6a9; early 12th century)

11608 Stepped head. L.87, W.4mm 17699 sf15221 (C6c1; early 12th century)

11609 Slightly curved, stepped head. L.102, W.6mm 4540 sf15227 (C6e13; mid 13th century)

11610 Tip missing. L.109, W.6mm 4141 sf15246 (C6i2; 17th/18th century)

11611 Stepped head. L.92, W.6mm 3235 sf15278 (A6g1; 13th/14th century)

11612 Head corroded. L.79, W.5mm 11656 sf15287 (B6g4; early 15th century)

11613 Stepped head. L.76, W.5mm 11632 sf15304 (B6a6; 11th/12th century)

11614 Stepped head. L.72, W.6mm 13902 sf15350 (B6c3; 12th/13th century)

11615 Stepped head. L.84, W.5mm 13568 sf15395 (B6a5; 11th/12th century)

11616 Tip missing. L.84, W.5mm 1283 sf15414 (C6z1; late 14th–early 15th century)

11617 L.71, W.5mm 6258 sf15798 (C6c3, D6a5; late11th/early 12th century)

11618 L.78, W.7mm u/s sf6091

11619 Stepped head. L.90, W.4mm u/s sf9061

11620 Bent, tip missing. L.74, W.6mm u/s sf16259

Rounded cross-section

6598 Stepped head. L.137, W.5mm 18331 sf4854 (B6a5, C6c3; early 12th century) (*Fig.802*)

6599 Stepped head. L.180, W.6mm 9330 sf1861 (Da25-6; 12th/13th century) (*Fig.1342*)

6600 Flattened head. L.142, W.7mm 11507 sf2754 (B6c6; early 13th century) (*Fig.802*)

6602 L.164, W.7mm 15040 sf3751 (B6c5; early 13th century) (*Fig.802*)

6603 L.131, W.5mm 9248 sf1072 (D6c1; mid 13th century) (*Fig.802*)

6604 L.145, W.6mm 9122 sf1045 (D6e1; 13th/14th century) (*Fig.802*)

6605 L.166, W.6mm 4620 sf1194 (C6e9; mid 13th century) (*Fig.802*)

6606 Upper 22mm slightly flattened. L.186, W.8mm 9224 sf1322 (C6e9; mid 13th century) (*Fig.802*)

6607 Stepped head. L.181, W.8mm 9224 sf1410 (C6e9; mid 13th century) (*Fig.802*)

11621 Stepped head. L.118, W.5mm 4243 sf345 (C6h1; 15th/16th century)

11622 Corroded. Flattened head, tip missing. L.83, W.6mm 1790 sf581 (D6f8; 15th/16th century)

11623 Tip missing. L.122, W.4mm 4661 sf753 (C6h1; 15th/16th century)

11624 Lower end missing. L.73, W.5mm 4570 sf758 (C6e13; mid 13th century)

11625 Broken at each end. L.85, W.5mm 4850 sf862 (C6e1; 12th/13th century)

11626 Stepped head. L.132, W.5mm 9057 sf865 (C6e11, D6e3; mid 13th century)

11627 Corroded, tip missing. L.98, W.4mm 1502 sf969 (C6e11, D6e3; mid 13th century)

11628 L.165, W.7mm 9188 sf971 (D6d3; late 13th century)

11629 L.88, W.6mm 9208 sf981 (D6e1; 13th/14th century)

11630 Head missing. L.75, W.5mm 9215 sf1022 (D6e3; 13th/14th century)

11631 Tip missing. L.119, W.6mm 9078 sf1128 (D6e1; 13th/14th century)

11632 Stepped head. L.130, W.5mm 4620 sf1146 (C6e9; mid 13th century)

11633 Stepped head, tip missing. L.182, W.6mm 5241 sf1214 (D6d3; late 13th century)

11634 Stepped head. L.154, W.6mm 5264 sf1412 (D6c1; mid 13th century)

11635 Head missing. L.94, W.5mm 9224 sf1450 (C6e9; mid 13th century)

11636 Stepped head. L.147, W.7mm 9224 sf1457 (C6e9; mid 13th century)

11637 L.136, W.5mm 5348 sf1488 (C6e1, D6a16; 12th–13th century)

11638 Tip missing, slight curve towards the tip. L.103, W.6mm 9224 sf1491 (C6e9; mid 13th century)

11639 L.116, W.4mm 9224 sf1553 (C6e9; mid 13th century)

11640 L.147, W.7mm 5373 sf1644 (C6e7; early 13th century)

11641 Tip bent at 90°, stepped head. L.109, W.6mm 9305 sf1660 (D6a24; 12th/13th century)

11642 Head missing. L.132, W.6mm 3405 sf1815 (A6f1; 13th century)

11643 Tip missing. L.83, W.6mm 5395 sf1893 (C6c6, D6a7; mid 12th century)

11644 Stepped head. L.102, W.6mm 1404 sf1953 (C6y1; late 13th–early 14th century)

11645 Stepped head. L.111, W.8mm 10333 sf2551 (B6g13, C6g15; late 15th/early 16th century)

11646 Stepped head. L.127, W.7mm 10633 sf2627 (B6g6; 15th century)

11647 Stepped head. L.98, W.6mm 11514 sf2757 (B6c2; 12th/13th century)

11648 L.93, W.5mm 11458 sf2770 (B6c7; late 11th–early 12th century)

11649 Head missing. L.97, W.7mm 11417 sf2774 (B6c7; late 11th–early 12th century)

11650 Stepped head. L.100, W.6mm 11402 sf2783 (B6g3; early 15th century)

11651 Flattened head. L.144, W.8mm 9224 sf2931 (C6e9; mid 13th century)

11652 L.141, W.6mm 9224 sf2966 (C6e9; mid 13th century)

11653 Incomplete. L.72, W.5mm 9224 sf2969 (C6e9; mid 13th century)

11654 Flattened head. L.154, W.7mm 12422 sf3066 (D6e1; 13th/14th century)

11655 L.112, W.5mm 13244 sf3242 (B6c2–6; 12th/13th century)

11656 Stepped head. L.100, W.6mm 13532 sf3592 (A6n3, B6c1; late 12th/early 13th century)

11657 Stepped head. L.153, W.7mm 13861 sf3636 (C6e7; early 13th century)

11658 Flattened and stepped head, tip missing. L.141, W.7mm 12785 sf3698 (C6e4; 12th/13th century)

11659 L.108, W.6mm 13951 sf3703 (B6c5; early 13th century)

11660 Badly corroded. L.128, W.7mm 12870 sf3711 (C6d23; late 12th century)

11661 Head missing. L.128, W.5mm 16069 sf3743 (C6e3; 12th/13th century)

11662 Tip missing. L.88, W.6mm 15106 sf3749 (B6c5; early 13th century)

11663 Lower part missing. L.86, W.5mm 12572 sf3824 (C6e1; 12th/13th century)

11664 Stepped head. L.176, W.10mm 16404 sf4132 (D6a18; late 12th century)

11665 Incomplete. L.48, W.3mm 16705 sf4327 (D6a9; early 12th century)

11666 Bent at 90° in centre. Stepped head. L.120, W.4mm 18153 sf4756 (B6c3; 12th/13th century)

11667 Head badly corroded. L.128, W.5mm 17539 sf4763 (C6d4; mid 12th century)

11668 Stepped head. L.165, W.7mm 18171 sf4769 (B6c1; 12th/13th century)

11669 Stepped head. L.86, W.5mm 17551 sf4877 (C6c3; early 12th century)

11670 Head missing. L.125, W.5mm 18172 sf4883 (B6c1; 12th/13th century)

11671 Head corroded. L.150, W.6mm 13902 sf5120 (B6c3; 12th/13th century)

11672 Head missing. L.108, W.6mm 18982 sf5587 (C6b2; 11th/12th century)

11673 Incomplete. L.60mm 16612 sf6168 (D6a1; late 11th century)

11674 Stepped head. L.75, W.6mm 17890 sf6590 (B6a1, C6a1; late 11th century)

11675 Stepped head. L.95, W.6mm 17890 sf6654 (B6a1, C6a1; late 11th century)

11676 Stepped head. L.87, W.8mm 17526 sf6874 (D6a5; 11th/12th century)

11677 Stepped head, bent at head, tip missing. L.80, W.7mm 13964 sf6984 (B6c8; early 13th century)

11678 Stepped head. L.97, W.7mm 15285 sf7229 (B6a1; late 11th century)

11679 Cross-section becomes sub-rectangular towards the tip which is missing, flattened towards the head which is stepped. L.103, W.9mm 3382 sf14655 (A6f2; 13th century)

11680 Head and tip missing. L.108, W.5mm 9252 sf14694 (D6e1; 13th/14th century)

11681 Fragment. L.62, W.5mm 9229 sf14722 (C6e9; mid 13th century)

11682 Cross-section becomes rectangular towards the head. L.113, W.7mm 5000 sf14732 (C6c6; mid 12th century)

11683 Head and tip missing. L.67, W.5mm 5786 sf14792 (C6e8; early 13th century)

11684 Cross-section becomes rectangular towards the head which is stepped, tip missing. L.97, W.5mm 6344 sf14800 (D6a1; late 11th century)

11685 Tip missing. L.98, W.6mm 6291 sf14817 (C6c1, D6a3; late 11th/early 12th century)

11686 Curved, tip missing. L.94, W.5mm 12018 sf14865 (D6e9; mid 14th century)

11687 Stepped head. L.61, W.6mm 12274 sf14876 (D6e1; 13th/14th century)

11688 Tip missing. L.67, W.5mm 5604 sf14878 (C6e2–6; 12th/13th century)

11689 Tip missing. L.82, W.6mm 13686 sf14939 (B6c5; early 13th century)

11690 Stepped head. L.104, W.6mm 9305 sf15008 (D6a24; 12th/13th century)

11691 L.107, W.6mm 9224 sf15014 (C6e9; mid 13th century)

11692 L.122, W.5mm 9224 sf15015 (C6e9; mid 13th century)

11693 Corroded. L.90, W.8mm 16462 sf15150 (C6d22; late 12th century)

11694 Head missing. L.88, W.7mm 16734 sf15179 (C6a1, D6a1; late 11th century)

11695 Lower part only. L.51, T.4mm 17786 sf15184 (C6c2; early 12th century)

11696 L.90, W.6mm 17397 sf15188 (B6a5; 11th/12th century)

11697 Stepped head, tip missing. L.66, W.7mm 10039 sf15190 (D6g1; early–mid 16th century)

11698 Cross-section becomes rectangular towards the tip, stepped head. L.87, W.7mm 17697 sf15209 (B6a4, C6c2; late 11th/early 12th century)

11699 Head missing. L.91, W.5mm 4691 sf15214 (C6g9–17; early 15th–15th/16th century)

11700 Stepped head. L.79, W.7mm 17699 sf15223 (C6c1; early 12th century)

11701 Stepped head. L.86, W.8mm 17360 sf15230 (C6d1; mid 12th century)

11702 Stepped head, tip missing. L.82, W.5mm 3051 sf15234 (A6j31; early 17th century)

11703 Stepped head. L.114, W.6mm 3359 sf15267 (A6f3; 13th century)

11704 Incomplete. L.72, W.5mm 1909 sf15300 (D6f3; mid–late 15th century)

11705 Incomplete. L.74, W.5mm 1506 sf15317 (D6e9; mid 14th century)

11706 Curved. L.100, W.6mm 1121 sf15356 (D6e10; mid 14th century)

11707 Fragment. L.55, T.5mm 10974 sf15527 (D6e7; early 14th century)

11708 L.93, W.5mm 7782 sf15851 (D6y1; late 12th–13th century)

11709 Stepped head, tip missing. L.62, W.6mm 17890 sf16107 (B6a1, C6a1; late 11th century)

11710 L.150, W.6mm u/s sf3118

11711 Stepped head. L.138, W.6mm u/s sf3651

11712 Base only. L.60, W.4mm u/s sf8713

Sub-rectangular cross-section

6601 Immediately below the head there is a fragment of binding plate around it. L.99, W.7mm 11726 sf3448 (B6c1; 12th/13th century) (*Fig.800*)

11713 Tip missing. L.74, W.4mm 4457 sf617 (C6f1; late 13th century)

11714 Stepped head. L.95, W.5mm 5415 sf1902 (C6c6, D6a7; mid 12th century)

11715 Stepped head, curved. L.92, W.5mm 11018 sf2392 (C6e6; early 13th century)

11716 Tip missing. L.102, W.5mm 13299 sf3310 (B6f4; early 14th century)

11717   Bent into L-shape. Tip missing. L.85, W.5mm 18143 sf4749 (B6c3; 12th/13th century)

11718   Stepped head. L.93, W.5mm 18366 sf4903 (B6a5; 11th/12th century)

11719   Stepped head. L.109, W.7mm 17699 sf5393 (C6c1; early 12th century)

11720   Stepped head. L.102, W.6mm 16612 sf5414 (D6a1; late 11th century)

11721   Stepped head. L.86, W.8mm 17890 sf5473 (B6a1, C6a1; late 11th century)

11722   Bent, tip missing. Stepped head. L.85, W.5mm 6339 sf5593 (D6a1; late 11th century)

11723   Stepped head, lower part missing. L.69, W.5mm 18486 sf6114 (C6b2; 11th/12th century)

11724   Stepped head, tip missing. L.113, W.7mm 3462 sf14611 (A6c1; 12th century)

11725   Incomplete, stepped head. L.70, W.6mm 6258 sf14805 (C6c3, D6a5; late11th/early 12th century)

11726   Stepped head. L.87, W.6mm 5348 sf14895 (C6e1, D6a16; 12th–13th century)

11727   Incomplete, stepped head. L.76, W.6mm 5348 sf14899 (C6e1, D6a16; 12th–13th century)

11728   Incomplete. L.64, W.8mm 17699 sf15224 (C6c1; early 12th century)

Indeterminate cross-section

11729   Very corroded. L.73mm 7782 sf3167 (D6y1; late 12th–13th century)

In addition to these spikes, there are three other iron objects from medieval contexts recorded as spikes on YAT's finds database (IADB). These are no longer available for study so are simply listed here: sf1533 (context 9224, C6e9, mid 13th century); sf15103 (context 10974, D6e7, early 14th century); sf15508 (context 4484, C6g18, 15th/16th century).

Toothed weft-beater blade

6608   A plate which widens slightly from one side to the other; the wider side is serrated with teeth c.2mm long, c.5 per cm. Traces of plating show all over one face and in a band 13mm wide along the serrated side on the other. L.175, W.40, T.2mm 3407 sf2593 (A6e1; early 13th century) (*Fig.1345*)

Tenter hooks

6609   Flattened at corner. Arms: L.51 and 29, W.13, T.6mm 12368 sf3188 (D6e3; 13th/14th century) (*Fig.1346*)

6610   One arm incomplete, flattened at corner. Arms: L.19 and 23, T.2mm 9058 sf884 (D6e8; early 14th century) (*Fig.825*)

6611   Arms: L.38 and 13, T.4mm 12147 sf2892 (D6e7; early 14th century) (*Fig.1346*)

6612   Arms: L.33 and 17, T.5mm 3083 sf15232 (A6i2; 14th/15th century)

11730   Arms: L.31 and 12, T.5mm 11507 sf3189 (B6c6; early 13th century)

Needles

Eyes round unless stated.

Heads with punched eyes

6613   Head incomplete. L.40, W.1mm 17322 sf4715 (C6c6; mid 12th century) (*Fig.830*)

6614   Head has rounded top. L.106, W.5mm 17627 sf5000 (C6c6; mid 12th century) (*Fig.830*)

6616   Head incomplete. L.115, W.3mm 16790 sf4417 (C6d14; late 12th century)

6617   Head has flattened triangular top, tip missing. L.109, W.4mm 9224 sf1367 (C6e9; mid 13th century)

6618   Head has rounded top. L.31, W.3mm 18172 sf4806 (B6c1; 12th/13th century) (*Fig.830*)

6619   Head has rounded top. L.167, W.5mm 13690 sf3575 (B6c4; 12th/13th century)

11731   Head incomplete. L.62, W.3mm 2193 sf64 (A6z5; mid 12th century)

11732   Head incomplete. L.47, W.3mm 5238 sf1454 (C6e5, D6a24; early 13th century)

11733   Oval head with countersunk eye. Shank has sub-rectangular cross-section, tip missing. L.115, W.5mm 9224 sf1521 (C6e9; mid 13th century) (*Fig.1347*)

11734   Head has triangular top. L.48, W.3mm 5238 sf1529 (C6e5, D6a24; early 13th century)

11735   Rounded top, tip missing. L.52, W.2mm 5415 sf1725 (C6c6, D6a7; mid 12th century)

11736   Lozenge-shaped eye, head has flattened triangular top, tip missing. L.63, W.4mm 5484 sf1779 (C6e1, D6a16; later 12th century)

11737   Curved. Head incomplete, oval eye, tip missing. L.34, W.3mm 5348 sf2072 (C6e1, D6a16; 12th–13th century)

11738   Curved, oval eye. L.52, T.2mm 1404 sf2125 (C6y1; late 13th–early 14th century)

11739   Complete. L.40, W.2mm 1404 sf2130 (C6y1; late 13th–early 14th century) (*Fig.1347*)

11740   Incomplete head, tip missing. L.59, W.3mm 5485 sf2313 (D6a16; mid 12th century)

11741   Head incomplete. L.51, W.2mm 5348 sf2605 (C6e1, D6a16; 12th–13th century)

11742   Curved, head incomplete. L.48, W.2mm 11332 sf2744 (B6f3; early 14th century)

11743   Head incomplete. L.42, W.1mm 12274 sf2984 (D6e1; 13th/14th century)

11744   Rectangular eye, head has flattened triangular top. L.48, W.2mm 12368 sf2993 (D6e3; 13th/14th century)

11745   Oval eye. L.53, W.2mm 13454 sf3819 (B6d2; mid 13th century)

11746   Head incomplete, tip missing. L.126, W.5mm 12578 sf4057 (D6a16–18; mid–late 12th century)

11747   Head has flattened triangular top, tip missing. L.36, W.3mm 17552 sf4787 (C6d2; mid 12th century)

11748   Head has rounded top. L.50, W.2mm 17397 sf4807 (B6a5; 11th/12th century)

11749   Head incomplete. L.39, W.2mm 6339 sf5117 (D6a1; late 11th century)

11750   Head has rounded top. L.63, W.2mm 17627 sf5690 (C6c6; mid 12th century)

11751   Head has triangular top. L.48, W.3mm 13886 sf5998 (B6a3; 11th/12th century)

11752   Oval eye, rounded top. L.50, T.2mm 13964 sf6203 (B6c8; early 13th century)

11753   Head incomplete, tip missing. L.34, T.3mm 10822 sf15119 (D6f1; mid–late 14th century)

11754   Tip missing. L.29, W.2mm u/s sf221

11755   Head incomplete, bent near tip which is missing. L.48, W.3mm u/s sf5778

11756   Head incomplete, tip missing. L.28, W.3mm u/s sf6156

11757   Head incomplete. L.37, W.2mm u/s sf12127

Heads with Y-eyes

11758 L.47, W.2mm 5484 sf1805 (C6e1, D6a16; later 12th century)

11759 Incomplete. L.9mm 11656 sf2483 (B6g4; early 15th century)

11760 L.34, T.2mm 16612 sf6005 (D6a1; late 11th century)

Uncertain head form

11761 Head largely missing; upper part of shank has a rounded cross-section and the lower part a triangular cross-section. L.70, W.2mm 1783 sf666 (D6f8; 15th/16th century) (*Fig.1347*)

11762 Head largely missing, tip missing. L.37, W.1mm 4620 sf1012 (C6e9; mid 13th century)

11763 Head incomplete. L.50, W.3mm 5415 sf1675 (C6c6, D6a7; mid 12th century)

11764 Head largely missing. L.22, W.1mm 6339 sf5147 (D6a1; late 11th century)

11765 Fragment with part of eye surviving. 18256 sf5509 (B6a7; early 12th century)

11766 Curved. Head incomplete, tip missing. L.41, W.2mm 17890 sf5547 (B6a1, C6a1; late 11th century)

Needle shanks

6615 L.16mm 18256 sf11421 (B6a7; early 12th century)

11767 L.47mm 9134 sf988 (D6e3–9; 13th/14th–mid 14th century)

11768 L.38mm 1404 sf1635 (C6y1; late 13th–early 14th century)

11769 L.27mm 11818 sf3276 (B6c2–6; 12th/13th century)

11770 L.35mm 12791 sf4114 (C6e3; 12th/13th century)

11771 L.21mm 16135 sf4260 (C6e2–4; 12th/13th century)

11772 L.31mm 17332 sf4666 (B6a5; 11th/12th century)

11773 L.15mm 18256 sf4915 (B6a7; early 12th century)

11774 L.32, T.1mm 17787 sf5220 (C6c1; early 12th century)

11775 L.65mm 18321 sf5333 (B6c6, C6e6; early 13th century)

11776 L.22mm 16612 sf5428 (D6a1; late 11th century)

11777 L.35mm 17890 sf5439 (B6a1; C6a1; late 11th century)

11778 L.10mm 18256 sf5487 (B6a7; early 12th century)

11779 L.37mm 6258 sf5727 (C6c3, D6a5; late11th/early 12th century)

11780 L.28mm 17890 sf6038 (B6a1, C6a1; late 11th century)

11781 L.40mm u/s sf7146

Agricultural tools

Spade sheaths

11782 Blade has a rounded tip and is slightly curved in cross-section; originally a lug on each side of the head, one now missing. L.140, W.75mm 9224 sf2980 (C6e9; mid 13th century) (*Fig.1351*)

11783 Exists as half the blade and a little of the upper sheathing. The tip was slightly convex and the surviving side slopes inwards. L.79, W.23, T.12mm u/s sf2850

Pitchfork tine

11784 Tapers to a point at one end, curves slightly at the other where it is broken; diamond-shaped cross-section. L.167, W.10, T.9mm 4604 sf736 (C6g19; mid 14th century)

Fishing

Fish hooks

The shanks have rounded cross-sections unless stated.

11785 Terminal and hook tip missing. L.43, W.12, T.2mm 5245 sf1211 (D6d3; late 13th century)

11786 Flattened terminal, pointed tip. L.59, W.30, T.3mm 9252 sf1397 (D6e1; 13th/14th century) (*Fig.1352*)

11787 Looped eye terminal in plane at 90° to hook, pointed tip. L.79, W.14, T.4mm 5348 sf1683 (C6e1, D6a16; 12th–13th century) (*Fig.1352*)

11788 Looped eye terminal in plane at 90° to hook. L.47, W.16, T.4mm 9224 sf2978 (C6e9; mid 13th century)

11789 Terminal and tip missing. L.24, W.9, T.2mm 12544 sf3367 (D6a25; 12th/13th century)

11790 Incomplete flattened terminal. L.28, W.8, T.1mm 13902 sf5166 (B6c3; 12th/13th century) (*Fig.1352*)

11791 Flattened terminal, barbed tip. L.49, W.18, T.3mm 16612 sf5985 (D6a1; late 11th century) (*Fig.1352*)

11792 Looped-eye terminal in same plane as hook, barbed tip. L.35, W.13, T.2mm u/s sf5873

Other tools

Shears

6620 Blade and stub of stem. Blade bent at 90° near tip. Shoulder roughly concave; back slightly convex to a point c.22mm from the tip and then slopes inwards to it. Tip rounded. L.138; blade: L.125, W.26mm 5415 sf1616 (C6c6, D6a7; mid 12th century)

6621 Complete. Bow looped. Stems have a rounded cross-section. Blade shoulders have a U-shaped notch in the centre; backs slightly convex, cutting edges straight. X-radiograph shows a butt-weld between back and cutting edge on one blade. L.158; bow: W.35; stem: W.6; blades: L.75, W.16mm 9224 sf1387 (C6e9; mid 13th century) (*Figs.1353–4*)

6622 In two pieces and badly corroded. Bow looped and has a flattened triangular cross-section. Stems have a rounded cross-section. Blade shoulders concave with an additional cusp. Neither blade is complete, but the back of one appears to be straight before curving in at the tip. L.79; bow: W.17, T.7; stem: W.4; blade: L.35, W.11mm 10394 sf2603 (C6g13; mid 15th century) (*Fig.1354*)

11793 Blade, stem and bow fragment in three pieces. Bow and stem have a D-shaped cross-section. Blade shoulder concave with an additional cusp; back straight before curving in to the tip. L.152; stem: W.8; blade: L.75, W.20mm 5484 sf1713 (C6e1, D6a16; later 12th century) (*Figs.1353–4*)

11794 Blade only. Back and cutting edge straight before curving in to the tip; sloping shoulder. L.64, W.12, T.3mm 17890 sf5578 (B6a1, C6a1; late 11th century)

11795 Incomplete bow and stub of stem only. L.25, W.24, T.7mm 11584 sf15306 (B6c5; early 13th century)

11796 Incomplete and badly corroded. Internal nibs at the base of the bow. Stems have a rounded cross-section. Blades missing. L.65; bow: W.16, T.5; stem: W.5mm 7788 sf3082 (modern)

11797 Blade and stub of stem. Blade shoulder concave, back straight before curving in at the tip. L.59; stem: W.6; blade: L.55, W.13mm u/s sf3412

Knives

Whittle tang knives

Blade back form A: blade back straight before sloping down to the tip

A1: blade back straight part horizontal

11798 Very corroded. Blade back appears horizontal for c.29mm and then slopes down, at c.20°, towards the tip which is missing. Cutting edge straight. Tang tip pointed. L.69; blade: L.45, W.11, T.6mm 1034 sf200 (C6h3–4; early–mid 16th century)

11799 Blade only. Back horizontal for 66mm and then slopes down, at c.10°, to the tip. Cutting edge has a very slight S shape. A groove runs along the top of each blade face. Tang severed at the shoulder. L.100; blade: L.96, W.11, T.5mm 16734 sf4455 (C6a1, D6a1; late 11th century) (*Fig.1355*)

11800 Blade only. Back probably horizontal for c.40mm and then slopes down, at c.15°, to the tip which is at the blade's mid-point. Cutting edge slightly convex. Tang severed at the shoulder. L.78, W.21, T.5mm 17457 sf4791 (B6a5; 11th/12th century)

A2: blade back straight part upward sloping

11801 Blade only, badly corroded. Back slopes up for c.54mm and then slopes down, at c.25°, towards the tip, now missing. Cutting edge now irregular. L.90, W.24, T.4mm 2329 sf105 (B6v1; 13th–early 14th century)

11802 Badly corroded. Blade back slopes up for c.35mm and then slopes down, at c.20°, towards the tip, now missing. Cutting edge irregular. Tang tip missing. L.79; blade: L.58, W.11, T.4mm 4620 sf2110 (C6e9; mid 13th century)

11803 Incomplete blade only, broken a little above the shoulder. c.39mm from the break the back slopes down, at c.12°, to the tip and becomes slightly concave. Cutting edge slightly convex. L.89, W.13, T.5mm 5620 sf2113 (C6c5, D6a6; early 12th century) Metallurgy report (*Fig.1355*)

11804 Incomplete corroded blade only. Back slopes up and then slopes down, at c.20°, towards the tip which is missing. Cutting edge very corroded. L.54, W.12mm 7782 sf3083 (D6y1; late 12th–13th century)

11805 Blade back slopes up for 42mm and then slopes down, at c.15°, towards the tip which is missing. Cutting edge badly corroded, but has a rough S shape. Tang tip missing. L.76; blade: L.56, W.12, T.7mm 12412 sf3353 (C6e5; early 13th century)

Ai: form of straight part of blade back indeterminate

11806 Back straight for 40mm and then slopes down at c.4° towards the tip which is missing. Cutting edge irregular. Tang incomplete, fragment of wooden handle. L.144; blade: L.128, W.21, T.4mm 9305 sf1704 (D6a24; 12th/13th century)

Blade back form B: blade back straight before becoming concave and curving to the tip

11807 Blade back slopes up slightly for 69mm and then becomes concave. Blade is at its widest just before this change. Cutting edge convex. There is a slight vertical ridge on either side of the blade at the shoulder. Tang tip pointed. L.133; blade: L.90, W.21, T.6mm 5406 sf1962 (C6e2; 12th/13th century) (*Fig.1355*)

Blade back form C: blade back straight before becoming convex and curving down to the tip

C1: straight part of blade back horizontal

11808 Blade back horizontal for 39mm, tip corroded, but was at blade's mid-point. Cutting edge badly corroded, but was slightly S-shaped. Tang bent slightly downwards, squared-off wedge tip. L.114; blade: L.66, W.11, T.4mm 4850 sf855 (C6e1; 12th/13th century)

11809 Blade back horizontal for 50mm, tip at one-third of the blade's width from the shoulder. Cutting edge convex. Tang bent slightly upwards, tip squared off. X-radiograph shows a butt weld between back and cutting edge. L.128; blade: L.90, W.14, T.5mm 5238 sf1493 (C6e5, D6a24; early 13th century) (*Fig.1356*)

11810 Blade back horizontal for c.36mm, tip at blade's mid-point. Cutting edge slightly S-shaped. Tang incomplete. L.116; blade: L.71, W.13, T.3mm 5348 sf1544 (C6e1, D6a16; 12th–13th century) (*Fig.1356*)

11811 Blade slightly bent, back horizontal for c.91mm, tip missing, but may have been at blade's mid-point. Cutting edge also corroded, but was horizontal before curving up to tip. Tang tapers to a point. L.175; blade: L.104, W.17, T.4mm 10118 sf2449 (C6g17; 15th/16th century) Metallurgy report (*Fig.1356*)

11812 Corroded. Blade back horizontal for c.43mm, tip missing. Cutting edge irregular. Horizontal weld between back and cutting edge visible on X-radiograph. Tang tip missing. L.99; blade: L.63, W.12, T.3mm 7782 sf3110 (D6y1; late 12th–13th century)

11813 Blade only. Back horizontal for c.61mm, tip missing. A shallow channel c.5mm wide runs along the middle of each face of the blade from shoulder towards tip. Cutting edge straight and parallel to the back before curving up towards tip. Tang broken off a little below the shoulder. L.129; blade: L.123, W.21, T.5mm 13501 sf3464 (B6c9; 13th century) (*Fig.1356*)

11814 Blade incomplete. Back horizontal for c.31mm. Cutting edge concave up to the break. Tang tip pointed. L.83; blade: L.50, W.13, T.6mm 3551 sf3466 (A6c4; 12th century) Metallurgy report

11815 Blade back horizontal for 51mm, tip missing, but was at blade's mid-point. Cutting edge convex. Tang incomplete. L.82; blade: L.66, W.14, T.5mm 12725 sf3527 (D6a26–b1; late 12th–early 13th century)

11816 Blade back horizontal for 42mm, tip at blade's mid-point. Cutting edge slightly S-shaped. Tang tapers a little away from the shoulder but is then parallel sided and has wedge-shaped tip. L.116; blade: L.56, W.10, T.5mm 18486 sf5063 (C6b2; 11th/12th century)

11817 Blade back horizontal for 43mm, tip at blade's mid-point. Cutting edge corroded, but was convex. Concave shoulder. L.114; blade: L.78, W.15, T.4mm 6339 sf5096 (D6a1; late 11th century) Metallurgy report

11818 Blade back horizontal for 60mm, tip at blade's mid-point. Cutting edge S-shaped. Sloping shoulder. Tang largely missing. L.90; blade: L.84, W.12, T.5mm 6339 sf5111 (D6a1; late 11th century) Metallurgy report

11819 Blade back horizontal for c.37mm, tip at blade's mid-point. Cutting edge S-shaped. Tang bent slightly downwards, tip squared off. L.107; blade: L.69, W.13, T.4mm 13886 sf5999 (B6a3; 11th/12th century) (*Fig.1356*)

11820 Blade back roughly horizontal for c.68mm, tip at blade's mid-point. Cutting edge badly corroded, but appears slightly S-shaped. Tang incomplete. L.118; blade: L.89, W.13, T.4mm u/s sf3044

11821 Blade back horizontal for 58mm, tip one-third of blade's width from the shoulder. Cutting edge straight before curving up. Tang tip missing. L.114; blade: L.79, W.15, T.4mm u/s sf4982

C3: straight part of blade back downward sloping

11822 Back slopes down for c.85mm, tip missing, but clearly at blade's mid-point. Cutting edge very slightly S-shaped. Tang bent slightly downwards, tip pointed. L.153; blade: L.111, W.17, T.6mm 1748 sf577 (D6i3; mid–late 17th century)

11823 Back slopes down for 45mm, tip at blade's mid-point. Cutting edge S-shaped. Tang tip wedge-shaped. L.148; blade: L.58, W.10, T.6mm 1502 sf974 (C6e11, D6e3; mid 13th century) (*Fig.1357*)

11824 Blade back slopes down slightly for 33mm, tip at blade's mid-point. Cutting edge S-shaped. Tang tip missing. L.96; blade: L.53, W.9, T.4mm 9330 sf1671 (D6a25–6; 12th/13th century)

11825 Back slopes down for c.21mm, tip at blade's mid-point. Cutting edge steps up at the rear and is then convex. Vertical shoulder. Tang tapers to a point. L.77; blade: L.48, W.10, T.4mm 5398 sf2197 (C6c6; mid 12th century)

11826 Back slopes down for c.40mm, tip slightly rounded and at its mid-point. Cutting edge has a pronounced S shape. Tang tip squared off. L.117; blade: L.66, W.11, T.6mm 11106 sf2401 (B6c8; early 13th century) (*Fig.1357*)

11827 Blade back slopes down for 53mm, tip at blade's mid-point. Cutting edge corroded, but was straight before curving up to the tip. Tang bent slightly downwards, tip pointed. L.107; blade: L.76, W.13, T.5mm 10511 sf2562 (C6g8; 14th/15th century)

11828 Blade back slopes down for 30mm, tip at blade's mid-point. Cutting edge slightly S-shaped. Shoulder very slight. Tang tip pointed. L.90; blade: L.44, W.12, T.5mm 11045 sf2599 (B6c8; early 13th century)

11829 Blade back somewhat corroded, slopes down slightly for c.31mm, tip missing, but was at half the blade's width. Cutting edge slightly S-shaped. Tang incomplete. L.79; blade: L.55, W.12, T.3mm 11458 sf2771 (B6c7; late 11th–early 12th century)

11830 Blade back slopes down for 45mm, tip missing. Cutting edge slightly S-shaped. Tang tip squared off and burred. L.96; blade: L.62, W.13, T.4mm 13160 sf3433 (B6c9; 13th century) Metallurgy report (*Fig.1357*)

11831 Blade back slopes down for c.23mm, tip at blade's mid-point. Cutting edge slightly S-shaped. Slightly sloping shoulder. Tang tip missing. L.57; blade: L.35, W.8, T.6mm 3493 sf3555 (A6c1; 12th century)

11832 Blade back slopes gently down for 45mm, tip at blade's mid-point. Cutting edge straight before curving up to the tip. Tang tip pointed. L.104; blade: L.68, W.12, T.4mm 18366 sf4942 (B6a5; 11th/12th century)

11833 Corroded. Back appears to slope down for c.48mm, tip at blade's mid-point. Cutting edge has a pronounced S-shape. Vertical shoulder. Tang tip wedge-shaped. L.112; blade: L.60, W.13, T.5mm 2284 sf4966 (B6v1; 13th–early 14th century) (*Fig.1357*)

11834 Blade back slopes down for c.46mm, tip at blade's mid-point. Cutting edge S-shaped, sloping shoulder. Tang tip squared off. L.103; blade: L.65, W.9, T.3mm 6339 sf5107 (D6a1; late 11th century) Metallurgy report

11835 Blade back slopes down for c.54mm, tip at one third blade's width from the shoulder. Cutting edge S-shaped. Vertical shoulder. Tang tip wedge-shaped. L.164; blade: L73, W.9, T.4mm 6339 sf5154 (D6a1; late 11th century)

11836 Blade back, which has a triangular cross-section, slopes down for 50mm, tip rounded. Cutting edge S-shaped. Tang tip missing, but was probably bent over. L.213; blade: L.106, W.17, T.7mm 16734 sf5371 (C6a1, D6a1; late 11th century) (*Fig.1357*)

11837 Blade corroded and incomplete, back slopes up for c.30mm before it originally would have come to an angle, although it is damaged in this area, and then sloped down towards the tip which is missing. Cutting edge irregular. Two grooves run along the top of both blade faces; each is inlaid with copper wire twisted in a herringbone pattern. Traces of copper plating on the tang. L.84; blade: L.59, W.16, T.5; tang: W.12, T.3mm 2300 sf15329 (B6v1; 13th–early 14th century) (*Figs.1357, 1359*)

11838 Badly corroded. Blade back slopes down for c.25mm, tip approximately at blade's mid-point. Cutting edge slightly S-shaped. Tang incomplete. L.72; blade: L.46, W.10mm u/s sf2860

11839 Blade back slopes down for c.43mm, tip at blade's mid-point. Cutting edge S-shaped. Tang incomplete. L.75; blade: L.57, W.12, T.4mm u/s sf5396

Ci: straight part of blade back has indeterminate form

11840 Blade back straight for c.45mm, tip at blade's mid-point. Cutting edge slightly S-shaped. Concave shoulder, tang tip squared off. L.102; blade: L.57, W.11, T.4mm 1304 sf266 (C6y1; late 13th–early 14th century)

11841 Blade only. Back straight for 45mm, tip missing. Cutting edge slightly S-shaped. Tang severed at shoulder. L.59, W.11, T.5mm 9305 sf2057 (D6a24; 12th/13th century)

11842 Blade only, badly corroded. Back was probably straight for c.45mm, tip at blade's mid-point. Cutting edge probably convex. Tang broken off immediately below the shoulder. L.76; blade: L.70, W.17, T.7mm 11458 sf3091 (B6c7; late 11th–early 12th century)

11843 Corroded blade, bent near the end, tip missing. Cutting edge straight before curving up at the tip. Sloping shoulder. L.114; blade: L.55, W.14, T.3mm 7791 sf3113 (C6z1; late 14th–early 15th century)

11844 Blade only. Back probably straight for 45mm, tip missing due to corrosion. Cutting edge was probably slightly S-shaped. L.77; blade: L.70, W.13mm 9813 sf5039 (D6a25; 12th/13th century)

11845 Blade only, now a little twisted. Cutting edge probably straight before curving gently up to the tip. Tang severed at the shoulder. L.90, W.10, T.4mm 12063 sf14851 (C6e11; mid 13th century)

11846 Blade back straight for 30mm, tip at blade's mid-point. Cutting edge slightly S-shaped. Tang incomplete. L.59; blade: L.50, W.9, T.4mm 1019 sf15967 (modern) (*Fig.1357*)

Blade back form D: blade back slightly convex and curves gently from the shoulder to the tip

11847 Blade's tip rounded off and at its mid-point. Cutting edge badly corroded, but was slightly S-shaped. Tang tip pointed. L.114; blade: L.75, W.15, T.5mm 4915 sf905 (C6e11; mid 13th century)

11848 Blade's tip at its mid-point. Cutting edge slightly convex. Tang tip probably pointed but badly corroded. L.125; blade: L.91, W.17, T.6mm 4693 sf973 (C6e13; mid 13th century)

11849 Incomplete blade. Cutting edge irregular, but was roughly straight. Tang tip pointed. L.105; blade: L.69, W.15, T.4mm 9122 sf1044 (D6e1; 13th/14th century)

11850 Blade's tip at its mid-point. Cutting edge has a slight S-shape. Tang incomplete. L.87; blade: L.60, W.13, T.7mm 4620 sf1189 (C6e9; mid 13th century)

11851 Blade only. Tip at blade's mid-point. Cutting edge straight before curving up to the tip. Tang broken off at the shoulder. L.72, W.15, T.6mm 9224 sf1335 (C6e9; mid 13th century)

11852 Blade only, badly corroded. Tip at the mid-point. Cutting edge convex. Tang severed immediately below the shoulder. L.83; blade: L.75, W.15, T.9mm 9224 sf1379 (C6e9; mid 13th century)

11853 Tip was at blade's mid-point. Cutting edge very slightly S-shaped. Tang bent slightly downwards, tip squared off. L.108; blade: L.65, W.10, T.4mm 5331 sf1442 (D6a17; late 12th century) (*Fig.1358*)

11854 Blade tip at its mid-point. Cutting edge slightly convex. At the top of both blade faces there is a line of nine incised semicircles. Sloping shoulder, tang largely missing. L.93; blade: L.83, W.19, T.5mm 9249 sf1469 (D6d2; late 13th century) (*Fig.1358*)

11855 Cutting edge slightly S-shaped, tip at the mid-point. Tang tip squared off. L.115; blade: L.74, W.13, T.5mm 5348 sf1495 (C6e1, D6a16; 12th–13th century) (*Fig.1358*)

11856 Blade tip at mid-point. Cutting edge S-shaped. Tang tip pointed. L.63; blade: L.42, W.7, T.3mm 5348 sf1552 (C6e1, D6a16; 12th–13th century)

11857 Blade tip missing. Cutting edge was probably convex. Tang tip pointed. L.61; blade: L.40, W.9, T.3mm 5415 sf1755 (C6c6, D6a7; mid 12th century)

11858 Cutting edge slightly concave. Little perceptible shoulder. Tang squared off. L.87; blade: L.50, W.15, T.4mm 3447 sf2596 (A6c1; 12th century)

11859 Blade tip at mid-point. Cutting edge convex. Tang tip pointed. L.112; blade: L.75, W.16, T.7mm 11416 sf2837 (B6c2–6; 12th/13th century)

11860 Blade only. Tip at mid-point. Cutting edge badly corroded but was probably S-shaped. Tang severed at the shoulder. L.93, W.18, T.5mm 11886 sf3038 (B6f4; early 14th century) Metallurgy report

11861 Slightly bent in the centre. Cutting edge slightly S-shaped. Tang tip missing. L.70; blade: L.45, W.9, T.4mm 13244 sf3389 (B6c2–6; 12th/13th century)

11862 Bent slightly in the centre. Cutting edge slightly S-shaped. Vertical shoulder. Groove runs along the top of both blade faces. L.78; blade: L.50, W.8, T.3mm 15840 sf4624 (B6c7, C6e7; early 13th century) Metallurgy report

11863 Blade's tip at its mid-point. Cutting edge S-shaped. Tang parallel sided, tip missing, but was wedge-shaped. L.93; blade: L.56, W.11, T.4mm 17322 sf4784 (C6c6; mid 12th century)

11864 Blade's tip at its mid-point. Cutting edge slightly S-shaped. Tang tip pointed. L.84; blade: L.57, W.10, T.5mm 17375 sf4834 (C6d1; mid 12th century)

11865 Blade's tip at its mid-point. Cutting edge slightly S-shaped. Sloping shoulder. Tang tip missing. L.101; blade: L.62, W.14, T.7mm 15285 sf5255 (B6a1; late 11th century) (*Fig.1358*)

11866 Blade bent at c.45° in the centre. Blade's tip at its mid-point. Cutting edge S-shaped. Thickening between the blade and tang. Tang tip rounded off. X-radiograph shows pattern-welding in the form of horizontal stripes. L.213; blade: L.159, W.18, T.3mm 15285 sf5321 (B6a1; late 11th century) (*Fig.1358*)

Back form E: blade back near straight from shoulder to tip

11867 Blade back slopes down for c.90mm and then slopes down very slightly more sharply to the tip. Cutting edge slightly worn near back, from centre curves strongly upwards. Tang tip wedge-shaped. L.215; blade: L.151, W.31, T4mm 5104 sf932 (C6e8; early 13th century, D6d3; late 13th century) (*Fig.1358*)

11868 Blade only, bent in the middle, tip was at the mid-point. Cutting edge roughly straight. Tang severed at the shoul-

der. L.105; blade: L.97, W.15, T.5mm 10739 sf2644 (C6f1; late 13th century)

Knives of indeterminate blade back form

11869 Incomplete blade, back straight up to the break. Cutting edge very worn. Tang tapers to a point. L.83; blade: L.42, W.18, T.3mm 2254 sf53 (A6z1; 11th/12th century)

11870 Incomplete blade. Back straight up to the break. Cutting edge was probably S-shaped. Brass collar at the junction of the blade and tang. Tang tapers to wedge-shaped tip. L.118; blade: L.52, W.15, T4mm 1020 sf164 (C6i3; 17th–18th century) (*Fig.1363*)

11871 Badly corroded. Blade narrows sharply and back slopes down from shoulder towards the tip which is missing, but was at the blade's mid-point. Cutting edge worn, but roughly straight. Tang tip squared off. L.110; blade: L.84, W.13, T.5mm 4915 sf924 (C6e11; mid 13th century)

11872 Incomplete blade only, badly corroded. L.48, W.25, T.4mm 9190 sf1017 (D6e8; early 14th century)

11873 Blade incomplete and bent in the centre at c.90°. Blade back slopes down slightly from shoulder to break. Cutting edge slopes up before running roughly horizontal up to the break. L.98; blade: L.56, W.24, T.3mm 3356 sf1070 (A6g1; 13th/14th century)

11874 Incomplete blade, back straight up to break. Cutting edge parallel to the back. Tang tip missing. L.69; blade: L.32, W.15, T.3mm 4620 sf1259 (C6e9; mid 13th century)

11875 Blade fragment, tang largely missing. L.45, W.20, T.2mm 9224 sf1329 (C6e9; mid 13th century)

11876 Incomplete blade, back straight up to the break. Cutting edge slightly concave. Tang tapers slightly and rounded off. L.67; blade: L.34, W.10, T.5mm 9481 sf1979 (D6a14; mid 12th century)

11877 Badly corroded. Blade back roughly straight, tip missing. Cutting edge may have been roughly parallel to the back. X-radiograph shows an inlaid cutler's mark in the centre of one blade face. Tang tip missing. L.74; blade: L.43, W.13, T.3mm 10101 sf2455 (C6i2; 17th/18th century) (*Fig.1363*)

11878 Blade incomplete and bent over twice at 90°. Tang complete. L. (unbent) 100; blade: (unbent) L.47, W.25, T.3mm 10979 sf2817 (D6e7; early 14th century)

11879 Blade fragment. L.45, W.10mm 11656 sf2858 (B6g4; early 15th century)

11880 Blade back straight, end missing. Groove runs along one face of the blade. Cutting edge pitted, but is basically slightly S-shaped. Tang severed a little below the shoulder. L.155; blade: L.148, W.16, T.3mm 9224 sf2988 (C6e9; mid 13th century) (*Fig.1363*)

11881 Corroded fragments only. 7782 sf3119 (D6y1; late 12th–13th century)

11882 Blade largely missing, concave shoulder. Tang incomplete. L.38; blade: W.17, T.7mm 5975 sf3284 (C6c6; mid 12th century)

11883 Incomplete blade only. Back straight. Cutting edge badly corroded, but was convex. L.53, W.15, T.4mm 13243 sf3296 (B6a7; early 12th century)

11884 Blade only, badly corroded. Back was possibly straight before curving down to the tip which is missing. Cutting edge may have been roughly parallel to the back. Tang was severed at the shoulder. L.90, W.16, T.3mm 13557 sf3470 (B6c6; early 13th century)

11885 Blade largely missing. Surviving part has a straight back. Tang tapers to a point. L.118; blade: L.15, W.11, T.6mm 13568 sf3545 (B6a5; 11th/12th century)

11886 In two pieces and badly corroded. Blade of indeterminate form, tang tip missing. L.83; blade: L.19, W.11mm 13120 sf3682 (B6y1; 16th–17th century)

11887   Tang and fragment of blade. L.77; blade: W.17, T.6mm 13581 sf3753 (A6n3, B6c5; early 13th century)

11888   Incomplete blade. Back straight up to the break and cutting edge roughly straight. Tang missing. X-radiograph shows pattern-welding. L.58; blade: L.55, W.18, T.5mm 12327 sf4013 (D6e1–3; 13th/14th century) Metallurgy report

11889   Incomplete blade, back straight up to the break. Cutting edge appears worn, but is straight and roughly parallel with the back. Sloping shoulder. Tang tip wedge-shaped. L.117; blade: L.34, W.29, T.2mm 15124 sf4120 (B6a7; early 12th century)

11890   Incomplete blade, back straight up to the break. Cutting edge was probably S-shaped. Between blade and tang is a bolster which expands towards the latter. Tang tip missing. L.71; blade: L.30, W.13, T.4; bolster: W.16mm 15202 sf4155 (B6a1; late 11th century)

11891   End of blade only, back straight and slopes downwards. Cutting edge convex. L.48, W.26, T.2mm 16535 sf4355 (D6a9; early 12th century)

11892   Blade only. Tip missing. A serrated possible weld-line runs along the back of the blade. Cutting edge badly corroded and appears irregular. Tang broken off at the shoulder. L.80, W.19, T.3mm 18194 sf4786 (B6c2; 12th/13th century) (Fig.1363)

11893   Incomplete blade. Back probably sloped up slightly from the shoulder to the break. Cutting edge appears worn, but is roughly straight. There are two holes 9mm apart at the rear of the blade, one has a small rivet in situ. Tang tip pointed. L.80; blade: L.57, W.19, T.2mm 18331 sf5184 (B6a5, C6c3; early 12th century) (Fig.1363)

11894   Blade back straight and becomes slightly concave before the tip which is at blade's mid-point. Cutting edge S-shaped. Tang tip missing. L.95; blade: L.60, W.13, T.6mm 13902 sf5271 (B6c3; 12th/13th century) Metallurgy report

11895   Incomplete blade. Back slopes up to the break after which it curved or sloped down. Cutting edge very irregular. Groove runs along the top of both faces. Vertical shoulder. Tang tip missing. L.114; blade: L.73, W.16, T.4mm 6285 sf5802 (D6a4; late 11th century)

11896   Incomplete blade. Back straight and cutting edge slightly concave. Rounded shoulder. Tang tip wedge-shaped. L.93; blade: L.27, W.14, T.4mm 18477 sf5828 (A6f1; 13th century)

11897   Blade largely missing, tang tip missing. L.50, W.12, T.3mm 5230 sf14780 (D6a7; 11th/12th century)

11898   Blade fragment. L.35, W.25mm 11867 sf15295 (B6f3; early 14th century)

11899   Very corroded incomplete blade. Back straight up to the break. Groove cut into one face. Cutting edge irregular. Tang tapers to a point. L.66; blade: L.34, W.15, T.5mm 11554 sf15341 (B6g9; 15th/16th century) (Fig.1363)

11900   Incomplete blade. Back straight. Cutting edge irregular. Butt weld between the back and cutting edge visible on X-radiograph. Concave shoulder. Tang tip missing. L.76; blade: L.40, W.12, T.6mm 1072 sf15971 (C6i1, D6z1; late 17th century)

11901   Somewhat corroded. Blade incomplete and separated from tang by a bolster of oval cross-section. Tang tapers to a point and set in a handle made of bone/ivory which has an oval cross-section and expands towards the end. L.99; blade: L.19, W.13, T.3; handle: W.16, T.13mm u/s sf2369

11902   Very badly corroded; only a fragment of the blade and tang survives. L.90; blade: L.73, W.16, T.8mm u/s sf3074

11903   Badly corroded and bent. Back roughly straight, blade tip missing. Cutting edge straight before curving up to the tip. Tang largely missing. L.54; blade: L.44, W.10, T.5mm u/s sf5309

11904   Incomplete blade and tang. Two small notches cut into each side of back near shoulder. Butt weld between back and cutting edge visible on X-radiograph. Concave shoulder. L.42, W.15, T.4mm u/s sf15362

Knife tangs

11905   Tapers to a point. L.49, W.11, T.4mm 5348 sf1989 (C6e1, D6a16; 12th–13th century)

11906   Tip rounded off. L.60, W.13, T.6mm 10391 sf15096 (D6g1; early–mid 16th century)

Pivoting knives

In each case the blades are of unequal length.

11907   Bent in the centre. Back roughly straight in the centre, at both ends it curves down towards the tips. Longer blade's cutting edge is straight and parallel to the back from the pivot to the centre before curving up to the tip which is at approximately one-third the blade width from the back. Shorter blade's cutting edge straight and slopes up; tip missing. L.85, W.10, T.2; blades: L.45 and 19mm 5348 sf1920 (C6e1, D6a16; 12th–13th century) (Fig.1380)

11908   Incomplete. Back slightly convex and curves gently down to tip at one end. Cutting edge of the complete blade has a slight S shape; other is straight up to the break. L.50, W.11, T.5; blades: L.26 and 9mm 3493 sf2919 (A6c1; 12th century)

11909   Bent towards the wider end. Back straight in centre, curves down towards the tip, now missing, of the shorter blade and becomes concave towards the tip, now missing, of the longer blade. On one face of the latter are the remains of two parallel grooves inlaid with copper and brass wires. L.77, W.13, T.3; blades: L.48 and 18mm 6258 sf5054 (C6c3, D6a5; late11th/early 12th century) (Fig.1380)

11910   Back very slightly concave in the centre; towards the end of the shorter blade it slopes down, at c.15°, to the tip, remaining very slightly concave, while towards the end of the longer blade it becomes concave, tip missing. Cutting edges slightly convex. L.164, W.20, T.3; blades: L.91 and 54mm 17890 sf5430 (B6a1, C6a1; late 11th century) (Fig.1380)

11911   Incomplete and corroded. Back slightly convex for most of its length, but on the longer blade, at a point where the knife is widest, it becomes concave. Tips of both blades missing. Cutting edges are convex. L.122, W.25, T.2; blades: L.82 and 33mm u/s sf3030

Other knives

11912   Consists of a thin tapering blade attached to an incomplete pierced component (on which it may have swivelled), a second blade may have projected beyond this. L.53, W.16, T.2mm 9067 sf890 (C6e11; mid 13th century) (Fig.1380)

11913   Incomplete blade with a convex back which continues as the top of the tang. This curves below the level of the cutting edge and thickens to a wedge-shaped tip. Cutting edge straight. L.59, W.18, T.5mm 18668 sf5317 (C6d6; mid 12th century) (Fig.1380)

Domestic equipment
Flesh hook

11914   Shank largely missing. The part that survives has three arms, the two outer arms, one incomplete, curve outwards and the central one is straight. The complete outer arm curves over at the tip and tapers to a point. L.53, W. (at base of arms) 13, T.4mm 18047 sf4764 (B6c3; 12th/13th century) (Fig.1388)

Strike-a-lights

11915 L-shaped; striking plate pierced in centre and tip rounded, corner slightly flattened. Arm: L.79, W.9; striking plate: L.50, W.18mm 11763 sf2925 (B6g4; early 15th century)

11916 Incomplete. Surviving end of the striking plate has a looped-over terminal. L.55, W.25, T.3mm 13454 sf3589 (B6d2; mid 13th century) (*Fig.1388*)

Shovels

11917 Incomplete. Handle and blade made in one piece. Blade incomplete, but was probably rectangular and the sides are turned up. Handle at a slight angle to the blade and has a rectangular cross-section. L.125; blade: W.102, T.6; handle: L.50, W.29, T.8mm 4385 sf554 (C6i4; 16th–19th century) (*Fig.1388*)

11918 Blade is rectangular and the sides are turned up. Handle was attached by being nailed twice to a roughly oval expansion at the back of the blade. Handle has a rectangular cross-section and narrows towards the head, except for a slight expansion near its base. This expansion is pierced and set in it is the rounded head of a short strip which is set at 90° to the handle. The strip has a rectangular cross-section and widens away from the head. Handle head is drawn out into a loop. L.425; blade: L.126, W.200, T.27; handle: W.20, T.5; strip: L.38, W.15, T.6mm 9254 sf1077 (D6e1; 13th/14th century) (*Figs.1388, 1390*)

Vessels

Wooden bucket with iron fittings

8742 Oak; radially split staves and base; nine staves, two with raised rounded upper ends perforated by augered circular holes. H.424, D. (top) 365, D. (bottom) 265, T. (staves) 21–8, T. (base) 16mm

Two iron suspension fittings: U-shaped loop at the head between two attachment plates with convex shoulders and rounded ends; pierced twice. a) L.133, W.76, T.12; b) L.127, W.78, T.14mm

Handle: U-shaped, widened around a suspension hole at the top, short out-turned arms at the ends which fitted into the suspension fittings. Rectangular cross-section with chamfered edges. W.360, H.200, T.16mm

Swivelling suspension fitting, set in the handle: a pear-shaped loop at the head develops into the shank, the base of which has a domed terminal. Rounded cross-section. L.125, W.58, T.13mm

Chain links: three linked together and attached to the swivelling suspension fitting. Figure-of-eight-shaped with sub-rounded or sub-rectangular cross-sections. a) L.185, W.45, T.12; b) L.171, W.45, T.10; c) L.210, W.45, T.13mm

Three iron bands run around the bucket at top, centre and base. D. not measurable, W.40mm

15300 sf4176 (B6g4; early 15th century) (*Figs.1391–2*)

Vessel handles   (see also 8742)

11919 Incomplete and somewhat corroded. Made from a slightly curved spirally twisted strip. One incomplete surviving terminal. L.154, W.8; terminal: W.16mm 12619 sf3365 (D6a24; 12th/13th century)

11920 Made from a slightly curved spirally twisted strip; the surviving looped terminal has a rolled tip. L.200, T.6; terminal: L.16, T.3mm 16734 sf5367 (C6a1, D6a1; late 11th century) (*Fig.1393*)

Structural items and fittings

Nails

Nails from medieval contexts have been quantified by context (data available in archive).

Plated nails

Complete length survives unless stated. Plating details, where available, given in parenthesis before dimensions. W = width of head.

11921 (Lead) L.40, W.16, T.5mm 1034 sf198 (C6h3–4; early–mid 16th century)

11922 (Tin) L.50, W.16, T.4mm 9204 sf931 (D6e10; mid 14th century)

11923 (Tin, a little lead) L.50, W.16, T.4mm 5981 sf2127 (C6c3, D6a5; late 11th/early 12th century)

11924 Shank bent at 90° in centre. L.85, W.24, T.4mm 5348 sf15751 (C6e1, D6a16; 12th–13th century)

11925 Shank incomplete, domed head. L.32, W.23, T.6mm 5126 sf15752 (C6h1; 15th/16th century)

11926 Shank U-shaped, tip missing. (Tin, small amount of lead) L.64, W.27, T.6mm 6423 sf15753 (C6b1; 11th/12th century)

11927 Tip missing, domed head. L.59, W.22, T.6mm 5977 sf15756 (D6a7; 11th/12th century)

11928 Domed head. L.69, W.22, T.6mm 5000 sf15757 (C6c6; mid 12th century)

11929 Low domed head. L.32, W.18, T.4mm 5245 sf15758 (D6d3; late 13th century)

11930 Domed head, shank bent a little in centre and at tip. L.56, W.20, T.6mm 5484 sf15760 (C6e1, D6a16; later 12th century)

11931 Tip missing, neatly rounded head. L.47, W.24, T.6mm 5000 sf15771 (C6c6; mid 12th century)

11932 Tip missing, neatly rounded head. L.21, W.12, T.4mm 5000 sf15772 (C6c6; mid 12th century)

11933 Shank incomplete. L.31, W.17, T.5mm 5413 sf15774 (D6a16; mid 12th century)

11934 Shank bent at 90° near tip and clenched. L.77, W.26, T.7mm 8305 sf15803 (A6z4; 13th century)

11935 Tip missing. L.32, W.15, T.4mm 13964 sf15807 (B6c8; early 13th century)

11936 Shank tip missing. L.33, W.19, T.6mm 3549 sf15812 (A6c4; 12th century)

11937 Curved shank. L.37, W.12, T.5mm 3537 sf15816 (A6c4; 12th century)

11938 L.35, W.12, T.5mm 3537 sf15817 (A6c4; 12th century)

11939 Shank set in concave head, tip missing. L.44, W.20, T.6mm 18486 sf15960 (C6b2; 11th/12th century) (*Fig.1408*)

11940 Roughly rounded, domed head, shank bent at 90° in centre and clenched. (Tin-lead) L.76, W.25, T.5mm 18366 sf15961 (B6a5; 11th/12th century) (*Fig.1408*)

11941 Neatly rounded, domed head, shank bent at 90° near head and tip clenched. (Tin and possible trace of lead) L.60, W.21, T.4mm 18256 sf15962 (B6a7; early 12th century) (*Fig.1408*)

11942 Neatly rounded head. (Lead) L.38, W.19, T.6mm 18152 sf15963 (B6c4; 12th/13th century)

11943 Domed head, shank bent at 90° near head. (Tin and trace of lead) L.64, W.26, T.6mm 18668 sf15964 (C6d6; mid 12th century)

11944 Domed head, shank incomplete. (Tin and trace of copper and lead) L.30, W.23, T.7mm 1506 sf15970 (D6e9; mid 14th century)

11945 Domed head, shank incomplete. (Tin and trace of lead and copper) L.40, W.22, T.6mm 9224 sf15972 (C6e9; mid 13th century)

11946 Neatly rounded, domed head, shank bent at 90° in centre. (Tin-lead) L.55, W.21, T.5mm 9224 sf15973 (C6e9; mid 13th century)

11947 Neatly rounded domed head, shank becomes U-shaped towards the base. (Tin and possible trace of lead) L.76, W.21, T.6mm 9224 sf15976 (C6e9; mid 13th century)

11948 Domed head. (Tin and trace of lead) L.60, W.30, T.6mm 3414 sf15979 (A6e1; early 13th century)

11949 L.69, W.24, T.5mm 9302 sf15980 (D6a26; 12th/13th century)

11950 Shank tip missing. (Tin) L.38, W.18, T.4mm 3258 sf15981 (A6g1; 13th/14th century)

11951 Shank tip missing. (Tin-lead) L.30, W.13, T.3mm 3407 sf16007 (A6e1; early 13th century)

11952 Shank curved slightly near base. L.80, W.10, T.5mm 3059 sf16008 (A6j28; early 17th century)

11953 Low domed head. (Tin) L.38, W.20, T.3mm 4013 sf16012 (C6j1; early–mid 18th century)

11954 (Tin-lead). L.29, W.11, T.3mm 4724 sf16014 (C6g17; 15th/16th century)

11955 L.37, W.17, T.6mm 4020 sf16015 (C6i3; 17th–18th century)

11956 Shank bent at 45° in centre and tip clenched. L.78, W.25, T.6mm 4043 sf16016 (C6z1; late 14th–early 15th century)

11957 Low domed head, shank curved. (Tin) L.35, W.13, T.4mm 12662 sf16017 (D6a26–d1; late 12th–mid 13th century)

11958 Neatly rounded, domed head, shank bent in centre at 90° and tip clenched. (Tin) L.67, W.22, T.5mm 12699 sf16018 (C6e1; 12th/13th century) (Fig.1408)

11959 Neatly rounded, domed head. (Tin with a trace of lead) L.56, W.21, T.6mm 12579 sf16019 (C6e4; 12th/13th century) (Fig.1408)

11960 Neatly rounded, domed head. Shank bent at 90° in centre, tip clenched. (Tin with a trace of lead) L.66, W.22, T.6mm 12794 sf16020 (C6e1; 12th/13th century)

11961 Head damaged, tip missing. (Tin with a trace of lead) L.59, W.25, T.5mm 12011 sf16021 (C6e11; mid 13th century)

11962 Sub-rectangular, low, domed head, shank tip missing. (Tin with a trace of lead) L.46, W.16, T.5mm 4000 sf16013 (modern)

11963 Shank incomplete. L.29, W.17, T.6mm u/s sf15811

11964 (trace lead) L.42, W.20, T.6mm u/s sf16104

Stud

11965 Thin elliptical domed head. L.80; head: W.50mm u/s sf4788

Bosses

11966 Exists as a boss of 'turk's head' shape which is hexagonal in cross-section. It is pierced and set on a shaft of rectangular cross-section which is plated (copper, lead and trace zinc). Copper alloy collar around the tip at the head. L.66; boss: L.18, D.16mm 11867 sf2979 (B6f3; early 14th century) (Fig.1408)

11967 Domed centre with a flange around the edge which slopes down. The flat underside had a projecting shank now largely missing. T.15, D.35mm 17890 sf5548 (B6a1, C6a1; late 11th century) (Fig.1408)

Clench bolts

All have roughly rounded heads and shanks of rectangular cross-section, except where stated.

Diamond-shaped roves

11968 L.53; head: W.22; shank: T.6; rove: L.23, W.21mm 1005 sf100 (D6y1; late 12th–13th century)

11969 Incomplete rove. L.44; head: W.20; shank: T.6; rove: L.20, W.15mm 4852 sf856 (C6e12; mid 13th century)

11970 Incomplete rove. L.31, W.20mm 9037 sf916 (C6e11; mid 13th century)

11971 L.45; head: W.26; shank: T.6; rove: L. 35, W.20mm 9122 sf1018 (D6e1; 13th/14th century)

11972 Head largely missing. L.53; shank: T.11; rove: L.32, W.30mm 3237 sf1064 (A6i2; 14th/15th century)

11973 L.40; head: W.19; shank: T.6; rove: L.19, W.18mm 4620 sf1154 (C6e9; mid 13th century)

11974 Head and rove incomplete. L.37; head: W.23; shank: T.6; rove: L.20, W.15mm 4620 sf1176 (C6e9; mid 13th century)

11975 Incomplete rove. L.39; head: W.24; shank: T.7; rove: L.31, W.30mm 5241 sf1212 (D6d3; late 13th century)

11976 Incomplete rove. L.29, W.25mm 9302 sf1357 (D6a26; 12th/13th century)

11977 Shank bent. L.47; head: W.21; shank: T.7; rove: L.24, W.19mm 9252 sf1374 (D6e1; 13th/14th century)

11978 Incomplete head and rove. L.40; head: W.12; shank: T.4; rove: L.23, W.23mm 9224 sf1409 (C6e9; mid 13th century)

11979 Incomplete head and rove. L.45; head: W.17; shank: T.4; rove: L.24, W.23mm 5238 sf1504 (C6e5, D6a24; early 13th century)

11980 Incomplete rove. L.51; head: W.28; shank: T.6; rove: L.21, W.20mm 9305 sf1575 (D6a24; 12th/13th century)

11981 L.36; head: W.23; shank: T.5; rove: L.27, W.25mm 5671 sf1786 (C6e6; early 13th century)

11982 L.50; head: W.28; shank: T.6; rove: L.28, W.18mm 5397 sf1826 (C6c6; mid 12th century) (Fig.1408)

11983 Somewhat corroded, head largely missing. Shank has a rounded cross-section. L.39; head: W.14; shank: T.7; rove: L.18, W.18mm 5348 sf1931 (C6e1, D6a16; 12th–13th century)

11984 Incomplete head and rove. L.54; head: W.20; shank: T.6; rove: L.53, W.21mm 3344 sf2245 (A6g1; 13th/14th century)

11985 Badly corroded, fragmentary. Head: W.17; shank: T.8; rove: L.31, W.29mm 9224 sf2297 (C6e9; mid 13th century)

11986 L.35; head: W.22; shank: T.4; rove: L.21, W.19mm 11052 sf2706 (B6c7; late 11th–early 12th century)

11987 L.30; head: W.19; shank: T.6; rove: L.36, W.25mm 3494 sf2893 (A6e1; early 13th century)

11988 Incomplete rove. L.36; head: W.20; shank: T.6mm; rove: L.32mm 3494 sf2895 (A6e1; early 13th century)

11989 Incomplete rove. L.48; head: W.21; shank: T.6; rove: L.33mm 10974 sf2910 (D6e7; early 14th century)

11990 Head largely missing. L.32; shank: T.6; rove: L.22, W.18mm 3406 sf2913 (A6e2; early 13th century)

11991 Incomplete rove. L.36; rove: L.31, W.23, T.6mm 9224 sf2952 (C6e9; mid 13th century)

11992 Incomplete head. L.66; head: W.19; shank: T.6; rove: L.35, W.26mm 9224 sf2953 (C6e9; mid 13th century)

11993 L.38; head: W.20; shank: T.7; rove: L.36, W.23mm 3555 sf2997 (A6c4; 12th century)

11994 Incomplete head and rove. L.43; head: W.17; shank: T.6; rove: L.21, W.20mm 3558 sf3026 (A6c4; 12th century)

11995 Somewhat corroded. L.45; head: W.22; shank: 6; rove: L.28, W.23mm 11966 sf3039 (B6c9; 13th century)

11996 L.41; head: W.22; shank: T.5; rove: L.25, W.18mm 9224 sf3049 (C6e9; mid 13th century)

11997 Roughly rectangular head. L.35; head: W.18; shank: T.6; rove: L.25, W.20mm 12412 sf3150 (C6e5; early 13th century)

11998 Head and most of shank missing. L.26; shank: T.5; rove: L.29, W.27mm 11514 sf3245 (B6c2; 12th/13th century)

11999 Incomplete rove. L.36; head: W.15; shank: T.6; rove: L.21, W.20mm 13416 sf3390 (B6f1; early 14th century)

12000 L.45; head: W.24; shank: T.6; rove: L.24, W.22mm 9215 sf3398 (D6e3; 13th/14th century)

12001 L.48; head: W.20; shank: T.4; rove: L.26, W.21mm 12789 sf3685 (C6e4; 12th/13th century)

12002 L.43; head: W.28; shank: T.7; rove: L.29, W.23mm 12364 sf3820 (C6e6; early 13th century)

12003 Incomplete head and rove. L.55; head: W.24; shank: T.7; rove: L.25, W.22mm 13501 sf3899 (B6c9; 13th century)

12004 Head missing. L.33; shank: T.7; rove: L.31, W.22mm 12635 sf4043 (D6a18; late 12th century)

12005 L.45; head: W.19; shank: T.6; rove: L.30, W.28mm 16072 sf4071 (C6e1; 12th/13th century)

12006 L.38; head: W.19; shank: T.5; rove: L.23, W.22mm 15136 sf4108 (A6n2, B6a5; early 12th century)

12007 L.34; head: W.12; shank: T.6; rove: L.20, W.20mm 16170 sf4119 (D6a16; mid 12th century)

12008 Head missing. L.35; shank: T.4; rove: L:23, W.22mm 16170 sf4320 (D6a16; mid 12th century)

12009 Head and shank badly corroded. L.39; shank: T.5; rove: L.26, W.20mm 16872 sf4506 (C6d9–11; mid–late 12th century)

12010 Head missing. L.34; shank: T.5; rove: L.25, W.23mm 16923 sf4549 (C6d9; mid–late 12th century)

12011 L.38; head: W.23; shank: T.5; rove: L.26, W.18mm 16797 sf4554 (C6d17; late 12th century)

12012 L.35; head: W.22; shank: T.6; rove: L.25, W.21mm 16950 sf4615 (C6d8, D6a8; mid 12th century)

12013 Incomplete rove. L.43; head: W.22; shank: T.7; rove: L.27, W.24mm 17009 sf4634 (B6a7; early 12th century)

12014 L.29; head: W.21; shank: T.8; rove: L.34, W.26mm 17532 sf4775 (C6c4, D6a6; early 12th century)

12015 L.42; head: W.20; shank: T.8; rove: L.40, W.23mm 17380 sf4922 (C6d4; mid 12th century)

12016 L.38; head: W.20; shank: T.7; rove: L.36, W.22mm 17627 sf5005 (C6c6; mid 12th century)

12017 Shank has sub-rounded cross-section. L.36; head: W.16; shank: T.6; rove: L.30, W.18mm 17740 sf5177 (C6c3; early 12th century)

12018 Shank has rounded cross-section. L.31; head: W.15; shank: T.5; rove: L.25, W.19mm 17787 sf5463 (C6c1; early 12th century)

12019 L.28; head: W.18; shank: T.6; rove: L.20, W.15mm 16612 sf6352 (D6a1; late 11th century) (Fig.1408)

12020 L.20; head: W.20; shank: T.4; rove: L.19, W.18mm 9794 sf14708 (D6a25; 12th/13th century)

12021 Rove and stub of shank. L.27, W.26mm 5230 sf14779 (D6a7; 11th/12th century)

12022 Head and part of shank missing. L.23; shank: T.5; rove: L.26, W.24mm 12412 sf14849 (C6e5; early 13th century)

12023 Incomplete rove. L.30; head: W.20 shank: T.7; rove: L.12, W.11mm 3493 sf15262 (A6c1; 12th century)

12024 Incomplete rove. Shank has roughly rounded cross-section. L.32; head: W.16; shank: T.6; rove: L.17, W.15mm 11867 sf15294 (B6f3; early 14th century)

12025 Rove badly corroded and in three pieces, shank has a rounded cross-section. L.42mm u/s sf429

12026 L.50; head: W.24; shank: T.8; rove: L.25, W.21mm u/s sf645

12027 L.24; head: W.17; shank: T.6; rove: L.18, W.18mm u/s sf2755

12028 L.43; head: W.22; shank: T.7; rove: L.24, W.22mm u/s sf4785

Rectangular roves

12029 In two pieces. L.36; head: W.18; shank: T.8; rove: L.22, W.17mm 1283 sf424 (C6z1; late 14th–early 15th century)

12030 L.39; head: W.17; shank: T.5; rove: L.22, W.19mm 1897 sf816 (D6e9; mid 14th century)

12031 L.38; head: W.23; shank: T.6; rove: L.26, W.23mm 5238 sf1474 (C6e5, D6a24; early 13th century)

12032 Incomplete rove. L.42; head: W.24; shank: T.7; rove: L.22, W.18mm 5348 sf1513 (C6e1, D6a16; 12th–13th century)

12033 Shank has sub-rectangular cross-section. L.40; head: W.18; shank: T.7; rove: L.16, W.15mm 3258 sf1752 (A6g1; 13th/14th century)

12034 Incomplete head. L.39; head: W.19; shank: T.6; rove: L.24, W.24mm 5333 sf1820 (D6a17; late 12th century)

12035 Head incomplete. L.30; head: W.25; shank: T.7; rove: L.25, W.24mm 9305 sf1845 (D6a24; 12th/13th century)

12036 L.35; head: W.19; shank: T.5; rove: L.26, W.20mm 5348 sf1899 (C6e1, D6a16; 12th–13th century) (Fig.1408)

12037 Rove has one convex side. L.36; head: W.22; shank: T.7; rove: L.26, W.22mm 9397 sf2265 (D6a17–23; late 12th–12th/13th century)

12038 Head incomplete. L.44; head: W.22; shank: T.8; rove: L.24, W.23mm 12422 sf3073 (D6e1; 13th/14th century)

12039 L.46; head: W.25; shank: T.4; rove: L.24, W.21mm 11342 sf3182 (B6f7; 14th century)

12040 Head missing. L.43; shank: T.8; rove: L.27, W.26mm 11514 sf3241 (B6c2; 12th/13th century)

12041 L.53; head: W.33; shank: T.7; rove: L.29, W.29mm 5668 sf3256 (C6e6; early 13th century)

12042 L.34; head: W.18; shank: T.7; rove: L.29, W.23mm 11583 sf3394 (B6c5; early 13th century)

12043 Rove has been pushed up the shank. L.51; head: W.24; shank: T.8; rove: L.23, W.22mm 3493 sf3673 (A6c1; 12th century)

12044 L.40; head: W.24; shank: T.6; rove: L.28, W.20mm 16104 sf3822 (D6a18; late 12th century)

12045 L.45; head: W.26; shank: T.5; rove: L.26, W.20mm 16117 sf3835 (D6a15–23; mid 12th–12th/13th century)

12046 L.32; head: W.19; shank: T.8; rove: L.22, W.20mm 12671 sf4277 (D6a16; mid 12th century)

12047 Rove has one convex side; shank has rounded cross-section. L.34; head: W.18; shank: T.6; rove: L.23, W.19mm 18366 sf5272 (B6a5; 11th/12th century)

12048 L.37; head: W.18; shank: T.7; rove: L.16, W.16mm 18331 sf5394 (B6a5, C6c3; early 12th century)

12049 Corroded and bent. Incomplete head. L.24; head: W.17; shank: T.5; rove: L.17, W.14mm 13964 sf6140 (B6c8; early 13th century)

12050 Corroded rove. L.38; head: W.18; shank: T.6; rove: L.19, W.16mm 1346 sf14828 (C6z1; late 14th–early 15th century)

12051 L.43; head: W.20; shank: T.6; rove: L.21, W.21mm 4752 sf15237 (C6g19; mid 14th century)

12052 L.32; head: W.16; shank: T.4; rove: L.20, W.14mm 3493 sf15256 (A6c1; 12th century)

12053 L.33; head: W.18; shank: T.6; rove: L.21, W.13mm u/s sf5685

12054 L.37; head: W.18; shank: T.5; rove: L.19, W.17mm u/s sf5686

12055 L.40; head: W.23; shank: T.4; rove: L.18, W.18mm u/s sf9400

12056 L.37; head: W.17; shank: T.4; rove: L.24, W.16mm u/s sf15363

Other clench bolts

12057 Head incomplete, rove missing. L.39; head: W.17; shank: T.5mm 1115 sf201 (D6e9; mid 14th century)

12058 Roughly rounded rove. L.38; head: W.20; shank: T.7; rove: W.20mm 4620 sf1145 (C6e9; mid 13th century)

12059 Rove missing. L.34; head: W.19; shank: T.5mm 5238 sf1371 (C6e5, D6a24; early 13th century)

12060 Rove missing. L.37; head: W.24; shank: T.6mm 5373 sf1505 (C6e7; early 13th century)

12061 Fragmentary head and rove. Head: W.14; shank: T.7; rove: L.46mm 5415 sf1636 (C6c6, D6a7; mid 12th century)

12062 In five pieces and somewhat corroded. L.41; head: W.29; shank: T.10 rove: L.19, W.18mm 11304 sf2707 (B6c7; late 11th–early 12th century)

12063 Rove fragmentary. L.59; head: W.17; shank: T.6mm 3235 sf2788 (A6g1; 13th/14th century)

12064 Head rectangular with rounded corners, rove has two straight sides at 90°, rest rounded. L.55; head: W.19; shank: T.7; rove: L.26, W.21mm 12108 sf2812 (C6e9; mid 13th century)

12065 Rove largely missing. L.60; head: W.30; shank: T.10; rove: W.22mm 5177 sf2891 (C6e11; mid 13th century)

12066 Head and rove largely incomplete. L.54; head: W.20; shank: T.7mm 12190 sf2934 (D6e3; 13th/14th century)

12067 Rove missing. L.50; head: W.21; shank: T.6mm 12467 sf3086 (C6f1; late 13th century)

12068 Rove largely missing, oval head. L.30; head: W.25; shank: T.5mm 11994 sf3104 (B6y2, C6i2; 17th/18th century)

12069 Head and rove incomplete. L.48; head: W.15; shank: T.7; rove: L.28, W.26mm 13227 sf3325 (B6d5, C6f6; 13th century)

12070 Irregularly shaped rove. L.33; head: W.17; shank: T.5; rove: L.16, W.15mm 6257 sf3330 (C6c4; early 12th century)

12071 Head missing, sub-rectangular rove. L.32; shank: T.7; rove: L.26, W.25mm 11583 sf3396 (B6c5; early 13th century)

12072 Irregularly shaped head. L.44; head: W.27; shank: T.6; rove: L.26, W.25mm 13861 sf3604 (C6e7; early 13th century)

12073 Incomplete rove. L.63; head: W.27; shank: T.7; rove: L.63, W.25mm 13862 sf3650 (B6d2; 13th century)

12074 Rove, sub-rectangular, and another nail or clench bolt. L.52; head: W.23; shank: T.6; rove: L.34, W.26mm 12725 sf3693 (D6a26–b1; late 12th–early 13th century)

12075 Head and part of shank missing. L.30; shank: T.5; rove: L.50, W.35mm 12647 sf3928 (D6c1; mid 13th century)

12076 Incomplete rove. L.29; head: W.15; shank: T.5; rove: L.18mm 13800 sf4718 (B6d2, C6e8; mid 13th century)

12077 Fragments. 18047 sf4743 (B6c3; 12th/13th century)

12078 Incomplete, irregularly shaped rove which has been pushed up the shank. L.50; head: W.23; shank: T.4; rove: L.50, W.25mm 3214 sf14652 (A6i2; 14th/15th century)

12079 Head and rove largely missing. L.34mm 13964 sf14931 (B6c8; early 13th century)

12080 Badly corroded. L.60mm 10507 sf15093 (C6g5–7; late 14th–14th/15th century)

12081 Fragmentary rove and part of shank. 10739 sf15108 (C6f1; late 13th century)

12082 Rove missing. L.30; head: W.17; shank: T.7mm 17551 sf15213 (C6c3; early 12th century)

12083 Rove fragmentary, lead lump below head and spots of lead on shank. L.43; head: W.24; shank: T.8mm 9224 sf15977 (C6e9; mid 13th century)

12084 Rove fragmentary. L.40; head: W.29; shank: T.6mm u/s sf3118

Clench bolt roves

Diamond-shaped

12085 Incomplete. L.18, W.13mm 5978 sf2186 (D6a6; 11th/12th century)

12086 L.17, W.15mm 3344 sf2293 (A6g1; 13th/14th century)

12087 Incomplete. L.33, W.30mm 5981 sf2333 (C6c3, D6a5; late 11th/early 12th century)

12088 L.25, W.20mm 18134 sf5110 (B6c5; early 13th century)

12089 Incomplete. L.22, W.18mm 5536 sf14912 (C6e1; 12th/13th century)

Rectangular

12090 L.34, W.24mm 4164 sf388 (C6z1; late 14th–early 15th century)

12091 L.22, W.19mm 11007 sf2389 (C6e6; early 13th century)

12092 L.28, W.26mm 10334 sf2654 (C6g3, mid 14th century)

12093 L.22, W.22mm 6258 sf5026 (C6c3, D6a5; late11th/early 12th century)

Staples

All have rectangular cross-sections and tapering arms with wedge-shaped tips, unless otherwise stated.

Rectangular

Wider faces of arms at 90° to wider faces of the staple itself

12094 One arm incomplete, other out-turned. L.31, W.64, T.11mm 1693 sf498 (D6f2; early 15th century)

12095 Now bent flat. One arm missing, complete arm tip pointed. L.39, W.76, T.12mm 4591 sf655 (C6g19; mid 14th century)

12096 One arm missing, other inturned and clenched. L.25, W.32, T.6mm 3253 sf966 (A6g1; 13th/14th century)

12097 One arm missing, surviving arm tapers to a point. L.28, W.63, T.7mm 9215 sf1023 (D6e3; 13th/14th century)

12098 Arms taper to a point, and are inturned and clenched. L.50, W.37, T.6mm 4620 sf1122 (C6e9; mid 13th century)

12099 Incomplete, head bent, arm inturned. L.16, W.22, T.7mm 4620 sf1197 (C6e9; mid 13th century)

12100 Surviving arm tip pointed. L.20, W.38, T.5mm 5262 sf1251 (D6d1; late 13th century)

12101 Badly corroded. Both arms incomplete. L.18, W.34, T.4mm 4620 sf19633 (C6e9; mid 13th century)

12102 One arm missing, surviving arm tapers to a point. L.20, W.39, T.6mm 4620 sf1261 (C6e9; mid 13th century)

12103 Arms taper to a point, one tip is slightly inturned. L.27, W.29, T.6mm 4620 sf1310 (C6e9; mid 13th century)

12104 One arm missing, one arm twisted, was inturned. L.20, W.35, T.5mm 9224 sf1414 (C6e9; mid 13th century)

12105 Arms inturned and overlap. L.39, W.59, T.8mm 5238 sf1500 (C6e5, D6a24; early 13th century)

12106 One arm, tip out-turned. L.45, W.7, T.2mm 9305 sf1662 (D6a24; 12th/13th century)

12107 One arm, tip out-turned. L.50, W.5, T.4mm 9330 sf1672 (D6a25–6; 12th/13th century)

12108 Arms taper to a point and are inturned. L.24, W.35, T.4mm 5348 sf1986 (C6e1, D6a16; 12th–13th century)

12109 In two pieces. Arms inturned and clenched. L.21, original W.40, T.2mm 5981 sf2192 (C6c3, D6a5; late 11th/early 12th century)

12110 One arm missing, the other has pointed tip. L.56, W.26, T.4mm 5981 sf2231 (C6c3, D6a5; late 11th/early 12th century)

12111 Arms incomplete. L.20, W.55, T.10mm 10397 sf2535 (C6g15; late 15th century)

12112 One arm incomplete, the other bent, both were inturned. L.14, W.63, T.7mm 11298 sf2626 (A6e5, B6e1; late 13th century)

12113 One arm inturned, the other out-turned. L.32, W.75, T.6mm 11045 sf2630 (B6c8; early 13th century)

12114 One arm. L.30, T.7mm 11332 sf2670 (B6f3; early 14th century)

12115 One arm incomplete. L.47, W.54, T.10mm 11344 sf2762 (B6f7; 14th century)

12116 One half, arm end inturned. L.25, W.29, T.7mm 9224 sf2813 (C6e9; mid 13th century)

12117 One arm and head fragment. L.60, W.22, T.7mm 11344 sf2859 (B6f7; 14th century)

12118 One arm inturned, the other missing. L.18, W.53, T.10mm 12018 sf2886 (D6e9; mid 14th century)

12119 Half. L.24, W.18, T.2mm 12180 sf2911 (D6e5; early 14th century)

12120 Arms splayed. L.29, W.39, T.7mm 9224 sf2929 (C6e9; mid 13th century)

12121 One arm longer than the other, tips pointed. L.34, W.27, T.6mm 5981 sf2943 (C6c3, D6a5; late 11th/early 12th century)

12122 L.29, W.55, T.6mm 11376 sf2963 (B6f1; early 14th century)

12123 One arm missing. L.20, W.30mm 12223 sf2971 (C6f6; late 13th century)

12124 One arm missing, the other has inturned tip. L.15, W.34, T.5mm 11867 sf2986 (B6f3; early 14th century)

12125 Arms inturned. L.18, W.30, T.9mm 12365 sf3020 (C6e6; early 13th century)

12126 Very corroded, arm missing. L.21, W.35mm 13039 sf3126 (B6y1; 16th–17th century)

12127 One arm, tip clenched. L.52, T.7mm 13202 sf3200 (B6f4; early 14th century)

12128 One arm curved forwards, the other bent, but was inturned and clenched. L.25, W.51, T.7mm 5975 sf3201 (C6c6; mid 12th century)

12129 L.38, W.79, T.7mm 12507 sf3292 (C6e3; 12th/13th century)

12130 One arm missing, one incomplete, head appreciably wider than the arms. L.34, W.60, T.10mm 12276 sf3411 (D6e5; early 14th century)

12131 Arms incurving. L.24, W.54, T.13mm 13243 sf3438 (B6a7; early 12th century)

12132 L.32, W.68, T.6mm 12619 sf3443 (D6a24; 12th/13th century)

12133 Arms splayed, one arm tip missing, the other bent in. L.45, W.49, T.6mm 13465 sf3507 (B6c1; 12th/13th century)

12134 Arms splayed. L.32, W.41, T.5mm 16074 sf3809 (C6d20; late 12th century)

12135 L.26, W.34, T.3mm 13554 sf3825 (B6a5; 11th/12th century)

12136 One arm missing. L.28, W.78, T.8mm 16362 sf4160 (B6c7; late 11th–early 12th century)

12137 L.27, W.39, T.5mm 16470 sf4169 (C6d5–12; mid–late 12th century)

12138 One arm missing, head distorted, surviving arm inturned and clenched. L.27, W.50, T.6mm 16170 sf4314 (D6a16; mid 12th century)

12139 Arms splayed. L.32, W.48, T.5mm 16925 sf4516 (C6d9; mid–late 12th century)

12140 L.29, W.31, T.5mm 16925 sf4530 (C6d9; mid–late 12th century)

12141 L.30, W.36, T.5mm 16925 sf4534 (C6d9; mid–late 12th century)

12142 One arm missing, the other inturned. L.29, W.28, T.5mm 16925 sf4544 (C6d9; mid–late 12th century)

12143 Arms splayed. L.30, W.32, T.5mm 16967 sf4546 (C6d10; mid–late 12th century)

12144 Arms splayed. L.28, W.37, T.5mm 17217 sf4626 (C6d4; mid 12th century)

12145 Bent. Arms inturned. L.16, W.39, T.5mm 18048 sf4759 (B6c4; 12th/13th century)

12146 L.20, W.38, T.7mm 18172 sf4779 (B6c1; 12th/13th century)

12147 Arms inturned, one incomplete, one clenched. L.16, W.41, T.4mm 3537 sf4851 (A6c4; 12th century)

12148 Overlapping inturned arms. L.45, W.39, T.5mm 16734 sf5012 (C6a1, D6a1; late 11th century)

12149 Head straight, arms curve inwards, tips missing. L.23, W.18, T.3mm 17551 sf5021 (C6c3; early 12th century)

12150 One arm missing, the other inturned and clenched. L.11, W.23, T.3mm 6258 sf5030 (C6c3, D6a5; late11th/early 12th century)

12151 Arms inturned and clenched. L.47, W.63, T.4mm 16734 sf5033 (C6a1, D6a1; late 11th century)

12152 One arm missing, the other inturned. L.17, W.24, T.4mm 17786 sf5199 (C6c2; early 12th century)

12153 Both arms were inturned; one now bent flat, the other incomplete. Original L.26, W.50, T.7mm 18331 sf5324 (B6a5, C6c3; early 12th century)

12154 Flattened out, one arm missing, the other arm tip out-turned. L.30, W.60, T.5mm 16612 sf5337 (D6a1; late 11th century)

12155 One arm missing, the other has tip inturned. L.20, W.31, T.5mm 17890 sf5445 (B6a1, C6a1; late 11th century)

12156 Arms inturned. L.20, W.35, T.4mm 17890 sf5639 (B6a1, C6a1; late 11th century)

12157 One arm missing, surviving arm inturned and incomplete. L.19, W.52, T.6mm 6339 sf5701 (D6a1; late 11th century)

12158 One arm, tip inturned. L.30, W.4mm 16615 sf7378 (D6a3–9, late 11th century–early 12th century)

12159 Both arms are largely missing. L.8, W.42, T.6mm 3362 sf14639 (A6ef; 13th century)

12160 Corroded. One arm missing, surviving arm incomplete. L.30, W.77, T.7mm 3214 sf14653 (A6i2; 14th/15th century)

12161 L.31, W.35, T.6mm 9252 sf14693 (D6e1; 13th/14th century)

12162 One arm missing, the other inturned. L.20, W.38, T.8mm 3237 sf14703 (A6i2; 14th/15th century)

12163 One arm. L.57, W.10, T.3mm 5262 sf14726 (D6d1; late 13th century)

12164 One arm missing; complete arm slightly inturned, tip pointed. L.52, W.42, T.7mm 5263 sf14833 (D6c1; mid 13th century)

12165 One arm missing; complete arm tip pointed and inturned. L.25, W.32, T.6mm 9224 sf14990 (C6e9; mid 13th century)

12166 One arm missing; surviving arm incomplete. L.16, W.36, T.4mm 11658 sf15302 (B6c7; late 11th–early 12th century)

12167 One arm missing; surviving arm tapers to a point, diamond-shaped cross-section. L.38, W.23, T.6mm 13501 sf15426 (B6c9; 13th century)

12168 One arm missing, the other has an inturned tip. L.17, W.40, T.8mm 5395 sf15836 (C6c6, D6a7; mid 12th century)

12169 Two arms. L.41 and 40mm 5975 sf15838 (C6c6; mid 12th century)

Wider faces of arms in same plane as staple itself

12170 One arm incomplete. L.36, W.84, T.6mm 5021 sf866 (C6e10–11; mid 13th century)

12171 One arm incomplete. L.55, W.46, T.7mm 5000 sf14731 (C6c6; mid 12th century)

U-shaped

Wider faces of arms at 90° to faces of staple itself

12172 Head has rounded cross-section. L.83, W.60, T.9mm 4105 sf265 (C6h2; early 16th century)

12173 One arm tip missing, other bent forwards. L.82, W.39, T.6mm 1455 sf356 (C6x2–6; 11th/13th century)

12174 One arm tip missing. L.36, W.17, T.6mm 4698 sf764 (C6f1; late 13th century)

12175 Arms taper to a point. L.46, W.25, T.6mm 5037 sf887 (C6e10; mid 13th century)

12176 Arms splay out, tips pointed. L.40, Original W.24 (now 55), T.5mm 5262 sf1296 (D6d1; late 13th century)

12177 L.49, W.27, T.2mm 9224 sf1403 (C6e9; mid 13th century)

12178 One arm largely missing. L.62, W.23, T.4mm 9224 sf1447 (C6e9; mid 13th century)

12179 One arm; tapers to a rounded tip. L.56, W.10, T.4mm 5348 sf1555 (C6e1, D6a16; 12th–13th century)

12180 Arms wedge-shaped, tips rounded; head is unusually wide, convex sides. L.55, W.33, T.6mm 9302 sf1556 (D6a26; 12th/13th century)

12181 Head now bent, but was slightly curved; arms curve inwards, clenched at tips. L.20, W.135, T.10mm 9302 sf1609 (D6a26; 12th/13th century)

12182 Arm tips bent forwards. L.32, W.23, T.7mm 5397 sf1797 (C6c6; mid 12th century)

12183 L.47, W.30, T.5mm 5348 sf1900 (C6e1, D6a16; 12th–13th century)

12184 Arms tips missing. L.30, W.27, T.6mm 5811 sf1948 (D6a10–15; early–mid 12th century)

12185 One arm and part of the head are missing. 5348 sf1974 (C6e1, D6a16; 12th–13th century)

12186 Arm tips bent forwards. L.50, W.23, T.4mm 9305 sf2045 (D6a24; 12th/13th century)

12187 One arm incomplete, the other has an out-turned tip. L.48, W.24, T.6mm 5981 sf2142 (C6c3, D6a5; late 11th/early 12th century)

12188 One arm incomplete, diamond-shaped cross-section. L.37, W.27, T.6mm 10532 sf2614 (C6g7–9; 14th/15th century)

12189 One arm incomplete; complete arm tapers to a point, diamond-shaped cross-section. L.68, W.30, T.9mm 10678 sf2635 (D6g2; mid 16th century)

12190 One arm longer than the other and bent out at the end. L.48, W.25, T.8mm 11291 sf2758 (B6f7; 14th century)

12191 Lower part of arms bent outwards, one tip bent forwards. L.56, W.50, T.8mm 11760 sf2876 (B6g2; 14th/15th century)

12192 Arms have pointed tips. L.45, W.18, T.6mm 11654 sf2883 (B6c7; late 11th–early 12th century)

12193 L.55, W.33, T.7mm 10974 sf2909 (D6e7; early 14th century)

12194 Arms splayed. L.33, W.35, T.6mm 11376 sf2965 (B6f1; early 14th century)

12195 One arm tip out-turned and one inturned. L.47, W.21, T.8mm 5981 sf3034 (C6c3, D6a5; late 11th/early 12th century)

12196 L.48, W.19, T.6mm 11284 sf3052 (B6f7; 14th century)

12197 One arm missing. L.60, W.35, T.7mm 9802 sf3078 (D6y1; late 12th–13th century)

12198 Arms splayed, one longer than the other. L.43, W.35, T.4mm 12485 sf3172 (D6c1; mid 13th century)

12199 One arm tip out-turned, the other curved forwards. L.50, W.28, T.6mm 13465 sf3413 (B6c1; 12th/13th century)

12200 One arm missing. L.37, W.31, T.5mm 13245 sf3441 (B6a7; early 12th century)

12201 One arm longer than the other. L.66, W.23, T.6mm 9224 sf3534 (C6e9; mid 13th century)

12202 L.69, W.29, T.9mm 13454 sf3813 (B6d2; mid 13th century)

12203 One arm has been severed, the other is bent inwards. L.51, W.33, T.7mm 12840 sf3913 (C6d23; late 12th century)

12204 L.38, W.20, T.6mm 12944 sf3914 (B6c4, C6e6; early 13th century)

12205 L.56, W.37, T.7mm 16612 sf4561 (D6a1; late 11th century)

12206 Diamond-shaped cross-section. One arm incomplete, the other has pointed tip. L.36, W.31, T.6mm 16879 sf4686 (C6c5–d17; early–late 12th century)

12207 One arm incomplete. L.22, W.17, T.3mm 18366 sf4927 (B6a5; 11th/12th century)

12208 Incomplete. L.25, W.16, T.4mm 13902 sf4940 (12th/13th century)

12209 One arm longer than the other, both tips pointed. L.37, W.22, T.5mm 13902 sf5158 (B6c3; 12th/13th century)

12210 L.37, W.21, T.4mm 15285 sf5258 (B6a1; late 11th century)

12211 Arms taper; one tip missing, the other pointed. L.42, W.27, T.7mm 3362 sf14638 (A6ef; 13th century)

12212 Corroded. L.34, W.32, T.4mm 5186 sf14787 (C6e7; early 13th century)

12213 One arm missing. L.26, W.40, T.8mm 12501 sf14843 (C6e7; early 13th century)

12214 Arm. L.53, W.5mm 12113 sf14945 (C6e11; mid 13th century)

12215 L.58, W.27, T.2mm 10617 sf15120 (B6g10; 15th/16th century)

12216 One arm. L.60, W.8mm 10531 sf15121 (C6g1; early–mid 14th century)

12217 Arms taper to a point, rounded cross-section. L.31, W.18, T.5mm 17699 sf15220 (C6c1; early 12th century)

12218 Arms taper to a point. L.45, W.34, T.7mm 3235 sf15276 (A6g1; 13th/14th century)

12219 One arm incomplete; surviving arm tapers to a point. L.37, W.24, T.5mm 11758 sf15305 (B6g9; 15th/16th century)

12220 One arm. L.79, W.8, T.7mm 3362 sf15985 (A6ef; 13th century)

12221 One arm tip out-turned. L.38, W.24, T.4mm 1037 sf205 (modern)

12222 One arm tip missing. L.48, W.25, T.8mm u/s sf4713

Arms' wider faces in same plane as staple itself

12223 Arms have pointed tips. L.70, W.29, T.7mm 4043 sf213 (C6z1; late 14th–early 15th century)

12224 Arm and incomplete head. L.60, W.19, T.6mm 10335 sf2537 (C6g12–14; mid 15th century)

12225 L.69, W.29, T.10mm 12106 sf2960 (C6e9, D6e1; mid 13th century)

12226 L.48, W.21, T.6mm 12501 sf4006 (C6e7; early 13th century)

12227 L.43, W.37, T.6mm 15124 sf4122 (B6a7; early 12th century)

12228 One arm incomplete. L.55, W.46, T.7mm 9252 sf14696 (D6e1; 13th/14th century)

12229 L.31, W.20, T.7mm 3235 sf15277 (A6g1; 13th/14th century)

Looped

12230 Half. L.59, W.5, T.2mm 17890 sf6035 (B6a1, C6a1; late 11th century)

Staple fragments

12231 One arm missing, the other inturned and clenched. L.11, W.34mm 5348 sf1498 (C6e1, D6a16; 12th–13th century)

12232 5348 sf2503 (C6e1, D6a16; 12th–13th century)

12233 One arm missing, the other curved inwards. L.7. W.49mm 7782 sf3108 (D6y1; late 12th–13th century)

12234 Arm. L.65, W.7mm 12496 sf3199 (D6a24; 12th/13th century)

12235 Arm; inturned at end. L.30mm 13302 sf3304 (B6f5, C6f6; early 14th century)

12236 Arm. L.58, W.8, T.2mm 2305 sf15847 (B6v1; 13th–early 14th century)

12237 Arm. L.50, W.9, T.2mm u/s sf2852

12238 Arm. L.37, W.7, T.2mm u/s sf15142

Small iron collars or clips

These objects are similar to staples, but their arms overlap.

12239 Oval, rounded cross-section. Arms twisted around each other. D.28, T.2mm 9129 sf960 (D6e9; mid 14th century) (Fig.1408)

12240 In two pieces, originally round. L.40, W.28, T.2.5mm 9122 sf1046 (D6e1; 13th/14th century) (Fig.1408)

12241 Incomplete, was oval. L.28, W.19, T.4mm 9793 sf3005 (D6a25; 12th/13th century)

12242 Incomplete, round. D.24, W.7mm 12485 sf3135 (D6c1; mid 13th century)

12243 L.14, W.13, T.10mm 11995 sf3140 (B6y1; 16th–17th century)

12244 Oval. L.20, W.13, T.2mm 16170 sf4323 (D6a16; mid 12th century)

Wall anchors

12245 Bent, widens at one end, where rounded pierced terminal. Other end probably originally similar, but now broken. Pinched in the centre to form a projection from one face. L.76, W.18, T.12mm 4915 sf943 (C6e11; mid 13th century) (Fig.1409)

12246 One half consists of a tang which tapers to a wedge-shaped tip; the other steps in on one face and is flattened to a rounded terminal. L.129, W.13, T.8mm 10527 sf2576 (B6g11; early 16th century)

Hinge pivots

All shanks taper and have rectangular cross-sections; all guide arms have a rounded cross-section unless stated.

12247 Guide arm: L.44, W.12; shank: L.85, W.23; bracket: L.170, T.10mm 1097 sf127 (C6i1; late 17th century)

12248 Shank incomplete, corner flattened. Guide arm: L.63, W.14; shank: L.58, W.24mm 4497 sf633 (C6e13; mid 13th century)

12249 Shank incomplete, corner markedly rounded. Guide arm: L.40, W.14; shank: L.43, W.13mm 4001 sf760 (C6i3; 17th–18th century)

12250 Shank tip missing. Guide arm: L.57, W.11; shank: L.76, W.21mm 5051 sf902 (C6e10; mid 13th century)

12251 Guide arm has a sub-rectangular cross-section, corner slightly flattened. Guide arm: L.55, W.12; shank: L.73, W.21mm 4620 sf925 (C6e9; mid 13th century)

12252 Guide arm has a sub-rectangular cross-section, corner slightly flattened. Guide arm: L.48, W.9; shank: L.71, W.18mm 5021 sf1033 (C6e10–11; mid 13th century) (Fig.1413)

12253 Guide arm largely missing, shank tip pointed, corner slightly flattened. Guide arm: L.20, W.10; shank: L.79, W.16mm 4620 sf1226 (C6e9; mid 13th century)

12254 Guide arm has a sub-rectangular cross-section, shank tip missing. Guide arm: L.31, W.6; shank: L.47, W.9mm 3258 sf1420 (A6g1; 13th/14th century)

12255 Shank incomplete. Guide arm: L.46, W.10; shank: L.47, W.18mm 4620 sf1446 (C6e9; mid 13th century)

12256 Corner roughly flattened, guide arm incurved. Guide arm: L.45, W.8; shank: L.61, W.16mm 5348 sf1480 (C6e1, D6a16; 12th–13th century) (Fig.1413)

12257 Guide arm has a sub-rectangular cross-section. Shank tip pointed and clenched. Corner flattened. Guide arm: L.29, W.5; shank: L.57, W.12mm 9305 sf2011 (D6a24; 12th/13th century)

12258 Shank tip pointed. Guide arm: L.65, W.13; shank: L.70, W.13mm 5348 sf2080 (C6e1, D6a16; 12th–13th century)

12259 Shank largely missing, corner slightly flattened. Guide arm: L.48, W.11; shank: L.22, W.16mm 10553 sf2653 (C6g2; early–mid 14th century)

12260 Shank flattened towards tip and squared off. Guide arm: L.28, W.10; shank: L.70, W.10mm 10531 sf2683 (C6g1; early–mid 14th century)

12261 Shank tip squared off. Guide arm: L.74, W.14; shank: L.114, W.19mm 10923 sf2720 (C6g1; early–mid 14th century)

12262 Corroded; shank incomplete. Guide arm: L.34, W.10; shank: L.32, W.12mm 11612 sf2794 (B6g3, C6g7; early 15th century)

12263 Shank incomplete, corner roughly flattened. Guide arm: L.36, W.7; shank: L.37, W.12mm 10797 sf2795 (D6h1; late 16th century)

12264 Shank tip pointed; corner slightly flattened. Guide arm: L.41, W.11; shank: L.79, W.17mm 12018 sf2800 (D6e9; mid 14th century)

12265 Shank flattened towards the tip and squared off. Guide arm: L.31, W.15; shank: L.59, W.15mm 11626 sf2809 (B6g4; early 15th century)

12266 Corroded; guide arm has sub-rectangular cross-section, shank tip pointed. Guide arm: L.51, W.11; shank: L.82, W.15mm 11378 sf2894 (C6e2; 12th/13th century)

12267 Shank tip missing; corner slightly flattened. Guide arm: L.36, W.9; shank: L.56, W.15mm 11820 sf2968 (B6g2; 14th/15th century)

12268 Guide arm has a sub-rectangular cross-section, shank largely missing. Guide arm: L.47, W.10; shank: L.22, W.9mm 12368 sf3055 (D6e3; 13th/14th century)

12269 Shank incomplete, corner slightly flattened. Guide arm: L.56, W.12; shank: L.67, W.22mm 12485 sf3228 (D6c1; mid 13th century)

12270 Guide arm has sub-rectangular cross-section, shank tip missing, corner slightly flattened. Guide arm: L.41, W.10;

shank: L.81, W.15mm 13244 sf3238 (B6c2–6; 12th/13th century)

12271 Guide arm: L.61, W.11; shank: L.96, W.20mm 7895 sf3346 (C6x3; early 13th century)

12272 Shank incomplete, corner slightly flattened. Guide arm: L.46, T.8; shank: L.31, W.18mm 12544 sf3358 (D6a25; 12th/13th century)

12273 Guide arm only. L.41, W.13mm 13140 sf3393 (B6v1; 13th–early 14th century)

12274 Shank tip missing, corner slightly flattened. Guide arm: L.65, W.15; shank: L.99, W.22mm 13454 sf3405 (B6d2; mid 13th century)

12275 Shank tip squared off, corner slightly flattened. Guide arm: L.46, W.9; shank: L.62, W.16mm 13501 sf3463 (B6c9; 13th century)

12276 Corroded. Shank incomplete. Guide arm: L.39, W.8; shank: L.36, W.9mm 16616 sf4258 (D6a12; early 12th century)

12277 Guide arm has sub-rectangular cross-section, corner slightly flattened. Guide arm: L.46, W.10; shank: L.81, W.14mm 16642 sf4296 (C6d12; late 12th century)

12278 Corner flattened; shank tip curled over. Guide arm: L.66, W.14; shank: L.100, W.25mm 16774 sf4418 (C6d20; late 12th century) (Fig.1413)

12279 Shank tip pointed, corner slightly flattened. Guide arm: L.66, W.14; shank: L.99, W.19mm 16782 sf4461 (C6d9; mid–late 12th century)

12280 Guide arm has a sub-rectangular cross-section, shank tip pointed. Guide arm: L.55, W.12; shank: L.96, W.19mm 17048 sf4577 (C6d8; mid–late 12th century)

12281 Shank tip pointed, corner slightly flattened. Guide arm: L.55, W.14; shank: L.87, W.19mm 18153 sf4750 (B6c3; 12th/13th century)

12282 Shank tip pointed, corner slightly flattened. Guide arm: L.31, W.8; shank: L.43, W.11mm 18366 sf4944 (B6a5; 11th/12th century)

12283 Shank tip squared off, corner slightly flattened. Guide arm: L.37, W.5; shank: L.51, W.14mm 17695 sf5024 (B6a5, C6c6; mid 12th century)

12284 Shank tip rounded, corner slightly flattened. Guide arm: L.45, W.11; shank: L.97, W.11mm 6339 sf5113 (D6a1; late 11th century)

12285 Guide arm has a sub-rectangular cross-section, shank tip rounded and clenched. Guide arm: L.30, W.7; shank: L.56, W.13mm 16612 sf5421 (D6a1; late 11th century)

12286 Guide arm has sub-rectangular cross-section, shank tip squared off. Guide arm: L.47, W.14; shank: L.63, W.12mm 5263 sf14834 (D6c1; mid 13th century)

12287 Shank tip missing. Guide arm: L.32, W.7; shank: L.52, W.12mm 10735 sf15126 (C6e11, D6e3; 13th/14th century)

12288 Shank tip pointed and clenched. Corner appears worn. Guide arm: L.34, W.8; shank: L.65, W.10mm 11776 sf15307 (B6f3; early 14th century)

12289 Guide arm has a sub-rectangular cross-section, tip missing, shank tip also missing, corner slightly flattened. Guide arm: L.41, W.9; shank: L.60, W.12mm 1506 sf15313 (D6e9; mid 14th century)

12290 Very corroded. Guide arm: L.45, T.11; shank: L.95, W.18mm 1097 sf15403 (C6i1; late 17th century)

12291 Fragmentary. L.30, W.30mm 1034 sf15869 (C6h3–4; early–mid 16th century)

12292 Guide arm has sub-rectangular cross-section. Shank tip clenched. Guide arm: L.70, W.8; shank: L.92, W.17mm u/s sf1602 (Fig.1413)

12293 Guide arm has a sub-rectangular cross-section, shank tip pointed, corner slightly flattened. Guide arm: L.46, W.7; shank: L.87, W.15mm u/s sf6244

12294 Guide arm has a sub-rectangular cross-section, shank tip missing. Guide arm: L.38, W.9; shank: L.56, W.9mm u/s sf6458

Latch rests

In each case the catch is triangular and formed by the widening and flattening the shank, and creating a shoulder which is usually vertical; the tip is squared off. Shanks, where complete, have wedge-shaped tips.

12295 L.105; catch: L.29, W.17, T.8mm 1506 sf87 (D6e9; mid 14th century)

12296 L.98; catch: L.23, W.18, T.6mm 5141 sf1222 (C6e10; mid 13th century) (Fig.1413)

12297 Shank incomplete. The catch tip droops down slightly. L.67; catch: L.32, W.19, T.5mm 9248 sf1286 (D6c1; mid 13th century)

12298 Shank incomplete. L.63; catch: L.9, W.13, T.7mm 10490 sf2577 (C6g10; early 15th century)

12299 Shank tip missing. L.63, W.15, T.5mm 12662 sf3458 (D6a26–d1; late 12th–mid 13th century)

12300 Shank incomplete. There is a concave shoulder between the shank and catch. The tip droops slightly downwards. L.62; catch: L.27, W.21, T.9mm u/s sf2464

Hooks

All have shanks of rectangular cross-section unless stated.

Wall hooks

12301 Tapering shank, tip missing. Hook stepped at base. Shank: L.71, W.10, T.6; hook: L.35, W.5mm 10355 sf2531 (C6g14–15; mid–late 15th century) (Fig.1413)

12302 Shank incomplete. Shank: L.25, W.11, T.6; hook: L.42mm 3493 sf3556 (A6c1; 12th century)

12303 Tapering shank with pointed tip. The hook is made from a strip of sub-rectangular cross-section which was welded to the side of the shank and there is a step at its base. Shank: L.103, W.7, T.7; hook: W.48mm 15107 sf3770 (B6c3; 12th/13th century) (Fig.1413)

12304 Shank flattened and widened in the centre and then tapers to a wedge-shaped tip. One of the faces of the wider part has five vertical indentations in it. Hook arm has a sub-rectangular cross-section and tapers to a point. Shank: L.165, W.25, T.14; hook: L.76, W.14, T.11mm 16584 sf4128 (C6d12–19; late 12th century) (Fig.1413)

12305 Shank incomplete, slight step at the base of the hook arm which tapers to wedge-shaped tip. Hook arm: L.34, W.9; shank: L.26, W.5mm 16734 sf6004 (C6a1, D6a1; late 11th century)

12306 Shank incomplete. Hook: L.46, T.5; shank: L.25, W.11mm 1502 sf15513 (C6e11, D6e3; mid 13th century)

12307 L-shaped; tapering shank and hook. Shank: L.132; hook: L.35, W.9mm u/s sf8

S-hooks

12308 Slanted shank and U-shaped hooks, tips missing. L.68, W.6; hooks: W.26mm 9224 sf1340 (C6e9; mid 13th century)

12309 Straight shank with shallow U-shaped hooks, tips flattened to a wedge shape. L.91, W.13, T.4; hook: W.21mm 10466 sf2546 (C6g14–15; mid–late 15th century)

12310 Straight shank with shallow U-shaped hooks, tips flattened to a wedge shape. L.116, W.13, T.3mm 12619 sf3417 (D6a24; 12th/13th century) (Fig.1414)

12311 L.38, T.4mm 13191 sf3435 (B6c3; 12th/13th century)

12312 Slanted shank which tapers into U-shaped hooks at each end; the hooks taper to a point. L.83, W.7, T.7; hooks: L.27, W.23mm 13902 sf5146 (B6c3; 12th/13th century) (*Fig.1414*)

12313 Slanted shank of rounded cross-section, U-shaped hooks, one of which is largely missing. L.33, W.4; hook: W.11mm 9224 sf15017 (C6e9; mid 13th century)

12314 Narrows from one end to the other. L.53, W.8, T.3mm 6258 sf15797 (C6c3, D6a5; late11th/early 12th century)

Swivel hook

12315 Shank has a rounded cross-section, hook has a rectangular cross-section, head domed. Plated (tin-rich tin-lead alloy). L.30, W.5; head: D.13mm 9305 sf1594 (D6a24; 12th/13th century) (*Fig.1414*)

Other hook

12316 Possible boat hook. Consists of a socket, pierced for attachment, which is flattened at the head into a wide L-shaped arm. L.103; socket: D.20; hook: L.35, W.18mm 13147 sf3976 (B6v1; 13th–early 14th century)

Hinge straps

Large straps

9056 Two hinge straps attached to shutter. Both taper to rounded, pierced terminal. Main body pierced three times. L.310mm 3270 sf19521 (A6i3; early 15th century) (*Fig.1415*)

12317 Broken at one end. It narrows towards the complete end where it widens into a rounded, pierced terminal. L.71, W.16, T.4; terminal: W.21mm 1502 sf447 (C6e11, D6e3; mid 13th century)

12318 Broken at one end where it starts to curve over and flatten out; strap pierced three times and narrows towards a rounded, pierced terminal which tapers to a pointed tip. L.224, W.36, T.5mm 4385 sf534 (C6i4; 16th–19th century) (*Fig.1416*)

12319 Broken at one end. At the complete end the strap is drawn out into a narrow strip and curved over to form a loop. Pierced near the broken end. L.70, W.39, T.4mm 4915 sf944 (C6e11; mid 13th century)

12320 Incomplete. At one end an incomplete loop; the other end broken. Pierced twice. L.175, W.15, T.4mm 1502 sf977 (C6e11, D6e3; mid 13th century) (*Fig.1416*)

12321 Bent, broken at one end over a hole. It narrows towards the complete end where it is flattened and widened, the sides becoming briefly convex. There is a bifurcated terminal, arms have looped ends. L.134, W.22; terminal: W.55mm 11867 sf2948 (B6f3; early 14th century) (*Fig.1416*)

12322 Broken at each end. Widens slightly towards one end where it narrows again before the break. Pierced twice, nail stubs in situ. L.166, W.37, T.7mm 11883 sf3161 (B6f3; early 14th century) (*Fig.1416*)

12323 Broken at one end, a bifurcated scrolled terminal at the other. L.61, W.19, T.7mm 13243 sf3449 (B6a7; early 12th century) (*Fig.1416*)

12324 Sides concave; at one end there was probably a rounded terminal, broken over piercing, at the other end it is pierced before tapering into a curved arm with a looped terminal. L.119, W.32, T.5mm 16410 sf4230 (D6a12; early 12th century)

Strap terminal

12325 One arm of bifurcated hinge strap terminal. L.44, W.31, T.4mm 4784 sf937 (C6g19; mid 14th century) (*Fig.1416*)

Small straps

12326 Incomplete link at the head, narrows towards the base, but broken, pierced once. Plated (tin). L.39, W.17, T.1mm 9122 sf1019 (D6e1; 13th/14th century) (*Fig.1416*)

12327 Link at the head, strap incomplete, pierced with a rectangular hole at the break. Short grooves along the sides on one face and two diagonal grooves cut into one shoulder at the base of the link. Plated (tin with possible trace of lead). L.44, W.34mm 9305 sf1624 (D6a24; 12th/13th century) (*Fig.1416*)

12328 Incomplete eye or link at head, of D-shaped cross-section. The strap is pierced at each end. One face covered with criss-cross grooves. Plated (tin). L.54, W.10, T.3mm 5348 sf2036 (C6e1, D6a16; 12th–13th century) (*Fig.1416*)

U-eyed hinges

On each side of the eye are a strap and terminal or two terminals or two straps. The terminals are all rounded and pierced, unless stated.

Strap and terminal

12329 Badly corroded. Strap (in three pieces) has convex shoulders, pierced twice. L.70, W.16; eye: W.13, T.3; strap: W.32mm 9020 sf1134 (D6e11; mid 14th century)

12330 Strap broken over piercing. Terminal bent outwards and has a pointed tip. L.69, W.31; eye: W.14; strap: L.45, W.22mm 3385 sf1463 (A6f2; 13th century) (*Fig.1418*)

12331 Corroded. Strap in three pieces, narrows slightly, pierced. Terminal has a pointed tip. L.209, W.44; eye: W.12; strap: W.22mm 9057 sf2468 (C6e11, D6e3; mid 13th century)

12332 Incomplete. Terminal has a pointed tip. L.65; eye: W.7, strap: W.21mm 10974 sf2785 (D6e7; early 14th century)

12333 Strap incomplete, but pierced twice, one nail in situ. Terminal has a pointed tip. L.99, W.23; eye: W.9; strap: W.49mm 3558 sf3023 (A6c4; 12th century)

12334 Strap has a slightly rounded expansion below the eye; it is then straight-sided and has a rounded end. Pierced twice, nails in situ, both tips clenched, one around a piece of carbonised wood. Terminal has a pointed tip. L.89, W.20; eye: W.8; strap: W.18; nails: L.32, W.16mm 3558 sf3024 (A6c4; 12th century) (*Fig.1418*)

12335 Strap widens, narrows at the end before a bifurcated end with scrolled terminals; pierced once, nail in situ. Terminal had a pointed tip, now missing, nail in situ. L.77, W.21; eye: W.7; strap: W.21; nail: L.25, W.12mm 13665 sf3602 (A6c5, B6a7; mid 12th century) (*Fig.1418*)

12336 Strap largely missing. L.36, W.33; eye: W.10; strap: W.27mm 5975 sf3893 (C6c6; mid 12th century)

Two terminals

12337 One terminal largely missing. Other terminal is oval. L.68, W.28; eye: W.10; strap: W.24mm 11784 sf3343 (B6c2–6; 12th/13th century)

12338 Nail in situ. L.29, W.11; terminals: W.12mm 13638 sf3495 (B6c7; late 11th–early 12th century)

Two straps

12339 One strap, now incomplete, was shorter than the other. Both straps pierced twice, nails in situ. L.89, W.23; eye: W.13; strap: W.19; nails: L.54, W.17mm 4620 sf1234 (C6e9; mid 13th century)

12340 Straps incomplete and widen away from the eye, both pierced. L.50, W.27; eye: W.10; strap: W.34mm 11789 sf3042 (B6c4; 12th/13th century)

12341 Straps widen below the eye, one incomplete, the other largely missing, both pierced, nail in situ. L.83, W.24; eye: W.8; strap: W.24; nail: L.30, W.20mm 16734 sf5684 (C6a1, D6a1; late 11th century)

12342 Straps are incomplete and pierced twice, nails in situ. L.78, W.27; eye: T.9; strap: W.27mm 1283 sf15413 (C6z1; late 14th–early 15th century)

Incomplete U-eyed hinges

12343 Eye incomplete; surviving strap incomplete, it has convex shoulders and is pierced. L.55; strap: W.36, T.7mm 9641 sf3253 (D6e1; 13th/14th century) (*Fig.1418*)

12344 On one side of the eye an incomplete strap with convex shoulders, pierced. On the other side the strap or terminal is missing. L.53, W.62; eye: W.11; strap: W.36mm 16736 sf4442 (B6a5; 11th/12th century)

Hasps
Figure-of-eight-shaped

The attachment links are all simple loops.

Made from strips of rectangular cross-section

12345 One loop larger than the other, slightly bent at the waist. Link largely missing. L.139, W.33, T.8mm 4454 sf909 (C6h1; 15th/16th century)

12346 Incomplete. One loop is larger than the other. Slightly bent at the waist. Link has a small rolled tip. L.152, W.31, T.7mm 3509 sf2790 (A6e1; early 13th century)

12347 Incomplete and slightly bent out of shape. One loop was longer than the other. Link survives. L.130, W.39, T.8mm 12190 sf2933 (D6e3; 13th/14th century) (*Fig.1419*)

12348 One loop longer than the other, bent through c.45° at the waist. Link survives. L.76, W.20, T.5mm 11376 sf2964 (B6f1; early 14th century) (*Fig.1419*)

Made from spirally twisted strips

12349 One loop larger than the other, slightly bent at the waist. Link incomplete. L.137, W.35, T.6mm 4620 sf987 (C6e9; mid 13th century) (*Fig.1419*)

12350 Loops approximately the same size, slightly curved. Link survives. L.115, W.29, T.8mm 9224 sf1394 (C6e9; mid 13th century) (*Fig.1419*)

12351 Link has a rolled tip. U-shaped staple in situ. L.116, W.29, T.5; staple: L.43, W.21, T.6mm 5415 sf1756 (C6c6, D6a7; mid 12th century) (*Fig.1419*)

12352 One loop is larger than the other, slightly bent at the waist. Link has a rolled tip. L.139, W.31, T.8mm 3484 sf2648 (A6e3; 13th century) (*Fig.1419*)

12353 Incomplete. Was slightly curved at the waist. L.58, W.20, T.5mm 11458 sf3098 (B6c7; late 11th–early 12th century) (*Fig.1419*)

12354 One loop missing. Slightly curved at the waist. Link survives. L.89, W.32, T.6mm 17259 sf4648 (C6d8; mid–late 12th century)

12355 One link larger than the other, bent through 90° at the waist. Link survives. L.89, W.19, T.4mm 9813 sf4994 (D6a25; 12th/13th century)

T-shaped hinge

12356 Originally attached to a hinge strap. Damaged, but was rectangular with a semi-circular projection from the centre of one side, an attachment loop developed from this. Now pierced twice. L.110, W.70, T. (over loop) 13mm 4089 sf254 (C6h7; mid 17th century) (*Fig.1420*)

Casket and chest fittings
Small U-eyed hinge fitting

12357 Rounded terminal each side of the eye. Plated (tin, trace copper). L.35; eye: W.14mm 16535 sf4211 (D6a9; early 12th century) (*Fig.1420*)

Pinned hinge

12358 The first component (a) is a plate folded in two, broken at the narrower end, pierced nearby; a rectangular notch at the wider end. Between the arms thus created is a pin on which the rounded terminal of the second component (b) is articulated. The faces of the terminal are at 90° to those of the body which narrows away from the head and is broken. (a) L.22, W.14, T.5; (b) L.29, W.13mm 5084 sf963 (C6e11; mid 13th century)

Corner brackets

12359 One arm incomplete, the other has a rounded, pierced terminal which tapered to a pointed tip. Arms: L.56 and 37, W.16, T.2mm 3235 sf2336 (A6g1; 13th/14th century) (*Fig.1420*)

12360 One arm largely missing; the complete arm narrows a little before widening again at the end. Pierced twice, one nail (unbroken) with rectangular head in situ. L.90, W.24, T.3; nail L.33mm 12413 sf4761 (B6c1; 12th/13th century)

Stapled hasps

The staples are always fixed to the widest part unless stated; they are always U-shaped and have a rectangular cross-section.

12361 It narrows and thickens slightly from the centre towards head and base. At the head there is a rounded eye terminal. At the tip of the base there is a rounded knob. L.62, W.10, T.3; staple: L.9, W.9mm 4924 sf827 (C6f1; late 13th century) (*Fig.1421*)

12362 It thickens and narrows gradually towards the head which is missing. It also narrows by means of two sloping shoulders towards the base which develops into a strip with a relief moulding at the tip, probably a stylised animal head. L.82, W.12, T.6; staple: L.13, W.9mm 4620 sf978 (C6e9; mid 13th century) (*Figs.1421–2*)

12363 It narrows gradually towards the head where it is slightly thickened and it probably developed into a looped terminal which is now largely missing. It also narrows towards the base where there is a rounded knob. Shallow triangular notches run along both edges of the upper faces. Plated (tin with a low level of lead). L.73, W.15, T.4; staple: L.12, W.11mm 4620 sf1011 (C6e9; mid 13th century) (*Figs.1421–2*)

12364 It narrows slightly from a point near the centre towards the head where it widens again by means of two sloping shoulders below a looped terminal. It also narrows towards the base, both sides being slightly convex. At the tip there is a rounded knob. The staple is sited a little above the widest part. Plated. L.89, W.16, T.4; staple: L.13, W.9mm 10977 sf2730 (D6g2; mid 16th century) (*Fig.1421*)

12365 It is slightly bent, but was originally straight. It narrows very slightly from a point a little above the base towards the head where it widens slightly and is rounded off; pierced a little below the head. Narrows sharply towards the base which is straight. L.104, W.11, T.3; staple: L.13, W.13, T.4mm 15040 sf3746 (B6c5; early 13th century) (*Fig.1421*)

12366 Incomplete, being broken above the staple. Slightly convex sides and narrows gently towards the base where there is a domed knob at the tip. Slightly curved cross-section. On the upper face there are the remains of a cross-hatched pattern formed by incised triple grooves. Plated (tin with trace copper, lead, zinc). L.73, W.19, T.4; staple: L.20, W.13, T.3mm 16465 sf4166 (D6a19; late 12th century) (*Figs.1421–2*)

12367 It is curved and the body is formed from three spirally twisted strips; the outer two form an eye at the head. There is a copper alloy animal head below the eye and at the tip. They are similar, but not identical. At the tip (numbers of ring-and-dot motifs in brackets): collar (3), ears, forehead (3), snout (3); below the eye: collar (2), ears, forehead, foreshortened snout (2). L.117, W.16; T. (in centre) 6mm 6281 sf5338 (D6a4; late 11th century) (*Figs.1421–2*)

12368 Short upper arm has an eye formed by drawing out the head and making a loop, linked to U-shaped staple or collar. Lower arm largely missing. Hasp: L.35, W.16; staple: L.30, W.22mm 1346 sf14829 (C6z1; late 14th–early 15th century) (*Fig.1421*)

Drop handles

12369 Corroded and in two pieces. It has L-shaped tapering arms set at 90° to a straight head, rounded cross-section. L.95, W.55, T.5; arm: L.18mm 4620 sf1260 (C6e9; mid 13th century)

12370 L-shaped arms set at c.90° to a straight head, rounded cross-section. L.70, W.19, T.4mm 18193 sf4777 (B6c2; 12th/13th century) (*Fig.1423*)

Fittings

They are described as either 'strips' or 'plates' using the same criteria as for bar iron, blanks and scrap (see p.3025). Those which were probably part of hinges or corner brackets are described as 'straps'. The strips and plates are also divided into 'large' or 'small' according to whether their surviving area is greater or smaller than c.1000mm².

All have a rectangular cross-section and are pierced once unless stated.

Large plates, straps and strips

Plates

12371 S-shaped, U-shaped cross-section, broken at each end. Not pierced. Plated (tin). L.140, W.11, W. across 11mm 4867 sf820 (C6g6; late 14th century) (*Fig.1424*)

12372 Narrows slightly, sides irregular, broken over piercing at each end. L.67, W.28, T.2mm 9122 sf1020 (D6e1; 13th/14th century)

12373 Originally from a larger curved plate, broken at both ends. Sides somewhat irregular. Pierced twice. L.47, W.22, T.3mm 9078 sf1132 (D6e1; 13th/14th century)

12374 Broken at both ends. Narrows for most of its length, but begins to widen again at the narrower end. Pierced at each end and at the narrowest point, nail in situ. L.77, W.22, T.3; nail: L.23, W.6, T.5mm 9249 sf1458 (D6d2; late 13th century)

12375 Bent out of shape. L.35, W.33, T.2mm 5484 sf1744 (C6e1, D6a16; later 12th century)

12376 Slightly curved over, one side convex, the others irregular. L.71, W.35, T.3mm 5777 sf2159 (D6a17–23; late 12th–12th/13th century)

12377 Curved and narrows from one end to the other. Curved over at the narrow end, pierced at the wider. Possibly a catch. L.88, W.12, T.2mm 5348 sf2335 (C6e1, D6a16; 12th–13th century) (*Fig.1424*)

12378 Broken at each end. L.57, W.24, T.5mm 10532 sf2631 (C6g7–9; 14th/15th century)

12379 Slightly curved, one end rounded, the other broken, pierced by three rectangular holes, nail fragments in situ. L.124, W.27, T.4mm 10334 sf2656 (C6g3; D6g1; early–mid 16th century)

12380 One end rounded, the other broken. L.76, W.22, T.3mm 11332 sf2669 (B6f3; early 14th century)

12381 One half consists of a tapering shank with wedge-shaped tip, the other half is an oval plate. Not pierced. L.61, W.24, T.7mm 11332 sf2702 (B6f3; early 14th century) (*Fig.1424*)

12382 Broken at each end, slightly curved, narrows to one end where there may be remains of a rounded terminal. L.88, W.33, T.3mm 12237 sf2937 (B6f4; early 14th century)

12383 Broken at each end, narrows slightly, pierced twice. L.107, W.27, T.3mm 11789 sf3027 (B6c4; 12th/13th century)

12384 Broken at each end. L.70, W.30, T.5mm 13390 sf3469 (B6c4; 12th/13th century)

12385 Incomplete. Now L-shaped and develops into an arm at each end, both broken. Corner rounded on the outside. Inner edge bevelled and concave before becoming L-shaped. Pierced in the corner. L.60, W.57, T.5mm 13579 sf3476 (B6c2; 12th/13th century) (*Fig.1424*)

12386 Broken at both ends. Pierced four times. L.122, W.19, T.3mm 13638 sf3576 (B6c7; late 11th–early 12th century)

12387 Curved over at 90° into two arms, one incomplete and pierced, nail in situ. Arms: L.28 and 16, W.35, T.3mm 16123 sf3845 (C6d22; late 12th century)

12388 Broken at each end, sides irregular and folded over in places. L.90, W.33, T.3mm 9815 sf4041 (D6a22; 12th/13th century)

12389 Broken at each end, slightly curved over. Pierced twice, one nail in situ. L.108, W.25, T.5mm 16604 sf4215 (B6b4; late 12th century)

12390 Broken at each end, pierced three times, two nails in situ, heads missing. L.86, W.18, T.3; nail: L.48mm 18119 sf4731 (B6c3; 12th/13th century)

12391 Broken at each end, pierced twice. L.85, W.37, T.3mm 6291 sf5061 (C6c1, D6a3; late 11th/early 12th century)

12392 Narrows slightly, C-shaped in cross-section. One end slightly concave, the other irregular due to breakage. Surviving corners rounded. L.77, W.70, T.2mm 18134 sf5108 (B6c5; early 13th century) (*Fig.1424*)

12393 Broken each end, one starts to curve over. L.50, W.20, T.2mm 17740 sf15172 (C6c3; early 12th century)

12394 One end rounded, other broken. Pierced twice. L.145, W.25, T.4mm 3085 sf15268 (A6j24; 16th century)

12395 Folded in two, distorted at one end. L.45, W.27, T.9mm 1908 sf15326 (D6f5; early 15th century)

12396 Broken across rectangular hole, the other end has rounded corners, slightly curved in cross-section, sides curved over, one smooth, the other rough. L.64, W.39, T.3mm 5104 sf15506 (C6e8; early 13th century, D6d3; late 13th century)

Straps

12397 Rounded strap terminal, nail fragment in situ. L.27, W.27, T.3mm 5484 sf1849 (C6e1, D6a16; later 12th century)

12398 Curved strip broken at one end with leaf-shaped strap terminal at the other. L.125, W.15, T.3mm u/s sf2370 (*Fig.1424*)

12399 Pierced twice with incomplete pierced, rounded terminal. L.148, W.18, T.2mm u/s sf2383

Strips

12400 Broken at one end, narrows towards the other where there is an incomplete looped terminal. The wider half is slightly curved and slightly curved in cross-section. Plated (tin). L.86, W.13, T.3mm 4620 sf1196 (C6e9; mid 13th century) (*Fig.1424*)

12401 Broken at both ends and widens slightly at one. Pierced four times, one nail in situ. L.124, W.16, T.4; nail: L.17, W.9mm 5348 sf1930 (C6e1, D6a16; 12th–13th century)

12402 L-shaped, both arms incomplete, the shorter pierced near the corner. Arms: L.82 and 31, W.15, T.5mm 10560 sf2587 (B6g10; 15th/16th century)

12403 Broken at each end and slightly curved. Not pierced. Plated (tin). L.48, W.4, T.1mm 10726 sf2640 (B6g4; early 15th century)

12404 Narrows from one end to the other, broken over a piercing at each end. L.88, W.31, T.4mm 3537 sf2829 (A6c4; 12th century)

12405 Curved with triangular cross-section. Rounded terminal at one end, probably had similar terminal at the other, now largely missing. Not pierced. Plated (tin, trace lead and copper). L.108; terminal: W.24, T.8mm 12106 sf2949 (C6e9, D6e1; mid 13th century) (*Fig.1424*)

12406 Corroded, in two pieces and broken at both ends. It begins to curve and narrow towards one end. Pierced four times. L.90, W.26, T.2mm 11793 sf3021 (B6c3; 12th/13th century)

12407 Bifurcated strap terminal, one arm incomplete. Not pierced. L.37, W.68, T.2mm 13110 sf3134 (B6c1; 12th/13th century)

12408 Broken at one end and rounded at the other, pierced near the rounded end. L.117, W.18, T.6mm 6111 sf3273 (D6a18; late 12th century)

12409 Broken at one end, at the other there is a looped terminal. L.179, W.11, T.3mm 18256 sf4832 (B6a7; early 12th century)

12410 Curved, broken at one end, at the other a rounded, pierced terminal. Plated (tin). L.65, W.18mm 11868 sf15290 (B6f3; early 14th century) (*Fig.1424*)

Small plates and strips

Plates

12411 Pierced twice. L.40, W.18mm 4693 sf891 (C6e13; mid 13th century)

12412 Nail fragment in situ. L.38, W.12, T.2mm 9224 sf1316 (C6e9; mid 13th century)

12413 Broken at one end; at the other it curves over into a simple loop. Not pierced. L.34, W.10, T.3; loop: D.15mm 5484 sf1712 (C6e1, D6a16; later 12th century)

12414 Parallel sides. One end rounded, other has angled corners, pierced at each end, nail fragments in situ. L.72, W.14, T.1mm 3344 sf1729 (A6g1; 13th/14th century) (*Fig.1424*)

12415 Broken at each end over piercings. L.42, W.10, T.2mm 5978 sf2184 (D6a6; 11th/12th century)

12416 One straight side, others broken, pierced twice. L.55, W.30mm 5348 sf2330 (C6e1, D6a16; 12th–13th century)

12417 Narrows, broken over piercing at wider end, sides irregular. L.49, W.19, T.2mm 11545 sf2797 (B6g10; 15th/16th century)

12418 Curved over and broken at one end. L.41, W.13, T.2mm 11416 sf2838 (B6c2–6; 12th/13th century)

12419 Fragment, pierced twice. L.35, W.15mm 11621 sf2905 (B6g4–8; early–late 15th century)

12420 Twisted in centre so that faces of the two halves are at 90° to each other. One half is pierced twice. L.61, W.14, T.3mm 13160 sf3481 (B6c9; 13th century) (*Fig.1424*)

12421 Pierced at one end, broken at other. Plated (tin). L.49, W.11, T.2mm 16535 sf4440 (D6a9; early 12th century)

12422 Broken at each end. L.48, W.20, T.2mm 16734 sf4990 (C6a1, D6a1; late 11th century)

12423 Broken at one end and slightly curved. One side is roughly straight, the other is somewhat irregular and slopes in towards the first. Pierced twice, one incomplete nail in situ. L.45, W.14, T.2mm 17787 sf5210 (C6c1; early 12th century) (*Fig.1424*)

12424 Broken at one end, the other is rounded. Nail tip in hole. L.36, W.14, T.3; nail: L.25, W.16mm 18668 sf5368 (C6d6; mid 12th century)

12425 Broken at each end, sides curved over, nail fragments in situ. L.37, W.26, T.2mm 17396 sf7405 (C6d1; mid 12th century)

12426 Ragged ends, pierced twice. L.47, W.21, T.2mm 5000 sf14736 (C6c6; mid 12th century)

12427 Triangular cross-section. Not pierced. Plated (tin). L.61, W.5, T.4mm 5238 sf14778 (C6e5, D6a24; early 13th century)

12428 Fragment (possible rove), nail fragment in situ. L.28, W.25mm 10951 sf15115 (D6e9–f2; mid 14th–early 15th century)

12429 Fragment of plate with applied strip, perhaps part of a padlock case. L.32, W.25mm u/s sf5086

Strips

12430 At one end flattened into a rounded, pierced terminal; at the other broken. L.138, W.5; terminal: L.18, W.16mm 1002 sf95 (D6y1; late 12th–13th century) (*Fig.1424*)

12431 Upper face has bevelled edges. At one end a roughly rectangular pierced terminal, rivet in situ, at the other a pierced oval area beyond which is more of the strip, corroded and broken. Two transverse grooves either side of the hole in the terminal and groove before oval area. Plated (tin with a trace of lead). L.47, W.5, T.3; terminal: D.9mm 4125 sf317 (C6z1; late 14th–early 15th century) (*Fig.1424*)

12432 Tapers slightly, broken at each end. Small D-shaped loop attached at centre. L.70, W. (at loop) 5; T.3mm 9213 sf999 (D6e1; 13th/14th century) (*Fig.1424*)

12433 Rounded, pierced strip terminal. L.30, W.23mm 4620 sf1245 (C6e9; mid 13th century)

12434 D-shaped cross-section; at one end a pierced, rectangular terminal, at the other an incomplete terminal. Transverse grooves each side of the hole in the terminal. Plated (tin). L.41, W.10, T.2mm 4620 sf1309 (C6e9; mid 13th century) (*Fig.1424*)

12435 Broken at one end, at the other it narrows and curves over into a loop with a rolled tip. Not pierced. L.30, W.15, T.3mm 5345 sf1345 (C6e5, D6a24; early 13th century)

12436 Pierced at one end, pinched and probably broken at the other; perhaps a padlock spring. Plated (leaded copper). L.51, W.6, T.2mm 9305 sf1549 (D6a24; 12th/13th century)

12437　Broken at each end. D-shaped cross-section, pierced twice. L.109, W.5, T.3mm 9302 sf1610 (D6a26; 12th/13th century)

12438　One end broken, the other narrows to a rounded, pierced terminal. L.71, W.12, T.6mm 9305 sf1956 (D6a24; 12th/13th century)

12439　At each end there is a pierced lobed terminal. One copper rivet and one iron rivet in situ. The strip has short diagonal grooves arranged alternately on both edges of its upper face. Plated (tin-lead alloy). L.49, W.16, T.2mm 5348 sf1957 (C6e1, D6a16; 12th–13th century) (*Fig.1424*)

12440　Folded over at one end. L.28, W.5, T.1mm 5981 sf2172 (C6c3, D6a5; late 11th/early 12th century)

12441　Triangular, pierced strip terminal. L.18, W.15, T.1mm 3235 sf2240 (A6g1; 13th/14th century)

12442　Bent in the centre and broken at both ends. One face of one half has chamfered edges and a recessed area running down the centre; the other half is thinner than the first. The recessed area is pierced by an oval hole. Plated (brass — copper, zinc and lead detected). L.79, W.10, T.4mm 10123 sf2466 (B6g14; 16th–17th century) (*Fig.1424*)

12443　D-shaped cross-section; at one end a rounded, pierced terminal, at the other remains of another. Plated (tin). L.43, W.5, T.3; terminal: D.9mm 12126 sf2792 (D6e9; mid 14th century) (*Fig.1424*)

12444　D-shaped cross-section. At one end an incomplete round, pierced terminal, rivet in situ, at the other the fragment of second terminal. Around the edge of the upper face of the terminal are 6–7 small indentations. Plated (tin). L.87; terminal: W.18mm 12051 sf2810 (C6f1; late 13th century)

12445　Fitting in the form of a cross. One arm complete with rounded pierced terminal, one with incomplete terminal and two arms incomplete. Arms have bevelled edges. L.45, W.41; complete arm: L.25, T.4mm 9224 sf3013 (C6e9; mid 13th century) (*Fig.1424*)

12446　Bent over at one end which is rounded and pierced, broken over a piercing at the other. L.65, W.13mm 12411 sf3053 (C6e5; early 13th century)

12447　Corroded. It consists of two rectangular panels and then a roughly oval panel joined by strips. The oval panel is folded over a ring and riveted to the central rectangular panel. The other rectangular panel also has a rivet hole in it and the strip between it and the central panel is thinner than the folded strip and has chamfered edges. The rectangular panels have a transverse groove on either side of the rivet holes. Plated (tin with trace of lead). L.52, W.9; ring:D.24mm 11687 sf3060 (B6g4; early 15th century) (*Fig.1424*)

12448　Broken at one end; at the other it narrows, and is curved over, tip looped. On one side of the strip near the curved-over end is a pierced U-shaped projection. One face of the strip has three fields separated by three sets of transverse grooves and within the fields are criss-cross grooves. Plated (tin-lead alloy). Possibly part of *12452*. L.88mm 12412 sf3154 (C6e5; early 13th century) (*Fig.1425*)

12449　Strip terminal, rounded end. L.26, W.25, T.2mm 5975 sf3218 (C6c6; mid 12th century)

12450　Pierced, rectangular terminal at each end, one incomplete. Each hole is flanked by a pair of transverse grooves. Plated (tin, trace copper). L.35, W.9, T.2mm 11979 sf3314 (B6d4; 13th century) (*Fig.1425*)

12451　From its broken end the object widens towards the other end, each side of the first two-thirds has four rectangular cuts taken out of it. From widest point object curves and tapers to a point. Transverse grooves across one face. Not pierced. Plated (tin). L.65, W.13, T.4mm 12619 sf3432 (D6a24; 12th/13th century) (*Fig.1425*)

12452　Incomplete, but perhaps originally U-shaped with identical arms. D-shaped cross-section. The surviving arm narrows slightly to the base where it is looped over; near the base there is a U-shaped pierced projection from the inner side. The head is slightly curved before the break; it has a U-shaped, pierced projection on the outer side. There are four sets of three transverse grooves: on the arm above its projection, in the centre, at the top of the arm and at the point of the projection from the head. Between these grooves are others in criss-cross pattern. Plated (tin-lead). Complete arm: L.103mm; W. across projection 16mm 12363 sf3647 (C6e5; early 13th century) (*Fig.1425*)

12453　Incomplete with rectangular, pierced terminal, rivet in situ. Plated (silver). L.28, W.6, T.2mm 11965 sf3984 (B6e1; late 13th century) (*Fig.1425*)

12454　One part has a D-shaped cross-section and tapers slightly towards one end where there is a roughly rounded and pierced terminal. The other part has a rectangular cross-section and tapers from the centre to a broken end. L.56, W.8, T.3; terminal: W.13mm 9641 sf14755 (D6e1; 13th/14th century)

12455　Rounded cross-section; at one end it has been folded over and welded to create an eye, rivet in situ, other end broken. L.33, W.2mm 9224 sf15018 (C6e9; mid 13th century)

12456　Rounded, pierced terminal at one end, curved over and broken at the other. L.38, W.11, T.4mm 17699 sf15225 (C6c1; early 12th century) (*Fig.1425*)

12457　Two pieces. One end broken, the other rounded. L.103, W.9, T.2mm 11341 sf15337 (B6f7; 14th century)

12458　Tapers to a point at one end, curved and flattened towards the wider end where a second strip, now fragmentary, is riveted on. Plated (copper, trace tin). L.72, W.10, T.3mm 1046 sf15373 (C6i3; 17th–18th century)

Fittings with a spirally twisted strip

12459　Strip curved over at each end presumably to make terminals, but they are now missing. L.94, W.9, T.5mm 4620 sf975 (C6e9; mid 13th century)

12460　Slightly curved strip, at one end is a rounded, pierced terminal, now incomplete; perhaps a handle. L.102, W.9, T.6mm 3359 sf1343 (A6f3; 13th century) (*Fig.1426*)

12461　Slightly curved strip flattened at each end into roughly rounded, pierced terminals; one is incomplete. L.152, W.13, T.5mm 11165 sf2407 (B6a6; 11th/12th century) (*Fig.1426*)

12462　Strip bent through c.45° near the centre; at one end it is flattened into a terminal which is largely incomplete, broken at the other. The spiral is tighter towards the ends. L.170, W.10, T.4mm 12412 sf3185 (C6e5; early 13th century) (*Fig.1426*)

Spirally twisted strips

12463　L.40, T.2mm 9305 sf1543 (D6a24; 12th/13th century)

12464　Roughly C-shaped, ends flattened out and broken; perhaps a handle or suspension loop. L.94, W.49, T.4mm 9305 sf1548 (D6a24; 12th/13th century) (*Fig.1426*)

12465　Broken at each end. L.49, W.3mm 17890 sf5438 (B6a1, C6a1; late 11th century)

12466　Broken at one end, rectangular cross-section near the other which tapers to a wedge-shaped tip. L.60, W.5mm 6258 sf7196 (C6c3, D6a5; late 11th/early 12th century)

12467　Broken at one end, rectangular cross-section near the other which tapers to point. L.86, W.4mm 16734 sf7205 (C6a1, D6a1; late 11th century)

12468　Tapers at one end and is turned over slightly and squared off; the other end is broken. L.126, W.7mm 9269 sf14754 (D6e8; early 14th century)

Small U-eyed fitting and hook

12469 The hook has a looped end and a domed head. The hinge is missing most of one strap. The surviving strap has bevelled edges and two rectangular expansions to accommodate nail holes, one below the eye and one at the end. Plated (tin). Hinge: L.42, W.8; hook: L.29, W. (head) 13, T.5mm 5348 sf1985 (C6e1, D6a16; 12th–13th century) (*Fig.1428*)

Eyed fitting

12470 Half of loop and one triangular terminal survive. Terminal pierced three times, rivets in situ. Plated (leaded tin). L.40; terminal: W.20mm 1137 sf15968 (C6h3; early 16th century) (*Fig.1428*)

Suspension fittings

Consist of a U-shaped eye each end of which widens out into a strap.

See also *8742*.

12471 One strap is pierced three times and broken at the end across one of the holes, the other is broken a little below the eye. L.47, W.30, T.4; strap: W.10mm 9305 sf2074 (D6a24; 12th/13th century) (*Fig.1428*)

12472 Both straps largely missing. L.37, W.40, T.3; strap: W.19mm 13946 sf3665 (B6c8; early 13th century)

12473 One half missing. Surviving strap pierced twice, end broken. L.69, W.25, T.3mm 9813 sf7394 (D6a25; 12th/13th century)

Possible suspension fittings

12474 U-shaped loop, one arm of which widens before the break. L.33, W.23, T.2mm 5981 sf2209 (C6c3, D6a5; late 11th/early 12th century)

12475 U-shaped strip, both arm ends flattened out and incomplete. L.31, W.23, T.5mm 13585 sf3671 (B6d6; 13th century)

Linch pins

12476 Shank has a rounded cross-section and tapers to a point. The head iis looped. L.70, W.13, T.6mm 5186 sf15857 (C6e7; early 13th century) (*Fig.1428*)

12477 Shank has a sub-rectangular cross-section and tapers to a point; the head is an oval loop. L.90, W.24, T.10mm u/s sf2527 (*Fig.1428*)

Chain links

All have a rectangular cross-section unless otherwise stated.

Figure-of-eight-shaped

See also *8742*.

12478 Incomplete. Made from spirally twisted strip, bent at waist where broken. L.53, W.20, T.3mm 4620 sf1191 (C6e9; mid 13th century)

12479 Sides touch at the waist where curved over through c.65°. L.54, W.15, T.4mm 5415 sf1667 (C6c6, D6a7; mid 12th century) (*Fig.1429*)

12480 Incomplete. Made from spirally twisted strip, bent through c.45° at waist. L.69, W.20, T.5mm 5398 sf1906 (C6c6; mid 12th century) (*Fig.1429*)

12481 Sides lie parallel at the waist. Sub-rectangular cross-section. L.118, W.29, T.6mm 10592 sf2607 (D6j1; late 17th century) (*Fig.1429*)

12482 Half a link. L.75, W.20, T.3mm 9801 sf3141 (D6y1; late 12th–13th century)

12483 Sides lie parallel in the centre. One loop incomplete. L.59, T.4mm 3493 sf3605 (A6c1; 12th century)

12484 A group of nine small joined links. Each link has a small strip wrapped around its waist. Each link: L.16, W.7mm 12748 sf3659 (D6a22; 12th/13th century) (*Fig.1429*)

12485 A group of five links. Each has sides touching at the waist. The link cross-sections are varied: in some places they are round, in others rectangular, and in others irregular. One link, now incomplete, has two links attached to it. Each link: L.52, T.5mm 16464 sf4170 (D6a19; late 12th century) (*Fig.1429*)

12486 Incomplete. L.39, W.10, T.2mm 5000 sf15866 (C6c6; mid 12th century)

12487 Incomplete. L.55, W.18, T.6mm 9630 u/s sf3187

12488 Incomplete. L.62, W.20, T.6mm u/s sf12945

Other forms

12489 Incomplete object which consists of a looped eye with its arms wrapped spirally by wire. L. 33, T.5; loop: W.9mm 12186 sf2824 (C6e9; mid 13th century)

12490 S-shaped with looped eye at each end, one incomplete, surviving eye has rolled tip. L.64; eye: W.12, T.4mm 12496 sf3321 (D6a24; 12th/13th century) (*Fig.1429*)

12491 Sub-oval ring. L.42, W.27, T.7mm 3493 sf19634 (A6c1; 12th century)

12492 Straight sides and rounded ends; rounded cross-section. L.50, W.17, T.3mm 16465 sf4354 (D6a19; late 12th century) (*Fig.1429*)

Rings

All made from a single strip curved around, the ends may be welded together or not.

Rectangular cross-section

12493 One half survives. D.36, T.3mm 9213 sf1207 (D6e1; 13th/14th century)

12494 Somewhat distorted. The strip ends are pointed and may originally have met in a scarf joint. D.28, T.4mm 9224 sf1604 (C6e9; mid 13th century)

12495 Oval, broken unfused scarf joint. L.28, W.21, T.3mm 1404 sf1915 (C6y1; late 13th–early 14th century)

12496 One-third survives, the surviving tip is pointed. L.38, T.7mm 13244 sf3230 (B6c2–6; 12th/13th century)

12497 Half. Unbroken end tapers to wedge-shaped tip. L.47, T.7mm 13302 sf3320 (B6f5, C6f6; early 14th century)

12498 D.37, T.4mm 16797 sf4568 (C6d17; late 12th century)

12499 Bent out of shape. Made from strip tapered at each end. D.65, W.10, T.3mm 5484 sf7397 (C6e1, D6a16; later 12th century)

12500 Strip ends overlapped but are not now welded together. D.13, T.3mm 18331 sf11415 (B6c7; early 13th century) (*Fig.1430*)

12501 Half. D.27, T.5mm 13674 sf15440 (C6g4; mid 14th century)

12502 Oval, the strip ends meet in a scarf joint. L.33, W.28, T.4mm u/s sf1288

Sub-rectangular cross-section

12503 Strip ends overlap in an unfused scarf joint. D.38, T.6mm 9078 sf874 (D6e1; 13th/14th century)

12504 D.33, T.4mm 11683 sf2868 (B6g3; early 15th century)

12505 Roughly oval. Strip ends overlap and the tips are pointed. L.30, W.25, T.5mm 13568 sf3544 (B6a5; 11th/12th century)

12506 Strip ends overlap and have pointed tips. D.24, T.3mm 16465 sf4357 (D6a19; late 12th century)

12507 Strip ends overlap and have pointed tips. D.28, T.4mm 18172 sf4802 (B6c1; 12th/13th century)

12508 Strip ends overlap and have pointed tips. D.30, T.4mm 18366 sf4931 (B6a5; 11th/12th century)

Rounded cross-section

12509 D.11, T.2mm 4830 sf1472 (C6g6; late 14th century)

12510 Two-thirds complete. D.41, T.7mm 9224 sf2250 (C6e9; mid 13th century)

12511 Strip ends did not meet; surviving tip tapers to a point. D.25, T.3mm 10532 sf2613 (C6g7–9; 14th/15th century)

12512 Strip ends did not meet; surviving tip tapers to a point. D.30, T.4mm 11416 sf2721 (B6c2–6; 12th/13th century)

12513 Strip ends overlapped. D.8, T.1mm 12018 sf2739 (D6e9; mid 14th century) (Fig.1430)

12514 Strip ends overlap and are unfused; tips are pointed. D.28, T.4mm 11784 sf2908 (B6c2–6; 12th/13th century)

12515 Strip ends overlap and the tips are pointed. D.28, T.3mm 3495 sf3213 (A6c2; 12th century)

12516 D.9, T.2mm 12662 sf3455 (D6a26–d1; late 12th–mid 13th century)

12517 Half. D.54, T.8mm 15136 sf4092 (A6n2, B6a5; early 12th century)

12518 Strip ends do not meet and the tips are pointed. D.23, T.3mm 12671 sf4212 (D6a16; mid 12th century)

12519 Bent out of shape, possibly a collar. W.38, T.2mm 9105 sf14685 (D6e1; 13th/14th century)

12520 Half, corroded, and smaller fragment. D.56mm 5395 sf14910 (C6c6, D6a7; mid 12th century)

12521 One-quarter survives. D.38, T.6mm 4182 sf15081 (C6e13; mid 13th century)

12522 Half. D.35, T.5mm 1214 sf15407 (C6h4; early–mid 16th century)

Diamond-shaped cross-section

12523 D.17, T.3mm 9137 sf465 (D6f2; early 15th century)

12524 Strip ends did not meet, surviving tip is pointed. D.2, T.3mm 11674 sf2855 (B6c5; early 13th century)

12525 Strip ends do not meet, tips are pointed. D.28, T.2mm 18668 sf5204 (C6d6; mid 12th century)

Made from spirally twisted strips

12526 Strip ends do not meet and are roughly pointed. Plated (leaded tin). D.38, T.3mm 9122 sf1028 (D6e1; 13th/14th century)

12527 D.50, T.6mm 9224 sf1337 (C6e9; mid 13th century)

Fragments

12528 L.18, T.2mm 5348 sf2068 (C6e1, D6a16; 12th–13th century)

12529 L.30, T.5mm 4012 sf15242 (C6i3; 17th–18th century)

Washers

12530 Disc with a hole in the centre, formed by curving a strip around and butt joining the ends. Grooves cut into the edge of one face. Plated (tin with a small amount of copper). D.33, T.4; central hole: D.12mm 9078 sf993 (D6e1; 13th/14th century) (Fig.1430)

12531 Lap joint. D.50, W.11, T.3mm u/s sf2380

Perforated disc

12532 Corroded and incomplete. D.36mm 13964 sf6372 (B6c8; early 13th century)

Tubes

12533 Broken at each end, pierced with rivet in situ. L.48, D.19mm 2346 sf252 (A6z1; 11th/12th century)

12534 Broken at each end and corroded. Tapers and is pierced; open seam. L.43, D.10, T.1mm 5241 sf1246 (D6d3; late 13th century)

12535 L.18, D.41mm 11401 sf2779 (B6g3; early 15th century)

12536 Crudely made. Overlapping seam secured by a nail, the head of which is inside the tube; the shank lies flush to the outside. L.32, D.34, T.3mm 16130 sf4308 (D6a16; mid 12th century)

12537 L.160, D.12mm u/s sf9

Ferrules

12538 Tip missing, trace of rivet near socket mouth. Fragment of wooden shaft in situ. Plated (tin). Wood is *ilex* (holly). L.119, D.15; socket: L.85mm 9122 sf989 (D6e1; 13th/14th century) (Fig.1431)

12539 Consists of a conical socket which may have developed into a ring at the tip, but this is largely missing. L.30, D.9mm 3493 sf15264 (A6c1; 12th century) (Fig.1431)

Candleholders

Socketed

All shanks have rectangular cross-section which taper to a point.

12540 L-shaped shank. Tang largely missing, socket welded onto other arm and is open at the base. Tang: L.10; socket arm: L.53; socket: L.21, W.18mm 10979 sf15091 (D6e7; early 14th century) (Fig.1432)

12541 L-shaped shank. Tang tapers to a point and the corner is pinched. Socket is welded on and tapers towards its base. Tang: L.47; socket arm: L.58; socket: L.33, W.19mm 10531 sf15123 (C6g1; early–mid 14th century) (Figs.1432–3)

Bifurcated

12542 Shank bent and bifurcates; both arms have a looped terminal. L.86, W.23, T.7mm 4693 sf942 (C6e13; mid 13th century)

12543 L-shaped. Both arms have rolled terminals. Arms: L.57 and 47, W.20, T.7mm 9305 sf1840 (D6a24; 12th/13th century) (Figs.1432–3)

12544 Spirally twisted shank, arms incomplete. L.91, T.6mm 11284 sf2725 (B6f7; 14th century) (Fig.1432)

12545 Corroded. One arm has a rolled terminal, the other incomplete. Possible pricket. L.132, W.29, T.9mm 18153 sf4766 (B6c3; 12th/13th century)

12546 L-shaped and has a spirally twisted shank. Each of the component strips becomes an arm, both incomplete. L.59, T.5mm 13466 sf4907 (B6c3; 12th/13th century)

12547 Shank unusually short, both arms have looped terminals. L.96, W.23, T.7mm 18331 sf5772 (B6a5, C6c3; early 12th century) (*Figs.1432–3*)

Prickets

12548 Shank and one of the arms made from a single strip to which the central spike and other arm are welded. Both arms have looped terminals. L.92, W.41, T.8mm 9092 sf992 (D6e8; early 14th century) (*Figs.1432–3*)

12549 Shank spirally twisted and incomplete. One arm survives and has a looped terminal; central spike is incomplete. L.56, T.7mm 9078 sf1181 (D6e1; 13th/14th century)

12550 Shank is spirally twisted and S-shaped, tip missing. Each of the shank's component strips become arms and the central spike is welded on between them. One arm has a looped and one a rolled terminal. L.90, W.32, T.6mm 5545 sf1684 (D6a17–23; late 12th–12th/13th century) (*Figs.1432–3*)

12551 Shank incomplete. One arm has a small, rolled terminal; the other arm and central spike are largely missing. L.52, T.6mm 5484 sf1982 (C6e1, D6a16; later 12th century)

12552 Central spike welded into the gap between the arms, both of which are incomplete, but one probably had a looped terminal. L.119, W.32, T.8mm 13454 sf3580 (B6d2; mid 13th century)

12553 Shank L-shaped and pinched at the corner. Central spike was welded on between the arms, both of which are incomplete. Spike: L.78; tang: L.69; T.7mm 13585 sf3676 (B6d6; 13th century) (*Fig.1432*)

12554 Central spike welded on between the arms, both of which have rolled terminals. L.69, T.6mm 13454 sf3829 (B6d2; mid 13th century)

12555 Central spike was welded on between the arms, tip missing. Both arms narrow and are incomplete, but one probably had a looped terminal. L.76, T.11mm 18172 sf4809 (B6c1; 12th/13th century)

12556 L-shaped. Above the corner the shank bifurcates, but the arms and central spike are only stubs. Tang: L.48; spike: 27, T.10mm 4885 sf15193 (C6f5; 13th/14th century)

12557 Corroded and crushed. Central spike was probably welded on between the arms, one of which has a looped terminal and the other is incomplete. L.94, W.13, T.7mm 1070 sf15377 (modern)

Locks and keys

Mounted locks

Lock mounted in wooden housing

9045 Corroded. Consists of bolt, tumbler, plate at rear of lock with projecting spindle. Strap across either end of bolt channel. Bolt: L.150mm 4385 sf561 (iron) and sf18997 (wood) (C6i4; 16th–19th century) (*Fig.1440*)

Lock bolts

12558 Two U-shaped projections and a retaining notch. L.207, W.22, T.4mm 4570 sf643 (C6e13; mid 13th century) (*Fig.1441*)

12559 Incomplete. Two rounded projections and a retaining notch. L.112, W.26mm 4620 sf1276 (C6e9; mid 13th century)

Bolt for lock with springs

12560 Roughly triangular plate with a central slot. There is a hole each side of the slot at wider end of plate where shoulders curve over to form a ridge on the inner face. Arms incomplete. L.80, W.31, T.4mm 6344 sf5088 (D6a1; late 11th century) (*Fig.1441*)

Padlocks

Barrel padlocks with U-shaped bolts

The bolts consist of a spring arm and a free arm; the latter is present unless stated. All bolts have a rectangular cross-section unless stated.

Cases with end key holes

12561 Somewhat crushed. End-plates recessed and the free arm tube welded on. Strips running longitudinally and around the ends are brazed on. Free arm tube has a strip running around it at its mouth. A second spring arm is attached by a strip to the underside of the bolt; closing-plate present. Plated with brazing metal (copper-tin alloy with a small amount of lead). L.64, W.34; case: L.47, W.26mm 18076 sf4804 (B6c3; 12th/13th century) (*Figs.1442, 1447*)

12562 Incomplete and somewhat crushed. Remains of the free arm tube survive on the part of the case which has been crushed. End-plates slightly recessed. Longitudinal strips and strips around the end are brazed on. Plated with brazing metal (copper-tin alloy with small amounts of lead and zinc). L.80, W.33mm 18256 sf4835 (B6a7; early 12th century) (*Fig.1442*)

Cases with a T-shaped key hole

12563 End-plates recessed, free arm tube attached by a fin which is pierced twice. Strips running longitudinally and around the ends of the case are brazed on. Free arm tube has a strip around its centre. Plated (quaternary). L.79, W.54; case: D.30mm 11900 sf2982 (B6f4; early 14th century) (*Figs.1442, 1445*)

12564 Tube for free arm is missing. End-plates recessed. Strips running longitudinally and around the ends were brazed on, but now largely missing. Plated with brazing metal (copper-tin alloy with some lead). L.64, W.29mm 16797 sf4425 (C6d17; late 12th century) (*Figs.1442, 1446*)

Case fragments

12565 Fragment of the end-plate and tip of the free arm tube. Plated (copper-tin alloy with trace of lead). L.40, W.9mm 5238 sf1424 (C6e5, D6a24; early 13th century)

12566 Exists as two spirally twisted strips joined by a fragment of plate. Plated (quaternary: copper, tin, lead, zinc). L.56, W.11mm 5186 sf1695 (C6e7; early 13th century)

12567 Free arm tube. On one side are two parallel fins which attached it to the case. Plated (copper-tin alloy with a little lead). L.77, W.12mm 15285 sf7230 (B6a1; late 11th century)

12568 Fin attached to case fragment on one side and along the other runs a strip which narrows slightly to a rounded tip. L.53; fin: W.8, T.2; strip: W.7, T.3mm 5000 sf14734 (C6c6; mid 12th century)

12569 Corroded and incomplete free arm tube and fin fragment. Plated. L.36, W.19mm 1502 sf15512 (C6e11, D6e3; mid 13th century)

Bolts

12570 Rounded cross-section. With closing plate, spring arm missing. L.57, W.36, T.9mm 4178 sf384 (C6z1; late 14th–early 15th century)

12571 Spring arm only with two springs welded on. L.35mm 1914 sf941 (D6e4; 13th/14th century)

12572 With closing plate and loop above it which joined the two spring arms. Faces of the spring arms are at 90° to each other. Both have two springs welded on at the base, one spring has a strip welded on to its face. Plated (copper-tin alloy with a small amount of lead). L.88; spring arms: L.58, W.15 and 7mm 9188 sf968 (D6d3; late 13th century) (*Figs.1447–8*)

12573 With closing plate and spring arm which has two springs made from a single strip wrapped around and welded to the base. L.57, W.25, T.6; spring arm: L.34mm 4620 sf1139 (C6e9; mid 13th century)

12574 Sub-rectangular cross-section. With incomplete closing plate and incomplete spring arm. L.82, W.49, T.8mm 4620 sf1168 (C6e9; mid 13th century)

12575 Spring arm only, pinched at the head, two springs welded to base. L.51mm 9224 sf1324 (C6e9; mid 13th century)

12576 With closing plate and incomplete spring arm. L.72, W.50, T.11mm 9305 sf1327 (D6a24; 12th/13th century)

12577 Spring arm missing. Plated (quaternary). L.68, W.35, T.7mm 5238 sf1393 (C6e5, D6a24; early 13th century)

12578 With closing plate and three spring arms. Rounded cross-section. Two spring arms are formed out of the bolt; one has a spring welded to the base and another riveted on, the other has the remains of two springs which were welded on. The third spring arm is attached by a strip to the underside of the bolt. Its faces are at 90° to the those of other arms, two springs are welded to the base. L.48, W.36, T.6; spring arms: L.24, W.5mm 5539 sf1642 (C6e2–6; 12th/13th century) (*Figs.1447–8*)

12579 Spring arm has two springs riveted to the base, the upper part of one spring is split into two. Plated (copper with a small amount of tin and zinc). L.67, W.35; spring arm: L.41, W.12mm 9305 sf2015 (D6a24; 12th/13th century) (*Fig.1448*)

12580 With closing plate and spring arm which has two springs welded to the base; one spring is divided into two for half its length. Plated. L.62, W.24, T.5; spring arm: L.36mm 5348 sf2087 (C6e1, D6a16; 12th–13th century)

12581 Spring, pierced at base, split in two at the head. L.43, W.9mm 5348 sf2320 (C6e1, D6a16; 12th–13th century)

12582 Spring arm only, pinched at the head, remains of two springs riveted to base. Plated (brass). L.64, W.9mm 10597 sf2621 (B6g7; late 15th century)

12583 Spring arm missing. Plated. L.50, W.20mm 13037 sf3162 (B6f4, C6g1; mid 14th century)

12584 Rounded cross-section. Free arm missing, spring arm incomplete. Above the closing plate are three small loops. Plated (copper-tin alloy with small amount of lead). L.59, T.9; spring arm: L.24mm 13554 sf3528 (B6a5; 11th/12th century)

12585 Incomplete free arm and head of spring arm. Plated (leaded bronze). L.40, W.47, T.7mm 5671 sf3802 (C6e6; early 13th century)

12586 Two spring arms, one of which has the remains of spring attached to it. L.69, W.45; spring arm: L.56mm 12501 sf3904 (C6e7; early 13th century)

12587 Spring arm only with two incomplete springs welded to the base. L.59, W.6mm 16399 sf4112 (C6e6; early 13th century)

12588 Rounded cross-section. With closing plate and spring arm. Immediately above the closing plate is a small loop and the remains of another. Spring arm has four springs, two (on the wider faces) made from a strip wrapped around the base; the other two are welded to edges of the arm, and are both divided in two towards the top. Plated (copper and tin). L.85, W.37, T.6; spring arm: L.53mm 18256 sf4819 (B6a7; early 12th century) (*Figs.1447–8*)

12589 A free arm of rounded cross-section with a closing plate, spring arm missing. Plated (copper-tin alloy with a small amount of lead). L.88mm 18366 sf4904 (B6a5; 11th/12th century)

12590 Rounded cross-section. With closing plate and spring arm which has two springs made of one strip wrapped around the base. Plated (copper-tin alloy with a trace of lead). L.88, W.34; spring arm: L.54mm 13465 sf4992 (B6c1; 12th/13th century)

12591 Rounded cross-section. Spring arm has the vestiges of a spring at the base which was attached by a rivet. L.57; spring plate: W.12mm 17786 sf5201 (C6c2; early 12th century)

12592 Spring arm only. Two springs welded to the base. L.52, W.6mm 12915 sf14970 (D6a16; mid 12th century)

12593 Rounded cross-section. Below the closing plate spring arm has a short ridge at the top of each face; the two springs are made from one strip wrapped around the base, they bifurcate at the top. Plated (copper). L.89, W.36mm u/s sf5179 (*Fig.1448*)

Spring arms from padlocks with shackles

12594 Spring arm and closing plate only. Spring arm has three springs; two are made from a strip wrapped around the base, the third is at 90° and welded to the side of the arm. Plated. L.47; spring arm: W.11mm 5348 sf2037 (C6e1, D6a16; 12th–13th century) (*Fig.1448*)

12595 Spring arm only with remains of closing plate and two springs welded to the base. L.51, W.13mm 16490 sf4325 (C6d18; late 12th century)

Padlocks with L-shaped bolts

12596 Spring arm missing. At the end of the case where the spring arm would be withdrawn the end plate is recessed and pierced twice. At other end T-shaped slot in case. Plated (copper). L.54, W.27; case: D.12mm 9252 sf1368 (D6e1; 13th/14th century) (*Figs.1447–8*)

12597 End-plate recessed and made in one piece with the free arm. Its tip slots into pierced projection from the spring arm which has two springs made from a single strip wrapped around its base. Plated (quaternary: copper, zinc, tin, lead). L.54, W.38; case: D.16mm 5484 sf1714 (C6e1, D6a16; later 12th century) (*Figs.1447–8*)

Keys

Keys for mounted locks

Keys with hollow stems

12598 Bow pear-shaped. Bit was rectangular with two ward cuts in the outer side. L.65; bow: L.22, W.20; stem: T.6; bit: L.9, W.12mm 1034 sf203 (C6h3–4; early–mid 16th century)

12599 Bow circular, has a rounded cross-section and was welded onto the stem. Stem has a moulding at its head and four groups of three grooves running around it: one is immediately below the moulding, one is near the middle of the stem, one above the bit and one at the tip. Bit has a five-chambered ward cut into its outer side and a small ward cut in the lower side. Small triangular notches are cut into both faces of the bit along its inner side. Plated (tin). L.115; bow: L.33, W.33; stem: T.11; bit: L.33, W.23mm 9248 sf1073 (D6c1; mid 13th century) (*Figs.1449, 1451*)

12600 Corroded. Bow a pear-shaped loop, tip tucked into the head of the stem which is incomplete, bit missing. L.67; bow: L.25, W.22mm 3407 sf2573 (A6e1; early 13th century)

12601 Corroded. Bow incomplete, but was circular. Stem has a moulding at the head and two groups of two grooves: between the bit and the bow, and at the tip. Bit has a three-chambered ward cut in the outer side. L.93; stem: T.9; bit: L.22, W.12mm 18047 sf4741 (B6c3; 12th/13th century) (*Fig.1449*)

12602 Bow lozenge-shaped with a roughly circular hole in the centre. Bit has a ward cut in the lower side. L.63; bow: L.21, W.9; stem: T.5; bit: L.15, W.10mm 18331 sf5391 (B6a5, C6c3; early 12th century) (*Fig.1449*)

12603 Bow circular and has a rounded cross-section. Stem has two groups of three grooves running around it: one immediately below the bow, one in the centre. There are also two grooves around the tip. Bit has a two-chambered ward cut in the outer side and a simple ward cut in the lower side. Small triangular notches are cut into the bit faces along its sides. Plated (leaded tin, trace copper). L.102; bow: L.41, W.38; stem: T.11; bit: L.19, W.15mm u/s sf2716 (*Fig.1449*)

12604 Bow a pear-shaped loop, stem incomplete. L.59; bow: L.30, W.28; stem: T.9mm u/s sf2853a

12605 Stub of stem and incomplete bit. May be part of same object as 12604. L.40; stem: T.9mm u/s sf2853b

Keys with solid stems which project beyond the bit with a central channel

12606 Bow circular with a sub-rectangular cross-section. Stem solid and tapers to a moulded knop at the tip which projects beyond the bit. There is a moulding at the head of the stem and three groups of two grooves run around it: below the bow, midway between the bow and the bit, near the bow and over the bit. A single groove runs around the stem over the outer end of the bit and before the knop. Bit has a ward cut in both the outer and inner sides and three in the lower side, the central one dividing the bit in two. The outer side has small grooves cut into it. L.141; bow: L.36, W.35; stem: T.12; bit: L.29, W.24mm 12062 sf2777 (C6e10; mid 13th century) (*Figs.1451–2*)

12607 Corroded, bow missing. Stem tapers towards the tip which projects beyond the bit. Bit probably incomplete, one ward cut survives in the outer side. Plated (tin). L.89; stem: T.12; bit: L.14, W.8mm 12066 sf2778 (C6g18, D6f8; late 15th/early 16th century)

Incomplete keys

12608 Bow and head of stem only. Bow kidney-shaped, solid stem is moulded at the head before the break. L.46; bow: L.24, W.44; stem: T.11mm 4385 sf545 (C6i4; 16th–19th century) (*Fig.1452*)

12609 Corroded. Survives as bit and solid stem fragment. L.35, W.24mm 17551 sf15210(C6c3; early 12th century)

12610 It survives largely as a shadow in the corrosion products and consists of a piece of bow and solid stem. L.48, W.6mm 5231 sf15862 (C6c6, D6a7; mid 12th century)

Barrel padlock keys

Bit at angle to stem

12611 Stem slightly bent. Bit roughly circular and set at 70° to the stem. From c.78mm above the bit the stem is gradually flattened and becomes a roughly diamond-shaped plate. Terminal largely missing, but was probably pierced with faces at 90° to those of the upper part of stem. L.114; bit: D.18; stem: W.15, T.8mm 4520 sf653 (C6e13; mid 13th century)

12612 In two pieces. Bit roughly oval and set at c.70° to the stem, the lower part of which has a rounded cross-section. 93mm above the bit the stem is flattened and widened, by upward sloping shoulders, into a plate which narrows slightly to the head. Looped terminal. L.134; bit: L.21, W.28; stem: W.16; terminal: L.10, W.12mm 4620 sf985 (C6e9; mid 13th century)

12613 Bit missing. 72mm from its base the stem is thickened by stepping out and then tapers to the head; this upper part has a sub-rectangular cross-section. Five notches are cut into the edges of the lower part of the stem opposite the side from which the bit projected. At the base of the upper part of the stem a group of three grooves run around it and towards the head a group of two. Terminal is an eye of rounded cross-section. L.116; stem: W.16, T.11; terminal: D.16mm 9252 sf1109 (D6e1; 13th/14th century) (*Figs.1453–4*)

12614 Bit roughly circular and set at 90° to the stem. 79mm from the bit the stem is flattened and widens to become a triangular plate which narrows sharply at the head with rounded shoulders. Looped terminal. L.116; bit: D.20; stem: W.15, T.4; terminal: D.9mm 9224 sf1363 (C6e9; mid 13th century) (*Fig.1453*)

12615 Stem bent in the centre. Bit largely missing, but appears to have been round and set at c.45° to the stem. c.67mm from the bit the stem is flattened and widened to become an irregular oval plate before narrowing sharply at the head. Looped terminal. L.102; stem: W.16, T.5; terminal: L.10, W.9mm 9224 sf1440 (C6e9; mid 13th century)

12616 Bit incomplete, but was clearly rounded and set at 90° to the stem. From a point 61mm from the bit the stem is gradually flattened and widened to become a triangular plate which narrows sharply at the head. Looped terminal. L.100; bit: W.19; stem: W.13, T.5; terminal: L.10, W.9mm 9224 sf1517 (C6e9; mid 13th century)

12617 Bit roughly circular and set at c.80° to the stem. From a point 57mm from the bit the stem is gradually flattened and widened to become a roughly diamond-shaped plate. Looped terminal. L.97; bit: W.19; stem: W.13, T.5mm 5484 sf1643 (C6e1, D6a16; later 12th century)

12618 The bit, now detached from the stem, is roughly oval and was set at c.45° to the stem. c.70mm from the bit the stem is flattened and widened to become a triangular plate which narrows at the head. Terminal missing. L.120; bit: L.19, W.22; stem: W.14, T.7mm 5442 sf1892 (C6e5; early 13th century)

12619 Slightly curved stem with sub-rectangular cross-section, bit and pierced terminal largely missing. L.77, W.5mm 5484 sf1980 (C6e1, D6a16; later 12th century)

12620 Bit roughly circular and set at c.60° to the stem. 65mm from the bit the stem is flattened slightly and widened to become a small diamond-shaped plate. The pierced terminal widens upwards to a rounded top, with faces at 90° to those of the stem. L.111; bit: D.15; plate: W.11; stem: W.4, T.2.5mm 11007 sf2390 (C6e6; early 13th century) (*Fig.1453*)

12621 Bit roughly circular and set at c.80° to the stem which is incomplete. At a point 93mm from the bit the stem is flattened and begins to widen. L.106; bit: D.20; stem: W.6mm 12106 sf2957 (C6e9, D6e1; mid 13th century)

12622 Bit circular and at 90° to the stem. c.90mm from the bit the stem is flattened and widened to become a triangular plate which narrows sharply at the head. Looped terminal with a rolled tip. L.170; bit: D.27; stem: W.15, T.9; terminal: L.28, W.11mm 6245 sf3265 (D6a6; 11th/12th century) (*Figs.1453–4*)

12623 Bit missing and stem incomplete. 68mm from the base the stem is flattened and widened to become an irregular diamond-shaped plate which narrows at the head. Looped terminal. L.102; stem: W.21, T.5; terminal: L.12, W.9mm 12412 sf3270 (C6e5; early 13th century)

12624 Bit roughly circular and set at c.50° to the stem. Looped terminal. L.84; bit: W.17; stem: W.5; terminal: L.10, W.9mm 6257 sf3375 (C6c4; early 12th century)

12625 Bit rectangular with rounded corners and set at c.80° to the stem. c.47mm from the bit the stem is flattened and widened to become a somewhat irregular elongated plate which narrows at its head. Looped terminal with a rolled tip. L.100; bit: L.13, W.17; stem: W.10, T.4mm 13568 sf3493 (B6a5; 11th/12th century) (Fig.1453)

12626 Bit roughly circular and set at 40° to the stem. 40mm from the bit the stem is flattened and widened by means of two horizontal shoulders; it then narrows towards the head. Rounded, pierced terminal, now incomplete, with faces at 90° to those of the upper part of the stem. L.76; bit: W.15; stem: W.11, T.4; terminal: D.11mm 13662 sf3549 (B6c2; 12th/13th century)

12627 Bit incomplete, but was clearly rounded. c.70mm from the bit the stem is flattened and widened to become an irregular oval plate which narrows sharply at the head. Looped terminal. L.109; stem: W.14, T.4; terminal: L.11, W.6mm 13245 sf3917 (B6a7; early 12th century)

12628 Bit set at 90° to the stem, basically rounded, but has two rectangular cuts taken out of each side. c.71mm from the bit the stem is stepped out and then tapers to the head. Cut into the edges of the stem on the face opposite that from which the bit projects there are small notches. Terminal is rounded and pierced, with faces in the same plane as those of the lower part of the stem. L.105; bit: W.13; stem: W.7; terminal: D.11mm 15136 sf4047 (A6n2, B6a5; early 12th century) (Figs.1453–4)

12629 Bit rounded with two rectangular cuts taken out of it. Lower part of the stem has a sub-rectangular cross-section and 42mm from the bit it is flattened slightly and widened by means of two upward sloping shoulders before narrowing to the head; the sides are now slightly concave. Terminal rounded and pierced, with faces in the same plane as those of the stem. L.78; bit: W.10; stem: W.11, T.5; terminal: D.12mm 13454 sf4064 (B6d2; mid 13th century) (Figs.1453–4)

12630 Bent in centre of stem. Bit roughly oval and set at 90° to the stem. From a point c.66mm from the bit the stem is flattened and widened by means of two sloping shoulders to form a roughly triangular plate which narrows to the head. Terminal rounded and pierced plate, with faces at 90° to those of the stem. L.94; bit: L.14, W.17; stem: W.9, T.3; terminal: D.8mm 15136 sf4073 (A6n2, B6a5; early 12th century)

12631 Bit basically oval, but has three rectangular cuts taken out of it and is set at c.90° to the stem. 61mm from the bit the stem widens by means of two upward sloping shoulders before narrowing to the head. Terminal, now incomplete, is rounded and pierced and in the same plane as the faces of the lower part of the stem. L.111; bit: L.17, W.13; stem: W.10, T.6; terminal: D.14mm 16612 sf4499 (D6a1; late 11th century)

12632 Bit roughly circular and set at c.80° to the stem. c.74mm from the bit the stem is flattened and widened to become a roughly triangular plate which narrows at the head. This plate is slightly curved over and has shallow grooves cut into the edge of each side of the face opposite that from which the bit projects. Looped terminal. L.124; bit: W.21; stem: W.16, T.7; terminal: L.15, W.8mm 18331 sf4873 (B6a5, C6c3; early 12th century) (Figs.1453–4)

12633 Bit roughly circular and set at c.90° to the stem. 72mm from the bit the stem is flattened and widened to become a roughly oval plate which narrows at the head. Looped

terminal. L.113; bit: W.20; stem: W.17, T.6; terminal: L.9, W.7mm 18331 sf4919 (B6a5, C6c3; early 12th century)

12634 Bit largely missing but was rounded and at 90° to the stem which has a rounded cross-section up to a point 70mm from base after which it is flattened with a step and widens. Head broken but largely complete. Looped terminal. L.120; stem: W.16, T.6mm 6336 sf5043 (D6a4–5; late 11th–11th/12th century) (Fig.1453)

12635 Bit circular and set at 90° to the stem. c.79mm from the bit the stem is flattened and widened to become a triangular plate which narrows again at the head. Looped terminal. L.130; bit: D.25; stem: W.20, T.6; terminal: L.11, W.13mm 6258 sf5052 (C6c3, D6a5; late11th/early 12th century)

12636 Bit gripping spine of padlock bolt, bit circular and at c.65° to the stem which is incomplete. L.36; bit: D.20mm 18331 sf5413 (B6a5, C6c3; early 12th century)

12637 Bit and lower part of stem missing. Stem widens by means of upward sloping shoulders before narrowing slightly to the head. Looped terminal. L.56; stem: W.14, T.7; terminal: L.12mm 3083 sf15233 (A6i2; 14th/15th century)

12638 Incomplete circular bit. Stem largely missing. L.30; bit: W.16; shank: T.5mm 5000 sf15865 (C6c6; mid 12th century)

12639 Bit sub-rectangular. At its head the stem is widened with sloping shoulders before narrowing to the terminal. This is pierced and has its wider faces at 90° to the head of stem. Plated (tin). L.108; bit: W.16; stem: W.10mm u/s sf2381 (Figs.1453–4)

Bit in line with stem

All stems have rounded cross-section, unless stated, and expand slightly in the centre. All terminals are, or were, pierced for attachment.

12640 Bit comprises four short projections, two on each side, from a spine at the base of the stem. Stem has a spiral groove inlaid with brass (with traces of lead and tin) running around it and there is a collar at its head. Terminal widens upwards and has a triangular top. L.82; bit: L.10, W.10; stem: T.9; terminal: W.10mm 4620 sf1184 (C6e9; mid 13th century) (Fig.1456)

12641 Bit composed of four short projections, two on each side, from a spine at the base of the stem. Stem has a moulding at the base and head. Terminal oval. L.78; bit: W.14; stem: T.8; terminal: L.15, W.10mm 5245 sf1232 (D6d3; late 13th century) (Fig.1456)

12642 Bit, now incomplete, was circular with a rectangular extension towards the stem. Stem has a spiral groove inlaid with brass (with traces of lead and tin) running around it and a moulding at the head. Terminal hexagonal, with faces at 90° to those of the bit; a suspension ring is attached. L.100; bit: W.36; stem: W.10; terminal: W.10mm 9305 sf1612 (D6a24; 12th/13th century) (Fig.1456)

12643 Bit circular and has two chambers. Stem has an inlaid spiral groove running around it, cuboid moulding at each end. Incomplete, pierced terminal. Plated (tin-lead). L.89; bit: W.16; stem: T.7mm 5415 sf1617 (C6c6, D6a7; mid 12th century) (Figs.1456–7)

12644 Bit largely missing. Stem has a spiral groove running around it and a moulding at the head. Terminal roughly hexagonal, with faces at 90° to those of the bit. L.87; stem: T.11; terminal: L.14, W.10mm 9305 sf1686 (D6a24; 12th/13th century) (Fig.1456)

12645 Bit consists of a roughly circular element and a polygonal extension towards the stem which has a moulding at the head. Terminal, now incomplete, has faces at 90° to those of the bit. L.85; bit: L.34, W.20; stem: T.9; terminal:

L.16, W.10mm 12485 sf3130 (D6c1; mid 13th century) (*Figs.1456–7*)

12646 Bit circular, multi-chambered cut. Stem has a sub-rectangular cross-section. Terminal widens upwards and has a triangular top. L.58; bit: D.19; stem: T.4; terminal: L.9, W.7mm 11514 sf3515 (B6c2; 12th/13th century) (*Figs.1456–7*)

12647 Bit consists of an inverted T-shaped element which projects from flat base of a D-shaped element. Stem has a sub-rounded cross-section. Terminal rounded. L.68; bit: L.16, W.12; stem: T.5; terminal: D.11mm 12791 sf4116 (C6e3; 12th/13th century) (*Figs.1456–7*)

12648 Bit circular with a rectangular extension towards the stem which has a sub-rectangular cross-section. Terminal rounded, with faces at 90° to those of the bit. L.98; bit: L.33, W.20; stem: W.6; terminal: W.12mm 18047 sf4740 (B6c3; 12th/13th century) (*Figs.1456–7*)

12649 Bit oval. Stem has a collar at the base and a slight moulding at the head. Stem and one face of the bit are covered with fine criss-cross grooves. Terminal widens upwards, has a triangular top, and faces at c.90° to those of the bit. L.74; bit: L.18, W.15; stem: T.6; terminal: L.18, W.9mm 16612 sf7237 (D6a1; late 11th century) (*Fig.1456*)

12650 Very corroded. Fragment of a rounded bit; head of stem missing. L.57, T.8mm 12309 sf14957 (C6e9; mid 13th century)

12651 Upper part of stem and incomplete terminal only. Stem has a spiral groove inlaid with copper and a moulding at the head. L.55, T.10mm 9224 sf15974 (C6e9; mid 13th century)

12652 Fragment of rounded multi-chambered bit and lower part of stem. Moulding between them. L.32, W.19, T.4mm 9224 sf15975 (C6e9; mid 13th century)

12653 Bit circular with multi-chambered ward cut. Stem has a spiral groove inlaid with brass wire running around it and there is a moulding at the base and head. Terminal widens upwards and possibly had a rounded top, with faces at 90° to those of the bit. L.107; bit: D.26; stem: T.11; terminal: L.20, W.11mm u/s sf800 (*Fig.1456*)

Bits composed of short projections

All these bits are, or probably were (*12657*), composed of four short projections from the base of the stem, two on each face. All terminals are, or were, pierced for attachment.

12654 In two pieces. 35mm from the base the stem is stepped out and then tapers to the head. Terminal rounded. L.63; stem: W.7, T.6; terminal: D.11mm 1030 sf129 (C6i1; late 17th century)

12655 Stem narrows upwards for 67mm and then steps out before tapering to the head where there is a rounded pierced terminal. A spiral groove inlaid with brass (with small amount of tin) runs around the upper part of the stem. L.100; stem: W.10, T.7mm 5484 sf2029 (C6e1, D6a16; later 12th century) (*Fig.1456*)

12656 37mm from the base the stem steps out and then tapers to the head; this upper part has a rounded cross-section. Rounded terminal, with faces at 90° to those of the lower part of the stem. L.67; bit: W.6; stem: W.8, T.7; terminal: D.9mm 16525 sf4353 (D6a13–14; mid 12th century) (*Figs.1455–6*)

12657 Badly corroded. Bit damaged. Stem steps out before tapering to the head. Terminal roughly circular, with faces in same plane as those of the stem. L.99; bit: L.11; stem: L.76, W.12; terminal: L.19, W.18mm u/s sf2384

Box padlock key

12658 Bit in line with stem. The central shaft of the stem has a rectangular cross-section immediately above the bit, but

then becomes a spiral. At the point where the change occurs and at the head of the stem there is a moulded strip wrapped around it. Between these two strips run three strips which are roughly convex in relation to the central shaft. A disc encircles the centre of the stem on which the mid-points of the convex strips rest. Each of the convex strips has a raised ridge running longitudinally down the centre of it and on either side of that is a low-relief rope-work pattern. Terminal is a loop of rounded cross-section, the base of which is set in the moulded strip at the head of the stem. Plated (tin). L.92; bit: L.20, W.22; terminal: L.19, W.11mm 5415 sf1911 (C6c6, D6a7; mid 12th century) (*Fig.1458*)

Dress, dress accessories and personal ornament

Buckles

All frames have rectangular cross-sections unless stated.

Buckles with buckle-plates

12659 Buckle: oval frame. Pin widened and flattened to form the loop, D-shaped cross-section, curved over at the tip. Buckle-plate: rectangular folded plate; the two halves are held together by a single rivet. Rectangular notches are cut into each half in the centre of the sides. Surface of one half crossed near folded end by two grooves and by three short triangular grooves on the edge of the open end. Both objects plated (tin with copper, zinc and lead also detected). L.35; buckle frame: L.25, W.14, T.3; pin: L.18, W.6, T.3; buckle-plate: L.24, W.18, T.5mm 9302 sf1613 (D6a26; 12th/13th century) (*Fig.1466*)

12660 Buckle: hexagonal frame (two straight sides and triangular ends) with a central bar. The sides have a rectangular cross-section and the ends have a D-shaped cross-section. There is a moulding at the tip of the ends and at the junction of the sides and ends. Two transverse grooves on each side of one face of the frame at the junction with the central bar. Buckle-plate: attached to central bar and formed from folded plate, each half narrows slightly towards the open end which is rounded. Held together by a dome-headed rivet. Both objects plated (tin-lead). Buckle: L.49, W.28, T.6; buckle-plate: L.47, W.20, T.8mm 10791 sf2756 (D6f1–g2; mid 14th–mid 16th century) (*Fig.1471*)

12661 Buckle: D-shaped frame with a rounded cross-section. A triangular notch serves as a pin rest. The pin has a simple loop, D-shaped cross-section, tapers to a point, and curves over at the tip. Buckle-plate: badly corroded, but was formed from a rectangular folded plate. The two halves are held together by two rivets near the open end. In the centre of one half is a stud with a head, the face of which resembles a flower with four petals around a central stamen. Plated (tin). L.51; buckle: L.20, W.33, T.5; pin: L.20, W.7, T.5; buckle-plate: L.36, W.29, T. (over stud) 8mm 16465 sf4351 (D6a19; late 12th century) (*Fig.1468*)

D-shaped buckle frames

12662 Pin widened to form the loop, shank of D-shaped cross-section which expands slightly in the centre and tapers to a point. Frame: L.58, W.43, T.7; pin: L.45, W.11, T.7mm 1020 sf159 (C6i3; 17th–18th century) (*Fig.1468*)

12663 Oblique rectangular cross-section and notched pin rest. Pin has simple loop, shank D-shaped cross-section, slightly kinked, tapers to a point. Frame: L.38, W.32, T.5; pin: L.34, W.6, T.3mm 4385 sf557 (C6i4; 16th–19th century) (*Fig.1468*)

12664 Somewhat corroded. Cross-section is probably oblique rectangular. Fused scarf joint on the straight side. L.43, W.34, T.7mm 5263 sf1224 (D6c1; mid 13th century)

12665 Slightly bent. Pin rest in form of small eye projects from the centre of the curved side. Cross-section flattened sub-rectangular on convex side and rounded on straight side. L.54, W.43, T.5mm 9305 sf1541 (D6a24; 12th/13th century) (Fig.1468)

12666 Unfused scarf joint on the straight side and a notched pin rest on the convex side. L.24, W.19, T.4mm 9305 sf1551 (D6a24; 12th/13th century) (Fig.1468)

12667 Curved side has a wedge-shaped cross-section, straight part a rounded cross-section. Pin has a simple loop, tapers, curved over at end. L.80, W.46, T.10mm 1404 sf2100 (C6y1; late 13th–early 14th century) (Fig.1468)

12668 Elongated frame with a rounded cross-section which becomes rectangular on the straight side. Pin has a D-shaped cross-section, tapers slightly, tip missing. Plated (tin). Frame: L.39, W.51, T.7; pin: L.54, W.9, T.7mm 12407 sf3046 (B6c9; 13th century) (Fig.1468)

12669 Incomplete frame. There was a scarf joint on the straight side. L.15, W.17, T.4mm 13124 sf3992 (B6x1; 15th–16th century)

12670 Flattened and widened on convex side to make a pin rest. Cross-section on the straight side is sub-rectangular. Pin has a simple loop, shank tapers and is slightly kinked. Frame: L.48, W.48, T.10; pin: L.48, W.10, T.7mm 16532 sf4238 (D6a10; early 12th century) (Fig.1468)

12671 Incomplete frame made from a spirally twisted strip. L.31, W.25, T.4mm 16734 sf5020 (C6a1, D6a1; late 11th century)

12672 Straight side is thinner than the curved side. Plated (tin). L.53, W.39mm 18255 sf5229 (B6c1; 12th/13th century) (Fig.1468)

12673 Unfused scarf joint on the straight side. L.25, W.17, T.4mm u/s sf11399

Rectangular buckle frames

12674 Rounded corners. Pin widened to form a loop, tip missing. Frame: L.25, W.29, T.5; pin: L.24, W.8, T.4mm 9224 sf1405 (C6e9; mid 13th century) (Fig.1469)

12675 Rounded corners. L.28, W.25, T.5mm 5484 sf1987 (C6e1, D6a16; later 12th century) (Fig.1469)

12676 Rounded corners. L.35, W.23, T.5mm 11484 sf2745 (B6g10; 15th/16th century) (Fig.1469)

12677 Incomplete frame with part of pin adhering. L.28, W.20, T.2mm 12258 sf2917 (D6e5; early 14th century)

12678 Incomplete frame of rounded cross-section. Plated (tin, trace lead and copper). L.31, W.17, T.1mm 9224 sf3004 (C6e9; mid 13th century)

12679 Incomplete frame with sub-rectangular cross-section. L.36, W.22, T.4mm 13310 sf3423 (B6f1; early 14th century)

12680 Incomplete frame. One face has D-section mouldings running around it. Plated (copper with zinc, lead and tin detected). L.48, W.21, T.6mm 16170 sf4101 (D6a16; mid 12th century)

12681 Rounded corners. One side has a notched pin rest. L.32, W.28, T.5mm 17302 sf4423 (C6d8; mid–late 12th century) (Fig.1469)

Other buckle frames

12682 Incomplete frame, probably circular. Pin has a widened loop, tip missing. Frame: W.55, T.7; pin: L.47, W.12, T.8mm 5484 sf1710 (C6e1, D6a16; later 12th century) (Fig.1465)

12683 Probable incomplete oval frame, diamond-shaped cross-section in thicker part. L.51, W.29, T.3mm 9396 sf1722 (D6a25; 12th/13th century)

12684 Irregular oval frame. Pin tapers to a point. Plated (tin-lead alloy with trace of copper). Frame: L.24, W.29, T.5; pin: L.33, W.8, T.5mm 5975 sf3223 (C6c6; mid 12th century) (Fig.1466)

12685 Incomplete frame. It may have been round or D-shaped. Notched pin rest flanked by two transverse relief strips. Plated (tin). L.47, W.34, T.4mm 11818 sf3371 (B6c2–6; 12th/13th century)

12686 Half of frame only. It may have been rounded. Surviving piece expands slightly in the centre and has a sub-rectangular cross-section. L.27, T.4mm 13410 sf3384 (B6c1; 12th/13th century)

12687 Frame, of which about two-thirds survives. It may have been D-shaped and has a diamond-shaped cross-section. L.29, W.21, T.6mm 12619 sf3420 (D6a24; 12th/13th century)

12688 Incomplete frame. One side a has rectangular cross-section, the other a rounded cross-section. L.45, W.25, T.4mm 16410 sf14445 (D6a12; early 12th century)

Buckles with rotating arms

12689 Rotating arm only. Roughly rounded cross-section and expands slightly in the centre. One end has a five-faceted dome-headed terminal, other end missing. L.65, W.7mm 5484 sf1895 (C6e1, D6a16; later 12th century)

12690 Rotating arm expands in the centre and has its tips set in protrusions from the side of the frame. Central T-shaped pin, the ends of which also are set in protrusions from the side of the frame. The shank tapers, has a kinked shaft and is curved over at the tip. Plated (tin with small amounts of lead and copper). Frame: L.63, W.47, T.13; pin: L.60, W.26, T.9mm 10620 sf2608 (B6g10; 15th/16th century)

12691 Rotating arm only. Rounded cross-section and tapers at each end, one is slightly burred. L.66, W.9mm 10596 sf2639 (D6f–h1; mid 14th–mid 16th century)

12692 Rectangular frame. Rotating arm slightly expanded in the centre and has domed terminals held in place by loops at the ends of the frame sides. Frame sides have a D-shaped cross-section. The fixed end is narrower than the sides and has a sub-rectangular cross-section. There are four diagonal grooves in the convex face of the sides immediately above the looped ends. Pin shank tapers and curves over slightly at the tip. Frame: L.60, W.51, T.10; pin: L.58, W.11, T.7mm 16291 sf4003 (C6d20; late 12th century) (Fig.1469)

12693 Rectangular frame. Rotating arm slightly expanded in the centre and has a four-faceted domed head at each end held by loops at the ends of the frame sides. Plated (tin with trace of lead and copper). L.52, W.46, T.8mm 17532 sf4745 (C6c4, D6a6; early 12th century) (Fig.1469)

12694 Rotating arm only, slightly expanded in the centre, four-faceted domed terminal at each end. L.62, T.8mm 18366 sf4946 (B6a5; 11th/12th century)

12695 Fragment of frame with pierced, rounded terminal and rotating arm in situ. L.79, T.7mm 10450 sf15095 (C6g13; mid 15th century)

Buckle with integral buckle-plate

12696 Frame D-shaped. Buckle-plate incomplete, but narrows to the break. Pierced below frame for pin, bevelled upper edges, grooves cut into sides. Plated (tin). L.30, W.18mm 9252 sf1125 (D6e1; 13th/14th century) (Fig.1467)

Buckle-pins

They exist as a simple loop, have a rectangular cross-section and taper to a point unless stated. W. = width of loop.

12697 Widened to form the loop. L.58, W.9, T.4mm 1020 sf169 (C6i3; 17th–18th century)

12698 Shank spirally twisted, now incomplete. L.30, W.9, T.2mm 1506 sf278 (D6e9; mid 14th century)

12699 Tip missing. L.47, W.8, T.3mm 1455 sf362 (C6x2–6; 11th/13th century)

12700 Tip missing. L.47, W.11, T.3mm 5245 sf1230 (D6d3; late 13th century)

12701 Kink at head of shank. L.31, W.8, T.5mm 5264 sf1413 (D6c1; mid 13th century) (Fig.1472)

12702 Diamond-shaped cross-section. L.53, W.14, T.6mm 5348 sf2096 (C6e1, D6a16; 12th–13th century)

12703 Rolled loop, diamond-shaped cross-section, tip missing. L.36, W.14, T.8mm 5981 sf2418 (C6c3, D6a5; late 11th/early 12th century)

12704 Loop formed by flattening, D-shaped cross-section, curved over at the tip. L.50, W.13, T.7mm 9641 sf3103 (D6e1; 13th/14th century)

12705 Rounded cross-section. L.45, W.6, T.2mm 5975 sf3202 (C6c6; mid 12th century)

12706 D-shaped cross-section. L.45, W.16, T.7mm 12759 sf3739 (D6a18; late 12th century)

12707 L.35, W.12, T.3mm 17184 sf4617 (C6d5; mid 12th century)

12708 A widened loop made by flattening, rounded cross-section. L.57, W.13, T.5mm 18668 sf5334 (C6d6; mid 12th century)

12709 Tip missing. L.14, W.5, T.3mm 18256 sf5530 (B6a7; early 12th century)

12710 Loop distorted. Plated (tin, trace lead). L.38, W.13, T.9mm 18331 sf6163 (B6a5, C6c3; early 12th century)

12711 Curves over slightly at the tip. L.40, W.8, T.3mm 17627 sf15152 (C6c6; mid 12th century)

12712 L.53, W.11, T.6mm 17787 sf15202 (C6c1; early 12th century)

12713 L.40, W.5mm 10532 sf15205 (C6g7–9; 14th/15th century)

Buckle-plate

See also 12659–61.

Made from plates folded over into two and pierced for attachment to a belt at the open end.

12714 One half is incomplete, but both were clearly triangular. The complete half narrows towards the open end and has chamfered sides before becoming an elongated strip, tip missing. There are two pointed protrusions on each side of the strip: one at the base of the triangle and one near the tip. It was originally held together by a single rivet. Unidentified remains inside. Plated (tin). L.29, W.21, T.10mm 12647 sf4065 (D6c1; mid 13th century) (Fig.1473)

Belt fitting

12715 At the head a pierced rectangular terminal; on one face there is a groove on each side of the hole. The shank tapers and is curved over at the tip. Plated (tin). L.26, W.9, T.2mm 13568 sf15396 (B6a5; 11th/12th century) (Fig.1472)

Belt hasps

12716 Rectangular; each end is recessed on one face. Attached to a length of leather strap by means of a U-shaped fitting. Plated (front: quaternary; back: leaded tin, a little copper; attachment: leaded tin, a little copper). L.17, W.10; L. (with fitting) 30mm 5333 sf1759 (D6a17; late 12th century) (Fig.1475)

12717 Nearly rectangular frame, ends of which have triangular cross-section. Diagonal grooves cut into one face of the ends, longer side has a roller around it, also with diagonal grooves. Plated. L.28, W.17, T.7mm 5755 sf2306 (D6a17–23; late 12th–12th/13th century) (Fig.1475)

12718 Rectangular cross-section with an elongated projection from the convex sides and little block projections at the junction of the convex and straight sides. L.53, W.23, T.4mm 3494 sf2686 (A6e1; early 13th century) (Fig.1475)

12719 D-shaped frame, oval cross-section. Attachment fitting rectangular, held together by two rivets. Plated (tin-rich alloy with lead and copper). L.52; frame: L.41, W.25, T.7; attachment plate: L.35, W.28mm 15840 sf5228 (B6c7, C6e7; early 13th century) (Fig.1475)

12720 Nearly rectangular frame; grooves run ?spirally around it. Attached to one side, now projecting at 90°, is an elongated loop. Plated. L.26; frame: L.21, W.15mm 5494 sf15759 (C6e2, D6a17; late 12th century) (Fig.1475)

Strap-guides

12721 Head narrow and has a relief pattern cut across it: central channel flanked on each side by groove/groove/groove/rounded protrusion/groove. Arms straight. L.25, W.31, T.8mm 10416 sf2540 (C6g14–16; mid–late 15th century) (Fig.1477)

12722 The head is composed of three rectangular panels: the two outer panels narrow inwards slightly and are wider than the central panel which is recessed. The junction between the panels is marked by a groove and relief strip. Clasp butt-jointed at the base. Plated (tin-lead). Head: L.22, W.15; clasp: T.4mm 16734 sf5010 (C6a1, D6a1; late 11th century) (Fig.1477)

Pins

12723 Looped head. Plated (tin) head. L.45, T.1mm 6245 sf3316 (D6a6; 11th/12th century)

12724 Flattened and pierced head, spirally twisted shank, squared-off wedge-shaped tip. L.100, W.19, T.4mm 16603 sf4226 (D6a3–7; late 11th century–11th/12th century) (Fig.1489)

12725 Spirally twisted shank, squared-off tip, head missing. L.99, T.3mm 6282 sf5268 (D6a4; late 11th century) (Fig.1489)

Bracelet

12726 Originally penannular, oval cross-section. One tip missing, the other corroded, but there appears to have been a relief collar before an expanded terminal. Plated (tin). D.c.100, W.7, T.5mm 9641 sf3305 (D6e1; 13th/14th century) (Fig.1492)

Medical and toilet implements

Fleams

Blades semi-circular and the shanks are spirally twisted with small looped terminals.

12727 L.46; blade: L.11, W.10; shank: T.2mm 9028 sf1164 (D6e9; mid 14th century)

12728   L.48; blade: L.11, W.11; shank: T.2mm 5362 sf1848 (C6d8, D6a8; mid 12th century) (*Fig.1500*)

Tweezers

12729   Arms welded together at the head. They are both flat strips which widen and thicken away from the head before stepping in and becoming short tapering spikes with a D-shaped cross-section. On the outer face of each arm at the step there is a small triangular indentation. L.123; arm: L.94, W.13mm 9224 sf1432 (C6e9; mid 13th century) (*Fig.1501*)

Funerary and devotional objects

Pendant

12730   Cross-shaped. Arms cross a little off-centre; one arm end is curved over into a looped terminal. L.33, W.25, T.3mm 13465 sf3416 (B6c1; 12th/13th century) (*Fig.1492*)

Riding equipment

Spurs

Prick spurs

12731   Part of one arm survives. Straight part exists as three rounded panels, one broken, joined by two short strips of D-shaped cross-section. This part develops into a curved part of rounded cross-section which has incised grooves which possibly formed a spiral. Plated (tin). L.135, W.22, T.8mm 1502 sf504 (C6e11, D6e3; mid 13th century) (*Fig.1522*)

12732   Arms (one bent) have triangular cross-sections, taper away from the back and curve up at the tips to double-eyed terminals. One eye of each terminal is linked to a short fitting which has a loop at one end and a pierced terminal at the other, rivet in situ on the complete example. Goad is incomplete and has a diamond-shaped cross-section. Plated (tin with lead and copper also detected). L.105, W.62, T.18; goad: L.23; fitting: L.21mm 4385 sf550 (C6i4; 16th–19th century) (*Fig.1522*)

12733   Goad and incomplete neck. L.35, T.11mm 12578 sf3981 (D6a16–18; mid 12th century)

12734   Arms curve gently downwards, have a D-shaped cross-section and figure-of-eight-shaped terminals. Neck slightly down-curved and has a D-shaped cross-section. Goad octahedral. Plated (tin-lead). L.119, W.118, T.15; neck and goad: L.36; terminal: L.16mm 15287 sf4330 (A6n1; late 11th century) (*Fig.1522*)

12735   One arm largely missing. Surviving arm has a D-shaped cross-section and rectangular terminal which is pierced twice, rivets with brass domed heads in situ. A groove on upper face, each side of base of neck. Neck has a rounded cross-section; a collar runs around it at the base of the goad which is octahedral. Plated (tin, trace lead). L.134, T.8; neck and goad: L.34mm 16612 sf4370 (D6a1; late 11th century) (*Fig.1522*)

12736   Neck and goad. The goad is a biconical expansion flanked on each side by a thin collar. The top of the neck has a rounded cross-section but at the base it is flattened and widened before the break. L.40, T.12mm 12237 sf14853 (B6f4; early 14th century) (*Fig.1522*)

12737   Incomplete arm. Markedly curved or bent, D-shaped cross-section. Figure-of-eight-shaped terminal, pierced twice, rivets in situ. Plated (tin-lead). L.46; terminal: W.12, T.4mm 9641 sf16102 (D6e1; 13th/14th century) (*Fig.1522*)

Hooked spur fitting

12738   It consists of a tapering hook with a sub-rectangular cross-section. At its base it widens out into two plates between which a strap would have been gripped. The plates have convex sides and the open end is straight. Each plate is pierced twice, rivets in situ; one has a round head and the other a rectangular head. Plated (tin). L.51, W.23, T.8mm 12485 sf3129 (D6c1; mid 13th century) (*Fig.1523*)

Spur fitting

12739   Consists of a ring between two small opposing hooks, one incomplete. L.27; ring: D.14; hook: L.10, W.10mm 11397 sf2740 (B6g4; early 15th century) (*Fig.1523*)

Horse equipment

Bits

Snaffle bit

12740   Consists of two joined links and two ring cheek pieces. Link eyes formed by flattening the ends of the shanks and curving them over into loops. Shanks have rounded cross-sections and eyes rectangular cross-sections. Cheek pieces have oval cross-sections. Plated (tin, ?trace copper). Links: L.84 and 72; shanks: T.8; cheek pieces: D.39, T.8mm 9274 sf1281 (D6a5–24; 11th/12th–13th/14th century) (*Fig.1524*)

Snaffle links

12741   With cheek piece. Link slightly curved, rounded cross-section. At one end folded over to grip the eye of the cheek piece, tapers towards the other end where there is an incomplete eye. Cheek piece, now incomplete, was a bar of rounded cross-section, tapering towards each end with a D-shaped eye in the centre. Plated (tin-lead alloy). Link: L.98, W.9; cheek piece: L.65, W.25, T.5mm 4385 sf535 (C6i4; 16th–19th century) (*Fig.1524*)

12742   Incomplete link. Shank has a sub-rectangular cross-section and tapers from one end to the other; at the thinner end a round looped eye survives. L.83, W.7, T.7; eye: W.20mm 4620 sf1157 (C6e9; mid 13th century)

12743   Badly corroded. One eye survives and was made by tapering the shank and curving it over into a loop. Plated. L.60; shank: W.7mm 9073 sf14704 (D6f4; late 14th century)

12744   Badly corroded. The shank has a sub-rectangular cross-section. One eye survives and was made by tapering the shank and curving it over into a loop. Plated (brass with trace lead). L.78; shank: W.10mm 1229 sf14929 (C6z1; late 14th–early 15th century) (*Fig.1524*)

12745   Shank has rounded cross-section, eye at each end. L.86, T.8, link W.19mm u/s sf11042

Cheek pieces

12746   From bar bit. Strip with rounded cross-section, domed knop at one end, flattened before break at other. L.98, W.10mm 1763 sf641 (D6g3; mid–late 16th century) (*Fig.1524*)

12747   From a bar bit. It has a D-shaped loop at the centre and two incomplete arms, with sub-rectangular cross-sections, at a slight angle to each other. One arm flattened and widened before the break. Transverse grooves on the arms. Plated (copper with zinc and tin, also lead detected).

L.72; eye: W.30mm 12366 sf3017 (D6e4–5; 13th/14th–early 14th century) (*Fig.1524*)

Curb bit parts

12748   Shank of D-shaped cross-section with eye at each end, faces at 90° to each other. Collar at the base of the smaller eye, incomplete projection from the larger eye at angle to shank. Plated (tin-rich tin-lead alloy). L.72, T.7mm; eyes: D.14 and 10mm 2259 sf50 (B6w2; early 15th century) (*Fig.1526*)

12749   Consists of a mouth piece which from the surviving corner has a spirally twisted strip projecting at c.90° before curving over in a near U-shape and terminating in an eye. Running vertically upwards from the eye were three spikes (the central and most robust is broken) which project above the U. The other end of the plate is broken. A fragment of a small ring was found in the eye. L.145; plate: L.96, W.29, T.5mm 4811 sf837 (C6g6; late 14th century) (*Fig.1526*)

12750   Somewhat bent out of shape. Originally U-shaped and made from a strip of roughly D-shaped cross-section which at each end is flattened, widened and curved over into a looped terminal. There are transverse diagonal grooves on the face. Plated (tin). L.241, T.3; terminal: D.12, T.1mm 13568 sf3454 (B6a5; 11th/12th century) (*Fig.1526*)

Probable bit components

12751   A spirally twisted strip, broken at one end; at the other it is formed into a T, one arm end is looped over, the other bifurcates into two short tapering prongs. L.81, T.6; crosspiece: L.47mm 13005 sf3093 (B6e1; late 13th century) (*Fig.1526*)

Harness pendant

12752   It consists of a looped terminal below which a plate of triangular cross-section widens by means of two sloping shoulders and then narrows towards the base. Upper surface has incised grooves in a diamond pattern. Attached to the terminal is a small triangular plate which has a short rivet-like protrusion at its narrow end. Plated (tin with trace of copper). L.50, W.17, T.3mm 4620 sf1143 (C6e9; mid 13th century) (*Fig.1529*)

Horseshoes

All branches narrow towards their tips. Thickness measurement is over the main part of the branch not the calkin. Horseshoes designated left or right based on view from top, i.e. hoof side.

Wavy outer side

Complete or near complete

12753   Right branch incomplete. Left branch has turned-over calkin. Both branches have three countersunk holes, three with nails in situ, worn flat heads. L.90, W.92; branch: W.20, T.5; nails: L.30, W.16mm 4059 sf304 (C6z1; late 14th–early 15th century)

12754   Left branch incomplete. Three countersunk holes in right branch, two survive in left, one nail in situ, flattened head. L.83, W.101; branch: W.17, T.3; nail: L.20, W.6mm 9213 sf1003 (D6e1; 13th/14th century) (*Fig.1530*)

12755   Part of left branch missing. Right branch has turned-over calkin. Each branch has or had three countersunk holes, one nail in situ. L.110, W.105; branch: W.20, T.6mm 9224 sf1375 (C6e9; mid 13th century) (*Fig.1530*)

12756   Near complete, but worn at tip and end of left branch missing. Right branch has folded-over calkin. Each arm has or had three countersunk holes and at the front of each is a fourth and larger countersunk hole. L.111, W.107; branch: W.28, T.7; calkin: T.13mm 9224 sf1470 (C6e9; mid 13th century) (*Fig.1530*)

12757   Complete. Turned-over calkins, three countersunk holes in each arm. L.112, W.103; branch: W.26, T.6mm 9224 sf1516 (C6e9; mid 13th century)

12758   Right branch incomplete. Left branch has turned-over calkin and three countersunk holes; right branch has two. L.95, W.90; branch: W.19, T.5mm 9305 sf1967 (D6a24; 12th/13th century)

Single branches and branch fragments

12759   End of left branch. Incomplete countersunk hole, turned-over calkin. L.40, W.16, T.4mm 1115 sf178 (D6e9; mid 14th century)

12760   Corroded right branch. Turned-over calkin, three countersunk holes. L.86, W.24, T.4mm 4505 sf661 (C6e13; mid 13th century)

12761   End of left branch. Turned-over calkin, countersunk hole, nail with sloping shoulders and convex head in situ. L.58, W.18, T.4; nail: L.32, W.13mm 4850 sf899 (C6e1; 12th/13th century)

12762   Left branch. Turned-over calkin, three countersunk holes. L.103, W.26, T.7mm 1692 sf1098 (C6e9, D6e1; mid 13th century)

12763   Incomplete left branch. Three countersunk holes, turned-over calkin. L.91, W.24, T.6mm 9252 sf1120 (D6e1; 13th/14th century)

12764   End of right branch. Turned-over calkin, one countersunk hole. L.54, W.19, T.5mm 4620 sf1271 (C6e9; mid 13th century)

12765   Branch fragment. Countersunk hole. L.59, W.19, T.6mm 9274 sf1301 (D6a5–24; 11th/12th–13th/14th century)

12766   Tip of left branch. Two countersunk holes. L.62, W.17mm 1502 sf1323 (C6e11, D6e3; mid 13th century)

12767   End of left branch. Two countersunk holes, folded-over calkin. L.60, W.19, T.5mm 5348 sf1523 (C6e1, D6a16; 12th–13th century)

12768   End of left branch. Turned-over calkin, countersunk hole. L.50, W.19, T.7mm 5348 sf1542 (C6e1, D6a16; 12th–13th century)

12769   End of right branch. Countersunk hole. L.50, W.20, T.7mm 9305 sf1680 (D6a24; 12th/13th century)

12770   Left branch. Folded-over calkin, three countersunk holes. L.102, W.21, T.7mm 5545 sf1687 (D6a17–23; late 12th–12th/13th century)

12771   Tip of right branch. Two countersunk holes. L.59, W.17, T.4mm 5348 sf1970 (C6e1, D6a16; 12th–13th century)

12772   Right branch. Two countersunk holes, turned-over calkin. L.63, W.17, T.5mm 5348 sf2318 (C6e1, D6a16; 12th–13th century)

12773   Left branch. Folded-over calkin, three countersunk holes. L.108, W.23, T.6mm 3414 sf2649 (A6e1; early 13th century) (*Fig.1530*)

12774   Tip of left branch. Turned-over calkin, two countersunk holes. L.56, W.17, T.5mm 11332 sf2713 (B6f3; early 14th century)

12775   Right branch. Turned-over calkin. Three countersunk holes, two with nails in situ, heads rectangular with convex tops. L.103, W.24, T.6; nail: L.43, W.13mm 10845 sf2760 (C6e11; mid 13th century)

12776   Left branch. Thickened calkin, three countersunk holes. L.100, W.23, T.9mm 7782 sf3100 (D6y1; late 12th–13th century)

12777 Branch. Turned-over calkin, three countersunk holes, three nails in situ, wedge-shaped heads. L.99, W.21; nails: L.34, 27, 21, W.13mm 11458 sf3106 (B6c7; late 11th–early 12th century)

12778 Incomplete left branch. Turned-over calkin, two countersunk holes. L.83, W.27, T.6mm 12485 sf3232 (D6c1; mid 13th century)

12779 End of right branch. Calkin, and one countersunk hole. L.50, W.23mm 12631 sf3428 (D6a26–e3; early–late 13th century)

12780 Right branch. Turned-over calkin, three countersunk holes. L.88, W.20, T.5mm 13523 sf3467 (B6a3; 11th/12th century)

12781 End of left branch. Turned-over calkin, two countersunk holes. L.63, W.21, T.5mm 9641 sf4021 (D6e1; 13th/14th century)

12782 Left branch. Turned-over calkin, three countersunk holes. L.98, W.18mm 15126 sf4084 (B6b1; 12th century)

12783 Left branch. Two incomplete countersunk holes. L.72, W.20, T.5mm 15136 sf4089 (A6n2, B6a5; early 12th century)

12784 Right branch. Turned-over calkin, three countersunk holes. L.80, W.21, T.7mm 16686 sf4317 (C6e2–6; 12th/13th century)

12785 Left branch. Turned-over calkins, three countersunk holes, two nails in situ, wedge-shaped heads. L.98, W.25, T.6; nails: L.20, W.17mm 16170 sf4496 (D6a16; mid 12th century)

12786 Left branch with fragment of right branch. Three countersunk holes. L.104; branch: W.25, T.6mm 13902 sf4871 (B6c3; 12th/13th century)

12787 Very corroded branch. Calkin, three countersunk holes. L.105 13902 sf4872 (B6c3; 12th/13th century)

12788 Right branch. Turned-over calkin, one countersunk hole. L.49, W.20, T.7mm 15285 sf5267 (B6a1; late 11th century)

12789 Right branch. Turned-over calkin, four countersunk holes, two nails in situ. L.100, W.21, T.6; nails: L.37, 34, W.14, 17mm 18331 sf5392 (B6a5, C6c3; early 12th century)

12790 Right branch. Turned-over calkin, three countersunk holes, one nail in situ, convex head. L.99, W.23, T.7; nail: L.36, W.17mm 17890 sf5464 (B6a1, C6a1; late 11th century)

12791 Fragment. 9252 sf14692 (D6e1; 13th/14th century)

12792 Tip of right branch. Turned-over calkin, incomplete hole. L.46, W.23, T.5mm 3509 sf14808 (A6e1; early 13th century)

12793 End of left branch. Folded-over calkin, two countersunk holes. L.60, W.19, T.6; calkin: T.14mm 12113 sf14946 (C6e11; mid 13th century)

12794 End of branch. Turned-over calkin, part of one hole. L.46, W.24, T.11mm 1073 sf15371 (D6f9; mid 14th century)

Smooth outer side

12795 Complete. Remains of one turned-over calkin. Four holes in one arm and three in the other, one nail in situ. L.117, W.119; branch: W.28, T.6mm 4292 sf516 (C6i4; 16th–19th century) (Fig.1530)

12796 Left branch. Turned-over calkin, Two rectangular holes. L.77, W.28, T.5mm 3384 sf2031 (A6f2; 13th century)

12797 Tip of left branch. Incomplete sub-rectangular hole. L.45, W.21, T.7mm 13383 sf3351 (B6d5, C6f6; 13th century)

12798 Right branch. Three countersunk holes, nail in situ. L.88, W.20, T.4; nail: L.43, W.10mm 13175 sf3362 (D6e1; 13th/14th century)

12799 Right branch. Turned-over calkin, two small rectangular holes. L.119, W.30, T.9mm 13577 sf5080 (B6g4; early 15th century)

12800 Left branch. Three holes. L.99, W.26, T.5mm 18331 sf5408 (B6a5, C6c3; early 12th century)

12801 Complete. Left branch much more worn than the right especially at the tip. Left branch has turned-over calkin. Three rectangular holes in each branch, one nail in situ. L.108, W.98; branch: W.20, T.15mm u/s sf529

12802 Complete. Right branch has turned-over calkin, and is wider than the left which tapers markedly towards the tip where it is thickened. Three rectangular holes in each branch and one at the top, two nails in situ. L.112, W.103; branch: W.29, T.7; nails: L.27mm u/s sf2768

Outer side indeterminate

12803 Tip of left branch. Turned-over calkin. L.45, W.22, T.4mm 9252 sf1113 (D6e1; 13th/14th century)

12804 End of right branch. Turned-over calkin, countersunk hole. L.56, W.22, T.8mm 9224 sf1321 (C6e9; mid 13th century)

12805 Tip of left branch. Turned-over calkin, countersunk hole. L.55, W.20, T.5mm 9252 sf1370 (D6e1; 13th/14th century)

12806 Tip of left branch. Turned-over calkin. L.42, W.16, T.6mm 9252 sf1385 (D6e1; 13th/14th century)

12807 Tip of right branch. Turned-over calkin, incomplete rectangular hole. L.37, W.25, T.4mm 5975 sf2248 (C6c6; mid 12th century)

12808 Incomplete left branch. Three rectangular holes, one nail in situ. L.76, W.25, T.5; nail: L.31mm 12011 sf2776 (C6e11; mid 13th century)

12809 Tip of right branch. Turned-over calkin, incomplete rectangular hole. L.58, W.26, T.5mm 11886 sf3037 (B6f4; early 14th century)

12810 Incomplete right branch. Two countersunk holes, nail in situ. L.62, W.25, T.6mm 11514 sf3244 (B6c2; 12th/13th century)

12811 Corroded branch fragment. Two countersunk holes. L.65, W.25, T.5mm 16148 sf3930 (C6d19–21; late 12th century)

12812 End of left branch. Turned-over calkin, one countersunk hole, nail in situ, D-shaped head. L.54, W.17, T.8mm 17103 sf4817 (C6c6; mid 12th century)

12813 End of right branch. Curled-over calkin, countersunk hole. L.53, W.24, T.4mm 18133 sf5050 (B6c5; early 13th century)

12814 End of left branch. Turned-over calkin. L.35, W.20, T.5mm 17787 sf5239 (C6c1; early 12th century)

12815 End of right branch. Turned-over calkin. L.35, W.20, T.5mm 5000 sf14737 (C6c6; mid 12th century

12816 End of branch with calkin. L.40, W.11, T.9mm 9305 sf15009 (D6a24; 12th/13th century)

12817 Corroded. Branch fragment, pierced once. L.87, W.37, T.7mm 10394 sf15906 (C6g13; mid 15th century)

Horseshoe nails

346 horseshoe nails were recorded, details of which are available in archive.

Curry combs

12818 It consists of a half-cylindrical 'blade' which is broken at one end and damaged along its edges. It has one complete handle arm which has a spirally twisted shank and is riveted to the blade through a rounded terminal; the arm tip is curved over at 90°. There is the terminal of another arm. Blade: L.61, D.42, T.4; handle: L.80mm 12671 sf3461 (D6a16; mid 12th century) (*Fig.1530*)

12819 Arm only. At one end curved over and has a wedge-shaped tip; at the other it is widened and flattened into a rounded, pierced terminal, now incomplete. L.77, W.3; terminal: W.12mm 13532 sf3838 (A6n3, B6c1; late 12th/early 13th century) (*Fig.1530*)

12820 Tapering spirally twisted arm with hook at the tip. At the head an incomplete rounded pierced terminal with rivet through it set in a fragment of the cylinder. L.111; terminal: W.18; rivet: L.19mm 12364 sf3881 (C6e6; early 13th century) (*Fig.1530*)

Weapons and armour
Sword blade

12821 Tip. L.40, W.18mm 3498 sf3217 (A6c5; 12th century) (*Fig.1532*)

Arrowheads

All are socketed and have a rivet hole in the side unless otherwise stated.

Tapering blades of rectangular cross-section

12822 Head of tang is waisted and socket is incomplete. L.117, T.11; socket: L.37, D.12mm 4640 sf1076 (C6e10; mid 13th century) (*Fig.1532*)

12823 L.81; socket: L.26, D.10mm 5777 sf1904 (D6a17–23; late 12th–12th/13th century) (*Fig.1532*)

12824 L.79, T.5; socket: D.10mm 12274 sf3084 (D6e1; 13th/14th century) (*Fig.1532*)

12825 L.110; socket: L.20, D.8mm u/s sf40

Triangular blades

These blades have straight sides and horizontal shoulders at base unless stated.

12826 L.87; blade: L.49, W.23; socket: D.13mm 5238 sf1401 (C6e5, D6a24; early 13th century)

12827 Blade has upward sloping shoulders and an elliptical cross-section. L.76; blade: L.42, W.14; socket: D.9mm 5348 sf2038 (C6e1, D6a16; 12th–13th century) (*Fig.1532*)

12828 Blade has concave upward sloping shoulders and an elliptical cross-section. L.71; blade: L.52, W.20; socket: D.7mm 5777 sf2044 (D6a17–23; late 12th–12th/13th century) (*Fig.1532*)

12829 Blade has convex sides and an elliptical cross-section. The base of the socket is irregular either due to burring or heat. Wood in socket. L.60; blade: L.17, W.17; socket: D.8mm 6257 sf3407 (C6c4; early 12th century) (*Fig.1532*)

12830 Blade has upward sloping shoulders. Triangular cross-section. L.63; blade: L.23, W.12; socket: D.9mm 17275 sf4895 (C6d11; late 12th century) (*Fig.1532*)

12831 Blade has convex sides and stepped shoulders. Triangular cross-section. L.58; blade: L.18, W.10; socket: D.9mm 17699 sf5223 (C6c1; early 12th century) (*Fig.1532*)

12832 Blade has convex sides and concave upward sloping shoulders. L.60; blade: L.29, W.16; socket: D.9mm 17699 sf5237 (C6c1; early 12th century) (*Fig.1532*)

Barbed blades

These blades have straight sides unless stated.

12833 Blade has convex sides. Lozenge-shaped cross-section. L.62; blade: L.41, W.16; socket: L.35, D.10mm 1981 sf829 (D6e9; mid 14th century) (*Fig.1532*)

12834 Incomplete. Elliptical cross-section. L.69; blade: L.38, W.18; socket: D.12mm 9078 sf1008 (D6e1; 13th/14th century)

12835 Blade has slightly convex sides and an elliptical cross-section. L.65; blade: L.40, W.19; socket: L.37, D.11mm 10355 sf2538 (C6g14–15; mid–late 15th century) (*Fig.1532*)

12836 Socket missing. Blade has convex sides and an elliptical cross-section. L.36, W.13mm 9224 sf2816 (C6e9; mid 13th century) (*Fig.1532*)

12837 Blade has lozenge-shaped cross-section. Wood in the socket. L.56; blade: L.30, W.8mm 9224 sf2825 (C6e9; mid 13th century)

12838 Blade has convex sides and an elliptical cross-section. No hole in the socket, but wood in situ. L.74; blade: L.61, W.22; socket: L.43, D.12mm 9224 sf2976 (C6e9; mid 13th century) (*Fig.1532*)

12839 Blade has one short rounded barb surviving and collar at junction of blade and socket. L.67; blade: L.27, W.17; socket: D.12mm 12422 sf3387 (D6e1; 13th/14th century) (*Fig.1532*)

12840 Blade has convex sides and an elliptical cross-section. Tip appears to have been deliberately cut off. L.57; blade: L.46, W.19; socket: L.39, D.11mm 12619 sf3422 (D6a24; 12th/13th century) (*Fig.1532*)

12841 Blade has short rounded barbs and a lozenge-shaped cross-section; collar at junction of blade and socket. L.58; blade: L.31, W.17; socket: D.8mm 12274 sf3426 (D6e1; 13th/14th century) (*Fig.1532*)

Other

12842 It has two conical arms which are joined at their narrower ends. One arm is tubular and is slightly longer and thinner than the other which is solid. L.75; arms: L.48, 27, W.16, 11mm 9305 sf1988 (D6a24; 12th/13th century) (*Fig.1532*)

Chain mail

12843 Two pieces, (a) and (b). Links have rounded cross-section, some have lapped joints visible. Pattern of links: (a) 1-1-2-1-2-1-1-1-2; (b) 1-1-3. Links: D.12, T.1mm 11332 sf2668 (B6f3; early 14th century) (*Fig.1533*)

Copper alloy
Textile tools
Needles

6626 With circular eye, top of head rounded, shank of circular section. D.0.7, L.26.4mm 9305 sf1678 (D6a24; 12th/13th century) (*Fig.830*)

6627 With circular eye, top of head rounded, shank of circular section. D.0.7, L.28mm 5484 sf1739 (C6e1, D6a16; later 12th century) (*Fig.830*)

6628 With flattened head, top pointed, circular eye, shank of circular section. D.2.2, L.80.7mm; head: W.4.2mm 5484 sf2030 (C6e1, D6a16; later 12th century) (*Fig.830*)

6629 Upper shaft flattened and widened, oval-shaped eye punched or drilled through. Rounded top to shaft, sub-rounded section, tapering. D.2, L.65mm 5348 sf1944 (C6e1, D6a16; 12th–13th century) (*Fig.830*)

6630 With expanded oval head, top flat, elongated oval eye, shank of circular section. D.1.3, L.50.7mm; head: W.2.4mm 5064 sf933 (C6e9; mid 13th century) (*Fig.830*)

6631 With expanded oval head, top flat, elongated oval eye, shank of circular section. D.2, L.84.9mm; head: W.2.9mm 9057 sf901 (C6e11, D6e3; mid 13th century) (*Fig.830*)

6632 Incomplete, head broken across eye, upper three-quarters of shank of circular section, lower quarter of triangular section. D.2.4, L.103mm 10333 sf2554 (B6g13, C6g15; late 15th/early 16th century) (*Fig.830*)

6633 Incomplete, top broken off through eye. Originally the top flattened with grooves punched into front and back to form long narrow eye, shaft section circular. D.0.8, L.38mm u/s sf6941 (*Fig.830*)

12844 Extreme tip broken off, drilled circular eye in flattened head, pointed at top, of oval section. D.2, L.74.3mm; head: W.4.2mm 4179 sf399 (C6z1; late 14th–early 15th century)

12845 With elongated oval head, oval eye, top of head flat, with shank of circular section. D.1.8, L.62.7mm 1502 sf970 (C6e11, D6e3; mid 13th century)

12846 Broken through oval eye at upper end, shank of circular section. D.1.4, L.78.8mm 9105 sf1068 (D6e1; 13th/14th century)

12847 Large, with split oval eye, shank bent up. D.1.8, L.132.6mm 9224 sf1430 (C6e9; mid 13th century)

12848 Incomplete, broken through circular eye drilled through flattened top, shank of oval section. D.2, L.61mm 5415 sf1877 (C6c6, D6a7; mid 12th century)

12849 Of sub-circular section, upper end of shank flattened, large oval eye, top of head tapers to flattened tip, top half of shank bent up, tip of shank broken off. D.2, L.66.1mm; head: W.3.8mm 9305 sf2117 (D6a24; 12th/13th century)

12850 Incomplete, broken across eye at upper end, of sub-oval section, tapering to tip. L.55.4, W.3.4, T.2mm 5536 sf2258 (C6e1; 12th/13th century)

12851 Incomplete, broken through eye, tip also broken off, of circular section. D.1, L.41.5mm 10022 sf2436 (C6i1; late 17th century)

12852 Shank only, of circular section, broken at upper end. D.1.1, L.83mm 10560 sf2589 (B6g10; 15th/16th century)

12853 Complete apart from tip which is broken off, of circular section, upper end flattened with circular eye. D.2.3, L.82mm; head: D.3.4mm 10039 sf2759 (D6g1; early–mid 16th century)

12854 Incomplete, broken across eye in flattened head, shank of sub-circular section, bent at both ends. D.1.3, L.140.9mm 11670 sf2870 (B6g1; 14th/15th century)

12855 Incomplete, broken across eye in flattened head, shank of sub-circular section. D.1.5, L.52.2mm 11458 sf3125 (B6c7; late 11th–early 12th century)

12856 Incomplete, broken across circular eye in flattened head, shank of circular section. D.2.5, L.97mm 12412 sf3145 (C6e5; early 13th century)

12857 Of sub-circular section, flattened head, top pointed, oval eye, lower half of shank bent up. D.2.2, L.67.9mm; head: W.3.4mm 16535 sf4414 (D6a9; early 12th century)

Netting needle

6634 Of circular section, with elongated split at each end, one end bent up. D.1, L.108.6mm; split end: L.15.2mm 10464 sf2575 (C6g7; 14th/15th century) (*Fig.1349*)

Other tools
Knives
Knife hilt-plates

12858 Of rectangular section, cropped lenticular shape, one end cut square, the other rounded, with central rectangular perforation. L.17.5, W.12.1, T.0.7mm 5348 sf2181 (C6e1, D6a16; 12th–13th century)

12859 Of rectangular section, cropped lenticular shape, one end cut square, the other pointed, with irregular rectangular cut-out. L.19.2, W.11.6, T.1.5mm 17421 sf4711 (B6a6; 11th/12th century) (*Fig.1364*)

Domestic equipment
Vessels
Rim

12860 Fragment, of sheet, outer edge curved, rounded over and slightly thickened, other edge and both ends broken. L.121.7, W.33.9, T.3.2mm 10490 sf2567 (C6g10; early 15th century) (*Fig.1395*)

Patch of sheet

12861 Incomplete, sub-rectangular, part of one edge and end survive, rest broken away, sub-lenticular holes run along the surviving edges. L.63.3, W.39, T.0.7mm 11554 sf2815 (B6g9; 15th/16th century) (*Fig.1399*)

Structural items and fittings

12862 Tack with circular domed head, shank of square section. L.20.3, W.3, T.2.4mm; head: D.7.9mm 1020 sf168 (C6i3; 17th/18th century)

12863 Staple rectangular, of rectangular section, both tips incomplete. L.14.3, W.2.4, T.0.9mm 18256 sf4821 (B6a7; early 12th century)

Binding strips

12864 Or mount, strip of plano-convex section, one end broken across perforation, other end with shallow sub-circular domed terminal with perforation just above, second perforation at point where strip curves round. L.93.5, W.5.3, T.2.3mm; terminal: D.7.8mm 11938 sf3062 (B6f3; early 14th century) (*Fig.1427*)

12865 Or mount, a narrow rectangular strip of rectangular section incorporating two complete open circles and broken across one partial open circle, the other end broken across rivet hole. L.70.6, W.3.8, T.3mm; hole: D.15.4mm 17551 sf4896 (C6c3; early 12th century) (*Fig.1427*)

Swivel fitting

12866 With shank of sub-circular section, projecting from looped terminal of plano-convex section. D.10.3, L.20.9, T.6.9mm 3158 sf806 (A6j16; late 15th century) (*Fig.1428*)

Chains

12867 Six lengths, comprising one, two or three links of twisted triple wire of circular section, all looped at ends, all lengths with one end broken. Longest: L.131.8, W.4.2, T.2.3mm;

wire: D.0.8mm 1687 sf503 (D6f–h; mid 14th–mid 16th century) (*Fig.1429*)

12868   Three S-shaped links, of circular section. L.62.6, W.9.6mm; section: D.2.2mm 18075 sf4725 (B6c7; early 13th century) (*Fig.1429*)

Rings

12869   Circular, of sub-hexagonal section. D.20.8mm; section: W.3.7, T.2.6mm 3053 sf148 (A6j21; 16th century) (*Fig.1430*)

12870   Incomplete, of flat, rectangular section. D.7.5mm; section: W.1.8, T.0.8mm 4032 sf196 (C6i3; 17th/18th century)

12871   Incomplete, ends broken, of flattened wire, decorated with punched transverse grooves on both sides. D.15.3mm; section: W.1.6, T.1.1mm 9260 sf1359 (D6a26; 12th/13th century)

12872   Incomplete, of sub-circular section. D.16.7mm; section: D.2.2mm 10119 sf2457 (C6h9; 16th–17th century)

12873   Sub-circular band, of sheet metal. D.10.3mm; section: W.2, T.0.5mm 10123 sf2467 (B6g14; 16th/17th century) (*Fig.1430*)

12874   Oval, of irregular thickness and sub-rectangular section. L.26.1, W.23.8mm; section: W.2.9, T.2.1mm 10464 sf2545 (C6g7; 14th/15th century)

12875   Circular but now split, of sub-circular section. D.17.5mm; section: D.2.2mm 10266 sf2625 (D6i1; early–mid 17th century) (*Fig.1430*)

Disc

12876   Sub-discoidal, centrally perforated. D.11.7, T.2.1mm 9572 sf2359 (D6a9; early 12th century)

Ferrule

9161   Incomplete, upper edge roughly broken, tapering to lower end, seam formed by folding one edge over the other, enclosing wood (beech) remains. L.53.6, W.19, T.10.7mm 10096 sf2525 (ferrule), sf19012 (wood) (B6g13; 16th–17th century) (*Fig.1431*)

Miscellaneous fitting

12877   Discoidal, with shank of sub-square section, rectangular terminal close to shank end. D.25.6, T.3mm; shank: L.32, W.6.7, T.5mm 1390 sf961 (C6x4–6; early–mid 13th century) (*Fig.1431*)

Locks and keys

Barrel padlock key

12878   With loop terminal at upper end, stem below of octagonal section, lower two-thirds of rectangular section, sub-H-shaped bit projecting at 90° to stem. L.63.5, W.4.6, T.5.4mm; bit: L.7, W.5.7mm 12791 sf4113 (C6e3; 12th/13th century) (*Figs.1453, 1455*)

Dress, dress accessories and personal ornament

Buckles

12879   Annular, of circular section, with square butted ends, pin looped around. D.14.7mm; section: D.1.3mm 3344 sf1082 (A6g1; 13th/14th century)

12880   Annular, frame of sub-circular section, pin looped around frame, moulding just below loop, tip bent up. D.41.5mm; pin: L.45.2, W.6.5, T.4.3mm; section: D.4.7mm 10546 sf2578 (C6g6; late 14th century) (*Fig.1465*)

12881   Oval with narrowed bar, of sub-rectangular section, slight bow to front at recess for pin, notch at each end of bar. L.37.3, W.22.7, T.3.3mm 10096 sf2453 (B6g13; 16th–17th century) (*Fig.1466*)

12882   Oval with offset narrowed bar, of D-shaped section, pin missing. L.28.2, W.15.5, T.2.6mm 18170 sf5180 (B6c1; 12th/13th century) (*Fig.1466*)

12883   Trapezoidal-shaped frame with integral plate, frame of plano-convex section, pin looped through hole with rivet hole just behind in plate which is slightly recessed with transverse grooving across it. A narrow rectangular projection from here also has transverse grooving, and expands into a terminal with notched edges and a central rivet hole. L.40.8, W.23.6, T.2.5mm 9224 sf1318 (C6e9; mid 13th century) (*Fig.1467*)

12884   Fragment, originally with integral plate, oval bow now bent up, slight rectangular projection for pin tip to rest on, perforation for pin, plate broken across rivet hole. L.28.6, W.16.3, T.2.9mm 3258 sf1352 (A6g1; 13th/14th century) (*Fig.1467*)

12885   Rectangular frame, of D-shaped section, with globular projections at each corner, notched lip for missing pin, narrowed bar, frame decorated with pairs of transverse incised lines. L.37, W.22.1, T.4.4mm 12710 sf3677 (D6a26; 12th/13th century) (*Fig.1469*)

Buckle-plates

12886   Made of sheet, rectangular, folded, with two loops, one broken, three rivet holes along lower edges of both plates, front plate with square field containing cross-hatching, lower edge of plate scallopped, back plate undecorated. Two copper alloy rivets survive, not in situ. L.27.9, W.15.6, T.4.8mm; sheet: T.0.7mm 12561 sf3306 (D6a3–25; late 11th–12th/13th century) (*Fig.1473*)

12887   Two fragments, made of sheet, both broken at one end, rectangular, with two rivet holes close to surviving ends. L.29.9, W.13, T.0.8mm 13390 sf3475 (B6c4; 12th/13th century)

12888   Fragment, made of sheet, sub-rectangular, one end and one edge survive, perforated close to complete end, other end slightly curved up, broken across perforation. L.21, W.7, T.0.6mm 15286 sf4162 (A6n1; late 11th century)

Strap-ends

12889   Two adjoining fragments, from two-piece strap-end, single rivet hole in each plate close to one end, one fragment with incised line decoration along edge. L.23.9, W.9.5, T.0.6mm 3258 sf1037 (A6g1; 13th/14th century)

12890   Forked spacer plate fragment, of sheet, sub-rectangular, terminal and sides incomplete. L.22.7, W.10.7, T.1.2mm 5348 sf2477 (C6e1, D6a16; 12th–13th century)

Chape

12891   Made of sheet, tapering to rounded tip, seam slightly overlapped, upper end slightly damaged, with traces of a band around the upper end which is now lost. L.47.8, W.16.4, T.0.9mm 4689 sf2544 (C6g9–17; early 15th–15th/16th century) (*Fig.1478*)

Mounts

12892 Fragmentary, originally rectangular with central and corner rivet holes. L.40.4, W.20.4, T.1.1mm 3047 sf149 (A6j28; early 17th century) (*Fig.1480*)

12893 Made of sheet, incomplete, one end broken away, sub-rectangular, with two rivet holes close to surviving end. L.21.1, W.13.4, T.0.7mm 1506 sf578 (D6e9; mid 14th century) (*Fig.1480*)

12894 Of sheet, lozenge-shaped, domed, with lead backing. L.16.5, W.15.5, T. (sheet) 0.9mm 6101 sf3059 (C6e9; mid 13th century) (*Fig.1480*)

12895 Incomplete, originally rectangular, of rectangular section, broken along one edge and at one end, rivet survives in one corner. L.15.2, W.5.7, T.0.9mm; rivet: L.5.1mm 1019 sf71 (modern)

12896 Rectangular, of rectangular section, with a separate rivet in each corner, deeply incised line along lateral central axis. L.17.4, W.12.3, T.1.2mm; rivet: L.5.6mm u/s sf23 (*Fig.1480*)

Annular brooches

12897 In two adjoining fragments, of plano-convex section, with seven circular raised settings containing vitreous enamel of outer opaque blue ring, opaque white ring and red chips in centre. Analysis: copper, trace lead. D.23.7, T.2.2mm 12412 sf3157 (C6e5; early 13th century) (*Fig. 1486*)

12898 Of circular section, with constriction for pin which is looped around. D.12.9mm; pin: L.11.8mm; section: D.1.6mm 12498 sf3329 (D6e1; 13th/14th century) (*Fig.1486*)

12899 Composed of three spirally twisted wires of sub-circular section, pin looped around frame. D.21.9, T.2.6mm; pin: L.20, W.1.9mm; section: D.1.3mm 12496 sf3355 (D6a24; 12th/13th century) (*Fig.1486*)

12900 Of square section, with constriction for pin, back face flat, front decorated with notches on inner and outer circumferences. Looped pin separated from brooch, of rectangular section, tapering to tip which is broken off. D.23.2mm; section: W.3, T.3.1mm; pin: L.17.7mm 13410 sf3383 (B6c1; 12th/13th century) (*Fig.1486*)

12901 With constriction for pin which is missing, of rectangular section, cusped edge with sub-oval projections from each cusp, incised line decoration around inner and outer edges on one face. D.35.9mm; section: W.6.3, T.2.3mm u/s sf2983 (*Figs.1486*)

Possible dress pin

12902 With circular head, centrally domed, surrounded by flat multi-lobed frill, each lobe perforated, perforations at the cardinal points being smaller than the others. A shank of sub-square section tapers to tip and lower two-thirds is bent up. Shank: L.69.1, W.3.1, T.1.8mm; head: D.36, T.1.6mm; boss: D.21.1 H. 10mm 16170 sf4095 (D6a16; mid 12th century) (*Fig.1489*)

Pins

With wire-wound head

12903 With double-twist wire-wound head, shank of circular section, half bent up, tip broken off. D.1.2, L.52.7mm; head: D.3.4mm u/s sf2377 (*Fig.1490*)

With sub-globular head

12904 Shank of circular section. D.1, L.49.4mm; head: D.2.1mm 4448 sf625 (C6h2; early 16th century)

12905 Shank of circular section, tapering to point. D.1, L.141.2mm; head: D.7mm 10464 sf2574 (C6g7; 14th/15th century) (*Fig.1490*)

12906 Shank of circular section, lower half bent up. D.0.8, L.77.7mm; head: D.2.8mm 10768 sf2645 (B6g4; early 15th century) (*Fig.1490*)

12907 Sides flattened, shank of circular section, tip bent. D.1.1, L.57.1mm; head: W.2.7mm 10903 sf2676 (C6g14; mid 15th century) (*Fig.1490*)

12908 Shank of circular section tapering to tip which is bent up. D.1.3, L.158.8mm; head: D.6.5mm 11626 sf2807 (B6g4; early 15th century) (*Fig.1490*)

With lead alloy head

12909 With lead alloy head cast onto top of pointed shank fragment, of circular section. D.0.7, L.48.2mm 9030 sf863 (D6g2; mid 16th century)

With lens-shaped head

12910 Shank of circular section tapering to point. D.0.7, L.45.7mm; head: D.4mm 11016 sf2512 (C6e6; early 13th century)

12911 Shank of circular section. D.0.6, L.53.3mm; head: D.5.3mm 13698 sf3522 (B6a5; 11th/12th century) (*Fig.1490*)

Lace tag

12912 Type E, rolled up, edge-to-edge seam, open at lower end, upper end broken through perforation on one side. D.2.4, L.27.1mm 11525 sf2761 (B6g10; 15th/16th century)

Possible lace tags

12913 With edge to edge seam, slightly tapering, distorted by twisting, lower end open, traces of rivet hole at upper end. D.2.6, L.83.8mm 11300 sf2617 (B6c7; early 13th century) (*Fig.1491*)

12914 Slightly tapering to open lower end, with edge to edge seam. D.7.9, L.84.6mm 13058 sf3195 (B6c7; early 13th century) (*Fig.1491*)

12915 Slightly tapering, with edge to edge seam, lower end sealed by one edge being folded over other. D.8.3, L.82.1mm 13228 sf3255 (B6f5; early 14th century) (*Fig.1491*)

12916 Tapering to sealed lower end, seam open on reverse, front face decorated with transverse grooving. D.3.9, L.39.3mm 18668 sf5369 (C6d6; mid 12th century) (*Fig.1491*)

Finger-rings

12917 Incomplete, part of hoop missing, oval bezel with decorative notched edge containing blue glass setting, moulding on each shoulder. Analysis: copper, zinc (v. high), trace lead and tin. D.24.6mm; bezel: L.8.9, W.7.3mm; section: W.2.9, T.2.1mm 5348 sf2200 (C6e1, D6a16; 12th–13th century) (*Figs.1492, 1497*)

12918 Of irregular D-shaped section. Analysis: copper, trace lead. D.17.3mm; section: W.1.8, T.1.8mm 13638 sf3497 (B6c7; early 13th century)

12919 Of plano-convex section, hoop with three pairs of decorative rectangular mouldings, largest pair in the centre, flanked by other pairs decreasing in size away from centre, all extending to both sides of hoop, each decorated with lozenges containing saltire. Analysis: copper, zinc, trace tin. D.20.2, W.2.1, T.1.4mm; largest moulding: W.3.4mm 15136 sf4099 (A6n2, B6a5; early 12th century) (*Fig.1492*)

12920 Of D-shaped section, decorated on outer face with vertical grooving. Analysis: copper, zinc, trace lead and tin. D.17.8mm; section: W.1.6, T.1.2mm 18172 sf4770 (B6c1; 12th/13th century) (*Fig.1492*)

12921 Plain band of sheet, oval, with ragged edges, the ends lapped and forged. Analysis: copper, zinc. L.19.8, W.16.3mm; section: T.0.5mm 17890 sf5607 (B6a1, C6a1; late 11th century)

12922 Plain band of sheet, shape now distorted, ends tapering. Analysis: copper, zinc, lead. L.15.7mm; section: W.3.6, T.0.7mm u/s sf6257

Toilet implements

12923 Double-ended, one end with circular scoop, the other end narrow lozenge shape of rectangular section, with twisted mid-section to the stem. D.5.7, L.83.5mm 10904 sf2766 (C6g6–10; late 14th–early 15th century) (*Fig.1501*)

Tweezers

12924 Now in two fragments, loop at upper end of rectangular section, arms thinning and broadening out towards the tips, upper half decorated on both faces with squared wave design. L.63, W.5, T.0.9mm 9224 sf1466 (C6e9; mid 13th century)

12925 Incomplete, part of one side broken off just below the slide, oval loop of rectangular section, with wire ring through, upper ends decorated with square notched design, below slide, surviving tip decorated with graved rocker tracery. L.70, W.5.0, T.2.5mm; ring: D.6.2mm 11507 sf2765 (B6c6; early 13th century) (*Fig.1501*)

12926 Complete apart from one tip which has broken off, small oval loop of rectangular section, sides gradually widening from loop to squared tips, upper end decorated with deeply cut squared wave design. Below the slide, the tips are flattened and decorated with incised zig-zag design. L.95.7, W.5.4, T.3.5mm 12865 sf3705 (D6a21; 12th/13th century) (*Fig.1501*)

12927 Formed from strip of rectangular section, looped at upper end, clip at lower end, below which tips are splayed out, decorated on both faces with lateral rouletted lines and along both edges with three pairs of notches on both faces. L.77.5, W.4, T.2mm 16410 sf4336 (D6a12; early 12th century) (*Fig.1501*)

Literacy
Book mount or boss

12928 Incomplete, made of sheet, a hollow cone with the remains of two projecting basal lobes, perforated for attachment, third lobe broken off. L.21.2, W.14, H.17.6mm 1506 sf292 (D6e9; mid 14th century) (*Fig.1506*)

Trade and exchange
Scale pan

12929 Of sheet, circular, dished, with three suspension holes. D.52.1, T.0.8mm 13200 sf3378 (B6c5; early 13th century) (*Fig.1519*)

Balance chain

12930 Two lengths, of S-shaped loops linked to ring of square section tapering to ends, now separated. L.151.9mm; ring: D.11.7, W. (section) 1.6mm 4736 sf763 (C6g10–16; early–late 15th century) (*Fig.1519*)

Riding equipment
Spur rowel

12931 Of rectangular section, with 14 points, central perforation. D.34.9, T.2.6mm 4399 sf573 (C6g18; 15th/16th century) (*Fig.1523*)

Weapons and armour
Finger-joint covers from plate armour gauntlets

12932 A curved rectangular plate made of sheet, with a repoussé lenticular ridge in the centre and a rivet hole to each side, one rivet hole broken through. D.24.5, W.18.4, T.1.3mm 11455 sf2844 (B6e1; late 13th century) (*Fig.1533*)

12933 A curved rectangular plate made of sheet, with a repoussé lenticular ridge, and a rivet hole to each side, one torn through. D.28.8, W.22.5, T.1mm 11633 sf2845 (B6c6; early 13th century) (*Fig.1533*)

Unidentified objects

12934 Incomplete, one end broken off, of plano-convex section, sub-rectangular, surviving end bent up and perforated, upper face with triangular facets and ring-and-dot motif decoration. L.54.7, W.6.4, T.2.5mm 5415 sf1669 (C6c6, D6a7; mid 12th century) (*Fig.1535*)

12935 Fragmentary, made up of five layers, one end broken away, other end with sub-globular terminal with single collar below, sub-cross-shaped projection on top, central layer extends beyond broken edges of others, widening out just below collar to form thin sub-rectangular strip, lower edge broken at oblique angle. L.20.1, T.3.7mm; projection: L.11, W.4.4, T.0.5mm 18119 sf16105 (B6c3; 12th/13th century) (*Fig.1535*)

Gold

12936 Brooch pin of rectangular section, with looped eye at one end, tapering to point at other which is slightly bent up. L.27.9, W.3, T.0.9mm; loop: D.2.9mm 10464 sf2571 (C6g7; 14th/15th century) (*Fig.1489*)

12937 Finger-ring set with central round pearl and four pink garnets on high turret-shaped collets at the cardinal points, shoulders decorated with nielloed lines. D.22.6mm; hoop: W.3, T.1.1mm; bezel: W.13.6, H.6.5mm 5029 sf872 (C6e10; mid 13th century) (*Figs.1492–4*)

Lead alloy
Building tools
Plumb-bob

12938 Sub-spherical, with small axial perforation. D.30.2mm, Wt.150.14g 11416 sf2841 (B6c2–6; 12th/13th century) (*Fig.1317*)

Fishing

Net weights

12939 Sub-triangular, of irregular plano-convex section and with a perforation towards one corner. L.62.6, W.61.9, T.18.8mm, Wt.386g 18169 sf4968 (B6g4; early 15th century) (*Fig.1352*)

12940 Triangular, of rectangular section, with two rounded corners and two perforations, one torn, on the vertical axis. L.22, W.15.2, T.1.3mm 18171 sf5264 (B6c1; 12th/13th century) (*Fig.1352*)

Domestic equipment

Spoon handle fragment

Previously published in *AY* 17/7 as a pin.

4279 Bowl broken away, ball knop, handle stem decorated on each side with raised chevron pattern. Traces of the casting flash remain. L.44.0mm; knop: D.5.0mm 10974 sf2827 (D6e7; early 14th century) (*Fig.1387*)

Vessels

12941 Rim fragment, of sheet, shape distorted, with two decorative circumferential rings on outer face close to rim, torn along broken lower edge. There are turning marks on the interior face. L.51, W.23.7, T.2.7mm 5262 sf1290 (D6d1; late 13th century) (*Fig.1395*)

Stuctural items and fittings

Cames

12942 Fragment, of H-shaped section, bent double. L.63.4mm; section: W.6.4, T.5.6mm; original L.142.5mm 10407 sf2539 (D6f1; mid–late 14th century)

12943 Fragment, of H-shaped section, with another piece soldered on at right angles at the lower end. L.47.3, W.23.9, T.4.9mm; section: W.6.8mm 10107 sf2647 (D6h2; 16th/17th century)

12944 Two fragments, H-shaped section, both with join at one end. L.98.1, W.14.5, T.8.7mm; section: W.9mm 10743 sf2681 (C6f1–g1; late 13th century–mid 14th century)

12945 Fragment, of H-shaped section, bent. L.95, W.4.8, T.2.7mm 12018 sf2789 (D6e9; mid 14th century)

12946 Of H-shaped section, twisted and crushed. L.91.6, W.6.9, T.4.4mm 9224 sf2928 (C6e9; mid 13th century)

12947 Of H-shaped section, split along most of length. L.124.4, W.8.6, T.6.5mm 18256 sf4813 (B6a7; early 12th century)

Dress, dress accessories and personal ornament

Ring

12948 Sub-circular, of rectangular section, tapering towards the ends which are overlapped. D.23.7mm; hoop: W.9.5, T.4.4mm 5975 sf3208 (C6c6; mid 12th century)

Annular brooches

12949 Broken at constriction for missing pin, of sub-plano-convex section, cable decoration around outer circumference, and with two collets. D.22.9, T.1.7mm 11054 sf2705 (B6e1; late 13th century) (*Fig.1486*)

12950 Complete but with pin separated, frame of sub-circular section, pin with moulding below loop, tip broken off. D.18.6mm; section: D.2.6mm; pin: L.14.6mm 13438 sf3409 (B6c7; early 13th century)

12951 Broken at constriction for pin which is missing, distorted, of bi-convex section, decorated with moulded transverse ridges. D.24, T.3.2mm 13862 sf3657 (B6d2; 13th century)

12952 In two fragments, broken across perforation for pin which is missing, of flat sheet, decorated with alternate fields of transverse and lateral lines, two opposing oval bosses on decorated face. D.23.5mm; section: W.4.4, T.1.3mm 15136 sf4067 (A6n2, B6a5; early 12th century) (*Figs.1486, 1488*)

Finger-ring

12953 Fragment, hoop of plano-convex section, lozenge-shaped bezel filled with cross-hatching, with single projection at east and west cardinal points, two projections at north and south, hoop decorated with oblique transverse grooves, and single moulding. L.16.9, W.6.5, T.1.4mm 16153 sf4192 (C6d22; late 12th century) (*Fig.1492*)

Literacy

Points

12954 With shaft of circular section, tapering to point at lower end which has been bent up, slightly expanded spatulate head. D.6.5, L.111.3mm; spatulate end: W.8.4mm 11953 sf3184 (B6f3; early 14th century) (*Fig.1502*)

12955 With shaft of square section, tapering to lower end, tip broken off, expanded spatulate head, top of head broken away, whole curved up. L.57.7mm; head: W.10.2mm; shank: W.4.1, T.3.9mm 13567 sf3459 (B6a3; 11th/12th century)

Funerary and devotional objects

Possible pilgrim badges

12956 Formed from sheet, in shape of equal-armed Maltese cross, all arms bent back, centre circular, containing equal-armed cross in relief, with bosses between cardinal points, border around centre and edges of arms decorated with transverse lines in relief. On the reverse are the remains of the catch plate and pin attachment loop. L.19.7, W.19.5, T.2mm 1586 sf324 (D6e3; 13th/14th century) (*Fig.1512*)

12957 Openwork, of triangular section, one side broken away, the other side with scroll within sub-oval cutaway. L.36.4, W.23.2, T.2.6mm 10977 sf2742 (D6g2; mid 16th century) (*Fig.1512*)

Bell

12958 Of sheet, sub-hemispherical with four triangular projections (vandykes) developing from the lower edge and folded to form base, incomplete suspension loop, bell decorated with ridges across seams, axial rows of dots on both faces, pea within. D.13.4, L.19.9mm 16410 sf4324 (D6a12; early 12th century) (*Fig.1515*)

Trade and exchange

Weights

12959 Bell-shaped, base with raised lip. L.57, W.47 H.57mm, Wt.600.05g 4620 sf1267 (C6e9; mid 13th century) (*Fig.1521*)

12960 Sub-circular, of plano-convex section, surfaces irregular. D.25, T.11mm, Wt.35.36g 9224 sf1423 (C6e9; mid 13th century)

1296 Sub-discoidal, of rectangular section. D.19.2, T.3.5mm, Wt.8.5g 12067 sf2775 (C6e10; mid 13th century) (*Fig.1520*)

12962 Circular, of plano-convex section. D.24.1, T.7mm, Wt.20.9g 9224 sf2926 (C6e9; mid 13th century)

12963 Discoidal. D.31.6, T.4.3mm, Wt.27.18g 15285 sf5273 (B6a1; late 11th century) (*Fig.1520*)

12964 Discoidal, of rectangular section. D.17.7, T.2.4mm, Wt.5.82g u/s sf945

Tin

Funerary and devotional objects

Ampullae

12965 Incomplete, part of flask-shaped ampulla and circular openwork frame broken away. The ampulla has a constricted neck, originally crimped closed, with single loops to each side, and most of the figure on it has been lost, but a hand can be seen apparently gripping his pallium. The openwork frame contains the figures of St Peter on the left, and St Paul with his sword on the right, the bottom part of the frame has been broken away. The border of the frame is billeted. The reverse appears undecorated Analysis: tin. D.61.9, L. (flask) 54.5, T.6.5mm 11886 sf3581 (B6f4; early 14th century) (*Figs.1512–13*)

12966 Flask-shaped, with double-looped handle to either side, set within sub-trapezoidal plate, with triangular projection at the bottom. The upper end of the ampulla was originally crimped closed. On one face of the flask is the figure of a bearded archbishop wearing his mitre, his right hand up in benediction, his left holding his crozier and gripping the edge of his pallium. He is flanked on the plate by two bearded figures, both with haloes, the figure on the left holding a large key (St Peter), that on right holding a sword (St Paul). The heads of both are in higher relief than the rest. The border of the plate is decorated with small bosses. On the reverse, within the flask, is an angel with four wings and a striped body. On this face, a band goes across the neck of the flask. Analysis: tin, trace copper. L.60.7, W.48.3, T.2.7mm u/s sf2353 (*Figs.1512, 1514*)

Finds from the earlier Anglo-Scandinavian occupation on Coppergate which occurred residually in medieval deposits (Period 6) have been published in *AY* 17/14. These are grouped according to material and listed by catalogue number below.

Stone
Ingot moulds: *4001 (AY 17/7), 9248*
Rotary grindstones: *9636–8*
Chalk cores: *9658–60*
Vessels: *9689–92*
Beads: *9779–81*
Porphry slab: *9821*

Jet
Playing piece: *9840*
Pendants: *9862–3*

Amber
Roughouts: *9872–4*
Beads: *9896–7*
Ring: *9912*
Pendant roughout: *9917*
Pendants: *9936–9*
Fragments: *9949–51*

Fired clay
Loomweight: *6589 (AY 17/11)*

Glass
Glassworking debris: *9980–2*
Vessel glass: *10017*
Finger-rings: *10065–6*
Beads: *10086–99, 10155–87, 10215–33, 10246–63, 10276–81, 10289–300, 10336–8, 10343–4, 10349, 10352–3*

Copper alloy
Balance: *10415–16*
Strap-end: *10424*
Hooked tag: *10437*
Dress pins: *10452, 10467, 10472, 10475*
Twisted wire ring: *10506*
Finger-ring: *10524*

Gold
Twisted wire ring: *10537*

Lead alloy
Badges: *4277–8 (AY 17/7)*
Clench bolts: *10576–8*
Weights: *10594–8*

Finds from the Coppergate watching brief site (1982.22)

Iron

Blanks and scrap

See p.3025 for a definition of terms used.

Strips

12967   Curved and turned over at each end. L.105, W.12, T.3mm 1546 sf79

12968   Expands towards one end, both ends taper to point. L.280, W.18, T.10mm 1546 sf103

12969   L.69, W.2mm 2077 sf255

12970   Tapers; curved over and widened further at wider end. L.44, W.22, T.6mm u/s sf16

Plates

12971   Narrows, one straight side, rest irregular. L.67, W.12, T.2mm 1546 sf75

12972   Folded over, rounded ends. L.32, W.9mm 1777 sf16

Metalworking tool

Punch

12973   Shaft has a rectangular cross-section. Upper part tapers slightly towards the head which is burred. L.142, W.8mm 1745 sf154 (*Figs.1327–8*)

Woodworking tool

Axe

12974   In face view the socket tapers to a waist, the blade is symmetrical with convex shoulders and a convex cutting edge. H.150, W.110mm 1384 sf151 (*Fig.1332*)

Textile tools

Fibre processing spikes

12975   Rectangular cross-section. Curved, tip missing, stepped head. L.100, W.6mm 1546 sf99

12976   Two spikes, both with rounded cross-sections, one with tip missing and the other with a stepped head. L.72, W.4mm 2077 sf256

12977   Rounded cross-section. Stepped head, bent near head. L.107, W.5mm 2077 sf258

12978   Rounded cross-section. Stepped head. L.73, W.4mm u/s sf30

12979   Sub-rectangular cross-section. Stepped head. L.107, W.6mm u/s sf41

Agricultural tool

Sickle

12980   Tanged, C-shaped tapering blade with a serrated cutting edge. Serrations angled back towards the tang. L.410; blade: W.46, T.3; tang: L.84, T.6mm 1506 sf143 (*Fig.1351*)

Other tools

Knives

Whittle tang knives

Blade back form C: blade back straight before becoming convex and curving down to the tip

C1: straight part of blade back horizontal

12981   Blade back straight for 36mm. Cutting edge straight and curves up slightly at the tip. Butt weld between the back and cutting edge visible on X-radiograph. Tang tip wedge-shaped. L.85; blade: L.56, W.9, T.3mm 1793 sf179 (*Fig.1356*)

C3: straight part of blade back downward sloping

12982   Blade back slopes down for 41mm, tip at blade's mid-point. Cutting edge S-shaped. Sloping shoulder. Tang pointed at tip where it is badly twisted and was probably curved over; set in a wooden handle which is somewhat decayed. L.135; blade: L.51, W.15, T.3mm u/s sf19 (*Fig.1357*)

Domestic equipment

Shovel

12983   Handle only. Turned through 30° near base where broken. Lower part is pierced and a short downward projecting rod is set in the hole. At the head is a looped terminal. L.200, W.15, T.5mm 1618 sf147 (*Fig.1388*)

Structural items and fittings

Clench bolts

Rectangular roves

12984   L.95; head: W.31, shank: T.9; rove: L.36, W.35mm 1477 sf145

12985   Tapering shank. L.87; head: W.32; shank: T.10; rove: L.30, W.27mm 1618 sf146

12986   L.88; head: W.35; shank: T.11; rove: L.33, W.30mm 1477 sf149

Staples

Rectangular

12987   One arm. L.55, W.8mm 1384 sf61

12988   Head widens in centre. L.16, W.72, T.10mm 1546 sf81

Hinge pivot

12989   Shank tip squared off, corner slightly flattened and burred. Guide arm: L.39, W.8; shank: L.69, W.15mm u/s sf239

Wall hook

12990 Consists of U-shaped hook with short tapering projection at 90° from head of shank. L.86, W.50, T.7; tang: L.38mm 1546 sf74 (*Fig.1413*)

Possible incomplete S-hook

12991 (a) Figure-of-eight-shaped, incomplete; (b) oval loop, plated (lead). Hook: L.115, W.24, T.6mm; loop: D.75, W.7, T.4mm 1874 sf176 (*Figs.1414, 1429*)

Corner brackets

12992 Complete arm is flattened and widened to a terminal with rounded corners; other arm incomplete. L.85, W.21, T.9mm 1546 sf134

12993 Curved over at one end and broken, at other end widens and has 'fish tail' end. Raised fillet runs along centre of outer face. Pierced twice. L.81, W.31, T.6mm 1384 sf220 (*Fig.1420*)

Fittings

Plates

12994 Broken at each end, widens and broken over hole at wide end. L.37, W.25, T.2mm 1384 sf60

12995 Broken at one end, one side becomes concave from centre to one end. L.100, W.37, T.4mm 1546 sf73

12996 Slightly curved, pierced at one end where broken. L.86, W.26, T.4mm 1546 sf107

12997 Fragment, nail head in situ. L.40, W.23mm 1777 sf158

Locks and keys

Barrel padlock

Case fragment

12998 One end only. End-plate recessed and made in one piece with what was probably the tip of the free arm tube. Two brazed-on strips run around the case, one at the surviving end. Plated (copper). L.28, W.50; case: W.29mm u/s sf9 (*Fig.1442*)

Barrel padlock key

Bit at an angle to the stem

12999 Bit circular and at c.90° to the stem which is flattened and widened above the mid-point into a triangular plate. Looped terminal. L.169, W.16, T.4mm 1055 sf175 (*Fig.1453*)

Dress, dress accessories and personal ornament

Buckle-plate

13000 Open end rounded, originally held together by single rivet. L.30, W.16mm 1205 sf7 (*Fig.1473*)

Horse equipment

Curb bit

13001 The object is an incomplete component of a curb bit which originally consisted of a Y-shaped strip with curving upper arms, one now missing; from the top edge of each arm was a small, pierced projection and at the ends of each arm were rounded eyes from which straight arms projected downwards to terminate in eyes in a plane at 90° to the first pair. Immediately above these terminal eyes the straight arms each had a pierced projection on their inner edge. Joining the two projections and also riveted in the centre to the base of the curving arms of the Y was a strip, now incomplete, widened and pierced in the centre and at each end. Plated (tin and trace lead). L.121, W.76, T.9mm 1906 sf178 (*Fig.1526*)

Weapons and armour

Arrowhead

13002 Blade, now very corroded, with socket running up the centre. L.60, W.25, D.19mm 1546 sf82

Copper alloy

Wire

13003 Folded in half and bent up. L.124mm, section D.1.6mm 1478 sf68

Box

13004 Incomplete, rectangular, part of one end and one side broken away, with sub-cylindrical leg in each corner, one broken off, each flattening out into paw-shaped foot. The surviving end of the box is decorated on the exterior face in relief with a snouted animal with a tail; the sides and other end have traces of openwork decoration, the intact side also having a transverse row of punched ring-and-dot motifs at each end. The rim along the sides is turned over with a ledge beneath and there is a perforation just below this in the centre of the intact side, and the rim of the intact end is also turned over at the same height as the ledge of the side. L.113.7, W.63.7, T.7.8, H.79.7mm 1736 sf180 (*Fig.1398*)

Rings

13005 Two, distorted, of sub-circular section. D.45.8mm, section: D.4mm 1056 sf138

Lead alloy

Candlestick drip tray

13006 Incomplete, discoidal, slightly distorted, with slightly raised rim on upper face, central hole for spike torn, flange around centre on lower face. D.52.2, T.4.3mm 1478 sf70 (*Fig.1434*)

Finds from 22 Piccadilly (1987.21)

Stone

Hones

13007 Fragment, sub-rectangular, broken at one end across slight waist, section thinning towards broken end. All faces very smooth, broad sharpening groove on one side. Phyllite, medium to dark grey, very fine-grained, quartzitic, micaceous (mainly or all muscovite), Purple Phyllite type, although slightly darker than normal. L.53.2, W.18.4, T.9.4mm 2089 sf213 (P4.2)

13008 Fragment, part of one face and edge surviving, both smooth. Purple Phyllite type, as *13007*. L.64.3, W.21.4, T.16mm 2146 sf538 (P4.2)

Haematite

13009 Fragment. Pale red, of reddle type. L.25, W.18, T.7mm 4004 sf834 (P5.1)

Rotary quern

13010 Fragment, tool marks on one face, other face worn. Lava, medium grey, very fine-grained, highly vesicular. Mayen type. L.91.6, W.66, T.48.9mm 2049 sf461 (P6)

Mortar

13011 Rim and body fragment, with rectangular projection and possible remains of pierced handle beneath. Limestone, brownish-cream, relict oolitic, mainly dolomitic. Lower Magnesian Limestone. T.40, H.148, internal D.144mm 1001 sf26 (P6) (*Fig.1385*)

Fired clay

Counters

13012 Sub-discoidal, made from vessel of Brandsby type, green glaze on one face. D.24.5, T.6.8mm 2041 sf112 (P6)

13013 Sub-discoidal, crudely cut from tile. D.53.6, T.16.8mm 1001 sf118 (P6)

Vessel glass

Flask/urinal

13014 Widely everted rim fragment of thick weathered opaque mottled brown, originally green, glass. Slightly distorted, probably by heat or fire. Rim diameter not measurable. At rim edge T.3.5–5.5mm 2011 sf66 (P6)

Iron

Blanks and scrap

Strips

13015 Pear-shaped loop, tips taper to point. L.31, W.21mm 1002 sf185 (P4.2)

13016 Tapers to a rough point, slightly curved. L.113, W.7mm 3009 sf132 (P5.2)

13017 L-shaped, possibly an incomplete buckle frame. Plated. Arms: L.17 and 11mm 3006 sf1139 (P5.2)

Metalworking tools

Punches

13018 Tapers to a point, sub-rectangular cross-section. L.112, W.7, T.7mm 3048 sf1039 (P4.3) (*Fig.1328*)

13019 Lower part of shank. Blade wedge-shaped. Near the break the shank is slightly twisted and the edges are folded in. L.53, W.9, T.8mm 2042 sf290 (P6) (*Fig.1328*)

Woodworking tool

Axe

13020 Asymmetrical cross-section. Socket incomplete, but has a flat top and D-shaped eye; tapering projections, incomplete, to rear and stub projection from surviving front edge. Blade longer at front than rear, sides slightly concave, cutting edge convex. L.178; socket: W.42; blade: W.99, T.30mm 2042 sf276 (P6) (*Figs.1332, 1334*)

Leatherworking tools

Awls

13021 Arms have diamond-shaped cross-section. Bent near one end. L.130, T.4mm 3013 sf167 (P5.1)

13022 Arms have diamond-shaped cross-section, one incomplete. Bent in the centre. L.121, W.6mm 3006 sf128 (P5.2)

13023 One arm, rectangular cross-section. L.73, W.3mm 1001 sf155 (P6)

Textile tools

Fibre processing spikes

13024 Sub-rectangular cross-section. L.120, W.4mm 3012 sf157 (P5.2) (*Fig.1342*)

13025 Rounded cross-section. Slightly curved at the head. L.101, W.5mm 2048 sf101 (P6)

13026 Rectangular cross-section. L.100, W.6mm 2042 sf272 (P6)

13027 Rounded cross-section. L.156, W.6mm 4000 sf620 (P7) (*Fig. 1342*)

Needles

13028 Punched round eye. L.58, T.2mm 3016 sf173 (P5.1)

13029 Punched eye, broken at upper end across eye, tip missing. L.33, T.0.9mm 3013 sf212 (P5.1) (*Fig.1348*)

13030 Punched oval eye. L.37, T.1mm 4004 sf677 (P5.1) (*Fig.1348*)

13031 Punched oval eye. L.30, T.1mm 3012 sf216 (P5.2) (*Fig.1348*)

13032 Y-eyed. Shank bent, tip missing. L.c.67, T.2mm 2079 sf121 (P6)

Needle shank

13033 L.39mm 3012 sf145 (P5.2)

Other tools

Knives

Whittle tang

Blade back form A: blade back straight before sloping down to the tip

A3: blade back straight part downward sloping

13034   Blade back straight and slopes down to a point 22mm from the shoulder and then slopes down at 10° towards the tip which is at half the blade's width. Cutting edge is straight before curving up to the tip. Notch cut into back at angle. Sloping shoulder, tang incomplete. L.59; blade: L.40, W.8, T.4mm u/s sf558 (*Fig.1355*)

Ai: form of straight part of blade back indeterminate

13035   Blade back straight to a point c.35mm from the shoulder and then slopes down at c.20° towards the tip which is missing. Cutting edge irregular. Tang largely missing. L.60; blade: L.51, W.12, T.5mm 2000 sf7 (P7)

Blade back form C: blade back straight before becoming convex and curving down to the tip

C1: straight part of blade back horizontal

13036   Blade back straight and horizontal to a point 44mm from the shoulder and then curves down to the tip. Cutting edge straight before curving up slightly at the tip. Back edges chamfered. Sloping shoulder, tang incomplete. L.103; blade: L.83, W.12, T.3mm 1014 sf234 (P4.2) (*Fig.1356*)

Domestic equipment

Vessels

Handle

13037   Incomplete, made of plate which widens towards the top from both sides before stepping in to a short spirally twisted section. L.184, W.25, T.1.5mm 1014 sf235 (P4.2) (*Fig.1393*)

Structural items and fittings

Nails

Data on nails are available in archive

Plated nail

13038   Shank only. L.28, T.5mm 3006 sf1138 (P5.2)

Clench bolts

Diamond-shaped roves

13039   Shank of rounded cross-section. L.35; shank: T.5; head: W.16; rove: L.15, W.13mm u/s sf964

13040   Shank of rounded cross-section and bent near rove. L.33; shank: T.6; head: W.18; rove: L.17, W.14mm u/s sf965

Staples

Rectangular

13041   One arm missing. L.25, W.40, T.6mm 2045 sf97 (P6)

U-shaped

13042   One arm. L.66, W.10mm 2041 sf87 (P6)

Fitting

13043   Pierced plate (terminal). One end broken, other has diagonal corners. On one face below the piercing are three transverse grooves and then on one side two short diagonal grooves and on the other one groove. Plated (tin). L.34, W.16mm 2083 sf263 (P6) (*Fig.1425*)

Ferrule

13044   A socket with open seam for half its length, then slightly bent and tapers with a rectangular cross-section to a blunt tip. L.158; socket: D.32mm 1000 sf2 (P7)

Locks and keys

Barrel padlock

13045   Case. One end-plate missing; the other, pierced by the bolt-hole, is recessed into the case. Free arm joined to the case by a fin. Case has applied strips around it at each end and wavy strips run between them. Plated (leaded bronze). L.63, W.36; case: D.23mm 3086 sf474 (P4.2) (*Figs.1442, 1447*)

Key for mounted lock

13046   Half of bow only. L.26, W.20, T.7mm 2042 sf203 (P6)

Barrel padlock key

Bit in line with stem

13047   Bit circular with a rectangular central chamber; stem has rounded cross-section and expands in the centre. Incomplete rounded, pierced terminal in plane at 90° to bit. L.92; bit: W.24; stem: T.7mm 3009 sf133 (P5.2) (*Fig.1456*)

Dress, dress accessories and personal ornament

Bracelet

13048   Fragment. Curved, rounded cross-section, broken at each end. Plated. L.32, T.6mm 3071 sf369 (P4.2)

Horse equipment

Bit

13049   Fragment of double-eyed strap joiner. Oval eye with knop at the top; below is a shank, of rounded cross-section, which steps out in the centre of the outer face and leads to the second eye which is largely missing. Plated. L.45, W.25, T.9mm 3053 sf511 (P4.3) (*Fig.1524*)

Horseshoe nails

Six horseshoe nails were found, details available in archive.

Weapons and armour

Arrowhead

Socketed tapering blade of rectangular cross-section

13050   Socket damaged. L.60; socket: D.12mm 2042 sf79 (P6)

Arrow tip

13051   Plated. L.28, D.8mm 2083 sf220 (P6)

Copper alloy

Manufacturing waste

13052   Sheet fragment, sub-trapezoidal, folded along both edges. L.38.7, W.23.1, T.7.4mm; sheet: T.2.1mm 3010 sf143 (P5.2)

13053   Strip fragment, sub-rectangular, both ends broken. L.34.9, W.15.2, T.0.9mm 2001 sf8 (P6)

13054   Strip fragment, irregularly shaped. L.25.4, W.2.7, T.0.7mm 2049 sf211 (P6)

13055   Strip in two adjoining fragments, one end and part of one edge broken away. L.35, W.4.2, T.0.7mm 2079 sf1252 (P6)

13056   Wire fragment, both ends broken, circular section, curved. D.0.8, L.54.1mm 2007 sf21 (P6)

13057   Wire or pin shank fragment, broken at both ends. D.1.2, L.59.4mm 2012 sf33 (P6)

13058   Wire fragment, both ends broken. D.0.9, L.57.3mm 2048 sf86 (P6)

13059   Wire or pin shank fragment, both ends broken. D.0.7, L.30.7mm 2042 sf941 (P6)

Structural items and fittings

Swivel fitting

13060   Incomplete, lower end of shank broken off, shank of sub-oval section, upper end hammered flat and eye punched through, irregular collar below. L.28.7, W.14.4, T.3mm 3006 sf196 (P5.2) (*Fig.1428*)

Ring

13061   Sub-circular, of sub-circular section, ends sprung apart. D.12.9, T.1mm; section: D.1mm 4004 sf679 (P5.1)

Dress, dress accessories and personal ornament

Pins

13062   With single twist wire-wound head. D.0.8 L.32.7mm; head: D.2.4mm 2041 sf93 (P6)

13063   With single twist wire-wound head. D.0.7, L.27.3mm; head: D.2.1mm 2041 sf109 (P6)

13064   With double twist wire-wound head. D.1.1, L.36.8mm; head: D.2.4mm 2042 sf206 (P6)

13065   With single twist wire-wound head. D.1.1, L.64.6mm; head: D.1.5mm 3000 sf58 (P7)

13066   With globular head, shank of circular section, tapering to tip. D.0.9, L.62.5mm; head: D.2.6mm 2010 sf41 (P6)

13067   With globular head, shank of circular section, bent up, tip broken off. D.1.3, L.121.2mm; head: D.3.5mm 3003 sf100 (P6)

13068   With sub-biconical head, shank of circular section, bent up. D.1.2, L.96.9mm 2083 sf175 (P6)

Lace tag

13069   Edge-to-edge seam, tapering slightly from upper end which has a perforation. L.26.8, W.2.3, T.1.9mm 2009 sf28 (P6)

Twisted wire loop

13070   Complete. D.0.8, L.30.2mm; eye: D.3mm 2042 sf80 (P6)

Lead alloy

Manufacturing waste

13071   Bar of rectangular section, both ends flattened, one broken across perforation, other partially split and folded up. L.73.1, W.7.5, T.5.4mm 2042 sf274 (P6)

13072   Rod fragment, of sub-circular section, broken at both ends. D.4.9, L.29.4mm 2042 sf309 (P6)

13073   Sheet fragment, irregularly shaped, bent up. L.29.7, W.17.7, T.3.5mm; sheet: T.1mm 3006 sf198 (P5.2)

Vessels

Patch of sheet

13074   Folded up, retaining iron rivets around edge, also perforations. L.49.1, W.18.9, T.4.6mm; sheet: T.1.1mm 1001 sf156 (P6)

Structural items and fittings

Came

13075   Fragment, of H-shaped section, twisted, both ends broken. L.32.7, W.3.0, T.2.8mm 2006 sf15 (P6)

Funerary and devotional objects

Pilgrim badge

13076   Two adjoining fragments, all edges irregular, depicting bearded head and part of body of figure of St Christopher, one hand holding a staff, part of a smaller figure (the Christ Child) on other shoulder, who is holding an orb. There is a bent clasp of lozenge-shaped section on reverse. L.20, W.18.5, T.1.5mm, clasp: L.18.2, W.2.9, T.1.9mm 2001 sf9 (P6) (*Fig.1512*)

Trade and exchange

Weight

13077   Discoidal. D.27.2, T.2.3mm, Wt.11.02g 3006 sf197 (P5.2)

Textiles

13078   Fibre, three tufts of calf hair, straight and pointed; fibres are 37–75 microns diameter, moderately pigmented (brown), with medullas in all fibres. The scale pattern is irregular mosaic, with smooth margins which are rippled on some coarse fibres. L.40–60mm 2012 sf32 (P6)

13079   Two fragments of textile made from an animal fibre in tabby weave, in plied yarn, 2/S2Z.2.0–3.0 x2/S2Z/2.0–3.0. L.150, W.130mm 3048 sf326 (P4.3)

Finds from the earlier Anglo-Scandinavian occupation on Piccadilly which occurred residually in medieval deposits (Period 4.2 onwards) have been published in *AY* 17/14. These are grouped according to material and listed by catalogue number below.

Stone
Haematite: *10636*

Glass
Glassworking debris: *10642*
Vessel glass: *10643*
Beads: *10651–2, 10658–60, 10664–6, 10674–7*

Copper alloy
Penannular ring: *10689*

Finds from Bedern Foundry (1973–6.13.II)

Stone

Spindle whorls

Form A1/C

13080　Rounded biconical, flattened; spindle hole D.8–9mm, drilled from either end. Chalk, greyish-white, very fine-grained. Chalk Group. D.30.5, H.11.7mm, Wt.14.5g 4114 sf1743 (P2)

Form C

13081　Fragment, flattened globular, spindle hole D.7–8mm, drilled from either end. Chalk, white, very fine-grained. Chalk Group. D.27.4, H.17.5mm, Wt.[9.8, est. 18]g 2912 sf1501 (P2)

13082　Globular; spindle hole D.8–9mm, drilled from either end; encircling grooves from lathe-turning. Chalk, greyish-white, fine-grained. Ferriby Chalk Formation of Chalk Group. D.28.8, H.18.8mm, Wt.19.5g 2778 sf1576 (P2) (*Fig.1344*)

13083　Rounded barrel-shape with spindle hole D.8–9.5mm, drilled from either end. Chalk, greyish-white, very fine-grained. Chalk Group. D.27.4, H.20.4mm, Wt.19.8g 212 sf297 (P6) (*Fig.1344*)

Hones

Norwegian Ragstone type

13084　Incomplete, one edge and one end roughly broken off, of trapezoidal section, surviving end is irregularly shaped, the other broken, originally slightly waisted. Schist, pale grey, fine-grained, quartzitic, micaceous (mainly muscovite). L.88.4, W.20.8, T.12.2mm 2522 sf1375 (P3)

13085　Incomplete, roughly broken at both ends, of sub-oval section, slightly waisted. Schist, as 13084. L.73.3, W.28.6, T.18.5mm 977 sf1186 (P4)

13086　Incomplete, roughly broken at one end, of rectangular section, tapering from broken end to other end which is rounded. Schist, as 13084. L.77.2, W.28, T.22.3mm 2551 sf1359 (P4)

Purple Phyllite type

13087　Incomplete, one edge dressed flat, other faces and both ends roughly broken or cleaved, of irregular section. Phyllite, medium grey, very fine-grained, quartzitic, micaceous (mainly muscovite). L.115.2, W.31.2, T.17mm 2888 sf1493 (P2)

Rotary querns

Lava of Mayen type

13088　Seven adjoining fragments of upper stone, damaged in antiquity, with three handle holes; surface of upper face damaged around, and one break through, one hole, stone thinning rapidly from circumference towards centre, signs of wear on grinding surface, and small depression, also incomplete rectangular cut-out for rynd. Lava, pale to medium grey, vesicular. Original D.680mm; L.273.8, W.181.4, T.28.8mm 4172 sf1678 (P1)

13089　Fragment, irregularly shaped, no original edges. Lava, as 13088. L.56.6, W.49.9, T.45mm 2528 sf3097 (P3)

13090　Fragment from circumference, other edges roughly broken, slight traces of wear on the grinding surface, other face pecked and with striations. Lava as 13088. L.202.2, W.180.5, T.42.3mm; original D.720mm 624 sf1413 (P5)

13091　Two fragments from upper stone, one from circumference, other irregular, with part of central perforation, trapezoidal cut-out for rynd, little trace of wear. Lava as 13088. Perforation: D.120; L.182.2, W.165.8, T.54.7mm; original D.620mm 443 sf619 (P6)

Native stones

13092　Fragment, from part of the circumference, other edges roughly broken. Sandstone, pale to medium grey and greyish-brown, medium- to (slightly) coarse-grained with sub-angular to sub-rounded grains, moderately sorted and moderately compacted, with abundant muscovite concentrated on parallel laminae. Millstone Grit or Coal Measures. L.105, W.62.4, T.20.2mm; original D.280mm 2377 sf1458 (P3)

13093　Fragment from the circumference, other edges broken, traces of heavy wear on the grinding surface, other face pecked. Sandstone, pale to medium grey, medium- to coarse-grained with sub-angular to sub-rounded grains, poorly sorted and poorly compacted, with a few rounded quartz pebbles up to 18mm long. Millstone Grit. L.227.9, W.167.9, T.60.4mm 2228 sf1418 (P4)

Mortars

13094　Fragment, with one surviving edge and face, which is slightly convex, other faces and edges roughly broken. Sandstone, pale grey, fine-grained with sub-angular to (more abundantly) sub-rounded grains, well sorted and well compacted, with sparse scattered muscovite and one small fish scale. Coal Measures or, more likely, Middle Jurassic of north-eastern Yorkshire. L.67.3, W.55.4, T.32.4mm; original D.160mm 2377 sf1460 (P3)

13095　Two adjoining fragments of rim with broad band below, part of a corner with a moulding of triangular section, and a shield-shaped projection on one side. Sandstone, pale brown, fine-grained with sub-angular to sub-rounded grains, well sorted and moderately compacted. Coal Measures or other Upper Carboniferous source, or Middle Jurassic of north-eastern Yorkshire. T.64, H.232mm 57 sf1774 (P5)

13096　Fragment, with polygonal base, flat rim with broad band below, rectangular lug with shallow sub-rectangular runnel, triangularly shaped projection below lug tapering to base, bowl circular. Limestone, cream, relict oolitic to microcellular, dolomitic. Lower Magnesian Limestone. T.40, H.200mm; internal D.180mm 57 sf1775 (P5) (*Fig.1385*)

13097　Rim fragment, rim flat with band below, rectangular rib running down from rim, vertical tooling marks on outer face of body. Limestone, cream, microcellular with a few relict ooliths, mainly dolomitic. Lower Magnesian Limestone. T.51.9, H.118.7mm; internal D.200mm 988 sf1777 (P5)

13098　Rim fragment, part of pierced handle with rounded profile survives, rim flat. Limestone, cream, microcellular, dolomitic. Lower Magnesian Limestone. T.52.9, H.133mm; handle W.59.3mm; internal D.140mm 157 sf1776 (P6)

Lamps

13099 Cuboid, with five reservoirs in the upper face, each tapering slightly to a rounded base. Limestone, creamy white, mainly fine-grained but finely relict oolitic/microcellular in places, variably dolomitic. Lower Magnesian Limestone. L.267.6, W.239.8, T.158.2mm 2801 sf1419 (P4) (*Fig.1436*)

13100 Fragment, originally rectangular, with remains of two circular reservoirs, one surviving edge, others roughly broken. Limestone, cream, microcellular, dolomitic, with part of vugh lined with dolomite crystals. Lower Magnesian Limestone. L.112.6, W.82.2, H.78mm; reservoir D.70mm u/s sf1444

Counters

13101 Sub-discoidal with the edge roughly chipped. Sandstone, pale brownish-grey, fine-grained with sub-angular to sub-rounded grains, well sorted and fairly well compacted, thin bedded, with sparse muscovite and traces of laminae. Coal Measures of Elland Flags type. D.58.8, T.21.3mm 2850 sf1449 (P3)

13102 Sub-discoidal, with roughly chipped edges. Sandstone, as *13101*, Coal Measures of Elland Flags type. D.52.4, T.20.9mm 698 sf1214 (P5)

Fossil

13103 Crinoid ossicle, calcitic. Carboniferous Limestone, Wensleydale Group (formerly Yoredale sequence) or Harrogate Roadstone. D.5.5, T.1.3mm 13 sf66 (P6)

Jet

13104 Offcut of sub-rectangular section, sub-rectangular, three sides and both faces cut flat. L.63.5, W.27, T.6.4mm 1 sf26 (P7)

13105 Fragment or offcut of sub-rectangular section, irregularly shaped, one edge roughly broken, others roughly shaped and smoothed, both faces appear sawn and smoothed. L.26.6, W.16, T.4.5mm 71 sf253 (P7)

Jet-like material

13106 Offcut of sub-rectangular section, rectangular, two sides and both faces cleft, other sides sawn or knife cut. L.14.3, W.10.9, T.9.6mm 62 sf78 (P6)

Fired clay

Loom weight

13107 Fragment; originally circular with central hole. L.28, W.23.5, T.18.9mm 45 sf190 (P6)

Counters

13108 Sub-discoidal, roughly chipped out of a plain medieval roof tile. D.53, T.17.2mm 4036 sf1572 (P1)

13109 Sub-discoidal, roughly chipped out of a plain medieval roof tile. D.41, T.12mm 617 sf983 (P5)

13110 Discoidal, chipped out of a plain medieval roof tile, edges and faces ground smooth. D.49.3, T.14mm 69 sf99 (P7) (*Fig.1518*)

Vessel glass

Tableware and other decorated vessels

Beaker

13111 Two adjoining rim and two body fragments probably from a beaker. Greenish glass with black and brown opaque surface weathering. Vertical wall profile, with faint optic-blown wrythen ribbing below the rim. Rim: D.72, T.1.5–2.0mm. 663 sf998 (P4) (*Fig.1402*)

Bowl

13112 Fragment of applied base ring from around basal angle of vessel of greenish colourless glass. Tooled to form small feet or prunts. Base rim: D.60–70; wall: T.0.7mm 81 sf119 (P5) (*Fig.1402*)

Bowl or goblet

13113 Curved body fragment of blue glass from a bowl, or goblet bowl, with two mould-blown vertical ribs. Iridescent weathering on the surface. L.35, W.29, T.1mm; ribs: T. to 4mm. 22 sf115 (P7) (*Fig.1402*)

Undiagnostic green glass fragments

13114 Rim fragment, slightly everted at edge, too small to measure diameter. 656 sf1079 (P5)

13115 Small rim fragment of greenish colourless glass, with brown weathered surfaces. Slightly everted rim. D.70–80, T.2mm. 22 sf3088 (P7)

13116 Body fragment, now weathered opaque brown/cream. T.2.2mm 621 sf1317 (P4)

13117 Body fragment, possibly from shoulder or similar curve. T.c.2mm. 986 sf1353 (P4)

Iron

Blanks and scrap

See p.3025 for definition of terms used.

Plates

Cast iron

13118 L.70, W.30mm 51 sf462 (P7)

13119 Triangular. L.68, W.35mm 166 sf478 (P7)

13120 L.125, W.60mm 140 sf566 (P7)

Wrought iron

13121 Two semi-circular cuts out of one side. L.50, W.20mm 2970 sf3283 (P2)

13122 L.35, W.20mm 4115 sf3302 (P2)

13123 In two pieces; possibly knife blade. L.75, W.15mm 2349 sf3244 (P3)

13124 Broken at each end. L.98, W.16, T.2mm 2073 sf1307 (P4)

13125 L.25, W.25mm 729 sf3228 (P4)

13126 L.58, W.22mm 690 sf992 (P5)

13127 Central rounded area with opposing pointed projections. L.69, W.39mm 698 sf997 (P5) (*Fig.1318*)

13128 Broken at each end. L.35, W.20mm 205 sf449 (P6)

13129 Possible casing. L-shaped cross-section, sides irregular. L.56; arms: W.22 and 20mm 70 sf470 (P6)

13130 Possible casing. Was folded, now crushed along long axis. L.68; arms: L.21 and 19mm 70 sf471 (P6)

13131 Roughly L-shaped. Arms: L.69 and 53, T.6mm 218 sf521 (P6)

13132 L.35, W.18mm 223 sf3206 (P6)

13133 L.55, W.35, T.10mm 224 sf3208 (P6)

13134 Curved. Corrosion contains non-ferrous material. L.173, W.18, T.c.10mm 211 sf498 (P7)

13135 Broken at each end. L.41, W.22mm 215 sf511 (P7)

Strips

13136 Broken at each end. L.47mm 2891 sf3272 (P2)

13137 Plated (leaded tin). L.55, W.7, T.2mm 2897 sf3275 (P2)

13138 Slightly curved. Droplet of lead adheres. L.69, T.3mm 2993 sf3285 (P2)

13139 Narrows, thickens to narrow end, semi-circular cut out of wide end. L.70, W.20, T.4mm 4008 sf3295 (P2)

13140 Curved. L.60, W.6mm 4065 sf3298 (P2)

13141 Burred at each end. Plated. L.40, T.5mm 4077 sf3299 (P2)

13142 Narrows, one side concave, bevelled edges on one face. L.57, W.17, T.3mm 2571 sf1374 (P3)

13143 Flattened towards each end in opposing planes. L.20, W.20, T.8mm 2377 sf3253 (P3)

13144 Narrows, one end irregular. L.38, W.15mm 2552 sf3255 (P3)

13145 Irregular. L.80, W.35, T.8mm 2910 sf3277 (P3)

13146 L.148, T.10, W.10mm 729 sf3227 (P4)

13147 Two pieces. L.96 and 50, W.14mm 2636 sf3256 (P4)

13148 L.80, W.12mm 2806 sf3264 (P4)

13149 Very corroded. Plated (tin, trace lead). L.52, W.7mm 924 sf3108 (P5)

13150 L.55, W.10mm 2360 sf3252 (P5)

13151 Corroded. Tapers at each end. L.100, W.10mm 51 sf463 (P7)

Wire

13152 Several pieces, two spirally twisted together. L.100mm 187 sf575 (P7)

Spikes

13153 Curves and tapers, rounded cross-section. L.142, T.4mm 4116 sf3303 (P2)

13154 Wedge-shaped tip. L.105, W.10, T.5mm 726 sf3225 (P3)

13155 In three pieces, two of which fit together. L.172, W.11, T.11; third piece: L.92mm 2698 sf3258 (P4)

Building tool
Pickaxe head

13156 The socket does not penetrate the object fully. Arms become thinner and flare out towards the ends. L.218, W.27, T.20mm 2948 sf1592 (P3) (*Fig.1316*)

Metalworking tools
Hammer heads

13157 Very corroded. One arm has a rounded cross-section; other tapers to a point. Rectangular haft hole. L.100, W.15, T.15mm 2971 sf3284 (P2)

13158 Very corroded. One arm and the socket survive. Arm has parallel sides and a straight end; haft hole is rectangular. L.90, W.40mm 994 sf3111 (P4)

Punches

13159 In two pieces, corroded. Rounded cross-section, probably a burred head and rounded tip. L.240, T.13mm 2950 sf1569 (P2)

13160 Burred head, rectangular cross-section, tip missing. L.103, W.10, T.9mm 2915 sf3279 (P3) (*Fig.1328*)

Chisel

13161 Or punch. Damaged probable wedge-shaped tip. At the head possibly deliberately pinched. L.155, W.18, T.12mm 143 sf514 (P7)

Woodworking tools
Spoon auger

13162 Triangular tang. L.105; blade: L.23, W.7mm 342 sf892 (P6)

Wedge

13163 Corroded. Bent in centre. L.86, W.22, T.15mm u/s sf3100

Leatherworking tools
Awl
Both arms with rectangular cross-sections

13164 Arms incomplete. L.61, W.6mm 870 sf3105 (P4)

Slicker

13165 One end broken, other end broken at base of tang. L.118, W.25, T.3mm 729 sf1206 (P4) (*Fig.1341*)

Textile tools
Fibre processing spikes
Rectangular cross-section

13166 Stepped head. L.106, T.5mm 2891 sf3270 (P2)

13167 L.115, T.4mm 2352 sf3247 (P3)

13168 Incomplete with fragment of binding plate adhering. L.40mm 911 sf1133 (P4)

13169 Slightly curved, tip missing. L.117, T.5mm 729 sf1225 (P4)

Rounded cross-section

13170 Stepped head, bent near tip. L.97, T.4mm 4016 sf3297 (P3)

13171 Bent in centre, stepped head, tip missing. L.108, T.5mm
729 sf3541 (P4)

13172 Incomplete. L.80, T.5mm 663 sf3221 (P7)

Indeterminate cross-section

13173 L.90mm 621 sf3214 (P4)

Tenter hook

13174 Arms: L.40 and 30, T.6mm u/s sf3115 (*Fig.1346*)

Needle

13175 Distorted, head form indeterminate. L.48, T.1mm 51 sf17
(P7)

Agricultural tools

Spade iron

13176 Rectangular blade. One arm missing. L.165; blade: L.95,
W.160mm 4239 sf1800 (P8) (*Fig.1351*)

Other tools

Knives

Whittle tang knives

Blade back form C: blade back straight before becoming convex and curving down to the tip

C1: straight part of blade back horizontal

13177 Straight for 53mm. Cutting edge S-shaped. Sloping shoulder. Tang bent. L.115; blade: L.73, W.10, T.6mm 1151
sf1054 (P7)

C3: straight part of blade back downward sloping

13178 Blade back slopes down for 37mm, tip at half blade's
width. Cutting edge S-shaped. Sloping shoulder. Tang
incomplete. L.67; blade: L.48, W.12, T.4mm 4122 sf3306
(P1)

Ci: straight part of blade back has indeterminate form

13179 Corroded. Blade back straight before curving down
slightly before the break. Cutting edge convex. Tang
largely missing. L.51, W.16, T.3mm 585 sf3211 (P5)

Knives of indeterminate back form

13180 Back straight to break, cutting edge slightly concave. Tang
complete. L.51; blade: L.22, W.13, T.4mm 2892 sf3274 (P2)

13181 Tip missing. L.83, W.12, T.1mm 4016 sf1623 (P3)

13182 Tip at blade's mid-point. Cutting edge convex. L.108,
W.12, T.2mm 729 sf1197 (P4)

13183 Corroded. L.70mm 78 sf481 (P6)

13184 Incomplete. On both faces immediately below the back
is a concave channel inlaid with wire in a running loop
pattern. The back is bevelled and also inlaid. Inlay is
mercury gilded silver. L.36, W.12, T.2mm 363 sf542 (P6)
(*Figs.1362–3*)

13185 Broken below the shoulder, tip missing. L.76, W.16, T.3mm
223 sf3207 (P6)

Scale tang knives

7985 Back slightly convex from shoulder to tip. Cutting edge
convex and rounded at the rear. Inlaid cutler's mark. Tang
widens from junction with blade. Remains of horn scale
plates held in place by five rivets. L.194; blade: L.111,
W.14, T.4mm 143 sf1151 (P7) (*Fig.1365*)

13186 Tang only. Non-ferrous shoulder plates (L-section). Widens towards the end, bone scale plates attached by four
tubular non-ferrous rivets, triangular non-ferrous end cap.
L.73, W.15, T.10mm 979 sf1166 (P4) (*Fig.1365*)

13187 Tang only. Non-ferrous shoulder plates. Widens to the
end where there is a non-ferrous end-cap. Four tubular
non-ferrous rivets. Traces of wooden scale plates. L.95,
W.13mm 309 sf390 (P6) (*Fig.1365*)

13188 Fragment of tang, pierced once. Plated. L.45, W.11, T.3mm
83 sf520 (P6)

13189 Blade widens slightly towards tip which is rounded. Bolster between blade and tang. Bone scale plates of D-
shaped cross-section attached by four ferrous rivets with
split ends. L.130; blade: L.50; tang: W.15, T.10mm 223
sf529 (P6)

13190 Tang fragment, three non-ferrous rivets. L.30, W.10mm
43 sf554 (P6)

13191 Corroded. Blade and tang incomplete. L.51; blade: L.25,
W.17mm 22 sf459 (P7)

13192 Blade incomplete. Cutting edge has rounded rear. Tang
incomplete, two iron rivets. L.54; blade: L.19, W.16, T.3mm
116 sf474 (P7)

13193 Very corroded. Blade incomplete. Non-ferrous shoulder
plates riveted on. Stub of tang. L.70, W.22, T.6mm 143
sf3202 (P7)

Blade fragments

13194 L.42, W.20, T.5mm 212 sf504 (P6)

13195 L.22, W.15, T.5mm 188 sf525 (P6)

13196 Tip only. L.35, W.15mm 177 sf544 (P6)

13197 227 sf551 (P7)

13198 227 sf553 (P7)

Pivoting knife

13199 Very corroded. Both blades incomplete, one has concave
back and convex cutting edge. L.87, W.10, T.4mm 281
sf579 (P6)

Domestic equipment

Strike-a-lights

13200 Elongated oval with central slot. L.75, W.20mm 2352
sfs3248–9 (P3)

13201 Plate incomplete. Looped terminal with recurved tip.
Plate: L.40, T.8; terminal: L.75mm 711 sf1143 (P4)
(*Fig.1388*)

Structural items and fittings

Nails

Details of nails available in archive.

Plated nails

Complete length survives unless stated. Plating details, where available, given in parenthesis before dimensions. W = width of head.

13202   Tip curled. Domed head. L.40, W.20mm 2898 sf3276 (P2)

13203   L.30, W.10mm 2850 sf3266 (P3)

13204   Shank tip missing. L.40, W.20mm 2876 sf3269 (P3)

13205   L.30, W.15mm 998 sf3112 (P4)

13206   Fragments. 2641 sf3257 (P4)

13207   In two pieces. Domed head. L.33, W.20mm 538 sf3102 (P5)

13208   Shank tip missing. (Lead and silver) L.40, W.12mm 641 sf3219 (P5)

13209   L.33, W.22mm 666 sf3222 (P5)

Staples

Rectangular

Pinched corners, wider faces in same plane as staple itself

13210   One arm incomplete. L.71, W.45, T.6mm 729 sf1185 (P4)

U-shaped

Wider faces of arms at 90° to faces of staple itself

13211   L.28, W.16, T.4mm 4072 sf1636 (P2)

13212   One arm incomplete. L.48, W.35mm 2352 sf3250 (P3)

13213   Arms incomplete. L.25, W.25mm 2764 sf3260 (P3)

13214   L.55, W.21mm 2145 sf3241 (P4)

13215   L.55, W.27mm 696 sf3224 (P5)

13216   One arm incomplete. L.40, W.20mm 227 sf410 (P7)

13217   L.67, W.30, T.5mm u/s sf913

Looped

13218   Bent, tips out-turned. Original L.88, W.18mm u/s sf1164

Hinge pivots

13219   Shank incomplete. Guide arm: L.50, W.10; shank: L.55, W.17mm 2352 sf3246 (P3)

13220   Guide arm: L.40, W.8; shank: L.47, W.20mm 2737 sf3259 (P3)

Wall hooks

L-shaped

13221   Shank bent down at tip. Hook: L.25; shank: L.45, T.5mm 902 sf3107 (P4)

13222   Hook arm largely missing, pinched elbow. L.90, W.12mm u/s sf3212

Shank projects at elbow

13223   Hook: L.34, T.8; shank: L.80, T.10mm 218 sf522 (P6) (*Fig.1413*)

U-eyed hinge

13224   One incomplete strap survives. L.90, W.32, T.5; eye: W.25mm 2319 sf3245 (P4)

Corner bracket

13225   One arm. Widens slightly at the end where pierced. L.65, W.22, T.3mm 2551 sf1360 (P4)

Fittings

They are described as either strips or plates using the same criteria as for bar iron, blanks and scrap (see p.3025). Those which were probably parts of hinges or corner brackets are described as straps.

All have a rectangular cross-section and are pierced once unless stated.

Plates

13226   Broken at one end, pierced near the other. L.53, W.25mm 2891 sf3271 (P2)

13227   Two pieces, perhaps adjoining. Plated (tin). L.48 and 40, W.23mm 649 sf3218 (P3)

13228   L.63, W.27mm 2865 sf3268 (P3)

13229   Broken at one end. Pierced in centre. Plated (tin). L.38, W.23, T.4mm 873 sf1091 (P4)

13230   In two pieces. Largest is broken at each end, one side straight, other has four lobes. Plated. L.54, W.19mm 2304 sf1318 (P4) (*Fig.1425*)

13231   Broken at one end. L.45, W.30mm 746 sf3229 (P4)

13232   Fragment. L.33, W.16mm 2145 sf3242 (P4)

13233   Very corroded and in two pieces. One end broken, at the other a rounded, pierced terminal. L.125, W.30mm 2934 sf3281 (P4)

13234   Corroded. L.110, W.33mm 329 sf326 (P5)

13235   In two pieces. Pierced twice. Largest piece: L.60, W.18mm 850 sf1098 (P5)

13236   One end broken, other rounded. L.35, W.16mm 573 sf3209 (P5)

13237   One end rounded, other broken. Pierced three times. Plated (tin). L.160, W.23, T.4mm 47 sf182 (P6) (*Fig.1425*)

13238   Possible casing/binding. Was folded, now crushed, along long axis. L.85, W.15mm 90 sf502 (P6)

13239   Possible casing. L-shaped cross-section, sides irregular. L.43, W.20mm 205 sf505 (P6)

13240   Nail in situ. L.53, W.40; nail: L.55mm 90 sf541 (P6)

13241   One end rounded, other broken. Pierced twice. L.70, W.35mm 77 sf562 (P6)

13242   Cast iron. L.79, W.34mm 1 sf54 (P7)

13243   Roughly L-shaped, pierced in centre. Arms: L.85 and 60, W.33mm 227 sf437 (P7)

13244   Very corroded. Pierced twice. L.101, W.15mm u/s sf3199

13245   One end broken, other rounded. Pierced twice. L.98, W.26mm u/s sf3307

Straps

13246   Broken at one end, at the other a pierced rounded terminal, now damaged. L.125, W.26, T.2mm 2925 sf1610 (P3)

13247   Broken at one end. Narrows and is slightly curved and then thickened to form roughly rounded terminal with eye in which there is a fragment of nail or link. Nicks along one edge. L.91, W.25, T.7mm 4034 sf1611 (P3) (*Fig.1425*)

13248 Narrows to form a link at the head, now missing; other end probably broken. L.81, W.21, T.5mm 4165 sf3305 (P3)

13249 One arm of bifurcated terminal. Tapers, at end a nail with clenched tip. L.50, W.11, T.3; nail: L.22mm 2440 sf1339 (P4)

Strip

13250 One end has pierced, rounded terminal, the other is broken. L.23, W.10mm 77 sf3543 (P6)

Suspension fitting

13251 U-shaped eye, each end of which widens out into a strap, both pierced twice. L.95, W.50mm 729 sf1204 (P4)

Chain link

Figure-of-eight-shaped

13252 Half link. L.28, W.15mm 652 sf3220 (P4)

Rings

13253 Half. D.40mm 13 sf65 (P6)

13254 Incomplete, rounded cross-section. D.15mm 1 sf44 (P7)

Collar

13255 Incomplete. Plated (brass). L.22, D.57mm u/s sf1261

Washer

13256 Flange around central hole, pierced twice, two opposing semi-circular cuts out of edge. D.55, T.10mm 63 sf558 (P7)

Tubes

13257 In three pieces. Pierced near one end. Plated. L.105, D.14mm 2049 sf1239 (P4)

13258 Tapers, broken at each end. L.33, D.16mm 425 sf532 (P6)

Candleholders

Socketed

13259 L-shaped. Flattened elbow. Shank: L.31; arm: L.77; socket: D.19mm 4116 sf3304 (P2)

13260 Straight. L.95, W.24mm 2049 sf1315 (P4)

13261 Straight. L.66; socket: D.7mm 90 sf535 (P6)

13262 L-shaped. Shank: L.40; arm: L.65; socket: D.19mm u/s sf3230

Prickets

13263 Two arms with looped terminals welded to central spine. L.51, W.38, T.7mm 740 sf1302 (P4)

Locks and keys

Barrel padlocks

13264 Very corroded and crushed case. L.80, W.30mm u/s sf1194

U-shaped bolt

13265 Part of bolt, closing plate, stub of spine. Welded to bolt and passing through closing plate two strips with looped heads which became spines. Plated (quaternary: copper, zinc, tin, lead). L.56, W.35, T.10mm 4016 sf3296 (P3) (*Fig.1448*)

Keys for mounted locks

Key with hollow stem

13266 Bow D-shaped, expanded on curved side. Stem incomplete, moulding at head. Bit missing. L.60; bow: L.25, W.33; stem: T.12mm 43 sf461 (P6)

Solid stem which does not project beyond bit

13267 Bow kidney-shaped. Bit has horizontal cut below stem. L.88; bow: L.16, W.25; bit: L.12, W.20mm 116 sf132 (P7)

Solid stem projects beyond a bit which does not have central channel

13268 Circular bow. Stem steps in after bit, collar below bow. Grooves around centre of stem and on inner side of bit. Plated (leaded tin). L.49; bow: D.18; stem: T.6; bit: L.10, W.17mm 2891 sf1505 (P2) (*Fig.1449*)

Barrel padlock key

Bit at 90° to stem

13269 Bit circular. Stem flattened near the head and becomes a plate, now incomplete. L.165; bit: D.28mm 4008 sf1666 (P2)

Dress, dress accessories and personal ornament

Buckles

Buckle and buckle-plate

13270 Frame: trapezoidal with central bar. Ends convex, on one a pin rest. In centre of each side on either side of rotation point a low ridge. Sides rectangular and ends rounded cross-section. L.44, W.30, T.7mm. Buckle-plate: folded plate. Groove runs across face near inner end. L.43, W.20mm. Both plated. 2172 sf1301 (P4) (*Fig.1471*)

Rectangular frame with rounded corners

13271 Incomplete. Cross bar of rounded cross-section set off-centre. L.21, W.28mm 143 sf515 (P7)

Rectangular frame with central bar

13272 Slightly curved in section at 90° to the bar. Outside the frame on one side an eye continues the line of the bar. L.32, W.30mm 163 sf145 (P6)

Trapezoidal frame

13273 One side has rounded cross-section. L.31, W.32mm 145 sf197 (P6) (*Fig.1469*)

Buckles with rotating arms

13274 Rotating arm only. Dome-headed terminals expands in centre. L.69, T.8mm 2912 sf3278 (P2)

13275 Rotating arm only. Plated (leaded tin). L.64, T.8mm u/s sf3114

Buckle-pin

13276 L.42, D.7mm 2779 sf3262 (P2)

Possible button

13277 Pierced disc with 'rope work' around the edge. Plated (tin trace lead). D.19mm 641 sf3215 (P5) (*Fig.1491*)

Cleat

13278 Oval. L.20, W.9mm 176 sf549 (P7)

Horse equipment
Possible bit component

13279 Originally a U-shaped strip of rounded cross-section, one arm now largely missing. Surviving arm has looped eye at the end; it expanded to form another eye near the top and another where the second arm is broken. Plated (mercury gilded silver). L.135, T.7mm 2047 sf1344 (P4) (*Fig.1526*)

Horseshoes
Wavy outer side

13280 Left branch. Slightly wavy side. Turned-over calkin. Four countersunk holes. L.145, W.29, T.6mm 2985 sf1503 (P2)

13281 Very corroded. One branch largely missing. Turned-over calkin. Three holes, possibly countersunk. L.115, W.25mm 4114 sf3301 (P2)

13282 Branch fragment. One countersunk hole. L.63, W.18mm 999 sf3113 (P4)

Smooth outer side

13283 Complete. Worn at toe end. Three countersunk holes per arm. L.102, W.100; branch: W.25, T.6mm 2975 sf1690 (P2) (*Fig.1530*)

13284 Complete, but very corroded. Three holes in each arm. L.120, W.105mm 2169 sf1334 (P4)

13285 Very corroded. Left branch. L.100, W.30, T.4mm 625 sf1159 (P7)

Indeterminate outer side

13286 End of right branch. Turned-over calkin. Two rectangular holes. L.72, W.28, T.4mm 2779 sf1626 (P2)

13287 End of branch. L.81, W.33, T.6mm 2861 sf3267 (P2)

13288 Incomplete branch. Two rectangular holes. L.85, W.30mm 2065 sf1242 (P4)

13289 Branch fragment, three rectangular holes. L.90, W.29, T.7mm 224 sf513 (P6)

Curry comb

13290 Very corroded. Part of cylinder and head of both **arms** with rounded pierced terminals. L.125mm 674 sf3223 (P5)

Weapons and armour
Spearhead

13291 Incomplete blade, triangular cross-section. L.102, W.18mm 2892 sf3273 (P2)

Arrowheads

All are socketed and have a rivet hole in the side unless stated.

Tapering blade with rectangular cross-section

13292 L.60, D.12mm 4088 sf3300 (P2)

Triangular blade

13293 Blade largely missing, convex shoulders at base. Socket projects into blade. L.49; socket: D.14mm 206 sf3205 (P6)

Barbed blades

13294 Socket projects into blade. L.83, W.32; socket: D.13mm 206 sf3210 (P6)

13295 Most of blade missing. L.39; socket: D.10mm u/s sf1316

Socketed bolt

13296 Blade has square cross-section. L.115; blade: L.63, T.14; socket: D.18mm 2014 sf1233 (P4) (*Fig.1532*)

Arrow tip

13297 L.39, D.10mm 227 sf539 (P7)

Copper alloy
Textile tools
Needles

13298 Sharply bent, broken through eye which is set in a groove. D.2, L.61mm 75 sf130 (P6)

13299 Incomplete, shank of triangular section, head broken away. L.67, W.2.5, T.2.5mm 195 sf286 (P6)

13300 Incomplete, head broken across eye in flattened upper end, lower end of shank of triangular section. L.70, W.1.5, T.1.5mm 342 sf380 (P6)

13301 Oval eye set in flattened upper end, top of eye and tip of shank both slightly bent. D.1.5, L.72mm 287 sf388 (P6)

Thimbles

13302 Fragment, open-topped, pits arranged in vertical rows, incised line around upper and lower edges. D.20.5, T.1.5, H.17.2mm 4040 sf1583 (P2) (*Fig.1347*)

13303 Open-topped, with makers mark H stamped towards lower edge. D.21.1, T.2.1, H.18.6mm 18 sf91 (P6) (*Fig.1347*)

Knitting needle

13304 Fragment, of circular section, one end broken off, other end pointed. D.2.6, L.133.2mm 1 sf7 (P7) (*Fig.1350*)

Domestic equipment

Vessels

Cast vessels

Legs

13305 Fragment of leg with central rib, damaged foot, possibly failed casting. L.58.1, W.38.6, T.13.3mm 2804 sf1421 (P4) (*Fig.1394*)

13306 Leg or handle fragment, of sub-trapezoidal section, possibly failed casting. L.33, W.12.8, T.10.2mm 13 sf62 (P6)

13307 Leg and foot, of sub-rectangular to oval section, possibly failed casting. L.15, W.6.7, T.6mm 305 sf338 (P6) (*Fig.1394*)

Rims

13308 Fragment. L.71.9, W.23.2, T.2.6mm 579 sf1219 (P5)

13300 Fragment, rough casting. L.29.2, W.20.8, T.5.5mm 85 sf334 (P6)

13310 Fragment, flaring, outer face rough and blackened, possibly failed casting. L.32.5, W.25.7, T.3mm 202 sf432 (P6)

13311 Fragment, outer face soot blackened, possibly failed casting. L.42.2, W.35.3, T.4.5mm 229 sf438 (P6)

Body fragments

13312 Soot blackening on outer face, possibly failed casting. L.63.7, W.58.8, T.2.8mm 4057 sf1578 (P1)

13313 Cast, remains of raised rib on inner surface, one edge broken, others much abraded, possibly failed casting. L.50.6, W.24.5, T.3.4mm 870 sf1094 (P4)

13314 Possibly failed casting. L.38.5, W.27.6, T.3.8mm 2477 sf1343 (P4)

13315 Possibly failed casting. L.39.7, W.15, T.3.2mm 63 sf175 (P7)

Sheet vessel

13316 Incomplete shallow dish, parts of edge and centre broken away, four irregularly spaced perforations close to circumference, and two pairs of cut circles in edge. D.129, T.1.3mm 623 sf972 (P4) (*Fig.1395*)

Patches and rivets

13317 Patch, sub-rectangular with six slots for rivets around edge, three retaining rivets cut from sheet and folded to form clips. L.55.3, W.29.6, T.1.6mm 652 sf1087 (P4) (*Fig.1399*)

13318 Rivet fragment, made from folded sheet. L.9, W.4.9, T.2.8mm 2380 sf1370 (P3)

Structural items and fittings

13319 Tack or rivet, shank incomplete. D.7 L.8.9mm 145 sf200 (P6)

13320 Staple rectangular, made from strip, tips bent inwards and upwards. L.43, W.7.5, H.13.5mm; section: T.1.3mm 2950 sf1557 (P2)

Binding strips

13321 Or decorative strip, rectangular, in two adjoining fragments, decorated with incised borders and axial row of punched dots, rivet at one end. L.50.6, W.5.7, T.1.2mm 2881 sf1469 (P3) (*Fig.1427*)

13322 Fragment, one edge notched, with traced and punched decoration, riveted to second strip (possibly part of *13323*). L.34.1, W.7.4, T.0.7mm 163 sf144 (P6) (*Fig.1427*)

13323 Fragment, ornamental, one end broken, with angled scalloped edge, traced and punched decoration similar to *13322*, a series of rivet holes above scalloped edge, one rivet in situ. L.34.8, W.10.5, T.0.6mm 163 sf147 (P6) (*Fig.1427*)

13324 Fragment, one end broken, other with decorative repoussé roundel containing rivet. L.18.6, W.11.2, T.1.5mm; rivet: L.8mm 195 sf372 (P6) (*Fig.1427*)

Chains

13325 Length, rope-like, made from links of wire bent through 180°. L.38, W.5.1, T.5mm; wire section: D.0.6mm 2552 sf1371 (P3)

13326 Length, links of small circular coils of fine wire. L.7, W.2.9, T.2.7mm 525 sf956 (P5)

13327 Two fragments with S-shaped links joined alternately to near or further loop. L.16.2, W.4.4mm; wire section: D.1.2mm 223 sf344 (P6) (*Fig.1429*)

Rings

13328 Fragment, rectangular in section. D.17.7, W.2, T.1.6mm 4065 sf1604 (P2)

13329 D-sectioned with raised ridge around inner face. D.24.5mm; hoop section: W.3.1, T.2.9mm 2377 sf1486 (P3) (*Fig.1430*)

13330 Fragment, of sub-circular section. L.23.8mm; section: D.3.3mm 794 sf1049 (P4)

Cylinder

13331 Incomplete, both ends broken, made from rolled sheet, overlapping seam. D.6.3, L.45.8mm; sheet: T.0.5mm 2950 sf1563 (P2)

Eyelet

13332 Or washer for securing stud or mount, annular with convex section. D.7.5, T.1.1mm 979 sf1167 (P4)

Perforated strip

13333 Sub-rectangular, ends rounded, one end broken across two holes, further holes in centre and at other end. L.56.6, W.13.3, T.1.2mm 881 sf1093 (P4) (*Fig.1431*)

Dress, dress accessories and personal ornament

Buckles

Oval frame

13334 Fragment, with narrowed offset pin bar with pin. L.12.9, W.28, T.3mm 2742 sf1432 (P3)

13335 Moulded front, offset pin bar, pin missing, fragmentary, folded over buckle plate, and remains of leather strap with copper alloy rivet. L.22.6, W.13.5, T.5.4mm 854 sf1083 (P4)

13336 Sub-oval frame with integral D-sectioned plate, perforation immediately below frame for pin which is missing, two perforations for attachment to strap, foliate terminal. L.43, W.14.5, T.3.5mm 729 sf1201 (P4) (*Fig.1467*)

13337 Deep pin rest on outer edge is flanked on each side by ridge and projecting knop, with sharply moulded stops at ends of offset pin bar, pin lost. L.23, W.27.7, T.5.6mm 559 sf910 (P5) (*Fig.1466*)

With forked spacers

13338 Sub-circular frame with pointed front, pin lost, very long forked spacer and plates attached, roughly broken at far end. L.60.6, W.15, T.5.3mm; buckle frame: L.15.5, T.3mm 868 sf1085 (P5) (*Fig.1467*)

13339 Incomplete oval frame with forked spacer and plates, upper plate with decoratively shaped end, wire pin. L.30.2, W.15.9, T.4.2mm u/s sf982

With forked spacers, unfinished

13340 Crudely cast and unfinished oval frame with lip, some casting flashes still attached, forked spacer, rectangular plates, small hole below frame for pin which is not present. L.46.2, W.25.6, T.4.5mm 77 sf155 (P6) (*Fig.1322*)

13341 Faulty casting with oval frame with pointed front, part of incompletely formed forked spacer, and irregular fragment projecting from one side of frame. L.35.5, W.17.7, T.3.5mm u/s sf991 (*Fig.1322*)

D-shaped frame

13342 With moulded stops at ends of pin bar, and incomplete folded-over plate. One side has three rivet holes for attachment and rectangular pattern of two lines of rouletting, other side fragmentary with square perforation. L.28.6, W.31.5, T.3.3mm; plate: T.2.2mm 4114 sf1642 (P2) (*Fig.1468*)

13343 With pointed front. L.13, W.17.7, T.3.5mm 2881 sf1477 (P3)

Rectangular frame

13344 In two adjoining fragments, with remains of pin corroded to frame. L.26, W.33, T.6.5mm 574 sf938 (P5)

13345 Trapezoidal-shaped, of square section, with off-centre pin bar with constriction for pin, front bar of frame with revolving cylinder. L.21.3, W.18.3, T.4mm 2071 sf1243 (P4) (*Fig.1469*)

Buckle-pins

13346 Incomplete, hooked end broken off. L.35.9, W.4, T.2.4mm 2945 sf1577 (P2)

13347 Fragment, of sheet. L.23.4, W.3.1, T.1.4mm 77 sf151 (P6)

Buckle-plate

13348 Fragment, front plate only survives, tongue-shaped with three rivet holes, front face gilded and decorated with a fine traced zig-zag line forming a border pattern. L.30.1, W.16.6, T.1mm 104 sf75 (P6) (*Fig.1473*)

Clasps

13349 Rectangular plate with longitudinal slot in centre, rivet at each end with convex washer beneath, folded plate with semi-circular openings cut into sides has been passed through the slot. Rectangular plate: L.35.8, W.12.1, T.2.1mm; folded plate: L.17.8, W.13.4, T.3.3mm 2810 sf1605 (P3) (*Fig.1474*)

13350 Rectangular plate with central rectangular slot, cast pivoting device of keyhole shape for locking pivots on one of two rivets used to secure plate. L.25.2, W.11.5, T.2.5mm 711 sf1142 (P4) (*Fig.1474*)

Strap-ends

13351 One-piece, folded lengthways, sub-rectangular, tapering to lower end, upper end split with central rivet. L.64.4, W.12.3, T.1.5mm; split end: T.4.9mm 4016 sf1515 (P3) (*Fig.1475*)

13352 Two plates attached to forked spacer with small knop at tip, single rivet at upper end which is incomplete, remains of leather strap inside. L.31.5, W.8.7, T.4mm 794 sf1036 (P4)

13353 Fragment, with forked spacer, terminal broken away, rivet remains at lower end, where a fragment of leather strap survives. L.25.5, W.14.3, T.4.3mm; strap: L.9.1, W.8.3, T.2.2mm 977 sf1171 (P4)

13354 Two plates with pointed ends held together by rivet at each end, leather strap remains within. L.27.6, W.7.9, T.2.2mm 729 sf1209 (P4)

13355 Two plates attached to forked spacer with small knop at lower end, one rivet at upper end which is incomplete, traces of second rivet at other end. L.60.2, W.15.1, T.3.3mm 877 sf1090 (P5)

13356 Made from two plates with ornamental cut-out at upper end and separated by a spacer plate, spacer forked at upper end. At lower end, a U-shape has been crudely cut out, there are two rivets. L.50, W.13.8, T.5.2mm; plate: T.1.5mm 85 sf337 (P6)

13357 Narrow, made of two plates with pointed tips, forked spacer between plates, one rivet at upper end which is damaged on both faces. L.29.5, W.7.4, T.3.6mm 523 sf877 (P6) (*Fig.1476*)

Strap-guide

13358 Sub-circular with external projecting shank. L.17.9, W.13.7, T.2.3mm 188 sf417 (P6)

Chape

13359 Narrow, made from sheet, overlapping seam, lower end closed, decorative shaping at the top and traces of two rivet holes. D.11.3, L.46.9, T.0.7mm 2567 sf1366 (P4) (*Fig.1478*)

Mounts

Discoidal

13360 Cut from sheet, two peripheral rivet holes, one containing rivet, large central perforation. D.24.8, T.1.6mm 2119 sf1300 (P5) (*Fig.1479*)

13361 Incomplete, in three fragments, concentric repoussé moulding, central hole. L.13.8, W.9.6, T.1.8mm 804 sf1092 (P4)

Domed

13362 Circular, of plano-convex section, shank broken off. D.10.8, H.3.6mm 2950 sf3044 (P2)

13363 Two, with central rivets. D.8.7, H.5.3mm 794 sf1038 (P4)

13364 Circular, separate central rivet. Head: D.7.7, T.0.7mm; rivet: L.5.1mm 854 sf1082 (P4)

13365 Fragment, originally domed, hollow, decorated with three groups of perforations, one group of three, other two groups damaged, of which one may have had only two perforations. L.25.8, W.23.3, T.1.4mm 2047 sf1354 (P4) (*Fig.1479*)

13366 Incomplete, central rivet hole. D.8.6, T.0.5, H.3.5mm 2804 sf1422 (P4)

13367 Sub-circular. D.14, T.0.5, H.2.5mm 82 sf172 (P6)

13368 Fragment, with integral rivet. D.5.3, T.1mm 83 sf264 (P6)

Lobed

13369 Three adjoining fragments made of thin repoussé sheet, originally triple-lobed, two lobes survive, one open, other outlined with cable border, containing sheet with central rivet hole. L.29.0, W.14.7, T.1.7mm 83 sf281 (P6) (*Fig.1479*)

Sexfoil

13370 Domed, with two pairs of rivet holes at edge, two holes containing rivets, central rectangular perforation. D.20, T.0.7, H.5.5mm 543 sf924 (P5) (*Fig.1479*)

13371 Distorted rosette shape, with central rivet hole. D.10.4, T.2.3mm 83 sf282 (P6)

13372 With remains of two peripheral rivet holes, also central hole, tin plated. D.14.5, T.0.5, H.3.7mm u/s sf1107 (*Fig.1479*)

Rosette

13373 Repoussé rosette, eight petals, central rivet hole. D.15, T.1.3mm 780 sf1047 (P4) (*Fig.1479*)

Other

13374 Square, with central rivet. L.11.2, W.8, T.1.3mm; rivet: L.9.6mm 83 sf345 (P6)

13375 Fragment, sub-trapezoidal, one end broken, with iron rivet close to other end, and wood adhering to back. L.21.9, W.15, T.1.2mm 4079 sf1622 (P2)

Bar mount

13376 Cast, rectangular, D-sectioned, one rivet at each end. L.14.6, W.4.2, T.2mm 2380 sf1368 (P3) (*Fig.1480*)

Figurative mounts

13377 In three adjoining fragments, cast fleur-de-lys, with possible rivet hole in centre, shank on back of upper part, gilded on front face. L.40.5, W.25.3, T.5.5mm 729 sf1224 (P4) (*Figs.1480–1*)

13378 Cast with openwork decoration, upper end scalloped, middle portion has bird within crocketed and scrolled frame, foliate terminal at lower end, holes for attachment visible on back. L.54.9, W.25.3, T.3.9mm 2682 sf1388 (P4) (*Fig.1480*)

Pins

Wire-wound heads

13379 D.0.8, L.32mm; head: D.2.2mm 2712 sf1396 (P3)

13380 D.1.4, L.67.9mm; head: D.2.8mm 559 sf903 (P5)

13381 With stamped wire-wound head. D.0.9, L.29.9mm; head: D.2mm 205 sf379 (P6) (*Fig.1490*)

Globular heads

13382 D.0.8, L.36mm; head: D.2mm 208 sf284 (P6)

13383 With sub-globular head. D.0.8, L.40.5mm; head: D.3.3mm 83 sf255 (P6) (*Fig.1490*)

13384 With sub-globular head and incomplete shank. D.0.7, L.34.4mm; head: D.3.4mm u/s sf986

Lens-shaped head

13385 D.1.5, L.47.5mm; head: D.5.7mm 625 sf973 (P7)

Lace tags

Type E

13386 With edge-to-edge seam, lower end open. D.1.9, L.25.8mm 283 sf245 (P6)

Type F

13387 With inward folded seam, lower end compressed closed, decorated with stamped cross-hatching. L.21, W.2, T.2mm 224 sf370 (P6) (*Fig.1491*)

Type O

13388 With overlapped seam, lower end closed, rivet hole at upper end. D.2.8, L.23.6mm 77 sf171 (P6) (*Fig.1491*)

Type U

13389 Sub-rectangular in section, decorated on three sides with crossed lines, containing silk braid fragment, possibly tablet-woven. Warp Z-twist, two types: fine D.0.2–0.3mm, coarse D.0.6–0.7mm, weft S-twist, D.0.3–0.4mm. Tag: L.30, W.3.1, T.3mm 22 sf116 (P7) (*Fig.1491*)

Wire loop fasteners

13390 With ends twisted together. D.5.2mm; wire: D.0.7mm 79 sf213 (P6)

13391 Ends twisted together. D.8.2mm; wire: D.1mm 281 sf269 (P6) (*Fig.1491*)

13392 In two adjoining fragments. D.11mm; wire: D.1.4mm 177 sf378 (P6)

13393 Incomplete, twisted ends broken. L.16, W.10, T.1mm 215 sf317 (P7)

Twisted wire loops

13394 Complete. L.31.6, W.2.6, T.2mm; loop: D.4.6mm 96 sf585 (P5) (*Fig.1491*)

13395 With incomplete loop. L.25.3mm; wire: D.0.7mm 83 sf256 (P6)

13396 With distorted loop. D.4.9, L.26.1mm 83 sf275 (P6)

Finger-ring

13397 Narrow hoop of sub-circular section, with small oval collet for missing stone, slight moulding at junction of hoop and collet. D.21.4mm; collet: L.5.8, W.4.5, T.3.3mm; section: D.1.6mm 2850 sf1504 (P3) (*Fig.1492*)

Literacy
Book clasps

13398 Hinge plate, unfinished, in two adjoining fragments, made from sheet, cut and folded, with rectangular slot between, decorated on one face with incisions along edge, two countersunk rivet holes. L.19.9, W.13.4, T.5mm; sheet: T.1.2mm 147 sf243 (P6) (*Fig.1503*)

13399 Hinge plate, folded over pin at one end, both sides secured by two axial rivets, one side cut short, other with third rivet hole, end slightly chamfered. L.45.7, W.19, T.3.6mm u/s sf1048 (*Fig.1503*)

Bells

13400 Fragment, incomplete upper hemisphere, with slit for loop. D.22.5, T.0.6, H.7.3mm 66 sf108 (P6)

13401 Made from two pieces of sheet metal, loop missing from upper half, lower half with slit opening, the whole compressed flat. D.20.8, H.6.7mm u/s sf1588

Trade and exchange
Balances

13402 Folding, complete apart from suspension stirrup, triangular pointer pierced at base, arms of rectangular section, folded up, perforated at ends. Pointer: L.31.6, W.6.6mm; arm: L.51.4, W.4.8, T.3.3mm; beam: L.30.9, W.4.7, T.4.1mm 729 sf1177 (P4) (*Fig.1519*)

13403 Fragment, of rectangular section, surviving end pointed and perforated. L.20.3, W.4.2, T.1.5mm u/s sf1100 (*Fig.1519*)

Unidentified object

13404 In three fragments, two circular plates, small fragment of sheet adhering to one, with crescent-shaped spacer now separate, forming hinge, incomplete wire loops on each end of hinge pin, one end of pin terminating in washer. Plate: D.26.1, T.1.3mm; hinge pin: D.2.9 L.11mm; spacer: D.27.5, section: W.3.9, T.2.8mm; 964 sf1208 (P4) (*Fig.1535*)

Gold

13405 Brooch pin of circular section, tapering to point at lower end, other end hammered flat on two opposing sides, tip broken, pointed end slightly bent up. D.1.1, L.37.1mm 227 sf423 (P7) (*Fig.1489*)

Lead alloy
Domestic equipment
Vessels

13406 Rim fragment, cast. L.60.7, W.24.2, T.2.9mm 623 sf3043 (P4)

13407 Fragments (c.35), all probably from shallow bowl with out-turned rim and concave base. L.64.3, W.40.7, T.2mm 90 sf396 (P6)

13408 Plug used to repair late 12th–13th century York ware highly decorated vessel sherd. L.23.9, W.17.6, T.7.2mm 595 sf1022 (P4)

Structural items and fittings
Cames

13409 Two fragments. L.40.3, W.7.6, T.4.1mm 538 sf3102 (P5)

13410 Fragment. L.79.4, W.6.9, T.5.3mm 4 sf49 (P6)

13411 Fragment, with broad flange, tangled and squashed. L.20.9, W.20.8, T.9.3mm 223 sf348 (P6)

13412 Two fragments, with narrow flange, largest with Y-shaped junction. L.73.7, W.7.5, T.4.7mm 225 sf377 (P6)

13413 Fragment with narrow flange, twisted up. L.75.3, W.10.3, T.5.6mm 49 sf385 (P6)

13414 Fragment, possibly window tie. L.96.1, W.4.2, T.3.9mm 281 sf485 (P6)

13415 Fragment, with broad flange, flattened. L.41, W.8.4, T.3.3mm 1 sf39 (P7)

13416 Fragment with broad flange, compressed. L.83.4, W.10.3, T.3.6mm 227 sf404 (P7)

13417 Fragment, compressed. L.23.6, W.3.8, T.3.5mm 22 sf466 (P7)

Disc

13418 Perforated. D.13.6, T.0.3mm 2691 sf1392 (P4)

Dress, dress accessories and personal ornament
Buckles

13419 Circular, of sub-lozenge-shaped section, pin lost. D.14.9mm; section: W.3, T.3.3mm 522 sf890 (P5)

13420 Circular, of lozenge-shaped section, pin lost. D.17.9mm; section: W.3.6, T.3.6mm 556 sf906 (P6) (*Fig.1465*)

13421 Two, both incomplete, both originally oval, of sub-lozenge-shaped section, pins lost. L.15.5, W.14.5mm; section: W.3.2, T.3.3mm 405 sf442 (P6)

13422 Incomplete, originally circular or oval, lozenge-shaped section. L.12.3, W.14.3mm; section: W.3.4, T.3.4mm u/s sf599

Trade and exchange
Weights

13423 Of rectangular section, approximately square with chamfered sides. L.16.9, W.16.3, T.5.6mm, Wt.14.9g 2975 sf1618 (P2) (*Fig.1520*)

13424 Sub-circular, of plano-convex section. L.21, W.19, H.7mm, Wt.12.7g u/s sf68

13425 Circular, cast, with relief decoration of cross and pellets on upper face, lower face slightly concave. D.32.3, T.7.9mm, Wt.50.9g u/s sf835

Riding equipment

Pendant

13426 Cast, with suspension loop, cross-shaped, ends of arms splayed as heraldic cross form. Cross: L.60, W.56; loop: 17mm 2982 sf1509 (P2) (*Fig.1529*)

Textiles

Tabby with coloured bands

13427 Fragment of wool textile in tabby weave, wa/10/Z/0.6 x we/12/S/0.5, with a band, 12.5mm deep, of closely woven stripes in extended tabby weave. Stripes are red and green wool, S-spun, and natural-coloured silk, plied I2S or Z2S. Ground weave and red stripe both dyed with madder, derived from *Rubia tinctorum*; green not identified. Wool is Generalised Medium fleece-type in warp and weft of ground. L.112, W.85mm 2573 sf1384 (P3) (*Fig.1463*)

Linens

13428 Several fragments of linen textile in tabby weave, 17–20/Z/0.2–0.5 x 12–14/Z/0.4–0.5. Much folded and in places mineralised. Largest fragment L.68, W.55mm 2666 sf1381 (P2)

13429 Mineralised. Fragment of folded textile in tabby weave, 14/Z/0.4 x 12/Z/0.5. Plant-stem fibre such as flax or hemp. L.85, W.69mm 77 sf153 (P6)

Sacking

13430 Fragments of poorly preserved plant-fibre textile in extended tabby weave, 2/Z/2.0 x 6 (3 pairs)/Z/2.0. (b) Coarse sewing thread, some on (a), most loose, plied Z2S, 3.0mm diameter. L.135, W.35mm; tertiary size (a): L.37, W.27mm; second size (a): L.46, W.18mm 2666 sf1380 (P2)

13431 Fragments of textile and plied thread, identical with *13430*. Largest fragment of textile L.44, W.26mm 2701 sf1395 (P2)

13432 Fragment of wool textile in tabby weave, made from plied yarn, 2/S2Z/3.0 x 2–3/S2Z/2.5. Not tested for dye. Fibre too poorly preserved to identify fleece-type. L.33, W.27.5mm 2990 sf1506 (P2)

Silk

13433 Two fragments of black silk textile in tabby weave, 40/Z/0.1 x 36/I/0.2. Dyed with a mordant dye, probably tannin(s). Folds and stitch-holes present. L.60, W.55mm; secondary size: L.40, W.30mm 2674 sf1385 (P3)

Half-silks

13434 Eleven lengths of silk yarn, each plied Z2S, 0.3–0.4mm diameter. Dyed with red mordant dye, perhaps madder. Yarn is kinked as if once used in weaving. L.315mm 2574 sf1379 (P3)

13435 Many parallel silk threads, plied Z2S or I2S, 0.4mm diameter. Imprint of crossways threads (now decomposed) indicates the threads were once woven in extended tabby weave, the crossways threads having been worked in pairs. Silk dyed with madder, derived from *Rubia tinctorum*. Maximum L.615mm 2571 sf1382 (P3)

Finds from the College of the Vicars Choral, Bedern

(site areas specified at the end of each entry)

Stone

Moulds

13436 Originally sub-rectangular, one corner and part of one edge broken away through keying holes, of rectangular section, with indents for casting on both faces. On one face channels lead from one edge to circular indents; the central channel leads to the largest indent which is inscribed with various decorative motifs concentrically arranged; to one side another channel leads to a smaller circle containing concentric circles and divided into quadrants, and to the other side a channel leads to three ring-and dot motifs. Close to the larger circles is a circle containing a metal deposit and a shallow unused ring-and-dot motif. On the other face the channel leads to a circle containing cross-hatching and divided into quadrants by lines and dots. To one side is a smaller crudely cut circle, unused, with lines, and the channel falls short of the indent. To the other is a circle containing concentric circles but also possibly unused as one of three keying holes has been cut through it. Chalk, greyish-white, fine-grained. Ferriby Chalk Formation of Chalk Group. L.66.9, W.48.7, T.13.6mm; largest indent: D.28.3mm 1973–5.13.IV, 1643 sf778 (P1) (*Fig.1321*)

13437 Incomplete, part of one long edge and corners of two others survive, of rectangular section, originally trapezoidal in shape; both large faces have been used for casting. One has a single runner dividing into five smaller runners each flowing into sub-rectangular convex cut-outs with incised surfaces producing ribbed or hatched decoration; there are four semi-circular notches below the cut-outs, and remains of two keying holes or notches, one to each side of the smaller runners. There is a further circular notch in the edge below. The other face has a single runner dividing into four smaller runners which flow into rectangular convex cut-outs. There are traces of two keying holes or notches, one to each side of the runners, and one containing possible traces of metal. Chalk, greyish-white, very fine-grained. Chalk Group. L.45, W.40.4, T.16.7mm 1976–9.13.X, 6342 sf2628 (P4) (*Fig.1321*)

Spindle whorls

Where whorls are incomplete, measurement of the incomplete dimension is given in brackets [ ]. In these cases an estimated original weight has been added after the present weight.

Form B

13438 Doughnut-shaped with flat upper and lower faces; spindle hole D.11–12mm, drilled from either end. Chalk, white, very fine-grained with a few forams. Chalk Group. D.37, H.17mm, Wt.24g 1973–5.13.IV, 1504 sf608 (P9)

Form C

13439 Globular with spindle hole, D.8mm, drilled from either end. Chalk, white, very fine-grained, with a few ?forams. Chalk Group. D.26.3, H.16.4mm, Wt.13.8g 1976–9.13.X, 5298 sf1964 (P7) (*Fig.1344*)

13440 Almost complete, globular; spindle hole D.9–10mm, drilled from either end; encircling lathe marks. Limestone, pale yellowish-grey, fine-grained. Middle or Upper Jurassic. D.30.5, H.21mm, Wt.[22.9g est.24]g 1976–9.13.X, 7096 sf2406 (P7) (*Fig.1344*)

Hones

Norwegian Ragstone type

13441 Incomplete, of rectangular section, broken at both ends and across two faces. Schist, pale grey, fine-grained, quartzitic, micaceous (mainly or all muscovite). L.198.2, W.33.4, T.22.9mm 1978–9.14.II, 1608 sf486 (P2) (*Fig.1381*)

13442 Incomplete, roughly broken at one end, of sub-square section, tapering slightly from broken end, groove worn across all faces close to surviving end which has been roughly cut square. Schist, as *13441*. L.41.7, W.12.9, T.11.7mm 1978–9.14.II, 1595 sf437 (P5) (*Fig.1381*)

13443 Fragment, of rectangular section, broken at both ends with two faces cleaved, sides roughly broken. Schist, pale grey, fine-grained, quartzitic, micaceous (mainly or all muscovite). L.62, W.18.9, T.12mm 1976–9.13.X, 7509 sf2779 (P5)

13444 Of sub-triangular section, broken at each end, one face grooved. Schist, as *13441*. L.131.2, W.27.2, T.21.5mm 1978–9.14.II, 1561 sf391 (P6)

13445 Of sub-trapezoidal section, one end irregularly shaped, tapering sharply to other end which is roughly broken, one face grooved. Schist, as *13443*. L.93.7, W.33.2, T.23mm 1976–9.13.X, 7522 sf2785 (P6)

13446 Of sub-square section, irregularly shaped, chamfered at one end, tapering to other end, grooves on all faces. Schist, as *13441*. L.133.5, W.27.9, T.26.4mm 1978–9.14.II, 1347 sf268 (P7)

13447 Fragment, roughly broken at both ends, of trapezoidal section, one face with groove of V-shaped section running close to one edge. A shallower groove runs parallel, and two other faces also have shallow grooves. Schist, as *13443*. L.66.4, W.24, T.16.5mm 1976–9.13.X, 6271 sf2390 (P7) (*Fig.1381*)

13448 Incomplete, both ends roughly broken, of rectangular section, one face grooved. Schist, pale to medium grey, fine-grained, quartzitic, micaceous (mainly muscovite with traces of ?biotite). L.87, W.29.7, T.15.9mm 1976–9.13.X, 6271 sf2394 (P7)

13449 Incomplete, roughly broken at upper end and split laterally along one long face, of rectangular section, sub-rectangular, tapering slightly from surviving end which is sub-rounded, traces of an unfinished suspension hole close to upper end. Schist, as *13443*. L.70, W.16, T.6.8mm 1976–9.13.X, 6174 sf2447 (P7)

13450 Incomplete, broken at one end, of rectangular section. Schist, as *13443*. L.53.9, W.15, T.10.3mm 1976–9.13.X, 6137 sf2207 (P8)

13451 Incomplete, one end roughly broken, of irregular sub-trapezoidal section, other end sub-rounded. Schist, as *13448*. L.104.8, W.30.4, T.11.4mm 1976–9.13.X, 5027 sf1865 (P9)

13452 Incomplete, one end roughly broken off, of trapezoidal section, surviving end rounded. Schist, as *13448*. L.87.2, W.54.8, T.17.4mm 1976–9.13.X, u/s sf198

Purple Phyllite type

13453 Fragment from one edge, originally of square or rectangular section, faces smoothed. Phyllite, medium grey, very fine-grained, quartzitic, micaceous (mainly or all muscovite). L.38.5, W.12, T.5.1mm 1978–9.14.II, 1668 sf471 (P4)

13454 Fragment, of triangular section, broken at each end and with the faces cleaved. Phyllite, medium grey, very fine-grained, quartzitic, micaceous (mainly or all muscovite). L.49.9, W.12.4, T.12mm 1976–9.13.X, 7271 sf2713 (P7)

13455 Of rectangular section, sub-trapezoidal in shape, bevelled at one end, broken at the other, faces smoothed, one with a deep groove. Phyllite, as 13453. L.105, W.19.6, T.6.4mm 1979–80.14.IV, 4113 sf525 (P8)

Native stones

13456 Of rectangular section, one end rounded, other roughly broken, traces of unfinished perforation on one face. Sandstone, pale greyish-brown, fine-grained with sub-angular to sub-rounded grains, fairly well sorted and fairly well compacted, with sparse minute muscovite and traces of laminar bedding. Coal Measures or other Upper Carboniferous source. L.61.8, W.23.4, T.18.5mm 1976–9.13.X, 7584 sf3081 (P2)

13457 Fragment, roughly broken at both ends, of rectangular section. Sandstone, pale brownish-grey (discoloured brown on original surfaces), fine-grained with sub-angular to sub-rounded grains, well sorted and well compacted. Coal Measures or other Upper Carboniferous source. L.33.6, W.37.3, T.18.1mm 1976–9.13.X, 6359 sf2574 (P6)

1345 Incomplete, one end broken, of plano-convex section, rounded at the other end, lower face with groove. Sandstone, medium grey, very fine- to fine-grained (i.e. almost siltstone), well sorted and well compacted. Probably Coal Measures or other Upper Carboniferous source, but conceivably Lower Palaeozoic. L.89, W.30.9, T.26mm 1976–9.13.X, 5146 sf1955 (P7)

Rotary querns

13459 Fragment of circumference, slight traces of wear on grinding surface, other surface heavily pecked. Lava, pale to medium grey, vesicular, Mayen type. L.208.5, W.175.1, T.68.8mm; original D.600mm 1973–5.13.III, 1122 sf1414 (P1)

13460 Fragment of circumference, upper surface irregularly convex and pecked, with traces of mortar on broken edges. Lava, as 13459. L.162.5, W.120.2, T.46.7mm; original D.580mm 1976–9.13.X, 6003 sf2216 (P9)

Mortars

13461 Fragment of hollowed rim, outer face smooth, upper face of rim polished smooth. Limestone, pale grey, bioclastic, consisting of well-compacted, small (1–4mm wide) globose shells with fine-grained limestone within and between the shells. Most of the shells are almost planispiral gastropods, but a few of the smaller ones may be ostracods. Middle or Upper Jurassic, probably from southern England; the lithology and freshwater or brackish-looking fauna are suggestive of some limestones in the Upper Jurassic Purbeck sequence in Dorset. L.88.1, W.29.6, T.34.3mm; internal D.120mm 1978–9.14.II, 1740 sf679 (P1)

13462 Fragment, single moulding survives, of triangular section supporting a polygonal projection with pouring lip, outer face dressed. Limestone, pale grey, fine-grained, with scattered minute pellets, minute fossils (including ?forams) and fossil fragments, and a gastropod cast on one worked surface. Middle or Upper Jurassic, possibly

from southern England. T.50, H.252mm; internal D.240mm 1976–9.13.X, 7606 sf2856 (P3) (*Fig.1386*)

13463 Fragment, part of the side and rim with sub-rectangular lug with runnel of irregular U-shaped section, lug tapering into the bowl side, with triangular projection below at base, outer face with tooling marks. Limestone, pale brown, minutely relict oolitic, mainly dolomitic, with a few small bivalve casts, minute spicules and small calcite-lined vughs. Lower Magnesian Limestone. L.130, T.28.5, H.97.6mm; internal D.140mm, lug: W.44.5mm 1978–9.14.II, 1447 sf339 (P6)

13464 Rim fragment with flat rim and remains of lug, vertical tooling on rim and on band below rim, also some tooling marks below band. Limestone, creamy white, microcellular with a few relict ooliths, mainly dolomitic. Lower Magnesian Limestone. L.100.6, T.28.2, H.79.4mm; internal D.140mm 1976–9.13.X, 7313 sf2700 (P7)

13465 Rim fragment, with rectangular lug with runnel of irregular U-shaped section, with triangular moulding below. Limestone, cream, fine relict oolitic, mainly dolomitic. Lower Magnesian Limestone. T.34.8, H.124.1mm; internal D.180mm 1976–9.13.X, 6061 sf2707 (P7)

13466 Rim and body fragment, rim flat with broad band below, rectangular lug with runnel of U-shaped section, and broad rib running down side from rim, with convex outer face at rim, of pentagonal section on side. Sandstone, pale greyish-brown, medium- to (mainly) coarse-grained with sub-angular to (less abundantly) sub-rounded grains, poorly sorted and poorly to moderately compacted, with appreciable pink and white feldspar grains and a few small (<0.7mm long) rounded quartz and feldspar pebbles. Millstone Grit. L.355.8, T.67.5mm; bowl: D.240, H.146.5mm; base: T.112.1mm 1976–9.13.X, 6060 sf2858 (P7)

13467 Rim fragment, with moulded rim, rectangular lug with runnel of rectangular section, lug tapering into the sides of the bowl, tooling on outer face. Limestone, cream, relict oolitic to (slightly) microcellular, mainly dolomitic. Lower Magnesian Limestone. L.123.1, T.32, H.100.3mm; internal D.140mm; lug: W.67mm 1978–9.14.II, 1156 sf267 (P8)

13468 Fragment of base with one angle surviving from an originally polygonal mortar with a circular bowl. Limestone, cream, otherwise as 13464, Lower Magnesian Limestone. L.129.5, W.117.6, T.45.6, H.102mm; original D.140mm 1973–5.13.IV, 1514 sf650 (P8)

13469 Two adjoining base fragments, with broad rib or handle of pentagonal section rising from base, bowl curved but standing on square base. Limestone, cream, medium to coarse relict, oolitic, mainly dolomitic, with small to minute bivalve fragments and spicules. Lower Magnesian Limestone. Internal D.170mm; external D.320, H.62.3mm 1976–9.13.X, 7006 sf2862 (P8)

13470 Rim fragment with moulded rim, and vertical projection of sub-plano-convex section, vertical tooling on outer face, much of the fragment encrusted with plastering mortar. Limestone, cream, mainly microcellular with some minute relict ooliths, mainly dolomitic. Lower Magnesian Limestone. L.180.7, T.49.5, H.122.7mm; internal D.200mm; projection: W.64.8mm 1979–80.14.IV, 4000 sf759 (P9)

13471 Rim fragment, rim moulded with broad rectangular lug tapering downwards, vertical tooling on outer face, rim and outer face encrusted with plastering mortar. Limestone, cream, fine to medium relict oolitic, mainly dolomitic, with traces of ?algal laminar structures. Lower Magnesian Limestone. L.196.7, T.70.7, H.95.4mm; internal D.220mm; lug: W.86mm 1979–80.14.IV, 4000 sf823 (P9)

13472 Fragment, with one angle of square or rectangular base remaining, circular bowl, rim flat with broad band below, broad rib of polygonal section running from rim to base, vertical tooling marks on band and body, diagonal marks on rim. Limestone, cream, relict oolitic to microcellular, dolomitic. Lower Magnesian Limestone. T.28, H.124mm; internal D.134mm 1976–9.13.X, u/s sf2193 (*Fig.1386*)

Pestle

13473 Base fragment, of circular section, lower face convex, tapering up towards handle which is broken away. Limestone, greyish-white, minutely pelletal and oolitic, fairly well sorted and moderately compacted, with open intergranular spaces, scattered minute pale bluish-grey particles (possibly glauconite), a few small shell fragments (including some ?ostreiids) and small tubercular structures. Middle or Upper Jurassic, probably from southern England; lithologically comparable to some varieties of the Upper Jurassic Portland stone in Dorset. D.62.4, L.56mm 1979–80.14.IV, 4489 sf922 (P2) (*Fig.1386*)

Trough

13474 Five fragments, largest being corner of originally rectangular trough; flat rim with diagonal tooling marks on outer faces of sides and on rim edge. Limestone, cream; relict fine to medium oolitic, mainly dolomitic. Lower Magnesian Limestone. L.188.4, W.146.7, T.51, H.103.1mm 1976–9.13.X, 7347 sf2740 (P6) (*Fig.1407*)

Lamps

13475 Incomplete, originally rectangular with square containers, one container surviving, tooling marks on base and one face. Limestone, creamy white, microcellular, mainly dolomitic. Lower Magnesian Limestone. L.80.6, W.68.9, H.38.2mm; container: L.54, W.53.7, H.21.3mm 1978–9.14.II, 1055B sf135 (P7) (*Fig.1435*)

13476 Approximately half surviving, originally circular with flat banded rim, moulded handle with a scrolled upper end, narrow mouldings around sides drawn up from eight-pointed platform on base, deep circular central well. Limestone, yellowish-cream, microcellular, dolomitic. Lower Magnesian Limestone. T.22, H.57mm; internal D.50.5mm 1976–9.13.X, 5132 sf1967 (P8) (*Fig.1435*)

Gemstones

13477 Table-cut rock crystal, clear, colourless, sub-rectangular, all faces slightly convex, chipped. L.10.5, W.7, T.4mm 1976–9.13.X, 6326 sf2845 (P5) (*Fig.1498*)

13478 Rock crystal, clear and colourless, with convex base, tapering sides, biconvex upper face, chamfered on each side, chipped. L.23.7mm 1976–9.13.X, 5011 sf1672 (P9)

Seal matrix

13479 Sub-circular, of sub-triangular section, crudely shaped, incised on one face with a circular stylised male face with beard encircled by inscription ...+PUPUGR CORITS. Two further concentric circles around the design are divided up into six roughly equal fields by inscribed transverse lines. On the opposite face a quadrant has been crudely incised. Limestone, creamy white, microcellular, mainly dolomitic. Lower Magnesian Limestone. D.35.2, T.16.6mm 1978–9.14.II, 1392A sf294 (P7) (*Fig.1507*)

Disc

13480 Circular, with a central perforation. Limestone or marble, variegated brownish-yellow coarse-grained (with interlocking crystalline texture) and subsidiary greyish-white fine-grained (containing minute dark inclusions); the two varieties have a vaguely nodular-linear structure, probably biogenic or foliated. Provenance uncertain. D.12.2, T.1.4mm 1976–9.13.X, 6321 sf2469 (P5)

Counters

13481 Sub-circular, edges chipped and then ground smooth, faces also ground smooth. Sandstone, medium grey, fine-grained with sub-angular to sub-rounded grains, well sorted and fairly well compacted, thin bedded, with sparse muscovite and traces of laminae and with a few minute carbonaceous particles. Coal Measures of Elland Flags type. D.45.6, T.7.9mm 1978–9.14.II, 1793 sf730 (P1)

13482 Sub-discoidal, with roughly chipped edges, one face smoothed. Sandstone, pale to medium grey, fine-grained with sub-angular to sub-rounded grains, well sorted and fairly well compacted, thin bedded, with sparse muscovite and traces of laminae. Coal Measures of Elland Flags type. D.54.1, T.17.4mm 1973–5.13.III, 1099 sf841 (P1)

13483 Sub-circular, of plano-convex section. Sandstone or congealed sand, pale brown, apparently fine- to medium-grained but other features obscured by dark brown crustal impregnation. Source unknown. D.16, T.7.4mm 1978–9.14.II, 1459 sf383 (P5)

13484 Sub-discoidal with edges chipped, some edges and faces ground smooth. Sandstone, pale brownish-grey, otherwise as *13482*, Coal Measures of Elland Flags type. D.64.4, T.15mm 1973–5.13.III, 1065 sf805 (P6) (*Fig.1518*)

13485 Sub-discoidal, edges roughly chipped, faces smoothed. Limestone, creamy white, fine-grained, mainly dolomitic, with traces of ?algal laminar structures. Lower Magnesian Limestone. D.36.4, T.14.6mm 1976–9.13.X, 5466B sf2505 (P6)

13486 Sub-discoidal with edges roughly chipped. Limestone, pale to medium grey, very fine-grained/porcellanous. Middle or Upper Jurassic. D.55, T.18mm 1976–9.13.X, 5347G sf2073 (P7)

13487 Discoidal with irregular edges, edges and faces ground smooth. Sandstone, medium grey, otherwise as *13482*, Coal Measures of Elland Flags type. D.46.5, T.10.2mm 1973–5.13.III, u/s sf848

Fossils

13488 Crinoid ossicles (four articulated), calcitic. Carboniferous Limestone, Wensleydale Group (formerly Yoredale sequence) or Harrogate Roadstone. D.2.3, L.3mm 1978–9.14.II, 1784B sf937 (P1)

13489 *Gryphaea* sp., calcitic. Shape suggests the Lower Jurassic *Gryphaea arcuata*, Lamarck, but greyish-white colour is more typical of Middle Jurassic limestones, which are characterised by *Gryphaea bilobata* (J. de C. Sowerby). L.25, W.18.2, T.11.6mm 1976–9.13.X, 7584 sf2853 (P2)

13490 *Gryphaea arcuata*, Lamarck, calcitic. Lower Jurassic. D.21, T.11mm 1978–9.14.II, 1708 sf583 (P3)

13491 Fragment, broken at one end, one face worked. Belemnite, calcitic. Jurassic or Cretaceous. D.17.3, L.37.7mm 1979–80.14.IV, 4036 sf374 (P9)

Jet

Offcut

13492 Of sub-rectangular section, sub-rectangular, one face slightly concave and polished, other faces appear sawn or cut, one end cut square, other chamfered. L.70.8, W.20.9, T.18.6mm 1973–5.13.III, 1225 sf953 (P1A)

Handles

13493 Incomplete, from whittle tang knife, roughly broken at join with blade, of oval section, expanding towards outer end with drooping shoulder, highly polished. L.70, W.28.6, T.18.5mm 1976–9.13.X, 5497B sf2566 (P6)

13494 Fragment, for a whittle tang, of polygonal section with chamfered edges, roughly broken at both ends, split longitudinally, all original faces polished. L.26.1, W.13.7, T.9.6mm 1979–80.14.IV, 4295 sf763 (P7) (Fig.1364)

Rosary beads

13495 Globular, end facets flattened, polished. D.14, H.12mm 1976–9.13.X, 7102 sf2412 (P6)

13496 Globular, polished. D.14.1, H.10.1mm 1976–9.13.X, 7102 sf2413 (P6)

13497 Globular, end facets flattened, polished. D.15.9, H.11.9mm 1976–9.13.X, 7102 sf2414 (P6) (Fig.1516)

13498 Fragment, half surviving, globular, with turning marks visible on outer face. D.12.6, H.11mm 1978–9.14.II, 1359B sf274 (P8)

13499 Fragment, half surviving, globular, polished. D.16.6, H.13.3mm 1978–9.14.II, 1022 sf113 (P9) (Fig.1516)

13500 Barrel-shaped with concave end facets, polished. D.14.8, H.21.2mm 1976–9.13.X, u/s sf2114 (Fig.1516)

Object

13501 Discoidal, part of edge broken away, one face dished and decorated with crudely carved raised scene of the crucifixion with figure to either side, probably the Virgin Mary and St John, with traces of crude inscription on reverse face. D.26.6, T.7mm 1976–9.13.X, u/s sf2601 (Fig.1518)

Jet-like material

Rosary beads

13502 Incomplete, globular, broken obliquely across perforation, decorated with all-over basket work. D.8.6, H.8.7mm 1976–9.13.X, 7116 sf2542 (P5) (Fig.1516)

13503 Fragment, irregularly shaped, all edges roughly broken. L.10.3, W.8.5, T.4.8mm 1978–9.14.II, 1505B sf953 (P6)

Shale

Rosary beads

13504 Discoidal, with rounded edge and roughly drilled perforation. D.10.4, H.1.9mm 1973–5.13.IV, 1592 sf744 (P5) (Fig.1516)

13505 Fragment, irregularly shaped, one face dressed smooth, others roughly broken. L.21.7, W.14, T.8.3mm 1979–80.14.IV, u/s sf714

Amber

Rosary beads

13506 Globular, axially perforated, matt surface. D.8, H.7.6mm 1976–9.13.X, 7098 sf2409 (P6) (Fig.1516)

13507 Annular. D.8.1, H.4mm 1978–9.14.II, 1117 sf215 (P8) (Fig.1516)

Fired clay

Crucibles

13508 Virtually complete, fabric too vitrified to be identified. D.30, H.45mm 1975–6.13.III, 1225 sf932 (P1A)

13509 Thin-walled fine bodysherd, possibly overfired Stamford crucible. L.24, W.21, T.5mm 1978–9.14.II 1740 sf5013 (P1)

13510 Thin-walled fine bodysherd, possibly overfired Stamford crucible. L.30, W.13, T.5mm 1979–80.14.IV 4384 sf5002 (P2)

13511 Rim sherd, Stamford ware. L.24, W.20, T.6mm 1976–9.13.X 7287 sf 2909 (P4)

13512 Complete, with pouring lip, suspension holes, evidence of burning on the exterior and interior surface, made from gritty, unglazed fabric. D.50, H.40mm 1976–9.13.X 7587 sf2825 (P6) (Fig.1320)

13513 Thin-walled fine bodysherd, Stamford ware. L.30, W.24, T.6mm 1978–9.14.II 1447 sf5005 (P6)

13514 Possible crucible sherd, fabric too vitrified to be identified. L.61, W.34, T.15mm 1973–5.13.IV 1583 sf2882 (P7)

13515 Small body sherd, vitrified sandy fabric. L.28, W.19, T.8mm 1978–9.14.II 4118 sf3042 (P7)

Counters

Cut from a Roman sherd

13516 Circular, chipped from a Roman colour-coat vessel base, with grafitto on the underside. D.30.8, T.7.3mm 1978–9.14.II, 1451 sf334 (P6)

Cut from medieval sherds

13517 Sub-discoidal, roughly chipped out of a glazed vessel sherd of Humber ware. D.43.9, T.7.6mm 1978–9.14.II, 1122 sf5039 (P1)

13518 Discoidal, chipped out of an unglazed Brandsby-type ware jug, edges and faces ground smooth. D.37.2, T.6mm 1978–9.14.II, 1339 sf275 (P7) (Fig.1518)

13519 Sub-discoidal, roughly chipped out of a York glazed ware vessel sherd..D.23.3, T.5.8mm 1978–9.14.II, 1249 sf249 (P7)

Cut from roof tiles

13520 Sub-discoidal, chipped out of a plain medieval roof tile. D.45.3, T.16.9mm 1979–80.14.IV, 4370 sf887 (P5)

13521 Sub-discoidal, roughly chipped out of a plain medieval peg roof tile. D.68.9, T.13.6mm 1979–80.14.IV, 4370 sf888 (P5)

13522 Sub-discoidal, roughly chipped out of a plain medieval roof tile. D.56, T.14.9mm 1979–80.14.IV, 4059 sf536 (P6)

13523 Sub-discoidal, roughly chipped out of a plain medieval roof tile. D.64, T.14.8mm 1976–9.13.X, 5472 sf2494 (P6)

13524 Sub-discoidal, roughly chipped out of a plain medieval roof tile. D.34, T.14.1mm 1976–9.13.X, 7330 sf2722 (P6)

13525 Sub-discoidal, roughly chipped out of a plain medieval roof tile. D.60, T.15.7mm 1976–9.13.X, 7522 sf2789 (P6)

13526 Sub-discoidal, roughly chipped out of a plain medieval roof tile. D.58.6, T.13.5mm 1976–9.13.X, 5220 sf2021 (P8)

13527 Sub-discoidal, roughly chipped out of a plain medieval roof tile. D.36.1, T.14.6mm 1978–9.13.II, 1055 sf147 (P9)

13528 Sub-discoidal, roughly chipped out of plain medieval roof tile. D.49.5, T.16.3mm 1976–9.13.X, 5000 sf2125 (P9)

13529 Counter or pot lid, sub-discoidal, roughly chipped out of a plain medieval roof tile. D.75, T.16.5mm 1976–9.13.X, 5170 sf2105 (P7)

Bead

13530 Annular, pale pink, with worn and irregular surface. D.13.4, H.8mm; perforation: D.4mm 1976–9.13.X, 7072 sf2560 (P7)

Vessel glass

Tableware and other decorated vessels

Beakers

13531 Body fragment of colourless glass beaker, with painted enamel decoration. Two parallel red border lines at the top of fragment, with trace of yellow-brown line between. Above is the edge of a white letter from an inscription. Below the border lines is part of an unidentifiable white motif. These are typical of the inscription band and border lines around the upper part of the 'Aldrevandin' type of enamelled beakers. The inscription and border part are painted on the external surface, as is usual with this type of beakers. Other parts of the beaker which have not survived were probably also painted on the internal surface. L.16, W.9, T.0.8mm 1973–5.13. III, 1086 sf757 (P6) (*Fig.1402*)

13532 Enamelled body fragment of colourless glass, probably from a beaker of the 'Aldrevandin' type. Enamelled on both sides: white and yellow-green on the external surface; red on inner surface. Too small to identify the depiction, which consists of a red elongated feature rounded at the end with two white parallel lines across it at right angles towards the end and a white outline. A yellow-green patch surrounds the end of the motif. L.18, W.12, T.0.8mm 1978–9.14.II, 1256 sf323 (P7) (*Fig.1402*)

Bowls

13533 Three adjoining rim fragments of a bowl of colourless glass with a little iridescent surface weathering. Thin blue trail applied around the rim edge. Body turns inwards a little below the rim. Originally had an S-shaped profile, narrowing towards the base. Rim: D.150, T.0.9mm; body: T.0.8mm 1976–9.13.X, 6223 sf2274 (P7) (*Fig.1402*)

13534 One rim and three body fragments of a bowl of colourless glass. Thin blue trail applied around the rim edge. Sharp turn on body fragments indicates an S-shaped profile, narrowing towards the base. Late 13th to 14th century style. Rim: D.147mm; body: T.0.8mm 1976–9.13.X, 7456 sf2765 (P7) (*Fig.1402*)

13535 Blue glass body fragment, probably from the flattened centre of a bowl or dish which turns upwards at the edge. Painted on the inner surface with a black pigment, which now has a greenish tinge. The surviving painted decoration shows the edge of a hexagram (or pentagram) of two interlacing triangles, originally with six (or possibly five) points, with some foliate decoration in and between the points, within a circular border with 'zig-zagging' edges. Small scratches on external surface. 13th to 14th century style. H.9, W.24, T.1.5–2.0mm 1978–9.14.II, 1117 sf227 (P8) (*Figs.1402–3*)

Goblet

13536 Yellow high-lead glass fragment from the base rim of a hollow flared stem of a goblet. Blue trail applied around

the upper edge of the base rim. Base rim D.96, T.0.4–4.0mm 1979–80.14.IV, 4140 sf513 (P9) (*Fig.1402*)

Jugs or pouring flasks

13537 Yellow high-lead glass rim fragment from a jug or serving flask. Slightly everted rim, Part of a green-blue trail remains on lower break, 10mm below rim. Slightly cloudy condition. May come from the same vessel as the fragments *13538*. Irregular D.c.34mm; T.2.0–2.5mm 1976–9.13.X, 6152 sf2214 (P7) (*Fig.1402*)

13538 Fragments of a yellow high-lead glass jug or flask with pouring lip, and at least three horizontal blue-green trails at intervals of c.10mm. Rim diameter not measurable, but approximate diameter of body fragment sf2632 is c.40mm.

a) Yellow body fragment with applied horizontal blue-green trail across centre. T.0.3mm 1976–9.13.X, 6357 sf2615 (P6) (*Figs.1402, 1404*)

b) Two yellow body fragments and one pouring lip fragment. Pouring lip fragment adjoins sf2619. Body fragments each have a horizontal blue-green trail applied 5mm below rim, 2mm wide. T.0.6–0.8mm 1976–9.13.X, 6371 sf2617 (P5) (*Figs.1402, 1404*)

c) Yellow body fragment, adjoins the pouring lip of sf2617. Three parallel applied horizontal blue-green trails. T.1–2mm 1976–9.13.X, 6356 sf2619 (P6) (*Figs.1402, 1404*)

d) Yellow cylindrical body fragment with three parallel applied horizontal blue-green trails. Trails 9–10mm apart, 0.8–1mm wide. Extant height of fragment 33mm. D.c.40mm at lowest trail. Body T.< 1mm 1976–9.13.X, 6342 sf2632 (P4) (*Figs.1402, 1404*)

e) Yellow body fragment with applied horizontal blue-green trail across centre. T.0.4mm 1976–9.13.X, u/s sf2657 (*Fig.1404*)

Other tableware/decorated vessels

13539 Body fragment of originally green glass, now weathered opaque brown, with trace of thin curvilinear trail. T.1.5mm 1978–9.14.II, 1784 sf717 (P1)

13540 Colourless body fragment with slight greenish tint and some surface weathering. Undiagnostic form. T.0.8mm 1978–9.14.II, 1212 sf252 (P7)

13541 Dark translucent red-purple body fragment. T.1.3mm 1976–9.13.X, 5451 sf2404 (P7)

13542 Flattish pale greenish body fragment, with a trace of an applied trail on the edge. T.0.8mm 1976–9.13.X, 6058 sf2607 (P7)

13543 Tiny fragment from a blue glass rib or trail. Undiagnostic form. L.8.9, W.4.5, T.2.0mm 1976–9.13.X, 6058 sf3045 (P7)

Flasks/urinals

13544 Fragment of kicked base from flask, with large pontil mark on underside. Originally green glass, now weathered opaque brown. L.30.0, W.24.5, T.7.9mm 1976–9.13.X, 5498 sf2541 (P1)

13545 Two horizontally flared flask/urinal rims, inturned at the edges, and four body fragments. Originally green glass, now weathered opaque beige. Rim D.c.80, T.2.5mm 1978–9.14.II, 1774 sf933 (P2)

13546 Convex flask/urinal base or alembic dome, with small pontil mark on external surface. Originally green glass, now weathered opaque beige. L.31.0, W.21.0, T.4.4mm 1976–9.13.X, 6361 sf2561 (P3)

13547 Two adjoining fragments of a convex flask/urinal base or alembic dome. Pontil mark visible on external surface.

Originally green glass, now weathered opaque brown. Extant D.45mm 1979–80.14.IV, 4428 sf893 (P4)

13548 Everted rim fragment of thick originally green glass now weathered opaque brown. Rim D.c.140, T.c.6mm 1976–9.13.X, 7287 sf2672 (P4)

13549 Flask fragments including a kicked base with a large pontil mark on underside. Horizontally everted rim fragment. Originally green glass, now weathered opaque beige. Rim: D.c.140, T.2.2mm; base: D.>50mm 1976–9.13.X, 6324 sf2458 (P6) (*Fig.1402*)

13550 Convex flask/urinal base or alembic dome, with pontil mark on external surface. Originally green glass, now weathered opaque brown. L.40.7, W.30.3, T.5.3mm 1976–9.13.X, 6347 sf2555 (P6)

13551 Kicked base from flask, with pontil mark on underside. Green glass, weathered mottled brown and black. D.>50mm 1976–9.13.X, 6367 sf2606 (P6)

13552 Fragment of kicked base from flask, with pontil mark on underside. Originally green glass, now weathered opaque brown. Base D.>100mm 1976–9.13.X, 6372 sf2683 (P6)

13553 Kicked base fragment of flask. Faint pontil mark visible on underside. Greenish colourless glass visible beneath thick beige surface weathering. Base D.>50mm 1979–80.14.IV, 4345 sf831 (P7)

13554 Two kicked bases from flasks of glass with green centres, but beige surface weathering. Pontil marks on underside of each. Also four small detached body fragments. Largest base D.c.100mm 1976–9.13.X, 6193 sf2466 (P7)

13555 Fragments of a flask including a kicked base with a pontil mark on the underside, tiny body fragments, and a slightly inverted, almost vertical, rim fragment. Originally green glass, now weathered opaque brown. Rim D.c.50mm 1978–9.14.II, 1141 sf206 (P8)

13556 Body fragments of weathered potash glass probably from the same vessel as *13555*. L.18.6, W.13.6, T.3.6mm 1978–9.14.II, 1141 sf208 (P8)

13557 Kicked base from flask. Thick green glass with iridescent surface weathering. L.39.2, W.30.5, T.5.3mm 1976–9.13.X, 5399 sf2265 (P8)

13558 Horizontally flared flask/urinal rim inturned at the edge. Green glass centre visible beneath brown surface weathering. Rim: D.c.80, T.2; body: T.1mm 1978–9.14.II, 1054 sf185 (P9) (*Fig.1402*)

13559 Convex flask/urinal base or alembic dome fragment, and many small body fragments. Pontil mark on external surface. Originally green glass, now weathered opaque beige. L.38.0, W.35.4, T.1.5mm 1979–80.14.IV, 4140 sf527 (P9)

13560 Convex flask/urinal base or alembic dome, and small body fragments. Pontil mark visible on external surface. Originally green glass, now weathered opaque brown/cream. Extant D.c.60mm u/s sf850 (*Fig.1402*)

Tubing

13561 Fragment, from an alembic spout or a flask neck. Green glass with opaque brown weathering. Small diameter, not measurable. L.12, T.1.0–3.5mm 1979–80.14.IV, 4348 sf836 (P7) (*Fig.1402*)

Undiagnostic green glass fragments

13562 Green glass rim fragment, with iridescent surface weathering. D. not measurable, T.3mm 1976–9.13.X, 5333 sf2283 (P9)

13563 Body fragment of originally green glass, now weathered opaque brown. T.c.2mm 1978–9.14.II, 1725 sf573 (P3)

13564 Sage green glass body fragment with iridescent surface weathering. T.4mm 1976–9.13.X, 7613 sf2861 (P3)

13565 Body fragments of green glass now weathered opaque brown. Five large fragments, many small fragments. T.<7mm 1979–80.14.IV, 4380 sf867 (P5)

13566 Two adjoining body fragments. Originally green glass, now weathered opaque brown. T.c.2mm 1978–9.14.II, 1690 sf508 (P6)

13567 Four body fragments of opaque beige weathered potash glass. T. <3mm 1976–9.13.X, 6365 sf2565 (P6)

13568 Eight originally green glass body fragments, now weathered opaque brown. T.c.1.5mm 1976–9.13.X, 6372 sf2664 (P6)

13569 Body fragment of green glass with surface weathering. T.2mm 1979–80.14.IV, 4202 sf644 (P7)

13570 Fifteen small weathered originally green glass body fragments, now weathered opaque brown. T.1.7mm 1976–9.13.X, 7297 sf2689 (P7)

13571 Six body fragments of green glass. T.<3mm 1976–9.13.X, 7285 sf2706 (P7)

13572 Sage green glass body fragment with surface weathering. T.3mm 1976–9.13.X, 7410 sf2746 (P7)

13573 Two adjoining body fragments. Originally green glass, now weathered opaque brown. T.>5mm 1978–9.14.II, 1134 sf191 (P8)

13574 Body fragment of originally green glass, now weathered opaque brown. T.2.8mm 1976–9.13.X, u/s sf3046

Hanging lamps

13575 Hanging lamp base stub of originally green glass, now weathered opaque brown and cream. Flares out slightly above base. Flat pontil mark on underside. H.35, D. at break 30mm 1976–9.13.X, 6342 sf2537 (P4) (*Fig.1437*)

13576 Two adjoining fragments from the base stub of an originally green potash glass hanging lamp. Weathered condition, now appears brown/black. Flat pontil mark on the underside. Extant H.c.18mm 1978–9.14.II, 1447 sf338 (P6)

Hanging lamps or flasks

13577 Rim and body fragments from a green glass vessel. Vessel has a flaring neck, turned in at an sharp angle to vertical c.10mm below the rim edge. Thick originally green glass, now weathered opaque brown. Either from an unusual hanging lamp type, or a flask. Five rim fragments, 20 large body fragments, and many more small body fragments. Rim D.c.100, T.5–6mm 1978–9.14.II, 1436 sf329 (P8) (*Fig.1437*)

13578 Two rim and two body fragments from a vessel similar to *13577*. Vessel has a flaring neck, turned in at a sharp angle to vertical c.10mm below the rim edge. Thick originally green glass, now weathered opaque brown. Rim D.c.90, T.5–6mm 1978–9.14.II, 1161 sf853 (P8)

Pin heads

13579 Hemispherical, with hole in lower surface for attachment, blue. D.9.7, H.7mm 1976–9.13.X, 7577 sf2813 (P2) (*Fig.1489*)

13580 Incomplete, globular, opaque dark blue, split in half. D.10.8, H.8.7mm 1979–80.14.IV, 4400 sf878 (P5) (*Fig.1489*)

Iron

Blanks and scrap

See p.3025 for definition of terms used.

Bars

13581 Irregular shape. Rectangular cross-section except at one end where it curves, tapers and has a rounded cross-section. L.245, W.26, T.26mm 1978–9.14.II, 1427 sf386 (P7) (*Fig.1318*)

13582 L.77, W.30mm 1976–9.13.X, 5144 sf1853 (P8)

13583 L.64, W.39, T.13mm 1976–9.13.X, 5254 sf3310 (P8)

13584 Tapered at one end. L.103, W.39, T.7mm 1979–80.14.IV, 4000 sf747 (P9)

Plates

Cast iron

13585 L.105, W.40, T.4mm 1976–9.13.X, 5248 sf1927 (P8)

Wrought iron

13586 Slightly curved , broken at each end. L.46, W.12, T.2mm 1978–9.14.II, 1784 sf704 (P1)

13587 Irregular shape and curved. L.71, W.35mm 1973–5.13.III, 1216 sf923 (P1)

13588 Bent at 90°. Arms: L.25, 12, W.13mm 1976–9.13.X, 5498 sf3384 (P1)

13589 L.50, W.11mm 1979–80.14.IV, 4445 sf5084 (P2)

13590 Possible casing. L-shaped. Arms: L.50 and 30, W.35mm 1979–80.14.IV, 1504 sf5180 (P2)

13591 L-shaped. Plated. Arms: L.30 and 22mm 1979–80.14.IV, 1549 sf5188 (P3)

13592 L.20, W.18mm 1978–9.14.II, 1549 sf5190 (P3)

13593 L.44, W.28mm 1976–9.13.X 7369 sf2743 (P4)

13594 L.45, W.28mm 1979–80.14.IV, 1544 sf5186 (P5)

13595 Irregular. L.45, W.38mm 1978–9.14.II, 1588 sf5221 (P5)

13596 L.62, W.15, T.4mm 1976–9.13.X, 6372 sf2649 (P6)

13597 L.35, W.30mm, 1976–9.13.X, 5503 sf3388 (P6)

13598 L-shaped. L.30, W.30mm 1976–9.13.X, 7379 sf3448 (P6)

13599 L.33, W.24mm 1976–9.13.X, 7491 sf3453 (P6)

13600 One straight side. L.37, W.25mm 1976–9.13.X, 6305 sf2475 (P7)

13601 L.38, W.11mm 1976–9.13.X, 5146 sf3330 (P7)

13602 One curved side, rest irregular. Possibly part of disc. Flecks of plating. L.60, W.40mm 1976–9.13.X, 5204 sf3337 (P7)

13603 L.30, W.11mm 1976–9.13.X, 5292 sf3351 (P7)

13604 Possible casing. In two pieces. L-shaped cross-section at one end and then arms pinched together towards the other. L.76; arms: L.21 and 20mm 1976–9.13.X, 5320 sf3357 (P7)

13605 Curves at one end. L.70, W.35, T.10mm 1976–9.13.X, 5367 sf3364 (P7)

13606 Two plates. Largest narrows. L.60, W.25mm 1976–9.13.X, 5410 sf3372 (P7)

13607 Large number of fragments of plated plate, possibly part of more than one object including perhaps a bell. 1976–9.13.X, 6163 sf3488 (P7)

13608 L.30, W.15mm 1976–9.13.X, 6262 sf3496 (P7)

13609 One rounded corner, rest irregular. L.40, W.23mm 1979–80.14.IV, 4275 sf5087 (P7)

13610 Triangular. L.47, W.40mm 1979–80.14.IV, 4180 sf5137 (P7)

13611 Irregular. L.58, W.58mm 1976–9.13.X, 5144 sf3328 (P8)

13612 One straight side. L.42, W.27mm 1976–9.13.X, 5354 sf3363 (P8)

13613 L.35, W.15, T.15mm 1976–9.13.X, 6009 sf3399 (P8)

13614 Sides irregular. L.65, W.19mm 1976–9.13.X, 6009 sf3400 (P8)

13615 L.49, W.20mm 1976–9.13.X, 6069 sf3413 (P8)

13616 L.30, W.15mm 1976–9.13.X, 6143 sf3477 (P8)

13617 Roughly triangular. L.50, W.20mm 1976–9.13.X, 6165 sf3486 (P8)

13618 L.33, W.13mm 1978–9.14.II, 1156 sf5223 (P8)

13619 Curved, possibly a knife blade. L.40, W.20mm 1978–9.14.II, 1117 sf5265 (P8)

13620 Broken at each end. L.40, W.33mm 1978–9.14.II, u/s sf5197

Strips

13621 L-shaped. Plated. Arms: L.54 and 20, W.11, T.2mm 1978–9.14.II, 1784 sf744 (P1)

13622 Flattened and widened at one end. L.79, W.14, T.6mm 1973–5.13.III, 1216 sf914 (P1)

13623 Spirally twisted. L.69, T.5mm 1978–9.14.II, 1662 sf463 (P2)

13624 Plated. L.25mm 1976–9.13.X, 7597 sf3470 (P2)

13625 Tapers, curved slightly, rounded cross-section except at one end. L.41, T.10mm 1978–9.14.II, 1732 sf5055 (P2)

13626 L.40, W.15mm 1979–80.14.IV, 4483 sf5085 (P2)

13627 Rounded cross-section. L.63, T.8mm 1979–80.14.IV 4441 sf5092 (P2)

13628 Narrows, broken at each end. L.52, W.11, T.3mm 1978–9.14.II, 1774 sf5238 (P2)

13629 Plated at each end. L.40, W.5mm 1978–9.14.II, 1743 sf5058 (P3)

13630 L.50mm 1976–9.13.X, 7287 sf3441 (P4)

13631 Twisted. L.45, W.9mm 1976–9.13.X, 7528 sf3460 (P4)

13632 L-shaped. Arms: L.42, W.15mm 1978–9.14.II, 1650 sf5045 (P4)

13633 Curved. L.61, W.10mm 1976–9.13.X, 7418 sf2753 (P5)

13634 Bent at 90°. Edges bevelled and two channels of V-shaped cross-section run down centre. Plated (tin). Arms: L.68 and 34, W.17mm 1976–9.13.X, 7126 sf3426 (P5)

13635 Irregular. L.50mm 1976–9.13.X, 7446 sf3452 (P5)

13636 L.86, W.9, T.2mm 1976–9.13.X, 5465 sf2448 (P6)

13637 Broken at one end, expands towards the other where there is a looped terminal. L.85, T.7; loop: W.30mm 1976–9.13.X, 6372 sf2644 (P6)

13638 L-shaped. Arms: L.50, W.20mm 1976–9.13.X, 7110 sf3423 (P6)

13639 L.30, W.13mm 1976–9.13.X, 7229 sf3434 (P6)

13640 L.37mm 1978–9.14.II, 1502 sf5178 (P6)

13641 Tapers; possibly a wedge. L.72, W.13, T.7mm 1978–9.14.II, 1561 sf5193 (P6)

13642 Tapers at each end. L.186, T.6mm 1978–9.14.II, 1225 sf254 (P7)

13643 Corroded. Widened at one end and broken. L.105, W.10, T.10mm 1979–80.14.IV, 4235 sf749 (P7)

13644 Cross-section rounded except at one end, other end slightly burred. L.197, T.9mm 1976–9.13.X, 5146 sf1856 (P7)

13645 L.70, W.14, T.6mm 1976–9.13.X, 7263 sf2636 (P7)

13646 Tapers slightly, curves at one end, broken at both. Plated (tin). L.74, T.7mm 1976–9.13.X, 5146 sf3335 (P7)

13647 L.72, W.6mm 1976–9.13.X, 5292 sf3352 (P7)

13648 Very corroded. Lead solder adheres. L.40mm 1976–9.13.X, 5292 sf3353 (P7)

13649 Bent. Plated (tin). L.51, W.6mm 1976–9.13.X, 6162 sf3544 (P7)

13650 L-shaped. Arms: L.45mm 1976–9.13.X, 6271 sf3502 (P7)

13651 Damaged at both ends. L.70, T.10mm 1979–80.14.IV, 4232 sf5088 (P7)

13652 One end curved over, at the other it widens out before being broken. L.70, W.22mm 1979–80.14.IV, 4163 sf5131 (P7)

13653 L-shaped. Lead solder adheres. Arms: L.42 and 15, T.8mm 1979–80.14.IV, 4180 sf5135 (P7)

13654 Broken at each end. L.60mm 1978–9.14.II, 1308 sf5159 (P7)

13655 Broken at each end. Cross-section with rounded corners. L.147, W.10, T.10mm 1978–9.14.II, 1220 sf5227 (P7)

13656 Corroded. L.c.105mm 1976–9.13.X, 5134 sf1843 (P8)

13657 L.70, W.10mm 1976–9.13.X, 5210 sf1898 (P8)

13658 Tapers. L.135, T.5mm 1976–9.13.X, 5211 sf1932 (P8)

13659 Tapers to a wedge-shaped tip. L.103, W.11mm 1976–9.13.X, 5268 sf3315 (P8)

13660 Tapers towards each end, one pointed, other broken. Plated (brass). L.60, T.16mm 1976–9.13.X, 5268 sf3318 (P8)

13661 L-shaped, both arms broken, shorter arm thicker. May have been a hook. Arms: L.45 and 18, T.12mm 1976–9.13.X, 5268 sf3320 (P8)

13662 Irregular. L.55, W.23, T.11mm 1976–9.13.X, 5268 sf3321 (P8)

13663 L.52mm 1976–9.13.X, 5144 sf3324 (P8)

13664 L.65, W.15, T.10mm 1976–9.13.X, 5144 sf3326 (P8)

13665 Bent at 90° in centre and tapers in irregular manner. Arms: L.45 and 30, W.14mm 1976–9.13.X, 6008 sf3396 (P8)

13666 Spirally twisted, broken at one end, at the other tapers to a point and has a rounded cross-section. L.99, W.8mm 1979–80.14.IV, 4076 sf5121 (P8)

13667 L.40, W.13, T.6mm 1978–9.14.II, 1123 sf5198 (P8)

13668 Tapers and is slightly curved. L.71, W.13, T.8mm 1978–9.14.II, 1481 sf368 (P9)

13669 Curved, rounded cross-section. L.40, T.9mm 1978–9.14.II, 1487 sf434 (P9)

13670 Rounded cross-section, one end slightly widened, other missing. L.325, T.9mm 1976–9.13.X, 5141 sf1931 (P9)

13671 L.21, W.7mm 1979–80.14.IV, u/s sf893

13672 L.160, T.3mm 1973–5.13.III, u/s sf1000

Wire

13673 Spirally intertwined wires. L.30mm 1978–9.14.II, 1108 sf5252 (P8)

Spike

13674 Tapers. L.260, T.9mm 1978–9.14.II, 1340 sf273 (P8)

Building tools

Trowels

13675 Triangular blade, tang missing. L.115, W.130, T.7mm 1979–80.14.IV, 4268 sf740 (P6)

13676 Triangular blade and crank-shaped tang. Blade: L.122, W.110; tang: L.70mm 1976–9.13.X, 5340 sf2042 (P7) (Fig.1316)

Metalworking tools

Tongs

13677 Mouthpieces curved in cross-section (concave inner face), and straight ends. Arms rounded in cross-section with ball expansions at the tip. L.160; mouthpieces: L.38, W.17mm 1976–9.13.X, 5339 sf2070 (P7) (Figs.1326–7)

Hammer head

13678 One arm. Widened and flattened slightly to a rounded wedge-shaped tip. L.57, W.16, T.15mm 1976–9.13.X, 7191 sf2586 (P7)

Punches

13679 Corroded. Slightly curved, head burred. L.140, W.20mm 1976–9.13.X, 7594 sf2826 (P3)

13680 Tapered near the head which is broken off. L.105, W.12, T.12mm 1978–9.14.II, 1561 sf5194 (P6) (Fig.1328)

13681 Upper one-third of the shank has a rounded cross-section. Lower two-thirds tapers to wedge-shaped tip and has a rectangular cross-section. Facets. L.155, T.17mm 1976–9.13.X, 6271 sf2392 (P7) (Figs.1327–8)

13682 Rounded cross-section. Tapers from the mid-point. L.53, W.10mm 1976–9.13.X, 5410 sf3377 (P7)

13683 Curved at the head, rounded cross-section. L.80, T.10mm 1976–9.13.X, 5202 sf1882 (P8)

13684 Tip damaged. Cross-section rectangular at the base, rounded at the top. L.126, T.11mm 1976–9.13.X, 6009 sf3393 (P8)

13685 Tapers for most of its length, rounded cross-section near the tip which is damaged; also tapers towards a pointed head, perhaps a tang. L.108, W.16, T.14mm 1976–9.13.X, u/s sf2280

Tanged punch

13686 One end has wedge-shaped tip, the other is pointed. L.99, W.20mm 1979–80.14.IV, 4477 sf5068 (P2)

File

13687 Incomplete blade. One face has fine cross-cut teeth, also teeth on both edges. L.50, W.8, T.2mm 1976–9.13.X, 7074 sf3421 (P8) (Fig.1331)

Chisel

13688 Broken at one end, wedge-shaped tip at the other. L.81, W.8, T.6mm 1976–9.13.X, 5155 sf1861 (P7)

Woodworking tools

Spoon augers

13689 Broken at head? L.46, W.14, T.7mm 1979–80.14.IV, 4462 sf5108 (P3)

13690 Complete. L.124, T.5; blade: L.42, T.26mm 1976–9.13.X, 5488 sf2544 (P5) (Fig.1335)

13691 Tang missing. L.75, W.10, T.7mm 1976–9.13.X, 5404 sf3371 (P7)

13692 Tang incomplete, blade tip missing. L.79; tang: W.12; blade: W.8, T.7mm 1976–9.13.X, 6008 sf3395 (P8)

13693 Complete. Remains of wooden handle (oak). L.93; blade: L.38, W.6, T.4mm 1978–9.14.II, u/s sf5253 (Figs.1335, 1337)

Wedges

13694 Rounded tip. L.55, W.18, T.8mm 1978–9.14.II, 1634 sf5195 (P5)

13695 Burred head. L.58, W.27mm 1976–9.13.X, 5431 sf3378 (P6)

13696 Very corroded. L.72, W.14, T.7mm 1978–9.14.II, 1402 sf5207 (P6)

13697 Wedge or knife tang. L.62, W.15, T.7mm 1978–9.14.II, 1442 sf5210 (P6)

13698 Tip damaged. L.74, W.26, T.8mm 1978–9.14.II, 1233 sf244 (P7)

13699 L.94, W.21, T.7mm 1976–9.13.X, 5392 sf2213 (P7)

13700 Burred head, rounded tip. L.64, W.26, T.20mm 1976–9.13.X, 5410 sf2269 (P7) (*Figs.1336–7*)

13701 Flattened and widened to the tip, heavily burred head. L.104, W.33, T.25mm 1976–9.13.X, 5149 sf3336 (P7) (*Figs.1336–7*)

13702 L.38, W.9mm 1976–9.13.X, 7308 sf3444 (P7)

13703 Very corroded. Tapers to a point, head burred. L.100, W.35, T.c.20mm 1978–9.14.II, 1233 sf5230 (P7)

13704 Tapers to a narrow tip, now broken. L.89, W.20, T.10mm 1973–5.13.IV, 1513 sf1807 (P9)

13705 L.72, W.11, T.9mm 1976–9.13.X, u/s sf2082

Saw blade

13706 Broken at both ends. Set teeth. L.64, W.17, T.5mm 1976–9.13.X, 7075 sf2456 (P7) (*Fig.1336*)

Leatherworking tools

Awls

Both arms of rectangular cross-section

13707 Arms of unequal length. Tang expanded in the centre. L.64, T.5mm 1973–5.13.III, 1203 sf837 (P1) (*Fig.1338*)

13708 Slightly twisted in centre. L.120, T.4mm 1973–5.13.III, 1215 sf875 (P1) (*Fig.1338*)

13709 Arms incomplete, rectangular collar in centre. L.42, W.5mm 1976–9.13.X, 7561 sf3462 (P5)

13710 L.104, W.5mm 1978–9.14.II, 1117 sf5269 (P8)

Other awls

13711 Working arm a rectangular cross-section, steps in at base before a short length with a rounded cross-section which expands before stepping in at the base of the tang. L.98, T.6mm 1973–5.13.III, 1200 sf871 (P1) (*Fig.1338*)

13712 Corroded and in three pieces. L.101, T.5mm 1978–9.14.II, 1501 sf5177 (P2)

13713 Rounded cross-section. One arm incomplete, other has tip missing. L.63, T.5mm 1976–9.13.X, 5320 sf3359 (P7)

Textile tools

Wool comb binding

13714 Incomplete. Two rows of five holes. L.51, W.28mm 1976–9.13.X, 5292 sf3344 (P7) (*Fig.1342*)

Fibre processing spikes

Rectangular cross-section

13715 Bent. L.103, T.5mm 1973–5.13.III, 1115 sf816 (P1) (*Fig.1342*)

13716 L.86, T.4mm 1973–5.13.III, 1131 sf944 (P1A)

13717 L.95mm 1978–9.14.II, 1702 sf5051 (P2)

13718 Base missing. L.70, T.4mm 1976–9.13.X, 7569 sf3463 (P3)

13719 L.95, T.5mm 1979–80.14.IV, 4457 sf5105 (P3)

13720 Widened at head. L.100, T.11mm 1979–80.14.IV, 4439 sf897 (P4) (*Fig.1342*)

13721 L.90mm 1978–9.14.II, 1660 sf5046 (P4)

13722 Stepped head. L.100, T.5mm 1978–9.14.II, 1450 sf5171 (P7)

13723 L.98mm 1976–9.13.X, 7008 sf3415 (P8)

Rounded cross-section

13724 Bent. L.c.85mm 1978–9.14.II, 1668 sf5047 (P4)

13725 Stepped head, tip missing. L.84, T.5mm 1978–9.14.II, 1561 sf5192 (P6)

13726 L.115, T.6mm 1973–5.13.III, 1095 sf718 (P7)

13727 Flattened head. L.86, W.9, T.2mm 1976–9.13.X, 5410 sf2452 (P7)

13728 Tip missing. L.75, T.6mm 1973–5.13.III, 1055 sf3232 (P7)

13729 Tip missing. L.79, T.5mm 1976–9.13.X, 6162 sf3481 (P7)

13730 Stepped head. L.121, W.6mm 1979–80.14.IV, 4047 sf5117 (P8)

13731 L.110, T.6mm 1978–9.14.II, u/s sf516

Indeterminate cross-section

13732 L.108mm 1978–9.14.II, 1318 sf5160 (P7)

Tenter hook

13733 Arms: L.29 and 23, T.4mm 1976–9.13.X, 5292 sf3345 (P7) (*Fig.1346*)

Needles

Punched eye

13734 Head incomplete. L.50, T.3mm 1973–5.13.III, 1225 sf919 (P1A) (*Fig.1348*)

13735 Head incomplete. L54, T.3mm 1973–5.13.III, 1225 sf957 (P1A)

13736 Widened head. L.53, W.4mm 1973–5.13.III, 1205 sf832 (P2) (*Fig.1348*)

Other needle

13737 Head missing. L.39mm 1976–9.13.X, 7546 sf2816 (P3)

Shanks

13738 L.38mm 1978–9.14.II, 1792 sf707 (P1) (*Fig.1348*)

13739 L.58mm 1978–9.14.II, 1453 sf340 (P5)

13740 L.33mm 1976–9.13.X, 7522 sf3458 (P6)

Scissors

13741 Oval finger loops. Stems expand slightly in centre, rounded cross-section. Blades hinged on rivet near top, bevelled edges, tips missing. L.125, W.49, T.9mm 1976–9.13.X, 6320 sf2483 (P5) (*Figs.1347, 1354*)

Agricultural tools

Pitchfork

13742   One straight tine survives, other a stub; incomplete tang of rounded cross-section. L.c.200, W.c.40, T.13mm 1973–5.13.IV, 1552 sf689 (P8)

Other tools

Shears

13743   Blade and stem. Cusped shoulder. Blade tip missing, back straight, bevelled edge. Star-shaped inlaid cutler's mark. L.109; blade: L.70, W.11, T.3mm 1976–9.13.X, 5180 sf1969 (P7)

13744   Looped bow and one stem of rounded cross-section. L.72, W.24, T.6mm 1976–9.13.X, 5180 sf1970 (P7)

13745   Blade and stub of stem. Blade has cusped shoulder and bevelled edge. L.80, W.11, T.3mm 1976–9.13.X, 5283 sf2024 (P7)

13746   Blade only. L.108, W.15, T.5mm 1976–9.13.X, 6262 sf2502 (P7)

13747   Incomplete blade, concave shoulder. Stub of stem. L.68, W.17, T.2mm 1976–9.13.X, 5146 sf3334 (P7)

13748   Blade, tip missing, and stub of stem. L.79, W.11, T.3mm 1976–9.13.X, 6246 sf3491 (P7)

13749   Two fragments of blade fused together. Shoulder of one blade cusped, other indistinct. Cusped blade: L.52, W.8, T.2mm 1976–9.13.X, 5132 sf1826 (P8)

13750   Blade and stub of stem. Back slightly convex, cutting edge convex. Concave shoulder. L.68, W.14, T.3mm 1976–9.13.X, 5132 sf1832 (P8)

13751   Looped bow with central rib. Blade tips missing, shoulders cusped. Cutting edge butt welded on. L.124; blades: L.70, W.11, T.3mm 1976–9.13.X, 6068 sf2164 (P8) (*Figs.1353–4*)

Knives

Whittle tang knives

Blade back form A: blade back straight before sloping down to the tip

A2: straight part of blade back upward sloping

13752   Incomplete blade only. L.44, W.13, T.2mm 1979–80.14.IV, 4479 sf925 (P2)

Blade back form C: blade back straight before becoming convex and curving down to the tip

C1: straight part of blade back horizontal

13753   Back horizontal for 27mm, tip at blade's mid-point. Cutting edge slightly S-shaped. Shoulder vertical. L.87; blade: 50, W.11mm 1978–9.14.II, 1418 sf336 (P7)

C2: straight part of blade back upward sloping

13754   Blade incomplete, thickened at the point where it curves down to the tip which is at mid-point. Cutting edge straight before curving up at the tip. Tang missing. L.94, W.25, T.6mm 1976–9.13.X, 6041 sf3404 (P8)

C3: straight part of blade back downward sloping

13755   Back straight for 72mm. Tip at blade's mid-point. Cutting edge S-shaped. L.202; blade: L.149, W.19, T.6mm 1978–9.14.II, 1740 sf622 (P1) (*Fig.1357*)

13756   Blade back slopes down for 25mm, tip missing. Cutting edge S-shaped. Parted weld line runs horizontally. L.94; blade: L.47, W.11, T.4mm 1973–5.13.III, 1200 sf866 (P1)

13757   Back straight for 30mm. Cutting edge S-shaped. Sloping shoulder. L.78; blade: L.51, W.10, T.4mm 1978–9.14.II, 1702 sf703 (P2)

13758   Back straight for c.25mm. Tip at blade's mid-point. Sloping shoulder. Cutting edge straight before curving up to tip; at rear it is continuous with the tang. L.58; blade: 39, W.10, T.4mm 1979–80.14.IV, 4404 sf894 (P4) (*Fig.1357*)

Ci: straight part of blade back has indeterminate form

13759   Corroded. Blade tip missing. Cutting edge convex. Stub of tang. L.57, W.10, T.4mm 1976–9.13.X, 7621 sf2857 (P3)

13760   Back horizontal for 51mm, tip missing. Cutting edge S-shaped. Vertical shoulder. Tang largely missing. L.72; blade: L.64, W.13, T.5mm 1976–9.13.X, 7493 sf2773 (P4)

13761   Blade and tang incomplete. Blade back straight to break, cutting edge was S-shaped. L.60, W.14, T.6mm 1978–9.14.II, 1281 sf262 (P6)

13762   Blade back straight for 51mm, blade tip missing. Cutting edge S-shaped. Groove on each face below the back. Tang largely missing. L.79, W.13, T.3mm 1976–9.13.X, 5458 sf2417 (P7)

13763   Back horizontal for c.77mm. Tip at mid-point. Cutting edge S-shaped. Sloping shoulder. Tang missing. L.96, W.14, T.5mm 1976–9.13.X, 5292 sf2424 (P7)

13764   Blade only. Tip at mid-point. Convex cutting edge. L.61, W.13mm 1976–9.13.X, 7020 sf3417 (P7)

13765   Back straight for c.90mm, tip at blade's mid-point. Cutting edge convex. Tang bent down. L.146; blade: L.108, W.13, T.6mm 1978–9.14.II, 1117 sf221 (P8) (*Fig.1357*)

13766   Cutting edge convex, tip at mid-point. Tang tip missing. L.93; blade: L.70, W.10, T.5mm 1978–9.14.II, 1007 sf124 (P9) Metallurgy report (*Fig.1357*)

Blade back form D: blade back slightly convex and curves gently from the shoulder to the tip

13767   Incomplete blade only. Convex cutting edge. Horizontal pattern-welded strip near back. Tang missing. L.50, W.11mm 1973–5.13.IV, 1640 sf772 (P1) Metallurgy report (*Fig.1358*)

13768   Tip at blade's mid-point. Cutting edge convex. Vertical shoulder. Tang incomplete. L.79; blade: L.68, W.13, T.5mm 1979–80.14.IV, 4469 sf912 (P2)

13769   Very corroded. Tip at blade's mid-point. Cutting edge convex. Tang incomplete. L.66; blade: L.57, W.9mm 1976–9.13.X, 7493 sf2778 (P4)

13770   Blade tip missing. Cutting edge slightly S-shaped. Stub of tang. L.72, W.12, T.6mm 1979–80.14.IV, 4162 sf581 (P7)

13771   Blade tip missing. Cutting edge straight. Inlaid (brass) cutler's mark. Tang largely missing. L.83; blade: L.73, W.16, T.4mm 1976–9.13.X, 6262 sf2365 (P7) (*Fig.1358*)

Knife blade of unusual form

13772   Back straight for 15mm and then slopes down sharply before sloping more gently to the tip which is at blade's mid-point. Cutting edge S-shaped. Two clear horizontal weld lines. Mineralised remains of handle. L.88; blade: L.57, W.15, T.5mm 1979–80.14.IV, 4457 sf918 (P3) (*Fig.1358*)

Knives of indeterminate blade back form

13773 Stub of blade, tang tip missing. L.83; blade: W.17, T.6mm 1979–80.14.IV, 4482 sf930 (P1)

13774 Incomplete. Form indistinct. L.65, W.9, T.3mm 1979–80.14.IV, 4457 sf908 (P3)

13775 Corroded. Cutting edge slightly S-shaped. Tang missing. L.74, W.13, T.3mm 1979–80.14.IV, 4457 sf929 (P3)

13776 Blade tip missing. Cutting edge convex. Tang largely missing. L.52, W.10, T.5mm 1976–9.13.X, 7582 sf3465 (P3)

13777 Blade incomplete. Two horizontal grooves run along the back of one face between which are eleven inlaid crosses. Vertical shoulder. L.96; blade: L.38, W.23, T.3mm 1978–9.14.II, 1544 sf408 (P5) (*Figs.1360, 1363*)

13778 Blade incomplete. Back straight to break. Pattern-welded strip near back set in a recessed channel. Vertical shoulder. Tang incomplete. L.55; blade: L.40, W.13, T.4mm 1978–9.14.II, 1494 sf492 (P5) (*Fig.1363*)

13779 Corroded. Back and cutting edge parallel as far as the break. Concave shoulder. L.64; blade: L.36, W.14mm 1976–9.13.X, 7382 sf3449 (P5)

13780 Corroded. Back and cutting edge indistinct, tip at blade's mid-point. Stub of tang. L.81, W.16, T.8mm 1978–9.14.II, 1238 sf245 (P7)

13781 Blade incomplete. Tang missing. L.72, W.12, T.2mm 1976–9.13.X, 5147 sf1834 (P7)

13782 Blade bent and incomplete, back form indistinct, tip missing. Two inlaid cutler's marks. Sloping shoulder. L.116; blade: L.61, W.15mm 1976–9.13.X, 5146 sf1951 (P7) Metallurgy report (*Fig.1363*)

13783 Incomplete blade. Back and cutting edge convex. Tang missing. L.62, W.12, T.4mm 1976–9.13.X, 5292 sf2421 (P7)

13784 Blade incomplete. Cutting edge curved at rear. Sloping shoulder. Tang tip missing. L.45, W.21, T.4mm 1976–9.13.X, 6254 sf3492 (P7)

13785 Blade incomplete. Cutting edge was S-shaped. Sloping shoulder. Tang largely missing. L.56, W.14, T.4mm 1976–9.13.X, 6271 sf3504 (P7)

13786 Blade incomplete, tang largely missing. L.42, W.13mm 1979–80.14.IV, 4180 sf5136 (P7)

13787 Blade incomplete, tang largely missing. L.41, W.12, T.3mm 1978–9.14.II, 1337 sf5162 (P7)

13788 Incomplete. Back and cutting edge convex. Tang missing. L.74, W.17, T.2mm 1976–9.13.X, 5132 sf1839 (P8)

13789 Very corroded. Blade incomplete, tang largely missing. L.72, W.14, T.2mm 1976–9.13.X, 5268 sf3312 (P8)

13790 Blade incomplete, rear of cutting edge rounded. Remains of non-ferrous shoulder plate welded on (tin with a little lead). Vertical shoulder, tang complete. L.53; blade: L.24, W.13, T.2mm 1976–9.13.X, 5268 sf3319 (P8)

13791 Blade and tang incomplete. Back and cutting edge parallel as far as the break. L.60, blade: L.35, W.15mm 1976–9.13.X, 5268 sf3322 (P8)

13792 Blade incomplete. Back straight up to the break, possibly sloped down to tip. Cutting edge slightly concave. Vertical shoulder, tang tip missing. On left face inlaid incised panel: between two pairs of horizontal lines a row of lozenges with curvilinear additions. Inlay is mercury gilded silver. L.78; blade: W.19, T.7mm 1979–80.14.IV, 4165 sf5133 (P8) (*Figs.1361, 1363*)

13793 Tang only. L.69, W.13, T.6mm 1979–80.14.IV, 4181 sf5139 (P8)

13794 Blade incomplete, back and cutting edge straight. Tang largely missing. Fragment of lead adheres. L.65, W.17, T.2mm 1978–9.14.II, 1117 sf5256 (P8)

13795 Back straight. Tip missing. Cutting edge convex. Tang missing. L.80, W.13mm 1979–80.14.IV, 4125 sf524 (P9)

13796 Blade incomplete. Bolster expands towards the tang which is set in an antler handle. It expands towards the end which is rounded and has a rounded cross-section. L.90; blade: L.22, W.12, T.4; handle: D.13mm 1976–9.13.X, 5027 sf1996 (P9) (*Fig.1363*)

Scale tang knives

8117 Blade in two pieces which do not join. Blade probably had a straight back which curved down towards the tip, now missing. Cutting edge convex. Blade has an inlaid cutler's mark and is pierced twice at the rear. Tang incomplete, widens, one non-ferrous rivet. On one side an ivory scale plate, on the other a short ivory plate and then part of another of glass or amber. L.c.140; blade: L.c.85, W.18, T.4mm 1978–9.14.II, 1267 sf261 (P6) (*Fig.1365*)

13797 Tang fragment, one tubular non-ferrous rivet. L.33mm 1979–80.14.IV, 4102 sf511 (P7)

13798 Tang only. Eye at end. Bone scale plates have chamfered edges and are attached by at least 14 non-ferrous rivets. L.81, W.18, T.13mm 1976–9.13.X, 5372 sf2182 (P7) (*Fig.1365*)

13799 Tang only. Slopes down at the end, pierced twice. L.58, W.15, T.3mm 1976–9.13.X, 7313 sf2716 (P7)

13800 Blade incomplete; inlaid cutler's mark in the form of a 'P' on the left face (inlay metal: brass, trace lead). Non-ferrous shoulder plate (brass, trace lead) riveted on. Tang incomplete, pierced twice, one brass rivet. Trace of wooden scale-plates. L.50; blade: L.33, W.13, T.2mm 1979–80.14.IV, 4121 sf5129 (P7) (*Fig.1365*)

13801 Tang only. Expands slightly at the end which is rounded. Bone scale plates have chamfered edges and are attached by four tubular non-ferrous rivets. L.95, W.16, T.6mm 1976–9.13.X, 6068 sf2170 (P8) (*Fig.1365*)

13802 Horn handle. L.95, W.24, T.10mm 1976–9.13.X, 7010 sf3416 (P8)

13803 Three pieces. Blade incomplete. Non-ferrous shoulder plate (ternary) riveted on. Three non-ferrous rivets (brass with little lead). Non-ferrous oval end cap (ternary with a little lead). Remains of wooden scale plates (oak). L.c.100; blade: L.30, W.13, T.2mm 1976–9.13.X, 6109 sf3480 (P8)

13804 Tang only. Widens slightly. Three non-ferrous tubular rivets. L.80, W.23, T.7mm 1976–9.13.X, 7036 sf2351 (P9)

13805 Tang only. Widens to an angled end which projects downwards slightly. Bone scale plates with small punched dots in groups of four attached by non-ferrous rivet. L.79, W.19, T.11mm 1976–9.13.X, u/s sf1950 (*Fig.1365*)

Knives with openwork tangs

13806 Stub of blade. Tang widens and is pierced by four chambers, each rectangular with a cusped head; they are arranged longitudinally side by side in two groups. L.134, W.20, T.7mm 1976–9.13.X, 5334 sf3360 (P8) (*Fig.1365*)

13807 Blade largely incomplete. Tang also incomplete but now appears as two broken projections. L.74, W.17, T.7mm 1976–9.13.X, 6008 sf3392 (P8) (*Fig.1365*)

Blade fragments

13808 From large blade. L.54, W.28, T.7mm 1978–9.14.II, 1688 sf497 (P1)

13809 L.28, W.16mm 1976–9.13.X, 7280 sf2666 (P6)

13810 L.70, W.25, T.3mm 1978–9.14.II, 1268 sf260 (P7)

13811 L.47, W.13, T.2mm 1976–9.13.X, 5403 sf3369 (P7)

13812 Tip of blade. L.36, W.12, T.2mm 1976–9.13.X, 6148 sf3478 (P7)

13813 L.74, W.12mm 1976–9.13.X, 5268 sf3313 (P8)

13814 L.35, W.13mm 1976–9.13.X, 6065 sf3412 (P8)

Knife tang

13815 L.55mm 1978–9.14.II, 1321 sf5199 (P7)

Folding knife

13816 Blade only. Back straight for c.65mm, slopes down at 20° and becomes concave as it approaches the tip. At rear it is broken, but probably pivoted on a rivet set on the end of which on one blade face (other obscured by corrosion) is an octahedral brass washer. L.101, W.22, T.4mm 1978–9.14.II, 1427 sf398 (P7) (*Fig.1380*)

Pierced blade

13817 Slightly curved blade broken at one end, narrows towards a pointed tip at the other, shortly before which there is a rounded pierced expansion. L.138, W.15, T.5mm 1979–80.14.IV, 4112 sf538 (P8) (*Fig.1380*)

Domestic equipment

Vessel

13818 Irregularly shaped fragment of a vessel with an everted rim. Rim appears folded over into a socket on inner face. L.78, W.68mm 1979–80.14.IV, 4016 sf862 (P5)

Structural items and fittings

Nails

Details of nails available in archive.

Plated nails

Plating details, where available, given in parenthesis before dimensions. W = width of head.

13819 Complete length. L.35, W.28mm 1979–80.14.IV, 4470 sf5156 (P2)

13820 Complete length. Domed head. L.22mm 1973–5.13.III, 1055 sf3231 (P3)

13821 Complete length. L.64, W.24, T.5mm 1973–5.13.III, 1055 sf3233 (P3)

13822 Shank incomplete, domed head. L.18, W.14mm 1976–9.13.X, 7613 sf3473 (P3)

13823 Shank tip missing. Domed head. L.58, W.25mm 1979–80.14.IV, 4457 sf5104 (P3)

13824 Complete length. Domed head. L.60, W.32mm 1979–80.14.IV, 4462 sf5107 (P3)

13825 Complete length, curved shank. Domed head. L.c.75, W.25, T.5mm 1979–80.14.IV, 4446 sf5157 (P3)

13826 Shank largely missing. W.20mm 1978–9.14.II, 1744 sf5237 (P3)

13827 Complete length. L.30, W.20mm 1976–9.13.X, 7588 sf3467 (P4)

13828 Complete length. Slightly domed and neatly rounded head. L.33, W.19mm 1976–9.13.X, 7588 sf3468 (P4)

13829 Shank curved and incomplete. Pointed head. (Tin) L.c.65, W.26, T.5mm 1976–9.13.X, 7589 sf3469 (P4)

13830 Shank largely missing. W.18mm 1978–9.14.II, 1726 sf5240 (P4)

13831 Complete length. L.30, W.23mm 1976–9.13.X, 5477 sf3381 (P5)

13832 Shank incomplete. L.30, W.20mm 1976–9.13.X, 5488 sf3382 (P5)

13833 Head only. W.20mm 1976–9.13.X, 7123 sf3425 (P5)

13834 L.15, W.16mm 1976–9.13.X, 7126 sf3427 (P5)

13835 Fragment. 1976–9.13.X, 7231 sf3436 (P5)

13836 Complete length. L.40, W.22mm 1976–9.13.X, 7561 sf3461 (P5)

13837 Complete length. L.34, W.22mm 1976–9.13.X, 6303 sf3507 (P5)

13838 Shank tip missing. Domed head. L.40, W.26mm 1978–9.14.II, 1595 sf5094 (P5)

13839 Tip missing. L.17, W.25mm 1978–9.14.II, 1457 sf5213 (P5)

13840 Complete length. Domed head. L.45, W.20mm 1978–9.14.II, 1647 sf5235 (P5)

13841 Shank tip missing. Domed head. L.32, W.28mm 1978–9.14.II, 1650 sf5236 (P5)

13842 Fragment. 1973–5.13.IV, 1590 sf3236 (P6)

13843 Complete length. L.60, W.15mm 1976–9.13.X, 5497A sf3383 (P6)

13844 Complete length. L.23, W.12mm 1976–9.13.X, 7336 sf3446 (P6)

13845 Domed head, shank incomplete. L.32, W.24mm 1976–9.13.X, 7522 sf3457 (P6)

13846 Shank incomplete. L.31, W.29mm 1976–9.13.X, 6347 sf3516 (P6)

13847 L.45, D.25mm 1979–80.14.IV, 1561 sf5010 (P6)

13848 Shank largely missing. L.20, W.16mm 1979–80.14.IV, 4395 sf5154 (P6)

13849 Complete length. Domed head. L.28, W.15mm 1979–80.14.IV, 4395 sf5155 (P6)

13850 Shank only. L.37mm 1978–9.14.II, 1446 sf5169 (P6)

13851 Complete length, shank L-shaped. L.30, W.15, T.4mm 1978–9.14.II, 1506 sf5179 (P6)

13852 Shank incomplete. L.30, W.20mm 1978–9.14.II, 1505 sf5181 (P6)

13853 Shank fragment. 1978–9.14.II, 1526 sf5185 (P6)

13854 Shank incomplete. Domed head. L.17, W.12mm 1978–9.14.II, 1505 sf5214 (P6)

13855 Head only. W.20mm 1978–9.14.II, 1230 sf5229 (P6)

13856 Complete length. L.23, W.18mm 1976–9.13.X, 5292 sf3343 (P7)

13857 Shank tip missing. L.32, W.21mm 1976–9.13.X, 5292 sf3350 (P7)

13858 Shank tip missing. L.23, W.14mm 1976–9.13.X, 5383 sf3367 (P7)

13859 Shank largely missing. W.20mm 1976–9.13.X, 5383 sf3368 (P7)

13860 Complete length. Slightly domed head. L.56, W.16, T.5mm 1976–9.13.X, 5403 sf3370 (P7)

13861 Complete length. L.35, W.20mm 1976–9.13.X, 5410 sf3373 (P7)

13862 Shank incomplete. L.24, W.13mm 1976–9.13.X, 6162 sf3482 (P7)

13863 Complete length. L.37, W.15mm 1976–9.13.X, 6162 sf3484 (P7)

13864 Complete length. L.25, W.18mm 1976–9.13.X, 6267 sf3499 (P7)

13865 In two pieces. Shank incomplete. L.30, W.17mm 1976–9.13.X, 6279 sf3505 (P7)

13866 Shank largely missing. W.20mm 1979–80.14.IV, 4152 sf5128 (P7)

13867 Neatly rounded head, shank incomplete. L.27, W.17mm 1979–80.14.IV, 4152 sf5130 (P7)

13868 Two with incomplete shanks. L.15, D.13mm 1979–80.14.IV, 4187 sf5144 (P7)

13869 Shank tip missing. L.34, W.27mm 1979–80.14.IV, 4194 sf5147 (P7)

13870 Shank incomplete. L.18, W.13mm 1978–9.14.II, 1366 sf5164 (P7)

13871 Shank largely missing. W.17mm 1978–9.14.II, 1242 sf5231 (P7)

13872 Shank tip missing. Domed head. L.45, W.18mm 1978–9.14.II, 1270 sf5234 (P7)

13873 Shank incomplete. L.26, W.19mm 1976–9.13.X, 5210 sf3309 (P8)

13874 Shank largely missing. L.16, W.16mm 1976–9.13.X, 6009 sf3394 (P8)

13875 Shank largely missing. Domed head. L.15, W.25mm 1979–80.14.IV, 4037 sf5116 (P8)

13876 Domed head. L.35, D.20mm 1979–80.14.IV, 4112 sf5123 (P8)

13877 Shank only. (Leaded tin) L.57mm 1979–80.14.IV, 4112 sf5124 (P8)

13878 Shank incomplete. L.20, W.20mm 1978–9.14.II, 1293 sf5158 (P8)

13879 Shank largely missing. L.20, W.27mm 1978–9.14.II, 1338 sf5201 (P8)

13880 Head only. W.13mm 1978–9.14.II, 1151 sf5222 (P8)

13881 Shank largely missing. W.30mm 1978–9.14.II, 1116 sf5254 (P8)

13882 Complete length. L.35, W.23mm 1978–9.14.II, 1117 sf5259 (P8)

13883 Shank largely missing. W.14mm 1978–9.14.II, 1117 sf5261 (P8)

13884 Rectangular head, shank incomplete. L.12, W.20mm 1978–9.14.II, 1117 sf5267 (P8)

13885 Shank incomplete. L.18, W.20mm 1978–9.14.II, 1117 sf5268 (P8)

13886 Complete length. Domed head. L.30, W.18mm 1978–9.14.II, 1117 sf5270 (P8)

13887 Shank largely missing. L.20, W.20mm 1978–9.14.II, 1117 sf5272 (P8)

13888 Complete length. L.35, W.16mm 1978–9.14.II, 1117 sf5271 (P8)

13889 Shank incomplete. L.13, W.15mm 1978–9.14.II, 1117 sf5276 (P8)

Studs

13890 Domed head, shank incomplete. L.30, D.45mm 1976–9.13.X, 7183 sf3431 (P6)

13891 Dished and in the form of a six-petalled flower, grooves radiate from centre running between and down the centre of each petal. Shank incomplete. Plated. L.14, D.39mm 1976–9.13.X, 5180 sf1984 (P7) (Fig.1408)

Bolt

13892 In two pieces. Curved with large domed head at one end. L.c.155, T.10; head: W.28mm 1978–9.14.II, 1588 sfs5219–20 (P5)

Clench bolt

13893 L.48mm 1973–5.13.III, 1216 sf966 (P1)

Staples

All have rectangular cross-sections and tapering arms with wedge-shaped tips, unless otherwise stated.

Rectangular

13894 Overlapping inturned arms. L.20, W.40mm 1976–9.13.X, 5498 sf2539 (P1)

13895 One arm missing. Head has convex sides and is unusually wide. L.31, W.50; head: W.21mm 1978–9.14.II, 1539 sf5216 (P4) (Fig.1408)

13896 Overlapping inturned arms. L.30, W.39, T.10mm 1976–9.13.X, 5292 sf1987 (P7)

13897 One arm. L.62mm 1976–9.13.X, 5292 sf1989 (P7)

13898 One arm incomplete, other clenched. L.25, W.38mm 1976–9.13.X, 5379 sf2208 (P7)

13899 L.41, W.91, T.9mm 1976–9.13.X, 5292 sf2420 (P7)

13900 One arm tip is bent forward and clenched, other arm incomplete. L.31, W.65mm 1976–9.13.X, 5146 sf3332 (P7)

13901 Arms inturned and clenched. L.12, W.48mm 1976–9.13.X, 5340 sf3361 (P7)

13902 One arm incomplete. L.44, W.52mm 1978–9.14.II, 1450 sf5172 (P7)

13903 One arm missing. L.28, W.72mm 1976–9.13.X, 6041 sf3406 (P8)

13904 One arm bent in, other largely missing. L.30, W.68mm 1976–9.13.X, 6064 sf3411 (P8)

Rectangular with pinched corners

Wider faces in same plane as the staple itself

13905 L.66, W.61, T.10mm 1976–9.13.X, 7584 sf2860 (P2)

13906 L.50, W.25mm 1978–9.14.II, 1537 sf5215 (P2)

13907 One arm missing, other incomplete. L.33, W.65, T.9mm 1976–9.13.X, 7436 sf3451 (P3)

13908 Both arms incomplete. L.54, W.47, T.8mm 1976–9.13.X, 7287 sf2670 (P4)

13909 Arms incomplete. L.51, W.61, T.9mm 1976–9.13.X, 7536 sf2793 (P5)

13910 One arm incomplete. L.99, W.48, T.7mm 1976–9.13.X, 7435 sf2754 (P6)

13911 One arm incomplete. L.51, W.60, T.11mm 1976–9.13.X, 6271 sf2400 (P7)

13912 L.66, W.65, T.10mm 1976–9.13.X, 6009 sf2197 (P8) (Fig.1408)

U-shaped

13913 L.50, W.22, T.5mm 1973–5.13.III, 1131 sf967 (P1)

13914 Arms bent forwards. L.53, W.26, T.9mm 1979–80.14.IV, 4472 sf911 (P2)

13915 L.55, W.24, T.5mm 1978–9.14.II, 1668 sf522 (P4)

13916 L.43, W.20mm 1973–5.13.IV, 1609 sf3239 (P5)

13917 One arm incomplete. L.55, W.45mm 1978–9.14.II, 1595 sf5093 (P5)

13918 Diamond-shaped cross-section. L.58, W.33, T.6mm 1979–80.14.IV, 4059 sf572 (P6)

13919 One arm missing. L.75, W.33mm 1976–9.13.X, 5292 sf3349 (P7)

13920 One arm incomplete. L.50, W.22mm 1978–9.14.II, 1456 sf5212 (P7)

13921 Arm tips bent forwards. L.32, W.16mm 1979–80.14.IV, 4037 sf5114 (P8)

13922   One arm largely missing. L.40, W.21mm 1978–9.14.II, 1341 sf5203 (P8)

Looped

13923   Tips out-turned. L.31, W.18mm 1979–80.14.IV, 4395 sf5153 (P6)

Other

13924   Arm: L.19mm 1973–5.13.III, 1131 sf870 (P1)

13925   Arm: L.55mm 1979–80.14.IV, 4407 sf890 (P5)

Wall anchors

13926   Tapering tang flattened at thicker end to form oval terminal which is corroded, but presumably pierced. L.165, T.22; terminal: W.37mm 1978–9.14.II, 1032 sf118 (P9)

13927   Tapering tang, flattened at thicker end to form oval terminal, pierced twice. L.104, T.14; terminal: W.30mm 1979–80.14.IV, 4136 sf653 (P9) (*Fig.1409*)

Eyed bar

13928   Round eye at the thicker end of a tapering spike. L.98, W.28mm 1978–9.14.II, 1156 sf265 (P8) (*Fig.1409*)

Window bar

13929   Central pierced oval area with projecting arm on each side. L.133, W.22, T.6mm 1978–9.14.II, 1123 sf198 (P8) (*Fig.1409*)

Hinge pivots

13930   Flattened elbow. Guide arm: L.47, W.11; shank: L.87, W.13mm 1979–80.14.IV, 4475 sf926 (P3)

13931   Nipped at elbow. Guide arm: L.32, W.8; shank: L.63, W.11mm 1978–9.14.II, 1644 sf443 (P5)

13932   Guide arm: L.33, W.8; shank: L.57, W.10mm 1976–9.13.X, 6303 sf3508 (P5)

13933   Shank tip missing. Guide arm: L.47, W.11; shank: L.68, W.13mm 1978–9.14.II, 1427 sf399 (P7)

13934   Guide arm: L.39, W.5; shank: L.52, W.10mm 1979–80.14.IV, 4185 sf686 (P7)

13935   Shank incomplete. Guide arm: L.32, W.7; shank: L.27, W.11mm 1978–9.14.II, 1360 sf5163 (P7)

13936   Corroded. Guide arm: L.40; shank: L.90, W.7mm 1973–5.13.IV, 1544 sf677 (P8)

13937   Shank largely missing. Guide arm: L.33, W.15; shank: L.41, W.14mm 1976–9.13.X, 5268 sf3317 (P8)

13938   Shank largely missing. Guide arm: L.40, T.9mm 1976–9.13.X, 6165 sf3485 (P8)

13939   Shank incomplete. Guide arm: L.45, W.10; shank: L.46, W.14mm 1979–80.14.IV, 4181 sf5140 (P8)

13940   Shank largely missing. Guide arm: L.40, W.10mm 1978–9.14.II, 1156 sf5224 (P8)

13941   Shank largely missing. Guide arm: L.63, W.15; shank: W.23mm 1978–9.14.II, 1117 sf5255 (P8)

Latch rests

13942   Tip of head missing. L.50, W.13, T.6mm 1978–9.14.II, 1402 sf5206 (P6)

13943   Shank incomplete. L.52, W.33mm 1979–80.14.IV, u/s sf5070

Hooks

All have shanks of rectangular cross-section.

Wall hooks

Shank projects at elbow

13944   Incomplete. L.40mm 1976–9.13.X, 7130 sf3428 (P5)

13945   Shank expands in the centre. Hook: L.21; shank: L.64, T.6mm 1976–9.13.X, 5422 sf2266 (P6) (*Fig.1413*)

13946   Shank: L.72, W.13; hook: L.39, W.15mm 1976–9.13.X, 5410 sf2243 (P7)

Other

13947   The rear half of the shank is widened out into a plate in one face of which there are four indentations; that nearest the hook is cross-shaped. Hook: L.37; shank: L.139, W.27, T.12mm 1973–5.13.III, 1104 sf808 (P1) (*Fig.1413*)

Double hook

13948   Shank head missing, hooks at 90° to each other. L.102, W.52, T.9mm 1976–9.13.X, 6008 sf2090 (P8) (*Fig.1388*)

Swivel hook

13949   Domed head, hook tip missing. L.57; head: D.16mm 1978–9.14.II, 1774 sf656 (P2)

Hinge straps

Pierced once unless stated.

13950   Looped eye at one end which widens out to form strap, pierced twice. L.57, W.23; eye: D.18mm 1978–9.14.II, 1634 sf433 (P5)

13951   Strap terminal. Diamond-shaped; at one end begins to curve over but is broken, at the other expands and is then broken, pierced in centre. L.71, W.21, T.6mm 1978–9.14.II, 1595 sf539 (P5) (*Fig.1417*)

13952   Bifurcated terminal with central arm which widens outwards. Broken over hole. L.61, W.71, T.5mm 1973–5.13.III, 1055 sf731 (P7) (*Fig.1417*)

13953   Closed eye at one end. Pierced four times, two nails in situ. L.119, W.25, T. (across loop) 6; nails: L.25mm 1976–9.13.X, 5180 sf1864 (P7) (*Fig.1417*)

13954   Looped eye at one end, narrows and has rounded tip at the other. Pierced five times. L.110, W.16; eye: D.13mm 1976–9.13.X, 7312 sf2686 (P7) (*Fig.1417*)

13955   Incomplete looped eye at the head, strap incomplete. Plated (tin, little lead). L35, W.20mm 1976–9.13.X, 6152 sf3479 (P7)

13956   Looped eye and fragment of strap. L.30, W.21mm 1976–9.13.X, 6271 sf3501 (P7)

Small hinge straps

13957   Strap stepped in and curves over perhaps to form loop or eye at one end; widens slightly towards the other. Plated. L.36, W.12mm 1979–80.14.IV, 4116 sf534 (P4)

13958   Narrows in to a short stub at one end where broken. Pierced at the other. Two transverse grooves above the hole. Short angled nicks in the face on each side. Plated (tin). L.55, W.13, T.7mm 1976–9.13.X, 5287 sf3338 (P7) (*Fig.1417*)

U-eyed hinges

13959 Stubs of the straps survive. L.53, W.38; eye: W.25mm 1978–9.14.II, 1681 sf518 (P3)

13960 On one side of eye a pierced terminal, other side missing. L.77; terminal: L.29, W.18mm 1978–9.14.II, 1544 sf593 (P5) (*Fig.1418*)

13961 Stubs of the straps survive. L.50; strap: W.46; eye: W.33, T.16mm 1976–9.13.X, 5237 sf2249 (P8)

13962 Two hinges. Stubs of the straps survive on one; the other is corroded, but one incomplete strap survives, pierced twice. L.80, W.33mm 1976–9.13.X, u/s sf2331

Hasp

13963 Incomplete, probably figure-of-eight-shaped. L.66, W.26, T.6mm 1979–80.14.IV, 4462 sf907 (P3)

Pinned hinges

13964 Both members incomplete. The longer narrows towards the base, pierced near head and has a slightly curved cross-section; small notches on each edge. Plated (tin). Members: L.48 and 24, W.27mm 1978–9.14.II, 1406 sf5167 (P6) (*Fig.1420*)

13965 One incomplete strap. It had been folded over the pin at one end. Pierced twice. Plated (tin). L.62, W.22, T.9mm 1976–9.13.X, 7308 sf2691 (P7) (*Fig.1420*)

13966 Second member missing. Surviving member is curved near the hinge. Lower half becomes a thin strip which is incomplete. Upper half is pierced twice and has chamfered edges and small incised triangles in the shoulders at the junction with lower half. Plated. L.83, W.15, T.2mm 1976–9.13.X, u/s sf2763 (*Fig.1420*)

Corner bracket

13967 One arm, in three pieces. At the end, where pierced, it is straight with rounded corners. Largest piece: L.43, W.20, T.2mm 1979–80.14.IV, 4206 sf667 (P7)

Stapled hasps

13968 Hinged. Upper member L-shaped, its upper arm pierced, nail in situ. Lower member has a six lobed 'floreate' panel at the head and then widens with convex sides to the point where staple is attached, after which it begins to narrow before a break. Surface of both arms convex. Plated. Upper member: arms L.20 and 17, W.12; lower member: L.42, W.12mm 1976–9.13.X, 6321 sf2473 (P5) (*Figs.1421–2*)

13969 Incomplete loop at head, below is a circular panel with six grooves around the edge. Below is a plate which widens towards base, but is incomplete. Plated (tin). L.45, W.20mm 1976–9.13.X, 7123 sf3424 (P5) (*Fig.1421*)

13970 Hinged. Upper member incomplete. Lower member has rounded base and is slightly curved in cross-section giving a convex face. Plated. L.82, W.10, T.3mm 1976–9.13.X, 6372 sf2674 (P6) (*Fig.1421*)

13971 Base with rounded end. L.46, W.18mm 1976–9.13.X, 7271 sf2645 (P7)

13972 Very corroded. Survives as plate with convex sides, staple at widest point, and recurved tip; upper part missing. L.c.78, W.25mm 1976–9.13.X, 7257 sf3439 (P7)

13973 Head missing. Now consists of a thin strip which widens near its base with rounded shoulders before narrowing to the tip which is recurved. The staple is set horizontally. L.86, W.22, T.4mm 1976–9.13.X, 5297 sf1961 (P8) (*Fig.1421*)

13974 It has a small loop at the head. The body steps forwards slightly at about one-third of its length. At about mid-point the sides step in, nicks in the face at the corners thus created. Pierced at base. Staple held in one hole in the narrower part. Above step forward the face has punched dots. Plated (tin-lead). L.84, W.28, T.2mm 1976–9.13.X, 6034 sf2097 (P9) (*Figs.1421–2*)

Drop handle

13975 At each end there is a looped terminal with recurved tip. L.29, W.87, T.8mm 1973–5.13.III, 1216 sf918 (P1) (*Fig.1423*)

Fittings

They are described as either strips or plates using the same criteria as for bar iron, blanks and scrap (see p.3025). Those which were probably parts of hinges or corner brackets are described as straps.

All have a rectangular cross-section and are pierced once unless stated.

Plates

13976 Originally U-shaped, both arms incomplete. One arm a strip with diagonal grooves cut into surface. Other arm, now distorted, widens out into a plate, waisted near broken end, pierced in centre, punched dots on surface. Plated. Original L.61, W.25mm 1973–5.13.III, 1099 sf815 (P1) (*Fig.1425*)

13977 Broken at each end, slightly curved in cross-section. Plated (tin, trace of lead). L.46, W.21mm 1976–9.13.X, 7521 sf3456 (P3)

13978 In two pieces. Hole at one end. L.70, W.22mm 1979–80.14.IV, 1743 sf5063 (P3)

13979 Roughly rectangular, pierced in one corner. L.90, W.83mm 1978–9.14.II, 1588 sf412 (P5)

13980 Pierced at one end, shallow channel along the centre of one face. L.133, W.25, T.5mm 1978–9.14.II, 1455 sf342 (P6)

13981 Irregular shape, small rectangular slot/hole cut out of one side. L.50, W.47mm 1976–9.13.X, 7303 sf2692 (P6)

13982 Rounded end, nail head in situ. Plated (tin, some lead: solder). L.21, W.18mm 1976–9.13.X, 6322 sf3512 (P6)

13983 Semi-circular, straight side broken. Pierced twice. Plated (tin). L.68, W.46mm 1979–80.14.IV, 4275 sf743 (P7)

13984 Corroded. L.147, W.22, T.10mm 1979–80.14.IV, 4121 sf796 (P7)

13985 Pierced at one end, broken at the other. L.88, W.17, T.3mm 1976–9.13.X, 5162 sf1852 (P7)

13986 Corroded. Broken at each end, narrows towards one end where broken across a hole. L.90, W.22mm 1976–9.13.X, 7393 sf2748 (P7)

13987 Curved over and broken at one end. Pierced twice, hole at broken end larger. L.52, W.25mm 1976–9.13.X, 5292 sf3347 (P7)

13988 Broken at one end. Pierced twice. L.68, W.10mm 1976–9.13.X, 5292 sf3348 (P7)

13989 One side irregular. Hole near other side, rivet in situ. L.33, W.22mm 1976–9.13.X, 5367 sf3365 (P7)

13990 Rounded at one end, possibly broken at the other. L.65, W.15mm 1976–9.13.X, 7316 sf3445 (P7)

13991   One end rounded, other broken. Large hole at rounded end, smaller hole nearby. L.50, W.30mm 1979–80.14.IV, 4332 sf5079 (P7)

13992   L.28, W.22mm 1979–80.14.IV, 4185 sf5143 (P7)

13993   One end rounded, other broken. Slightly curved in cross-section. Pierced twice. Plated. L.47, W.23mm 1978–9.14.II, 1601 sf427 (P8)

13994   Narrows, broken at each end. L.69, W.20, T.4mm 1979–80.14.IV, 4060 sf487 (P8)

13995   Two, largest broken at each end. Largest: L.126, W.23, T.2mm 1979–80.14.IV, 4154 sf535 (P8)

13996   Broken at each end, nail in situ. L.65, W.22mm 1976–9.13.X, 5268 sf3314 (P8)

13997   Two pieces which do not join. Curved in cross-section. L.35 and 33, W.30mm 1976–9.13.X, 6064 sf3410 (P8)

13998   Pierced four times, holes of various sizes. L.36, W.35mm 1978–9.14.II, 1326 sf5200 (P8)

13999   Broken over hole at one end. L.43, W.23mm 1978–9.14.II, 1117 sf5263 (P8)

14000   Broken over hole at each end. L.35, W.20mm 1117 sf5266 (P8)

14001   Pierced in the centre. L.66, W.38mm 1976–9.13.X, 6201 sf2254 (P9)

14002   Corroded. L.100, W.35mm 1978–9.14.II, u/s sf187

14003   L.115, W.35mm 1978–9.14.II, u/s sf326

Straps

14004   Slightly rounded and pierced terminal at one end; had bifurcated and scrolled terminals at the other, one survives. L.124, W.22, T.6mm 1976–9.13.X, 7519 sf2784 (P3) (Fig.1425)

14005   Incomplete strap terminal existing as two plates. Upper plate has fragment of strap surviving, groove across head. Terminal round with a dome on upper face, pierced near the tip. Plated (tin-lead alloy). Lower plate similar but fragmentary, terminal flat. Between plates remains of ?leather. Wood remains on lower face of lower plate. L.36, W.19mm 1976–9.13.X, 6262 sf3497 (P7) (Fig.1425)

Strips

14006   A rounded pierced terminal at each end, one slightly larger than the other, nail fragments in situ. Each has incised grooves cut radially. Plated (tin). L.52, W.21mm 1976–9.13.X, 7609 sf3471 (P2) (Fig.1425)

14007   Curved, narrows and broken across piercing at wider end. L.60, W.20mm 1978–9.14.II, 1608 sf5098 (P2)

14008   Tapers, pierced at the thicker end. L.133, W.9, T.5mm 1978–9.14.II, 1668 sf523 (P4)

14009   D-shaped, pierced terminal at each end. L.19, T.2mm 1976–9.13.X, 6342 sf2631 (P4)

14010   Tapers, pierced at one end, rivet in situ. L.54, W.7, T.2mm 1978–9.14.II, 1614 sf5101 (P6)

14011   Pierced rounded terminal and stub. Plated (tin). L.23mm 1978–9.14.II, 1424 sf5208 (P6)

14012   Corroded. Pierced oval terminal at one end. L.45, W.8mm 1976–9.13.X, 5292 sf3340 (P7)

14013   Broken over holes at each end. L.31, W.3mm 1976–9.13.X, 5292 sf3354 (P7)

14014   Round terminal only, nail head in situ, and stub. L.20, W.14, T.4mm 1976–9.13.X, 5144 sf3327 (P8)

14015   Broken at each end. Plated (tin-lead). L.40, W.8mm 1976–9.13.X, 6009 sf3398 (P8)

14016   In two pieces. Widens from the centre towards one end which is cut in a deep zig-zag and pierced. At other end an incomplete rounded terminal. D-shaped cross-section. Plated (tin). L.113, W.13mm 1979–80.14.IV, 4165 sf5132 (P8) (Fig.1425)

14017   In two pieces, both broken at each end; at end of one a pierced lozenge-shaped expansion. Plated (tin). L.69, W.10, T.2mm 1978–9.14.II, 1189 sf5228 (P8)

14018   Spirally twisted fitting, at one end an incomplete rounded pierced terminal, other end missing. L.65; terminal: W.16mm 1976–9.13.X, 5348 sf3362 (P7)

Mount

14019   Pierced disc in centre with short 'ears' on opposite sides, pierced with non-ferrous rivets in situ. L.21, W.11mm 1978–9.14.II, 1340 sf5202 (P8)

Suspension fitting

14020   In three pieces. U-shaped eye, each end of which widens out into a strap, both pierced twice. L.90, W.50mm 1978–9.14.II, 1584 sf5218 (P5)

Swivel fitting

14021   Consists of an incomplete link which at one end (probably the base) appears to have a smaller eye set in it and at the other (probably the head) it is pierced. Set in the piercing is a strip with a spirally twisted loop at the head and a domed knop at the base. L.88mm 1978–9.14.II, 1486 sf405 (P5) (Fig.1428)

Chain links

Figure-of-eight-shaped

14022   Incomplete. L.58, W.10, T.2mm 1976–9.13.X, 5147 sf1847 (P7)

14023   Incomplete. L.55, W.12mm 1976–9.13.X, 5341 sf2247 (P7)

14024   Half. L.30, W.20mm 1979–80.14.IV, 4112 sf5122 (P8)

Other forms

14025   Incomplete oval link. L.60mm 1979–80.14.IV, 4493 sf5074 (P1)

14026   Oval link in two pieces. L.c.75, W.45mm 1978–9.14.II, 1588 sf5032 (P5)

14027   Small incomplete link? Eye at one end of shank (?rounded cross-section), other broken. Collar around base of eye. L.20, T.5mm 1978–9.14.II, 1606 sf5097 (P5)

14028   Strip wrapped around with wire, eye at one end, other missing. L.39; eye: W.10mm 1976–9.13.X, 5293 sf1959 (P7) (Fig.1429)

14029   Incomplete oval link. L.75, W.48, T.10mm 1976–9.13.X, 5268 sf3316 (P8)

Rings

14030   Oval. Rounded cross-section. W.26, T.4mm 1973–5.13.III, 1216 sf965 (P1)

14031   Half. D.40, T.5mm 1979–80.14.IV, 4482 sf5083 (P1)

14032   Incomplete. Rounded cross-section. Plated (bronze) — perhaps made from brazed iron strips. L.56, T.10mm 1973–5.13.IV, 1592 sf3237 (P5)

14033   D.31, T.4mm 1976–9.13.X, 5237 sf2190 (P8)

14034   Half and roughly formed. D.78, W.11mm 1976–9.13.X, 5268 sf3311 (P8)

14035 Fragment. L.45, T.10mm 1978–9.14.II, 1159 sf5225 (P8)

14036 Half. D.20mm 1978–9.14.II, 1117 sf5258 (P8)

Collars

14037 Circular; overlapping arms. D.20mm 1979–80.14.IV, 4405 sf883 (P4)

14038 One side straight. Possibly plated. L.5, D.17, T.2mm 1978–9.14.II, 1543 sf401 (P5)

14039 Rolled. D.23mm 1976–9.13.X, 5403 sf2426 (P7)

Tubes

14040 Tapers slightly, rectangular cross-section. Plated (quaternary: copper, zinc, tin, lead). L.38, W.16mm 1979–80.14.IV, 4388 sf5152 (P6)

14041 Damaged, widened into a crude flange at one end, broken at the other. L.85, D.20; flange: W.40mm 1976–9.13.X, 7179 sf3430 (P7)

Candleholders

Socketed

14042 L-shaped. Shank: L.30; arm: L.22; socket: D.10mm 1976–9.13.X, 7287 sf3442 (P4)

14043 L-shaped. Shank: L.24; arm: L.29; socket: D.12mm 1976–9.13.X, 7287 sf3443 (P4) (Fig.1432)

14044 L-shaped. Shank: L.60; arm L.80; socket: D.16mm 1976–9.13.X, 5146 sf1854 (P7) (Fig.1432)

14045 T-shaped (tang projects at 90° from the base of the socket). L.74; shank: L.45, T.9; socket: D.16mm 1976–9.13.X, 5146 sf3331 (P7) (Figs.1432–3)

14046 Shank incomplete, but projects above socket. L.50; socket: D.20mm 1976–9.13.X, 6200 sf3489 (P7)

14047 Straight, tang projects above the socket. L.78; socket: D.17mm 1976–9.13.X, 6268 sf3500 (P7)

14048 L-shaped. Shank: L.70; arm: L.30; socket: D.20mm 1976–9.13.X, 6280 sf3506 (P7)

14049 Socket and stub of shank. L.50, D.20mm 1976–9.13.X, 6305 sf3509 (P7)

14050 L-shaped, in two pieces. Shank: L.60; arm: L.40; socket: D.20mm 1976–9.13.X, 6310 sf3510 (P7)

14051 Straight. Near the base two curving arms and another behind the socket at top. L.143; socket: D.17mm 1976–9.13.X, 7193 sf2591 (P8)

Prickets

14052 L-shaped, flattened at elbow, all three arms incomplete. Shank: L.46; arm: L.59mm 1976–9.13.X, 7514 sf2780 (P3)

Locks and keys

Locks

Lock ward plate

14053 Tapers to each end, central hole. L.40, W.10, T.3mm 1976–9.13.X, 6331 sf3513 (P6)

Barrel padlock case

14054 End of case, was recessed into cylinder which has an applied strip around the end. Plated (quaternary: copper, zinc, tin, lead). L.13, D.40mm 1979–80.14.IV, 4188 sf5146 (P8) (Fig.1442)

Barrel padlock spring

14055 Two arms. L.20, W.7mm 1979–80.14.IV, 4343 sf839 (P6)

Barrel padlock bolts

14056 Bolt and closing plate, spine with spring. Brazed to the top of the bolt is a strip which passes through the closing plate to form a second spine. Plated (leaded bronze). L.65, W.25mm 1978–9.14.II, 1575 sf5217 (P4) (Fig.1448)

14057 Part of bolt, rectangular closing plate. Welded to the bolt is a strip which bifurcates before passing through closing plate. Therefore originally three spines. Welded to base of bolt are three small eyes. Plated (leaded bronze). L.37, W.23, T.7mm 1979–80.14.IV, 4353 sf5151 (P7) (Fig.1448)

14058 Part of bolt. Plated (bronze with a little lead). L.51, T.8mm 1978–9.14.II, 1427 sf5209 (P7)

14059 Stub of bolt, closing plate and two spines with faces at 90° to each other, pierced for springs. L.47, W.30mm 1978–9.14.II, 1066 sf5251 (P8)

L-shaped barrel padlock bolt

14060 Incomplete L-shaped bolt. End of shorter arm flattened and widened originally form closing plate to which springs attached. Plated (ternary: copper, zinc, tin, trace lead). Arms L.59, W.26, T.6mm 1976–9.13.X, 7585 sf3466 (P3)

Keys

Keys for mounted locks

Keys with hollow stem

14061 Bit missing. Bow pear-shaped, formed in one piece with stem. L.75; bow: W.20; stem: T.10mm 1979–80.14.IV, 1677 sf5048 (P1)

14062 Bow pear-shaped, oval cross-section. Moulding and collar at head of stem, two grooves around the centre, three grooves around the tip. Bit corroded, but clearly bifurcated. Plated (tin, trace of lead). L.78, bow: W.28; stem: T.12; bit: W.27mm 1976–9.13.X, 7493 sf3454 (P4)

14063 Circular bow. L.100; bow: D.26; stem: T.10; bit: L.23, W.26mm 1979–80.14.IV, 4327 sf816 (P6)

14064 Lozenge-shaped bow. Stem has four groups of encircling grooves. Bit crank-shaped in cross-section. Plated. L.108; bow: L.35, W.40; stem: T.12; bit: L.27, W.29mm 1976–9.13.X, 5292 sf1991 (P7) (Figs.1449, 1451)

14065 Oval bow. Stem has moulding at head and encircling grooves in centre and above the bit. Bit has been slotted into the stem. Plated. L.57; bow: L.20, W.27; bit: L.15, W.26mm 1976–9.13.X, 6200 sf2323 (P7) (Fig.1449)

14066 Incomplete hollow stem and bit, made as one piece. L.35mm 1976–9.13.X, 5292 sf3342 (P7)

14067 Bow incomplete, stem a stub. Grooves around the head of the stem. L.31, T.7mm 1976–9.13.X, 5292 sf3346 (P7)

14068 Circular bow. Stem has a moulding at the head. L.102; bow: D.31, stem: T.13; bit: L.24, W.30mm 1978–9.14.II, 1156 sf263 (P8) (Fig.1449)

14069 Oval bow. L.60; bow: L.19, W.27; stem: T.8; bit: L.18, W.24mm 1976–9.13.X, 6008 sf2160 (P8) (Fig.1449)

Hollow stem, bit with central channel

14070 Bow missing. Bit made in one piece with stem. L.60; stem: T.10; bit: L.24, W.27mm 1976–9.13.X, 5268 sf2045 (P8)

Solid stem projects beyond a bit which does not have a central channel

14071 Bow circular. Stem slightly expanded in the centre and has a moulding at the head; tip projects beyond the bit. Bit has a ward cut in the inner and outer sides, set asymmetrically. L.39; bow: L.15, W.15, T.6; bit: L.10, W.8mm 1978–9.14.II, 1734 sf599 (P1) (*Fig.1449*)

14072 Bow missing. Three groups of three grooves around the stem. Bit incomplete, grooves on the inner side. Plated. L.130; stem: T.10; bit: W.c.30mm 1978–9.14.II, 1141 sf204 (P8)

14073 Oval bow with pinched-out tip. L.93; bow: L.13, W.22; bit: L.19, W.18mm 1976–9.13.X, 5268 sf2065 (P8) (*Fig.1449*)

Solid stem projects beyond a bit which has a central channel

14074 Incomplete D-shaped bow. Stem has moulding at head and encircling grooves over bit and at tip (all indistinct). L.145; stem: T.12; bit: L.32, W.30mm 1976–9.13.X, 5399 sf2235 (P8) (*Fig.1452*)

14075 Incomplete oval bow. Stem has grooves around it at head, in centre and above rear of bit. Plated (tin, trace of lead and copper). L.99; stem: T.10; bit: L.30, W.28mm 1976–9.13.X, 7060 sf3419 (P8) (*Fig.1452*)

14076 Incomplete oval bow. Stem has moulding below bow; three encircling grooves above rear of bit, two near tip. Bit has grooves on inner and outer side. Plated (tin and trace of lead). L.119; stem: T.8; bit: L.31, W.26mm 1973–5.13.IV, 1513 sf1806 (P9) (*Figs.1451–2*)

14077 D-shaped bow. Bit incomplete. L.150; bow: L.30, W.45; stem: T.8mm 1976–9.13.X, 5333 sf2236 (P9)

14078 Corroded. D-shaped bow. Plated. L.195; bow: L.25, W.50; stem: T.8, bit: L.36, W.30mm 1976–9.13.X, u/s sf2262

Solid stem which does not project beyond bit

14079 Bit and stem fragment. L.23, W.14mm 1979–80.14.IV, 4455 sf5106 (P3)

14080 Bow D-shaped. Short stem has a thickened collar (with saltire) above the bit. Bit has horizontal cut below the stem. L.72; bow: L.19, W.32; stem: T.9; bit: L.34, W.27mm 1979–80.14.IV, 4268 sf736 (P6) (*Figs.1451–2*)

14081 Bow incomplete. Stem has double moulding at the head on first of which there are diagonal grooves. Bit has horizontal cut below stem; grooves on the outer side. Plated (tin). L.90; stem: T.10; bit: L.28, W.33mm 1976–9.13.X, 5292 sf2029 (P7) (*Fig.1452*)

14082 Bow missing. Bit has horizontal cut below stem. L.42, W.26, T.7mm 1973–5.13.III, 1055 sf3234 (P7) (*Fig.1452*)

14083 Corroded. D-shaped bow. Bit has horizontal cut below the stem. 1978–9.14.II, 1116 sf192 (P8)

14084 Bow largely missing, but may have had openwork design. Stem rectangular cross-section, thickened slightly at head. Bit has horizontal cut below stem, six teeth along base. Plated (tin). L.56; stem: T.7; bit: L.24, W.22mm 1976–9.13.X, 6195 sf3487 (P8) (*Fig.1452*)

Incomplete keys

14085 Bow fragment. Plated (tin, trace lead). L.25, T.6mm 1976–9.13.X, 5292 sf3355 (P7)

14086 Incomplete D-shaped bow. Plated (tin). L.39, T.5mm 1979–80.14.IV, 4202 sf5149 (P7)

Barrel padlock keys

Bits at 90° to stem

14087 Upper part only. Stem flattened and widened into an oval plate, looped terminal. Plated. L.86, W.19, T.5mm 1978–9.14.II, 1215 sf378 (P6)

14088 Rounded, pierced terminal with faces in same plane as the wider faces of the stem. L.107, W.10; bit: D.20mm 1976–9.13.X, 5125 sf2241 (P8) (*Fig.1453*)

14089 Bit circular. Stem was attached in the centre, stub survives. D.22, L.11mm 1973–5.13.IV, u/s sf764

Latch keys

14090 D-shaped bow. Short stem, multi-chambered bit, now incomplete. Plated. L.79, T.6; bow: L.20, W.39mm 1976–9.13.X, 5204 sf1906 (P7) (*Fig.1459*)

14091 Bow rounded, but with pointed end. Stem steps in just above bit which has a projection from the base. L.92, W.20, T.5mm 1976–9.13.X, 5170 sf2071 (P7) (*Fig.1459*)

Dress, dress accessories and personal ornament

Buckles

D-shaped frame

14092 Convex part has flattened rectangular cross-section, straight part rounded cross-section. Pin in situ. L.53, W.84, T.7mm 1976–9.13.X, 5523 sf3389 (P6) (*Fig.1468*)

14093 Widens outwards slightly from straight side, thickest on the curved side. Plated. L.45, W.41, T.5mm 1979–80.14.IV, 4206 sf681 (P7)

14094 One end missing. Straight part has rectangular cross-section. Curved part thickened in centre and has rounded cross-section. L.33, W.42, T.6mm 1976–9.13.X, 5146 sf3333 (P7)

14095 Rounded cross-section. L.26, T.4mm 1976–9.13.X, 6029 sf2152 (P8)

14096 Widens outwards slightly from straight side. Straight side has rounded cross-section; rest rectangular cross-section. Pin has looped eye. L.32, W.33, T.3mm 1978–9.14.II, 1117 sf5274 (P8)

Rectangular frame

14097 In two pieces. Sides flattened towards outer edge and have diagonal incised grooves on one face. Plated (tin). L.66, W.31, T.11mm 1978–9.14.II, 1608 sfs5099–100 (P2) (*Fig.1469*)

Circular frame

14098 D.15mm 1976–9.13.X, 6008 sf3391 (P8)

T-shaped frame

14099 Incomplete. Originally shorter end rotated, looped terminal survives on one side. L.51, W.88mm 1976–9.13.X, 5486 sf2515 (P6) (*Fig.1469*)

Frames with rotating arm

14100 Arm only. Plated (leaded tin). L.48, W.11mm 1978–9.14.II, 1366 sf5165 (P7)

14101 Incomplete. Survives as rotating arm and terminal at the head of one side. Arm: L.71; side: L.31mm 1976–9.13.X, 5144 sf1838 (P8)

14102 Frame incomplete. Plated. L.44, W.36mm 1978–9.14.II, 1117 sf211 (P8)

Rectangular frame with rotating tube

14103 Sides rounded cross-section, ends rectangular cross-section. Pin. L.55, W.71mm 1979–80.14.IV, 4059 sf5119 (P6) (*Fig.1469*)

Buckle with integral buckle-plate

14104 Frame widens outwards, pierced for pin at junction with buckle-plate, now largely missing. Plated (tin, trace lead). L.21, W.14, T.3mm 1976–9.13.X, 6321 sf3511 (P5) (*Fig.1467*)

Incomplete frames

14105 Half a frame which was oval or D-shaped. Groove in centre of the thickest part. Possibly plated. W.24, T.6mm 1979–80.14.IV, 4482 sf5082 (P1)

Frame fragments

14106 Plated (leaded tin). 1976–9.13.X, 5204 sf3308 (P7)

14107 Diamond-shaped cross-section. Plated. L.51, T.4mm 1976–9.13.X, u/s sf2480

Buckle-pin

14108 Looped eye. L.30, D.15mm 1973–5.13.III, u/s sf1015

Strap-end

14109 Rectangular with a kink in the middle, folded over at one end, two semi-circular cuts one on each side near opposite end. Pierced three times, twice near folded end and once at other, rivets in situ. Diagonal grooves on the surface of the kink. Plated (tin). Leather remains at folded end. L.46, W.18mm 1978–9.14.II, 1606 sf5095 (P5) (*Fig.1476*)

Pin

14110 Ball head, collar at head of stem which is incomplete. Plated (tin). L.26, T.8mm 1976–9.13.X, 7245 sf3437 (P8)

Boot plates

14111 Two rectangular holes in each arm. L.53, W.58; branch: W.11mm 1976–9.13.X, 6000 sf2048 (P9)

14112 One arm incomplete, the other a stub. Five rectangular holes. L.53, W.14, T.5mm 1978–9.14.II, 1000 sf852 (P9)

Medical and toilet implements

Fleam

14113 Shank incomplete. L.40; blade: W.16mm 1979–80.14.IV, 4185 sf5142 (P7)

Tweezers

14114 U-shaped head, wedge-shaped arms. L.38, W.18mm 1976–9.13.X, 7087 sf3422 (P7)

Literacy

Styli

14115 Short flattened triangular eraser. Shank of rounded cross-section. L.100, W.12, T.7mm 1976–9.13.X, 5451 sf2387 (P7)

14116 The eraser is rounded with an open kidney-shaped centre and a straight top on which there are zig-zag grooves in pairs. The stem tapers, but the tip is missing. At the head is a block collar each face with incised saltire and in centre a nick out of the edges. Around the stem traces of criss-cross grooves. Plated (tin). L.78; eraser: L.23, W.25; stem: T.8mm 1976–9.13.X, u/s sf2801 (*Fig.1502*)

Music and recreation

Jew's harp

14117 One arm tip broken. Copper alloy pin. L.57, W.26, T.6mm 1976–9.13.X, u/s sf3380 (*Fig.1517*)

Riding equipment

Spurs

Rowel spurs

14118 Curved arms, one incomplete. Complete arm has a D-shaped cross-section and at tip recurves to a double-eyed terminal. Rowel box formed from two U-shaped projections with pierced terminals. Below the rowel box is a projecting oval plate. Set in the terminal is a hooked fitting with a central disc. Plated. L.126; arm: T.10; rowel box: L.42; fitting: L.27mm 1976–9.13.X, 6174 sf2446 (P7) (*Fig.1523*)

14119 Fragment of back, rowel box and rowel. Plated (tin). L.35mm 1976–9.13.X, 6162 sf3483 (P7)

14120 Back and crank-shaped rowel chamber with six-pointed rowel. Plated. L.32, W.31mm 1979–80.14.IV, 4189 sf626 (P8) (*Fig.1523*)

Arm terminal

14121 Looped terminal with stub of arm. Plated (tin). L.34, W.8, T.5mm 1979–80.14.IV, 4047 sf5115 (P8)

Horse equipment

Bits

14122 Possible cheek piece. Consists of two circular elements connected by a short strip of D-shaped cross-section. The first element has one slightly concave face, a central hole and three equally spaced projections from the edge. The second is incomplete, but was originally pierced four times. Plated (mercury gilded silver). L.60, W.31, T.8mm 1973–5.13.III, 1131 sf858 (P1) (*Fig.1524*)

14123 Possible cheek piece from bar bit. Domed head, shank flattened to wedge tip. Plated. L.113, T.9; head: D.12mm 1978–9.14.II, 1470 sf367 (P7) (*Fig.1524*)

Horseshoes

Wavy outer side

14124 Complete except for end of right branch. Slightly wavy side. Thickened calkin. Three countersunk holes in each arm, one nail in situ, D-shaped head. L.89, W.93, T.7; nail: L.30mm 1973–5.13.IV, 1640 sf777 (P1)

14125 Branch fragment. Two countersunk holes, thickened calkin. L.75, W.18mm 1976–9.13.X, 5498 sf3387 (P1)

14126 End of branch. One countersunk hole, thickened calkin. L.70, W.30mm 1978–9.14.II, 1774 sf5062 (P2)

14127 Left branch. Slightly wavy side. Turned-over calkin. Three countersunk holes. L.100, W.26mm 1979–80.14.IV, 4200 sf658 (P5)

14128 End of right branch, one countersunk hole. L.74, W.19, T.3mm 1973–5.13.III, 1100 sf804 (P5)

14129 One complete branch and part of second. Three countersunk holes, one with nail, and additional hole at head, tapers to tip. L.107, W.21mm 1976–9.13.X, 5523 sf3390 (P6)

14130 Fragment of small horseshoe. One countersunk hole. L.63, W.21mm 1978–9.14.II, 1117 sf5257 (P8)

Smooth outer side

14131 Branch fragment. Two rectangular holes. Lower face convex. L.60, W.26, T.4mm 1976–9.13.X, 7519 sf2782 (P3)

14132 Part of branch, three rectangular holes. L.90, W.30mm 1976–9.13.X, 7613 sf3472 (P3)

14133 Part of branch. One rectangular hole. L.83, W.30mm 1978–9.14.II, 1634 sf5196 (P5)

14134 Branch. Three rectangular holes. L.100, W.30mm 1978–9.14.II, 1266 sf5233 (P6)

14135 Left branch. Two rectangular holes. L.100, W.23, T.5mm 1976–9.13.X, 7297 sf2682 (P7)

14136 Part of branch, one possible hole. L.95, W.30mm 1976–9.13.X, 6262 sf3494 (P7)

14137 End of right branch. Nail in rectangular hole. L.64, W.26mm 1979–80.14.IV, 4275 sf5089 (P7)

14138 Upper part of both branches, two countersunk holes in one, one in the other. L.50, W.80, T.6; branch: W.33mm 1979–80.14.IV, 4189 sf631 (P8)

14139 Fragment, one rectangular hole. L.50, W.25, T.4mm 1978–9.14.II, 1117 sf5275 (P8)

14140 Left branch. Three small rectangular holes. L.120, W.30, T.5mm 1976–9.13.X, 6003 sf2098 (P9)

Indeterminate outer side

14141 Branch fragment, one rectangular hole. L.60, W.30mm 1979–80.14.IV, 4479 sf5076 (P2)

14142 Branch fragment two possibly elliptical holes, nail in one. L.66, W.23mm 1976–9.13.X, 6345 sf3514 (P3)

14143 End of branch. Turned-over calkin. L.38, W.22, T.11mm 1978–9.14.II, 1606 sf5096 (P5)

14144 Branch fragment. One rectangular hole. L.52, W.26mm 1978–9.14.II, 1420 sf5168 (P6)

14145 End of branch. Part of one countersunk hole. Tapered and thickened at tip. L.59, W.18, T.17mm 1979–80.14.IV, 4206 sf677 (P7)

14146 End of right branch. Turned-over calkin, two countersunk holes, one with nail in situ. L.72, W.26, T.6mm 1976–9.13.X, 5404 sf2232 (P7)

14147 End of branch. L.65, W.30mm 1976–9.13.X, 6256 sf3493 (P7)

14148 Corroded fragment. 1978–9.14.II, 1183 sf234 (P8)

14149 End of right branch. One countersunk hole, recurved calkin. L.60, W.29, T.5mm 1976–9.13.X, 5125 sf2238 (P8)

14150 Branch fragment. One incomplete rectangular hole. L.60, W.35mm 1976–9.13.X, 6089 sf3414 (P8)

14151 Very corroded. L.100, W.28mm 1976–9.13.X, 6003 sf3542 (P9)

14152 Very corroded. L.99, W.30, T.6mm 1973–5.13.IV, u/s sf713

Horseshoe nails

22 horseshoe nails were recorded, details available in archive.

Weapons and armour

Arrowheads

Tanged

14153 Leaf-shaped blade, lozenge-shaped cross-section. L.148; blade: L.140, W.22, T.8mm 1976–9.13.X, 7287 sf2669 (P4) (*Fig.1532*)

Socketed leaf-shaped blade

14154 Blade incomplete, rivet hole in socket. L.53; blade: L.27, W.11; socket: D.11mm 1979–80.14.IV, 4200 sf5148 (P5)

Socketed tapering blade

14155 Small rivet in socket. L.50, D.10mm 1978–9.14.II, 1341 sf5204 (P8)

Socketed barbed blade

14156 Barbs reach to end of socket, rivet hole in socket. L.52, W.20; socket: D.10mm 1979–80.14.IV, 4445 sf5065 (P2)

14157 Barbs extend almost to base of socket. L.90; blade: W.28; socket: D.10mm 1978–9.14.II, 1560 sf428 (P5) (*Fig.1532*)

14158 Lozenge-shaped cross-section. L.51, W.13; socket: D.10mm 1976–9.13.X, 7231 sf3435 (P5) (*Fig.1532*)

14159 Short barbs, lozenge-shaped cross-section. L.88; blade: L.49, W.21, T.6; socket: D.11mm 1973–5.13.III, 1075 sf740 (P6) (*Fig.1532*)

14160 Short barbs. Rivet in socket (not drawn). L.71; blade: W.17; socket: D.12mm 1976–9.13.X, 5379 sf2211 (P7) (*Fig.1532*)

14161 Barbs reach to mid-point of socket. L.38, W.11, D.6mm 1976–9.13.X, 6271 sf3503 (P7)

14162 Blade tip missing. Short barbs. L.37, W.15; socket: D.9mm 1979–80.14.IV, 4206 sf5081 (P7)

14163 Socket reaches to tip. Short little barbs lie flat against side of blade. L.41, D.14mm 1976–9.13.X, 6041 sf3405 (P8)

14164 Short barbs. L.43; blade: W.11; socket: D.10mm 1978–9.14.II, 1117 sf5262 (P8)

Socket of bolt

14165 L.48, D.8mm 1979–80.14.IV, u/s sf5086

Arrow tips

14166 L.34, D.10mm 1976–9.13.X, 7229 sf3433 (P6)

14167 Plated (leaded bronze). L.44, D.10mm 1976–9.13.X, 7622 sf3474 (P6) (*Fig.1532*)

14168 Possibly plated. L.35, D.12mm 1979–80.14.IV, 4202 sf5073 (P7)

14169 Plated (leaded bronze). L.49, D.11mm 1976–9.13.X, 5145 sf3329 (P8)

14170 Plated (bronze with a little lead). L.25, D.9mm 1978–9.14.II, 1117 sf5260 (P8)

Copper alloy

Manufacturing waste

14171 Bar, irregularly shaped, of irregular section. L.49.1, W.5.3, T.4.7mm 1976–9.13.X, 6009 sf2196 (P8) (*Fig.1324*)

14172 Offcut or strip, one end bent up. L.107.3, W.3.1, T.1.9mm 1976–9.13.X, 7450 sf2762 (P5) (*Fig.1324*)

Textile tools

Needles

14173 Incomplete, broken across eye. D.2, L.64.7mm 1973–5.13.III, 1131 sf822 (P1A)

14174 Incomplete, head broken away. D.1.8, L.60.6mm 1973–5.13.III, 1131 sf889 (P1A) (*Fig.1348*)

14175 Flat lozenge-shaped head with punched circular eye. L.74.6, W.4.5mm; shank: D.2.6mm 1978–9.14.II, 1606 sf500 (P5) (*Fig.1348*)

14176 With eye made by splitting end of shank, head bent up, tip of triangular section. D.1.5, L.44.6mm 1978–9.14.II, 1193 sf239 (P7)

14177 With triangular-sectioned tip, flattened head broken across pierced eye. D.2.1, L.80.1mm 1976–9.13.X, 6271 sf2370 (P7) (*Fig.1348*)

14178 Made from folded or rolled strip, drawn to point at one end, head flattened and cut to lozenge shape with round eye. D.1.7, L.38mm 1976–9.13.X, 6271 sf2384 (P7) (*Figs.1347–8*)

14179 Large, with large sub-oval eye punched into flattened head. D.2.8, L.109mm 1976–9.13.X, 5125 sf2008 (P8) (*Fig.1347–8*)

14180 Of circular section, head sub-lozenge-shaped with circular pierced eye. D.2.3, L.77mm 1978–9.14.II, 1603 sf414 (P9) (*Fig.1348*)

14181 Oval eye set in a groove, lower end of shank of triangular section. L.87,W.3, T.2.5mm 1973–5.13.IV, 1512 sf629 (P9)

14182 Broken across eye which is set in a groove, shank bent in four places. D.3, L.110mm 1976–9.13.X 6000 sf2260 (P9)

14183 Circular eye set into flattened upper end, short shank. D.2, L.33mm 1976–9.13.X 7291 sf2712 (P9)

Netting needle

14184 Split at each end to make open-ended eyes. D.1.4, L.86.9mm 1973–5.13.III, 1034 sf679 (P9) (*Fig.1349*)

Thimbles

14185 Small, thin with low sides, conical cap, two grooves around mouth, lower pits arranged in vertical rows, others in rings. D.16.8, T.0.9, H.14.6mm 1976–9.13.X, 5268 sf2063 (P8) (*Fig.1347*)

14186 Tall, narrow with tapering sides, pits seem arranged in irregular spiral. D.14.5, T.0.9, H.18.4mm 1976–9.13.X, 6008 sf2066 (P8) (*Fig.1347*)

14187 Two fragments with large spiral pits. W.17.5, T.1, H.17.7mm 1976–9.13.X, 6015 sf2072 (P8)

14188 Open-topped, ornamental band at top and mouth, pits arranged in a spiral. D.19.2, T.1.8, H.14.8mm 1976–9.13.X, 7013 sf2324 (P8)

Other tools

Knives

Knife hilt-plate

14189 Sub-rectangular, one end rounded, of sheet, with rectangular hole for attachment of scale tang. L.15, W.10, T.1.2mm 1978–9.14.II, 1595 sf515 (P5) (*Fig.1364*)

Domestic equipment

Spoon

14190 In three adjoining fragments, with flat, leaf-shaped bowl and long tapering handle of circular section. L.161.5mm; handle section: D.3mm; bowl: L.35.8, W.16.5, T.1.4mm 1973–5.13.IV, 1607 sf734 (P6) (*Fig.1387*)

Vessels

Cast vessels

Bases

14191 Fragment, sub-circular, sides splayed out. D.45.4, H.9.5mm; section: T.3.9mm 1979–80.14.IV, 4369 sf857 (P6) (*Fig.1394*)

14192 Or casting debris fragment, flat bottomed, no soot blackening. L.75.9, W.42.9, T.6.7mm 1976–9.13.X, 5146 sf1976 (P7)

Legs

14193 Leg and foot fragment from skillet or ewer, well made with small collar above foot. L.66.8, W.23.6, T.16.8mm 1973–5.13.IV, 1552 sf697 (P8) (*Fig.1394*)

14194 Fragment, foot and part of leg with flattened section and shallow midrib. L.52.4, W.34.9, T.12.1mm 1976–9.13.X, 5114 sf1801 (P8) (*Fig.1394*)

Rims

14195 Nine fragments, all distorted, four from rim with large perforations close to rim, all with ragged, thin and pitted lower edges. L.44.4, W.23.1, T.1.8mm 1976–9.13.X, 6246 sf2349 (P7)

14196 Fragment, with angular upper edge. L.71.5, W.14.4, T.5.2mm 1976–9.13.X, 6262 sf2492 (P7)

14197 Fragment, possibly from cooking vessel. L.75, W.56.8, T.6.7mm 1973–5.13.IV, 1544 sf662 (P8) (*Fig.1394*)

14198 Fragment from shallow vessel, one edge broken across perforation just below rim. L.44.7, W.23.8, T.2mm 1976–9.13.X, 6064 sf2154 (P8) (*Fig.1394*)

14199 Fragment, possibly cast, irregularly shaped, with remains of perforation in one edge. L.38.2, W.15.2, T.2.3mm 1978–9.14.II, u/s sf595

Handle

14200 Fragment, of oval section, slightly curved. L.36.8, W.23.6, T.5.9mm 1978–9.14.II, 1034 sf123 (P8) (*Fig.1394*)

14201 Fragment with ridged moulding. L.53.1, W.21.7, T.10.1mm 1976–9.13.X, 5245 sf1949 (P8) (*Fig.1394*)

Body fragments

14202 L.58, W.41.7, T.3.1mm 1976–9.13.X, 5326 sf2014 (P6)

14203 From thin cast cooking pot, soot blackening on outer face. L.49.2, W.31.9, T.1.7mm 1976–9.13.X, 5326 sf2027 (P6)

14204 L.80, W.29, T.1.7mm 1976–9.13.X, 5465 sf2500 (P6)

14205 L.26.3, W.13.3, T.2.8mm 1976–9.13.X, 6200 sf2279 (P7)

14206 Or bell fragment, with angled profile. L.27.4, W.19.6, T.5.4mm 1976–9.13.X, 6262 sf2499 (P7)

14207 Soot blackening on outer surface. L.50.6, W.30.4, T.2.2mm 1976–9.13.X, 5163 sf1858 (P8)

14208 Sub-rectangular, one edge rounded, with raised lug. L.23.2, W.16.3, T.12.7mm 1976–9.13.X, 5237 sf1892 (P8) (*Fig.1394*)

Sheet vessels

14209 Fragment, bent up. L.64.6, W.18.2, T.1.7mm 1973–5.13.IV, 1067 sf724 (P8)

14210 Rim fragment. L.39.8, W.15.7, T.1.3mm 1973–4.13.III, 1034 sf664 (P9)

Patches

14211 Of sheet, sub-trapezoidal, with rectangular slot close to one corner. L.40.5, W.24, T.2mm 1978–9.13.X, 7488 sf2775 (P4)

14212 Lozenge-shaped plate with slots in corners, one containing rivet made from folded sheet. L.49.6, W.40, T.1mm 1978–9.13.X, 5292 sf1985 (P7)

14213 Two fragments, larger with slots for rivets, smaller retains one rivet made from folded sheet. L.35.2, W.30, T.1.4mm 1978–9.13.X, 5403 sf2419 (P7)

14214 Fragment, originally circular plate of sheet, slots for rivets round edge and two rivets made from folded sheet in body of plate. D.165.8, T.1.3mm 1978–9.13.X, 5211 sf1910 (P8)

14215 Four fragments of copper sheet, all with slots for folded sheet rivets around the edge, some still containing rivets. L.54.3, W.27.6, T.1.6mm 1978–9.13.X, 5084 sf1833 (P9)

Rivets

14216 Sub-square, made from folded strip. L.10.3, W.10, T.3.5mm 1979–80.14.IV, 4438 sf898 (P3)

14217 Made from folded sheet. L.26.3, W.16.6, T.2.8mm 1978–9.13.X, 5354 sf2178 (P8)

14218 Made from folded sheet, unused. L.24.0, W.17.0, T.1.6mm 1978–9.13.X, 7163 sf2589 (P8) (*Fig.1399*)

Structural items and fittings

Tacks

14219 Or rivet shank, of circular section. D.1.4, L.6.7mm 1978–9.14.II, 1486 sf385 (P5)

14220 With sub-oval head, irregular shank. L.8.1mm; head: L.2.6, W.2.4mm 1978–9.14.II, 1505A sf949 (P6) (*Fig.1408*)

14221 Or rivet, with flat sub-circular head, shank of circular section. L.12.3mm; shank section: D.1.2mm; head: D.3.6mm 1976–9.13.X, 7435 sf2756 (P6)

14222 Two nail shank fragments. L.19.8, W.4, T.3.5mm 1979–80.14.IV, 4345 sf829 (P7)

14223 Shank fragment, head broken off. L.11.3, W.1.8, T.1.8mm 1976–9.13.X, 7264 sf2641 (P7)

Staples

14224 Made from strip with pointed ends, bent into trapezoidal shape. L.25.2mm, W.3.5, T.1.3mm 1976–9.13.X, 5488 sf2520 (P5)

14225 Sub-rectangular, cut from sheet, pointed ends. L.44.6, W.11.4, T.1.3mm 1976–9.13.X, 5180 sf1979 (P7)

14226 U-shaped, of circular section, with pointed tips. L.16.2, W.11.5, T.2.9mm 1976–9.13.X, 6065 sf2180 (P8) (*Fig.1408*)

14227 Or fitting, made from strip bent at centre with out-turned forked ends. L.26.8, W.11.7, T.1mm 1976–9.13.X, 6143 sf2228 (P8) (*Fig.1408*)

Knops

14228 Or stud, collared globular head on short shank. D.5.7, L.11.3mm 1978–9.14.II, 1215 sf372 (P6) (*Fig.1408*)

14229 Or mount, domed, of rectangular section, collared, short shank. L.10.4, W.8.2, H.13mm; shank section: D.3mm 1979–80.14.IV, 4191 sf670 (P7) (*Fig.1408*)

14230 Incomplete, terminal and part of circular-sectioned shank survive, terminal with collared knop at end and another below, shank broken below second knop. Terminal: D.4.6mm; shank: D.2.6, L.24.5mm 1979–80.14.IV, 4102 sf5021 (P7)

Binding strips

14231 Five adjoining fragments, of U-shaped section, one with rivet. L.12, W.4.1, T.0.3mm; rivet: D.2.2, L.10.2mm 1973–5.13.III, 1099 sf828 (P1)

14232 U-sectioned. L.45.2, W.2.5, T.0.4mm 1973–5.13.III, 1225 sf945 (P1A) (*Fig.1427*)

14233 Three fragments, of U-shaped section. L.31.5, W.2.5, T.0.2mm 1973–5.13.III, 1225 sf948 (P1A)

14234 Two fragments, of U-shaped section. L.25.7, W.3.3, T.0.4mm 1973–5.13.III, 1138 sf3533 (P1A)

14235 Of D-shaped section with flattened ends; incised line and beaded decoration. L.62.9, W.3.3, T.2.3mm 1978–9.14.III, 1560 sf424 (P5)

14236 Fragment, of D-shaped section, with mercury silvering, rivet at one end, other end broken. L.22.2, W.3.5, T.1.7mm 1978–9.14.III, 1494 sf507 (P5)

14237 Fragment of U-shaped section with rivet. L.6.5, W.4.7, T.0.5mm 1978–9.14.III, 1245 sf343 (P6)

14238 Fragment, made from folded-over strip, curved. L.18.6, W.5.3, T.3.4mm 1973–5.13.III, 1065 sf769 (P6)

14239 Bent up into rectangle, one end broken, other with perforation. L.13, W.10.9mm; section: W.4, T.0.7mm 1979–80.14.IV, 4073 sf473 (P7)

14240 With ring terminal, incomplete D-sectioned strip. L.10.3, W.2.5, T.1.4mm; terminal: D.5.2mm 1979–80.14.IV, 4068 sf467 (P9)

Hinges

14241 Plate fragment, irregularly shaped, both ends broken, one obliquely across two perforations. L.20.2, W.14.5, T.0.8mm 1976–9.13.X, 7606 sf3536 (P3)

14242 Incomplete, sub-rectangular, folded over longitudinally to form tube along one long edge, other long edge decorated with cut out trefoils and incised zig-zags between. Two rectangular but incomplete strips have been attached at back by pairs of rivets which perforate both sides. L.46.4, W.12.1mm; plate: T.0.4mm; tubular side: D.3.5mm 1976–9.13.X, 5486 sf2519 (P6) (*Fig.1420*)

14243 A pair of folded plates, both pairs incomplete, one containing two iron rivets, the other with three rivet holes. L.30.7, W.12.1, T.3.1mm; plate: T.1mm 1976–9.13.X, 7349 sf2729 (P7) (*Fig.1420*)

Hook

14244 Of rectangular section, with flattened and pierced sub-triangular terminal, shaft tapering and curving up to other end. L.49.4, W.7.7, T.2.7mm; stem: W.3.5mm 1973–9.13.III, 1216 sf928 (P1A)

Swivel fitting

14245 Pierced terminal, trapezoidal collar, shank of circular section broken at lower end. L.15.1, W.6.7, T.4.1mm; shank section: D.2.4mm 1976–9.13.X, 7550 sf2798 (P6) (*Fig.1428*)

Chains

14246 Link fragment, made of wire, one end curved round. L.15.9mm; section: D.1.3mm 1976–9.13.X, 7548 sf2795 (P2)

14247 Fragment of two S-shaped links of circular section. L.12.4mm; link section: D.1.2mm 1976–9.13.X, 7569 sf2806 (P3)

14248 Two links, incomplete, S-shaped. L.13.3, W.5.7, T.1mm; section: D.1.2mm 1973–5.13.IV, 1552 sf700 (P8)

Collar

14249 Incomplete, originally circular, of sub-triangular section, with ridge moulding on outer face. D.25, T.5.7, H.15mm 1976–9.13.X, 7087 sf2543 (P7) (*Fig.1430*)

Rings

14250 Made from fine wire with butted ends. D.16.5mm; section: D.1.1mm 1973–5.13.IV, 1611 sf749 (P1) (*Fig.1430*)

14251 Of circular section. D.31.6mm; section: D.3.5mm 1976–9.13.X, 6342 sf2518 (P4)

14252 Incomplete, narrow band. D.24.6mm; band: W.2.7, T.1mm 1976–9.13.X, 7287 sf2673 (P4)

14253 Fragment, of irregular oval section. D.34.4mm; section: W.3.6, T.2.7mm 1979–80.14.IV, 4383 sf872 (P5)

14254 Of irregular rectangular section. D.21.9mm; section: W.3.3, T.2.3mm 1976–9.13.X, 7098 sf2408 (P6) (*Fig.1430*)

14255 Of sub-plano-convex section. D.18mm; section: W.2.6, T.2.9mm 1976–9.13.X, 6304 sf2445 (P6)

14256 Of sub-plano-convex section. D.22.7mm; section: W.2.9, T.2.9mm 71976–9.13.X, 7280 sf2655 (P6)

14257 Of sub-square section. D.21.5mm; section: W.3.6, T.2.6mm 1973–5.13.IV1577 sf717 (P7)

14258 Of irregular section. D.18.2mm; section: W.3.2, T.2.2mm 1976–9.13.X, 6295 sf2436 (P7)

14259 Of sub-rectangular section. D.21mm; section: W.2.7, T.2mm 1976–9.13.X, 7308 sf2685 (P7)

14260 Sub-circular, of sub-rectangular section. D.18.7mm; section: W.2.8, T.2.3mm 1978–9.14.III, 1117 sf214 (P8)

14261 Of sub-rectangular section. D.14mm; section: W.2.6, T.2.2mm 1979–80.14.IV, 4171 sf574 (P8)

14262 Of sub-circular section, irregular thickness. D.20.2mm; section: D.3mm 1976–9.13.X, 5237 sf1891 (P8)

14263 Of oval section. D.44.7mm; section: W.4.6, T.3.2mm 1976–9.13.X, 5237 sf2033 (P8)

14264 Penannular, of rectangular section, tapering towards one end, other end broken. D.17.8mm; section: W.2.3, T.2mm 1976–9.13.X, 5268 sf2145 (P8)

Discs

14265 With perforation close to edge. D.24.2, T.1.3mm 1979–80.14.IV, 4377 sf866 (P5)

14266 With small central perforation. D.16.4, T.0.5mm 1979–80.14.IV, 4183 sf621 (P7)

14267 With four irregularly spaced perforations, one side bent up. D.32.2, T.1mm 1976–9.13.X, 6162 sf2217 (P7) (*Fig.1430*)

14268 With small central perforation. D.26.2, T.1mm 1976–9.13.X, 6253 sf2344 (P7) (*Fig.1430*)

14269 With small central perforation. D.23.3, T.1mm 1976–9.13.X, 6271 sf2396 (P7)

14270 Broken through central perforation. D.10.8, T.1mm 1976–9.13.X, 7087 sf2525 (P7)

14271 Plain. D.27.2, T.1.1mm 1976–9.13.X, 7087 sf2531 (P7)

14272 Two, identical, both broken through perforation close to the edge. D.18, T.1.4mm 1976–9.13.X, 7349 sf2727 (P7)

14273 Plain. D.25.3, T.1.4mm 1978–9.14.II, 1067 sf139 (P8)

14274 Plain. D.24.2, T.1.2mm 1978–9.14.II, 1116 sf184 (P8)

14275 Slightly dished, with irregular, large central perforation. D.19.7, T.0.6mm 1976–9.13.X, 6143 sf2201 (P8)

Ferrule

14276 Made from rolled sheet, with irregular overlapping seam, tapering to open lower end. D.5.6, L.38.4mm; sheet: T.0.8mm 1978–9.14.II, 1740 sf588 (P1)

Cylinders

14277 Made from rolled sheet, butted seam, tapering slightly to one end which is broken. D.10.8, L.107.8mm; sheet: T.0.8mm 1976–9.13.X, 7440 sf2758 (P3) (*Fig.1431*)

14278 Incomplete, roughly broken at both ends, made from rolled up sheet, with overlapped seam. D.7, L.41.8mm; sheet: T.0.9mm 1976–9.13.X, 7594 sf2831 (P3)

14279 Tapering and thinning from one end which is cut square to the other which is rounded, rivet hole close to squared end. L.2, W.4.2, T.2.2mm 1978–9.14.II, 1480 sf620 (P5)

14280 Made from rolled sheet, overlapped seam, one end broken. D.7.1, L.27.5mm; sheet: T.0.9mm 1976–9.13.X, 7234 sf2654 (P5)

14281 In two fragments, incomplete, formed from rolled sheet, overlapping seam. D.7.2, L.28.9mm; sheet: T.1.3mm 1978–9.14.II, 1395 sf299 (P6)

Perforated strips

14282 Two fragments, larger clasped around sides of smaller, both joined by two rivets with hole for another, all ends broken. T.2, L.26, W.10.8mm 1976–9.13.X, 7087 sf2551 (P7)

14283 Fragment, one end curved round, other broken across perforation. L.18.4, W.9.2, T.1mm 1976–9.13.X, 7308 sf2680 (P7)

14284 Fragment, perforated at one end, other end broken. L.36.4, W.10.8, T.1mm 1976–9.13.X, 7393 sf2745 (P7)

14285 Slightly curved, both ends broken across perforations. L.41.8, W.12.6, T.0.6mm 1978–9.14.II, 1341 sf270 (P8)

14286 Two fragments, both curved and tapering to one broken end, one strip fits over the other, both with axial rows of punched slots. L.56.3, W.7.5, T.1mm 1976–9.13.X, 6038 sf2151 (P8)

Candleholders

14287 Fragment, a slightly tapering socket of rectangular section, one side with remains of projection of rectangular section. D.18.8, H.15.2mm; lug: L.10.5, W.9mm; section: T.3.5mm 1976–9.13.X, 7123 sf2548 (P5) (*Fig.1434*)

14288 Socket from portable folding candlestick, made of sheet, with incised zig-zag decoration round socket mouth, other end open, attached from midway to hinge plate of folded sheet by two rivets, sides of plate decoratively notched. L.46.5mm; socket: D.11.0, L.28.0, T.0.8mm 1979–80.14.IV, 4206 sf662 (P7) (*Figs.1433–4*)

Locks and keys

14289 Padlock with polygonal case, bolt of circular section, in position with spring inside, separate front face with keyhole with pivoting cover. Two rivets hold the case together. L.41.3, W.20, H.17.9mm; bolt section: D.2.5mm 1976–9.13.X, 7459 sf2768 (P5) (*Fig.1448*)

14290 Key with broken and distorted bow, with collar, incomplete bit projecting to one side of solid stem with pointed projecting end. L.43mm; bit: L.10.8, W.7.6, T.3.2mm; stem section: D.4.5mm 1973–5.13.III, 1055 sf720 (P7) (*Figs.1451, 1460*)

14291 Key, incomplete, bow broken away above double collar moulding, bit projecting to one side of solid stem, projecting end of stem broken. D.4.8, L.30.3mm 1976–9.13.X, u/s sf2534 (*Figs.1451, 1460*)

Dress, dress accessories and personal ornament

Buckles

Annular frame

14292 Two adjoining fragments, of triangular section. D.37mm; section: W.5.8, T.2.7mm 1976–9.13.X, 7124 sf2552 (P5)

14293 Of circular section, with broad pin. D.45.1mm; section: D.4.4mm 1976–9.13.X, 5346B sf2083 (P7)

14294 Of circular section, with pin with transverse moulding. D.44.7mm; frame section: D.5.3mm 1978–9.14.II, 1000 sf104 (P9) (*Fig.1465*)

Oval frame

14295 With moulded front and exaggerated knops, narrowed and offset bar, wire pin. L.23.1, W.23.7mm; frame section: W.5.4, T.3.6mm 1978–9.14.II, 1540 sf406 (P2) (*Fig.1466*)

14296 With incised transverse lines on front, offset narrowed pin bar, pin missing. L.15.5, W.17.1, T.2.8mm 1976–9.13.X, 7576 sf2809 (P2)

14297 With broad central projection decorated with incised lines, offset narrowed pin bar, part of pin survives. L.21, W.22.4, T.4.6mm 1976–9.13.X, 7577 sf2812 (P2) (*Fig.1466*)

14298 With moulded front with central sheet roller, decorated with incised lines, tip of pin broken off, sub-rectangular plate with traced border decoration and five rivet holes. L.56.3, W.21.5, T.4.3mm; buckle-plate: L.39.4, W.15.3, T.0.8mm 1976–9.13.X, 7591 sf2850 (P3) (*Fig.1466*)

14299 Sub-oval frame of D-shaped section, narrowed offset bar with pin. L.11.3, W.14.9, T.2.8mm 1979–80.14.IV, 4278 sf751 (P6)

14300 Sub-oval frame with ogee pointed front with groove for pin, offset pin bar with part of pin surviving, folded over buckle-plate with single rivet. L.25.1, W.15.9, T.3.5mm 1976–9.13.X, 7324 sf2708 (P6) (*Fig.1466*)

14301 Frame fragment, originally oval, of triangular section. W.24, T.2.3mm 1976–9.13.X, 7342 sf2725 (P6)

14302 Offset pin bar with groove, pin lost. L.21.4, W.26.1, T.2.9mm 1976–9.13.X, 5156 sf1851 (P7) (*Fig.1466*)

14303 Heavily moulded front bar, sheet roller on front decorated with punched or traced lines, offset and narrowed pin bar, wire pin. L.19, W.20.3, T.5mm 1979–80.14.IV, 4049 sf446 (P9) (*Fig.1466*)

14304 With recurved projections at ends of narrowed pin bar, groove for pin on front of frame, pin lost. L.33.4, W.28, T.2.3mm 1976–9.13.X, 7036 sf2576 (P9) (*Fig.1466*)

14305 Sub-oval frame, of sub-rectangular section, frame expanded at front, folded sub-rectangular plate with rivet at end, wire pin. L.32.4, W.18.9, T.2mm; frame section: W.7, T.4.5mm 1978–9.14.II, u/s sf394

14306 Narrow oval frame with heavily moulded front, with knop at each end, pin missing, but slight constriction for it on offset narrowed pin bar. L.56.9, W.25.7, T.5.9mm u/s sf825 (*Fig.1466*)

With integral plate

14307 Sub-oval, heavy front bar moulding protruding beyond each side, plate with remains of five iron rivets with domed heads, sixth perforation just below frame for pin, now lost. L.57.3, W.30.5, T.6.7mm; integral plate: L.29.8, W.23.2, T.2.7mm 1976–9.13.X, 6347 sf2583 (P6) (*Fig.1467*)

14308 Incomplete, end rounded with two projections, rivet hole, frame originally circular with iron pin. L.35, W.15, T.3mm 1979–80.14.IV, 4185 sf5141 (P6)

With forked spacer

14309 Fragment, frame originally circular, hole for pin just below, forked spacer with plates which may have been tinned, rivet hole at far end which is decoratively curved. L.33.3, W.16.5, T.5mm 1976–9.13.X, 6271 sf2411 (P7)

14310 Sub-circular frame of sub-triangular section, with square projection or lip to front, notch on frame to receive pin tip, forked spacer with plates, notched to accommodate wire pin. L.42.4, W.15.1, T.6mm; buckle frame: T.2.7mm; buckle-plates: L.26.4, W.10.8mm 1976–9.13.X, 6218 sf2268 (P7) (*Fig.1467*)

14311 Oval frame with pointed ogee front, offset pin bar with pin, forked spacer broken off. L.23.1, W.20.6, T.3mm 1976–9.13.X, 5146 sf1941 (P7)

14312 Fragmentary circular frame with pin surviving, forked spacer with plates, single rivet at far end; textile between plates. L.45.5, W.16.1, T.4.8mm 1976–9.13.X, 5131 sf1808 (P8)

14313 Frame, of sub-triangular section, oval with lip, forked spacer with moulding just below buckle frame, plates missing. L.26.5, T.2.5mm; frame: W.15.5mm 1976–9.13.X, 5254 sf1896 (P8)

14314 Incomplete oval frame with pronounced lip, remains of fine wire pin and incomplete forked spacer. L.39.5, W.17.2, T.2.6mm 1976–9.13.X, 6008 sf2188 (P8)

14315 Frame of sub-triangular section, oval with pointed front, and incompletely cast forked spacer. L.33.3, W.25, T.4mm 1978–9.14.II, 1039 sf121 (P9)

D-shaped frame

14316 Of sub-circular section, with devolved zoomorphic heads at ends of narrowed pin bar. L.15.9, W.22, T.5.7mm 1978–9.14.II, 1537 sf403 (P2) (*Fig.1468*)

14317 Fragment, flat irregular casting. L.31.9, W.22.2, T.2mm 1976–9.13.X, 5243 sf1918 (P8)

14318 With pin and remains of folded-over plates. L.23, W.15.2, T.6mm 1976–9.13.X, 5255 sf1915 (P8)

Square, rectangular or trapezoidal frame

14319 Square frame, with sheet roller on front, pin missing. L.15.3, W.15, T.4.8mm 1979–80.14.IV, 4444 sf899 (P5) (*Fig.1469*)

14320 Frame fragment, of sub-square section, frame originally rectangular with rectangular projection below pin bar. L.30.7, W.6.8, T.3.4mm 1976–9.13.X, 7072 sf2633 (P7)

14321 Incomplete, originally trapezoidal with off-centred bar, of rectangular section. L.15, W.23.7, T.4.9mm 1978–9.14.II, 1146 sf212 (P8)

14322 Trapezoidal frame made from strip with separate pin bar inserted into it, part of folded-over plates remain. L.20.8, W.11.4, T.5.1mm 1976–9.13.X, 5144 sf1836 (P8)

14323 Frame, of sub-rectangular section, sub-rectangular with slightly convex sides and heavily moulded front, narrow rectangular buckle-plates retain single rivet at far end and contain remains of leather strap. L.40.7, W.11.4, T.3.5mm; plate: L.27.8, W.9, T.0.7mm 1978–9.14.II, 1000 sf101 (P9)

14324 Trapezoidal frame, with pin, notch on front of frame for pin tip, remains of folded-over buckle-plate attached. L.28, W.11.7, T.4.3mm; frame: L.15.4, W.11.7, T.2.6mm 1976–9.13.X, u/s sf2612 (*Fig.1469*)

Double-looped

14325 With straight bars at ends, folded buckle-plate, tinned. L.15, W.9, T.2mm 1978–9.14.II, 1389 sf318 (P5) (*Fig.1471*)

14326 Fragment, originally double-looped, one loop of flattened triangular section survives, rest broken away at point of central bar, one side of frame broken through perforation, other just beyond perforation which contains remains of iron. L.15.5, W.23.7, T.1.3mm 1973–5.13.IV, 1545 sf674 (P8)

14327 Oval frame, of plano-convex section, loops decorated with notches to each side of iron bar which carries copper alloy pin. L.23.2, W.18.4, T.2mm; section: W.2.3, T.2mm 1978–9.14.II, 1092 sf168 (P9) (*Fig.1471*)

14328 Oval frame, with iron pin. L.16, W.12.3, T.1mm; frame section: W.2.3, T.1.5mm 1978–9.14.II, u/s sf395 (*Fig.1471*)

Buckle pins

14329 Tip fragment. L.17.2, W.3.9, T.1.5mm 1978–9.14.II, 1668 sf475 (P4)

14330 With ridged moulding below hooked end. L.46.8, W.4.7, T.4.4mm 1976–9.13.X, 6367 sf2604 (P6)

14331 Hooked end broken off just beyond transverse mouldings. L.37.5, W.4.1, T.4.8mm 1976–9.13.X, 7432 sf2759 (P6) (*Fig.1472*)

14332 Of rectangular section, slightly tapering, roughly broken at both ends. L.30.6, W.4.6, T.1.7mm 1979–80.14.IV, 4102 sf504 (P7)

14333 Of rectangular section, one end looped, tapering to tip. L.30.9, W.2.7, T.1mm 1979–80.14.IV, 4037 sf376 (P8)

14334 Upper end of rectangular section, decorated with five impressed rings, originally gilded; below this section changes to sub-plano-convex. L.54, W.7.9, T.4.2mm 1976–9.13.X, 5239 sf2220 (P8) (*Fig.1472*)

14335 Decorated with transverse lines and group of four punched dots below hooked end. L.49.6, W.5.3, T.3.2mm 1976–9.13.X, 5003 sf1729 (P9)

14336 With moulded boss below hooked end. L.49.7, W.4.6, T.7.7mm 1976–9.13.X, u/s sf2605 (*Fig.1472*)

14337 Or nail shank, of rectangular section, tip bent. L.26.6, W.3.5, T.2.3mm 1976–9.13.X, 7072 sf2626 (P7)

14338 Or wire hook, of square section, incomplete. L.24.2mm; section: W.2, T.2mm 1976–9.13.X, 7579 sf2814 (P7)

Buckle-plates

14339 Fragment, broken at fold, slot for pin, rivet hole in each corner and central one with rivet. L.44.6, W.13.4, T.0.6mm 1978–9.14.II, 1611 sf418 (P5)

14340 Fragment, broken at fold and across slot for pin, with five rivet holes and traced or punched border decoration, back face scratched. L.42, W.15.4, T.0.7mm 1978–9.14.II, 1560 sf430 (P5) (*Fig.1473*)

14341 Incomplete, in two fragments, broken at one end across loop, slot for pin, plates joined by two dome-headed rivets. L.22, W.9.6, T.0.7mm 1979–80.14.IV, 4200 sf655 (P5)

14342 Incomplete, folded-over sheet with gap for pin, single rivet, end of one side broken off. L.18.4, W.8.3, T.3.1mm 1976–9.13.X, 7120 sf2545 (P5)

14343 Made from folded-over sheet, loops broken, with single rivet at lower end. L.17, W.9.1, T.2.6mm; sheet: T.0.8mm 1976–9.13.X, 7131 sf2558 (P5)

14344 Incomplete, folded with four dome-headed rivets. L.39.3, W.17.3, T.7mm; plate: T.1.2mm 1976–9.13.X, 7344 sf2767 (P5)

14345 Two fragments, joined with single rivet, both broken at both ends. L.17.9, W.9.3, T.1.5mm 1979–80.14.IV, 4278 sf752 (P6)

14346 Folded with two rivets, retaining buckle pin, part of leather strap survives within plates. L.17, W.9.6, T.2.7mm; buckle pin: L.13.4mm 1976–9.13.X, 7347 sf2739 (P6)

14347 Two adjoining fragments, rectangular, larger with central rivet hole. L.26.2, W.8.4, T.1mm 1979–80.14.IV, 4102 sf505 (P7)

14348 Rectangular, with fragment of buckle frame, offset pin bar, slot for pin behind bar, corners cut away for ends of pin bar, two rivets at lower end. L.42.6, W.17, T.3.7mm; plate: T.0.9mm 1976–9.13.X, 6310 sf2455 (P7)

14349 With pin bar of buckle frame, two rivets survive, third rivet hole broken through, traced zig-zag border along intact edge. L.33.5, W.17.3, T.2.8mm 1976–9.13.X, 5410 sf2474 (P7)

14350 Fragment, single plate broken at fold, with punched border decoration, five rivet holes, two broken through at lower end. L.28.2, W.12.9, T.0.8mm 1976–9.13.X, 5317 sf2011 (P8)

14351 Fragment of sheet, sub-rectangular, broken across attachment loops, rivet hole just below on each side. L.22.4, W.21.4, T.0.9mm 1976–9.13.X, 5399 sf2234 (P8)

14352 Incomplete, folded with notch for pin, part of buckle frame survives with slight moulding just above pin bar, single rivet hole at lower end of plate, end of one side broken away. L.29, W.17, T.3.9mm 1976–9.13.X, 5041 sf1675 (P9)

Folding strap clasps

14353 Frame with convex sides, folding end with separate bar-mount attached by three rivets, forked spacer and strap-end plates with ornamental opening at end and two rivets. L.51.4, W.21.4, T.6.7mm 1976–9.13.X, 5144 sf1948 (P8) (*Fig.1474*)

14354 Clasp, sub-circular plate with bar mount attached, plate and mount each riveted onto textile with rivet secured by washer on underside. Textile is silk tablet-woven braid with corded outer borders and central patterned area of tabby with diagonal warp-float pattern. Worked on two-hole tablets apart from single outermost cord which is four-hole. Warp S-ply, 30–35 per cm (in tabby), weft paired, ?no twist, 24 per cm. Shades of brown and black in outer cords. Underneath braid, threads of S-ply silk, probably the end of the braid folded back. L.17.2, W.12.4, T.3.2mm; bar mount: W.4.8, T.3.1mm 1976–9.13.X, 7074 sf2675 (P8) (*Fig.1474*)

Clasps

14355 Plate, rectangular with fragment of sub-oval frame, single rivet at far end with two decorative notches cut into end, remains of leather strap. L.35.7, W.11.6, T.3.6mm; plate: T.1.4mm; buckle frame: L.7.7, W.15.3, T.3.5mm 1978–9.14.II, 1215 sf371 (P6)

14356 Or buckle-plate fragment, sub-trapezoidal with broad hook at narrower end, rivet holes in each corner at wider end, one rivet survives, with axial row of two larger perforations. L.36.4, W.24.7, T.1.6mm 1978–9.14.II, 1192 sf235 (P7) (*Fig.1474*)

14357 Hooked at one end, cut from sheet with three rivet holes, two containing rivets, one secured by convex washer with leather between layers of metal, unidentified plating or solder around one rivet hole. L.35.3, W.13.3, T.1.1mm 1978–9.14.II, 1151 sf210 (P8)

14358 Fragment, with incomplete plate decorated with incised saltire within rectangular frame, grooved around loop which is attached to rectangular frame fragment. L.26.2, W.13, T.4.9mm; plate: T.1.1mm 1978–9.14.II, 1137 sf220 (P8) (*Fig.1474*)

Strap-ends

Made of one or two pieces of sheet

14359 Tapering from upper end, made from sheet folded widthways, with single rivet at top and remains of leather strap. L.19.6, W.7.8, T.2.6mm; sheet: T.0.5mm 1979–80.14.IV, 4389 sf873 (P2) (*Fig.1475*)

14360 Or buckle-plate, folded, with two rivets at far end, tapering slightly to folded end. L.29.8, W.14.6, T.4.6mm 1976–9.13.X, 7613 sf2848 (P3)

14361 Or buckle-plate, incomplete, with one rivet and part of another rivet hole. L.14.1, W.16.1, T.1.5mm 1976–9.13.X, 7276 sf2650 (P6)

14362 Two plates with ends cut to ogee shape at tip, rivet close to tip, two rivets at upper end, all finished flush with surface of plates, remains of leather strap within. L.23.8, W.11.8, T.2.5mm 1979–80.14.IV, 4206 sf664 (P7) (*Fig.1475*)

14363 Made up of two circular plates with mineralised leather between, held together by single peripheral rivet with large domed head which is gilded. D.20.9, T.6.8mm; plate: T.0.8mm; rivet head: D.9.1mm 1976–9.13.X, 7087 sf2398 (P7)

14364 Plate, of sheet, sub-rectangular, one end with ornamental opening and two rivet holes, other end with corner broken away. L.24.5, W.15.4, T.1mm 1976–9.13.X, 6193 sf2457 (P7)

14365 Or buckle-plate, sub-rectangular, folded with one rivet and enclosing end of leather strap. L.32.5, W.16.9, T.6.6mm; plate: T.0.7mm 1976–9.13.X, 7170 sf2526 (P7)

14366 Or clasp fragment, two sub-rectangular plates, one narrow and straight-sided, with small central rectangular projection at upper end, other broader and flaring on one side, broken off at upper end across rivet, two further rivets hold two plates together. L.29.8, W.14.1, T.1.8mm 1976–9.13.X, 7285 sf2668 (P7)

With spacer plate

14367 Made from three thicknesses of sheet, with flat spacer with open panel, projections from outer and inner plates join to form loop or hinge, openwork decoration on upper plate with cruciform terminal at lower end, and two transverse bar-mounts flanking openwork are held on with rivets. L.31.6, W.9.6, T.4.1mm 1976–9.13.X, 5320 sf2012 (P7) (*Fig.1476*)

14368 Fragment, forked spacer only, with central annular expansion. L.42, W.15.6mm; section: W.5.2, T.2.5mm 1976–9.13.X, 5363 sf2165 (P7) (*Fig.1476*)

14369 Incomplete, made from two plates with spacer plate between, cut to ogee shape at bottom, tinned on one face, other face corroded, two outer plates incomplete, spacer intact. L.17.8, W.11.9, T.3mm 1976–9.13.X, 7087 sf2556 (P7)

14370 Forked spacer plate, unfinished, roughly cut from sheet with pointed end, cut obliquely across fork. L.23.4, W.15.6, T.1.4mm 1978–9.14.II, 1141 sf197 (P8) (*Fig.1476*)

14371 Two plates with ornamental opening at top and two rivets, forked spacer between with well-formed acorn knop with decorative cross-hatching at lower end, all surfaces silvered. L.67.5, W.11.8, T.4mm 1976–9.13.X, 5131 sf1809 (P8) (*Fig.1476*)

14372 Two plates with a rounded expansion at the lower end, upper ends of both incomplete, one retaining a rivet hole, forked spacer now separate, with similar round expansion and acorn knop with cross-hatching on 'cup'. L.56.7, W.16, T.4.4mm 1976–9.13.X, 5163 sf1872 (P8) (*Fig.1476*)

14373 Forked spacer, faulty casting, tips of fork broken off, terminal unfinished. L.57.4, W.8.9, T.3.6mm 1976–9.13.X, 5210 sf1938 (P8) (*Figs.1322, 1476*)

14374 Fragment, sub-rectangular forked spacer with pointed end. L.28.2, W.11.7, T.1.4mm 1976–9.13.X, 6069 sf2174 (P8)

14375 Made from two plates with spacer plate between, cut to ogee shape at lower end, upper end irregularly convex, three rivets finished flush with surface of plate, remains of strap inside. L.27.8, W.14.6, T.3mm 1976–9.13.X, u/s sf2581

Strap-guides

Rectangular/trapezoidal frame with internal lugs

14376 Trapezoidal, of sub-square section, with internal lugs. L.12.3, W.13, T.2.2mm 1976–9.13.X, 6345 sf2846 (P3)

14377 Of sub-square section, incomplete, originally rectangular, now in two adjoining fragments, front bar with collar and boss mouldings, one internal lug survives. L.21.5, W.31.2mm; section: W.4.1, T.4.8mm 1976–9.13.X, 6346 sf2516 (P4) (*Fig.1477*)

14378 Trapezoidal, of sub-rectangular section, with internal lugs, small boss on front bar. L.20, W.26.5mm; section: W.2.5, T.3.2mm 1976–9.13.X, 5540 sf2637 (P5) (*Fig.1477*)

14379 Trapezoidal with internal lugs, frame of rectangular section apart from front bar of sub-triangular section. L.26.9, W.20mm; section: W.3.2, T.2.2mm 1976–9.13.X, 5292 sf2135 (P7) (*Fig.1477*)

14380 Incomplete, originally trapezoidal, frame of square section, moulding in centre of one edge, slight inward projection on one side close to frame corner. L.22, W.18.1, T.3.6mm 1976–9.13.III, 1034 sf682 (P9)

Oval/rectangular/trapezoidal loops with external rivets

14381 Faulty casting of two strap-guides, both sub-oval with external rivets, of irregular plano-convex section, loops still attached to each other. Single loop: L.16, W.12.4, T.3.2mm 1978–9.14.II, 1605 sf415 (P4) (*Figs.1322, 1477*)

14382 D-shaped, of D-shaped section, with external stud for attachment. L.14.4, W.16.1mm; section: W.1.7, T.2.6mm 1976–9.13.X, 5477 sf2508 (P5) (*Fig.1477*)

14383 Or swivel, trapezoidal loop with remains of integral external rivet. L.12.4, W.11.7mm; section: W.2.3, T.3.6mm 1978–9.14.II, 1215 sf373 (P6)

14384 Sub-circular, with knopped front and integral external rivet. L.26.9, W.15.3, T.3mm; section: W.2.2, T.3.8mm 1978–9.14.II, 1212 sf257 (P7)

14385 Sub-oval with knopped front and integral external rivet for attachment. L.27.5, W.13.4mm; section: W.2, T.3.3mm 1979–80.14.IV, 4206 sf673 (P7)

14386 D-shaped with incomplete ornamental knop, projecting shank broken away at other end. L.23.2, W.15mm; section: W.1.9, T.3mm 1976–9.13.X, 5349 sf2116 (P7)

14387 D-shaped with ornamental knop. L.21.8, W.14.5mm; section: W.3.2, T.2.1mm 1976–9.13.X, 5292 sf2162 (P7) (*Fig.1477*)

Possible strap-guides

14388 Pentagonal in shape, made from strip with ends cut diagonally, rivet or pin joins ends of strip together. L.14.8, W.12.7mm; section: W.5.4, T.0.7mm 1979–80.14.IV, 4198 sf649 (P7)

14389 Made from strip with diagonally cut ends, bent into rectangle, rivet or pin forms central bar. L.12.1, W.10.8mm; section: W.4.5, T.0.7mm 1979–80.14.IV, 4146 sf709 (P7) (*Fig.1477*)

14390 Frame fragment, with part of internal bar surviving. L.10.4, W.4.2, T.1mm; bar: L.8.2, W.3.7, T.2.5mm 1979–80.14.IV, 4295 sf767 (P7)

14391 Made from strip bent to approximately pentagonal shape, with separate bar. L.14.6, W.17.1, T.0.8mm; bar: T.1.7mm 1976–9.13.X, 6340 sf2532 (P7)

Chapes

14392 Made from sheet with long edges soldered at back, two rivet holes at top edge at back, lower end slit and closed, traces of leather inside. L.52, W.17, T.6mm 1978–9.14.II, 1524 sf389 (P6)

14393 Made from sheet metal with edges overlapped, ornamental opening at mouth, rivet hole on one face. D.13.2 L.32.7mm; sheet: T.1mm 1976–9.13.X, 6262 sf2489 (P7) (*Fig.1478*)

14394 Or ferrule, in two adjoining fragments, tapering slightly to rounded lower end. L.18.4, W.10.5, T.1.1mm 1976–9.13.X, 6262 sf2514 (P7)

14395 From scabbard, made from sheet metal with edges soldered, bottom edge with triangular notches cut out and remaining points folded in to close end, part of leather scabbard remaining inside. L.37, W.19, T.10mm 1973–5.13.IV, u/s sf848 (*Fig.1478*)

14396 In four fragments, with folded-over seam, rivet hole at upper end, lower end sealed, traces of tinning. Lower end fragment: L.15, W.7.7, T.5.9mm; sheet: T.0.3mm 1976–9.13.X, u/s sf2620

Purse hanger frame

14397 Or arched pendant mount, with three semi-circular hoops of sub-triangular section, projecting terminal at one end, other end broken. L.37.1mm; section: W.3, T.2.9mm 1976–9.13.X, 7127 sf2697 (P7) (*Fig.1479*)

Mounts

Flat and circular

14398 Inserted into leather with shank clenched over washer. D.9mm; washer: D.6.2mm; rivet: L.5.6mm 1978–9.14.II, 1581 sf439 (P2)

14399 Shallowly domed, central rivet hole, repoussé decoration of concentric rings of pellets. D.16.8, H.3mm 1976–9.13.X, 5146 sf2023 (P7) (*Fig.1479*)

14400 Incomplete, one edge torn through central perforation. D.12, T.0.5mm 1976–9.13.X, 6162 sf2386 (P7)

14401 Centrally perforated. D.5, T.1.1mm 1976–9.13.X, 7285 sf2710 (P7)

14402 Made of thin foil, three peripheral rivet holes, decoration cast in shallow relief, border with inward-facing fleurs-de-lys and shield in centre. D.33.9, T.0.3mm 1976–9.13.X, 5327 sf2050 (P8) (*Fig.1479*)

14403 Slightly convex, decorated with incised chequer pattern within plain border, three rivet holes. D.35.4, T.1.1mm 1976–9.13.X, 5268 sf2074 (P8) (*Fig.1479*)

Domed

14404 Fragment, slightly convex, originally sub-circular. L.13.2, W.10.8, T.2.3mm 1978–9.14.II, 1774 sf652 (P2)

14405 Circular, with central rivet. D.9mm; rivet: L.5.6mm 1976–9.13.X, 7585 sf2823 (P3)

14406 Fragment, originally circular with raised central perforation. L.8.7, W.7, T.3.2mm 1978–9.14.II, 1649 sf448 (P5)

14407 Circular. D.7.7, T.0.6mm 1976–9.13.X, 7418 sf2731 (P5)

14408 Circular, slightly domed, with central rivet hole. D.11.5, T.0.4mm 1976–9.13.X, 7148 sf2634 (P6)

14409 Two adjoining mount or boss fragments, sub-discoidal, convex. D.22.2, T.0.6mm 1979–80.14.IV, 4187 sf633 (P7)

14410 Two, circular, dome-headed, gilded, attached to leather strap by rivets with traces of washers at lower ends. D.7.8mm; rivet: L.9.9mm; strap: L.15, W.7, T.3.1mm 1976–9.13.X, 5292 sf2137 (P7)

14411 Dome-headed, central rivet. D.12.2, T.0.8, H.4.5mm; rivet: L.5.5mm 1976–9.13.X, 6271 sf2403 (P7) (*Fig.1479*)

14412 Circular, with central rivet hole. D.8.8, T.1mm 1976–9.13.X, 7072 sf2627 (P7)

14413 Circular, rivet clenched over rectangular washer at lower end. D.7.2, T.0.7mm; rivet: L.4.7mm 1979–80.14.IV, 4171 sf576 (P8)

14414 Six fragments, of sheet, originally circular and convex. L.25, W.15.3, T.0.7mm 1979–80.14.IV, 4189 sf632 (P8)

14415 Fragment, originally circular, slightly domed. D.30, T.0.8mm 1976–9.13.X, 5131 sf1818 (P8)

14416 Circular, with central rivet, washer on underside, with remains of leather. D.11.8, H.6.5mm 1976–9.13.X, 5219 sf1900 (P8)

14417 Two, both circular, dome-headed with rivets. D.7.3, H.3mm 1976–9.13.X, 7006 sf2320 (P8)

Triple-lobed

14418 Fragment of repoussé sheet with three lobes outlined with cable decoration, two outer lobes with rivet holes, all lobes incomplete. L.24.3, W.11.7, T.1mm 1976–9.13.X, 6008 sf2210 (P8)

Petalled

14419 Quatrefoil with remains of central rivet. L.11.5, W.11.5, T.1.3mm 1976–9.13.X, 7427 sf2751 (P3) (*Fig.1479*)

14420 Sub-square. L.10, W.9.8, T.1.1mm 1976–9.13.X, 7203 sf2593 (P6)

14421 Fragment, repoussé, originally quatrefoil or trefoil, broken through central rivet hole. L.9.4, W.7.5, T.0.5mm 1976–9.13.X, 6009 sf2085 (P8)

14422 Repoussé, quatrefoil with central rivet hole. L.8, W.7.5, T.0.7mm 1976–9.13.X, 5166 sf1866 (P9)

14423 Sexfoil, repoussé, with central rivet. D.9.7, T.1mm 1976–9.13.X, 5144 sf1841 (P8)

14424 Sexfoil, two rivet holes, central perforation damaged. D.15.9, T.0.6, H.2.8mm 1976–9.13.X, 5337 sf2200 (P8) (*Fig.1479*)

14425 Sexfoil, centrally domed, rivet now separate. D.13.6, T.0.8mm; rivet: D.1.3 L.7mm 1976–9.13.X, 7232 sf2602 (P8)

14426 Rosette, incomplete, made from sheet, with repoussé decoration of three whorls of six petals punched from back using tool with C-shaped end, one central and three peripheral rivet holes. D.33.4, T.0.9mm 1979–80.14.IV, 4210 sf669 (P6) (*Fig.1479*)

Possibly petalled

14427 Fragment, of thin sheet, irregularly shaped, gilded with repoussé decoration, one rivet hole. L.15.9, W.10.2, T.0.8mm 1979–80.14.IV, 4377 sf864 (P5)

Rectangular/lozenge-shaped

14428 Fragment, of sheet, sub-rectangular, both ends broken across rivet holes. L.12.8, W.9, T.1.1mm 1976–9.13.X, 7573 sf2807 (P2)

14429 Rectangular, of U-shaped section, with central rivet. L.8, W.6.4, T.1.5mm; rivet: L.6.2mm 1979–80.14.IV, 4295 sf770 (P7)

14430 Incomplete, lozenge-shaped with large central perforation and rivet hole at each end, one end broken through hole. L.15.7, W.7.5, T.0.8mm 1976–9.13.X, 5267 sf1924 (P8) (*Fig.1480*)

14431 Fragment, of sheet, rectangular, rivet at one end, other end broken across rivet hole. L.11.9, W.6.7, T.0.6mm; rivet: L.3.3mm 1976–9.13.X, 7048 sf2352 (P8)

14432 Sub-rectangular plate with large slightly off-centre perforation, rivet holes in each corner. L.25.2, W.21.2, T.1.1mm 1973–5.13.IV, u/s sf902

Bar mounts

14433 Rectangular, of plano-convex section, with rivet at each end. L.14.5, W.4.4, T.2.4mm 1979–80.14.IV, 4462 sf919 (P3)

14434 Sub-rectangular, with decorative pelleted edge, incised transverse lines and rivet at each end. L.15, W.5.6, T.1.6mm 1976–9.13.X, 7521 sf2788 (P3) (*Fig.1480*)

14435 Sub-rectangular, of U-shaped section with two rivets, one missing. L.12.6, W.3.8, T.0.6mm 1978–9.14.II, 1651 sf458 (P4)

14436 Or binding fragment, of D-shaped section, with rivet. L.7.8, W.4.6, T.2mm 1979–80.14.IV, 4149 sf530 (P7)

14437 Of D-shaped section, with circular central perforated expansion, rivet holes in terminals, one containing a rivet,

transverse mouldings on bars. L.16.5, W.6.5, T.2mm 1976–9.13.X, 5376 sf2202 (P7) (*Fig.1480*)

Other mounts

14438 S-shaped, made from repoussé sheet, raised decoration of lines and pellets on the S, rivet at each end. L.26.1, W.28, T.0.7mm 1978–9.14.II, u/s sf203 (*Fig.1480*)

14439 Or eyelet, with separate perforated scallop-shaped head of repoussé sheet, and tubular shank, splayed at upper end. D.12.1, T.0.6mm; shank: D.5.8 L.5.5mm 1979–80.14.IV, 4304 sf784 (P7) (*Fig.1480*)

14440 Sub-cruciform, of rectangular section, with foliate terminals and central boss, two terminals with rivet holes, others corroded. L.51.7, W.48.5mm; arm section: W.4.6, T.6mm 1978–9.14.II, 1560 sf422 (P5) (*Fig.1480*)

14441 Fragment, made of sheet, one end sub-circular, other broken, traces of iron rivet and two other rivet holes, the whole embedded in organic material. L.19.3, W.19mm 1979–80.14.IV, 4457 sf924 (P3)

Brooches

14442 Annular, incomplete, broken at constriction for pin which is missing, of circular section, one half of hoop with twisted ornament, traces of mercury gilding. D.22mm; section: D.2.2mm 1978–9.14.II, 1708 sf579 (P3) (*Fig.1486*)

14443 Incomplete, a curved strip, both ends broken, with rivet hole close to outer edge. D.40, T.0.5mm; section: W.6.5mm 1976–9.13.X, 6141 sf2199 (P7) (*Fig.1486*)

Brooch pin

14444 With expansion below hooked end, slightly curved profile, possibly mercury gilded. L.32.3, W.8.7, T.2.3mm 1976–9.13.X, 7406 sf2766 (P6) (*Fig.1489*)

Pins

Wire-wound headed

14445 Incomplete, with stamped wire-wound head. D.1.1, L.29.8, W.1.0, T.1.0mm; head: D.2.2mm 1978–9.14.II, 1064 sf140 (P7)

14446 Complete, with moulded wire-wound head. D.0.9, L.30.5mm; head: D.1.8mm 1973–5.13.IV, 1500 sf661 (P7)

14447 Complete. D.1.0, L.43.4mm; head: D.1.8mm 1976–9.13.X, 7087 sf2535 (P7)

Globular headed

14448 Incomplete. D.1.5, L.22.7, W.1, T.1mm; head: D.2.5mm 1978–9.14.II, 1643 sf438 (P5)

14449 Complete, with decoratively ridged globular head. D.0.9, L.30.6, W.1.0, T.1.0mm; head: D.1.4mm 1978–9.14.II, 1595 sf457 (P5) (*Fig.1490*)

14450 Complete. Analysis of pin: brass with tin-lead solder. D.0.9, L.38.3mm; head: D.4.1mm 1976–9.13.X, 5410 sf2244 (P7)

Buttons

14451 Sub-spherical, much corroded. D.9.9, T.7.5mm 1976–9.13.X, 7585 sf2820 (P3)

14452 Solid spherical, with loop. D.9.6mm 1973–5.13.IV, 1619 sf750 (P4) (*Fig.1491*)

14453 Made from two convex discs, now separated, one disc with central loop. Sheet: T.0.5mm; D.8.8, H.3.2mm 1976–9.13.X, 7435 sf2757 (P6) (*Fig.1491*)

14454 Or badge, appears to depict ecclesiastical figure, loop on reverse. L.25.5, W.16.3, T.3.5mm 1976–9.13.X, 5269 sf1944 (P8) (*Fig.1491*)

Lace tags

Type E

14455 With edge-to-edge seam, lower end open, rivet hole at upper end. D.5, L.28.4mm 1978–9.14.II, 1595 sf454 (P5)

14456 With edge-to-edge seam, slightly tapering. D.6.3, L.48.6mm 1978–9.14.II, 1156 sf264 (P8)

14457 With edge-to-edge seam, lower end open, upper end incomplete .D.1.9, L.22.6mm 1976–9.13.X, 6181 sf2233 (P8)

14458 With edge-to-edge seam, slightly overlapped at end. D.2.8, L.29mm 1976–9.13.X, 6009 sf3168 (P8)

Type F

14459 With folded-in seam. D.3.5, L.23mm 1973–5.13.IV, 1513 sf659 (P9)

14460 Incomplete, lower end broken away, with inward-folded seam. Folded braid visible in end view, made from coarse S-spun threads of plant-stem fibre, probably hemp. D.3.1, L.20.7mm 1976–9.13.X, 7000 sf2292 (P9)

Type O

14461 With overlapped seam, rivet hole at upper end, lower end closed. D.2.3, L.25.1mm 1978–9.14.II, 1428 sf328 (P8)

14462 With folded-over seam, rivet hole at upper end, lower end closed. D.2.2, L.26.6mm 1976–9.13.X, 7167 sf2578 (P8)

Wire loop fasteners

14463 Oval, ends twisted together. L.16.3mm; wire: T.0.9mm 1976–9.13.X, 5233 sf1933 (P8)

14464 Incomplete, twisted ends broken. L.16, T.1mm 1976–9.13.X, 5327 sf2020 (P8)

14465 Ends twisted together. L.13, W.9.1mm; section: D.1.2mm 1978–9.14.II, 1018 sf177 (P9)

Twisted wire loops

14466 Complete. L.25.4mm; loop: D.2.6mm; wire section: D.0.8mm 1976–9.13.X, 5291 sf1966 (P7)

14467 Complete. D.5.4, L.20.4mm; wire section: D.1.2mm 1976–9.13.X, 6247 sf2366 (P7)

14468 Complete, with long twisted ends. L.19.6mm; wire section: D.1mm; eye: D.3.1mm 1976–9.13.X, 7285 sf2699 (P7)

14469 Loop incomplete. L.24.2mm; wire section: D.0.9mm 1976–9.13.X, 5237 sf2248 (P8)

Part of hook and eye

14470 Fastener hook of wire. L.15.5, T.1.1mm 1976–9.13.X, 6029 sf2091 (P8)

Possible hair accessory

14471 Two wire lengths, coiled into spring. D.4.7, L.30.5mm; wire: D.1.2mm 1976–9.13.X, 7189 sf2592 (P7) (*Fig.1491*)

Finger-rings

14472 Originally stirrup-shaped, now distorted and hoop of plano-convex section broken at end opposite bezel, hoop rises up to pointed bezel originally set with oval stone which is now missing. L.23.1, W.21, T.3mm; hoop section: W.3.3, T.3.2mm 1978–9.14.II, 1606 sf449 (P5) (*Fig.1492*)

14473 Band, outer face with slight ridge moulding running round centre, inner face flat, irregular width. D.21.2mm; section: W.3.1, T.1.4mm 1978–9.14.II, 1552 sf688 (P8)

Toilet implements

14474 Fragment, narrow leaf-shaped blade and part of twisted handle. L.36.4, W.2.7, T.1.6mm 1979–80.14.IV, 4073 sf474 (P7) (*Fig.1501*)

14475 Spoon/ear-scoop, shaft of circular section, one end spatulate, tapering to point at other. L.48.6, W.4mm; shaft section: D.1.6mm 1979–80.14.IV, 4112 sf519 (P8) (*Fig.1501*)

14476 Tweezers made from two cast strips of trapezoidal section, now separated, broadening out slightly at tips, originally held together by rivet and solder. Strip: L.69.8, W.5.8, T.1.8mm 1979–80.14.IV, 4059 sf558 (P6)

Literacy

Book fittings

14477 Tweezers or parchment holder tip fragment, sub-trapezoidal, with incised line decoration along edges of outer face, scar showing point of attachment to rest of object. Analysis: alloy, copper-tin (arsenic-antimony), lead; coating; tin. L.19.8, W.25.7, T.1.2mm 1976–9.13.X, 7486 sf2776 (P6) (*Fig.1503*)

Book clasps

14478 A folded plate with two rivet holes, hinged end with vertical perforation and terminal with transverse perforation. L.29.7, W.8.7, T.3.4mm 1979–80.14.IV, 4094 sf482 (P7) (*Fig.1503*)

14479 Incomplete, hooked end broken off, part of back plate and leather strap survive, two rivets in broad end, decorated with three punched dots and parallel incised lines. L.21.7, W.13, T.4mm 1976–9.13.X, 5403 sf2416 (P7)

14480 Sub-rectangular, hooked at upper end, other end splayed, lower edge decoratively cut and decorated with triangular arrangement of three perforations close to two rivets. An incised ring-and-dot motif fills the centre of the plate. L.49, W.30, T.1.6mm 1976–9.13.X, 6000 sf2100 (P9) (*Fig.1503*)

Book mounts

14481 Incomplete, made of sheet, domed with remains of four perforated lugs, centrally perforated, surface tinned. L.23.2, W.20.2, T.0.8mm 1979–80.14.IV, 4374 sf861 (P6)

14482 Conical hexafoil with shaped edge and central rivet hole. D.23.1, H.15.6mm; sheet: T.1mm 1976–9.13.X, 6271 sf2393 (P7)

14483 Incomplete, repoussé sheet with domed centre, four projecting pierced square lugs, one retaining a rivet, larger perforation on one side. L.21.0, W.20.5, T.1, H.4.3mm 1976–9.13.X, 7087 sf2554 (P7) (*Fig.1506*)

Seal matrices

14484 Faceted conical shape with loop handle, matrix circular showing squirrel surrounded by inscription 'I CRAKE NOTIS'. D.12.1, H.15.3mm 1976–9.13.X, 7130 sf2805 (P5) (*Fig.1507*)

14485 Conical, faceted with quatrefoil loop handle above collar moulding, oval matrix, device shows kneeling virgin and robed man; below them, a small kneeling figure. Inscribed 'S' THOME D' SWIN CEMENTARI'. H.31.2mm; handle: T.8.5mm; matrix: L.27.2, W.21.5mm 1976–9.13.X, 7010 sf2327 (P8) (*Fig.1507*)

14486 Incomplete, shaft originally conical with facets, upper part missing, lower face sub-circular, design crudely incised, showing stag surrounded by inscription '...(E)SV SEL...'. D.18.7, H.10.5mm 1976–9.13.X, 5084 sf2264 (P9) (*Fig.1507*)

Bells

14487 Clapper, with pierced end, gilded. L.23, W.8, T.8mm 1978–9.14.II, 1550 sf426 (P4) (*Fig.1515*)

14488 Fragment, upper hemisphere, compressed out of shape, with remains of loop. L.25.6, W.10.5, T.1mm 1976–9.13.X, 7308 sf2678 (P7)

14489 Two, made of sheet metal, corroded and associated with wood and ferrous corrosion from iron peas. One is virtually complete, position of loop obscured by wood, squashed. The other is fragmentary, being part of one side; inside the outer shell is a bundle of mineralised S-plied threads. D.23.4, L.20.2mm 1976–9.13.X, 6220 sf2286 (P7) (*Fig.1515*)

14490 Pendant, bell sub-globular, made from sheet, with stud mounting, mercury gilded. D.11.3, L.25.1mm 1978–9.14.IV, 4084 sf483 (P8) (*Fig.1515*)

Loops

14491 Oval, made from strip of plano-convex section. L.6.8mm; section: W.1.8, T.1mm 1976–9.13.X, 7559 sf2838 (P2)

14492 Sub-circular, made from strip, ends appear stuck together. D.8.8mm; strip: W.2.1, T.0.8mm 1976–9.13.X, 7271 sf2647 (P7)

Trade and exchange

Balances

14493 Scale pan, triangular, with suspension hole in each corner, one incomplete, and traced zig-zag border decoration. L.33.6, W.33.3, T.0.8mm 1976–9.13.X, 5237 sf2219 (P8) (*Fig.1519*)

Riding equipment

Harness pendants

14494 Fragment, originally shield-shaped with loop, gilded. L.53.5, W.32.7, T.0.9mm 1978–9.14.II1795 sf737 (P1)

14495 Quatrefoil with leaf shapes outlined in traced zig-zags and pierced decoration of five irregularly spaced holes, gilded on front face. L.44.8, W.34.6, T.3mm 1979–80.14.IV, 4475 sf913 (P3) (*Fig.1529*)

14496 Circular, convex, with perforated lug for attachment, traces of gilding. D.17.8, T.1.1mm; lug: L.12.7, W.5.1, T.2.3mm 1976–9.13.X, 7259 sf2621 (P5) (*Fig.1529*)

14497 Lozenge-shaped with loop, of rectangular section, and of irregular thickness being thicker at upper end, showing white enamelled lion 'passant guardant'. L.46, W.31.1, T.5mm 1976–9.13.X, 5194 sf1883 (P8) (*Figs.1528–9*)

Harness mounts

14498 Cruciform with shaped and perforated terminals for attachment, larger central hole, one arm missing, mercury gilded. L.45, W.9.5, T.2mm; W. unbent 25.5mm 1978–9.14.II, 1595 sf413 (P5) (*Fig.1529*)

14499 Shield-shaped, with long projecting shank, unclear enamelled design on front face, original colour of enamel unidentifiable, gilding on edges. Shank: L.19.4mm; mount: L.21, W.18.3, T.3mm 1979–80.14.IV, 4261 sf732 (P7) (*Fig.1529*)

Unidentified objects

14500 Rod of circular section with bulbous expansion at one end, pierced lozenge-shaped expansion close to other. L.60.2mm; section: D.4mm 1976–9.13.X, 5522 sf2643 (P1) (*Fig.1535*)

14501 Strip of irregular triangular section, with central flattened area with mouldings to either side and at each end, both of which are broken. L.116.5, W.3.7, T.2.2mm 1973–5.13.II, 1225 sf976 (P1A) (*Fig.1535*)

14502 Incomplete, stem of circular section with collared finial at one end, other end damaged by corrosion. D.4.7, L.37.3mm 1979–80.14.IV, 4094 sf484 (P7)

14503 Tongue-shaped, of sheet, with rectangular notch cut into upper end, longitudinal slot cut close to lower end. L.25, W.16.5, T.1.7mm 1976–9.13.X, 7029 sf2341 (P7) (*Fig.1535*)

14504 Mount or fitting, annular with projections on opposing sides which have incomplete rivets for attachment. D.23.7mm; section: W.4.9, T.2.8mm; rivet: L.7.0mm 1976–9.13.X, 5237 sf2223 (P8) (*Fig.1535*)

Silver

14505 Annular brooch of sub-circular section, with incomplete pin looped over. D.12.3, T.2mm 1978–9.14.II, 1766 sf635 (P1) (*Fig.1486*)

14506 Annular brooch, flat, with recess for missing pin, inscribed 'INRI', with mercury or fire gilding, more visible on back than front face. D.14.1, T.1mm 1976–9.13.X, 6008 sf2183 (P8) (*Fig.1486*)

Gold

14507 Annular brooch, complete, formed from 16 strands of wire S-twisted and soldered in pairs to form eight strands, which in turn are Z-twisted around a solid core and soldered at the ends. The pin tapers to a point where it rests on the brooch, and has a gripped or clasped hand design where it pivots around the brooch. D.15.5mm; frame: D.2.4mm 1976–9.13.X, 7612 sf2847 (P3) (*Fig.1486*)

14508 Finger-ring with circular band made in two parts: head and shoulders, and shank. Shoulders taper to shank, hexagonal bezel with watery, bluish, natural sapphire. Bezel and stone: W.7.6, H.5.6mm; band: D.18.9, T.0.5mm 1978–9.14.II, 1561 sf390 (P6) (*Figs.1492, 1495–6*)

Lead alloy

Manufacturing waste

14509 Litharge cake. L.100, W.70, T.14mm 1976–9.13.X 5221, sf1937 (P8)

14510 Bar of lozenge-shaped section, folded in half, both ends cut square. L.86.8, W.25.4, T.12.1mm; bar: W.11mm 1976–9.13.X, 7300D sf2684 (P7) (*Fig.1325*)

Building tools
Plumb-bobs

14511 Sub-biconical, with copper alloy staple passing through and forming hook for suspension. D.34.1, H.33.9mm 1976–9.13.X, 7543 sf2792 (P4) (*Fig.1317*)

14512 Conical with perforation running through it, two indentations in flat end. D.29, H.37.9mm, Wt.141.5g 1978–9.14.II, 1592 sf410 (P9) (*Fig.1317*)

Fishing

14513 Weight, sub-leaf-shaped with two perforations, smaller in centre, larger at pointed end. L.40.1, W.18, T.3.1mm, Wt.10.4g 1976–9.13.X, 5503 sf2550 (P6) (*Fig.1352*)

Domestic equipment
Vessels

14514 Rim fragment with internal thickening. L.39, W.16.9, T.4.9mm 1976–9.13.X, 5342 sf2106 (P7)

14515 Fragment, a zoomorphic clawed foot with fringe of hair running down back of leg. L.34.1, W.14.7, T.9mm 1979–80.14.IV, 4084 sf477 (P8) (*Fig.1394*)

Plugs

14516 Of fused lead, sub-circular, double thickness. D.21.9, T.11.8mm 1979–80.14.IV, 4027 sf766 (P7)

14517 Irregularly shaped, double thickness. L.30, W.21.3, T.3.7mm 1979–80.14.IV, 4027 sf5000 (P7)

Offcuts

14518 Of sheet, rectangular, with three perforations showing impressions of nail heads on one face. L.83.1, W.20.5, T.2.2mm 1979–80.14.IV, 4010 sf465 (P6)

14519 Of sheet, tightly folded up, nail holes around all edges with impressions of nail heads. L.66.2, W.31, T.12.7mm; sheet: T.2mm 1976–9.13.X, 5466B sf2504 (P6)

14520 Five offcuts of sheet, all irregularly shaped and partially folded up, three largest with nail holes at the edge. L.91.5, W.63.3, T.8.1mm; sheet: T.1.4mm 1976–9.13.X, 5309 sf1990 (P7)

Structural items and fittings
Perforated strip

14521 Incomplete, both ends appear broken through perforations. L.31, W.13.6, T.3.6mm 1976–9.13.X, 5367 sf2184 (P7)

Cames

14522 Narrow. L.50.5, W.8, T.5.4mm 1978–9.14.II, 1607 sf425 (P5)

14523 Fragment, compressed and twisted. L.70.6, W.7.7, T.3.5mm 1979–80.14.IV, 4313 sf804 (P6)

14524 Two fragments. L.16.2, W.4.2, T.3.4mm 1979–80.14.IV, 4323 sf811 (P6)

14525 Fragment. L.68.2, W.7.5, T.3.3mm 1976–9.13.X, 4077 sf3139 (P6)

14526 Fragment, one end bent up. L.83.9, W.5, T.5.1mm 1979–80.14.IV, 4121 sf502 (P7)

14527 Fragment. L.30.1, W.5.5, T.4.5mm 1979–80.14.IV, 4152 sf537 (P7)

14528 Narrow. L.60.5, W.3.4, T.6.9mm 1979–80.14.IV, 4121 sf578 (P7)

14529 Fragment, broad. L.62, W.10.9, T.3.3mm 1976–9.13.X, 7254 sf2610 (P7)

14530 Two lengths joined to form Y-shape. L.101.7, W.6.4, T.7.6mm 1978–9.14.II, 1602 sf420 (P8)

14531 Fragment, narrow. L.46.2, W.4.6, T.1.6mm 1973–5.13.IV, 1544 sf683 (P8)

14532 Two fragments. L.40, W.9.2, T.4.3mm 1976–9.13.X, 6126 sf2189 (P8)

14533 Fragment. L.70.8, W.7, T.2.6mm 1976–9.13.X, 7054 sf2376 (P8)

14534 Five fragments, from square or diamond-shaped panes. L.111, W.11, T.4.1mm 1978–9.14.II, 1000 sf105 (P9)

14535 Fragment, broad, with transverse milling. L.69.1, W.6, T.3mm 1973–5.13.IV, 1512 sf625 (P9)

14536 Fragment, H-sectioned. L.58, W.6.9, T.4.2mm 1973–5.13.III, 1031 sf646 (P9)

14537 Fragment, narrow. L.80.9, W.5.4, T.2.7mm 1973–5.13.IV, u/s sf647

Discs

14538 Oval, cut out of sheet, scratched lines on one face. L.14.4, W.10.8, T.1.3mm 1973–5.13.III, 1115 sf813 (P1)

14539 Perforated, made of sheet. D.13.5, T.1mm 1979–80.14.IV, 4392 sf874 (P2)

14540 With tiny central perforation. D.33.2, T.2mm 1976–9.13.X, 7357 sf2741 (P6)

14541 Sub-circular, cut from sheet. D.17.8, T.1.4mm, Wt.1.8g 1979–80.14.IV, 4176 sf596 (P7)

Knop

14542 Sub-spherical head, collar below, with projecting rectangular flanges. D.15.2, L.24.7mm; flange: W.9.8, T.1mm 1978–9.14.II, 1444 sf375 (P2) (*Fig.1408*)

Dress, dress accessories and personal ornament
Brooch

14543 Shaped like a long-necked bird with raised head, stylised feathers forming base, two loops on dimpled base for attachment. L.23.4, W.17.3, T.0.8mm; bird's neck: H.15mm 1978–9.14.II, 1760 sf610 (P1) (*Fig.1486*)

Shoe buckles

14544 Sub-circular frame of lozenge-shaped section, remains of iron pin. D.17.5mm; section: W.4.1, T.4.1mm 1979–80.14.IV, 4175 sf797 (P7)

14545 Oval frame, of sub-circular section, incomplete. L.16.4, W.14.4mm; section: D.2.8mm 1976–9.13.X, 7164 sf2577 (P7)

14546 Oval frame, pin missing. L.18.2, W.17.1mm; section: W.3.6, T.3.3mm 1976–9.13.X, 5269 sf1945 (P8)

14547 Oval frame, of lozenge-shaped section, pin lost. L.16.7, W.15.1mm; section: W.3.3, T.3.4mm 1976–9.13.X, 5027 sf1829 (P9)

Mount

14548 Lozenge-shaped, of plano-convex section, one edge torn through from central perforation. L.19.6, W.11.2, T.3.3mm 1976–9.13.X, 7591 sf2829 (P3)

Literacy
Points
Class I

14549 With shaft of circular section, lower end tapering to point, upper end rounded, slightly flattened and perforated. D.4.9, L.54mm 1979–80.14.IV, 4375 sf901 (P6)

14550 Of sub-circular section, lower end tapering to point, upper end cut square. D.5.1, L.76mm 1978–9.14.II, 1117 sf213 (P8) (*Fig.1502*)

Class II

14551 With shaft of circular section, lower end tapering to point, upper end chamfered and spatulate. L.97.1mm; shaft section: D.8mm 1976–9.13.X, 7548 sf2799 (P2)

14552 With shaft of circular section, lower end tapering to point, spatulate upper end incomplete. L.90.1mm; shaft section: D.6.1mm 1976–9.13.X, 7577 sf2811 (P2)

14553 With shaft of sub-circular section, tapering to point at one end, upper end chamfered to spatulate. D.5.6, L.62.9mm 1979–80.14.IV, 4466 sf906 (P3)

14554 With shaft of circular section, tapering to point at lower end, upper end chamfered and squared off. L.46.8mm; shaft section: D.5.4mm 1976–9.13.X, 7594 sf2794 (P3)

14555 Incomplete, point broken away, shaft of circular section, upper end chamfered to spatulate. L.42.9mm; shaft section: D.5.1mm 1979–80.14.IV, 4314 sf805 (P6)

14556 With shaft of circular section, tapering to point at lower end, chamfered to spatulate at upper end which is incomplete. L.78.7mm; shaft section: D.5.2mm 1978–9.14.II, 1319 sf304 (P7)

14557 Of sub-circular section, tip incomplete, upper end chamfered and squared. L.62.6mm; shaft section: D.6.2mm 1976–9.13.X, 5410 sf2451 (P7)

14558 Shaft of circular section, tapering to point at lower end, upper end flattened spatulate. L.84.3mm; shaft section: D.5.1mm; head: W.11, T.1.3mm 1979–80.14.IV, 4065 sf464 (P9)

Class III

14559 Incomplete, in two fragments, one being the spatulate end, the other part of the shaft of sub-square section. Spatulate end: L.31.2, W.11, T.4.5mm 1979–80.14.IV, 4275 sf741 (P7)

14560 Incomplete, tip broken off, shaft of sub-rectangular section, upper end flat spatulate. L.45.2mm; shaft section: W.5, T.4.1mm; head: W.9.6, T.2mm 1979–80.14.IV, 4372 sf860 (P7)

14561 Of sub-square section, tapering to point at lower end, upper end flattened to sub-square spatulate, upper half of point bent through 90°. L.83.6mm; head: W.16.3, T.2.3mm; shaft section: W.6.9, T.5.3mm 1976–9.13.X, 6271 sf2391 (P7) (*Fig.1502*)

Unclassed

14562 Incomplete, upper end broken off, shaft of circular section, tapering to point at lower end. D.4.9, L.75.8mm 1978–9.14.II, 1702 sf700 (P2)

14563 Upper end chamfered to spatulate, lower end notched or broken across perforation. L.25.2mm; shaft section: D.5.3mm 1976–9.13.X, 7582 sf2833 (P3) (*Fig.1502*)

14564 Incomplete, upper end broken off, shaft of circular section, lower end tapering to point. L.59.5mm; shaft section: D.3.9mm 1979–80.14.IV, 4313 sf808 (P6)

14565 With shaft of sub-circular section, upper end irregularly spatulate, lower end notched to from two short prongs. L.64mm; shaft section: D.6.4mm; head: W.12.3, T.3.4mm 1976–9.13.X, 7342 sf2726 (P6) (*Fig.1502*)

14566 In two adjoining pieces, shaft of sub-circular section, one end with knop-like moulding, other end chamferred but incomplete. L.87.7mm; shaft section: D.5.6mm 1976–9.13.X, 7403 sf2749 (P6)

14567 Or stylus, shaft of circular section, lower end sharply pointed, upper chamfered with two V-shaped notches cut into it. D.5.5, L.66mm 1979–80.14.IV, 4293 sf765 (P7) (*Fig.1502*)

Funerary and devotional objects
Pilgrim badges

14568 Or ampulla, incomplete, in five fragments, of plano-convex section, three adjoining to form central stem with branching or foliate design at upper end, fourth broken across perforation at upper end. L.51.7, W.23.6, T.3mm 1976–9.13.X, 7531 sf2791 (P5)

14569 Fragment, irregularly shaped with possible drapery, traces of catch for pin on reverse. L.33.5, W.16.5, T.4.2mm 1979–80.14.IV, 4198 sf672 (P7)

Trade and exchange
Weights

14570 Sub-discoidal, faces uneven. D.29.4, T.3.2mm, Wt.18.1g 1979–80.14.IV, 4010 sf460 (P6)

14571 Incomplete, sub-discoidal, faces uneven. D.25.5, T.3.2mm, Wt.10.7g 1979–80.14.IV, 4193 sf645 (P7)

14572 Sub-discoidal with illegible stamped motifs on one face. D.22, H.9.3mm, Wt.31.5g 1976–9.13.X, 5292 sf2204 (P7)

14573 Sub-discoidal. D.27.3, H.10mm, Wt.38.2g 1979–80.14.IV, 6262 sf2482 (P7)

14574 Oval, of plano-convex section. L.22, W.19.5, T.2.8mm, Wt.8.15g 1979–80.14.IV, 4462 sf904 (P3)

14575 Sub-oval, of rectangular section. L.24.9, W.20.3, T.3.9mm, Wt.12.4g 1976–9.13.X, 5497 sf2567 (P6) (*Fig.1520*)

14576 Oval, of plano-convex section. L.25.8, W.23.3, T.7mm, Wt.23.54g 1976–9.13.X, 7048 sf2353 (P8) (*Fig.1520*)

14577 Sub-oval disc with scratches on one face. L.23.6, W.20.9, T.4.4mm, Wt.16.9g 1976–9.13.X, 5001 sf1565 (P9)

14578 Sub-octagonal, of rectangular section, upper face impressed with eight-petalled daisy. D.35.6, T.9.8mm, Wt.53.5g 1979–80.14.IV, 4189 sf629 (P8) (*Fig.1520*)

Possible weights

14579 Circular, with shallow domed centre, flat back, front face decorated with group of nine punched dots or stars in centre, tiny holes regularly spaced around edge. D.52.8, T.9.2mm, Wt.113.1g 1976–9.13.X, 7479 sf2771 (P5) (*Fig.1521*)

14580 Sub-discoidal, with one rough surface, notch cut into other smoother face. D.62.3, H.13mm, Wt.391.7g 1976–9.13.X, 6069 sf2158 (P8) (*Fig.1521*)

14581 Circular, central area recessed and edges much thickened. D.37.5, T.11.1mm, Wt.68.4g 1976–9.13.X, 7013 sf2325 (P8) (*Fig.1521*)

Unidentified objects

14582 Sub-discoidal, one thickness folded onto other, sides intermittently sealed, both faces stamped with possible rosette or fleur-de-lys motifs. D.20.8, T.8mm 1978–9.14.II, 1717 sf565 (P2) (*Fig.1536*)

14583 Incomplete, shaft of sub-circular section, both ends roughly broken. D.3.8, L.43.7mm 1978–9.14.II, 1668 sf466 (P4)

14584 Tapering cylinder made from folded sheet, edge-to-edge seam, wider end closed by an attached flap, whole compressed flat. L.82.7, W.19, T.6.8mm 1976–9.13.X, 5338 sf2031 (P8) (*Fig.1536*)

Textiles

Yarns

14585 Less than 1g of short lengths of black, carbonised yarn, Z-spun, 0.2–0.5mm diameter. Torn ends, some slubs. Plant-stem fibre L.70mm 1973–5.13.III, 1221 sf908 (P1A)

14586 Several coarse S-spun threads, now matted together, perhaps originally woven. A trace of an unidentified red mordant dye present. Wool is Generalised Medium fleece-type. Largest fragment L.15.5mm 1976–9.13.X, 5339 sf2038 (P7)

14587 Several S-spun threads, 1.0–1.5mm diameter, matted together, possibly originally woven. Too poorly preserved to identify fleece-type. Largest fragment L.23mm 1976–9.13.X, 5347G sf2917 (P7)

Wool

14588 Several fragments of wool textile woven in 2/1 twill, 15/Z/0.3 x 10/S/0.5–0.6. Slightly matted, perhaps fulled. A trace of a red mordant dye, perhaps madder. Wool is Generalised Medium fleece-type in warp and weft. L.80, W.40mm 1976–9.13.X, 6372F sf2677 (P6)

14589 Several fragments of poorly preserved wool textile in tabby weave, 14/Z x 14–16/S. Trace of a yellow mordant dye, perhaps luteolin (from weld). Fibres too poorly preserved to identify fleece-type. Largest fragment L.80, W.55mm 1976–9.13.X, 5339 sf2030 (P7)

14590 Fragment of wool textile in tabby weave, 7–9/S and Z/0.7–1.1 x 5/S.0–1.5. Threads in one system are spun both Z and S in haphazard order: 2Z, 2S, 2Z, 11S, 1Z, 2S. An unidentified red mordant dye detected. Matted on one face, perhaps from wear. Possible remains of seam. L.120, W.50mm 1976–9.13.X, 5219 sf1905 (P8)

14591 Several small fragments of mineralised textile in twill weave, probably 2/1 twill, 30–36/Z/0.2 x18–20/?S/?. Fibre mineralised wool. L.10, W.10mm 1973–5.13.IV, 1503 sf610 (P9)

Linen

14592 Fragments of mineralised textile in loose, open, tabby weave, 12/Z/0.5 x 12–14/Z/0.4. Plant-stem fibre. Largest fragment L.25, W.7mm 1976–9.13.X, 5346C sf2111 (P7)

Raw fibres

Animal hair identifications by H.M. Appleyard

14593 Less than 0.2g of fine, straight animal fibres, 12–28mm long. Identified as resembling fine goat hair. L.28mm 1976–9.13.X, 5292 sf2003 (P7)

14594 Less than 0.3g of fine, straight animal fibre, identified as resembling goat hair. L.48mm 1976–9.13.X, 5292 sf2004 (P7)

14595 A single staple of straight, dark brown animal fibre, with roots and tips present. Identified as horse hair. L.55mm 1976–9.13.X, 5309 sf2081 (P7)

14596 0.1g of animal fibre, identified as resembling goat hair. L.47mm 1976–9.13.X, 5292 sf2118 (P7)

14597 Less than 2g of dark brown animal fibre, now matted together, but some intact staples present. Staples are pointed, wavy. Identified as cattle hair. L.42mm 1976–9.13.X, 5367C sf2179 (P7)

Silk

14598 Fragment of folded, mineralised textile in loose tabby weave, 18–20/Z/0.3 x 16–18/Z or I/0.3. Fibre not identified, but very fine, so perhaps silk. In association some animal fibres, identified (by H.M. Appleyard) as dog hair. L.34, W.23mm 1978–9.14.II, 1774 sf5033 (P2)

Cordage

14599 Single length of silk cord, plied Z2S. Tested for dye but none detected. D.1, L.70mm 1978–9.14.II, 1505B sf955 (P6)

14600 A single length of wool cord, plied S2S. Too poorly preserved to identify fleece-type. L.70, D.3mm 1976–9.13.X, 5292 sf2131 (P7)

Finds from the earlier Anglo-Scandinavian occupation on the site of the College of Vicars Choral at Bedern which occurred residually in medieval deposits have been published in *AY* 17/14. These are grouped according to material and listed by catalogue number below.

Jet
Bracelet fragment: *10698*

Glass
Beads: *10699–707*

Copper alloy
Mount fragment: *10708*
Dress pins: *10709–10*

Finds from Bedern Chapel (1980.20)

Stone

Spindle whorls

Where whorls are incomplete, measurement of the incomplete dimension is given in brackets [ ]. In these cases an estimated original weight has been added after the present weight.

Form C

14601 Incomplete, globular, slightly ovoid; axial hole, D.9–10mm, drilled from either end. Chalk, white, very fine-grained, with a few forams. Chalk Group. D.35, H.21.6mm, Wt.[24, est. 30]g 9071 sf148 (P7)

Iron

Blanks and scrap

See p.3025 for definition of terms used.

Plate

14602 L-shaped. L.54, W.43mm 9014 sf83 (P9)

Strips

14603 Curved with a short projection from the centre. L.60, W.35mm 9059 sf165 (P7)

14604 L.40mm 9014 sf94 (P9)

Tools

Knives

Scale tang knife

8120 Blade incomplete. Between blade and tang is a bolster. Bone scale plates with chamfered edges attached by three rivets. Handle widens to the end where it is rounded. L.123; blade: L.42, W.16, T.4mm 9022 sf143 (P9) (*Fig.1365*)

Blade fragment

14605 L.48, W.15mm 9022 sf142 (P9)

Structural items and fittings

Staples

U-shaped

14606 One arm incomplete. L.38, W.25mm sf166 9059 (P7)

Other

14607 Arm. L.60mm sf169 9027 (P9)

U-eyed hinge

14608 On one side of eye a rounded pierced terminal and on the other a strap which has rounded shoulders and con-cave sides, pierced three times. L.116, W.24; eye: W.20mm 8005 sf114 (P5)

Fittings

Plate

14609 Pierced at each end. L.78, W.14mm 9049 sf167 (P9)

Ring

14610 Rounded cross-section. D.32, T.4mm sf40 9008 (P9)

Keys

Keys for mounted locks

Solid stem projects beyond a bit which has a central channel

14611 Incomplete oval bow. Moulded stem. L.124; stem: T.15; bit: L.22, W.36mm u/s sf2864 (*Fig.1452*)

Solid stem which does not project beyond bit

14612 Pear-shaped bow. Moulding and collar at head of stem. Bit bifurcated. Plated (tin). L.50; bow: W.17; stem: T.9; bit: L.10, W.18mm 9087 sf164 (P5)

Dress, dress accessories and personal ornament

Buckles

Circular frame

14613 Shoe buckle; rounded cross-section, stub of pin. Plated. D.31, T.4mm 9014 sf82 (P9)

Rectangular frame with rotating tube

14614 Half of frame missing. L.33mm 9008 sf41 (P9)

Horse equipment

Horseshoe

Indeterminate outer side

14615 Very corroded. L.110, W.105, T.7; branch: W.24mm 9000 sf161 (P9)

Copper alloy

Structural items and fittings

14616 Ring of sub-plano-convex section. D.16.5mm; section: W.2.7, T.3mm 9084 sf157 (P7)

14617 Cylinder with overlapped seam, lower end broken off. D.7.4, L.19mm 9087 sf151 (P5)

14618 Eyelet of U-shaped section with central rivet hole. D.6.6, T.0.5, H.1.6mm 9059 sf136 (P7)

14619 Mount, incomplete, originally circular, slightly domed, with central rivet hole. D.6.8, T.0.4, H.1.5mm 9067 sf158 (P5)

Dress, dress accessories and personal ornament

Buckle pin

14620 One end looped, tapering to the other end. L.16.5, W.4.4, T.2.5mm 9059 sf137 (P7)

Chape

14621 From scabbard, made from sheet metal with edges soldered at back, lower edge notched and folded in to close. L.21, W.11mm 9004 sf4 (P9)

Mounts

14622 Made from repoussé sheet, triple lobed, outer lobes with decoratively frilled edges and central rivet holes, one still containing rivet, central lobe with larger central perforation. L.24.8, W.12, T.2.3mm 9019 sf106 (P9)

14623 Rectangular, cut from thick sheet, notch cut midway along each side to form angular quatrefoil, central rivet hole. L.14.2, W.13.8, T.2.3mm 9011 sf69 (P9) (*Fig.1479*)

14624 Fragment, originally sexfoil, with central rivet hole. L.15, W.11.7, T.0.7mm 9016 sf50 (P9)

14625 Belt or book mount, two rectangular plates with leather between, rivet in each corner and larger perforation in centre, upper plate with decorative notches cut into ends of plate and traces of large circle around central perforation. L.33.3, W.21.5, T.5mm; plate: T.1mm 9000 sf139 (P9) (*Fig.1480*)

Pins

14626 Two, with moulded wire-wound heads. D.0.9, L.28.3mm; head: D.1.8mm 9008 sf32 (P9)

14627 Thirteen, complete or partial, all with stamped wire-wound heads. Also three pins with wire-wound heads. D.0.9, L.30.3mm; head: D.2.4mm 9008 sf33 (P9)

14628 With stamped wire-wound head. D.0.8, L.25.5mm; head: D.1.6mm 9040 sf67 (P9)

14629 With wire-wound head. D.0.7, L.23.7mm; head: D.1.6mm 9014 sf80 (P9)

14630 With stamped wire-wound head. D.1, L.23.2mm; head: D.1.5mm 9014 sf81 (P9)

14631 Two, both with wire-wound heads. D.0.7, L.35mm; head: D.1.7mm 9004 sf87 (P9)

14632 With stamped wire-wound head. D.0.8, L.24.8mm; head: D.1.7mm 9010 sf101 (P9)

14633 With stamped wire-wound head. D.0.8, L.26.5mm; head: D.1.7mm 9019 sf102 (P9)

14634 Three, one complete with stamped wire-wound head, other two lacking heads. D.0.5, L.24.5mm; head: D.1.6mm 9014 sf111 (P9)

Lace tags

14635 With inward folded seam, lower end open. D.2, L.28.7mm 9008 sf60 (P9)

14636 With edge-to-edge seam, lower end open, rivet hole at upper end. D.2.6, L.33mm 9011 sf70 (P9)

14637 Two, one complete, with overlapped seam, lower end closed, the other fragmentary with inward-folded seam. D.2.2, L.26mm 9004 sf88 (P9)

14638 With overlapped seam, lower end open, rivet hole at upper end. D.2.3, L.20.7mm 9014 sf112 (P9)

Twisted wire loop

14639 Complete. D.3.1, L.24.3mm; wire section: D.0.7mm 9051 sf131 (P8)

Literacy

Book clasps

14640 Two sub-square plates, upper one extended to form hook, two rivets attaching plates onto remains of leather strap, upper plate decorated with two pairs of incised lines, each pair flanking central rivet, notches in edges, and rocked tracer decoration in field betwen rivets. L.18, W.16, T.3.6mm; plate: T.1.1mm 9027 sf129 (P8) (*Fig.1503*)

14641 Or strap-end, hinged double-sided plate with two pairs of rivet holes, two rivets surviving, with cast loop of plano-convex section, centrally perforated with looped terminal at right angles. L.40.0, W.15.5, T.4.9mm 9027 sf130 (P8) (*Fig.1503*)

Book mount

14642 Conical sexfoil with central perforation, two peripheral rivet holes, deeply incised radial lines separate petals. D.18.5, T.0.9, H.6.5mm 9051 sf132 (P8) (*Fig.1506*)

Silver

14643 Wire fragment, curved. D.1.0, L.11.1mm 9059 sf138 (P7) (*Fig.1324*)

Lead alloy

Structural items and fittings

Came

14644 Fragment. L.67, W.8.3, T.7.1mm 9071 sf159 (P7) (*Fig.1412*)

14645 Fragments, a tangled mass, one containing glass fragment. L.131, W.9.8, T.5.4mm 9000 sf3 (P9)

14646 Two fragments. L.44, W.7.2, T.3.7mm 9008 sf42 (P9)

14647 Fragment. L.25.1, W.4.2, T.3.9mm 9004 sf86 (P9)

14648 Three fragments. L.40.6, W.5.9, T.3.2mm 9014 sf100 (P9)

14649 Two fragments. L.79, W.7.3, T.5mm 9014 sf109 (P9)

14650 Fragment. L.101.9, W.8.3, T.4.5mm 8000 sf118 (P9)

Dress, dress accessories and personal ornament

Buckle

14651 Sub-circular, of irregular section, no pin. D.17.9mm; section: W.3.3, T.3.1mm 9014 sf37 (P9)

Trade and exchange

Weights

14652   Made from sub-rectangular plate with raised edges, ends rounded, folded in half and perforated with concentric circle of decorative dots around perforation on upper face. L.34.2, W.27.5, T.5.7mm, Wt.33.8g 9085 sf150 (P5) (*Fig.1520*)

14653   Sub-discoidal. D.31.5, T.3.8mm, Wt.24.5g 9027 sf38 (P8)

Textiles

14654   Fragments of silk and silver-thread textile woven in tabby weave, wa/18 x we/70 per cm. Warp is a silver strip S-twisted around a Z-twist silk core. Weft is Z-twist silk, with occasional inserts of flat strip silver. No dye detected. Largest fragment L.24, W.10mm 9014 sf75 (P9)

14655   Fibre, less than 1g of poorly preserved wool, fibres at present approximately 8mm long, soft and crimpy. Too poorly preserved to identify fleece-type. Largest fragment L.20.5mm 9017 sf90 (P9)

Finds from 2 Aldwark (1978–80.14.III)

Stone

Hones

Norwegian Ragstone type

14656 Incomplete, broken at one end, of rectangular section, sub-rectangular, thinning from complete end towards other, faces smoothed. Schist, pale grey, fine-grained, quartzitic, micaceous (mainly muscovite). L.71, W.12.6, T.9.8mm 3073 sf762 (PA3)

14657 Incomplete, broken at both ends, of rectangular section, tapering from one end to the other. Schist, as *14656*. L.101, W.30.8, T.19mm u/s sf663

Fossil

14658 *Pentacrinites sp.* ossicles (seven articulated), calcitic. Jurassic. D.6.7, L.11.9mm 3086 sf781 (PA3)

Vessel glass

Undiagnostic green glass fragments

14659 Six green glass body fragments, now weathered opaque brown. T.<3mm 3086 sf780 (PA3)

14660 Two body fragments: one heavily weathered green glass, the other iridescent and weathered. T.2mm 3023 sf641 (PA5)

14661 Iridescent weathered body fragment. T.c.1.5mm u/s sf691

Iron

Blanks and scrap

See p.3025 for definition of terms used.

Plates

14662 Irregular. L.40, W.40mm 3089 sf5250 (PA3)

14663 Narrows. L.49, W.14, T.2mm 3068 sf742 (PA4)

14664 L.41, W.25mm 3022 sf5241 (PA5)

14665 L.51, W.28mm 3087 sf5248

Strip

14666 L.50mm 3072 sf5247 (PA4)

Leatherworking tools

Awl

Arms of diamond-shaped cross-section

14667 Ends of the arms of two awls fused together. L.31, T.4mm 3095 sf5103

Textile tools

So-called couching needle

14668 Rectangular slit near shank tip. Head moulded: on each of four faces a relief flower with four triangular petals and a stalk towards shank. Tip of head pointed. Plated. L.100, T.7mm 3090 sf790 (PA3) (*Fig.1349*)

Other tools

Shears

14669 Blade and stem. Blade back straight before curving in to the tip, cutting edge straight. Cusped shoulder. Stem has rounded cross-section. L.113; blade: L.80, W.10, T.3mm 3063 sf715 (PA6)

14670 Looped bow, stem and fragment of blade. L.50, W.17mm 3113 sf5111 (PA2)

Knife

14671 Incomplete blade only. Back straight to break. Cutting edge convex. L.88, W.12, T.3mm 3090 sf815 (PA3)

Structural items and fittings

Nails

Details of nails available in archive.

With pointed head

14672 Head sub-rectangular in cross-section. L.47mm 3101 sf5110 (PA3) (*Fig.1408*)

Staples

Rectangular

14673 One arm missing. L.21, W.35, T.9mm 3000 sf699

Rectangular with pinched corners

Wide faces outwards

14674 One incomplete arm. L.60, W.10mm 3087 sf5249

U-shaped

14675 One arm incomplete. L.47, W.27, T.5mm 3116 sf5112 (PA1)

Hinge pivot

14676 Guide arm: L.32, W.7; shank: L.62, W.10mm 3114 sf855 (PA2)

Hooks

S-hook

14677 Slanted shank, one end widened into convex-sided terminal. L.74, W.20mm 3039 sf792 (*Fig.1414*)

Fittings

Plate

14678 One end broken, other rounded. L.40, W.32mm 3054 sf5246 (PA5)

Strip

14679 Broken at one end and pierced, rounded terminal at the other. L.95, W.7; terminal: W.30mm 3100 sf835

Ring

14680 Incomplete, possibly a fragment of key bow. Plated (tin). L.43, W.10mm 3095 sf5109

Tube

14681 Broken at one end. L.58, D.17mm 3000 sf698

Locks and keys

Barrel padlock

14682 Case fragment and base of bolt. Plated (copper, trace of lead). 3022 sf5242 (PA5)

Keys for mounted locks

Key for lock with sprung sliding bolt

14683 Bit only (L- or T-shaped). L.34, W.26mm 3054 sf5245 (PA5)

Solid stem projects beyond bit which does not have central channel

14684 Bow missing. L.74; bit: W.29mm 3023 sf5244 (PA5)

Dress, dress accessories and personal ornament

Buckles

Circular frame

14685 Shoe buckle; rounded cross-section. Pin bent. Plated. D.33, T.3mm 3118 sf838 (PA2) (*Fig.1465*)

Horse equipment

Bits

14686 Complete snaffle bit with ring cheek pieces. The head of each link is pierced and has a flat top, grooves around at head and a little below head only on what would have been outer face. Notches at head of links. Plated (tin with a little lead). Links: L.c.93; cheek pieces: D.70, T.7mm 3063 sf708 (PA6) (*Fig.1524*)

14687 Two snaffle links. Spirally twisted shanks which develop into an eye at each end. Plated. L.72, T.6mm 3000 sf734 (*Fig.1524*)

Horseshoes

Indeterminate outer side

14688 End of left branch. Turned-over calkin. One countersunk hole. L.45, W.20mm 3116 sf5113 (PA1)

14689 Very corroded branch. Turned-over calkin. Three countersunk holes. L.130, W.32, T.5mm 3115 sf840 (PA3)

14690 Corroded branch with two rectangular holes and turned-over calkin. L.75, W.20mm 3006 sf5239 (PA5)

14691 Fragment. L.50, W.20mm 3022 sf5243 (PA5)

Copper alloy

Manufacturing waste

14692 Offcut of sheet, irregularly shaped. L.19, W.14, T.2mm 3063 sf710 (PA6)

14693 Sheet fragment, one edge and both ends broken, slightly curved. L.40.5, W.17, T.1.7mm 3117 sf846 (PA2)

14694 Sheet fragment, irregularly shaped. L.27.1, W.30.2, T.2.4mm 3001 sf738 (PA6)

14695 Strip fragment, curved. L.11.4, W.5.8, T.0.7mm 3054 sf5036 (PA5)

14696 Two adjoining wire fragments. D.2.2 L.33.1mm 3090 sf788 (PA3)

Textile tools

Knitting needles

14697 Bent rod, both points rounded. D.2.5, L.181mm 3090 sf783 (PA3) (*Figs.1349–50*)

14698 Rod of sub-circular section, slightly bent, both points rounded. D.1.9, L.176.8mm 3090 sf787 (PA3) (*Fig.1350*)

Domestic equipment

Vessels

Patch of sheet

14699 Originally rectangular, one corner folded down, with folded sheet rivets and slits for others around edge, one face with inscribed decoration of concentric semi-circles, inner one containing remains of central compass-drawn daisy motif. L.105.8, W.42.8, T.1.4mm 3022 sf627 (PA5) (*Fig.1399*)

Structural items and fittings

Rings

14700 Of irregular sub-square section. D.22, T.2.9mm 3089 sf782 (PA3)

14701 Oval, of sub-oval section. L.27.3, W.23.6mm; section: W.3, T.2.1mm 3006 sf174 (PA5)

14702 Made from wire loop of circular section, one end pointed. L.19.9, W.17mm; section: D.2.5mm 3016 sf612 (PA5)

Disc

14703 With perforation close to edge. D.17.2, T.1mm 3073 sf755 (PA3)

Dress, dress accessories and personal ornament

Buckles

14704 Frame or chain link, oval, of sub-rectangular section. L.52.3, W.30mm; section: W.4.6, T.3.6mm 3047 sf779 (PA3)

14705 Frame with pointed front and forked spacer, pin with curved profile. L.40, W.17, T.2mm 3104 sf817 (PA3) (*Fig.1467*)

14706 Double-looped, loops oval, frame of sub-square section. L.22.5, W.15.9, T.3mm u/s sf711

Buckle-plate

14707 With single rivet at one end. L.23, W.10, T.1mm 3106 sf818 (PA2)

Hinges

14708 Incomplete, made from a pair of folded plates hinged around central cylinder, one roughly broken, other sub-trapezoidal, with decorative notch on each side, perforated through both thicknesses of plate close to end, appearing square on reverse, round on obverse, entire surface tin-plated with incised line decoration. L.28, W.17.3, T.5mm 3073 sf777 (PA3) (*Fig.1475*)

14709 Made from sub-trapezoidal folded plates which are pointed at the ends, hinged around central bar, sub-triangular notches cut out of sides, perforation at each end. L.35, W.15.1, T.6.2mm 3022 sf630 (PA5) (*Fig.1475*)

Strap-ends

14710 Made from a pair of tongue-shaped plates soldered onto spacer of uncertain form, single rivet at upper end attaching plates to remains of leather strap. L.29.7, W.12.9, T.3.9mm; plate: T.1mm 3104 sf820 (PA3) (*Fig.1476*)

14711 Forked spacer with terminal knop, complete apart from one tip of fork. L.44.6, W.19.4, T.1.8mm; knop: T.4mm u/s sf754 (*Fig.1476*)

14712 Consisting of two tongue-shaped plates soldered onto forked spacer with acorn-shaped terminal knop, upper plate decorated with rocker traced zig-zag lines, circular cut-out and groove at top of plate where it is attached by two rivets to textile strap. L.73.6, W.21.8, T.5mm; plate: T.0.8mm u/s sf827 (*Fig.1476*)

Possible strap-end

14713 Two-piece, annular, with flat back and convex upper face, with incomplete sub-rectangular projection on one side, two iron rivets adjacent, upper face with worn incised geometric decoration. Grass, Z-spun textile and a looped iron pin are attached. D.40.1mm; section: W.9.4, T.4mm 3073 sf764 (PA3) (*Fig.1476*)

Belt loop

14714 Made from strip bent into a square, ends butted, with rivet hole in each side close to this end. L.16.7, W.16.7, T.0.9mm 3112 sf834 (PA1)

Mounts

14715 Repoussé disc, fragmentary, with one rivet, another missing. D.24, T.0.8mm u/s sf692

Domed

14716 Incomplete, circular, with remains of rivet. D.16.6, T.1.4mm 3089 sf814 (PA3)

14717 Four, circular domed heads and central rivets secured to leather by convex washers on underside. D.8.3, H.6.2mm u/s sf178

Petalled

14718 Two fragments, quatrefoil, with repoussé decoration, one with rivet hole. L.13.8, W.10.9, T.1.2mm 3090 sf791 (PA3)

14719 Incomplete sexfoil, made of sheet, with raised centre. D.13.4, T.0.5mm u/s sf605

14720 Fragment, with repoussé decoration and rivet. L.13.6, W.10.9, T.0.8mm u/s sf843

Pins

14721 Incomplete, with moulded wire-wound head. D.1.1, L.23, W.1, T.1.0mm; head: D.2.5mm 3004 sf167 (PA5)

14722 Incomplete, with wire-wound head. D.1.3, L.20.7, W.1.0, T.1.0mm; head: D.2.3mm 3054 sf701 (PA5)

14723 Incomplete, with moulded wire-wound head. D.0.7, L.12.7, W.1.0, T.1.0mm; head: D.2.0mm 3003 sf155 (PA6)

14724 Incomplete, wire-wound head. D.1.2, L.13.7, W.1.0, T.1mm; head: D.2.8mm u/s sf171

14725 Incomplete, sub-globular head. L.3.0, W.3.0, T.3.0mm; head: D.5.7mm 3004 sf38 (PA5)

14726 Or rivet head, dome shaped, incomplete. Head: D.3.6mm 3047 sf800 (PA3)

Bell

14727 Now in three fragments, made from two hemispheres of sheet, strip loop inserted into top half, iron pea inside, dumbbell-shaped opening in lower half. Top half: D.18.5, T.1.2 H.16.7mm 3052 sf688 (PA6)

Trade and exchange

Weight

14728 Square, of pentagonal section, top edges bevelled. L.12.4, W.11.6, T.4.6mm; Wt.4.2g u/s sf842 (*Fig.1520*)

Lead alloy

14729 Offcut of sheet, twisted. L.36.2, W.14.2, T.4.3mm 3072 sf753 (PA4)

14730 Net sinker rolled up into irregular cylinder, overlapped seam. D.19.1 L.41mm; sheet: T.2.8mm 3047 sf809 (PA3)

14731 Patch of sheet, sub-rectangular with regularly perforated edges, slightly curved. L.161.4, W.64.4, T.1.9mm 3090 sf798 (PA3)

14732 Weight, discoidal, upper face decorated with raised pellets. D.27.7, T.6.5mm; Wt.19.8g u/s sf844

14733 Object, possibly a weight, circular, domed, solid. D.29.7, T.10.1mm, Wt.39.65g 3116 sf837 (PA1)

Finds from 46–54 Fishergate (1985.9)

Stone

Mould

14734 A flat, sub-rectangular stone, one end rounded, the other cut square, with a fragment split off from the underside. Towards the squared end, a cruciform shape has been cut into the surface, with a keying hole in each arm and in the centre. Incised lines splay out from these holes towards the edges of the cross, and at the bottom, two small sub-oval fields stand in relief. Sandstone, medium greenish-grey, very fine-grained, possibly erratic, probably pre-Carboniferous. L.76.3, W.44.8, T.9.2mm; cross: L.26.9, W.21.9mm 9100 sf8654 (P11) (*Fig.1321*)

Hones

Norwegian Ragstone type

14735 Fragment, of rectangular section, both ends roughly broken. One face and one edge dressed flat, others natural cleavages. Schist, pale to medium silvery grey, very fine-grained (almost phyllite) mica with some very fine-grained quartz. L.50.8, W.19, T.14.5mm 5261 sf5791 (P6a) (*Fig.1381*)

14736 Sub-rectangular, of rectangular section, lower end bevelled from upper surface, upper end broken across perforation. All faces and edges dressed flat. Schist, pale to medium silvery grey, very fine-grained (almost phyllite) mica with some very fine-grained quartz. L.89.8, W.22, T.7.9mm 5261 sf5961 (P6a) (*Fig.1381*)

14737 Fragment, of triangular section, tapering from one partially sawn end to the other, which is roughly broken. Faces natural cleavages. Schist, pale silvery grey, mica (muscovite), with some quartz. L.61.4, W.21.5, T.15.9mm 5518 sf7639 (P6a/b) (*Fig.1381*)

14738 Sub-rectangular, of square section, tapering to rounded lower end, upper end squared off. All faces and edges dressed flat. There is an incompletely drilled perforation on one face close to upper end. Schist, pale slightly silvery grey, mica, with some quartz. L.81.9, W.12.1, T.11.4mm 3185 sf3377 (P7a) (*Fig.1381*)

14739 Fragment, rectangular section, tapering from one broken end to the other end, partly sawn. Both edges and one face dressed flat. Schist, pale silvery grey, quartz-mica. L.34.8, W.15.4, T.10mm 4023 sf324 (P7b)

14740 Fragment, of square section, one end roughly broken, the other partially sawn. All faces and edges dressed flat. Schist, pale silvery grey, quartz-mica. L.42.2, W.22.4, T.20.7mm 8024 sf1313 (P7c) (*Fig.1381*)

14741 Of rectangular section, expanding towards roughly broken end which has a sharpening groove, the other end partly sawn. All faces and edges dressed flat. Schist, pale silvery grey, quartz-mica. L.125.4, W.32.1, T.18.3mm 5011 sf801 (P8) (*Fig.1381*)

Native stones

14742 Two adjoining fragments, of rectangular section, rear face and lower end roughly broken, upper end with perforation partially broken. Sandstone (greywacke), dark grey, fine- to medium-grained, pre-Carboniferous. L.87.4, W.43.7, T.24mm 4680 sf3722 (P6a) (*Fig.1382*)

14743 Of irregular section, very worn, tapering to point at lower end, perforation at broken upper end. All faces and edges dressed flat. Siltstone (greywacke), medium grey, pre-Carboniferous. L.75.7, W.6.2, T.11.8mm 5261 sf5594 (P6a) (*Fig.1382*)

14744 Fragment, of rectangular section, faces, edges and one end dressed flat, other end sawn. Scratch marks on one face. Sandstone, pale grey, fine-grained Middle or Upper Jurassic. L.44.2, W.40.3, T.20.4mm 1402 sf3656 (P10) (*Fig.1382*)

14745 Of rectangular section, tapering from one end to the other, deep groove on one face. Sandstone, pale grey, fine-grained, probably Upper Carboniferous, but could be Middle Jurassic. L.86.2, W.43.5, T.51.7mm u/s sf5112 (*Fig.1382*)

Rotary grindstone

14746 Fragment of cylindrical stone, broken across axial perforation. Circumference smooth, faces roughly dressed flat, pinkish colour due to heat. Sandstone, pale slightly pinkish-grey, fine- to (mainly) medium-grained Millstone Grit or, less probably, Coal Measures. L.163, W.87, T.89.8mm; original D.175mm 8024 sf8784 (P7c) (*Fig.1383*)

Haematite fragments

14747 Two, brick red. L.16.3, W.9.5, T.7.6mm 4710 sf5121 (P6a)

14748 Three, brick red. L.9, W.8, T.5.2mm 4680 sf6772 (P6a)

14749 Two, brick red. L.16.7, W.14.9, T.9.2mm 4710 sf7411 (P6a)

14750 Brick red. L.11.8, W.10.3, T.4.4mm 4710 sf8268 (P6a)

14751 Brick red. L.8, W.7, T.3.6mm 2381 sf6216 (P6c)

14752 Dark greyish-red to brick red. L.11, T.2mm 1386 sf9351 (P6e)

14753 Partially roasted haematite and/or limonite, part of clay-ironstone concretion. Mudstone sequence in Upper Carboniferous (i.e. Millstone Grit or Coal Measures) or Jurassic. 7065 sf3357 (P6z)

Weights

14754 Or net sinker, naturally ovoid, with natural perforation towards one end. Flint, medium to dark grey, possibly an erratic cobble, Welton or Burnham Chalk Formations of Chalk Group. L.85.5, W.54.5, T.61.3mm, Wt.287g 2259 sf6922 (P6a) (*Fig.1352*)

14755 Incomplete, with drilled perforation. Chalk, white, very fine-grained, beach cobble, Chalk Group. L.67.4, W.58.2, T.30mm, Wt.104g 5013 sf825 (P6a/b) (*Fig.1352*)

Pestle

14756 Conical, flat surface cut at angle to top, very smooth. Outer surface tooled all over. Limestone, greyish-white, Middle or Upper Jurassic. D.114.1, H.77.5mm 1391 sf2445 (P6e) (*Fig.1386*)

Gemstones

14757 Cornelian, orange, sub-triangular, of sub-oval section, surfaces convex. L.12.9, W.10.2, T.7.5mm 5429 sf6389 (P6a) (*Fig.1498*)

14758 Amethyst, translucent purple, rounded biconical, with convex faces, one slightly chipped. D.10.7, T.6.2mm 5242 sf4465 (P6a/b) (*Fig.1498*)

14759 Incomplete, being just over half of originally octagonal object, broken transversely, of rectangular section. Black, with light blue layer forming one face. L.20, W.13.8, T.2.9mm 1304 sf1337 (P6z) (*Fig.1498*)

Die

14760 Sub-cuboidal, one corner missing, digits represented by simple holes, unconventional numbering of one opposite three, two opposite six and four opposite five. Chalk, white, very fine-grained, Chalk Group. L.13.3, W.12.9, T.12mm 5198 sf7272 (P6c) (*Fig.1518*)

Counter

14761 Sub-discoidal. Sandstone, pale brownish-grey, fine- to (slightly) medium-grained, Middle or Upper Jurassic. D.24.4, T.5.2mm 3145 sf6377 (P6b)

Fossils

14762 Five, comprising crinoid ossicles in silicified limestone (2), indeterminate shell debris in silicified limestone (2), all Carboniferous limestone or Yoredale sequence; crinoid ossicles in grey chert (1), Yoredale sequence. 10076 sf9389 (P6a)

14763 Crinoid ossicles, brachiopod and coral fragments in pale grey silicified limestone. Carboniferous limestone or Yoredale sequence. L.44, W.35, T.13mm 5211 sf4561 (P6a/b)

14764 Crinoid ossicle in silicified limestone, Carboniferous limestone or Yoredale sequence. D.3.7, L.2.4mm 5091 sf6689 (P6a/b)

14765 Crinoid ossicles (3), calcite, Carboniferous limestone or Yoredale sequence. 4058 sf9370 (P6e)

14766 Mould of indeterminate shell fragment in silicified limestone, Carboniferous limestone or Yoredale sequence. L.5, W.3, T.2mm 1386 sf9353 (P6e)

14767 Ammonite or gastropod in fine-grained ironstone, probably Lower Jurassic Cleveland Ironstone. L.92.6, W.52.3, T.15.7mm 1053 sf247 (P6z)

Unidentified object

14768 Rectangular, of rectangular section, one end rounded, other partially sawn. One face and one edge cut, surfaces polished. Igneous rock, probably basalt, black, very finely crystalline. L.29.8, W.18.2, T.13.2mm 4802 sf8254 (P6a)

Jet

Finger-ring

14769 Fragment, of plano-convex section, both ends roughly broken, both inner and outer faces polished. L.19.3, W.5.4, T.3.6mm 2296 sf5575 (P6a) (*Fig.1492*)

Rosary beads

14770 Discoidal, with slightly raised lip around perforation on both end facets, outer surface polished. D.5, H.1.9mm 4694 sf5130 (P6a) (*Fig.1516*)

14771 Two, both sub-globular, end facets flattened and unpolished, outer surface polished. D.5.9, H.4.4mm 4068 sfs3699–70 (P6b) (*Fig.1516*)

Jet-like material

14772 Fragment, heptagonal, of rectangular section, one face unworked, other polished but laminated, edges knife cut and polished. L.43, W.41.9, T.6.3mm 3012 sf556 (P7a)

Amber

Fragments

14773 With one face and one edge worked, other faces and edges roughly broken. L.10.2, W.4.8, T.6.6mm 3518 sf7312 (P7a)

14774 Two, adjoining, of unworked amber. L.11.9, W.9.3, T.8.4mm 1663 sf6714 (P6a)

Rosary beads

14775 Two, both globular, both chipped close to the axial perforation at one end facet. D.7.5, H.8.3mm 3282 sf7815 (P7a) (*Fig.1516*)

Fired clay

14776 Counter or pot lid, discoidal, chipped out from a plain unglazed tile. D.76, T.15.4mm 8023 sf1302 (P7c)

Vessel glass

Hanging lamp

14777 Part of the base of the stem. Originally green glass, now weathered opaque mottled grey with some yellow crystallisation. Flat pontil scar on the underside. H.25, T.1.4mm 8019 sf1274 (P7c)

Undiagnostic green glass fragments

14778 Many small body fragments of heavily weathered iridescent and opaque brown, originally green, glass. T.1–3mm 3256 sf3837 (P6d)

14779 Widely everted rim fragment of originally green glass, now heavily weathered with an opaque mottled brown/iridescent surface. From either a wide-necked flask or urinal, or a lamp bowl. Fire-rounded edge. H.c.22mm; rim: D.c.68, T.1.8–2.5mm u/s sf2824

Iron

Blanks and scrap

See p.3025 for definition of terms used.

Bars

14780 Tapers slightly. L.46, W.22, T.22mm 5551 sf9270 (P6a/b)

14781 L.42, W.15, T.15mm 1478 sf4706 (P6z)

14782 Narrows. L.154, W.25, T.10mm 1448 sf3809 (P7a)

Plates

14783 One end irregular. L.47, W.26, T.3mm 4479 sf3093 (P6a)

14784 Fragments. 4649 sf3486 (P6a)

14785 Irregular. L.36, W.30. T.3mm 4649 sf3487 (P6a)

14786 Two sides at 90°, rest irregular. L.20, W.20, T.3mm 10089 sf3670 (P6a)

14787 One end has angled corners, other end one angled corner. Plated (copper alloy; not analysed). L.35, W.16, T.2mm 4693 sf4360 (P6a)

14788 L.37, W.25, T.6mm 4710 sf5058 (P6a)

14789 Irregular. L.35, W.30, T.3mm 4710 sf9266 (P6a)

14790 L.22, W.15, T.2mm 3352 sf9350 (P6a)

14791 Broken at each end. L.52, W.30, T.3mm 3313 sf9480 (P6a)

14792 Fragment. L.35, W.15, T.2mm 2185 sf5025 (P6b)

14793 Folded over on its long axis. L.48, W.20, T.4mm 5293 sf5149 (P6b)

14794 Broken at each end, narrows irregularly, possibly an arrowhead. L.75, W.17, T.2mm 1443 sf6943 (P6b)

14795 L.90, W.41, T.5mm 5013 sf971 (P6a/b)

14796 Broken at each end. L.57, W.42, T.8mm 5155 sf3969 (P6a/b)

14797 Irregular. L.35, W.16, T.2mm 5242 sf4487 (P6a/b)

14798 Bent in two and broken at each end. L.43, W.31, T.2mm 10138 sf8436 (P6a/b)

14799 Narrows, sides turned over. L.40, W.30, T.2mm 5091 sf8754 (P6a/b)

14800 Narrows. L.35, W.22, T.3mm 5205 sf9506 (P6a/b)

14801 L.41, W.24, T.3mm 2166 sf4947 (P6c)

14802 Irregular. L.50, W.20, T.3mm 2015 sf9468 (P6c)

14803 Bent, irregular. L.56, W.50, T.3mm 7001 sf2222 (P6z)

14804 L.47, W.22mm 3007 sf730 (P7a)

14805 In two pieces. L.72, W.20mm 4086 sf2443 (P7a)

14806 Two straight sides at 90° with rounded corner, edges curved over; rest irregular. L.30, W.26mm 2001 sf8881 (P7a)

14807 L.38, W.15mm 4429 sf2558 (P7b)

14808 Cast iron plate of irregular shape. L.95, W.85mm 4429 sf2763 (P7b)

14809 L.34, W.27mm 8023 sf1211 (P7c)

14810 L.56, W.26mm 8023 sf1212 (P7c)

14811 One end rounded. L.25, W.15mm 8024 sf1254 (P7c)

Strips

Rectangular cross-section unless stated.

14812 L.31, W.8mm 1237 sf1623 (P6a)

14813 Slightly flattened at one end. L.53, W.10, T.9mm 3227 sf3626 (P6a)

14814 Slightly curved, rounded cross-section, possibly a pin shank. Plated. L.65, T.3mm 3250 sf3797 (P6a)

14815 Tapers. L.82, W.6, T.6mm 3342 sf4221 (P6a)

14816 L.62, W.8, T.2mm 1527 sf4392 (P6a)

14817 L.35, W.7, T.5mm 4710 sf4467 (P6a)

14818 Corroded at one end, D-shaped cross-section. L.53, W.9, T.6mm 4710 sf4562 (P6a)

14819 Corroded. Tapers towards each end. L.75, W.9, T.7mm 4694 sf5166 (P6a)

14820 Flattened to one end, other bent over. L.40, W.6, T.3mm 4716 sf5325 (P6a)

14821 L.49, W.6, T.3mm 3334 sf5360 (P6a)

14822 Narrows. L.38, W.9, T.4mm 4789 sf5471 (P6a)

14823 Tapers, thick end roughly finished, sub-rectangular cross-section. L.63, W.7, T.7mm 5139 sf6944 (P6a)

14824 Curved, broken at each end. Plated. L.70, W.9, T.6mm 2429 sf7104 (P6a)

14825 Curves slightly, broken each end. L.40, W.7, T.4mm 1832 sf7697 (P6a)

14826 Broken at one end, looped terminal at the other. L.44, W.16, T.5mm 4097 sf602 (P6b)

14827 L.60, W.6, T.2mm 5013 sf991 (P6a/b)

14828 Rounded cross-section, broken at each end. L.48, T.6mm 5205 sf4175 (P6a/b)

14829 Rounded cross-section. L.34, T.9mm 5289 sf5319 (P6a/b)

14830 L.47, W.11, T.6mm 5345 sf5995 (P6a/b)

14831 Curved, broken at each end, possibly a ring fragment. L.43, W.7, T.2mm 10002 sf2273 (P6c)

14832 L.63, W.7, T.7mm 5073 sf3266 (P6c)

14833 Possible wedge. L.60, W.11, T.2mm 5073 sf3369 (P6c)

14834 Tapers, chisel cut at head, wedge-shaped tip. Possibly a wedge. L.77, W.9, T.5mm 5104 sf3393 (P6c)

14835 Tapers to a rounded wedge-shaped tip, chisel-cut at the wider end. Possibly a wedge. L.84, W.12, T.15mm 5104 sf3395 (P6c)

14836 L.42, W.8, T.7mm 5073 sf3506 (P6c)

14837 L.46, W.11, T.3mm 5113 sf3646 (P6c)

14838 Tapers, chisel cut at the wider end, broken at the other. L.61, W.15, T.6mm 5117 sf3948 (P6c)

14839 L.21, W.8, T.7mm 5147 sf3949 (P6c)

14840 Corroded. L.55mm 2126 sf4149 (P6c)

14841 Tapers slightly, spirally twisted. L.69, W.5mm 5243 sf5030 (P6c)

14842 L.51, W.9, T.5mm 6096 sf5416 (P6c)

14843 Rounded cross-section, possibly an incomplete punch. L.52, T.7mm 2302 sf5574 (P6c)

14844 Curved, broken at each end. L.37, W.4, T.3mm 2381 sf6198 (P6c)

14845 Flattened and widened slightly at one end, tapers and flattened slightly at the other; possibly a comb tooth. L.120, W.5, T.2mm 3240 sf3819 (P6d)

14846 D-shaped cross-section, broken at each end. L.80, W.10, T.5mm 3240 sf3821 (P6d)

14847 Curved. L.57, W.12, T.3mm 3275 sf3998 (P6d)

14848 L.38, W.9, T.5mm 2304 sf5823 (P6d)

14849 Tapers. L.56, W.9, T.4mm 4604 sf9204 (P6d)

14850 L-shaped, one arm incomplete, rounded cross-section. Arms: L.40, T.10 and 8mm 1386 sf2331 (P6e)

14851 Pinched at one end, tapers to other where broken. L.76, W.6, T.6mm 7001 sf2026 (P6z)

14852 Tapers, flattened at the wider end. L.72, W.7, T.4mm 7001 sf2077 (P6z)

14853 Three strips of cast iron with round section fused together. L.115mm 2061 sf2548 (P7a)

14854 Narrows slightly. L.85, W.15, T.6mm 3215 sf3373 (P7a)

14855 L-shaped, diamond-shaped cross-section, possibly an awl. Arms: L.45 and 40mm 2062 sf3429 (P7a)

14856 Curved over and broken at each end. L.71, W.13, T.13mm 8023 sf1278 (P7c)

14857 L-shaped. Arms: L.29 and 20mm 8003 sf1488 (P7c)

Building tools

Trowel

14858 Blade is incomplete, but was triangular. Tang crank-shaped with remains of the wooden handle in situ. Blade: L.108, W.95; handle: H.76, L.75mm 4691 sf3920 (P6a)

Pickaxe head

14859 Wedge-shaped blade at one end, pointed tip at the other. Widened in centre to accommodate shaft hole. L.435mm 3002 sf245 (P7a)

Metalworking tools

Tongs

14860   Arms articulate on a pin; at the mouth flat tips, for the handle rounded cross-sections, one tip has a loop to which an incomplete figure-of-eight-shaped chain link is attached. L.112, W. across mouth 19; T. of mouth 11mm 5131 sf3856 (P6c) (*Figs.1326–7*)

Punches

14861   Punch, wedge or bar. Tapers to a wedge-shaped tip. Broken at the top? L.94, W.29, T.18mm 3157 sf7207 (P6b)

14862   Possible punch. Tapering bar which is distorted at base, tip (which may have been wedge-shaped) now missing. Roughly finished at the thicker end. L.92, W.16, T.11mm 5073 sf3454 (P6c)

14863   Tapers slightly to a rounded wedge-shaped tip; head slightly burred; X-ray suggests non-ferrous metal adheres. L.109, W.15, T.8mm 1386 sf2329 (P6e) (*Figs.1327–8*)

14864   Tapers from just below the mid-point to a rounded tip, lower part has a rounded cross-section. Burred head. L.114, W.24; shank: W.16, T.13mm 4093 sf621 (P6z) (*Figs.1327–8*)

Possible tanged punch

14865   Both arms taper, tang has a wedge-shaped tip. L.55, W.11, T.7mm 4281 sf1109 (P6z)

File

14866   Blade incomplete. Tang largely missing. Visible face has fine diagonal grooves. L.91, W.47mm 1448 sf3843 (P7a)

Chisels

14867   Burred head. Rectangular/sub-rectangular cross-section. L.250, head: W.32; shank: W.20, T.20mm 2096 sf3098 (P6a/b)

1486   Rectangular blade attached to stub of stem of rounded cross-section. L.74, W.20, T.11mm 3050 sf2282 (P7a)

Woodworking tools

Spoon augers

14869   Tang, shaft and top of blade. Tang widens upwards from shaft before tapering to wedge-shaped tip. Shaft has a sub-rectangular cross-section. L.63, W.14, T.6mm 5103 sf3195 (P6c)

14870   Tang widens upwards from shaft before tapering to wedge-shaped tip. Shaft has a sub-rectangular cross-section. Blade has a rounded tip. L.83; blade: L.25, W.7, T.6mm 5644 sf7791 (P6c) (*Figs.1335, 1337*)

14871   Tang widens upwards from shaft before tapering to wedge-shaped tip. Blade incomplete. L.76, W.10mm 8003 sf1400 (P7c)

Wedges

14872   Flares a little at the tip which is damaged. Sub-rectangular cross-section. L.30, W.6, T.4mm 2234 sf5724 (P6c)

14873   Blade flares near cutting edge. Head burred. L.67, W.17, T.10mm 1384 sf2209 (P7a) (*Fig.1336*)

14874   L.101, W.18, T.8mm 2061 sf2547 (P7a)

14875   Tip damaged. L.55, W.15, T.5mm 2061 sf2810 (P7a)

Rasp

14876   Blade back straight before curving down to a rounded tip; edge slightly convex, teeth slant towards tang, 4 per cm. Tang continuous with blade back and curves up slightly to wedge-shaped tip. L.127; blade: L.56, W.11, T.5mm 4659 sf3807 (P6a) (*Figs.1336–7*)

Leatherworking tools

Awls

Both arms have diamond-shaped cross-section

14877   One arm incomplete. L.81, W.7mm 3262 sf3984 (P6a)

Both arms have rectangular cross-section

14878   One arm incomplete. L.47, W.5, T.3mm 5073 sf3269 (P6c)

14879   Both ends have wedge-shaped tip, one narrower than the other. L.74, W.6, T.3mm 7065 sf5422 (P6z)

One arm has rectangular cross-section, other a rounded cross-section

14880   L.81, W.8, T.7mm 5155 sf5874 (P6a/b) (*Fig.1338*)

Other awls

14881   Possible sub-rectangular cross-section. L.57, T.3mm 3342 sf4426 (P6a)

14882   Possible rounded cross-section. L.48, W.3mm 7060 sf3256 (P6z)

Textile tools

Fibre processing spikes

Rectangular cross-section

14883   Stepped head, tip missing. L.72, W.6mm 3342 sf4403 (P6a)

14884   L.93, W.5mm 3342 sf4411 (P6a)

14885   In two pieces. Stepped head. L.82, W.5mm 3342 sf4449 (P6a)

14886   L.106, T.5mm 10004 sf2732 (P6a/b)

14887   Curves slightly, head missing. L.85, T.5mm 5091 sf2858 (P6a/b)

14888   Stepped head. L.99, W.5mm 5237 sf4318 (P6a/b)

14889   Slightly curved; stepped head. L.105, W.5mm 5184 sf5713 (P6a/b)

14890   L.87, W.5mm 5349 sf7422 (P6a/b)

Rounded cross-section

14891   Stepped head, lower part missing. L.70, W.3mm 1211 sf740 (P6a)

14892   L.150, T.5mm 1075 sf781 (P6a)

14893   Head only, rounded cross-section. L.43, W.7mm 2357 sf7850 (P6a)

14894 L.92, T.4mm 5242 sf4486 (P6a/b)

14895 Incomplete and twisted. L.60, W.6mm 5242 sf4617 (P6a/b)

14896 Stepped head. L.83, W.4mm 10140 sf4658 (P6a/b)

14897 Stepped head, tip missing. L.71, W.5mm 5273 sf4988 (P6a/b)

14898 L.97, W.5mm 5518 sf7263 (P6a/b)

14899 Twisted. L.72, W.5mm 5110 sf5608 (P6c)

14900 Stepped head. L.97, W.6mm 5600 sf7618 (P6c)

Sub-rectangular cross-section

14901 L.78, W.6mm 1084 sf3206 (P6b)

14902 L.114, W.4mm 5295 sf5263 (P6b)

14903 Stepped head. End missing. L.60, W.6mm 2381 sf6201 (P6c)

Sub-rounded cross-section

14904 Stepped head, tip missing. L.92, T.6mm 1080 sf359 (P6a)

14905 L.112, W.6mm 5640 sf7773 (P6a)

Indeterminate cross-section

14906 Stepped head. L.90, W.5mm 1080 sf254 (P6a)

14907 Curved; head and tip missing. L.86, W.4mm 3342 sf4198 (P6a)

14908 L.97, W.5mm 4789 sf5469 (P6a)

14909 Curved near head. L.98, W.4mm 4789 sf5470 (P6a)

14910 Stepped head, tip missing. L.82, T.6mm 5184 sf4119 (P6a/b)

Tenter hooks

14911 Arms: L.32 and 15, T.3mm 1386 sf2319 (P6e)

14912 Rounded elbow. Arms: L.38 and 35, W.10 and 6mm 7001 sf2030 (P6z)

14913 Shank has wedge-shaped tip with face in plane at 90° to that of object. Arms: L.35 and 26, T.4mm 7047 sf3862 (P6z)

Needles

Punched eye

14914 Round eye. L.50, T.3mm 3335 sf4181 (P6a)

14915 Head incomplete, tip missing. L.50, T.2mm 5261 sf5954 (P6a)

14916 Head largely missing, tip missing. L.24, T.2mm 3227 sf9380 (P6a)

14917 Head incomplete and tip missing. L.24, T.3mm 5184 sf4029 (P6a/b)

14918 Round eye. Tip missing. L.41, T.3mm 3054 sf1038 (P7a)

Shanks

14919 L.36mm 5195 sf4130 (P6a/b)

14920 L.36mm 4254 sf1071 (P6z)

Agricultural tools

Possible pruning hook

14921 Corroded. It has an incomplete curved blade and a stub of tang. L.82, W.21, T.7mm 1055 sf109 (P6a)

Other tools

Shears

14922 Blade and stub of stem. Blade back straight, tip missing, shoulder concave. L.71, W.10, T.5mm 10092 sf4091 (P6a)

14923 Blade and stub of stem. Blade back straight before curving in to tip, sloping shoulder. L.61; blade: L.34, W.9, T.4mm 4802 sf5592 (P6a)

14924 Incomplete blade and stub of stem. Concave shoulder. L.51, W.13, T.2mm 10004 sf8387 (P6a/b)

14925 Blade and stub of tang. Shoulder concave, blade tip missing. L.84, W.15, T.4mm 3182 sf3258 (P7a)

Knives

Whittle tang knives

Blade back form A: blade back straight before sloping down to the tip

A1: blade back straight part horizontal

14926 Back straight for 40mm and then slopes down at c.14°. Cutting edge S-shaped. Slight vertical shoulder, tang bent over at 90°, but complete. L.83; blade: L.56, W.11, T.3mm 4694 sf5640 (P6a)

A2: blade back straight part upward sloping

14927 Back straight for 35mm and then slopes down at c.15°, tip missing. Cutting edge S-shaped. Vertical shoulder, tang tip wedge-shaped. L.112; blade: L.80, W.13, T.4mm 3342 sf4223 (P6a)

14928 Back straight for 15mm and then slopes down at c.25°. Cutting edge straight and then curves up to the tip. Slight shoulder, tang tip wedge-shaped. Non-ferrous metal located by conservation (not identified). L.59; blade: L.34, W.10, T.4mm 3409 sf5310 (P6a) (Fig.1355)

14929 Blade incomplete. Back straight for 52mm and then slopes down at c.25°. Cutting edge irregular. Vertical shoulder, tang tip wedge-shaped. L.95; blade: L.52, W.14, T.3mm 2182 sf5049 (P6a/b)

Ai: form of straight part of blade back indeterminate

8169 Blade back horizontal for 42mm and then slopes down at c.5° towards the tip which is missing due to corrosion. Cutting edge is S-shaped, but curves up markedly towards the tip. Ivory handle with round cross-section. At the head a copper alloy collar with an incised line around each margin, the one nearest the blade decorated with notches. Plated. L.228; knife: L.178; blade: L.120, W.20, T.5mm 2162 sf4945 (P6b) (Fig.1355)

14930 Back straight for 40mm and then slopes down at c.15°. Cutting edge S-shaped. Shoulder concave, tang largely missing. L.64; blade: L.60, W.12, T.4mm 5184 sf4051 (P6a/b)

14931 End of blade. Angle between two parts of back 20°. Cutting edge straight before curving up to tip. L.35, W.9, T.4mm 2283 sf5499 (P6c)

14932 Corroded. Blade tip missing. Tang a stub. L.49, W.12, T.5mm 6130 sf6203 (P7a)

Blade back form C: blade back straight before becoming convex and curving down to the tip

C1: straight part of blade back horizontal

4983   Blade back straight for 33mm. Cutting edge has a very slight S-shape. At shoulder back steps down before coming to a triangular end. Tang tip a rounded wedge-shape. L.90; blade: L.54, W.10, T.4mm 3342 sf4203 (P6a) (*Fig.1356*)

14933   Bent at junction of blade and tang. Blade back straight for 46mm, tip at blade's mid-point. Cutting edge has a slight S-shape. Notch cut into back at shoulder. Sloping shoulder, tang tip wedge-shaped. Butt weld between back and cutting edge visible on X-radiograph. L.127; blade: L.82, W.10, T.3mm 5353 sf5867 (P6a) (*Fig.1356*)

14934   Blade back straight for 23mm. Cutting edge straight before curving up to the tip which is at the blade's mid-point. Groove on each blade face. Notch cut into back at shoulder. Sloping shoulder, tang incomplete L.63; blade: L.39, W.9, T.4mm 5375 sf6912 (P6a)

14935   Blade back straight for 67mm. Cutting edge has a slight S-shape, tip at blade's mid-point. Concave shoulder, tang has wedge tip. Mineralised remains of handle, material unidentified. L.121; blade: L.90, W.11, T.4mm 5375 sf7044 (P6a)

14936   Blade back straight for 48mm. Cutting edge straight and curves up to the tip which is at blade's mid-point. Two grooves on one face and one on the other. Sloping shoulder, tang complete. L.121; blade: L.87, W.15, T.4mm 3242 sf5443 (P6b) (*Fig.1356*)

14937   Blade slightly bent. Back straight to a point 40mm from the shoulder, tip at half the blade's width. Cutting edge straight before curving up to the tip. Sloping shoulder, tang tip missing. L.84; blade: L.58, W.10, T.4mm 5254 sf4707 (P6a/b) Metallurgy report (*Fig.1356*)

14938   Cutting edge straight before curving up at the tip. Tang slightly bent. L.145; blade: L.91, W.14, T.3mm 1408 sf2909 (P7a)

C2: straight part of blade back upward sloping

14939   Blade tip missing, back straight for 45mm, edges chamfered. Butt weld between back and cutting edge visible on X-radiograph. Sloping shoulder, tang largely missing. L.82; blade: L.79, W.12, T.4mm 5640 sf7707 (P6a)

C3: straight part of blade back downward sloping

14940   Back straight to a point 52mm from the shoulder, tip at half the blade's width. Cutting edge convex. Sloping shoulder, tang tip missing. L.109; blade: L.82, W.19, T.9mm 5131 sf3994 (P6c) Metallurgy report

Ci: straight part of blade back has indeterminate form

14941   Blade only, narrows towards tip. Back straight for much of its length. Cutting edge straight. L.53, W.15, T.3mm 3283 sf4063 (P6a)

14942   Blade tip missing. Cutting edge convex. Sloping shoulder, tang tip pointed. L.85; blade: L.57, W.12, T.4mm 3342 sf4187 (P6a)

14943   Tip of blade. Cutting edge straight. L.39, W.12mm 2167 sf4902 (P6a)

14944   Blade and stub of tang. Back straight for 41mm. Cutting edge S-shaped, tip at blade's mid-point. Sloping shoulder. L.96; blade: L.91, W.13, T.3mm 7065 sf5420 (P6z)

Knives of indeterminate blade back form

14945   Tang and stub of blade. L.57; blade: L.18, W.13, T.5mm 1055 sf118 (P6a)

14946   Tang and stub of blade. L.60; blade: L.15, W.18, T.2mm 1055 sf125 (P6a)

14947   Very corroded, bent blade fragment. L.49mm 2167 sfs5005–6 (P6a)

14948   Tip of blade. L.12, W.10mm 3334 sf5394 (P6a)

14949   Corroded. Blade tip missing, tang largely missing. L.62, W.10, T.4mm 1663 sf6581 (P6a)

14950   Corroded. Blade back form uncertain, tip missing, cutting edge irregular. Slight shoulder, tang incomplete. L.129; blade: L.107, W.17, T.8mm 3146 sf7000 (P6b)

14951   Very corroded and bent in two. L.(unbent) 60mm 10140 sf4610 (P6a/b)

14952   Blade incomplete. Cutting edge was S-shaped. Sloping shoulder, tang complete. L.78; blade: L.43, W.11, T.4mm 5273 sf4833 (P6a/b)

14953   Very corroded. Incomplete blade and stub of tang. Vertical shoulder. L.58, W.13, T.3mm 5551 sf7419 (P6a/b)

14954   Tang bent at the junction with the blade and again after c.23mm so that it is at 90° to the blade. Blade tapers towards the tip, now missing. The back is straight, but irregular near tip due to corrosion. Cutting edge was probably slightly convex, but is pitted by corrosion. Vertical shoulder, tang swells in centre, tip missing. L.296; blade: L.188, W.14, T.6mm 5104 sf3300 (P6c) (*Fig.1363*)

14955   Blade incomplete, back straight before possibly curving down to the tip. At the junction with the tang a trace of non-ferrous shoulder plates. L.59, W.15, T.4mm 1390 sf9322 (P6e)

14956   Corroded. Blade tapers sharply. Cutting edge a marked S-shape. Sloping shoulder, tang incomplete. L.62; blade: L.45, W.8, T.4mm 1558 sf4695 (P6z)

14957   Corroded. Cutting edge irregular. Sloping shoulder, tang largely missing. L.51; blade: L.47, W.9, T.3mm 7178 sf5530 (P6z)

Other tanged knife

14958   Blade back straight to a point 47mm from the shoulder, then develops into a curled-over tip. Cutting edge is slightly convex and finishes where a tip at blade's mid-point would be. Sloping shoulder, tang tapers to point, wood remains. L.163; blade: L.66, W.13, T.5mm 5261 sf5451 (P6a) (*Fig.1358*)

Knife tang

14959   Wood remains. L.57mm 1386 sf2301 (P6e)

Scale tang knife

14960   Blade tip missing, back straight as far as break. Cutting edge irregular. Bent at junction with tang which is incomplete. What survives is pierced twice, non-ferrous metal around one of the holes. L.138; blade: L.103, W.13, T.3mm 2061 sf2979 (P7a)

Paring knife

14961   Blade has straight back and is curved over into a C-shape near the tip. Tang incomplete. L.90; blade: W.19, T.4mm 8023 sf1276 (P7c) (*Fig.1380*)

Knife mood

14962   Parallel-sided 'blade' and tang. L.69; blade: L.44, W.13, T.4mm 5073 sf3484 (P6c)

Possible sharpening steel

14963   Consists of a tang of rounded cross-section which tapers to point and a 'blade' which is parallel-sided with a rounded end. L.182; blade: L.85, W.12, T.3; tang: T.7mm 5375 sf6045 (P6a) (*Fig.1380*)

Structural items and fittings

Stud

14964   C-shaped solid head. Shank incomplete. L.30, W.40, T.8mm 1392 sf9857 (P7a)

Clench bolts

Diamond-shaped roves

14965   Head missing, incomplete rove. L.36; shank: T.8; rove: L.32, W.20mm 4716 sf5140 (P6a)

14966   L.42; head: W.19; shank: T.8; rove: L.35, W.27mm 5261 sf5165 (P6a)

14967   L.20; head: W.15; shank: T.4; rove: L.28, W.19mm 1663 sf6582 (P6a)

14968   Rove pushed up shank. L.45; head: W.39; shank: T.7; rove: L.60, W.32mm 1686 sf6662 (P6a)

14969   L.41; head: W.16; shank: T.6; rove: L.28, W.17mm 5242 sf4464 (P6a/b)

14970   L.56; head: W.22; shank: T.7; rove: L.37, W.26mm 5254 sf4694 (P6a/b)

14971   Incomplete rove. L.30; head: W.15; shank: T.5; rove: L.20, W.15mm 5642 sf7681 (P6a/b)

14972   Incomplete rove, head missing. L.42; shank: T.8; rove: L.22, W.12mm 2026 sf248 (P6c)

14973   Bent shank. L.41; head: W.20; shank: T.6; rove: L.37, W.30mm 5073 sf3056 (P6c)

14974   L.59; head: W.30; shank: T.9; rove: L.36, W.22mm 5110 sf5596 (P6c)

14975   Very corroded, in two pieces. L.50; head: W.24; shank: T.6; rove: L.45, W.25mm 5131 sf9437 (P6c)

14976   L.37; head: W.19; shank: T.5; rove: L.27, W.20mm 7001 sf2025 (P6z)

14977   L.35; head: W.18; rove: L.25, W.20mm 7002 sf1998 (P7a)

14978   Head missing, elongated rove. L.40, W.33mm 2062 sf3553 (P7a)

Rectangular roves

14979   L.32; head: W.16; shank: T.8; rove: L.36, W.25mm 4190 sf814 (P6a)

14980   Chisel marks on rove ends. L.31; head: W.18; shank: T.6; rove: L.17, W.14mm 5139 sf6951 (P6a)

14981   Head missing. L.34; shank: T.9; rove: L.22, W.18mm 1758 sf7600 (P6a)

14982   Two, both with heads incomplete. Largest: L.43; shank: T.5; rove: L.23, W.20mm 4694 sf9747 (P6a)

14983   Head missing. L.32; shank: T.5; rove: L.22, W.14mm 2214 sf5245 (P6a/b)

14984   L.43; head: W.26; shank: T.6; rove: L.30, W.26mm 5110 sf5473 (P6c)

Square roves

14985   Head missing. L.44; shank: T.5; rove: L.14, W.14mm 3342 sf4188 (P6a)

14986   L.35; head: W.17; shank: T.6; rove: L.16, W.16mm 4710 sf5064 (P6a)

14987   Unusual thin head. L.26; head: W.16; shank: T.6; rove: L.16, W.16mm 1419 sf3153 (P6b)

Others

14988   Rove incomplete. L.43; head: W.21; shank: T.6mm 4716 sf5445 (P6a)

14989   Rove missing. L.40; head: W.26; shank: T.6mm 1527 sf4263 (P6a)

14990   Very corroded. Possibly rectangular rove. L.c.30; head: W.27; shank: T.6; rove: L.30mm 6255 sf6919 (P6a)

14991   Head and rove largely missing. L.30; shank: T.5mm 5521 sf9264 (P6a)

14992   Head largely missing. Possibly rectangular rove. L.34; shank: T.7; rove: L.35, W.28mm 1456 sf3917 (P6b)

14993   Rove largely missing. L.31; head: W.24; shank: T.6mm 1463 sf3923 (P6b)

14994   In two pieces. Possibly diamond-shaped rove. L.63; head: W.30; rove: L.32, W.30mm 5084 sf2625 (P6a/b)

14995   Rove missing. L.36; head: W.26; shank: T.7mm 5132 sf3794 (P6a/b)

14996   Rove fragmentary, shank rounded cross-section. L.42; head: W.22; shank T.7mm 8030 sf1367 (P7c)

Roves

14997   Diamond-shaped. L.42, W.33mm 2324 sf5795 (P6a)

14998   Rectangular. L.22, W.16mm 1760 sf7635 (P6a)

14999   Rectangular. L.20, W.20mm 1792 sf7693 (P6a)

15000   Fragment, rectangular. L.30, W.20mm 6346 sf8032 (P6a)

15001   Rectangular. L.33, W.24mm 5295 sf9483 (P6b)

15002   Rectangular. L.30, W.20mm 5155 sf3955 (P6a/b)

15003   Rectangular. L.27, W.21mm 2260 sf5504 (P6a/b)

15004   Rectangular. L.25, W.20mm 5073 sf3443 (P6c)

15005   Rectangular. L.24, W.22mm 2305 sf5654 (P6c)

15006   Diamond-shaped. L.33, W.25mm 2103 sf3114 (P6b/c)

15007   Square. L.30, W.30mm 1052 sf733 (P6z)

15008   Diamond-shaped. L.40, W.25mm 1478 sf4139 (P6z)

15009   Diamond-shaped. L.40, W.24mm 1478 sf4140 (P6z)

15010   Square. L.30, W.25mm 7040 sf3062 (P7a)

15011   Rectangular. L.28, W.22mm 7054 sf3176 (P7a)

Staples

Rectangular

15012   One arm was bent back and broken off. L.22, W.65, T.6mm 2259 sf6411 (P6a)

15013   Arm tips missing, one was inturned. L.30, W.25, T.2mm 6242 sf7958 (P6a)

15014   One arm missing, other incomplete. L.22, W.48mm 1584 sf6146 (P6b)

15015   One arm missing, other inturned tip. L.15, W.35, T.5mm 1390 sf2391 (P6e)

15016   Both arms incomplete. Head at its widest in centre. L.63; head: W.11, T.2mm 4099 sf1515 (P7b)

U-shaped

15017   One arm tip missing. L.56, W.42, T.10mm 3197 sf3264 (P6d)

15018   L.50, W.37, T.9mm 8023 sf10003 (P7c)

Other staples

15019   Rectangular with rounded corners. Wider faces of arms in same plane as wider face of staple. One arm incomplete. L.103, W.63, T.12mm 3281 sf3945 (P6c)

15020   Staple arm. L.46, W.8mm 2158 sf4676 (P6c)

15021   Staple arm. L.55, W.8, T.8mm 2122 sf9738 (P6c)

15022   Staple arm. L.50mm 8003 sf1429 (P7c)

15023   Staple arm. L.48mm 8003 sf1467 (P7c)

Collars

15024   Roughly rectangular. L.31, W.20, T.3mm 2343 sf5870 (P6a)

15025   Bent into L-shape, was rectangular. Arms: L.52 and 40, W.6, T.2mm 5375 sf5931 (P6a)

15026   Incomplete, was rectangular. L.27, W.20, T.3mm 2381 sf6169 (P6c)

Wall anchor

15027   Shank incomplete, at the thicker end it is flattened into a rounded terminal, pierced in centre with nail in situ. L.84, W.25, T.20mm 3180 sf3047 (P7a)

Gutter support

15028   Long tapering shank with, at the thicker end, a downward projecting tapered S-shaped arm and an upward projecting oval plate attached. L.400mm 3010 sf2541 (P7a) (Fig.1409)

Hinge pivots

15029   Very corroded. Guide arm: L.69, W.15; shank: L.35, W.6mm 5073 sf3149 (P6c)

15030   Shank incomplete. Guide arm: L.35, T.9; shank: L.23, W.13mm 2120 sf4274 (P6d)

15031   Slight step below the guide arm. Guide arm: L.28, T.3; shank: L.39, W.12mm 7060 sf3308 (P6z)

15032   Hinge pivot or hook. Guide arm bent outwards. Shank narrows sharply to pointed tip. Guide arm: L.30, T.4; shank: L.36, W.11mm 7047 sf3858 (P6z)

Latch rests

15033   L.96, W.28, T.7mm 1385 sf2227 (P6e) (Fig.1413)

15034   Shank incomplete. L.62, W.26, T.7mm 4478 sf3070 (P6e)

Hooks

Wall hook

15035   Hook arm curves back slightly over the shank. Arms: L.80 and 33, W.8, T.7mm 5640 sf7807 (P6a) (Fig.1413)

S-hook

15036   One end missing. L.65, W.25, T.10mm 4694 sf5643 (P6a)

Swivel hooks

15037   Fragment. Domed head and stub of hook. Plated (tin). L.29mm 5199 sf4323 (P6a/b)

15038   Domed head, sub-rounded cross-section. Plated (tin). L.40, W.24, T.5, head: D.13mm 4478 sf3099 (P6e) (Fig.1414)

Hinge straps

15039   It has a pivot arm at the wider end of the strap which is pierced twice and narrows to what had been a rounded, pierced terminal, now largely missing. Plated (tin-lead). L.142, W.20, T.6mm 1386 sf2326 (P6e) (Fig.1416)

15040   Link at head largely missing. Strap has convex shoulders and is incomplete, pierced twice, nails in situ, neatly rounded heads. Plated (possibly solder, not identified). L.76, W.20, T.3; nail heads: D.7mm 1390 sf9321 (P6e)

Hasp

15041   Figure-of-eight-shaped, rounded cross-section, links of unequal size, sides touch. L.61, W.18, T.4mm 4478 sf3108 (P6e) (Fig.1419)

Pinned hinge strap

15042   Head of strap with loop in the centre. Plated (tin-lead). L.42, W.33, T.2mm 4505 sf4296 (P6e)

Stapled hasp

15043   At the head is a pierced rectangular terminal. The body is leaf-shaped and the staple is attached at the widest point. Small grooves in the edges of the upper face. L.52, W.10, T.2; staple: L.13, W.8mm 5312 sf5938 (P6b) (Figs.1421–2)

Handles

15044   Ring handle and staple. Ring has sub-rectangular/sub-rounded cross-section. Staple U-shaped. Ring: D.88, T.7; staple: L.44, W.18, T.5mm 3342 sf4184 (P6a)

15045   Consists of: (a) tube with strip brazed around it at head and base; (b) a ring from which a prong projects to hold it into the top of the tube. Within the ring is a cross member supported by two curved members. Plated (brass). L.86; tube: D.10; ring: D.29mm 1385 sf2195 (P6e) (Fig.1423)

15046   Drop handle (found with fragment of staple). Incomplete, one looped terminal survives. Plated. L.50, T.8mm 1052 sf720 (P6z)

Catch

15047   Exists as a small fitting with an eye at one end of a lozenge-shaped plate which has a rectangular notch in one side and is curled over at tip. L.37, W.13mm 8014 sf8109 (P7c)

Fittings

They are described as either strips or plates using the same criteria as for bar iron, blanks and scrap (see p.3025). Those which were probably part of hinges or corner brackets are described as straps. All have a rectangular cross-section and are pierced once unless stated.

Plates

15048   Strap terminal with pointed end, sides curved over slightly, pierced twice. L.41, W.15, T.3mm 3352 sf9237 (P6a)

15049 Irregular. L.30, W.20, T.2mm 3347 sf9438 (P6a)

15050 Curved at 90° in the centre and irregular in shape. Pierced at the end of one arm. A strip is brazed to it on its long axis (perhaps some form of casing). Plated (brass). Arms: L.44 and 39; W.28, T.5mm 5047 sf1823 (P6a/b)

15051 Narrows, broken at each end, pierced twice, one with rivet in situ. L.29, W.23mm 1077 sf145 (P6b)

15052 Slightly curved, narrows to a point at one end, rest irregular. Pierced twice, nail heads in situ on concave face, one holds a fragment of another plate. ?Leather adheres to concave face. Possibly armour. L.64, W.40, T.5mm 3187 sf3198 (P6b)

15053 Bent over at one end, broken at both. L.33, W.24, T.4mm 4475 sf9478 (P6c)

15054 Perhaps from hasp or hinge strap. Narrows at one end, broken at both, one face convex. Unpierced. Plated (tin). L.47, W.19, T.4mm 3240 sf9479 (P6d)

15055 Broken at both ends, widened at one. L.47, W.34, T.4mm 4478 sf3102 (P6e)

15056 Irregular fragment. Domed head of nail in situ, shank missing. Possibly plated. L.32, W.22mm (see 15067) 4695 sf3913 (P6e)

15057 Pierced, rounded end, perhaps of corner bracket. L.20, W.15, T.3mm 1391 sf9214 (P6e)

15058 Two plates, longer incomplete, held together at one end by a nail. L.68, W.23, T.3mm 9001 sf1811 (P6z)

15059 Pierced at one end. L.47, W.35mm 3003 sf1320 (P7a)

Strips

15060 Broken at one end; at the other a pierced, rounded terminal. L.54, T.3; terminal: W.18mm 4802 sf5582 (P6a)

15061 Flattened at each end to form a pierced, rounded terminal, one incomplete, one with rivet in situ. Grooves cut into the face of strip. Plated (tin-lead). L.53, T.4; terminal: W.19mm 5302 sf5877 (P6b)

15062 Y-shaped. The ends of the two shorter arms are made thinner by a step and are pierced. L.29, W.28, T.6mm 5205 sf4183 (P6a/b)

15063 Pierced at one end. L.32, W.7, T.3mm 10034 sf9277 (P6a/b)

15064 Broken at one end; at the other an incomplete pierced, rounded terminal. One face of the strip has notches punched into it. Plated (tin). L.77, W.5; terminal: W.11mm 5158 sf4532 (P6c)

15065 L-shaped, both arms incomplete. Shorter arm plated. Arms: L.51 and 28, W.11, T.5mm 5114 sf3541 (P6e)

15066 One end broken; other has a pierced trapezoidal terminal. L.62, T.7; terminal: W.19mm 1386 sf3754 (P6e) (Fig.1425)

15067 Small bifurcated terminal of a possible hinge strap. Exists as an incomplete curved strip which tapers and is looped back on itself. In the loop a dome-headed nail, shank fragmentary. Plated. Wood remains on one face (see 15056). L.32, W.20, T.2; nail: W.20mm 4695 sf3908 (P6e)

15068 Slightly S-shaped strip, broken at one end and flattened to form a rounded pierced terminal at the other. L.70; terminal: W.25mm 1395 sf2921 (P7a) (Fig.1425)

15069 Curved strip, broken at one end with rounded pierced terminal at other which has seven small domed protrusions around its perimeter. L.58; terminal: W.28mm 3182 sf3261 (P7a) (Fig.1425)

15070 In two pieces; at each end an incomplete pierced terminal, one has small punched dots on the surface. L.70; terminal: W.28mm 8024 sfs1233–4 (P7c) (Fig.1425)

Fitting with spirally twisted strip

15071 Curved strip with an incomplete terminal at each end. Possibly a handle. L.95, T.5mm 4798 sf6831 (P6a)

Suspension fitting

15072 Consists of link and stub of strap, broken across piercing. L.37, W.25, T.6mm 5261 sf7086 (P6a)

Chain links
Figure-of-eight-shaped

15073 L.118, W.43, T.8mm 1385 sf2225 (P6e) (Fig.1429)

Other forms

15074 Incomplete. Oval with rounded cross-section. L.45, W.33, T.5mm 5375 sf7088 (P6a)

15075 Oval with rounded cross-section. L.32, W.28, T.3mm 10138 sf4308 (P6a/b)

15076 One eye larger than the other, faces at 90° to each other. Shank has rounded cross-section, slight expansion in the centre. L.65, T.5; eyes: L.20 and 13, W.13 and 12mm 2026 sf5968 (P6c) (Fig.1429)

Rings

15077 Overlapping tips in unfused scarf joint. D.42, W.11, T.2mm 5013 sf968 (P6a/b) (Fig.1430)

15078 Very corroded. Half. D.59mm 3256 sf3922 (P6d)

Collar

15079 In two pieces. Tapers very slightly, nail shank fused to interior. Possibly plated. Wood remains. L.27, D.23mm 4694 sf4753 (P6a) (Fig.1430)

Tubes

15080 One end broken. Around the complete end runs spiral groove. Seam held with brazing metal which covers the object. L.54, D.10mm 1052 sf579 (P6z) (Fig.1431)

15081 Fragment. L.78, D.16mm 8034 sf9054 (P7c)

Locks and keys
Lock bolt

15082 Two short curved projections from base, notch in top. L.178, W.17, T.7mm; W. (across projections) 29mm 1385 sf2224 (P6e) (Fig.1441)

Lock ward plate

15083 Ends broken. Triangular with central key hole. L.65, W.25mm 8034 sf1853 (P7c) (Fig.1441)

Barrel padlocks

Case fragments

15084 Fragment. Plated (bronze). L.31, W.25mm 5013 sf900 (P6a/b)

15085 Crushed and incomplete (original length survives). Surviving end-plate recessed into case, rectangular bolt hole. Plain strip brazed around the case end and two spirally twisted strips brazed onto the body. Free arm tube attached by wide fin. L.67, W.42; case: D.25mm 5638 sf7676 (P6a/b) (*Fig.1442*)

15086 Half an end-plate which had been recessed into case. Plated (copper, some tin and lead = brass). L.30, W.15, T.5mm 2290 sf5514 (P6d)

Bolts and springs

15087 Probable padlock spine, now incomplete, pierced at one end to which a spring, now fragmentary, is riveted. L.56, W.10mm 5261 sf5910 (P6a) (*Fig.1448*)

15088 Spine to which two springs are riveted. Plated (brass). L.58, W.11, T.6mm 2092 sf3086 (P6b/c) (*Fig.1448*)

15089 Stub of bolt, closing plate and two spines each with two springs fused to them. Closing plate plated. L.29, W.11, T.11mm 3240 sf3930 (P6d)

15090 Spine with fragment of a spring which was riveted on. L.62, W.8, T.3mm 2304 sf5796 (P6d)

Keys for mounted locks

Keys with hollow stem

15091 Bow bent and incomplete, was formed from flattening the head of stem, pierced in centre. Stem incomplete. L.32; bow: W.16; stem: D.7mm 3342 sf7143 (P6a)

15092 Stub of stem and bit. Stem hollow. Bit has a single cut, with two chambers, in outer side. L.34; stem: D.8; bit: L.15, W.21mm 3194 sf3458 (P6b)

15093 Bow largely missing, was made by flattening the head of the stem and piercing. Stem hollow, tapers slightly. Bit reverse S-shaped in cross-section. L.38; stem: D.10; bit: L.10, W.19mm 2110 sf3252 (P6b/c) (*Fig.1449*)

15094 Bow oval, rounded cross-section, has a prong by which it is held in the head of the stem. Bit S-shaped. L.70; bow: L.25, W.28; stem: D.10; bit: L.13, W.22mm 3276 sf3933 (P6d) (*Figs.1449, 1451*)

Solid stem projects beyond bit which has a central channel

15095 Very corroded. Bow and part of stem missing. Bit channel is cross-shaped and each side has two cuts into its base. Plated (not identified). L.120; stem: T.15; bit: L.47, W.50mm 3256 sf3921 (P6d)

15096 Bow kidney-shaped, flattened tip. Stem swells in the centre and has knop at tip. Grooves around stem: two at tip flanking knop, two or three at rear of bit, two between bit and bow. Bit largely missing. L.127; stem: T.6; bow: L.22, W.38mm 1386 sf2295 (P6e) (*Figs.1451–2*)

15097 Bow D-shaped, flattened tip, sub-rounded cross-section. Stem has sub-rounded cross-section, starts to taper as it approaches the rear of the bit, stepped in above the middle of the bit and ends in a knop. Three grooves behind the bit, two in the centre. Each side of the bit has a cut in base. L.139; bow: L.26, W.36; stem: D.8; bit: L.26, W.27mm 1390 sf2338 (P6e) (*Figs.1451–2*)

15098 Bow largely missing. Bit channel is cross-shaped. L.115; bit: W.28; stem: T.9mm 4048 sf524 (P7b) (*Fig.1452*)

Barrel padlock keys

15099 Upper part only. Lower part of stem, largely missing, is stepped out on its wider faces and the upper part then tapers to the head and has a rounded cross-section. At the head a ring terminal. X-radiograph shows fragment of suspension ring in situ. L.53, W.7, T.5mm 3535 sf7720 (P6a)

Bit and stem in line

15100 Bit incomplete, but was round with a trapezoidal extension at the top. Stem expands in the centre and has a rounded cross-section. Terminal missing. L.77; bit W.25; stem: T.10mm 3163 sf2256 (P7a) (*Fig.1456*)

Dress, dress accessories and personal ornament

Buckles

Frames have rectangular cross-section unless stated.

Buckles and buckle-plates

15101 Buckle: D-shaped, looped pin. Buckle-plate: rectangular, pierced once for attachment. L.32; buckle: L.23, W.13; buckle-plate: L.22, W.13mm 5238 sf4337 (P6a/b)

15102 Buckle frame, incomplete. Surviving end a cylinder set in the ends of the sides, also a smaller cylindrical central member around which buckle-plate is folded. Buckle-plate has a rounded end and was attached by two rivets. Buckle: L.21, W.30; buckle-plate: L.26mm 3282 sf8180 (P7a)

Shoe buckles with circular frames

15103 Rounded cross-section, looped pin. D.16, T.3mm 2190 sf5088 (P6a/b)

15104 Rounded cross-section, looped pin. D.15, T.3mm 1386 sf3769 (P6e)

15105 Sub-rounded cross-section. Pin a strip folded in the centre. Plated. D.28, T.4; pin: L.40, W.11mm 4505 sf4293 (P6e) (*Fig.1465*)

Other buckle frames

15106 Oval frame. Pin a strip folded in the centre. L.40, W.21, T.3; pin: L.29, W.8mm 1075 sf775 (P6a) (*Fig.1466*)

15107 Incomplete frame has straight sides and rounded ends. Side on which pin was set incomplete, but had scarf joint; other side has slight kink in centre. L.64, W.31, T.3mm 5245 sf4938 (P6a/b) (*Fig.1466*)

Frame with rotating arm

15108 Arm has rounded cross-section, pinched at each end where set in the frame sides, now fragmentary. Arm has recessed pin rest in centre. Groups of three encircling grooves at each end and either side of pin rest. Plated (tin). L.45, T.8mm 4448 sf2692 (P7b) (*Fig.1469*)

Buckle-pin

15109 Looped eye, pointed tip. L.67, T.6; loop: W.13mm 3287 sf8192 (P6a) (*Fig.1472*)

Pins

15110 Spherical head. Plated (tin-lead). L.39; head: D.5; shank: T.2mm 4694 sf5628 (P6a)

15111 Small roughly spherical head. L.39; head: D.3; shank: T.2mm 1831 sf7684 (P6a)

15112 In fragments. Lead sub-spherical head with flat top. L.40; head: D.8; shank: T.2mm 10076 sf9227 (P6a)

15113 Pointed head, shank tip missing. Plated (tin). L.39; head: D.5; shank: T.3mm 5254 sf4751 (P6a/b)

15114 Lead sub-spherical head with flat top, shank incomplete. L.29; head: D.6; shank: T.2mm 10085 sf4953 (P6a/b)

15115 Roughly spherical head, shank bent and has sub-rectangular cross-section, tip missing. Plated (tin-lead) L.50; head: D.10; shank: T.4mm 4253 sf1066 (P6z)

Dress hook

15116 Pierced twice at the top and narrows slightly before stepping in to taper to a pointed tip. L.37, W.13mm 3282 sf10051 (P7a)

Riding equipment

Spur fitting

15117 Consists of central domed element with opposing hooked terminals. Plated (tin). L.37, W.25mm 8008 sf1196 (P7c) (*Fig.1523*)

Horse equipment

Horseshoes

Wavy outer edge

15118 One branch incomplete. Complete arm has three countersunk holes and thickened calkin; other arm has two countersunk holes. L.110, W.113mm 4085 sf1363 (P6a)

15119 End of branch. Slightly thickened calkin, one and a half countersunk holes. L.60, W.19, T.6mm 4694 sf6551 (P6a)

15120 End of branch. Turned-over calkin, part of countersunk hole. L.40, W.18mm 3525 sf7597 (P6a)

15121 End of branch. Folded-over calkin, one incomplete countersunk hole. L.50, W.18, T.13mm 3310 sf4020 (P6d)

Smooth outer edge

15122 Tip worn. One branch incomplete, other narrows sharply to tip where there is a slightly thickened calkin. Complete arm has three rectangular holes, other arm two. L.102, W.105, T.7mm 1033 sf13 (P6z)

15123 Complete. Three countersunk holes in each arm and one at the tip. Turned-over calkins. L.120, W.105; branch: W.25mm 1395 sf2980 (P7a)

15124 Complete. Fullered groove through which there are three holes in one branch and four in the other. End of each branch stamped 'H'. L.135, W.115; branch: W.34mm 5060 sf2142 (P8)

Indeterminate outer edge

15125 Tip of branch. Curves and tapers to wedge tip. L.70, W.13, T.4mm 3334 sf9495 (P6a)

15126 End of branch, broken over hole. L.71, W.21, T.12mm 1081 sf3248 (P6b)

15127 End of branch, broken over a hole, L.55, W.30mm 8023 sf1277 (P7c)

Horseshoe nails

Four horseshoe nails were recovered, details available in archive.

Weapons and armour

Arrowheads

All are socketed.

Leaf-shaped blade

15128 Socket incomplete. Blade has low triangular cross-section. L.63; socket: D.6; blade: W.13mm 3334 sf4235 (P6a) (*Fig.1532*)

15129 Corroded. Tang incomplete. Tip broken off. Lozenge-shaped cross-section. L.101, W.13, T.6; blade: L.46mm 3145 sf6505 (P6b)

Tapering blade of rectangular cross-section

15130 L.64; socket: D.9mm 5312 sf5670 (P6b) (*Fig.1532*)

Barbed blade

15131 Triangular blade, socket largely missing. L.39, W.16mm 5582 sf7480 (P6c) (*Fig.1532*)

Uncertain blade shape

15132 Incomplete socket and blade. L.37; blade: W.17; socket: D.10mm 4694 sf9231 (P6a)

Arrow tips

15133 Corroded. Plated (brass). Wood remains. L.31, D.10mm 4549 sf3503 (P6b)

15134 Plated (copper). Wood remains. L.25, D.11mm 1385 sf2199 (P6e) (*Fig.1532*)

15135 Has a thin fin on opposing sides. L.34, D.14mm 1386 sf2309 (P6e) (*Fig.1532*)

15136 Plated (copper, trace of zinc). L.38, D.14mm 1386 sf3753 (P6e)

15137 Has a thin fin on opposing sides. Plated (brass). L.40, D.13mm 1386 sf9334 (P6e)

15138 L.27, W.12mm 8024 sf1257 (P7c) (*Fig.1532*)

Unidentified object

15139 Strip with at the head a small hook or eye; strip tapers towards the base and is drawn out into a loop with a long tail. Possibly from a chatelaine. L.79, W.5, T.2mm 3352 sf4438 (P6a) (*Fig.1535*)

Copper alloy

Manufacturing waste

15140 Rod of sub-circular section, one end hammered flat, both ends broken. D.7.2, L.38.9, W.9.9, T.5.9mm 5521 sf7095 (P6a) (*Fig.1324*)

15141 Wire, long length, of circular section, bent up. D.1.5, L.393.8mm 5013 sf974 (P6a/b) (*Fig.1324*)

15142 Offcut, tapering from one end to other which is looped up. L.39.0, W.7.4, T.1.2mm 2327 sf5763 (P6a/b) (*Fig.1324*)

Textile tools

Needles

15143   Incomplete, head broken across lower part of eye, shank of circular section, lower half of shank bent up. D.1.0, L.35.1mm 5518 sf7246 (P6a/b)

15144   Incomplete, head broken off across eye, shank of circular section. D.0.8, L.30.3mm 7001 sf1983 (P6z)

So-called couching needle

15145   Object with long shaft of sub-circular section, tapering to one end, other end roughly squared off. Towards the tip there is a large sub-oval eye with deep grooves of V-shaped section on each side of eye and on both faces of shaft. At the other end there are the remains of the head, an incomplete inverted dome with out-turned rim, centrally perforated, end of shaft projecting through perforation, upper dome of head missing. D.3.4, L.162.4mm; head: D.14, T.0.5mm 4185 sf786 (P6a) (*Fig.1349*)

Thimbles

15146   Complete, slightly squashed on one side, with detachable leather lining, dome-shaped, with incised transverse line just above rim, and with D-shaped indentations in slightly oblique rows on sides and in radial rows on the crown. The leather lining is also dome-shaped, with a hole at the top and a longitudinal seam on one side, with seam holes visible. D.21.7, T.1, H.21.6mm 1386 sf2248 (P6e) (*Fig.1347*)

15147   Largely complete, dome-shaped, cracked at rim on one side, small piece broken off rim on other, with incised transverse line just above rim, with deep indentations all over sides and crown in slightly irregular lines. D.19.9, T.1.2, H.20.2mm 3162 sf2099 (P7a)

Domestic equipment

Vessels

15148   Two adjoining fragments, part of everted rim. L.44.2, W.33.2, T.1.2mm 3335 sf4169 (P6a)

15149   Fragment, possibly of base, sub-rectangular, of sub-rectangular section of irregular thickness, one face flat with scratches, other face uneven, with incomplete concentric rings radiating out from one edge. L.26, W.15.3, T.2.5mm 1430 sf3217 (P6e)

15150   Bowl, complete, originally hemispherical but now slightly misshapen, with flat out-turned rim, outer face relatively unworn, slightly damaged with holes in base and one on side. D.210.8, T.1.7mm 4560 sf3284 (P6a) (*Figs.1395–7*)

Patches

15151   Of sheet, sub-rectangular, two edges cut, two broken, one corner torn, sheet rivet in each corner, one with iron fragment attached. L.27.4, W.23.8, T.0.8mm; corner: T.4mm 3214 sf5007 (P6a) (*Fig.1399*)

15152   Of sheet, sub-rectangular, one long edge partially cut and partially folded over, other long edge folded over, one end cut, other broken, two sheet rivets survive on one long edge. L.49.2, W.31.5, T.2.9mm 4476 sf3043 (P6b)

15153   Sub-rectangular, of sheet, corners cut obliquely, irregular transverse slot at each end for sheet rivets. L.41.1, W.28.4, T.1mm 1390 sf3777 (P6e) (*Fig.1399*)

15154   Sub-triangular, one edge folded over, rivet hole close to edge. L.28.5, W.19.3, T.7.1mm 7035 sf4205 (P6z) (*Fig.1399*)

Structural items and fittings

Rivets

15155   Shank, of sub-square section. D.3.2, L.11.6mm 2325 sf5650 (P6a)

15156   Fragment, irregularly shaped, of sub-oval section. L.9.3, W.5.3, T.3.3mm 2305 sf5638 (P6c)

Tacks

15157   Shallowly domed, gilt, curved shank tapering to tip. L.11, W.1.9, T.1.3mm; head: D.6.8mm 1527 sf4254 (P6a) (*Fig.1408*)

15158   Shank of sub-square section, tapering, both ends flattened. L.22.8, W.3.9, T.3.3mm 5096 sf2907 (P6e)

15159   Shank of square section, lower half bent up. L.31, W.2.9, T.2.3mm 7065 sf4725 (P6z)

15160   Or plug, with flat sub-oval head, and stem of sub-circular section, tapering to pointed tip, with seam visible on top and down stem. L.15.5; head: D.10.0mm 6242 sf7200 (P6a) (*Fig.1408*)

Staples

15161   Sub-rectangular, of rectangular section, tapering to both ends, which are bent under, slightly bent centrally. L.29.1, W.4, T.1.5mm 5117 sf3973 (P6c) (*Fig.1408*)

15162   Sub-rectangular, of square section. L.66.5, W.2, T.2mm 4253 sf1173 (P6z)

15163   U-shaped, both ends cut at an angle. D.1.3, L.13.4mm 8023 sf1203 (P7c)

Collar

15164   Incomplete and misshapen, cut transversely at one side, torn and folded over at other. Along the top and bottom edges, there are irregularly spaced short slits, some V-shaped, others rectangular, all narrow. There are hammer marks on the outer face, and signs of filing on the inner. L.37.6, W.29.7, T.0.7mm 1456 sf3918 (P6b)

Binding strips

15165   Rectangular with obliquely cut corners, both ends and central square hammered down producing two square raised areas, the three lower areas each with traces of an iron rivet, the rivet head still surviving at one end. There are traces of probable tin plating in grooves on the upper face, and mineralised wood remains around one rivet on the underside. L.70.3, W.14, T.1mm; rivet: L.5.6mm 2201 sf5232 (P6a) (*Fig.1427*)

15166   Fragment, one end bent round at approximately 90°, broken across rivet hole close to one edge, and punched hole close to the other, with lateral incised line decoration on outer face of this side, possible solder on outer face of other side. L.12.1, W.11.8, T.0.6mm; shorter side: L.6.4mm 4473 sf3293 (P6c) (*Fig.1427*)

15167   Rectangular, with axial lines of perforations at each end, four at one end, three at the other, central area unperforated. L.85.6, W.13.3, T.0.9mm 3310 sf4013 (P6d) (*Fig.1427*)

15168   Originally curved, transverse crack where strip has been bent back into current slight wave, decorated with two parallel longitudinal lines, one end broken across rivet hole, other appears roughly cut. L.32.4, W.7.6, T.0.7mm 3003 sf123 (P7a)

Chains

15169 Four figure-of-eight links of circular section, a link at one end having been forced open. L.39.6, W.4.8mm; section: D.1.6mm 3017 sf1272 (P7a) (*Fig.1429*)

15170 Link, made from wire, folded transversely, the two lengths compressed together, hooked up at fold, diverging at the other end. D.1.4, L.19mm 7002 sf1931 (P7a)

15171 Link, incomplete, originally twisted figure-of-eight, of plano-convex section. L.9.6, W.1.3, T.1.3mm 3282 sf8177 (P7a)

15172 Link fragment, of circular section, one end looped up, the upper part curves away, the end being roughly broken. D.1.6, L.14.6mm 8013 sf572 (P7c)

Rings

15173 Fragment, both ends broken, of circular section, slight thickening of diameter towards one end. Section: D.5.3mm; internal D.35mm 4206 sf885 (P6a) (*Fig.1430*)

15174 Fragment, tiny, of D-shaped section, both ends roughly broken. L.8.2, W.4.6, T.1.5mm 1663 sf6587 (P6a)

15175 Fragment, narrow, of square section, both ends broken. L.14.6, W.1.6, T.1.6mm 4680 sf9366 (P6a)

15176 Penannular, complete but broken, tiny, misshapen, with ends forced apart, of circular section. D.8.6mm; wire: D.1mm 2219 sf5250 (P6b)

15177 Incomplete, annular, of circular section, small fragment broken away. D.15.6mm; section: D.1.1mm 5312 sf5627 (P6b)

Cylinder

15178 Incomplete, one end roughly broken, rolled up with one edge overlapping, and unsealed. L.27.1, W.9.4mm; sheet: T.0.6mm 3154 sf7128 (P6b) (*Fig.1431*)

Ferrule

15179 Tubular, with oval looped eye of D-shaped section at upper end, tube formed from plate of semi-circular section, which has been folded round forming loop, rivet through tube at lower end. D.11, L.48.5, T.1.2mm; loop: L.14.2, W.14, T.3.5mm 6296 sf7375 (P6a) (*Fig.1431*)

Perforated strips

15180 Fragment, rectangular, both ends broken across perforations. L.30.1, W.5.2, T.0.7mm 3269 sf3982 (P6a)

15181 Fragment, sub-rectangular, one end broken, irregular off-centre perforation near cut end. L.13.8, W.6, T.0.6mm 3194 sf3462 (P6b)

15182 Fragment, thin, sub-rectangular, one end broken across perforation, folded. L.13.1, W.12.9, T.0.4mm 4689 sf3903 (P6c)

Fitting

15183 Formed by small sub-square sheet, with central rivet which projects through sheet slightly on one face, having circular section, the rest is of square section, and there are the remains of second sheet fragment at other end. A

second rivet of similar length survives in one corner, and there are traces of rivets in the other corners, all with ends hammered flat. There are mineralised wood remains on upper face of square sheet close to central rivet. Sheet: L.13.8, W.13.7, T.1mm; central rivet: L.15.3, W.2.8, T.2.6mm 1390 sf2285 (P6e) (*Fig.1431*)

Candlestick

15184 Socket, cylindrical, of irregular thickness, tapering in and then flaring out symmetrically at lower end, with narrower solid circular stub, decorated with two bands of incised transverse lines. There are some ?Z-spun threads inside, made from a plant stem fibre, almost certainly flax. D.22.0, L.38.0, T.2.5mm 3163 sf2367 (P7a) (*Fig.1434*)

Dress, dress accessories and personal ornament

Buckles

15185 Incomplete, originally D-shaped, of sub-trapezoidal section, pin and part of bar broken off. L.28.3, W.15.2, T.2.5mm; frame: W.3.4mm 7001 sf2157 (P6z) (*Fig.1468*)

15186 Incomplete, originally with D-shaped frame, of sub-trapezoidal section, at one end a pentagonal knop of D-shaped section and small collar below. W.17, T.3.9mm; terminal: L.8.3, W.6.9, T.3.9mm 5060 sf2133 (P8) (*Fig.1468*)

15187 Square, with slightly convex sides, broad far end with deep groove for reception of pin, incised line on each side of groove, pin broken off. L.17.4, W.14.2, T.2.9mm 8008 sf1842 (P7c) (*Fig.1469*)

15188 Square, with slightly convex sides, broad end with deep groove to receive tip of pin and incised line on either side. Strap attachment plates are folded around the bar, ends of both broken, holding pin looped around bar. Organic remains between the plates are probably leather, and a small rivet goes through this from one plate to other. L.40.4, W.15.1, T.4.1mm; plate: L.27.7, W.12.8, T.0.5mm 4000 sf3291 (P11) (*Fig.1469*)

15189 Incomplete, originally trapezoidal, of sub-rectangular section, decorated on upper face along all sides with rocker-arm tracery, gilded on upper face and on edges. L.46.3, W.16.9, T.3.1mm; bow: W.4.8mm 3234 sf3554 (P6a) (*Figs.1469–70*)

15190 Sub-oval frame, of sub-convex section, thickness varying greatly, thickest in centre of frame opposite bar, thinning out on each side, projections or remains of second loop on each side of bar. A piece of sheet is curved around the bar, partially torn at one corner and bent back, and a very corroded iron pin is looped over the sheet. D.17.5, T.5.5mm 1663 sf7024 (P6a) (*Fig.1471*)

15191 'Spectacle' or double-looped, butterfly-shaped, central bar lost, but traces on bow show it was of iron. Of sub-rectangular section at one side where pin was situated, overlapping join on frame is visible. Decorative incised lines in corners of bow. L.33.4, W.26, T.5mm; bow: W.4.9mm 4000 sf1985 (P11) (*Fig.1471*)

Buckle-pins

15192 Of sub-plano-convex section, incomplete upper end flattened, tapering towards other flattened end, upper two-thirds convexly curved and decorated with incised saltire. L.41.1, W.9, T.4.9mm 10004 sf2607 (P6a/b)

15193 Or brooch pin, of plano-convex section, one end rounded, other end flattened, of rectangular section, hooked over. L.34.2, W.5, T.3.1mm 3004 sf7627 (P7a) (*Fig.1472*)

Possible buckle-plates

15194 Incomplete, in two adjoining fragments, formed from two rectangular strips, attached at one end by rivet. The strips are each broken at the same end; other ends rounded or cut square. There is possible organic material near the rivet, and one fragment has incised line decoration on one face. L.39.3, W.10.4, T.0.5mm; rivet: L.3.3mm 10077 sf3401 (P6a) (*Fig.1473*)

15195 Fragment, sub-rectangular, long edges straight, others broken. There are two rivet holes at one end, one of which still contains a rivet. L.39, W.18.2, T.0.8mm; rivet: D.2.2 L.3.9mm 4048 sf526 (P7b) (*Fig.1473*)

15196 Fragment, rectangular plate broken at one end, two perforations at other end, one placed slightly lower than other. L.30.4, W.11.3, T.0.5mm 8024 sf1839 (P7c) (*Fig.1473*)

Clasp

15197 Rectangular, of rectangular section, front plate with hooked projection at upper end, riveted to back plate close to upper end. There are two rivets on lower edge, which has short incised slightly oblique grooves along it on upper face, and there are organic remains between the plates. There is a rectangular perforated loop on the upper plate. L.37.0, W.22.1, T.4.2mm; projection: L.5.0, W.6.7, T.2.5mm; plate: T.1mm 2060 sf1997 (P8) (*Fig.1474*)

Strap-ends

15198 Fragment, from two-piece strap-end, irregularly shaped, one edge broken across rivet hole, a rivet surviving where part of edge is folded under. Close to one edge, there is incised leaf design, incorporating two leaves joined at ends of stems. L.33.4, W.15.9, T.0.8mm; rivet: D.2.2, L.1.9mm 5097 sf2987 (P6a/b) (*Fig.1475*)

15199 Plate from two-piece strap-end, sub-rectangular, one end rounded, rivet hole close to other square end. L.22.6, W.6.9, T.1.2mm 2182 sf5138 (P6a/b) (*Fig.1475*)

15200 Two adjoining fragments which form folded rectangular strip, one fragment with one end bent up and broken, perforation close to other end, other fragment with both ends roughly broken. L.24.9, W.9.7, T.0.5mm 7047 sf3836 (P6z)

15201 Formed from two sub-rectangular plates, soldered together at one end, now broken apart, with remains of two iron rivets at far end of each plate. L.17.4, W.12.2, T.0.6mm 8014 sf9377 (P7c)

Chape

15202 Sub-triangular, tapering from upper edge to rounded tip, soldered longitudinal seam on reverse and tip, closed end formed by three short longitudinal cuts, ends folded in and sealed. Upper edge is scalloped on front face, horizontal on reverse, with perforation on one side close to edge, fragment broken away across perforation on other side. There is incised decoration on the front face with tapering panel enclosing axial line of crude six-pointed stars with short oblique lines on either side. L.41, W.20.8, T.1.5mm 4002 sf100 (P9) (*Fig.1478*)

Mounts

15203 Incomplete, sub-discoidal, slightly convex, with central perforation. D.8.3, T.0.2mm 6255 sf6863 (P6a)

15204 Incomplete, sub-discoidal, perforated off-centre. D.16.4, T.1.4mm 10140 sf4493 (P6a/b)

15205 Domed, with internal traces of solder. D.14.5, T.0.4mm 1374 sf1812 (P6b) (*Fig.1479*)

15206 Hollow dome, with central perforation punched through from underside. The circumference has been crimped, and there are traces of tin-lead plating on the upper face. D.8.9, T.0.4mm 4450 sf2695 (P6b)

15207 Circular, hollow, domed. D.10.6, T.0.7mm 6217 sf7354 (P6c) (*Fig.1479*)

15208 Incomplete, originally sexfoil, centrally domed and perforated. There are small projections at the ends of the lobes, one lobe is roughly broken, another partially torn through from perforation. There are rivets for attachment in two lobes, one of which retains part of a rivet. D.24.9, T.0.9mm; rivet: L.4.9mm 3010 sf2507 (P7a) (*Fig.1479*)

15209 Two, both rectangular strips, made from same piece of sheet split into two, both with a small rivet hole in each corner along one long side. L.23.7, W.10.5, T.0.2mm 5175 sfs4378–9 (P6c) (*Fig.1480*)

15210 Sub-rectangular, with central perforation, and a smaller hole close to each end, one still containing rivet. L.17.6, W.9.9, T.0.9mm; rivet: D.1.3, L.3.7mm 7054 sf3037 (P7a) (*Fig.1480*)

Pins

15211 With wire-wound head, single twist, tapering shank to tip. D.0.8, L.27.9mm; head: D.2mm 7014 sf2136 (P7a) (*Fig.1490*)

15212 With wire-wound head, globular, shank of circular section, slightly bent. D.0.7, L.23.5mm; head: D.1.3mm 4041 sf400 (P10)

15213 With hemispherical head, top convex, shank of circular section, tapering to tip, traces of solder between head and shank. Analysis: copper, zinc and lead. More lead at head, and ?tin, possibly solder. D.1.0, L.45.6mm; head: D.2.1mm 5253 sf4655 (P6a/b)

15214 Incomplete, tip broken off, head globular, with irregular sub-radial grooves cut in. D.0.9, L.22.4mm; head: D.1.7mm 2138 sf4199 (P7a)

15215 Complete, with globular head, shank of circular section, bent close to tip. D.0.8, L.28.5mm; head: D.1.7mm 8003 sf1462 (P7c)

15216 Head incomplete, appears to have been formed by attaching small blobs to shank at top, roughly cut to have lozenge-shaped facets, one blob lost. Shank of circular section, drawing lines visible, tip bent up. D.0.9, L.39mm; head: D.1.4mm 5312 sf5641 (P6b)

15217 With sub-spherical head, decorated with lozenge-shaped facets standing proud, shank of circular section. D.1.9, L.38.1mm; head: D.1.7mm 2079 sf2739 (P7a) (*Fig.1490*)

15218 With trapezoidal head, longitudinally faceted, top rounded, shank of circular section, bent up from centre, extreme tip broken off. D.1.2, L.90.3mm; head: D.4.4mm 4077 sf581 (P7b)

Lace tags

15219 Two, one complete. The complete tag has overlapped seam. Incomplete tag has edge-to-edge seam, is corroded, has a securing rivet and contains organic material identified as the remains of silk cord or braid. D.2.0, L.24.3mm 1386 sf9328 (P6e)

15220 With edge-to-edge seam, one end closed. D.2.0, L.20.5mm 8003 sf1375 (P7c) (*Fig.1491*)

Lace or ribbon threader

15221 Incomplete, with at one end a globular terminal, quadruple hexagonal collar, short stem of hexagonal section, and second single collar. Main stem is of rectangular section with longitudinal facet cuts on both sides of each face, the end is broken across a rectangular perforation. L.59.8, W.4.7, T.4.3mm; terminal: D.7mm 4402 sf1461 (P6f) (*Fig.1491*)

Dress fastener

15222 Double-hooked, made from strip, central area flattened and slightly expanded, decorated with ribbing on both faces. L.34, W.1.9, T.1mm; across hook: W.4.3mm 4016 sf270 (P7b) (*Fig.1491*)

Wire loop fastener

15223 Oval, ends joined by single twist and broken. D.1.2, L.18.3, W.7.9mm 2003 sf10 (P7a) (*Fig.1491*)

Twisted wire loop

15224 Complete. D.2.1, L.24mm; loop: D.10.5mm; loop wire: D.1.1mm 1386 sf3755 (P6e)

Finger-ring

15225 Fragment, both ends broken, of sub-oval section, with relief decoration of line running along each side. W.2.4, T.3.9mm; original D.20mm 10265 sf6023 (P6a/b)

Medical and toilet implements
Medical plate

15226 Two fragments, both probably originally discoidal, with perforations arranged in concentric circles. There are the fragmentary remains of leather over the copper alloy. D.73.5, T.0.9mm 10265 sf6025 (P6a/b) (*Figs.1499–500*)

Toilet set

15227 Incomplete, comprising unguent spoon or ear scoop, one side of bifurcated upper end broken off. Each side of the upper end is of a different section: the incomplete side is of circular section; the other, which is curved convexly, is of sub-pentagonal section. The stem below is of hexagonal section, broadening out slightly to a square area of rectangular section which is centrally perforated, and decorated with two lateral grooves on each side. Below this, the stem tapers and the section becomes sub-circular, the end broadening out again and being scooped. L.67.5, W.15.5, T.3.8mm 3187 sf3202 (P6b) (*Fig.1501*)

Tweezers

15228 Of rectangular section, with arms slightly tapering from tips to loop, both arms decorated with incised line along both edges on both faces, incomplete rectangular slide close to tips, which are inturned. There are traces of iron within the loop. L.48.5, W.6.2, T.3.9mm; arm: T.0.7mm 3366 sf4497 (P6a) (*Fig.1501*)

15229 Of rectangular section, with oval loop, arms tapering slightly to tips, which are inturned, extreme tip of one arm broken off. L.45.2, W.3.6, T.0.5mm 10004 sf2562 (P6a/b) (*Fig.1501*)

15230 Incomplete, loop broken off at top, of rectangular section, arms taper slightly from tips to top, with wire slide towards upper end, both arms decorated with rocker-arm ornament in zig-zag pattern. L.36, W.10, T.6mm 3222 sf3364 (P6d) (*Fig.1501*)

15231 Of rectangular section, complete apart from small piece missing from loop, rectangular slide close to loop, tip of one arm slightly bent out. L.40.0, W.4.0, T.3.6mm; arm (sheet): T.0.8mm 4552 sf3280 (P6e) (*Fig.1501*)

15232 Incomplete, of rectangular section, arms bent out, ends of both broken off. L.27.2, W.5.2, T.0.8mm 3532 sf7696 (P7a)

Spoon

15233 Complete apart from end of stem, with shallow oval or leaf-shaped bowl, stem of rectangular section, slightly bent, decorated at junction of stem and bowl with saltire between transverse lines. L.75.8, T.1.2mm; stem: L.50.9, W.3.3mm; bowl: L.24.9, W.14.6mm 1075 sf236 (P6a) (*Fig.1501*)

Literacy
Book clasps

15234 Incomplete, front plate only, sub-rectangular, splayed out at base with central indentation and wavy edge, one corner broken off, two rivets at the lower end. There is a hook at the upper end, an iron sheet is attached to the back of the plate. The front of the plate has a punched hole, and is decorated with incised concentric circles. L.36.3, W.15.6, T.1.3mm 1386 sf9335 (P6e) (*Fig.1503*)

15235 Incomplete, front plate only, sub-rectangular, of rectangular section, with flat hooked projection at one end, plate broadening towards other end, from which a projection has been broken off. L.49.1, W.14.2, T.1.2mm 1448 sf3826 (P7a) (*Fig.1503*)

15236 In two pieces, with pair of rectangular plates, made in one piece, looped at one end through which passes pin attaching clasp. The plates have rivets at other end, with remains of leather strap between them, and notched decoration on upper face at end of upper plate. The clasp is of plano-convex section, of rectangular shape at the end where the plates are attached; below this it has a circular shape, with central perforation, and with projecting loop perforated transversely. Plates: L.14.1, W.11, T.0.7mm; pendant: D.11.0, L.22.6, T.4.1mm 3161 sf2905 (P7a) (*Fig.1503*)

Book mounts

15237 Incomplete, of sheet, shaped like gable end of building with inverted T-shaped projection, broken at lower end. There are two rivet holes arranged axially below the projection. Notches are marked and occasionally cut through on edges, the front of the mount is decorated with two incised concentric circles circumscribing a quatrefoil cutout, the decoration perforated by a third rivet hole. L.59, W.32.8, T.0.9mm 3387 sf4684 (P4z) (*Fig.1506*)

15238 Circular disc with central hollow projection of truncated cone shape, three rivet holes in broad rim, one still containing remains of iron rivet. D.36.9, T.2mm; projection: H.13.4mm 3050 sf2239 (P7a) (*Fig.1506*)

15239 Square, made of sheet, edges irregularly pinked, with central perforation, edges curved slightly. L.28.9, W.28.1, T.0.9mm 2114 sf3361 (P7a) (*Fig.1506*)

15240 An L-shaped piece of sheet, with rounded corner with large perforation, with impression of rivet head on one face. Close to ends are small perforations with slits to them from edge. L.41.2, W.39.6, T.1.5mm 8003 sf1425 (P7c) (*Fig.1506*)

Seal matrix

15241 Incomplete, originally discoidal, but subsequently cut in half. Surviving half depicts hand holding jesses of bird of prey with part of second bird also visible. Around scene within billeted border is legend OME: DEBELEBIO. D.27.4, T.3.4mm 5117 sf3870 (P6c) (*Fig.1507*)

Bell

15242 Incomplete, upper half only, slightly misshapen, hollow dome with hole punched through top from underside, corrosion hole in side. Part of out-turned rim on lower edge survives, most of this edge has been roughly broken. D.22.3, T.0.7mm 7001 sf1960 (P6z)

Trade and exchange

Scale pan

15243 Incomplete, circular, shallowly dished, with three equally spaced suspension holes on circumference. D.42, T.0.8mm 1391 sf2366 (P6e) (*Fig.1519*)

Riding equipment

Harness pendants

15244 Sub-circular, partially cut away close to upper end, with trapezoidal attachment loop of rectangular section on reverse face, perforated by punched hole. D.27.9, T.2.3mm; loop: D.3.2, L.9.6, W.8.4, T.2.5mm 5155 sf5878 (P6a/b) (*Fig.1529*)

15245 Discoidal, centrally perforated, with a suspension loop. The upper face is decorated with a low-relief six-pointed star within an incised circle, with arms of unequal width and unequally spaced, fields between arms filled with punched circles. There are traces of gilding on the decorated face. D.28.2, T.1mm; loop: D.7.2mm 3000 sf2066 (P11) (*Figs.1528–9*)

Possible harness pendant

15246 Incomplete, a sub-shield shape, of plano-convex section, with bulbous projection at one end, sub-circular projection on one side close to opposite end, complementary projection on other side broken away, the piece between these two tapering up to the top which is roughly broken. An incomplete attachment loop of convex section projects out from reverse face, and begins to curve up before being broken transversely. The entire object appears to have been tinned. L.35.6, W.20.8, T.6.3mm; loop: L.23.6, W.6.4, T.3.2mm 5047 sf1798 (P6a/b) (*Fig.1529*)

Unidentified objects

15247 Slightly convex strip of rectangular section, slightly expanded centrally, one end flattened, other end scooped with raised sides, extreme ends broken. L.59.5, W.6, T.1.8mm; scoop: T.3mm 1075 sf776 (P6a) (*Fig.1535*)

15248 Decorative strip fragment, sub-rectangular, broken transversely at one end, other end cut obliquely, both twisted up. One long edge is horizontal, the other has been roughly cut in a dog-tooth pattern. The fragment is decorated with double lines of rouletting along the straight edge, and at 90° to this down every other dog-tooth. There are traces of solder on the reverse face. L.41.0, W.10.3, T.1.2mm 4694 sf4572 (P6a) (*Fig.1535*)

15249 Incomplete, with shaft of circular section, one end appears rounded, other end rectangular, of rectangular section, extreme end broken off. D.1.6, L.32.3, W.3.8, T.2.5mm 4710 sf4662 (P6a)

15250 Or offcut, narrow strip of irregular width, curved up into U-shape, both ends rounded and out-turned. L.63.3; section: W.3.7, T.1.1mm 3145 sf6496 (P6b) (*Fig.1535*)

15251 Sub-rectangular, originally tubular, one end open, main body flattened and of rectangular section, other end solid and cut square. D.2.7, L.25.6, W.3.3, T.1.4mm 2072 sf2434 (P7a)

Silver

Dress, dress accessories and personal ornament

Brooch pin

15252 Of square section, one end rolled up to form looped eye, tapering to other end which is bent. L.27.5, W.1.9, T.1.3mm; eye: D.3.1mm 4789 sf5477 (P6a) (*Fig.1489*)

Finger-ring

15253 Bezel, sub-discoidal, with traces of breaks from hoop on either side. D.9.0, T.1.5mm 3334 sf4284 (P6a)

Lead alloy

Manufacturing waste

15254 Run-off fragment. L.85.3, W.18.2, T.4.7mm 8003 sf1430 (P7c) (*Fig.1325*)

15255 Offcut of sheet, rectangular, tapering slightly to one end, twisted, cut mark at edge on one face. L.66.2, W.10, T.2.9mm 1456 sf3904 (P6b) (*Fig.1325*)

15256 Two narrow strips, tightly folded up together. L. (unfolded) 29.1, W.4.5, T.6.3mm 3183 sf3064 (P6a) (*Fig.1325*)

Building tools

Plumb-bobs

15257 Of convex cone shape, of circular section, with a sub-rectangular apex, partially broken, of sub-rectangular section, having been drawn out and pinched flat, and with two small perforations through it. There is a hollow in the base, and various knife cuts on the body, with a D-shaped notch cut close to the base. D.18.9, H.27.7mm, Wt.34.9g 4693 sf4004 (P6a) (*Fig.1317*)

15258 An elongated oval, of circular section, lower end with fragment cut off at angle, upper end with copper alloy suspension wire with collar. D.11.9 L.34.4mm; wire: L.6.3, T.0.6mm, Wt.25.9g 5312 sf5774 (P6b) (*Fig.1317*)

Fishing

Net sinkers

15259 Cylindrical, of sub-circular section, formed from sheet rolled leaving central hole, seam visible. D.18.6, L.28mm, Wt.38.7g 3334 sf4286 (P6a)

15260 Irregularly cylindrical, of plano-convex section, both ends roughly torn. Formed from folded sheet. L.44.5, W.13.8, T.10.5mm, Wt.24.5g 3334 sf5393 (P6a) (*Fig.1352*)

15261 Of sub-rectangular section, formed from tightly folded sheet, overlapping edge visible. L.49.4, W.15.6, T.12mm, Wt.63.4g 2259 sf6403 (P6a) (*Fig.1352*)

15262 Cylindrical, compressed to sub-rectangular section. Formed from sheet rolled leaving central hole. L.30.1, W.10, T.8.8mm, Wt.12.2g 5375 sf6823 (P6a)

15263 Elongated oval, of circular section, axially perforated, one end pinched closed, formed from tightly rolled sheet. L.38, W.11.3, T.10mm, Wt.19.5g 7060 sf3267 (P6z) (*Fig.1352*)

15264 Elongated oval, of circular section, formed from rolled sheet, with smoothed overlapped seam. D.14.6, L.37.0mm, Wt.35.5g 5588 sf7805 (P7a) (*Fig.1352*)

Structural items and fittings

Nail

15265 With broad, flat, sub-circular head, shank of hexagonal section, tip broken off. L.38mm; head: L.35, W.33mm 5689 sf7813 (P6c) (*Fig.1408*)

Flashing

15266 Fragment, irregularly shaped strip, one edge cut, other edges and ends roughly broken. L.520, W.135, T.5mm 3222 sf3366 (P6d) (*Fig.1412*)

Offcuts of roof lead

15267 Strip of sheet, rectangular, with four perforations close to one end, two square, two irregular, the other end folded over. L.115.7, W.56.2, T.5.5mm; strip: T.2.6mm 1084 sf2659 (P6b)

15268 Offcut of sheet, one end cut square, other roughly broken across perforation, one-third of strip folded over, five other perforations with nail head impressions. L. (unfolded) 135.7, W.11.8, T.2.8mm 1384 sf2212 (P7a) (*Fig.1412*)

15269 Strip of sheet, rectangular, one corner removed at angle, with two roughly central perforations, one still containing a nail. L.97.9, W.44.9, T.2.8mm 2070 sf2351 (P7a)

15270 Strip of sheet, rectangular, one end folded over, with two roughly central square perforations. L. (unfolded) 129.3, W.50.1, T.8.6mm; strip: T.3mm 2064 sf3345 (P7a) (*Fig.1412*)

15271 Strip of sheet, rectangular, broken at one end across two perforations. L.34.4, W.28.7, T.2.9mm 2114 sf3359 (P7a)

15272 Strip of sheet, rectangular, with two perforations close to one end, one with nail, this end folded over, trapping glass fragment. L. (unfolded) 110.4, W.52.9, T.13.5mm; strip: W.40.3, T.2.8mm 2114 sf3727 (P7a) (*Fig.1412*)

15273 Strip perforated by rectangular nail hole near one edge, with impression of circular nail head. L.29.8, W.28.1, T.3.3mm 8003 sf1415 (P7c)

15274 Strip, one edge partially bent, perforated by small nail hole, small stab marks on both faces. L.83.5, W.65.6, T.11.8mm 8003 sf1833 (P7c)

15275 Offcut of strip, perforated by nail, part folded over nail head, torn at one corner. L.49mm; strip (folded): L.24.8, W.22.2, T.1.5mm u/s sf7347

Came

15276 Fragment, H-shaped section, split longitudinally, twisted, with visible casting ridges. L.154.8, W.9.4, T.6.7mm 3283 sf4062 (P6a) (*Fig.1412*)

15277 Three fragments, H-shaped sections, largest being two lengths with two crosspieces. L.63.1, W.40.5, T.9.3mm 3162 sf2076 (P7a) (*Fig.1412*)

Star

15278 With seven wavy rays, of triangular section, each tapering to curved end, ends bent up on three rays. There is a central perforation, punched through from the upper face, which has traces of gilding all over it. L.67.6, W.53.5, T.3.2mm; ray: W.11.5mm 3010 sf500 (P7a) (*Fig.1412*)

Discs

15279 Circular, of irregular thickness, perforated off-centre, with traces of a previous attempt to make hole near perforation. D.35,6, T.3.1mm, Wt.25.6g 1386 sf2247 (P6e) (*Fig.1430*)

15280 Sub-circular, both faces slightly uneven, cut mark at circumference. D.38, T.4mm, Wt.31.4g 8003 sf1390 (P7c)

Dress, dress accessories and personal ornament

Buckle

15281 Circular, of sub-triangular section, with iron pin. One end of the bar has become detached from the frame and rests against it. D.16.7, T.3mm; pin: D.1.4 L.17.1mm 8023 sf1831 (P7c) (*Fig.1465*)

Literacy

Points

Class II

15282 With shaft of circular section, tapering to point at one end, widening to other flattened spatulate end which is bent over. D.5, L.69.5mm 4185 sf803 (P6a) (*Fig.1502*)

15283 Incomplete, with shaft of circular section, broken transversely at one end, other end flattened spatulate, part of shaft bent up. D.6, L.85.0mm 4639 sf3425 (P6b) (*Fig.1502*)

15284 Incomplete, shaft of sub-circular section, broken mid-shaft, surviving end chamfered asymmetrically. D.6.4, L.36mm 3194 sf3441 (P6b) (*Fig.1502*)

15285 With shaft of sub-circular section, tapering from just below midpoint to point at one end, widening out and thinning to other end which is flattened spatulate. D.6.3, L.56.7mm 3146 sf6682 (P6b) (*Fig.1502*)

Class IV

15286 Incomplete, broken across one end, which is forked, with shaft of circular section, tapering to a pointed tip at other end. L.52.4, W.7.2, T.5.8mm u/s sf2744 (*Fig.1502*)

Funerary and devotional objects

Chalice and paten

15287 Chalice incomplete, bowl slightly angled on stem, with out-turned rim, much lost, hollow stem with single beaded knop, flaring out from here, and broken transversely below, fragments of circular flared foot survive separately, inner surface of bowl bubbly. Paten has beaded rim, and is slightly dished, with patched central hole. Paten: D.112.1, T.2.8mm; chalice bowl: D.102.5, T.2, H.28.6mm; foot: D.72.4, T.3mm; stem: D.27.9, T.1.5, H.39mm 6127 sf5712 (P6a) (*Figs.1509–11*)

15288 Chalice fragments, largest fragment cylindrical, solid, upper and lower faces flat, with added circumferential band. Also many smaller fragments, unidentifiable. D.24.2, T.13.5mm 1427 sf3332 (P6b)

Trade and exchange

Weights

15289 Discoidal, with cast and turned copper alloy shell, one face with three stepped concentric rings, the inner circle with the remains of the turning hole. The reverse face is heavily corroded with traces of iron staining. There is a split on one side of the shell. D.32.8, T.13.7mm, Wt.73.4g 3342 sf4517 (P6a) (*Fig.1520*)

15290 Discoidal, both faces uneven, perforated slightly off-centre. D.29.4, T.3.7mm, Wt.14.5g 8024 sf1300 (P7c)

Unidentified objects

15291 Sub-rectangular, of plano-convex section, one end spatulate, shaft broadening to other end which is bevelled and slightly bent up. L.78.3, W.15, T.3.7mm 3347 sf4250 (P6a)

15292 With shaft of hexagonal section, tapering and curving slightly to one end with expanded biconical head with pointed tip, other end broken. L.65.2, W.8.2, T.6.7mm 4448 sf2753 (P7b) (*Fig.1536*)

Textiles

Wool

15293 Two fragments, wool in 2/1 twill, 15/S/0.6 x 10/S/0.8. Finer system paler than coarser, single blue thread in finer system, no dye detected, fleece-type unidentifiable. L.15, W.3mm 6019 sf9703 (P6z)

15294 Two fragments of wool textile in 2/1 twill, with single blue thread in finer system, 16/S/0.6 x 10/S/0.8, no dye detected L.20, W.10mm 6019 sf9704 (P6z)

Linen

15295 Fragment, mineralised, in tabby weave, two layers deep, 18/Z/0.4 x 16/Z/0.5. L.10, W.8, T.1mm 1386 sf9352 (P6e)

Fibre not known

15296 Mineralised, in 2/2 twill, 24–26/Z/0.4 x 24–26/Z/0.4. L.7, W.7mm 3282 sf7818 (P7a)

Finds from the earlier Anglian or Anglo-Scandinavian occupation on Fishergate which occurred residually in medieval deposits (Period 6 onwards) have been published in *AY* 17/9. These are grouped according to material and listed by catalogue number below.

Stone
Spindle whorls: *4428–9; 4432–5*
Hones: *4448–51*
Rotary querns: *4528–44*

Fired clay
Crucibles: *4606–11*
Mould: *4620*
Loomweights: *4628–31*

Glass
Vessel glass: *4635, 4639, 4645–9, 4653–5, 4663, 4665, 4667–9, 4673, 4676, 4678, 4682, 4685–6, 4699, 4712–14, 4722–4, 4728–9*
Window glass: *4737, 4741, 4744*
Waste: *4753-7*
Tesserae: *4758–9*
Mount: *4761*
Beads: *4777-83, 4789, 4805–10, 4815–18, 4821–2, 4826–7, 4836*

Frit
Beads: *4843–5*

Iron
Knives: *4983, 4999*
Pins: *5059–63, 5066–7, 5088–97*
Keys: *5238–9, 5242*
Swords: *5261–3*

Copper alloy
Vessel fragment: *5310*
Buckles: *5312–14*
Strap-ends: *5318–21*
Brooches: *5328, 5333*
Dress pins: *5344–9, 5354–5, 5358–9, 5362, 5365, 5371–2, 5378–87, 5400–10*
Ear-ring: *5414*
Finger-ring: *5416*
Twisted wire ring: *5418*

Silver
Garment hook: *5435*
Finger-ring: *5436*

Lead alloy
Pendant: *5486*

Bone
Tooth plate blanks: *5499–501*
Connecting plate blank: *5510*
Spindle whorl: *5526*
Pin-beater: *5527*
Pins: *5556–67*
Combs: *5577–9, 5582–3*
Tooth plates: *5586–7*
Decorated connecting plates: *5597–9*
Undecorated connecting plates: *5606–8*
Comb case: *5609*

Antler
Pedicles: *5615–17*
Burrs: *5629–31*
Crown offcuts: *5634–6*
Tines: *5648–54*
Medullary tissue offcuts: *5665–9*
Tooth plate blank: *5679*
Connecting plate blank: *5683*
Objects: *5691–4*
Handle: *5696*
Comb: *5699*
End plates: *5706–8*
Tooth plates: *5723–6*
Connecting plates: *5734–8*
End plate: *5740*
Tooth plates: *5749–50*
Decorated connecting plates: *5771–5*
Undecorated connecting plates: *5782–3*

Catalogue of Anglo-Scandinavian additions

A small number of iron artefacts were recovered from the upper levels of three sites which were originally thought to be medieval but have since been rephased as Anglo-Scandinavian. The objects from these levels are now considered to be Anglo-Scandinavian, too. However, those from 16–22 Coppergate and the Coppergate watching brief had not been rephased at the time *AY* 17/6 was written and so were not included in that fascicule. Those from 22 Piccadilly were not available for inclusion in *AY* 17/14 with other Anglo-Scandinavian finds from that site. It has therefore been decided that this group of material should be published here.

16–22 Coppergate

Awl

15299 Arms have diamond-shaped cross-section. Slightly expanded in the centre. L.111, W.8mm 13887 sf6177 (P5Cr)

Fibre processing spikes

15300 Head corroded. Sub-rectangular cross-section, stepped head. L.100, W.7mm 18744 sf5656 (P5Cr)

15301 Stepped head. L.95, W.7mm 15311 sf5755 (P5Cr)

15302 Somewhat corroded. Rectangular cross-section, stepped head. L.88, W.5mm 18744 sf5759 (P5Cr)

15303 Rectangular cross-section. L.95, W.6mm 18744 sf5831 (P5Cr)

15304 Rectangular cross-section, stepped head. L.85, W.5mm 18744 sf5858 (P5Cr)

15305 Rectangular cross-section, pinched head. L.85, W.5mm 18744 sf5939 (P5Cr)

15306 Stepped head. L.87, W.7mm 6789 sf6101 (P5Cr)

Knives

Blade back form C3

15307 Blade back slopes down from the shoulder for c.50mm. Tip at the blade's mid-point. Cutting edge has a slight S shape. Tang tip missing. L.81; blade: L.54, W.15, T.6mm 6054 sf2717 (P5B) (Metallurgy report) (*Fig.1555*)

Indeterminate back form

15308 Incomplete blade, tip missing. Cutting edge probably had a slight S shape. Tang tapers a little from the shoulder but is then parallel sided, tip missing. L.105; blade: L.53, W.13, T.5mm 6350 sf5051 (P5B) (Metallurgy report)

Clench bolt

15309 Incomplete diamond-shaped rove. L.41; head: W.20; shank: T.6; rove: L.20, W.18mm 3658 sf3025 (P4/5)

Staples

15310 Rectangular, wider faces in same plane as staple. One arm incomplete. L.54, W.30, T.9mm 5258 sf1263 (P5B)

15311 Rectangular. One arm missing, other arm out turned at tip. L.23, W.26, W.5mm 13968 sf6007 (P5Cr)

15312 One arm; very sturdy. L.81, W.10, T.8mm 16878 sf6867 (P5B)

Pierced plate

15313 A bit crumpled, roughly U-shaped in cross-section. Pierced eight times in an irregular pattern, one end rounded, broken over two holes at other. L.60, W.17, T.2mm 1611 sf368 (P5B) (*Fig.1556*)

Ferrule

15314 Tapers. L.63, D.17mm 7390 sf1305 (P5B)

Pin

15315 Biconical head, at the top of shank is a small moulding. Plated (tin). L.57; head: L.7, W.8; shank: T.2mm 15639 sf4529 (P5B) (*Fig.1558*)

Horseshoes

15316 Tip of left branch, wavy outer side. Turned-over calkin, incomplete countersunk hole. L.41, W.20, T.6mm 9772 sf2806 (P5B)

15317 Tip of right branch, smooth outer side. Turned-over calkin. L.42, W.22, T.6mm 3526 sf2391

Arrowhead

15318 Tanged blade, somewhat misshapen, but basically leaf-shaped. Roughly triangular cross-section. L.83, W.17; tang: T.7mm 1310 sf319 (P5B) (*Fig.1558*)

Coppergate Watching Brief (1982.22)

Knife

Blade back form C3

15319 Blade back slopes down for 50mm, tip at blade's mid-point. Cutting edge S-shaped. Tang tip missing. L.130; blade: L.79, W.12, T.4mm 1205 sf29 (*Fig.1554*)

22 Piccadilly (1987.21)

Strips

15320 Looped over. L.49, W (over loop) 11, T.4mm 1041 sf312 (P3)

15321 L.35, W.5, T.2mm 1031 sf649 (P3)

Punches

15322 Slightly burred head, rectangular cross-section, pointed tip. L.47, W.5, T.5mm 2162 sf486 (P4) (*Fig.1554*)

15323 Lower part of shank. Cross-section rectangular with rounded corners, tapers at the base to a blunt tip. Trace lead and copper on the broken end. L.45, W.8, T.7mm 2187 sf568 (P4) (*Fig.1554*)

Shears

15324 Half surviving. Bow slightly looped; below it is a pointed nib. Stem has a rounded cross-section and incised into it are three groups of three grooves; between the lower two is an incised saltire cross. The blade has a sloping shoulder and a back which is straight before curving into the tip; cutting edge straight. L.152; stem: T.4; blade: L.55, W.9mm 1058 sf352 (P3) (*Figs.1354, 1554*)

Comb teeth

15325 Rounded cross-section, flattened head. L.98, W.6mm 1058 sf353 (P3)

15326 Rounded cross-section, short pointed projection from head. L.95, W.7, T.4mm 2192 sf531 (P4)

15327 Rounded cross-section, stepped head. L.97, W.6mm 2291 sf770 (P3)

15328 Rectangular cross-section, stepped head. L.97, W.5mm 2113 sf855 (P4)

Strike-a-light

15329 Incomplete tapering plate with recurved arm at wider end which tapers to point. L.70, W.48; plate: W.20, T.7mm 3112 sf785 (P3)

Knives

Blade back form A2

15330 Blade back straight and upward sloping to a point 20mm from the shoulder and then slopes down at 20° to the tip. Cutting edge slightly S-shaped. Back edges chamfered. Vertical shoulder. Tang has expansion near junction with blade, tip wedge-shaped and rounded. L.70; blade: L.39, W.10, T.3mm 1041 sf856 (P3) (*Fig.1554*)

Blade back form C1

15331 Blade back straight to a point 34mm from the shoulder and then curves down to the tip which is at half the blade's width. Cutting edge irregular before curving up to the tip. Tang bent upwards and tip clenched. L.142; blade: L.51, W.11, T.3mm 2146 sf329 (P4)

Blade back form C3

15332 Blade back straight and slopes down to a point 39mm from the shoulder from where it curves down to the tip which is at half the blade's width. Cutting edge S-shaped. Tang bent upwards, wedge-shaped tip. L.120; blade: L.55, W.10, T.3mm 2112 sf256 (P4)

15333 Blade back roughly straight and downward sloping to a point 43mm from the shoulder and then curves down to the tip. Cutting edge slightly S-shaped. Sloping shoulder. On each face a short fine groove runs along the top of the tang and top of the blade either side of the junction of tang and blade. L.103; blade: L.52, W.11, T.5mm 3080 sf436 (P4) (*Fig.1554*)

Other knives

15334 Corroded, blade and tang tip missing. L.84; blade: L.56, W.13, T.4mm 2112 sf506 (P4)

Paring knife

15335 Blade only, curved. Back straight to a point c.67mm from the shoulder and then curves down to the tip. Cutting edge slightly S-shaped. Vertical shoulder. Butt weld visible on X-radiograph. L.c.82, W.11, T.3mm 1015 sf421 (P3) (*Fig.1554*)

Plated nail

15336   Shank incomplete. L.22, W.19, T.8mm 3080 sf479 (P4)

Clench bolts

15337   Rove only. Diamond-shaped. L.23, W.17mm 2192 sf532 (P4)

15338   Diamond-shaped rove and stub of shank. L.24; rove:L.37, W.18mm 3130 sf954 (P3)

Staple

15339   Rectangular. One arm distorted, other inturned. Originally: L.17, W.50mm 2204 sf573 (P4)

Spirally twisted strip

15340   L.146, T.5mm 2089 sf232 (P4)

U-eyed hinges

15341   Strap bifurcates and each arm has a recurved tip; pierced below the eye. Terminal incomplete. L.195, W.145; strap: W.34; eye: W.33, T.7mm 3129 sf583 (P3) (*Fig.1557*)

15342   Strap bifurcates and each arm has a recurved tip; pierced below the eye. Terminal rounded and pierced. Nail in situ, shank bent at 90°. L.200, W.133; strap: W.31; eye: W.33, T.7; nail: L.55; head: W.14mm 3129 sf585 (P3) (*Figs.1556–7*)

Stapled hasp

15343   Strap incomplete and bent at c.45°, but originally at 90°. Eye at the head formed by drawing out. Short grooves cut into the edges of the outer face. Plated (tin, a little lead). U-shaped staple with overlapping arms linked to

head. L.43, W.14, T.3; staple: L.21, W.10mm 2280 sf741 (P4) (*Fig.1556*)

Chain link

15344   Oval. L.!8, W.11, T.2mm 2089 sf188 (P4)

Rings

15345   Incomplete. D.48, W.6, T.2mm 2086 sf172 (P4)

15346   Oval cross-section. D.40, T.5mm 1058 sf1041 (P3)

Padlock key

15347   Oval bit with two chambers, at 90° to the stem which is incomplete; near the top it is flattened and widened into a plate. L.125; bit: W.23; stem: W.14, T.5mm 2087 sf179 (P4)

Buckle

15348   D-shaped frame, butt joint on straight side, rounded cross-section. L.21, W.12, T.3mm 1058 sf372 (P3) (*Fig.1558*)

Pin

15349   Tin head, shank expands slightly in the centre. Plated (tin). L.63; head: W.4mm 1043 sf328 (P3) (*Fig.1558*)

Horseshoe

15350   One branch. Outer side. Two countersunk holes and part of third. Hammering marks on upper face. L.85, W.28, T.3mm 3116 sf565 (P4)

Horseshoe nails

15351   Triangular head. L.40, W13mm 2113 sf835 (P4)

15352   Thin triangular head. L.42, W.16mm 2112 sf1187 (P4)

Provenances

Finds were recovered from contexts on the sites as follows; context numbers are given in Roman type, catalogue numbers in italics.

16–22 Coppergate

1002: *12430;* 1005: *11968;* 1019: *11846, 12895;* 1020: *11870, 12662, 12697, 12862;* 1030: *11063, 12654;* 1034: *11440, 11798, 11921, 12291, 12598;* 1037: *12221;* 1046: *12458;* 1070: *12557;* 1072: *11900;* 1073: *12794;* 1096: *10977;* 1097: *12247, 12290;* 1106: *6551;* 1114: *10881;* 1115: *12057, 12759;* 1121: *11706;* 1137: *12470;* 1141: *11399;* 1207: *11033;* 1213: *10884;* 1214: *12522;* 1219: *11226;* 1229: *10938, 12744;* 1263: *10829;* 1283: *10882, 10966, 11173, 11616, 12029, 12342;* 1284: *11240;* 1304: *11840;* 1332: *10885;* 1346: *12050, 12368;* 1390: *12877;* 1404: *11055, 11644, 11738, 11739, 11768, 12495, 12667;* 1440: *10939;* 1442: *11052;* 1445: *11539;* 1455: *12173, 12699;* 1472: *10983;* 1502: *11092, 11108, 11178, 11627, 11823, 12306, 12317, 12320, 12569, 12731, 12766, 12845;* 1506: *10853, 11250, 11705, 11944, 12289, 12295, 12698, 12893, 12928;* 1550: *11540;* 1572: *11282;* 1585: *10846, 11122;* 1586: *12956;* 1609: *11244;* 1687: *12867;* 1692: *12762;* 1693: *12094;* 1748: *11822;* 1763: *12746;* 1765: *10984;* 1783: *11761;* 1790: *11622;* 1897: *12030;* 1908: *12395;* 1909: *11704;* 1914: *12571;* 1981: *12833;* 2128: *11085;* 2192: *11232;* 2193: *11172, 11731;* 2254: *11869;* 2259: *12748;* 2284: *11084, 11214, 11833;* 2286: *10876, 10930, 10954, 11141;* 2300: *11837;* 2305: *12236;* 2329: *11801;* 2336: *10838;* 2346: *12533;* 2901: *6564, 10847;* 3047: *12892;* 3051: *11702;* 3053: *12869;* 3059: *11952;* 3083: *6612, 10960, 12637;* 3085: *12394;* 3093: *11106, 11169;* 3098: *10890, 11030;* 3101: *11445;* 3109: *11035;* 3158: *12866;* 3165: *11107;* 3190: *11245;* 3208: *11327;* 3214: *12078, 12160;* 3225: *11158;* 3232: *11249;* 3233: *11588;* 3235: *11190, 11230, 11231, 11286, 11437, 11487, 11611, 12063, 12218, 12229, 12359, 12441;* 3237: *11972, 12162;* 3253: *12096;* 3256: *10900, 10962, 10975;* 3257: *11180;* 3258: *6577, 10974, 11950, 12033, 12254, 12884, 12889;* 3270: *9056;* 3344: *11229, 11984, 12086, 12414, 12879;* 3356: *11873;* 3359: *11703, 12460;* 3362: *10863, 11135, 11375, 11493, 12159, 12211, 12220;* 3364: *11089;* 3382: *11377, 11679;* 3384: *12796;* 3385: *12330;* 3392: *10866;* 3401: *11040;* 3405: *11642;* 3406: *11990;* 3407: *6608, 11951, 12600;* 3414: *11500, 11501, 11948, 12773;* 3447: *11858;* 3460: *11317;* 3462: *11724;* 3484: *12352;* 3493: *6565, 11060, 11074, 11436, 11518, 11831, 11908, 12023, 12043, 12052, 12302, 12483, 12491, 12539;* 3494: *11987, 11988, 12718;* 3495: *12515;* 3498: *12821;* 3509: *11392, 12346, 12792;* 3537: *6550, 11937, 11938, 12147, 12404;* 3539: *11300;* 3549: *11043, 11936;* 3551: *11814;* 3555: *11993;* 3558: *11994, 12333, 12334;* 3561: *10831;* 4000: *11962;* 4001: *12249;* 4008: *10845;* 4012: *11434, 11435, 12529;* 4013: *11953;* 4020: *11955;* 4032: *12870;* 4043: *11242, 11243, 11418, 11956;* 4057: *10980;* 4059: *12753;* 4060: *11417;* 4074: *11489;* 4081: *11469;* 4087: *10981;* 4089: *10982, 12356;* 4105: *12172;* 4125: *11241, 12431;* 4141: *11610;* 4164: *12090;* 4178: *12570;* 4179: *12844;* 4182: *12521;* 4243: *11621;* 4252: *11457, 11458, 11496;* 4289: *11470;* 4292: *12795;* 4304: *11029;* 4385: *9045, 11917, 12318, 12608, 12663, 12732, 12741;* 4399: *11419, 12931;* 4409: *11246;* 4448: *12904;* 4454: *12345;* 4457: *11713;* 4497: *12248;* 4505: *12760;* 4520: *12611;* 4540: *11433, 11609;* 4570: *11624, 12558;* 4571: *10883;* 4591: *11432, 12095;* 4604: *10886, 11174, 11247, 11784;* 4620: *6574, 6605, 10857, 10888, 10889, 10891, 11046, 11081, 11109, 11181, 11183, 11234, 11254, 11255, 11258, 11259, 11260, 11261, 11267, 11462, 11497, 11498, 11632, 11762, 11802, 11850, 11874, 11973, 11974, 12058, 12098, 12099, 12101, 12102, 12103, 12251, 12253, 12255, 12339, 12349, 12362, 12363, 12369, 12400, 12433, 12434, 12459, 12478, 12559,* 12573, 12574, 12612, 12640, 12742, 12752, 12764, 12959; 4640: *12822;* 4658: *10854;* 4661: *11623;* 4689: *12891;* 4691: *11699;* 4692: *11175;* 4693: *11848, 12411, 12542;* 4698: *12174;* 4724: *11954;* 4736: *12930;* 4752: *12051;* 4784: *12325;* 4788: *8189;* 4811: *12749;* 4830: *12509;* 4850: *8190, 11625, 11808, 12761;* 4851: *11176;* 4852: *11969;* 4858: *11155;* 4867: *12371;* 4874: *10940;* 4875: *11251;* 4885: *12556;* 4915: *10972, 11091, 11156, 11847, 11871, 12245, 12319;* 4924: *12361;* 4931: *11527;* 5000: *11224, 11382, 11383, 11384, 11385, 11386, 11482, 11511, 11682, 11928, 11931, 11932, 12171, 12426, 12486, 12568, 12638, 12815;* 5009: *11150;* 5021: *11179, 11542, 12170, 12252;* 5029: *12937;* 5037: *12175;* 5051: *12250;* 5064: *6630, 10855, 11157;* 5084: *11524, 12358;* 5104: *11867, 12396;* 5126: *11925;* 5141: *12296;* 5177: *12065;* 5186: *11390, 11592, 12212, 12476, 12566;* 5206: *11380;* 5230: *11389, 11591, 11897, 12021;* 5231: *6543, 12610;* 5238: *10893, 10904, 11285, 11479, 11547, 11590, 11732, 11734, 11809, 11979, 12031, 12059, 12105, 12427, 12565, 12577, 12826;* 5239: *11034;* 5241: *11633, 11975, 12534;* 5245: *10843, 11184, 11785, 11929, 12641, 12700;* 5262: *11381, 12100, 12163, 12176, 12941;* 5263: *11396, 11397, 11595, 12164, 12286, 12664;* 5264: *11526, 11634, 12701;* 5330: *11268;* 5331: *11225, 11391, 11447, 11853;* 5333: *11275, 12034, 12716;* 5345: *12435;* 5348: *6629, 8170, 8193, 10839, 10867, 10894, 10901, 10903, 10942, 11133, 11134, 11136, 11168, 11278, 11279, 11376, 11405, 11463, 11490, 11520, 11525, 11546, 11548, 11549, 11557, 11596, 11597, 11637, 11726, 11727, 11737, 11741, 11787, 11810, 11855, 11856, 11905, 11907, 11924, 11983, 12032, 12036, 12108, 12179, 12183, 12185, 12231, 12232, 12256, 12258, 12328, 12377, 12401, 12416, 12439, 12469, 12528, 12580, 12581, 12594, 12702, 12767, 12768, 12771, 12772, 12827, 12858, 12890, 12917;* 5362: *10959, 12728;* 5373: *11269, 11272, 11640, 12060;* 5395: *10976, 11053, 11554, 11643, 12168, 12520;* 5397: *11982, 12182;* 5398: *10897, 11825, 12480;* 5404: *11530;* 5406: *11807;* 5412: *11037;* 5413: *11933;* 5415: *6620, 11073, 11094, 11274, 11388, 11552, 11714, 11735, 11763, 11857, 12061, 12351, 12479, 12643, 12658, 12848, 12934;* 5442: *6570, 12618;* 5484: *6627, 6628, 6569, 10840, 10864, 10865, 10896, 10985, 11088, 11185, 11276, 11400, 11736, 11758, 11793, 11930, 12375, 12397, 12413, 12499, 12551, 12597, 12617, 12619, 12655, 12675, 12682, 12689;* 5485: *10906, 11740;* 5494: *12720;* 5536: *12089, 12850;* 5539: *11448, 12578;* 5545: *11273, 12550, 12770;* 5604: *11688;* 5620: *11803;* 5668: *12041;* 5671: *10899, 11981, 12585;* 5755: *11125, 12717;* 5777: *10905, 12376, 12823, 12828;* 5779: *11508;* 5786: *11683;* 5811: *12184;* 5906: *11056;* 5975: *6568, 11198, 11202, 11334, 11882, 12128, 12169, 12336, 12449, 12684, 12705, 12807, 12948;* 5977: *11195, 11927;* 5978: *12085, 12415;* 5981: *10849, 10943, 10944, 10963, 11281, 11464, 11559, 11923, 12087, 12109, 12110, 12121, 12187, 12195, 12440, 12474, 12703;* 6034: *10933, 11057;* 6101: *12894;* 6111: *12408;* 6245: *12622, 12723;* 6257: *11442, 11443, 11446, 12070, 12624, 12829;* 6258: *10934, 11051, 11217, 11349, 11365, 11372, 11593, 11617, 11725, 11779, 11909, 12093, 12150, 12314, 12466, 12635;* 6269: *10919;* 6281: *11441, 11576, 12367;* 6282: *11010, 12725;* 6285: *11895;* 6291: *11371, 11685, 12391;* 6336: *12634;* 6339: *10878, 11014, 11351, 11364, 11580, 11722, 11749, 11764, 11817, 11818, 11834, 11835, 12157, 12284;* 6344: *10923, 11684, 12560;* 6423: *11926;* 7782: *11321, 11708, 11729, 11804, 11812, 11881, 12233, 12776;* 7788: *11538, 11796;* 7791: *11843;* 7895: *12271;* 8304: *10830, 11086, 11132;* 8305: *11934;* 9017: *10880;* 9020: *12329;* 9028: *12727;* 9030: *12909;* 9037: *11177, 11970;* 9057: *6631, 10961, 11090, 11248, 11626, 12331;* 9058: *6610;* 9067: *11912;* 9073: *12743;* 9078: *11182, 11257, 11631, 12373, 12503, 12530, 12549, 12834;* 9092: *10856, 12548;* 9105: *12519, 12846;* 9116: *11031;* 9122: *6604, 10973, 11082, 11378, 11849, 11971, 12240, 12326, 12372, 12526, 12538;* 9129: *10887, 12239;* 9134: *11767;* 9137: *12523;* 9188: *11628, 12572;* 9190:

11872; 9204: *11922*; 9208: *11629*; 9213: *10858, 11541, 12432, 12493, 12754*; 9215: *11630, 12000, 12097*; 9219: *11528*; 9224: *6575, 6576, 6606, 6607, 6617, 6621, 10860, 10892, 10941, 10958, 10967, 11026, 11032, 11099, 11104, 11151, 11227, 11262, 11263, 11264, 11265, 11266, 11303, 11304, 11305, 11308, 11320, 11411, 11412, 11413, 11414, 11415, 11416, 11506, 11529, 11543, 11556, 11599, 11600, 11635, 11636, 11638, 11639, 11651, 11652, 11653, 11691, 11692, 11733, 11782, 11788, 11851, 11852, 11875, 11880, 11945, 11946, 11947, 11978, 11985, 11991, 11992, 11996, 12083, 12104, 12116, 12120, 12165, 12177, 12178, 12201, 12308, 12313, 12350, 12412, 12445, 12455, 12494, 12510, 12527, 12575, 12614, 12615, 12616, 12651, 12652, 12674, 12678, 12729, 12755, 12756, 12757, 12804, 12836, 12837, 12838, 12847, 12883, 12924, 12946, 12960, 12962*; 9229: *11681*; 9248: *6603, 11038, 11223, 12297, 12599*; 9249: *11256, 11854, 12374*; 9252: *11080, 11188, 11252, 11253, 11379, 11680, 11786, 11977, 12161, 12228, 12596, 12613, 12696, 12763, 12791, 12803, 12805, 12806*; 9254: *11918*; 9260: *12871*; 9269: *12468*; 9274: *11545, 12740, 12765*; 9302: *10861, 11095, 11544, 11949, 11976, 12180, 12181, 12437, 12659*; 9305: *6626, 10895, 10898, 10986, 11036, 11042, 11093, 11271, 11277, 11409, 11410, 11513, 11551, 11555, 11641, 11690, 11806, 11841, 11980, 12035, 12106, 12186, 12257, 12315, 12327, 12436, 12438, 12463, 12464, 12471, 12543, 12576, 12579, 12642, 12644, 12665, 12666, 12758, 12769, 12816, 12842, 12849*; 9323: *10859*; 9330: *6599, 10902, 11270, 11280, 11387, 11491, 11550, 11824, 12107*; 9346: *11519*; 9362: *10835, 10862*; 9396: *12683*; 9397: *11283, 11553, 12037*; 9481: *11284, 11471, 11876*; 9572: *6544, 11186, 11499, 12876*; 9641: *8191, 12343, 12454, 12704, 12726, 12737, 12781*; 9789: *11083*; 9793: *12241*; 9794: *12020*; 9801: *12482*; 9802: *12197*; 9813: *11575, 11844, 12355, 12473*; 9815: *11330, 12388*; 10022: *11187, 11485, 12851*; 10039: *11697, 12853*; 10096: *9161, 11096, 12881*; 10097: *11126*; 10101: *11877*; 10107: *12943*; 10118: *11811*; 10119: *10907, 12872*; 10123: *12442, 12873*; 10264: *11293*; 10265: *11604*; 10266: *12875*; 10280: *11421*; 10333: *6632, 11460, 11645*; 10334: *12092, 12379*; 10335: *12224*; 10355: *12301, 12835*; 10391: *11906*; 10394: *6622, 12817*; 10397: *12111*; 10407: *12942*; 10416: *12721*; 10450: *12695*; 10464: *6634, 11237, 12874, 12905, 12936*; 10466: *12309*; 10490: *12298, 12860*; 10507: *12080*; 10511: *11827*; 10527: *11236, 11290, 12246*; 10531: *12216, 12260, 12541*; 10532: *12188, 12378, 12511, 12713*; 10546: *11291, 12880*; 10553: *12259*; 10560: *11292, 12402, 12852*; 10592: *12481*; 10596: *12691*; 10597: *12582*; 10617: *12215*; 10620: *12690*; 10633: *11646*; 10634: *11295*; 10641: *11424*; 10678: *12189*; 10726: *12403*; 10735: *12287*; 10739: *11868, 12081*; 10743: *12944*; 10758: *11110, 11422*; 10766: *11111*; 10768: *12906*; 10771: *11601*; 10779: *11420*; 10791: *12660*; 10797: *12263*; 10813: *10841*; 10822: *11294, 11753*; 10824: *11097, 11112*; 10832: *11423*; 10845: *12775*; 10847: *11228*; 10880: *11113*; 10903: *12907*; 10904: *12923*; 10923: *11098, 12261*; 10944: *11191*; 10951: *12428*; 10974: *4279, 11707, 11989, 12193, 12332*; 10977: *12364, 12957*; 10979: *11878, 12540*; 11007: *12091, 12620*; 11016: *12910*; 11018: *11715*; 11045: *11828, 12113*; 11052: *11986*; 11053: *10868*; 11054: *12949*; 11106: *11287, 11826*; 11165: *12461*; 11284: *12196, 12544*; 11291: *12190*; 11298: *10968, 11488, 12112*; 11300: *12913*; 11304: *12062*; 11332: *11742, 12114, 12380, 12381, 12774, 12843*; 11341: *12457*; 11342: *12039*; 11344: *11047, 12115, 12117*; 11376: *12122, 12194, 12348*; 11378: *12266*; 11397: *12739*; 11401: *12535*; 11402: *11650*; 11415: *11152*; 11416: *11461, 11859, 12418, 12512, 12938*; 11417: *11649*; 11440: *11001*; 11447: *11192*; 11455: *11102, 12932*; 11458: *10945, 11153, 11507, 11558, 11648, 11829, 11842, 12353, 12777, 12855*; 11484: *12676*; 11507: *6600, 11296, 11730, 12925*; 11514: *11159, 11647, 11998, 12040, 12646, 12810*; 11525: *12912*; 11530: *10834*; 11545: *12417*; 11554: *11101, 11899, 12861*; 11565: *11298*; 11570: *11233*; 11577: *11438*; 11583: *12042, 12071*; 11584: *11795*; 11612: *12262*; 11621: *12419*; 11626: *11100, 12265, 12908*; 11632: *11613*; 11633: *12933*; 11654: *12192*; 11656: *11612, 11759, 11879*; 11658: *12166*; 11670:

12854; 11674: *12524*; 11680: *11299*; 11683: *10908, 12504*; 11687: *12447*; 11726: *6601*; 11758: *12219*; 11760: *12191*; 11763: *11114, 11915*; 11776: *12288*; 11784: *12337, 12514*; 11789: *12340, 12383*; 11793: *12406*; 11803: *11160, 11302*; 11818: *10873, 11769, 12685*; 11820: *12267*; 11857: *11315*; 11867: *11898, 11966, 12024, 12124, 12321*; 11868: *12410*; 11870: *11066*; 11879: *11025, 11403*; 11883: *11194, 11516, 12322*; 11886: *10870, 11860, 12809, 12965*; 11900: *12563*; 11913: *11309*; 11938: *12864*; 11940: *11197*; 11951: *11439*; 11953: *11067, 12954*; 11958: *11130*; 11965: *10914, 10946, 11318, 12453*; 11966: *11995*; 11979: *12450*; 11994: *12068*; 11995: *12243*; 12011: *11961, 12808*; 12018: *11193, 11401, 11402, 11686, 12118, 12264, 12513, 12945*; 12051: *12444*; 12054: *11297*; 12062: *11404, 12606*; 12063: *11845*; 12066: *12607*; 12067: *12961*; 12097: *11048*; 12106: *11307, 12225, 12405, 12621*; 12108: *12064*; 12113: *12214, 12793*; 12125: *11406*; 12126: *12443*; 12147: *6611, 11288, 11289*; 12148: *11560*; 12165: *10869*; 12179: *11407*; 12180: *11103, 11394, 12119*; 12186: *12489*; 12190: *12066, 12347*; 12191: *11444*; 12223: *12123*; 12237: *12382, 12736*; 12257: *11301*; 12258: *12677*; 12274: *11105, 11196, 11306, 11515, 11687, 11743, 12824, 12841*; 12276: *11146, 12130*; 12278: *11395*; 12309: *12650*; 12327: *11888*; 12363: *10916, 11139, 11332, 11534, 12452*; 12364: *11117, 12002, 12820*; 12365: *12125*; 12366: *12747*; 12368: *6609, 11115, 11465, 11744, 12268*; 12407: *12668*; 12411: *11563, 12446*; 12412: *11311, 11316, 11561, 11562, 11805, 11997, 12022, 12448, 12462, 12623, 12856, 12897*; 12413: *12360*; 12422: *10850, 11310, 11654, 12038, 12839*; 12467: *12067*; 12485: *11200, 12198, 12242, 12269, 12645, 12738, 12778*; 12489: *11314*; 12494: *11199*; 12496: *6571, 11478, 12234, 12490, 12899*; 12498: *12898*; 12501: *10911, 10947, 11333, 11503, 12213, 12226, 12586*; 12503: *11589*; 12507: *12129*; 12544: *11789, 12272*; 12561: *11189, 11564, 12886*; 12563: *10987*; 12572: *11566, 11663*; 12578: *11313, 11335, 11746, 12733*; 12579: *11959*; 12619: *11331, 11919, 12132, 12310, 12451, 12687, 12840*; 12631: *12779*; 12635: *12004*; 12647: *10949, 11203, 12075, 12714*; 12662: *11205, 11957, 12299, 12516*; 12671: *11206, 12046, 12518, 12818*; 12699: *11958*; 12710: *12885*; 12725: *11815, 12074*; 12727: *10910, 11087, 11486*; 12745: *11398*; 12748: *12484*; 12759: *12706*; 12762: *11138*; 12785: *11658*; 12789: *12001*; 12791: *11148, 11408, 11770, 12647, 12878*; 12794: *11960*; 12839: *11336*; 12840: *12203*; 12841: *11162*; 12851: *10833*; 12853: *10989, 11328, 11509*; 12863: *11207*; 12865: *12926*; 12870: *11660*; 12912: *11143*; 12915: *11505, 12592*; 12928: *10991, 10992, 10993, 10994, 10995, 10996, 10997, 11473*; 12944: *10978, 12204*; 12982: *11326*; 12985: *10990*; 13005: *12751*; 13037: *11147, 11466, 12583*; 13039: *12126*; 13058: *12914*; 13110: *12407*; 13119: *10832*; 13120: *11886*; 13124: *10912, 12669*; 13140: *12273*; 13147: *11059, 11064, 12316*; 13160: *11154, 11830, 12420*; 13175: *12798*; 13188: *10909*; 13191: *11127, 12311*; 13200: *12929*; 13202: *12127*; 13215: *11325*; 13227: *12069*; 13228: *12915*; 13242: *11140*; 13243: *11329, 11883, 12131, 12323*; 13244: *11655, 11861, 12270, 12496*; 13245: *10872, 12200, 12627*; 13299: *11716*; 13302: *11312, 12235, 12497*; 13310: *12679*; 13315: *11201*; 13331: *10871*; 13383: *12797*; 13385: *11116*; 13390: *12384, 12887*; 13410: *12686, 12900*; 13416: *11999*; 13427: *11068*; 13434: *11472*; 13438: *12950*; 13442: *10913, 11510*; 13454: *11161, 11204, 11323, 11467, 11492, 11502, 11514, 11532, 11567, 11745, 11916, 12202, 12274, 12554, 12629*; 13465: *11324, 11568, 12133, 12199, 12590, 12730*; 13466: *12546*; 13492: *10964*; 13501: *11813, 12003, 12167, 12275*; 13523: *12780*; 13527: *11129, 11517, 13532: *11075, 11078, 11656, 12819*; 13554: *12135, 12584*; 13557: *11884*; 13567: *10988, 12955*; 13568: *11615, 11885, 12505, 12625, 12715, 12750*; 13571: *10948*; 13577: *12799*; 13579: *12385*; 13581: *11887*; 13585: *12475, 12553*; 13591: *11319*; 13638: *11069, 12338, 12386, 12918*; 13660: *11322*; 13662: *12626*; 13663: *10874*; 13665: *11531, 12335*; 13674: *12501*; 13686: *11598, 11689*; 13690: *6619*; 13698: *12911*; 13800: *11344, 12076*; 13861: *11657, 12072*; 13862: *10851, 12073, 12951*; 13886: *11477, 11751, 11819*; 13899: *10879*;

13902: *6572, 6573, 11023, 11079, 11167, 11352, 11357, 11537, 11573, 11614, 11671, 11790, 11894, 12208, 12209, 12312, 12786, 12787;* 13912: *11468;* 13946: *12472;* 13949: *10915;* 13951: *11659;* 13964: *10935, 11368, 11369, 11584, 11677, 11752, 11935, 12049, 12079, 12532;* 15033: *10922;* 15040: *6602, 12365;* 15043: *11041, 11128;* 15106: *11163, 11565, 11662;* 15107: *12303;* 15124: *11337, 11889, 12227;* 15126: *12782;* 15136: *8171, 11123, 11495, 11533, 12006, 12517, 12628, 12630, 12783, 12919, 12952;* 15166: *11015, 11212;* 15202: *11338, 11890;* 15285: *10852, 11216, 11577, 11678, 11865, 11866, 12210, 12567, 12788, 12963;* 15286: *12888;* 15287: *12734;* 15300: *8742;* 15594: *11061;* 15840: *11121, 11862, 12719;* 16069: *11661;* 16072: *10998, 10999, 12005;* 16074: *12134;* 16104: *12044;* 16112: *10971;* 16117: *12045;* 16123: *12387;* 16135: *11771;* 16148: *12811;* 16153: *12953;* 16170: *11535, 12007, 12008, 12138, 12244, 12680, 12785, 12902;* 16219: *11119;* 16291: *12692;* 16311: *11000;* 16362: *12136;* 16399: *12587;* 16404: *11664;* 16410: *11208, 11425, 11602, 12324, 12688, 12927, 12958;* 16456: *10875;* 16462: *11693;* 16464: *11339, 12485;* 16465: *10917, 12366, 12492, 12506, 12661;* 16470: *12137;* 16490: *12595;* 16501: *11118;* 16508: *10965;* 16518: *11002;* 16525: *11340, 11474, 12656;* 16532: *12670;* 16534: *8192;* 16535: *11426, 11427, 11891, 12357, 12421, 12857;* 16556: *11004;* 16584: *12304;* 16603: *12724;* 16604: *12389;* 16612: *10918, 10928, 10979, 11070, 11210, 11360, 11370, 11571, 11585, 11673, 11720, 11760, 11776, 11791, 12019, 12154, 12205, 12285, 12631, 12649, 12735;* 16615: *11373, 12158;* 16616: *12276;* 16617: *11003;* 16642: *12277;* 16686: *12784;* 16705: *11665;* 16722: *11058;* 16731: *11341;* 16734: *10926, 10950, 11049, 11149, 11209, 11348, 11374, 11428, 11481, 11512, 11522, 11583, 11603, 11694, 11799, 11836, 11920, 12148, 12151, 12305, 12341, 12422, 12467, 12671, 12722;* 16736: *12344;* 16761: *11005;* 16774: *11006, 12278;* 16782: *12279;* 16790: *6616;* 16797: *11342, 12011, 12498, 12564;* 16799: *11007;* 16872: *12009;* 16879: *12206;* 16884: *2431;* 16891: *11021;* 16892: *11020;* 16923: *12010;* 16925: *12139, 12140, 12141, 12142;* 16950: *12012;* 16967: *12143;* 17009: *10951, 12013;* 17024: *10842;* 17033: *11027;* 17040: *11430, 11572, 11607;* 17048: *12280;* 17065: *11008;* 17103: *11016, 11019, 11164, 12812;* 17129: *10957, 11221;* 17184: *12707;* 17217: *12144;* 17241: *11120;* 17253: *11211;* 17259: *12354;* 17275: *11044, 12830;* 17302: *12681;* 17322: *6613, 11863;* 17332: *11772;* 17344: *11009;* 17360: *10969, 11039, 11701;* 17375: *11864;* 17380: *12015;* 17396: *12425;* 17397: *11028, 11343, 11429, 11605, 11606, 11696, 11748;* 17421: *12859;* 17457: *11071, 11800;* 17511: *11012;* 17518: *11011;* 17526: *11676;* 17532: *12014, 12693;* 17537: *11144;* 17539: *11667;* 17551: *8172, 11165, 11347, 11366, 11367, 11582, 11669, 12082, 12149, 12609, 12865;* 17552: *11747;* 17587: *11018, 11024;* 17591: *10921, 11022;* 17627: *6614, 11581, 11750, 12016, 12711;* 17695: *12283;* 17697: *10877, 11698;* 17699: *11586, 11608, 11700, 11719, 11728, 12217, 12456, 12831, 12832;* 17740: *11076, 11353, 12393;* 17786: *10924, 11695, 12152, 12591;* 17787: *10936, 11215, 11218, 11355, 11431, 11774, 12018, 12423, 12712, 12814;* 17788: *11579;* 17890: *10927, 10931, 10955, 10956, 11054, 11065, 11358, 11359, 11362, 11363, 11475, 11587, 11674, 11675, 11709, 11721, 11766, 11777, 11780, 11794, 11910, 11967, 12155, 12156, 12230, 12465, 12790, 12921;* 18047: *10920, 11013, 11914, 12077, 12601, 12648;* 18048: *12145;* 18074: *10970;* 18075: *12868;* 18076: *12561;* 18119: *12390, 12935;* 18133: *12813;* 18134: *11350, 12088, 12392;* 18143: *11521, 11717;* 18152: *11942;* 18153: *11666, 12281, 12545;* 18169: *12939;* 18170: *12882;* 18171: *11668, 12940;* 18172: *6618, 11062, 11670, 12146, 12507, 12555, 12920;* 18193: *12370;* 18194: *11131, 11222, 11892;* 18255: *12672;* 18256: *6615, 11166, 11213, 11346, 11765, 11773, 11778, 11941, 12409, 12562, 12588, 12709, 12863, 12947;* 18284: *10952;* 18285: *11017;* 18321: *11775;* 18331: *6598, 10844, 10932, 11050, 11072, 11235, 11354, 11361, 11393, 11480, 11578, 11594, 11893, 12048, 12153, 12500, 12547, 12602, 12632, 12633, 12636, 12710, 12789, 12800;* 18366: *10953, 11045, 11145, 11345, 11356, 11504, 11523,*

11536, 11574, 11718, 11832, 11940, 12047, 12207, 12282, 12508, 12589, 12694; 18477: *11896;* 18486: *11723, 11816, 11939;* 18668: *10925, 11913, 11943, 12424, 12525, 12708, 12916;* 18982: *10929, 11476, 11672;* 19844: *11137;* 29325: *11484*

Unprovenanced: *6566, 6578, 6633, 10836, 10837, 10848, 10937, 11077, 11142, 11170, 11171, 11238, 11239, 11449, 11450, 11451, 11452, 11453, 11454, 11455, 11456, 11459, 11483, 11494, 11618, 11619, 11620, 11710, 11711, 11712, 11754, 11755, 11756, 11757, 11781, 11783, 11792, 11797, 11820, 11821, 11838, 11839, 11901, 11902, 11903, 11904, 11911, 11963, 11964, 11965, 12025, 12026, 12027, 12028, 12053, 12054, 12055, 12056, 12084, 12222, 12237, 12238, 12292, 12293, 12294, 12300, 12307, 12398, 12399, 12429, 12477, 12487, 12488, 12502, 12531, 12537, 12593, 12603, 12604, 12605, 12639, 12653, 12657, 12673, 12745, 12801, 12802, 12825, 12896, 12901, 12903, 12922, 12964, 12966*

Watching Brief

1055: *12999;* 1056: *13005;* 1205: *13000;* 1384: *12974, 12987, 12993–4;* 1477: *12984, 12986;* 1478: *13003, 13006;* 1506: *12980;* 1546: *12967–8, 12971, 12975, 12988, 12990, 12992, 12995, 12996, 13002;* 1618: *12983, 12985;* 1736: *13004;* 1745: *12973;* 1777: *12972, 12997;* 1793: *12981;* 1874: *12991;* 1906: *13001;* 2077: *12969, 12976, 12977*

Unprovenanced: *12970, 12978–9, 12982, 12989, 12998*

22 Piccadilly

1000: *13044;* 1001: *13011, 13013, 13023, 13074;* 1002: *13015;* 1014: *13036, 13037;* 2000: *13035;* 2001: *13053, 13076;* 2006: *13075;* 2007: *13056;* 2009: *13069;* 2010: *13066;* 2011: *13014;* 2012: *13057, 13078;* 2041: *13012, 13042, 13062–3;* 2042: *13019–20, 13026, 13046, 13050, 13059, 13064, 13070–2;* 2045: *13041;* 2048: *13025, 13058;* 2049: *13010, 13054;* 2079: *13032, 13055;* 2083: *13043, 13051, 13068;* 2089: *13007;* 2146: *13008;* 3000: *13065;* 3003: *13067;* 3006: *13017, 13022, 13038, 13060, 13073, 13077;* 3009: *13016, 13047;* 3010: *13052;* 3012: *13024, 13031, 13033;* 3013: *13021, 13029;* 3016: *13028;* 3048: *13018, 13079;* 3053: *13049;* 3071: *13048;* 3086: *13045;* 4000: *13027;* 4004: *13009, 13030, 13061*

Unprovenanced: *13034, 13039–40*

Bedern Foundry

1: *13104, 13242, 13254, 13304, 13415;* 4: *13410;* 13: *13103, 13253, 13306;* 18: *13303;* 22: *13113, 13115, 13191, 13389, 13417;* 43: *13190, 13266;* 45: *13107;* 47: *13237;* 49: *13413;* 51: *13118, 13151, 13175;* 57: *13095, 13096;* 62: *13106;* 63: *13256, 13315;* 66: *13400;* 69: *13110;* 70: *13129–30;* 71: *13105;* 75: *13298;* 77: *13241, 13250, 13340, 13347, 13388, 13429;* 78: *13183;* 79: *13390;* 81: *13112;* 82: *13367;* 83: *13188, 13368–9, 13371, 13374, 13383, 13395–6;* 85: *13300, 13356;* 90: *13238, 13240, 13261, 13407;* 96: *13394;* 104: *13348;* 116: *13192, 13267;* 140: *13120;* 143: *7985, 13161, 13193, 13271;* 145: *13273, 13319;* 147: *13398;* 157: *13098;* 163: *13272, 13322–3;* 166: *13119;* 176: *13278;* 177: *13196, 13392;* 187: *13152;* 188: *13195, 13358;* 195: *13299, 13324;* 202: *13310;* 205: *13128, 13239, 13381;* 206: *13293–4;* 208: *13382;* 211: *13134;* 212: *13083, 13194;* 215: *13135, 13393;* 218: *13131, 13223;* 223: *13132, 13185, 13189, 13327, 13411;* 224: *13133, 13289, 13387;* 225: *13412;* 227: *13197–8, 13216, 13243, 13297, 13405, 13416;* 229: *13311;* 281: *13199, 13391, 13414;* 283: *13386;* 287: *13301;* 305: *13307;*

309: *13187;* 329: *13234;* 342: *13162, 13300;* 363: *13184;* 405: *13421;* 425: *13258;* 443: *13091;* 522: *13419;* 523: *13357;* 525: *13326;* 538: *13207, 13409;* 543: *13370;* 556: *13420;* 559: *13337, 13380;* 573: *13236;* 574: *13344;* 579: *13308;* 585: *13179;* 595: *13408;* 617: *13109;* 621: *13116, 13173;* 623: *13316, 13406;* 624: *13090;* 625: *13285, 13385;* 641: *13208, 13277;* 649: *13227;* 652: *13252, 13317;* 656: *13114;* 663: *13111, 13172;* 666: *13209;* 674: *13290;* 690: *13126;* 696: *13215;* 698: *13102, 13127;* 711: *13201, 13350;* 726: *13154;* 729: *13125, 13146, 13165, 13169, 13171, 13182, 13210, 13251, 13336, 13354, 13377, 13402;* 740: *13263;* 746: *13231;* 780: *13373;* 794: *13330, 13352, 13363;* 804: *13361;* 881: *13333;* 850: *13235;* 854: *13335, 13364;* 868: *13338;* 870: *13164, 13313;* 873: *13229;* 877: *13355;* 902: *13221;* 911: *13168;* 924: *13149;* 964: *13404;* 977: *13085, 13353;* 979: *13186, 13332;* 986: *13117;* 988: *13097;* 994: *13158;* 998: *13205;* 999: *13282;* 1151: *13177;* 2014: *13296;* 2047: *13279, 13365;* 2049: *13257, 13260;* 2065: *13288;* 2071: *13345;* 2073: *13124;* 2119: *13360;* 2145: *13214, 13232;* 2169: *13284;* 2172: *13270;* 2228: *13093;* 2304: *13230;* 2319: *13224;* 2349: *13123;* 2352: *13167, 13200, 13212, 13219;* 2360: *13150;* 2377: *13092, 13094, 13143, 13329;* 2380: *13318, 13376;* 2440: *13249;* 2477: *13314;* 2522: *13084;* 2528: *13089;* 2551: *13086, 13225;* 2552: *13144, 13325;* 2567: *13359;* 2571: *13142, 13435;* 2573: *13427;* 2574: *13434;* 2636: *13147;* 2641: *13206;* 2666: *13428, 13430;* 2674: *13433;* 2682: *13378;* 2691: *13418;* 2698: *13155;* 2701: *13431;* 2712: *13379;* 2737: *13220;* 2742: *13334;* 2764: *13213;* 2778: *13082;* 2779: *13276, 13286;* 2801: *13099;* 2804: *13305, 13366;* 2806: *13148;* 2810: *13349;* 2850: *13101, 13203, 13397;* 2861: *13287;* 2865: *13228;* 2876: *13204;* 2881: *13321, 13343;* 2888: *13087;* 2891: *13136, 13166, 13226, 13268;* 2892: *13180, 13291;* 2897: *13137;* 2898: *13202;* 2910: *13145;* 2912: *13081, 13274;* 2915: *13160;* 2925: *13246;* 2934: *13233;* 2945: *13346;* 2948: *13156;* 2950: *13159, 13320, 13331, 13362;* 2970: *13121;* 2971: *13157;* 2975: *13283, 13423;* 2982: *13426;* 2985: *13280;* 2990: *13432;* 2993: *13138;* 4008: *13139, 13269;* 4016: *13170, 13181, 13265, 13351;* 4034: *13247;* 4036: *13108;* 4040: *13302;* 4057: *13312;* 4065: *13140, 13328;* 4072: *13211;* 4077: *13141;* 4079: *13375;* 4088: *13292;* 4114: *13080, 13281, 13342;* 4115: *13122;* 4116: *13153, 13259;* 4122: *13178;* 4165: *13248;* 4172: *13088;* 4239: *13176*

Unprovenanced: *13100, 13163, 13174 13217, 13218, 13222, 13244, 13245, 13255, 13262, 13264, 13275, 13295, 13339, 13341, 13372, 13384, 13399, 13401, 13403, 13422, 13425*

College of the Vicars Choral, Bedern

Bedern North-East (1978–9.14.II, 1979–80.14.IV)

1000: *14112, 14294, 14323, 14534;* 1007: *13766;* 1018: *14465;* 1022: *13499;* 1032: *13926;* 1034: *14200;* 1039: *14315;* 1054: *13558;* 1055: *13527;* 1055B: *13475;* 1064: *14445;* 1066: *14059;* 1067: *14273;* 1092: *14327;* 1108: *13673;* 1116: *13881, 14083, 14274;* 1117: *13507, 13535, 13619, 13710, 13765, 13794, 13882–9, 13941, 13999, 14000, 14036, 14096, 14102, 14130, 14139, 14164, 14170, 14260, 14550;* 1122: *13517;* 1123: *13667, 13929;* 1134: *13573;* 1137: *14358;* 1141: *13555–6, 14072;* 1146: *14321;* 1151: *13880, 14357;* 1156: *13467, 13618, 13928, 13940, 14068, 14456;* 1159: *14035;* 1161: *13578;* 1183: *14148;* 1189: *14017;* 1192: *14356;* 1193: *14176;* 1212: *13540, 14384;* 1215: *14087, 14228, 14355, 14383;* 1220: *13655;* 1225: *13642;* 1230 : *13855;* 1233: *13698, 13703;* 1238: *13780;* 1242: *13871;* 1245: *14237;* 1249: *13519;* 1256: *13532;* 1266: *14134;* 1267: *8117;* 1268: *13810;* 1270: *13872;* 1281: *13761;* 1293: *13878;* 1308: *13654;* 1318: *13732;* 1319: *14556;* 1321: *13815;* 1326: *13998;* 1337: *13787;* 1338: *13879;* 1339: *13518;* 1340: *13674, 14019;* 1341: *13922, 14155, 14285;* 1347: *13446;* 1359B: *13498;* 1360: *13935;* 1366: *13870, 14100;* 1389: *14325;* 1392A: *13479;* 1395: *14281;* 1402: *13696, 13942;* 1406: *13964;* 1418: *13753;* 1420: *14144;* 1424: *14011;* 1427: *13581, 13816, 13933, 14058;* 1428: *14461;*

1436: *13577;* 1442: *13697;* 1444: *14542;* 1446: *13850;* 1447: *13463, 13513, 13576;* 1450: *13722, 13902;* 1451: *13516;* 1453: *13739;* 1455: *13980;* 1456: *13920;* 1457: *13839;* 1459: *13483;* 1470: *14123;* 1480: *14279;* 1481: *13668;* 1486: *14021, 14219;* 1487: *13669;* 1494: *13778, 14236;* 1501: *13712;* 1502: *13640;* 1504: *13590;* 1505: *13852, 13854;* 1505A: *14220;* 1505B: *13503, 14599;* 1506: *13851;* 1524: *14392;* 1526: *13853;* 1537: *13906, 14316;* 1539: *13895;* 1540: *14295;* 1543: *14038;* 1544: *13594, 13777, 13960;* 1549: *13591–2;* 1550: *14487;* 1552: *14473;* 1560: *14157, 14235, 14340, 14440;* 1561: *13444, 13641, 13680, 13725, 13847, 14508;* 1575: *14056;* 1581: *14398;* 1584: *14020;* 1588: *13595, 13892, 13979, 14026;* 1592: *14512;* 1595: *13442, 13838, 13917, 13951, 14189, 14449, 14455, 14498;* 1601: *13993;* 1602: *14530;* 1603: *14180;* 1605: *14381;* 1606: *14027, 14109, 14143, 14175, 14472;* 1607: *14522;* 1608: *13441, 14007, 14097;* 1611: *14339;* 1614: *14010;* 1634: *13694, 13950, 14133;* 1643: *14448;* 1644: *13931;* 1647: *13840;* 1649: *14406;* 1650: *13632, 13841;* 1651: *14435;* 1660: *13721;* 1662: *13623;* 1668: *13453, 13724, 13915, 14008, 14329, 14583;* 1677: *14061;* 1681: *13959;* 1688: *13808;* 1690: *13566;* 1702: *13717, 13757, 14562;* 1708: *13490, 14442;* 1717: *14582;* 1725: *13563;* 1726: *13830;* 1732: *13625;* 1734: *14071;* 1740: *13461, 13509, 13755, 14276;* 1743: *13629, 13978;* 1744: *13826;* 1760: *14543;* 1766: *14505;* 1774: *13545, 13628, 13949, 14126, 14404, 14598;* 1784: *13539, 13586, 13621;* 1784B: *13488;* 1792: *13738;* 1793: *13481;* 1795: *14494;* 4000: *13470–1, 13584;* 4010: *14518, 14570;* 4016: *13818;* 4027: *14516–17;* 4036: *13491;* 4037: *13875, 13921, 14333;* 4047: *13730, 14121;* 4049: *14303;* 4059: *13522, 13918 , 14103, 14476;* 4060: *13994;* 4065: *14558;* 4068: *14240;* 4073: *14239, 14474;* 4076: *13666;* 4084: *14490, 14515;* 4094: *14478, 14502;* 4102: *13797, 14230, 14332, 14347;* 4112: *13817, 13876–7, 14024;* 4113: *13455;* 4116: *13957;* 4118: *13515;* 4121: *13800, 13984, 14526, 14528;* 4125: *13795;* 4136: *13927;* 4140: *13536, 13559;* 4146: *14389;* 4149: *14436;* 4152: *13866–7, 14527;* 4154: *13995;* 4162: *13770;* 4163: *13652;* 4165: *13792, 14016;* 4171: *14261, 14413;* 4175: *14544;* 4176: *14541;* 4180: *13610, 13653, 13786;* 4181: *13793, 13939;* 4183: *14266;* 4185: *13934, 13992, 14113, 14308;* 4187: *13868, 14409;* 4188: *14054;* 4189: *14120, 14138, 14414, 14578;* 4191: *14229;* 4193: *14571;* 4194: *13869;* 4198: *14388, 14569;* 4200: *14127, 14154, 14341;* 4202: *13569, 14086, 14168;* 4206: *13967, 14093, 14145, 14162, 14288, 14362, 14385;* 4210: *14426;* 4232: *13651;* 4235: *13643;* 4261: *14499;* 4268: *13675, 14080;* 4275: *13609, 13983, 14137, 14559;* 4278: *14299, 14345;* 4293: *14567;* 4295: *13494, 14390, 14429;* 4304: *14439;* 4313: *14523, 14564;* 4314: *14555;* 4323: *14524;* 4327: *14063;* 4332: *13991;* 4343: *14055;* 4345: *13553, 14222;* 4348: *13561;* 4353: *14057;* 4369: *14191;* 4370: *13520, 13521;* 4372: *14560;* 4374: *14481;* 4375: *14549;* 4377: *14265, 14427;* 4380: *13565;* 4383: *14253;* 4384: *13510;* 4388: *14040;* 4389: *14359;* 4392: *14539;* 4395: *13848–9, 13923;* 4400: *13580;* 4404: *13758;* 4405: *14037;* 4407: *13925;* 4428: *13547;* 4438: *14216;* 4439: *13720;* 4441: *13627;* 4444: *14319;* 4445: *13589, 14156;* 4446: *13825;* 4455: *14079;* 4457: *13719, 13772, 13774–5, 13823, 14441;* 4462: *13689, 13824, 13963, 14433, 14574;* 4466: *14553;* 4469: *13768;* 4470: *13819;* 4472: *13914;* 4475: *13930, 14495;* 4477: *13686;* 4479: *13752, 14141;* 4482: *13773, 14031, 14105;* 4483: *13626;* 4489: *13473;* 4493: *14025;* 6262: *14573*

Unprovenanced: *13505, 13620, 13671, 13693, 13731, 13943, 14002–3, 14108, 14165, 14199, 14305, 14328, 14438*

Bedern South-East (1976–9.13.X)

4077: *14525;* 5000: *13528;* 5001: *14577;* 5003: *14335;* 5011: *13478;* 5027: *13451, 13796, 14547;* 5041: *14352;* 5084: *14215, 14486;* 5114: *14194;* 5125: *14088, 14149, 14179;* 5131: *14312, 14371, 14415;* 5132: *13476, 13749–50, 13788;* 5134: *13656;* 5141: *13670;* 5144: *13582, 13611, 13663–4, 14014, 14101, 14322, 14353, 14423;* 5145: *14169;* 5146: *13458, 13601, 13644, 13646, 13747, 13782, 13900, 14044–5, 14094, 14192, 14311, 14399;* 5147: *13781, 14022;* 5149: *13701;* 5155:

13688; 5156: *14302;* 5162: *13985;* 5163: *14207, 14372;* 5166: *14422;*
5170: *13529, 14091;* 5180: *13743–4, 13891, 13953, 14225;* 5194:
14497; 5202: *13683;* 5204: *13602, 14090, 14106;* 5210: *13657, 13873,*
14373; 5211: *13658, 14214;* 5219: *14416, 14590;* 5220: *13526;* 5221:
14509; 5233: *14463;* 5237: *13961, 14033, 14208, 14262–3, 14469,*
14493, 14504; 5239: *14334;* 5243: *14317;* 5245: *14201;* 5248: *13585;*
5254: *13583, 14313;* 5255: *14318;* 5267: *14430;* 5268: *13659–62,*
13789–91, 13813, 13937, 13996, 14029, 14034, 14070, 14073, 14185,
14264, 14403; 5269: *14454, 14546;* 5283: *13745;* 5287: *13958;* 5291:
14466; 5292: *13603, 13647–8, 13714, 13733, 13763, 13783, 13856–*
7, 13896–7, 13899, 13919, 13987–8, 14012–13, 14064, 14066–7,
14081, 14085, 14212, 14379, 14387, 14410, 14572, 14593–4, 14596,
14600; 5293: *14028;* 5297: *13973;* 5298: *13439;* 5309: *14520, 14595;*
5317: *14350;* 5320: *13604, 13713, 14367;* 5326: *14202–3;* 5327: *14402,*
14464; 5333: *13562, 14077;* 5334: *13806;* 5337: *14424;* 5338: *14584;*
5339: *13677, 14586, 14589;* 5340: *13676, 13901;* 5341: *14023;* 5342:
14514; 5346B: *14293;* 5346C: *14592;* 5347G: *13486, 14587;* 5348:
14018; 5354: *13612, 14217;* 5363: *14368;* 5367: *13605, 13989, 14521;*
5367C: *14597;* 5372: *13798;* 5376: *14437;* 5379: *13898, 14160;* 5383:
13858–9; 5392: *13699;* 5399: *13557, 14074, 14351;* 5403: *13811,*
13860, 14039, 14213, 14479; 5404: *13691, 14146;* 5410: *13606, 13682,*
13700, 13727, 13861, 13946, 14349, 14450, 14557; 5422: *13945;* 5431:
13695; 5451: *13541, 14115;* 5458: *13762;* 5465: *13636, 14204;* 5466B:
13485, 14519; 5472: *13523;* 5477: *13831, 14386;* 5486: *14099, 14242;*
5488: *13690, 13832, 14224;* 5497: *14575;* 5497A: *13843;* 5497B:
13493; 5498: *13544, 13588, 13894, 14125;* 5503: *13597, 14513;* 5522:
14500; 5523: *14092, 14129;* 5540: *14378;* 6000: *14111, 14182, 14480;*
6003: *13460, 14140, 14151;* 6008: *13665, 13692, 13807, 13948, 14069,*
14098, 14186, 14314, 14418, 14506; 6009: *13613–14, 13684, 13874,*
13912, 14015, 14171, 14421, 14458; 6015: *14187;* 6029: *14095, 14470;*
6034: *13974;* 6038: *14286;* 6041: *13754, 13903, 14163;* 6058: *13542–*
3; 6060: *13466;* 6061: *13465;* 6064: *13904, 13997, 14198;* 6065: *13814,*
14226; 6068: *13751, 13801;* 6069: *13615, 14374, 14580;* 6089: *14150;*
6109: *13803;* 6126: *14532;* 6137: *13450;* 6141: *14443;* 6143: *13616,*
14227, 14275; 6148: *13812;* 6152: *13537, 13955;* 6162: *13649, 13729,*
13862–3, 14119, 14267, 14400; 6163: *13607;* 6165: *13617, 13938;*
6174: *13449, 14118;* 6181: *14457;* 6193: *13554, 14364;* 6195: *14084;*
6200: *14046, 14065, 14205;* 6201: *14001;* 6218: *14310;* 6220: *14489;*
6223: *13533;* 6246: *13748, 14195;* 6247: *14467;* 6253: *14268;* 6254:
13784; 6256: *14147;* 6262: *13608, 13746, 13771, 14005, 14136, 14196,*
14206, 14393–4; 6267: *13864;* 6268: *14047;* 6271: *13447, 13650,*
13681, 13785, 13911, 13956, 14161, 14177–8, 14269, 14309, 14411,
14482, 14561; 6279: *13865;* 6280: *14048;* 6295: *14258;* 6303: *13837,*
13932; 6304: *14255;* 6305: *13600, 14049;* 6310: *14050, 14348;* 6320:
13741; 6321: *13480, 13968, 14104;* 6322: *13982;* 6324: *13549;* 6326:
13477; 6331: *14053;* 6340: *14391;* 6342: *13437, 13538d, 13575, 14009,*
14251; 6345: *14142, 14376;* 6346: *14377;* 6347: *13550, 13846, 14307;*
6356: *13538c;* 6357: *13538a;* 6359: *13457;* 6361: *13546;* 6365: *13567;*
6367: *13551, 14330;* 6371: *13538b;* 6372: *13552, 13568, 13596, 13637,*
13970; 6372F: *14588;* 7000: *14460;* 7006: *13469, 14417;* 7008: *13723;*
7010: *13802, 14485;* 7013: *14188, 14581;* 7020: *13764;* 7029: *14503;*
7036: *13804, 14304;* 7048: *14431, 14576;* 7054: *14533;* 7060: *14075;*
7072: *13530, 14320, 14337, 14412;* 7074: *13687, 14354;* 7075: *13706;*
7087: *14114, 14249, 14270–1, 14282, 14363, 14369, 14447, 14483;*
7096: *13440;* 7098: *13506, 14254;* 7102: *13495–7;* 7110: *13638;* 7116:
13502; 7120: *14342;* 7123: *13833, 13969, 14287;* 7124: *14292;* 7126:
13634, 13834; 7127: *14397;* 7130: *13944, 14484;* 7131: *14343;* 7163:
14218; 7164: *14545;* 7167: *14462;* 7170: *14365;* 7179: *14041;* 7183:
13890; 7189: *14471;* 7191: *13678;* 7193: *14051;* 7203: *14420;* 7229:
13639, 14166; 7231: *13835, 14158;* 7232: *14425;* 7234: *14280;* 7245:
14110; 7254: *14529;* 7257: *13972;* 7259: *14496;* 7263: *13645;* 7264:
14223; 7271: *13454, 13971, 14492;* 7276: *14361;* 7280: *13809, 14256;*
7285: *13571, 14366, 14401, 14468;* 7287: *13511; 13548, 13630, 13908,*
14042–3, 14153, 14252; 7291: *14183;* 7297: *13570, 14135;* 7300D:

14510; 7303: *13981;* 7308: *13702, 13965, 14259, 14283, 14488;* 7312:
13954; 7313: *13464, 13799;* 7316: *13990;* 7324: *14300;* 7330: *13524;*
7336: *13844;* 7342: *14301, 14565;* 7344: *14344;* 7347: *13474, 14346;*
7349: *14243, 14272;* 7357: *14540;* 7369: *13593;* 7379: *13598;* 7382:
13779; 7393: *13986, 14284;* 7403: *14566;* 7406: *14444;* 7410: *13572;*
7418: *13633, 14407–8;* 7427: *14419;* 7432: *14331;* 7435: *13910, 14221;*
14453; 7436: *13907;* 7440: *14277;* 7446: *13635;* 7450: *14172;* 7456:
13534; 7459: *14289;* 7479: *14579;* 7486: *14477;* 7488: *14211;* 7491:
13599; 7493: *13760, 13769, 14062;* 7509: *13443;* 7514: *14052;* 7519:
14004, 14131; 7521: *13977, 14434;* 7522: *13445, 13525, 13740, 13845;*
7528: *13631;* 7531: *14568;* 7536: *13909;* 7543: *14511;* 7546: *13737;*
7548: *14246, 14551;* 7550: *14245;* 7559: *14491;* 7561: *13709, 13836;*
7569: *13718, 14247;* 7573: *14428;* 7576: *14296;* 7577: *13579, 14297,*
14552; 7579: *14338;* 7582: *13776, 14563;* 7584: *13456, 13489, 13905;*
7585: *14060, 14405, 14451;* 7587: *13512;* 7588: *13827–8;* 7589: *13829;*
7591: *14298, 14548;* 7594: *13679, 14278, 14554;* 7597: *13624;* 7606:
13462, 14241; 7609: *14006;* 7612: *14507;* 7613: *13564, 13822, 14132,*
14360; 7621: *13759;* 7622: *14167;*

Unprovenanced: *13452, 13472, 13500–1, 13538e, 13560, 13574,*
13685, 13705, 13805, 13962, 13966, 14078, 14107, 14116–17, 14306,
14324, 14336, 14375, 14396

Bedern long trench (1973–5.13.III/IV)

1031: *14536;* 1034: *14184, 14210, 14380;* 1055: *13728, 13820–1,*
13952, 14082, 14290; 1065: *13484, 14238;* 1067: *14209;* 1075: *14159;*
1086: *13531;* 1095: *13726;* 1099: *13482, 13976, 14231;* 1100: *14128;*
1104: *13947;* 1115: *13715, 14538;* 1122: *13459;* 1131: *13716, 13913,*
13924, 14122, 14173–4; 1138: *14234;* 1200: *13711, 13756;* 1203:
13707; 1205: *13736;* 1215: *13708;* 1216: *13587, 13622, 13893, 13975,*
14030, 14244; 1221: *14585;* 1225: *13492, 13508, 13734–5, 14232–3,*
14501; 1500: *14446;* 1503: *14591;* 1504: *13438;* 1512: *14181, 14535;*
1513: *13704, 14076, 14459;* 1514: *13468;* 1544: *13936, 14197, 14531;*
1545: *14326;* 1552: *13742, 14193, 14248;* 1577: *14257;* 1583: *13514;*
1590: *13842;* 1592: *13504, 14032;* 1607: *14190;* 1609: *13916;* 1611:
14250; 1619: *14452;* 1640: *13767, 14124;* 1643: *13436*

Unprovenanced: *13487, 13672, 14089, 14108, 14152, 14395, 14432,*
14537

Bedern Chapel

8000: *14650;* 8005: *14608;* 9000: *14615, 14625, 14645;* 9004: *14621,*
14631, 14637, 14647; 9008: *14610, 14614, 14626–7, 14635, 14646;*
9010: *14632;* 9011: *14623, 14636;* 9014: *14602, 14604, 14613, 14629–*
30, 14634, 14638, 14648–9, 14651, 14654; 9016: *14624;* 9017: *14655;*
9019: *14622, 14633;* 9022: *8120, 14605;* 9027: *14607, 14640–1, 14653;*
9040: *14628;* 9049: *14609;* 9051: *14639, 14642;* 9059: *14603, 14606,*
14618, 14620, 14643; 9067: *14619;* 9071: *14601, 14644;* 9084: *14616;*
9085: *14652;* 9087: *14612, 14617*

Unprovenanced: *14611*

2 Aldwark

3000: *14673, 14681, 14687;* 3001: *14694;* 3003: *14723;* 3004: *14721,*
14725; 3006: *14690, 14701;* 3016: *14702;* 3022: *14664, 14682, 14691,*
14699, 14709; 3023: *14660, 14684;* 3039: *14677;* 3047: *14704, 14726,*
14730; 3052: *14727;* 3054: *14678, 14683, 14695, 14722;* 3063: *14669,*
14686, 14692; 3068: *14663;* 3072: *14666, 14729;* 3073: *14656, 14703,*
14708, 14713; 3086: *14658–9;* 3087: *14665, 14674;* 3089: *14662,*
14700, 14716; 3090: *14668, 14671, 14696–8, 14718, 14731;* 3095:

14667, 14680; 3100: *14679;* 3101: *14672;* 3104: *14705, 14710;* 3106: *14707;* 3112: *14714;* 3113: *14670;* 3114: *14676;* 3115: *14689;* 3116: *14675, 14688, 14733;* 3117: *14693;* 3118: *14685*

Unprovenanced: *14657, 14661, 14706, 14711–12, 14715, 14717, 14719–20, 14724, 14728, 14732*

46–54 Fishergate

1033: *15122;* 1052: *15007, 15046, 15080;* 1053: *14767;* 1055: *14921, 14945–6;* 1075: *14892, 15106, 15233, 15247;* 1077: *15051;* 1080: *14904, 14906;* 1081: *15126;* 1084: *14901, 15267;* 1211: *14891;* 1237: *14812;* 1304: *14759;* 1374: *15205;* 1384: *14873, 15268;* 1385: *15033, 15045, 15073, 15082, 15134;* 1386: *14752, 14766, 14850, 14863, 14911, 14959, 15039, 15066, 15096, 15104, 15135–7, 15146, 15219, 15224, 15234, 15279, 15295;* 1390: *14955, 15015, 15040, 15097, 15153, 15183;* 1391: *14756, 15057, 15243;* 1392: *14964;* 1395: *15068, 15123;* 1402: *14744;* 1408: *14938;* 1419: *14987;* 1427: *15288;* 1430: *15149;* 1443: *14794;* 1448: *14782, 14866, 15235;* 1456: *14992, 15164, 15255;* 1463: *14993;* 1478: *14781, 15008–9;* 1527: *14816, 14989, 15157;* 1558: *14956;* 1584: *15014;* 1663: *14949, 14967, 15174, 15190;* 1686: *14968;* 1758: *14981;* 1760: *14998;* 1792: *14999;* 1831: *15111;* 1832: *14825;* 2001: *14806;* 2003: *15223;* 2015: *14802;* 2026: *14972, 15076;* 2060: *15197;* 2061: *14853, 14874–5, 14960;* 2062: *14855, 14978;* 2064: *15270;* 2070: *15269;* 2072: *15251;* 2079: *15217;* 2092: *15088;* 2096: *14867;* 2103: *15006;* 2110: *15093;* 2114: *15239, 15271–2;* 2120: *15030;* 2122: *15021;* 2126: *14840;* 2138: *15214;* 2158: *15020;* 2162: *8169;* 2166: *14801;* 2167: *14943, 14947;* 2182: *14929, 15199;* 2185: *14792;* 2190: *15103;* 2201: *15165;* 2214: *14983;* 2219: *15176;* 2234: *14872;* 2259: *14754, 15012, 15261;* 2260: *15003;* 2283: *14931;* 2290: *15086;* 2296: *14769;* 2302: *14843;* 2304: *14848, 15090;* 2305: *15005, 15156;* 2324: *14997;* 2325: *15155;* 2327: *15142;* 2343: *15024;* 2357: *14893;* 2381: *14751, 14844, 14903, 15026;* 2429: *14824;* 3000: *15245;* 3002: *14857;* 3003: *15059, 15168;* 3004: *15193;* 3007: *14804;* 3010: *15028, 15208, 15278;* 3012: *14772;* 3017: *15169;* 3050: *14868, 15238;* 3054: *14918;* 3145: *14761, 15129, 15250;* 3146: *14950, 15285;* 3154: *15178;* 3157: *14861;* 3161: *15236;* 3162: *15147, 15277;* 3163: *15100, 15184;* 3180: *15027;* 3182: *14925, 15069;* 3183: *15256;* 3185: *14738;* 3187: *15052, 15227;* 3194: *15092, 15181, 15284;* 3197: *15017;* 3214: *15151;* 3215: *14854;* 3222: *15230, 15266;* 3227: *14813, 14916;* 3234: *15189;* 3240: *14845–6, 15054, 15089;* 3242: *14936;* 3250: *14814;* 3256: *14778, 15078, 15095;* 3262: *14877;* 3269: *15180;* 3275: *14847;* 3276: *15094;* 3281: *15019;* 3282: *14774–5, 15102, 15116, 15171, 15296;* 3283: *14941, 15276;* 3287: *15109;* 3310: *15121, 15167;* 3313: *14791;* 3334: *14821, 14948, 15125, 15128, 15253, 15259–60;* 3335: *14914, 15148;* 3342: *4983, 14815, 14881, 14883–5, 14907, 14927, 14942, 14985, 15044, 15091, 15289;* 3347: *15049, 15291;* 3352: *14790, 15048, 15139;* 3366: *15228;* 3387: *15237;* 3409: *14928;* 3518: *14773;*

3525: *15120;* 3532: *15232;* 3535: *15099;* 4000: *15188, 15191;* 4002: *15202;* 4016: *15222;* 4023: *14739;* 4041: *15212;* 4048: *15098, 15195;* 4058: *14765;* 4068: *14771;* 4077: *15218;* 4085: *15118;* 4086: *14805;* 4093: *14864;* 4097: *14826;* 4099: *15016;* 4185: *15145, 15282;* 4190: *14979;* 4206: *15173;* 4253: *15115, 15162;* 4254: *14920;* 4281: *14865;* 4402: *15221;* 4429: *14807–8;* 4448: *15108, 15292;* 4450: *15206;* 4473: *15166;* 4475: *15053;* 4476: *15152;* 4478: *15034, 15038, 15041, 15055;* 4479: *14783;* 4505: *15042, 15105;* 4549: *15133;* 4552: *15231;* 4560: *15150;* 4604: *14849;* 4639: *15283;* 4649: *14784–5;* 4659: *14876;* 4680: *14742, 14748, 15175;* 4689: *15182;* 4691: *14858;* 4693: *14787, 15257;* 4694: *14770, 14819, 14926, 14982, 15036, 15079, 15110, 15119, 15132, 15248;* 4695: *15056, 15067;* 4710: *14747, 14749–50, 14788–9, 14817–18, 14986, 15249;* 4716: *14820, 14965, 14988;* 4789: *14822, 14908, 14909, 15252;* 4798: *15071;* 4802: *14768, 14923, 15060;* 5011: *14741;* 5013: *14755, 14795, 14827, 15077, 15084, 15141;* 5047: *15050, 15246;* 5060: *15124, 15186;* 5073: *14832–3, 14836, 14862, 14878, 14962, 14973, 15004, 15029;* 5084: *14994;* 5091: *14764, 14799, 14887;* 5096: *15158;* 5097: *15198;* 5103: *14869;* 5104: *14834, 14835, 14954;* 5110: *14899, 14974, 14984;* 5113: *14837;* 5114: *15065;* 5117: *14838, 15161, 15241;* 5131: *14860, 14940, 14975;* 5132: *14995;* 5139: *14823, 14980;* 5147: *14839;* 5155: *14796, 14880, 15002, 15244;* 5158: *15064;* 5175: *15209;* 5184: *14889, 14910, 14917, 14930;* 5195: *14919;* 5198: *14760;* 5199: *15037;* 5205: *14800, 14828, 15062;* 5211: *14763;* 5237: *14888;* 5238: *15101;* 5242: *14758, 14797, 14894–5, 14969;* 5243: *14841;* 5245: *15107;* 5253: *15213;* 5254: *14937, 14970, 15113;* 5261: *14735, 14736, 14743, 14915, 14958, 14966, 15072, 15087;* 5273: *14897, 14952;* 5289: *14829;* 5293: *14793;* 5295: *14902, 15001;* 5302: *15061;* 5312: *15043, 15130, 15177, 15216, 15258;* 5345: *14830;* 5349: *14890;* 5353: *14933;* 5375: *14934–5, 14963, 15025, 15074, 15262;* 5429: *14757;* 5518: *14737, 14898, 15143;* 5521: *14991, 15140;* 5551: *14780, 14953;* 5582: *15131;* 5588: *15264;* 5600: *14900;* 5638: *15085;* 5640: *14905, 14939, 15035;* 5642: *14971;* 5644: *14870;* 5689: *15265;* 6019: *15293–4;* 6096: *14842;* 6127: *15287;* 6130: *14932;* 6217: *15207;* 6242: *15013, 15160;* 6255: *14990, 15203;* 6296: *15179;* 6346: *15000;* 7001: *14803, 14851–2, 14912, 14976, 15144, 15185, 15242;* 7002: *14977, 15170;* 7014: *15211;* 7035: *15154;* 7040: *15010;* 7047: *14913, 15032, 15200;* 7054: *15011, 15210;* 7060: *14882, 15031, 15263;* 7065: *14753, 14879, 14944;* 7178: *14957;* 8003: *14857, 14871, 15022–3, 15215, 15220, 15240, 15254, 15273, 15280;* 8008: *15187;* 8013: *15172;* 8014: *15047, 15201;* 8019: *14777;* 8023: *14776, 14809–10, 14856, 14961, 15018, 15127, 15163, 15274, 15281;* 8024: *14740, 14746, 14811, 15070, 15138, 15196, 15290;* 8030: *14996;* 8034: *15081, 15083;* 9001: *15058;* 9100: *14734;* 10002: *14831;* 10004: *14886, 14924, 15192, 15229;* 10077: *15194;* 10034: *15063;* 10076: *14762, 15112;* 10085: *15114;* 10089: *14786;* 10092: *14922;* 10138: *14798, 15075;* 10140: *14896, 14951, 15204;* 10265: *15225–6*

Unprovenanced: *14745, 14779, 15275, 15286*

Appendix One

Data used in the chronological analysis of the ironwork (pp.2976–85)

Table 332 16–22 Coppergate: numbers of iron objects by group for the Anglo-Scandinavian and medieval periods (see Fig.1537, p.2977)

| | Object group | | | | | | | | | |
	A	B	C	D	E	F	G	H	I	Total
Period										
3	139	46	21	45	99	12	25	6	8	401
4A	36	28	7	7	20	2	12	2	3	117
4B	228	163	40	74	161	29	71	11	12	789
5A	73	40	16	14	48	8	20	0	1	220
5B	131	85	75	67	162	26	24	17	12	599
5C	50	29	24	10	39	2	6	29	0	189
All Anglo-Scan.	657	391	183	217	529	79	158	65	36	2315
6i	89	54	61	37	151	32	31	134	6	595
6ii	104	72	91	47	247	49	26	153	9	798
6iii	57	26	25	12	151	9	13	56	7	356
6iv	43	12	14	13	66	7	13	25	2	195
All medieval	293	164	191	109	615	97	83	368	24	1944
All	950	555	374	326	1144	176	241	433	60	4259

Table 333 16–22 Coppergate: numbers of iron objects by group for the Anglo-Scandinavian and medieval periods expressed as percentages of the period totals (see Fig.1538, p.2978)

| | Object group | | | | | | | | |
	A	B	C	D	E	F	G	H	I
Period									
3	35.0	11.5	5.0	11.0	25.0	3.0	6.0	1.5	2.0
4A	30.5	24.0	6.0	6.0	17.0	2.0	10.5	1.5	2.5
4B	29.0	20.5	5.0	9.5	20.5	3.5	9.0	1.0	1.0
5A	33.0	18.0	7.5	6.5	22.0	3.5	9.0	0	<1.0
5B	22.0	14.0	12.0	11.0	27.0	5.0	4.0	3.0	2.0
5C	26.5	15.5	12.5	5.5	20.5	1.0	3.0	15.5	0
All Anglo-Scan.	28.5	17.0	8.0	9.5	23.0	3.0	7.0	3.0	1.0
6i	15.0	9.0	10.5	6.0	25.5	6.0	5.0	22.0	1.0
6ii	13.0	9.0	11.5	6.0	31.0	6.0	3.5	19.0	1.0
6iii	16.0	7.5	7.0	3.5	42.5	2.5	3.5	15.5	2.0
6iv	22.0	6.0	7.0	6.5	34.0	4.0	6.5	13.0	1.0
All medieval	15.0	8.5	10.0	5.5	31.5	5.0	4.5	19.0	1.0
All	22.5	13.0	9.0	7.5	27.0	4.0	5.5	10.0	1.5

Table 334 16–22 Coppergate: numbers and percentages of iron objects in the Anglo-Scandinavian and medieval periods in Groups B with D, and E with F (see Fig.1539, p.2979)

| | Object group Numbers | | | Percentages | |
	B+D	E+F	Total	B+D	E+F
Period					
3	91	111	202	45.0	55.0
4A	35	22	57	61.5	38.5
4B	237	190	427	55.5	44.5
5A	54	56	110	49.0	51.0
5B	152	188	340	44.5	55.5
5C	39	41	80	49.0	51.0
6i	91	151	242	37.5	62.5
6ii	119	296	415	28.5	71.5
6iii	38	160	198	19.0	81.0
6iv	25	73	98	25.5	74.5

Table 335 46–54 Fishergate: numbers of iron objects by group for the Anglian and medieval periods (see Fig.1540, p.2980)

| | Object group | | | | | | | | | |
	A	B	C	D	E	F	G	H	I	Total
Period										
3	44	18	4	29	46	6	23	1	0	171
4	44	20	11	26	89	4	16	13	0	220
6a–c	71	32	40	32	69	12	12	21	10	299
6d–e	7	2	1	2	21	6	2	3	4	48
Total	166	72	56	89	225	28	53	38	14	743

Table 336 46–54 Fishergate: numbers of iron objects by group for the Anglian and medieval periods expressed as percentages of the period totals (see Fig.1541, p.2981)

| | Object group | | | | | | | | |
	A	B	C	D	E	F	G	H	I
Period									
3	25.5	10.5	2.5	17.0	27.0	3.5	13.5	<1.0	0
4	19.5	9.0	5.0	11.5	40.0	2.0	7.0	6.0	0
6a–c	23.5	10.5	14.0	10.5	23.0	4.0	4.0	7.0	3.5
6d–e	15.0	4.0	2.0	4.0	44.0	13.0	4.0	6.0	8.0
All	22.5	9.5	7.5	12.0	30.5	4.0	7.0	5.0	2.0

Table 337 46–54 Fishergate: numbers and percentages of iron objects from the Anglian and medieval periods in Groups B with D and E with F (see Fig.1542, p.2981)

| | Object group Numbers | | | Percentages | |
	B+D	E+F	Total	B+D	E+F
Period					
3	47	52	99	47.5	52.5
4	46	93	139	33.0	67.0
6a–c	64	81	145	44.0	56.0

Table 338 Bedern: numbers of iron objects by group for the medieval and late medieval/post-medieval periods (see Fig.1543, p.2982)

| | Object group | | | | | | | | | |
	A	B	C	D	E	F	G	H	I	Total
FP										
1	28	14	11	18	38	8	6	23	4	150
2	23	14	4	7	44	8	5	16	6	127
3	30	26	9	24	65	14	7	9	5	189
4	43	16	7	43	76	17	17	16	7	242
Total	124	70	31	92	223	47	35	54	22	708

Table 339 Bedern: numbers of iron objects by group for the medieval and late medieval/post-medieval periods expressed as percentages of the Finds Period totals (see Fig.1544, p.2982)

| | Object group | | | | | | | | |
	A	B	C	D	E	F	G	H	I
FP									
1	18.0	9.0	7.0	12.0	25.0	6.0	5.5	15.5	2.0
2	18.0	11.0	3.0	5.5	34.5	6.5	4.0	12.5	5.0
3	16.0	14.0	5.0	12.5	34.5	7.5	3.5	5.0	2.0
4	18.0	6.5	3.0	18.0	31.5	7.0	7.0	6.0	3.0

Table 340 Bedern: numbers and percentages of iron objects in the medieval and late medieval/post-medieval periods in Groups B with D and E with F (see Fig.1545, p.2983)

| | Object group Numbers | | | Percentages | |
	B+D	E+F	Total	B+D	E+F
Period					
1	32	46	78	41.0	59.0
2	21	52	76	27.5	72.5
3	50	79	129	39.0	61.0
4	59	93	152	39.0	61.0

Table 341 Coppergate, Bedern, Fishergate: a) ironwork assemblages in descending order of scores for tools and implements, and knives (Groups B and D) as a percentage of the total numbers of objects in Groups B, D, E and F; b) percentage of knives (D) in Groups B and D (see Figs.1546–7, pp.2984–5)

Period assemblage	Date	% Group B+D	% D in B+D
Coppergate 4A	Anglo-Scandinavian	61.5	20.0
Coppergate 4B	Anglo-Scandinavian	55.5	31.0
Coppergate 5A	Anglo-Scandinavian	49.0	26.0
Coppergate 5C	Anglo-Scandinavian	49.0	25.5
Fishergate 3	Anglian	47.0	61.5
Coppergate 3	Anglo-Scandinavian	45.0	49.5
Coppergate 5B	Anglo-Scandinavian	44.5	44.0
Fishergate 6a–c	Medieval	44.0	50.0
Bedern FP 1	Medieval	41.0	56.0
Bedern FP 3	Medieval	39.0	48.0
Bedern FP 4	Medieval	39.0	73.0
Coppergate 6i	Medieval	37.5	40.5
Fishergate 4	Anglo-Scan./Medieval	33.0	56.5
Coppergate 6ii	Medieval	28.5	39.5
Bedern FP 2	Medieval	27.5	33.5
Coppergate 6iv	Medieval	25.5	52.0
Coppergate 6iii	Medieval	19.0	31.0

Appendix Two

Data used in the inter- and intra-site spatial analysis of the ironwork (pp.2992–8)

Table 342 16–22 Coppergate: numbers of medieval iron objects in each group by tenement (see Fig.1548, p.2992)

	Tenements							
	A	AB	B	BC	C	CD	D	Total
Object group								
A	23	1	42	18	105	19	86	294
B	7	5	28	15	49	19	40	163
C	7	1	34	12	63	17	57	191
D	7	1	28	5	30	10	28	109
E	40	5	123	20	181	55	149	573
F	2	2	15	6	37	13	22	97
G	2	0	14	1	20	10	36	83
H	33	1	63	16	113	27	114	367
I	0	0	1	0	10	3	10	24
Totals	121	16	348	93	608	173	542	1901

Table 343   16–22 Coppergate: object group percentages for each tenement assemblage (see Fig.1549, p.2993)

| | Object group | | | | | | | | |
	A	B	C	D	E	F	G	H	I
Tenement									
A	19.0	6.0	6.0	6.0	33.0	1.5	1.0	27.5	0
B	12.0	8.0	10.0	8.0	35.5	4.5	4.0	18.0	<1.0
BC	19.0	16.0	13.0	5.5	21.5	7.0	1.0	17.0	0
C	17.5	8.0	10.5	5.0	30.0	6.0	3.5	18.5	1.0
CD	11.0	11.0	10.0	6.0	32.0	7.5	6.0	15.5	1.0
D	16.0	7.5	10.5	5.0	27.5	4.0	6.5	21.0	2.0
All	16.0	8.5	10.0	5.5	30.0	5.0	4.5	19.5	1.0

Table 344   16–22 Coppergate: iron object group breakdown by tenement (percentages) (see Fig.1550, p.2993)

| | Tenement | | | | | | |
	A	AB	B	BC	C	CD	D
Object group							
A	8.0	<1.0	14.5	6.0	36.0	6.5	28.5
B	4.5	3.0	17.0	9.0	30.0	11.5	25.0
C	3.5	<1.0	18.0	6.5	33.0	9.0	30.0
D	7.0	<1.0	25.5	4.5	28.0	9.0	25.5
E	7.0	<1.0	22.0	3.5	32.0	9.5	26.0
F	2.0	2.0	15.5	6.0	38.0	13.5	23.0
G	2.5	0	17.0	<1.0	25.0	12.0	43.5
H	9.0	<1.0	17.0	4.5	31.0	7.5	31.0
I	0.0	0	4.0	0	41.5	13.0	41.5
All	7.0	<1.0	18.5	5.0	32.0	9.0	28.5

Table 345   Bedern: medieval iron objects, numbers in each object group by area (see Fig.1551, p.2995)

| | | Area | | |
	Foundry	South-west	North-east	All
Object group				
A	31	54	47	132
B	14	46	21	81
C	8	14	10	32
D	23	37	33	93
E	61	99	81	241
F	6	25	21	52
G	9	15	12	36
H	13	23	33	69
I	7	9	9	25
Totals	172	322	267	761

Table 346   Bedern: object group percentages for each area (see Fig.1552, p.2995)

| | Object group | | | | | | | | |
	A	B	C	D	E	F	G	H	I
Area									
Foundry	18.0	9.0	4.5	13.5	35.5	4.0	5.0	7.5	4.0
South-west	16.5	14.5	4.5	12.0	30.0	8.0	4.5	7.0	3.0
North-east	17.5	8.0	3.0	12.5	30.5	8.0	4.5	12.5	3.5
All	17.5	10.5	4.0	12.0	32.0	7.0	4.5	9.0	3.5

Table 347   Bedern: medieval iron objects, percentage of objects by group in each area (see Fig.1553, p.2996)

| | | Area | |
	Foundry	South-west	North-east
Object group			
A	23.5	41.0	35.5
B	17.5	57.5	25.0
C	25.0	44.0	31.0
D	24.0	40.5	35.5
E	25.5	41.0	33.5
F	11.5	48.0	40.5
G	25.0	41.5	33.5
H	19.0	33.5	47.5
I	28.0	36.0	36.0
All	22.5	42.5	35.0

Appendix Three

Analysis of non-ferrous platings and deposits on ironwork from Coppergate, the Foundry and Bedern

By Tim Horsley

Following conservation at the YAT Conservation Laboratory, a number of iron objects from Coppergate, the Foundry and Bedern with indications of metal plating were submitted for analysis by qualitative X-ray fluorescence (XRF) to identify the metals present in the platings.

The XRF spectrometer used was a Link Analytical XR400 energy dispersive system. Analyses were carried out under the following conditions: a tube voltage of 35kV; a current of 30–50μA; a collimator size of 4mm; and a collection time of 100 seconds. This size of collimator allows the analysis of a fairly large area, about 1cm^2, which is often necessary when dealing with the non-homogeneous tracings of metal platings. The greater the analysis area, the better the detection of these metals. For each analysis, both peak height and peak area were recorded as a measure of elemental signal strength.

Low levels of copper were detected on most objects, even in areas where no non-ferrous metal was apparently present. As pointed out by Wilthew (1984), this is likely to be the result of contamination during burial, and therefore is not evidence that the object was originally plated. This trace level of copper was often detected with both the tin and tin-lead platings, and so was also assumed to be due to contamination and ignored.

The results obtained were qualitative in nature, necessitating a level of interpretation before the original ratios of the metals could be arrived at. The strength of signal (peak height) is affected by many factors, including the shape, size and surface texture of the object, its position during analysis, the concentration and distribution of the metal plating, and the analytical conditions used. Any corrosion processes may have altered the relative proportions of metals in an alloy, adding further complications (*AY* 17/6, 724). The combination of these factors makes it impossible to give the exact percentage compositions of metals in a plating, although a rough idea of their ratios can be achieved.

The analyses of a number of different tin-lead alloy and copper alloy standards allowed the identification of mathematical relationships between the recorded peak heights and the percentage of metals present in the different alloys. These findings were then used as a guide in giving an indication of the proportions of non-ferrous metals present on the analysed ironwork.

Details of the platings identified have been incorporated in the catalogue and the terms used have the following meanings.

Tin alloy platings

tin: tin was the only non-ferrous metal detected, and therefore the plating was essentially pure tin.

tin, trace lead: a trace of lead was detected, probably representing a lead level of about 1%. At such a low level, this may well be the result of contamination, during either manufacture or burial.

tin, a little lead: the level of lead was up to about 10%, and is more likely to represent the deliberate addition of lead to the tin, rather than contamination.

leaded tin: the amount of lead was 'significant', that is, greater than 10%.

tin-lead alloy: this term has been used where both lead and tin were detected, but since the levels of both were extremely low, no attempt has been made to estimate their relative proportions.

lead: lead was the only non-ferrous metal detected. Most of the objects which gave this result were not coated. The lead was present as lumps or droplets of metal adhering to the object.

Copper alloy platings

copper: copper was the only non-ferrous metal detected, the plating essentially being pure copper.

leaded copper: 'significant' amounts of lead were detected in addition to the copper.

bronze: copper and significant amounts of tin were detected.

leaded bronze: bronze with significant lead.

brass: copper with significant levels of zinc.

ternary: in addition to copper, significant amounts of zinc and tin were detected. This is effectively a gunmetal, though the term 'ternary' has been used instead to indicate that the relative proportions of these three metals in the alloy appear to vary considerably.

quaternary: a ternary alloy with significant amounts of lead (leaded gunmetal).

Any other non-ferrous metals detected are mentioned by their elemental name.

A full report on the non-ferrous platings and deposits on ironwork may be consulted in archive: T. Horsley, 'Analysis of Platings and Deposits on Ironwork from Bedern and Coppergate, York' (AML Report 87/97).

Acknowledgements

York Archaeological Trust and the authors wish to express their thanks to all those who have helped in the preparation of this fascicule.

The excavation at 16–22 Coppergate was directed by R.A. Hall, with supervision by David T. Evans (1976–81), Shahed Power (1976–8), Mick Humphreys (1976–7) and Ian Lawton (1978–81). Post-excavation work has been under the overall direction of R.A. Hall. The excavation was made possible through the generous co-operation of York City Council, the site owners, and the financial support of the then Department of the Environment and a number of generous benefactors and donors.

The excavation at 22 Piccadilly was directed by N.F. Pearson, assisted by R. Finlayson who undertook the post-excavation analysis. The project was financed by Wimpey Property Holdings Limited.

The excavation at 46–54 Fishergate was directed by R.L. Kemp, with supervision by M.C. Whyman and J.M. Lilley, and K.C. Jones was post-excavation assistant . Funding for the excavation was provided by English Heritage, the City of York and Costain Homes (North-Eastern) Limited.

The Bedern excavations were initially directed for York Archaeological Trust by B. Whitwell, then by M.J. Daniells, and finally by M. Stockwell. The Foundry site was supervised in 1973 by P. Mills (Trench I) and I. Reed (Trench II), in 1974 by P. Mills, and from 1975–6 by R. Bartkowiak. The latter also conducted some post-excavation ordering of the Foundry site archive. For Bedern south-west and Bedern northeast, initial post-excavation analysis and production of the archive report was undertaken by A. Clarke and M. Stockwell. York Archaeological Trust is most grateful to the original owner of the site, York City Council, and the subsequent owner, Simons of York, and also to the Dean and Chapter of York Minister who own the Chapel, for making the land available for excavation, and for giving every assistance during the work. The excavations were supported by grants from the Department of the Environment, now English Heritage. Many of the excavation assistants were employed on a STEP scheme administered by the Manpower Services Commission, whilst the su-pervisory staff were financed directly by the Department of the Environment. From 1976 to 1978 the excavation was staffed with DOE-funded excavation assistants and supervisors who were supplemented by Manpower Services Commission Job Creation Programme staff from 1978 to 1979. Later all employees were replaced with MSC Special Temporary Employment Programme personnel although the DOE continued to provide funding for supervision. Until 1979 additional summer help was provided by many hardworking volunteers, students from the University of Pennsylvania and the College of Ripon and York St John, and inmates from HM Open Prison at Askham Bryan.

The project has been managed at the Trust by P.J. Ottaway, N.S.H. Rogers and F.P. Mee, and by P. Wilson for English Heritage.

Thanks are expressed to the staff, students and volunteers of the YAT Conservation Department both past and present, in particular Margaret Brooks, Kate Buckingham, Julie Jones, Sonia O'Connor, Ian Panter, Erica Paterson, Sue Rees and Jim Spriggs; to Christine McDonnell and the Trust Finds Department staff, especially Gill Woolrich, Annie Jowett, Bev Shaw and Renée Gajowskyj who supervised the transport of artefacts for study and illustration. Thanks are also due to all contributors to the text, and to Alison and Ian Goodall for their early work on the finds. Thom Richardson of the Royal Armouries, Elizabeth Hartley of the Yorkshire Museum, Geoff Egan of MOLAS, and John Cherry and David Gaimster of the British Museum all provided useful advice and access to their collections. Analyses of metals and specialist metallurgy reports were carried out at the Ancient Monuments Laboratory by Justine Bayley, David Starley and Tim Horsley, and also by Gerry McDonnell and Karen Wiemer. Emma Bowron undertook analysis of the plated nails, Ian Panter analysed the jet, Ailsa Mainman identified crucible and pottery fabrics, and Sandra Garside-Neville identified ceramic tile types. The authors are grateful to Christopher Knüsel for drawing attention to the possible function of the medical plate from Fishergate, to Edwin Holmes for discussion about the thimbles, to Hugh Murray for advice on heraldry, to Charmian Ottaway for interpretation of the horse bits and to

Jim Halliday for supplying information relating to local metal detector finds. Current and former colleagues at the Trust who provided both encouragement and scholarly advice include Ian Carlisle, Chris Daniell, Richard Hall and Dominic Tweddle. Rhona Finlayson, Kurt Hunter-Mann, Richard Kemp and Julian D. Richards all helped with contextual queries.

The majority of the iron objects have been drawn by Charlotte Bentley, the majority of the objects of other materials by Lesley Collett, with others by Kate Biggs, Glenys Boyles, Sheena Howarth and Helen Humphreys. Weave diagrams and leather straps with copper alloy mounts are by Paula Chew. Reconstructions of horse harness, padlocks and structural fittings were prepared by Simon Chew, with Fig.1439 finalised by Glenys Boyles, and Figs.1525 and 1527 finalised by Lesley Collett. Other reconstructions, charts, diagrams, maps and plans are by Charlotte Bentley, Lesley Collett and Terry Finnemore. The illustrations were prepared for press by Charlotte Bentley, Glenys Boyles, Lesley Collett and Terry Finnemore.

The principal photographer was Simon I. Hill, FRPS (Scirebröc). Figs.1366–9 were taken by David Starley and Figs.1372–3, 1375–8 and 1555 are reproduced from Karen Wiemer's PhD thesis. Other photographs are reproduced with permission from the Bodleian Library (Figs.1319, 1333 and 1438), Bibliothèque nationale de France (Fig.1343), the British Library (Figs.1384, 1389, 1401, 1405 and 1531), York Minster Archive, © Dean and Chapter of York (Figs.1450, 1485, 1508 and 1534), the Yorkshire Museum (Fig.1505).

The summary was translated into French by Charlette Sheil-Small and into German by Mrs K. Aberg. This fascicule was edited by Frances Mee, who also prepared the text for publication. The project has been funded and the fascicule published with the assistance of a generous subvention by English Heritage.

Summary

This report is the definitive publication of some 6,000 objects made in a wide range of materials, but including a substantial number of iron and non-ferrous metals. They come from contexts dated, for the most part, to between c.1066 and 1600, excavated at four major and a few minor sites in the medieval city. The major sites are 16–22 Coppergate (medieval tenements), Bedern Foundry (bronze-working workshop), Bedern (College of the Vicars Choral of York Minster) and 46–54 Fishergate (Gilbertine Priory).

A brief description of the sites from which the objects were recovered is followed by a discussion of conservation techniques. The main body of the report is divided into two parts: 'Craft and Industry' and 'Everyday Life'. The first part describes tools and implements, including those used in metalworking, leatherworking and textile manufacture, and the debris from craft activity. In respect of the latter there is a report on the analysis of non-ferrous metalworking waste at the Bedern Foundry and College sites, which supplements data presented in *AY* 10/3. In addition, there is a full report on the metallurgy of seventeen iron knives to set alongside analyses of Anglian (*AY* 17/9) and Anglo-Scandinavian (*AY* 17/6) specimens from York

The second part of the fascicule, 'Everyday Life', presents a wide range of objects, many of which were used on the sites where they were found. They provide a vivid insight into aspects of life as it was experienced in medieval York and include items of personal dress and clothing, jewellery, glass and other vessels, equipment for horse and rider, and a substantial assemblage of objects which illustrate the character of buildings and their fittings and furnishings.

The concluding discussion evaluates the assemblage as a whole in terms of the character of the activity and occupation on the principal sites, and summarises the evidence it has revealed for the economy and society of the medieval city. There is also a review of medieval finds from York in the context of comparable medieval assemblages from England, which is followed by remarks on the future direction of finds research.

Résumé

Ce rapport est la publication définitive de quelque 6000 objets fabriqués de matières très diverses mais comprenant un grand nombre de fer et de métaux non ferreux. Ils proviennent de contextes dont la date remonte, pour la plupart, entre environ 1066 et 1600, découverts dans quatre grands sites et quelques petits sites de la ville médiévale. Les grands sites sont ceux du 16–22 Coppergate (habitations médiévales), de Bedern Foundry (atelier de travail du bronze), de Bedern (College of the Vicars Choral of York Minster) et du 46–54 Fishergate (Prieuré des Gilbertins).

Une discussion sur les techniques de conservation fait suite à une brève description des sites où les objets ont été découverts. La principale partie du rapport est divisée en deux parties: 'Artisanat et industrie' et 'Vie quotidienne'. La première partie décrit les outils et le matériel, y compris le matériel utilisé pour le travail du métal, le travail du cuir et la fabrication des textiles et les débris de l'activité artisanale. En ce qui concerne ces derniers, il existe un rapport sur l'analyse des déchets du travail des métaux non ferreux sur les sites de Bedern Foundry et du College, lequel rapport s'ajoute aux données présentées dans *AY* 10/3. En outre, il y a un rapport complet sur la métallurgie de dix-sept couteaux en fer à mettre en parallèle avec des analyses des spécimens angliens (*AY* 17/9) et anglo-scandinaves (*AY* 17/6) d'York.

Le deuxième partie du fascicule, 'Vie quotidienne', présente une grande variété d'objets, dont nombre ont été utilisés sur les sites où ils ont été découverts. Ils révèlent une vision précise des aspects de la vie médiévale au quotidien à York et comprennent des vêtements et des accessoires, des bijoux, du verre et autres récipients, le nécessaire pour chevaux et cavaliers, et un important ensemble d'objets qui illustrent le caractère des bâtiments ainsi que leur équipement et leurs meubles.

La discussion récapitulative évalue l'ensemble dans sa totalité au niveau de l'activité et de l'occupation des sites principaux et donne un résumé des indices révélés par cet ensemble concernant l'économie et la société de la cité médiévale. Il y a également un bilan des découvertes médiévales d'York dans le contexte d'ensembles médiévaux comparables découverts en Angleterre, bilan suivi de remarques sur l'orientation future de la recherche sur les découvertes.

Zusammenfassung

Dieser Bericht ist die definitive Veröffentlichung von rund 6000 aus verschiedenstem Material gefertigten Gegenständen, unter denen sich jedoch eine beträchtliche Anzahl von Funden aus Eisen und Nichteisenmetallen befanden. Sie entstammen datierten Horizonten, zum größten Teil zwischen circa 1066 und 1600, und wurden auf vier Großgrabungsstellen und mehreren kleineren Fundstellen in der mittelalterlichen Stadt ausgegraben. Die Großgrabungen sind 16–22 Coppergate (mittelalterliche Grundstücke), die Gießerei in Bedern (Bronze verarbeitende Werkstatt), Bedern (Kolleg der Vicars Choral des Münsters von York) und 46–54 Fishergate (gilbertinische Priorei).

An die kurze Beschreibung der Fundstellen, in denen die Objekte gefunden wurden, schließt sich eine Diskussion der Konservationstechniken an. Der Hauptteil des Berichtes ist in zwei Abschnitte unterteilt: 'Handwerk und Industrie' und 'tägliches Leben'. Der erste Teil beschreibt die Werkzeuge und Geräte, einschließlich jener die in der Metallverarbeitung, Lederverarbeitung und Textilherstellung benutzt wurden sowie den Abfall aus diesen handwerklichen Tätigkeiten. Mit Bezug auf den letzteren ist hier ein Bericht über die Analyse des Abfalles von Nichteisenmetallen aus den Grabungen in der Gießerei und dem Kolleg in Bedern beigefügt, der die Daten, die in *AY* 10/3 vorgelegt wurden ergänzt. Weitenhin eingefügt ist ein Bericht über die Metallurgie von siebzehn Eisenmessern, der Analysen von anglischen (*AY* 17/9) und anglo-skandinavischen (*AY* 17/6) Beispielen aus York gegenübergestellt werden.

Der zweite Abschnitt des Fasciküls, 'tägliche Leben', stellt eine weitreichende Anzahl von Objekten vor, von denen viele am Fundort in Gebrauch gewesen waren. Sie erlauben einen klaren Einblick in die Lebensweise im mittelalterlichen York. Unter ihnen befinden sich persönliches und Kleidungszubehör, Ausrüstung für Pferd und Reiter sowie eine beträchtliche Sammlung von Gegenständen, die den Charakter von Gebäuden, deren Austattung und Mobiliar veranschaulichen.

Die abschließende Diskussion bewertet die Fundgruppen als Einheit in Zusammenhang mit dem Charakter der Aktivität und Nutzung auf den Hauptfundstellen, und faßt den Befund, der für Wirtschaft und Gesellschaft in der mittelalterlichen Stadt vorgelegt wurde zusammen. Weiterhin werden die mittelalterlichen Funde aus York im Zusammenhang mit vergleichbaren, mittelalterlichen Fundgruppen aus England betrachtet. Daran schließen sich dann einige Bemerkungen über die zukünftige Forschungsrichtung im Bezug auf Funde an.

Abbreviations

Most abbreviations are those recommended by the Council for British Archaeology, but the following are used in addition. Other abbreviations used in bibliographic references in the text are explained in the Bibliography below.

RCHM   Royal Commission on Historical Monuments

SS   Surtees Society

YAT   York Archaeological Trust

YM   Yorkshire Museum

YMA   York Minster Archives

Bibliography

Addyman, P.V. and Priestley, J., 1977. 'Baile Hill, York: a report on the Institute's excavations', *Archaeol. J.* **134**, 115–56

Alexander, J. and Binski, P. (eds), 1987. *Age of Chivalry. Art in Plantagenet England 1200–1400* (London)

Allan, J.P., 1984. *Medieval and Post-Medieval Finds from Exeter, 1971–1980*, Exeter Archaeol. Rep. **3** (Exeter)

Alldritt, D.M., Carrott, J.B., Hall, A.R. and Kenward, H.K., 1991. 'Environmental evidence from 17–21 Piccadilly (Reynard's Garage)', *Reports from the Environmental Archaeology Unit, York* 91/1

Ancient Monuments Laboratory, 1995. *A Strategy for the Care and Investigation of Finds*

Andersen, H.H., Crabb, P.J. and Madsen, H.J., 1971. *Århus Søndervold: en Byarkeologisk Undersøgelse*, Jysk Arkaeologisk Selskabs Skrifter **9** (Århus)

Archer, M., 1985. *English Stained Glass* (HMSO)

Armitage, K.H., Pearce, J.E. and Vince, A.G., 1981. 'A late medieval 'bronze' mould from Copthall Avenue, London', *Antiq. J.* **61** (2), 362–4

Armstrong, P. and Ayers, B., 1987. *Excavations in High Street and Blackfriargate*, E. Riding Archaeol. **8**

Armstrong, P., Tomlinson, D. and Evans, D.H., 1991. *Excavations at Lurk Lane, Beverley, 1979–82*, Sheffield Excavation Rep. **1** (Sheffield)

Arwidsson, G. and Berg, G.G., 1983. *The Mästermyr Find: a Viking Age Tool Chest from Gotland* (Stockholm)

Ashurst, J. and Dimes, F.G., 1990. *Conservation of Building and Decorative Stone*, 2 vols (London)

Atkin, M., Carter, A. and Evans, D.H., 1985. *Excavations in Norwich 1971–1978, Part II*, E. Anglian Archaeol. Rep. **26** (Norwich)

Attwater, W.A., 1961. *Leathercraft* (London)

Axworthy Rutter, J.A., 1990. 'Window lead' in S.W. Ward, *Excavations at Chester: The Lesser Medieval Religious Houses, Sites Investigated 1964–83* (Chester), 118–19

AY. Addyman, P.V. (ed.) *The Archaeology of York* (York)

3 *The Legionary Fortress*:

  3 P.J. Ottaway, 1996. *Excavations and Observations on the Defences and Adjacent Sites, 1971–90*

7 *Anglian York (AD 410–876)*:

  1 R.L. Kemp, 1996. *Anglian Settlement at 46–54 Fishergate*

8 *Anglo-Scandinavian York*:

  4 D. Evans and R.A. Hall, in prep. *Anglo-Scandinavian Structures at Coppergate*

10 *The Medieval Walled City north-east of the Ouse*:

  2 R.A. Hall, H. MacGregor and M. Stockwell, 1988. *Medieval Tenements in Aldwark, and Other Sites*

  3 J.D. Richards, 1993. *The Bedern Foundry*

  4 D.A. Stocker, 2000. *The College of the Vicars Choral of York Minster at Bedern: Architectural Fragments*

  5 J.D. Richards, 2001. *The Vicars Choral of York Minster: The College at Bedern*

  6 R.A. Hall and K. Hunter-Mann, 2001. *Buildings and Land Use at and around Medieval Coppergate*

11 *The Medieval Defences and Suburbs*:

  2 R.L. Kemp with C.P. Graves, 1996. *The Church and Gilbertine Priory of St Andrew, Fishergate*

  3 C.P. Graves, 2000. *The Window Glass of the Order of St Gilbert of Sempringham: A York-based Study*

12 *The Medieval Cemeteries*:

  2 G. Stroud and R.L. Kemp, 1993. *Cemeteries of St Andrew, Fishergate*

3 J.M. Lilley et al., 1994. *The Jewish Burial Ground at Jewbury*

14 *Past Environment of York:*

5 H.K. Kenward, A.R. Hall and A.K.G. Jones, 1986. *Environmental Evidence from a Roman Well and Anglian Pits in the Legionary Fortress*

7 H.K. Kenward and A.R. Hall, 1995. *Biological Evidence from Anglo-Scandinavian Deposits at 16–22 Coppergate*

15 *The Animal Bones:*

3 T.P. O'Connor, 1989. *Bones from Anglo-Scandinavian Levels at 16–22 Coppergate*

4 T.P. O'Connor, 1991. *Bones from 46–54 Fishergate*

5 J.M. Bond and T.P. O'Connor, 1999. *Bones from Medieval Deposits at 16–22 Coppergate and Other Sites in York*

16 *The Pottery:*

3 C.M. Brooks, 1987. *Medieval and Later Pottery from Aldwark and Other Sites*

5 A.J. Mainman, 1990. *Anglo-Scandinavian Pottery from 16–22 Coppergate*

6 A.J. Mainman, 1993. *Pottery from 46–54 Fishergate*

8 J. Monaghan, 1997. *Roman Pottery from York*

9 A.J. Mainman, in prep. *Medieval Pottery from York*

17 *The Small Finds:*

1 A. MacGregor, 1976. *Finds from a Roman Sewer and an Adjacent Building in Church Street*

3 A. MacGregor, 1982. *Anglo-Scandinavian Finds from Lloyds Bank, Pavement and Other Sites*

4 D. Tweddle, 1986. *Finds from Parliament Street and Other Sites in the City Centre*

5 P. Walton, 1989. *Textiles, Cordage and Raw Fibre from 16–22 Coppergate*

6 P.J. Ottaway, 1992. *Anglo-Scandinavian Ironwork from 16–22 Coppergate*

7 J. Bayley, 1992. *Non-Ferrous Metalworking from 16–22 Coppergate*

8 D. Tweddle, 1992. *The Anglian Helmet from Coppergate*

9 N.S.H. Rogers, 1993. *Anglian and Other Finds from 46–54 Fishergate*

10 H.E.M. Cool, G. Lloyd-Morgan and A.D. Hooley, 1995. *Finds from the Fortress*

11 P. Walton Rogers, 1997. *Textile Production at 16–22 Coppergate*

12 A. MacGregor, A.J. Mainman and N.S.H. Rogers, 1999. *Craft, Industry and Everyday Life: Bone, Antler, Ivory and Horn from Anglo-Scandinavian and Medieval York*

13 C.A. Morris, 2000. *Craft, Industry and Everyday Life: Wood and Woodworking in Anglo-Scandinavian and Medieval York*

14 A.J. Mainman and N.S.H. Rogers, 2000. *Craft, Industry and Everyday Life: Finds from Anglo-Scandinavian York*

16 Q. Mould, I. Carlisle and E. Cameron, in prep. *Craft, Industry and Everyday Life: Leather and Leatherworking in Anglo-Scandinavian and Medieval York*

18 *The Coins:*

1 E.J.E. Pirie, 1986. *Post-Roman Coins from York Excavations, 1971–81*

2 R. Brickstock in prep. *Roman Coins from York*

Baart, J. et al., 1977. *Oppgravingen in Amsterdam* (Amsterdam)

Bakka, E., 1965. 'Ytre Moa', *Viking* **29**, 121–46

Barclay, K. and Biddle, M., 1990. 'Stone and pottery lamps' in Biddle (ed.) 1990, ii, 983–1000

Barlow, F., Biddle, M., von Feilitzen, O. and Keene, D.J., 1976. *Winchester in the Early Middle Ages: An Edition and Discussion of the Winton Domesday*, Winchester Studies (Oxford)

Barraclough, K.C., 1976. 'The Development of the Cementation Process for the Manufacture of Steel', *J. Post-Medieval Archaeol.* **10**, 66–88

Baumgartner, E. and Krueger, I., 1988. *Phönix aus Sand und Asche: Glas des Mittelalters* (Munich)

Bayley, J., 1992. 'Metalworking ceramics', *Medieval Ceramics* **16**, 3–10

—— 1993. 'Assessment of metalworking debris from the Bedern excavations, York', AML Rep. 73/93

Bayley, J., Freestone, I., Jenner, A. and Vince, A., 1991. 'Metallurgy' in Vince (ed.) 1991, 389–405

Beck, S.W., 1886. *The Draper's Dictionary* (London)

Beresford, G., 1975. *The Medieval Clay-Land Village: Excavations at Goltho and Barton Blount*, Soc. for Medieval Archaeol. Monogr. Ser. **6** (London)

—— 1987. *Goltho: The Development of an Early Medieval Manor c.850–1150*, English Heritage Archaeol. Rep. **4** (London)

Bergman, K. and Billberg, I., 1976. 'Metallhantverk' in A.W. Mårtensson (ed.), *Uppgrävt förflutet för PKBanken i Lund*, Archaeol. Lundensia 7, 199–213

Biddle, M. (ed.), 1990. *Object and Economy in Medieval Winchester*, Winchester Studies 7, 2 vols (Oxford)

Biddle, M. and Barclay, K., 1990. '"Sewing pins" and wire' in Biddle (ed.) 1990, ii, 560–71

Biddle, M. and Brown, D., 1990. 'Writing equipment' in Biddle (ed.) 1990, ii, 729–47

Biddle, M. and Cook, L., 1990. 'Buttons' in Biddle (ed.) 1990, ii, 571–81

Biddle, M. and Creasey, S., 1990. 'Beads' in Biddle (ed.) 1990, ii, 659–65

Biddle, M. and Elmhirst, L., 1990. 'Sewing equipment' in Biddle (ed.) 1990, ii, 804–15

Biddle, M. and Hinton, D.A., 1990a. 'Copper-alloy bells' in Biddle (ed.) 1990, ii, 725–28

—— 1990b. 'Book-clasps and page-holder' in Biddle (ed.) 1990, ii, 755–8

—— 1990c. 'Points' in Biddle (ed.) 1990, ii, 581–9

Biddle, M. and Kjølbye-Biddle, B., 1990. 'Chalices and patens in burials' in Biddle (ed.) 1990, ii, 791–9

Biddle, M. and Smith, D., 1990. 'The querns' in Biddle (ed.) 1990, ii, 881–90

Biggs, N., 1992. *English Weights. An Illustrated Survey* (Llanfyllin)

Blades, N., 1995. (unpublished) *Copper Alloys from English Archaeological Sites 400–1600 AD: An Analytical Study Using ICP-AES*, PhD thesis, University of London

Blair, J. and Ramsay, N., 1991. *English Medieval Industries* (London)

Bowron, E.L., 1996. (unpublished) *The Analysis of Tin, Lead and Tin/Lead Plating on Iron Knives*, BA dissertation, University of Bradford

Bradley, J. and Manning, C., 1981. 'Excavations at Duiske Abbey, Graiguenamanagh, Co. Kilkenny', *Proc. Royal Irish Academy* **81C**, 397–426

Brisbane, T., 1990. 'Later medieval spoons' in Biddle (ed.) 1990, **ii**, 828–32

Brown, D., 1990. 'Dice, a games-board and playing pieces' in Biddle (ed.) 1990, **ii**, 692–706

Brownsword, R., 1985. *English Latten Domestic Candlesticks*, Finds Research Group 700–1700 Datasheet **1**

Brownsword, R. and Pitt, E.E.H., 1981. 'Medieval "bell metal" mortars — a misnomer', *Metallurgist and Materials Technologist* **13**(4), 184–5

Brownsword, R., Pitt, E.E.H. and Richardson, C., 1981. 'Medieval tripod ewers in Carlisle Museum', *Trans. Cumberland Westmorland Archaeol. Antiq. Soc.* **81**, 49–55

Bruce-Mitford, R., 1976. 'The Chapter-House Vestibule graves at Lincoln, and the body of St Hugh of Avalon' in F. Emmison and R. Stephens, *Tribute to an Antiquary; Essays presented to Marc Fitch by some of his friends* (London), 127–40

Buckland, K., 1979. 'The Monmouth cap', *Costume: The Journal of the Costume Society* **13**, 23–37

Buckland, P.C., 1988. 'The stones of York: building materials in Roman Yorkshire' in J. Price, P.R. Wilson and C.S. Briggs (eds), *Recent Research in Roman Yorkshire*, Brit. Archaeol. Rep. **193** (Oxford), 237–87

Butler, L.A.S., 1983. 'Domestic mortars' in Mayes and Butler 1983, 330–3

Buyse, L.J., 1955. (unpublished) *The Market for Flemish and Brabantine Cloth in England from the 12th to the 14th Century*, MA thesis, University of London

Calendar of the Patent Rolls: Vol.7, Edward III, AD 1345–1348 (Rolls Series)

Callander, J.G., 1924. 'Fourteenth century brooches and other ornaments in the National Museum of Antiquities of Scotland', *Proc. Soc. Antiq. Scot.* **58**, 160–84

Camden, W., 1695. *Britannia* (ed. E. Gibson)

Caple, C., 1991. 'The detection and definition of an industry: the English medieval and post medieval pin industry', *Archaeol. J.* **148**, 241–55

Cardon, D., 1993. *Fils Renoués, Trésors Textiles du Moyen Âge en Languedoc-Rousillon* (Carcassonne)

Carrott, J., Dobney, K., Hall, A.R., Issitt, M., Jacques, D., Kenward, H., Large, F., Miles, A. and Shaw, T., 1995. 'Assessment of biological remains from excavations at

22 Piccadilly (ABC Cinema) York (YAT/YM site code 1987.21)', *Reports from the Environmental Archaeology Unit, York* 95/53

Carter, A., 1977. 'Tiles and Other Baked Clay Objects' in Clarke and Carter 1977, 298–311

Charleston, R.J., 1975. 'The Glass' in C. Platt and R. Coleman-Smith, *Excavations in Medieval Southampton: Volume 2: The Finds* (Leicester), 204–26

—— 1984. 'The Glass' in Allan 1984, 258–78

—— 1990. 'Vessel Glass of the Late Medieval and Modern Periods' in Biddle (ed.) 1990, **ii**, 934–47

—— 1991. 'Vessel Glass' in Blair and Ramsay 1991, 237–64

Cherry, J., 1981. 'Medieval Rings 1100–1500' in Ward et al. 1981, 51–86

—— 1991. *Medieval Decorative Art* (London)

—— 1992. 'The breaking of seals', *Medieval Europe 1992, pre-printed papers* **7**, 23–7

Childs, W.R., 1981. 'England's iron trade in the fifteenth century', *Economic History Review* **33**, 25–7

Clark, J., 1983. 'Medieval Enamelled Glasses from London', *Medieval Archaeology* **27**, 152–6

—— (ed.), 1995. *The Medieval Horse and Its Equipment c.1150–c.1450*, Medieval Finds from Excavations in London **5** (London, HMSO)

Clarke, H. and Carter, A., 1977. *Excavations in King's Lynn 1963–1970*, Soc. Medieval Archaeol. Monogr. **7**

Clay, P., 1981. 'The small finds — copper alloy' in Mellor and Pearce 1981, 130–7

Cook, G.H., 1961. *English Monasteries in the Middle Ages* (London)

Cowgill, J., de Neergaard, M. and Griffith, N., 1987. *Knives and Scabbards*, Medieval Finds from London: **1** (London, HMSO)

Crosby, D.D.B. and Mitchell, J.G., 1987. 'A survey of British metamorphic honestones of the 9th to 15th centuries AD in the light of potassium-argon and natural remanent magnetisation studies', *J. Archaeol. Sci.* **14**, 483–506

Crowfoot, E., 1976. 'The Textiles' in T.G. Hassall, 'Excavations at Oxford Castle, 1965–1973', *Oxoniensia* **41**, 271–4

—— 1979. 'Textiles' in M.O.H. Carver, 'Three Saxo-Norman tenements in Durham City', *Medieval Archaeol.* **23**, 36–9

Crowfoot, E., Pritchard, F. and Staniland, K., 1992. *Textiles and Clothing c.1150–c.1450*, Medieval Finds from Excavations in London **4** (London, HMSO)

Crowfoot, G., 1950. 'A medieval tablet woven braid from a buckle found at Felixstowe', *Proc. Suffolk Instit. Archaeol.* **225**/2, 202–4

—— 1954. 'Tablet-woven braid from a thirteenth-century site', *Antiq. J.* **34**, 234–5

Crowfoot, G.M. and Harden D.B., 1931. 'Early Byzantine and Later Glass Lamps', *J. Egyptian Archaeol.* **17**, 196–208

Crummy, N., 1983. *The Roman Small Finds from Excavations in Colchester 1971–9*, Colchester Archaeol. Rep. **6** (Colchester)

Dale, M.K., 1934. 'The London silkwomen of the fifteenth century', *Economic History Review* 1st ser. **4**, 324–35

Drinkwater, N., 1991. 'Domestic stonework' in Saunders and Saunders (eds) 1991, 169–83

Dunning, G.C., 1962. 'The bronze skillet from Stanford in the Vale, Berkshire', *Berkshire Archaeol. J.* **60**, 98–100

—— 1974. 'Comparative material' in L.A.S. Butler and G.C. Dunning, 'Medieval Finds from Castell-y-Bere, Monmouth', *Archaeol. Cambrensis* **123**, 101–6

—— 1977. 'Mortars' in Clarke and Carter 1977, 320–47

—— 1991. 'A Note on Stone Pestles' in Saunders and Saunders (eds) 1991, 172

Durham, B., 1977. 'Archaeological Investigations in St Aldates, Oxford', *Oxoniensia* **42**, 83–203

Eames, E.S., 1980. *Catalogue of Medieval Lead-Glazed Earthenware Tiles in the Department of Medieval and Later Antiquities, British Museum, Vol 2: The Plates* (London)

Edge, D. and Paddock, J.M., 1988. *Arms and Armour of the Medieval Knight* (London)

Egan, G., 1995. 'Buckles, hasps and strap hooks' in Clark (ed.) 1995, 55–61

—— (ed.) 1998. *The Medieval Household, Daily Living c.1150–c.1450*, Medieval Finds from Excavations in London **6** (London, HMSO)

Egan, G. and Pritchard, F., 1991. *Dress Accessories c.1150–c.1450*, Medieval Finds from Excavations in London **3** (London)

Ellis, B., 1995. 'Spurs and spur fittings' in Clark (ed.) 1995, 124–56

Ellis, S.E., 1969. 'The petrography and provenance of Anglo-Saxon and Medieval English honestones, with notes on some other hones', *Bull. Brit. Mus. (Nat. Hist.), Mineralogy* **2**, 135–87

Ellis, S.E. and Moore, D.T., 1990. 'The hones' in Biddle (ed.) 1990, **ii**, 868–81

Espinas, G., 1913. *La Vie Urbaine de Douai au Moyen Age*, 4 vols (Paris)

Evans, K.J., 1969. 'A discovery of two unusual objects in New Shoreham', *Sussex Archaeol. Collections* **107**, 79–86

EYC. Clay, C.T. (ed.), *Early Yorkshire Charters*, YASRS, Extra Series

Farley, M., 1976. 'Saxon and medieval Walton, Aylesbury: excavations 1973–4', *Records of Buckinghamshire* **20**, 153–290

Fell, V. and Starley, D., forthcoming. 'Metallographic Analysis of Selected Knives' in A. Hardy, A. Dodd and G. Keevil, *Excavations at Eynsham Abbey 1989–1992*, Oxford Archaeol. Unit Thames Valley Landscapes Monogr.

Fingerlin, I., 1971. *Gürtel des Hohen und Späten Mittelalters* (Munich)

Flury-Lemberg, M., 1988. *Textile Conservation and Research* (Bern)

Foreman, M., 1991. 'The lead and lead alloy' in Armstrong, Tomlinson and Evans 1991, 155–63

Fowler, J.T. (ed.), 1903. *Rites of Durham, Being a Description or Brief Declaration of All the Ancient Monuments, Rites, and Customs Belonging or Being Within the Monastical Church of Durham Before the Suppression. Written 1593*, SS **107** (Durham)

Foy, D., 1985, 'Essai de Typologie des Verres Medievaux d'Après les Fouilles Provençales et Languedoçiennes', *J. Glass Studies* **27**, 18–71

Foy, D. and Sennequier, G., 1989. *A Travers le Verre du Moyen Âge à la Renaissance* (Rouen)

French, T.W, 1999. *York Minster: The St William Window*, Corpus Vitrearum Medii Aevi Great Britain (Oxford)

Furnivall, F.J., 1868. *Early English Meals and Manners*, Early English Text Society, Original Series **32** (London)

Geake, H., 1995. (unpublished) *The Use of Grave Goods in Conversion Period England, c.600–c.850*, PhD thesis, University of York

Geddes, J., 1985. 'The small finds' in Hare 1985, 147–77

Geddes, J. and Carter, A., 1977. 'Objects of Non-Ferrous Metal, Amber and Paste' in Clarke and Carter 1977, 287–91

Geijer, A., 1979. *A History of Textile Art* (London)

Gibson, P., 1989. 'Architectural glass' in R. Newton and S. Davison, *Conservation of Glass* (London), 241–74

Goldberg, P.J.P., 1992. *Women, Work and Life Cycle in a Medieval Economy: Women in York and Yorkshire c.1300–1520* (Oxford)

Goodall, A.R., 1979. 'Copper-alloy objects' in D.D. Andrews and G. Milne (eds), *Wharram: A Study of Settlement on the Yorkshire Wolds*, Soc. Medieval Archaeol. Monogr. Ser. **8** (London), 108–14

—— 1982. 'Objects of copper alloy' in J.G. Coad and A.D.F. Streeten, 'Excavations at Castle Acre Castle, Norfolk, 1972–77', *Archaeol. J.* **139**, 235–9

—— 1983a. 'Objects of copper alloy' in A. Streeten, *Bayham Abbey*, Sussex Archaeol. Soc. Monogr. **2**, 109–10

—— 1983b. 'Non-ferrous metal objects (except military finds, spurs and pins)' in Mayes and Butler 1983, 231–9

—— 1984. 'Objects of non-ferrous metal' in Allan 1984, 337–48

—— 1987a. 'Objects of copper alloy' in Armstrong and Ayers 1987, 202–6

—— 1987b. 'Medieval copper alloy' in Beresford 1987, 172–6

—— 1991. 'The copper alloy and gold' in Armstrong, Tomlinson and Evans 1991, 148–54

Goodall, I.H., 1977. 'Iron objects' in Clarke and Carter 1977, 291–8

—— 1979a. 'Iron objects' in G.H. Smith, 'The excavation of the hospital of St Mary of Ospringe, commonly called Maison Dieu', *Archaeol. Cantiana* **95**, 129–37

—— 1979b. 'Iron objects' in D.D. Andrews and G. Milne, *Wharram. A Study of Settlement on the Yorkshire Wolds 1, Domestic Settlement, Areas 10 and 6,* Soc. Medieval Archaeol. Monogr. **8**, 115–23

—— 1979c. 'Iron objects' in P.A. Rahtz, *The Saxon and Medieval Palaces at Cheddar: Excavations 1960–2,* Brit. Archaeol. Rep. Brit. Ser. **65** (Oxford)

—— 1980a. 'The iron objects' in P. Wade-Martins, *Excavations in North Elmham Park, 1967–72,* E. Anglian Archaeol. **9** (Gressenhall) 509–16

—— 1980b. (unpublished) *Ironwork in Medieval Britain: An Archaeological Study,* PhD thesis, University College Cardiff

—— 1983. 'Iron objects' in Mayes and Butler 1983, 240–52

—— 1984. 'Iron objects' in A. Rogerson and C. Dallas, *Excavations in Thetford 1948–59 and 1973–80,* E. Anglian Archaeol. **2** (Gressenhall) 76–106

—— 1987. 'Objects of iron' in Beresford 1987, 177–87

—— 1990a. 'Knives' in Biddle (ed.) 1990, **ii**, 835–60

—— 1990b. 'Chains, Links, Chain Fittings, Rings and Washers' in Biddle (ed.) 1990, **ii**, 821–8

—— 1990c. 'Locks and Keys' in Biddle (ed.) 1990, **ii**, 1001–36

—— 1993. 'Structural ironwork' in Margeson 1993, 143–8

—— 2000. 'Iron objects' in P. Ellis (ed.), *Ludgershall Castle Wiltshire: A Report on Excavations by P.V. Addyman 1964–1972,* Wiltshire Archaeol. and Nat. Hist. Soc. Monogr. Ser. **2**, 143–56

Goodall, I.H. and Carter, A., 1977. 'Iron objects' in Clarke and Carter 1977, 291–8

Goodall, I.H, Ellis, B. and Oakley, G.E., 1979. 'The iron objects' in Williams 1979, 268–77

Goodall, I.H. and Hinton, D., 1977. 'Iron and bronze' in B. Durham 1977, 135–50

Graham, R., 1901. *St. Gilbert of Sempringham and the Gilbertines* (London)

Gray, H., St George, 1930. 'A Medieval Spoon Found at Taunton Castle', *Antiq. J.* **10**, 156–8

Grew, F. and de Neergaard, M., 1988. *Shoes and Pattens,* Medieval Finds from Excavations in London **2** (London)

Griffiths, N., 1989. *Shield-Shaped Mounts,* Finds Research Group 700–1700 Datasheet **12** (Oxford)

—— 1990. 'Finger-joint cover from a plate armour gauntlet' in Biddle (ed.) 1990, **ii**, 1084–5

—— 1995. 'Harness pendants and associated fittings' in Clark (ed.) 1995, 61–71

Groves, S., 1973 (1st edn 1966). *The History of Needlework Tools and Accessories* (London)

Hall, A.R., Kenward, H., Robertson, A., 1993a. 'Investigation of medieval and post-medieval plant and invertebrate remains from Area X of the excavations in The Bedern (south-west), York (YAT/Yorkshire Museum sitecode 1973–81.13 X): Technical Report', AML Rep. 93/56

—— 1993b. 'Investigation of medieval and post-medieval plant and invertebrate remains from Area II of the excavations in The Bedern (south-west), York (YAT/Yorkshire Museum sitecode 1976–81.14 II): Technical Report', AML Rep. 93/58

Hall, R.A., 1984. *The Viking Dig* (London)

Hall, R.A. and Coppack, G., 1972. 'Excavations at Full Street, Derby 1972', *Derbyshire Archaeol. J.,* 29–77

Hare, J.N., 1985. *Battle Abbey: The Eastern Range and the Excavations of 1978–80,* HBMCE Rep. **2** (London)

Harrison, F., 1952. *Life in a Medieval College* (London)

Hartley, M. and Ingilby, J., 1978. *The Old Hand-Knitters of the Dales* (Clapham, N.Yorks., *The Dalesman*)

Harvey, Y., 1975. 'The bronze' in C. Platt and R. Coleman-Smith, *Excavations in Medieval Southampton 1953–69 : 2 The Finds,* 254–68 (Leicester)

Haslam, J., 1993. 'Glass Vessels' in Margeson 1993, 97–117

Hawthorne, J.G. and Smith, C.S., 1963. *Theophilus, On Divers Arts* (Chicago)

Hayward, J.F., 1957. *English Cutlery, Sixteenth–Eighteenth Century* (London)

Heaton, H., 1965. *Yorkshire Woollen and Worsted Industries* (Oxford, 2nd edn)

Henderson, J., 1992. 'The Glass' in D.H. Evans, D.G. Tomlinson, *Excavations at 33–35 Eastgate, Beverley, 1983–86,* Sheffield Excavation Rep. **3**, 135–7

—— 2000. 'The vessel glass' in P. Ellis (ed.), *Ludgershall Castle, Wiltshire. A Report on the Excavations by Peter Addyman, 1964–1972,* Wilts. Archaeol. and Nat. Hist. Soc. Monogr. **2**, 168–77

Henig, M., 1974. 'Medieval Finds' in T.W.T. Tatton-Brown, *Excavations at the Custom House site, City of London, 1973,* Trans. London Middlesex Archaeol. Soc. **25**, 189–201

—— 1988. 'Small Finds' in Sherlock and Woods 1988, 177–231

Henisch, B.A., 1976. *Fast and Feast* (Pennsylvania)

Heslop, T.A., 1987. 'English seals in the thirteenth and fourteenth centuries' in Alexander and Binski 1987, 114–18

Hinton, D.A., 1977. 'Objects of iron' in B. Cunliffe, *Excavations at Portchester Castle 3: Medieval, the Outer Bailey and its Defences,* Soc. Antiq. Res. Rep. **34**, 196–203

—— 1990a. 'Buckles and buckle-plates' in Biddle (ed.) 1990, **ii**, 506–26

—— 1990b. 'Belt hasps and other belt-fittings' in Biddle (ed.) 1990, **ii**, 539–42

—— 1990c. 'Belt- and strap-mounts' in Biddle (ed.) 1990, **ii**, 542–5

—— 1990d. 'Gold, silver, lead or pewter, and copper-alloy fittings' in Biddle (ed.) 1990, **ii**, 762–81

—— 1990e. 'Handles' in Biddle (ed.) 1990, **ii**, 864-8

—— 1990f. 'Harness pendants and swivels' in Biddle (ed.) 1990, **ii**, 1047–53

—— 1990g. 'Copper-alloy and tin chains' in Biddle (ed.) 1990, ii, 1089–91

—— 1990h. 'Copper-alloy, lead and pewter rings' in Biddle (ed.) 1990, ii, 1095–7

—— 1990j. 'Unidentified Copper Alloy Objects' in Biddle (ed.) 1990, ii, 1115–26

Hirst, S.M., Walsh, D.J. and Wright, S.M., 1983. *Bordesley Abbey* ii *2nd Report on Excavations at Bordesley Abbey, Redditch, Hereford-Worcestershire*, Brit. Archaeol. Rep. **23**

Holmes, E., 1985. *Thimbles*, Finds Research Group 700–1700 Datasheet **5**

Hopkins, H.J., 1970. *A Span of Bridges* (Newton Abbot)

Horsman, V., Milne, C. and Milne, G., 1988. *Aspects of Saxo-Norman London: 1, Building and Street Development*, London Middlesex Archaeol. Soc. Special Paper **11**

Hurst, H.R., 1986. *Gloucester, the Roman and Later Defences*, Gloucester Archaeol. Rep. **2** (Gloucester)

James, M.R., 1902. *Western Manuscripts in the Library at Trinity College, Cambridge* iii (Cambridge)

Jennings, S., 1991. 'Just Part of the Story', *Interim: Archaeology in York* **16**/2, 30–4

Jessop, O., 1996. 'A new artefact typology for the study of medieval arrowheads', *Medieval Archaeol.* **40**, 192–205

Jones, V., 1990. 'Plumb-bobs' in Biddle (ed.) 1990, i, 304–6

Kenyon, G.H., 1967. *The Glass Industry of the Weald* (Leicester)

Kisch, B., 1965. *Scales and Weights. A Historical Outline,* Yale Studies in the History of Science and Medicine **1**

Knight, B., 1986. 'Window lead can be interesting!', *Conservation News* **29**, 31

Knüsel, C.J., Kemp, R.L. and Budd, P., 1995. 'Evidence for remedial medical treatment of a severe knee injury from the Fishergate Gilbertine Monastery in the City of York', *J. Archaeol. Sci.* **22**, 369–84

Leggett, J.I., 1971. 'The 1371 poll tax return for the City of York', *YAJ* **43**, 128–46

Lewis, J.M. 1987. 'A Collection of Medieval Artefacts found near Holywell, Clwyd', *Bulletin of Board of Celtic Studies* **34**, 270–82

Liber Custumarum, H.T. Riley (ed.), 1860. Vols 1 and 2 of the series *Munimenta Guildhallae Londoniensis; Liber Alba, Liber Custumarum et Liber Horn* (1859–62) (Rolls Series)

Lloyd-Morgan, G., 1990. 'Copper alloy' in S.W. Ward, *Excavations at Chester. The Lesser Medieval Religious Houses — Sites Investigated 1964–83*, Grosvenor Museum Archaeol. Excav. and Survey Rep. **6**, 166–73

Macdonald, A.D.S. and Laing, L.R., 1974–5. 'Excavations at Lochmaben Castle, Dumfriesshire', *Proc. Soc. Antiq. Scot.* **106**, 124–57

MacGregor, A., 1974. 'Sites Review February–June', *Interim: Archaeology in York* **2**/1, 9–17

Manley, J.F. and Lewis, J.M., 1987. 'A collection of medieval artefacts found near Holywell, Clwyd', *Bulletin of Board of Celtic Studies* **34**, 270–82

Mann, J.E., 1982. *Early Medieval Finds from Flaxengate — Objects of Antler, Bone, Stone, Horn, Ivory, Amber and Jet*, The Archaeology of Lincoln **14**/1

Manning, W.H., 1985. *Catalogue of the Romano-British Iron Tools, Fittings and Weapons in the British Museum* (London)

Margeson, S., 1985. 'The Small Finds' in Atkin, Carter and Evans 1985, 52–67

—— 1993. *Norwich Households: The Medieval and Post-Medieval Finds from Norwich Survey Excavations 1971–78*, E. Anglian Archaeol. **58** (Gressenhall)

May, F.L., 1957. *Silk Textiles of Spain* (New York)

Mayes, P. and Butler, L.A.S., 1983. *Sandal Castle Excavations 1964–73* (Wakefield)

Mead, V.K., 1977. *Evidence for the manufacture of amber beads in London in the 14th–15th Century*, Trans. London Middlesex Archaeol. Soc. **28**, 211–15

Mellor, J.E. and Pearce T., 1981. *The Austin Friars, Leicester*, Counc. Brit. Archaeol. Res. Rep. **35** (London)

Mentasti, R.B, Dorigato, A., Gasparetto, A. and Toninato, T., 1982. *Mille Anni di Arte del Vetro a Venezia* (Venezia)

Michaelis, R.F., 1978. *Old Domestic Base-Metal Candlesticks from the 13th to 19th Century* (Woodbridge)

Miller, E., 1961. Medieval York, in P.M. Tillott (ed.), *A History of Yorkshire, The City of York* (London), 25–116

Mills, J.M., 1993. 'Non-ferrous metalwork' in J.W. Hawkes and M.J. Heaton, *A Closed-shaft Garderobe and Associated Medieval Structures at Jennings Yard, Windsor, Berkshire*, Wessex Archaeol. Rep. **3**, 38–9

Mitchiner, M., 1986. *Medieval Pilgrim and Secular Badges* (Sanderstead)

Moore, D.T., 1978. 'The petrography and archaeology of English honestones', *J. Archaeol. Sci.* **5**, 61–73

Moorhouse, S.A., 1983. 'Vessel Glass' in Mayes and Butler 1983, 225–30

—— 1993. 'Pottery and Glass in the Medieval Monastery' in R. Gilchrist and H. Mytum (eds.), *Advances in Mon-astic Archaeology*, Brit. Archaeol. Rep. **227** (Oxford), 127–48

Moorhouse, S. and Wrathmell, S., 1987. *Kirkstall Abbey I. The 1950–64 Excavations: a Reassessment*, Yorkshire Archaeol. **1** (Wakefield)

Moorhouse, S.A., Greenaway, F., Moore, C.C., Bellamy, C.V., Nicholson,W.E. and Biek, L., 1972. 'Medieval Distilling-Apparatus of Glass and Pottery', *Medieval Archaeol.* **16**, 79–121

Morris, C.A. and Margeson, S., 1993. 'Spoons' in Margeson 1993, 136–7

Murdoch, T., 1991. *Treasures and Trinkets. Jewellery in London from pre-Roman times to the 1930s* (London)

Murray, H.K. and Murray, J.C., 1993. 'Excavations at Rattray, Aberdeenshire. A Scottish deserted burgh', *Medieval Archaeol.* **37**, 109–219

Musty, J. and Algar, D., 1986. 'Excavations at the deserted medieval village of Gomeldon, near Salisbury', *Wilts. Archaeol. and Nat. Hist. Magazine* **80**, 127–69

Mynard, D.C., 1969. 'Excavations at Somerby, Lincs 1957', *Lincolnshire History and Archaeology* **4**, 63–91

Mårtensson, A.W. (ed.), 1976. *Uppgrävt Förflutet för PKbanken i Lund*, Archaeologia Lundensia **7** (Lund)

Nahlik, A., 1963. 'Textiles from the excavation' in A.V. Artsikhovsky and B.A. Kolchin (eds), *Dwellings of Ancient Novgorod Excavation Reports* **4**, 228–313

Nelson, P., 1936. 'Some British medieval seal-matrices', *Archaeol. J.* **93**, 13–44

Newton, S.M., 1980. *Fashion in the Age of the Black Prince. A Study of the Years 1340–65* (Woodbridge)

Nielsen, E.L., 1968. 'Pedersstraede i Viborg', *Kuml*, 23–82

Oakley, G.E., 1979. 'The copper alloy objects' in Williams 1979, 248–64

Oakley, K., 1965. 'Folklore of fossils: parts 1 and 2', *Antiquity* **39**, 117–25

Oman, C., 1957. *English Church Plate 597–1830* (London)

—— 1974. *British Rings 800–1914* (London)

—— 1990. 'Chalices and Patens — Backgound and Typology' in Biddle (ed.) 1990, ii, 789–91

O'Neil, B.H. St J., 1953. 'Some seventeenth century houses in Great Yarmouth', *Archaeologia* **95**, 141–80

Ottaway, P., 1990. (unpublished) *Anglo-Scandinavian Ironwork from 16–22 Coppergate, York, c.850–1100 AD*, PhD thesis, York University

—— 1992. *Archaeology in British Towns* (London)

—— 1996. 'The ironwork' in R.A. Hall and M. Whyman, 'Settlement and Monasticism at Ripon, North Yorkshire, from the 7th–11th centuries AD', *Medieval Archaeol.* **40**, 99–113

—— forthcoming. 'Domestic Cutlery including Scissors and Knives: Knives' in A. Hardy, A. Dodd and G. Keevil, *Excavations at Eynsham Abbey 1989–1992*, Oxford Archaeol. Unit Thames Valley Landscapes Monogr.

—— in prep. 'Iron Objects' in C.P. Loveluck (ed.), *Excavations at Flixborough*, Oxbow Archaeol. Monogr. Series (Oxford)

Pritchard, F., 1991. 'Small Finds' in Vince (ed) 1991, 120–278

Radley, J., 1971. 'Economic aspects of Anglo-Danish York', *Medieval Archaeol.* **15**, 37–57

Rahtz, P. A., 1983. 'Copper alloy' in Hirst, Walsh and Wright 1983, 175–81

Ranson, D.M. 1977. (unpublished) *An analysis of medieval moulds and casting debris from the Bedern, York*, MA dissertation, University of Bradford

RCHMY. Royal Commission on Historical Monuments (England). *An Inventory of the Historical Monuments in the City of York.* **1**: *Eburacum, Roman York* (1962) (HMSO, London)

Reddaway, T.F. and Walker, L.E.M., 1975. *The Early History of the Goldsmiths' Company 1327–1509* (London)

Rhodes, M., 1984. 'Slate writing implements' in A. Thompson, F. Grew and J. Schofield, 'Excavations at Aldgate 1974', *Post-Medieval Archaeology* **18**, 120–2

Robins, F.W., 1937. *The Story of the Lamp (and the Candle)* (Oxford)

Roesdahl, E., Graham-Campbell J., Connor P. and Pearson K., 1981. *The Vikings in England*

Rogers, N.S.H., 1997. 'Other artefacts' in M. Whyman, 'Excavations in Deanery Gardens and Low St Agnesgate, Ripon, North Yorkshire', *Yorkshire Archaeol. J.* **69**, 149–52

Rogerson, A., 1976. 'Excavations on Fuller's Hill, Great Yarmouth', E. Anglian Archaeol. **2** (Gressenhall)

Rollins, J.G., 1981. *Needlemaking*, Shire Album **71**

Rutt, R., 1987. *A History of Hand Knitting* (London)

Saunders, A.D., 1978. 'Excavations in the Abbey Church of St Augustine's Abbey, Canterbury 1955–8', *Medieval Archaeol.* **22**, 25–63

Saunders, P. and Saunders, E., 1991. *Salisbury Museum Medieval Catalogue 1* (Salisbury)

Schäfer, H. and Gross, U., 2000. 'Kein Einschnitt erkennbar', *Archäologie in Deutschland*, Heft 1/2000, 30–3

Schjølberg, E., 1984. 'The hair products', *The Bryggen Papers* (Supplementary Series No.1),

Schmedding, B., 1978. *Mittelalterliche Textilien in Kirchen und Klostern der Schweiz* (Bonn)

Scully, O.M.B., 1997. 'Metal artefacts' in M.F. Hurley and O.M.B. Scully, *Late Viking Age and Medieval Waterford. Excavations 1986–92* (Waterford), 438–89

Sellers, M., 1974. 'Textile industries', *Victoria History of the County of Yorkshire* **2** (London), 406–29

Sherlock, D. and Woods, H., 1988. *St Augustine's Abbey: Report on Excavations 1960–78*, Monogr. Series of Kent Archaeol. Soc. **4** (Maidstone)

Sneyd, C.A. (ed. and transl.), 1847. *A Relation, or Rather a True Account, of the Island of England; with Sundry Particulars of the Customs of these People, and of the Royal Revenues under King Henry the Seventh, About the Year 1500*, London: Camden Society **37**

Spencer, B., 1983. 'The Pewter Brooch' in K.S. Jarvis (ed.), *Excavations in Christchurch 1969–1980*, Dorset Nat. History and Archaeol. Soc. Monogr. **4**, 81–3

—— 1985. 'Fifteenth Century Collar of SS and a Hoard of False Dice and their Container from the Museum of London', *Antiq. J.* **64** (2), 376–82

—— 1998. *Pilgrim Badges and Secular Souvenirs,* Medieval Finds from Excavations in London **7** (London)

Sprott, G., 1984. 'Pearl Fishing in Scotland' in B. Gunda (ed.), *The Fishing Culture of the World* (Budapest)

Starley, D.E., 1992. (unpublished) *Medieval Iron and Steel Production: An Assessment of the Changing Technology of European Ferrous Alloy Production through the Analysis of Medieval and Renaissance Armour*, PhD thesis, University of Bradford

Steane, J.M. and Bryant, G.F., 1975. 'Excavations at the Deserted Medieval Settlement at Lyveden, Fourth Report', *J. Northampton Museums* **12**

Steane, J.M. and Foreman, M., 1988. 'Medieval fishing tackle' in M. Aston (ed.), *Medieval Fish, Fisheries and*

Fishponds in England, Brit. Archaeol. Rep. Brit. Ser. **182/**
1 (Oxford), 137–86

Strutt, J., 1842 (reprinted 1970). *A Complete View of the Dress and Habits of the People of England*, 2 vols (London)

Swanson, H., 1989. *Medieval Artisans* (Oxford)

Tait, H., 1979. *The Golden Age of Venetian Glass* (London)

Taylor, R., 1974. *Weoley Castle. Hand List of Exhibits* (Birmingham)

Theuerkauff-Liederwald, A.-E., 1975. 'Die Formen der Messingkannen im 15. und 16. Jahrhundert', *Rotterdam Papers* **2** (Rotterdam)

Thomas, C., Sloane, B., and Phillpotts, C., 1997. *Excavations at the Priory and Hospital of St Mary Spital, London* (London)

Thompson, F.H., 1960. 'The deserted medieval village of Riseholme, near Lincoln', *Medieval Archaeol.* **4**, 95–108

Tidow, K., 1990. 'Spatmittelalterliche und fruhneuzeitliche Textilfunde aus Lubeck und ihre fruheren Verwendungen' in P. Walton and J.P. Wild (eds), *Textiles in Northern Archaeology: NESAT III* (London), 165–74

Tringham, N.J., 1993. *Charters of the Vicars Choral of York Minster: City of York and its Suburbs to 1546* (Leeds)

Turgoose, S., 1982. 'The Nature of Surviving Iron Objects' in R.W. Clarke and S. Blackshaw (eds), *Conservation of Iron*, Maritime Monographs and Reports **53**, 1–7

Turnau, I., 1983. 'The diffusion of knitting in medieval Europe' in N. Harte and K. Ponting, *Cloth and Clothing in Medieval Europe (Pasold Studies in Textile History)*, 368–89

Tylecote, R.F., 1972. 'A contribution to the Metallurgy of 18th and 19th century Brass Pins', *Post-Medieval Archaeol.* **6**, 183–90

—— 1976. *A History of Metallurgy*, The Metals Society (London)

—— 1990. 'Scientific examination and analysis of iron objects' in Biddle (ed.), 140–59

Tylecote, R.F. and Gilmour B.J.J., 1986. *The Metallography of Early Ferrous Edge Tools and Edged Weapons*, Brit. Archaeol. Rep. Brit. Ser. **155** (Oxford)

Tyson, R., 2000. *Medieval Glass Vessels found in England c. AD 1200–1500*, Counc. Brit. Archaeol. Res. Rep. **121** (York)

Vince, A.G. (ed.), 1991. *Aspects of Saxon and Norman London 2: Finds and Environmental Evidence*, London Middlesex Archaeol. Soc. Special Paper **12**

Vons-Comis, S., 1982. 'Medieval textile finds from the Netherlands' in K. Tidow (ed.) *Textil-symposium Neumünster: Archaologische Textilfunde* (Neumünster), 151–62

Walton, P., 1981. 'The Textiles' in B. Harbottle and M. Ellison 1981, 'An excavation in the Castle ditch, Newcastle upon Tyne, 1974–76', *Archaeologia Aeliana* 5th series **9**, 190–228

—— 1987. 'Medieval and 17th century textiles from High Street/Blackfriargate' in Armstrong and Ayers 1987, 227–231

—— 1988. 'Caulking, cordage and textile' in C. O'Brien, L. Bown, S. Dixon and R. Nicholson, *The Origins of the Newcastle Quayside*, Soc. Antiq. Newcastle upon Tyne Monogr. Series **3**, 78–85

Walton Rogers, P., 1993. 'Post-Medieval Aiglets (Lace Tags) with Remains of Laces from Miscellaneous Sites', *Textiles from the City of Lincoln, 1972–1989*, City of Lincoln Archaeol. Rep. (Lincoln)

—— 2001. 'The Re-appearance of an Old Roman Loom in Medieval England' in P. Walton Rogers, L. Bender Jørgensen and A. Rast-Eicher, *The Roman Textile Industry and its Influence* (Oxford)

—— unpublished. 'Textiles from Dudley Castle, West Midlands'

Ward, A., Cherry, J., Gere, C. and Cartlidge, B., 1981. *The Ring from Antiquity to the Twentieth Century* (London)

Ward Perkins, J.B., 1940. *London Museum Medieval Catalogue* (London)

Waterer, J.W., 1981. *Leather and the Warrior* (Northampton)

Waterman, D.M., 1954. 'Excavations at Clough Castle Co. Down', *Ulster J. Archaeol.* **17**, 103–63

—— 1959. 'Late Saxon, Viking and early medieval finds from York', *Archaeologia* **97**, 59–105

Watkin, J., 1987. 'Objects of stone, fired clay, jet and mica' in Armstrong and Ayers 1987, 191

Webster, L.E. and Cherry, J., 1974. 'Medieval Britain in 1973', *Medieval Archaeology* **18**, 174–223

Wedepohl, K.H., Krueger, I, Hartmann, G., 1995. 'Medieval Lead Glass from Northwestern Europe', *J. Glass Studies* **37**, 65–82

Wheeler, R.E.M., 1930. *London in Roman Times*, London Museum Catalogue **3**

Wheeler-Holohan, V., 1931. *Boutell's Manual of Heraldry* (London)

Whitehouse, D., 1981. 'Notes on Late Medieval Glass in Italy', *Annales du 8e Congrès Internationale d'Etudes Historique du Verre 1979*, Association Internationale pour l'Histoire du Verre, Liège: Centre de Public de l'AIHV, 165–77

Wiemer, K., 1993. (unpublished) *Early British Iron Edged Tools: A Metallurgical Study*, PhD thesis, University of Cambridge

Williams, J.H., 1978. 'Excavations at Greyfriars, Northampton 1972', *Northants Archaeol.* **13**, 96–180

—— 1979. *St Peter's Street, Northampton: Excavations 1973–76*, Northampton Archaeol. Monogr. **2** (Northampton)

Williams, V., 1997. 'The small finds' in B. Morley and D. Gurney, *Castle Rising Castle, Norfolk*, E. Anglian Archaeol. Rep. **81**, 87–110

Wilkins, E., 1969. *The Rose-Garden Game. The Symbolic Background to the European Prayer-Beads* (London)

Wilson, C., 1977. *The Shrines of St William of York* (York)

Wilson, C. and Burton, J., 1988. *St Mary's Abbey, York* (York)

Wilthew, P., 1984. 'Analysis of inlays and fittings on medieval knives and shears from the Museum of London', AML Rep. 4311

—— 1986. 'Examination of a mould from Prudhoe Castle, Northumberland', AML Rep. 4818

Wood, C.J. and Smith, E.G., 1978. 'Lithostratigraphical classification of the chalk in North Yorkshire, Humberside and Lincolnshire', *Proc. Yorkshire Geol. Soc.* **42**, 263–87

Wood, E.S., 1965. 'A medieval glasshouse at Blunden's Wood, Hambledon , Surrey', *Surrey Archaeol. Collections* **62**, 54–79

YMA, VC 6/2. Vicars Choral chamberlains' rolls and rent rolls

YMB. Sellers, M. (ed.), 1912, 1915. *York Memorandum Book* **1**, **2**, SS **120**, **125**

Ypey, J., 1981. 'Wapen of werktuig?', *Liber Castellorum, 40 Varieties op het Thema Kasteel* (Zutphen), 367–75

Zarnecki, G., Holt, J. and Holland, T., 1984. *English Romanesque Art 1066–1200* (London)

Øye, I., 1988. 'Textile equipment and its working environment, Bryggen in Bergen c1150–1500', *The Bryggen Papers, Main Series* **2** (Oslo)

Index

By Susan Vaughan

Illustrations are denoted by page numbers in *italics*. Places are in York unless indicated otherwise. The following abbreviations have been used in this index: B and NES – Bath and North-East Somerset; Beds – Bedfordshire; Berks – Berkshire; Bucks – Buckinghamshire; Ches – Cheshire; Corn – Cornwall; Derbys – Derbyshire; Dum and Gall – Dumfries and Galloway; E Riding – East Riding of Yorkshire; Glos – Gloucestershire; Hants – Hampshire; Herts – Hertfordshire; Leics – Leicestershire; Lincs – Lincolnshire; N Yorks – North Yorkshire; Northants – Northamptonshire; Northumb – Northumberland; Notts – Nottinghamshire; Oxon – Oxfordshire; Som – Somerset; W Mids – West Midlands; Wilts – Wiltshire; Worcs – Worcestershire.